American Casebook Series
Hornbook Series and Basic Legal Texts
Nutshell Series

of

WEST PUBLISHING COMPANY
P.O. Box 64526
St. Paul, Minnesota 55164–0526

Accounting

FARIS' ACCOUNTING AND LAW IN A NUT-SHELL, 377 pages, 1984. Softcover. (Text)

FIFLIS, KRIPKE AND FOSTER'S TEACHING MATERIALS ON ACCOUNTING FOR BUSINESS LAWYERS, Third Edition, 838 pages, 1984. (Casebook)

SIEGEL AND SIEGEL'S ACCOUNTING AND FINANCIAL DISCLOSURE: A GUIDE TO BASIC CONCEPTS, 259 pages, 1983. Softcover. (Text)

Administrative Law

BONFIELD AND ASIMOW'S CASES AND MATERIALS ON STATE AND FEDERAL ADMINISTRATIVE LAW, Approximately 800 pages, March, 1989 Pub. (Casebook)

DAVIS' CASES, TEXT AND PROBLEMS ON ADMINISTRATIVE LAW, Sixth Edition, 683 pages, 1977. (Casebook)

GELLHORN AND BOYER'S ADMINISTRATIVE LAW AND PROCESS IN A NUTSHELL, Second Edition, 445 pages, 1981. Softcover. (Text)

MASHAW AND MERRILL'S CASES AND MATERIALS ON ADMINISTRATIVE LAW—THE AMERICAN PUBLIC LAW SYSTEM, Second Edition, 976 pages, 1985. (Casebook) (1989 Supplement)

ROBINSON, GELLHORN AND BRUFF'S THE ADMINISTRATIVE PROCESS, Third Edition, 978 pages, 1986. (Casebook)

Admiralty

HEALY AND SHARPE'S CASES AND MATERIALS ON ADMIRALTY, Second Edition, 876 pages, 1986. (Casebook)

MARAIST'S ADMIRALTY IN A NUTSHELL, Second Edition, 379 pages, 1988. Softcover. (Text)

SCHOENBAUM'S HORNBOOK ON ADMIRALTY AND MARITIME LAW, Student Edition, 692 pages, 1987. (Text)

Agency—Partnership

FESSLER'S ALTERNATIVES TO INCORPORATION FOR PERSONS IN QUEST OF PROFIT, Second Edition, 326 pages, 1986. Softcover. Teacher's Manual available. (Casebook)

HENN'S CASES AND MATERIALS ON AGENCY, PARTNERSHIP AND OTHER UNINCORPORATED BUSINESS ENTERPRISES, Second Edition, 733 pages, 1985. Teacher's Manual available. (Casebook)

REUSCHLEIN AND GREGORY'S HORNBOOK ON THE LAW OF AGENCY, PARTNERSHIP AND OTHER UNINCORPORATED BUSINESS ORGANIZATIONS, 625 pages, 1979, with 1981 pocket part. (Text)

SELECTED CORPORATION AND PARTNERSHIP STATUTES, RULES AND FORMS. Softcover. 621 pages, 1987.

STEFFEN AND KERR'S CASES ON AGENCY-PARTNERSHIP, Fourth Edition, 859 pages, 1980. (Casebook)

STEFFEN'S AGENCY-PARTNERSHIP IN A NUTSHELL, 364 pages, 1977. Softcover. (Text)

Agricultural Law

MEYER, PEDERSEN, THORSON AND DAVIDSON'S AGRICULTURAL LAW: CASES AND MATERIALS, 931 pages, 1985. Teacher's Manual available. (Casebook)

Alternative Dispute Resolution

KANOWITZ' CASES AND MATERIALS ON ALTERNATIVE DISPUTE RESOLUTION, 1024 pages, 1986. Teacher's Manual available. (Casebook)

RISKIN AND WESTBROOK'S DISPUTE RESOLUTION AND LAWYERS, 468 pages, 1987. Teacher's Manual available. (Casebook)

RISKIN AND WESTBROOK'S DISPUTE RESOLUTION AND LAWYERS, Abridged Edition, 223 pages, 1987. Softcover. Teacher's Manual available. (Casebook)

TEPLE AND MOBERLY'S ARBITRATION AND CONFLICT RESOLUTION, (The Labor Law Group). 614 pages, 1979. (Casebook)

American Indian Law

CANBY'S AMERICAN INDIAN LAW IN A NUTSHELL, Second Edition, 336 pages, 1988. Softcover. (Text)

GETCHES AND WILKINSON'S CASES AND MATERIALS ON FEDERAL INDIAN LAW, Second Edition, 880 pages, 1986. (Casebook)

Antitrust—see also Regulated Industries, Trade Regulation

GELLHORN'S ANTITRUST LAW AND ECONOMICS IN A NUTSHELL, Third Edition, 472 pages, 1986. Softcover. (Text)

GIFFORD AND RASKIND'S CASES, PROBLEMS AND MATERIALS ON FEDERAL ANTITRUST LAW, 694 pages, 1983. (Casebook) (1985 Supplement)

HOVENKAMP'S BLACK LETTER ON ANTITRUST, 323 pages, 1986. Softcover. (Review)

HOVENKAMP'S HORNBOOK ON ECONOMICS AND FEDERAL ANTITRUST LAW, Student Edition, 414 pages, 1985. (Text)

OPPENHEIM, WESTON AND MCCARTHY'S CASES AND COMMENTS ON FEDERAL ANTITRUST LAWS, Fourth Edition, 1168 pages, 1981. (Casebook) (1985 Supplement)

POSNER AND EASTERBROOK'S CASES AND ECONOMIC NOTES ON ANTITRUST, Second Edition, 1077 pages, 1981. (Casebook) (1984–85 Supplement)

SULLIVAN'S HORNBOOK OF THE LAW OF ANTITRUST, 886 pages, 1977. (Text)

Appellate Advocacy—see Trial and Appellate Advocacy

Architecture and Engineering Law

SWEET'S LEGAL ASPECTS OF ARCHITECTURE, ENGINEERING AND THE CONSTRUCTION PROCESS, Third Edition, 999 pages, 1985. Teacher's Manual available. (Casebook)

Art Law

DUBOFF'S ART LAW IN A NUTSHELL, 335 pages, 1984. Softcover. (Text)

Banking Law

LOVETT'S BANKING AND FINANCIAL INSTITUTIONS LAW IN A NUTSHELL, Second Edition, 464 pages, 1988. Softcover. (Text)

SYMONS AND WHITE'S TEACHING MATERIALS ON BANKING LAW, Second Edition, 993 pages, 1984. Teacher's Manual available. (Casebook) (1987 Supplement)

Business Planning—see also Corporate Finance

PAINTER'S PROBLEMS AND MATERIALS IN BUSINESS PLANNING, Second Edition, 1008 pages, 1984. (Casebook) (1987 Supplement)

See also Selected Securities and Business Planning Statutes

SELECTED SECURITIES AND BUSINESS PLANNING STATUTES, RULES AND FORMS. Softcover. 493 pages, 1987.

Civil Procedure—see also Federal Jurisdiction and Procedure

AMERICAN BAR ASSOCIATION SECTION OF LITIGATION—READINGS ON ADVERSARIAL JUSTICE: THE AMERICAN APPROACH TO ADJUDICATION, 217 pages, 1988. Softcover. (Coursebook)

CASAD'S RES JUDICATA IN A NUTSHELL, 310 pages, 1976. Softcover. (Text)

CLERMONT'S BLACK LETTER ON CIVIL PROCEDURE, Second Edition, 332 pages, 1988. Softcover. (Review)

COUND, FRIEDENTHAL, MILLER AND SEXTON'S CASES AND MATERIALS ON CIVIL PROCEDURE, Fourth Edition, 1202 pages, 1985. Teacher's Manual available. (Casebook)

COUND, FRIEDENTHAL, MILLER AND SEXTON'S CIVIL PROCEDURE SUPPLEMENT. 455 pages, 1987. Softcover. (Casebook Supplement)

EHRENZWEIG, LOUISELL AND HAZARD'S JURISDICTION IN A NUTSHELL, Fourth Edition, 232 pages, 1980. Softcover. (Text)

Civil Procedure—Cont'd

FEDERAL RULES OF CIVIL-APPELLATE PROCEDURE—EDUCATIONAL EDITION. Softcover. 574 pages, 1988.

FRIEDENTHAL, KANE AND MILLER'S HORNBOOK ON CIVIL PROCEDURE, 876 pages, 1985. (Text)

KANE'S CIVIL PROCEDURE IN A NUTSHELL, Second Edition, 306 pages, 1986. Softcover. (Text)

KOFFLER AND REPPY'S HORNBOOK ON COMMON LAW PLEADING, 663 pages, 1969. (Text)

MARCUS, REDISH AND SHERMAN'S CIVIL PROCEDURE: A MODERN APPROACH, Approximately 1100 pages, February, 1989 Pub. Teacher's Manual available. (Casebook)

MARCUS AND SHERMAN'S COMPLEX LITIGATION–CASES AND MATERIALS ON ADVANCED CIVIL PROCEDURE, Teacher's Manual available. (Casebook)

PARK'S COMPUTER-AIDED EXERCISES ON CIVIL PROCEDURE, Second Edition, 167 pages, 1983. Softcover. (Coursebook)

SIEGEL'S HORNBOOK ON NEW YORK PRACTICE, 1011 pages, 1978, with 1987 pocket part. (Text)

Commercial Law

BAILEY AND HAGEDORN'S SECURED TRANSACTIONS IN A NUTSHELL, Third Edition, 390 pages, 1988. Softcover. (Text)

EPSTEIN, MARTIN, HENNING AND NICKLES' BASIC UNIFORM COMMERCIAL CODE TEACHING MATERIALS, Third Edition, 704 pages, 1988. Teacher's Manual available. (Casebook)

HENSON'S HORNBOOK ON SECURED TRANSACTIONS UNDER THE U.C.C., Second Edition, 504 pages, 1979, with 1979 pocket part. (Text)

MURRAY'S COMMERCIAL LAW, PROBLEMS AND MATERIALS, 366 pages, 1975. Teacher's Manual available. Softcover. (Coursebook)

NICKLES' BLACK LETTER ON COMMERCIAL PAPER, 450 pages, 1988. Softcover. (Review)

NICKLES, MATHESON AND DOLAN'S MATERIALS FOR UNDERSTANDING CREDIT AND PAYMENT SYSTEMS, 923 pages, 1987. Teacher's Manual available. (Casebook)

NORDSTROM, MURRAY AND CLOVIS' PROBLEMS AND MATERIALS ON SALES, 515 pages, 1982. (Casebook)

NORDSTROM, MURRAY AND CLOVIS' PROBLEMS AND MATERIALS ON SECURED TRANSACTIONS, 594 pages, 1987. (Casebook)

SELECTED COMMERCIAL STATUTES. Softcover. 1544 pages, 1988.

SPEIDEL'S BLACK LETTER ON SALES AND SALES FINANCING, 363 pages, 1984. Softcover. (Review)

SPEIDEL, SUMMERS AND WHITE'S COMMERCIAL LAW: TEACHING MATERIALS, Fourth Edition, 1448 pages, 1987. Teacher's Manual available. (Casebook)

SPEIDEL, SUMMERS AND WHITE'S COMMERCIAL PAPER: TEACHING MATERIALS, Fourth Edition, 578 pages, 1987. Reprint from Speidel et al., Commercial Law, Fourth Edition. Teacher's Manual available. (Casebook)

SPEIDEL, SUMMERS AND WHITE'S SALES: TEACHING MATERIALS, Fourth Edition, 804 pages, 1987. Reprint from Speidel et al., Commercial Law, Fourth Edition. Teacher's Manual available (Casebook)

SPEIDEL, SUMMERS AND WHITE'S SECURED TRANSACTIONS: TEACHING MATERIALS, Fourth Edition, 485 pages, 1987. Reprint from Speidel et al., Commercial Law, Fourth Edition. Teacher's Manual available. (Casebook)

STOCKTON'S SALES IN A NUTSHELL, Second Edition, 370 pages, 1981. Softcover. (Text)

STONE'S UNIFORM COMMERCIAL CODE IN A NUTSHELL, Second Edition, 516 pages, 1984. Softcover. (Text)

UNIFORM COMMERCIAL CODE, OFFICIAL TEXT WITH COMMENTS. Softcover. 1155 pages, 1987.

WEBER AND SPEIDEL'S COMMERCIAL PAPER IN A NUTSHELL, Third Edition, 404 pages, 1982. Softcover. (Text)

WHITE AND SUMMERS' HORNBOOK ON THE UNIFORM COMMERCIAL CODE, Third Edition, Student Edition, 1386 pages, 1988. (Text)

Community Property

MENNELL AND BOYKOFF'S COMMUNITY PROPERTY IN A NUTSHELL, Second Edition, 432

Community Property—Cont'd

pages, 1988. Softcover. (Text)

VERRALL AND BIRD'S CASES AND MATERIALS ON CALIFORNIA COMMUNITY PROPERTY, Fifth Edition, 604 pages, 1988. (Casebook)

Comparative Law

BARTON, GIBBS, LI AND MERRYMAN'S LAW IN RADICALLY DIFFERENT CULTURES, 960 pages, 1983. (Casebook)

GLENDON, GORDON AND OSAKWE'S COMPARATIVE LEGAL TRADITIONS: TEXT, MATERIALS AND CASES ON THE CIVIL LAW, COMMON LAW AND SOCIALIST LAW TRADITIONS, 1091 pages, 1985. (Casebook)

GLENDON, GORDON AND OSAKWE'S COMPARATIVE LEGAL TRADITIONS IN A NUTSHELL. 402 pages, 1982. Softcover. (Text)

LANGBEIN'S COMPARATIVE CRIMINAL PROCEDURE: GERMANY, 172 pages, 1977. Softcover. (Casebook)

Computers and Law

MAGGS AND SPROWL'S COMPUTER APPLICATIONS IN THE LAW, 316 pages, 1987. (Coursebook)

MASON'S USING COMPUTERS IN THE LAW: AN INTRODUCTION AND PRACTICAL GUIDE, Second Edition, 288 pages, 1988. Softcover. (Coursebook)

Conflict of Laws

CRAMTON, CURRIE AND KAY'S CASES–COMMENTS–QUESTIONS ON CONFLICT OF LAWS, Fourth Edition, 876 pages, 1987. (Casebook)

SCOLES AND HAY'S HORNBOOK ON CONFLICT OF LAWS, Student Edition, 1085 pages, 1982, with 1989 pocket part. (Text)

SCOLES AND WEINTRAUB'S CASES AND MATERIALS ON CONFLICT OF LAWS, Second Edition, 966 pages, 1972. (Casebook) (1978 Supplement)

SEIGEL'S CONFLICTS IN A NUTSHELL, 470 pages, 1982. Softcover. (Text)

Constitutional Law—Civil Rights—see also Foreign Relations and National Security Law

ABERNATHY'S CASES AND MATERIALS ON CIVIL RIGHTS, 660 pages, 1980. (Casebook)

ALEINIKOFF AND GARVEY'S READINGS ON

MODERN CONSTITUTIONAL THEORY, May 1989 Pub. Softcover (Reader)

BARRON AND DIENES' BLACK LETTER ON CONSTITUTIONAL LAW, Second Edition, 310 pages, 1987. Softcover. (Review)

BARRON AND DIENES' CONSTITUTIONAL LAW IN A NUTSHELL, 389 pages, 1986. Soft cover. (Text)

COHEN'S CASES AND MATERIALS ON THE LAW OF DEPRIVATION OF LIBERTY: A STUDY IN SOCIAL CONTROL, 755 pages, 1980. (Casebook)

ENGDAHL'S CONSTITUTIONAL FEDERALISM IN A NUTSHELL, Second Edition, 411 pages, 1987. Softcover. (Text)

LOCKHART, KAMISAR, CHOPER AND SHIFFRIN'S CONSTITUTIONAL LAW: CASES–COMMENTS–QUESTIONS, Sixth Edition, 1601 pages, 1986. (Casebook) (1988 Supplement)

LOCKHART, KAMISAR, CHOPER AND SHIFFRIN'S THE AMERICAN CONSTITUTION: CASES AND MATERIALS, Sixth Edition, 1260 pages, 1986. Abridged version of Lockhart, et al., Constitutional Law: Cases–Comments–Questions, Sixth Edition. (Casebook) (1988 Supplement)

LOCKHART, KAMISAR, CHOPER AND SHIFFRIN'S CONSTITUTIONAL RIGHTS AND LIBERTIES: CASES AND MATERIALS, Sixth Edition, 1266 pages, 1986. Reprint from Lockhart, et al., Constitutional Law: Cases–Comments–Questions, Sixth Edition. (Casebook) (1988 Supplement)

MANNING'S THE LAW OF CHURCH-STATE RELATIONS IN A NUTSHELL, 305 pages, 1981. Softcover. (Text)

MARKS AND COOPER'S STATE CONSTITUTIONAL LAW IN A NUTSHELL, 329 pages, 1988. Softcover. (Text)

MILLER'S PRESIDENTIAL POWER IN A NUTSHELL, 328 pages, 1977. Softcover. (Text)

NOWAK, ROTUNDA AND YOUNG'S HORNBOOK ON CONSTITUTIONAL LAW, Third Edition, 1191 pages, 1986 with 1988 pocket part. (Text)

ROTUNDA'S MODERN CONSTITUTIONAL LAW: CASES AND NOTES, Third Edition, Approximately 1000 pages, May, 1989 Pub. (Casebook)

VIEIRA'S CIVIL RIGHTS IN A NUTSHELL, 279

Constitutional Law—Civil Rights—Cont'd
pages, 1978. Softcover. (Text)

WILLIAMS' CONSTITUTIONAL ANALYSIS IN A NUTSHELL, 388 pages, 1979. Softcover. (Text)

Consumer Law—see also Commercial Law

EPSTEIN AND NICKLES' CONSUMER LAW IN A NUTSHELL, Second Edition, 418 pages, 1981. Softcover. (Text)

SELECTED COMMERCIAL STATUTES. Softcover. 1544 pages, 1988.

SPANOGLE AND ROHNER'S CASES AND MATERIALS ON CONSUMER LAW, 693 pages, 1979. Teacher's Manual available. (Casebook) (1982 Supplement)

Contracts

CALAMARI, AND PERILLO'S BLACK LETTER ON CONTRACTS, 397 pages, 1983. Softcover. (Review)

CALAMARI AND PERILLO'S HORNBOOK ON CONTRACTS, Third Edition, 1049 pages, 1987. (Text)

CALAMARI, PERILLO AND HADJIYANNAKIS' CASES AND PROBLEMS ON CONTRACTS, Second Edition, approximately 1100 pages, May 1989 Pub. (Casebook)

CORBIN'S TEXT ON CONTRACTS, One Volume Student Edition, 1224 pages, 1952. (Text)

FESSLER AND LOISEAUX'S CASES AND MATERIALS ON CONTRACTS—MORALITY, ECONOMICS AND THE MARKET PLACE, 837 pages, 1982. Teacher's Manual available. (Casebook)

FRIEDMAN'S CONTRACT REMEDIES IN A NUTSHELL, 323 pages, 1981. Softcover. (Text)

FULLER AND EISENBERG'S CASES ON BASIC CONTRACT LAW, Fourth Edition, 1203 pages, 1981 (Casebook)

HAMILTON, RAU AND WEINTRAUB'S CASES AND MATERIALS ON CONTRACTS, 830 pages, 1984. (Casebook)

JACKSON AND BOLLINGER'S CASES ON CONTRACT LAW IN MODERN SOCIETY, Second Edition, 1329 pages, 1980. Teacher's Manual available. (Casebook)

KEYES' GOVERNMENT CONTRACTS IN A NUTSHELL, 423 pages, 1979. Softcover. (Text)

SCHABER AND ROHWER'S CONTRACTS IN A NUTSHELL, Second Edition, 425 pages,

1984. Softcover. (Text)

SUMMERS AND HILLMAN'S CONTRACT AND RELATED OBLIGATION: THEORY, DOCTRINE AND PRACTICE, 1074 pages, 1987. Teacher's Manual available. (Casebook)

Copyright—see Patent and Copyright Law

Corporate Finance

HAMILTON'S CASES AND MATERIALS ON CORPORATE FINANCE, 895 pages, 1984. (Casebook) (1986 Supplement)

Corporations

HAMILTON'S BLACK LETTER ON CORPORATIONS, Second Edition, 513 pages, 1986. Softcover. (Review)

HAMILTON'S CASES ON CORPORATIONS—INCLUDING PARTNERSHIPS AND LIMITED PARTNERSHIPS, Third Edition, 1213 pages, 1986. Teacher's Manual available. (Casebook) (1986 Statutory Supplement)

HAMILTON'S THE LAW OF CORPORATIONS IN A NUTSHELL, Second Edition, 515 pages, 1987. Softcover. (Text)

HENN'S TEACHING MATERIALS ON THE LAW OF CORPORATIONS, Second Edition, 1204 pages, 1986. Teacher's Manual available. (Casebook)

See Selected Corporation and Partnership Statutes

HENN AND ALEXANDER'S HORNBOOK ON LAWS OF CORPORATIONS, Third Edition, Student Edition, 1371 pages, 1983, with 1986 pocket part. (Text)

JENNINGS AND BUXBAUM'S CASES AND MATERIALS ON CORPORATIONS, 1180 pages, 1979. (Casebook)

SELECTED CORPORATION AND PARTNERSHIP STATUTES, RULES AND FORMS. Softcover. 621 pages, 1987.

SOLOMON, SCHWARTZ AND BAUMAN'S MATERIALS AND PROBLEMS ON CORPORATIONS: LAW AND POLICY, Second Edition, 1391 pages, 1988. Teacher's Manual available. (Casebook)

See also Selected Corporation and Partnership Statutes

Corrections

KRANTZ' CASES AND MATERIALS ON THE LAW OF CORRECTIONS AND PRISONERS' RIGHTS,

Corrections—Cont'd

Third Edition, 855 pages, 1986. (Casebook) (1988 Supplement)

KRANTZ' THE LAW OF CORRECTIONS AND PRISONERS' RIGHTS IN A NUTSHELL, Third Edition, 407 pages, 1988. Softcover. (Text)

POPPER'S POST-CONVICTION REMEDIES IN A NUTSHELL, 360 pages, 1978. Softcover. (Text)

ROBBINS' CASES AND MATERIALS ON POST-CONVICTION REMEDIES, 506 pages, 1982. (Casebook)

Creditor's Rights

BANKRUPTCY CODE, RULES AND FORMS, LAW SCHOOL EDITION, Softcover. 792 pages, 1988.

EPSTEIN'S DEBTOR-CREDITOR RELATIONS IN A NUTSHELL, Third Edition, 383 pages, 1986. Softcover. (Text)

EPSTEIN, LANDERS AND NICKLES' CASES AND MATERIALS ON DEBTORS AND CREDITORS, Third Edition, 1059 pages, 1987. Teacher's Manual available. (Casebook)

LOPUCKI'S PLAYER'S MANUAL FOR THE DEBTOR-CREDITOR GAME, 123 pages, 1985. Softcover. (Coursebook)

NICKLES AND EPSTEIN'S BLACK LETTER ON CREDITOR'S RIGHTS AND BANKRUPTCY, Approximately 500 pages, 1989. (Review)

RIESENFELD'S CASES AND MATERIALS ON CREDITORS' REMEDIES AND DEBTORS' PROTECTION, Fourth Edition, 914 pages, 1987. (Casebook)

WHITE'S CASES AND MATERIALS ON BANKRUPTCY AND CREDITOR'S RIGHTS, 812 pages, 1985. Teacher's Manual available. (Casebook) (1987 Supplement)

Criminal Law and Criminal Procedure—see also Corrections, Juvenile Justice

ABRAMS' FEDERAL CRIMINAL LAW AND ITS ENFORCEMENT, 866 pages, 1986. (Casebook) (1988 Supplement)

CARLSON'S ADJUDICATION OF CRIMINAL JUSTICE: PROBLEMS AND REFERENCES, 130 pages, 1986. Softcover. (Casebook)

DIX AND SHARLOT'S CASES AND MATERIALS ON CRIMINAL LAW, Third Edition, 846 pages, 1987. (Casebook)

FEDERAL RULES OF CRIMINAL PROCEDURE—EDUCATIONAL EDITION. Softcover. 560 pages, 1988.

GRANO'S PROBLEMS IN CRIMINAL PROCEDURE, Second Edition, 176 pages, 1981. Teacher's Manual available. Softcover. (Coursebook)

HEYMANN AND KENETY'S THE MURDER TRIAL OF WILBUR JACKSON: A HOMICIDE IN THE FAMILY, Second Edition, 347 pages, 1985. (Coursebook)

ISRAEL, KAMISAR AND LAFAVE'S CRIMINAL PROCEDURE AND THE CONSTITUTION: LEADING SUPREME COURT CASES AND INTRODUCTORY TEXT, 734 pages, 1989. Softcover. (Casebook)

ISRAEL AND LAFAVE'S CRIMINAL PROCEDURE—CONSTITUTIONAL LIMITATIONS IN A NUTSHELL, Fourth Edition, 461 pages, 1988. Softcover. (Text)

JOHNSON'S CASES, MATERIALS AND TEXT ON CRIMINAL LAW, Third Edition, 783 pages, 1985. Teacher's Manual available. (Casebook)

JOHNSON'S CASES AND MATERIALS ON CRIMINAL PROCEDURE, 859 pages, 1988. (Casebook)

KAMISAR, LAFAVE AND ISRAEL'S MODERN CRIMINAL PROCEDURE: CASES, COMMENTS AND QUESTIONS, Sixth Edition, 1558 pages, 1986. (Casebook) (1988 Supplement)

KAMISAR, LAFAVE AND ISRAEL'S BASIC CRIMINAL PROCEDURE: CASES, COMMENTS AND QUESTIONS, Sixth Edition, 860 pages, 1986. Softcover reprint from Kamisar, et al., Modern Criminal Procedure: Cases, Comments and Questions, Sixth Edition. (Casebook) (1988 Supplement)

LAFAVE'S MODERN CRIMINAL LAW: CASES, COMMENTS AND QUESTIONS, Second Edition, 903 pages, 1988. (Casebook)

LAFAVE AND ISRAEL'S HORNBOOK ON CRIMINAL PROCEDURE, Student Edition, 1142 pages, 1985, with 1988 pocket part. (Text)

LAFAVE AND SCOTT'S HORNBOOK ON CRIMINAL LAW, Second Edition, 918 pages, 1986. (Text)

LANGBEIN'S COMPARATIVE CRIMINAL PROCEDURE: GERMANY, 172 pages, 1977. Softcover. (Casebook)

Criminal Law and Criminal Procedure—Cont'd

LOEWY'S CRIMINAL LAW IN A NUTSHELL, Second Edition, 321 pages, 1987. Softcover. (Text)

LOW'S BLACK LETTER ON CRIMINAL LAW, 433 pages, 1984. Softcover. (Review)

SALTZBURG'S CASES AND COMMENTARY ON AMERICAN CRIMINAL PROCEDURE, Third Edition, 1302 pages, 1988. Teacher's Manual available. (Casebook) (1988 Supplement)

UVILLER'S THE PROCESSES OF CRIMINAL JUSTICE: INVESTIGATION AND ADJUDICATION, Second Edition, 1384 pages, 1979. (Casebook) (1979 Statutory Supplement) (1986 Update)

VORENBERG'S CASES ON CRIMINAL LAW AND PROCEDURE, Second Edition, 1088 pages, 1981. Teacher's Manual available. (Casebook) (1987 Supplement)

Decedents' Estates—see Trusts and Estates

Domestic Relations

CLARK'S CASES AND PROBLEMS ON DOMESTIC RELATIONS, Third Edition, 1153 pages, 1980. Teacher's Manual available. (Casebook)

CLARK'S HORNBOOK ON DOMESTIC RELATIONS, Second Edition, Student Edition, 1050 pages, 1988. (Text)

KRAUSE'S BLACK LETTER ON FAMILY LAW, 314 pages, 1988. Softcover. (Review)

KRAUSE'S CASES, COMMENTS AND QUESTIONS ON FAMILY LAW, Second Edition, 1221 pages, 1983. (Casebook) (1986 Supplement)

KRAUSE'S FAMILY LAW IN A NUTSHELL, Second Edition, 444 pages, 1986. Softcover. (Text)

KRAUSKOPF'S CASES ON PROPERTY DIVISION AT MARRIAGE DISSOLUTION, 250 pages, 1984. Softcover. (Casebook)

Economics, Law and—see also Antitrust, Regulated Industries

GOETZ' CASES AND MATERIALS ON LAW AND ECONOMICS, 547 pages, 1984. (Casebook)

Education Law

ALEXANDER AND ALEXANDER'S THE LAW OF SCHOOLS, STUDENTS AND TEACHERS IN A NUTSHELL, 409 pages, 1984. Softcover. (Text)

MORRIS' THE CONSTITUTION AND AMERICAN EDUCATION, Second Edition, 992 pages, 1980. Teacher's Manual available. (Casebook)

Employment Discrimination—see also Women and the Law

JONES, MURPHY AND BELTON'S CASES AND MATERIALS ON DISCRIMINATION IN EMPLOYMENT, (The Labor Law Group). Fifth Edition, 1116 pages, 1987. (Casebook)

PLAYER'S CASES AND MATERIALS ON EMPLOYMENT DISCRIMINATION LAW, Second Edition, 782 pages, 1984. Teacher's Manual available. (Casebook)

PLAYER'S FEDERAL LAW OF EMPLOYMENT DISCRIMINATION IN A NUTSHELL, Second Edition, 402 pages, 1981. Softcover. (Text)

PLAYER'S HORNBOOK ON EMPLOYMENT DISCRIMINATION LAW, Student Edition, 708 pages, 1988. (Text)

Energy and Natural Resources Law—see also Oil and Gas

LAITOS' CASES AND MATERIALS ON NATURAL RESOURCES LAW, 938 pages, 1985. Teacher's Manual available. (Casebook)

RODGERS' CASES AND MATERIALS ON ENERGY AND NATURAL RESOURCES LAW, Second Edition, 877 pages, 1983. (Casebook)

SELECTED ENVIRONMENTAL LAW STATUTES—EDUCATIONAL EDITION. Softcover. 772 pages, 1988.

Environmental Law—see also Energy and Natural Resources Law; Sea, Law of

BONINE AND McGARITY'S THE LAW OF ENVIRONMENTAL PROTECTION: CASES—LEGISLATION—POLICIES, 1076 pages, 1984. Teacher's Manual available. (Casebook)

FINDLEY AND FARBER'S CASES AND MATERIALS ON ENVIRONMENTAL LAW, Second Edition, 813 pages, 1985. (Casebook) (1988 Supplement)

FINDLEY AND FARBER'S ENVIRONMENTAL LAW IN A NUTSHELL, Second Edition, 367 pages, 1988. Softcover. (Text)

RODGERS' HORNBOOK ON ENVIRONMENTAL LAW, 956 pages, 1977, with 1984 pocket part. (Text)

Environmental Law—Cont'd

SELECTED ENVIRONMENTAL LAW STATUTES—EDUCATIONAL EDITION. Softcover. 772 pages, 1988.

Equity—see Remedies

Estate Planning—see also Trusts and Estates; Taxation—Estate and Gift

LYNN'S AN INTRODUCTION TO ESTATE PLANNING IN A NUTSHELL, Third Edition, 370 pages, 1983. Softcover. (Text)

Evidence

BROUN AND BLAKEY'S BLACK LETTER ON EVIDENCE, 269 pages, 1984. Softcover. (Review)

BROUN, MEISENHOLDER, STRONG AND MOSTELLER'S PROBLEMS IN EVIDENCE, Third Edition, 238 pages, 1988. Teacher's Manual available. Softcover. (Coursebook)

CLEARY, STRONG, BROUN AND MOSTELLER'S CASES AND MATERIALS ON EVIDENCE, Fourth Edition, 1060 pages, 1988. (Casebook)

FEDERAL RULES OF EVIDENCE FOR UNITED STATES COURTS AND MAGISTRATES. Softcover. 378 pages, 1989.

GRAHAM'S FEDERAL RULES OF EVIDENCE IN A NUTSHELL, Second Edition, 473 pages, 1987. Softcover. (Text)

KIMBALL'S PROGRAMMED MATERIALS ON PROBLEMS IN EVIDENCE, 380 pages, 1978. Softcover. (Coursebook)

LEMPERT AND SALTZBURG'S A MODERN APPROACH TO EVIDENCE: TEXT, PROBLEMS, TRANSCRIPTS AND CASES, Second Edition, 1232 pages, 1983. Teacher's Manual available. (Casebook)

LILLY'S AN INTRODUCTION TO THE LAW OF EVIDENCE, Second Edition, 585 pages, 1987. (Text)

MCCORMICK, SUTTON AND WELLBORN'S CASES AND MATERIALS ON EVIDENCE, Sixth Edition, 1067 pages, 1987. (Casebook)

MCCORMICK'S HORNBOOK ON EVIDENCE, Third Edition, Student Edition, 1156 pages, 1984, with 1987 pocket part. (Text)

ROTHSTEIN'S EVIDENCE IN A NUTSHELL: STATE AND FEDERAL RULES, Second Edition, 514 pages, 1981. Softcover. (Text)

SALTZBURG'S EVIDENCE SUPPLEMENT: RULES,

STATUTES, COMMENTARY, 245 pages, 1980. Softcover. (Casebook Supplement)

Federal Jurisdiction and Procedure

CURRIE'S CASES AND MATERIALS ON FEDERAL COURTS, Third Edition, 1042 pages, 1982. (Casebook) (1985 Supplement)

CURRIE'S FEDERAL JURISDICTION IN A NUTSHELL, Second Edition, 258 pages, 1981. Softcover. (Text)

FEDERAL RULES OF CIVIL-APPELLATE PROCEDURE—EDUCATIONAL EDITION. Softcover. 574 pages, 1988.

FORRESTER AND MOYE'S CASES AND MATERIALS ON FEDERAL JURISDICTION AND PROCEDURE, Third Edition, 917 pages, 1977. (Casebook) (1985 Supplement)

REDISH'S BLACK LETTER ON FEDERAL JURISDICTION, 219 pages, 1985. Softcover. (Review)

REDISH'S CASES, COMMENTS AND QUESTIONS ON FEDERAL COURTS, Second Edition, 1122 pages, 1989. (Casebook)

VETRI AND MERRILL'S FEDERAL COURTS PROBLEMS AND MATERIALS, Second Edition, 232 pages, 1984. Softcover. (Coursebook)

WRIGHT'S HORNBOOK ON FEDERAL COURTS, Fourth Edition, Student Edition, 870 pages, 1983. (Text)

Foreign Relations and National Security Law

FRANCK AND GLENNON'S FOREIGN RELATIONS AND NATIONAL SECURITY LAW, 941 pages, 1987. (Casebook)

Future Interests—see Trusts and Estates

Health Law—see Medicine, Law and

Human Rights—see International Law

Immigration Law

ALEINIKOFF AND MARTIN'S IMMIGRATION PROCESS AND POLICY, 1042 pages, 1985. (Casebook) (1987 Supplement)

WEISSBRODT'S IMMIGRATION LAW AND PROCEDURE IN A NUTSHELL, 345 pages, 1984, Softcover. (Text)

Indian Law—see American Indian Law

Insurance Law

DOBBYN'S INSURANCE LAW IN A NUTSHELL,

Insurance Law—Cont'd

281 pages, 1981. Softcover. (Text)

KEETON'S CASES ON BASIC INSURANCE LAW, Second Edition, 1086 pages, 1977. Teacher's Manual available. (Casebook)

KEETON AND WIDISS' INSURANCE LAW, Student Edition, 1359 pages, 1988. (Text)

WIDISS AND KEETON'S COURSE SUPPLEMENT TO KEETON AND WIDISS' INSURANCE LAW, 502 pages, 1988. Softcover. (Casebook)

YORK AND WHELAN'S CASES, MATERIALS AND PROBLEMS ON GENERAL PRACTICE INSURANCE LAW, Second Edition, 787 pages, 1988. Teacher's Manual available. (Casebook)

International Law—see also Sea, Law of

BUERGENTHAL'S INTERNATIONAL HUMAN RIGHTS IN A NUTSHELL, 283 pages, 1988. Softcover. (Text)

BUERGENTHAL AND MAIER'S PUBLIC INTERNATIONAL LAW IN A NUTSHELL, 262 pages, 1985. Softcover. (Text)

FOLSOM, GORDON AND SPANOGLE'S INTERNATIONAL BUSINESS TRANSACTIONS—A PROBLEM-ORIENTED COURSEBOOK, 1160 pages, 1986. Teacher's Manual available. (Casebook) (Documents Supplement)

FOLSOM, GORDON AND SPANOGLE'S INTERNATIONAL BUSINESS TRANSACTIONS IN A NUTSHELL, Third Edition, 509 pages, 1988. Softcover. (Text)

HENKIN, PUGH, SCHACHTER AND SMIT'S CASES AND MATERIALS ON INTERNATIONAL LAW, Second Edition, 1517 pages, 1987. (Casebook) (Documents Supplement)

JACKSON AND DAVEY'S CASES, MATERIALS AND TEXT ON LEGAL PROBLEMS OF INTERNATIONAL ECONOMIC RELATIONS, Second Edition, 1269 pages, 1986. (Casebook) (Documents Supplement)

KIRGIS' INTERNATIONAL ORGANIZATIONS IN THEIR LEGAL SETTING, 1016 pages, 1977. Teacher's Manual available. (Casebook) (1981 Supplement)

WESTON, FALK AND D'AMATO'S INTERNATIONAL LAW AND WORLD ORDER—A PROBLEM-ORIENTED COURSEBOOK, 1195 pages, 1980. Teacher's Manual available. (Casebook) (Documents Supplement)

Interviewing and Counseling

BINDER AND PRICE'S LEGAL INTERVIEWING AND COUNSELING, 232 pages, 1977. Teacher's Manual available. Softcover. (Coursebook)

SHAFFER AND ELKINS' LEGAL INTERVIEWING AND COUNSELING IN A NUTSHELL, Second Edition, 487 pages, 1987. Softcover. (Text)

Introduction to Law—see Legal Method and Legal System

Introduction to Law Study

DOBBYN'S SO YOU WANT TO GO TO LAW SCHOOL, Revised First Edition, 206 pages, 1976. Softcover. (Text)

HEGLAND'S INTRODUCTION TO THE STUDY AND PRACTICE OF LAW IN A NUTSHELL, 418 pages, 1983. Softcover (Text)

KINYON'S INTRODUCTION TO LAW STUDY AND LAW EXAMINATIONS IN A NUTSHELL, 389 pages, 1971. Softcover. (Text)

Jurisprudence

CHRISTIE'S JURISPRUDENCE—TEXT AND READINGS ON THE PHILOSOPHY OF LAW, 1056 pages, 1973. (Casebook)

Juvenile Justice

FOX'S CASES AND MATERIALS ON MODERN JUVENILE JUSTICE, Second Edition, 960 pages, 1981. (Casebook)

FOX'S JUVENILE COURTS IN A NUTSHELL, Third Edition, 291 pages, 1984. Softcover. (Text)

Labor Law—see also Employment Discrimination, Social Legislation

GORMAN'S BASIC TEXT ON LABOR LAW— UNIONIZATION AND COLLECTIVE BARGAINING, 914 pages, 1976. (Text)

GRODIN, WOLLETT AND ALLEYNE'S COLLECTIVE BARGAINING IN PUBLIC EMPLOYMENT, (The Labor Law Group). Third Edition, 430 pages, 1979. (Casebook)

LESLIE'S LABOR LAW IN A NUTSHELL, Second Edition, 397 pages, 1986. Softcover. (Text)

NOLAN'S LABOR ARBITRATION LAW AND PRACTICE IN A NUTSHELL, 358 pages, 1979. Softcover. (Text)

Labor Law—Cont'd

OBERER, HANSLOWE, ANDERSEN AND HEINSZ' CASES AND MATERIALS ON LABOR LAW—COLLECTIVE BARGAINING IN A FREE SOCIETY, Third Edition, 1163 pages, 1986. (Casebook) (Statutory Supplement)

RABIN, SILVERSTEIN AND SCHATZKI'S LABOR AND EMPLOYMENT LAW: PROBLEMS, CASES AND MATERIALS IN THE LAW OF WORK, (The Labor Law Group). 1014 pages, 1988. Teacher's Manual available. (Casebook) (1988 Statutory Supplement)

Land Finance—Property Security—see Real Estate Transactions

Land Use

CALLIES AND FREILICH'S CASES AND MATERIALS ON LAND USE, 1233 pages, 1986. (Casebook) (1988 Supplement)

HAGMAN'S CASES ON PUBLIC PLANNING AND CONTROL OF URBAN AND LAND DEVELOPMENT, Second Edition, 1301 pages, 1980. Teacher's Manual available. (Casebook)

HAGMAN AND JUERGENSMEYER'S HORNBOOK ON URBAN PLANNING AND LAND DEVELOPMENT CONTROL LAW, Second Edition, Student Edition, 680 pages, 1986. (Text)

WRIGHT AND GITELMAN'S CASES AND MATERIALS ON LAND USE, Third Edition, 1300 pages, 1982. Teacher's Manual available. (Casebook) (1987 Supplement)

WRIGHT AND WRIGHT'S LAND USE IN A NUTSHELL, Second Edition, 356 pages, 1985. Softcover. (Text)

Legal History—see also Legal Method and Legal System

PRESSER AND ZAINALDIN'S CASES AND MATERIALS ON LAW AND AMERICAN HISTORY, 855 pages, 1980. Teacher's Manual available. (Casebook)

Legal Method and Legal System—see also Legal Research, Legal Writing

ALDISERT'S READINGS, MATERIALS AND CASES IN THE JUDICIAL PROCESS, 948 pages, 1976. (Casebook)

BERCH AND BERCH'S INTRODUCTION TO LEGAL METHOD AND PROCESS, 550 pages, 1985. Teacher's Manual available. (Casebook)

BODENHEIMER, OAKLEY AND LOVE'S READINGS AND CASES ON AN INTRODUCTION TO THE

ANGLO-AMERICAN LEGAL SYSTEM, Second Edition, 166 pages, 1988. Softcover. (Casebook)

DAVIES AND LAWRY'S INSTITUTIONS AND METHODS OF THE LAW—INTRODUCTORY TEACHING MATERIALS, 547 pages, 1982. Teacher's Manual available. (Casebook)

DVORKIN, HIMMELSTEIN AND LESNICK'S BECOMING A LAWYER: A HUMANISTIC PERSPECTIVE ON LEGAL EDUCATION AND PROFESSIONALISM, 211 pages, 1981. Softcover. (Text)

GREENBERG'S JUDICIAL PROCESS AND SOCIAL CHANGE, 666 pages, 1977. (Coursebook)

KELSO AND KELSO'S STUDYING LAW: AN INTRODUCTION, 587 pages, 1984. (Coursebook)

KEMPIN'S HISTORICAL INTRODUCTION TO ANGLO-AMERICAN LAW IN A NUTSHELL, Second Edition, 280 pages, 1973. Softcover. (Text)

MURPHY'S CASES AND MATERIALS ON INTRODUCTION TO LAW—LEGAL PROCESS AND PROCEDURE, 772 pages, 1977. (Casebook)

REYNOLDS' JUDICIAL PROCESS IN A NUTSHELL, 292 pages, 1980. Softcover. (Text)

Legal Profession

ARONSON, DEVINE AND FISCH'S PROBLEMS, CASES AND MATERIALS IN PROFESSIONAL RESPONSIBILITY, 745 pages, 1985. Teacher's Manual available. (Casebook)

ARONSON AND WECKSTEIN'S PROFESSIONAL RESPONSIBILITY IN A NUTSHELL, 399 pages, 1980. Softcover. (Text)

MELLINKOFF'S THE CONSCIENCE OF A LAWYER, 304 pages, 1973. (Text)

PIRSIG AND KIRWIN'S CASES AND MATERIALS ON PROFESSIONAL RESPONSIBILITY, Fourth Edition, 603 pages, 1984. Teacher's Manual available. (Casebook)

ROTUNDA'S BLACK LETTER ON PROFESSIONAL RESPONSIBILITY, Second Edition, 414 pages, 1988. Softcover. (Review)

RYAN'S STATING YOUR CASE: HOW TO INTERVIEW FOR A JOB AS A LAWYER, 190 pages, 1982. Softcover. (Text)

SCHWARTZ AND WYDICK'S PROBLEMS IN LEGAL ETHICS, Second Edition, 341 pages, 1988. (Coursebook)

SELECTED STATUTES, RULES AND STANDARDS ON THE LEGAL PROFESSION. Softcover. 449

Legal Profession—Cont'd

pages, 1987.

SMITH'S PREVENTING LEGAL MALPRACTICE, 142 pages, 1981. Softcover. (Text)

WOLFRAM'S HORNBOOK ON MODERN LEGAL ETHICS, Student Edition, 1120 pages, 1986. (Text)

Legal Research

COHEN'S LEGAL RESEARCH IN A NUTSHELL, Fourth Edition, 452 pages, 1985. Softcover. (Text)

COHEN AND BERRING'S HOW TO FIND THE LAW, Eighth Edition, 790 pages, 1983. (Coursebook)

Legal Research Exercises, 2nd Ed., for use with Cohen and Berring, 1986. Teacher's Manual available.

COHEN AND BERRING'S FINDING THE LAW, 600 pages, 1984. Softcover reprint from Cohen and Berring's How to Find the Law, Eighth Edition. (Coursebook)

ROMBAUER'S LEGAL PROBLEM SOLVING—ANALYSIS, RESEARCH AND WRITING, Fourth Edition, 424 pages, 1983. Teacher's Manual with problems available. (Coursebook)

STATSKY'S LEGAL RESEARCH AND WRITING, Third Edition, 252 pages, 1986. Softcover. (Coursebook)

TEPLY'S PROGRAMMED MATERIALS ON LEGAL RESEARCH AND CITATION, Second Edition, 358 pages, 1986. Softcover. (Coursebook)

Student Library Exercises, 2nd ed., 1986. Answer Key available.

Legal Writing

CHILD'S DRAFTING LEGAL DOCUMENTS: MATERIALS AND PROBLEMS, 286 pages, 1988. Softcover. Teacher's Manual available. (Coursebook)

DICKERSON'S MATERIALS ON LEGAL DRAFTING, 425 pages, 1981. Teacher's Manual available. (Coursebook)

FELSENFELD AND SIEGEL'S WRITING CONTRACTS IN PLAIN ENGLISH, 290 pages, 1981. Softcover. (Text)

GOPEN'S WRITING FROM A LEGAL PERSPECTIVE, 225 pages, 1981. (Text)

MELLINKOFF'S LEGAL WRITING—SENSE AND NONSENSE, 242 pages, 1982. Softcover.

Teacher's Manual available. (Text)

PRATT'S LEGAL WRITING: A SYSTEMATIC APPROACH, Approximately 300 pages, March, 1989 Pub. (Coursebook)

RAY AND RAMSFIELD'S LEGAL WRITING: GETTING IT RIGHT AND GETTING IT WRITTEN, 250 pages, 1987. Softcover. (Text)

SQUIRES AND ROMBAUER'S LEGAL WRITING IN A NUTSHELL, 294 pages, 1982. Softcover. (Text)

STATSKY AND WERNET'S CASE ANALYSIS AND FUNDAMENTALS OF LEGAL WRITING, Third Edition, 424 pages, 1989. (Text)

WEIHOFEN'S LEGAL WRITING STYLE, Second Edition, 332 pages, 1980. (Text)

Legislation

DAVIES' LEGISLATIVE LAW AND PROCESS IN A NUTSHELL, Second Edition, 346 pages, 1986. Softcover. (Text)

ESKRIDGE AND FRICKEY'S CASES AND MATERIALS ON LEGISLATION: STATUTES AND THE CREATION OF PUBLIC POLICY, 937 pages, 1988. Teacher's Manual available. (Casebook)

NUTTING AND DICKERSON'S CASES AND MATERIALS ON LEGISLATION, Fifth Edition, 744 pages, 1978. (Casebook)

STATSKY'S LEGISLATIVE ANALYSIS AND DRAFTING, Second Edition, 217 pages, 1984. Teacher's Manual available. (Text)

Local Government

FRUG'S CASES AND MATERIALS ON LOCAL GOVERNMENT LAW, 1005 pages, 1988. (Casebook)

MCCARTHY'S LOCAL GOVERNMENT LAW IN A NUTSHELL, Second Edition, 404 pages, 1983. Softcover. (Text)

REYNOLDS' HORNBOOK ON LOCAL GOVERNMENT LAW, 860 pages, 1982, with 1987 pocket part. (Text)

VALENTE'S CASES AND MATERIALS ON LOCAL GOVERNMENT LAW, Third Edition, 1010 pages, 1987. Teacher's Manual available. (Casebook)

Malpractice—see Medicine, Law and; Legal Profession

Mass Communication Law

GILLMOR AND BARRON'S CASES AND COMMENT

Mass Communication Law—Cont'd

ON MASS COMMUNICATION LAW, Fourth Edition, 1076 pages, 1984. Teacher's Manual available. (Casebook)

GINSBURG'S REGULATION OF BROADCASTING: LAW AND POLICY TOWARDS RADIO, TELEVISION AND CABLE COMMUNICATIONS, 741 pages, 1979 (Casebook) (1983 Supplement)

ZUCKMAN, GAYNES, CARTER AND DEE'S MASS COMMUNICATIONS LAW IN A NUTSHELL, Third Edition, 538 pages, 1988. Softcover. (Text)

Medicine, Law and

FURROW, JOHNSON, JOST AND SCHWARTZ' HEALTH LAW: CASES, MATERIALS AND PROBLEMS, 1005 pages, 1987. Teacher's Manual available. (Casebook)

KING'S THE LAW OF MEDICAL MALPRACTICE IN A NUTSHELL, Second Edition, 342 pages, 1986. Softcover. (Text)

SHAPIRO AND SPECE'S CASES, MATERIALS AND PROBLEMS ON BIOETHICS AND LAW, 892 pages, 1981. (Casebook)

SHARPE, FISCINA AND HEAD'S CASES ON LAW AND MEDICINE, 882 pages, 1978. (Casebook)

Military Law

SHANOR AND TERRELL'S MILITARY LAW IN A NUTSHELL, 378 pages, 1980. Softcover. (Text)

Mortgages—see Real Estate Transactions

Natural Resources Law—see Energy and Natural Resources Law, Environmental Law

Negotiation

EDWARDS AND WHITE'S PROBLEMS, READINGS AND MATERIALS ON THE LAWYER AS A NEGOTIATOR, 484 pages, 1977. (Casebook)

GIFFORD'S LEGAL NEGOTIATION: THEORY AND APPLICATIONS, Approximately 300 pages, March, 1989 Pub. Softcover. (Text)

PECK'S CASES AND MATERIALS ON NEGOTIATION, (The Labor Law Group). Second Edition, 280 pages, 1980. (Casebook)

WILLIAMS' LEGAL NEGOTIATION AND SETTLEMENT, 207 pages, 1983. Softcover. Teacher's Manual available. (Coursebook)

Office Practice—see also Computers and Law, Interviewing and Counseling, Negotiation

HEGLAND'S TRIAL AND PRACTICE SKILLS IN A NUTSHELL, 346 pages, 1978. Softcover (Text)

STRONG AND CLARK'S LAW OFFICE MANAGEMENT, 424 pages, 1974. (Casebook)

Oil and Gas—see also Energy and Natural Resources Law

HEMINGWAY'S HORNBOOK ON OIL AND GAS, Second Edition, Student Edition, 543 pages, 1983, with 1986 pocket part. (Text)

KUNTZ, LOWE, ANDERSON AND SMITH'S CASES AND MATERIALS ON OIL AND GAS LAW, 857 pages, 1986. Teacher's Manual available. (Casebook) (Forms Manual) Revised.

LOWE'S OIL AND GAS LAW IN A NUTSHELL, Second Edition, 465 pages, 1988. Softcover. (Text)

Partnership—see Agency—Partnership

Patent and Copyright Law

CHOATE, FRANCIS, AND COLLINS' CASES AND MATERIALS ON PATENT LAW, INCLUDING TRADE SECRETS, COPYRIGHTS, TRADEMARKS, Third Edition, 1009 pages, 1987. (Casebook)

MILLER AND DAVIS' INTELLECTUAL PROPERTY—PATENTS, TRADEMARKS AND COPYRIGHT IN A NUTSHELL, 428 pages, 1983. Softcover. (Text)

NIMMER'S CASES AND MATERIALS ON COPYRIGHT AND OTHER ASPECTS OF ENTERTAINMENT LITIGATION ILLUSTRATED—INCLUDING UNFAIR COMPETITION, DEFAMATION AND PRIVACY, Third Edition, 1025 pages, 1985. (Casebook) (1989 Supplement)

Products Liability

FISCHER AND POWERS' CASES AND MATERIALS ON PRODUCTS LIABILITY, 685 pages, 1988. Teacher's Manual available. (Casebook)

NOEL AND PHILLIPS' CASES ON PRODUCTS LIABILITY, Second Edition, 821 pages, 1982. (Casebook)

PHILLIPS' PRODUCTS LIABILITY IN A NUTSHELL, Third Edition, 307 pages, 1988. Softcover. (Text)

Property—see also Real Estate Transactions, Land Use, Trusts and Estates

BERNHARDT'S BLACK LETTER ON PROPERTY, 318 pages, 1983. Softcover. (Review)

BERNHARDT'S REAL PROPERTY IN A NUTSHELL, Second Edition, 448 pages, 1981. Softcover. (Text)

BOYER'S SURVEY OF THE LAW OF PROPERTY, Third Edition, 766 pages, 1981. (Text)

BROWDER, CUNNINGHAM AND SMITH'S CASES ON BASIC PROPERTY LAW, Fourth Edition, 1431 pages, 1984. (Casebook)

BRUCE, ELY AND BOSTICK'S CASES AND MATERIALS ON MODERN PROPERTY LAW, Second Edition, approximately 1000 pages, February 1989 Pub. Teacher's Manual available. (Casebook)

BURKE'S PERSONAL PROPERTY IN A NUTSHELL, 322 pages, 1983. Softcover. (Text)

CUNNINGHAM, STOEBUCK AND WHITMAN'S HORNBOOK ON THE LAW OF PROPERTY, Student Edition, 916 pages, 1984, with 1987 pocket part. (Text)

DONAHUE, KAUPER AND MARTIN'S CASES ON PROPERTY, Second Edition, 1362 pages, 1983. Teacher's Manual available. (Casebook)

HILL'S LANDLORD AND TENANT LAW IN A NUTSHELL, Second Edition, 311 pages, 1986. Softcover. (Text)

KURTZ AND HOVENKAMP'S CASES AND MATERIALS ON AMERICAN PROPERTY LAW, 1296 pages, 1987. Teacher's Manual available. (Casebook) (1988 Supplement)

MOYNIHAN'S INTRODUCTION TO REAL PROPERTY, Second Edition, 239 pages, 1988. (Text)

UNIFORM LAND TRANSACTIONS ACT, UNIFORM SIMPLIFICATION OF LAND TRANSFERS ACT, UNIFORM CONDOMINIUM ACT, 1977 OFFICIAL TEXT WITH COMMENTS. Softcover. 462 pages, 1978.

Psychiatry, Law and

REISNER'S LAW AND THE MENTAL HEALTH SYSTEM, CIVIL AND CRIMINAL ASPECTS, 696 pages, 1985. (Casebook) (1987 Supplement)

Real Estate Transactions

BRUCE'S REAL ESTATE FINANCE IN A NUT-SHELL, Second Edition, 262 pages, 1985. Softcover. (Text)

MAXWELL, RIESENFELD, HETLAND AND WARREN'S CASES ON CALIFORNIA SECURITY TRANSACTIONS IN LAND, Third Edition, 728 pages, 1984. (Casebook)

NELSON AND WHITMAN'S BLACK LETTER ON LAND TRANSACTIONS AND FINANCE, Second Edition, 466 pages, 1988. Softcover. (Review)

NELSON AND WHITMAN'S CASES ON REAL ESTATE TRANSFER, FINANCE AND DEVELOPMENT, Third Edition, 1184 pages, 1987. (Casebook)

NELSON AND WHITMAN'S HORNBOOK ON REAL ESTATE FINANCE LAW, Second Edition, 941 pages, 1985 with 1989 pocket part. (Text)

OSBORNE'S CASES AND MATERIALS ON SECURED TRANSACTIONS, 559 pages, 1967. (Casebook)

Regulated Industries—see also Mass Communication Law, Banking Law

GELLHORN AND PIERCE'S REGULATED INDUSTRIES IN A NUTSHELL, Second Edition, 389 pages, 1987. Softcover. (Text)

MORGAN, HARRISON AND VERKUIL'S CASES AND MATERIALS ON ECONOMIC REGULATION OF BUSINESS, Second Edition, 666 pages, 1985. (Casebook)

Remedies

DOBBS' HORNBOOK ON REMEDIES, 1067 pages, 1973. (Text)

DOBBS' PROBLEMS IN REMEDIES. 137 pages, 1974. Teacher's Manual available. Softcover. (Coursebook)

DOBBYN'S INJUNCTIONS IN A NUTSHELL, 264 pages, 1974. Softcover. (Text)

FRIEDMAN'S CONTRACT REMEDIES IN A NUTSHELL, 323 pages, 1981. Softcover. (Text)

LEAVELL, LOVE AND NELSON'S CASES AND MATERIALS ON EQUITABLE REMEDIES, RESTITUTION AND DAMAGES, Fourth Edition, 1111 pages, 1986. Teacher's Manual available. (Casebook)

MCCORMICK'S HORNBOOK ON DAMAGES, 811 pages, 1935. (Text)

O'CONNELL'S REMEDIES IN A NUTSHELL, Second Edition, 320 pages, 1985. Softcover. (Text)

Remedies—Cont'd

YORK, BAUMAN AND RENDLEMAN'S CASES AND MATERIALS ON REMEDIES, Fourth Edition, 1029 pages, 1985. Teacher's Manual available. (Casebook)

Sea, Law of

SOHN AND GUSTAFSON'S THE LAW OF THE SEA IN A NUTSHELL, 264 pages, 1984. Softcover. (Text)

Securities Regulation

HAZEN'S HORNBOOK ON THE LAW OF SECURITIES REGULATION, Student Edition, 739 pages, 1985, with 1988 pocket part. (Text)

RATNER'S MATERIALS ON SECURITIES REGULATION, Third Edition, 1000 pages, 1986. Teacher's Manual available. (Casebook) (1989 Supplement)

See Selected Securities and Business Planning Statutes

RATNER'S SECURITIES REGULATION IN A NUTSHELL, Third Edition, 316 pages, 1988. Softcover. (Text)

SELECTED SECURITIES AND BUSINESS PLANNING STATUTES, RULES AND FORMS. Softcover. 493 pages, 1987.

Social Legislation

HOOD AND HARDY'S WORKERS' COMPENSATION AND EMPLOYEE PROTECTION IN A NUTSHELL, 274 pages, 1984. Softcover. (Text)

LaFRANCE'S WELFARE LAW: STRUCTURE AND ENTITLEMENT IN A NUTSHELL, 455 pages, 1979. Softcover. (Text)

MALONE, PLANT AND LITTLE'S CASES ON WORKERS' COMPENSATION AND EMPLOYMENT RIGHTS, Second Edition, 951 pages, 1980. Teacher's Manual available. (Casebook)

Sports Law

SCHUBERT, SMITH AND TRENTADUE'S SPORTS LAW, 395 pages, 1986. (Text)

Tax Practice and Procedure

GARBIS, STRUNTZ AND RUBIN'S CASES AND MATERIALS ON TAX PROCEDURE AND TAX FRAUD, Second Edition, 687 pages, 1987. (Casebook)

Taxation—Corporate

KAHN AND GANN'S CORPORATE TAXATION AND TAXATION OF PARTNERSHIPS AND PART-

NERS, Second Edition, 1204 pages, 1985. Teacher's Manual available. (Casebook)

WEIDENBRUCH AND BURKE'S FEDERAL INCOME TAXATION OF CORPORATIONS AND STOCKHOLDERS IN A NUTSHELL, Third Edition, approximately 325 pages, 1989. Softcover. (Text)

Taxation—Estate & Gift—see also Estate Planning, Trusts and Estates

McNULTY'S FEDERAL ESTATE AND GIFT TAXATION IN A NUTSHELL, Fourth Edition, approximately 479 pages, 1989. Softcover. (Text)

PENNELL'S CASES AND MATERIALS ON INCOME TAXATION OF TRUSTS, ESTATES, GRANTORS AND BENEFICIARIES, 460 pages, 1987. Teacher's Manual available. (Casebook)

Taxation—Individual

DODGE'S CASES AND MATERIALS ON FEDERAL INCOME TAXATION, 820 pages, 1985. Teacher's Manual available. (Casebook)

GUNN AND WARD'S CASES, TEXT AND PROBLEMS ON FEDERAL INCOME TAXATION, Second Edition, 835 pages, 1988. Teacher's Manual available. (Casebook)

HUDSON AND LIND'S BLACK LETTER ON FEDERAL INCOME TAXATION, Second Edition, 396 pages, 1987. Softcover. (Review)

KRAGEN AND McNULTY'S CASES AND MATERIALS ON FEDERAL INCOME TAXATION—INDIVIDUALS, CORPORATIONS, PARTNERSHIPS, Fourth Edition, 1287 pages, 1985. (Casebook)

McNULTY'S FEDERAL INCOME TAXATION OF INDIVIDUALS IN A NUTSHELL, Fourth Edition, 503 pages, 1988. Softcover. (Text)

POSIN'S HORNBOOK ON FEDERAL INCOME TAXATION, Student Edition, 491 pages, 1983, with 1987 pocket part. (Text)

ROSE AND CHOMMIE'S HORNBOOK ON FEDERAL INCOME TAXATION, Third Edition, 923 pages, 1988. (Text)

SELECTED FEDERAL TAXATION STATUTES AND REGULATIONS. Softcover. 1519 pages, 1989.

SOLOMON AND HESCH'S PROBLEMS, CASES AND MATERIALS ON FEDERAL INCOME TAXATION OF INDIVIDUALS, 1068 pages, 1987. Teacher's Manual available. (Casebook)

Taxation—International

KAPLAN'S FEDERAL TAXATION OF INTERNATIONAL TRANSACTIONS: PRINCIPLES, PLANNING AND POLICY, 635 pages, 1988. (Casebook)

Taxation—Partnership

BERGER AND WIEDENBECK'S CASES AND MATERIALS ON PARTNERSHIP TAXATION, Approximately 800 pages, 1989. (Casebook)

Taxation—State & Local

GELFAND AND SALSICH'S STATE AND LOCAL TAXATION AND FINANCE IN A NUTSHELL, 309 pages, 1986. Softcover. (Text)

HELLERSTEIN AND HELLERSTEIN'S CASES AND MATERIALS ON STATE AND LOCAL TAXATION, Fifth Edition, 1071 pages, 1988. (Casebook)

Torts—see also Products Liability

CHRISTIE'S CASES AND MATERIALS ON THE LAW OF TORTS, 1264 pages, 1983. (Casebook)

DOBBS' TORTS AND COMPENSATION—PERSONAL ACCOUNTABILITY AND SOCIAL RESPONSIBILITY FOR INJURY, 955 pages, 1985. Teacher's Manual available. (Casebook)

KEETON, KEETON, SARGENTICH AND STEINER'S CASES AND MATERIALS ON TORT AND ACCIDENT LAW, 1360 pages, 1983. (Casebook)

KIONKA'S BLACK LETTER ON TORTS, 339 pages, 1988. Softcover. (Review)

KIONKA'S TORTS IN A NUTSHELL: INJURIES TO PERSONS AND PROPERTY, 434 pages, 1977. Softcover. (Text)

MALONE'S TORTS IN A NUTSHELL: INJURIES TO FAMILY, SOCIAL AND TRADE RELATIONS, 358 pages, 1979. Softcover. (Text)

PROSSER AND KEETON'S HORNBOOK ON TORTS, Fifth Edition, Student Edition, 1286 pages, 1984 with 1988 pocket part. (Text)

ROBERTSON, POWERS AND ANDERSON'S CASES AND MATERIALS ON TORTS, Approximately 1000 pages, April, 1989 Pub. Teacher's Manual available. (Casebook)

Trade Regulation—see also Antitrust, Regulated Industries

MCMANIS' UNFAIR TRADE PRACTICES IN A NUTSHELL, Second Edition, 464 pages, 1988. Softcover. (Text)

OPPENHEIM, WESTON, MAGGS AND SCHECHTER'S CASES AND MATERIALS ON UNFAIR TRADE PRACTICES AND CONSUMER PROTECTION, Fourth Edition, 1038 pages, 1983. (Casebook) (1986 Supplement)

SCHECHTER'S BLACK LETTER ON UNFAIR TRADE PRACTICES, 272 pages, 1986. Softcover. (Review)

Trial and Appellate Advocacy—see also Civil Procedure

APPELLATE ADVOCACY, HANDBOOK OF, Second Edition, 182 pages, 1986. Softcover. (Text)

BERGMAN'S TRIAL ADVOCACY IN A NUTSHELL, 402 pages, 1979. Softcover. (Text)

BINDER AND BERGMAN'S FACT INVESTIGATION: FROM HYPOTHESIS TO PROOF, 354 pages, 1984. Teacher's Manual available. (Coursebook)

CARLSON AND IMWINKELRIED'S DYNAMICS OF TRIAL PRACTICE: PROBLEMS AND MATERIALS, Approximately 800 pages, March 1989 Pub. Teacher's Manual available. (Coursebook)

GOLDBERG'S THE FIRST TRIAL (WHERE DO I SIT? WHAT DO I SAY?) IN A NUTSHELL, 396 pages, 1982. Softcover. (Text)

HAYDOCK, HERR, AND STEMPEL'S FUNDAMENTALS OF PRE-TRIAL LITIGATION, 768 pages, 1985. Softcover. Teacher's Manual available. (Coursebook)

HEGLAND'S TRIAL AND PRACTICE SKILLS IN A NUTSHELL, 346 pages, 1978. Softcover. (Text)

HORNSTEIN'S APPELLATE ADVOCACY IN A NUTSHELL, 325 pages, 1984. Softcover. (Text)

JEANS' HANDBOOK ON TRIAL ADVOCACY, Student Edition, 473 pages, 1975. Softcover. (Text)

MARTINEAU'S CASES AND MATERIALS ON APPELLATE PRACTICE AND PROCEDURE, 565 pages, 1987. (Casebook)

MCELHANEY'S EFFECTIVE LITIGATION, 457 pages, 1974. (Casebook)

NOLAN'S CASES AND MATERIALS ON TRIAL PRACTICE, 518 pages, 1981. (Casebook)

SONSTENG, HAYDOCK AND BOYD'S THE TRI-

Trial and Appellate Advocacy—Cont'd

ALBOOK: A TOTAL SYSTEM FOR PREPARATION AND PRESENTATION OF A CASE, 404 pages, 1984. Softcover. (Coursebook)

Trusts and Estates

ATKINSON'S HORNBOOK ON WILLS, Second Edition, 975 pages, 1953. (Text)

AVERILL'S UNIFORM PROBATE CODE IN A NUTSHELL, Second Edition, 454 pages, 1987. Softcover. (Text)

BOGERT'S HORNBOOK ON TRUSTS, Sixth Edition, Student Edition, 794 pages, 1987. (Text)

CLARK, LUSKY AND MURPHY'S CASES AND MATERIALS ON GRATUITOUS TRANSFERS, Third Edition, 970 pages, 1985. (Casebook)

DODGE'S WILLS, TRUSTS AND ESTATE PLANNING–LAW AND TAXATION, CASES AND MATERIALS, 665 pages, 1988. (Casebook)

KURTZ' PROBLEMS, CASES AND OTHER MATERIALS ON FAMILY ESTATE PLANNING, 853 pages, 1983. Teacher's Manual available. (Casebook)

MCGOVERN'S CASES AND MATERIALS ON WILLS, TRUSTS AND FUTURE INTERESTS: AN INTRODUCTION TO ESTATE PLANNING, 750 pages, 1983. (Casebook)

MCGOVERN, KURTZ AND REIN'S HORNBOOK ON WILLS, TRUSTS AND ESTATES–INCLUDING TAXATION AND FUTURE INTERESTS, 996 pages, 1988. (Text)

MENNELL'S WILLS AND TRUSTS IN A NUTSHELL, 392 pages, 1979. Softcover. (Text)

SIMES' HORNBOOK ON FUTURE INTERESTS,

Second Edition, 355 pages, 1966. (Text)

TURANO AND RADIGAN'S HORNBOOK ON NEW YORK ESTATE ADMINISTRATION, 676 pages, 1986. (Text)

UNIFORM PROBATE CODE, OFFICIAL TEXT WITH COMMENTS. 578 pages, 1987. Softcover.

WAGGONER'S FUTURE INTERESTS IN A NUTSHELL, 361 pages, 1981. Softcover. (Text)

WATERBURY'S MATERIALS ON TRUSTS AND ESTATES, 1039 pages, 1986. Teacher's Manual available. (Casebook)

Water Law—see also Energy and Natural Resources Law, Environmental Law

GETCHES' WATER LAW IN A NUTSHELL, 439 pages, 1984. Softcover. (Text)

SAX AND ABRAMS' LEGAL CONTROL OF WATER RESOURCES: CASES AND MATERIALS, 941 pages, 1986. (Casebook)

TRELEASE AND GOULD'S CASES AND MATERIALS ON WATER LAW, Fourth Edition, 816 pages, 1986. (Casebook)

Wills—see Trusts and Estates

Women and the Law—see also Employment Discrimination

KAY'S TEXT, CASES AND MATERIALS ON SEX–BASED DISCRIMINATION, Third Edition, 1001 pages, 1988. (Casebook)

THOMAS' SEX DISCRIMINATION IN A NUTSHELL, 399 pages, 1982. Softcover. (Text)

Workers' Compensation—see Social Legislation

WEST'S LAW SCHOOL
ADVISORY BOARD

JOHN A. BAUMAN
Professor of Law, University of California, Los Angeles

CURTIS J. BERGER
Professor of Law, Columbia University

JESSE H. CHOPER
Dean and Professor of Law,
University of California, Berkeley

DAVID P. CURRIE
Professor of Law, University of Chicago

DAVID G. EPSTEIN
Dean and Professor of Law, Emory University

YALE KAMISAR
Professor of Law, University of Michigan

MARY KAY KANE
Professor of Law, University of California,
Hastings College of the Law

WAYNE R. LaFAVE
Professor of Law, University of Illinois

RICHARD C. MAXWELL
Professor of Law, Duke University

ARTHUR R. MILLER
Professor of Law, Harvard University

JAMES J. WHITE
Professor of Law, University of Michigan

CHARLES ALAN WRIGHT
Professor of Law, University of Texas

*

ADMINISTRATIVE LAW

THE AMERICAN PUBLIC LAW SYSTEM

CASES AND MATERIALS

Second Edition

Jerry L. Mashaw

William Nelson Cromwell Professor
Yale Law School

Richard A. Merrill

Dean and Daniel Caplin Professor
University of Virginia Law School

AMERICAN CASEBOOK SERIES

WEST PUBLISHING CO.
ST. PAUL, MINN., 1985

COPYRIGHT © 1975 By WEST PUBLISHING CO.
COPYRIGHT © 1985 By WEST PUBLISHING CO.
                              50 West Kellogg Boulevard
                              P.O. Box 43526
                              St. Paul, Minnesota 55164

Library of Congress Cataloging in Publication Data
Mashaw, Jerry L.
  Cases and materials on administrative law.

  (American casebook series)
  Rev. ed. of: Introduction to the American public law
system. 1975.
  Includes index.
  1. Administrative law—United States—Cases. 2. Public
law—United States—Cases. I. Merrill, Richard A.
II. Mashaw, Jerry L. Introduction to the American public
law system. III. Title. IV. Series.
KF5402.A4M35 1985   342.73'066   84–27068
ISBN 0–314–87702–9   347.30266

M. & M.—Cs. & Mats. on Admin.Law, 2d Ed. ACB
1st Reprint—1989

*For Jay and Mark
and for Patty and John*

*

Preface to the
Second Edition

When the first edition of these materials appeared a decade ago, under a different title, the Preface * discussed the authors' two major aims:

First, we wanted a casebook that combined functional analysis of specific administrative programs with conceptual analysis of administrative law doctrine. As a matter of pedagogy we were convinced (1) that conceptualism without context was an arid exercise but also (2) that examination of specific questions of administrative policy or procedure must be informed by understanding of the broader issues of legality and institutional legitimation that traditionally have defined the field of administrative law. We thus struck a compromise between organization by doctrinal category and organization by case study of agency tasks or functions. This "compromise" was not so schizophrenic as it may sound. Case studies presented doctrinal issues, and doctrinal analysis of particular legal concepts could often be pursued through cases reviewing the actions of a single agency.

Our second objective was to "contextualize" administrative law itself. This purpose was pursued in two different ways. First, we wanted to expose the student to the intimate connection between administrative and legislative action. We saw the administrative lawyer operating in a world of statutes, whose creator, the Congress, perceived administration to be largely an extension of legislation. Some sophisticated awareness of legislation and legislative process, therefore, seemed essential to understanding the administrative process, and we accordingly devoted three chapters primarily to issues of statutory creation and design and legislative oversight of program implementation.

Second, we thought it important to pursue linkages between those remedial issues that have formed so large a part of the traditional study of federal administrative law (standing, reviewability, governmental and official immunities, primary jurisdiction, and the like) and the broader remedial system that further defines the citizen's bundle of rights in the modern administrative state. Private rights and public law have many points of contact and continuous reciprocal influence, intersections that previously had been ignored by administrative law texts. The first edition, thus, added materials on implied rights of action under federal statutes, on regulatory supercession of

---

* An edited version of the original, omitting descriptive materials that are no longer relevant, is reproduced below.

the common law, and on actions based on 42 U.S.C. § 1983 to the standard doctrinal fare of judicial remedies against administrators. Perhaps carried away by the breadth and novelty of our approach, we titled the first edition an "Introduction to the American Public Law System."

Major changes have taken place in the general arena of federal administrative law since 1975. The apparent enthusiasm of the 1960's and early 1970's for federal regulation as a strategy of social management, with prescriptive administrative rulemaking as its primary legal technique, has abated. It has been replaced by demands for deregulation and for the use of market-like regulatory incentives. Central executive oversight has assumed increased importance as cost-benefit analysis has been institutionalized within agencies and made subject to the supervision of the Office of Management and Budget. The ambitious proceduralist impulses of the Court of Appeals for the District of Columbia Circuit have been sharply constrained by a Supreme Court, which is reluctant either to "constitutionalize" administrative procedure or to exercise a creative interpretive role in its development. An emerging federal common law of remedies "implied" under federal regulatory statutes has yielded to renewed concern for primary administrative jurisdiction and for the prerogatives of both Congress and the states. Separation of powers doctrine has experienced a reinvigoration few would have predicted.

These developments have not, however, caused us to reject the fundamental orientation of the first edition in preparing this volume. Revised ideas, different emphases, and new primary legal materials are abundant in this edition, but many are basically variations on prior themes. The most significant structural changes are the abbreviation of the materials on legislation and the legislative process and the addition of a new chapter on "Executive Supervision of Administrative Action." These changes recognize that we had originally provided more legislative materials than most instructors could (or wanted to) use and less on the role of the Chief Executive (and Executive Office staff) than contemporary developments warranted.

Thus, while reorganized (twelve chapters have been reduced to eight), updated, and in some instances featuring different illustrations, the second edition owes much to the pedagogic and substantive convictions of the first. Two interstitial novelties are nevertheless worth noting. The first is more frequent reference to, and occasional use of, materials from related disciplines—particularly political science, organization theory, and public choice theory. The past decade has witnessed a remarkable outpouring of literature in these fields that is of interest to administrative lawyers. Second, we have attempted to give greater emphasis to the informal processes of agencies than in the first edition—to questions of internal organization, routine, staffing and departmental location that subtly yet powerfully influence the realities of administration and, therefore, the operational meaning of administrative law.

J.L.M.
R.A.M.

New Haven, Conn.,
and Charlottesville, Va.,
May, 1985

*

Preface to the
First Edition

The core of these materials is a course-book on administrative law. . . .

Within this compass teachers of administrative law will find much that is familiar. We have attempted to include, or at least discuss, most of what can be described as the "standard" administrative law cases. Teachers will also find special emphasis devoted to issues that the editors consider to be of growing contemporary importance, e.g., procedural and substantive limitations on agency rulemaking and judicial remedies for administrative inaction. Furthermore, the materials reflect a consistent attention to the functional implications of administrative procedure. We are persistently asking what difference it makes—for agency power, for efficient governmental operation, for the protection of private interests, or for the preservation of democratic values and the rule of law—that administrative action is accomplished in a particular fashion. . . .

While we are concerned with function, however, we are simultaneously attentive to concept. The lawyer who will deal with administrative bodies as dissimilar as the Federal Environmental Protection Agency and the local building inspector requires an intellectual framework in which to order the random pieces of administrative law material that are cast his way. Accordingly, our functional analysis of administrative procedure goes on primarily in the setting of materials organized in accordance with traditional conceptual categories. . . .

Supplying a functionally oriented, contemporary course book on administrative law, however, is a subordinate part of our purpose in assembling this text. Our larger and primary aim is to begin an integration of administrative law into the larger fabric of the legal order. This objective is approached in two ways.

First, the materials attempt to integrate analysis of the administrative process with ways of thinking about the legislative process. Administrative law practitioners would probably agree that the separation of the study of legislation and the legislative process from the study of administrative law is artificial and unsatisfactory. Administrative law deals with the pursuit of objectives defined with various degrees of precision by statutes, and most contemporary statutes rely primarily on administrative implementation to achieve legislated objectives. Moreover, the functional relationship between legislatures and administrative agencies is often close. Much legislation, or the occasion for its adoption, is generated by existing administrative bodies. And many policies developed in the implementation of statutes are inspired by legislative oversight committees. The lawyer who fails to perceive the administrative process as an extension of the process of legislation, or to recognize the constraints placed upon legislative action by the necessity of devising methods of implementation that comport with governing principles of administrative law, has only a partial understanding of either subject. Many traditional concepts of administrative law, e.g., judicial review of the sufficiency of standards and procedures for administrative action, can as easily be viewed as constraints on the exercise of legislative power as limits on administrative process.

Furthermore, viewing administrative action as an extension of the legislative process affords distinct advantages. This perspective sharpens issues of the appropriate role of courts in reviewing the legality of legislative and administrative policies. For example, courts confronted with legislative action demand only the barest showing of the rationality of the legislature's judgments and seem largely indifferent to the regularity of the process by which legislation was produced. Yet when administrators make policy, judges increasingly demand empiric justification and insist upon procedural regularity. Can these sharply divergent legal and political postures be justified? If not, around which model of review should further judicial development coalesce?

Much current ferment in administrative law is related to this fundamental issue of appropriate legal controls over legislative action. For example, the power (and in some contexts the duty) of administrative bodies to adopt "legislative" rules has become a point of controversy in recent years. Recognition that ubiquitous administrators are not mere appliers of law, but are in important ways "legislators", heightens awareness of the implications of conferring legislative power and provides a fresh perspective on judicial attempts to find an appropriate posture from which to review administrative legislation. Should courts circumscribe explicit, and reject implicit, administrative rulemaking authority in order to curb the political power of the administrative state? Or should they welcome attempts to frame general policy as clarifying and thereby making fairer administrative controls that would otherwise emerge through adjudication or informal action? Should courts attempt to impose procedural safeguards for administrative rulemaking that are to substitute for the political accountability of the legislature? Or should they acknowledge that familiar safeguards, usually derived from the judicial model, often produce a form of proceeding that can stifle effective development of policy?

As the preceding questions suggest, our view is that courses in administrative law should increasingly be courses in "legal civics," and we have therefore assembled materials that emphasize the relationship between administrative and legislative functions . . .

The second organizing idea for these materials is that the public law system—the institutional structure that defines the legal relationship of citizens with their government—shares important points of connection, reenforcement, and tension with the private law system. First, public law often represents an attempt to solve private law problems, a phenomenon that is illustrated by our opening case study of the 1899 Rivers and Harbors Act. The development of a statutory and regulatory regime employing criminal sanctions, forfeitures, and licenses was a response to the inadequacy of the private law of nuisance, or, more correctly, filled a gap created by the absence of a private common law of nuisance at the federal level.

Second, to the extent that public law institutions have been empowered to resolve or manage aspects of social conduct, a citizen's concern will shift from the direct pursuit of remedies against other private parties who interfere with the accomplishment of his desires, to the availability of remedies for government interference with his plans or government failure to protect his legitimate expectations. For example, given public regulation of water quality, an entrepreneur who proposes to discharge waste into a navigable waterway may perceive his legal situation not as one in which he must attempt to make acceptable arrangements with downstream users or forestall their lawsuits, but as one in which he must negotiate acceptable discharge permit conditions with the responsible government agency. Similarly, parties desiring to avoid or prevent damaging discharges may look to the agency, rather than to the private law of property or tort, for protection of their interests. Thus there inevitably emerges a system of rights and remedies that citizens possess vis-a-vis public officers and institutions. This remedial side of public law has developed rapidly in recent years as both courts and the Congress have perceived the need for legal protection of interests created or affected by an increasingly interventionist governmental system. Remedies in the public law system are examined primarily in Chapters 10 and 11, which treat actions for compensation based on the Constitution, statutes, or common law and non-compensatory suits to review the legality of governmental action or inaction.

Third, public law may alter the rights and remedies private citizens have against each other. Among the general questions raised in this area of conjunction, two warrant particular attention: (1) To what extent do standards of conduct established by public regulatory legislation give rise to private remedies for their breach? (2) To what extent does the enactment of a system of governmental remedies for violation of statutory standards indicate the abolition or migitation of pre-existing private remedies for the same conduct? Analysis of these questions requires an appreciation, not only of traditional approaches to harmonization of statutory and common law, but also of the role of discretionary enforcement and of controls over that discretion in the public law system generally.

Our aim then, is to provide the student with materials that illustrate the major facets of what has come to be called "Administrative Law" and to locate that collection of legal issues within the broader context of a general concern with public decision processes and legal remedies in the administrative state. Our central conception is that administrative law should not be studied as a separate and narrow segment of the legal order. Rather, the proliferating activities of administrators and agencies define the arena in which fundamental issues of institutional interrelationship and of political legitimacy in the American legal system increasingly are focused and, for better or worse, resolved.

J.L.M.
R.A.M.

Charlottesville, Virginia
May, 1975

Acknowledgements

We gratefully acknowledge our debt to the pioneer teachers of administrative law, Professors Walter Gellhorn and Clark Byse, Louis Jaffe and Nathanial Nathanson, and Kenneth Culp Davis. We also thank numerous colleagues, at our own and other schools, who contributed to the preparation of these materials through criticism, suggestion, and classroom use.

The list of University of Virginia and Yale law students who assisted us during the life of the project is long. Many who have been exposed in class to earlier versions have contributed by calling our attention to errors of both substance and style, by supplying answers to questions that demand many minds to resolve, and by suggesting the issues that should be examined. During preparation of the first edition six research assistants struggled with us through proofreading, cite-checking, and occasional periods of despair: Anne MacClintock, Christopher Kennedy, Alvin Lorman, David Baker, Rob Hawkins, and Mac Norton, all from the University of Virginia. The roster of student collaborators on this second edition includes, from Yale, Lynn Baker, Mark Barnes, Peter Benda, Victor Diaz, Daniel Esty, and Peter Swire; and from Virginia, Roland DuBois, Vernon Dunbar, Kevin Gallagher, Kathy Hess, and Janet Mahairas Pollan (officially of New York University Law School), in addition to James Ritter, whom we thank specially for preparing the index. To all these we express our deep appreciation.

Finally, we express our appreciation to Diane Moss and her splendid staff for typing revisions too numerous to recall.

None of the foregoing friends and supporters, nor others unnamed, bear responsibility for any errors that remain in the final product or, of course, for its underlying concept. We acknowledge with appreciation the following authors, publishers, and journals which have generously granted permission to reprint excerpts from their publications:

(1) Arizona Law Review: Rosenberg, *Presidential Control of Agency Rulemaking*, 23 Ariz.L.Rev. 1199 (1981). Copyright © 1981 by the Arizona Board of Regents. Reprinted by permission.

(2) Boston University Law Review: Mashaw, *Administrative Due Process: The Quest for a Dignitary Theory*, 61 Boston U.L.Rev. 885 (1981).

(3) Brigham Young University Law Review: Orme, *Tucker Act Jurisdiction Over Breach of Trust Claims*, 1979 B.Y.U.L.Rev. 855.

(4) The Brookings Institution: S. MELNICK, REGULATION AND THE COURTS (1983); L. LAVE, THE STRATEGY OF SOCIAL REGULATION: DECISION FRAMEWORKS FOR POLICY (1981). Copyright © 1981 and 1983, by the Brookings Institution, Washington, D.C.

(5) California Law Review: Hamilton, *Procedures for the Adoption of Rules of General Applicability: The Need for Procedural Innovation in Administrative Rulemaking,* 60 Calif.L.Rev. 1276 (1972). Copyright © 1972, California Law Review, Inc.

(6) Columbia Law Review: Strauss, *Rules, Adjudications, and Other Sources of Law in an Executive Department: Reflections on the Interior Department's Administration of the Mining Law,* 74 Colum.L.Rev. 1231 (1974). Copyright © 1974 by the Directors for the Columbia Law Review Association, Inc. All rights reserved.

(7) Environmental Law: Rodgers, *Judicial Review of Risk Assessments: The Role of Decision Theory in Unscrambling the Benzene Decision,* 11 Environ.L. 301 (1981).

(8) Federal Law Review: Robinson, *Access to Government Information: The American Experience,* 14 Federal L.Rev. 35 (1983).

(9) Georgetown Law Journal: Harter, *Negotiating Regulations: A Cure for Malaise,* 71 Geo.L.J. 1 (1982); Note, *Drug Efficacy and the 1962 Drug Amendments,* 60 Geo.L.J. 185 (1971). Reprinted with the permission of The Georgetown Law Journal Association.

(10) Harvard Journal on Legislation: Klonoff, *The Congressman as Mediator Between Citizens and Government Agencies: Problems and Prospects,* 16 Harv.J.Legis. 701 (1979).

(11) Harvard Law Review: Scott, *Standing in the Supreme Court—A Functional Analysis,* 86 Harv.L.Rev. 645 (1973); Note, *The Irrebuttable Presumption Doctrine in the Supreme Court,* 87 Harv.L.Rev. 1534 (1974). Copyright © 1973 and 1974 by the Harvard Law Review Association.

(12) Michigan Law Review: Boyer, *Alternatives to Administrative Trial-Type Hearings for Resolving Complex Scientific, Economic, and Social Issues,* 71 Mich.L.Rev. 111 (1972); Burt, *Forcing Protection on Children and Their Parents: The Impact of Wyman v. James,* 69 Mich.L.Rev. 1259 (1971); Rosenberg, *Beyond the Limits of Executive Power: Presidential Control of Agency Rulemaking Under Executive Order 12,291,* 80 Mich.L.Rev. 193 (1981).

(13) National Center for Administrative Justice: J. NYNART & M. CARROW, Els., LAW AND SCIENCE IN COLLABORATION (1983). Copyright © by Lexington Books.

(14) Northwestern University Law Review: Fuchs, *Development and Diversification in Administrative Rule Making,* 72

Nw.U.L.Rev. 83 (1977). Reprinted by permission of the Northwestern University Law Review, © by Northwestern School of Law.

(15) Oklahoma Law Review: Sax, *The Unhappy Truth About NEPA*, 26 Okla.L.Rev. 239 (1973). Reprinted with permission of Oklahoma Law Review © 1973.

(16) Political Science Quarterly: Fisher, *A Political Context for Legislative Vetoes*, 93 Pol.Sci.Q. 241 (1978).

(17) The Public Interest: Bardach and Pugliaresi, *The Environmental Impact Statement vs. The Real World*, The Public Interest, Fall 1977.

(18) Regulation: Scalia, *The Legislative Veto: A False Remedy for System Overload*, 3 Regulation 19 (Nov./Dec. 1979); Scalia, *The Freedom of Information Act Has No Clothes*, 6 Regulation 14 (Mar./Apr. 1982). Reprinted with permission of the American Enterprise Institute.

(19) Supreme Court Review: Karl, *Executive Reorganization and Presidential Power*, 1977 Sup.Ct.Rev. 1; Scalia, *Vermont Yankee: The APA, the D.C. Circuit, and the Supreme Court*, 1978 Sup.Ct.Rev. 345; Winter, *Judicial Review of Agency Decisions: The Labor Board and the Court*, 1968 Sup.Ct.Rev. 53. Reprinted with permission of the University of Chicago Press.

(20) Tulane Law Review: Mashaw, *Constitutional Deregulation: Notes Toward a Public, Public Law*, 54 Tul.L.Rev. 849 (1980).

(21) University of California Press: J. PRESSMAN & A. WILDARSKY, IMPLEMENTATION (2d ed. 1981).

(22) University of Chicago Law Review: Davis, *The Liberalized Law of Standing*, 37 U.Chi.L.Rev. 450 (1970); Mashaw, *The Supreme Court's Due Process Calculus for Administrative Adjudication in Mathews v. Eldridge: Three Factors in Search of a Theory of Value*, 44 U.Chi.L.Rev. 28 (1976).

(23) University of Colorado Law Review: Engdahl, *Immunity and Accountability for Positive Governmental Wrongs*, 44 U.Colo.L.Rev. 1 (1972).

(24) University of Pennsylvania Law Review: Robinson, *The Making of Administrative Policy: Another Look at Rulemaking and Adjudication and Administrative Procedure Reform*, 118 U.Pa.L.Rev. 485 (1970).

(25) Virginia Law Review: Robinson, *The Federal Communications Commission: An Essay on Regulatory Watchdogs*, 64 Va.L.Rev. 169 (1978).

(26) The Washington Post: Vaughan, *Our Government Stymies Open Government*, The Washington Post (July 1, 1984).

(27) W.W. Norton and Company, Inc.: T. LOWI, THE END OF LIBERALISM (1969).

(28) Yale Law Journal: Diver, *The Optimal Precision of Administrative Rules*, 93 Yale L.J. 65 (1983); Bernstein, *The NLRB's Adjudication-Rule Making Dilemma Under the Administrative Procedure Act*, 79 Yale L.J. 571 (1970); Pedersen, *Formal Records and Informal Rulemaking*, 85 Yale L.J. 38 (1975). Reprinted by permission of The Yale Law Journal and Fred B. Rothman & Company.

(29) Yale University Press: J. MASHAW, BUREAUCRATIC JUSTICE (1983).

Summary of Contents

	Page
Preface to Second Edition	xvii
Preface to First Edition	xxi
Acknowledgements	xxv
Table of Cases	xxxix

PART I. POLITICAL CONTROL OF ADMINISTRATION

Chapter 1. The Legislative Connection 2
A. Statutory Vagueness and Its Antidotes 2
B. Pervasive Methods of Legislative Control 48
C. Statutory Precision and Its Consequences 83

Chapter 2. Executive Supervision of Administrative Action 110
A. Appointment and Removal of Officers 112
B. Executive Direction of Agency Policy 132

PART II. ADMINISTRATIVE PROCEDURE AND JUDICIAL OVERSIGHT

Chapter 3. Formal Agency Adjudication 174
A. The Right to Trial-Type Hearings 176
B. Bureaucratic Decisionmaking and Formal Adjudication 224
C. Judicial Review of Agency Adjudication 250
D. Avoiding Formal Adjudication by Making Rules 273

Chapter 4. Administrative Rulemaking 317
A. Judicial Review of the Substance of Agency Rules 318
B. The Choice Between Rulemaking and Adjudication 385
C. Procedures for Agency Rulemaking 413

Chapter 5. Government Information and Disclosure 508
A. Investigation and Discovery 508
B. Access to Information Held by the Federal Government 561

PART III. PUBLIC LAW REMEDIES

Chapter 6. Suits to Review Administration Action 623
A. Introduction 623
B. Standing to Obtain Review 639

Page

Chapter 6. Suits to Review Administration Action—Continued
C. Reviewability _____ 688
D. Timing of Judicial Review _____ 746

Chapter 7. Damage Actions Against the Federal Government and Its Officers _____ 783
A. Damage Actions Against the Government _____ 783
B. Suits Against Federal Officers _____ 783

Chapter 8. Beneficiary Enforcement of Public Law _____ 844
A. Explicit Remedies _____ 844
B. Implied Rights of Action _____ 847
C. Beneficiary Enforcement Under 42 U.S.C.A. § 1983 _____ 878
D. Substitution of Public for Private Rights _____ 910

Appendices

App.
A. The Constitution of the United States of America _____ 935
B. Selected Provisions of Title 28, U.S.C. _____ 939
C. Administrative Procedure Act 5 U.S.C., Chapter 5 _____ 943

INDEX _____ 967

Table of Contents

	Page
PREFACE TO SECOND EDITION	xvii
PREFACE TO FIRST EDITION	xxi
ACKNOWLEDGEMENTS	xxv
TABLE OF CASES	xxxix

PART I. POLITICAL CONTROL OF ADMINISTRATION

	Page
Chapter 1. The Legislative Connection	2
A. Statutory Vagueness and Its Antidotes	2
1. The "Non-Delegation" Doctrine	2
Amalgamated Meat Cutters v. Connally	6
Economic Stabilization Act of 1970	15
Notes	16
Sun Ray Drive-In Dairy, Inc. v. Oregon Liquor Control Commission	19
Notes	23
Delegation, Representation, and Good Government	24
2. The "Legislative Veto"	31
Immigration and Naturalization Service c. Chadha	31
Notes	43
B. Pervasive Methods of Legislative Control	48
1. The Statutory Environment of Federal Administration	48
Procedure Statutes	49
Administrative Procedure Act	49
Federal Register Act	51
Freedom of Information Act	51
Government in the Sunshine Act	53
Federal Advisory .Committee Act	54
Privacy Act	55
General Statutes Addressed to the Substance of Agency Decisions	55
National Environmental Policy Act	56
Regulatory Flexibility Act	58
Paperwork Reduction Act	60
Statutes Safeguarding the Integrity of Agency Decisionmakers	60
2. Congressional Choice of Agency Structure and Location	64
"Independent" Status	66
Collegial Form	69
Departmental Location	69
Designation of Authority	69
Budgetary Oversight	71
Power to Conduct Litigation	71
Other Structural Choices	72

Chapter 1. The Legislative Connection—Continued   **Page**
  3. Legislative Oversight, Casework, and Influence _____   74
       Pillsbury Co. v. FTC _____   *78*
       D.C. Federation of Civic Ass'ns v. Volpe _____   *80*
       American Public Gas Assoc. v. Federal Power Commission   *81*
C. Statutory Precision and Its Consequences _____   83
  1. Irrebuttable Presumptions_____   83
       *U.S. Department of Agriculture v. Murry*_____   *83*
          Note, The Irrebuttable Presumption Doctrine in the
             Supreme Court _____   *88*
          Notes _____   *91*
  2. The Decisive Delaney Clause _____   92
       Saccharin Ban Moratorium: House Report 95–658 _____   *92*
          Notes _____   *95*
       Hearing Before the Subcommittee on Health and Environ-
          ment of the House Committee on Interstate and Foreign
          *Commerce (6/27/77)*_____   *98*
       Hearing Before the Subcommittee on Health and the Envi-
          ronment of the House Committee on Interstate and For-
          *eign Commerce (4/11/79)*_____   *100*
          Problem _____   *103*
       L. Lave, The Strategy of Social Regulation _____   *103*

Chapter 2. Executive Supervision of Administrative Action ___ **110**
A. Appointment and Removal of Officers _____   112
     Humphrey's Executor v. United States _____   *112*
        *Notes*_____   *116*
     Buckley v. Valeo _____   *119*
        *Notes*_____   *125*
B. Executive Direction of Agency Action_____   132
     *Youngstown Sheet & Tube Co. v. Sawyer*_____   *132*
        Notes _____   *139*
     Executive Order 12,291 _____   *143*
     The Constitutional Status of Executive Order No. 12,291 _____   *146*
     Memorandum for Honorable David Stockman _____   *150*
     Administrative Organization and the Chief Executive _____   *155*

**PART II. ADMINISTRATIVE PROCEDURE AND
JUDICIAL REVIEW**

Chapter 3. Formal Agency Adjudication_____ **174**
A. The Right to Trial-Type Hearings _____   176
     Goldberg v. Kelly _____   *182*
        *Notes*_____   *191*
     Mathews v. Eldrige _____   *195*
        *Notes*_____   *204*
     *Califano v. Yamasaki*_____   *207*
        Notes _____   *211*
     O'Bannon v. Town Court Nursing Center _____   *212*
     *"Live, Liberty or Property"*_____   *219*

Chapter 3. Formal Agency Adjudication—Continued **Page**
B. Bureaucratic Decisionmaking and Formal Adjudication _____ 224
    1. General Concerns _____ 224
        Mashaw, _Bureaucratic Justice_ _____ 225
    2. Tensions Between Administration and Adjudication _____ 228
        Hierarchy Versus Personal Judgment _____ 228
        Factual Context Versus Policy Implementation _____ 229
        Neutrality Versus Institutional Intelligence _____ 232
        Attorney General's Committee on Administrative Procedure,
           Administrative Procedure in Government Agencies _____ 233
           Notes _____ 236
    3. The Social Security Administration and Its Administrative
        Law Judges _____ 239
        Nash v. Califano _____ 241
           Notes _____ 245
        Heckler v. Campbell _____ 246
           Notes _____ 249
C. Judicial Review of Agency Adjudication _____ 250
    NLRB v. Hearst Publications _____ 252
    National Labor Relations Board v. Bell Aerospace Co. _____ 262
    The Impact of Judicial Review of Agency Adjudication _____ 267
D. Avoiding Formal Adjudication by Making Rules _____ 273
    1. The Effect of Agency Rules _____ 273
        National Petroleum Refiners Ass'n v. Federal Trade Commis-
           sion _____ 274
           Notes _____ 281
    2. FDA Implementation of the 1962 Drug Amendments ____ 285
        The Regulatory Scheme for Therapeutic Drugs _____ 285
        The NAS–NRC Efficacy Review _____ 288
        Legal Impediments to FDA Implementation _____ 294
        Hynson, Westcott and Dunning, Inc. v. Richardson _____ 294
           Notes _____ 296
        The Attempt to Accelerate FDA Action _____ 298
        Weinberger v. Hynson, Westcott and Dunning, Inc. _____ 300
        Weinberger v. Bentex Pharmaceuticals, Inc. _____ 304
           Notes _____ 306
        FDA's Subsequent Experience With Summary Judgment _____ 307
        Status of the NAS–NRC Review _____ 311
        Administrative Summary Judgment Without Rules _____ 313

Chapter 4. Administrative Rulemaking _____ 317
A. Judicial Review of the Substance of Agency Rules _____ 318
    1. Constitutional Limits on the Rationality of Agency Rules 319
        Pacific States Box & Basket Co. v. White _____ 319
           Notes _____ 321
    2. Substantive Review of Agency Rules Under the APA __ 322
        Automotive Parts & Accessories Ass'n. v. Boyd _____ 323
           Notes _____ 333
        National Tire Dealers & Retreaders Ass'n v. Brinegar _____ 335
           Notes _____ 340

Chapter 4. Administrative Rulemaking—Continued   **Page**

Motor Vehicles Mfrs. Ass'n. v. State Farm Mutual Insurance Co. _____ 343

     Notes _____ 352

Industrial Union Dept., AFL–CIO v. American Petroleum Inst. _____ 354

     Notes _____ 374

Rogers, Judicial Review of Risk Assessments: The Role of Decision Theory in Unscrambling the Benzine Decision _____ 381

Congressional Proposals to Intensify Judicial Review of Agency Decisions _____ 383

B. The Choice Between Rulemaking and Adjudication _____ 385

   1. The NLRB's Proclivity for Adjudication _____ 385

     National Labor Relations Board v. Wyman-Gordon Co. _____ 387

       Notes _____ 393

   2. Required Rulemaking _____ 399

     Morton v. Ruiz _____ 399

       Notes _____ 402

     Implementing Policy Without Making Rules _____ 406

     Agencies' Obligations to Comply With Their Own Rules _____ 408

C. Procedures for Agency Rulemaking _____ 413

   1. Introduction _____ 413

   2. The APA's Dichotomous Rulemaking Models _____ 415

   3. Rulemaking on a Record _____ 418

     Wirtz v. Baldor Electric Co. _____ 418

       Notes _____ 422

     United States v. Florida East Coast Ry. Co. _____ 425

       Note _____ 431

   4. Evolution of Informal Rulemaking Under Section 553 _____ 432

     Coverage of Section 553 _____ 432

     The Evolving Judicial Understanding of Section 553 _____ 439

     United States v. Nova Scotia Food Products Corp. _____ 440

       Notes _____ 446

     Persistent Issues in Federal Agency Rulemaking _____ 447

     Judicial Demands for Oral Hearings _____ 458

     Vermont Yankee Nuclear Power Corp. v. Natural Resources Defense Council, Inc. _____ 461

       Notes _____ 466

     Ex Parte Contracts and Adversarial Comment _____ 470

       Notes _____ 473

     White House Oversight and Ex Parte Contracts _____ 475

     Sierra Club v. Costle _____ 476

       Notes _____ 489

     Official Bias and Prejudgment _____ 489

     Association of National Advertisers, Inc. v. FTC _____ 489

     Reforms of Federal Agency Rulemaking _____ 498

Page

Chapter 5. Government Information Acquisition and Disclosure **508**

A. Investigation and Discovery 508
   1. Authority to Subpoena Witnesses and Documents 509
      The Judicial Role in Enforcement of Agency Subpoenas *514*
      Germane to a Lawful Subject of Inquiry *517*
      Specific and Not Unreasonably Burdensome *518*
      Issued by Proper Authority *519*
      Notice of Investigation *520*
      Recognition of Constitutional and Other Privileges *521*
      Responsibility for Enforcement *523*
   2. Reporting and Record-Keeping Requirements 523
      Basic Doctrine *524*
      Fifth Amendment Limits *526*
         Notes *528*
      Required Records of Unlawful Activity *529*
         Notes *531*
      Costs of Government-Mandated Records and Reports *533*
   3. Physical Inspections 537
      Basic Premises *538*
         Notes *541*
      Exceptions and Elaborations *542*
         Notes *545*
      Contemporary Doctrine *546*
      Marshall v. Barlow's, Inc. *546*
         Notes *555*
      Donovan v. Dewey *557*
         Notes *560*
B. Access to Information Held by the Federal Government 561
   1. Claims to Access to Government Information 562
   2. The Federal Freedom of Information Act 564
      G. Robinson, *Access to Government Information: The American Experience* *565*
   3. Balancing Government Interests in Confidentiality 569
      NLRB v. Sears, Roebuck & Co. *569*
         Notes *579*
      Executive Privilege *585*
      Judicial Techniques for Monitoring Agency Compliance With the FOIA *587*
      Scope of Judicial Discretion to Refuse to Order Mandatory Disclosures *589*
      NLRB v. Robbins Tire & Rubber Co. *591*
         Notes *599*
   4. Protecting Private Interests in Information in the Government's Possession 600
      Chrysler Corp. v. Brown *600*
         Notes *606*
      Exemption of Proprietary Information *606*
      Protection of Personal Privacy *608*

Chapter 5. Government Information Acquisition and Disclosure—Continued

Page

5. Impact and Reform of the FOIA_____ 610

Robinson, *Access to Government Information: The American Experience* _____ *613*

PART III. PUBLIC LAW REMEDIES

Chapter 6. Suits to Review Administrative Action_____ 623

A. Introduction _____ 623

1. Sovereign Immunity, Jurisdiction, and Modes of Judicial Review _____ 624

2. Presumptive Review _____ 628

*Citizens to Preserve Overton Park, Inc. v. Volpe*_____ *629*

*Notes*_____ *633*

B. Standing to Obtain Review_____ 639

1. Standing Prior to the APA _____ 639

*Notes*_____ *644*

2. Standing Under the APA_____ 645

*Association of Data Processing Service Organizations, Inc. v. Camp*_____ *645*

Barlow v. Collins _____ *648*

*Notes*_____ *652*

Sierra Club v. Morton _____ *653*

*Notes*_____ *656*

3. Causality, Nexus, and Redressability _____ 658

*Simon v. Eastern Ky. Welfare Rights Organization*_____ *660*

*Notes*_____ *665*

Valley Forge Christian College v. Americans United For Separation of Church and State _____ *671*

*Notes*_____ *675*

*Havens Realty Corp. v. Coleman*_____ *676*

*Notes*_____ *681*

C. Reviewability _____ 688

1. Statutory Preclusion of Review _____ 688

*Johnson v. Robinson*_____ *690*

*Notes*_____ *692*

Constitutional Restraints on Statutory Preclusion of Review *694*

Exclusive Routes of Judicial Review _____ *696*

2. Decisions "Committed to Agency Discretion" by Law ___ 698

*Discretionary Grants and Government Contracts*_____ *701*

Public Lands and NEPA _____ *703*

Defense and Foreign Affairs _____ *704*

Presidential Powers and Political Questions _____ *705*

*Certification of Bargaining Units*_____ *705*

3. Review of Agency Inaction _____ 706

Enforcement Discretion _____ *706*

Dunn v. Retail Clerks International Ass'n _____ *706*

*Notes*_____ *708*

Bachowski v. Brennan _____ *712*

Chapter 6. Suits to Review Administrative Action—Continued Page

   Dunlop v. Bachowski _____ *715*

    Notes _____ *717*

   Chaney v. Heckler _____ *723*

    Notes _____ *727*

   Heckler v. Chaney _____ *727*

   Discretion to Regulate _____ *733*

   Natural Resources Defense Council v. S.E.C. _____ *733*

    Notes _____ *739*

 D. Timing of Judicial Review _____ 746

  1. The "Final Order" Doctrine _____ 746

   Environmental Defense Fund, Inc. v. Hardin _____ *746*

    Notes _____ *749*

   Environmental Defense Fund, Inc. v. Ruckelshaus _____ *750*

    Notes _____ *753*

  2. Pre-Enforcement Review _____ 754

   Abbott Laboratories v. Gardner _____ *754*

   Toilet Goods Ass'n v. Gardner _____ *761*

    Notes _____ *766*

  3. Exhaustion of Administrative Remedies _____ 769

   Federal Trade Commission v. Standard Oil Co. _____ *769*

    Notes _____ *776*

   McKart v. United States _____ *779*

Chapter 7. Damage Actions Against the Federal Government and Its Officers _____ 783

 A. Damage Actions Against the Government _____ 783

  1. The Tucker Act _____ 784

   United States v. Mitchell _____ *785*

  2. The Federal Tort Claims Act _____ 791

   United States v. S.A. Empresa de Viacao Aerea Rio Grandense (Varig Airlines) et al. _____ *792*

    Notes _____ *801*

 B. Suits Against Federal Officers _____ 805

  1. Common Law Actions Against Government Officers: Official Immunity _____ 805

   Gregoire v. Biddle _____ *807*

   Barr v. Matteo _____ *809*

    Notes _____ *815*

  2. Constitutional Actions Against Federal Officers _____ 817

   Bivens v. Six Unknown Named Agents of the Federal Bureau of Narcotics _____ *818*

    Notes _____ *827*

   Butz v. Economou _____ *827*

    Notes _____ *840*

Chapter 8. Beneficiary Enforcement of Public Law _____ 844

 A. Explicit Remedies _____ 844

 B. Implied Rights of Action _____ 847

  1. The Borak Doctrine _____ 847

   J. I. Case Co. v. Borak _____ *847*

Chapter 8. Beneficiary Enforcement of Public Law—Continued   **Page**

Implication Analysis and Federal Common Law _____ 851
National R.R. Passenger Corp. v. National Ass'n of R.R.
  Passengers _____ 855
Cort v. Ash _____ 861
  Notes _____ 865
Cannon v. University of Chicago _____ 866
  Notes _____ 876
C. Beneficiary Enforcement Under 42 U.S.C.A. § 1983 _____ 878
  Maine v. Thiboutot _____ 878
    Notes _____ 889
  Penhurst State School and Hospital v. Halderman _____ 893
D. Substitution of Public for Private Rights _____ 910
  1. Primary Jurisdiction _____ 910
    Nader v. Allegheny Airlines, Inc. _____ 910
    Origins and Rationales of Primary Jurisdiction _____ 916
  2. Legislative Supersession of Common Law Rights _____ 920
    Middlesex Cty. Sewerage Authority v. National Sea Clammers
      Ass'n _____ 920
        Notes _____ 929

Appendices

App.
A. The Constitution of the United States of America _____ 935
B. Selected Provisions of Title 28, U.S.C. _____ 939
C. Administrative Procedure Act 5 U.S.C., Chapter 5 _____ 943

INDEX _____ 967

Table of Cases

The principal cases are in italic type. Cases cited or discussed are in roman type. References are to Pages.

Abbott Laboratories v. Gardner, 322, 633, 688, *754*, 766, 767

Accardi, United States ex rel. v. Shaughnessy, 408, 410, 412

Action for Children's Television v. F.C.C., 471, 746

Action on Safety and Health v. FTC, 718

Adamo Wrecking Co. v. United States, 696, 767

Adams v. Richardson, 742

Addington v. Texas, 207

Air Line Pilots Association, Intl. v. Quesada, 307

Air New Zealand Ltd. v. CAB, 767

Air Pollution Variance Board v. Western Alfalfa Corp., 560

Alabama Association of Insurance Agents v. Board of Governors, 334

Alascom, Inc. v. FCC, 766

Albertson v. Subversive Activities Control Board, 528, 529

Alexander Sprunt & Son v. United States, 639, 640, 642, 643

Allen v. McCurry, 909

Allen v. Wright, 682, 706

Almeida-Sanchez v. United States, 560

Amalgamated Meat Cutters v. Connally, 6, 16, 17, 19, 23, 270, 317, 318

American Airlines, Inc. v. Civil Aeronautics Board, 705

American Bus Association v. United States, 434

American Civil Liberties Union v. Rabun County Chamber of Commerce, 676

American College of Neuropsychopharmacology v. Weinberger, 434

American Cyanamid Co. v. FDA, 316

American Cyanamid v. FTC, 237

American Farm Lines v. Black Ball Freight Service, 410

American Federation of Government Employees v. Acree, 778

American Federation of Government Employees, AFL–CIO v. Block, 438

American Home Products Corp. v. Finch, 290

American Mail Line, Limited v. Gulick, 579, 580

American Optometric Association v. Federal Trade Commission, 284

American Petroleum Institute v. EPA, 377

American Public Gas Association v. Federal Power Commission, 81

American Public Health Association v. Harris, 312

American Public Health Association v. Veneman, 298, 300, 312

American Textile Manufacturers Institute v. Donovan, 25, 377, 455

Amoco Oil Co. v. EPA, 377

AMP, Inc. v. Gardner, 777

Andresen v. Maryland, 533

Anglo-American & Overseas Corp. v. United States, 802

Animal Health Institute v. FDA, 452, 453

Appalachian Power Co. v. EPA, 459

Application of (see name of party)

Arizona v. California, 5

Arnett v. Kennedy, 221

Ash Grove Cement Co. v. FTC, 589

Associated Industries of New York State, Inc. v. Ickes, 644

Associated Merchandising Corp., United States v., 518

Association of Data Processing Service Organizations, Inc. v. Camp, 639, *645*, 652, 657, 671, 686, 893

Association of National Advertisers, Inc. v. FTC, 489

Automotive Parts & Accessories Association v. Boyd, 323, 334, 340, 342, 447

Bachowski v. Brennan, 712, 717, 718, 727

Bailey v. Richardson, 220

Bailey v. Van Buskirk, 816

Balanyi v. Local 1031, p. 709

Baldwin County Electric Membership Corp. v. Price Commission, 19

Baltimore Gas & Electric Co. v. NRDC, 468

Banzhaf v. Smith, 127

Barlow v. Collins, 556, 557, 559, 561, 639, 648

Barr v. Matteo, 809, 815, 816, 843

Barrett v. Kunzig, 560

Becker v. Philco Corp., 816

Bell v. Burson, 91, 92

Bell v. Hood, 817

Bentex Pharmaceuticals, Inc. v. Richardson, 219, 297, 300

Berry v. Reagen, 116

Birnbaum v. United States, 804

Bishop v. Wood, 223

Biswell, United States v., 542, 543, 546, 557

Bivens v. Six Unknown Named Agents of the Federal Bureau of Narcotics, 818, 827, 847, 865, 866, 933

Board of Curators of the University of Missouri v. Howowitz, 410

Board of Regents of State Colleges v. Roth, 220, 221

Bob Jones University v. United States, 321

Bolling v. Sharpe, 410

Bradley v. Fisher, 807

Brandenfels v. Heckler, 311

Braniff Master Executive Council v. CAB, 54

Brig Aurora, The, 3

Brotherhood of Railroad Trainmen v. Central of Georgia Railway Co., 692

Brotherhood of Railway and Steamship Clerks v. Association for Benefit of Non-Contract Employees, 705

Brown v. United States, 804

Buckley v. Valeo, 119, 125

Bunny Bear, Inc. v. Peterson, 341

Burks v. Lasker, 852

Burma Oil Co., United States v., 845

Burr v. New Rochelle Municipal Housing Authority, 414

Bush v. Lucas, 933

Butz v. Economou, 827, 840, 842, 843, 892

CAB v. Air Transport Association, 522

CAB v. Hermann, 519

Caceres, United States v., 411

Califano v. Yamasaki, 207, 211, 227

California v. Sierra Club, 877

California Bankers Association v. Shultz, 528, 532

Camara v. Municipal Court, 538, 541, 542, 543, 544, 559, 560

Cannon v. University of Chicago, 866, 877

Carlson v. Green, 827

Caulfield v. United States Department of Agriculture, 692

Center for Auto Safety v. National Highway Traffic Safety Administration, 740, 741

Cerro Metal Products v. Marshall, 557

Chaney v. Heckler, 723

Chapman v. Houston Welfare Rights Organization, 892

Chevron U.S.A. Inc. v. Natural Resources Defense Council, 26, 27

Chicago Junction Case, The, 641

Chicago & Northwestern Transportation Co. v. Kalo Brick & Tile Co., 918

Chicago & Southern Air Lines v. Waterman Steamship Corp., 704, 705

Chisholm v. Georgia, 902

Chris-Craft Industries, Inc. v. Piper Aircraft Corp., 853

Chromalloy American Corp. v. Marshall, 555, 556

Chrysler Corp. v. Brown, 52, 600, 606

Chrysler Corp. v. EPA, 698

Ciba-Geigy Corp. v. Richardson, 294

Cinderella Career and Finishing Schools, Inc. v. FTC, 239

Cities of Anaheim, Riverside, Banning, Colton and Azusa v. FERC, 398

Citizens to Preserve Overton Park v. Brinegar, 635

Citizens to Preserve Overton Park, Inc. v. Volpe, 342, 629, 633, 634, 636, 637, 638, 688, 727

City of (see name of city)

Claus v. Gyorkey, 843

Cleveland Board of Education v. LaFleur, 91, 92

Clinkscales v. Carver, 852

Cogwell, United States v., 546

Colonnade Catering Corp. v. United States, 542, 546, 557

Community Nutrition Institute v. Block, 686

Communist Party of the United States v. Subversive Activities Control Board, 529

Communist Party of the United States v. United States, 529

Consolidated Edison Co. v. NLRB, 256

Consumer Energy Council of America v. Federal Energy Regulatory Commission, 45, 46

Consumers Union v. Department of HEW, 745

Consumers Union v. Federal Trade Commission, 46, 284

Consumers Union v. Veterans Administration, 590

Continental Air Lines, Inc. v. CAB, 769

Control Data Corp. v. Baldrige, 686

Cooper Laboratories, Inc. v. Commissioner, 308

Cort v. Ash, 861, 865, 866, 877, 878

Couch v. Steel, 853, 854

Couch v. United States, 533

Council of the Southern Mountains, Inc. v. Donovan, 438

Courts v. Economic Opportunity Authority, 410

Crafts v. FTC, 516

Crowell v. Benson, 695

Cudahy Packing Co. v. Holland, 519

Curlott v. Campbell, 414

Curran v. Laird, 704

D.C. Federation of Civic Associations v. Volpe, 80

DaCosta v. Laird, 705

Dalehite v. United States, 802, 803

Dames & Moore v. Regan, 142

Damico v. California, 909

Daniel International Corp. v. OSHRC, 767

Davidson v. New Orleans, 180

Davis v. Passman, 827

Davis, United States v., 560

De Haen v. Rockwood Sprinkler Co., 852

Deering Milliken, Inc. v. OSHRC, 767

Degge v. Hitchcock, 625

Department of Health v. Owens-Corning Fiberglass Co., 19

Department of the Air Force v. Rose, 609

Doe v. Norton, 545

Donaldson v. United States, 517

Donovan v. Dewey, 557

Dow Chemical Co. v. Ruckelshaus, 753

Duke Power Co. v. Carolina Environmental Study Group, Inc., 667, 671, 675

Dunlop v. Bachowski, 715

Dunn v. Retail Clerks International Association, 706, 708, 709, 717, 718

E. R. Squibb & Sons, Inc. v. Weinberger, 311

East Oakland-Fruitvale Planning Council v. Rumsfeld, 702, 703

Edelman v. Jordan, 902, 904, 907, 908

Edison Pharmaceutical Co. v. Food and Drug Administration, 288, 311

Edward Hines Yellow Pine Trustees v. United States, 640

EEOC v. CBS, Inc., 44, 47

Elmo Division of Drive-X Co. v. Dixon, 778

Employees v. Department of Public Health and Welfare, 902, 903, 906

Endicott Johnson Corp. v. Perkins, 511, 514

Environmental Defense Fund, Inc. v. Hardin, 746, 749

Environmental Defense Fund, Inc. v. Ruckelshaus, 750

Environmental Protection Agency v. Mink, 579, 587, 588

Erie Railroad Co. v. Tompkins, 852

Establishment Inspection of Gilbert & Bennett Manufacturing Co., In re, 555, 556

Establishment Inspection of Northwest Airlines, Inc. In re, 556

Establishment Inspection of Urick Property, In re, 556

Estate of (see name of party)

Ethyl Corp. v. EPA, 375, 413, 414, 466

Ex parte (see name of party)

Excelsior Underwear, Inc., 393, 398, 402

Exxon Corp., United States v., 515

Far East Conference v. United States, 916, 919

FCC v. Allentown Broadcasting Corp., 231

Federal Communications Commission v. Sanders Brothers, 643, 644, 681

Federal Open Market Committee v. Merrill, 582, 589

Federal Trade Commission v. Standard Oil Co., 514, 769

Fein v. Selective Service System Local Board No. 7, p. 692

Feres v. United States, 801

Ferry v. Udall, 703

Field v. Clark, 3, 318

Fisher v. United States, 521

Fitzpatrick v. Bizer, 905

Flast v. Cohen, 659

Fleming v. Mohawk Wrecking & Lumber Co., 519

Florida Department of State v. Treasure Salvors, Inc., 906, 907

Florida East Coast Railway Co., United States v., 425, 431, 432, 459, 468

Florida Medical Association v. Department of Health, Education and Welfare, 610

Ford Motor Co. v. Department of Treasury, 903, 905

Ford Motor v. FTC, 403

Forsham v. Califano, 590

Forsham v. Harris, 590

FPC v. Texaco, Inc., 306

Frank v. Maryland, 538, 559

Freed, United States v., 531

Freeman v. Brown Brothers Harriman & Co., 515

Friedman v. Rogers, 236

FTC v. American Tobacco Co., 510

FTC v. Cement Institute, 236

FTC v. Crowther, 413

FTC v. Texaco, Inc., 518, 519

FTC v. Universal-Rundle Corp., 727
FTC Line of Business Report Litigation, In re, 526, 533

Gardner v. FCC, 412
Garner v. Rathburn, 816
General Motors Corp., 394
General Services Administration v. Benson, 579, 590
Getman v. NLRB, 590, 608
Gibson v. Berryhill, 236, 489
Gideon v. Wainwright, 890
Gladstone v. Realtors, 681
GM Leasing Corp. v. United States, 560
Goldberg v. Kelly, 177, 182, 191, 192, 194, 195, 204, 220, 224, 267, 718
Gonzalez v. Freman, 702
Gorris v. Scott, 852
Gray v. FAA, 307
Great Northern Railway v. Merchants Elevator Co., 918
Greater Boston Television Corp. v. FCC, 251, 342
Greenholtz v. Inmates, 207
Greentree v. United States Customs Service, 609
Gregoire v. Biddle, 807
Griffin v. United States, 802, 803
Grimaud, United States v., 3
Griswold v. Connecticut, 509
Grosso v. United States, 531

Hagans v. Lavine, 626, 892
Hahn v. Gottlieb, 698, 700, 701
Haig v. Agee, 19
Hanly v. Kleindienst, 56, 703
Hannah v. Larche, 125
Hansen v. Norfolk & Western Railway, 919
Hardin v. Kentucky Utilities Co., 641
Haring v. Prosise, 909
Harlow v. Fitzgerald, 840, 843
Harris County Commissioners Court v. Moore, 910
Hatahley v. United States, 802
Havens Realty Corp. v. Coleman, 675, 676, 681, 682
Hawaii Housing Authority v. Midkiff, 910
Haynes v. United States, 531
Heckler v. Campbell, 246, 249, 267, 268, 273, 306
Heckler v. Chaney, 727
Heine v. Raus, 816
Hellenic Lines Ltd. v. Federal Maritime Board, 517, 518
Hennen, Ex parte, 126
Hercules, Inc. v. EPA, 472, 742
Hess & Clark v. Food and Drug Administration, 309, 314

Hill v. Philpott, 532, 533
Hi-Ridge Lumber Co. v. United States, 702
Holmes v. New York Housing Authority, 23, 402
Home Box Office, Inc. v. F.C.C., 470, 471, 475
Hornsby v. Allen, 23, 402
Houghton v. Shafer, 909
Humphrey's Executor v. United States, 112, 116, 117, 118, 119
Huron Valley Hospital v. City of Pontiac, 919
Hurtado v. California, 223
Hutto v. Finney, 905
Hynson, Westcott and Dunning, Inc. v. Richardson, 294, 300, 306, 307, 308, 312, 313, 385, 418

Illinois v. Milwaukee, 929
Imbler v. Pachtman, 892
Immigration and Naturalization Service v. Chadha, 31, 43, 44, 45, 46, 47, 284, 402
In re (see name of party)
Independent U.S. Tanker Owners Committee v. Lewis, 398
Indian Towing v. United States, 801, 803
Industrial Union Department v. American Petroleum Institute, 6, 25, 26, 354
Industrial Union Department AFL–CIO v. Hodgson, 342, 374, 375
Ingraham v. Wright, 206
International Business Machines v. United States, 413
International Harvester Co. v. Ruckelshaus, 377, 451, 458, 461
Investment Co. Institute v. FDIC, 721, 741
Israel v. Baxter Laboratories, Inc., 919
ITT World Communications, Inc. v. FCC, 54

J. B. Kramer Grocery Co., United States v., 544
J.I. Case Co. v. Borak, 847, 851, 852, 853, 866
Jacobsen v. NLRB, 709
Jaffee v. United States, 628
Jefferson Parish School Board, United States v., 18
Johnson v. Robison, 690, 692, 693, 694, 695
Jones v. United States, 802
Jones, United States v., 784
Joseph G. Moretti, Inc., United States v., 920

Kahriger, United States v., 530
Kastigar v. United States, 522
Katherine Gibbs School v. FTC, 284, 473
Kelley v. Dunne, 816
Kelly v. Wyman, 191

Kendall v. Stokes, 807
Kendall v. United States ex rel. Stokes, 141
Kennecott Copper Corp. v. EPA, 335
Kent v. Dulles, 18, 19
Kerr Steamship Co. v. United States, 518
Kesselhaut v. United States, 63
King, United States v., 784
Kissinger v. Reporters Committee for Freedom of the Press, 591
Kixmiller v. SEC, 710, 718
Kletschka v. Driver, 701
Knox, United States v., 531

Laird v. Nelms, 802
Laird v. Tatum, 232
Lake Carriers' Association v. MacMullan, 910
Lake Country Estates v. Tahoe Regional Planning Agency, 892, 905
Langevin v. Chenango Court, Inc., 698, 699, 700, 701
Larson v. Domestic and Foreign Commerce Corp., 627, 902, 906, 908
LaSalle National Bank, United States v., 516, 533
Laveson v. Trans World Airlines, 919
Leary v. United States, 91, 531
Lee, United States v., 626
Leedom v. International Bhd. of Electrical Workers, Local 108, p. 394
Leedom v. Kyne, 777
Lefkowitz v. Turley, 522
Lewis v. United States, 530
Lieb, United States v., 18
Linda R.S. v. Richard B., 659
Linmark Associates, Inc. v. Willingboro, 682
Littell v. Morton, 627
Litton Industries, Inc., United States v., 516
Local 814, International Brotherhood of Teamsters v. NLRB, 638
Local 1219, American Federation of Government Employees v. Donovan, 719
Lochner v. New York, 321
Love v. United States Department of HUD, 414
Lowe v. Conroy, 806

McKart v. United States, 779
McLennan, United States ex rel. v. Wilbur, 625
McMann v. SEC, 522
McNeese v. Board of Education, 909
Mackey v. United States, 531
Maclean v. Huddleston, 876
Maine v. Thiboutot, 878, 891, 892, 893, 905
Manhattan-Bronx Postal Union v. Gronouski, 142

Mapp v. Ohio, 890
Marbury v. Madison, 49
Marchetti v. United States, 529, 531
Marshall v. Barlow's, Inc., 514, 546
Marshall v. Pool Offshore Co., 556
Marshall v. Union Oil Co., 767
Marshall v. W & W Steel Co., 557
Marshall v. Weyerhauser, 556
Marshall v. Wollaston Alloys, Inc., 556
Martinez-Fuente, United States v., 560
Mathews v. Eldridge, 179, 195, 204, 205, 206, 207, 211, 219, 239, 240, 778, 779
Matlovich v. Secretary of the Air Force, 307
Mayer v. Ordman, 709
Medical Committee for Human Rights v. SEC, 710, 718
Memphis Light, Gas and Water Division v. Craft, 206
Merrill Lynch, Pierce, Fenner & Smith v. Curran, 876
Metropolitan Washington Coalition for Clear Air v. District of Columbia, 846
Michigan v. Tyler, 561
Middlesex County Sewerage Authority v. National Sea Clammers Association, 846, 920, 929, 931
Midwest Oil Co., United States v., 142
Miller v. Horton, 806
Milwaukee v. Illinois, 929
Minker, United States v., 516
Minnesota State Board for Community Colleges v. Knight, 414
Mitchell, United States v., 785, 804
Mizokami v. United States, 802
Mobil Oil Corp. v. FPC, 459
Monell v. Department of Social Services of the City of New York, 892, 905
Monroe v. Pape, 890, 891, 908, 909
Montanye, United States ex rel. Terraciano v., 532
Montrose Chemical Corp. v. Train, 579
Montship Lines Ltd. v. Federal Maritime Board, 517, 518
Moog Industries, Inc. v. FTC, 727, 731
Moragne v. United States, 852
Morgan v. United States, 228, 229
Morgan, United States v., 229
Morris v. Gressette, 688, 693, 694
Morton v. Ruiz, 51, 399, 406, 408, 434
Morton Salt Co., United States v., 524, 526
Motor Vehicle Manufacturers Association v. State Farm Mutual Insurance Co., 343, 354, 404, 413
Mourning v. Family Publications Service, Inc., 91
Muller Optical Co. v. EEOC, 44, 47

Muniz, United States v., 801
Myers v. Bethlehem Shipbuilding Corp., 117, 514, 776, 777

Nadelson, Application of, 531
Nader v. Allegheny Airlines, Inc., 910
Nader v. Bork, 126, 410
Nash v. Califano, 241
National Automatic Laundry and Cleaning Council v. Schultz, 769
National Congress of Hispanic American Citizens (El Congreso) v. Marshall, 449, 743
National Congress of Hispanic American Citizens v. Usery, 742
National Forest Preservation Group v. Butz, 703
National Industrial Constructors, Inc. v. OSHRC, 767
National Labor Relations Board v. Bell Aerospace Co., Division of Textron, Inc., 262, 268, 386, 395, 403, 404
National Labor Relations Board v. Tennessee Products & Chemical Corp., 709
National Labor Relations Board v. Wyman-Gordon Co., 387, 393, 395, 396, 398
National Nutritional Foods Association v. FDA, 424
National Nutritional Foods Association v. Kennedy, 424, 436
National Parks and Conservation Association v. Morton, 599, 607
National Petroleum Refiners Association v. Federal Trade Commission, 274, 282, 283, 285, 306, 313, 385, 417, 418, 452
National Railroad Passenger Corp. v. National Association of Railroad Passengers, 855
National Tire Dealers & Retreaders Association v. Brinegar, 335, 340, 341, 342, 446, 453
Natural Resources Defense Council v. Costle, 744, 745
Natural Resources Defense Council v. EPA, 439
Natural Resources Defense Council v. Ruckelshaus, 408, 745
Natural Resources Defense Council v. SEC, 733, 740, 741
Neustadt, United States v., 802
New Jersey, State of v. United States Environmental Protection Agency, 438
New Motor Vehicle Board v. Orrin W. Fox Co., 223
New York Stock Exchange, Inc. v. Bloom, 768, 769
Ng Fung Ho v. White, 695
Nixon v. Fitzgerald, 840

Nixon v. Sirica, 586, 587
Nixon, United States v., 586
NLRB v. Columbian Enameling and Stamping Co., 257
NLRB v. Guy F. Atkinson Co., 394
NLRB v. Hearst Publications, 252, 256, 384, 386
NLRB v. James Thompson & Co., 231
NLRB v. Lewis, 519
NLRB v. Majestic Weaving Co., 394
NLRB v. Robbins Tire & Rubber Co., 591, 599
NLRB v. Sears, Roebuck & Co., 52, 569, 579
NLRB v. Standard Oil Co., 257
NLRB v. Universal Camera Corp., 230
Nolan v. Ramsey, 414
Nor-Am Agricultural Products, Inc. v. Hardin, 749
North American Pharmacal, Inc. v. Department of HEW, 311
Northern Pipeline Construction Co. v. Marathon Pipe Line Co., 119
Northwest Airlines, Inc. v. Transport Workers Union of America, AFL–CIO, 877
Nova Scotia Food Products Corp. v. United States, 452, 453, 469, 470
Nova Scotia Food Products Corp., United States v., 440, 447, 590
NRDC v. NRC, 467
NRDC v. Train, 742

O'Bannon v. Town Court Nursing Center, 212, 219, 223
O'Connor, United States v., 516
Ohio Valley Water Co. v. Ben Avon Borough, 695
Oklahoma Press Publishing Co. v. Walling, 512, 514
Ortwein v. Schwab, 695
Owen v. City of Independence, 892, 905

Pacific Coast Ass'n of Pulp & Paper Mfrs., 394
Pacific Gas & Electric Co. v. FPC, 435
Pacific Legal Foundation v. Goyan, 454
Pacific States Box & Basket Co. v. White, 319, 321
Pacific Westbound Conference v. United States, 517
Packwood v. Briggs & Stratton Corp., 269
Painter v. FBI, 609
Pan American World Airways v. CAB, 54
Pan American World Airways, Inc. v. United States, 919
Panama Refining Co., v. Ryan, 4, 6
Parden v. Terminal Railway, 903

Parham v. J.R., 206, 223

Parratt v. Taylor, 892

Patel v. Immigration and Naturalization Service, 402

Patsy v. Board of Regents, 909

Paul v. Davis, 892

Pax Co. v. United States, 75, 753

Payton v. United States, 803

Pearson v. Zehr, 806

Pennhurst State School and Hospital v. Halderman, 893, 902, 905, 907, 908

Perkins v. Luken Steel Co., 220, 642

Perry v. Sinderman, 221

Pfizer, Inc. v. Richardson, 294

Pharmaceutical Manufacturers Association v. Finch, 292, 434

Pharmaceutical Manufacturers Association v. Gardner, 424

Pharmaceutical Manufacturers Association v. Richardson, 293

Pharmaceutical Manufacturers Association v. Weinberger, 606

Pickus v. United States Board of Parole, 435

Pillsbury Co. v. FTC, 78

Port of Boston Marine Terminal Association v. Rederiaktiebolaget Transatlantic, 919

Porter v. United States Department of Justice, 609

Portland Cement Association v. Ruckelshaus, 377, 460

Powell, United States v., 516, 517, 520

Praylou, United States v., 802

Process Gas Consumers Group v. Consumers Energy Council of America, 46

Public Citizen v. Department of Health and Human Services, 439

Public Citizen Health Research Group v. FDA, 607

Public Interest Research Group v. FCC, 413

Public Service Commission v. FPC, 460

Queen v. Tennessee Valley Authority, 843

Quern v. Jordan, 905

Railroad Commission v. Pullman Co., 909

Rayonier, Inc. v. United States, 801, 803

Red Lion Broadcasting Co. v. FCC, 321

Reiff, United States v., 532

Renegotiation Board v. Bannercraft Clothing Co., 590

Renegotiation Board v. Grumman Aircraft Engineeering Corp., 581

Republic Steel Corp., United States v., 877

Reynolds, United States v., 562, 586, 587

Ricci v. Chicago Mercantile Exchange, 919, 920

Richardson, United States v., 659, 660, 675, 683

Robles v. Environmental Protection Agency, 608, 609

Rochester, City of v. Bond, 698

Rodway v. United States Department of Agriculture, 335

Roe v. Norton, 545

Roe v. Wade, 321

Rombough v. FAA, 307

Rosado v. Wyman, 778, 893, 920

Rosen v. Hursh, 545

Ruckelshaus v. Monsanto Co., 608

Rylander, United States v., 522

S., Linda R. v. Richard D., 659, 660

S.A. Empresa De Viacao Aerea Rio Grandense (Varig Airlines), United States v., 792, 801, 802

S & E Contractors, Inc. v. United States, 523

Saez v. Goslee, 709

St. Joseph Stock Yards v. United States, 695

Scanwell Laboratories v. Shaffer, 702

Schechter Poultry Corp. v. United States, 5, 6, 281

Scheuer v. Rhodes, 892, 904

Schilling v. Rogers, 692

Schlesinger v. Reservists Committee to Stop the War, 659, 660, 675, 683

Schmidt, In re, 907

SEC v. Chenery Corp., 393, 395

SEC v. Dresser Industries, Inc., 521

SEC v. Jerry T. O'Brien, Inc., 520

SEC v. Wheeling-Pittsburgh Steel Corp., 516

Secretary of Agriculture v. United States, 413

See v. Seattle, 538, 539, 541, 542, 543, 560

Serr v. Sullivan, 515

Service v. Dulles, 409, 410, 412

Shapiro v. Drug Enforcement Administration, 609

Shapiro v. United States, 526, 528, 529, 530, 531, 532

Shasta Minerals & Chemical Co. v. SEC, 516

Shaughnessy v. Pedreiro, 692

Shaughnessy, United States ex rel. Accardi v., 408

Siebold, Ex parte, 126, 127

Sierra Club v. Costle, 476

Sierra Club v. Morton, 653, 656, 657, 659, 681

Silverman, United States v., 532

Simon v. Eastern Kentucky Welfare Rights Organization, 660, 684
Singleton v. Wulff, 666
Small Refiner Lead Phase-Down Task Force v. EPA, 59
Smiertka v. United States Department of Treasury, 55
Smith v. United States, 706, 803
Smithkline Corp. v. FDA, 309
Soucie v. David, 579, 590
South Terminal Corp. v. EPA, 451
Southern California District Council v. Ordman, 709, 718
Stanley v. Illinois, 91, 92
Stark v. Connally, 532
Starr v. FAA, 307
State of (see name of state)
Stephenson Enterprises, Inc. v. Marshall, 544, 561
Sterling Drug, Inc. v. FTC, 580
Sterling Drug, Inc. v. Weinberger, 311
Stevens v. Carey, 142
Stiftung, Carl Zeiss v. V.E.B. Carl Zeiss, Jena, 562
Stoddard Lumber Co. v. Marshall, 557
Storer Broadcasting Co., United States v., 306, 313, 418
Strycker's Bay Neighborhood Council v. Karlen, 56
Student Public Interest Research Group of New Jersey v. Fritzsche, Dodge and Olcott, Inc., 846
Students Challenging Regulatory Agency Procedures (SCRAP), United States v., 657, 658, 660, 675
Sun Ray Drive-In Dairy, Inc. v. Oregon Liquor Control Commission, 19, 23, 402
Switchmen's Union v. National Mediation Board, 705

T.I.M.E., Inc. v. United States, 916
Tabor v. Joint Board for Enrollment of Actuaries, 335
Tax Analysts and Advocates v. Blumenthal, 686
Telecommunications Research and Action Center v. FCC, 448, 698
Tennessee Electric Power Co. v. TVA, 641
Terminal Freight Handling Co. v. Solien, 718
Terraciano, United States ex rel. v. Montanye, 532
Testan, United States v., 784, 785
Texas v. California, 905
Texas and Pacific Railway Co. v. Abilene Cotton Oil Co., 917, 918
Theodore, United States v., 519
Thompson v. Clark, 59

Thriftimart, Inc., United States v., 543
Toilet Goods Association v. Gardner, 745, 761, 766.
Touche Ross & Co. v. Redington, 876
Tower v. Glover, 892
Tracy v. Gleason, 689
Trafficante v. Metropolitan Life Insurance Co., 681
Train v. New York, 705
Transamerica Mortgage Advisors, Inc. (TAMA) v. Lewis, 877
Twining v. New Jersey, 889

Ullmann v. United States, 522
United States v. _____ (see opposing party)
United States Coin and Currency, United States v., 531
United States Department of Agriculture v. Murry, 83, 92
United States ex rel. v. _____ (see opposing party)
United States Lines, Inc. v. Federal Maritime Commission, 472
United Steelworkers v. Marshall, 452, 455
Universal Camera Corp. v. NLRB, 230, 231, 232, 258, 260, 261
University of Southern Cal. v. Cost of Living Council, 18
Upjohn Co. v. Finch, 290, 293
Upjohn Co. v. United States, 523
USV Pharmaceutical Corp. v. Richardson, 289
USV Pharmaceutical Corp. v. Secretary of HEW, 296

Valley Forge Christian College v. Americans United for Separation of Church and State, 671, 675, 684
Vaughan v. Rosen, 588, 612
Vermont Yankee Nuclear Power Corp. v. Natural Resources Defense Council, Inc., 414, *461,* 466, 468, 469
Vigil v. Andrus, 433
Vitarelli v. Seaton, 409, 410, 412
Vitek v. Jones, 206
Vlandis v. Kline, 92

Wagner Electric Corp. v. Volpe, 450, 451, 452, 453
WAIT Radio v. FCC, 307
Walker, United States v., 703
Walter Holm & Co. v. Hardin, 459, 460
Warren, United States v., 532, 533
Warth v. Seldin, 665, 666, 681, 684
Washington, Virginia & Maryland Coach Co. v. NLRB, 256
Watson, Estate of v. Blumenthal, 628

Weinberger v. Bentex Pharmaceuticals, Inc., 304, 920
Weinberger v. Carlos Romero-Barcelo, 846
Weinberger v. Hynson, Westcott and Dunning, Inc., 300
Weinberger v. Salfi, 692, 779
Wellford v. Hardin, 589, 590
Wellman v. Whittier, 689
Western Pacific Railway, United States v., 918
Weyerhaeuser Co. v. Costle, 377
Weyerhaeuser Co. v. Marshall, 544
Wheeldin v. Wheeler, 817
Wiener v. United States, 117, 118, 119
Wilbur, United States ex rel. McLennan v., 625
Williamette Iron Bridge Co. v. Hatch, 877
Williams v. Barry, 414
Williams, United States v., 889
Williamson v. Lee Optical Co., 318, 321
Wilson & Co. v. NLRB, 257

Windsor v. The Tennessean, 843
Wirtz v. Baldor Electric Co., 418, 562, 590
Withrow v. Larkin, 236, 489
Wolfe v. Weinberger, 458
Work v. United States ex rel. Rives, 692
WWHT Inc. v. Federal Communications Commission, 739
Wyman v. James, 544, 545, 546

Yakus v. United States, 696
Young, Ex parte, 902, 904, 905, 906, 907, 908
Youngberg v. Romeo, 905
Younger v. Harris, 909
Youngstown Sheet & Tube Co. v. Sawyer, 132, 141, 142

Zicarelli v. New Jersey State Commission of Investigation, 522
Zwickler v. Koota, 910

*

ADMINISTRATIVE LAW

THE AMERICAN PUBLIC LAW SYSTEM

CASES AND MATERIALS

Second Edition

*

Part I

POLITICAL CONTROL OF ADMINISTRATION

Chapter 1

THE LEGISLATIVE CONNECTION

Virtually all agency action begins with a statute. Indeed, as we shall see, administrators are adrift in a sea of statutes and legislative contacts that guide and shape their efforts at implementation. More importantly for purposes of administrative law, statutes provide the legitimating standard for much of agency decisionmaking. Save for a few executive functions specified in the Constitution, the agent—the administrative agency, —has only those powers provided by its principal—the legislature. Legislative specification of agency jurisdiction, purposes, and powers thus provides both democratic legitimation for the exercise of administrative authority and an instrumental conception of administration as essentially the task of implementing policy choices made in the political process.

It is hardly surprising, therefore, that one of the concerns of administrative law should be to regulate the linkage between legislative and administrative action. But, as it struggles to do so, legal doctrine confronts a world wonderfully more complex than the one our simplistic principal-agent analogy suggests. In that world, agencies may appear to behave more like independent entrepreneurs seeking capital support from the Congress for projects of their own than like well-instructed agents implementing their congressional principal's orders. Whether administrative law should seek to provide a structure within which this and many other sorts of legislative-administrative connections can flourish, or should seek to reinforce the principal-agent model, is but one of several related issues that these pages pursue.

A. STATUTORY VAGUENESS AND ITS ANTIDOTES

1. THE "NON-DELEGATION" DOCTRINE

Article I, section 1 of the United States Constitution provides: "All legislative Powers herein granted shall be vested in a Congress of the United States, which shall consist of a Senate and House of Representatives." Similar provisions appear in virtually every state constitution. For at least 150 years the Supreme Court's decisions were replete with categorical statements suggesting that Congress may not relinquish any of its power to enact legislation through grants of policy-making power to administrators.   The following statement by the first Justice Harlan in *Field v. Clark*, 143 U.S. 649 (1892), is typical:

> That Congress cannot delegate legislative power to the President is a principle universally recognized as vital to the integrity and maintenance of the system of government ordained by the constitution.

Yet in that case the Court upheld a provision of the Tariff Act of 1890 which authorized the President to suspend favorable tariff treatment for nations that imposed on American products "any duties or other exactions * * * which * * * [he] may deem to be reciprocally unequal and unreasonable."   The Court theorized that the Act simply accorded the President the authority to make the factual determination requisite for implementation of the policy prescribed by Congress.   "He was the mere agent of the law-making department to ascertain and declare the event upon which * * * [the legislature's] expressed will was to take effect."   143 U.S. at 692–93.

In decisions both before and after *Field v. Clark* the Supreme Court upheld, against attack as invalid delegations of legislative power, statutes that accorded the President, or occasionally other executive officers, a large role in formulating as well as implementing national policy.   Many of these laws dealt with foreign affairs, a field in which, perhaps more than in others, Congress might have believed the President should have wide discretion in effectuating legislative judgment.   The Court offered a variety of rationales for upholding such delegations of authority. Some laws were said merely to accord the President authority to determine the "contingency"—*e.g.*, violation of the nation's neutral rights by a foreign power—that brought congressional policy into force. *E.g., The Brig Aurora*, 11 U.S. (7 Cranch) 382 (1813).   In other statutes, the Court suggested Congress had firmly established the general contours of public policy and simply left the President to "fill up the details" of regulation, even though such "filling up" might involve the power to declare conduct criminal.   *E.g., United States v. Grimaud*, 220 U.S. 506 (1911).   It was clear to the Court, of course, that Congress could not feasibly prescribe in detail the rules governing every facet of federally regulated activity, but it nonetheless purported to demand that Congress establish a "discernible standard" for administrative implementation of its policies.

In all these early decisions, the Court kept insisting that the Constitution forbade delegation of Congress' monopoly of legislative power.   But not once did it invalidate any delegation Congress saw fit to make, and it upheld phrases such as "just and reasonable rates" for railroad regulation and "public interest, convenience, or necessity" for the issuance of broadcast licenses as establishing "meaningful standards" for agencies to apply.   It therefore is not surprising that by the early 1930's, the "nondelegation doctrine" was thought to have become an empty formalism.   L. JAFFE, JUDICIAL CONTROL OF ADMINISTRATIVE ACTION 51–62 (1965).   However, in 1935, the Court for the first—and last—time struck down congressional enactments as unlawful delegations of legislative power.   The Court did so in two cases dealing with separate sections of the National Industrial Recovery Act, an early piece of New Deal legislation that soon fell into disfavor with most elements of the Roosevelt constituency.

In *Panama Refining Co. v. Ryan*, 293 U.S. 388 (1935) the provision at issue was Section 9(c) of the National Industrial Recovery Act.* That section authorized the President to exclude from interstate commerce oil products "produced or withdrawn from storage in excess of the amount permitted to be produced or withdrawn from storage by any state law or valid regulation. * * * " Disobedience to an exclusion order was made a crime punishable by fine and imprisonment. Section 9(c) provided no criteria on which the President was to base his action, and the Court refused to find the requisite guiding principles in the Act's declaration of policy, which listed many competing objectives apparently without preference.** Nor did the Act require the President "to ascertain and proclaim the conditions prevailing in the industry which made the prohibition necessary." Canvassing its previous precedents, which without exception had upheld congressional delegations of lawmaking power, the Court declared:

> Thus, in every case in which the question has been raised, the Court has recognized that there are limits of delegation which there is no constitutional authority to transcend. We think that § 9(c) goes beyond those limits. As to the transportation of oil production in excess of state permission, the Congress has declared no policy, has established no standard, has laid down no rule. There is no requirement, no definition of circumstances and conditions in which the transportation is to be allowed or prohibited.

> If § 9(c) were held valid, it would be idle to pretend that anything would be left of limitations upon the power of the Congress to delegate its law-making function. The reasoning of the many decisions we have reviewed would be made vacuous and their distinctions nugatory. Instead of performing its law-making function, the Congress could at will and as to such subjects as it chose transfer that function to the President or other officer or to an administrative body. The question is not of the intrinsic importance of the particular statute before us, but of the constitutional processes of legislation which are an essential part of our system of government.

---

*The Petroleum Code of Fair Competition, promulgated under the NIRA, was also challenged in this suit. The Court did not pass on the validity of the Petroleum Code, however, because the offending section had been amended out of existence, unknown to the prosecuting authorities and the lower courts. This embarrassing event led to the enactment of the Federal Register Act of 1935, 44 U.S.C.A. §§ 301–335. See L. JAFFE, JUDICIAL CONTROL OF ADMINISTRATIVE ACTION 61–62 (1965).

** The declaration of policy, set out in section 1 of Title I of the Act, provided in part:

It is hereby declared to be the policy of Congress to remove obstructions to the free flow of interstate and foreign commerce which tend to diminish the amount thereof; and to provide for the general welfare by promoting the organization of industry for the purpose of cooperative action among trade groups, to induce and maintain united action of labor and management under adequate governmental sanctions and supervision, to eliminate unfair competitive practices, to promote the fullest possible utilization of the present productive capacity of industries, to avoid undue restriction of production (except as may be temporarily required), to increase the consumption of industrial and agricultural products by increasing purchasing power, to reduce and relieve unemployment, to improve standards of labor, and otherwise to rehabilitate industry and to conserve natural resources.

293 U. S. at 430.   With but a single dissent, the Court thus struck down the "hot oil" provisions of the NIRA.

Four months after the *Panama Refining* decision, in *Schechter Poultry Corp. v. United States*, 295 U.S. 495 (1935), the Court invalidated section 3 of the same Act, which empowered the President to approve industry codes of "fair competition" upon submission by trade associations or business groups. The only conditions limiting the President's power were that the groups submitting codes for approval had to be "truly representative" of the industry and could impose no "inequitable restrictions on admission to membership," and that no code could "be designed to promote monopolies or to eliminate or oppress small enterprises * * * [or] operate to discriminate against them. * * *"   Upon adoption a code became the standard of fair competition for an industry, and violation became a criminal misdemeanor, carrying a fine of up to $500.   The Schechter brothers had been prosecuted under the Act. Again the Supreme Court, this time without dissent, found the statements of congressional policy in section 1 of Title I wholly insufficient as criteria for the President's exercise of his wide authority.   The Court specifically noted that the Act, unlike other statutes upheld as valid delegations of legislative authority, provided no procedural safeguards—such as notice, hearing, and findings based on evidence—for the adoption of codes of fair competition.

Justice Cardozo, who had been the lone dissenter in *Panama Refining*, joined the majority in *Schechter*.   "The delegated power of legislation which has found expression in this Code," he declared, "is not canalized within banks that keep it from overflowing.   It is unconfined and vagrant. * * *"   295 U.S. at 551.

Since the *Schechter* case the Supreme Court has not invalidated a single Congressional delegation of law-making authority to an administrative agency or executive officer.   This result—not surprising, of course, given the history of the doctrine—cannot be explained by improvements since 1935 in the drafting of statutes.   Many subsequent grants of authority have been upheld in the face of plausible charges that they were no more specific than those found wanting in 1935.   See, e.g., *Arizona v. California*, 373 U.S. 546 (1963), upholding a grant of essentially standardless power to the Secretary of the Interior to apportion the waters of the Colorado River.   Even statutes of major political and economic significance, containing provisions of great detail and complexity, often exhibit vagueness precisely at the point of critical policy choice.   The Resource Conservation and Recovery Act of 1976 (RCRA) is exemplary.   After conferring authority on the Administrator of the Environmental Protection Agency (EPA) to regulate the generation, transportation, treatment and disposal of all "hazardous materials" (the quoted term to be defined by EPA), section 304 of the statute merely instructs the Administrator to promulgate such regulations for treatment and disposal of "hazardous wastes * * * as may be necessary to protect human health and the environment."   42 U.S.C.A. § 6924.   Another illustration is section 6(b)(5) of the Occupational Safety and Health Act, 29 U.S.C.A. § 655(b)(5), which directs the Secretary of Labor, "to the extent feasible" to eliminate worker exposure to toxic substances capable of causing material health impairment.   See *Industrial Union Department, AFL-CIO v. American Petroleum Institute*, 448 U. S. 607 (1980), infra p. 354.

One can argue, therefore, that the *Schechter* and *Panama Refining* cases are "sports," better explainable in terms of the politics of the justices of the Supreme Court in 1935 than in terms of legal doctrine.   This explanation, however, does not give sufficient weight to other factors at work in those cases, nor does it, even if substantially accurate, necessarily detract from the importance of the non-delegation doctrine.   That doctrine is admittedly political, for it deals explicitly with the fundamental political organization of the state.   The Court's reiteration of the non-delegation principle, coupled with its very sparing use to strike down legislation, illustrates a continuing judicial concern with the spectre of administrative absolutism—combined with a sense that legal techniques short of declaring statutes invalid are generally preferable means for accommodating the necessities of public policy with effective control of administrative discretion.

AMALGAMATED MEAT CUTTERS v. CONNALLY

United States District Court, District of Columbia, 1971.
337 F. Supp. 737.

LEVENTHAL, CIRCUIT JUDGE.

In this litigation Plaintiff Union, the Amalgamated Meat Cutters suing on its own behalf and on behalf of its affiliated local unions, attacks the constitutionality of the Economic Stabilization Act of 1970.*

Two different actions are consolidated in the complaint. Count II seeks to require the major meat packing companies to perform their obligations, under their 1970 collective bargaining agreements with the Union, to grant a general wage increase of twenty-five cents an hour effective September 6, 1971. * * * The employers respond that the implementation of the wage increase obligation would violate Executive Order 11615, promulgated by President Nixon August 15, 1971 * * * .   This Executive Order, Stabilization of Prices, Rents, Wages and Salaries, establishes a 90-day price-wage freeze, a requirement that "prices, rents, wages and salaries shall be stabilized for a period of 90 days" at levels no greater than the highest rates pertaining to a substantial volume of actual transactions by the seller of commodities or services involved in a specified base period preceding August 15. The Union's position is that this defense is insufficient as a matter of law because the Act is unconstitutional and the Executive Order invalid.

The broader aspect of the controversy before us appears in Count I of the Complaint, an action brought against John B. Connally, who as Secretary of the Treasury is Chairman of the Cost of Living Council, and the other officials constituting the Council.   In Executive Order 11615 Presi-

*[Reproduced following this case. Eds.]

dent Nixon established the Cost of Living Council "which shall act as an agency of the United States," specified that it shall be composed of certain designated officials as members and "delegated to the Council all of the powers conferred on the President by the Economic Stabilization Act of 1970."

In Count I the Union seeks a declaratory judgment that the Act and Executive Order 11615 are illegal and unconstitutional, and also an injunction against the officials named as defendants, individually and as members of the Council, restraining and enjoining them from administering or giving any force or effect to the Executive Order and the Act. * * *

The main claim of the Union is that the Act unconstitutionally delegates legislative power to the President, in violation of the general constitutional principle of the Separation of Powers, and in contravention of Article I, Section I of the Constitution * * * .

The Union's position is that the Act's broad authority to the President "to issue such orders and regulations as he may deem appropriate to stabilize prices, rents, wages and salaries" vests "unbridled legislative power in the President," a "naked grant of authority" to determine whether they "will be controlled, and the scope, manner and timing of those controls."

* * *

The matter has been argued to us on principle and precedent. The divergences in the principles perceived by the litigants are matched by divergences in the precedents they summon. The Government cites numerous authorities but relies most heavily on *Yakus v. United States*, 321 U.S. 414 (1944), sustaining the grant in the Emergency Price Control Act of 1942 of broad price-fixing authority. The Union particularly invokes the 1935 decisions in *Schechter Corp. v. United States* and *Panama Refining Co. v. Ryan*, holding invalid provisions of the National Industrial Recovery Act.

We are of the view that the *Yakus* ruling and principles there applied provide the more meaningful guidance for the novel problem at hand, and that this constitutional assault cannot be sustained. * * *

* * * There is no analytical difference, no difference in kind, between the legislative function—of prescribing rules for the future—that is exercised by the legislature or by the agency implementing the authority conferred by the legislature. The problem is one of limits.

An agency assigned to a task has its freedom of action circumscribed not only by the constitutional limitations that bind Congress but by the perimeters described by the legislature as hedgerows defining areas open to the agency. The question is the extent to which the Constitution limits a legislature that may think it proper and needful to give the agency broad flexibility to cope with the conditions it encounters.

* * *

Concepts of control and accountability define the constitutional requirement. The principle permitting a delegation of legislative power, if there has been sufficient demarcation of the field to permit a judgment whether the agency has kept within the legislative will, establishes a principle of accountability under which compatibility with the legislative design may be ascertained not only by Congress but by the courts and the public. That principle was conjoined in *Yakus* with a recognition that the burden is on the party who assails the legislature's choice of means for effecting its purpose, a burden that is met "[o]nly if we could say that there is an absence of standards for the guidance of the Administrator's action, so that it would be impossible in a proper proceeding to ascertain whether the will of Congress has been obeyed."

Rule

These doctrines have been applied to sustain legislation that delegated broad authority indeed in order to assure requisite flexibility to the officials or agencies designated to discharge the tasks assigned by the Congress. *New York Central Securities Corp. v. United States*, 287 U. S. 12, 24 (1932) (permitting consolidation of carriers when "in the public interest"); *FPC v. Hope Natural Gas Co.*, 320 U.S. 591, 600 (1944) ("just and reasonable" rates for natural gas); *Nat'l Broadcasting Co. v. United States*, 319 U.S. 190, 225–226 (1943) (licensing of radio communications "as public convenience, interest or necessity requires"); *Lichter v. United States*, 334 U.S. 742, 785–786 (1948) (recovery of "excessive profits" earned on war contracts). But perhaps the broadest delegation yet sustained and the one closest to the case before us came in *Yakus*, for the ultimate standard in the 1942 statute was only that the maximum prices be "generally fair and equitable."

Reason

Under these governing concepts we cannot say that in the Act before us there is such an absence of standards that it would be impossible to ascertain whether the will of Congress has been obeyed.

In some respects, indeed, Congress has been precise in its limitations. The President is given an authority to stabilize prices and wages by § 202(a) of the act, but not at levels less than those prevailing on May 25, 1970.

Moreover the legislation is not as vulnerable as it would have been prior to the amendment adopted earlier in 1971, under which the President is precluded by § 202(b) from singling out "a particular industry or sector of the economy upon which to impose controls" unless he makes a specific finding that wages or prices in that industry or sector have increased at a rate disproportionate to the rate for the economy as a whole. * * *

The limitation on the President's power to take action in particular industries or sectors made this authority more narrow than the authority over prices in the 1942 legislation.[14] It also clarified the will of Con-

---

14. That Act * * * permitted the administrator to set maximum prices in a particular industry where prices, in his judgment, "have risen or threaten to rise to an extent or in a manner inconsistent with the purposes of this Act." The administrator issued maximum price regulations for particular industries until the General Maximum Price Regulation, issued April 30, 1942, 7 F.R. 3153, forbade the sale of most commodities at prices in excess of the highest price charged by the seller during March 1942.

gress.   Congress gave the President broad authority to stabilize prices, rents, wages and salaries, but in effect it contemplated that controls to achieve broad stabilization would begin with a regulation applicable to the entire economy. * * * The House Banking and Currency Committee Report specifically envisaged a 3-month "freeze" to get "a handle on inflation."

This ascertainment of the contours of the power to "stabilize" is fortified by explicit legislative history.   But even the text of the law, the starting point of analysis, must not be taken in a vacuum.   In rejecting claims of invalid delegation of legislative power the Court has made clear that the standards of a statute are not to be tested in isolation and derive "meaningful content from the purposes of the Act, its factual background, and the statutory context."

The historical context of the 1970 law is emphasized in the Government's submission:

> "In enacting the legislation in question here, Congress was, of course, acting against a background of wage and price controls in both wars.   The administrative practice under both of those Acts was the subject of extensive judicial interpretation and review.   This substantial background of prior law and practice provides a further framework for assessing whether the Executive has stayed within the bounds authorized by Congress and provides more than adequate standards for the exercise of authority granted by the Act."

We think this contention is sound.   The context of the 1970 stabilization law includes the stabilization statutes passed in 1942, and the stabilization provisions in Title IV of the Defense Production Act of 1950, and the "common lore" of anti-inflationary controls established by the agency approaches and court decisions, including the probing analyses of the Emergency Court of Appeals.   We do not suggest that the 1970 law was intended as or constitutes a duplicate of the earlier laws.   But those laws and their implementation do provide a validating context as against the charge that the later statute stands without any indication to the agencies and officials of legislative contours and contemplation.

* * *

An undeniably prominent feature of the earlier stabilization programs was the adoption thereunder of across-the-board wage and price controls, typically with "freeze" and "hold-the-line" approaches, subject to relaxation for hardships and inequities under implementing standards.   There can be no doubt that in its broad outlines the general freeze ordered by the President conforms to the legislative intention. Even a rudimentary recourse to available legal materials readily permits a court to ascertain at least to this extent the contours of the legislative will and the conformance of the Executive action to it.

The Union challenges the thesis that the 1970 Act can be sustained by reference to the earlier stabilization laws and rulings thereunder, complaining that unlike the earlier statutes the present law is "shorthand legislation," devoid of any statement of policy or objectives, or of conditions under which action is to be taken, or findings of Congressional intent.

The Act is obviously different in its structure from the law upheld in *Yakus*, which was replete with just such statements of policy, objectives and findings. The difference is largely one of drafting style, ascribable perhaps to the circumstance that the 1942 law was proposed by the Executive, and introduced on that basis after scrutiny by the legislature's drafting staffs. * * *

The purposes of the 1970 law, to a considerable extent inherent in the very authority to "stabilize," are set forth more explicitly in the Report of the House Committee on Banking and Currency which inserted these provisions into the legislative process. H.R. Rep. No. 91-1330 (hereafter cited as House Report). * * *

Whether legislative purposes are to be obtained from committee reports, or are set forth in a separate section of the text of the law, is largely a matter of drafting style. Plainly the 1970 legislative purpose set forth in the House Report does not differ in material degree from the statement of legislative purpose in the 1942 legislation upheld in *Yakus*. This purpose was reiterated in debate on the 1970 Act.

We see no merit in the contention that the Act is constitutionally defective because the timing of the imposition of controls was delegated to the President. * * *

The House Report clarifies that this delegation was not an abdication by Congress, but the product of a reasoned analysis that only such delegation as to timing would further the legislative purpose of stabilization. * * *

The issue whether the delegation before us is excessive must be considered in the light of the unique situation, with the President not in accord with the conclusion of Congress as to the need or desirability of the power entrusted to him. Thus the Speaker, supporting the law, put it that the President and his advisers "are prescribing the wrong medicine for the particular inflationary virus now affecting the Nation," that restrictive fiscal and monetary policies are appropriate for combating traditional "demand-pull inflation" but the country was now beset by "cost-push inflation" for which direct controls were needed. It is not our place to review the merits of these differences. But the physician-virus metaphor is revealing. Viewing the President as a physician in charge, Congress could advise but not mandate his diagnosis. It sought in the national interest to have the right remedy available on a standby basis, if the President should wish to adopt that prescription, following his further reflection and taking into account future developments and experience.

* * *

Finally the House Report takes cognizance, in support of delegation of "timing" to the President, that Congress might not be in session when action was requisite.

* * *

The need felt by Congress to delegate broadly to the President is not undercut by the circumstance that the country was not experiencing and Congress did not contemplate a sudden or dramatic price rise, such as sometimes accompanies a war or shooting emergency, but only a "creeping" inflation.   Continuing the medical analogy a cost-push inflation is no less malignant than a demand-pull inflation.   On the issue of delegation, Congress had reason to authorize the President to begin prompt treatment with direct controls whenever he concluded this was the proper course and regardless of the prior rate of spread of the disease.   The matter was reconsidered in debate on the occasion of the 1971 extension, when some legislators argued that Congress should abandon a "Gulf of Tonkin" approach to the problem that delegated broadly to the President. Other legislators reasoned in response that the "creeping" nature of inflation required a broad delegation to the President to precipitate an effective counter-action.   We have no basis or warrant for holding that what purported to be a reasoned assignment of authority was only an abdication of responsibility.

This is a suitable juncture to refer to the undoubted and substantial significance of the interrelation between the domestic wage and price controls and the actions taken by the President on August 15, 1971, in the field of international trade and monetary adjustments.   The President's message identifies the existence of such an interrelation though not its exact nature.   The House Report's recount of legislative policy includes its recital that the current inflation malady is significantly responsible for the balance-of-payments crisis and liquidity squeeze.   This was a 1970 problem and a legislative objective not known at the time of the 1942 and 1950 legislation.   The consequence for international trade, liquidity and monetary relationships, enhances the range of power Congress may permissibly delegate to the President. * * * And it particularly substantiates the legitimacy of delegating to the President the authority as to the timing for the blending of actions with international consequences.

It is also material, though not dispositive, to note the limited time frame established by Congress for the stabilization authority delegated to the President.   The Act as enacted on August 15, 1970 expired February 28, 1971, establishing a lifespan of about six months.   Two subsequent extensions provided even shorter durations.   When the current expiration date of April 30, 1972, was set on May 18, 1971, Congress rejected the administration request for a two-year extension.   Thus, in the words of the Government's memorandum, Congress established a "close control."   It conjoined flexibility in the President to act promptly with an obligation in Congress to undertake an affirmative review without prolonged delay, without the option of acquiescence by inaction.

However Congress cannot delegate unlimited authority to the Executive over prices and wages even for a period limited to say, the 8-9 months between the President's Order of August 15, 1971, and the April 30, 1972 expiration date.

P/cont.   The Union says that during this period the President has been given a "blank check" for internal affairs which is intolerable in our constitutional system. The Union notes that the order exempted from controls the prices charged for raw agricultural products without statutory authority for the exemption. It claims that the failure of Congress to require, as in the 1942 and 1950 legislation that ongoing regulations be "fair and equitable" is tantamount to a delegation to the President of the power to be unfair and inequitable. The Union complains that there was a failure to provide a system for testing these orders, administratively and by judicial review, as in the earlier legislation.

The net result, charges the Union, is a legislative initiation of control by bare executive fiat, with completely unlimited authority put at the disposal of the President.

This is a formidable fusillade, devastating verbally and not without force analytically. When the smoke clears away, however, we conclude that the Rule of Law has been beleaguered but not breached.

We begin with the observation that we cannot stand on the analysis put to us by the Government. The Government does say, correctly, that the doors of the courts remain open. But the question is, whether the courts can apprise the claim that the stabilization actions do not conform to the legislative will, measured by an intelligible standard. If the courts are open only nominally, they would enhance rather than inhibit executive absolutism.

In the last analysis Government counsel seem to meet these contentions by relying on, and reiterating, the limited duration of the President's powers. That is material, as we have noted, but it is not itself a sufficient answer to the Union's contentions.

If the Act gives the President authority to be unfair and inequitable, as the Union claims, this legislative vessel may indeed founder on a constitutional rock. But we do not reach this constitutional issue because we do not think the Act can be given the extremist interpretation offered by the Union.

We take this view not only because of the doctrine that statutes are to be construed so as to avoid serious constitutional questions, but more directly because we do not think it can sensibly or fairly be said that this extremist approach was what was intended by the legislature. * * *

* * * The ultimate standard for follow-on controls replacing the freeze is a standard of fairness and equity. This standard of removal of "gross inequities" is voiced as an authority of the President in § 202 of the Act. We think there is fairly implicit in the Act the duty to take whatever action is required in the interest of broad fairness and avoidance of gross inequity, although presumably his range of discretion means there may be inequities that a President may remove that he is not compelled by law to remove. * * *

Another feature that blunts the "blank check" rhetoric is the requirement that any action taken by the Executive under the law, subsequent to the freeze, must be in accordance with further standards as developed by the Executive. This requirement, inherent in the Rule of Law and implicit in the Act, means that however broad the discretion of the Executive at the outset, the standards once developed limit the latitude of subsequent executive action.

The importance in present context of this self-limiting aspect of executive and agency discretion is brought out in *Yakus v. United States,* supra.   After noting that the Constitution does not demand the impossible, that the essentials of the legislative function are preserved with a determination of legislative policy, Chief Justice Stone continues:

> * * * [T]he standards prescribed by the present Act, with the aid of the "statement of the considerations" required to be made by the Administrator, are sufficiently definite and precise to enable Congress, the Courts and the public to ascertain whether the Administrator, in fixing the designated prices, has conformed to those standards.   [Citation] Hence we are unable to find in them an unauthorized delegation of legislative power.

The requirement of subsidiary administrative policy, enabling Congress, the courts and the public to assess the Executive's adherence to the ultimate legislative standard, is in furtherance of the purpose of the constitutional objective of accountability.   This 1970 Act gives broadest latitude to the Executive.   Certainly there is no requirement of formal findings.   But there is an on-going requirement of intelligible administrative policy that is corollary to and implementing of the legislature's ultimate standard and objective.   This requirement is underscored by the consideration that the exercise of wide discretion will probably call for "imaginative interpretation," leaving the courts to see whether the executive, using its experience, "has fairly exercised its discretion within the vaguish, penumbral bounds" of the broad statutory standard. * * *

The claim of undue delegation of legislative power broadly raises the challenge of undue power in the Executive and thus naturally involves consideration of the interrelated questions of the availability of appropriate restraints through provisions for administrative procedure and judicial review.   These components of fairness are themselves elements of statutory and constitutional rights but it is appropriate to discuss them in present context because they bear on the issue whether there has been undue delegation to the Executive.

The safeguarding of meaningful judicial review is one of the primary functions of the doctrine prohibiting undue delegation of legislative powers. * * *

The Government concedes and we agree that the Executive's actions under the 1970 Act are not immune from judicial review. * * *

The Government's position rests on the proposition that since the Act provides for enforcement either by way of fine (§ 204) or by way of injunction restraining violations (§ 205), and the person charged with violation is able to obtain judicial review by inserting a defense to either type of enforcement proceeding, this provides ample judicial review for constitutional purposes.

We need not consider whether under conditions of modern life the Constitution permits a restriction to enforcement proceedings of judicial review of Executive discretion as broad in range and significant in impact as that provided by this law, requiring citizens with substantial doubts concerning the validity of the exercise of such broad discretion to run the risk of criminal proceedings. * * *

It is our conclusion that in addition to the judicial reviews noted by the Government, challenges may be made under the provisions for judicial review in the Administrative Procedure Act, 5 U.S.C.A. § § 701–706. These provisions contemplate an action for declaratory judgment or injunction, assuming pertinent requirements for these forms of action are met, as well as a defense in civil or criminal proceedings, see 5 U.S.C.A. § 703. They provide that a person suffering legal wrong because of agency action is entitled to review thereof, 5 U.S.C.A. § 702. Judicial review is provided for final agency action for which there is no other adequate remedy in court, 5 U.S.C.A. § 704.

When the impact of regulations is direct and immediate, so that the controversy is "ripe" for judicial resolution, these provisions of 5 U.S.C.A. § § 701–706, permit pre-enforcement judicial review. * * *

By the same token actions under this 1970 Act are subject to the administrative procedure provisions of the Administrative Procedure Act, 5 U.S.C.A. § 551 ff. It may well be that the applicability of these provisions will have no practical consequence. The rule-making provisions of 5 U.S.C.A. § 553, requiring notice and opportunity for participation by interested persons, are subject to the provision in subsection (b) removing those requirements "(B) when the agency for good cause finds (and incorporates the finding and a brief statement of reasons therefor in the rules issued) that notice and public procedure thereon are impracticable, unnecessary, or contrary to the public interest." The adjudication provisions of 5 U.S.C.A. § 554 are applicable only when an agency hearing is required by the statute, or by compulsion of general law. * * * And *Yakus* upheld the validity of the failure to provide for such hearings in the 1942 maximum price law.

* * *

We turn finally to precedents cited by the Union. They remind us that Separation of Powers is a doctrine with vitality. It is the force that motivated *Youngstown Sheet & Tube Co. v. Sawyer*, 343 U.S. 579 (1952)— where however the executive order seizing the nation's steel mills was without any authorization in legislation. Given a legislative enactment, there have not been any Supreme Court rulings holding statutes unconstitutional for excessive delegation of legislative power since the *Panama Refining* and *Schechter* cases invalidated provisions of the National Industrial Recovery Act of 1933.

These cases express a principle that has validity—reserved for the extremist instance. These precedents were referred to in *Fahey v. Mallonee*, 332 U.S. 245, 249 (1947):

> Both cited cases dealt with delegation of a power to make federal crimes of acts that never had been such before and to devise novel rules of law in a field in which there had been no settled law or custom.

They are without vigor for a case like the one before us, where the delegation is in a context of historical experience with anti-inflation legislation.

The particular application of the delegation principle in *Panama Refining* was colored, as students of the Court's decisions have noted, by the circumstance that the regulation in that case was not generally available and had been inadvertently amended out of effect—a circumstance that led to the creation of the Federal Register.

In *Schechter*, which held invalid the provisions of the National Industrial Recovery Act that authorized the fixing of codes of fair conduct, the "function of formulating the codes was delegated, not to a public official responsible to Congress or the Executive, but to private individuals engaged in the industries to be regulated." * * * The "corporate state" aspects of the Blue Eagle codes that emerged in practice were made possible and reinforced by a legal context of authority to prescribe "codes of fair competition" that covered the entire range of economic life, going beyond even the broad subject matter before us.

A supplemental memorandum in another lawsuit has raised the question that the President's plans for a Price Commission and a Pay Board present the very kind of delegation of government power to private groups that was involved in *Schechter*. That claim has not been put forward by the plaintiff in this case, possibly because the Union has a different litigating interest. We note the point only to say that we do not and are not required to pass on it. We have no way of knowing whether or to what extent the President will delegate authority to persons who are not, at least pro tanto, part of a government agency, or will provide for review of their exercise of such authority. More important, any such delegation is not inherent in the Act as passed. The presumption must be that Congress, in vesting power in the President, contemplated only such further delegation as would be consistent with law, including the requirement that the orders providing for stabilization be issued on a basis that accords with general fairness and avoids gross inequity, and provide for administration and procedures that are meaningfully consistent with that standard. If there should be a problem with the administration provided by the President, whether as to structure or procedure it may be subject to attack as not consistent with the Act, but it does not render the Act void *ab initio*, which is the Union's core claim.

* * *

* * * Our view of the applicable law makes it clear that plaintiff's motion for injunctive relief must be denied.

So ordered.

ECONOMIC STABILIZATION ACT OF 1970
TITLE II—COST OF LIVING STABILIZATION

§ 202. Presidential Authority

(a) The President is authorized to issue such orders and regulations as he may deem appropriate to stabilize prices, rents, wages, and salaries at levels not less than those prevailing on May 25, 1970.   Such orders and regulations may provide for the making of such adjustments as may be necessary to prevent gross inequities.

(b) The authority conferred on the President by this section shall not be exercised with respect to a particular industry or segment of the economy unless the President determines, after taking into account the seasonal nature of employment, the rate of employment or under-employment, and other mitigating factors, that prices or wages in that industry or segment of the economy have increased at a rate which is grossly disproportionate to the rate at which prices or wages have increased in the economy generally.

§ 203. Delegation

The President may delegate the performance of any function under this title to such officers, departments, and agencies of the United States as he may deem appropriate.

§ 204. Penalty

Whoever willfully violates any order or regulation under this title shall be fined not more than $5,000.

§ 205. Injunctions

Whenever it appears to any agency of the United States, authorized by the President to exercise the authority contained in this section to enforce orders and regulations issued under this title, that any person has engaged, is engaged or is about to engage in any acts or practices constituting a violation of any regulation or order under this title, it may in its discretion bring an action, in the proper district court of the United States or the proper United States court of any territory or other place subject to the jurisdiction of the United States to enjoin such acts or practices, and upon a proper showing a permanent or temporary injunction or restraining order shall be granted without bond.   Upon application of the agency, any such court may also issue mandatory injunctions commanding any person to comply with any regulation or order under this title.

§ 206. Expiration

The authority to issue and enforce orders and regulations under this title expires at midnight April 30, 1972, but such expiration shall not affect any proceeding under section 204 for a violation of any such order or regulation, or for the punishment for contempt committed in the violation of any injunction under section 205, committed prior to May 1, 1972.

Notes

One of the healthy impediments to "delegation run riot" that Judge Leventhal found in the *Amalgamated Meat Cutters (AMC)* case was the shortness of the period for which Presidential authority was conferred.   This provided some assurance that executive action would not continue long without Congressional review of performance that presumably would accompany a decision whether to extend the Act.   Indeed, within two months of the *AMC* decision Congress again extended and amended the 1970 legislation, 85 Stat. 743 (1971). The amendments included a detailed statement of national policy, extensive congressional findings to justify wage and price controls, and more detailed standards to be followed in administering the Act. Among these standards was the duty to be "generally fair and equitable." The amendments also established specific administrative procedures and, as Judge Leventhal had already held, expressly stipulated that the rulemaking provisions of the Administrative Procedure Act (APA) applied to administration of the Act. Congress also provided for judicial review of wage and price orders, including appellate review of district court decisions by a Temporary Emergency Court of Appeals. See generally Leventhal, *Principled Fairness and Regulatory Urgency*, 25 Case W. Res. L. Rev. 66 (1974).

In addition to the prospect of periodic congressional oversight, Judge Leventhal found safeguards against administrative arbitrariness (1) in the requirement that power be exercised generally rather than by singling out particular industries, (2) in the availability of judicial review, (3) in the prior history of wage-price controls, (4) in the procedural safeguards of the APA, and (5) in the notion that the administration of the Act would be self-confining as policy was developed and expressed in regulatory form. The court thus shifted the focus of discussion away from debate over whether the power conferred was "legislative" to the issue of whether the legal order could, consistent with the rule of law, accommodate the legislative judgment that the choice of anti-inflation strategy and the timing of its application should, for reasons both of coordination and expedition, reside largely with the executive branch. However sensible this approach generally, consider whether Judge Leventhal may have been too sanguine about the prospects for effective legal control of the authority conferred by the Economic Stabilization Act.

Judicial Review. The availability of judicial review is comforting, but it is hardly a panacea. Courts can exercise effective control over specific administrative acts only where there are relatively clear standards against which to measure administrative performance. To be sure, it is not essential that those standards appear in legislation—they can be promulgated in regulations or emerge from the pattern of agency decisions. But there was no guarantee that either basis for judicial review would develop quickly under the Economic Stabilization Act. Neither the President nor his delegates were required to issue regulations setting forth their policies for its administration. In fact, they produced a welter of regulations, circulars, orders, releases and question-and-answer statements whose legal status was often uncertain. See Gellhorn, *The Legal Effect of Anti-Inflation Advice from Government Agencies*, 17 Prac. Law. 13 (Dec. 1971). Moreover, courts could certainly be expected to have difficulty discerning patterns until a larger number of potential reviewable decisions had been implemented. The program of emergency wage-price controls might be over before a firm basis for review emerged in the "common law" generated by agency activity.

Nor was the *AMC* court necessarily correct in believing that there was only limited room for individualized judgment under the statute. The basic action before the court was general—a ninety-day freeze on wages and prices—but its implementation required many specific decisions interpreting exactly what was frozen and when. The President conferred on the Cost of Living Council (CLC) the power to define any terms in the freeze order, to make exceptions and exemptions, and to issue any other appropriate order. 3 C.F.R. § 199 (1971). Thus, even if controls were general, individualized action was clearly possible by way of interpretation, exemption, or other "appropriate" action. During the ninety days of the freeze the CLC received 50,000 complaints of violations, 6,000 formal requests for exceptions, and 750,000 requests for interpretations. See generally R. KAGAN, REGULATORY JUSTICE: IMPLEMENTING A WAGE-PRICE FREEZE (1978). How were the courts to review these individual determinations?

The answer of the few cases that reached the Temporary Emergency Court of Appeals seems to be, "on the basis of the desire of the Congress to give the executive broad discretion." For example, a landlord who contended that the Cost of Living Council had misconstrued the President's freeze order was rebuffed in part by the remarkable statement that his argument ignored the fact that the order had delegated to the Council all the power of the President under the act—including presumably the power to change the meaning of the order. *United States v. Lieb*, 426 F.2d 1161 (Em. App. 1972). And, when the University of Southern California appealed an order that required it to refund an increase in the price of 1971 season football tickets (although the tickets had been sold prior to August 17, 1971) on the theory that the "transaction" occurred with the post-freeze playing of the football games, it was met with the response that the court must give great weight to the interpretations of the agency charged with administrative responsibility, particularly where, as here, "the broadest possible delegation of power was given." *University of Southern Cal. v. Cost of Living Council*, 472 F.2d 1065 (Em. App. 1972), *cert. denied* 410 U.S. 928 (1973). In the latter case, the court was discomforted by the fact that the Council had previously decided that universities could charge higher tuition and dormitory prices scheduled, but not collected, before August 17 and had apparently decided the "date of transaction" question both ways with respect to teachers' salaries. See *United States v. Jefferson Parish School Board*, 333 F. Supp. 418 (E.D. La. 1971). However, recognizing that the Council was faced with a "gargantuan task," the court of appeals found "any inconsistencies in interpretation—[to be] reasonable." 472 F.2d at 1072.

The Force of History. Nowhere in the judicial decisions under the 1970 act does one find serious reference to the OPA experience as a source of limiting standards for administrative action. Indeed, one wonders whether that prior experience, with "demand-pull" inflation in wartime, should be made concretely applicable to decisions directed at "cost-push" inflation in peacetime. The prior experience with direct controls may have seemed more pertinent to Judge Leventhal, who was Assistant General Counsel of the OPA during World War II and chief counsel of the price control apparatus during the Korean War, than it proved for other judges who reviewed the CLC's decisions.

In other contexts, however, judicial reliance on prior experience has been influential. In *Kent v. Dulles*, 357 U.S. 116 (1958), for example, a wholly open-ended delegation of power to the Secretary of State to issue or deny passports was, in response to an improper delegation challenge, judicially confined to a determination of whether the applicant was a citizen or owed allegiance to the United States and was engaged in lawful conduct. The Supreme Court found these standards for the exercise of the Secretary's discretion in the historic practice of the Department of State, implicitly approved by the Congress. Given these precise limits, it rejected the power assumed by the Secretary—to refuse issuance of passports to Communists—and the constitutional question of improper delegation thus was "not reached." The disposition both to search for standards and to find quite narrow discretion under a seemingly broad delegation is accentuated in cases, like *Kent*, which implicate personal freedoms. But cf. *Haig v. Agee*, 453 U.S. 280 (1981).

The courts' familiarity with historically operative standards has, however, often helped sustain legislative delegations. Regulation of common carriers on the basis of "public interest, convenience and necessity" is a common, well-understood, and judicially accepted administrative function, although the statutory formula appears vacuous. Here and elsewhere a long history of governmental regulation, or a common-law heritage, may both sustain a delegation and provide a reasonably firm basis for judicial review. See, e.g., *Department of Health v. Owens-Corning Fiberglass Co.*, 100 N.J. Super. 366, 242 A.2d 21, (1968), *affirmed* 53 N.J. 248, 250 A.2d 11 (1969), which upholds a delegation of authority to regulate "air pollution" where that term is defined to correspond roughly with the common-law definition of nuisance. Judge Leventhal's recourse to history was neither novel nor inappropriate generally; it is merely the technique's utility in these circumstances that may be questioned.

Procedural Safeguards. Judge Leventhal's assurance in *AMC* that the 1970 Stabilization Act fits within a well-defined system of administrative law-making rests mainly on the Federal Administrative Procedure Act (APA), which is discussed at length at pp. 49–51 infra. Yet again, as Judge Leventhal obliquely concedes, the APA's procedural safeguards lacked force in the *AMC* context. The APA's exceptions from required public rulemaking procedures probably covered most CLC regulations, and the Economic Stabilization Act did not mandate formal adjudication for any executive decisions, including individual exemptions or orders. Indeed, the CLC was later accused of employing highly secretive procedures that impeded both effective participation by affected parties and judicial review. See *Baldwin County Electric Membership Corp. v. Price Commission*, 481 F.2d 920, 924–28 (Em. App. 1973) (dissent of Judge Hastie). See also Note, *The Administration of Economic Controls: The Economic Stabilization Act of 1970*, 29 Case W. Res. L. Rev. 458 (1979).

Moreover, even if strict procedural formalities had been mandated and followed, procedures may not be a total substitute for substantive standards. The opportunity to present evidence, cross-examine witnesses, and make oral argument can be effective only to the extent that the bases for an eventual decisions are reasonably well understood. Before contestants can exercise their procedural rights sensibly they must know what facts are relevant, what portions of opposing testimony are crucial, and what issues of policy or precedent are important. The APA would have required publication of any adopted regulatory standards, but neither it nor the Stabilization Act required that standards be adopted.

SUN RAY DRIVE-IN DAIRY, INC. v. OREGON LIQUOR CONTROL COMMISSION

Court of Appeals of Oregon, 1973.
16 Or. App. 63, 517 P.2d 289.

TANZER, JUDGE.

Petitioner appeals from an order of the Oregon Liquor Control Commission denying its application for a Class B Package Store liquor license for its store in Ontario, Oregon. The commission based its refusal on

ORS 471.295(1) which provides that the Commission may refuse to license an applicant if it has reasonable ground to believe that there are "sufficient licensed premises in the locality" or that the granting of the license is "not demanded by public interest or convenience." * * *

Various persons employed by the licensing division of the commission testified at the hearing on petitioner's application. Mr. William Alexander, a liquor control officer, * * * initially testified that he recommended refusal of petitioner's application because of (1) objections of area residents; (2) the large number of existing outlets; and (3) the fact that petitioner's store did not have a broad inventory of groceries. However, he subsequently abandoned the last ground. He testified that even if the petitioner's store had been a Safeway, he would have recommended refusal because of the number of outlets already in the area. * * *

Mr. Alexander's [2] * direct superior, Mr. Charles Miller, * * * testified that he reviewed Mr. Alexander's report and agreed that the application should be denied. Mr. Miller's reasons * * * [were the same as] Mr. Alexander's. * * * Mr. Miller testified that he had no "yardstick" to go by and that his recommendation was based on his "past experience and judgment."

Mr. Miller's recommendation was * * * passed on to Mr. Don Church, the commission's director of licensing. Mr. Church testified [3] that the number of other licensees in a particular area was not a factor in deciding whether to issue a license. * * * Mr. Church stated that if a store is deemed by the Commission to be a "legitimate grocery store," the commission's policy is to grant the store a Class B Package Store license, regardless of how many other licenses are in the immediate area. The reason for his recommendation of denial to the Commission, Mr. Church said, was that petitioner's store had been represented to him in the reports from his subordinates as a "gasoline station with dairy products." Mr. Church concluded from the evidence he heard at the hearing that petitioner's store more closely approximated a "legitimate grocery store" than he had supposed, but that there would have to be still greater expansion of the scope of petitioner's inventory and the number of items of each type before he would recommend approval. Mr. Church expressed concern, for example, that the store's inventory listed only three packages of Birdseye creamed peas.

Petitioner gave evidence that several similar businesses in the Ontario area and neighboring cities, some with significantly smaller grocery inventories and one that appears to be an ordinary gas station, had package licenses.

The commission then made the following findings of fact and ultimate facts upon which the denial of license is based:

"FINDINGS OF FACT

"Sun Ray Drive-In Dairy, Inc., * * * factually demonstrated that * * * their Sun Ray Dairy store in Ontario during the month of January, 1973, made gross sales of $15,797.25 plus sales of dairy and food items of

$8,909.18; that theirs is a 'convenient convenience' store with inventory running about 6 to $7,000.00 which inventories are refilled weekly.   There were local objectors to the issuance of PB license to the applicants.   There are fifteen licensed outlets for beer sales in Ontario, with five outlets within four blocks of the applicant.   The listed inventory was not sufficient for a grocery store.   The Commission particularly noted applicant's inventory listed one can of beef stew, three—twelve ounce packages of weiners, two cans of chili, three cans of pork and beans and one Quaker Oats together with other groceries and dairy products.?

"ULTIMATE FACTS

"There are sufficient licensed premises in the locality of the application.   There were local objections to the issuance of Package Store Class B license to the applicant.   The applicant's inventory is not sufficient for a grocery store."

Petitioner asks that we reverse the findings of fact, contending that the proof of each ultimate fact was otherwise.   We are unable to review for substantial evidence because we are unable to ascertain the issues or the standards against which the evidence is to be measured.   How many licensed premises are "sufficient" in the "locality"?   Is sufficiency to be measured by population density, supply and demand, geographical area to be covered, other factors, or a combination of factors?   How are public objections to be weighed?   What ratio of acceptability should be required?   Within what area of the license applicant?   Finally, are all grocery stores entitled to a package license?   If so, how is "grocery store" defined?

The legislature has not answered these questions by statute.   * * *

The commission has not published rules or regulations establishing standards by which the statutory grounds for refusal for "sufficient licensed premises in the locality" or that the license "is not demanded by public interest or convenience," are to be applied.   Instead, the licensing personnel of the commission testified at the hearing as to the "policy" of the commission.   Those policies * * * have the quality of folklore in that unwritten rules are passed on orally by culture carriers from one generation of employees to another, from one level of employees to another, without the stabilizing effect of the written word.

A legislative delegation of power in broad statutory language such as the phrase "demanded by public interest or convenience" places upon the administrative agency a responsibility to establish standards by which that law is to be applied.   The legislature has provided for such rule making in the [Oregon] Administrative Procedures Act.

Compliance with the Administrative Procedures Act is much more than an act of technical legal ritual.   Unwritten standards and policies are no better than no standards and policies at all.   Without written, published standards, the entire system of administrative law loses its keystone.   The ramifications affect every party and every procedure involved in the fulfillment of the agency's responsibility under the law, e.g., the public, the applicant, agency personnel, the participants in the hearing, the commission, the legislature and the judiciary.

The policies of an agency in a democratic society must be subject to public scrutiny. Published standards are essential to inform the public. Further, they help assure public confidence that the agency acts by rules and not from whim or corrupt motivation. In addition, interested parties and the general public are entitled to be heard in the process of rule adoption under the Administrative Procedures Act.

An applicant for a license should be able to know the standards by which his application will be judged before going to the expense in time, investment and legal fees necessary to make application. Thereafter, he is entitled to even treatment by rule of law and reasonable confidence that he has received such treatment. This cannot be achieved without published rules.

Cases are usually disposed of without litigation. In most situations, the law and the agency policy are expressed in the actions of agency personnel who deal with the public. Written standards and policies are essential to assure an acceptable degree of consistency of practice among the personnel of the agency. In this case, as an example of what occurs in the absence of rules, the field investigator and his supervisor each recommended against approval because of the number of licensees already in the area, but the director of licensing who was in charge of their activities testified that the number of pre-existing outlets was not significant. He recommended disapproval because applicant was not a grocery store. The order of the commission, however, adopts both reasons as grounds for its denial. An administrative agency cannot properly perform its duty under the law unless employees at all levels work toward the same objectives under a clear direction of policy from the head of that agency, in this case the commission. The public is entitled to consistency of enforcement from the agency. That situation cannot be achieved in the absence of written standards.

The parties to a hearing of a contested case must know what is to be heard in the hearing. The agency and the applicant are entitled to know what they are required to prove and disprove in order to gather and present their evidence. The hearings officer must have standards so that he can determine questions of materiality and relevance and propose appropriate findings and conclusions to the commission.

Written standards enable the decision-making body, in this case the commission, to make its decisions by rule of law rather than for subjective or ad hominem reasons. In this case, for example, the applicant introduced evidence of several similar businesses in the area which had package licenses. There is no way for him or for us to know whether he was singled out for discriminatory treatment or whether he was subjected to the same policy standards which were employed when the other comparable outlets were licensed and renewed. We recognize the wide discretion vested in the commission by its enabling legislation, but that discretion is not unbridled. It is discretion to make policies for even application, not discretion to treat each case on an ad hoc basis. The danger of inconsistent, subjective and ad hominem decision making is minimized by the deliberate adoption of written, published policy standards applicable alike to all applicants.

The legislature is entitled to know whether or not the policies and practices of the agency are consistent with the legislative policies upon which the delegation of legislative power to the agency is based. In the absence of published rules, members of the legislature must form their judgments instead upon rumor, individual cases, isolated news reports and other fragmentary, impressionistic and often unreliable sources of information. Published standards are necessary to the proper performance of the duty of legislative oversight of executive agencies operating under legislative delegations of power.

Finally, and most directly applicable to this case, the parties to a contested case are entitled to judicial review. Judicial review is among the safeguards which serve to legitimatize broad legislative delegations of power to administrative agencies. In the absence of standards, however, the courts are unable to perform that task of judicial review. We cannot determine whether substantial evidence supported the findings because we cannot know what was in issue at the hearing. * * * It is not for the court, but for the administrative agency with its statutory mandate and its expertise to develop standards. Were we to decide this case in the absence of administratively adopted standards, we would necessarily either be imposing court-made standards on the agency or we would ourselves be guilty of subjective decision making. Either role would be deleterious to the ability of the agency to fulfill its proper administrative role. Until the commission adopts appropriate rules, we cannot perform our judicial function.

Therefore, we vacate the order, remand this case and direct that the Oregon Liquor Control Commission not act on petitioner's application until it has first adopted rules pursuant to the Administrative Procedures Act, designed to accomplish the legislative purposes of the [licensing statute] which will be applicable to this applicant as well as to all other applicants for issuance or renewal of licenses alike.

* * *

Notes

Like the *Sun Ray* decision, several federal courts have gone beyond Judge Leventhal's gentle suggestion in *AMC* that agency standards might ultimately substitute for legislative standards, by insisting, as an aspect of procedural due process rather than the nondelegation doctrine, that agencies develop policies and criteria for making particularized judgments. See, e.g., *Holmes v. New York Housing Authority*, 398 F.2d 262 (2d Cir. 1968); *Hornsby v. Allen*, 326 F.2d 605 (5th Cir. 1964). In *Hornsby*, the district court was instructed to enjoin the denial of liquor licenses by the City of Atlanta unless and until "ascertainable standards" for such denials had been established by the Board of Aldermen. In *Holmes* the court held that a complaint alleging that the Housing Authority had established no standards governing the selection of nonpreference applicants for public housing in New York City stated a cause of action under the due process clause. See *Judicial Review of Public Housing Admissions*, 1971 Urban L. Ann. 228.

Delegation, Representation, and Good Government

In THE END OF LIBERALISM 125, 126, 148–49, 155 (1969), Theodore Lowi argues that modern toleration of broad delegations of policymaking authority to administrators is part of a political tradition that is antithetical to *law* (that is, to rules or standards as distinguished from procedures) and that the legislature's failure to prescribe policy inevitably results in a failure of government to develop coherent policy and ultimately in the replacement of law by ad hoc bargaining.

Professor Lowi further contends that broad delegations will generally result, not in administrative rulemaking to determine policy, but in policy remaining permanently indeterminate. This is true, he argues, because in individual cases it will be too costly for affected parties to insist upon a clear statement of policy:

> Interest-group liberalism has little place for law because laws interfere with the political process. * * *
>
> In brief, law, in the liberal view, is too authoritative a use of authority. Authority has to be tentative and accessible to be acceptable. If authority is to be accommodated to the liberal myth that it is "not power at all," it must emerge out of individual bargains.
>
> * * * Delegation of power provides the legal basis for rendering a statute tentative enough to keep the political process in good working order all the way down from Congress to the hearing examiner, the meat inspector, the community action supervisor, and the individual clients with which they deal. Everyone can feel that he is part of one big policy-making family. * * *
>
> *Wages and Hours Regional:* Mr. Employer, we find that you owe your ten employees a total of $10,000 in back wages, plus fines, for having them take telephone messages while having lunch on the premises.
>
> *Employer:* I object. You interrogated my employees without my knowledge, and did not interrogate me at all. And, besides, where do you get off saying my boys were "on call" because they heard the phone ring? Talk to my lawyer.
>
> *Regional:* How about $5,000 in back pay and no fines?
>
> *Employer:* Good God, now I'm really disgusted. I want in writing your official interpretation governing such a case: And aren't there rules about notice and hearings?
>
> *Regional:* How about $2,500 in back pay?
>
> *Employer:* Well, hell, I * * *
>
> *Regional:* How about an exchange of memoranda indicating future compliance?
>
> *Employer:* Mmm * * * [aside: Lawyers' fees * * * trips to testify * * * obligations to that damned congressman of ours * * *]
>
> *Official memo from Regional, weeks later:* You are hereby directed to cease * * *

Posted in employees' toilet: You are hereby directed to eat lunch off the premises.

This drama could have taken place in one long-distance call or in half a dozen letters strung out over many weeks. However, the demoralizing part is not what one might expect. It isn't "bureaucracy." * * * Disgust, disappointment, and distrust would arise in such a case because the agency appears "gutless." Its effort to avoid enunciating a rule may be rationalized as flexibility, but to most intelligent people directly involved in such a problem it can end in reduced respect—for the agency and for government. And meanwhile, no rule. * * *

* * * Admittedly the complexity of modern life forces Congress into vagueness and generality in drafting its statutes. Admittedly the political pressure of social unrest forces Congress and the President into premature formulations that make delegation of power inevitable. But to take these causes and effects as natural and good, and then to build the system around them, is to doom the system to remaining always locked into the original causes and effects.

Professor Lowi is by no means alone in believing that the practice of broad delegation is a formula for bad government. In DEMOCRACY AND DISTRUST (1980), John Hart Ely views the failure of the "legislature [i.e., Congress] to legislate [i.e., decide policy questions]" as one of the major obstacles to a truly representative democracy. "There can be little point in worrying about the distribution of the franchise and other personal political rights unless the important policy choices are being made by elected officials." Id. at 133. In Ely's view, restricting legislative delegations will not produce perfect, only democratic, governance. "I'm not saying we may not still end up with a fair number of clowns as representatives, but at least then it will be because clowns are what we deserve." Id. at 134.

Similar sentiments seem to underlie recent dissenting opinions by Justices Rehnquist and Burger. See *Industrial Union Department, AFL-CIO v. American Petroleum Institute*, 448 U.S. 607, 671 (1980); *American Textile Manufacturers Institute v. Donovan*, 452 U.S. 490, 543 (1981). Both would apparently send section 6(b)(5) of the Occupational Safety and Health Act, 29 U.S.C.A. § 655(b)(5) back to Congress for further specification of the criteria by which the Occupational Safety and Health Administration should balance the objectives of protecting worker health and maintaining a healthy economy. The pertinent language of section 6(b)(5) directs OSHA, in regulating worker exposure to toxic chemicals, to prescribe the standard that "most adequately assures, to the extent feasible * * * that no employee will suffer material impairment of health or functional capacity even if such employee has regular exposure to the hazard * * * for the period of his working life." Union representatives claimed that this instruction obliged OSHA to mandate the use of whatever available technology an industry can afford to install without bankrupting itself, while employer groups contended that the agency is required to weigh the costs of controls against health benefits in deciding what standard is "feasible." Adoption of the first interpretation could in some instances force employers to spend hundreds of millions of dollars, while acceptance of the latter version would reduce protection for workers in industries where control technology was expensive.

According to Justice Rehnquist's dissent in *Industrial Union Dept.*, a challenge to OSHA's standard for benzene, a known human carcinogen:

> In drafting § 6(b)(5), Congress was faced with a clear, if difficult, choice between balancing statistical lives and industrial resources or authorizing the Secretary to elevate human life above all concerns save massive dislocation. * * * That Congress chose * * * to pass this difficult choice on to the Secretary is evident from the spectral quality of the standard it selected.

448 U.S. at 685. In the later case Rehnquist and the Chief Justice suggested that the "spectral" language of section 6(b)(5) masked a policy disagreement so profound that had the Congress been required to resolve it "there would have been no bill for the President to sign." 452 U.S. at 546.

The Lowi-Ely-Rehnquist critique dramatizes an apparently serious flaw in American government—a legislature fleeing from choice on critical issues, not by postponing action but by adopting vacuous statutes conferring policy-making power on administrators who will themselves be deeply compromised by their lack of clear statutory authority. Thus, it is suggested, we blunder our way into an administrative state that has traded its democratic values for little or no increase in effective governance.

Yet before accepting this depressing vision, and the judicial insistence on statutory specificity that it apparently entails, consider some critical questions. First, are you convinced that Congress should decide all basic policy issues *by statute* when it launches any public program? For example, are you as confident as Justice Rehnquist that there should be no OSHA program absent an initial Congressional decision firmly establishing priorities between health and economic well-being? Do you agree with Professor Lowi that the lack of a clear rule for making such tradeoffs in specific industries will be demoralizing? Is it clear, as Professor Ely would seem to suggest, that this sort of ambiguity about basic values is "unrepresentative" of the electorate, or otherwise interferes with republican government? See generally G. CALABRESI & P. BOBBITT, TRAGIC CHOICES (1978).

In at least some instances, the Supreme Court has seemed perfectly content with statutory formulations that confer significant policy discretion on administrators even assuming, hypothetically, that Congress' loose language was an evasion made necessary by the legislators' inability to decide. *Chevron U.S.A. Inc. v. Natural Resources Defense Council*, ___ U.S. ___, 104 S.Ct. 2778 (1984), involved review of the Environmental Protection Agency's so-called "bubble policy." Pursuant to regulations the agency adopted in 1981, facilities were permitted to install new equipment not meeting all the conditions in their air quality permits so long as they made offsetting reductions elsewhere in the facility that prevented deterioration of the overall quality of the emissions from their plants. Respondents claimed that each source of pollution within an existing plant was a "stationary source" under the Clean Air Act. Because the Act prohibits any increase in emissions from any "stationary source" in so-called "non-attainment" areas, NRDC argued that the flexibility sought to be introduced by the "bubble" regulations was impermissible in areas of the country that were required to improve, not merely maintain, air quality.

The Supreme Court held that the EPA could treat a whole plant as one "stationary source" for purposes of the bubble policy in all geographic areas even though for other purposes the agency treated each emitting location as a stationary source. After parsing the statute and its legislative history, the Court concluded that the Congress had no specific intent either to encourage or to inhibit use of the bubble interpretation. More generally, the Clean Air Act sought to accommodate in some fashion demands for both environmental quality and economic vitality. Because the Administrator seemed to have reached a reasoned accommodation of those interests adopting the bubble policy, the Court concluded that its reviewing function was at an end. Without ever mentioning the potential non-delegation issue raised by a statute that, as interpreted, clearly conferred administrative power to make critical value choices, the Court said:

> Congress intended to accommodate both [economic and environmental] interests, but did not do so itself on the level of specificity presented by this case. Perhaps that body consciously desired the Administrator to strike the balance at this level, thinking that those with great expertise and charged with responsibility for administering the provision would be in a better position to do so; perhaps it simply did not consider the question at this level; and perhaps Congress was unable to forge a coalition on either side of the question, and those on each side decided to take their chances with the scheme devised by the agency. For judicial purposes, it matters not which of these things occurred.

> Judges are not experts in the field, and are not part of either political branch of the Government. Courts must, in some cases, reconcile competing political interests, but not on the basis of the judges' personal policy preferences. In contrast, an agency to which Congress has delegated policy-making responsibilities may, within the limits of that delegation, properly rely upon the incumbent administration's views of wise policy to inform its judgments. While agencies are not directly accountable to the people, the Chief Executive is, and it is entirely appropriate for the political branch of the Government to make such policy choices—resolving the competing interests which Congress itself either inadvertently did not resolve, or intentionally left to be resolved by the agency charged with the administration of the statute in light of everyday realities.

___ U.S. at ___, 104 S.Ct. at 2793. Perhaps significantly, Justice Rehnquist did not participate in the *Chevron* decision.

Second, even if we were to agree that Congress *should* determine the basic social values that are to be implemented by public programs, to what extent can statutory language realistically control subsequent events? Consider the following excerpt from J. PRESSMAN & A. WIL-DAVSKY, IMPLEMENTATION 182–84 (2d ed. 1979):

> We begin by observing that the essential constituents of any policy are objectives and resources.   In most policies of interest, objectives are characteristically multiple (because we want many things, not just one), conflicting (because we want different things), and vague (because that is how we can agree to proceed without having to agree also on exactly what to do).   So if the objectives are not uniquely determined, neither are the modes of implementation for them.

> Because of the cognitive limitations and the dynamic quality of our environment, moreover, there is no way for us to understand at first all the relevant constraints on resources.   We can discover and then incorporate them into our plans only as the implementation process unfolds.   As long as we cannot determine what is feasible, we cannot carry out any well-defined policy univocally; all we can do is carry along a cluster of potential policies.   Implementation begins neither with words nor deeds, but with multiple dispositions to act or to treat certain situations certain ways.   * * *

> Now Webster's definition of disposition ("the tendency of something to act in a certain manner under given circumstances") obscures the important point that many dispositions—and certainly those relevant to the present discussion—are generic rather than specific.   They do not find expression in a unique function or activity, and it may even be impossible to determine, a priori, the specific forms in which they will be realized.   * * *

> Policies grow out of ideas, and ideas are inexhaustible.   What can be done with them depends as much on their intrinsic richness as on the quality of the minds and the nature of their environment.   As problems are truly understood only after they have been solved, so the full implications of an idea can often be seen only from hindsight, only after the idea has been used and adapted to a variety of circumstances.   Hence the beginnings of an idea are, generally speaking, an insufficient measure of its capabilities or its scope.

> Any new idea, Cardinal Newman once observed, has unknown amplitude:

> It will, in proportion of its native vigour and subtlety, introduce itself into the framework and details of social life, changing public opinion and supporting or undermining the foundations of established order. Thus in time it has grown into an ethical code, or into a system of government or into a theology, or into a ritual, according to its capabilities; and this system, or a body of thought, theoretical and practical * * * will after all be only the adequate representation of the original idea, being nothing else than what that very idea meant from the first—its exact image as seen in a combination of the most diversified aspects, with the suggestions and corrections of many minds, and the illustration of many trials.

What might it mean to make a policy choice separated from policy implementation?   Is the policy to be implemented, then, what was conceived or what it became, or what it might have been?   And how do we credit the contributions of those "many minds" and "many trials?" What exactly is it that the vague delegation critics would have the Congress—or the courts—do?

Third, are there reasons to believe that explicit legislative choices among competing policies will produce decisions that are either socially beneficial or representative of majoritarian preferences? Stripped of its sometimes forbidding formal proofs and elaborate notation systems, modern public choice theory seems to suggest that the answer is "no."

Imagine, for simplicity, a three person legislature composed of A, B and C. These representatives are asked to vote on alternative specific policies, X, Y, and Z, for addressing public issue N. Our representatives have the following preference orderings among the alternatives: A prefers X to Y to Z; B prefers Y to Z to X; and C prefers Z to X to Y. These preference orderings can be depicted tabularly as follows:

Representative	Preference Ordering (N)		
A	X	Y	Z
B	Y	Z	X
C	Z	X	Y

Obviously, no policy has a majority of first place votes. Moreover, these preferences result in a "vicious" circle when voted on in pairs. When X is paired against Y, X wins (A and C vs. B). When X is paired against Z, Z wins (B and C vs. A). When Z is paired against Y, Y wins (A and B vs. C). That is, X beats Y, which beats Z, which beats X.

How is our legislature to decide? In a now-famous theorem, Kenneth Arrow demonstrated (or rediscovered) that if the representatives have equally weighted votes, cannot make side payments to alter the preference orderings, make decisions by majority rule, and cannot manipulate the agenda to exclude any pairwise vote, there can be no stable legislative decision. Moreover, since Arrow's initial article on the subject in 1950, he and others have demonstrated that, unhappily, this "paradox of voting" may apply to a large number of the run-of-the-mill issues that come before electorates or assemblies. See generally A. SEN, COLLECTIVE CHOICE AND SOCIAL WELFARE (1970); Sen, *Social Choice Theory: A Re-Examination*, 45 Econometrica 53 (1977).

The means for avoiding the voting paradox, implicit in the Arrow theorem's conditions, are not attractive. We can abandon majority rule, allow the agenda to be rigged, give one representative extra votes, or permit side payments. Since the first three devices obviously give special power to someone (what the public choice theorists sometimes call a "dictatorship result"), they hold little appeal as means for rescuing representative democracy. The fourth, however, might be.

Suppose there were another set of alternative policies relating to a second public issue N_1, among which A, B and C had the following preferences:

Representative	Preference Ordering (N_1)		
A	X_1	Y_1	Z_1
B	Y_1	Z_1	X_1
C	Z_1	X_1	Y_1

Now suppose that A has a very strong preference for X over Y and Z, but a very weak preference for X_1, over Y_1, and Z_1. Conversely, B has a very weak preference for Y over Z and X, but a very strong preference for Y_1 over Z_1 and X_1. It would surely make sense for A and B to swap votes across issues N and N_1, with both voting for X and for Y_1. If they did, the voting paradox would disappear in favor of stable majorities on both issues. This result might also be considered satisfactory from a public welfare perspective. A and B both increased their welfare (or, hopefully, that of their constituents) by trading lesser valued policies for greater valued ones.

But, alas such vote-trading ("logrolling") may as easily have unfortunate public welfare effects. For once we allow *intensity* of preference to enter the picture we can hardly forget about C. What if C's preferences for Z and Z_1 are much stronger than A and B's combined intensity for X and Y_1? If so, general welfare will have been reduced.

Although we cannot know what the welfare effects will be (because we have no way of measuring A, B and C's preference intensities on the same scale), a number of scholars in the public choice tradition suspect that majority rule with logrolling systematically decreases general welfare. The logic of their hypothesis is straightforward: Shifting legislative majorities enact multiple programs, each of which has costs that exceed its benefits, but each of which distributes more benefits than costs to the (bare) majority that voted for it. Over time the excess of costs over benefits grows. William Riker and Steven Brams have called this—you guessed it—*The Paradox of Vote Trading*, 67 Am. Pol. Sci. Rev. 1235 (1973).

Having come this far we might now believe that there are some rather good arguments for permitting, even favoring, broad delegations of legislative authority. Statutory vagueness avoids ubiquitous voting cycles and random or contrived "dictatorship" results through agenda influence, see generally Levine and Plott, *Agenda Influence and its Implications*, 63 Va. L. Rev. 561 (1977), and may make welfare-reducing logrolling across issues less attractive. A vague statutory mandate at least suggests that a majority wants *something* done, the *status quo* altered. And perhaps subsequent development of policy by administrators, under the watchful eyes of Congress, the President, and the courts, is at least as socially beneficial *and* representative of popular sentiment as any legislatively prescribed policy outcomes.

Many scholars in the public choice tradition would almost certainly dissent from this sanguine suggestion. For example, in *Legislative Choice of Regulatory Forms: Legal Process or Administrative Process?*, 39 Pub. Choice 33 (1982), Morris Fiorina argues that delegation to administrators is a useful device for reelection-oriented legislators to shift the responsibility for the focused costs of regulation, such as environmental regulation, that has only diffuse—and, therefore, electorally irrelevant—benefits. Conversely, Fiorina would expect legislators to enact specific "legally" (meaning "judicially") enforceable norms where benefits are concentrated (and electorally valuable credit can be claimed) and costs are diffuse.   For further discussion, see Aronson, Gellhorn, and Robinson, *A Theory of Legislative Delegation,* 68 Corn.L.Rev.1 (1982); Mashaw, *Pro-Delegation: Why Administrators Should Make Political Decisions,* 1 T. Law, Econ. & Org. ___ (1985).   See Generally R. ABRAMS, FOUNDATIONS OF POLITICAL ANALYSIS (1980).

2. THE "LEGISLATIVE VETO"

IMMIGRATION AND NATURALIZATION SERVICE v. CHADHA

Supreme Court of the United States, 1983.
462 U.S. 919, 103 S.Ct. 2764, 77 L.Ed. 2d 317

CHIEF JUSTICE BURGER delivered the opinion of the Court.

* * *

Chadha is an East Indian who was born in Kenya and holds a British passport.   He was lawfully admitted to the United States in 1966 on a nonimmigrant student visa. His visa expired on June 30, 1972.   On October 11, 1973, the District Director of the Immigration and Naturalization Service ordered Chadha to show cause why he should not be deported for having "remained in the United States for a longer time than permitted." Pursuant to § 242(b) of the Immigration and Nationality Act (Act), 8 U.S.C. § 1254(b), a deportation hearing was held before an immigration judge on January 11, 1974.   Chadha conceded that he was deportable for overstaying his visa and the hearing was adjourned to enable him to file an application for suspension of deportation under § 244(a)(1) of the Act. Section 244(a)(1) provides:

> "(a) As hereinafter prescribed in this section, the Attorney General may, in his discretion, suspend deportation and adjust the status to that of an alien lawfully admitted for permanent residence, in the case of an alien who applies to the Attorney General for suspension of deportation and—
>
> "(1) is deportable under any law of the United States except the provisions specified in paragraph (2) of this subsection; has been physically present in the United States for a continuous period of not less than seven years immediately preceding the date of such application, and proves that during all of such period he was and is a person of good moral character; and is a person whose deportation would, in the opinion of the Attorney General, result in extreme hardship to the alien or to his spouse, parent, or child, who is a citizen of the United States or an alien lawfully admitted for permanent residence."

* * *

Pursuant to § 244(c)(1) of the Act, the immigration judge suspended Chadha's deportation and a report of the suspension was transmitted to Congress.   Section 244(c)(1) provides:

> "Upon application by any alien who is found by the Attorney General to meet the requirements of subsection (a) of this section the Attorney General may in his discretion suspend deportation of such alien.   If the deportation of **any**

alien is suspended under the provisions of this subsection, a complete and detailed statement of the facts and pertinent provisions of law in the case shall be reported to the Congress with the reasons for such suspension.   Such reports shall be submitted on the first day of each calendar month in which Congress is in session."

Once the Attorney General's recommendation for suspension of Chadha's deportation was conveyed to Congress, Congress had the power under § 244(c)(2) of the Act to veto[2] the Attorney General's determination that Chadha should not be deported.   Section 244(c)(2) provides:

"(2) In the case of an alien specified in paragraph (1) of subsection (a) of this subsection—if during the session of the Congress at which a case is reported, or prior to the close of the session of the Congress next following the session at which a case is reported, either the Senate or the House of Representatives passes a resolution stating in substance that it does not favor the suspension of such deportation, the Attorney General shall thereupon deport such alien or authorize the alien's voluntary departure in the manner provided by law.   If, within the time above specified, neither the Senate nor the House of Representatives shall pass such a resolution, the Attorney General shall cancel deportation proceedings."

*   *   *

On December 12, 1975, Representative Eilberg, Chairman of the Judiciary Subcommittee on Immigration, Citizenship, and International Law, introduced a resolution opposing "the granting of permanent residence in the United States to [six] aliens," including Chadha.   The resolution was referred to the House Committee on the Judiciary.   On December 16, 1975, the resolution was discharged from further consideration by the House Committee on the Judiciary and submitted to the House of Representatives for a vote.   The resolution had not been printed and was not made available to other Members of the House prior to or at the time it was voted on.   So far as the record before us shows, the House consideration of the resolution was based on Representative Eilberg's statement from the floor that

"[i]t was the feeling of the committee, after reviewing 340 cases, that the aliens contained in the resolution [Chadha and five others] did not meet these statutory requirements, particularly as it relates to hardship; and it is the opinion of the committee that their deportation should not be suspended."

The resolution was passed without debate or recorded vote.   Since the House action was pursuant to § 244(c)(2), the resolution was not treated as an Article I legislative act; it was not submitted to the Senate or presented to the President for his action.   *   *   *

---

2. In constitutional terms, "veto" is used to describe the President's power under Art. I, § 7 of the Constitution.   See Black's Law Dictionary 1403 (5th ed. 1979).   It appears, however, that Congressional devices of the type authorized by § 244(c)2) have come to be commonly referred to as a "veto."   *   *   *   We refer to the Congressional "resolution" authorized by § 244(c)(2) as a "one-House veto" of the Attorney General's decision to allow a particular deportable alien to remain in the United States.

Pursuant to § 106(a) of the Act, Chadha filed a petition for review of the deportation order in the United States Court of Appeals for the Ninth Circuit. The Immigration and Naturalization Service agreed with Chadha's position before the Court of Appeals and joined him in arguing that § 244(c)(2) is unconstitutional. In light of the importance of the question, the Court of Appeals invited both the Senate and the House of Representatives to file briefs *amici curiae.*

After full briefing and oral argument, the Court of Appeals held that the House was without constitutional authority to order Chadha's deportation; accordingly it directed the Attorney General "to cease and desist from taking any steps to deport this alien based upon the resolution enacted by the House of Representatives." *Chadha v. INS,* 634 F.2d 408, 436 (CA9 1980). * * *

Explicit and unambiguous provisions of the Constitution prescribe and define the respective functions of the Congress and of the Executive in the legislative process. Since the precise terms of those familiar provisions are critical to the resolution of this case, we set them out verbatim. Art. I provides:

> "All legislative Powers herein granted shall be vested in a Congress of the United States, which shall consist of a Senate *and* a House of Representatives." Art. I, § 1. (Emphasis added).

> "Every Bill which shall have passed the House of Representatives *and* the Senate, *shall*, before it become a Law, be presented to the President of the United States; * * * " Art. I, § 7, cl. 2. (Emphasis added).

> "*Every* Order, Resolution, or Vote to which the Concurrence of the Senate and House of Representatives may be necessary (except on a question of Adjournment) *shall* be presented to the President of the United States; and before the Same shall take Effect, *shall be* approved by him, or being disapproved by him, *shall be* repassed by two thirds of the Senate and House of Representatives, according to the Rules and Limitations prescribed in the Case of a Bill." Art. I, § 7, cl. 3. (Emphasis added).

* * *

THE PRESENTMENT CLAUSES

The records of the Constitutional Convention reveal that the requirement that all legislation be presented to the President before becoming law was uniformly accepted by the Framers. Presentment to the President and the Presidential veto were considered so imperative that the draftsmen took special pains to assure that these requirements could not be circumvented. During the final debate on Art. I, § 7, cl. 2, James Madison expressed concern that it might easily be evaded by the simple expedient of calling a proposed law a "resolution" or "vote" rather than a "bill." As a consequence, Art. I, § 7, cl. 3 was added.

The decision to provide the President with a limited and qualified power to nullify proposed legislation by veto was based on the profound conviction of the Framers that the powers conferred on Congress were the powers to be most carefully circumscribed. It is beyond doubt that lawmaking was a power to be shared by both Houses and the President.   In The Federalist No. 73 (H. Lodge ed. 1888), Hamilton focused on the President's role in making laws:

> "If even no propensity had ever discovered itself in the legislative body to invade the rights of the Executive, the rules of just reasoning and theoretic propriety would of themselves teach us that the one ought not to be left to the mercy of the other, but ought to possess a constitutional and effectual power of self-defense."

See also The Federalist No. 51.   In his Commentaries on the Constitution, Joseph Story makes the same point.

The President's role in the lawmaking process also reflects the Framers' careful efforts to check whatever propensity a particular Congress might have to enact oppressive, improvident, or ill-considered measures. The President's veto role in the legislative process was described later during public debate on ratification:

> "It establishes a salutary check upon the legislative body, calculated to guard the community against the effects of faction, precipitancy, or of any impulse unfriendly to the public good which may happen to influence a majority of that body. * * * The primary inducement to conferring the power in question upon the Executive is to enable him to defend himself; the secondary one is to increase the chances in favor of the community against the passing of bad laws through haste, inadvertence, or design."   The Federalist No. 73 at 458 (A. Hamilton).

The Court also has observed that the Presentment Clauses serve the important purposes of assuring that a "national" perspective is grafted on the legislative process:

> "The President is a representative of the people just as the members of the Senate and of the House are, and it may be, at some times, on some subjects, that the President elected by all the people is rather more representative of them all than are the members of either body of the Legislature whose constituencies are local and not countrywide. * * * * "   *Myers v. United States*, 272 U.S. 52, 123 (1926).

BICAMERALISM

The bicameral requirement of Art, I, § § 1, 7 was of scarcely less concern to the Framers than was the Presidential veto and indeed the two concepts are interdependent.   By providing that no law could take effect without the concurrence of the prescribed majority of the Members of both Houses, the Framers reemphasized their belief, already remarked upon in connection with the Presentment Clauses, that legislation should not be enacted unless it has been carefully and fully considered by the Nation's elected officials.

> "Despotism comes on mankind in different shapes.   Sometimes in an Executive, sometimes in a military, one.   Is there danger of a Legislative despotism?   Theory & practice both proclaim it.   If the Legislative authority be not restrained, there can be neither liberty nor stability; and it can only be

restrained by dividing it within itself, into distinct and independent branches. In a single house there is no check, but the inadequate one, of the virtue & good sense of those who compose it." * * *

This view was rooted in a general skepticism regarding the fallibility of human nature later commented on by Joseph Story:

> "Public bodies, like private persons, are occasionally under the dominion of strong passions and excitements; impatient, irritable, and impetuous. * * * If [a legislature] feels no check but its own will, it rarely has the firmness to insist upon holding a question long enough under its own view, to see and mark it in all its bearings and relations to society." * * *

However familiar, it is useful to recall that apart from their fear that special interests could be favored at the expense of public needs, the Framers were also concerned, although not of one mind, over the apprehensions of the smaller states. Those states feared a commonality of interest among the larger states would work to their disadvantage; representatives of the larger states, on the other hand, were skeptical of a legislature that could pass laws favoring a minority of the people. It need hardly be repeated here that the Great Compromise, under which one House was viewed as representing the people and the other states, allayed the fears of both the large and small states.

We see therefore that the Framers were acutely conscious that the bicameral requirement and the Presentment Clauses would serve essential constitutional functions. * * * It emerges clearly that the prescription for legislative action in Art. I, § § I, 7 represents the Framers' decision that the legislative power of the Federal government be exercised in accord with a single, finely wrought and exhaustively considered, procedure.

* * * [We] must nevertheless establish that the challenged action under § 244(c)(2) is of the kind to which the procedural requirements of Art. I, § 7 apply. Not every action taken by either House is subject to the bicameralism and presentment requirements of Art. I. Whether actions taken by either House are, in law and fact, an exercise of legislative power depends not on their form but upon "whether they contain matter which is properly to be regarded as legislative in its character and effect."

Examination of the action taken here by one House pursuant to § 244(c)(2) reveals that it was essentially legislative in purpose and effect. In purporting to exercise power defined in Art. I, § 8, cl. 4 to "establish an uniform Rule of Naturalization," the House took action that had the purposes and effect of altering the legal rights, duties and relations of persons, including the Attorney General, Executive Branch officials and Chadha, all outside the legislative branch. Section 244(c)(2) purports to authorize one House of Congress to require the Attorney General to deport an individual alien whose deportation otherwise would be cancelled under § 244. The one-House veto operated in this case to overrule the Attorney General and mandate Chadha's deportation; absent the House action, Chadha would remain in the United States. Congress has *acted* and its action has altered Chadha's status.

The legislative character of the one-House veto in this case is confirmed by the character of the Congressional action it supplants. Neither the House of Representatives nor the Senate contends that, absent the veto provision in § 244(c)(2), either of them, or both of them acting together, could effectively require the Attorney General to deport an alien once the Attorney General, in the exercise of legislatively delegated authority,[16] had determined the alien should remain in the United States. Without the challenged provision in § 244(c)(2), this could have been achieved, if at all, only by legislation requiring deportation.[17] * * *

Finally, we see that when the Framers intended to authorize either House of Congress to act alone and outside of its prescribed bicameral legislative role, they narrowly and precisely defined the procedure for such action. There are but four provisions in the Constitution, explicit and unambiguous, by which one House may act alone with the unreviewable force of law, not subject to the President's veto:

(a) The House of Representatives alone was given the power to initiate impeachments. Art. I, § 2, cl. 6;

(b) The Senate alone was given the power to conduct trials following impeachment on charges initiated by the House and to convict following trial. Act. I, § 3, cl. 5;

(c) The Senate alone was given final unreviewable power to approve or disapprove presidential appointments. Art. II, § 2, cl. 2;

16. Congress protests that affirming the Court of Appeals in this case will sanction "lawmaking by the Attorney General. * * * Why is the Attorney General exempt from submitting his proposed changes in the law to the full bicameral process?" Brief of the United States House of Representatives 40. To be sure, some administrative agency action—rule making, for example—may resemble "lawmaking." See 5 U.S.C.A. § 551(4), which defines an agency's "rule" as "the whole or part of an agency statement of general or particular applicability and future effect designed to implement, interpret, or prescribe *law* or policy. * * * This Court has referred to agency activity as being "quasi-legislative" in character. *Humphrey's Executor v. United States*, 295 U.S. 602, 628 (1935). Clearly, however, "[i]n the framework of our Constitution, the President's power to see that the laws are faithfully executed refutes the idea that he is to be a lawmaker." *Youngstown Sheet & Tube Co. v. Sawyer*, 343 U. S. 579, 587 (1952). When the Attorney General performs his duties pursuant to § 244, he does not exercise "legislative" power. The bicameral process is not necessary as a check on the Executive's administration of the laws because his administrative activity cannot reach beyond the limits of the statute that created it—a statute duly enacted pursuant to Art. I, § § 1, 7. The constitutionality of the Attorney General's execution of the authority delegated to him by § 244 involves only a question of delegation doctrine. The courts, when a case or controversy arises, can always "ascertain whether the will of Congress has been obeyed, " *Yakus v. United States*, 321 U. S. 414, 425 (1944), and can enforce adherence to statutory standards. It is clear, therefore, that the Attorney General acts in his presumptively Art. II capacity when he administers the Immigration and Nationality Act. Executive action under legislatively delegated authority that might resemble "legislative" action in some respects is not subject to the approval of both Houses of Congress and the President for the reason that the Constitution does not so require. That kind of Executive action is always subject to check by the terms of the legislation that authorized it; and if that authority is exceeded it is open to judicial review as well as the power of Congress to modify or revoke the authority entirely. A one-House veto is clearly legislative in both character and effect and is not so checked; the need for the check provided by Art. I, § § 1, 7 is therefore clear. Congress' authority to delegate portions of its power to administrative agencies provided no support for the argument that Congress can constitutionally control administration of the laws by way of a Congressional veto.

17. We express no opinion as to whether such legislation would violate any constitutional provision.

(d) The Senate alone was given unreviewable power to ratify treaties negotiated by the President.   Art. II, § 2, cl. 2.

Clearly, when the Draftsmen sought to confer special powers on one House, independent of the other House, or of the President, they did so in explicit, unambiguous terms. * * *

Since it is clear that the action by the House under § 244(c)(2) was not within any of the express constitutional exceptions authorizing one House to act alone, and equally clear that it was an exercise of legislative power, that action was subject to the standards prescribed in Article I.
 * * * To accomplish what has been attempted by one House of Congress in this case requires action in conformity with the express procedures of the Constitution's prescription for legislative action: passage by a majority of both Houses and presentment to the President. * * *

The choices we discern as having been made in the Constitutional Convention impose burdens on governmental processes that often seem clumsy, inefficient, even unworkable, but those hard choices were consciously made by men who had lived under a form of government that permitted arbitrary governmental acts to go unchecked. There is no support in the Constitution or decisions of this Court for the proposition that the cumbersomeness and delays often encountered in complying with explicit Constitutional standards may be avoided, either by the Congress or by the President.   See *Youngstown Sheet & Tube Co. v. Sawyer*, 343 U.S. 579 (1952).   With all the obvious flaws of delay, untidiness, and potential for abuse, we have not yet found a better way to preserve freedom than by making the exercise of power subject to the carefully crafted restraints spelled out in the Constitution. * * *

Affirmed.

JUSTICE POWELL, concurring in the judgment.

The Court's decision, based on the Presentment Clauses, Art. I, § 7, cl. 2 and 3, apparently will invalidate every use of the legislative veto.   The breadth of this holding gives one pause.   Congress has included the veto in literally hundreds of statutes, dating back to the 1930s.   Congress clearly views this procedure as essential to controlling the delegation of power to administrative agencies.   One reasonably may disagree with Congress' assessment of the veto's utility, but the respect due its judgment as a coordinate branch of Government cautions that our holding should be no more extensive than necessary to decide this case.   In my view, the case may be decided on a narrower ground.   When Congress finds that a particular person does not satisfy the statutory criteria for permanent residence in this country it has assumed a judicial function in violation of the principle of separation of powers.   Accordingly, I concur in the judgment.

JUSTICE WHITE, dissenting. * * *

The prominence of the legislative veto mechanism in our contemporary political system and its importance to Congress can hardly be overstated.   It has become a central means by which Congress secures the accountability of executive and independent agencies.   Without the legislative veto, Congress is faced with a Hobson's choice: either to refrain from delegating the necessary authority, leaving itself with a hopeless task of writing laws with the requisite specificity to cover endless special circumstances across the entire policy landscape, or in the alternative, to abdicate its law-making function to the executive branch and independent agencies.   To choose the former leaves major national problems unresolved; to opt for the latter risks unaccountable policymaking by those not elected to fill that role.   Accordingly, over the past five decades, the legislative veto has been placed in nearly 200 statutes.   The device is known in every field of governmental concern: reorganization, budgets, foreign affairs, war powers, and regulation of trade, safety, energy, the environment and the economy.   * * *

The history of the legislative veto also makes clear that it has not been a sword with which Congress has struck out to aggrandize itself at the expense of the other branches—the concerns of Madison and Hamilton. Rather, the veto has been a means of defense, a reservation of ultimate authority necessary if Congress is to fulfill its designated role under Article I as the nation's lawmaker.   While the President has often objected to particular legislative vetoes, generally those left in the hands of congressional committees, the Executive has more often agreed to legislative review as the price for a broad delegation of authority.   To be sure, the President may have preferred unrestricted power, but that could be precisely why Congress thought it essential to retain a check on the exercise of delegated authority.

For all these reasons, the apparent sweep of the Court's decision today is regretable.   The Court's Article I analysis appears to invalidate all legislative vetoes irrespective of form or subject.   Because the legislative veto is commonly found as a check upon rulemaking by administrative agencies and upon broadbased policy decisions of the Executive Branch, it is particularly unfortunate that the Court reaches its decision in a case involving the exercise of a veto over deportation decisions regarding particular individuals.   * * *

The Court holds that the disapproval of a suspension of deportation by the resolution of one House of Congress is an exercise of legislative power without compliance with the prerequisites for lawmaking set forth in Art. I of the Constitution.   Specifically, the Court maintains that the provisions of § 244(c)(2) are inconsistent with the requirement of bicameral approval, implicit in Art. I, § I, and the requirement that all bills and resolutions that require the concurrence of both Houses be presented to the President, Art. I, § 7, cl. 2 and 3.

I do not dispute the Court's truismatic exposition of these clauses.   * * *

It does not, however, answer the constitutional question before us.   The power to exercise a legislative veto is not the power to write new law without bicameral approval or presidential consideration.   The veto must be authorized by statute and may only negative what an Executive department or independent agency has proposed.   On its face, the legislative veto no more allows one House of Congress to make law than does the presidential veto confer such power upon the President. Accordingly, the Court properly recognizes that it "must establish that the challenged action under § 244(c)(2) is of the kind to which the procedural requirements of Art. I, § 7 apply" and admits that "not every action taken by either House is subject to the bicameralism and presentation requirements of Art. I."

The terms of the Presentment Clauses suggest only that bills and their equivalent are subject to the requirements of bicameral pasage and presentment to the President.   Article I, § 7, cl. 2, stipulates only that "Every Bill which shall have passed the House of Representatives and the Senate, shall before it becomes a Law, be presented to the President" for approval or disapproval, his disapproval then subject to being overriden by a two-thirds vote of both houses.   Section 7, cl. 3 goes further:

> "Every Order, Resolution, or Vote to which the Concurrence of the Senate and House of Representatives may be necessary (except on a question of Adjournment) shall be presented to the President of the United States; and before the same shall take Effect, shall be approved by him, or being disapproved by him, shall be repassed by two-thirds of the Senate and House of Representatives, according to the Rules and Limitations prescribed in the Case of a Bill.

Although the Clause does not specify the actions for which the concurrence of both Houses is "necessary," the proceedings at the Philadelphia Convention suggest its purpose was to prevent Congress from circumventing the presentation requirement in the making of new legislation. James Madison observed that if the President's veto was confined to bills, it could be evaded by calling a proposed law a "resolution" or "vote" rather than a "bill."   Accordingly, he proposed that "or resolve" should be added after "bill" in what is now clause 2 of § 7.   After a short discussion on the subject, the amendment was rejected.   On the following day, however, Randolph renewed the proposal in the substantial form as it now appears, and the motion passed.   The chosen language, Madison's comment, and the brevity of the Convention's consideration, all suggest a modest role was intended for the Clause and no broad restraint on Congressional authority was contemplated.   This reading is consistent with the historical background of the Presentation Clause itself which reveals only that the Framers were concerned with limiting the methods for enacting new legislation.   The Framers were aware of the experience in Pennsylvania where the legislature had evaded the requirements attached to the passing of legislation by the use of "resolves," and the criticisms directed at this practice by the Council of Censors.   There is no record that the Convention contemplated, let alone intended, that these Article I requirements would someday be invoked to restrain the scope of Congressional authority pursuant to duly-enacted law.

When the Convention did turn its attention to the scope of Congress' lawmaking power, the Framers were expansive.   The Necessary and

Proper Clause, Art. I, § 8, cl. 18, vests Congress with the power "to make all laws which shall be necessary and proper for carrying into Execution the foregoing Powers [the enumerated powers of § 8], and all other Powers vested by this Constitution in the government of the United States, or in any Department or Officer thereof." It is long-settled that Congress may "exercise its best judgment in the selection of measures, to carry into execution the constitutional powers of the government," and "avail itself of experience, to exercise its reason, and to accommodate its legislation to circumstances." *McCulloch v. Maryland,* 4 Wheat. 316, 415–416, 420 (1819).

The Court heeded this counsel in approving the modern administrative state. The Court's holding today that all legislative-type action must be enacted through the lawmaking process ignores that legislative authority is routinely delegated to the Executive branch, to the independent regulatory agencies, and to private individuals and groups. * * *

This Court's decisions sanctioning such delegations make clear that Article I does not require all action with the effect of legislation to be passed as a law. * * *

If Congress may delegate lawmaking power to independent and executive agencies, it is most difficult to understand Article I as forbidding Congress from also reserving a check on legislative power for itself. Absent the veto, the agencies receiving delegations of legislative or quasi-legislative power may issue regulations having the force of law without bicameral approval and without the President's signature. It is thus not apparent why the reservation of a veto over the exercise of that legislative power must be subject to a more exacting test. In both cases, it is enough that the initial statutory authorizations comply with the Article I requirements.

Nor are there strict limits on the agents that may receive such delegations of legislative authority so that it might be said that the legislature can delegate authority to others but not to itself. While most authority to issue rules and regulations is given to the executive branch and the independent regulatory agencies, statutory delegations to private persons have also passed this Court's scrutiny. In *Currin v. Wallace,* 306 U.S. 1 (1939), the statute provided that restrictions upon the production or marketing of agricultural commodities was to become effective only upon the favorable vote by a prescribed majority of the affected farmers. *United States v. Rock Royal Co-operative,* 307 U.S. 533, 577 (1939), upheld an act which gave producers of specified commodities the right to veto marketing orders issued by the Secretary of Agriculture. Assuming *Currin* and *Rock Royal Co-operative* remain sound law, the Court's decision today suggests that Congress may place a "veto" power over suspensions of deportation in private hands or in the hands of an independent agency, but is forbidden from reserving such authority for itself. Perhaps this odd result could be justified on other constitutional grounds, such as the separation of powers, but certainly it cannot be defended as consistent with the Court's view of the Article I presentment and bicameralism commands. * * *

The Court also takes no account of perhaps the most relevant consideration: * * *

The central concern of the presentation and bicameralism requirements of Article I is that when a departure from the legal status quo is undertaken, it is done with the approval of the President and both Houses of Congress—or, in the event of a presidential veto, a two-thirds majority in both Houses. This interest is fully satisfied by the operation of § 244(c)(2). The President's approval is found in the Attorney General's action in recommending to Congress that the deportation order for a given alien be suspended. The House and the Senate indicate their approval of the Executive's action by not passing a resolution of disapproval within the statutory period. Thus, a change in the legal status quo—the deportability of the alien—is consummated only with the approval of each of the three relevant actors. The disagreement of any one of the three maintains the alien's pre-existing status: the Executive may choose not to recommend suspension; the House and Senate may each veto the recommendation. The effect on the rights and obligations of the affected individuals and upon the legislative system is precisely the same as if a private bill were introduced but failed to receive the necessary approval. * * *

Thus understood, § 244(c)(2) fully effectuates the purposes of the bicameralism and presentation requirements. I now briefly consider possible objections to the analysis.

First, it may be asserted that Chadha's status before legislative disapproval is one of nondeportation and that the exercise of the veto, unlike the failure of a private bill, works a change in the status quo. This position plainly ignores the statutory language. At no place in § 244 has Congress delegated to the Attorney General any final power to determine which aliens shall be allowed to remain in the United States. Congress has retained the ultimate power to pass on such changes in deportable status. By its own terms, § 244(a) states that whatever power the Attorney General has been delegated to suspend deportation and adjust status is to be exercisable only "as hereinafter prescribed in this section." Subsection (c) is part of that section. A grant of "suspension" does not cancel the alien's deportation or adjust the alien's status to that of a permanent resident alien. A suspension order is merely a "deferment of deportation," which can mature into a cancellation of deportation and adjustment of status only upon the approval of Congress—by way of silence—under § 244(c)(2). Only then does the statute authorize the Attorney General to "cancel deportation proceedings" § 244(c)(2), and "record the alien's lawful admission for permanent residence * * * " § 244(d). The Immigration and Naturalization Service's action, on behalf of the Attorney General, "cannot become effective without ratification by Congress." Until that ratification occurs, the executive's action is simply a recommendation that Congress finalize the suspension—in itself, it works no legal change.

Second, it may be said that this approach leads to the incongruity that the two-House veto is more suspect than its one-House brother. Although the idea may be initially counter-intuitive, on close analysis, it is not at all unusual that the one-House veto is of more certain constitution-ality than the two-House version.   If the Attorney General's action is a proposal for legislation, then the disapproval of but a single House is all that is required to prevent its passage.   Because approval is indicated by the failure to veto, the one-House veto satisfies the requirement of bi-cameral approval.   The two-House version may present a different ques-tion.   The concept that "neither branch of Congress, when acting sepa-rately, can lawfully exercise more power than is conferred by the Constitution on the whole body," is fully observed. * * *

The Court of Appeals struck § 244(c)(2) as violative of the constitutional principle of separation of powers. * * *

* * * *Nixon v. Administrator of Gen. Servs.*, 433 U.S. 425 (1977), * * * in rejecting a separation of powers objection to a law re-quiring that the Administrator take custody of certain presidential pa-pers, set forth a framework for evaluating such claims:

> "[I]n determining whether the Act disrupts the proper balance between the coordinate branches, the proper inquiry focuses on the extent to which it pre-vents the Executive Branch from accomplishing its constitutionally assigned functions.   Only where the potential for disruption is present must we then determine whether that impact is justified by an overriding need to promote objectives within the constitutional authority of Congress."   433 U.S., at 443.

Section 244(c)(2) survives this test.   The legislative veto provision does not "prevent the Executive Branch from accomplishing its constitu-tionally assigned functions."   First, it is clear that the Executive Branch has no "constitutionally assigned" function of suspending the deportation of aliens.* * * Nor can it be said that the inherent function of the Ex-ecutive Branch in executing the law is involved.   *The Steel Seizure Case* resolved that the Article II mandate for the President to execute the law is a directive to enforce the law which Congress has written.   *Youngs-town Sheet & Tube Co. v. Sawyer*, 343 U.S. 579 (1952) * * * .   Here, § 244 grants the executive only a qualified suspension authority and it is only that authority which the President is constitutionally authorized to execute. * * *

Nor does § 244 infringe on the judicial power, as JUSTICE POWELL would hold.   Section 244 makes clear that Congress has reserved it own judgment as part of the statutory process.   Congressional action does not substitute for judicial review of the Attorney General's deci-sions.   The Act provides for judicial review of the refusal of the Attorney General to suspend a deportation and to transmit a recommendation to Congress. * * *

I do not suggest that all legislative vetoes are necessarily consistent with separation of powers principles.   A legislative check on an inherent-ly executive function, for example that of initiating prosecutions, poses an entirely different question.   But the legislative veto device here—and in many other settings—is far from an instance of legislative tyranny over the Executive.   It is a necessary check on the unavoidably expanding power of the agencies, both executive and independent, as they engage in exercising authority delegated by Congress.

I regret that I am in disagreement with my colleagues on the fundamental questions that this case presents. But even more I regret the destructive scope of the Court's holding. It reflects a profoundly different conception of the Constitution than that held by the Courts which sanctioned the modern administrative state. Today's decision strikes down in one fell swoop provisions in more laws enacted by Congress than the Court has cumulatively invalidated in its history. I fear it will now be more difficult "to insure that the fundamental policy decisions in our society will be made not by an appointed official but by the body immediately responsible to the people." I must dissent.

JUSTICE REHNQUIST, with whom JUSTICE WHITE joins, dissenting. * * *

Section 244(c)(2) is an exception to the general rule that an alien's deportation shall be suspended when the Attorney General finds that statutory criteria are met. It is severable only if Congress would have intended to permit the Attorney General to suspend deportations without it. * * *

* * * [T]he history elucidated by the Court shows that Congress was unwilling to give the Executive Branch permission to suspend deportation on its own. Over the years, Congress consistently rejected requests from the Executive for complete discretion in this area. Congress always insisted on retaining ultimate control, whether by concurrent resolution, as in the 1948 Act, or by one-House veto, as in the present Act. Congress has never indicated that it would be willing to permit suspensions of deportation unless it could retain some sort of veto. * * *

Because I do not believe that § 244(c)(2) is severable, I would reverse the judgment of the Court of Appeals.

Notes

1. Debate over the "legislative veto," its utility and its constitutionality, has raged for a decade as Congress has become increasingly enamored of the device. Yet few thoughtful commentators imagined that the Court, when it finally faced the issue squarely, would write so sweeping an opinion as *Chadha.* An excellent article by Louis Fisher, *A Political Context for Legislative Vetoes,* 93 Pol. Sci. Q. 241 (1978), is exemplary. On his first page Fisher warns:

> The great danger at the present time is the temptation to join one of two rival camps. One choice: the legislative veto is an essential means of controlling the bureaucracy and maintaining representative government. Alternatively: the legislative veto violates the separation of powers doctrine and evades the president's veto power. My contention is that the issue, presented in this manner, is wrongly framed. The legislative veto is not a simple substance, to be disposed of one way or the other. No single constitutional theory can exonerate it or invalidate it. We confront not an element but many different compounds, some easier to justify legally and politically than others.

Fisher goes on to suggest four categories of legislative veto which, in his view, should have different political and constitutional significance. The first is the explicit *quid pro quo*. The Congress gives the President a power subject to "veto" that it otherwise would not confer. Authority to reorganize executive branch departments is a principal example. Because reorganization plans are few in number, are subjected to careful congressional scrutiny, and begin only by presidential initiative, Fisher views them as impairing neither the legislative function of the Congress nor the presentment clause protection of presidential power. The Second Circuit, however, has since interpreted *Chadha* as invalidating the veto provisions of the 1977 Reorganization Act, and with them the statute itself. *EEOC v. CBS, Inc.*, 743 F.2d 969 (2d Cir. 1984). Compare *Muller Optical Co v. EEOC*, 743 F.2d 380 (6th Cir. 1984).

In a second category Fisher identifies certain compromise solutions to problems in the perennial borderlands of congressional and presidential power. Here the executive is likely to feel that any delegation of legislative power is redundant while Congress views the retention of a veto as maintaining the status quo. Hence Fisher views the legislative veto included in the Impoundment Control Act of 1974, Pub. L. No. 93–344, 88 Stat. 297 (codified at 31 U.S.C.A. § § 665, 1400–1407), and the War Powers Resolution of 1973, Pub. L. No. 93–148, 87 Stat. 555 (codified at U.S.C.A. § § 1541–1548), for example, not as provisions for legislative nullification but as "a procedural link between two rival interpretations" of constitutional authority. And because each interpretation is both plausible and useful, the veto serves the beneficial constitutional function of maintaining these mutually contradictory perspectives. Here Fisher reminds us of James Madison's dictum in The Federalist No. 37 that the boundary between legislative and executive is as elusive as the line between the animal and vegetable kingdoms.

Congressional retention of a veto over administrative rulemaking is for Fisher a much more problematic case. Rulemaking initiatives do not imply presidential involvement, nor is a *quid pro quo* so obvious. Moreover, the possibility of constant revision of "legislative intent" via veto resolutions tends to undermine the distinction between legislative action and legislative oversight. In Fisher's view this blurring of distinct functions may compromise both legislative and administrative processes. While Fisher can imagine special cases in which a legislative veto over rules would be justified, he opposes, on both policy and constitutional grounds, a general congressional veto over administrative rulemaking.

Finally, Fisher views the *Chadha* case itself as involving one unconstitutional form of legislative veto. The section 244(c) procedure is, in his opinion, a legislative incursion into a specific adjudicatory function without any semblance of adjudicatory due process. To what extent does the *Chadha* opinion leave open the distinctions that Fisher urges? Are they worth preserving?

2. When considering the latter question take account of Professor, now Judge, Scalia's sardonic judgment. In *The Legislative Veto: A False Remedy for System Overload*, 3 Regulation 19, 26 (Nov./Dec. 1979), he suggests that a candid congressman would write the following open letter to constituents:

Fellow Citizens:

There is abroad in our land the feeling that we no longer control our government, but it controls us, through thousands of law-making functionaries in every field of life who are effectively beyond popular control. That feeling, I am sorry to tell you, is well founded.   And the cause is quite simply that your Congress has over the years delegated so many policy judgments of the sort once made by your elected representatives to the executive agencies that by now neither the Congress nor the President can realistically monitor or supervise the results.

We in Congress have done this not maliciously but with the best of intention.   We have wanted to give all of you a clean environment, a safe working place, safe consumer products, protection from deceptive merchandizing—and many other protections which were in earlier years the responsibility of elected bodies in your cities, counties, and states.   You have evidently approved what we have done, since you have continued to elect us on the basis of these programs.

But the time has come to tell you that all these benefits cannot be provided at the federal level and still be provided in a democratic fashion.   There are simply too many important policy judgments to be made.   Your elected President and your elected members of Congress cannot possibly make them all or even keep track of them all—and it is useless any longer to pretend that we can.

You must face the unhappy fact that democratic government implies—at least at any single level—limited government.   You cannot realistically continue to demand from us in Washington the constant stream of new programs we have become accustomed to providing and at the same time complain that these programs are governed, not merely in their details but in many of their basic directions, by individuals whom you have never had the chance to vote in or out of office.   The system is overloaded.   We are now at the point at which each major new program entails an overall diminution of democratic control.   You must keep this inevitable trade-off in mind.

Instead of writing this letter, I might have berated the unresponsive bureaucracy, or proposed encumbering the agencies with new procedures, or supported devices that give the appearance of "no-nonsense" congressional control.   But the truth is that the bureaucracy is not unresponsive, only unelected; that procedures are no substitute for the ballot box; and that congressional control is no longer possible.

I thought you would want to know the truth.

3. Prior to the Supreme Court's ruling in *Chadha*, the legislative veto had been at issue in two prominent cases before the D.C. Circuit Court of Appeals. In *Consumer Energy Council of America v. Federal Energy Regulatory Commission*, 673 F.2d 425 (D.C. Cir. 1982), petitioners challenged the constitutionality of a provision of the Natural Gas Policy Act of 1978 which authorized either House of Congress to veto a rule, mandated by the Act, extending "incremental pricing" of natural gas to new classes of industrial users.   Incremental pricing was to be a means of shifting the burden of partial deregulation of natural gas prices from residential to industrial users, and the concept was an important component of the legislative compromise that resulted in passage of the 1978 Act.   Writing for a unanimous court, Judge Wilkey struck down the veto provision as violative of both bicameralism and the presentation clause, inconsistent with principles of separation of powers, and an intrusion into the judiciary's authority to oversee administrative obedience to statutory law.   Judge Wilkey specifically rejected the suggestion that, as an independent regulatory agency with close ties to Congress, FERC stood on a footing different from executive

branch administrators.   Less than a year later, the D.C. Circuit, this time sitting *en banc,* sustained a similar challenge to a veto provision in the Federal Trade Commission Improvements Act of 1980.   *Consumers Union v. Federal Trade Commission,* 691 F.2d 575 (D.C. Cir. 1982).   That Act obligated the Commission to submit trade regulation rules for Congressional review, permitting a rule to become effective after 90 days unless previously disapproved by both Houses of Congress.

Applications for review of these decisions were pending at the time the Court decided *Chadha.*   Both Justice White and Justice Powell had argued that the institutional context of veto provisions should make a difference in assessing their constitutionality, but it quickly became clear that a majority of the Justices were not impressed by such distinctions.   On July 6, 1983, with Justice Powell not participating, the Court summarily affirmed the judgments in *Consumer Energy Council* and the FTC case, without any elaboration of *Chadha's* reasoning. While unsurprised by the result, Justice White commented:

> I cannot agree that the legislative vetoes in these cases violate the requirements of Article I of the Constitution.   Where the veto is placed as a check upon the actions of the independent regulatory agencies, the Article I analysis relied upon in *Chadha* has a particularly hollow ring. * * *
>
> The Court's opinion in *Chadha* has not convinced me otherwise.   Congress, with the President's consent, characteristically empowers the agencies to issue regulations.   These regulations have the force of law without the President's concurrence; nor can he veto them if he disagrees with the law that they make.   The President's authority to control independent agency lawmaking, which on a day-to-day basis is nonexistent, could not be affected by the existence or exercise of the legislative veto.   To invalidate the device, which allows Congress to maintain some control over the lawmaking process, merely guarantees that the independent agencies, once created, for all practical purposes are a fourth branch of the government not subject to the direct control of either Congress or the executive branch.   I cannot believe that the Constitution commands such a result.

Process Gas Consumers Group v. Consumers Energy Council of America, ___ U.S. ___, ___, 103 S.Ct. 3556, 3557–58 (1983).

4. There is a copious literature on the constitutionality and effects of legislative veto provisions.   Among the useful discussions of the practical consequences of veto arrangements are Bruff & Gellhorn, *Congressional Control of Administrative Regulation: A Study of Legislative Vetoes,* 90 Harv. L. Rev. 1369 (1977), and McGowan, *Congress, Court and Control of Delegated Power,* 77 Colum. L. Rev. 1119 (1977).   For further treatment of the institutional and constitutional issues, all pre-*Chadha,* see J. BOLTON, THE LEGISLATIVE VETO: UNSEPARATING THE POWERS (1977); Dixon, *The Congressional Veto and Separation of Powers: The Executive On a Leash?* 56 N.C.L. Rev. 423 (1978); Nathanson, *Separation of Powers and Administrative Law: Delegation, The Legislative Veto, and the "Independent" Agencies,* 75 Nw. U.L. Rev. 1064 (1981); Watson, *Congress Steps Out: A Look at Congressional Control of the Executive,* 63 Calif. L. Rev. 983 (1975).   For a post-*Chadha* discussion, see Elliott, *INS v. Chadha: The Administrative Constitution, the Constitution, and the Legislative Veto,* 1983 Sup. Ct. Rev. 125.

5. The Supreme Court's invalidation of the legislative veto has spurred the search for alternative means of Congressional control over the exercise of dele-

gated authority.   One obvious course is for Congress to take greater pains to define standards for administrative decisionmaking when it enacts legislation.   Some writers have suggested that the unavailability of veto will encourage rather than diminish Congressional interference with administrative decisionmaking.   See, e.g., Fisher, *Congress Can't Lose on Its Veto Power*, The Washington Post, Feb. 21, 1982, at D1.   Others speculate that the nullification of the veto will prevent the enactment of some laws altogether.   The suggestion here is that the assurance of an opportunity to reexamine discrete administrative actions has been critical to Congress' willingness to enact controversial legislation, such as the Natural Gas Policy Act of 1978.

Of more immediate concern is the severability of now vulnerable veto provisions found in over 200 existing laws, which underpin literally thousands of administrative rules and Presidential actions.   In *Chadha* the Court found that a severability clause in the act itself created a conclusive presumption that the Attorney General's authority survived invalidation of Congress' veto.   The 1978 Natural Gas Policy Act included no severability provision, but this oversight did not prevent the D.C. Circuit (or apparently the Supreme Court) from concluding that the veto provision was severable.   According to one lawyer who represented the Senate in *Chadha*, these decisions confirm that "there is hardly a case in which the courts will rule that delegated executive power is completely bound up with the veto that had superintended it."   Davidson, *Reflections from the Losing Side*, 7 Regulation 23 (July/Aug. 1983).   This prediction may yet prove accurate, but the U.S. Court of Appeals for the Second Circuit found the veto provision of the 1977 Reorganization Act was not severable and held the entire act unconstitutional in *EEOC v. CBS, Inc.*, 743 F.2d 969 (2d Cir. 1984).   The Sixth Circuit reached the contrary judgment in *Muller Optical Co. v. EEOC*, 743 F.2d 380 (6th Cir. 1984).

A variety of procedural and institutional arrangements have been put forward as substitutes for the legislative veto.   These include two mechanisms already familiar to Congress.   No general federal sunset legislation has been enacted, but Congress often limits the duration of major regulatory statutes, such as those administered by the EPA and the Consumer Product Safety Commission.   The scheduled expiration of authorizing legislation forces the legislature, or at least its relevant committees, to review an agency's performance and consider changes in its mandate.   While this process has rarely resulted in the death of a program and often leads to operation under continuing resolutions, it has frequently produced important changes in the standards or procedures an agency must follow.   See, e.g., Consumer Product Safety Amendments of 1981, Pub. L. No. 97–35, Title XII, § 1214, 95 Stat. 724 (amending 15 U.S.C.A. § 2081 (imposing substantial changes in the CPSC's rulemaking authority and procedures, its duty to respond to public petitions, and the Commission's scientific evaluation of products thought to present cancer hazards).   See also Merrill, *CPSC Regulation of Cancer Risks in Consumer Products: 1972–1981*, 67 U. Va. L. Rev. 1261, 1373–75 (1981); Klayman, *Standard Setting Under the Consumer Product Safety Amendments of 1981: A Shift in Regulatory Philosophy*, 51 Geo. Wash. L. Rev. 96 (1982).

Another approach elicits criticism even from defenders of Congressional prerogatives, but no one doubts its constitutionality.   This is the enactment of substantive limitations on agency activity as part of appropriations legislation.   It is not uncommon for Congress to specify that no funds budgeted for an agency **may** be expended in adopting or enforcing specific controversial rules.

In recent sessions of Congress three other proposals for more active legislative involvement in administrative rulemaking have commanded serious support.   The first would require, by general legislation or amendment of individual statutes, that agency rules receive affirmative approval by both Houses of Congress and by the President before they become effective.   The chief proponent of this idea, Congressman Elliot Levitas, has conceded that it might be limited either to "major" rules or to agencies that promulgate few rules, if only to spare Congress the nightmare of reviewing the thousands of new rules promulgated each year.   The Levitas proposal, obviously, would effect a fundamental realignment of governmental power for in substance it would force Congress to legislate twice before any new rule could become effective.   A more cautious proposal, likewise responsive to the Court's objections to the one- and two-house vetoes, would require agencies to submit their rules to Congress before they became effective, and permit any rule to be disapproved by joint resolution—a device that requires Presidential concurrence.   Thus, Congress could, by legislating again, prevent implementation of a rule it did not like.   A variation of this "report and wait" approach, urged by several Senators, would require an agency to allow Congress 30 legislative days before making a rule effective, and an additional 60 days if a committee of either House recommended disapproval.   This waiver period would give the two Houses and the President an opportunity to adopt a joint resolution disapproving the rule.   The proposal would also prevent committees to which a rule was referred from obstructing consideration by the full Congress by forcing the issue to the floor.

Each of the latter proposals purports to satisfy *Chadha's* objections to the legislative veto by requiring joint action by both Houses of Congress and participation by the President.   None has been included in specific legislation, but bills have been introduced to superimpose one or another of these approaches on administrative rulemaking generally or on specific agencies.   In 1983 the House went so far as to include both the Levitas "required approval" proposal and the "joint resolution of disapproval" proposal in legislation to reauthorize the CPSC.

B. PERVASIVE METHODS OF LEGISLATIVE CONTROL

1. THE STATUTORY ENVIRONMENT OF FEDERAL ADMINISTRATION

Despite the looseness of many Congressional delegations of power in organic statutes, and the apparent unavailability of the legislative veto as a mechanism for legislative control, it would surely be a mistake to view federal agencies as essentially free from legislative direction.   In reality, the substance, and especially the procedures of administrative decisions, are subject to multiple sets of Congressionally specified instructions.   An agency's organic act is thus only the starting place for exploring issues of legislative control of administrative action.   The numerous general laws that establish the current framework for federal administration, moreover, illustrate many of the dominant themes of American administrative law.

At the beginning of this century, there was no extensive body of federal administrative law—judicial or statutory.   To be sure, as early as *Marbury v. Madison*, the federal courts had enunciated and sometimes enforced principles establishing the legal accountability of federal officers (e.g., Monaghan, *Marbury and the Administrative State*, 83 Colum. L. Rev. 1 (1983)), and a smattering of federal statutes, such as the Interstate Commerce Act, the 1906 Pure Food and Drugs Act, and the Meat Inspection Act, created genuine regulatory programs.   But the landscape was barren of general legislation limiting the powers or defining the procedures of federal administrators.   During the next forty years, the number of new federal programs—each created by Congress—grew rapidly as the nation struggled to escape from the Depression.   By the time World War II broke out, the U.S. Code was full of authorizing legislation, accompanied by a relatively small number of laws addressed to administrators generally.   Most of the latter addressed prosaic matters, such as appointment and pay of employees and acquisition and use of property.

By 1980 the shape of this legal terrain had changed dramatically.   The accretion of new government programs had not slowed.   The 1970's produced a flowering of new statutes addressed to health, the environment, and public welfare, which substantially reoriented the federal approach to social regulation.   More importantly, for our purposes, commencing with the Administrative Procedure Act in 1946, 5 U.S.C.A. § § 551 *et seq.*, Congress had enacted a series of general statutes that speak to, and limit the discretion of most federal agencies.   Accordingly, if one attempts to describe the legal context in which any federal agency now operates—even one created to administer a brand-new organic law—one must discuss a long list of statutes that make no reference whatever to that program, yet by their terms embrace and limit it.

Procedure Statutes
Administrative Procedure Act   1946

Without doubt, the Administrative Procedure Act (APA) remains the most important of these statutes.   On first glance this influential law bears a resemblance to the Federal Rules of Civil Procedure, since it purports to establish uniform procedures for certain formal actions—rulemaking and adjudication—by any federal administrative tribunal or official.   But this analogy both overstates the APA's achievement in unifying agency procedures and ignores many quasi-substantive obligations that the Act imposes.

The APA was the product of almost a decade of efforts within Congress and the private bar to systematize the procedures employed by federal agencies whose number had grown so rapidly during the New Deal and, equally important, to curtail perceived abuses in the commingling of prosecutory and judging functions within the same organization.   See Williams, *Fifty Years of the Law of the Federal Administrative Agencies—And Beyond*, 29 Fed. Bar J. 267, 268 (1970).   The 1940 Walter-Logan bill, which would have abolished several of the so-called independent agencies, prescribed uniform procedures for formal administrative

actions, and enlarged judicial review of agency decisions, passed both
Houses of Congress before being vetoed.   The next year, the Roosevelt
administration created the Attorney General's Committee on Administrative Procedure, chaired by Dean Acheson and including many prominent administrative lawyers of the era, to evaluate the federal administrative process and recommend reforms.   Although delayed by the war
effort and compromised in important particulars, the ultimate 1946 registration embodied many of the Acheson Committee's recommendations.
Final Report of the Attorney General's Committee on Administrative
Procedure, U.S. Government Printing Office (1941); also printed as S.
Doc. No. 8, 88th Cong., 1st Sess. (1941).

The APA's basic structure is easily summarized.   Section 2 defines
terms, including the term "agency" which determines the law's coverage.
Section 3 prescribes an agency's obligations to make public information
about its organization, procedures, and substantive requirements.
Section 4 mandates minimum basic procedures for administrative rulemaking.   Sections 5 through 8 speak to the procedures an agency is obligated to follow in formal, usually case-by-case, decisionmaking, such as
the imposition of penalties or the issuance of licenses or permits.   Finally,
section 10 outlines the general conditions for judicial review of the decisions of federal administrators.

The APA's original text has been remarkably durable; most provisions
of sections 4 through 10 have remained unchanged, though in many instances judicial rulings have effected important transformations.   (The
APA's specific requirements receive more detailed attention in later
chapters.)   Congress has not since attempted a comprehensive recodification of federal administrative procedure.   Panel Discussion, *Time for a
New APA?* (Comments of Professor, now Judge, Scalia), 32 Ad. L. Rev.
357, 371 (1980).   It has, however, displayed strong continuing interest in
agency procedures in a variety of other ways.

From the beginning the APA was recognized as interstitial legislation;
it supplied the procedures an agency was obliged to follow if its organic
statute did not provide different instructions.   Thus Congress always
could, and with increasing frequency did, supplant the APA's requirements with more explicit directives for particular agencies or programs.
Most recent health and environmental statutes, for example, contain detailed instructions concerning procedure as well as substance.

Furthermore, while Congress has never undertaken a comprehensive
revision of the APA, it has made important additions to certain sections,
thus amplifying its instructions to the entire administrative apparatus.
One example is a 1976 amendment to section 10, which eliminated sovereign immunity as a barrier to suits seeking declaratory or injunctive relief against the government.   Pub. L. No. 94–574, 90 Stat. 2721.   More
notable examples are the Freedom of Information Act, enacted in 1966 as
a comprehensive rewriting of section 2 of the APA, 5 U.S.C.A. § 552, and
the Government in the Sunshine Act, Pub. L. No. 94–409, 90 Stat. 1241
(1976), likewise codified as a part of the APA.   5 U.S.C.A. § 552b.   These

and certain other statutes that are nominally a part of the APA justify separate treatment. They not only apply to all agencies, as defined by the APA; they also are rarely modified by the specific terms of an agency's organic legislation.

Federal Register Act

When enacted in 1935, the Federal Register Act, 49 Stat. 500, 44 U.S.C.A. § § 1501 *et seq.*, was the first general statute addressed to the public procedures of federal agencies. The Act's requirement that agencies publish their rules and its provisions for their codification in the Code of Federal Regulations have become such well-engrained parts of agency behavior that the law now rarely attracts much notice. But see *Morton v. Ruiz*, 415 U.S. 199 (1974), infra p. 399. See generally Note, *The Federal Register and the Code of Federal Regulations—A Reappraisal*, 80 Harv. L. Rev. 439, 451 (1966); L. SCHMECKEBIER AND R. EASTIN, GOVERNMENT PUBLICATIONS AND THEIR USE 300–29 (2d rev. ed. 1969).

Freedom of Information Act

The FOIA, Pub. L. No. 89–487, 80 Stat. 250 (codified at 5 U.S.C.A. § 552), has quickly become one of the most prominent features of the statutory landscape in which federal administrators function. Passed in 1966 and amended in 1974 and in 1976, the Act's obligations touch most activities of federal administrators and facilitate the activities of the many organizations and individuals who report on or advise about federal decisionmaking. We will consider the FOIA at several junctures during our study of the administrative process—just as administrative lawyers frequently encounter the statute as they perform other functions on behalf of government agencies or private clients who deal with them.

The Information Act's basic structure is straightforward. The Act requires an agency, in response to a request from any member of the public, to make available for examination (i.e., to copy and release) any "agency record" that does not fall within any of ten specified exempt categories. An agency also *may* release exempt documents unless some other law prohibits it from doing so or it would be "arbitrary" to do so. The FOIA thus embodies a presumption in favor of disclosure. The Act imposes no requirement that the person seeking access to a record have a good, or indeed any announced, reason for requesting it.

The FOIA was adopted in response to claims that many important documents and other information underlying important agency decisions were not available to the public, thereby impairing the rights of citizens to monitor government performance and impeding the functions of the Press. See Note, *The Freedom of Information Act: A Seven-year Assessment*, 74 Colum. L. Rev. 895 (1974); Project, *Government Information and the Rights of Citizens*, 73 Mich. L. Rev. 971 (1975). When Congress later concluded that many agencies were slow or even devious in responding to FOIA requests under the Act, it strengthened the legal remedies available to seekers of information. Twenty-first Report by the Committee on Government Operations, H.R. Rep. No. 92–1419, 92d Cong., 2d Sess. 8–9 (1972). Both in 1974 and in 1976 it narrowed the grounds for withholding certain categories of documents. See Pub. L. No. 93–502, 88 Stat. 156 (1974); Note, *The Freedom of Information Act Amendments of 1974: An Analysis*, 26 Syracuse L. Rev. 951 (1975); Pub. L. No. 94–409 § 5(b), 90 Stat. 1247 (1976); Note, *The Effect of the 1976 Amendment to Exemption Three of the Freedom of Information Act*, 76 Colum. L. Rev. 1029 (1976). Congress insisted upon prompt responses to FOIA requests, and it authorized persons whose requests were denied or neglected to initiate suit against the agency, giving such cases docket priority and requiring the agency to justify withholding of records. Attorney fees were authorized for plaintiffs who "substantially prevail" in such suits. Government officials who wrongfully withhold documents were exposed to disciplinary proceedings.

The FOIA exemptions to mandatory disclosure describe circumstances in which Congress found that other values outweigh the interest in public access to government records. These exemptions embrace material properly classified as confidential for national security reasons, material protected from disclosure by some other statute, material whose disclosure would constitute "an unwarranted invasion of personal privacy," law enforcement records whose disclosure could jeopardize pending actions or the safety of officers, as well as other categories of documents. Perhaps the most important exemption covers inter- and intra-agency memoranda, which represents a Congressional attempt to protect the deliberative processes of the executive. This exemption has become a battleground over the scope and continuing legitimacy of the doctrine of "executive privilege." It has been construed as protecting analysis and advice provided to decision makers but not documents—or portions of documents—that are largely factual in nature. See, e.g., *NLRB v. Sears, Roebuck & Co.*, 421 U.S. 132 (1975); Note, *Discovery of Government Documents and the Official Information Privilege*, 76 Colum. L. Rev. 142 (1976).

One result of the FOIA's elaborate legal structure for regulating access to government records has been a cascade of law suits. Most are brought by persons seeking documents, but some seek to enjoin administrators from disclosing information obtained from private sources, generally commercial enterprises. E.g., *Chrysler Corp. v. Brown*, 441 U.S. 281 (1979). See Clement, *The Rights of Submitters to Prevent Agency Disclosure of Confidential Business Information: The Reverse Freedom of Information Act Lawsuit*, 55 Tex. L. Rev. 587 (1977); *Reverse Freedom of Information Act Suits: Confidential Information in Search of Protection* 70 Nw. U.L. Rev. 995 (1976); Note, *Protection from Government Disclosure—The Reverse-FOIA Suit*, 1976 Duke L.J. 330. The FOIA has also inspired the establishment of firms whose sole business is obtaining government information for private clients, often including information about who is seeking information from the government about them.

Government in the Sunshine Act

The Sunshine Act, Pub. L. No. 94–409, 90 Stat. 1241 (codified at 5 U.S.C.A. § 552b), parallels the "open meetings" laws of many states and is similarly designed to prevent secrecy in government. Its reach and impact are more limited than the FOIA's. The Sunshine Act applies only to agencies headed by collegial bodies, such as the FTC, the SEC, and the CPSC. It obligates such agencies to provide advance notice of meetings at which agency business is to be conducted, and to meet in public unless the members, by majority vote, decide that the subject matter falls within one of nine statutory exemptions. These exemptions parallel those in the FOIA, except for the "inter- and intra-agency memoranda" exemption, which has no obvious application to oral discussions. But Congress recognized the legitimacy of protecting oral deliberations on issues whose resolution could be undermined by premature disclosure and thus section 9(B) of the Sunshine Act permits closure if discussion would

> disclose information the premature disclosure of which would * * * be likely to significantly frustrate implementation of a proposed agency action * * * but [this exception] shall not apply in any instance where the agency has already disclosed to the public the content or nature of its proposed action, or * * * is required by law to make such disclosure on its own initiative prior to taking final agency action on such proposal.

The narrow terms of this exception make closure of meetings problematical in most cases.

Suits to enforce the Sunshine Act have been less frequent than claims under the FOIA because they require knowledge of a pending meeting far enough in advance to prepare court papers. Agencies also sometimes neglect to provide advance notice of their meetings. Most agencies, however, have displayed surprising fidelity to the terms of the Act—even sacrificing opportunities for private discussion of controversial issues. See, e.g., Merrill, *CPSC Regulation of Cancer Risks in Consumer Products: 1972–1981*, 67 Va. L. Rev. 1261 (1981); Statler, *Let the Sunshine In?*, 67 A.B.A. J. 573 (1981); Tucker, *Sunshine—The Dubious New God*, 32 Ad. L. Rev. 537 (1980); Welborn, *Implementation and Effects of the Federal Government in the Sunshine Act*, Report to the U.S. Administrative Conference (Sept. 1983).

An additional impediment to suits under the Sunshine Act, which the statute authorizes, is uncertainty about the character and value of judicial relief. Even if a suit might force an agency to open a meeting that has not yet occurred, it is not obvious that the observed event will be the same as the discussions that would have occurred in private. Indeed, a meeting ordered to be rescheduled may never occur; the issue before the agency may get resolved in some other fashion. The Sunshine Act permits collateral review in the context of suits challenging the underlying agency action, generally long after the questioned meeting occurred. But the Act's instruction to grant whatever relief the court "deems appropriate" hardly provides much guidance in deciding what relief then makes sense.   Setting aside otherwise sustainable agency action seems excessive, but a mere declaration that the Act was violated may not deter future violations.   For examples of judicial handling of these cases, see, e.g., *Pan American World Airways v. CAB*, 684 F.2d 31 (D.C. Cir. 1982); *Braniff Master Executive Council v. CAB*, 693 F.2d 220 (D.C. Cir. 1982); *ITT World Communications, Inc. v. FCC*, 699 F.2d 1219 (D.C. Cir. 1983), *reversed* 104 S.Ct. 1936 (1984).   See also R. BERG & S. KLITZMAN, AN INTERPRETIVE GUIDE TO THE GOVERNMENT IN THE SUNSHINE ACT (1978).

Federal Advisory Committee Act

The FACA, 5 U.S.C.A. App. 1, was enacted in 1972, Pub. L. No. 92–463, 86 Stat. 770, and amended in 1976 to incorporate the Sunshine Act standards for open meetings, Pub. L. No. 94–409, 90 Stat. 1240 (1976).   The Act has several purposes.   It establishes requirements that agencies must follow when consulting groups of individuals who are not federal employees, and it prescribes how these groups—perforce "advisory committees"—shall proceed in rendering their service to the agency. The main requirements for the creation of an advisory committee are issuance of a charter, which must be approved by the General Services Administration; selection of members to assure diverse views on the issues to be considered; and forced expiration, or rechartering, after two years.   The main obligations of established committees are to provide advance public notice of their meetings and to deliberate in public, subject to the Sunshine Act exceptions permitting closure.   See Perritt and Wilkinson, *Open Advisory Committees and the Political Process: The Federal Advisory Committee Act After Two Years*, 63 Geo. L.J. 725 (1975).

The obvious objectives of the FACA are to facilitate public awareness of the advice an agency receives from outside persons and to inhibit preferential access by regulated firms.   A less obvious purpose of the original Act, authored by Senator Metcalf of Montana, was to discourage agency reliance on outside "experts" by making it difficult to create advisory committees.   118 Cong. Rec. S3529 (daily ed. Sept. 15, 1972).   Metcalf's investigations suggested that few committees performed important functions and most were expensive to maintain.   Recent administrations have also seized upon FACA's rechartering requirement to shrink the government's total number of advisory committees and, thereby, to justify claims that the roster of federal "agencies" had been sharply curtailed. Cardozo, *The Federal Advisory Committee Act*, 33 Ad. L. Rev. 1, 5 (1981).   The Act's requirements significantly affect agencies whose responsibilities require an understanding of modern science and technology. The FDA and the EPA, for example, have often used expert advisory committees as an inexpensive means of tapping the expertise of the academic community on sensitive regulatory issues.   Some recent organic laws, such as the 1981 amendments to the Consumer Product Safety Act, Pub. L. No. 97–35, 95 Stat. 357 (1981), mandate consultation with expert advisory committees as a step in the procedures for imposing controls over putative health hazards. See, NATIONAL ACADEMY OF SCIENCES, RISK ASSESSMENT IN THE FEDERAL GOVERNMENT: MANAGING THE PROCESS 91–93 (1983).

Privacy Act

The 1974 Privacy Act, Pub. L. No. 93–579, 88 Stat. 1896 (codified at 5 U.S.C.A. § 552a), is intended to provide individuals access to personal information in the government's possession. The FOIA excepts from mandatory disclosure records whose release would constitute an "unwarranted invasion of personal privacy." The Privacy Act makes this exemption mandatory and guarantees individuals—though not firms or associations—access to any personally identifiable records about them in an agency's possession. It also provides a procedure by which an individual may correct or supplement personal information in government files that he or she regards as inaccurate.

The Privacy Act grew out of a report by the Secretary of Health, Education and Welfare's Advisory Committee on Automated Personnel Data Systems, Records, Computers, and the Rights of Citizens (1973). The Act has stimulated thousands of requests for access or correction and several lawsuits, many of them from current or former employees of the federal government, but its impact has been less dramatic than the FOIA. "[T]he right of access afforded by the Privacy Act is not designed to free up public entry to the full range of government files. Rather, access * * * is merely a necessary adjunct to the broader objective of assuring information quality by obtaining the views of persons with interest and ability to contribute to the accuracy of agency records." *Smiertka v. United States Department of Treasury*, 447 F. Supp. 221, 226–27 (D.D.C. 1978). For useful discussions of the Act, see Note, *The Privacy Act of 1974: An Overview*, 1976 Duke L.J. 301; Hanus and Relyea, *A Policy Assessment of the Privacy Act of 1974*, 25 Am. U.L. Rev. 555 (1976).

General Statutes Addressed to the Substance of Agency Decisions

The APA was intended to unify the procedures that federal agencies follow in making rules and adjudicating cases. The FOIA, the Federal Register Act, and the Sunshine Act, among other laws, were intended to enhance public awareness of federal agency decisionmaking and to provide opportunities for affected individuals and organizations to participate in the process. While these laws have affected the content of administrative decisions by bringing new information and views to the attention of administrators and, more subtly, through exposure and delay, Congress did not intend through their enactment to affect specific substantive policies. Other statutes addressed generally to federal administrators, however, do have substantive objectives, though they sometimes utilize ostensibly "procedural" means.

National Environmental Policy Act

The National Environmental Policy Act of 1969 (NEPA), Pub. L. No. 91–190, 83 Stat. 852 (1970) (codified at 42 U.S.C.A. § § 4321 *et seq.*), is the best known of these statutes.   The Act enunciates a national concern for the environment and sets forth procedural requisites to assure agency consideration of environmental values in the formulation and implementation of policy.   NEPA's goals are framed in broad, constitutional terms, and its procedural directives leave room for agency adaptation.   See Cramton and Berg, *On Leading a Horse to Water: NEPA and the Federal Bureaucracy*, 71 Mich. L. Rev. 511 (1971).   But the Act's core is the requirement that, before taking any "major action" that may significantly affect "the quality of the human environment," an agency must prepare an environmental impact statement identifying those effects, assaying their significance, and evaluating alternatives.   NEPA does not direct that all actions harmful to the environment must be avoided, and it expressly applies only to the extent not inconsistent with an agency's organic law.   But it clearly was intended to increase administrative awareness of the environmental consequences of governmental actions and prompt rethinking of those whose effects seem disproportionate.

Entire volumes have been written about NEPA's procedural requirements and operational impact, and virtually every issue of the Federal Reporter and Federal Supplement contains cases that involve NEPA-based challenges to agency action.   See generally F. ANDERSON, NEPA IN THE COURTS; A LEGAL ANALYSIS OF THE NATIONAL ENVIRONMENTAL POLICY ACT (1973).   Most of the voluminous litigation under NEPA has concerned the circumstances under which an EIS must be prepared and, somewhat less frequently, the adequacy of those that are prepared.   See, e.g., *Hanly v. Kleindienst*, 471 F.2d 823 (2d Cir. 1972), *cert. denied* 412 U.S. 908 (1973).   There is substantial doubt whether a reviewing court can set aside an agency's action, taken after ventilation of its environmental effects, on the ground that these effects are excessive.   See *Strycker's Bay Neighborhood Council v. Karlen*, 444 U.S. 223 (1980).   NEPA authorizes the Council on Environmental Quality to coordinate the environmental consideration among federal agencies and, with Presidential support, the Council has periodically issued guidelines for the preparation of environmental impact statements.   See Note, *Implementation of the Environmental Impact Statement*, 88 Yale L.J. 596 (1979).

While we encounter NEPA again in examining other administrative law doctrines, space precludes comprehensive treatment.   Because it has served as a model for other proposals to broaden the range of values and the types of information administrators weigh in making decisions, however, it is appropriate to explore here NEPA's purported effects on governmental decisionmaking.

Cramton and Berg concluded in 1971 that NEPA had produced a "dramatic transformation" in the thinking of the Atomic Energy Commission (now the Nuclear Regulatory Commission) and the Army Corps of Engineers and "significant changes" in decisions by the Departments of Defense, Interior, and Transportation. See 71 Mich. L. Rev. 511, 512 n.4, supra. Bardach and Pugliaresi, in *The Environmental Impact Statement vs. The Real World*, The Public Interest, Fall 1977, 22–38, while acknowledging that NEPA has had important effects on the administrative process, suggest that they are not those Congress intended or, indeed, would now endorse:

> There can be no doubt that a major effect of the EIS requirement has been to give environmental groups a legal and political instrument to cancel, delay, or modify development projects that they oppose. * * *

> The legal and political effects of the EIS requirement were not, of course, those that Congress intended. * * * To put the case very baldly: Agencies cannot be penetrating or creative when their analyses are directed and mobilized for primarily defensive purposes. * * *

> The EIS has no method of locating the serious issues for the reader. In the worst traditions of bureaucracy and technocracy, the EIS appears in a very elaborate standardized format that simply drops the issues where it finds them. * * * And there is a reason for this: To highlight the 'critical' environmental issues in a summary section (or elsewhere in the EIS) would necessarily imply that others were not so critical. The solicitor's office worries that such judgments are 'conclusory' and in violation of NEPA. * * *

> Environmentalist critics believe that EIS's are turgid and undiscriminating because bureaucrats wish to camouflage the critical issues. Perhaps this is sometimes true. But the more severe problem is the opposite one: the reluctance to downgrade the noncritical issues.

> The routinization and bureaucratization of the EIS process has an even worse effect than obscuring issues: Sometimes the EIS misses them altogether. * * *

Another disappointed critic of NEPA is Professor Joseph Sax, *The (Unhappy) Truth about NEPA*, 26 Okla. L. Rev. 239, 245–46 (1973). His critique based on a review of impact statements proposed in connection with planning strategies to cope with airport noise and congestion, suggests impediments to generalized schemes for making administrators more sympathetic to values that have not historically been considered:

> * * * I know of no solid evidence to support the belief that requiring articulation, detailed findings or reasoned opinions enhances the integrity or propriety of the administrative decisions. I think the emphasis on the redemptive quality of procedural reform is about nine parts myth and one part coconut oil. * * *

> In my opinion * * * *as presently structured and enforced*, the NEPA will not lead to significant self-reform by agencies.

> The first, and probably most important, explanation is that of operational responsibility. People who run airports have their attention riveted on the day-to-day problems of their airport. Nothing is more important to them professionally than to assure that the airport is not bogged down in chaotic congestion or overwhelmed by noise complaints. From their perspective,

there is only one way by which they can have some assurance about, and control over, the prevention of such chaos: that is to get bulldozers moving out on the field to build new or expanded runways. * * *

A correlative point is that an agency with operative responsibility is going to favor the solution where the financing is the most certain. In the airport context, Congress has—unwittingly, perhaps—itself undermined the success of NEPA by enacting the Airport and Airways Development Act. That Act provides a federal trust fund to pay for a substantial share of new airport construction. Conversely, quiet engine programs, new traffic control improvements and other such technological alternatives depend on uncertain appropriations from time to time.

Another behavioral characteristic of major operative enterprises is a high degree of political sensitivity. They have friends and constituents, and they want to keep them as happy and friendly as possible. Proposals for flight consolidation, rescheduling and imposition of high fees for general aviation have a potential for alienating traditional allies, the airlines and private fliers.

Conversely, new construction generally provokes intense hostility from only a small group of persons who live quite close to the airport and are usually already unhappy; it frequently pleases nearby business property owners and labor unions, who see new construction as jobs; and the out-of-pocket costs of construction are diffused among a very broad taxpaying population that has only a dim awareness of the issues or alternatives that are available. * * *

The behavioral characteristics I have already cited suggest the limitations of staff or consultants, however environmentally well informed. It soon becomes obvious to such an employee or consultant that there is likely to be a strong inclination toward new construction as the favored solution. The favored solution is rarely likely to be so insupportable that it would rub against the expert's ethical responsibilities to his profession. * * *

Despite the criticism of NEPA, two recent federal statutes adopt variants of the model for guiding administrative discretion where decisions may affect small entities or impose unreasonable record-keeping and reporting burdens on affected parties.

Regulatory Flexibility Act

The Regulatory Flexibility Act (RFA), Pub. L. No. 96–354, 94 Stat. 1164 (1980) (codified at 5 U.S.C.A. § 601), was a product of mounting Congressional concern about the impact of regulation—particularly environmental and health regulation—on economic growth generally and on the vitality of small businesses specifically. Proponents of the Act observed that "regulations tend to be uniform in design, permit little discretion in their implementation and implicitly assume that all those subject to them are basically alike." 126 Cong. Rec. S10935 (August 6, 1980). According to the Senate Judiciary Committee, such uniform regulations frequently have a "disproportionately greater economic impact upon small businesses and thus upon their competitive conditions." S. Rep. No. 878, 96 Cong., 2d Sess. 3 (1980). The focus of the RFA is ostensibly procedural; it does not alter, or require any agency to alter, substantive regulations. Rather, it compels each agency to gather information about, and make findings concerning, the impact of regulatory requirements on small business. This obligation applies both in the issuance of new regulations and in the review, mandated by the Act, of existing regulations.

The RFA requires all federal agencies to modify their rulemaking procedures and to consider regulatory alternatives to rules "likely to have a significant economic impact on a substantial number of small entities." 5 U.S.C.A. § § 602, 603, and 604. Before initiating rulemaking an agency must assess the economic impact of a contemplated rule and, if it cannot certify that it will _not_ significantly affect a substantial number of small businesses, include the initiative on its biennial "regulatory flexibility agenda"—a public listing designed to elicit information from small businesses about the impact of, and alternatives to, new agency rules. Before issuing a proposal, the agency must prepare an "initial regulatory flexibility analysis" that estimates the proposed rule's impact on small entities and explores alternatives that would accomplish the same objectives. A final "flexibility analysis" must be part of the record of the agency's published rule.

AGENCY HAS BURDEN OF PROOF

The RFA's main impact may stem from its requirements that agencies (a) publish a plan for review of all existing rules and (b) complete within ten years their review of all rules existing on January 1, 1981. The Act imposes requirements for consideration of the effects on small business and identification of less burdensome alternatives that are comparable to those for new rules. This demand that agencies reexamine their existing rules could have important effects on administrative behavior. The diversion of resources required to accomplish it will almost certainly slow development of new initiatives. Furthermore, the review process will afford opportunities for new managers, as well as outside parties, to introduce considerations that may have been overlooked or rejected when the rules were initially adopted. See generally Stewart, *The New Regulatory Flexibility Act*, 67 A.B.A. J. 66 (January 1981); Verkuil, *A Critical Guide to the Regulatory Flexibility Act*, 1982 Duke L.J. 213.

How compliance with the RFA is to be assured is unclear. The Act specifies that an agency's failure to prepare a "regulatory flexibility analysis" for a rule not certified as exempt shall void the rule. But it goes on to provide that agency determinations of the Act's applicability as well as their analyses "shall not be subject to judicial review." At the same time, any analysis prepared for a rule whose validity is challenged "shall constitute part of the whole record of agency action in connection with the review." The sparse judicial references to the RFA betray little disposition to second-guess agency decisions that a rule's impact on small business is not excessive or could not be avoided by some alternative approach. See, e.g., *Small Refiner Lead Phase-Down Task Force v. EPA*, 705 F.2d 506 (D.C. Cir. 1983); *Thompson v. Clark*, 741 F.2d 401 (D.C. Cir. 1984). The RFA makes the Chief Counsel of the Small Business Administration responsible for coordinating compliance among the agencies and for encouraging participation in agency proceedings by representatives of small business. The SBA Chief Counsel is also authorized to appear as amicus curiae in judicial proceedings to review regulations to which the Act applies.

For further discussion of the RFA, see Davis, *Regulatory Reform and Congressional Control of Regulation*, 17 New Eng. L. Rev. 1199 (1982); Strauss, *Regulatory Reform in a Time of Transformation*, 15 Suffolk U.L. Rev. 903 (1981); Pashigian, *The Effect of Environmental Regulation on Optimal Plant Size and Factor Shares*, 27 J. Law & Econ. 1 (1984).

Paperwork Reduction Act

The Paperwork Reduction Act, Pub. L. No. 96–511, 94 Stat. 2812 (1980) (codified at 44 U.S.C.A. § § 3501 *et seq.*), was one of the last pieces of legislation signed by President Carter, and reflected concerns about the impact of regulation on economic vitality similar to those that inspired the RFA. See OMB, Paperwork and Red Tape (Sept. 1979). Unlike the RFA, however, the Paperwork Reduction Act included provisions that assured it would have immediate impact on the policies of administrative agencies.

The Paperwork Act amends the Federal Reports Act of 1942, which was likewise intended to systemize government information gathering activities and to minimize the burden of official record-keeping and reporting requirements. The 1942 Act, however, had been construed as inapplicable to three-quarters of all federal information demands on the private sector. See S. Rep. No. 96–930, 96th Cong., 2d Sess. 75 (1980). The 1980 legislation retains the basic format of the 1942 law, which purported to require central approval for agency information demands on businesses and individuals, but it eliminates virtually all agency exemptions and centralizes control in OMB.

Any agency that desires to impose a new demand for information on the private sector, whether in a proposed rule or independently, must first convince OMB that the information sought "is necessary for the proper performance of the functions of the agency, including whether the information will have practical utility." OMB's refusal to approve a request is final, unless the request comes from an independent agency and a majority of its members vote to override the "veto." OMB may not veto a proposal to obtain information that is demanded by an agency's organic legislation, but the Act still requires that OMB have an opportunity to review such proposals. The Act's clear thrust is to discourage new information demands and reduce the "paperwork burden" created by existing agency requirements for records and reports.

Statutes Safeguarding the Integrity of Agency Decisionmakers

Executive agency officials and employees of independent commissions function within a complex framework of legal restrictions designed both to assure competence and protect integrity. The very concept of a "civil service" implies a rejection of partisan affiliation as a criterion for public employment. The Pendleton (or the Civil Service) Act, now codified at 5 U.S.C.A. § § 1101–1105, an early victory for the Progressive Movement, was a response to perceived abuses in the hiring and removal of federal employees under Presidents Grant and Hayes. The original Act created the U.S. Civil Service Commission, which for more than 80 years oversaw the employment practices of the entire federal civilian establishment—except for employees of the courts and Congress.

This apparatus underwent far-reaching changes in 1978, when President Carter persuaded Congress to enact the Civil Service Reform Act, Pub. L. No. 95–454, 92 Stat. 1111. The new law's chief objectives were to foster conditions that rewarded able and conscientious civil servants and made it easier for dedicated managers to remove employees who performed poorly. The 1978 Act created a new Senior Executive Service (SES) which staffs executive positions throughout government, and gave supervisors substantial flexibility to adjust pay and reassign duties. 5 U.S.C.A. § 1101.

The 1978 law also restructured the system by which employees can contest discipline or removal. First, it divided the old CSC into two agencies: the Office of Personnel Management, whose functions are apparent from the title, 5 U.S.C.A. § § 1101—05, and the independent Merit System Protection Board, which oversees compliance with merit selection requirements and hears employee challenges to disciplinary actions. 5 U.S.C.A. § § 1201—05. We examine the history and current structure of civil service legislation in more detail in Chapter 2, infra p. 128 *et seq.*

The various civil service laws have been designed to stifle partisan influence in the appointment and removal of federal employees, save those at the upper tiers of government who must enjoy the administration's confidence. In recent years attention has shifted from political favoritism to the potential influence of private personal investment or the expectation of future private-sector employment. The U.S. Code has long prohibited a federal employee from participating in the disposition of any "particular matter" in which he has a financial interest, and barred former employees from representing private interests in any "particular matter" in which they were personally involved in government. 18 U.S.C.A. § § 205, 207. These well-established statutory prohibitions have been augmented by a blizzard of administrative regulations as well as by new legislation.

An employee's obligation to refrain from participating in the decision about a matter in which he or a family member has a financial interest is straightforward. Regulations also prohibit employees from accepting gifts of significant value from persons or organizations having dealings with their employer. Indeed, Executive Order No. 11,222 prohibits a government employee from engaging in any conduct "which might result in, or create the appearance of * * * affecting adversely the confidence of the public in the integrity of the Government." 3 C.F.R. 306, *reprinted in* 18 U.S.C.A. § 201. Concern that official actions may be compromised by even the appearance of private gratuity has led to some extreme measures. For example, the FDA forbids employees to accept free accommodations from groups they are invited to address, or even the difference between actual cost and the maximum reimbursement allowed by the government. In 1979 the FDA General Counsel cautioned lawyers on his staff against attending a Christmas cocktail party sponsored by a law firm whose members had once worked for, and represented clients regulated by, the agency. While few agencies would be so sensitive, the General Counsel correctly anticipated embarrassment if the party received press coverage, as in Washington it could. His sensitivity may have been heightened by the recent circulation of a study by Common Cause, which revealed that 11 of the last 12 lawyers to leave the FDA went to work for companies the agency regulated or for law firms representing them.

In the Ethics in Government Act of 1978, Pub. L. No. 95–521, 92 Stat. 1824 (1978) (codified at 5 U.S.C.A. App. § § 401–405), Congress attempted to insulate agencies from the supposedly malign effects of this "revolving door" and simultaneously tightened controls over incumbent federal employees. The Act imposed two new obligations on current employees. It broadened the requirement that management-level employees annually file statements of their financial holdings and those of close family members. 5 U.S.C.A. App. § § 202, 402. These statements were to help guide both employees and, in questionable cases, the Office of Government Ethics to identify decisions, or classes of decisions, in which their participation should be avoided. The Act's more controversial innovation was a provision making these financial statements available for public inspection. 5 U.S.C.A. App. § 402(b)(3). This disclosure requirement provoked cries of invaded privacy and caused some part-time government employees, generally academics serving on advisory committees, to terminate their government service.

The Ethics in Government Act also erected new barriers to the self-interested influence of former employees. It imposes a lifetime ban on an employee's formal or informal appearance in any "particular matter" in which he was "personally and substantially" involved while in the government. This category embraces any adjudicated dispute, grant, or contract, but a proceeding to establish a rule is not considered a "particular matter." The Act also forbids former employees, for two years, to counsel, aid, or advise others who do appear before the agency, thus closing a loophole in the former law which reached only appearances by the employee himself. 18 U.S.C.A. § 207(b). This two-year ban extends to all matters that fell within the employee's official responsibility as well as those in which he participated personally. Finally, the Ethics Act forbids a former high-level employee from approaching his old agency in order to influence the resolution of any particular matter—defined, for this purpose, to include rulemaking—whether or not the matter was pending during his government employment. 18 U.S.C.A. § 207(c). These prohibitions are enforceable through criminal prosecution, a rare event, and through disciplinary action by the agency to which an unlawful approach is made. 18 U.S.C.A. § 207(c), (i).

An issue that has troubled local bar officials stems from the personal character of these restrictions on former government employees. While the law's prohibitions now reach private assistance to others who appear before the agency, they speak only to the former employee; his partners and associates are not precluded from activities that would be forbidden to the employee himself. Bar officials in both the District of Columbia and New York have addressed the matter of institutional disqualification, and the D.C. Bar once gave serious consideration to a rule that would extend a former employee's disqualifications to all lawyers with whom he practices.   See *Former Government Attorneys in Private Practice: Final Legal Ethics Committee Proposal for Comment*, 3 District Lawyer 44 (1978); Note, *Ethical Problems for the Law Firm of a Former Government Attorney: Firm or Individual Disqualification?*, 1977 Duke L.J. 512.   See also *Kesselhaut v. United States*, 214 Ct. Cl. 124, 555 F.2d 791 (1977).   One argument against such an extension voiced by some senior government lawyers is that it would hamper the government's ability to compete for young attorneys, who could become unmarketable if their public service automatically disqualified all lawyers in any firm that hired them.   For a generally reassuring assessment of the impact on public officials' behavior and their expectations for private-sector employment, see P. QUIRK, INDUSTRY INFLUENCE IN FEDERAL REGULATORY AGENCIES 143–74 (1981).   For a more skeptical discussion of the value and costs of laws intended to curb unethical behavior by civil servants, see A. NEELY, ETHICS-IN-GOVERNMENT LAWS: ARE THEY TOO "ETHICAL"?   (AEI 1984).

The statutory restrictions on conflict of interest in government service and post-employment conduct of former employees are intended to insulate government decisions from improper private influence and personal ambition.   Other laws betray Congressional concern about excessive deference of executive employees to the wishes of the President and his appointees.   The appointment of Archibald Cox as Special Watergate Prosecutor revived Congressional interest in an institution that had enjoyed popularity at the state level.   In 1978 Congress passed legislation to institutionalize this method for enforcing limits on the conduct of executive officers, whom the Department of Justice may be unwilling to pursue.   A special prosecutor is to be appointed whenever the Attorney General concludes that charges of misconduct or criminality against a government official require independent exploration.   See Pub. L. No. 95–521, 92 Stat. 1824 (1978) (codified at 28 U.S.C.A. § § 591–598).   For a good discussion of the history of the Act, problems raised by its application, and proposals for change, see Kramer and Smith, *The Special Prosecutor Act: Proposals for 1983*, 66 Minn. L. Rev. 963 (1982).   Congressional demands for the appointment of a special prosecutor to investigate charges against high-ranking executive officers—such as President Carter's OMB Director and President Reagan's Secretary of Labor—are now common.   (Compare the Civil Service Reform Act of 1978, Pub. L. No. 95–454, which creates a Special Counsel within the new Merit System Protection Board to investigate and prosecute unlawful personnel practices, such as attempts to use promotion, transfer, and discipline to reward political favorites.)

In the same legislation Congress for the first time accorded statutory sanction for another common Washington practice—"whistleblowing," a term that embraces almost any effort by federal employees to expose the misjudgments or misfeasance of their superiors.   The willingness of subordinate civil servants to call attention to serious deficiencies or dishonesty may be independently praiseworthy, but "whistleblowing" enjoys special popularity in Congress, particularly among members who recognize its potential for embarrassing the party in power.

Statutory protection for "whistleblowers," in the form of prohibiting disciplinary action against employees who seek to expose mistakes and wrongdoing, thus became a precondition for many members' support of the Civil Service Reform Act of 1978. For a sympathetic analysis of this legislation, see Vaughn, *Statutory Protection of Whistleblowers in the Federal Executive Branch*, 1982 U. Ill. L. Rev. 615. See also discussion at pp. 131–32 infra.

Observers of Congressional oversight can confirm the popularity as witnesses of employees who can purport to speak from personal experience about deficiencies in their agencies' administration of the law. Where a member of Congress knows enough to provide such an employee a public forum, his public show of support ordinarily will forestall retaliatory discipline. The statute's protection provides additional assurance, however, that members will hear from employees whose accusations may or may not justify public discrimination. Encouragement of "whistleblowing" can thus be viewed as another means by which Congress exerts influence over administrators. The practice also enjoys popularity among members of the press. See Richburg, *Do We Really Want Britain's Secrecy Laws?*, The Washington Post, Jan. 29, 1984, at D1, D5.

2. CONGRESSIONAL CHOICE OF AGENCY STRUCTURE AND LOCATION

In conducting its examination of the federal administrative process, the 1941 Attorney General's Committee studied twenty-seven different agencies. The resulting staff monographs described a variety of administrative structures and revealed possibly important differences in governmental location within and outside the executive branch. S. Doc. 186, 76th Cong., 3d Sess. (1940); S. Doc. 8, 77th Cong., 1st Sess. (1941). Subsequent decades have brought increased organizational diversity as Congress has added to the arsenal of federal regulatory, promotional, and public benefits programs. While many new laws have simply enlarged the responsibilities of existing bodies, and thus often occasioned no debate over structure or location, in creating new agencies Congress has routinely given careful attention to such matters, recognizing their impact on administrative behavior and susceptibility to legislative control. A 1977 study prepared for the Senate Committee on Governmental Affairs concluded:

> It is our view that organizational structure is not neutral, that it is more than a game of moving boxes on an organizational chart, and that it is not devoid of policy implications. * * *

> Whether or not a given organizational structure for regulatory administration should be favored over all others will depend, in large part, on what political values are to be promoted. * * *

V Study on Federal Regulation: Regulatory Organization, U.S. Senate Committee on Governmental Affairs, 95th Cong., 1st Sess. 1, 21–22 (1977) (hereafter *1977 Study on Federal Regulation).*

Near the end of an illuminating essay on the necessity for maintaining, indeed strengthening, presidential power over bureaucratic institutions, *Executive Reorganization and Presidential Power,* 1977 Sup. Ct. Rev. 1, 33–34, Professor Karl makes the same point more trenchantly:

> The history of executive reorganization thus has a tendency to obscure the basic purpose of reorganization: to secure power over a bureaucracy whose real source of independence is congressional funding.   Congress has reason to protect that independence, and the bureaucracy has reason to respect the loose political oversight Congress is able to provide.   The president who seeks the power to reorganize must obtain it from a legislature that sees clear benefit in his not having the power.   The grounds for compromise are narrow, therefore, and depend upon couching the issue in language that conceals the no-win game actually being played.   While the arguments do tend to emphasize the gains in power the executive will achieve, the loss in power to the legislature is rarely, if ever, defined with any clarity.   Indeed, the terms used to describe that loss usually take the form of pejoratives no ambitious legislator would wish to use: logrolling, spoils, patronage, satisfaction of interest-group lobbyists, and the like.   * * *

Too many choices are involved in the creation of a new agency for us to catalog, much less illustrate, all of them here.   It is possible, however, to identify some general issues of structure or location that historically have loomed as significant for members of Congress.   In most cases the salient feature of structure or locational choice is subsequent agency susceptibility to legislative influence, or at least insulation from the competitive political influence of the President.

Until near the end of the 19th century, all administrative functions of the federal government were performed by officials within the executive branch under the supervision of some cabinet secretary or responsible to the President directly.   R. RABIN, PERSPECTIVES ON THE ADMINISTRATIVE PROCESS 207 (1979).   In the Interstate Commerce Commission, however, Congress fashioned a new regulatory entity that had both a distinctive location and structure: The ICC was considered to be outside and independent of the executive branch, yet not formally part of the legislature; and it was administered, not by a single head, but by a collegial body of five, ostensibly coequal, commissioners.   The first characteristic raises a persistent constitutional issue that we shall pursue further in Chapter 2.   The supposed unhappy practical consequences of the second— collegial administration—have been the focus of numerous proposed reforms of administrative government, particularly since World War II.   See, e.g., THE PRESIDENT'S ADVISORY COUNCIL ON EXECUTIVE ORGANIZATION: A NEW REGULATORY FRAMEWORK: REPORT ON SELECTED INDEPENDENT REGULATORY AGENCIES (1971) (the "Ash Council Report"); Robinson, *On Reorganizing the Independent Regulatory Agencies,* 57 Va. L. Rev. 947 (1971).   Both features, however, have implications for Congressional control.

"Independent" Status

The 1977 study for the Senate Committee on Governmental Affairs describes the evolution in Congressional perception of the "independent" status of the ICC and its numerous sister regulatory commissions. This group includes, for example, the FTC, the SEC, the CAB, and the FCC—the latter three creations of the New Deal—as well as the Consumer Product Safety Commission, the Commodity Futures Trading Commission, and the Federal Energy Regulatory Commission—all established since 1970.

There are * * * no fewer than 18 independent agencies which receive more than a third (or about $1 billion) of the total annual budget for federal regulation. * * * [I]n the past five years, Congress has created no fewer than four new regulatory commissions,* and all were expressly designed as "independent" in their organic acts. * * * Most recently the Department of Energy Organization Act * * * established such an agency fully within an executive department. The vitality of the independent commission is also apparent in Congressional determination to distinguish those agencies from other forms of government organizations. In March 1977, in granting the President broad powers to reorganize the federal government, Congress expressly prohibited any reorganization plan that would abolish, consolidate or wholly transfer the functions of independent regulatory commissions. Significantly no previous reorganization authority, granted by Congress to every President from Truman through Nixon, contained that limitation.

Several years ago Congress excepted the independent regulatory commissions from the requirement that all information-gathering forms first be cleared by the Office of Management and Budget, and instead transferred a more limited clearance authority for those agencies only to the Comptroller General. Further there have been a series of attempts, some of which have been successful as to particular agencies, to exempt the independent commissions from general executive branch-wide requirements, concerning: standards and process for the selection of top level, noncareer agency staff members; clearance by the OMB of the agencies' budget requests, legislative recommendations and testimony prior to submission to Congress; and the power to litigate in the courts independent of Justice Department supervision and control. * * *

* * * [W]hen first established [the ICC] was something short of fully independent, since [it] was originally placed within the Department of the Interior. * * *

Two years later in 1889, without a single hearing or a word of recorded debate, Congress significantly altered that relationship by lifting the Interstate Commerce Commission out of the Department of the Interior, and by granting the agency sole authority over its own budget, personnel and internal management. Thus was born the first independent regulatory commission. * * * [I]t is noteworthy that Congress adopted those and other amendments concerning the ICC just two days before the Presidential inauguration of a Republican railroad lawyer named Benjamin Harrison. * * *

*Commodity Futures Trading Commission, Consumer Product Safety Commission, Federal Energy Regulatory Commission and Nuclear Regulatory Commission.

Freedom from Presidential domination was within 20 years the principal justification voiced in Congress for the independent agency form.   In 1910, debate on ICC amendments was filled with references to the agency's independent status, which very simply meant that it should not be subjected to control by an executive official.   The ICC, it was reasoned, was exercising what were essentially legislative functions and was as such—an "arm of Congress," even a "committee of Congress."   In short, the agency was legislative in character, and thereby enjoyed a special relationship to Congress. * * *

* * *   In May 1973, the very same thought was expressed by the late Senator [Philip] Hart during the debate on a nominee to an independent commission:

> * * *   Congress, and more specifically the Senate, is subject to criticism for loss of sight over the years as to the purpose for which we established these commissions.   The commissions, if I may risk oversimplification, are ours.   We have concluded that certain regulatory activities have gotten to a point where, on a day-to-day basis, Congress itself is inept and ill-equipped to make decisions.   So we create a commission. * * *   In substance, we say to them, "Gentlemen * * * you do for us what we like to think we would do if we had your skill and the time to give attention to the problems that confront you."

* * *

Yet the notion has not gone unchallenged.   Certainly the most famous rebuttal in that regard was filed in 1937 by the Brownlow Commission [a study group created by President Roosevelt], which declared that independent commissions

> * * * are in reality miniature independent governments set up to deal with the railroad problem, the banking problem, or the radio problem. They constitute a headless "fourth branch" of the Government, a haphazard deposit of irresponsible agencies and uncoordinated powers.   They do violence to the basic theory of the American Constitution that there should be three branches of the Government and only three.[35]

* * *

Certainly the easiest way to identify an independent regulatory agency is when Congress, in the agency's organic act, labels it as such * * * .

The organizational situation does get rather confusing, and the structural location of an agency is not always a telling sign of its status.   For instance, there is an independent regulatory agency that is fully within an executive department; conversely there are regulatory agencies, located outside such departments, which are not "independent" in the traditional sense of that term.   The newly created Federal Energy Regulatory Commission is the exception contained in the former category.   FERC is located within the De-

---

35. The President's Committee on Administrative Management, "Report of the Committee with Studies of Administrative Management in the Federal Government (1937)", as printed in, Subcommittee on Separation of Powers, Committee on the Judiciary, U. S. Senate, *Separation of Powers and the Independent Agencies: Cases and Selected Readings*, 91st Cong., 1st sess., pp. 345–346 (1969).

partment of Energy, and there are * * * certain coordinating relationships between the commission and the Secretary of the Department of Energy. * * *

Conversely, simply because an agency is located *outside* an executive department does not necessarily mean it is independent in the sense of being an "arm of Congress." * * * For example, the Environmental Protection Agency is regulatory in character, and is not within any other agency or department. It was created in 1970 by a reorganization plan submitted by the President to Congress, rather than by statute. In submitting the plan, then President Nixon did indicate that EPA was intended to be an independent agency, and it was repeatedly so characterized in Congress. * * *

But the EPA is by no means free of general direction by the President. As illustrated by this exchange at the [Administrator Russell] Train confirmation hearing, the EPA is not independent in that sense:

> Senator [Hugh] SCOTT: * * * I want to be absolutely fair and absolutely clear. It is my conception that you are 100 percent subject to the President. Is that your impression?
>
> Mr. TRAIN. I think legally that is probably entirely right. * * *
>
> I am fully assured that the President agrees with my interpretation and at such time, of course—I do not serve for a fixed term—that my conduct is not acceptable to the President, I can be removed forthwith. * * *

Service at the pleasure of the President is one critical difference between "independent agencies within the executive branch," such as the EPA, and other independent regulatory agencies. The latter group can be identified by the unique structure concerning tenure of office, which Congress expressly created in order to assure independence from the executive branch. * * *

The size of the commission, the length of the terms, and the fact that they do not all lapse at one time are key elements of the independent structure. Because of those features, it was thought unlikely that any President would be able to influence the commissions, through the appointment power, in the same way as he could an executive department * * *. Congress placed other restrictions on the appointment power of the President. First no more than a simple majority of any commission's membership could come from a single political party; this would, it was thought, neutralize the number of commissioners selected from the President's party and assure bipartisan membership. In addition, Congress restricted the President's power to remove independent commissioners, by providing removal only for "inefficiency, neglect of duty, or malfeasance in office." * * *

In the early debates in Congress, the bipartisan requirement was viewed as a matter of "great moment" and a "vital point" in assuring agency independence; while the restriction on removal of independent commissioners either received no attention or was considered more as a protection against incompetent or objectionable commissioners than as a limitation upon the President. As it turned out, the reverse proved to be the case. The bipartisan requirement has been of comparatively little utility in either neutralizing partisanship or increasing independence; * * * so-called minority seats are typically filled by persons who are partisans of the President though not members of his party. On the other hand, the removal restriction is perhaps the single most important feature of regulatory independence. * * *

Collegial Form

All of the so-called "independent" agencies are collegial bodies. While Congress could presumably create an agency headed by a single administrator who was ostensibly independent of the executive branch, it has never done so. Collegial bodies, whose members' staggered terms are not co-extensive with the President's, may be thought inherently better equipped to resist White House pressures. But collegial form may not be an expression solely of Congress' desire to limit Presidential influence over administrative policy. As the previous excerpt suggests, a major function of the first commissions involved the adjudication of individual cases—license applications, rate proposals, unfair trade or labor practice charges—for which a collegial tribunal may have seemed appropriate.

Recent criticism of collegial bodies has focused on their asserted inability to visualize the need for and to formulate general policies (i.e., to make rules) and on their deficiencies as administrators. See, e.g., M. BERNSTEIN, REGULATING BUSINESS BY INDEPENDENT COMMISSION (Princeton, 1955); Ash Council Report, supra. Yet no student of governmental organization has ever been able conclusively to link regulatory success or failure to the collegial or non-collegial form of an agency. See R. NOLL, REFORMING REGULATION: AN EVALUATION OF THE ASH COUNCIL PROPOSALS 102–03 (1971). See also Noll, *The Economics and Politics Of Regulation*, 57 U. Va. L. Rev. 1016 (1971).

Departmental Location

Many executive branch agencies are components of cabinet-level departments and thus fall under the supervision of a secretary appointed, and subject to immediate removal, by the President. Notable examples include the Food and Drug Administration, which occupies a third tier in the Department of Health and Human Services, and OSHA, headed by an Assistant Secretary of Labor. These two agencies differ in one important way: the Assistant Secretary for Occupational Safety and Health is subject to Senate confirmation, while the Commissioner of Food and Drugs—a lower ranking position—owes his job only to the Secretary of HHS and, to the extent of White House interest, to the President.

Several executive branch agencies fall organizationally outside the cabinet-level departments. The best example is the Environmental Protection Agency, whose Administrator is subject to Senate confirmation and sometimes enjoys what is termed "Cabinet-level" status—an unofficial characterization that mainly denotes reputed ease of access to the President and his staff.

Designation of Authority

When legislation delegating lawmaking authority also creates a new entity to implement it, Congress' choice of delegate may be subsumed in discussions of the powers and structure of the new agency. But Congress often delegates new authority to an existing body, whose prior performance will surely be influential in its assignment of responsibility. The legislature may seek to affect the administration of delegated authority by sheltering it from political oversight within the executive branch, e.g., FERC, or by precluding its subdelegation to officials who may lack political sensitivity. For example, section 505(e) of the Federal Food, Drug, and Cosmetic Act, 21 U.S.C.A. § 355(e), permits only the Secretary of HHS summarily to suspend marketing of a drug that presents an "imminent hazard to health," though it allows all remaining authorities conveyed to be subdelegated to, and thus exercised by, the Commissioner of Food and Drugs.

Of course the President too may take account of the influence of location and perspective on the exercise of delegated authority. The EPA was created by executive order in 1970, and assigned responsibility for administering environmental laws previously disbursed among the Departments of Agriculture, the Interior, and HEW. One motive for reassigning responsibilities was the expectation that EPA would pursue policies different from those adopted by the original delegates. And without question, reassigning administration of the federal pesticide laws from USDA was followed by more aggressive concern for health and environmental effects though there had been no change in the statutory text. See generally Marcus, *Environmental Protection Agency*, ch. 8 in J. Q. WILSON, THE POLITICS OF REGULATION (1980).

While statutes routinely designate the officer or agency responsible for their administration, it is not always obvious what motives inspire Congress' choice. Surely the desire to take advantage of specialization and to promote coordination are powerful influences. Thus, for example, most laws governing public lands are administered by the Secretary of the Interior, although this may also betray a Congressional desire to sustain support from the constituencies served by the Interior Department. But there are also exceptions to the pattern of concentrating related laws and programs in a single department, which reflect other Congressional policies. Thus the U.S. Forest Service, which regulates public and private uses of the vast acres of the national forests, has remained within USDA despite periodic suggestions for its removal to Interior, a department sometimes regarded as more "conservation minded." See, e.g., G. ROBINSON, THE FOREST SERVICE: A STUDY IN PUBLIC LAND MANAGEMENT 276 (1975); J. SAX, MOUNTAINS WITHOUT HANDRAILS: REFLECTIONS ON THE NATIONAL PARKS (1980). USDA has also retained authority over the marketing of all food containing meat and poultry in the face of vigorous proposals to combine this program with those of the FDA. See, e.g., *1977 Study on Federal Regulation* at 113 *et seq.;* Commodities Futures Trading Commission Act of 1974, 7 U.S.C.A. § 13-1 (excepting sales of onions).

While one can generally discern from legislative history, text, or experience why Congress delegated primary authority to a specific agency, in recent years dispute has arisen over the implications of Congress' choice for participation by officials elsewhere in government—specifically officials acting on behalf of the President.   In both the Carter and Reagan administrations officials based in, or affiliated with, the Office of Management and Budget often attempted to influence choices made by the nominal delegates of Congressional authority, claiming to speak for presidential interest in curbing inflation, reducing costs of regulation, or effecting coordination among regulatory programs.   In Chapter 2 we consider whether Congress' delegation to a particular officer, e.g., the Secretary of the Interior, impliedly precludes OMB oversight, or even Presidential rejection, of that official's choices, save by the device of removal.   See, e.g., Rosenberg, *Beyond the Limits of Executive Power: Presidential Control of Agency Rulemaking Under Executive Order 12,291*, 80 Mich. L. Rev. 193 (1981).

Budgetary Oversight

In addition to its increasingly important function as the President's coordinator of policy-making by departments and agencies, OMB has played a central role in managing the executive's budgetary affairs.   As the title suggests—and its original name, Bureau of the Budget, made clear—OMB was established, by Franklin Roosevelt, to provide the President a means of controlling legislative initiatives and budgetary demands.   OMB has continued to perform the two main functions assumed by the old Bureau of the Budget, *viz.*, reviewing proposals for new legislation from, and annual budget requests by, all non-Congressional agencies. Congress has generally acquiesced in this role, though not without objection.   Congressional budget committees commonly ask agency officials to describe not only their OMB sanctioned budgetary needs but also those that OMB vetoed.   And occasionally Congress has enacted legislation specifically directing that an agency shall not be required to submit its budget requests to OMB or other Presidential officials.   E.g., 15 U.S.C.A. § 2076(k)(1), (2) (CPSC); 7 U.S.C.A. § 4a(h)(1), (2) (CTFC).

Power to Conduct Litigation

By statute, 28 U.S.C.A. § 516, Pub. L. No. 89–554, § 4(c), 80 Stat. 613 (1966), without explicit Congressional authorization only the Attorney General can represent the United States in court.   While the Department of Justice lacks the manpower to handle all of the cases to which the United States or some agency is a party, it nominally decides which cases shall be brought, defended, and appealed, and determines what arguments will be advanced on the government's behalf.   Given the usually close political relationship between the President and the Attorney General, Justice Department representation might appear to provide decisive leverage for the White House in the competition with Congress for control over agency action.   The reality, however, is more complex, and is explored in depth at pp. 162–72 infra.

Other Structural Choices

The foregoing illustrations of Congressional concern for agency structure, location, and relationships reiterate a single recurrent theme: the desire to limit the President's influence over the development and implementation of administrative policy. Often this desire is accompanied by an expectation that an agency insulated against Presidential influence will be more susceptible to Congressional overtures, e.g., from oversight and budget committees. Statutory specifications of structure or procedure may, however, have other important policy objectives.

One can find many instances where Congress, either initially or in the light of experience, has attempted to divorce governmental functions that it regarded as incompatible. The APA contains one illustration in its prohibition against the commingling of prosecutory and adjudicatory functions, save by the individuals who comprise the agency itself. See 5 U.S.C.A. § 554(d). This provision reflects a judgment that such a combination impairs the fairness of agency adjudications. An analogous perception is reflected in laws that assign the roles of policy-making prosecutor and judge to two separate agencies. The most recent example is the 1970 Occupational Safety and Health Act, 29 U.S.C.A. § 651, which assigned to OSHA responsibility for enforcing workplace health and safety standards, 29 U.S.C.A. § 659, and also created, within the Department of Labor, an independent tribunal for determining guilt and assessing penalties, the Occupational Safety and Health Review Commission. 29 U.S.C.A. § 661.

A variation on this theme appeared in the 1947 Taft-Hartley amendments to the National Labor Relations Act which, in addition to revising the rights of workers and employers, established the NLRB General Counsel as an office separate from the Board and subject to Presidential appointment and Senate confirmation. 29 U.S.C.A. § 153(d). This legislation did not separate the functions of case-deciding and policy-making, which remained with the Board members, but attempted to assure that the official who decided whether to challenge specific employer or union practices would be independent of a tribunal suspected of excessive sympathy for organized labor.

Pursuing a somewhat different concern about the commingling of incompatible functions, Congress in 1974 disassembled the old Atomic Energy Commission, which had been responsible both for supporting development of civilian nuclear power and for assuring the safety of new generating facilities. Congress concluded that the roles of promoter and regulator should be institutionally separate. *1977 Study on Federal Regulation* at 102-05. Congress made a similar judgment in 1958 when it removed responsibility for regulating the safety of commercial aviation equipment and facilities from the Civil Aeronautics Board and reassigned it to a new executive agency, the Federal Aviation Administration, which is now part of the Department of Transportation. See Hector, *Problems of the CAB and the Independent Regulatory Commissions*, 69 Yale L.J. 931 (1960).

These examples illustrate Congressional efforts to stifle the effects of potential bias in the development or enforcement of regulatory policy and eliminate potential prejudgment of facts in particular cases. In recent years Congress has responded to arguments that, in some fields, agency predeliction may combine with lack of sophistication to yield unsound policies. The notable examples come from the health and safety field. During the late 1960's and 1970's Congress enacted a series of laws addressed to threats to air and water and other elements of the environment and to product and workplace hazards to human health. It generally made clear, both in text and in oversight and budget hearings, that the new agencies—OSHA and CPSC—as well as the older ones—FDA and EPA—were to be zealous in their efforts to protect public health. But the controversy that accompanied many of their actions—against such compounds as DDT, vinyl chloride, and TRIS—sparked criticism that the agencies were unequipped to assess, or disposed to misinterpret, the complex scientific data on which their actions rested.

Congress responded by appending procedural requirements to enhance the quality and objectivity of agency scientific judgments. An early example appeared in the original Occupational Safety and Health Act, which also created the National Institute of Occupational Safety and Health (NIOSH) under the supervision of the Secretary of HEW (now HHS). NIOSH was to serve as OSHA's independent scientific arm, providing the expert assessments of occupational hazards that an action-oriented, field-based agency would require. See T. GREENWOOD, KNOWLEDGE AND DISCRETION IN GOVERNMENT REGULATION (1984). Later in both the Clean Air Act and the federal pesticide law, Congress specified that EPA must submit the scientific analyses prepared by its own staff to panels of outside scientists before initiating regulatory action. In 1981, troubled by accusations that the CPSC lacked the necessary trained personnel, Congress required the agency to establish an independent expert panel whenever it contemplated regulation of consumer products to control a risk of cancer or other chronic disease. See NATIONAL ACADEMY OF SCIENCES, RISK ASSESSMENT IN THE FEDERAL GOVERNMENT: MANAGING THE PROCESS 91–93 (1983).

Each of the Congressional actions cited here could, and most were intended to, influence the substance of agency policy. Yet legislative directives addressed to agency organization, location, and process have rarely produced, or been accompanied by, clarification of the standards for exercising delegated authority. Indeed, directives with respect to procedure or structure often are alternatives to clarification of the agency's substantive mission and sometimes appear to advance policies quite different from those enunciated in the agency's standards for decision. The full package of Congressional instructions to an agency will betray the compromises of objectives that characteristically are required to produce laws establishing regulatory or benefits programs. Thus an agency directed to regulate activities posing even slight risks of harm may be encumbered by a structure and procedures that assure dramatic actions will occur infrequently.   The student of health and safety legislation of the 1970's, for example, might well conclude that the proponents of regulation frequently prevailed in the battle over the standards for action, but just as often lost ground when debate shifted to structure or procedure.

It is important to remember that legislation typically embodies diverse, sometimes even conflicting, visions of desirable public policy, with individual provisions reflecting the demands of changing political coalitions.   Indeed, it may be more accurate to suggest that modern delegations to administrators do not enunciate national policy but rather shift the debate over its content to another arena.   E.g., Latham, *The Group Basis of Politics: Notes for a Theory*, 46 Am. Pol. Sci. Rev. 376 (1952); Greider, *Welcome to the Marketplace that is Washington, Mr. President*, The Washington Post, January 20, 1981, at Z28:

> Congress, after all, does not really enact laws in most areas * * *.   A law, one would think, tells all citizens or certain recognizable classes of citizens that they must do something (such as pay their taxes) or must not do something also (such as commit murders.)
>
> But so much of modern legislation does not do that.   It declares worthy intentions.   Let us end poverty.   Let there be literacy.   Let there be clean meat. * * *
>
> The legislative process has become a reflexive exercise in wishful thinking.   Congress concludes that too many workers are killed and maimed every year in American industry.   To general applause, it enacts a law that says industrial deaths and injuries are a grave national affliction and unsafe working conditions ought to be eliminated.
>
> Then the whole mess is turned over to an agency of the executive branch with vague instructions to work out the details. * * *

3. LEGISLATIVE OVERSIGHT, CASEWORK, AND INFLUENCE

While an agency's structure and location within government surely can affect its behavior, it is less clear that Congress' initial choices effectively preserve its influence over the development of administrative policy. The enactment of authorizing legislation, however, does not sever connections between Congress and its delegates.   Rather, relations assume a variety of new forms, which expose administrative performance to legislative observation—and influence—with irregular frequency and uncertain effect.   Congress is called upon each year to appropriate funds to sustain, enlarge, or curtail agency programs.   Legislative committees, through oversight hearings, monitor specific agency activities and, far less frequently, perform comprehensive reviews of agency performance, sometimes in the context of evaluating proposals for new legislation.   Individual members of both houses inquire about the status of cases or contemplated rules, often at the initiative of constituents or financial backers. And for many agencies the Senate ostensibly participates with the President in the appointment of top managers through its confirmation power.   In performing these various functions, members of Congress can call upon a substantial staff—whose rate of growth since 1970 substantially outpaces that of government generally—and several Congressionally-chartered agencies, such as the General Accounting Office, the Office of Technology Assessment, and the Congressional Research Service.

Political scientists have examined these diverse channels for the expression of Congressional preferences about agency performance in a vast literature; their conclusions are too complex to summarize here. Their recurrent themes, however, raise doubt whether existing connections between Congress and administrative bodies are effective means for accomplishing any of several plausible objectives, including assuring fidelity to Congressional intent, preserving the political responsiveness of government, or dispassionately assessing the strengths and weaknesses of regulatory programs. Traditional scholarship suggests that oversight and casework, for example, may be even less predictable instruments of congressional control than the organizational choices made in organic laws. One typical assessment of the impact of oversight concludes:

> Unless [the oversight activity] reveals a scandalous situation with possibilities for favorable publicity for the legislator, the work is considered dull and potentially troublesome * * * . For elected officials, the incentives favor looking ahead, not back. Responding to current concerns and working on legislation desired by inflential groups have more direct bearing on future elections—and political survival is paramount.

B. ROSEN, HOLDING GOVERNMENT BUREAUCRACIES ACCOUNTABLE 21 (1982). And studies of particular agencies tend to agree:

> Oversight and ad hoc monitoring activities seldom influence [FTC] activities, although they do cause the Commission to expend valuable resources in responding to them.

K. CLARKSON & T. MURIS, THE FEDERAL TRADE COMMISSION SINCE 1970: ECONOMIC REGULATION AND BUREAUCRATIC BEHAVIOR 34 (1981).

Although Congress since 1947 has assigned broad oversight responsibilities to all standing legislative and/or appropriations committees, established special committees on government operations in both houses, and increased its staff five-fold, oversight of administrative agency activity occupies only 11 percent of the agenda of committee hearings and meetings. Aberbach, *Changes in Congressional Oversight*, 22 Am. Behav. Scientist 493, 502 (1979). A recent Congressionally-funded (and authored) study concludes:

> The legislative committees have a formidable array of oversight tools. * * * But unlike the appropriations committees other committees do not systematically conduct oversight. Indeed, one of the most notable features of oversight by nonappropriating committees is its sporadic, unsystematic functioning.

> This *ad hoc* approach to oversight is particularly evident in the regulatory area. Only those agencies with a periodic authorization are actually guaran-

teed review by a legislative committee. Between authorization periods, there may or may not be regular oversight hearings called. While the appropriations committees respond to a set agenda, other committees rarely do. The wide range of techniques available to legislative committees are seldom marshalled for an annual review. An oversight hearing may be held every six months, but a careful analysis of the entire agency's operation may never occur. While the legislative committees have the freedom to define which issues to pursue, they also have the freedom to ignore close scrutiny of an agency.

Oversight tends to be done on a crisis basis only. * * * The oversight effort is usually initiated not in accordance with any preplanned set of priorities, but rather in response to a newspaper article, a complaint from a constituent or special interest group, or information from a disgruntled agency employee. * * *

The *ad hoc* approach to oversight is illustrated by committee treatment of agency regulations. Very few committees or committee staff members systematically review the regulations issued by agencies under their jurisdiction. Issues of the *Federal Register* containing proposed agency rules are not regularly scrutinized. One committee staff member explained that he did not have time to review all of the regulations issued by "his" agency. Only when complaints were registered about a particular rule did he inquire about it. * * *

II Study on Federal Regulation: Congressional Oversight of Regulatory Agencies, U.S. Senate Committee on Government Operations, 95th Cong., 1st Sess. 66–67 (1977).

So-called "casework" occupies a larger segment of legislative-agency interactions. As one member of Congress is said to have lamented, "I thought I was going to be Daniel Webster, but I found out that most of my work was personal work for constituents." C. CLAPP, THE CONGRESSMAN: HIS WORK AS HE SEES IT 51 (1963). Officials of agencies such as the Social Security Administration, which receives 100,000 congressional inquiries each year, would surely agree. Yet casework seldom seems to have relevance for general agency policy. An empirical study of its impact concluded:

> The quantity and variety of complaints received by congressional offices, provide a rich source of information upon which to base legislative reform of agencies. Although many congressional offices believe that casework already serves this function, in fact, individual cases handled by congressional offices rarely stimulate investigation and correction of administrative problems. Offices only infrequently perceive and almost never act upon the larger agency problems implied in citizens' allegations.

Klonoff, *The Congressman as Mediator Between Citizens and Government Agencies: Problems and Prospects*, 16 Harv. J. Legis. 701, 712–13 (1979).

More recent scholarship has begun to question the conventional wisdom that agencies are largely unaffected by informal Congressional expressions of preference. For example, in their study of the Federal

Trade Commission during the decade of the 1970's, Moran and Weingast conclude that the FTC "is remarkably sensitive to even small changes in the imposition of preferences represented on the [oversight] subcommittee and its subcommittee chairman." *Congress as a Source of Regulatory Decisions: The Case of the Federal Trade Commission*, 72 AEA Papers and Proceedings 109, 111 (1982). Moreover, they maintain this finding is true of both the FTC's general policy initiatives and its enforcement activities. See also Weingast and Moran, *Bureaucratic Discretion or Congressional Control? Regulatory Policymaking at the Federal Trade Commission*, 91 J. Pol. Econ. 765 (1983). The authors, who employ statistical techniques for associating changes in agency policy with changes in the voting profiles of oversight subcommittee members, do not question the prevalent findings that congressional-agency contacts are infrequent, sporadic, and superficial. But they contend those findings are consistent with substantial congressional influence over regulatory policy. Weingast and Moran thus "suggest that the mechanics of congressional influence are both subtle and indirect, so much so that even careful observers may not perceive their operation." *The Myth of the Runaway Bureaucracy*, 6 Regulation 33 (May/June 1982). And, of course, the more obvious sanctions of critical hearings and threatened appropriations may have much to do with an agency's responsiveness to the "subtle and indirect" signals it receives about the preferences of the members of Congress who sit on relevant subcommittees.

Should the Weingast and Moran thesis prove correct for most agencies over the long term, Congress' propensity for broad delegations, coupled with the unconstitutionality of the legislative veto, might seem less disconcerting. Neither would signal the demise of electoral accountability—so long as we can presume that "the Congress" is adequately represented by its committees and subcommittees. But that surely is an heroic assumption.

One reason to doubt the "representativeness" of Congressional committees and subcommittees is that they include only a small percentage of the membership of either house. Moreover, the sheer number of standing subcommittees—now more than 200 in the House of Representatives—in practice means that only the chairman and ranking minority member can remain informed about what an agency is doing. The process for selecting chairmen still gives weight to seniority as well as to constituent interest, neither of which may contribute to a balanced perspective of an agency's role or its performance. A member's performance as chairman apparently has little impact on personal reelection prospects, and, of course, committee chairmanships turn over whenever there is a change in party control, even when a chairman's constituents applaud his oversight activities and reelect him. The personalized character of committee management in both houses—the chairman usually chooses a committee's staff, dictates its agenda, and, to the extent any elected official does so, directs its investigations—undermines any notion that committees are microcosms of the whole or reliable amplifiers of current popular sentiment on matters within a committee's jurisdiction. Most expressions of "committee" interest—just like those of individual members—are unencumbered by any of the constraints of genuinely collegial decision-making. This does not mean, of course, that an agency will not be interested in, or even subservient to, the wishes of the chairmen of the committees in whose jurisdictions it falls, but simply that its willingness to be responsive will have little to do with its perception that the chairmen are reliable expositors of legislative intent or "representative" of current Congressional sentiment.

Yet we must remember that committee chairmen often can exercise nearly as much autonomous influence—and authority—over the drafting and passage of legislation. A powerful chairman can prevent, or at least substantially delay, votes on bills that would command overwhelming support. He can largely determine when and whether hearings will be scheduled on a bill, or a markup session held. The chairman's staff will determine who writes the important legislative history, sometimes even the history of legislation the chairman dislikes but declines to oppose. Thus final statutory language as well as the ostensibly authentic sources of legislative history, such as committee reports, can often reflect the decisive influence of a few powerful individuals. However, the necessity to secure votes of other members—within the committee, on the floor, and among the conferees—gives many members the opportunity to affect what "Congress" says. The more informal expressions of attitude or preference, reflected in letters, questions, even reports of hearings, are not subject to the same constraints.

Congressional inquiries can reach the entire range of an agency's activities, from decisions about budgetary choices, to the assignment of personnel, to the relocation of branch offices. Most decisions of these sorts are not the product of formal agency proceedings nor required by law to be based on some administrative record. But many of the more visible, and thus controversial, decisions of administrators are the product of procedures structured to avoid or nullify certain kinds of overtures. Members of Congress and their staffs, however, have sometimes displayed indifference, or insensitivity, towards such distinctions, prompting courts to intervene.

Pillsbury Co. v. FTC, 354 F.2d 952, 963–65 (5th Cir. 1966), is exemplary. In an interlocutory administrative ruling the Commission had taken the position—rejecting the argument of its prosecutorial staff—that the acquisition of active competitors by Pillsbury, a company with a substantial share of the milling market, was not a *per se* violation of the Clayton Act. The Commission had, however, reversed the trial examiner's finding that no prima facie case of monopolization had been made out and remanded the case for further hearings on whether Pillsbury's acquisitions had in fact substantially lessened competition. Ultimately, it resolved that issue against the firm, and ordered divestiture.

While the case was back before the trial examiner, Commission Chairman Howrey and several staff members were called to testify before Senator Estes Kefauver's Antitrust and Monopoly Subcommittee and its counterpart in the House.   At the Senate hearings the FTC witnesses were subjected to prolonged and hostile questioning concerning the Commission's initial rejection of the *per se* theory.   The case was referred to more than 100 times during the several sessions and Chairman Howrey thereafter disqualified himself from further participation in it.   In a statement before the House subcommittee he explained this action:

> I wrote the [interlocutory] opinion.   It is still a pending adjudication; and because of some of the penetrating questions over on the Senate side, I felt compelled to withdraw from the case because I did not think I could be judicial any more when I had been such an advocate of [the Commission's] views in answering questions.

On appeal from its divestiture order, the court of appeals determined that the persistent questioning during the Congressional hearings had so intruded into the Commission's decision processes that other commissioners who participated in the final decision should also be disqualified:

> In view of the inordinate lapse of time in this proceeding, brought to undo what was done by mergers completed in 1951, we are naturally loathe to frustrate the proceedings at this late date.   However, common justice to a litigant requires that we invalidate the order entered by a quasi-judicial tribunal that was importuned by members of the United States Senate, however innocent they intended their conduct to be, to arrive at the ultimate conclusion which they did reach.   * * *
>
> We are sensible of the fact that, pursuant to its quasi-legislative function, it frequently becomes necessary for a commission to set forth policy statements or interpretative rules   * * *   in order to inform interested parties of its official position on various matters.   This is as it should be.
>
> At times similar statements of official position are elicited in Congressional hearings.   In this context, the agencies are sometimes called to task for failing to adhere to the "intent of Congress" in supplying meaning to the often broad statutory standards from which the agencies derive their authority   * * *.   Although such investigatory methods raise serious policy questions as to the *de facto* "independence" of the federal regulatory agencies, it seems doubtful that they raise any constitutional issues.   However, when such an investigation focuses directly and substantially upon the mental decisional processes of a commission *in a case which is pending before it*, Congress is no longer intervening in the agency's *legislative* function, but rather, in its *judicial* function.   At this latter point, we become concerned with the right of private litigants to a fair trial and, equally important, with their right to the appearance of impartiality, which cannot be maintained unless those who exercise the judicial function are free from powerful external influences.   * * *
>
> It may be argued that such officials as members of the Federal Trade Commission are sufficiently aware of the realities of governmental, not to say "political," life as to be able to withstand such questioning as we have outlined here.   However, this court is not so "sophisticated" that it can shrug off such a procedural due process claim merely because the officials involved should be able to discount what is said and to disregard the force of the intrusion into the adjudicatory process.   * * *

* * * [But] we are convinced that the Commission is not permanently disqualified to decide this case. * * * [T]he passage of time, coupled with the changes in personnel on the Commission, sufficiently insulate the present members from any outward effect from what occurred in 1955.

Pressure by one or a few congressmen may also invalidate agency action that is not "quasi-judicial" in character, as *D.C. Federation of Civic Associations v. Volpe*, 459 F.2d 1231, 1245–49 (D.C. Cir. 1972), indicates. That case was a challenge to a decision by the Secretary of Transportation to proceed with the (later abandoned) "Three Sisters Bridge" project as a part of the interstate highway system in the District of Columbia. In the process of ordering a remand for further fact-finding by the trial court, Judge Bazelon had this to say about congressional influence in highway planning:

> As the District Court pointed out,
>> [t]here is no question that the evidence indicates that strong political pressure was applied by certain members of congress in order to secure approval of the bridge project. Congressman Natcher stated publicly and made no secret of the fact that he would do everything that he could to withhold Congressional appropriations for the District of Columbia rapid transit system, the need for which is universally recognized in the Washington metropolitan area, until the District complied with the 1968 Act.
>
> When funds for the subway were, in fact, blocked, Representative Natcher
>> made his position perfectly clear, stating that "as soon as the freeway project gets under way beyond recall then we will come back to the House and recommend that construction funds for rapid transit be approved." * * *

The District Court was surely correct in concluding that the Secretary's action was not judicial or quasi-judicial, and for that reason we agree that much of the doctrine cited by plaintiffs is inapposite. If he had been acting in such a capacity, plaintiffs could have forcefully argued that the decision was invalid because of the decisionmaker's bias, or because he had received ex parte communications. Well-established principles could have been invoked to support these arguments, and plaintiffs might have prevailed even without showing that the pressure had actually influenced the Secretary's decision. With regard to judicial decisionmaking, whether by court or agency, the appearance of bias or pressure may be less objectionable than the reality. But since the Secretary's action was not judicial, that rationale has no application here.

If, on the other hand, the Secretary's action had been purely legislative, we might have agreed with the District Court that his decision could stand in spite of a finding that he had considered extraneous pressures. Beginning with *Fletcher v. Peck* [10 U.S. (6 Cranch.) 87 (1810)], the Supreme Court has maintained that a statute cannot be invalidated merely because the legislature's action was motivated by impermissible considerations (except, perhaps, in special circumstances not applicable here). Indeed that very principle requires us to reject plaintiffs' argument that the approval of the bridge by the District of Columbia City Council was in some sense invalid. **We do** not sit in judgment of the motives of the District's legislative body, nor do we have authority to review its decisions. The City Council's action constituted, in our view, the approval of the project required by statute.

Thus, the underlying problem cannot be illuminated by a simplistic effort to force the Secretary's action into a purely judicial or purely legislative mold. His decision was not "judicial" in that he was not required to base it solely on a formal record established at a public hearing. At the same time, it was not purely "legislative" since Congress had already established the boundaries within which his discretion could operate. But even though his action fell between these two conceptual extremes, it is still governed by principles that we had thought elementary and beyond dispute. If, in the course of reaching his decision, Secretary Volpe took into account "considerations that Congress could not have intended to make relevant," his action proceeded from an erroneous premise and his decision cannot stand. The error would be more flagrant, of course, if the Secretary had based his decision solely on the pressures generated by Representative Natcher. But it should be clear that his action would not be immunized merely because he also considered some relevant factors. * * *

To avoid any misconceptions about the nature of our holding, we emphasize that we have not found—nor, for that matter, have we sought—any suggestion of impropriety or illegality in the actions of Representative Natcher and others who strongly advocate the bridge. They are surely entitled to their own views on the need for the Three Sisters Bridge, and we indicate no opinion on their authority to exert pressure on Secretary Volpe. Nor do we mean to suggest that Secretary Volpe acted in bad faith or in deliberate disregard of his statutory responsibilities. He was placed, through the action of others, in an extremely treacherous position. Our holding is designed, if not to extricate him from that position, at least to enhance his ability to obey the statutory command notwithstanding the difficult position in which he was placed.

In contexts not involving formal adjudication, however, the mere possibility of bias or prejudgment due to congressional influence apparently has never precipitated judicial invalidation. *American Public Gas Association v. Federal Power Commission*, 567 F.2d 1016, 1067–70 (D.C. Cir. 1977), involving a national proceeding to set rates for natural gas, is suggestive. Certain gas producers sought to upset the resulting rate order because of allegedly improper congressional pressure, described by the court of appeals as follows:

The factual basis for the producers' position, in brief, is that while the rehearing was pending the members of the Commission were summoned before an Oversight Subcommittee of the House Committee on Interstate and Foreign Commerce and were subjected, particularly Chairman Dunham, to an intensive examination by Subcommittee Chairman Moss and Subcommittee Counsel Atkisson. Congressman Moss and three other Subcommittee members were parties to the proceedings before the Commission and as such had an interest in the Commission's decision on rehearing. At the Subcommittee hearing, particularly during the examination by Congressman Moss and Subcommittee Counsel Atkisson, the rationale of several important decisions underlying the rates established by Opinion No. 770 came under attack.

These decisions were among those subject to reconsideration by the Commission, and this occurred notwithstanding warnings that the issues were pending before the Commission on the rehearing, and despite objections from other Subcommittee members. The questioning was not confined to explication of "what the Opinion means and what its implications are." Chairman Moss went further, stating:

> I am most committed as an adversary. I find that I am outraged by Order 770. I find it very difficult to comprehend any standard of just and reasonableness in the decision and I would not want the record to be ambiguous on that point for one moment.

Referring to the prior caselaw the court continued:

> We doubt the proper utility of classifying the ratemaking undertaken in the present proceedings by the Power Commission as entirely a judicial or a legislative function, or a combination of the two, for in any event the need for an impartial decision is obvious. Congressional intervention which occurs during the still-pending decisional process of an agency endangers, and may undermine, the integrity of the ensuing decision, which Congress has required be made by an impartial agency charged with responsibility for resolving controversies within its jurisdiction. Congress as well as the courts has responsibility to protect the decisional integrity of such an agency.

> Nevertheless, upon consideration of the whole setting in which the producers now present their claim of disqualification, we are led under settled principles to deny the producers the relief they seek. When Opinion No. 770 was pending on rehearing they concededly had knowledge of all the facts which they now assert had disqualified the Commission, except of course such changes as were made on the rehearing and stated in Opinion No. 770-A. Fully aware of the facts which are the only basis upon which the claim of disqualification can stand, the producers failed to call upon the Commission to disqualify itself. * * *

> We agree with the ruling of Judge Aldrich for his court in *In re United Shoe Machinery Corp.*, 276 F.2d 77, 79 (1st Cir. 1960):

>> a party, knowing of a ground for requesting disqualification, can not be permitted to wait and decide whether he likes subsequent treatment that he receives. * * *

> Our denial of relief at the instance of the producers does not dispose fully of the problem. Independent of the status of the parties seeking relief we think it is obvious that within the equitable relationship between the reviewing court and the agency there resides—there inheres—judicial jurisdiction, and responsibility in the public interest, to decide whether there occurred here such an inroad upon the integrity of the decisional function of the independent agency as to require the court sua sponte to set aside the whole or any part of Opinion No. 770-A. This necessitates our consideration of: the character and scope of the interference alleged; the fact that the parties who raise the disqualification question seem not to have deemed what occurred to impair the impartiality of the Commission itself independent of the result it reached; the fact that in one important respect, and indeed the issue that was most vehemently examined by the Congressmen, namely the correctness of the Commission's decision respecting the income tax component, the Commission left standing the disposition criticized at the Subcommittee hearing;

the fact that there is nothing to lead the court to find that actual influence affected Opinion No. 770-A; and the fact that insofar as any actions of the Commissioners themselves are concerned no appearance of partiality is evident.   In these circumstances we decline to set aside any part of Opinion No. 770-A sua sponte by reason of what occurred before the congressional Subcommittee.

In concluding as above we recognize the possibility, but not the probability, that what occurred may have influenced the Commission.   We consider the intervention through the Subcommittee regrettable and quite inconsistent with that due regard for the independence of the Commission which Congress and the courts must maintain.   Nevertheless, when weighed in the context of the record as a whole, the possibility of influence upon the Commission is too intangible and hypothetical a basis for this court of its own motion to nullify Opinion No. 770-A. * * *

By no means are all communications from members of Congress to federal administrators calculated to influence agency decisions, and only a small number smack of impropriety.   Yet in 1975 the Food and Drug Administration took a step that may have betrayed such suspicions.   In imposing a general obligation on top-ranking officials to document, and disclose, the content of meetings and telephone calls with third parties on pending matters, the agency specified that the new practice would cover communications from or on behalf of members of Congress.   It seems clear that the agency expected that some overtunes would not be made if the authors anticipated that their very occurrence would become public.   In other words, the FDA sought to discourage calls and letters from members of Congress by threatening to make them public.   Was this an appropriate attempt to curtail Congressional influence?

C. STATUTORY PRECISION AND ITS CONSEQUENCES

1. IRREBUTTABLE PRESUMPTIONS

UNITED STATES DEPARTMENT OF AGRICULTURE v. MURRY

Supreme Court of the United States, 1973.
413 U.S. 508, 93 S.Ct. 2832, 37 L.Ed.2d 767.

MR. JUSTICE DOUGLAS delivered the opinion of the Court.

* * *

Appellee Murry has two sons and ten grandchildren in her household.   Her monthly income is $57.50, which comes from her ex-husband as support for her sons.   Her expenses far exceed her monthly income.   By payment, however, of $11 she received $128 in food stamps. But she has now been denied food stamps because her ex-husband (who has remarried) had claimed her two sons and one grandchild as tax dependents in his 1971 income tax return.   That claim, plus the fact that her eldest son is 19 years old, disqualified her household for food stamps under § 5(b) of the Act.[1] * * *

* * * Section 5(b) makes the entire household of which a "tax dependent" was a member ineligible for food stamps for two years: (1) during the tax year for which the dependency was claimed and (2) during the next 12 months. During these two periods of time § 5(b) creates a conclusive presumption that the "tax dependent's" household is not needy and has access to nutritional adequacy.

* * *

The tax dependency provision was generated by congressional concern about nonneedy households participating in the Food Stamp program. The legislative history reflects a concern about abuses of the program by "college students, children of wealthy parents." But, as the District Court said, the Act goes far beyond that goal and its operation is inflexible. "Households containing no college student, that had established clear eligibility for Food Stamps and which still remain in dire need and otherwise eligible are now denied stamps if it appears that a household member 18 years or older is claimed by someone as a tax dependent."

Tax dependency in a prior year seems to have no relation to the "need" of the dependent in the following year. It doubtless is much easier from the administrative point of view to have a simple tax "dependency" test that will automatically—without hearing, without witnesses, without findings of fact—terminate a household's claim for eligibility of food stamps. Yet, as we recently stated in *Stanley v. Illinois:*

> "[I]t may be argued that unmarried fathers are so seldom fit that Illinois need not undergo the administrative inconvenience of inquiry in any case, including Stanley's. The establishment of prompt efficacious procedures to achieve legitimate state ends is a proper state interest worthy of cognizance in constitutional adjudication. But the Constitution recognizes higher values than speed and efficiency. Indeed, one might fairly say of the Bill of Rights in general, and the Due Process Clause in particular, that they were designed to protect the fragile values of a vulnerable citizenry from the overbearing concern for efficiency and efficacy that may characterize praiseworthy government officials no less, and perhaps more, than mediocre ones."

We have difficulty in concluding that it is rational to assume that a child is not indigent this year because the parent declared the child as a dependent in his tax return for the prior year. But even on that assumption our problem is not at an end. Under the Act the issue is not the indigency of the child but the indigency of a different household with which the child happens to be living. Members of the different household are denied Food Stamps if one of its present members was used as a tax de-

---

1. Section 5(b) of the Act provides in part: "Any household which includes a member who has reached his eighteenth birthday and *who is claimed as a dependent child for Federal income tax purposes by a taxpayer who is not a member of an eligible household,* shall be ineligible to participate in any food stamp program established pursuant to this chapter during the tax period such dependency is claimed and for a period of one year after expiration of such tax period. * * * " (Emphasis **added**.) * * *

duction in the past year by his parents even though the remaining members have no relation to the parent who used the tax deduction, even though they are completely destitute and even though they are one, or 10 or 20 in number.   We conclude that the deduction taken for the benefit of the parent in the prior year is not a rational measure of the need of a different household with which the child of the tax-deducting parent lives and rests on an irrebuttable presumption often contrary to fact.   It therefore lacks critical ingredients of due process found wanting in *Vlandis v. Kline*, 412 U.S. 441, 452 (1973); *Stanley v. Illinois*, 405 U.S. 645 (1972); and *Bell v. Burson*, 402 U.S. 535 (1971).

Affirmed.

[Justice Stewart's concurring opinion is omitted.]

MR. JUSTICE MARSHALL, concurring.

I join the opinion of the Court.   I wish to state briefly what I believe are the analytic underpinnings of that opinion.   One aspect of fundamental fairness, guaranteed by the Due Process Clause of the Fifth Amendment, is that individuals similarly situated must receive the same treatment by the Government. * * * It is a corollary of this requirement that, in order to determine whether persons are indeed similarly situated, "such procedural protections as the particular situation demands" must be provided.   Specifically, we must decide whether, considering the private interest affected and the governmental interest sought to be advanced, a hearing must be provided to one who claims that the application of some general provision of the law aimed at certain abuses will not in fact lower the incidence of those abuses but will instead needlessly harm him.   In short, where the private interests affected are very important and the governmental interest can be promoted without much difficulty by a well-designed hearing procedure, the Due Process Clause requires the Government to act on an individualized basis, with general propositions serving only as rebuttable presumptions or other burden-shifting devices.   That, I think, is the import of *Stanley v. Illinois*.

Is this, then, such a case?   Appellants argue that Congress could rationally have thought that persons claimed as tax dependents by a taxpayer himself not a member of an eligible household in one year could, during that year and the succeeding one, probably receive sufficient funds from the taxpayer to offset their need for food stamps.   If those persons received food stamps, they would be denying to the truly needy some of the limited benefits Congress has chosen to make available.   The statute, on this view, is aimed at preventing abuse of the program by persons who do not need the benefits Congress has provided.   Even if, as appellants urge, the statute is interpreted to make ineligible for food stamps only those persons validly claimed as tax dependents, I do not think that Congress adopted a method for preventing abuse that is reasonably calculated to eliminate only those who abuse the program.   In particular, it could not be fairly concluded that, because one member of the household had received half his support from a parent, the *entire* household's need for assistance in purchasing food could be offset by outside contributions.

It is, of course, quite simple for Congress to provide an administrative mechanism to guarantee that abusers of the program were eliminated from it. All that is needed is some way for a person whose household would otherwise be ineligible for food stamps because of this statute to show that the support presently available from the person claiming a member of the household as a tax dependent does not in fact offset the loss of benefits. Reasonable rules stating what a claimant must show before receiving a hearing on the question could easily be devised. We deal here with a general rule that may seriously affect the ability of persons genuinely in need to provide an adequate diet for their households. In the face of readily available alternatives that might prevent abuse of the program, Congress did not choose a method of reducing abuses that was "fairly related to the object of the regulation," by enacting the statute challenged in this case.

This analysis, of course, combines elements traditionally invoked in what are usually treated as distinct classes of cases, involving due process and equal protection. But the elements of fairness should not be so rigidly cabined. Sometimes fairness will require a hearing to determine whether a statutory classification will advance the legislature's purposes in a particular case so that the classification can properly be used only as a burden- shifting device, while at other times the fact that a litigant falls within the classification will be enough to justify its application. There is no reason, I believe, to categorize inflexibly the rudiments of fairness. Instead, I believe that we must assess the public and private interests affected by a statutory classification and then decide in each instance whether individualized determination is required or categorical treatment is permitted by the Constitution.

[Justice Blackmun's dissenting opinion is omitted.]

MR. JUSTICE REHNQUIST, with whom THE CHIEF JUSTICE and MR. JUSTICE POWELL concur, dissenting. * * *

Notions that in dispensing public funds to the needy Congress may not impose limitations which "go beyond the goal" of Congress, or may not be "inflexible," have not heretofore been thought to be embodied in the Constitution. In *Dandridge v. Williams*, 397 U.S. 471 (1970), the Court rejected this approach in an area of welfare legislation that is indistinguishable from the food stamp program here involved. There the District Court, in the words of this Court,

"while apparently recognizing the validity of at least some of these state concerns, nonetheless held that the regulation 'is invalid on its face for overreaching,' that it violates the Equal Protection Clause '[b]ecause it cuts too broad a swath on an indiscriminate basis as applied to the entire group of AFDC eligibles to which it purports to apply * * *.' "

Applying the Equal Protection Clause of the Fourteenth Amendment to state action, the Court reversed the District Court and held:

"[T]he concept of 'overreaching' has no place in this case. For here we deal with state regulation in the social and economic field, not affecting freedoms guaranteed by the Bill of Rights, and claimed to violate the Fourteenth

Amendment only because the regulation results in some disparity in grants of welfare payments to the largest FDC families.   For this Court to approve the invalidation of state economic or social regulation as 'overreaching' would be far too reminiscent of an era when the Court thought the Fourteenth Amendment gave it power to strike down state laws 'because they may be unwise, improvident, or out of harmony with a particular school of thought' * * *.

"In the area of economics and social welfare, a state does not violate the Equal Protection Clause merely because the classifications made by its laws are imperfect.   If the classification has some 'reasonable basis,' it does not offend the Constitution simply because the classification 'is not made with mathematical nicety or because in practice it results in some inequality.' "

In placing the limitations on the availability of food stamps which are involved in this case, Congress has not in any reasoned sense of that word employed a conclusive presumption as stated by the majority; it has simply made a legislative decision that certain abuses which it conceived to exist in the program as previously administered were of sufficient seriousness to warrant the substantive limitation which it enacted.   There is a qualitative difference between, on the one hand, holding unconstitutional on procedural due process grounds presumptions which conclude factual inquiries without a hearing on such questions as fault, *Bell v. Burson*, the fitness of an unwed father to be a parent, *Stanley v. Illinois*, or, accepting the majority's characterization in *Vlandis v. Kline*, residency, and, on the other hand, holding unconstitutional a duly enacted prophylactic limitation on the dispensation of funds which is designed to cure systemic abuses.

Thus, we deal not with the law of evidence, but with the extent to which the Fifth Amendment permits this Court to invalidate such a determination by Congress.   In *Williamson v. Lee Optical Co.*, 348 U.S. 483, 487–488 (1955), the Court said:

"But the law need not be in every respect logically consistent with its aims to be constitutional.   It is enough that there is an evil at hand for correction, and that it might be thought that the particular legislative measure was a rational way to correct it."

The majority concludes that a "deduction taken for the benefit of the parent in the prior year is not a rational measure of the need of a different household with which the child of the tax-deducting parent lives."   But judged by the standards of the foregoing cases, the challenged provision of the Food Stamp Act has a legitimate purpose and cannot be said to lack any rational basis. * * * [I]n order to disqualify a household for food stamps, the taxpayer claiming one of its members as a dependent must both provide over half of the dependent's support and must himself be a member of a household with an income large enough to disqualify that household for food stamps.   These characteristics indicate that the taxpayer is both willing and able to provide his dependent with a significant amount of support.   To be sure, there may be no perfect correlation between the fact that the taxpayer is part of a household which has income exceeding food stamp eligibility standards and his provision of enough support to raise his dependent's household above such standards.   But there is some correlation, and the provision is, therefore, not irrational.*

Nor is § 5(b) deprived of a rational basis because disqualification of the household extends one year beyond the year in which the dependency deduction is claimed.   Since income tax returns are not filed until after the termination of the tax year, the carryover provision is the only practical means of enforcing the congressional purpose unless Congress were to establish an administrative adjudication procedure wholly independent of the existing tax collection structure.   Such an alternative system would doubtless have its own delays, inefficiencies, and inequities.   Under these circumstances we cannot say that Congress acted irrationally in judging a person's need in one year by whether he was claimed as a tax dependent in the previous year.

Finally, the fact that the statute as presently administered may operate to deny food stamps on the basis of fraudulent as well as lawful dependency deduction claims does not, * * * render it unconstitutional.   A false dependency claim subjects the taxpayer to both civil and criminal penalties, and Congress may reasonably proceed on the assumption that taxpayers will obey the law.

NOTE, THE IRREBUTTABLE PRESUMPTION DOCTRINE IN THE SUPREME COURT

87 Harv. L. Rev. 1534, 1539–44, 1548–49 (1974).

The analysis employed in *Murry* was not entirely unprecedented; several provisions of tax statutes were invalidated by the Supreme Court more than forty years ago because they contained inaccurate irrebuttable presumptions.   Yet these cases seemed inextricably tied to disfavored intervention based on notions of substantive due process, and hence were largely ignored by the Court after 1937.   Within the past three years, however, four cases besides *Murry* have employed irrebuttable presumption analysis and invalidated statutes on that basis.   Thus, the doctrine has undergone somewhat of a renaissance, and similar analysis may become a regular basis for judicial intervention.

*The Court's opinion makes much of the facts that there may be no relationship between the tax dependent's parent and the remaining members of the household, that they may be completely destitute, and that they may be one or 10 or 20.   Section 3(e) of the Food Stamp Act, 7 U.S.C.A. § 2012(e), provides in relevant part:

"The term 'household' shall mean a group of * * * individuals * * * who * * * are living as one economic unit.* * * *"

In its instructions to the state agencies administering the Food Stamp Program, the Department of Agriculture's Food and Nutrition Service defines "economic unit" as meaning that "the common living expenses are shared from the income and resources of all members and that the basic needs of all members are provided for without regard to their ability or willingness to contribute."

The majority does not question that Congress could rationally so choose to dispense welfare benefits to "economic units" rather than to individuals.   Since the resources of the household member claimed as a tax dependent are by definition available to the entire household, it is rational to disqualify such units containing ineligible tax dependents.

Although neither employing the term "irrebuttable presumption" nor enunciating the standard eventually adopted, *Bell v. Burson* has rightly been identified by its progeny as the first of the recent irrebuttable presumption cases. The Georgia statute challenged in that case did not require that drivers be insured; instead, it provided that should an uninsured motorist be involved in an accident causing damage, his license would be suspended pending final determination of liability. The driver had no opportunity to prevent the suspension of his license by presenting evidence of his nonliability to a judicial or administrative tribunal.

The Court unanimously decided that the failure to grant a hearing deprived the uninsured motorist of due process of law. * * * Reasoning that the use of motor vehicles represented a cognizable property interest, the Court found that such use could be denied only after a motorist had been granted an opportunity to demonstrate his nonliability. Georgia had argued that the statutory scheme constituted a compromise measure and that if compulsory insurance were permissible, then the legislation would be a *fortiori* proper. But the Court found that since revocation of the privilege to drive ultimately depended on a finding of fault, the lack of a pre-suspension hearing represented merely a shortcut method of determining fault to further administrative convenience. And since the legislature could not presume that all uninsured motorists were at fault, a hearing had to be provided.

The Court's decision went beyond the rationale of the right-to-hearing cases. By focusing on the inaccuracy of the legislative means used in furthering what it declared to be the ends of the statute, the Court established the pattern for the future irrebuttable presumption cases. Its characterization of the statute as overinclusive moved the due process inquiry from the question of whether the individual belonged to the prescribed classification to whether the classification was properly drawn. The result of this shift would be far-reaching in the later cases.

The Court articulated the irrebuttable presumption analysis more clearly in *Stanley v. Illinois*. Stanley was the father of several illegitimate children whose mother had died. Under an Illinois statute a child could be declared a ward of the state if it had no surviving parents. "Parent" was defined to include both parents of a child born in wedlock and the mother of an illegitimate child. A child could be declared a ward over the objections of a "parent" only if the parent were adjudged to be unfit. The state had instituted proceedings seeking custody of Stanley's children without a determination of his unfitness. Stanley alleged that this application of the statute unconstitutionally discriminated against him.

The Supreme Court found that the Illinois statute violated the fourteenth amendment's due process clause. The Court reasoned that the statute established an irrebuttable presumption that illegitimate fathers are unfit. Noting that such fathers have parental rights cognizable under the due process clause, the Court rejected the state's argument that illegitimate fathers are so frequently uninterested in the welfare of their children that the statutory provisions were reasonable.   Declaring that "the Constitution recognizes higher values than speed and efficiency," the Court held that regardless of the general accuracy of the presumption that illegitimate fathers are not suitable parents, Stanley was entitled to a hearing to determine his fitness.

In *Vlandis v. Kline*, the Court declared unconstitutional a Connecticut statute which classified individuals as permanent nonresidents, for the purpose of determining tuition at a state university, on the basis of their past or present place of residence.   Married students whose legal address was outside the state at the time of their application to a state university, and unmarried students whose legal address was outside the state at any time in the twelve months prior to application, were deemed nonresidents, and thus were ineligible for reduced tuition.

The Court found this permanent classification to be an irrebuttable presumption.   In response to Connecticut's argument that in the absence of the provision the state's school system would be subjected to onslaughts of education prospectors, the Court responded as it had in *Stanley:* efficiency cannot outweigh individual rights to a judicial determination of entitlement.   The standard adopted by the Court was enormously exacting:

> [I]t is forbidden by the Due Process Clause to deny an individual the resident rates on the basis of a permanent and irrebuttable presumption of nonresidence, when that presumption is not necessarily or universally true in fact, and when the State has reasonable alternative means of making the crucial determination.

But the Court suggested that there would be no constitutional infirmity were students given an opportunity, after one year of residence in Connecticut, to establish that they were bona fide domiciliaries.   This suggestion undercut the standard of "universal truth" which the court had erected.

In the most recent of the irrebuttable presumption cases, *Cleveland Board of Education v. LaFleur* [414 U.S. 632 (1974)], the Court dealt with administrative regulations which required that teachers take leaves of absence in the fifth or sixth month of pregnancy.   The Court found that the regulations created irrebuttable presumptions of disability which were clearly not universally true.   Reiterating the *Vlandis* standard, the Court found that absent a hearing the regulations violated the due process clause of the fourteenth amendment.   Curiously, the Court again allowed the possibility that a more limited, although not totally accurate, presumption might be permissible if supported by a "consensus" of medical testimony, or a showing of administrative necessity.   * * *

This strange hybrid of due process and equal protection scrutiny seems to be applicable to any legislative classification.   * * *

Once a court determines the purpose toward which a classification is directed, it can always rephrase the statute as an irrebuttable presumption.   And since nearly all classifications contain some measure of inaccuracy, very few acts of legislation could survive the test of "necessarily or universally true in fact" promulgated by the irrebuttable presumption cases. Thus, this new basis for judicial intervention appears to have remarkably wide-ranging applicability.

Notes

1. Neither before, after, nor during the flurry of irrebuttable presumption cases in the early 1970's has the Court applied the doctrine wholesale. In *Mourning v. Family Publications Service, Inc.*, 411 U.S. 356, 376–77 (1973), for example, the Fifth Circuit had invalidated a Federal Reserve Board regulation promulgated under the Federal Truth-in-Lending Act, inter alia, because in requiring certain disclosures by all creditors who extended credit repayable in more than four installments the regulation had "conclusively presumed" that all such extensions of credit included a finance charge. In reversing, the Supreme Court referred back to the only comparable outburst of irrebuttable presumption reasoning, during the heyday of substantive rationality review, and said:

> Finally, the Four Installment Rule does not conflict with the Fifth Amendment under our holdings in *Schlesinger v. State of Wisconsin*, 270 U.S. 230 (1926), and *Heiner v. Donnan*, 285 U.S. 312 (1932). In *Schlesinger* and *Heiner* we held that certain taxing provisions violated the Due Process Clauses of the Fifth and Fourteenth Amendments because they conclusively presumed the existence of determinative facts. The challenged rule contains no comparable presumption. The rule was intended as a prophylactic measure; it does not presume that all creditors who are within its ambit assess finance charges, but, rather, imposes a disclosure requirement on all members of a defined class in order to discourage evasion by a substantial portion of that class.

Indeed, after *LaFleur* the Court quietly abandoned the irrebuttable presumption idea in cases not raising issues that the challenged statute characterized as evidentiary. See, e.g., *Leary v. United States*, 395 U.S. 6, 29–53 (1969). Both the Court's use and its silent abandonment of irrebuttable presumption analysis may be criticized. As one of us suggested in another context when discussing *Bell* and *Stanley:*

> * * * [The irrebuttable presumption] cases make hash of the prior procedural due process jurisprudence. It had been (indeed still is) thought obvious that there was no need for a hearing where there was nothing to talk about. And since the driver in *Bell* and the father in *Stanley* admitted that they fell squarely within the legislative disqualifications, "hearing" talk seems misplaced—substance and procedure have somehow been conflated.

> * * * [Moreover,] [t]he irrebuttable presumption doctrine has a voracious appetite for statutes. Left long at large it will gnaw its way through substantial portions of the codes of the fifty states and the U.S. Code as well. If the validity of some of our most ubiquitous legal rules—the fifty-five mile per hour speed limit, twenty-one years as the age of majority, statutes of limitations, formal requirements for testamentary disposition, for example—is to be tested by asking whether the general principle or purpose that underlies the rule (safety, knowing consent, etc.) is furthered *in every instance* of its application, then rules are no longer possible.

Because such a state of affairs is insupportable we need some way of avoiding this particular proceduralist perspective. But in the irrebuttable presumption cases the Court does not (and indeed cannot) tell us when an attack on legislative over-generality should be perceived for what it is—a substantive rationality claim that under current doctrine is a sure loser—and when it may be translated into a "right-to-hearing"/"irrebuttable presumption" claim that is a sure winner.   Confronted with an extremely important question (When is it permissible to generalize by rule rather than particularize by reference to a principle or standard?) the Court, having barred itself from considering the substantive rationality of legislative judgments, had nothing to say.

Mashaw, *Constitutional Deregulation: Notes Toward a Public, Public Law,* 54 Tul. L. Rev. 849, 863–64 (1980).

2. What are the institutional implications of rejecting overbroad, but clear and determinate statutory standards?   What substantive criteria and administrative decision process would be necessary to implement the legislative purposes that apparently underlie the statutes reviewed in *Murry, Bell, Stanley, Vlandis,* and *LaFleur?*   Should we rename the "irrebuttable presumption doctrine" the "pro-delegation doctrine"?

2. THE DECISIVE DELANEY CLAUSE

On March 9, 1977, the Food and Drug Administration announced its intention to initiate proceedings to ban the use of saccharin in all food products marketed in the United States.   The FDA's action was premised on a finding that saccharin had been determined to be carcinogenic in tests in laboratory animals.   Because saccharin had no approved substitutes as a non-nutritive sweetener, the FDA proposal predictably precipitated intense public controversy.   The ensuing debate focused on food safety, but it also explored the advantages and pitfalls of legislative efforts to enunciate general policy with unmistakable clarity.

The saccharin controversy was not generated by an agency run rampant under vague legislation, but by an agency that claimed its hands were tied by the combination of scientific findings and its governing statute.   The statutory framework for food safety regulation is reviewed in Merrill, *Regulating Carcinogens in Food: A Legislator's Guide to the Food Safety Provisions of the Federal Food, Drug and Cosmetic Act,* 77 Mich. L. Rev. 171 (1978).   An excellent and accessible discussion of scientific testing for carcinogenicity can be found in Maugh, *Chemical Carcinogens: The Scientific Basis for Regulation,* 201 Science 1200 (1978); and *Chemical Carcinogens: How Dangerous are Low Doses,* 202 Science 37 (1978).

SACCHARIN BAN MORATORIUM

House Report 95–658.
95th Congress, 1st Session (October 3, 1977).

On March 9, 1977, the Food and Drug Administration announced that it intended to initiate proceedings under the Federal Food, Drug, and Cosmetic Act to ban the use of saccharin and its salts in all food products sold in the United States.   Oversight hearings on the FDA proposal were conducted by the Subcommittee on Health and the Environment on March 21 and 22, 1977.   On April 15, the Food and Drug Administration published in the Federal Register its proposal to revoke the interim food additive regulation under which saccharin and its salts are currently permitted as ingredients in prepackaged foods and as tabletop nonnutritive sweeteners (42 F.R. 19996).   The notice also * * * solicited new drug applications to enable saccharin to be marketed as a single ingredient over-the-counter drug.   * * *

A "food additive" is defined in section 201(s) of the Federal Food, Drug, and Cosmetic Act (hereinafter, the Food and Drug Act) as any substance the intended use of which results or may reasonably be expected to result, directly or indirectly, in its becoming a component or otherwise affecting the characteristics of any food.   * * *

* * * Before a food additive may be marketed, there must be in effect for the additive a regulation prescribing the conditions under which it may be safely used.

* * * The Delaney clause requires that

> no (food) additive shall be deemed to be safe if it is found to induce cancer when ingested by man or animal, or if it is found, after tests which are appropriate for the evaluation of the safety of food additives, to induce cancer in man or animals.

* * * [A]ccording to FDA officials, the Delaney clause authorizes the agency to exercise scientific judgment in determining whether a test is an appropriate one.   Tests may be rejected on the basis that they were conducted improperly, or because the tests involved ingestion at dosage levels not widely accepted by the scientific community.   FDA is unable to cite examples of the agency having refused to consider test results because the dosage was too high.   However, a 1974 National Academy of Sciences study which evaluated the various tests involving saccharin was critical of the FDA test [concluded in 1972 which suggested saccharin caused cancer] which involved a feeding level of 7.5 percent because of a considerable depression of weight in the test animals.   * * *

* * * Once the agency has exercised scientific judgment with respect to the appropriateness of the test, however, the Delaney clause does not permit the agency to make further inquiry.   It may not, for example, establish a maximum level of safe use[7] or authorize further use of an additive based on a judgment that the benefits of continued use outweigh the risks involved.

Saccharin was first introduced in the United States in about 1900 and its use has steadily increased.   The Calorie Control Council, a trade association, estimates that in 1974 approximately 5 million pounds of saccharin were used in foods.   About 74 percent of this amount was used in diet soft drinks; 14 percent in dietetic foods such as canned fruits, gelatin des-

---

7. It is the position of the FDA and the National Cancer Institute—and most scientists—that a safe threshold level for a cancer-producing substance has not been established.

serts, jams, ice creams, and puddings; and 12 percent as tabletop sweeteners. * * *

* * * The [National] Academy [of Sciences in 1974] concluded that nine [of eleven] * * * studies demonstrated no association between bladder cancer and saccharin intake. The report noted the possible association between saccharin consumption and bladder tumors in rats in two studies (the Wisconsin study and one undertaken by the FDA) of second generation rats whose parents also were fed saccharin (thus exposing the second generation to saccharin *in utero*). Because both of these studies were conducted on saccharin which contained an impurity (orthotoluenesulfonamide, or OTS) * * * the Academy raised the question as to whether it was saccharin or the impurity in the saccharin that produced the bladder cancer. * * *

* * * [T]he Canadian government in February of 1974 undertook a long term study of the carcinogenicity of OTS in rats at three different levels (2.5, 25, and 250 milligrams per kilogram of body weight per day). A fourth group of rats was fed 250 milligrams of OTS per kilogram per day plus 1% sodium chloride in order to produce a more acidic urine (which decreases the production of bladder stones thought by some to be associated with bladder cancer in rats). In addition, because OTS-free saccharin was available at the time the study was initiated, a fifth group of 50 male and 50 female rats were fed 2,500 milligrams per kilogram of body weight of pure sodium saccharin (5 percent of their daily diet).

The results of the Canadian study of first and second generation rats show 3 of the first generation and 12 of the second generation male rats fed pure saccharin developed malignant bladder tumors. * * * None of the rats in the control group or in the groups fed OTS developed malignant tumors, thus implicating saccharin, and exonerating OTS, as a potential cancer-causing agent.

The announcement by the Food and Drug Administration on March 9, 1977, that it intended to exercise its authority under the Delaney Clause to ban saccharin as a food additive, was done in such a way as to produce an immediate and highly emotional response from the public and the diet food and beverage industry. By stating that cancer was observed in those test animals receiving "the equivalent of 800 cans of diet soda daily" without attempting to explain why high dose feeding studies in animals are generally accepted as a valid method of predicting the low dose effects in both animals and humans, the FDA unintentionally invited the wrath and ridicule of those who might have accepted a more rationally presented announcement. * * *

At oversight hearings held by the Subcommittee on Health and the Environment on March 21 and 22, 1977, the then Acting Director of the FDA, Sherwin Gardner, defended the FDA's proposed action and the validity of the Canadian rat studies. * * *

It * * * became clear during the hearing that there is a paucity of direct evidence linking bladder cancer in humans to the use of saccharin. Several epidemiological studies were cited, including studies on **diabetic** populations, which showed no correlation between saccharin usage and bladder cancer.   However, Dr. Sidney Wolfe, of the Public Citizen Health Research Group, pointed out that because of the population sizes used in the epidemiological studies, an increase in the incidence of bladder cancer of less than 30 to 40 percent would have been undetectable.   By way of contrast, extrapolation of the Canadian rat data to humans would result in an increase in the incidence of bladder cancer of only around 7 percent, an increase which would be unlikely to have been detected in a small scale epidemiological study.

It was further argued during the hearings by representatives of health organizations (as the American Heart Association, the Juvenile Diabetes Foundation, and the American Diabetes Association) that saccharin provides an enormous benefit to persons, such as diabetics, and the obese, who must restrict their intake of sugar.   It was contended that while saccharin is not essential to such individuals, it nevertheless has enabled them to enjoy the same quality of life as individuals who need not restrict their intake of sugar, and that this is a benefit which outweighs what is, at worst, a relatively low risk of bladder cancer. * * *

Legislative hearings were held on June 27, 1977, to evaluate, among other things, whether or not there was still the degree of disagreement among scientists as to the carcinogenicity of saccharin and to determine whether or not there was a need for Congressional action with respect to the proposed saccharin ban. * * * [T]he emotional climate of earlier months still prevailed and the scientific community remained divided on the carcinogenicity of saccharin in humans.   While the Committee recognizes that there appears to be an increasingly strong circumstantial case being mounted against the safety of saccharin, it is, at worst, a mild carcinogen.   The Committee further notes that there is still much disagreement among experts as to the actual risk to the human population due to the consumption of saccharin and whether or not the benefits from its use outweigh the risks.   Therefore, the reasons which prompted * * * H.R. 8518, as amended by the Committee, remain valid.

[The bill recommended by the committee, and ultimately enacted, Pub. L. No. 95–203, 91 Stat. 1451, (a) prohibited the FDA from restricting the sale of saccharin based on its potential carcinogenicity as demonstrated by any previously reported study, (b) authorized the agency to require label warnings on saccharin-sweetened foods, and (c) directed the Secretary of HHS to request the National Academy of Sciences to evaluate the data on saccharin's carcinogenicity and health benefits, if any, and to recommend reforms in the existing food safety law.   Eds.]

Notes

1. The Delaney Clause bears the name of Congressman James J. Delaney of New York, who in 1950 became chairman of a new House Select Committee to Investigate the Use of Chemicals in Foods and Cosmetics.   The Department of Health, Education, and Welfare (speaking for the FDA) at first opposed the singling out of carcinogens, primarily on the ground that it was unnecessary.   **As-**

sistant Secretary Elliot Richardson argued that evidence that an additive was carcinogenic would prevent its approval under the Amendment's general safety standard. However, Delaney was insistent that there be an explicit prohibition against the approval of carcinogens, and HEW ultimately acquiesced in the language that became the current clause—which it had redrafted to avoid the implication that a substance would automatically have to be disapproved if it caused cancer by a route other than ingestion.

The Delaney Clause was never the focus of prolonged discussion among members of Congress generally; it received no attention in the Senate debates and only brief mention in the relevant committee reports. According to one source, "the clause was essentially the personal hobbyhorse of James Delaney." Blank, *The Delaney Clause: Technical Naivete and Scientific Advocacy in the Formulation of Public Health Policies*, 62 Calif. L. Rev. 1084 (1974).

2. The FDA has consistently insisted that the Delaney Clause is redundant, i.e., that the law's general requirement that food additives be proved "safe" effectively precludes approval of one that has been shown, in appropriate tests, to induce cancer in laboratory animals. The agency's view is most forcefully stated in its 1977 proposal to ban saccharin:

> FDA has previously prohibited the use in food of ingredients found to cause cancer in laboratory animals to which the Delaney clause was not applicable. * * *
>
> Those actions, like this one, were based on certain well-recognized postulates about chemical carcinogesis: (1) there is reason to believe that those substances which cause cancer in animals may also cause cancer in man; (2) animal tests, despite inadequacies, provide the best evidence currently available about the potential of a chemical to cause cancer in humans; (3) there is no reliable basis for concluding that there is a completely "safe" level of a carcinogen, i.e., a threshold level that will not cause cancer in some members of the population; and (4) cancer appears to be an irreversible process in both test animals and in man.
>
> It is of course true that the present law would afford the Commissioner no choice but to prohibit the marketing of saccharin as an ingredient in foods even if he were not persuaded that the scientific evidence independently warranted such action. * * *

Saccharin and Its Salts: Proposed Rulemaking, 42 Fed. Reg. 19996, 20002 (April 15, 1977).

3. The FDA has interpreted the Delaney Clause as allowing it another sort of judgment, i.e., as to the appropriateness of tests for carcinogenicity. Thus, the FDA was exercising its own judgment when it determined that the Canadian two-generation study in rats, employing doses as high as 5 percent of their total diet, was "appropriate for the evaluation of the safety" of saccharin. Moreover, as one of us has explained, the Delaney Clause does not govern all substances used or found in food:

> Because they are not considered food additives, the natural constituents of agricultural commodities are beyond the reach of the Delaney Clause, though several have been found carcinogenic when administered to laboratory animals. * * * [A]nother statutory escape from no-risk regulation is

available for food constituents that FDA characterizes as unavoidable environmental contaminants of food.   These include polychlorinated biphenyls (PCBs) in fish and aflatoxins on peanuts and corn.   FDA regulates the marketing of foods containing these familiar carcinogens under a statutory provision that impliedly permits consideration of both the risk to health and the costs of limiting exposure. * * *

* * * Aflatoxin mold, a potent carcinogen in laboratory animals, contaminates much of the corn and peanuts grown in this country, though often at levels below the limit of reliable detection.   FDA has classified aflatoxin as an unavoidable contaminant of peanuts, which it has attempted to control by setting a tolerance under section 406 of the Act. * * * The agency regards aflatoxin as unavoidable, assuming that peanuts are to be consumed; and so it is, but one could avoid the risk by not eating peanuts, or, from FDA's vantage, prevent it by banning their sale. The latter result could be reconciled with the language of the Act, but clearly would not withstand scrutiny in Congress or, indeed, in the Department of Health and Human Services of which FDA is a part. * * *

* * * When peanuts are added as an ingredient of another food, e.g., candy bars or peanut butter, it is more difficult to characterize aflatoxin as "unavoidable."   Few foods, with the exception of peanut butter, require the use of peanuts. * * * Moreover, the Delaney Clause would appear to fit this case exactly: (1) peanuts are "added" ingredients; (2) peanuts contaminated with any amount of aflatoxin surely cannot be considered "generally recognized as safe"; and (3) aflatoxin is a frank carcinogen when fed to experimental animals.   Yet FDA has not so much as hinted that the addition of peanuts to other foods should be banned. * * *

Merrill, *Book Review: Regulation of Toxic Chemicals*, 58 Tex. L. Rev. 463, 474–78 (1980).

4. The Delaney Clause represents a Congressional statement of the policy to be followed in regulating carcinogenic food additives—a policy that reflects uncertainty about how cancer occurs, about whether the experience of small rodents can be extrapolated to man, and about whether carcinogens display a genuine "no effect" or "threshold" dose.   The FDA's effort to ban saccharin revived debate on all these issues.

Dr. Donald Kennedy, a reknowned biologist and FDA Commissioner at the time, later explained the relevance of high-dose animal tests:

In a typical experiment involving chronic exposure of 100 experimental animals to a test substance the 100 animals represent our population of over 200 million Americans. * * * An excess rate of cancer of 5 percent in the exposed group would be disastrous—the equivalent of 10 million additional cases of human cancer in the United States if the entire population were exposed. * * *

A 5 percent excess of tumors in the experimental group is close to the sensitivity limit of the test.   We could compensate for this insensitivity by increasing the number of animals, but the high costs involved make this an unrealistic option. * * * Instead of increasing the number of animals tested, however, we can increase the amount or dose of the test substance they receive.

This strengthening of the dose is responsible for a lot of confusion about the implications such animal tests have for human health and it commonly sparks two questions: Won't too much of anything produce cancer?   Aren't such massive overdoses irrelevant to human beings? * * *

The potential for causing cancer is not widespread among chemicals, and not an effect readily revealed upon heroic exposure.   Instead it is a rare property that behaves exactly as though it depended upon some specific (but yet undefined) relationship between the carcinogenic chemical and the chemistry of the living cell. * * *

One other important aspect of animal testing invites disbelief.   It is done on nonhuman organisms. * * * The similarities between cancer in animals and in human beings, such as the fact that cancer cells are capable of metastasizing—breaking away from the original cancer and seeding themselves elsewhere—together with the growing evidence that cancer-causing chemicals interfere with the biochemistry of genetic material, are powerful arguments for the appropriateness of using animals as models for people.   We strengthen the credibility of the experiment by using animals in whom the system or organ under investigation is as like ours as possible.   There is, finally, the persuasive comparison between the substances known to cause cancer in human beings and their effect on laboratory animals.   Of 18 such substances, all but two [arsenic and, then, but no longer, benzene] are also carcinogenic in animals. * * *

Kennedy, *What Animal Research Says About Cancer*, Human Nature, May 1978.

HEARING BEFORE THE SUBCOMMITTEE ON HEALTH AND ENVIRONMENT OF THE HOUSE COMMITTEE ON INTERSTATE AND FOREIGN COMMERCE

95th Congress, 1st Session.
(June 27, 1977).

Mr. WAXMAN [D. Cal.]. * * *

Gentlemen, a recent poll showed the people in this country fear cancer more than any other event, including war, and statistics show one out of four people is going to get cancer and two out of three of those people are going to die of cancer.   If we accept this latest Canadian study, we are talking about between 1,500 and 2,000 cancer cases a year in the United States could be attributed on the use to artificial sweeteners, primarily saccharin.

We are talking about preventable cases of cancer.   Doesn't the Government have a duty to prevent these cancers from striking our people?   Dr. Kennedy?

Dr. KENNEDY.   Congressman Waxman, obviously I think it does because I am in charge of a regulatory agency to which you and your colleagues in the Congress have given us the responsibility of doing exactly that. * * *

Mr. WAXMAN. Dr. Kennedy * * * [t]his ban brought more protests to Members of Congress than any issue since Nixon's Saturday night massacre. It resulted in House of Representatives' action last week forbidding the use of any of the funds in the appropriation bill for enforcement of this ban and the fact that we are holding these hearings in a very percipitous [sic] way.

All of this indicates that the public is furious over the idea saccharin is going to be taken away from them. Part of the reason is this * * * distrust of FDA when FDA tells them there is a danger, and then also tells them that the danger really exists only if you drink 800 cans of soda a day.

Dr. KENNEDY. * * *

I think it's unfair to put the entire burden of it on a regulatory agency that was basing a sound decision on sound science and was acting properly under the law. There are some public policy questions that people just aren't going to be very happy with the outcomes of and this may be one of them. * * *

Mr. SATTERFIELD [D. Va.]. Given all the facts, and let's assume we take them all for granted, why wouldn't it be a wise thing to do to just inform the public * * * of what the risks are and let them make their own decision as to whether or not they want to use saccharin?

Dr. KENNEDY. I think the question you are really asking, Mr. Satterfield, is why don't the food additive laws allow the balancing of risks and benefits? I think Congress had in mind, when they put in the provisions of the food safety laws, that it is not easy for all members of the public to determine what is in their foods. * * *

* * * Many of the people who consume diet soft drinks are youngsters who may not have the same access to understanding as other members of the public. I worry about making it freely available to them, and I wonder if their freedom of choice is as informed as you and I would like to see it be.

Mr. SATTERFIELD. What you are saying is that the considered judgment and opinion of government supersedes that of the individual?

Dr. KENNEDY. I wonder, Mr. Satterfield, if we don't owe a certain amount of protection to those members of society who consume soft drinks who are a little young to be making that kind of decision.

Mr. SATTERFIELD. You don't feel their parents have the capability of making it; the government can make a better decision than parents?

Dr. KENNEDY. Mr. Satterfield, I guess I would want to reemphasize at this point that we really are in the realm of philosophy.

Mr. SATTERFIELD. That is right; that is what this whole thing is all about.

Dr. KENNEDY. I think not. I think my Agency's responsibility is to carry out its statutory mandate and our statutory mandate does not allow us to consider those issues—

Mr. SATTERFIELD. I would like to see us rescind that mandate.

HEARING BEFORE THE SUBCOMMITTEE ON HEALTH AND THE ENVIRONMENT OF THE HOUSE COMMITTEE ON INTERSTATE AND FOREIGN COMMERCE

96th Congress, 1st Session.
(April 11, 1979).

MR. WAXMAN. The committee will come to order. * * *

Today, we will receive, firsthand, the recommendations from the National Academy of Sciences based upon the scientific findings.

The Academy recommends: One, a single policy be developed for all foodstuffs, food additives, and food contaminants.

Two, that the public officials responsible for implementation of that policy be given sufficient flexibility to factor risks, benefits, and other considerations into account when making a decision concerning a material that has been called into question.

Three, that regulatory officials have options available to them; and four, that questionable materials be categorized into low, moderate, or high risk.

Today we intend to delve into the findings of the National Academy of Sciences, including the arguments set forth by the 5 minority signatories as well as the position expounded by the majority 32 members.

Dr. [David] HAMBURG [President, Institute of Medicine, National Academy of Sciences]. * * *

We were fortunate indeed to be able to persuade one of the world's most distinguished scientists, Dr. Frederick Robbins, to head the effort requested by the Congress under Public Law 95–203. He is a Nobel laureate, a pediatrician and dean of one of our Nation's finest medical schools [Case Western Reserve University]. * * *

Dr. ROBBINS. * * *

I do not think anybody disagreed with the conclusion that saccharin is a carcinogen. The fact that it causes cancer in animals leads to the conclusion that it has to be assumed of being capable of causing cancer in man. It is not possible on the basis of modern techniques to precisely define the risk for man. No squeezing of the scientific facts will provide those data.

The evidence in regard to the benefits of saccharin is certainly far from overwhelming. There are no scientific studies that can be accepted as credible studies that prove a health benefit. The Chairman raised the question as to whether appropriate studies could be done. They could be done. They would be very difficult, expensive and they would not offer answers in the immediate future. * * *

[Dr. Robbins' prepared statement went on to outline the reforms in food safety regulation recommended by a majority of the NAS panel.]

A national food safety policy should encourage the establishment of reasonable goals for the reduction of risks of carcinogenic and other toxic substances in the food supply of the U.S. population. The policy should take into account the averages and the wide variations in food requirements, preferences, and exposures to particular foods in a heterogeneous society.   The policy should maximize public health advantage while protecting individual choice * * * .

The system should be comprehensive, applying to all foods and their constituents on a uniform and equitable basis.   However, it must also take into account that particular foods or food constituents are not usually consumed in isolation but rather in combinations that vary both geographically and culturally with diverse diets.

The system should discriminate among risk levels, and assign priorities among categories of risks (for example, high, moderate or low*), with emphasis on those that pose the greatest potential hazards.   It should apply severe and general constraints only to items involving the greatest, most frequent, and most certain dangers.   It should recognize that it is impossible to eliminate all risk.   As a matter of feasibility, the regulatory process cannot be applied individually to each of the great number of substances in the human diet.   The regulatory agency must have a way to set priorities * * * .

The committee * * * believes that Congress should modify the existing policy for food additive regulation.   Were the policy modified along the lines suggested in our report, the FDA could deal with the saccharin issue on a more discriminating basis with a wider range of available options.   If, however, the policy is not so modified, Congress has the alternative to deal with saccharin as a special issue by legislative enactment. Under these circumstances the committee sees a series of options, any of which might be chosen, in the light of the facts on saccharin presented in Part 1 of our report.   These options fall into three major categories: (1) a total ban; (2) some form of restriction and/or warning on use, for example, permitting it as a table-top sweetener but not as a food additive; (3) no restrictions on use in foods.

No committee members favored the first or third category, but no specific policy was selected from the several options in (2).   Under the system of risk categories proposed by the committee, saccharin could be assigned to either the high-risk or the moderate-risk category, depending on the regulatory agency's evaluation of saccharin's cancer-causing potency. Under this proposed system, saccharin could be banned in whole or in part.   If not entirely banned, saccharin and all foods to which it is added

---

High Risk foods or ingredients are materials demonstrated by experience, or suitable scientific testing, to be likely to result in severe (irreversible, incapacitating, or lethal) damage to humans, either in general or in susceptible sub-populations, with appreciable frequency.

Moderate Risk foods or ingredients are materials that, as shown by experience or suitable scientific tests, may cause appreciable harm to humans either in general or in susceptible subpopulations, with sufficient frequency to justify regulatory action designed to modify their use.

Low Risk foods or ingredients are those for which there is evidence of some risk, but the risk is neither serious nor frequent enough for placement in the moderate risk category.

Other food outside of these three categories would be food and food ingredients that, under current knowledge, individually neither pose known risk nor the presumption of any significant risk under reasonable patterns of consumption.

could be identified with an appropriate warning and with adequate information about risks made available to consumers.

In any case, research to develop alternatives to saccharin should be encouraged, to lead to a gradual phasing out of saccharin use. * * *

Dr. [Colin] CAMPBELL [Professor of Nutritional Biochemistry, Cornell University]. * * *

I participated in the panel II study on food safety policy and wish to present some views which disagree with several of the recommendations presented in that report. * * *

First, the recommendation that food additives should be evaluated in terms of risk categories and furthermore that such information should be made available in the marketplace for the consumer is unequivocally indefensible, in my view.

* * * [The recommendation's] proponents argue that people do make judgments about levels of risk all the time and that keeping the risk categories to a minimum of three levels is consonant with making such judgments. * * * Common sense would suggest that there would be a major economic and political difference between two neighboring categories, for example, even more so between a low risk and a high risk category. Yet scientific knowledge simply does not permit such discrimination.

To illustrate this dilemma, it is instructive to examine the case study with aflatoxin * * * where there is probably more knowledge on human experience than for any other significantly toxic food substance.

Experimental animal studies have shown that this is probably the most potent chemical carcinogen, molecule for molecule, of any that has ever been studied. Furthermore, human epidemiological studies in East Africa and Thailand, where liver cancer incidence is incidentally much higher than in the United States, appear to demonstrate a very impressive relationship between the incidence of primary liver cancer and the level of aflatoxin ingestion. Yet those same studies tell us nothing about the incidence rate which we see in the United States.

There is one interesting difference between the liver cancer cases in these two regions that may help us to explain the dilemma. The Asian and African cases appear to have been exposed to the hepatitis B virus suspected by some of playing a role in liver cancer etiology.

On the other hand, there is some evidence that American liver cancer cases were exposed to factors which apparently predispose toward liver cirrhosis, factors such as alcohol abuse for example.

In other words, for many individuals, particularly here in the United States, aflatoxin might be classified as low risk. For those who abuse alcohol or contract this type of hepatitis or use certain types of diets or who are associated with other as yet largely unknown predisposing factors, aflatoxin ingestion may incur a very high risk indeed. * * *

It is scientific nonsense now and in the foreseeable future to suggest that individual risks can be determined for the hundreds and perhaps thousands of other chemicals normally ingested in our food. It is **even** more ridiculous to ask the consumer to estimate their own individual risks. If those with the most significant expertise cannot do it, how can the lay public do it? * * *

The second point that I would like to make is that chemicals which initiate irreversible toxicities such as cancer, birth deformities, mutations, and the like should not be evaluated within the same context as with chemicals which are associated with reversible toxicities. * * *

The third point I wish to make is, food safety policy should allow only for a minimum of regulatory agency discretion or flexibility. * * * I recognize the exceedingly complex and rather trivial organization of chemicals based on such factors as (a) the history of marketplace introduction, (b) the type of food commodity containing the chemical, (c) its intended purpose and (d) whether or not a letter in the file sanctioned its sale before enabling legislation.

Surely a more comprehensive and scientifically consistent policy should be possible. However, after development of a more consistent regulatory policy, regulatory agency discretion should then be held at a minimum. Particularly for those chemicals which initiate irreversible toxicities, there should be an absolute minimum of discretion, otherwise, regulatory policy would be continually subjected to the political and economic pressures of the day. * * *

Problem

What should Congress do about the Delaney Clause as it applies to food additives? To other categories of food constituents?

When considering this question keep in mind some of the alternatives available to Congress to structure whatever further discretion might be given the FDA in regulating carcinogenic food constituents. Lester Lave, an economist, has depicted several of the alternatives, their advantages and disadvantages. After setting out alternative "decision frameworks," Lave suggests the results of applying them to various food constituents, including saccharin.

L. LAVE, THE STRATEGY OF SOCIAL REGULATION

9–26, 74–75 (1981).

Six frameworks for making regulatory decisions are currently being used and two have been proposed. The frameworks range, roughly, from those requiring the least theory, data, and analysis and offering the least flexibility to those at the opposite pole.

MARKET REGULATION

Economic theory has formalized the 200-year-old insight of Adam Smith that competitive markets are efficient. In particular (under a set of stringent assumptions including complete information, no transaction costs, rational consumers and producers, no economies of scale in production, and no externalities), a competitive market produces an efficient (or Pareto optimal) equilibrium in the sense that no one can be made better off without making at least one person worse off. This efficiency principle also holds for situations involving risk, such as hazardous products or jobs, although still more stringent assumptions are needed. * * *

An outstanding controversy concerns whether the current U.S. economy is essentially competitive and the consumers well informed. One side claims that the economy has hardly a hint of competition and that most consumers and workers are ignorant. The other side sees intense competition, even within such oligopolistic industries as automobiles and airlines. Each side can muster persuasive examples, although general proof is impossible. * * *

* * * [T]he decision to use the market to regulate risk puts faith in consumer information and judgments. It sees the costs of bureaucracy constraining private decisions as larger than costs arising from market imperfections and advises accepting current imperfections rather than creating regulatory morass.

No-Risk

* * *

The no-risk framework has the advantage of requiring little data and analysis and precludes agonizing about the decision to be made. According to the Delaney Clause, the only question is whether a food additive has been shown to be a carcinogen in humans or animals. Thus data (on the quality, variety, and price of food) concerning the consequences of banning may not be considered. * * *

If society were concerned solely or even principally with the safety of food, the no-risk approach would be an appropriate guide for regulation, but society is concerned with many other issues as well. People eat foods they know to be harmful to their health and they indulge in a range of habits indicating that health is neither their sole objective nor even a very important one. * * * Attempting to legislate safety by banning food additives that lower cost, enhance flavor and appearance, or increase convenience is like attempting to legislate morality: the rhetorical appeal is evident, but regulation can hope to affect only a tiny proportion of the relevant risk, and at rapidly increasing cost. * * *

Technology-Based Standards

Recognizing the difficulty of attempting to estimate the health and safety effects of a proposed standard (much less the problem of quantifying these effects), a number of agencies have placed their reliance on engineering judgments. The best available control technology has been required extensively by the Environmental Protection Agency in regulating air and water pollution. This framework has the simplicity of requiring the estimation of neither benefits nor costs. The data and analysis required are for identifying a hazard and then for making the engineering judgment as to the best available control technology. This framework requires a second set of information for determining the best available control technology in addition to the carcinogenicity data required for the no-risk framework.   * * *

* * * [T]he primary advantage of technology-based standards is that they require no formal evidence on costs or benefits; the only data required are those necessary for good engineering judgments.   The resulting standard, however, will depend on regulators' perceptions of industry profitability.   If an area is populated by an industry teetering on the brink of bankruptcy, best available control technology will be weak and few emissions will be abated.   If the industry is profitable, it will require large expenditures.   There is more than a theoretical possibility that the first regulation in an industry would press it to the limit of its ability to afford regulation, leaving no financial resources to handle later regulations that might be far more important.   Rather than being a framework for lowering risk or even for using engineering judgments, technology-based standards is a framework for regulating economic activity through imposing costs arbitrarily among industries until all are at the same minimal level of profit.

RISK-RISK: DIRECT

Even if maximum protection were desired, the Delaney Clause would be a poor framework because it requires banning carcinogens.   Some toxic substances, such as food additives and fungicides, prevent contamination of food, and thus it is desirable to weigh one risk against the other. * * *

RISK-RISK: INDIRECT

The advantage of the risk-risk framework over the no-risk framework is that it permits wider analysis of risks. . . . Yet it is evident that the direct risk-risk framework takes only the first step of considering the health of the person consuming the food.   People are also associated with the production and distribution of food; society desires to minimize the adverse health effects associated with producing as well as consuming bacon (for a fixed level of production).   * * *

The indirect risk-risk framework is an important generalization since it allows consideration of implied health risks to workers.   The difficulty is estimating health risks.   As a first step in the analysis, assume that the same quantity of a regulated product would be produced as had been produced before.   The immediate effect on workers might be estimated by assuming that the average rates of accidents and occupational disease in an industry would apply to the additional effort required by the proposed regulation, for example, additional feed grains to fatten steers because diethylstilbestrol is banned in particular, if banning it required a 10 percent increase in corn production, accidents and occupational disease among corn farmers would be estimated to increase by 10 percent. There are a series of ripple effects, however.   The additional farming will require more seed, fertilizer, machinery, and fuel; these in turn will require more steel, coal, and so forth, each of which will involve occupational accidents and disease. * * *

RISK-BENEFIT

Unlike the risk-benefit framework, the three previous ones do not allow consideration of nonhealth effects. The folly of refusing to consider these effects is illustrated by examining one's own choices. For example, most people are willing to risk the minute chance of biological contamination rather than to be bothered with boiling drinking water. They are willing to undertake additional risks in order to get rewards such as additional income and recreational stimulation. For example, there is a risk premium in the pay of workers in hazardous occupations to attract them in the face of the higher risks. These premiums can be extremely high, as for test pilots, steeplejacks, and divers working deep in the ocean. If the effect of a regulation is to lower risk minutely at the cost of a vast increase in price, a lessening of choice or convenience, harm to the environment, or a sacrifice in social goals generally, society should not be satisfied. The frameworks previously mentioned suffer from their lack of recognition of other social goals such as the ecosystem, endangered species, and individual freedoms. * * *

The intellectual difficulty with this framework is its lack of precise definition. Are only health risks to be considered, or are risks to the present and future environment (air, water, louseworts, snail darters, and tundra) relevant? If they are not, the framework is no more complete than the previous one, and if they are, how can the risks to louseworts be added to those to the health of our great grandchildren and of current workers? Similarly, there is no guidance about how to quantify benefits: what is the value of an increase in the supply of food or electricity?

This is the most general and flexible framework, but one despairs at its implementation. * * *

COST-EFFECTIVENESS

Many organizations, private and public, find themselves attempting to increase output even though their current budget is fixed. The intellectual contributions in defining this problem and developing rules to solve it have come from the Department of Defense. Although cost-effectiveness is often thought erroneously to refer to getting some specific project done at lowest cost, the concept is much broader, referring to accomplishing some general objective at lowest cost. * * *

Cost-effectiveness offers a major advantage over benefit-cost analysis in that it does not require an explicit value for the social cost of premature death (or other untraded goods). Assumptions about these values are built into the goal and budget (for example, maximize lives saved for a fixed budget) but need not be stated explicitly. The flip side of this advantage, however, is that errors in stating the goal or in determining the budget can lead to bad decisions, and there is no internal mechanism for showing the errors in these decisions and the changes in goals or budget that are necessary.

REGULATORY BUDGET

Cost-effectiveness is a good framework if the relevant costs are being measured in the analysis. Unfortunately when the only costs considered are those of the regulatory agency, the framework will misallocate resources because only one subset of the total costs of the regulation to the entire economy is being considered. * * *

An idea originating in the Council of Economic Advisers under Charles Schultz was to give each regulatory agency an implementation budget in the form of a limit on the total annual costs that its regulations could impose. For example, the Environmental Protection Agency might be given an implementation budget of $10 billion a year, which would mean that the costs of implementing its air, water, solid waste, radiation, and pesticide regulations could not exceed $10 billion in that year. Each agency would develop an implementation budget request, just as it currently develops its operating budget request. The administration would coordinate and impose priorities on the agencies, and then Congress would react to these requests, modifying them as necessary. * * *

The principal difficulties with the framework are in estimating the costs and effects of each regulation. * * * If there is a factor-of-five-or-ten difference between reasonable high and low estimates of implementation costs, the regulatory budget cannot provide a helpful constraint.

Discipline might be exerted by the use of ex post reviews of previous cost estimates and the resulting experience. Even for regulations that have been implemented, however, it is difficult to estimate the additional costs due to the regulation. In addition, several years would elapse before sufficient experience accumulated to estimate costs retrospectively; disciplining the agency for bad cost estimates during a previous administration would make little sense.

Excluding uncertain or indirect costs (while estimating only direct costs or those that can be confidently quantified) would give a terrible set of incentives to the regulatory agency. For example, banning a substance would minimize direct costs, even though it might impose very substantial indirect costs. Similarly, counting only current costs would lead the agency to design a regulation to impose costs in the future. * * *

A good deal of work remains to be done in exploring this framework. Seemingly subtle issues affect the outcome of the analysis. For example, the budget constraint can be stated for all regulatory agencies, for each division or program, or for "discretionary" funds. If trade-offs are made only within narrow programs, the overall result is unlikely to be satisfactory. For example, should the Food and Drug Administration be making trade-offs among food additives or among all activities under its purview that could enhance health?   If the Food and Drug Administration were permitted to allocate time and funds among all activities, it might focus on cigarette smoking and ignore food additives.   Some groups feel strongly about food additives and would protest a lack of regulatory attention to this area, even if the resources saved more lives by decreasing cigarette consumption. * * *

BENEFIT-COST

This framework is similar to the general balancing of risks against benefits; the principal difference is that it is more quantitative and formal. In addition to enumerating the various benefits of the regulation and then subjectively balancing benefits against costs, this framework would require quantification of the extent to which the benefits and costs vary with the level of regulation, and then would require each of these effects to be translated into dollars.

There are many controversial aspects to its application, including putting an explicit value on prolonging a life, quantifying other benefits, deciding the rate at which effects in the future are discounted to make them equivalent to current effects, and redistributing income.   Valuing benefits, or even deciding what is a benefit, runs into the diversity of cultural backgrounds, personal goals, fears, and time horizons. * * *   Benefit-cost analysis is the most general and quantitative of the frameworks, and thus elicits the most information and requires the most analysis.

Benefit-cost analysis is a sufficiently broad framework to be adapted to consider virtually any aspect of a regulation or public decision.   The implications for those who gain or lose can be folded into the analysis. None of the objections to the framewrok have the effect of showing an inherent bias or blind spot in the analysis.

In practice, however, the picture is quite different.   Benefit-cost analysis is often viewed, correctly, as a tool for defending the status quo.   It is rarely used to consider who benefits or pays, and it focuses on the present, giving short shrift to even the near-term future with no importance for events more than a few decades in the future. * * *

The eight frameworks stretch from simple solutions (let the market do it or accept no unnecessary risk) to elaborate ones (identify all effects and value them in dollars).   The range of problems is even greater, stretching from purely scientific ones (is nitrite a carcinogen?) to purely value conflicts (since so few people buckle their belts, should passive seat belts be required, even though they are more expensive and less effective than current belts?).   Only by appreciating the complexity of problems and frameworks can there be an intelligent analysis of how to improve standard settings. * * *

Table 1 summarizes the regulatory actions that would be implied by the application of each of the decision frameworks to four additives or contaminants (in addition to current FDA regulations).   Needless to say this table is highly tentative at best and incomplete because of the inability to survey the range of programs as required for the cost-effectiveness **and** regulatory budget frameworks.

Table 1.   Application of Decision Frameworks to Additives and Contaminants

Decision framework	Implied regulatory action for			
	Nitrite	DES	Aflatoxin	Saccharin
Market regulation	No action	No action	No action	No action
No risk	Ban	Ban	Levels as low as technologically feasible	Ban
Technology-based standards	Ban	Ban	Levels as low as technologically feasible	Ban
Risk-risk	Low amounts permitted	No action	No action	Ban
Risk versus benefits	No excess permitted	Careful use permitted	Fairly stringent	No action
Cost-effectiveness	No agency attention	No agency attention	More attention and control	No agency attention
Regulatory budget	No agency attention	No agency attention	More attention and control	No agency attention
Benefit-cost	No excess permitted	Careful use permitted	More stringent than present	No action

Chapter 2

EXECUTIVE SUPERVISION OF
ADMINISTRATIVE ACTION

The U.S. Constitution is more than usually delphic in describing the structure and the powers of the Executive Branch. Article II concerns itself primarily with the election, compensation, and removal of the President and Vice-President. Other executive branch officials are mentioned in two contexts: (1) The President is empowered, with the advice and consent of two-thirds of the Senate, to appoint and "commission" "officers of the United States;" and (2) the President is authorized to demand "the opinion, in writing, of the principal officer in each of the executive departments, upon any subject relating to the duties of their respective offices." The chief domestic power of the President is stated as a responsibility—"he shall take care that the laws be faithfully executed"—and is listed, almost as an afterthought, following instructions that the President make reports and recommendations to the Congress and "receive Ambassadors and other Public Ministers."

From these meager constitutional underpinnings the modern executive branch, with its multiple departments, hundreds of bureaus, and millions of employees, has gradually emerged. Yet the growth of administrative governance and power over these two hundred years has left undecided (if "decision" implies judicial interpretation) most of the constitutional questions that could have been asked in 1787. What is an "office" to which the President is authorized to appoint? How are "officers" who are not subject to impeachment to be removed? What is a "department"? How are they to be created, staffed, and managed? What techniques are available to the President, beyond demanding reports in writing, to "execute" the laws? In responding to these questions, as one author puts it, "[A]ppellate adjudications are, for the most part, replete with examples of issue-avoidance, purposeful equivocation, ambiguity and indecision. * * * " Burkoff, *Appointment and Removal Under the Federal Constitution: The Impact of Buckley v. Valeo*, 22 Wayne L. Rev. 1335 (1976).

This gap in our constitutional jurisprudence does not reflect continuous harmonious adjustment. Ambiguity or vagueness concerning the powers of the executive almost always suggests the *possibility* of legislative power. The brevity of Article II thus leads not to a power vacuum but to a power struggle. The battle began in the first Congress (see I ANNALS OF CONGRESS 473–608 (1789)) concerning the removal power (see Burkoff, *supra*, at 1379–83), and has been raging ever since, as the *Chadha* case in Chapter 1 attests. This is a political war with many truces but no possibility of a comprehensive, stable peace treaty. For neither the President nor the Congress are political lightweights; the political stakes are often high; and each has regular opportunities to encroach on domains claimed by the other.

Consider, for example, the techniques available to the modern President to shape administrative policy. First, there are the powers to appoint, and to remove, agency officials. These powers are amplified by the authority to issue executive orders, directives, or simple statements of policy. The President can also explore possibilities for agency organization and reorganization, impose requirements for inter-agency coordination, and demand central clearance of budget requests and legislative proposals. Lying behind these various carrots and sticks are others, ranging from the Attorney General's control over agency litigation to the President's unique access to the media.

Unlike the Pope, however, the Congress possesses its own divisions. Appointments can be blocked and removals prohibited or conditioned on "cause." The power to appoint and remove may be delegated to others. Agencies can be set up as "independent" or outside the Executive branch; agency budgets can be cut or expanded; statutory administrative powers can be altered, deleted, or withheld. Presidential ambitions for new legislation may be held hostage to congressional desires for administrative changes of direction. Congressional oversight hearings may be structured to embarrass the President politically, and even impeachment, while rare, is not unknown.

To be sure, not all the things the President and the Congress *might* do as they contend for political control of administration are necessarily constitutional. Indeed, because virtually every technique available to one contestant has implications for the reserved powers of the other, each thrust and parry necessarily raises an issue of separation of powers. Moreover, certain forms of interbranch competition for control of the federal bureaucracy may affect the constitutional, statutory, or common law rights of third parties. Thus some (and, with the decline of traditional barriers to justiciability, an increasing number of) disputes bearing on executive control of administrative action make their way into the courts.

In this chapter we concern ourselves with two related presidential powers—the power to appoint and to remove officers and the power to direct agency policy choice—that together define important aspects of executive branch control of administration. The pertinent jurisprudence will not supply definitive answers to many of our questions, but it is sufficient to outline the terms of the continuing debate.

A. APPOINTMENT AND REMOVAL OF OFFICERS

HUMPHREY'S EXECUTOR v. UNITED STATES

Supreme Court of the United States, 1935.
295 U.S. 602, 55 S.Ct. 869, 79 L.Ed. 1611.

MR. JUSTICE SUTHERLAND delivered the opinion of the Court.

Plaintiff brought suit in the Court of Claims against the United States to recover a sum of money alleged to be due the deceased for salary as a Federal Trade Commissioner from October 8, 1933, when the President undertook to remove him from office, to the time of his death on February 14, 1934. The court below has certified to this court two questions in respect of the power of the President to make the removal. The material facts which give rise to the questions are as follows:

William E. Humphrey, the decedent, on December 10, 1931, was nominated by President Hoover to succeed himself as a member of the Federal Trade Commission, and was confirmed by the United States Senate. He was duly commissioned for a term of seven years expiring September 25, 1938; and, after taking the required oath of office, entered upon his duties. On July 25, 1933, President Roosevelt addressed a letter to the commissioner asking for his resignation, on the ground "that the aims and purposes of the Adminstration with respect to the work of the Commission can be carried out most effectively with personnel of my own selection," but disclaiming any reflection upon the commissioner personally or upon his services. The commissioner replied, asking time to consult his friends. After some further correspondence upon the subject, the President on August 31, 1933, wrote the commissioner expressing the hope that the resignation would be forthcoming and saying:

"You will, I know, realize that I do not feel that your mind and my mind go along together on either the policies or the administering of the Federal Trade Commission, and, frankly, I think it is best for the people of this country that I should have a full confidence."

The commissioner declined to resign; and on October 7, 1933, the President wrote him:

"Effective as of this date you are hereby removed from the office of Commissioner of the Federal Trade Commission."

Humphrey never acquiesced in this action, but continued thereafter to insist that he was still a member of the commission, entitled to perform its duties and receive the compensation provided by law at the rate of $10,000 per annum. Upon these and other facts set forth in the certificate, which we deem it unnecessary to recite, the following questions are certified:

"1. Do the provisions of section 1 of the Federal Trade Commission Act, stating that 'any commissioner may be removed by the President for inefficiency, neglect of duty, or malfeasance in office,' restrict or limit the power of the President to remove a commissioner except under one or more of the causes named?

"If the foregoing question is answered in the affirmative, then—

"2. If the power of the President to remove a commissioner is restricted or limited as shown by the foregoing interrogatory and the answer made thereto, is such a restriction or limitation valid under the Constitution of the United States?" The Federal Trade Commission Act, at U.S.C.A. § § 41, 42, creates a commission of five members to be appointed by the President by and with the advice and consent of the Senate, and § 1 provides:

> "Not more than three of the commissioners shall be members of the same political party. The first commissioners appointed shall continue in office for terms of three, four, five, six, and seven years, respectively, from the date of the taking effect of this Act, the term of each to be designated by the President, but their successors shall be appointed for terms of seven years, except that any person chosen to fill a vacancy shall be appointed only for the unexpired term of the commissioner whom he shall succeed. The commission shall choose a chairman from its own membership. No commissioner shall engage in any other business, vocation, or employment. Any commissioner may be removed by the President for inefficiency, neglect of duty, or malfeasance in office." * * *

First. The question first to be considered is whether, by the provisions of § 1 of the Federal Trade Commission Act already quoted, the President's power is limited to removal for the specific causes enumerated therein. * * *

* * * [T]he fixing of a definite term subject to removal for cause, unless there be some countervailing provision or circumstance indicating the contrary, which here we are unable to find, is enough to establish the legislative intent that the term is not to be curtailed in the absence of such cause. But if the intention of Congress that no removal should be made during the specified term except for one or more of the enumerated causes were not clear upon the face of the statute, as we think it is, it would be made clear by a consideration of the character of the commission and the legislative history which accompanied and preceded the passage of the act.

The commission is to be non-partisan; and it must, from the very nature of its duties, act with entire impartiality. It is charged with the enforcement of no policy except the policy of the law. Its duties are neither political nor executive, but predominantly quasi-judicial and quasi-legislative. Like the Interstate Commerce Commission, its members are called upon to exercise the trained judgment of a body of experts "appointed by law and informed by experience."

The legislative reports in both houses of Congress clearly reflect the view that a fixed term was necessary to the effective and fair administration of the law. * * *

The debates in both houses demonstrate that the prevailing view was that the commission was not to be "subject to anybody in the government but * * * only to the people of the United States"; free from "political domination or control" or the "probability or possibility of such a thing"; to be "separate and apart from any existing department of the government—not subject to the orders of the President." * * *

Thus, the language of the act, the legislative reports, and the general purposes of the legislation as reflected by the debates, all combine to demonstrate the Congressional intent to create a body of experts who shall gain experience by length of service—a body which shall be independent of executive authority, *except in its selection,* and free to exercise its judgment without the leave or hindrance of any other official or any department of the government.   To the accomplishment of these purposes, it is clear that Congress was of the opinion that length and certainty of tenure would vitally contribute.   And to hold that, nevertheless, the members of the commission continue in office at the mere will of the President, might be to thwart, in large measure, the very ends which Congress sought to realize by definitely fixing the term of office.

We conclude that the intent of the act is to limit the executive power of removal to the causes enumerated, the existence of none of which is claimed here; and we pass to the second question.

Second.   To support its contention that the removal provision of § 1, as we have just construed it, is an unconstitutional interference with the executive power of the President, the government's chief reliance is on *Myers v. United States*, 272 U.S. 52 [1926].   That case has been so recently decided, and the prevailing and dissenting opinions so fully review the general subject of the power of executive removal, that further discussion would add little of value to the wealth of material there collected.   These opinions examine at length the historical, legislative and judicial data bearing upon the question, beginning with what is called "the decision of 1789" in the first Congress and coming down almost to the day when the opinions were delivered.   They occupy 243 pages of the volume in which they are printed.   Nevertheless, the narrow point actually decided was only that the President had power to remove a postmaster of the first class, without the advice and consent of the Senate as required by act of Congress.   In the course of the opinion of the court, expressions occur which tend to sustain the government's contention, but these are beyond the point involved and, therefore, do not come within the rule of *stare decisis*.   In so far as they are out of harmony with the views here set forth, these expressions are disapproved. * * *

The office of a postmaster is so essentially unlike the office now involved that the decision in the *Myers* case cannot be accepted as controlling our decision here.   A postmaster is an executive officer restricted to the performance of executive functions.   He is charged with no duty at all related to either the legislative or judicial power.   The actual decision in the *Myers* case finds support in the theory that such an officer is merely one of the units in the executive department and, hence, inherently subject to the exclusive and illimitable power of removal by the Chief Executive, whose subordinate and aid he is.   Putting aside *dicta*, which may be followed if sufficiently persuasive but which are not controlling, the **nec**essary reach of the decision goes far enough to include all purely **execu-**

tive officers. It goes no farther;—much less does it include an officer who occupies no place in the executive department and who exercises no part of the executive power vested by the Constitution in the President.

The Federal Trade Commission is an administrative body created by Congress to carry into effect legislative policies embodied in the statute in accordance with the legislative standard therein prescribed, and to perform other specified duties as a legislative or as a judicial aid. Such a body cannot in any proper sense be characterized as an arm or an eye of the executive. Its duties are performed without executive leave and, in the contemplation of the statute, must be free from executive control. In administering the provisions of the statute in respect of "unfair methods of competition"—that is to say in filling in and administering the details embodied by that general standard—the commission acts in part quasi-legislatively and in part quasi-judicially. In making investigations and reports thereon for the information of Congress under § 6, in aid of the legislative power, it acts as a legislative agency. Under § 7, which authorizes the commission to act as a master in chancery under rules prescribed by the court, it acts as an agency of the judiciary. To the extent that it exercises any executive function—as distinguished from executive power in the constitutional sense—it does so in the discharge and effectuation of its quasi-legislative or quasi-judicial powers, or as an agency of the legislative or judicial departments of the government.*

If Congress is without authority to prescribe causes for removal of members of the trade commission and limit executive power of removal accordingly, that power at once becomes practically all-inclusive in respect of civil officers with the exception of the judiciary provided for by the Constitution. The Solicitor General, at the bar, apparently recognizing this to be true, with commendable candor, agreed that his view in respect of the removability of members of the Federal Trade Commission necessitated a like view in respect of the Interstate Commerce Commission and the Court of Claims. We are thus confronted with the serious question whether not only the members of these quasi-legislative and quasi-judicial bodies, but the judges of the legislative Court of Claims, exercising judicial power, continue in office only at the pleasure of the President.

We think it plain under the Constitution that illimitable power of removal is not possessed by the President in respect of officers of the character of those just named. The authority of Congress, in creating quasi-legislative or quasi-judicial agencies, to require them to act in discharge of their duties independently of executive control cannot well be doubted; and that authority includes, as an appropriate incident, power to fix the period during which they shall continue in office, and to forbid their removal except for cause in the meantime. For it is quite evident that one who holds his office only during the pleasure of another, cannot be de-

---

*The provision of § 6(d) of the [FTC] act which authorizes the President to direct an investigation and report by the commission in relation to alleged violations of the anti-trust acts, is so obviously collateral to the main design of the act as not to detract from the force of this general statement as to the character of that body.

pended upon to maintain an attitude of independence against the latter's will.

The fundamental necessity of maintaining each of the three general departments of government entirely free from the control or coercive influence, direct or indirect, of either of the others, has often been stressed and is hardly open to serious question. So much is implied in the very fact of the separation of the powers of these departments by the Constitution; and in the rule which recognizes their essential co-equality. * * *

The result of what we now have said is this: Whether the power of the President to remove an officer shall prevail over the authority of Congress to condition the power by fixing a definite term and precluding a removal except for cause, will depend upon the character of the office; the *Myers* decision, affirming the power of the President alone to make the removal, is confined to purely executive officers; and as to officers of the kind here under consideration, we hold that no removal can be made during the prescribed term for which the officer is appointed, except for one or more of the causes named in the applicable statute.

To the extent that, between the decision in the *Myers* case, which sustains the unrestrictable power of the President to remove purely executive officers, and our present decision that such power does not extend to an office such as that here involved, there shall remain a field of doubt, we leave such cases as may fall within it for future consideration and determination as they may arise. * * *

Notes

1. The opinion in *Humphrey's Executor* is usually understood as making a sharp distinction between executive officers, removable at the President's will, and independent agency officers, removable by the President subject to statutory limitation. Because the power to remove is often thought to include the power to control, this distinction is of obvious consequence.

Yet one should not imagine that Presidents have either complete control over executive officers or none over officers in "independent" agencies. For example, Humphrey did not remain a functioning member of the Federal Trade Commission. Indeed, as one of our colleagues relished repeating to his class each year, "The lesson of the *Humphrey* case is in the title."

Nor do removals of nominally "executive" officials always proceed without contest. For example, President Reagan set off a political tempest in 1983 when he removed three members of the Civil Rights Commission, which by statute was an executive agency. 42 U.S.C.A. § 1975b(a). After several months of widely publicized debate, a compromise was reached which retained two of the three commissioners. A new enabling statute was enacted, expanding the number of commissioners from six to eight, and making the Commission independent. Pub. L. No. 98–183, 97 Stat. 1301 (1983). The clear language in the original act—"there is created in the executive branch"—obviously did not prevent claims by civil rights groups and some Congressmen that the Commission should be considered operationally independent, and that the removals were improper. Nor did this language convince the U.S. District Court for the District of Columbia which issued a preliminary injunction blocking the removals. *Berry v. Reagan,* 32

Empl. Prac. Dec. (CCH) ¶ 31, 304 (1983), *vacated as moot* 732 F.2d 949 (D.C. Cir. 1983).

Conversely, the President often need not remove officers in order ultimately to control the membership of independent agencies. Members of independent boards and commissions rarely serve their full terms. One study examined the history from 1945 to 1970 of seven important agencies, whose members were statutorily granted terms of office ranging from five to seven years. During this period the President had only once needed more than three years to name an actual majority of the Commissioners, and the average time from inauguration to appointment of a majority was 21 months. When the Presidency changed parties, the average time for the President to gain a *partisan* majority on a Commission was but 7 months. These figures illustrate that, even with limited removal authority, the President retains substantial power to shape the membership, and thus presumably the policies, of the independent agencies. Goodsell and Gayo, *Appointive Control of Federal Regulatory Commissions*, 23 Ad. L. Rev. 291 (1971).

2. Statutory provisions for the removal of officers are hardly uniform. Although many statutes provide that commissioners may be removed only for "cause," that cause is variously articulated. "Inefficiency, neglect of duty, or malfeasance in office" is a common formulation. But there is seldom any provision for determining whether a presidential removal on one of these grounds is in fact justified. The National Labor Relations Act may be unique in providing that in removing a member of the Board the President shall act "upon notice and hearing." Presumably the disappointed office holder removed under other statutes would test out the propriety of the removal in a suit for back pay.

Not all appointees to independent commissions enjoy statutory "for cause" limitations on their removal. During the time between the *Myers* case and *Humphrey's Executor*, the Congress created the Securities and Exchange Commission, the Federal Communications Commission and the Federal Power Commission. In each case, presumably on the basis of the *Myers* holding, the Congress provided no restrictions on the President's power of removal. Does this mean, following *Humphrey's* and *Wiener*, infra p. 118, that the President's power of removal with respect to these commissions is in fact unrestricted?

Some recent statutes seem to recognize a division between (1) policy formation and prosecutorial functions and (2) licensing and adjudicatory functions, both in the structure of agencies and in the provisions for the removal of officers. The Energy Reorganization Act of 1974, for example, replaced the Atomic Energy Commission with two agencies: one, the Energy Research and Development Administration, is described in the statute as "an independent executive agency," whatever that means, 42 U.S.C.A. § 5811; the other, the Nuclear Regulatory Commission, is styled "an independent regulatory commission." 42 U.S.C.A. § 5841. The ERDA, which has responsibility for military and production activities and for basic research, is headed by an Administrator who is appointed by the President, with the advice and consent of the Senate, for an indefinite term. 42 U.S.C.A. § 5812. There is no mention of the removal of the Administrator in the statute. The five NRC commissioners, on the other hand, are appointed by the President with the advice and consent of the Senate for five year terms and are made removable by the President for "inefficiency, neglect of duty, or malfeasance in office."

A similar separation of functions and differentiation of removal authority occurs in the Occupational Safety and Health Act, 29 U.S.C.A. § § 651–678. The Secretary of Labor, who exercises enforcement functions under the statute, is a cabinet level executive officer. Adjudication of contested cases under the Act is performed by the Occupational Safety and Health Review Commission. Commission members are appointed by the President with the advice and consent of the Senate for six year terms and are subject to removal on the same grounds as the members of the Nuclear Regulatory Commission.

3. *Humphrey's Executor* fails to indicate how the "independence" of an agency is to be determined or what that classification implies. Indeed, the opinion itself does not use the term "independent agency," but instead distinguishes between agencies that are "purely executive" and those established to "exercise * * * judgment without the leave or hindrance of any other official or any department of the government." 295 U.S. at 625–26. How are we to determine whether an agency is so established?

One possibility is to see whether the Congress says as much in the legislation creating the agency, or elsewhere. Congress has listed agencies it considers to be "independent" in 44 U.S.C.A. § 3502(10). But surely congressional choice cannot be the end of the matter. *Humphrey's Executor* stresses the "fundamental necessity" of maintaining the separation of powers. A Congress that could define the executive branch away, save for the constitutional officers—the President and Vice-President—would be supreme over, not coordinate with, the executive.

4. Twenty years later, in the next major case dealing with the President's removal power, *Wiener v. United States*, 357 U.S. 349 (1958), the Court embraced a more functional approach. This also was a suit for back pay, by a member of the War Claims Commission, a temporary Commission established to hear claims, "according to law," arising out of enemy activity during World War II. Wiener was removed by President Eisenhower six months prior to the expiration of the Commission's mandate for reasons virtually identical to those President Roosevelt offered Humphrey. The statute creating the War Claims Commission did not mention removal. Justice Frankfurter, for the Court, concluded (357 U.S. at 355–56):

> When Congress has for distribution among American claimants funds derived from foreign sources, it may proceed in different ways. Congress may appropriate directly; it may utilize the Executive; it may resort to the adjudicatory process. For Congress itself to have made appropriations for the claims with which it dealt under the War Claims Act was not practical in view of the large number of claimants and the diversity in the specific circumstances giving rise to the claims. The House bill in effect put the distribution of the narrow class of claims that it acknowledged into Executive hands, by vesting the procedure in the Federal Security Administrator. The final form of the legislation, as we have seen, left the widened range of claims to be determined by adjudication. Congress could, of course, have given jurisdiction over these claims to the District Courts or to the Court of Claims. The fact that it chose to establish a Commission to "adjudicate according to law" the classes of claims defined in the statute did not alter the intrinsic judicial character of the task with which the Commission was charged. The claims were to be "adjudicated according to law," that is, on the merits of each claim, supported by evidence and governing legal considerations, by a body that was

"entirely free from the control or coercive influence, direct or indirect," *Humphrey's Executor v. United States,* of either the Executive or the Congress. If, as one must take for granted, the War Claims Act precluded the President from influencing the Commission in passing on a particular claim, *a fortiori* must it be inferred that Congress did not wish to have hang over the Commission the Damocles' sword of removal by the President for no reason other than that he preferred to have on that Commission men of his own choosing.

For such is this case.   We have not a removal for cause involving the rectitude of a member of an adjudicatory body, nor even a suspensory removal until the Senate could act upon it by confirming the appointment of a new Commissioner or otherwise dealing with the matter.   Judging the matter in all the nakedness in which it is presented, namely, the claim that the President could remove a member of an adjudicatory body like the War Claims Commission merely because he wanted his own appointees on such a Commission, we are compelled to conclude that no such power is given to the President directly by the Constitution, and none is impliedly conferred upon him by statute simply because Congress said nothing about it.   The philosophy of *Humphrey's Executor,* in its explicit language as well as its implications, precludes such a claim.

5. What are we to make of *Humphrey's Executor* and *Wiener* in combination?   Is it "quasi-judicial" responsibility that defeats Presidential control? *Humphrey's Executor* will hardly bear so limited an interpretation.   And the *Wiener* opinion seems to presume that the Congress could have conferred the War Claims Commission functions on the Federal Security Administrator while leaving that a "purely executive" office.   The President's conceded ability to remove executive officials who exercise quasi-judicial functions, such as the Commissioner of Food and Drugs and the Commissioner of Social Security, has never been thought to encroach on the due process rights of license or benefits claimants (see infra pp. 228–50).   Nor would the protection of "good cause" removal prevent constitutional objection to the Commission's exercising the "judicial power," were the war claims involved in *Wiener* considered "private" rights, see *Northern Pipeline Construction Co. v. Marathon Pipe Line Co.,* 458 U.S. 50 (1982).   Perhaps the notion is that quasi-judicial, and quasi-legislative, functions form a sufficient constitutional predicate for a congressional judgment that the President's removal power should be circumscribed by statute, but do not compel such a choice.   But with respect to appointments the situation is not so malleable, as the next case illustrates.

BUCKLEY v. VALEO

Supreme Court of the United States, 1976.
424 U.S. 1, 96 S.Ct. 612, 46 L.Ed. 2d 659.

PER CURIAM.

These appeals present constitutional challenges to the key provisions of the Federal Election Campaign Act of 1971 (Act), and related provisions of the Internal Revenue Code of 1954, all as amended in 1974. * * *

* * * The statutes at issue summarized in broad terms, contain the following provisions: (a) individual political contributions are limited to

$1,000 to any single candidate per election, with an overall annual limitation of $25,000 by any contributor; independent expenditures by individuals and groups "relative to a clearly identified candidate" are limited to $1,000 a year; campaign spending by candidates for various federal offices and spending for national conventions by political parties are subject to prescribed limits; (b) contributions and expenditures above certain threshold levels must be reported and publicly disclosed; (c) a system for public funding of Presidential campaign activities is established by Subtitle H of the Internal Revenue Code; and (d) a Federal Election Commission is established to administer and enforce the legislation.

* * *

The 1974 amendments to the Act create an eight-member Federal Election Commission (Commission) and vest in it primary and substantial responsibility for administering and enforcing the Act. The question * * * is whether, in view of the manner in which a majority of its members are appointed, the Commission may under the Constitution exercise the powers conferred upon it. We find it unnecessary to parse the complex statutory provisions in order to sketch the full sweep of the Commission's authority. It will suffice for present purposes to describe what appear to be representative examples of its various powers.

Chapter 14 of Title 2 makes the Commission the principal repository of the numerous reports and statements which are required by that chapter to be filed by those engaging in the regulated political activities. Its duties under § 438(a) with respect to these reports and statements include filing and indexing, making them available for public inspection, preservation, and auditing and field investigations. It is directed to "serve as a national clearinghouse for information in respect to the administration of elections."

Beyond these recordkeeping, disclosure, and investigative functions, however, the Commission is given extensive rulemaking and adjudicative powers. Its duty under § 438(a)(10) is "to prescribe suitable rules and regulations to carry out the provisions of * * * chapter [14]." Under § 437(d)(8) the Commission is empowered to make such rules "as are necessary to carry out the provisions of this Act." Section 437d(a)(9) authorizes it to "formulate general policy with respect to the administration of this Act" and enumerated sections of Title 18's Criminal Code, as to all of which provisions the Commission "has primary jurisdiction with respect to [their] civil enforcement." § 437c(b). The Commission is authorized under § 437f(a) to render advisory opinions with respect to activities possibly violating the Act, the Title 18 sections, or the campaign funding provisions of Title 26, the effect of which is that "[n]otwithstanding any other provision of law, any person with respect to whom an advisory opinion is rendered * * * who acts in good faith in accordance with the provisions and findings [thereof] shall be presumed to be in compliance with the [statutory provision] with respect to which such advisory opinion is rendered." In the course of administering the provisions for Presidential campaign financing, the Commission may authorize convention expenditures which exceed the statutory limits.

The Commission's enforcement power is both direct and wide ranging. It may institute a civil action for (i) injunctive or other relief against "any acts or practices which constitute or will constitute a violation of this Act"; (ii) declaratory or injunctive relief "as may be appropriate to implement or con[s]true any provisions" of Chapter 95 of Title 26, governing administration of funds for Presidential election campaigns and national party conventions; and (iii) "such injunctive relief as is appropriate to implement any provision" of Chapter 96 of Title 26, governing the payment of matching funds for Presidential primary campaigns. If after the Commission's post-disbursement audit of candidates receiving payments under Chapter 95 or 96 it finds an overpayment, it is empowered to seek repayment of all funds due the Secretary of the Treasury. In no respect do the foregoing civil actions require the concurrence of or participation by the Attorney General; conversely, the decision not to seek judicial relief in the above respects would appear to rest solely with the Commission. With respect to the referenced Title 18 sections, § 437g(a)(7) provides that if, after notice and opportunity for a hearing before it, the Commission finds an actual or threatened criminal violation, the Attorney General "upon request by the Commission * * * shall institute a civil action for relief." Finally, as "[a]ldditional enforcement authority," § 456(a) authorizes the Commission, after notice and opportunity for hearing, to make "a finding that a person * * * while a candidate for Federal office, failed to file" a required report of contributions or expenditures. If that finding is made within the applicable limitations period for prosecutions, the candidate is thereby "disqualified from becoming a candidate in any future election for Federal office for a period of time begining on the date of such finding and ending one year after the expiration of the term of the Federal office for which such person was a candidate."

The body in which this authority is reposed consists of eight members. The Secretary of the Senate and the Clerk of the House of Representatives are *ex officio* members of the Commission without the right to vote. Two members are appointed by the President *pro tempore* of the Senate "upon the recommendations of the majority leader of the Senate and the minority leader of the Senate." Two more are to be appointed by the Speaker of the House of Representatives, likewise upon the recommendations of its respective majority and minority leaders. The remaining two members are appointed by the President. Each of the six voting members of the Commission must be confirmed by the majority of both Houses of Congress, and each of the three appointing authorities is forbidden to choose both of their appointees from the same political party.

* * *

The principle of separation of powers was not simply an abstract generalization in the minds of the Framers: it was woven into the document that they drafted in Philadelphia in the summer of 1787. Article I, § 1, declares: "All legislative Powers herein granted shall be vested in a Congress of the United States." Article II, § 1, vests the executive power "in a President of the United States of America," and Art. III, § 1, declares that "The judicial Power of the United States, shall be vested in one supreme Court, and in such inferior Courts as the Congress may from time to time ordain and establish." The further concern of the Framers of the Constitution with maintenance of the separation of powers is found in the so-called "Ineligibility" and "Incompatibility" Clauses contained in Art. I, § 6:

> "No Senator or Representative shall, during the Time for which he was elected, be appointed to any civil Office under the Authority of the United States, which shall have been created, or the Emoluments whereof shall have been encreased during such time; and no Person holding any Office under the United States, shall be a Member of either House during his Continuance in Office."

It is in the context of these cognate provisions of the document that we must examine the language of Art. II, § 2, cl. 2.   * * *

> "[The President] shall nominate, and by and with the Advice and Consent of the Senate, shall appoint Ambassadors, other public Ministers and Consuls, Judges of the supreme Court, and all other Officers of the United States, whose Appointments are not herein otherwise provided for, and which shall be established by Law: but the Congress may by Law vest the Appointment of such inferior Officers, as they think proper, in the President alone, in the Courts of Law, or in the Heads of Departments."

* * * We think [the] fair import [of this language] is that any appointee exercising significant authority pursuant to the laws of the United States is an "Officer of the United States," and must, therefore, be appointed in the manner prescribed by § 2, cl. 2, of the Article.

* * * [I]t is difficult to see how the members of the Commission may escape inclusion. If a postmaster first class, *Myers v. United States*, and the clerk of a district court, *Ex parte Hennen*, 38 U.S. 225, 13 Pet. 230 (1839), are inferior officers of the United States within the meaning of the Appointments Clause, as they are, surely the Commissioners before us are at the very least such "inferior Officers" within the meaning of that Clause.[162]

Although two members of the Commission are initially selected by the President, his nominations are subject to confirmation not merely by the Senate, but by the House of Representatives as well. The remaining four voting members of the Commission are appointed by the President *pro tempore* of the Senate and by the Speaker of the House. While the second part of the Clause authorizes Congress to vest the appointment of the officers described in that part in "the Courts of Law, or in the Heads of Departments," neither the Speaker of the House nor the President *pro tempore* of the Senate comes within this language.

* * *

162. *"Officers of the United States"* does not include all employees of the United States, but there is no claim made that the Commissioners are employees of the United States rather than officers. Employees are lesser functionaries subordinate to officers of the United States, see *Auffmordt v. Hedden*, 137 U.S. 310, 327 (1890); *United States v. Germaine,* 99 U.S. 508 (1879), whereas the Commissioners, appointed for a statutory term, are not subject to the control or direction of any other executive, judicial, or legislative authority.

The Appointments Clause specifies the method of appointment only for "Officers of the United States" whose appointment is not "otherwise provided for" in the Constitution. But there is no provision of the Constitution remotely providing any alternative means for the selection of the members of the Commission or for anybody like them. Appellee Commission has argued, and the Court of Appeals agreed, that the Appointments Clause of Art. II should not be read to exclude the "inherent power of Congress" to appoint its own officers to perform functions necessary to that body as an institution. But there is no need to read the Appointments Clause contrary to its plain language in order to reach the result sought by the Court of Appeals. Article I, § 3, cl. 5, expressly authorizes the selection of the President *pro tempore* of the Senate, and § 2, cl. 5, of that Article provides for the selection of the Speaker of the House. Ranking nonmembers, such as the Clerk of the House of Representatives, are elected under the internal rules of each House and are designated by statute as "officers of the Congress." There is no occasion for us to decide whether any of these member officers are "Officers of the United States" whose "appointment" is otherwise provided for within the meaning of the Appointments Clause, since even if they were such officers their appointees would not be. Contrary to the fears expressed by the majority of the Court of Appeals, nothing in our holding with respect to Art. II, § 2, cl. 2, will deny to Congress "all power to appoint its own inferior officers to carry out appropriate legislative functions."

* * *

The trilogy of cases from this Court dealing with the constitutional authority of Congress to circumscribe the President's power to *remove* officers of the United States is entirely consistent with this conclusion. In *Myers v. United States*, the Court held that Congress could not by statute divest the President of the power to remove an officer in the Executive Branch whom he was initially authorized to appoint. In explaining its reasoning in that case, the Court said:

> "The vesting of the executive power in the President was essentially a grant of the power to execute the laws. But the President alone and unaided could not execute the laws. He must execute them by the assistance of subordinates. * * * As he is charged specifically to take care that they be faithfully executed, the reasonable implication, even in the absence of express words, was that as part of his executive power he should select those who were to act for him under his direction in the execution of the laws.

* * *

"Our conclusion on the merits, sustained by the arguments before stated, is that Article II grants to the President the executive power of the Government, i.e., the general administrative control of those executing the laws, including the power of appointment and removal of executive officers—a conclusion confirmed by his obligation to take care that the laws be faithfully executed. * * * "

In the later case of *Humphrey's Executor,* where it was held that Congress could circumscribe the President's power to remove members of independent regulatory agencies, the Court was careful to note that it was dealing with an agency intended to be independent of executive authority *"except in its selection."* 295 U.S., at 625 (emphasis in original). *Wiener v. United States,* 357 U.S. 349 (1958), which applied the holding in *Humphrey's Executor* to a member of the War Claims Commission, did not question in any respect that members of independent agencies are not independent of the Executive with respect to their appointments.

* * *

Thus, on the assumption that all of the powers granted in the statute may be exercised by an agency whose members *have been* appointed in accordance with the Appointments Clause, the ultimate question is which, if any, of those powers may be exercised by the present voting Commissioners, none of whom *was* appointed as provided by that Clause. * * *

Insofar as the powers confided in the Commission are essentially of an investigative and informative nature, falling in the same general category as those powers which Congress might delegate to one of its own committees, there can be no question that the Commission as presently constituted may exercise them. * * *

But when we go beyond this type of authority to the more substantial powers exercised by the Commission, we reach a different result. The Commission's enforcement power, exemplified by its discretionary power to seek judicial relief, is authority that cannot possibly be regarded as merely in aid of the legislative function of Congress. A lawsuit is the ultimate remedy for a breach of the law, and it is to the President, and not to the Congress, that the Constitution entrusts the responsibility to "take Care that the Laws be faithfully executed." Art. II, § 3.

* * *

* * * Such functions may be discharged only by persons who are "Officers of the United States" within the language of that section.

All aspects of the Act are brought within the Commission's broad administrative powers: rulemaking, advisory opinions, and determinations of eligibility for funds and even for federal elective office itself. These functions, exercised free from day-to-day supervision of either Congress or the Executive Branch, are more legislative and judicial in nature than are the Commission's enforcement powers, and are of kinds usually performed by independent regulatory agencies or by some department in the Executive Branch under the direction of an Act of Congress. Congress viewed these broad powers as essential to effective and impartial administration of the entire substantive framework of the Act. Yet each of these functions also represents the performance of a significant governmental duty exercised pursuant to a public law. While the President may not insist that such functions be delegated to an appointee of his removable at will, *Humphrey's Executor v. United States,* 295 U.S. **602**

(1935), none of them operates merely in aid of congressional authority to legislate or is sufficiently removed from the administration and enforcement of public law to allow it to be performed by the present Commission.   These administrative functions may therefore be exercised only by persons who are "Officers of the United States."

Notes

1. *Buckley's* basic message is clear enough.   Congress may appoint only officials (not "officers") who perform internal legislative functions.   But the line between internal and external can be elusive.   The Civil Rights Commission, which as we noted earlier was originally established "in the Executive branch," was held in *Hannah v. Larche*, 363 U.S. 420 (1960), to be exercising a purely legislative investigatory function and therefore to be bound to provide only those procedures (arguably none) demanded of *legislative* bodies by the Due Process Clause. Does that mean that the Commission's members could have been appointed by Congress?   On the various techniques that Congress has used or attempted to use to influence particular appointments and removals, see Fisher, *Congress and the Removal Power*, 10 Cong. & Pres. 63 (1983).

2. The elusive internal-external dichotomy may appear a bright line, however, compared to the other distinctions apparently made necessary by the Appointments Clause.   "Officers" presumably must be distinguished from "mere employees" and "inferior" from "superior" officers.   Nor are these distinctions trivial.   Criminal sanctions, pay, tenure and pension rights have repeatedly turned on the classification appropriate to a particular person or post.   But the decided cases offer little critical guidance.   Supreme Court interpretation has oscillated between bald assertion and tautological deduction.   See generally Burkoff, *Appointment and Removal under the Federal Constitution: The Impact of Buckley v. Valeo*, 22 Wayne L. Rev. 1335, 1338–59 (1976).   Moreover, *Buckley* makes power to act conditional upon the propriety of the mode of appointment chosen, without in any significant degree clarifying the criteria for assigning particular posts to the various possible categories of appointment.

3. Consider, for example, the office of "special prosecutor" (now sometimes "independent counsel") to investigate possible illegalities in the executive branch.   Where may the authority to appoint such an "officer" (and surely pursuant to *Buckley* a special prosecutor is an officer) be lodged?   Current legislation in effect vests appointment authority jointly in the Attorney General and a special court.   The Attorney General determines *when* an independent counsel should be appointed; the court determines whom to appoint.   28 U.S.C.A. § § 591–594.   Presumably this represents a congressional belief that the independent counsel is an "inferior" officer, not necessarily subject to presidential appointment.

But why involve the Attorney General?   Modern practice virtually assures that the Attorney General will be the President's close political ally.   If the Attorney General cannot be trusted to investigate and prosecute executive corruption, why can we expect more of the Attorney General when called upon to determine whether someone else should do so?   There seems no particularly good answer to this question other than that a delegation to the Attorney General seems to have worked once and it avoids the constitutional uncertainties of a delegation elsewhere.

In a delicate political compromise Attorney General Elliott Richardson created the office of Special Watergate Prosecutor and appointed Archibald Cox to it.   Richardson acted pursuant to a preexisting and very general delegation of authority "to prescribe regulations for the governance of his department," but the action was upheld, at least by a district court.   *Nader v. Bork*, 366 F. Supp. 104 (D.D.C. 1973).   Subsequently, of course, Cox was removed at the direction of President Nixon, an action subsequently declared to be illegal on the sole ground that the removal violated Richardson's regulation establishing the office. Id.

Obviously Congress would have preferred a less problematic position for the Special Prosecutor.   Indeed, most of the proposals for establishing a permanent, if only occasionally operational, office after the Cox affair contemplated appointment by someone in the judicial branch.   Yet this alternative was of doubtful constitutionality.   Although the Constitution says that Congress may delegate the appointment of inferior officers to heads of departments and the judiciary, an early Supreme Court decision stated that such appointive power was "no doubt intended to be exercised by the department of the government to which the officer to be appointed most appropriately belonged."   *Ex parte Hennen*, 38 U.S. (13 Pet.) 225, 258 (1839).   In short, the bare words of the appointments clause authorizing Congress to delegate are to be read within the context of separation of powers principles.

Those principles are hardly inflexible, however, as *Ex parte Siebold* made clear some forty years later.   At issue were appointments of election commissioners vested by statute in the courts of appeals.   While upholding the statute the Supreme Court said (100 U.S. (10 Otto) 371, 397–98 (1879)):

It is no doubt usual and proper to vest the appointment of inferior officers in that department of the government, executive or judicial, or in that particular executive department to which the duties of such officers appertain.   But there is no absolute requirement to this effect in the Constitution; and, if there were, it would be difficult in many cases to determine to which department an office properly belonged.   * * *

* * * [A]s the Constitution stands, the selection of the appointing power, as between the functionaries named, is a matter resting in the discretion of Congress.   And, looking at the subject in a practical light, it is perhaps better that it should rest there, than the country should be harassed by the endless controversies to which a more specific direction on this subject might have given rise.   The observation in the case of *Hennen*, to which reference is made, that the appointing power in the clause referred to "was no doubt intended to be exercised by the department of the government to which the official to be appointed most appropriately belonged," was not intended to define the constitutional power of Congress in this regard, but rather express the law or rule by which it should be governed.   * * * [T]he duty to appoint inferior officers, when required thereto by law, is a constitutional duty of the courts; and in the present case there is no such incongruity in the duty required as to excuse the courts from its performance, or to render their acts void.   It cannot be affirmed that the appointment of the officers in question could, with any greater propriety, and certainly not with equal regard to convenience, have been assigned to any other depositary of official power capable of exercising it.   Neither the President, nor any head of department, could have been equally competent to the task.

Siebold was the principal authority debated by the numerous law professors who testified concerning the constitutionality of vesting appointment of a "permanent" special prosecutor in the judiciary.   Most seemed convinced that a special prosecutor—particularly one to investigate the executive branch—was not so "inherently executive" as to preclude judicial appointment.   See generally *Hearings on Special Prosecutor Before the Senate Committee on the Judiciary,* 93d Cong., 1st Sess., Pts. 1 and 2 (1973).   Yet some viewed such a delegation as vesting the appointment of the "vital officers" of one branch in another and, therefore, as unconstitutional.   E.g., id. at 351 (testimony of Dean Cramton).

In the end Congress adopted an elaborate compromise that is described in *Banzhaf v. Smith,* 737 F.2d 1167 (D.C. Cir. 1984) *(en banc)*:

Enacting the Ethics in Government Act in 1978, Congress established a neutral procedure for resolving the conflict of interest that arises when the Attorney General must decide whether to pursue allegations of wrongdoing leveled against high ranking federal officers who will typically be the Attorney General's close political associates.   The Act provides that the Attorney General "shall" conduct a "preliminary investigation" upon receipt of "information that the Attorney General determines is sufficient to constitute grounds to investigate."   28 U.S.C. § 592(a)(1).   The Act also establishes a special division of the federal court, comprised of three judges, to whom the Attorney General reports.   If the Attorney General decides, after investigation, that there exist "reasonable grounds to believe that further investigation or prosecution is warranted," or if 90 days pass after receipt of information without the Attorney General's making any determination, then "the Attorney General shall apply to the division of the court for the appointment of a *[sic]* independent counsel."   Upon such application the division of the court appoints "appropriate independent counsel" and determines his or her "prosecutorial jurisdiction."   If, after investigation, the Attorney General concludes there are "no reasonable grounds to believe that further investigation or prosecution is warranted," the Attorney General must report this determination to the division of the court, "and the division of the court shall have no power to appoint a *[sic]* independent counsel."

The court then went on to hold that the Attorney General's decision not to seek an appointment was not judicially reviewable:

We find in the Ethics in Government Act a specific congressional intent to preclude judicial review, at the behest of members of the public, of the Attorney General's decisions not to investigate particular allegations and not to seek appointment of independent counsel.   The Act contains provisions that severely delimit judicial review of the Attorney General's actions.   The decision to request appointment of independent counsel "shall not be reviewable in any court."   28 U.S.C. § 592(f).   The decision *not* to request appointment of independent counsel is explicitly made unreviewable in the special division of the court created in the statute.   Id. § 592(b)(1).   Though congressional preclusion of some review does not in itself force the conclusion that Congress intended to preclude all review, neither does it compel the conclusion that Congress intended to permit review wherever it did not explicitly preclude review.   With respect to the Attorney General's decision not to request independent counsel, we find it difficult to accept that Congress would have explicitly precluded review in the special division of the court established to handle issues under the Act and yet intended to permit review of such decisions, at the behest of members of the public, in any federal District Court.

Inferences of intent drawn from the statutory scheme and its legislative history compel us to conclude that Congress did intend to preclude review. The Act makes no provision for members of the public to petition the Attorney General to act, and in terms provides for no review of refusals to act. In contrast, the statute explicitly gives Congress power to "request in writing that the Attorney General apply for a [*sic*] independent counsel," when that request comes from a majority of either majority of minority party members of the Senate or House Judiciary Committees. 28 U.S.C.A. § 595(e). And "[n]ot later than thirty days after the receipt of such a request, or not later than fifteen days after the completion of a preliminary investigation of the matter with respect to which the request is made, whichever is later, the Attorney General shall provide written notification of any action the Attorney General has taken in response to such request and, if no application has been made to the division of the court, why such application was not made." Id. See 124 Cong. Rec. 36,464 (1978) ("if [the Attorney General] does not respond to a situation that appears to be appropriate," members of the House Judiciary Committee can request independent counsel under 28 U.S.C.A. § 595(e), thereby bringing "the political process" into play) (remarks of Rep. Mann). The lack of any authorization for petitions by the public or review at the behest of members of the public, when viewed in the context of the limits on review built into the statute and the explicit provision of congressional oversight as a mechanism to keep the Attorney General to his statutory duty, strongly suggests that Congress intended no review at the behest of the public. This view is buttressed by other structural considerations. Congress explicitly sought to prevent premature airing of criminal charges that might prove on investigation to be unfounded. "In most cases" Congress anticipated that the Attorney General would conduct a preliminary investigation "without the public being aware that review is taking place." S. Rep. No. 95–170, 95th Cong., 2d Sess. 62–63 (1977). Permitting judicial review of the Attorney General's decisions not to investigate or request independent counsel would severely undermine this policy by airing charges preliminarily in the District Courts. Congress could not have intended such a result.

4. What do any of these cases suggest about the constitutional position of Civil Service employees who, by the millions, are appointed by persons not mentioned in the Appointments Clause and who, by statute, may be removed only for "such cause as will promote the efficiency of the service"? 5 U.S.C.A. § 7513(a). The answer is far from clear, but the question surely justifies a brief look at the historical development of the civil service system.

The Pendleton (or Civil Service) Act of 1883, 22 Stat. 403, now codified at 5 U.S.C.A. §§ 1101–1105, was an early victory for the Progressive Movement. It initiated the development of a complex framework of legal restrictions designed both to assure the competence and protect the integrity of executive branch officials and employees of the independent commissions. Conceived as a response to perceived abuses flowing from an historical pattern of politically-motivated presidential appointments to and dismissals from federal service (a practice which, while in evidence from the early years of the republic, had assumed new dimensions under the post-Jackson "spoils system"), this landmark legislation enshrined the basic principles of merit selection and relative security of tenure for subordinate government officials. The Act also created the U.S. Civil Service Commission, which for more than 80 years oversaw the employment practices of the federal civilian establishment.   The creation of the modern civil service was, however, an event of ambiguous constitutional portent; the Pendleton Act was passed in a highly charged political context and reflected an uneasy compromise with respect to control of public personnel administration that left basic issues of presidential and congressional authority largely unresolved.   For general historical background on the events leading up to the passage of the Pendleton Act, see S. SKOWRONEK, BUILDING A NEW AMERICAN STATE 47–68 (1982), and sources cited therein.   On the appointment and removal policies of presidents up to 1829, see D. ROSENBLOOM, FEDERAL SERVICE AND THE CONSTITUTION 19–46 (1971).

The relatively limited protection initially afforded subordinate government officials by the terms of the Pendleton Act is understandable when viewed in light of the apparently widespread contemporary concern that even the attempt (via introduction of the new merit system) to place limitations or conditions upon the President's appointment power amounted to a congressional intrusion upon executive authority.   When a late change in the original Act reduced the number of Civil Service Commissioners from five to three and made their appointment subject to the Senate's advice and consent, the thorny question of whether the new merit system was ultimately intended as an arm of the President or of the Congress—a question civil service reformers had studiously sought to avoid— was inevitably thrown into sharp relief.   The unprecedented designation of the CSC itself as a "semi-independent" agency within the federal establishment, charged on the one hand with aiding the President in preparing "suitable rules and regulations" for public personnel action and with the enforcement of those regulations against executive branch officials on the other, served only to highlight this fundamental ambiguity.

Indeed, although subsequently driven underground, constitutional doubts bearing on the CSC's role were never decisively laid to rest.   The theory that sustains the constitutionality of those civil service laws bearing on the selection process seems to be that while "the officer to whom the appointing power is given retains the discretion which it was intended he should exercise in making appointments, * * * as an aid to his exercise of that power, another body may be given the power to determine the qualifications necessary for the position under consideration."   Oliver Field, as quoted in P. VAN RIPER, HISTORY OF THE UNITED STATES CIVIL SERVICE 107 (1958).   In any event, owing much no doubt to these constitutional scruples, Congress determined not to go too far in making the provisions of the Pendleton Act mandatory upon the President.   The original Act placed only ten percent of the 140,000-odd positions in the federal public service under the merit system to form the classified civil service, the remaining "unclassified" positions to be brought under the new regime by Executive Order when and if the President saw fit.

The Pendleton Act's compromise on the power to remove reflected even greater solicitude for the basic principles laid down in the "decision of 1789."   Indeed, as one historian has noted, "That the removal power of the President was left largely untouched was the outstanding difference between pre-Civil War attempts at [civil service] reform and the Act of 1883."   Id. at 102.   To be sure, the reformers were no less concerned than previously to restrain abuses in the exercise of the removal power, but the constitutional crisis precipitated by the Tenure of Office Act of 1867 counselled, if nothing else did, against any further attempts to assert direct legislative control over presidential authority in this context.   Hence, while provisions prohibiting removals of classified civil servants for failure to contribute money or to render service for political purposes were eventually included in the Pendleton Act, principal emphasis was placed on the regulation of the selection process on the theory that to the extent that appointments were made on a merit basis, the temptation for improper removals would be correspondingly diminished.   As George William Curtiss, a leading reformer, once declared: "[W]e hold that it is better to take the risk of occasional injustice from passion or prejudice [in the exercise of the dismissal authority], which no law or regulation can control, then to seal up incompetence, negligence, insubordination, insolence, and every other mischief in the system, by requiring a virtual trial at law before an unfit or incapable clerk can be removed." Id. at 102.

Though the Pendleton Act was effective for a time in preventing widespread removals from merit positions—during the first sixteen months of the Cleveland administration, the turnover rate for the 5,000-odd classified positions stood at 6.5%, as against 68% for unclassified positions and 90% for "presidential offices" (i.e. those whose appointments were subject to the Senate's advice and consent)—events were soon to disclose the limitations of the original system in preventing arbitrary dismissals.   While the CSC had been directed to prepare rules to implement the various prohibitions against the political manipulation and/or removal of competitive employees, the failure of the Act to attach criminal penalties for their violation (with the exception of the provisions prohibiting political assessments), and the fact that prosecution of the offenders was left to the discretion of the chief executive, left the Commission all but powerless with respect to enforcement.   By the mid-1890s, as evidence accumulated that neither purely arbitrary removals nor dismissals on the basis of an individual civil servant's political and religious opinions or affiliations had really been stymied, reform leader Carl Schurz and others disowned their initial "sanguine expectation" that the abusive practices of the past would cease with the introduction of the competitive system.   D. ROSENBLOOM, supra, at 88.   Calls for corrective action, specifically for the introduction of procedural safeguards, were issued with increasing regularity.

These calls were first answered when, on July 27, 1897, President McKinley provided by executive order that "no removal shall be made from any position subject to competitive examination except for just cause and upon written charges filed with the head of the Department, or other appointing officer, and of which the accused shall have full notice and an opportunity to make a defense."   18 CSC Annual Report 282 (1901).   This rule went through several modifications in the years that followed, but in essence, it was incorporated into law by the Lloyd-LaFollette Act of August 24, 1912 (37 Stat. 555), at which time the current locution, "except for such cause as will promote the efficiency of the service" was adopted.   ("Efficiency of the service," while somewhat vague, was a meaningful standard because there was a provision for rating efficiency.   See 37 Stat. 413 (August 23, 1912).)

Beginning with the administration of President Theodore Roosevelt (himself a former Civil Service Commissioner), the substantive supervisory authority of the Commission in dealing with merit employees was fortified by a series of executive orders, and steps were taken to ensure that the CSC would have adequate institutional resources to enforce a host of new rules (especially those having to do with "neutrality") regulating the nonpartisan realm of the civil service.   The efforts of Presidents Roosevelt and Taft to build a strong, stable, and professional arm of civil administration under executive control nevertheless provoked considerable controversy; for the adoption of the Lloyd-LaFollette Act had been prompted by Congress' desire to assert its role "as an equal and alternative ear for all administrative interests." On the political struggles in this context during the period 1900–1920, see SKOWRONEK, supra, at 177–211.

The nonpartisan realm of the civil service was greatly expanded, albeit in halting and uneven fashion, by executive order as Presidents exercised the discretionary authority granted them under the Pendleton Act. By 1920, over 70 percent of the executive civil service (then totalling roughly 560,000) was under the merit system. Id. at 210. Since 1947, by which time the civil service numbered some two million, the figure has been over 80 percent. ROSENBLOOM, supra, at 83. The removal provisions of the Lloyd-LaFollette Act remained in effect throughout this period, and the protections accorded classified individuals against arbitrary dismissal were augmented by additional procedural safeguards, including rights to a hearing and representation and occasionally to cross-examination as well. Id. at 83. These provisions were enforced through an elaborate system operated by the CSC for adjudicating disciplinary actions against civil servants who had completed probationary service. See, e.g., Merrill, *Procedures for Adverse Action Against Federal Employees*, 59 Va. L. Rev. 196 (1973).

If by mid-century the principle of protection against arbitrary removal for classified civil servants was firmly in place, traditional concerns about political manipulation of the civil service as a whole had by no means been laid to rest. The basic issues of presidential and congressional authority for public personnel administration which were left unsettled by the Pendleton Act had never been resolved. In the midst of continuing debate about what central authority, if any, should govern the system as a whole and over how responsibility for protecting it from political partisanship should be organized, the civil service remained "a precarious idea in an ambiguous organizational structure." H. HECLO, A GOVERNMENT OF STRANGERS, 23 (1977).

After four decades of truncated efforts at reform, far-reaching changes in the apparatus inherited from the nineteenth century were introduced in 1978, when President Carter persuaded Congress to enact the Civil Service Reform Act, Pub. L. No. 95–454, 92 Stat. 1111. The 1978 Act incorporated many of the suggestions that had been bandied about for years, including a proposal to divide the CSC into two units, a presidential agency to oversee civil service policies, the Office of Personnel Management, 5 U.S.C.A. § § 1101–1105, and a separate unit to police the civil service rules, the independent Merit Systems Protection Board, 5 U.S.C.A. § § 1201–1205.

More important for present purposes, the Civil Service Reform Act had some direct implications for the removal issue. One of the law's chief objectives, in fact, was to make it easier for dedicated managers to remove employees who performed poorly. Under the new ground rules, an agency need sustain an employee's removal for incompetence only by "substantial evidence," rather than a preponderance. 5 U.S.C.A. § 7701(c)(1). However, while the legislation generally strengthened the hand of government managers, it also afforded, as had the Ethics in Government Act, Pub. L. No. 95–521, 92 Stat. 1824 (1978) (codified at 5 U.S.C.A. App. § § 401–405), of the same year special protection for civil servants who report improprieties by their supervisors or agencies—"whistleblowers" in the Washington vernacular. 5 U.S.C.A. § 2301(b)(9). The Act's broad language prohibits a supervisor from taking, or failing to take, personnel action, i.e., disciplining or failing to reward, against an employee who discloses—to the press, Congress, or others—unclassified information which the employee "reasonably believes evidence a violation of law, rule, or regulation or mismanagement, a gross waste of funds, an abuse of authority, or a substantial and specific danger to public health and safety. * * * " For a sympathetic analysis of this legislation, see Vaughn, *Statutory Protection of Whistleblowers in the Federal Executive Branch*, 1982 U. Ill. L. Rev. 615.

B. EXECUTIVE DIRECTION OF AGENCY POLICY

Musing in the oval office on the difficulties of presidential leadership in a large and fragmented bureaucracy, President Truman is reported to have said, shortly before the Eisenhower inauguration, "Poor Ike. He'll sit here and say, 'Do this. Do that.', and nothing will happen." Although every President is perceived to possess enormous power, perhaps each sometimes also feels powerless—and is, as Truman himself discovered in *Youngstown Sheet and Tube Co. v. Sawyer*, 343 U.S. 579 (1952).

YOUNGSTOWN SHEET & TUBE CO. v. SAWYER

Supreme Court of the United States, 1952.
343 U.S. 579, 72 S.Ct. 863, 96 L.Ed. 1153

MR. JUSTICE BLACK delivered the opinion of the Court.

We are asked to decide whether the President was acting within his constitutional power when he issued an order directing the Secretary of Commerce to take possession of and operate most of the Nation's steel mills. The mill owners argue that the President's order amounts to lawmaking, a legislative function which the Constitution has expressly confided to the Congress and not to the President. The Government's position is that the order was made on findings of the President that his action was necessary to avert a national catastrophe which would inevitably result from a stoppage of steel production, and that in meeting this grave emergency the President was acting within the aggregate of his constitutional powers as the Nation's Chief Executive and the Commander in Chief of the Armed Forces of the United States. The issue emerges here from the following series of events:

In the latter part of 1951 [during the Korean War], a dispute arose between the steel companies and their employees over terms and conditions that should be included in new collective bargaining agreements. [Efforts to settle the dispute—including reference to the Federal Wage Stabilization Board—failed.] On April 4, 1952, the Union gave notice of a nation-wide strike called to begin at 12:01 A.M. April 9. The indispensability of steel as a component of substantially all weapons and other war materials led the President to believe that the proposed work stoppage would immediately jeopardize our national defense and that governmental seizure of the steel mills was necessary in order to assure the continued availability of steel.   Reciting these considerations for his action, the President, a few hours before the strike was to begin, issued Executive Order 10340 [directing] the Secretary of Commerce to take possession of most of the steel mills and keep them running.   The Secretary immediately issued his own possessory orders, calling upon the presidents of the various seized companies to serve as operating managers for the United States. * * * The next morning the President sent a message to Congress reporting his action. * * * Congress has taken no action.

Obeying the Secretary's orders under protest, the companies brought proceedings against him in the District Court, * * * [which] on April 30 issued a preliminary injunction restraining the Secretary from "continuing the seizure and possession of the plants * * * and from acting under *Procedure* the purported authority of Executive Order No. 10340."   On the same day the Court of Appeals stayed the District Court's injunction.   Deeming it best that the issues raised be promptly decided by this Court, we granted certiorari on May 3 and set the cause for argument on May 12. * * *

The President's power, if any, to issue the order must stem either from an act of Congress or from the Constitution itself.   There is no statute that expressly authorizes the President to take possession of property as he did here.   Nor is there any act of Congress to which our attention has been directed from which such a power can fairly be implied. * * * There are two statutes which do authorize the President to take both personal and real property under certain conditions.   [The Selective Service Act of 1948 and the Defense Production Act of 1950].   However, the Government admits that these conditions were not met and that the President's order was not rooted in either of the statutes.   The Government refers to the seizure provisions of one of these statutes [the 1950 Act] as "much too cumbersome, involved, and time-consuming for the crisis which was at hand."

Moreover, the use of the seizure technique to solve labor disputes in order to prevent work stoppages was not only unauthorized by any congressional enactment; prior to this controversy, Congress had refused to adopt that method of settling labor disputes.   When the Taft-Hartley Act was under consideration in 1947, Congress rejected an amendment which would have authorized such governmental seizures in cases of emergency. * * * Instead, the plan sought to bring about settlements by use of the customary devices of mediation, conciliation, investigation by boards of inquiry, and public reports.   In some instances temporary injunctions were authorized to provide cooling-off periods.   All this failing, unions were left free to strike * * * .

It is clear that if the President had authority to issue the order he did, it must be found in some provision of the Constitution.   And it is not claimed that express constitutional language grants this power to the President. The contention is that presidential power should be implied from the aggregate of his powers under the Constitution.   Particular reliance is placed on provisions in Article II which say that "The executive

Power shall be vested in a President * * * ;" that "he shall take Care that the Laws be faithfully executed"; and that he "shall be Commander in Chief of the Army and Navy of the United States."

The order cannot properly be sustained as an exercise of the President's military power as Commander in Chief of the Armed Forces. The Government attempts to do so by citing a number of cases upholding broad powers in military commanders engaged in day-to-day fighting in a theater of war. Such cases need not concern us here. Even though "theater of war" be an expanding concept, we cannot with faithfulness to our constitutional system hold that the Commander in Chief of the Armed Forces has the ultimate power as such to take possession of private property in order to keep labor disputes from stopping production. This is a job for the Nation's lawmakers, not for its military authorities.

Nor can the seizure order be sustained because of the several constitutional provisions that grant executive power to the President. In the framework of our Constitution, the President's power to see that the laws are faithfully executed refutes the idea that he is to be a lawmaker. The Constitution limits his functions in the law making process to the recommending of laws he thinks wise and the vetoing of laws he thinks bad. * * *

The President's order does not direct that a congressional policy be executed in a manner prescribed by Congress—it directs that a presidential policy be executed in a manner prescribed by the President. The preamble of the order itself, like that of many statutes, sets out reasons why the President believes certain policies should be adopted, proclaims these policies as rules of conduct to be followed, and again, like a statute, authorizes a government official to promulgate additional rules and regulations consistent with the policy proclaimed and needed to carry that policy into execution. The power of Congress to adopt such public policies as those proclaimed by the order is beyond question. It can authorize the taking of private property for public use. It can make laws regulating the relationships between employers and employees, prescribing rules designed to settle labor disputes, and fixing wages and working conditions in certain fields of our economy. The Constitution does not subject this lawmaking power of Congress to presidential or military supervision or control.

It is said that other Presidents without congressional authority have taken possession of private business enterprises in order to settle labor disputes. But even if this is true, Congress has not thereby lost its exclusive constitutional authority to make laws necessary and proper to carry out the powers vested by the Constitution "in the Government of the United States, or any Department or Officer thereof."

The Founders of this Nation entrusted the lawmaking power to the Congress alone in both good and bad times. It would do no good to recall the historical events, the fears of power and the hopes for freedom that lay behind their choice. Such a review would but confirm our holding that this seizure order cannot stand. * * *

Affirmed.*

MR. JUSTICE JACKSON, concurring in the judgment and opinion of the Court.

* * *

A judge, like an executive adviser, may be surprised at the poverty of really useful and unambiguous authority applicable to concrete problems of executive power as they actually present themselves.   Just what our forefathers did envision, or would have envisioned had they foreseen modern conditions, must be divined from materials almost as enigmatic as the dreams Joseph was called upon to interpret for Pharoh.   A century and a half of partisan debate and scholarly speculation yields no net result but only supplies more or less apt quotations from respected sources on each side of any question.   They largely cancel each other. And court decisions are indecisive because of the judicial practice of dealing with the largest questions in the most narrow way.

The actual art of governing under our Constitution does not and cannot conform to judicial definitions of the power of any of its branches based on isolated clauses or even single Articles torn from context. While the Constitution diffuses power the better to secure liberty, it also contemplates that practice will integrate the dispersed powers into a workable government.   It enjoins upon its branches separateness but interdependence, autonomy but reciprocity.   Presidential powers are not fixed but fluctuate, depending upon their disjunction or conjunction with those of Congress.   We may well begin by a somewhat oversimplified grouping of practical situations in which a President may doubt, or others may challenge, his powers, and by distinguishing roughly the legal consequences of this factor of relativity.

1. When the President acts pursuant to an express or implied authorization of Congress, his authority is at its maximum, for it includes all that he possesses in his own right plus all that Congress can delegate.   * * *   A seizure executed by the President pursuant to an Act of Congress would be supported by the strongest of presumptions and the widest latitude of judicial interpretation, and the burden of persuasion would rest heavily upon any who might attack it.

2. When the President acts in absence of either a congressional grant or denial of authority, he can only rely upon his own independent powers, but there is a zone of twilight in which he and Congress may have concurrent authority, or in which its distribution is uncertain.   Therefore, congressional inertia, indifference or quiescence may sometimes, at least as a practical matter, enable, if not invite, measures on independent presidential responsibility.   In this area, any actual test of power is likely to de-

* [The decision was 6 to 3.   Although all but one of the concurring Justices—Justice Clark—joined the opinion as well as the judgment announced by Justice Black, each also wrote a separate concurring opinion.   Only the most celebrated of those, Justice Jackson's is included here.   Eds.]

pend on the imperatives of events and contemporary imponderables rather than on abstract theories of law.

3. When the President takes measures incompatible with the expressed or implied will of Congress, his power is at its lowest ebb, for then he can rely only upon his own constitutional powers minus any constitutional powers of Congress over the matter. Courts can sustain exclusive presidential control in such a case only by disabling the Congress from acting upon the subject. Presidential claim to a power at once so conclusive and preclusive must be scrutinized with caution, for what is at stake is the equilibrium established by our constitutional system.

Into which of these classifications does this executive seizure of the steel industry fit? It is eliminated from the first by admission, for it is conceded that no congressional authorization exists for this seizure. * * * Can it then be defended under flexible tests available to the second category? It seems clearly eliminated from that class because Congress has not left seizure of private property an open field but has covered it by three statutory policies inconsistent with this seizure.

This leaves the current seizure to be justified only by the severe tests under the third grouping, where it can be supported only by any remainder of executive power after subtraction of such powers as Congress may have over the subject. In short, we can sustain the President only by holding that seizure of such strike-bound industries is within his domain and beyond control by Congress. * * *

The Solicitor General seeks the power of seizure in three clauses of the Executive Article, the first reading, "The executive Power shall be vested in a President of the United States of America." * * *

* * * I cannot accept the view that this clause is a grant in bulk of all conceivable executive power but regard it as an allocation to the presidential office of the generic powers thereafter stated.

The clause on which the Government next relies is that "The President shall be Commander in Chief of the Army and Navy of the United States." * * * [T]his loose appellation is sometimes advanced as support for any presidential action, internal or external, involving use of force, the idea being that it vests power to do anything, anywhere, that can be done with an army or navy.

That seems to be the logic of an argument tendered at our bar—that the President having, on his own responsibility, sent American troops abroad derives from that act "affirmative power" to seize the means of producing a supply of steel for them. * * *

* * * [N]o doctrine that the Court could promulgate would seem to me more sinister and alarming than that a President whose conduct of foreign affairs is so largely uncontrolled, and often even is unknown, can vastly enlarge his mastery over the internal affairs of the country by his own commitment of the Nation's armed forces to some foreign venture. I do not, however, find it necessary or appropriate to consider the legal status of the Korean enterprise to discountenance argument based on it. * * *

* * * The Constitution expressly places in Congress power "to raise and *support* Armies" and "to *provide* and *maintain* a Navy." (Emphasis supplied.) This certainly lays upon Congress primary responsibility for supplying the armed forces. Congress alone controls the raising of revenues and their appropriation and may determine in what manner and by what means they shall be spent for military and naval procurement. I suppose no one would doubt that Congress can take over war supply as a Government enterprise. * * *

That military powers of the Commander in Chief were not to supersede representative government of internal affairs seems obvious from the Constitution and from elementary American history.

We should not use this occasion to circumscribe, much less to contract, the lawful role of the President as Commander in Chief. I should indulge the widest latitude of interpretation to sustain his exclusive function to command the instruments of national force, at least when turned against the outside world for the security of our society. But, when it is turned inward, not because of rebellion but because of a lawful economic struggle between industry and labor, it should have no such indulgence. * * *

The third clause in which the Solicitor General finds seizure powers is that "he shall take Care that the Laws be faithfully executed." That authority must be matched against [the due process clause of the Fifth Amendment]. One gives a governmental authority that reaches so far as there is law, the other gives a private right that authority shall go no farther. These signify about all there is of the principle that ours is a government of laws, not of men, and that we submit ourselves to rulers only if under rules.

The Solicitor General lastly grounds support of the seizure upon nebulous, inherent powers never expressly granted but said to have accrued to the office from the customs and claims of preceding administrations. The plea is for a resulting power to deal with a crisis or an emergency according to the necessities of the case, the unarticulated assumption being that necessity knows no law.

Loose and irresponsible use of adjectives colors all nonlegal and much legal discussion of presidential powers. "Inherent" powers, "implied" powers, "incidental" powers, "plenary" powers, "war" powers and "emergency" powers are used, often interchangeably and without fixed or ascertainable meanings.

The vagueness and generality of the clauses that set forth presidential powers afford a plausible basis for pressures within and without an administration for presidential action beyond that supported by those whose responsibility it is to defend his actions in court. The claim of inherent and unrestricted presidential powers has long been a persuasive dialectical weapon in political controversy. While it is not surprising that counsel should grasp support from such unadjudicated claims of power, a judge cannot accept self-serving press statements of the attorney for one of the interested parties as authority in answering a constitutional question, even if the advocate was himself.* But prudence has coun-

---

*[Justice Jackson, named to the Court by President Franklin D. Roosevelt, was the At- torney General when he was nominated. Eds.]

seled that actual reliance on such nebulous claims stop short of provoking a judicial test. * * *

* * *

In view of the ease, expedition and safety with which Congress can grant and has granted large emergency powers, certainly ample to embrace this crisis, I am quite unimpressed with the argument that we should affirm possession of them without statute. * * *

MR. CHIEF JUSTICE VINSON, with whom MR. JUSTICE REED and MR. JUSTICE MINTON join, dissenting.

* * *

One is not here called upon even to consider the possibility of executive seizure of a farm, a corner grocery store or even a single industrial plant. Such considerations arise only when one ignores the central fact of this case—that the Nation's entire basic steel production would have shut down completely if there had been no Government seizure. * * *

* * * [I]f the President has any power under the Constitution to meet a critical situation in the absence of express statutory authorization, there is no basis whatever for criticizing the exercise of such power in this case. * * *

* * * [W]e are not called upon today to expand the Constitution to meet a new situation. For, in this case, we need only look to history and time-honored principles of constitutional law—principles that have been applied consistently by all branches of the Government throughout our history. It is those who assert the invalidity of the Executive Order who seek to amend the Constitution in this case.

A review of executive action demonstrates that our Presidents have on many occasions exhibited the leadership contemplated by the Framers when they made the President Commander in Chief, and imposed upon him the trust to "take Care that the Laws be faithfully executed." With or without explicit statutory authorization, Presidents have at such times dealt with national emergencies by acting promptly and resolutely to enforce legislative programs, at least to save those programs until Congress could act. Congress and the courts have responded to such executive initiative with consistent approval. [Chief Justice Vinson undertook a lengthy examination of historical episodes from George Washington to Franklin D. Roosevelt, including:]

Beginning with the Bank Holiday Proclamation and continuing through World War II, executive leadership and initiative were characteristic of President Franklin D. Roosevelt's administration. * * *

* * * [S]ix months before Pearl Harbor, a dispute at a single aviation plant at Inglewood, California, interrupted a segment of the production of military aircraft. * * * President Roosevelt ordered the seizure of the plant "pursuant to the powers vested in [him] by the Constitution and laws of the United States, as President of the United States of America and Commander in Chief of the Army and Navy of the United States." The Attorney General (Jackson) vigorously proclaimed that the Presi-

dent had the moral duty to keep this Nation's defense effort a "going concern." * * *

[Before and after Pearl Harbor], industrial concerns were seized to avert interruption of needed production. During the same period, the President directed seizure of the Nation's coal mines to remove an obstruction to the effective prosecution of the war. * * *

At the time of the seizure of the coal mines [a] bill to provide a statutory basis for seizures [was] before Congress. As stated by its sponsor, the purpose of the bill was not to augment Presidential power, but to "let the country know that the Congress is squarely behind the President. * * *

This is but a cursory summary of executive leadership. But it amply demonstrates that Presidents have taken prompt action to enforce the laws and protect the country whether or not Congress happened to provide in advance for the particular method of execution. * * * [T]he fact that Congress and the courts have consistently recognized and given their support to such executive action indicates that such a power of seizure has been accepted throughout our history. * * *

Much of the argument in this case has been directed at straw men. We do not now have before us the case of a President acting solely on the basis of his own notions of the public welfare. Nor is there any question of unlimited executive power in this case. The President himself closed the door to any such claim when he sent his Message to Congress stating his purpose to abide by any action of Congress, whether approving or disapproving his seizure action. Here, the President immediately made sure that Congress was fully informed of the temporary action he had taken only to preserve the legislative programs from destruction until Congress could act.

The absence of a specific statute authorizing seizure of the steel mills as a mode of executing the laws—both the military procurement program and the anti-inflation program—has not until today been thought to prevent the President from executing the laws. * * *

* * * [T]here is no statute prohibiting the action taken by the President in a matter not merely important but threatening the very safety of the Nation. Executive inaction in such a situation, courting national disaster, is foreign to the concept of energy and initiative in the Executive as created by the Founding Fathers.

The broad executive power granted by Article II to an officer on duty 365 days a year cannot, it is said, be invoked to avert disaster. Instead, the President must confine himself to sending a message to Congress recommending action. Under this messenger-boy concept of the Office, the President cannot even act to preserve legislative programs from destruction so that Congress will have something left to act upon. * * *

Notes

1. Assertions of "emergency" powers having domestic legal consequences but implicating issues of war and peace or foreign affairs comprise a large cate-

gory of problematic presidential action. For example, President Lincoln's Emancipation Proclamation, January 1, 1863, 12 Stat. 1268, states:

BY THE PRESIDENT OF THE UNITED STATES OF AMERICA
A Proclamation

Whereas, on the twenty-second day of September, A.D. 1862, a proclamation was issued by the President of the United States, containing, among other things, the following, to wit:

"That on the first day of January, A.D. 1863, all persons held as slaves within any state or designated part of a state the people whereof shall then be in rebellion against the United States, shall be then, thenceforward, and forever, free; and the Executive Government of the United States, including the military and naval authority thereof, will recognize and maintain freedom of such persons, and will do no act or acts to repress such persons, or any of them, in any efforts they may make for their actual freedom.

"That the Executive will, on the first day of January aforesaid, by proclamation, designate the states and parts of states, if any, in which the people thereof, respectively, shall then be in rebellion against the United States * * *

Now, therefore I, ABRAHAM LINCOLN, President of the United States, by virtue of the power in me vested as commander-in-chief of the army and navy of the United States in time of actual armed rebellion against the authority and Government of the United States, and as a fit and necessary war measure for suppressing said rebellion, do, on this first day of January, A.D. 1863, and in accordance with my purpose so to do, publicly proclaimed for the full period of one hundred days from the day first above mentioned, order and designate as the states and parts of states wherein the people thereof, respectively, are this day in rebellion against the United States, the following. * * *

And by virtue of the power and for the purpose aforesaid, I do order and declare that all persons held as slaves within said designated states and parts of states are, and henceforward shall be, free; and that the Executive Government of the United States, including the military and naval authorities thereof, will recognize and maintain the freedom of said persons.

And I hereby enjoin upon the people so declared to be free to abstain from all violence, unless in necessary self-defense; and I recommend to them that, in all cases when allowed, they labor faithfully for reasonable wages.

And I further declare and make known that such persons, of suitable condition, will be received into the armed service of the United States to garrison forts, positions, stations, and other places, and to man vessels of all sorts in said service.

And upon this act, sincerely believed to be an act of justice, warranted by the Constitution upon military necessity, I invoke the considerate judgment of mankind and the gracious favor of Almighty God.

2. The use of executive orders by American presidents long predates Lincoln's presidency. The power to insure that the laws are faithfully executed necessarily implies the power to issue instructions to executive officers, although ob-

viously, as the *Youngstown* case demonstrates, not a power to direct department heads to disregard statutes.   See *Kendall v. United States ex rel. Stokes*, 37 U.S. (12 Pet.) 524 (1839). And, as Jefferson's order to Secretary of State Madison to withhold delivery of Marbury's judicial commission illustrates, the use of executive orders has often been controversial.

Yet however ancient their lineage, there is no clear definition of what constitutes an executive order, nor a well-settled jurisprudence governing the extent of the president's power to act in this fashion.   Executive Order No. 10006, which establishes procedures for the issuance of executive orders, does not define the term.   Executive orders were not numbered until 1907 when the Department of State, in order to organize its files of presidential documents, began to give numbers to those that it could locate.   Executive Order No. 1 was assigned to President Lincoln's order of October 20, 1862.   Executive orders were then numbered chronologically from that date, although some were later discovered and had to be inserted out of order.   Various estimates put the total of unnumbered executive orders at between fifteen and twenty thousand.

The Federal Register Act contributed to regularity by requiring that all official executive documents including "any presidential proclamation or executive order and any order * * * issued * * * by a federal agency" be published in the Federal Register.   That statute also defined "federal agency" in a way that included the President of the United States.   In Executive Order No. 7,298 President Roosevelt, in 1936, first established a procedure for the issuance of executive orders and proclamations.   The basic procedure remains unchanged. Proposed executive orders are first submitted to and analyzed by the Office of Management and Budget.   They may originate with any federal agency.   If, after analysis, OMB approves an executive order, it is then submitted to the Department of Justice (Assistant Attorney General, Office of Legal Counsel) for consideration both as to its form and its legality.   If the order clears these two hurdles, and is signed by the President, it is then published in the Federal Register.

Over the years executive orders have had an enormous range of uses.   Most have been documents that can fairly be described as "internal" to the federal executive establishment.   They are directions to the whole or a part of the bureaucracy concerning the organization and conduct of their business.   Many concern personnel and budgetary matters and the use of public lands.

Yet from the beginning executive orders have used language suggesting effects on private parties.   George Washington, for example, issued a "proclamation" in 1793 for the purpose "of preventing interference of the citizens of the United States in the war between France and Great Britain.   "C. THOMAS, AMERICAN NEUTRALITY IN 1793, 26 (1931).   That proclamation enjoined United States citizens "from all acts and proceedings whatsoever, which * * * tend to contravene such disposition * * * [of] a conduct friendly and impartial toward the beligerant powers. * * * * "   Id.   The proclamation indicated that the sanction for failure to abide by its terms was prosecution.   Since Congress passed the first Neutrality Act in the following year, the president's power to issue a binding declaration of neutrality was never tested.   Washington's proclamation nevertheless precipitated a dispute between Hamilton and Madison in the press, with Hamilton supporting its constitutionality and Madison opposing.   See E. CORWIN, THE PRESIDENT, OFFICE AND POWERS 179 (4th Ed. 1957).

Executive orders have often been used in wartime to create necessary public agencies.   During World War I, for example, the War Trade Board, the Committee For Public Information, the Food Administration and the Grain Corporation were all established by Executive Order.   As might be imagined, Franklin Roosevelt used the device extensively during the 1930's.   In the three years 1933, 1934, and 1935, Roosevelt issued nearly fifteen hundred executive orders.   By contrast in the years 1953–56 there were a mere two hundred fifty executive orders issued.   (Perhaps interest in the executive order form was dampened by President Truman's experience in the *Youngstown Sheet & Tube* case.)

It seems clear, however, that the executive order has been used in the last few decades in circumstances where legislation would certainly have been equally appropriate.   In 1953, for example, President Truman ordered the heads of all federal contracting agencies to incorporate, and enforce, nondiscrimination clauses in all govenment contracts.   Executive Order No. 10,479, 18 Fed. Reg. 4899 (1953).   And President Kennedy issued a far-reaching executive order on non-discrimination in housing in 1962.   Executive Order No. 11,063, 27 Fed. Reg. 11527 (1962).   Subsequent presidents have revised the non-discrimination requirements from time to time, for example, to extend discrimination prohibitions to sexual discrimination.   Executive Order No. 11,375, 32 Fed. Reg. 14303 (1967).

As we noted in Chapter 1 the executive order has also been used as a device to institute wage and price controls through the government's power of procurement and its use of publicity.   And most recently, and controversially, President Carter used executive orders to implement his agreement with the government of Iran for the release of American hostages.   These orders appear as Executive Orders Nos. 12, 276–12, 285, 46 Fed. Reg. 7913–7932 (1981).

The provisions of the Carter executive orders that suspended all claims against the government of Iran then pending in United States' courts were tested and upheld in *Dames & Moore v. Regan*, 453 U.S. 654 (1981).   The Court's approach in *Dames & Moore* provides an interesting contrast with *Youngstown Sheet & Tube*.   The *Dames & Moore* majority in essence accepted the methodological premises of the *Youngstown* dissent.   After reviewing all of the statutes surrounding the president's power to negotiate and make agreements concerning the treatment of American nationals by foreign powers, the Court reluctantly concluded that none of the statutes provided precisely the power that President Carter had exercised in his claims suspension order.   It nevertheless found a long history of congressional acquiescence in the presidential settlement of disputes involving foreign claims.   And in the final analysis, it was this historic practice that legitimated the Carter executive order.   Nor is *Dames & Moore* the first case to uphold an exercise of executive power, expressed through an executive order and without statutory basis, on a finding of congressional acquiescence.   See *United States v. Midwest Oil Co.*, 236 U.S. 459 (1915).

Although, as *Dames & Moore* illustrates, executive orders clearly may affect private rights, courts are reluctant to find that an executive order "confers" a private right of action.   See, e.g. , *Manhattan-Bronx Postal Union v. Gronouski*, 350 F.2d 451 (D.C. Cir. 1965), *cert. denied* 382 U.S. 978 (1966), and *Stevens v. Carey*, 483 F. 2d 188 (7th Cir. 1973).   The jurisprudence is in fact rather confused in this area, sometimes declining to find a right of action because the executive order is not "intended" to provide such rights, sometimes suggesting that the order represents a policy or project which is "personal" to the president, and occasionally finding that executive orders without statutory basis are insufficient to confer federal court subject matter jurisdiction.

On the subject of executive orders generally, see Raven-Hansen, *Making Agencies Follow Orders: Judicial Review of Agency Violation of Executive Order 12, 291*, 1983 Duke L.J. 285; Note, *Presidential Power: Use and Enforcement of Executive Orders*, 39 Notre Dame Law. 44 (1963); House Committee on Government Operations, 85 Cong., 1st Sess., *Executive Orders and Proclamations: A Study of a Use of Presidential Powers* (Comm. Print 1957).

EXECUTIVE ORDER 12,291

46 Fed. Reg. 13193 (February 17, 1981)

Federal Regulation

By the authority vested in me as President by the Constitution and laws of the United States of America and in order to reduce the burdens of existing and future regulations, increase agency accountability for regulatory actions, provide for presidential oversight of the regulatory process, minimize duplication and conflict of regulations, and insure well-reasoned regulations, it is hereby ordered as follows:

Section 1. Definitions
For the purposes of this Order:

(a) "Regulation" or "rule" means an agency statement of general applicability and future effect designed to implement, interpret, or prescribe law or policy or describing the procedure or practice requirements of an agency, but does not include:

(1) Administrative actions governed by the provisions of Sections 556 and 557 of Title 5 of the United States Code;

(2) Regulations issued with respect to a military or foreign affairs function of the United States; or

(3) Regulations related to agency organization, management, or personnel.

(b) "Major rule" means any regulation that is likely to result in:

(1) An annual effect on the economy of $100 million or more;

(2) A major increase in costs or prices for consumers, individual industries, Federal, State, or local government agencies, or geographic regions; or

(3) Significant adverse effects on competition, employment, investment, productivity, innovation, or on the ability of United States-based enterprises to compete with foreign-based enterprises in domestic or export markets.

(c) "Director" means the Director of the Office of Management and Budget.

(d) "Agency" means any authority of the United States that is an "agency" under 44 U.S.C. 3502(1), excluding those agencies specified in 44 U.S.C. 3502(10). * * *

Section 2. General Requirements

In promulgating new regulations, reviewing existing regulations, and developing legislative proposals concerning regulation, all agencies, to the extent permitted by law, shall adhere to the following requirements:

(a) Administrative decisions shall be based on adequate information concerning the need for and consequences of proposed government action;

(b) Regulatory action shall not be undertaken unless the potential benefits to society for the regulation outweigh the potential costs to society;

(c) Regulatory objectives shall be chosen to maximize the net benefits to society;

(d) Among alternative approaches to any given regulatory objective, the alternative involving the least net cost to society shall be chosen; and

(e) Agencies shall set regulatory priorities with the aim of maximizing the aggregate net benefits to society, taking into account the condition of the particular industries affected by regulations, the condition of the national economy, and other regulatory actions contemplated for the future.

Section 3. Regulatory Impact Analysis and Review

(a) In order to implement Section 2 of this Order, each agency shall, in connection with every major rule, prepare, and to the extent permitted by law consider, a Regulatory Impact Analysis. * * *

(c) Except as provided in Section 8 of this Order, agencies shall prepare Regulatory Impact Analyses of major rules and transmit them, along with all notices of proposed rulemaking and all final rules, to the Director. * * *

(d) To permit each proposed major rule to be analyzed in light of the requirements stated in Section 2 of this Order, each preliminary and final Regulatory Impact Analysis shall contain the following information:

(1) A description of the potential benefits of the rule, including any beneficial effects that cannot be quantified in monetary terms, and the identification of those likely to receive the benefits.

(2) A description of the potential costs of the rule, including any adverse effects that cannot be quantified in monetary terms, and the identification of those likely to bear the costs;

(3) A determination of the potential net benefits of the rule, including an evaluation of effects that cannot be quantified in monetary terms;

(4) A description of alternative approaches that could substantially achieve the same regulatory goal at lower cost, together with an analysis of the potential benefit and costs and a brief explanation of the legal reasons why such alternatives, if proposed, could not be adopted; and

(5) Unless covered by the description required under paragraph (4) of this subsection, an explanation of any legal reasons why the rule cannot be based on the requirements set forth in Section 2 of this Order.

(e) (1) The Director * * * is authorized to review any preliminary or final Regulatory Impact Analysis, notice of proposed rulemaking, or final rule based on the requirements of this Order. * * *

(f)(1) Upon the request of the Director, an agency shall consult with the Director concerning the review of a preliminary Regulatory Impact Analysis or notice of proposed rulemaking under this Order, and shall, subject to Section 8(a)(2) of this Order, refrain from publishing its preliminary Regulatory Impact Analysis or notice of proposed rulemaking until such review is concluded. * * *

(i) Agencies shall initiate reviews of currently effective rules in accordance with the purposes of this Order, and perform Regulatory Impact Analyses of currently effective major rules. The Director * * * may designate currently effective rules for review in accordance with this Order, and establish schedules for reviews and Analyses under this Order. * * *

Section 6. * * * Office of Management and Budget

(a) To the extent permitted by law, the Director shall have authority * * * to:

(1) Designate any proposed or existing rule as a major rule in accordance with Section 1(b) of this Order;

(2) Prepare and promulgate uniform standards for the identification of major rules and the development of Regulatory Impact Analyses;

(3) Require an agency to obtain and evaluate, in connection with a regulation, any additional relevant data from any appropriate source;

(4) Waive the requirements of Sections 3, 4 or 7 of this Order with respect to any proposed or existing major rule;

(5) Identify duplicative, overlapping and conflicting rules, existing or proposed, and existing or proposed rules that are inconsistent with the policies underlying statutes governing agencies other than the issuing agency or with the purposes of this Order, and, in each such case, require appropriate interagency consultation to minimize or eliminate such duplication, overlap, or conflict;

(6) Develop procedures for estimating the annual benefits and costs of agency regulations, on both an aggregate and economic or industrial sector basis, for purposes of compiling a regulatory budget;

(7) In consultation with interested agencies, prepare for consideration by the President recommendations for changes in the agencies' statutes; and

(8) Monitor agency compliance with the requirements of this Order and advise the President with respect to such compliance. * * *

Section 7. Pending Regulations

(a) To the extent necessary to permit reconsideration in accordance with this Order, agencies shall, except as provided in Section 8 of this Order, suspend or postpone the effective dates of all major rules that they have promulgated in final form as of the date of this Order, but that have not yet become effective. * * *

(e) Except as provided in Section 8 of this Order, agencies shall, to the extent permitted by law, refrain from promulgating as a final rule any proposed major rule that has been published or issued as of the date of this Order until a final Regulatory Impact Analysis, in accordance with Section 3 of this Order, has been prepared for the proposed major rule. * * *

(i) This Section does not supersede the President's Memorandum of January 29, 1981, entitled "Postponement of Pending Regulations," which shall remain in effect until March 30, 1981.

(j) In complying with this Section, agencies shall comply with all applicable provisions of the Administrative Procedure Act, and with any other procedural requirements made applicable to the agencies by other statutes.

Section 8. Exemptions

(a) The procedures prescribed by this Order shall not apply to:

(1) Any regulation that responds to an emergency situation. * * *

(2) Any regulation for which consideration or reconsideration under the terms of this Order would conflict with deadlines imposed by statute or by judicial order. * * *

Section 9. Judicial Review

This Order is intended only to improve the internal management of the Federal government, and is not intended to create any right or benefit, substantive or procedural, enforceable at law by a party against the United States, its agencies, its officers or any person. The determinations made by agencies under Section 4 of this Order, and any Regulatory Impact Analysis for any rule, shall be made part of the whole record of agency action in connection with the rule. * * *

[signed] Ronald Reagan

The Constitutional Status of Executive Order No. 12,291

Executive Order No. 12,291 did not spring full blown upon the regulatory scene in the early days of 1981. President Nixon's OMB applied what it called a "quality of life review" to some federal regulatory activities, principally those of the Environmental Protection Agency. President Ford's Executive Order No. 11,821, 3A C.F.R. 203, required federal executive agencies to prepare "inflation impact statements" for major decisions. See Note, *The Inflation Impact Statement Program: An Assessment of the First Two Years*, 26 Am. U.L. Rev. 1138 (1977). President Carter was even more ambitious in his attempts to achieve economy and coordination in Executive Order No. 12,044, 3 C.F.R. 152, but stopped short of placing central compliance responsibility in any body outside of the program agencies themselves or an interagency council on which they were represented. See DeMuth, *Constraining Regulatory*

Costs—Part I: The White House Review Programs, 4 Regulation 13 (Jan./ Feb. 1980).   Each of these earlier efforts, as well as the Reagan order, employed techniques borrowed from prior experience with Environmental Impact Statements under the National Environmental Protection Act and from newer statutes such as the Regulatory Flexibility Act, 5 U.S.C.A. § 601, and the Paperwork Reduction Act of 1980, 44 U.S.C.A. § 3501, supra pp. 58–60.

In its scope, detail, and assertions of central authority, however, the Reagan program could claim to be novel.   A report prepared by Morton Rosenberg, a specialist in American public law at the Congressional Research Service, for the House Committee on Energy and Commerce, stated:

> The scheme of [Executive Order No. 12,291], in scope and substance, is a marked departure from previous Presidential efforts to control administrative lawmaking.   It does not appear to draw its authority from any specific congressional enactment.   Indeed, the order itself refers only to "the authority vested in me as President by the Constitution and laws of the United States of America."   * * *
>
> * * * [T]he question raised is whether the President in promulgating Executive order 12,291 has engaged in an exercise of Executive lawmaking without either constitutional or statutory authority and thereby violated the separation of powers doctrine.

Rosenberg, *Presidential Control of Agency Rulemaking*, 23 Ariz. L. Rev. 1199 (1981).

Relying on familiar authority—*Youngstown, Humphrey's Executor,* and *Wiener*—Rosenberg answers this question in the affirmative.   He rejects the notion that the President was ever intended to be an administrative manager sitting atop a centralized Executive Branch.   Officers, in his view, receive their authority to act from legislation; they are congressional delegates, not executive subordinates.

In *Beyond the Limits of Executive Power: Presidential Control of Agency Rulemaking Under Executive Order 12,291*, 80 Mich. L. Rev. 193 (1981), Rosenberg also challenges the notion that the central clearance functions of OMB suggest congressional acquiescence in the form of presidential direction to agencies contemplated by Executive Order No. 12,291.   Rosenberg offers the following portrayal of the relevant history (id. at 221–25):

> Since early in this century, the President, with Congress's blessing, has wielded a great deal of authority over the agency budget process.   Through his budget office, the President has been authorized to present a unified annual budget on behalf of federal agencies, clear agency information requests, and even decide which legislative proposals urged by the agencies should receive congressional attention.   * * *
>
> Presidential authority in the agency budget process began with the enactment of the Budget and Accounting Act of 1921, which allowed the President to formulate a national budget with the assistance of a newly created Bureau of the Budget (BOB).   Previously, each agency had submitted its annual budget request directly to Congress.   Finding this process inefficient and unwieldy, Congress created the BOB to review the morass of agency budgetry

information and to approve agency budget requests. By 1970, the BOB possessed an impressive array of legal authorities for supervision of nearly all departments and agencies. In addition to reviewing and approving agency budget requests, the Bureau was authorized to study agency organization, to clear agency proposals for legislation or agency comments on proposed legislation, and to control agencies' requests for information.

In granting these powers to the President, Congress intended—at least in part—that he would play a policy-neutral role; the President was to coordinate the vast tangle of administrative agencies. Through his authority to study agency organization and review budget requests, the President could identify overlapping efforts, eliminate needless duplication, and resolve interagency conflicts. One must recognize, however, that the powers that enabled the President to carry out his managerial responsibilities also gave him the capacity to influence administrative policy. In the threat of budget reductions, the President possesses a powerful tool that he can use to enforce his own policy designs. The President could, moreover, use his clearance powers to focus congressional attention on agency proposals or comments agreeable to him. Yet the BOB, notwithstanding its significant policy-influencing potential, maintained an image of bipartisan neutrality, and its Director was seen as a personal technical adviser on fiscal and organizational matters. Although, in principle, the President has long been able to influence substantively the policies formulated by administrative agencies, until recently the power was relatively dormant.

In 1970, however, President Nixon reconstituted the BOB as the OMB and sought to expand its role. Departing from the history of policy-neutrality, President Nixon began to use the OMB, together with his self-proclaimed impoundment powers, to alter or end established programs. As the OMB began to be viewed as a political instrument of the President, Congress's response to President Nixon's unprecedented efforts was far-reaching; the legislature severly limited the OMB's autonomy and forcefully asserted its own desire to control administrative policy-making. For the first time, Congress required Senate confirmation of the OMB's Director and Deputy Director. The OMB's monopoly on the processing of agency budget requests was ended as Congress created its own central budget evaluator, the Congressional Budget Office (CBO). Congress has, on a selective basis, either eliminated the requirement that the OMB clear agency budget requests or mandated that the requests be concurrently submitted to the CBO. Equally significant was the enactment of the Budget Impoundment and Control Act of 1974, which greatly limited the President's putative authority to impound agency funds and his concomitant power to shape policy. Finally, Congress countered the institutional development of the OMB by enhancing the authority of its watchdog audit agency, the General Accounting Office, with program evaluation functions and a special oversight role in preventing presidential impoundments. The spate of legislation following the politicization of the OMB conclusively demonstrates that Congress, rather than acquiescing to presidential policy-making, desired to maintain control over administrative agencies. Congress has empowered the President to act in the interests of coordination and organizational efficiency, but has carefully restrained such action, lest it assume substantive policy dimensions.

Congressional limitations on the President's reorganizational powers reiterate the theme that the President's managerial role does not encompass control of administrative policy-making.   Congress has several times delegated to the President extensive powers of governmental reorganization.   The policy-making potential stemming from these powers was great: The President typically could transfer, consolidate, or abolish agency functions, including rulemaking.   In principle, the President could have transferred rulemaking programs from one agency to another possessing a fundamentally different mission.   Hesitant to confer power with such potential substantive impact, Congress has imposed several conditions on the President's reorganizational authority.   First, all of the reorganization acts have been of limited duration, none being effective for more than four years.   Second, some of the acts specifically restricted reorganizational power.   Illustratively, the most recent reorganization act, which lapsed on April 7, 1981, expressly prohibited the President from abolishing "any enforcement or statutory program," creating any new executive departments, or consolidating two or more departments.   Third, with two short-lived exceptions, all of the reorganization acts adopted since 1932 have included provisions authorizing a legislative veto. Each of these restrictions, and particularly the provisions for a legislative veto, reflect Congress's intent to cabin even the potential for presidential control of administratively formulated policy.

Rosenberg takes comfort finally from *Kendall v. United States*, 37 U.S. (12 Pet.) 524 (1838), a suit for money due pursuant to an accounting by the Solicitor of the Treasury.   The Postmaster General defended his refusal to pay by invoking an express direction from the President.   The important issue was whether a court could direct the action of an executive official under these circumstances.   The Postmaster General argued that it could not.   His actions, he claimed, were discretionary and only the President could direct him to exercise his discretion in a particular way.   The Court disagreed:

> The executive power is vested in a President; and as far as his powers are derived from the constitution, he is beyond the reach of any other department, except in the mode prescribed by the constitution through the impeaching power.   But it by no means follows, that every officer in every branch of that department is under the exclusive direction of the President.   Such a principle, we apprehend, is not, and certainly cannot be claimed by the President.
>
> There are certain political duties imposed upon many officers in the executive department, the discharge of which is under the direction of the President.   But it would be an alarming doctrine, that congress cannot impose upon any executive officer any duty they may think proper, which is not repugnant to any rights secured and protected by the constitution; and in such cases, the duty and responsibility grow out of and are subject to the control of the law, and not to the direction of the President.   And this is emphatically the case, where the duty enjoined is of a mere ministerial character. * * *
>
> It was urged at the bar, that the postmaster general was alone subject to the direction and control of the President, with respect to the execution of the duty imposed upon him by this law, and this right of the President is claimed, as growing out of the obligation imposed upon him by the constitution, to take care that the laws be faithfully executed.   This is a doctrine that cannot receive the sanction of this court.   It would be vesting in the President a dispensing power, which has no countenance for its support in any part of the

constitution; and is asserting a principle, which, if carried out in its results, to all cases falling within it, would be clothing the President with a power entirely to control the legislation of congress, and paralyze the administration of justice.

To contend that the obligation imposed on the President to see the laws faithfully executed, implies a power to forbid their execution, is a novel construction of the constitution, and entirely inadmissible.

The Reagan Administration's contrasting view of the legal situation is well-summarized in an opinion submitted on February 12, 1981, by the Assistant Attorney General, Office of Legal Counsel to OMB Director Stockman.

UNITED STATES DEPARTMENT OF JUSTICE WASHINGTON, D.C. 20530

MEMORANDUM FOR HONORABLE DAVID STOCKMAN
Director
Office of Management and Budget

RE: PROPOSED EXECUTIVE ORDER ON FEDERAL REGULATION

The President is considering a proposed Executive Order designed to reduce regulatory burdens, to provide for presidential oversight of the administrative process, and to ensure well-reasoned regulations. The Order sets forth a number of requirements that Executive Branch agencies must adhere to in exercising their statutory rulemaking authority. Certain of the Order's procedural requirements would apply to the independent regulatory commissions as well. This memorandum discusses the legal basis for the proposed Order and examines issues that are raised by certain of its provisions. We conclude that the Order is within the President's authority. * * *

I. LEGAL AUTHORITY: EXECUTIVE BRANCH AGENCIES

The President's authority to issue the proposed Executive Order derives from his constitutional power to "take Care that the Laws be faithfully executed." U.S. Const., Art. II, § 3. It is well established that this provision authorizes the President, as head of the Executive Branch, to "supervise and guide" Executive officers in "their construction of the statutes under which they act in order to secure that unitary and uniform execution of the laws which Article II of the Constitution evidently contemplated in vesting general executive power in the President alone." *Myers v. United States*, 272 U.S. 52, 135 (1926).[1]

---

1. In *Buckley v. Valeo*, 424 U.S. 1, 140–41 (1976), the Supreme Court held that any "significant governmental duty exercised pursuant to a public law" must be performed by an "Officer of the United States," appointed by the President or the Head of a Department pursuant to Art. II, § 2, cl. 2. We believe that this holding recognizes the importance of preserving the President's supervisory powers over those exercising statutory duties, subject of course to the power of Congress to confine presidential supervision by appropriate legislation.

The supervisory authority recognized in *Myers* is based on the distinctive constitutional role of the President. The "take Care" clause charges the President with the function of coordinating the execution of many statutes simultaneously: "Unlike an administrative commission confined to the enforcement of the statute under which it was created * * * the President is a constitutional officer charged with taking care that a 'mass of legislation' be executed," *Youngstown Sheet & Tube Co. v. Sawyer,* 343 U.S. 579, 702 (1952) (Vinson, C.J., dissenting). Moreover, because the President is the only elected official who has a national constituency, he is uniquely situated to design and execute a uniform method for undertaking regulatory initiatives that responds to the will of the public as a whole.[2] In fulfillment of the President's constitutional responsibility, the proposed Order promotes a coordinated system of regulation, ensuring a measure of uniformity in the interpretation and execution of a number of diverse statutes. If no such guidance were permitted, confusion and inconsistency could result as agencies interpreted open-ended statutes in differing ways.

Nevertheless, it is clear that the President's exercise of supervisory powers must conform to legislation enacted by Congress.[3] In issuing directives to govern the Executive Branch, the President may not, as a general proposition, require or permit agencies to transgress boundaries set by Congress. It is with these basic precepts in mind that the proposed Order must be approached.

We believe that an inquiry into congressional intent in enacting statutes delegating rulemaking authority will usually support the legality of presidential supervision of rulemaking by Executive Branch agencies. When Congress delegates legislative power to Executive Branch agencies, it is aware that those agencies perform their functions subject to presidential supervision on matters of both substance and procedure. This is not to say that Congress never intends in a specific case to restrict presidential supervision of an Executive agency; but it should not be presumed to have done so whenever it delegates rulemaking power directly to a subordinate Executive Branch official rather than the President. Indeed, after *Myers* it is unclear to what extent Congress may insulate Executive Branch agencies from presidential supervision. Congress is also aware of the comparative insulation given to the independent regulatory agencies, and it has delegated rulemaking authority to such agencies when it has sought to minimize presidential interference. By contrast, the heads of non-independent agencies hold their positions at the pleasure of the President, who may remove them from office for any reason. It would be anomalous to attribute to Congress an intention to immunize from presidential supervision those who are, by force of Art. II, subject to removal when their performance in exercising their statutory duties displeases the President. * * *

---

2. See Bruff, *Presidential Power and Administrative Rulemaking,* 88 Yale L.J. 451, 461–62 (1978).

3. In certain circumstances, statutes could invade or intrude impermissibly upon the President's "inherent" powers, but that issue does not arise here.

Procedurally, [the order] would direct agencies to prepare an RIA assessing the costs and benefits of major rules. We discern no plausible legal objection to this requirement, which like most procedural requisites is at most an indirect constraint on the exercise of statutory discretion. * * *

Substantively, the Order would require agencies to exercise their discretion, within statutory limits, in accordance with the principles of cost-benefit analysis. More complex legal questions are raised by this requirement. Some statutes may prohibit agencies from basing a regulatory decision on an assessment of the costs and benefits of the proposed action. See, e.g., *EPA v. National Crushed Stone Ass'n*, 101 S.Ct. 295 (1980). The Order, however, expressly recognizes this possibility by requiring agency adherence to principles of cost-benefit analysis only "to the extent permitted by law." The issue is thus (whether, when cost-benefit analysis is a statutorily authorized basis for decision, the President may require Executive agencies to be guided by principles of cost-benefit analysis even when an agency, acting without presidential guidance, might choose not to do so.) We believe that such a requirement is permissible. First, there can be little doubt that, when a statute does not expressly or implicitly preclude it, an agency may take into account the costs and benefits of proposed action. * * *

Second, the requirement would not exceed the President's powers of "supervision." It leaves a considerable amount of decisionmaking discretion to the agency. Under the proposed Order, the agency head, and not the President, would be required to calculate potential costs and benefits and to determine whether the benefits justify the costs. * * *

We believe that the President would not exceed any limitations on his authority by authorizing * * * the Director to supervise agency rulemaking as the Order would provide. The Order does not empower the Director * * * to displace the relevant agencies in discharging their statutory functions or in assessing and weighing the costs and benefits of proposed actions. The function of * * * the Director would * * * include such tasks as the supplementation of factual data, the development and implementation of uniform systems of methodology, the identification of incorrect statements of fact, and the placement in the administrative record of a statement disapproving agency conclusions that do not appear to conform to the principles expressed in the President's Order. Procedurally, the Director * * * would be authorized to require an agency to defer rulemaking while it responded to their statements of disapproval of proposed agency action. This power of consultation would not, however, include authority to reject an agency's ultimate judgment, delegated to it by law, that potential benefits outweigh costs, that priorities under the statute compel a particular course of action, or that adequate information is available to justify regulation. * * *

II. INDEPENDENT REGULATORY COMMISSIONS

We now consider (whether the proposed Order may legally be applied to the independent regulatory commissions in certain respects. Principally, the Order would require independent agencies to prepare RIA's and would authorize the Director or the Task Force to exercise limited supervision over the RIA's. For reasons stated below, we believe that, under the best view of the law, these and some other requirements of the Order can be imposed on the independent agencies. We would emphasize, however, that an attempt to exercise supervision of these agencies through techniques such as those in the proposed Order would be lawful only if the Supreme Court is prepared to repudiate certain expansive dicta in the leading case on the subject, and that an attempt to infringe the autonomy of the independent agencies is very likely to produce a confrontation with Congress, which has historically been jealous of its prerogatives with regard to them. * * *

The holding of *Humphrey's Executor* is that Congress may constitutionally require cause for the removal of an FTC Commissioner; the Court's opinion, however, contains broad dicta endorsing a perceived congressional purpose to insulate the FTC almost entirely from Presidential supervision:

> The commission is to be non-partisan; and it must, from the very nature of its duties, act with entire impartiality. It is charged with the enforcement of no policy except the policy of the law. Its duties are neither political nor executive, but predominately quasi-judicial and quasi-legislative. Like the Interstate Commerce Commission, its members are called upon to exercise the trained judgment of a body of experts "appointed by law and informed by experience."

295 U.S. at 624 (quoting *Illinois Cent. Ry. v. ICC*, 206 U.S. 441 (1906)). The Court continued:

> Thus, * * * the Congressional intent to create a body of experts who shall gain experience by length of service—a body which shall be independent of executive authority *except in its selection*, and free to exercise its judgment without the leave or hindrance of any other official or any department of the government. * * * And to hold that, nevertheless, the members of the commission continue in office at the mere will of the President, might be to thwart, in large measure, the very ends which Congress sought to realize by definitely fixing the term of office.

Id. at 625–26 (emphasis in original).

If the dicta of *Humphrey's Executor* are taken at face value, the President's constitutional power to supervise the independent agencies is limited to his power of appointment, and none of the proposed Order's requirements may legally be applied to the independent agencies. We believe, however, that there are several reasons to conclude that the Supreme Court would today retreat from these dicta. First, the Court in *Humphrey's Executor* and *Wiener* focused primarily on the inappropriateness of Presidential interference in agency adjudication, a concern not pertinent to supervision of rulemaking. Second, insofar as the Court was concerned about rulemaking, it did not take account of the fact that Executive Branch and independent agencies engage in rulemaking in a functionally indistinguishable fashion. Third, the Court espoused what is now an outmoded view about the "apolitical" nature of regulation. It is now recognized that rulemaking may legitimately reflect political influences of certain kinds from a number of sources, including Congress and the affected public. Fourth, the President has today a number of statutory powers over the independent agencies, which recognize the legitimacy of his influence in their activities. * * *

It seems clear that Congress intends the independent agencies to be free of Presidential supervision on matters of substantive policy. * * * We believe that the holding of *Humphrey's Executor,* shorn of the Court's broad dicta that these agencies are independent "except in [their] selection," fully supports the view that Congress may remove some rulemaking from Presidential supervision of the sort that would be appropriate in the absence of such a provision. It remains necessary, then, to reconcile the holding of *Humphrey's Executor* with the President's duty under Article II, § 3, to "take Care that the Laws be faithfully executed." Certainly provisions requiring cause for removal must be read as expressing congressional intent to minimize Presidential supervision of these agencies. Accordingly, a frequent formulation of the President's power over the independent agencies has been that he may supervise them as necessary to ensure that they are faithfully executing the laws, although he may not displace their substantive discretion to decide particular adjudicative or rulemaking matters.[14] Such a formulation would allow for many types of procedural supervisions.

In addition to his constitutional powers, the President has been given some statutory powers that extend to independent as well as Executive Branch agencies. These powers include reorganization authority, OMB's budgetary and legislative request processes, the deferral or rescission of appropriations, and the selection of agency chairmen. We do not interpret these statutes to imply broad authority for presidential supervision of the independent agencies, because of the clear congressional intent to minimize presidential supervision that is expressed in removal restrictions. Nevertheless, we do believe that these statutes recognize the legitimacy of some presidential influence in the activities of independent agencies, especially when it consists of a coordinating role with only an indirect effect on substantive policymaking.

We believe that the foregoing constitutional and statutory analysis supports the application to the independent agencies of those portions of the Order that would be extended to them. The principal requirement is that independent agencies prepare RIA's. These analyses would have only an indirect effect on substantive discretion, since the identification of

---

14. See, e.g., Landis, *Regulatory Agencies to the President-Elect* 33 (1960):

The congestion of the dockets of the agencies, the delays incident to the disposition of cases, the failure to evolve policies pursuant to basic statutory requirements are all a part of the President's constitutional concern to see that the laws are faithfully executed. The outcome of any particular adjudicatory matter is, however, as much beyond his concern, except where he has a statutory responsibility to intervene, as the outcome off any cause pending in the courts and his approach to such matters before the agencies should be exactly the same as his approach to matters pending before the courts.

costs and benefits and the particular balance struck would be for the agency to make.   It should also be possible for OMB to prescribe criteria for independent agencies to follow in preparing their RIA's, to consult with them in the process, and to disagree with an independent agency's analysis on the administrative record.   None of these actions would directly displace the agencies' ultimate discretion to decide what rule best fulfills their statutory responsibilities. * * *

Administrative Organization and the Chief Executive

The original conception of the presidency was quite different from that conveyed to the modern mind by the words "chief executive."   Willoughby's authoritative constitutional law text said:

> It was undoubtedly intended that the President be little more than a political chief; that is to say, one whose function should, in the main consist in the performance of those political duties which are not subject to judicial control.   It was quite clear that it was intended that he should not, except as to these political matters, be the administrative head of the government, with general power of directing and controlling the acts of subordinate federal administrative agents.

3 W. WILLOUGHBY, CONSTITUTIONAL LAW 1479–80 (2d ed. 1929).   See also, 1 F. GOODNOW, COMPARATIVE ADMINISTRATIVE LAW 52–62 (1893).

Early statutes establishing various departments of the government seem to recognize this intention, at least with respect to domestic functions as distinguished from presidential power with respect to foreign affairs and military matters.   When establishing the departments of Foreign Affairs (Act of July 27, 1789, ch. 4, § 1, 1 Stat. 28), War (Act of August 7, 1789 ch. 7, § 1, 1 Stat. 49), and Navy (Act of April 30, 1798, ch. 35, § 1, 1 Stat. 553) legislation explicitly gave the President a power of direction. For example, the acts creating the departments of Foreign Affairs and War stipulated that the Secretaries "perform and execute such duties as shall from time to time be enjoined on or intrusted to [them] by the President" and "conduct the business of said department in such manner as the President . . . shall from time to time order or instruct."   Act of July 22, 1789, ch. 4, § 1 (1 Stat. 29); Act of August 7, 1789, ch. 7, § 1 (1 Stat. 50).   The Act establishing the Department of the Navy placed the Secretary even more firmly under direct control and supervision, instructing him simply "to execute such orders as he shall receive from the President." Act of April 30, 1798, ch. 35, § 1 (1 Stat. 553).

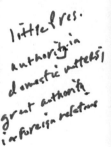

This power of direction was not included, however, in departments such as the Treasury (Act of September 2, 1789, ch. 12, § 1, 1 Stat. 65 (1789)) or in statutes establishing departments such as the Post Office (Act of May 8, 1794, ch. 23, § 3, 1 Stat. 357) and the Interior Department (Act of March 3, 1849, ch. 108, § 1, 9 Stat. 395).   The Treasury Department statute did not even mention the President, required the Secretary to make reports to Congress, and said that the Secretary of the Treasury should "generally * * * perform all those services relative to the finances, as he shall be directed to perform." Act of September 2, 1789, ch. 12, § 2, 1 Stat. 66 (1789). In the context, apparently, any "directions" were expected to come from Congress. During the early years of the republic, secretaries of departments seem to have been viewed as independent political actors often competing with each other, at odds with the President politically, and dependent upon the Congress for much of their power. See L. WHITE, THE FEDERALISTS 44–49, 68–87, 94–96, 218–252 (1948).

This vision of the non-managerial presidency was not unanimous. Alexander Hamilton had strong views on the need for centralized administration. And the Jackson presidency certainly emphasized the political accountability of office holders to the president. See L. WHITE, THE JACKSONIANS 23–28, 33–44, 50–124, 300–346, 552–567 (1954). It was not, however, until the vast increases in federal bureaucratic operations after the Civil War that administrative management became a significant issue for those concerned about federal government organization. See generally Karl, *Executive Reorganization and Presidential Power*, 1977 Sup. Ct. Rev. 1, 11–28. Interest in "managerial" questions increased steadily in response to increases in the scale of the private and public organizations in the late nineteenth and early twentieth centuries.

With the coming of the New Deal the management of the Executive Branch was recognized as a critical problem. President Roosevelt set up a Committee on Administrative Management to report to him on the organization and effectiveness of the executive branch. It is fair to say that the committee was appalled by the state of federal administrative organization. It urgently recommended, and the Congress enacted, legislation reorganizing and strengthening the role of the Bureau of the Budget and providing other central staff to assist the President in developing and coordinating the organization and financing of the government's administrative functions. REPORT OF PRESIDENT'S COMMITTEE ON ADMINISTRATIVE MANAGEMENT 5–6, 16–25, 33–38, 51–53 (Washington, U.S. Govt. Print. Ofc. 1937). Moreover, the Committee's report suggested that the operative constitutional conception of the chief executive had been radically transformed. The Committee referred quite unselfconsciously to "our constitutional ideal of a fully coordinated executive branch responsible to the president." Id. at 41. Moreover the Report viewed with alarm the growth of the so-called independent regulatory commissions. In the committee's words, "They constitute a headless fourth branch of the government, a haphazard deposit of irresponsible agencies and uncoordinated powers. They do violence to the basic theory of the American Constitution that there should be three major branches of the government and only three. The Congress has found no effective way of supervising them, they cannot be controlled by the president, and they are answerable to the courts only in respect to the legality of their activities. * * * Id. at 40.

Since 1937 there has been no lack of commissions, task forces, and reports on the organization of the Executive Branch, including the independent regulatory commissions.   Some of the more important include The Commission on Organization of the Executive Branch of Government (the Hoover Commission) (1947–1949); The United States Commission on Organization of the Executive Branch of the Government (Second Hoover Commission) (1953–1955); James M. Landis' Report on the Regulatory Agencies to the President-elect (Senate Committee on the Judiciary, 86th Cong., 2d Sess. (Committee print, 1960)); the President's Advisory Council on Executive Organization (the Ash Council Report, 1971); and the ABA Commission on Law and the Economy (Federal Regulation: Roads to Reform, 1979).   Virtually all have been critical of independent regulatory agencies and have been concerned about the incapacity of the president to supervise and direct their activities.

The reports of these commissions, task forces and individuals, have generated their own secondary literature both critical and supportive. See, e.g., Hector, *Problems of the CAB and the Independent Regulatory Commissions*, 69 Yale L.J. 931 (1960); Auerbach, *Some Thoughts on the Hector Memorandum*, 1960 Wis. L. Rev. 183; Elman, *A. Modest Proposal for Radical Reform*, 56 A.B.A. J. 1045 (1970); *Symposium on Federal Regulatory Agencies: A Response to the Ash Report*, 57 Va. L. Rev. 925 (1971); Redford, *The President and the Regulatory Commissions*, 44 Texas L. Rev. 288 (1965); H. FRIENDLY, THE FEDERAL ADMINISTRATIVE AGENCIES (1962); McFarland, *Landis' Report: The Voice of One Crying in the Wilderness*, 47 Va. L. Rev. 373 (1961).   In response to the various reports several presidents have proposed, and Congress has sometimes accepted, reorganization plans for various of the regulatory agencies.   These plans, by and large, have strengthened the internal structure of the agencies without adding much to the president's power of supervision, direction or control.   The power to appoint the chairmen of certain independent commissions, rather than having them selected by the commissions themselves, is perhaps the only exception to the foregoing generalization.

Yet, it is certainly possible to take issue with Rosenberg's characterization of the broad history of congressional authorizations to the president in the budgetary and reorganization contexts as evincing a Congress jealous of its institutional prerogatives and intent on maintaining control of administrative policy-making.   The pattern of broad delegations of reorganization authority has more typically been viewed as reflecting an acknowledgement (if only implicit) on Congress' part of its inability to fulfill what it has always claimed to be its responsibility—not the President's—to keep the organization and operations of government up to date.   See, e.g., J. SUNDQUIST, THE DECLINE AND RESURGENCE OF CONGRESS 51–55, 57–60 (1981).   The notion that the modern president's managerial role was not intended by Congress to reach substantive matters of policy may have some accuracy as a formal matter, but even if it has awakened to the realization only occasionally, Congress cannot have been entirely blind to the larger implications of its grants of reorganization authority.   Whatever misgivings it may currently entertain about its participation, and whatever the limitations it has endeavored to impose, the record suggests that Congress has generally been an obliging partner in a process whose "basic purpose" has been "to secure [presidential] power over a bureaucracy whose real source of independence is congressional funding."   Karl, *op cit.* at 33.

From the close of the second World War until April 1, 1973, the Congress—with occasional lapses, none of which lasted more than two years—consistently renewed the reorganization authority, and between 1939 and 1973 it accepted 83 of the 105 reorganization plans submitted to it by six presidents.   SUNDQUIST, *op cit.* at 54.   Events at the close of this era, moreover, would seem to belie the suggestion that an attentive Congress stood ready to hold the President to strict accountability if he sought to expand his managerial role to encompass control of adminstrative policy-making.   The Democratic Congress of 1970–71, for example, could not have been unaware of the fact (acknowledged by Rosenberg) that the BOB had been steadily developing its capacity as an agency for imposing presidential discipline on the policy-making processes of traditionally semiautonomous departments and agencies.   Yet when in 1971 it renewed the reorganization authority under which President Nixon had converted the BOB into the OMB only twenty members voted against the bill in the House and it was not even debated in the Senate.   Id. at 55.

There is some evidence to suggest that Rosenberg's contention regarding congressional determination to withstand presidential "aggrandizement" via the reorganization authority may have greater applicability in the post-Nixon era, but even here the record is ambiguous.   In recent years, attention has increasingly been devoted to the question of whether the reorganization authority process has really served the interests of either branch.   See, e.g., Fisher and Roe, *Presidential Reorganization Authority: Is It Worth the Cost?*, 96 *Pol. Sci. Q.* 301 (Winter 1981–82).   The Congress itself appears to have had some reservations on this score.   In 1980, it enacted Pub. L. No. 96–250, granting a one-year extension to the authority provided the President under the Reorganization Act of 1977 (5 U.S.C.A. § 901, *et. seq.*), but this action was not viewed as a ringing endorsement of the concept or of the law by the chairman of the Senate Governmental Affairs Committee, who emphasized that the renewal had been made "in case minor adjustments" were needed and that the year was to be used as a time for "further study" of the law and its procedures.   See id. at 301, n. 1.   That statement turned out to represent something of a death-knell (perhaps temporary) for the reorganization authority, which lapsed when the extension expired on April 6, 1981.   Several proposals have been introduced in the intervening period, however, and they afford some insight into the form the reorganization process is likely to assume should new authorization be provided.

Two of the recent proposals were adopted by one House.   The first of these, S. 893, the Reorganization Act of 1981, which offered a four-year grant of authority, was introduced on April 7, 1981 by Senator Roth (Del.) with the Reagan Administration's blessing and passed the Senate by voice vote on June 15th of the same year.   (A parallel proposal in the House, H.R. 3270, never came to a vote in the 97th Congress.)   Two years later, on April 10, 1984, the Reorganization Act Amendments of 1983, H.R. 1314, providing authorization only through the end of 1984, was approved by the House.   S. 893 and H.R. 1314 had certain important features in common.   Each sought to amend the Reorganization Act of 1977 by placing two new restrictions on the content of reorganization plans: one was designed to prohibit the President from renaming any existing department*, the second to preclude the creation of new agencies which are not made part of any existing department or independent agency. S. 893, § 5(a)(1)–(2); H.R. 1314, § 5(a)(1)–(2).   Ostensibly in the interest of speeding up implementation and avoiding delay or unforeseen costs, both pieces of legislation also called upon the President to submit, along with the message accompanying any given plan, any executive orders or other written directives that might be required to put the plan into effect.   S. 893, § 4; H.R. 1314, § 4.   Yet another significant similarity between the two bills were provisions to extend the period for congressional consideration of any reorganization plan submitted by the President from 60 to 90 days.   S. 893, § 3(a) (1); H.R. 1314; § 3(a) (1).

On the procedure for approving a plan, however, the bills differed radically.   The Senate proposal in effect retained the one-House legislative veto provision that had been incorporated in the Reorganization Act of 1977.   Section 6 of S. 893 provided, however, that reorganization proposals submitted by the President would become effective if any one of three conditions were satisfied during the 90-day period: (1) each House adopts a resolution of approval; (2) one House adopts such a resolution while the other House fails to act; or (3) neither House votes on an approving resolution.   S. 893, § 6.   As the Governmental Affairs Committee, which reported S. 893, was at pains to point out, the change in the voting procedure would not have altered the arrangement under the 1977 Act whereby a plan became effective "even if one or both Houses [did] not bring the proposal to a vote."   Senate Comm. on Governmental Affairs, *Reorganization Act of 1981*, S. Rep. No. 182, 97th Cong., 1st Sess. 11 (1981).

The change in congressional procedure contemplated by H.R. 1314 was considerably more far-reaching in its implications.   The bill abandoned the use of the legislative veto mechanism altogether, requiring instead the use (within the 90 day period) of a joint resolution of approval: affirmative action by both Houses and approval by the President would be required for a plan to go into effect.   Failure by either house to vote would be tantamount to disapproval.   H. 1314, § 3(a).

While the House Committee on Government Operations had recommended this approach prior to the Supreme Court's decision in *Chadha*, its report on the Reorganization Act Amendments of 1983 expressly noted

---

*This amendment was introduced to deal with a problem which had arisen during the Carter years, when the Adminstration forwarded a reorganization plan to establish a Department of Natural Resources that would absorb the Interior Department and include the Forest Service from the Agriculture Department and NOAA from the Commerce Department.   The Administration was accused of seeking to evade a provision of the 1977 Act prohibiting any plan "hav[ing] the effect of creating" a new executive department.

that "recent action in the courts appears to have tipped the balance in favor of requiring affirmative votes in both the House and the Senate to approve Presidential reorganization plans." House Comm. on Government Operations, *Reorganization Act Amendments of 1983*, H. Rep. No. 128, 98th Cong., 1st Sess. 3–4 (1983) (citing *Consumer Energy Council of America v. Federal Energy Regulatory Commission*, 673 F.2d 425 (1982), supra p. 45). The committee also had at its disposal the brief submitted in January of 1982 by the Department of Justice in the *Chadha* case, which expressed the view that all legislative vetoes, including those attached to Presidential reorganization plans, were unconstitutional.

Effects of OMB Oversight

One year after the issuance of Executive Order No. 12,291 the General Accounting Office conducted a study of OMB's operations. *Improved Quality, Adequate Resources, and Consistent Oversight Needed If Regulatory Analysis Is To Help Control Costs of Regulations* (November 2, 1982). The GAO found that in 1981 OMB had reviewed 2,679 rules, 62 of which were classed as "major." Over 90 percent of these rules were approved as submitted by the authoring agency. OMB approved 5 percent with "minor" changes and returned 2 percent unapproved. An additional 2 percent were withdrawn during the review process.

The GAO discovered little about OMB's operations, in part because most of the communications between OMB and the relevant agencies were <u>oral</u>. Without contemporaneous records the GAO could not measure the influence of OMB's review process on the substance of rules as they emerged. And it had no way to determine how many rules never saw the light of day because of the necessity of running the OMB gauntlet.

As would be expected in a high volume operation, most decisions for OMB were made by desk officers in its Office of Information and Regulatory Analysis. These decisions included determinations of whether rules were "major" and also "waivers" of OMB review for many of the rules so classified. In fact, designating a large number of rules (98 percent) as not major and granting waivers for nearly half the rest was probably essential. OMB was receiving nearly ten rules each working day and its Office of Information and Regulatory Analysis (OIRA) had been given few additional personnel to handle its new responsibilities.

OMB's review priorities remain mysterious. Nevertheless, it seems fair to assume that it devoted major effort to regulations "targeted" for review by the Task Force on Regulatory Relief, chaired by Vice President Bush. Thus, in specific policy areas it seems likely that the review process produced a shift in regulatory direction. See Olson, *The Quiet Shift of Power: Office of Management & Budget Oversight of Environmental Protection Agency Rulemaking Under Executive Order 12,291*, 4 Va. J. Nat. Res. L. 1 (1984).

The Reagan Administration's most significant and controversial actions in the name of regulatory relief involved the "auto package," which was announced in April of 1981.   Thirty-four specific regulatory actions comprised part of the administration's plan to "save" the domestic automobile industry.   The administration estimated the potential monetary savings of these actions to be $1.4 billion in capital costs for the industry and $9.3 billion for consumers over a period of five years.   See Wines, *Reagan Plan to Relieve Auto Industry of Regulatory Burden Gets Mixed Grade*, Nat'l J., July 23, 1983, 1534–35.   The lead agencies implementing the "auto package" were the National Highway Traffic Safety Administration and the Environmental Protection Agency, the two agencies whose regulatory actions most affect the automobile industry.   The administration had been careful to appoint at these agencies administrators who were committed to relief for the automobile industry.   And although under E.O. 12,291 relaxing regulations ostensibly had to undergo the same review as regulations that impose new costs, some observers believe that the new powers given to OMB, including its power to exempt "major" rules from the executive order's requirements, helped assure that the Reagan program for the automobile industry did indeed provide substantial assistance.   By contrast, the Carter Administration's almost identical proposals, administered by an Interagency Council, had foundered in bureaucratic infighting and delay.   See G. EADS & M. FIX, RELIEF OR REFORM? REAGAN'S REGULATORY DILEMMA 132 (1984).

The OMB review process has drawn praise in some quarters as a means for overcoming the bureaucratic and political inertia of entrenched regulatory systems.   Yet as OMB seeks to regulate the regulators, it seems plausible that it encounters many of the same problems and dilemmas that confront regulatory agencies themselves.   We have already noted the staggering potential caseload.   Perhaps more importantly, in most instances OMB confronts an agency with greater resources and expertise in the subject of the rule that OMB could hope to amass—a disadvantage most regulators have *vis a vis* regulated firms.

Finally, as in most stringent forms of regulatory programs (e.g., licensing), the agency (here OMB) sees mainly proposals for the future; it does not review the enormous body of existing regulations.   Like the new plants, products, and processes that become the focus of health and safety regulators, and that are also likely to be more benign than old plants, products, and processes, most new rules are likely to reflect greater sensitivity to regulatory costs and benefits than old rules.   In short, there is reason to believe that both regulators and OMB spend their time rendering more difficult and costly activities that are presumptively superior to those that they, of necessity, ignore, and that their interventions thus tend to preserve.

Whatever its impact on economic performance, the Reagan executive order has clearly energized Congress.   A bare two months after it was issued, legislation was introduced in the Senate aiming "to codify some of the excellent principles of E.O. 12,291, to extend such principles to independent agencies, and to accomplish other reforms which cannot be achieved through executive action." *Regulatory Reform Act: Hearings on S. 1080 Before the Subcomm. on Regulatory Reform of the Senate Comm. on the Judiciary,* 97th Cong., 1st Sess. 36 (1981) (Statement of Chairman Thurmond).

S. 1080, which garnered no less than 81 sponsors and was eventually passed by unanimous vote of the Senate on March 24, 1982, adopted almost verbatim the provisions of Executive Order No. 12,291 requiring the agencies to conduct cost-benefit analyses for any "major rule" and to submit "regulatory impact analyses" for central consideration at least 60 days prior to final publication. The legislation retained, indeed subtly augmented, the executive order's provision for executive oversight of the analysis and rule-making processess. A proposed amendment to the APA conferred on the President "the authority to establish procedures for agency compliance" and "to monitor, review, and ensure agency implementation of such procedures." And the President would have been empowered to "delegate this authority, in whole or in part, to the Vice President or to an officer, within the Executive Office of the President whose appointment has been subject to the advice and consent of the Senate." Under the legislation, this officer's exercise or failure to exercise this authority—as well as any determination that a rule is a major rule—was to be entirely exempt from judicial review.

The Senate Judiciary Committee's description of proposed APA § 624 warrants quotation in full:

> Section 624 is designed to achieve the important but limited goal of assuring effective Executive Branch oversight of agency compliance with the new procedures for major rules added to Chapter 6 by this bill. * * * [S]ection 624 is not intended to comprise a complete catalog or description of the President's authority vis-a-vis Executive Branch agencies and independent agencies. Nor is it intended to resolve all the questions—some of which are quite difficult—as to what the President's authority is under the Constitution and existing laws, or what it should be. It does not change the authority an agency is given by other laws to make substantive decisions in a rulemaking. Section 624 neither grants nor withholds from the President any authority to determine what the substance of the agency's rule should be.
>
> The Committee does believe, however, that effective coordination of compliance with the new procedure required for major rules is essential. The Committee also believes that this need extends to independent agencies as well. Particularly given the limited scope of judicial review of the regulatory analysis permitted under the bill, it is essential that the President have the authority to assure that there is effective coordination and implementation of this new process by the independent agencies as well as Executive Branch agencies.

The Regulatory Reform Act, S. Rep. No. 284, 97th Cong., 1st Sess. 158 (1981).

Despite the broad support for S. 1080 within the Senate, neither of two parallel pieces of legislation in the House came to a vote before the close of the 97th Congress. Concerns about OMB's activities under Executive Order No. 12,291 and about the implications of provisions to extend the order's reach to the independent agencies were voted both by

Congressmen and by representatives of the various commissions and evidently contributed to the impasse.   See, e.g., *Hearings on H.R. 746, The Regulatory Procedure Act, Before the Subcomm. on Administrative Law and Governmental Relations of the House Comm. on the Judiciary*, 97th Cong., 1st Sess. 113, 129 (1981).   Undeterred, Senators Grassley and Heflin introduced an amended S. 1080 for consideration during the first session of the 98th Congress.

Several distinctive features of the 1983 Senate proposals, and of two parallel proposals (H.R. 220 and H.R. 3939) introduced by Representatives Levitas and Lott, respectively, warrant mention.   First, while the 1981 legislation had not addressed directly the issue of congressional oversight of agency rulemaking, the new S. 1080 and each of the House bills proposed to authorize congressional review.

In the wake of the *Chadha* decision, all of the bills sought to assure effective congressional oversight by means other than that of the legislative veto.   Under the scheme contemplated by each of these bills, a "major rule" would not take effect absent a joint resolution of approval by the Congress within a specified period (60 or 90 days) after its initial submission to the Secretary of the Senate and Clerk of the House.   For all other agency rules, a joint resolution of disapproval within a specified period would be required to prevent a rule from taking effect.   The 98th Congress is now history, and, as this edition goes to press, Congress has not yet acted.   Meanwhile, however, President Reagan has reinforced OMB's role under Executive Order No. 12,291, by requiring that all agencies develop and obtain OMB approval of annual pleas describing their proposed regulatory activities.   Deviation from an approved plan requires independent approval by OMB.   See Executive Order No. 12,498, 50 Fed. Reg. 1036 (1985).

For other, sometimes novel, proposals to render agencies accountable to the President and the incumbent administration's general program, see, e.g., Cutler & Johnson, *Regulation and the Political Process*, 84 Yale L.J. 1395 (1975); ABA Comm. on Law & the Economy, *Federal Regulation: Road to Reform* (1979); Note, *Delegation and Regulatory Reform: Letting the President Change the Rules* 89 Yale L.J. 561 (1980); Bruff, Presidential Power and Administrative Rulemaking, 88 Yale L.J. 451 (1979); Cutler, *The Case for Presidential Intervention in Regulatory Rulemaking by the Executive Branch*, 56 Tul. L. Rev. 830 (1982).

Executive Control Through the Office of the Attorney General

The issuance of executive orders, ɪemoval of officials, and "technocratic" oversight by OMB do not by any means exhaust the chief executive's devices for shaping policy.   One other device, control over agency litigation, merits more extended treatment.

Although American government functioned initially with a single part-time legal counsel, see Bell, *The Attorney General: The Federal Government's Chief Lawyer and Chief Litigator, or One Among Many?*, 46 Fordham L. Rev. 1049, 1050–52 (1978), the Department of Justice has become one of the nerve centers of the Executive Branch. This central position is due largely to the statutory centralization in that Department of legal representation of the United States. 28 U.S.C.A. § 516; 5 U.S.C.A. § 3106. Because the responsibility to provide legal representation in court entails the power to withhold it as well, the President has, through the Attorney General, a powerful technique for assuring that at least some consultation takes place between the far-flung agencies of the U.S. Government and its central administration.

The possibilities for centralized coordination through the Department of Justice obviously vary enormously from agency to agency and function to function. One might imagine that Justice Department policy would be of crucial importance to agencies like the FTC and the NLRB, whose regulatory powers historically have been backed by sanctions available only through judicial enforcement and whose "clientele" is both recalcitrant and litigious. On the other hand, an agency like the National Science Foundation, whose chief function is to fund academic research projects, should have little concern about potential conflicts between its policies and those of the Justice Department, for it will rarely have occasion to request the latter's assistance. An agency responsible for "entitlement" programs, like the Social Security Administration, which is seldom a plaintiff but often a defendant, probably lies between these polar cases.

Yet general propositions reveal little about the real influence of the Justice Department on particular agencies. The need for legal representation depends too much on the interaction of formal and informal administrative powers in particular substantive domains. Even enforcement-oriented agencies accomplish most of their tasks without resort to the courts. The use of an agency's need for representation as a lever to move policies in a particular direction will also depend on the degree to which the Justice Department views its cases as important, troublesome, routine, or trivial. See Rabin, *Agency Criminal Referrals in the Federal System: An Empirical Study of Prosecutorial Discretion*, 24 Stan. L. Rev. 1036, 1045–67 (1972). Moreover, the Department itself is hardly monolithic. The ninety-four U.S. Attorneys in districts around the country operate with considerable autonomy. Id. at 1040–42, 1074–75. See also Comment, *Justice Department's Prosecution Guidelines of Little Value to State and Local Prosecutors*, 72 J. Crim. Law & Criminology 955, 957–59 (1981).

Experience Under the Freedom of Information Act. The administration of the Freedom of Information Act (FOIA) provides one example of the Justice Department's capacity to become the lead agency in the federal establishment by virtue of its role as exclusive representative of the United States in court. (For more detailed treatment of the FOIA and its implementation, see Chapter 5, infra p. 508 *et seq.*) The original FOIA envisaged private lawsuits in district courts as the primary mode for forcing recalcitrant federal agencies to disclose public records. In the view of the legislation's sponsors, and apparently most of those who supported it in Congress, the Executive Branch—which had vigorously opposed enactment, see, e.g., *Administrative Procedure Act: Hearings Before the Sub-comm. on Adminstrative Practice and Procedure of the Senate Comm. on the Judiciary,* 89th Cong., 1st Sess. 29, 192 (1965)—could hardly be expected to be the primary enforcer of its own responsibilities under the Act.

Within three years of the FOIA's enactment, the number of lawsuits, and judicial reversals of agency decisions withholding information, had grown enough to cause the Justice Department to assume an active role in the administration of the statute. In 1969, the Department established an informal "Freedom of Information Committee" to screen final denials by agencies of FOIA requests.   Memorandum to General Counsels of All Federal Departments and Agencies Re Coordination of Certain Administrative Matters Under the Freedom of Information Act (Dec. 8, 1969), reprinted in *Administration and Operation of the Freedom Information Act: Hearings Before the Subcomm. on U.S. Government Policies and Practices of the House Comm. on Government Operations,* 92nd Cong., 2nd Sess., Pt. 4, 1132–33 (1912).   In the memorandum the Department "requested" that the general counsels consult with the FOIA Committee before finally denying a FOIA request, "if there is any substantial possibility that such a denial might lead to a court decision adversely affecting the Government."   The Department indicated that the Committee would give the proposed denial a timely and careful review "in terms of litigation risks, government implications, and the policy of the act."   The underlying message was clear.   If a department or agency persisted in a FOIA denial against the Committee's advice, the Justice Department would withhold legal counsel should suit be brought to force disclosure.

Reliance on this "internal" technique of FOIA implementation has varied with the information policies of different administrations.   In July 1973, Attorney General Richardson announced explicitly that the Justice Department would refuse to defend any agency decisions to withhold information unless the agency had consulted with the FOIA Committee prior to a final denial.   38 Fed. Reg. 19123 (July 18, 1973).   Three years later, however, Attorney General Levi removed the requirement of consultation.   41 Fed. Reg. 10222 (March 10, 1976).   But following President Carter's election, and reflecting his emphasis on open government, Attorney General Bell announced to the heads of all federal departments and agencies that "the Justice Department will defend Freedom of Information Act suits only when disclosure is demonstrably harmful, even if the documents technically fall within the exemptions in the Act."   Attorney General's May 5, 1977, Memorandum on FOIA, reprinted in *Freedom of Information Act: Hearings Before the Subcomm. on Administrative Practice and Procedure of the Senate Comm. on the Judiciary,* 95th Cong., 1st Sess., 217–18 (1977).   See also Procedures and Standards on Refusals to Defend FOIA Suits, DOJ—OILP, January 29, 1979.

Perhaps more importantly, the Carter Justice Department took several non-coercive initiatives to reinforce compliance with the FOIA.   A new Office of Information Law and Policy (OILP) was formed.   43 Fed. Reg.

45991 (Oct. 5, 1978). With increased staff, the OILP took on considerable consultative responsibilities with respect to agency inquiries about information policy throughout the government. The Carter Administration also announced a departmental review of all six hundred pending FOIA cases to determine how many might be resolved without further litigation.

It is unclear how much influence the Justice Department's efforts have had on agency compliance with the FOIA. There is every reason to believe that their impact has been substantial, but there are no data from which we can demonstrate this. We do know that the FOIA is invoked frequently and that agencies generally fulfill requests for records; while suits under the Act are numerous, as a percentage of requests the number is low. Yet we have no way of knowing how much Justice's efforts (by comparison, for example, with judicial review and congressional oversight) contributed to this generally forthcoming attitude on the part of agencies. Moreover, one should not make too muc of this example of the Department's general influence.

Centralized Legal Administration in Historical Perspective. Statutory provisions vesting exclusive representational authority in the Attorney General and granting that office power to supervise the activities of federal law officers can be traced to the creation of the Department of Justice, Act of June 22, 1870, 16 Stat. 162. The desirability of centralizing litigating authority in a single official, however, has not always commanded assent. Departmental responsibility for criminal proceedings in any case involving the United States has never been seriously questioned, but Attorneys General have from the very outset had to struggle, with uneven success, to retain their exclusive prerogative in civil litigation. A number of 19th century cases purported to recognize the Attorney General's plenary power over all government litigation, see, e.g. *The Gray Jacket,* 72 U.S. (5 Wall.) 342 (1866), *Confiscation Cases,* 74 U.S. (7th Wall.) 454 (1868), *United States v. San Jacinto Tin Co.,* 125 U.S. 273 (1888), and in executive orders Presidents Wilson and Franklin Roosevelt later expressly reaffirmed the principle that all U.S. law officers were to exercise their functions under the A.G.'s supervision and control. Executive Order No. 2,877 (1918); Executive Order No. 6,616 (1933).

Yet throughout this period, with the apparent if not explicit sanction of Congress, solicitors in various executive branch departments steadily assumed litigation authority. By 1913 much of the legal work of the Departments of State, Treasury, Interior, Commerce, Labor, Agriculture, Navy, and Post Office, as well as that of the Internal Revenue Service, was being conducted in a manner "actually if not theoretically independent of the Department of Justice." Key, *The Legal Work of the Federal Government,* 25 Va. L. Rev. 165, 189 (1938). A similar process was at work with respect to the independent regulatory agencies. 1910 amendments to the ICC Act expressly authorized lawyers for the Commission—which had customarily handled much of its own litigation in the lower courts—to intervene "of their own motion and as of right" in all court challenges to its actions and to "prosecute, defend or continue [any such] action or proceeding unaffected by the action or nonaction of the Attorney General therein." 28 U.S.C.A. § § 2321, 2323. While their independent litigation authority was generally not as far-reaching, the FTC (1914), FCC (1934), FPC (1934), SEC (1934), and NLRB (1935) were all in turn either expressly, or through judicial interpretation, granted varying degrees of autonomy from Justice Department supervisions.

As commentators have frequently observed, it is difficult to discern a consistent pattern in the apportionment of responsibility for litigation. The division of labor has tended to vary, sometimes radically, particularly as concerns the power to initiate lawsuits. Thus while the FPC enjoyed a clear grant of Congressional authority to sue on its own initiative, 16 U.S.C.A. § 825m(c), the FCC has traditionally had to rely on Justice whenever it went to court to enforce its orders, 47 U.S.C.A. § 401. The situation at the FTC initially represented something of a median between these polar extremes. Prior to 1973, the Justice Department represented the Commission in injunction and mandamus proceedings as well as civil penalty suits in the district courts, while the agency through its own attorneys handled enforcement proceedings in the courts of appeals. Thus, the law has been and remains "a hodgepodge of exceptions to the general statutes" vesting control in the Attorney General. Senate Committee on Governmental Affairs, V *Study on Federal Regulation* 56, 95th Cong., 1st Sess. (Comm. Print 1977) (hereafter *1977 Study on Federal Regulation*).

With respect to both executive branch and independent agencies, the late 19th and early 20th centuries witnessed a steady deterioration in the Department of Justice's centralized control of litigation. Decentralization continued in the mid-twentieth century, particularly with respect to the regulatory commissions. The Administrative Orders Review Act of 1950, for example, applied almost verbatim the provisions of the 1910 ICC Act cited above to three other independent agencies—the FCC, FMC, and AEC (now NRC). 28 U.S.C.A. § 2341. And in 1949, in *United States v. ICC*, 337 U.S. 426, 431–32 (1949), the Supreme Court modified its earlier pronouncements recognizing Justice as the exclusive spokesman for the government and acknowledged that increasing governmental involvement in diverse regulatory controls sometimes demanded a division of representation.

Developments in the intervening period have only served to reaffirm the general historical pattern, noted by one scholar, of "a continuing effort by Attorneys General to centralize responsibility for all government litigation in Justice, a continuing effort by many agencies to escape from that control with respect to civil litigation, and a practice by Congress of accepting the position of the Attorneys General in principle and then cutting them to pieces by exemptions." Davis, *Justice Department Control of Agency Litigation* 17, Report to the U.S. Administrative Conference, August 14, 1975.

Following the statutory recodification in 1966 of the Attorney General's authority to "control" and "supervise" all litigation in which the United States or an agency is interested or is a party, 28 U.S.C.A. § § 516, 519, the historical struggle has evidently intensified. The concerted attempt on the part of the Nixon administration to bring the whole of the federal policy-making establishment more directly under Presidential supervision, see generally R. NATHAN, THE ADMINISTRATIVE PRESIDENCY (1983), included efforts to ensure the Justice Department's more effective control of litigation. On June 30, 1970, for example, the Bureau of the Budget issued Circular No. A99, expressly directing executive branch departments and agencies considering new legislation to include provisions vesting control of litigation in the Department of Justice and to "oppose provisions in pending legislation which infringe on the Attorney General's litigative responsibilities." *Hearings on Department of Justice Authorization and Oversight, 1981*, Senate Comm. on the Judiciary, 96th Cong., 2d sess., 435 (1980) (hereinafter *1981 DOJ Authorization*). While there is little to suggest that this circular had any appreciable long-term effect on executive branch agencies anxious to assert their independence, it symbolizes the determination of recent administrations to resist what Attorney General Bell in 1977 characterized as the "Balkanization" of the Justice Department's litigation authority. *New York Times*, Oct. 17, 1977 (cited in *1977 Study on Federal Regulation* at 55). And, for a time at least, the attempts of the Nixon Justice Department appear to have had some effect. Thus, the new Commodity Futures Trading Commission (CFTC) was authorized to control injunction proceedings and the Consumer Products Safety Commission to proceed on its own via injunction and seizure against "imminently hazardous products," but control of litigation in all other cases was placed firmly in the hands of the Attorney General. 7 U.S.C.A. § 13a–1; 15 U.S.C.A. § § 2071, 2076(b)(7). But apart from those notable exceptions, recent centralization efforts have generally proved unavailing. Indeed, most of the statutory exemptions currently in effect were granted by Congress during the 1970s.

The most serious challenge confronting Justice during the 1970s came from the independent regulatory agencies. As we know, Congress traditionally has been concerned to ensure that these commissions particularly operate outside the supervision of the President and other executive branch officials, including the Attorney General. And while the CFTC and CPSC had been granted narrow litigating autonomy in their initial enabling acts, both soon joined the chorus of demands for greater autonomy emanating from the other independent agencies and their congressional supporters.

In these recent struggles agency participation in judicial review proceedings has not been a major issue. Even before passage of the 1950 Administrative Orders Review Act, most commissions customarily participated as parties in judicial review proceedings. The courts had recognized this "ancillary power" as "essential" to the effective discharge of their responsibilities. *FTC v. Dean Foods*, 384 U.S. 597, 607 (1966). The agitation that surfaced during the 1970's thus focused on two other important aspects of their authority to litigate, *viz.*, the power to initiate lawsuits for the purposes of enforcement and investigation and the ability of the independent agencies to initiate and argue appeals before the Supreme Court.

While it would be illusory to suggest that any single event triggered this round of conflict, the case of *FTC v. Guignon*, 390 F. 2d 323 (8th Cir. 1968), is often cited as critical. At issue in *Guignon* was the question whether the FTC was obliged to appear through the Attorney General to enforce its subpoenas. For decades, pursuant to a provision in its organic act authorizing it to "invoke the aid of any court of the United States in requiring the attendance and testimony of witnesses and the production of documentary evidence," 15 U.S.C.A. § 49, the Commission had brought court actions to enforce subpoenas at its own initiative and represented by its own attorneys. That practice was overturned in *Guignon* by the Eighth Circuit, which found that the legislative history, when read in light of other sections of the FTC Act, indicated a Congressional intention that only the Justice Department represent the agency in court. 390 F. 2d at 329. The court's decision appears to have been much influenced by an *amicus curiae* brief submitted by the Attorney General— at the invitation of the court and after argument was concluded. The FTC's consternation peaked when its request to the Department of Justice to seek certiorari in *Guignon* was summarily refused. See Davis, supra, at 35 n. 146.

From the vantage point of the FTC and the other independent agencies, the events surrounding *Guignon* provided a particularly telling illustration of the frustrations inherent in Department of Justice centralized control of litigation. *Guignon*, however, proved to be something of a pyrrhic victory for the Department. A number of proposals soon emerged in Congress aimed not only at expanding the authority of the independent agencies to initiate and conduct suits but also permitting them independently to seek certiorari from the Supreme Court and to plead their own case in that forum.

The Justice Department eventually prevailed in the first serious challenge (by the SEC) to the hitherto exclusive authority of the Attorney and Solicitor Generals under 28 U.S.C.A. § 518 to "conduct and argue suits and appeals in the Supreme Court." In testimony during consideration of the 1973 Securities Exchange Act Amendments, Solicitor General Griswold stressed the importance of the policing function performed by his office and cited a 1971 letter in which Chief Justice Burger had expressed the "unanimous view" of the Justices as to the inadvisability of diluting the Solicitor General's authority. *Hearings on H.R. 5050 and H.R. 340 before the Subcomm. on Commerce and Finance of House Comm. on Interstate and Foreign Commerce*, 93d Cong., 1st sess., 272 (1973) (hereinafter *1973 House Hearings*). Provisions that would have greatly augmented the SEC's already-formidable independent litigating authority were eventually dropped from the legislation.

In the post-*Guignon* battle over the litigating authority of the FTC, however, the Justice Department was less fortunate. An amendment tacked on to the Trans-Alaska Pipeline Authorization Act of 1973 expressly empowered the Commission to appear for itself in any lower-court proceeding "after formally notifying and consulting with and giving the Attorney General 10 days to take the action proposed by the Commission," Pub. L. No. 93–153, § 408, 87 Stat. 591, 592, and the FTC Improvements Act of 1975, Pub. L. No. 93–637, § 204, went even further, not only giving the Commission exclusive representational authority in lower court subpoena enforcement, injunctive relief and consumer redress cases, but also conferring on it still unique authority to seek Supreme Court review if first it requests the Justice Department to take that action and, after the passage of 60 days, the Attorney General declines or does nothing.   15 U.S.C.A. § 56(a)(3)(A).

In 1974, the Justice Department confronted, in S. 704, the first of two sweeping proposals that would have conferred greatly enhanced litigative powers—apparently including the right of self-representation before the Supreme Court—upon a host of agencies.   Section 5 of the Regulatory Agencies Independence Act would have authorized the CAB, FCC, FMC, FTC, SEC, ICC, and FPC to act in their own name and through their own counsel and to supervise and conduct *all* litigation in *any* civil action "not-withstanding any other provision of law."   Three years later, the Senate Commerce Committee issued a series of reports advancing a slightly less daring proposal.   The relevant portions of the proposed Interim Regulatory Reform Acts stipulated (with respect to the FMC, ICC, FPC, FCC, and CAB) that if after 45 days the Attorney General had failed to act on the request of the commission or board on a matter over which the latter had an arguable statutory right of self-representation, then the agency "shall have authority to commence, defend or intervene and supervise the litigation of such action (or any appeal of such action) in its own name and by its own attorneys."

In the end, the Justice Department was able to weather each of these storms and to prevent substantial, across-the-board excisions of its authority.   And consequently pressures to permit agency self-representation, at least, before the Supreme Court, appear to have abated.   Thus, the Federal Energy Regulatory Commission (FERC) was expressly denied power to litigate before the Court when it was chartered in 1977, 42 U.S.C.A. § 7171(i); and the same year the Senate Study on Federal Regulation, conceding that on this particular issue there "does appear to be a special justification for a greater degree of coordination," recommended that the Attorney General and Solicitor General continue to control and argue cases before the Supreme Court.   *1977 Study on Federal Regulation* at 66.

On the broader questions of authority to initiate lawsuits and self-representation, however, the Justice Department lost ground during the mid- and late 1970s.   In 1977, Congress granted FERC the broad type of statutory authorization with respect to the initiation of suits and defense of orders originally contemplated for the commissions covered by § 704.   Having failed in their attempts to promote adoption of generic legislation, the various other independent agencies continued to press for individual statutory exemptions and/or informal arrangements with Justice that would enhance their litigating independence.   Evidently in the context of negotiations with other executive branch agencies during this period, Justice began the practice of entering into informal "memoranda of understanding" regarding the allocation of litigation responsibilities.

The negotiations needless to say, were often acrimonious, and the memoranda of understanding frequently reflected last-ditch efforts on Justice's part to fend off further statutory amputation of its litigation authority.

This at least was the Department's view of the matter as presented before the Senate Judiciary Committee in 1981. A number of current and former DOJ officials were asked to comment on the background and status of the informal agreements Justice had made over the years with executive branch and independent agencies (including the Departments of Labor and Energy, the CFTC, and the Federal Election Commission). The memoranda of understanding were "usually a result of a kind of blackmail procedure," according to one official; the arrangement with Energy was "a major loss" that had been consented to only because Justice "had a gun at its head," offered a second; the Department's 1975 agreement permitting Labor control over ERISA and OSHA cases had been entered into "under duress," with the threat of further statutory fragmentation looming "on the horizon," explained a third. *1981 DOJ Authorization and Oversight Hearings* at 383, 444. Needless to say, Justice's perception that these memoranda of understanding had invariably compromised its authority to supervise and control litigation was not universally shared. The 1977 Senate Study, for example, reviewed an arrangement then in place with EPA and concluded that it was unsatisfactory because by its terms the agreement "makes it clear that litigation authority remains within the province of the Attorney General." *1977 Study on Federal Regulation* at 66.

As of the late 1970's some 29 separate governmental entities (eighteen commissions, boards, or corporations and eleven executive branch departments or agencies) exercised some form of statutory litigation authority and exercised similar authority via informal delegations. With Justice continuing to warn of complete chaos, and with pressures building on all sides, the Carter Administration resolved to review the entire issue. In a directive issued in August 1977, the administration launched, what came to be known as the "PRP Federal Legal Representation Project," later to be described by an OMB official as "the first comprehensive study of the Federal Government's legal system since the Hoover Commission completed its 1955 report." *1981 DOJ Authorization and Oversight Hearings* at 428.

Despite the lofty aims, when this project had completed its work and Executive Order No. 12,146 was issued in 44 Fed. Reg. 42657 (July 18, 1979), the basic questions remained unsettled. The failure to confront the issue head-on—let alone definitely to resolve matters in its favor—clearly frustrated many within the Justice Department, see, e.g., *1981 DOJ Authorization* at 822 (Statement of Rex Lee, Former Assistant Attorney General and later Solicitor General). A principal in the project later frankly acknowledged that "the whole question of allocation of litigation authority is one that is so controversial, both in the Congress and between the executive branch and independent regulatory agencies, that we felt it was not fruitful to try to reach some kind of final decision in the Executive Order."   Id. at 433–34.

The principle initiative undertaken in Executive Order No. 12,146 reflected the conclusion of the project participants that, while decisions allocating litigation responsibilities had best "be handled administratively rather than prescribed in detail by statute," a more orderly mechanism than memorandums of understanding was clearly required for resolving some of the existing disputes.   For at least 458 lawsuits by one agency against another were filed in fiscal year 1977 alone.   The order thus called for the formation of a Federal Legal Council "composed of the Attorney General and the representatives of not more than 15 agencies" designed to promote (among other, lesser objectives) "coordination and communication among Federal legal offiices."   Executive Order No. 12,146 also prescribed a dispute resolution procedure whereby, in the event of non- negotiable conflict between them, "Executive agencies whose heads serve at the pleasure of the President" were required to submit their disagreement to the Attorney General "prior to proceeding in any court."   44 Fed. Reg. 42657–58.

Justice Department officials and others were quick to point out that while the Federal Legal Council included representatives of such major commissions as the FTC, ICC, and SEC, the failure to apply the dispute resolution mechanism across the board meant that the Council would have no authority over the many cases involving conflicts between the independent and executive branch agencies.   Defenders of the Council, anxious not to see its efforts undone by these criticisms, could only express the hope that the commissions would (as they were "encouraged" by the order to do) voluntarily agree to abide by the procedure.

Justice Department officials no doubt concurred in the judgment of Senator Baucus that the failure of Executive Order No. 12,146 to address the problems with the independent agencies, or to shore up the Attorney General's authority within the Council rendered likely continued statutory and informal erosion of centralized litigation authority.   Id. at 462.   Yet, important as they may be, the developments chronicled in the preceding paragraphs almost surely understate the Department's capacity to control litigation involving the federal government and to use that authority as a lever to move policies in a particular direction—just as the FOIA example may overstate the Department's influence.   Even at the worst of times, more than two-thirds of the 90-odd federal agencies within and outside the executive branch have had to rely exclusively on the Justice Department for representation in court.   And while Department attorneys are generally concerned to maintain good relations with their clients, when compliance with central directives is considered of sufficient importance the Department on its own, or the President acting through the Attorney General, can still use the threat of withholding representation as a means to bring agencies into line.

Part II

ADMINISTRATIVE PROCEDURE AND JUDICIAL OVERSIGHT

Chapter 3

FORMAL AGENCY ADJUDICATION

Formal adjudication is surely familiar to students who have been exposed to a basic course in civil procedure—indeed, to anyone exposed to American theater, television, or motion pictures. The courtroom trial is a ubiquitous part of our culture; a constant source of social fascination, dramatic inspiration, and political as well as legal commentary. But what of formal *administrative* adjudication? What is special here that should grasp our attention? The very term, administrative adjudication, threatens to dampen interest—until one recalls, for example, that it was an administrative tribunal which adjudicated Dr. Robert Oppenheimer's claim to a security clearance. Or that administrative adjudications comprise a governmental exercise vaster by far than the caseload of all civil and criminal courts. Moreover, the contexts in which administrative tribunals function are equally diverse.

While it is obvious that the judicial trial model could not be replicated in all administrative adjudications or even in all cases involving substantial or valuable interests, a central concern of this chapter is the appropriate extent of departures from that model in the non-judicial context. The responses to this question by American courts—and legislatures and administrators—are complex, for formal adjudication plays several roles in the history and the contemporary functioning of American government. The lawyer who would perform successfullly within this ostensibly familiar legal environment must see adjudication as performed by administrators not simply in a new light, but as bathed simultaneously in several new lights.

First, one must recognize that the administrative trial—or the "trial-type" hearing—is a legally, indeed a constitutionally, problematic undertaking. To be sure, the legal questions for administrative lawyers include familiar issues concerning the scope of the rights of parties in formal adjudicatory proceedings. The novelty of administrative adjudication lies in part in the law's responses to these issues, which vary both with agency function (e.g., licensing, rate-making, prosecution, dispute settlement) and with substantive program (e.g., trade regulation, income redistribution, environmental protection). Administrative lawyers, however, are as often preoccupied with a prior question: When must agency decisionmaking take the form of a trial-type proceeding? It is with this question that the chapter begins.

174

Why is the "right to hearing" question deemed so important?　In a trivial sense administrative lawyers, acting as litigators, ask the question because it is strategically advantageous.　Courts will treat it seriously, and sometimes they will reverse agency decisions for failure to provide an adequate hearing.　But why will the courts listen?　The answer is, of course, imbedded in our peculiar constitutional history and constitutional structure.　That history and structure make us skeptical both of administrative government *and* of judicial reexamination of legislative judgments.　And, somehow, through a process of evolution that cannot be captured in a volume, much less a line, we have discovered that the "right to hearing" question is the question to be put when we fear administrative governance and simultaneously wish to avoid actuating fears of an imperial judiciary.

Yet, even if historically justified, is the "right to hearing" question the correct question?　Can it be answered in ways that will both protect individual liberties and facilitate the achievement of collective ends?　Might the answers—perhaps even the incessant asking—somehow confuse and ultimately defeat the purposes of a government that is at once liberal and democratic, yet run largely by administrators?

To illuminate these issues we must examine the functioning of formal adjudication in the unfamiliar and often harsh light of administration.　We must consider what it means to implement government programs—to bend many hands and many minds to a common enterprise. What are the organizational imperatives of bureaucratic administration? With what attributes?　With what effects?　These are the sorts of issues that lurk beneath the surface of the "right to hearing" cases.　In Part B of this chapter we confront them directly, and from a "bureaucratic" perspective.

That not all administrative decisionmaking can be cast in the form of a trial seems obvious.　"Hearings" will inevitably be structured differently for different administrative functions and different legislative programs. Yet *how* these accommodations will be made and with what *significance* for the overall conception of administrative law are by no means obvious.

Many important administrative decisions are, however, the product of procedures similar to civil trials.　Accordingly, our spotlight shifts to judicial review of administrative adjudication.　What is the courts' role when reviewing formal agency adjudications?　If not the same as when reviewing trial court dispositions, what judicial posture is appropriate? And what are the effects of court review on agency behavior and on private interests? These are the issues for Part C.

Finally, we study how an agency with a specific mission, limited resources, and subject to explicit statutory requirements for formal hearings, tries to accomplish its job.　We focus illustratively on a single agency and examine how it "lawyers" its way through, in fact substantially around, obligations of formal administrative adjudication.　This is the concern of Part D, which deals with the implementation of the "new drug" licensing process by the Food and Drug Administration.

A.   THE RIGHT TO TRIAL-TYPE HEARINGS

Trial-type or "adjudicatory" process customarily includes several basic features: (1) timely and specific notice of the issues to be resolved at a hearing; (2) the right of affected parties to appear personally or through representatives for purposes of presenting evidence and arguing their positions; (3) confrontation and cross-examination of opposing witnesses; (4) public proceedings; (5) an impartial decisionmaker; (6) a decision based exclusively on the evidence and argument submitted at the hearing or otherwise made a part of the "record" of the proceeding; and (7) written findings of fact and conclusions of law.   The paradigm example of this process for contemporary American lawyers is perhaps the private civil action, tried without a jury, in a federal district court.

Although highly stylized, even ritualistic, complex considerations of "fairness" are thought to motivate the modern trial process.   Because each party is generally considered to have the same stake in the outcome, each participates on identical terms.   An opportunity is provided for each party to know about and to contest any assertion of fact or law made by another party.   The equal and extensive participation by affected parties in shaping the evidence, and their equal opportunities to persuade the deciding official, are sought to be assured by limiting the decisionmaker's sources of information to evidence submitted "on the record" in the proceeding and by requiring articulation of how the decision was reached on the basis of that record.

The APA incorporates this basic model of formal adjudication in 5 U.S.C.A. § § 554-57.   Note, however, that the APA itself does not make these procedures applicable to any activity other than the removal of administrative law judges. 5 U.S.C.A. § 7521.   The right to the procedures prescribed by sections 554-57 must flow from some other statute, e.g., an agency's organic act, requiring the agency to make decisions only "on the record after opportunity for hearing."   Moreover, an agency's authorizing statute might as easily prescribe the APA formal process for rulemaking as for adjudication.   From this abstract perspective the question of whether there is a right to a trial-type hearing before an administrative agency seems easily answered: Such a right exists if provided by statute.

This answer suffices in many standard situations.   Congress has specified trial-type processes for the core adjudicatory activities of agencies such as the Social Security Administration, the Federal Trade Commission, and the National Labor Relations Board.   However, many other agencies, and indeed those just named when making certain types of decisions, have been provided less clear instructions.   Often an agency's governing statute has virtually nothing to say about the procedures it should follow in making decisions, or simply enjoins the agency to act only after a "hearing."

Moreover, the constitutional concept of "due process" has long been considered to confer some independent right to procedural protections; a right entailing, but not necessarily satisfied by, the provision of those administrative procedures specified by particular statutes and by "due process," is hardly self-defining.   Thus, whether interpreting vague statutory directions or the Constitution's Due Process Clause, the courts have had to search for general principles to guide their analysis of "what process is due?"; who has a "right to trial-type hearing"; and what such a "right" entails.

General principles have not been easy to derive or to apply.   In a seminal essay, *Methodology and Criteria in Due Process Adjudication*, 66 Yale L.J. 319 (1957), Sanford Kadish reviewed the Supreme Court's due process jurisprudence with a sense of frustration.   One strain of the case law seemed reasonably coherent: it simply relied upon tradition. Processes that had close analogues in wide use, or that were historically sanctioned, were deemed legitimate; other processes—relatively uncommon—were deemed illegitimate.   Yet, as Kadish discovered, the tradition-based approach hardly exhausted the courts' repertoire of due process analysis.   Other cases spoke in terms of such concepts as "fundamental fairness" or "governmental necessity."   In the end Kadish could only suggest that beyond tradition-sanctioned procedures, the federal courts recognized a concept of "flexible due process" which lacked any apparent principle of similar generality.

Viewed from a more contemporary perspective due process doctrine does not display much more coherence.   It is now possible, however, to suggest that due process adjudication consists principally of variations on three central themes, which we can term "tradition," "natural rights," and "interest balancing."[3] Each theme is complex and richly embellished in the cases.   Each has its adherents and detractors.   See generally J. MASHAW, DUE PROCESS IN THE ADMINISTRATIVE STATE (1985).   Here we can only introduce the core ideas and suggest their limitations.

Tradition.   A tradition-based approach to due process analysis asks whether the procedures at issue conform to the customary processes of law.   As an historical matter this way of putting the due process question has much to recommend it.   The original understanding of the due process constraint may have been that it provided protection against oppressive governmental acts enforced through "special" proceedings.   The Due Process Clause is thus the constitutional heir of English concerns with Star Chamber proceedings and revolutionary resistance to an arbitrary colonial magistracy.

But tradition has serious limitations as a decisional guide.   As a jurisprudential technique, its weakness lies in the difficulty of identifying a single appropriate tradition.   When, for example, the Supreme Court in *Goldberg v. Kelly*, 397 U.S. 254 (1970), infra p. 182, confronted the distinctly Twentieth Century question of an appropriate process for terminating welfare benefits, it was required to choose from among competing traditions.   The long tradition of non-enforcement of gratuitous promises, including promises of continuous income support, suggested that there was no legal interest involved sufficient to actuate due process concern.   The tradition of commercial law remedies suggested that the welfare recipient (creditor) should have post-termination recourse to ordinary civil process to determine the legality of the government's (debtor) failure to perform. The tradition of governmental cancellation of other valuable privileges, such as common carrier certificates or professional licenses, suggested that, absent emergency, some form of pretermination proceeding was necessary. By what jurisprudential technique does a court decide which tradition is most relevant?

The value presuppositions of a tradition-focused approach to due process protection are also troublesome. If tradition implies adherence to the original understanding of "life, liberty and property," then many governmental activities that encroach on modern notions of humane values evade constitutional constraint. And, on one "original" understanding of due process—meaning the processes of the ordinary courts or of the legislature—much of the regulatory apparatus of the welfare state applicable to property interests would be unconstitutional (the national labor relations laws, all federal environmental legislation, most safety legislation, the anti-fraud activities of the Federal Trade and Securities and Exchange Commissions, to name a few). By modern standards the process constraints of such a traditional approach to due process (a choice limited to representative assemblies and judicial trials) are as over-protective as the traditional view's substantive values (protection only against death, incarceration, or invasion of common-law property) are underinclusive.

Natural Rights. A natural rights analysis takes a quite different view of the due process problem. It begins, not with the historical contingencies of tradition, but with a basic moral premise concerning individual autonomy. Each citizen is an end, not merely a means for the attainment of collective ends. The government cannot, therefore, pursue its purposes through processes that ignore the independent status and purposes of the individual. From the natural rights perspective this dignitary principle is what the Due Process Clause, like other portions of the Bill of Rights, protects. A conception of human dignity thus informs the historic demand for "fundamental fairness."

While this secular formulation of the natural rights approach has substantial support in liberal political theory (see, e.g., J. MASHAW, *op. cit.*; Pincoffs, *Due Process, Fraternity, and a Kantian Injunction,* DUE PROCESS, NOMOS XVIII 173 (J.R. Pennock and J. Chapman, eds. 1977)), and clear connections with the individualistic ethos of ordinary political discourse (see, e.g., E. REDFORD, DEMOCRACY IN THE ADMINISTRATIVE STATE (1969)), it also raises problems of application. The set of procedural rights necessary to preserve individual dignity seems infinitely expansive. See, e.g., Saphire, *Specifying Due Process Values: Toward a More Responsive Approach to Procedural Protection,* 127 U. Pa. L. Rev. 111 (1978); Tushnet, *The Newer Property: Suggestions for the Revival of Substantive Due Process,* 1975 Sup. Ct. Rev. 261. Any governmentally imposed disappointment provides an occasion for invocation of the principle. Moreover, autonomy implies that due process should be defined as those procedures freely accepted by the individuals affected. Because such a principle forecloses governance, limitations must be imposed. But, what are the principles of limitation? Where is the objective set of *truly important* human values and *sufficiently dignified* procedures for making collective decisions about them?

The judicial dilemma is apparent. Questions of value are crucial to the application of the Due Process Clause. The constitutional text requires that human interests be characterized as "life, liberty or property" concerns that either have or do not have sufficient status to trigger due process protection. And, substantive stakes in decisional outcomes aside, it is surely not irrelevant whether governmental processes do or do not respect individual interests in autonomy. Yet, in an increasingly secular and scientific society, confronting questions of moral value directly, and in an authoritative context, can be embarrassing. Because they have no attachment to revealed truth and no empirical underpinning, moral pronouncements *cum* constitutional interpretations appear radically subjective. Decisions based on "fundamental fairness" seem to measure justice, as in the old saw, by the length of the Chancellor's foot.

Interest Balancing. This, the dominant contemporary mode of due process analysis promises the functional criteria so conspicuously absent from natural rights propositions. Under the prevailing Supreme Court formulation, the assessment of process adequacy requires consideration of (1) the magnitude of the interests of private parties, (2) the governmental interest in procedural expedition, and (3) the likely contribution of various procedural ingredients to the correct resolution of disputes. See *Mathews v. Eldridge*, 424 U.S. 319 (1976). In short, the court performs a social welfare calculation to determine whether society will be better or worse off if it honors the claim to more formalized procedure.

The great advantages of the interest balancing approach are its adaptability to virtually any question of procedural adequacy and its recognition that judgments about process adequacy necessarily involve tradeoffs between collective and individual ends. But, as a constitutional theory this brand of utilitarianism has the defects of its virtues. For one thing, interest balancing suggests that, given a good enough reason, the government can use whatever process it pleases. The Bill of Rights is, however, not meant only to facilitate adaptation of constitutional constraints to changing governmental forms; its most obvious function is to protect against official encroachments on individual liberty. The interest balancing methodology thus seems to contradict the basic libertarian presuppositions of the text that it would implement. Moreover, the information requirements of a rigorous utilitarian calculus are very substantial, perhaps excessive. Mashaw, *Administrative Due Process As Social Cost Accounting*, 9 Hofstra L. Rev. 1423 (1981). Can the dignitary costs of individuals and the administrative costs of government, for example, be measured in the same currency? Is it really possible to predict the effect of any discrete changes in the decision process on the accuracy of decisions?

Given even this sketchy introduction to the strengths and weaknesses of the dominant due process methodologies, it is hardly surprising that the Supreme Court has never chosen a single approach and adhered to it.

GREAT RISE IN DUE PROCESS SUITS

Nor, even when operating ostensibly under one or another methodological tendency, has it achieved consistency. ✓Unhappily, this vagueness and vacillation combine with—some might say induce—a continuing high level of suits against government agencies claiming rights to some aspect of trial type process. We estimate that approximately three thousand administrative due process cases were *decided* by the federal courts during the 1970s. And thousands more cases may have been filed. This level of conflict over administrative procedure has been variously characterized as a "process explosion" or a "due process revolution." See, e.g., Friendly, *Some Kind of Hearing*, 123 U. Pa. L. Rev. 1267, 1268 (1975); Rendleman, *The New Due Process: Rights and Remedies*, 63 Ky. L.J. 531 (1975).

SUITS USED TO BE RARE

While "explosions" and "revolutions" are presumably a cause for concern, if not alarm, the continuing flow of due process claims should be kept in perspective. The emergence of due process cases as an important category of constitutional litigation seems to be directly related to the relative activism of government. Between 1787 and 1866 only one due process case was decided by the Supreme Court. And, for the next sixty-five years, until the New Deal, virtually all of the Supreme Court's due process jurisprudence was concerned with the activities of state government. Why? ·Because, prior to 1933, governmental activity directly affecting individual citizens and enterprises was carried on primarily by states and localities. And before the ratification of the Civil War amendments such state and local activity was not subject to due process review under the federal constitution. Following the adoption of the Fourteenth Amendment, such review was increasingly sought with respect to these relatively "activist" levels of government.

Indeed, in the mid-1870s the Supreme Court was making noises much like its contemporary critics. In *Davidson v. New Orleans*, 96 U.S. (6 Otto) 97, 103-04 (1877), the Court lamented:

> It is not a little remarkable, that while [the Due Process Clause] has been in the Constitution of the United States, as a restraint upon the authority of the Federal government, for nearly a century * * * this special limitation upon its powers has rarely been invoked in the judicial forum * * * . But while it has been a part of the Constitution, as a restraint upon the power of the States, only a very few years, the docket of this court is crowded with cases in which we are asked to hold that State courts and State legislatures have deprived their own citizens of life, liberty, or property without due process of law. There is here abundant evidence that there exists some strange misconception of the scope of this provision as found in the fourteenth amendment. In fact, it would seem, from the character of many of the cases before us, and the arguments made in them, that the clause under consideration is looked upon as a means of bringing to the test of the decision of this court the abstract opinions of every unsuccessful litigant in a State court of the justice of the decision against him, and of the merits of the legislation on which such a decision may be founded.

✓The New Deal reversed the balance of federal and state governmental activity. Where four of every five due process claims that reached the

Supreme Court between 1866 and 1933 concerned state action, from the New Deal to the Great Society four out of five involved the federal government. Thereafter, the proportions are again reversed. While new federal regulatory and subsidy programs were still being generated in abundance in the post-1965 period, those programs increasingly were implemented by state and local officials. And it is at the level of implementation that demands for procedural protection customarily arise.

The explanation for the historic association between due process litigation and governmental activism seems relatively straightforward. As government acts in new areas, or expands activity in older ones, it adopts new forms. While tradition has a strong hold on the legal imagination, legislation is an empiric business—experimentation is constant. Within the lifetime of many still living, for example, there has been a shift in the paradigmatic legal techniques of social control. Legislative rules of conduct, enforceable by criminal sanction in the courts, have been replaced by the more flexible techniques of regulatory commissions. *Post hoc* regulation of primary conduct through liability rules has given way to *ex ante* intervention, either to regulate harmful activities or to subsidize useful ones. *Laissez faire* has been replaced by the welfare state. Much of the citizen's wealth and security have come to be held, not in the currency of physical capital and familial attachment, but in the coin of government contract, license, regulation or subsidy. Legislative grants of individual licenses, charters or subsidies were replaced by legislative programs administered by specialized agencies.

These profound changes in our forms of governance generated two predictable legal responses: attacks on the constitutional legitimacy of change by those whose interests lay with the old regime and attempts to regularize and reinforce the legal relationships that reconstituted the citizen's portfolio of welfare state entitlements. Both responses are portentous for the evolution of hearing rights. The enticing vagueness of the Due Process Clause permits virtually any lament of "what sort of government is this anyway?" to be reformulated as a justiciable claim to process protection. Moreover, when cast in procedural terms, such claims invite the courts to interpose constraints on governmental action without confronting directly the substantive powers of the legislature. Process fairness can be zealously protected without exciting much alarm concerning the judiciary's constitutional mandate.

Given our peculiar governmental and constitutional history, procedural due process claims thus provide many of the occasions for our on-going conversation concerning the appropriate structure of an increasingly administrative state. Yet the central place of due process adjudication in any discussion of constitutional history, interpretive method, or administrative law cannot be portrayed here through rigorous analysis and historical and institutional contextualization of even the most important of the Supreme Court's due process decisions. Most of the great political issues of post-Civil War America—immigration, state economic regulation, communist subversion, welfare rights, the status of public employees, the treatment of prisoners and patients, to name but a few—have converged on the federal courts with due process claims leading the charge. Within only the last dozen years the Supreme Court has heard procedural challenges to the actions of administrators who implement programs of public assistance, unemployment insurance, medical insurance, and disability insurance; who license nursing homes, automobile drivers and nuclear reactors; who oversee institutions for public education, and for the custody and rehabilitation of the emotionally disturbed, mentally incompetent or socially deviant; who control access to alcoholic beverages, public employment, parole and electrical service; who regulate railroad rates; and who enforce public safety ordinances.

From this diverse and politically charged caseload—itself not fully representative of judicial activity—we must select an illustrative sample. We have chosen as our microcosm the domain of social welfare payments. Within this arena one finds contemporary cases of paramount doctrinal importance as well as illustrations of the central issues that pervade the due process jurisprudence generally. But no selection can do justice to the complexity displayed by the ubiquitous demand of litigants for an administrative "hearing," presumably the more "formal" the better.

GOLDBERG v. KELLY

Supreme Court of the United States, 1970.
397 U.S. 254, 90 S.Ct. 1011, 25 L.Ed.2d 287.

MR. JUSTICE BRENNAN delivered the opinion of the Court.

* * *

This action was brought in the District Court for the Southern District of New York by residents of New York City receiving financial aid under the federally assisted program of Aid to Families with Dependent Children (AFDC) or under New York State's general Home Relief program. Their complaint alleged that the New York State and New York City officials administering these programs terminated, or were about to terminate, such aid without prior notice and hearing, thereby denying them due process of law. At the time the suits were filed there was no requirement of prior notice or hearing of any kind before termination of financial aid. However, the State and city adopted procedures for notice and hearing after the suits were brought, and the plaintiffs, appellees here, then challenged the constitutional adequacy of those procedures.

* * *

* * * A caseworker who has doubts about the recipient's continued eligibility must first discuss them with the recipient. If the caseworker concludes that the recipient is no longer eligible, he recommends termination of aid to a unit supervisor. If the latter concurs, he sends the recipient a letter stating the reasons for proposing to terminate aid and notifying him that within seven days he may request that a higher official review the record, and may support the request with a written statement prepared personally or with the aid of an attorney or other person. If the reviewing official affirms the determination of ineligibility, aid is stopped immediately and the recipient is informed by letter of the rea-

P/c

sons for the action.   Appellees' challenge to this procedure emphasizes the absence of any provisions for the personal appearance of the recipient before the reviewing official, for oral presentation of evidence, and for confrontation and cross-examination of adverse witnesses.   However, the letter does inform the recipient that he may request a post-termination "fair hearing."   This is a proceeding before an independent state hearing officer at which the recipient may appear personally, offer oral evidence, confront and cross-examine the witnesses against him, and have a record made of the hearing.   If the recipient prevails at the "fair hearing" he is paid all funds erroneously withheld.   A recipient whose aid is not restored by a "fair hearing" decision may have judicial review.

The constitutional issue to be decided, therefore, is the narrow one (whether the Due Process Clause requires that the recipient be afforded an evidentiary hearing *before* the termination of benefits.)* * *   *ISSUE*

Appellant does not contend that procedural due process is not applicable to the termination of welfare benefits.   Such benefits are a matter of statutory entitlement for persons qualified to receive them.[8]   Their termination involves state action that adjudicates important rights.   The constitutional challenge cannot be answered by an argument that public assistance benefits are "a 'privilege' and not a 'right.'"   *Shapiro v. Thompson*, 394 U.S. 618, 627 n.6 (1969).   Relevant constitutional restraints apply as much to the withdrawal of public assistance benefits as to disqualification for unemployment compensation, *Sherbert v. Verner*, 374 U.S. 398 (1963); or to denial of a tax exemption, *Speiser v. Randall*, 357 U.S. 513 (1958); or to discharge from public employment, *Slochower v. Board of Higher Education*, 350 U.S. 551 (1956).   The extent to which procedural due process must be afforded the recipient is influenced by the extent to which he may be "condemned to suffer grievous loss," *Joint Anti-Fascist Refugee Committee v. McGrath*, 341 U.S. 123, 168 (1951) (Frankfurter, J., concurring), and depends upon whether the recipient's interest in avoiding that loss outweighs the governmental interest in summary adjudication.   Accordingly, as we said in *Cafeteria & Restaurant Workers Union v. McElroy*, 367 U.S. 886, 895 (1961), "consideration of what procedures due process may require under any given set of cir-

---

8. It may be realistic today to regard welfare entitlements as more like "property" than a "gratuity."   Much of the existing wealth in this country takes the form of rights that do not fall within traditional common-law concepts of property.   It has been aptly noted that

"[s]ociety today is built around entitlement.   The automobile dealer has his franchise, the doctor and lawyer their professional licenses, the worker his union membership, contract, and pension rights, the executive his contract and stock options; all are devices to aid security and independence.   Many of the most important of these entitlements now flow from government: subsidies to farmers and businessmen, routes for airlines and channels for television stations; long term contracts for defense, space, and education; social security pensions for individuals.   Such sources of security, whether private or public, are no longer regarded as luxuries or gratuities; to the recipients they are essentials, fully deserved, and in no sense a form of charity.   It is only the poor whose entitlements, although recognized by public policy, have not been effectively enforced."   Reich, Individual Rights and Social Welfare: The Emerging Legal Issues, 74 Yale L.J. 1245, 1255 (1965).   See also Reich, The New Property, 73 Yale L.J. 733 (1964).

cumstances must begin with a determination of the precise nature of the government function involved as well as of the private interest that has been affected by governmental action."

It is true, of course, that some governmental benefits may be administratively terminated without affording the recipient a pretermination evidentiary hearing. But we agree with the District Court that when welfare is discontinued, only a pretermination evidentiary hearing provides the recipient with procedural due process. For qualified recipients, welfare provides the means to obtain essential food, clothing, housing, and medical care. Thus the crucial factor in this context—a factor not present in the case of the blacklisted government contractor, the discharged government employee, the taxpayer denied a tax exemption, or virtually anyone else whose governmental entitlements are ended—is that termination of aid pending resolution of a controversy over eligibility may deprive an *eligible* recipient of the very means by which to live while he waits. Since he lacks independent resources, his situation becomes immediately desperate. His need to concentrate upon finding the means for daily subsistence, in turn, adversely affects his ability to seek redress from the welfare bureaucracy.[12]

Moreover, important governmental interests are promoted by affording recipients a pre-termination evidentiary hearing. From its founding the Nation's basic commitment has been to foster the dignity and well-being of all persons within its borders. We have come to recognize that forces not within the control of the poor contribute to their poverty. This perception, against the background of our traditions, has significantly influenced the development of the contemporary public assistance system. Welfare, by meeting the basic demands of subsistence, can help bring within the reach of the poor the same opportunities that are available to others to participate meaningfully in the life of the community. At the same time, welfare guards against the societal malaise that may flow from a widespread sense of unjustified frustration and insecurity. Public assistance, then, is not mere charity, but a means to "promote the general Welfare, and secure the Blessings of Liberty to ourselves and our Posterity." The same governmental interests that counsel the provision of welfare, counsel as well its uninterrupted provision to those eligible to receive it; pre-termination evidentiary hearings are indispensable to that end.

Appellant does not challenge the force of these considerations but argues that they are outweighed by countervailing governmental interests in conserving fiscal and administrative resources. These interests, the argument goes, justify the delay of any evidentiary hearing until after discontinuance of the grants. Summary adjudication protects the public fisc by stopping payments promptly upon discovery of reason to believe that a recipient is no longer eligible. Since most terminations are ac-

---

12. His impaired adversary position is particularly telling in light of the welfare bureaucracy's difficulties in reaching correct decisions on eligibility. See Comment, Due Process and the Right to a Prior Hearing in Welfare Cases, 37 Ford. L. Rev. 604, 610-611(1969).

cepted without challenge, summary adjudication also conserves both the fisc and administrative time and energy by reducing the number of evidentiary hearings actually held.

We agree with the District Court, however, that these governmental interests are not overriding in the welfare context. The requirement of a prior hearing doubtless involves some greater expense, and the benefits paid to ineligible recipients pending decision at the hearing probably cannot be recouped, since these recipients are likely to be judgment-proof. But the State is not without weapons to minimize these increased costs. Much of the drain on fiscal and administrative resources can be reduced by developing procedures for prompt pre-termination hearings and by skillful use of personnel, and facilities. * * * As the District Court correctly concluded: "[t]he stakes are simply too high for the welfare recipient, and the possibility for honest error or irritable misjudgment too great, to allow termination of aid without giving the recipient a chance, if he so desires, to be fully informed of the case against him so that he may contest its basis and produce evidence in rebuttal."

We also agree with the District Court, however, that the pre-termination hearing need not take the form of a judicial or quasi-judicial trial. We bear in mind that the statutory "fair hearing" will provide the recipient with a full administrative review.[14] Accordingly, the pre-termination hearing has one function only: to produce an initial determination of the validity of the welfare department's grounds for discontinuance of payments in order to protect a recipient against an erroneous termination of his benefits. Thus, a complete record and a comprehensive opinion, which would serve primarily to facilitate judicial review and to guide future decisions, need not be provided at the pre-termination stage. We recognize, too, that both welfare authorities and recipients have an interest in relatively speedy resolution of questions of eligibility, that they are used to dealing with one another informally, and that some welfare departments have very burdensome caseloads. These considerations justify the limitation of the pre-termination hearing to minimum procedural safeguards, adapted to the particular characteristics of welfare recipients, and to the limited nature of the controversies to be resolved. We wish to add that we, no less than the dissenters, recognize the importance of not imposing upon the States or the Federal Government in this developing field of law any procedural requirements beyond those demanded by rudimentary due process.

"The fundamental requisite of due process of law is the opportunity to be heard." *Grannis v. Ordean*, 234 U.S. 385, 394 (1914). The hearing must be "at a meaningful time and in a meaningful manner." *Armstrong v. Manzo*, 380 U.S. 545, 552 (1965). In the present context these principles require that a recipient have timely and adequate notice detailing the reasons for a proposed termination, and an effective opportunity to defend by confronting any adverse witnesses and by presenting his own ar-

---

14. Due process does not, of course, require two hearings. If, for example, a State simply wishes to continue benefits until after a "fair" hearing there will be no need for a preliminary hearing.

guments and evidence orally.   These rights are important in cases such as those before us, where recipients have challenged proposed terminations as resting on incorrect or misleading factual premises or on misapplication of rules or policies to the facts of particular cases.[15]

We are not prepared to say that the seven-day notice currently provided by New York City is constitutionally insufficient *per se*, although there may be cases where fairness would require that a longer time be given.   Nor do we see any constitutional deficiency in the content or form of the notice.   New York employs both a letter and a personal conference with a caseworker to inform a recipient of the precise questions raised about his continued eligibility.   Evidently the recipient is told the legal and factual bases for the Department's doubts.   This combination is probably the most effective method of communicating with recipients.

The city's procedures presently do not permit recipients to appear personally with or without counsel before the official who finally determines continued eligibility.   Thus a recipient is not permitted to present evidence to that official orally, or to confront or cross-examine adverse witnesses.   These omissions are fatal to the constitutional adequacy of the procedures.

The opportunity to be heard must be tailored to the capacities and circumstances of those who are to be heard.   It is not enough that a welfare recipient may present his position to the decision maker in writing or secondhand through his caseworker.   Written submissions are an unrealistic option for most recipients, who lack the educational attainment necessary to write effectively and who cannot obtain professional assistance. Moreover, written submissions do not afford the flexibility of oral presentations; they do not permit the recipient to mold his argument to the issues the decision maker appears to regard as important.   Particularly where credibility and veracity are at issue, as they must be in many termination proceedings, written submissions are a wholly unsatisfactory basis for decision.   The secondhand presentation to the decision maker by the caseworker has its own deficiencies; since the caseworker usually gathers the facts upon which the charge of ineligibility rests, the presentation of the recipient's side of the controversy cannot safely be left to him.   Therefore a recipient must be allowed to state his position orally. Informal procedures will suffice; in this context due process does not require a particular order of proof or mode of offering evidence.

In almost every setting where important decisions turn on questions of fact, due process requires an opportunity to confront and cross-examine adverse witnesses.   What we said in *Greene v. McElroy*, 360 U.S. 474, 496-497 (1959), is particularly pertinent here:

"Certain principles have remained relatively immutable in our jurisprudence.   One of these is that where governmental action seriously injures an

---

15. This case presents no question requiring our determination whether due process requires only an opportunity for written submission, or an opportunity both for written submission and oral argument, where there are no factual issues in dispute or where the application of the rule of law is not intertwined with factual issues.   See *FCC v. WJR*, 337 U. S. 265, 275-77 (1949).

individual, and the reasonableness of the action depends on fact findings, the evidence used to prove the Government's case must be disclosed to the individual so that he has an opportunity to show that it is untrue.   While this is important in the case of documentary evidence, it is even more important where the evidence consists of the testimony of individuals whose memory might be faulty or who, in fact, might be perjurers or persons motivated by malice, vindictiveness, intolerance, prejudice, or jealousy.   We have formalized these protections in the requirements of confrontation and cross-examination.   They have ancient roots.   They find expression in the Sixth Amendment * * * .   This Court has been zealous to protect these rights from erosion.   It has spoken out not only in criminal cases, * * * but also in all types of cases where administrative * * * actions were under scrutiny."

Welfare recipients must therefore be given an opportunity to confront and cross-examine the witnesses relied on by the department.

"The right to be heard would be, in many cases, of little avail if it did not comprehend the right to be heard by counsel."   *Powell v. Alabama,* 287 U.S. 45, 68-69 (1932).   We do not say that counsel must be provided at the pre-termination hearing, but only that the recipient must be allowed to retain an attorney if he so desires.   Counsel can help delineate the issues, present the factual contentions in an orderly manner, conduct cross-examination, and generally safeguard the interests of the recipient.   We do not anticipate that this assistance will unduly prolong or otherwise encumber the hearing. * * *

Finally, the decision maker's conclusion as to a recipient's eligibility must rest solely on the legal rules and evidence adduced at the hearing.   To demonstrate compliance with this elementary requirement, the decision maker should state the reasons for his determination and indicate the evidence he relied on, though his statement need not amount to a full opinion or even formal findings of fact and conclusions of law.   And, of course, an impartial decision maker is essential.   We agree with the District Court that prior involvement in some aspects of a case will not necessarily bar a welfare official from acting as a decision maker.   He should not, however, have participated in making the determination under review.

Affirmed.

MR. JUSTICE BLACK, dissenting.

In the last half century the United States, along with many, perhaps most, other nations of the world, has moved far toward becoming a welfare state, that is, a nation that for one reason or another taxes its most affluent people to help support, feed, clothe, and shelter its less fortunate citizens.   The result is that today more than nine million men, women, and children in the United States receive some kind of state or federally financed public assistance in the form of allowances or gratuities, generally paid them periodically, usually by the week, month, or quarter. Since these gratuities are paid on the basis of need, the list of recipients is not static, and some people go off the lists and others are added from time to time.   These ever-changing lists put a constant administrative burden on government and it certainly could not have reasonably anticipated that this burden would include the additional procedural expense imposed by the Court today.

* * *

The more than a million names on the relief rolls in New York, and the more than nine million names on the rolls of all the 50 States were not put there at random.   The names are there because state welfare officials believed that those people were eligible for assistance.   Probably in the officials' haste to make out the lists many names were put there erroneously in order to alleviate immediate suffering, and undoubtedly some people are drawing relief who are not entitled under the law to do so.   Doubtless some draw relief checks from time to time who know they are not eligible, either because they are not actually in need or for some other reason.   Many of those who thus draw undeserved gratuities are without sufficient property to enable the government to collect back from them any money they wrongfully receive. * * * In other words, although some recipients might be on the lists for payment wholly because of deliberate fraud on their part, the Court holds that the government is helpless and must continue, until after an evidentiary hearing, to pay money that it does not owe, never has owed, and never could owe.   I do not believe there is any provision in our Constitution that should thus paralyze the government's efforts to protect itself against making payments to people who are not entitled to them. * * *   The Court, however, relies upon the Fourteenth Amendment and in effect says that failure of the government to pay a promised charitable instalment to an individual deprives that individual of *his own property*, in violation of the Due Process Clause of the Fourteenth Amendment.   It somewhat strains credulity to say that the government's promise of charity to an individual is property belonging to that individual when the government denies that the individual is honestly entitled to receive such a payment.

* * * Although the majority attempts to bolster its decision with limited quotations from prior cases, it is obvious that today's result does not depend on the language of the Constitution itself or the principles of other decisions, but solely on the collective judgment of the majority as to what would be a fair and humane procedure in this case.

* * *

* * * Reduced to its simplest terms, the problem in this case is similar to that frequently encountered when two parties have an ongoing legal relationship that requires one party to make periodic payments to the other.   Often the situation arises where the party "owing" the money stops paying it and justifies his conduct by arguing that the recipient is not legally entitled to payment.   The recipient can, of course, disagree and go to court to compel payment.   But I know of no situation in our legal system in which the person alleged to owe money to another is required by law to continue making payments to a judgment-proof claimant without the benefit of any security or bond to insure that these payments can be recovered if he wins his legal argument.   Yet today's decision in no way obligates the welfare recipient to pay back any benefits wrongfully received during the pre-termination evidentiary hearings or post any bond, and in all "fairness" it could not do so.   These recipients are by definition too poor to post a bond or to repay the benefits that, as the majority assumes, must be spent as received to insure survival.

The Court apparently feels that this decision will benefit the poor and needy.   In my judgment the eventual result will be just the opposite. While today's decision requires only an administrative, evidentiary hearing, the inevitable logic of the approach taken will lead to constitutionally imposed, time-consuming delays of a full adversary process of administrative and judicial review.   In the next case the welfare recipients are bound to argue that cutting off benefits before judicial review of the agency's decision is also a denial of due process.   Since, by hypothesis, termination of aid at that point may still "deprive an *eligible* recipient of the very means by which to live while he waits," I would be surprised if the weighing process did not compel the conclusion that termination without full judicial review would be unconscionable.   After all, at each step, as the majority seems to feel, the issue is only one of weighing the government's pocketbook against the actual survival of the recipient, and surely that balance must always tip in favor of the individual.   Similarly today's decision requires only the opportunity to have the benefit of counsel at the administrative hearing, but it is difficult to believe that the same reasoning process would not require the appointment of counsel, for otherwise the right to counsel is a meaningless one since these people are too poor to hire their own advocates.   Thus the end result of today's decision may well be that the government, once it decides to give welfare benefits, cannot reverse that decision until the recipient has had the benefits of full administrative and judicial review, including, of course, the opportunity to present his case to this Court.   Since this process will usually entail a delay of several years, the inevitable result of such a constitutionally imposed burden will be that the government will not put a claimant on the rolls initially until it has made an exhaustive investigation to determine his eligibility.   While this Court will perhaps have insured that no needy person will be taken off the rolls without a full "due process" proceeding, it will also have insured that many will never get on the rolls, or at least that they will remain destitute during the lengthy proceedings followed to determine initial eligibility.

*   *   *

MR. CHIEF JUSTICE BURGER, with whom MR. JUSTICE BLACK joins, dissenting. * * *

The procedures for review of administrative action in the "welfare" area are in a relatively early stage of development: HEW has already taken the initiative by promulgating regulations requiring that AFDC payments be continued until a final decision after a "fair hearing" is held.   The net effect would be to provide a hearing prior to a termination of benefits.   Indeed, the HEW administrative regulations go far beyond the result reached today since they require that recipients be given the right to appointed counsel, a position expressly rejected by the majority. As the majority notes, these regulations are scheduled to take effect in July 1970.* Against this background I am baffled as to why we should engage in "legislating" via constitutional fiat when an apparently reasonable result has been accomplished administratively. * * *

The Court's action today seems another manifestation of the now familiar constitutionalizing syndrome: once some presumed flaw is observed, the Court then eagerly accepts the invitation to find a constitutionally "rooted" remedy. If no provision is explicit on the point, it is then seen as "implicit" or commanded by the vague and nebulous concept of "fairness." * * *

I would not suggest that the procedures of administering the Nation's complex welfare programs are beyond the reach of courts, but I would wait until more is known about the problems before fashioning solutions in the rigidity of a constitutional holding.

By allowing the administrators to deal with these problems we leave room for adjustments if, for example, it is found that a particular hearing process is too costly. The history of the complexity of the administrative process followed by judicial review as we have seen it for the past 30 years should suggest the possibility that new layers of procedural protection may become an intolerable drain on the very funds earmarked for food, clothing, and other living essentials.[3]

Aside from the administrative morass that today's decision could well create, the Court should also be cognizant of the legal precedent it may be setting. The majority holding raises intriguing possibilities concerning the right to a hearing at other stages in the welfare process which affect the total sum of assistance, even though the action taken might fall short of complete termination. For example, does the Court's holding embrace welfare reductions or denial of increases as opposed to terminations, or decisions concerning initial applications or requests for special assistance? The Court supplies no distinguishable considerations and leaves these crucial questions unanswered.

[Justice Stewart also dissented in a cryptic paragraph which merely described the question, for him, as "a close one." In a companion case, *Wheeler v. Montgomery*, 397 U.S. 280 (1970), the Court invalidated California's procedure for terminating old age assistance benefits because it failed to afford the recipient "an evidentiary hearing at which he may personally appear to offer oral evidence and confront and cross-examine the witnesses against him."]

---

* [The proposed regulations were withdrawn before they took effect and were redrafted to take account of the *Goldberg* decision; among other changes, the right to appointed counsel was eliminated. Eds.]

3. We are told, for example, that Los Angeles County alone employs 12,500 welfare workers to process grants to 500,000 people under various welfare programs. The record does not reveal how many more employees will be required to give this newly discovered "due process" to every welfare recipient whose payments are terminated for fraud or other factors of ineligibility or those whose initial applications are denied.

Notes

1. The Supreme Court in *Goldberg* speaks rather abstractly about the "brutal need" of welfare claimants. The District Court's description, *sub. nom. Kelly v. Wyman*, 294 F. Supp. 893, 899-900 (S.D.N.Y. 1968), is more graphic:

> * * * The case of Angela Velez * * * makes the point starkly. She was terminated on March 11, 1968, because her husband allegedly visited her home every night. She requested the post-termination state fair hearing in mid-March. The hearing was held in June, and, pursuant to the request of this court for expedition, the decision issued on July 10. The State Commissioner found that the information that caused suspension of benefits came from Mrs. Velez's landlady, that the information was untrue, that the husband does not live with his wife, that she had obtained a court order in 1966 to prevent his night visits, that he is allowed to visit the four small children only on Wednesday, and that at that time he brings his support money of $30 a week, but no more, in accordance with an agreement worked out in Family Court. Accordingly, the State Commissioner directed the local agency to reinstate assistance. However, in the four months between termination of AFDC benefits and the decision reversing the local agency, Mrs. Velez and her four children, ages one to six, were evicted from her apartment for non-payment of rent and went to live with her sister, who has nine children and is on relief. Mrs. Velez and three children have been sleeping in two single beds in a small room, and the youngest sleeps in a crib in the same room. Thirteen children and two adults have been living in one apartment, and Mrs. Velez states that she has been unable to feed her children adequately, so that they have lost weight and have been ill.

> The case of Mrs. Esther Lett * * * is also instructive. According to the affidavits of plaintiff Lett and her Legal Aid Society attorney: She and her four dependents, aged three months to fifteen years, were abruptly terminated for public assistance on February 1, 1968. The purported ground was that she had concealed her current employment by the Board of Education. In fact, she had worked for Operation Head Start in July and August 1967, but had not been employed by the Board of Education after August 20, 1967. Since that date and up to February 1968, she had worked at Day Care Centers on twenty-six different days, earning a total of $300, with the knowledge of the local welfare agency. As a result of termination of assistance, she and her dependents were forced to live on the handouts of neighbors. On February 18, she and her family had to go to the hospital for severe diarrhea, apparently brought on by the only means they had had that day—spoiled chicken and rice donated by a neighbor. She applied for emergency aid and a post-termination state "fair hearing" but the aid was refused and the fair hearing was not scheduled. Through the herculean efforts of The Legal Aid Society, including numerous telephone calls and three personal trips to local agencies, it was learned that the Board of Education had apparently made an error. However, the Board would not so inform the welfare agency until it requested a new verification. On Tuesday, February 27, Mrs. Lett went to a local center to seek emergency aid. Because she had not eaten all day, she fainted in the center, but when she awoke she was told that she could not get money for food immediately because it had not yet been authorized. Finally, after waiting eight hours, she was given $15 to feed herself and four depen-

dents and told to return on Friday.   After suit was brought, her assistance was apparently temporarily reinstated without prejudice.

Poignant though they are, these facts should not be taken as demonstrating the lack of concern of the welfare bureaucracy for accurate and fair determinations of eligibility for public assistance. Welfare law in the United States is enormously complex and also involves many subjective determinations.   The complexity results from our historic, and only partially successful attempt, to provide assistance to the "deserving poor" without trenching too heavily on the work incentives that are thought critical to the well-being of a market economy and on the public support politically necessary to continue public assistance. Subjectivity is the result of the attempt to tailor money payments and other social services to fit the needs of individuals or families.   As a consequence the often underpaid and undertrained welfare eligibility technician is faced with regulations which may fill a bookshelf four feet wide and yet also with the necessity of deciding such questions as whether an individual is "essential to the well-being" of a dependent child and therefore eligible to have his needs included in determining the need of the "family budget unit."   See generally Joint Economic Committee of the Congress, Studies in Public Welfare, Paper No. 5 (Part 1), *Issues in Welfare Administration: Welfare—An Administrative Nightmare*, 92d Cong., 2d Sess. (1972).   Of course not all "errors" in eligibility determinations are the result of complexity and work load.   See Mashaw, *Welfare Reform and Local Administration of Aid to Families with Dependent Children in Virginia*, 57 Va. L. Rev. 818 (1971).

2.   Assume that errors in the AFDC system may be the product of two factors—agency recalcitrance and simple inefficiency.   How will the hearing rights prescribed in *Goldberg* help prevent errors traceable to these causes?   Consider, for example, the prospects for consistent protection of claimants' rights through hearings where denials, limitations, reductions or terminations of assistance are a consequence of agency disagreement with state or federal policy.   The right to a prior hearing is likely to be effective in this context only to the extent that claimants are aware of their rights, are aggressive, and have legal assistance readily available.   For public assistance claimants none of these conditions is likely to exist.   First, although awareness of entitlements is considerably higher among recipients and potential recipients today than in the past, in a system that baffles the bureaucrat the applicant's or recipient's knowledge is almost certain to be too general to provide a basis for recognizing that a departmental decision is open to question.   Second, persons who are chronically or even temporarily dependent should not be expected to be aggressive in asserting their rights. Appeals are not likely to be forthcoming from those who remain attached to the welfare system except when the limitation or reduction of assistance is very substantial.   It is not sensible to challenge the decisions of administrators who make continuous highly discretionary judgments about one's basic necessities (e.g., whether to grant funds for a new mattress, a telephone, or an additional heating allowance) unless the issue is serious and the prospects for success are high. See generally Handler, *Controlling Official Behavior in Welfare Administration*, 54 Calif. L. Rev. 479 (1966); Handler and Hollingsworth, *Reforming Welfare: The Constraints of the Bureaucracy and the Clients*, 118 U. Pa. L. Rev. 1167 (1970).

Third, we should also recognize that the incentive to appeal resulting from the continuation of benefits under the prior-hearing requirement of *Goldberg* will **not** operate in the context of disputes raising only issues of policy or law.   A hearing prior to termination is required only where there is a disputed issue of fact or of application of law to fact.   Finally, the recalcitrant welfare agency has virtually complete control over the factors that make a hearing meaningful—adequate notice, access to evidence, aid in preparing an appeal, and convenient scheduling of hearings.   Ultimately a very detailed court order and vigilant monitoring for contempt may be necessary to realize the full benefits of a right to hearing in the face of a strong disapproval by local officials of the bases for an appellant's claim. Judicial enforcement, of course, requires the availability of free legal service—a commodity that is always in short supply.

Administrative hearing requirements might produce greater benefits where the likely contests involve claims of bureaucratic error rather than issues of official lawlessness.   Appeals are less threatening in this context.   Issues should often involve factual disputes or disputes over the application of policy to fact rather than policy disagreements and thus should often require a prior hearing with its attendant incentive for appeal.   And an intention to thwart effective exercise of hearing rights should not be presumed. It must be recognized, however, that the same overworked and under-trained bureaucracy that makes initial determinations is also heavily involved in the appeals process.   If initial decisions cannot be made correctly, there is reason to doubt that the hearing process will be run effectively.   These doubts were in part confirmed by an evaluation of the hearing process in New York City.   See Kirchheimer, *Community Evaluation of Fair Hearing Procedures Available to Public Assistance Recipients* (mimeo, New York City Human Resources Administration, May 1973).   Based on a random sample of appeals decided in October of 1972, the evaluation found: (1) Five percent of appellants had received no notice of a proposed adverse action; (2) 25 percent did not receive timely notice; (3) 63 percent of all notices failed to contain an adequate statement of what action was proposed to be taken and what the factual and policy bases for the action were; (4) in 12 percent of the cases aid had not been continued as required pending appeal; (5) only 25 percent of the appellants who requested access to relevant agency files prior to appeal were given such access; and (6) in only seven percent of the cases was an opportunity for cross-examination afforded by having opposing witnesses present.

No matter what the causes of underlying errors, hearings are not a major protection unless they are utilized.   AFDC hearings are requested sparingly.   According to HEW's National Center for Social Statistics, hearings seem to be running at a fairly constant rate of only two or three percent of the potentially appealable determinations.   And, over fifty percent of all appeals reported in some quarters are attributable to two or three states.   A determination favorable to the appellant results in about twenty percent of the reported appeals.

Of course, even if twenty percent is considered a relatively low success rate by appellants, those who get errors corrected derive tangible benefits, and even those who fail to obtain relief may develop a greater sense of fairness and therefore acceptance of results.   There is also the possibility that hearings will clarify policies, and their proper application, so that other decisions will be made correctly in the first instance.   However, in an administrative system which is overburdened, or which is staffed by recalcitrant officials, these latter benefits seem highly speculative.

The costs side of the equation is no less difficult to assess.   Obviously, there are the costs of the hearings themselves and the costs of continuing aid pending their completion.   The state of Michigan estimated its *"Goldberg"* payments at $450,000 in 1971, and in ninety-two percent of the Michigan appeals the hearing confirmed the initial decision.   In short, a very high percentage of the payments made between the notice of proposed action and the final decision after opportunity for hearing are made to ineligible persons.   *Hearings before the Subcommittee on Fiscal Policy of the Joint Economic Committee, Problems in Administration of Public Welfare Programs,* 687, 92d Cong., 2d Sess. (1972) [hereinafter *Hearings*].   In June of 1972 New York City's payments for cases noticed for reduction of termination had reached a rate of $5,000,000 per month.   Kihss, "Mayor Assails Relief Rule," Wall St. J., August 14, 1972, p. 3.

This may seem a small price to pay for basic fairness, but there is the nagging suspicion that the welfare claimants themselves are paying the price.   State appropriations for welfare payments are generally made in a lump sum.   If money runs short the state agency usually has the power to reduce the percentage of need covered by public assistance payments in order to make the books balance. Hence, an unexpectedly high number of pre-termination appeals may simply result in a reduction of welfare benefits to eligible recipients by the amount paid out to appellants who are determined not to have been entitled to benefits. Moreover, because welfare departments are required to continue payments pending hearings, the number of ineligibles on the rolls at any given time is increased.   And the more numerous such ineligibles ("welfare cheaters" in the political vernacular), the greater general disaffection with the welfare system is likely to be.   Such disaffection is at least as likely to manifest itself in reduced or static appropriations as in progressive welfare reform.

There is also the question of the effects of hearings on the ability of the welfare bureaucracy to provide benefits to which people are entitled.   The head of the Fulton County Department of Family and Children Services in Atlanta testified that while fair hearings were good "in themselves," they "drastically and negatively" affected services to other recipients because of the very large drain on staff time when hearings are properly prepared and conducted.   *Hearings* at 1042.

The difficulty of balancing the costs and benefits of procedural safeguards does not necessarily suggest that the courts should refrain from imposing procedural due process protections in the way that they have retreated from policing rationality via substantive due process.   What may be needed is an approach to due process that recognizes both the peculiarities of particular administrative systems and that techniques for assuring accuracy and fairness other than trial-type hearings might also be a part of due process of law.   See generally Mashaw, *The Management Side of Due Process: Some Theoretical and Litigation Notes on the Assurance of Accuracy, Fairness, and Timeliness in the Adjudication of Social Welfare Claims,* 59 Cornell L. Rev. 772 (1974).

3.   As the Fulton County administrator suggested, the *Goldberg* ruling presented welfare administrators with a significant problem.   First, if a substantial percentage of the recipients noticed for termination exercised their appeal rights, the welfare departments would simply be unable to process the cases without a large infusion of funds for administration.   Because of the complexity of welfare decisionmaking, adequate preparation of cases to prove the correctness of termination decisions was likely to be quite costly.   But the alternative would be even more expensive—leaving substantial numbers of persons believed to be ineligible on the rolls.   These administrative difficulties fed into and **rein-**

forced a political difficulty.   Welfare rolls were already increasing rapidly.   State legislators were simply unwilling to provide more funds either for well-constructed hearings or for welfare benefits themselves.   As Justice Black's dissent seems to recognize, a strategy was needed that would preserve fiscal integrity and produce defensible decisions.

Indeed the incremental changes that followed *Goldberg* went far beyond his speculation that welfare officials were likely to tighten up and slow down the initial eligibility determination process.   In addition many welfare departments moved to generalize and objectify their substantive eligibility criteria so that messy subjective judgments about individual cases would not have to be made and defended.   This in turn lead to the realization that well-trained or professionalized social welfare workers were no longer needed.   Costs could then be reduced further by reducing the quality of the staff and by depersonalizing staff-claimant encounters.   If these reactions were not sufficient to restore fiscal balance, then payment levels could be reduced or allowed to remain stable in the face of rising prices.   A tougher stance was also taken with respect to work requirements and prosecution of absent parents.   Moreover, because hearings presumably protected the claimants' interests, internal audit procedures were skewed to ignore nonpayment and underpayment problems and to concentrate on preventing overpayments and payments to ineligibles.   See generally D. BAUM, THE WELFARE FAMILY AND MASS ADMINISTRATIVE JUSTICE (1974); J. HANDLER, PROTECTING THE SOCIAL SERVICE CLIENT (1979); Simon, *Legality, Bureaucracy, and Class in the Welfare System,* 92 Yale L.J. 1198 (1983).

If this story of welfare since *Goldberg v. Kelly* is generally accurate, then the Supreme Court's legal reconceptualization of welfare recipients as rights-bearing citizens entitled to quasi-judicial processes for the protection of their rights has had very substantial effects.   Programs that were generally viewed as paternalistic, discretionary and individualized have been transformed into semi-adversary, impersonal, property-rights regimes.   There are surely some gains from such a transformation.   But do the benefits exceed the costs?   Are welfare claimants as a class better off?   Is the society well served by the elimination of the historic connection between income support and social services that attempted to ameliorate nonpecuniary sources of distress and to promote development towards self-reliance?   Are these questions and their answers relevant to what the Supreme Court decided in *Goldberg?*

MATHEWS v. ELDRIDGE

Supreme Court of the United States, 1976.
424 U.S. 319, 96 S.Ct. 893, 47 L.Ed.2d 18.

MR. JUSTICE POWELL delivered the opinion of the Court.

The issue in this case is whether the Due Process Clause of the Fifth Amendment requires that prior to the termination of Social Security disability benefit payments the recipient be afforded an opportunity for an evidentiary hearing.

Cash benefits are provided to workers during periods in which they are completely disabled under the disability insurance benefits program created by the 1956 amendments to Title II of the Social Security Act, 42 U.S.C.A. § 423.   Respondent Eldridge was first awarded benefits in

June 1968. In March 1972, he received a questionnaire from the state agency charged with monitoring his medical condition. Eldridge completed the questionnaire, indicating that his condition had not improved and identifying the medical sources, including physicians, from whom he had received treatment recently. The state agency then obtained reports from his physician and a psychiatric consultant. After considering these reports and other information in his file the agency informed Eldridge by letter that it had made a tentative determination that his disability had ceased in May 1972. The letter included a statement of reasons for the proposed termination of benefits, and advised Eldridge that he might request reasonable time in which to obtain and submit additional information pertaining to his condition.

In his written response, Eldridge disputed one characterization of his medical condition and indicated that the agency already had enough evidence to establish his disability.[2] The state agency then made its final determination that he had ceased to be disabled in May 1972. This determination was accepted by the Social Security Administration (SSA), which notified Eldridge in July that his benefits would terminate after that month. The notification also advised him of his right to seek reconsideration by the state agency of this initial determination within six months.

Instead of requesting reconsideration Eldridge commenced this action challenging the constitutional validity of the administrative procedures established by the Secretary of Health, Education, and Welfare for assessing whether there exists a continuing disability. He sought an immediate reinstatement of benefits pending a hearing on the issue of his disability. The Secretary moved to dismiss on the grounds that Eldridge's benefits had been terminated in accordance with valid administrative regulations and procedures and that he had failed to exhaust available remedies. In support of his contention that due process requires a pretermination hearing, Eldridge relied exclusively upon this Court's decision in *Goldberg v. Kelly*, which established a right to an "evidentiary hearing" prior to termination of welfare benefits. The Secretary contended that *Goldberg* was not controlling since eligibility for disability benefits, unlike eligibility for welfare benefits, is not based on financial need and since issues of credibility and veracity do not play a significant role in the disability entitlement decision, which turns primarily on medical evidence.

The District Court concluded that the administrative procedures pursuant to which the Secretary had terminated Eldridge's benefits abridged his right to procedural due process. The court viewed the interest of the disability recipient in uninterrupted benefits as indistin-

---

2. Eldridge originally was disabled due to chronic anxiety and back strain. He subsequently was found to have diabetes. The tentative determination letter indicated that aid would be terminated because available medical evidence indicated that his diabetes was under control, that there existed no limitations on his back movements which would impose severe functional restrictions, and that he no longer suffered emotional problems that would preclude him from all work for which he was qualified. In his reply letter he claimed to have arthritis of the spine rather than a strained back.

guishable from that of the welfare recipient in *Goldberg*. * * * Reasoning that disability determinations may involve subjective judgments based on conflicting medical and nonmedical evidence, the District Court held that prior to termination of benefits Eldridge had to be afforded an evidentiary hearing of the type required for welfare beneficiaries under Title IV of the Social Security Act.   Relying entirely upon the District Court's opinion, the Court of Appeals for the Fourth Circuit affirmed the injunction barring termination of Eldridge's benefits prior to an evidentiary hearing.   We reverse.

* * *

Procedural due process imposes constraints on governmental decisions which deprive individuals of "liberty" or "property" interests within the meaning of the Due Process Clause of the Fifth or Fourteenth Amendment.   The Secretary does not contend that procedural due process is inapplicable to terminations of Social Security disability benefits.   He recognizes, as has been implicit in our prior decisions, that the interest of an individual in continued receipt of these benefits is a statutorily created "property" interest protected by the Fifth Amendment.   Rather, the Secretary contends that the existing administrative procedures, detailed below, provide all the process that is constitutionally due before a recipient can be deprived of that interest.

This Court consistently has held that some form of hearing is required before an individual is finally deprived of a property interest. * * * Eldridge agrees that the review procedures available to a claimant before the initial determination of ineligibility becomes final would be adequate if disability benefits were not terminated until after the evidentiary hearing stage of the administrative process.   The dispute centers upon what process is due prior to the initial termination of benefits, pending review.

In recent years this Court increasingly has had occasion to consider the extent to which due process requires an evidentiary hearing prior to the deprivation of some type of property interest even if such a hearing is provided thereafter.   In only one case, *Goldberg v. Kelly*, has the Court held that a hearing closely approximating a judicial trial is necessary.   In other cases requiring some type of pretermination hearing as a matter of consitutional right the Court has spoken sparingly about the requisite procedures.

* * *

These decisions underscore the truism that " '[d]ue process,' unlike some legal rules, is not a technical conception with a fixed content unrelated to time, place and circumstances." * * * Accordingly, resolution of the issue whether the administrative procedures provided here are constitutionally sufficient requires analysis of the governmental and private interests that are affected.   More precisely, our prior decisions indicate that identification of the specific dictates of due process generally require consideration of three distinct factors: First, the private interest that will be affected by the official action; second, the risk of an erroneous deprivation of such interest through the procedures used, and the probable value, if any, of additional or substitute procedural safeguards, and finally, the Government's interest, including the function involved and the fiscal and administrative burdens that the additional or substitute procedural requirement would entail.

We turn first to a description of the procedures for the termination of Social Security disability benefits and thereafter consider the factors bearing upon the constitutional adequacy of these procedures.

*   *   *

In order to establish initial and continued entitlement to disability benefits a worker must demonstrate that he is unable

> "to engage in any substantial gainful activity by reason of any medically determinable physical or mental impairment which can be expected to result in death or which has lasted or can be expected to last for a continuous period of not less than 12 months   *   *   *   ." 42 U.S.C.A. § 423(d)(1)(A).

To satisfy this test the worker bears a continuing burden of showing, by means of "medically acceptable clinical and laboratory diagnostic techniques," § 423(d)(3), that he has a physical or mental impairment of such severity that

> "he is not only unable to do his previous work but cannot, considering his age, education, and work experience, engage in any other kind of substantial gainful work with which exists in the national economy, regardless of whether such work exists in the immediate area in which he lives, or whether a specific job vacancy exists for him, or whether he would be hired if he applied for work." § 423(d)(2)(A).

The principal reasons for benefits terminations are that the worker is no longer disabled or has returned to work. As Eldridge's benefits were terminated because he was determined to be no longer disabled, we consider only the sufficiency of the procedures involved in such cases.

The continuing-eligibility investigation is made by a state agency acting through a "team" consisting of a physician and a nonmedical person trained in disability evaluation. The agency periodically communicates with the disabled worker, usually by mail—in which case he is sent a detailed questionnaire—or by telephone, and requests information concerning his present condition, including current medical restrictions and sources of treatment, and any additional information that he considers relevant to his continued entitlement to benefits.

Information regarding the recipient's current condition is also obtained from his sources of medical treatment. If there is a conflict between the information provided by the beneficiary and that obtained from medical sources such as his physician, or between two sources of treatment, the agency may arrange for an examination by an independent consulting physician. Whenever the agency's tentative assessment of the beneficiary's condition differs from his own assessment, the beneficiary is informed that benefits may be terminated, provided a summary of the evidence upon which the proposed determination to terminate is based, and afforded an opportunity to review the medical reports and other evidence in his case file.[18]   He also may respond in writing and submit additional evidence.

The state agency then makes its final determination, which is reviewed by an examiner in the SSA Bureau of Disability Insurance.   If, as is usually the case, the SSA accepts the agency determination it notifies the recipient in writing, informing him of the reasons for the decision, and of his right to seek *de novo* reconsideration by the state agency.   Upon acceptance by the SSA, benefits are terminated effective two months after the month in which medical recovery is found to have occurred.

If the recipient seeks reconsideration by the state agency and the determination is adverse, the SSA reviews the reconsideration determination and notifies the recipient of the decision.   He then has a right to an evidentiary hearing before an SSA administrative law judge.   The hearing is nonadversary, and the SSA is not represented by counsel.   As at all prior and subsequent stages of the administrative process, however, the claimant may be represented by counsel or other spokesmen.   If this hearing results in an adverse decision, the claimant is entitled to request discretionary review by the SSA Appeals Council, and finally may obtain judicial review.

Should it be determined at any point after termination of benefits, that the claimant's disability extended beyond the date of cessation initially established, the worker is entitled to retroactive payments.   If, on the other hand, a beneficiary receives any payments to which he is later determined not to be entitled, the statute authorizes the Secretary to attempt to recoup these funds in specified circumstances.

Despite the elaborate character of the administrative procedures provided by the Secretary, the courts below held them to be constitutionally inadequate, concluding that due process requires an evidentiary hearing prior to termination.   In light of the private and governmental interests at stake here and the nature of the existing procedures, we think this was error.

Since a recipient whose benefits are terminated is awarded full retroactive relief if he ultimately prevails, his sole interest is in the uninterrupted receipt of this source of income pending final administrative decision on his claim.   His potential injury is thus similar in nature to that of the welfare recipient in *Goldberg,* the nonprobationary federal employee in *Arnett v. Kennedy,* 416 U.S. 134 (1974), and the wage earner in *Sniadach v. Family Finance Corp.,* 395 U.S. 337 (1969).

Only in *Goldberg* has the Court held that due process requires an evidentiary hearing prior to a temporary deprivation.   It was emphasized

---

18.   The disability recipient is not permitted personally to examine the medical reports contained in his file.   This restriction is not significant since he is entitled to have any representative of his choice, including a lay friend or family member, examine all medical evidence.   The Secretary informs us that this curious limitation is currently under review.

there that welfare assistance is given to persons on the very margin of subsistence. * * *

Eligibility for disability benefits, in constrast, is not based upon financial need.[24] Indeed, it is wholly unrelated to the worker's income or support from many other sources, such as earnings of other family members, workmen's compensation awards, tort claims awards, savings, private insurance, public or private pensions, veterans' benefits, food stamps, public assistance, or the "many other important programs, both public and private, which contain provisions for disability payments affecting a substantial portion of the work force * * *."

As *Goldberg* illustrates, the degree of potential deprivation that may be created by a particular decision is a factor to be considered in assessing the validity of any administrative decision-making process. The potential deprivation here is generally likely to be less than in *Goldberg*, although the degree of difference can be overstated. As the District Court emphasized, to remain eligible for benefits a recipient must be "unable to engage in substantial gainful activity." Thus, in contrast to the discharged federal employee in *Arnett*, there is little possibility that the terminated recipient will be able to find even temporary employment to ameliorate the interim loss.

As we recognized last Term in *Fusari v. Steinberg*, 419 U.S. 379, 389 (1975), "the possible length of wrongful deprivation of * * * benefits [also] is an important factor in assessing the impact of official action on the private interests." * * * [T]he delay between the actual cutoff of benefits and final decision after a hearing exceeds one year.

In view of the torpidity of this administrative review process, and the typically modest resources of the family unit of the physically disabled worker,[26] the hardship imposed upon the erroneously terminated disability recipient may be significant. Still, the disabled worker's need is likely to be less than that of a welfare recipient. In addition to the possibility of access to private resources, other forms of government assistance will become available where the termination of disability benefits places a worker or his family below the subsistence level.[27] In view of these po-

---

24. The level of benefits is determined by the worker's average monthly earnings during the period prior to disability, his age, and other factors not directly related to financial need, specified in 42 U.S.C.A. § 415 (1970 ed., Supp. III). See § 423(a)(2).

26. *Amici* cite statistics compiled by the Secretary which indicate that in 1965 the mean income of the family unit of a disabled worker was $3,803, while the median income for the unit was $2,836. The mean liquid assets—i. e., cash, stocks, bonds—of these family units was $4,862; the median was $940. These statistics do not take into account the family unit's nonliquid assets—i. e., automobile, real estate, and the like. Brief for AFL-CIO et al. as *Amici Curiae* App. 4a.

27. *Amici* emphasize that because an identical definition of disability is employed in both the Title II Social Security Program and in the companion welfare system for the disabled, Supplemental Security Income (SSI), the terminated disability-benefits recipient will be ineligible for the SSI Program. There exist, however, state and local welfare programs which may supplement the worker's income. In addition, the worker's household unit can qualify for food stamps if it meets the financial need requirements. Finally, in 1974, 480,000 of the approximately 2,000,000 disabled workers receiving Social Security benefits also received SSI benefits. Since financial need is a criterion for eligibility under the SSI program, those disabled workers who are most in need will in the majority of cases be receiving SSI benefits when disability insurance aid is terminated. And, under the SSI program, a pretermination evidentiary hearing is provided, if requested.

tential sources of temporary income, there is less reason here than in *Goldberg* to depart from the ordinary principle, established by our decisions, that something less than an evidentiary hearing is sufficient prior to adverse administrative action.

An additional factor to be considered here is the fairness and reliability of the existing pretermination procedures, and the probable value, if any, of additional procedural safeguards. Central to the evaluation of any administrative process is the nature of the relevant inquiry. In order to remain eligible for benefits the disabled worker must demonstrate by means of "medically acceptable clinical and laboratory diagnostic techniques," that he is unable "to engage in any substantial gainful activity by reason of any *medically determinable* physical or mental impairment. * * *" In short, a medical assessment of the worker's physical or mental condition is required. This is a more sharply focused and easily documented decision than the typical determination of welfare entitlement. In the latter case, a wide variety of information may be deemed relevant, and issues of witness credibility and veracity often are critical to the decision-making process.

* * *

By contrast, the decision whether to discontinue disability benefits will turn, in most cases, upon "routine, standard, and unbiased medical reports by physician specialists," *Richardson v. Perales*, 402 U.S., at 404, concerning a subject whom they have personally examined.[28] In *Richardson* the Court recognized the "reliability and probative worth of written medical reports," emphasizing that while there may be "professional disagreement with the medical conclusions" the "spectre of questionable credibility and veracity is not present." To be sure, credibility and veracity may be a factor in the ultimate disability assessment in some cases. But procedural due process rules are shaped by the risk of error inherent in the truth-finding process as applied to the generality of cases, not the rare exceptions. The potential value of an evidentiary hearing, or even oral presentation to the decision maker, is substantially less in this context than in *Goldberg*.

The decision in *Goldberg* also was based on the Court's conclusion that written submissions were an inadequate substitute for oral presentation because they did not provide an effective means for the recipient to communicate his case to the decision maker. Written submissions were viewed as an unrealistic option, for most recipients lacked the "educational attainment necessary to write effectively" and could not afford profes-

---

28. The decision is not purely a question of the accuracy of a medical diagnosis since the ultimate issue which the state agency must resolve is whether in light of the particular worker's "age, education, and work experience," he cannot "engage in any * * * substantial gainful work which exists in the national economy. * * *" Yet information concerning each of these worker characteristics is amenable to effective written presentation. The value of an evidentiary hearing, or even a limited oral presentation, to an accurate presentation of those factors to the decision maker does not appear substantial. Similarly, resolution of the inquiry as to the types of employment opportunities that exist in the national economy for a physically impaired worker with a particular set of skills would not necessarily be advanced by an evidentiary hearing. The statistical information relevant to this judgment is more amenable to written than to oral presentation.

sional assistance. In addition, such submissions would not provide the "flexibility or oral presentations" or "permit the recipient to mold his argument to the issues the decision maker appears to regard as important." In the context of the disability-benefits-entitlement assessment the administrative procedures under review here fully answer these objections.

The detailed questionnaire which the state agency periodically sends the recipient identifies with particularity the information relevant to the entitlement decision, and the recipient is invited to obtain assistance from the local SSA office in completing the questionnaire. More important, the information critical to the entitlement decision usually is derived from medical sources, such as the treating physician. Such sources are likely to be able to communicate more effectively through written documents than are welfare recipients or the lay witnesses supporting their cause. The conclusions of physicians often are supported by X-rays and the results of clinical or laboratory tests, information typically more amenable to written than to oral presentation.

A further safeguard against mistake is the policy of allowing the disability recipient's representative full access to all information relied upon by the state agency. In addition, prior to the cutoff of benefits the agency informs the recipient of its tentative assessment, the reasons therefor, and provides a summary of the evidence that it considers most relevant. Opportunity is then afforded the recipient to submit additional evidence or arguments, enabling him to challenge directly the accuracy of information in his file as well as the correctness of the agency's tentative conclusions. These procedures, again as contrasted with those before the Court in *Goldberg*, enable the recipient to "mold" his argument to respond to the precise issues which the decision maker regards as crucial.

Despite these carefully structured procedures, *amici* point to the significant reversal rate for appealed cases as clear evidence that the current process is inadequate. Depending upon the base selected and the line of analysis followed, the relevant reversal rates urged by the contending parties vary from a high of 58.6% for appealed reconsideration decisions to an overall reversal rate of only 3.3%.[29] Bare statistics rarely provide a satisfactory measure of the fairness of a decision making process. Their adequacy is especially suspect here since the administrative review system is operated on an open-file basis. A recipient may always submit new evidence, and such submissions may result in additional medical examinations. Such fresh examinations were held in approximately 30% to 40% of the appealed cases, in fiscal 1973, either at the reconsideration or evidentiary hearing stage of the administrative process.

---

29. By focusing solely on the reversal rate for appealed reconsideration determinations *amici* overstate the relevant reversal rate. [I]n order fully to assess the reliability and fairness of a system of procedure, one must also consider the overall rate of error for all denials of benefits. Here that overall rate is 12.2%. Moreover, about 75% of these reversals occur at the reconsideration stage of the administrative process. Since the median period between a request for reconsideration review and decision is only two months, the deprivation is significantly less than that concomitant to the lengthier delay before an evidentiary hearing. Netting out these reconsideration reversals, the overall reversal rate falls to 3.3%.

In this context, the value of reversal rate statistics as one means of evaluating the adequacy of the pretermination process is diminished. Thus, although we view such information as relevant, it is certainly not controlling in this case.

In striking the appropriate due process balance the final factor to be assessed is the public interest. This includes the administrative burden and other societal costs that would be associated with requiring, as a matter of constitutional right, an evidentiary hearing upon demand in all cases prior to the termination of disability benefits. The most visible burden would be the incremental cost resulting from the increased number of hearings and the expense of providing benefits to ineligible recipients pending decision. No one can predict the extent of the increase, but the fact that full benefits would continue until after such hearings would assure the exhaustion in most cases of this attractive option. Nor would the theoretical right of the Secretary to recover undeserved benefits result, as a practical matter, in any substantial offset to the added outlay of public funds. The parties submit widely varying estimates of the probable additional financial cost. We only need say that experience with the constitutionalizing of government procedures suggests that the ultimate additional cost in terms of money and administrative burden would not be insubstantial.

Financial cost alone is not a controlling weight in determining whether due process requires a particular procedural safeguard prior to some administrative decision. But the Government's interest, and hence that of the public, in conserving scarce fiscal and administrative resources is a factor that must be weighed. At some point the benefit of an additional safeguard to the individual affected by the administrative action and to society in terms of increased assurance that the action is just, may be outweighed by the cost. Significantly, the cost of protecting those whom the preliminary administrative process has identified as likely to be found undeserving may in the end come out of the pockets of the deserving since resources available for any particular program of social welfare are not unlimited.

But more is implicated in cases of this type than ad hoc weighing of fiscal and administrative burdens against the interests of a particular category of claimants. The ultimate balance involves a determination as to when, under our constitutional system, judicial-type procedures must be imposed upon administrative action to assure fairness. * * * The judicial model of an evidentiary hearing is neither a required, nor even the most effective, method of decision-making in all circumstances. * * * All that is necessary is that the procedures be tailored, in light of the decision to be made, to "the capacities and circumstances of those who are to be heard," *Goldberg v. Kelly,* 397 U.S., at 268-269 (footnote omitted), to insure that they are given a meaningful opportunity to present their case. In assessing what process is due in this case, substantial weight must be given to the good-faith judgments of the individuals charged by Congress with the administration of social welfare programs that the procedures they have provided assure fair consideration of the entitlement claims of individuals. This is especially so where, as here, the prescribed procedures not only provide the claimant with an effective process for asserting his claim prior to any administrative action, but also assure a right to an evidentiary hearing, as well as to subsequent judicial review, before the denial of his claim becomes final.

We conclude that an evidentiary hearing is not required prior to the termination of disability benefits and that the present administrative procedures fully comport with due process.

The judgment of the Court of Appeals is reversed.

* * *

MR. JUSTICE BRENNAN, with whom MR. JUSTICE MARSHALL concurs, dissenting.

For the reasons stated in my dissenting opinion in *Richardson v. Wright*, 405 U.S. 208, 212 (1972), I agree with the District Court and the Court of Appeals that, prior to termination of benefits, Eldridge must be afforded an evidentiary hearing of the type required for welfare beneficiaries under Title IV of the Social Security Act * * *. I would add that the Court's consideration that a discontinuance of disability benefits may cause the recipient to suffer only a limited deprivation is no argument. It is speculative. Moreover, the very legislative determination to provide disability benefits, without any prerequisite determination of need in fact, presumes a need by the recipient which is not this Court's function to denigrate. Indeed, in the present case, it is indicated that because disability benefits were terminated there was a foreclosure upon the Eldridge home and the family's furniture was repossessed, forcing Eldridge, his wife, and their children to sleep in one bed. Finally, it is also no argument that a worker, who has been placed in the untenable position of having been denied disability benefits, may still seek other forms of public assistance.

Notes

1. Justice Powell's careful formulation and application of the "three factor" test in *Eldridge* suggests an attempt to integrate and unify the Court's approach to the administrative due process questions that had been brought to it in increasing numbers since *Goldberg.* The generality of the *Eldridge* test seems to have been designed to lend consistency and principle to the Court's approach while permitting review of differing administrative functions in the light of their particular circumstances. Yet, the *Eldridge* formulation was immediately criticized as flawed in principle and incapable of coherent application. Mashaw, *The Supreme Court's Due Process Calculus for Administrative Adjudication in Mathews v. Eldridge: Three Factors in Search of a Theory of Value*, 44 U. Chi. L. Rev. 28, 47-49 (1976):

> * * * [T]he three-factor analysis enunciated in *Eldridge* appears to be a type of utilitarian, social welfare function. That function first takes into account the social value at stake in a legitimate private claim; it discounts that value by the probability that it will be preserved through the available admin-

istrative procedures, and it then subtracts from that discounted value and the social cost of introducing additional procedures. When combined with the institutional posture of judicial self-restraint, utility theory can be said to yield the following plausible decision-rule: "Void procedures for lack of due process only when alternative procedures would so substantially increase social welfare that their rejection seems irrational."

The utilitarian calculus is not, however, without difficulties. The *Eldridge* Court conceives of the values of procedure too narrowly: it views the sole purpose of procedural protections as enhancing accuracy, and thus limits its calculus to the benefits or costs that flow from correct or incorrect decisions. No attention is paid to "process values" that might inhere in oral proceedings or to the demoralization costs that may result from the grant-with-drawal-grant-withdrawal sequence to which claimants like Eldridge are subjected. Perhaps more important, as the Court seeks to make sense of a calculus in which accuracy is the sole goal of procedure, it tends erroneously to characterize disability hearings as concerned almost exclusively with medical impairment and thus concludes that such hearings involve only medical evidence, whose reliability would be little enhanced by oral procedure. As applied by the *Eldridge* Court the utilitarian calculus tends, as cost-benefit analyses typically do, to "dwarf soft variables" and to ignore complexities and ambiguities.

The problem with a utilitarian calculus is not merely that the Court may define the relevant costs and benefits too narrowly. However broadly conceived, the calculus asks unanswerable questions. For example, what is the social value, and the social cost, of continuing disability payments until after an oral hearing for persons initially determined to be ineligible? Answers to those questions require some technique for measuring the social value and social costs of government income transfers, but no such technique exists. Even if such formidable tasks of social accounting could be accomplished, the effectiveness of oral hearings in forestalling the losses that result from erroneous terminations would remain uncertain. In the face of these pervasive indeterminacies the *Eldridge* Court was forced to retreat to a presumption of constitutionality.

Finally, it is not clear that the utilitarian balancing analysis asks the constitutionally relevant questions. The due process clause is one of those Bill of Rights protections meant to insure individual liberty in the face of contrary collective action. Therefore, a collective legislative or administrative decision about procedure, one arguably reflecting the intensity of the contending social values and representing an optimum position from the contemporary social perspective, cannot answer the constitutional question of whether due process has been accorded. A balancing analysis that would have the Court merely redetermine the question of social utility is similarly inadequate. There is no reason to believe that the Court has superior competence or legitimacy as a utilitarian balancer except as it performs its peculiar institutional role of insuring that libertarian values are considered in the calculus of decision.

See also Mashaw, *Administrative Due Process as Social-Cost Accounting*, 9 Hofstra L. Rev. 1423 (1981), for a more elaborate development of the information demands of the *Eldridge* approach and of techniques for managing the imponderables of a social welfare calculus.

2. Doctrinal consistency (beyond repeated enunciation of the *Eldridge* test) has not characterized the post-*Eldridge* Supreme Court jurisprudence. To be sure, assessing the consistency of the application of a formulation as open-textured as the *Eldridge* criteria, especially to practices and claims as varied as those raised in administrative due process cases, is a problematic enterprise. However, some oscillations in the Court's approach are virtually impossible to reconcile on any persuasive ground.

Consider *Memphis Light, Gas and Water Division v. Craft*, 436 U.S. 1 (1978), a case involving the adequacy of a municipal utility's procedure for resolving disputes with customers. Craft complained that the utility had failed to notify him of the availablity of the company's pre-termination review procedure when threatening him with termination of services for non-payment. The company admitted its failure to notify, but argued that the available common-law remedies—pre-termination injunction, post-termination damages and a post-payment action for refund—made a pre-termination conference superfluous. The utility's argument rested on the decision, only one term earlier in *Ingraham v. Wright*, 430 U.S. 651 (1977). There the Court had held that there was no need for "pre-paddling" hearings in a school system employing corporal punishment precisely because, "the available civil and criminal sanctions for abuse * * * afford significant protection against unjustified corporal punishment." 430 U.S. at 678. Indeed, the Memphis utility seemed to have an *a fortiori* case. The holding in *Ingraham* emerged from a context in which (a) any common law remedy would have been available only for "abuse," not error; (b) no pre-punishment common law remedy was thought to exist; and (c) no court in the affected state had ever recognized a remedy against a teacher for corporal punishment. The utility must certainly have been surprised, therefore, to learn that common law remedies were not "an adequate substitute for a pre-termination review of the disputed bill with a designated employee." 436 U.S. at 20.

Nor does the significance to be accorded the existence or non-existence of common law remedies exhaust the Court's problems when analyzing the contribution of additional procedures to accurate decisionmaking. A brace of cases involving psychiatric assessment, and a similar pair relating to decisions based on character, intelligence, and good faith, continue an erratic jurisprudence. Consider first *Parham v. J.R.*, 442 U.S. 584 (1979), and *Vitek v. Jones*, 445 U.S. 480 (1980).

In *Parham* the issue was whether a minor was entitled to a hearing prior to commitment to an institution for treatment of mental illness. The Court thought not, in substantial part because a hearing would provide little additional protection from error: "Common human experience and scholarly opinions suggest that the supposed protections of an adversary hearing to determine the appropriateness of medical decisions for the commitment and treatment of mental and emotional illness may well be more illusory than real." 442 U.S. at 609. This sentiment seems quite consistent with the Court's view of medical evidence in *Eldridge*. Yet in *Vitek*, where the question was whether a prisoner should have a hearing prior to being transferred to a mental hospital, the suggestion that psychiatric judgment was involved elicited the following judicial response: "The medical nature of the inquiry * * * does not justify dispensing with due process requirements. *It is precisely "[t]he subtleties and nuances of psychiatric diagnoses" that justify the requirement of adversary hearings.*" 445

U.S. at 495 (quoting *Addington v. Texas*, 441 U.S. 418, 430 (1979)) (emphasis supplied).

Greenholtz v. Inmates, 442 U.S. 1 (1979), and *Califano v. Yamasaki*, 442 U.S. 682 (1979), are no less baffling.   *Greenholtz* holds that a face-to-face, oral hearing is not required in parole decisions based on an assessment of the offender's personality, readiness to undertake responsibilities, intelligence, training, "mental and physical makeup," attitude toward law and authority, and any other factors the parole board deems relevant.   Accuracy, the Court ruled, could be achieved by a review of the prisoner's files.   Yet *Yamasaki* requires an oral hearing (at least a conversation) before the Secretary of HHS declines to waive recoupment of overpaid disability benefits because the waiver standard, lack of fault, rests "on an evaluation of all 'pertinent circumstances' including the recipient's intelligence * * * and physical and mental condition as well as his good faith."   442 U.S. at 696-97 (quoting from 10 C.F.R. § 402.507).   Indeed, *Yamasaki*'s apparent inconsistency with *Eldridge* warrants a closer look.

CALIFANO v. YAMASAKI

Supreme Court of the United States, 1979.
442 U.S. 682, 99 S.Ct. 2545, 61 L.Ed.2d 176.

Mr. JUSTICE BLACKMUN delivered the opinion of the Court.

[Under section 204(a)(1) of the Social Security Act, recoupment of overpayments of disability benefits was to be accomplished by deductions from future payments.   However, Section 204(b) precludes recoupment where the Secretary finds that the recipient is without fault and adjustments or recovery would *either* "defeat the purposes" of the Act *or* "be against equity and good conscience."]

The Secretary has undertaken to define the terms employed in § 204(b). Under his regulations, "without fault" means that the recipient neither knew nor should have known that the overpayment or the information on which it was based was incorrect. * * *

The regulations say that to "defeat the purpose of the subchapter" is to "deprive a person of income required for ordinary and necessary living expenses." * * *   Recoupment is "against equity and good conscience" when the recipient "because of a notice that such payment would be made or by reason of the incorrect payment, relinquished a valuable right * * *   or changed his position for the worse." * * *

The Secretary's practice is to make an *ex parte* determination under § 204(a) that an overpayment has been made, to notify the recipient of that determination, and then to shift to the recipient the burden of either (i) seeking reconsideration to contest the accuracy of that determination, or (ii) asking the Secretary to forgive the debt and waive recovery in accordance with § 204(b).   If a recipient files a written request for reconsideration or waiver, recoupment is deferred pending action on that request. * * * The papers are sent to one of the seven regional offices where the request is reviewed.

If the regional office decision goes against the recipient, recoupment begins. The recipient's monthly benefits are reduced or terminated[3] until the overpayment has been recouped. Only if the recipient continues to object is he given an opportunity to present his story in person to someone with authority to decide his case. That opportunity takes the form of an on-the-record *de novo* evidential hearing before an independent hearing examiner. The recipient may seek subsequent review by the Appeals Council, and finally by a federal court. If it is decided that the Secretary's initial determination was in error, the amounts wrongfully recouped are repaid.

[After describing the lower court judgments finding the procedures constitutionally defective and requiring an oral hearing prior to recoupment the Court continued.]

A court presented with both statutory and constitutional grounds to support the relief requested usually should pass on the statutory claim before considering the constitutional question.

The District Courts and Court of Appeals in the cases now before us gave these principles somewhat short shrift in declining to pass expressly on respondents' contention that § 204 itself requires a pre-recoupment oral hearing. We turn to the statute first, and find that it fairly may be read to require a pre-recoupment decision by the Secretary. With respect to § 204(a) reconsideration as to whether overpayment occurred, we agree that the statute does not require that the decision involve a prior oral hearing, and we reject respondents' contention that the Constitution does so. With respect to § 204(b) waiver of the Secretary's right to recoup, however, because the nature of the statutory standards makes a hearing essential, we find it unnecessary to determine whether the Constitution would require a similar result.

On its face, § 204 requires that the Secretary make a pre-recoupment waiver decision, and that the decision, like that concerning the fact of the overpayment, be accurate. In the imperative voice,[9] it says "there shall

---

3. The Secretary has altered his procedures in several respects since the initiation of this litigation, including: (i) rather than terminate all benefits until recoupment is completed, the Secretary now in nonfraud cases usually reduces the recipient's monthly payments by only 25%, see Claims Manual § 5515 (January 1979); and (ii) recipients who report excessive earnings and are found to have been overpaid now receive notice before, rather than after, recoupment begins. See *Elliott v. Weinberger,* 564 F.2d 1219, 1223 (C.A.9 1977). Neither party contends that these changes moot this case.

9. A number of statutes authorizing the recovery of federal payments make an exception for cases that are "against equity and good conscience." Most are entirely permissive. They provide that recovery "is not required," e.g., 10 U.S.C.A. § § 1442, 1453 (ser-

viceman's family annuity and survivors' benefit); or that an agency "may waive" recovery if a proper showing is made, 5 U.S.C.A. § 4108(c) (civil service training expenses), 5 U.S.C.A. § 5922(b)(2) (foreign station allowances); or that the agency head "shall make such provision as he finds appropriate," 42 U.S.C.A. § 1383(b) (supplemental security income); or simply that recovery "may be waived," 10 U.S.C.A. § 2774(a) (military pay).

In contrast, § 204 is mandatory in form. It says "there shall be no" recovery when waiver is proper. In this regard it resembles the "equity and good conscience" waiver provisions found in only four other statutes: 38 U.S.C.A. § 3102(a) (veterans benefits); 42 U.S.C.A. § 1395gg(c) (Medicare); 45 U.S.C.A. § 231i(c) (Railroad Retirement Act); 45 U.S.C.A. § 231i(c) (Railroad Retirement Act of 1974); 45 U.S.C.A. § 352(d) (Railroad Unemployment Insurance Act). Even those statutes are **not**

be no adjustment of payments to, or recovery by the United States from, any person" who qualifies for waiver. See *Mattern v. Weinberger*, 519 F.2d, at 166, and n.32. Echoing this requirement, § 204(a) says that only "proper" adjustments or recoveries are to be made. The implication is that recoupment from a person qualifying under § 204(a) would not be "proper."

Insofar as § 204 is read to require a pre-recoupment decision, the reading is in accord with the manner in which the Secretary presently administers the statute. No recoupment is made until a preliminary waiver or reconsideration decision has taken place, either by default after the recipient has received proper notice, or by review of a written request. Claims Manual § § 5503.2(c), 5503.4(b). This interpretation is also reinforced by a comparison with other sections of the Social Security Act. Section 204 is strikingly unlike § 225,[10] which expressly permits suspension of disability benefits before eligibility is finally decided. See *Richardson v. Wright*, 405 U.S. 208 (1972). On the other hand, an analogy may be drawn between § 204 and § 303(a)(1), 42 U.S.C.A. § (a)(1), which this Court in *California Human Resources Dept. v. Java*, 402 U.S. 121 (1971), interpreted to require payment of unemployment benefits pending a final determination of eligibility.[11] Neither § 204 nor § 303(a)(1) expressly addresses the timing of a hearing, but both speak in mandatory terms and imply that the mandated act—here waiver of recoupment, there payment of benefits—is to precede other action.

The heart of the present dispute concerns not whether a pre-recoupment decision should be made, but whether making the decision by regional office review of the written waiver request is sufficient to protect the recipient's right not to be subjected to an improper recoupment.

In this regard, requests for reconsideration under § 204(a), as to whether overpayment occurred, may be distinguished from requests for waiver of the Secretary's right to recoup under § 204(b). * * * [R]equests under § 204(a) for reconsideration involve relatively straightforward matters of computation for which written review is ordinarily an

---

identical to § 204 in all material respects. While the use of the word "shall," particularly with reference to an equitable decision, does not eliminate all discretion, see *Hecht Co. v. Bowles*, 321 U. S. 321, 327-331 (1944), it at least imposes on the Secretary a duty to decide. And here where the provision for recovery, § 204(a), and the provision for waiver, § 204(b), are phrased in equally mandatory terms, it is reasonable to infer that in this particular statute Congress did not intend to exalt recovery over waiver.

The legislative history of § 204(b) indicates merely that Congress intended to make recovery more equitable by authorizing waiver.

10. Section 225 provides:

"If the Secretary, on the basis of information obtained by or submitted to him,

believes that an individual entitled to [disability benefits] * * * may have ceased to be under a disability, the Secretary may suspend the payment of benefits * * * until it is determined * * * whether or not such individual's disability has ceased or until the Secretary believes that such disability has not ceased."

11. Section 303(a) provides:

"The Secretary of Labor shall make no certification for payment to any State unless he finds that the law of such state * * * includes provisions for—

"(1) Such methods of administration * * * as are found by the Secretary of Labor to be reasonably calculated to insure full payment of unemployment compensation when due."

adequate means to correct prior mistakes. Many of the named respondents were found to have been overpaid based on earnings reports they themselves had submitted. But unlike the Court of Appeals in this case, we do not think that the rare instance in which a credibility dispute is relevant to a § 204(a) claim is sufficient to require the Secretary to sift through all requests for reconsideration and grant a hearing to the few that involve credibility. The statute authorizes only "proper" recoupment, but some leeway for practical administration must be allowed. Nor do the standards of the Due Process Clause, more tolerant than the strict language here in issue, require that pre-recoupment oral hearings be afforded in § 204(a) cases. The nature of a due process hearing is shaped by the "risk of error inherent in the truthfinding process as applied to the generality of cases, not the rare exceptions." *Mathews v. Eldridge.* It would be inconsistent with that principle to require a hearing under § 204(a) when review of a beneficiary's written submission is an adequate means of resolving all but a few § 204(a) disputes.

By contrast, written review hardly seems sufficient to discharge the Secretary's statutory duty to make an accurate determination of waiver under § 204(b). Under that subsection, the Secretary must assess the absence of "fault" and determine whether or not recoupment would be "against equity and good conscience." These standards do not apply under § 204(a). The Court previously has noted that a "broad 'fault' standard is inherently subject to factual determination and adversarial input." *Mitchell v. W. T. Grant Co.*, 416 U.S. 600, 617 (1974). As the Secretary's regulations make clear, "fault" depends on an evaluation of "all pertinent circumstances" including the recipient's "intelligence * * * and physical and mental condition" as well as his good faith." 20 C.F.R. § 404.507 (1978). We do not see how these can be evaluated absent personal contact between the recipient and the person who decides his case. Evaluating fault, like judging detrimental reliance, usually requires an assessment of the recipient's credibility, and written submissions are a particularly inappropriate way to distinguish a genuine hard luck story from a fabricated tall tale.

The consequences of the injunctions entered by the District Courts confirm the reasonableness of interpreting § 204(b) to require a pre-recoupment oral hearing. In compliance with those orders, the Secretary, beginning with calendar year 1977, has granted what respondents term "a short personal conference with an impartial employee of the Social Security Administration at which time the recipient presents testimony and evidence and cross-examines witnesses, and the administrative employee questions the recipient." Of the approximately 2,000 conferences held between January 1977 and October 1978, 30% resulted in a reversal of the Secretary's decision. This rate of reversal confirms the view that, without an oral hearing, the Secretary may misjudge a number of cases that he otherwise would be able to assess properly, and that the hearing requirement imposed by the Court of Appeals significantly furthers the statutory goal that "there shall be no" recoupment when waiver is appropriate. We therefore agree with the Court of Appeals that an opportunity for a pre-recoupment oral hearing is required when a recipient requests waiver under § 204(b).

Notes

1. Why should Congress want the recoupment of overpaid disability benefits by reductions in future payments to be accompanied by greater safeguards than the complete termination of disability benefits?

2. If the basis for the decision in *Yamasaki* is the mandatory language of the statute, how far short of perfection can the Secretary's judgments be and still comply with the "congressional instruction"?

3. Why does a 30% "reversal rate" in the newly instituted conference procedure suggest that the Secretary may otherwise "misjudge" the issue of fault? Why did an even higher 50% rate of reversal of disability terminations by Administrative Law Judges fail to persuade the Court in *Eldridge* that the disability determination process was wildly inaccurate absent face-to-face hearings?

4. Is "fault" a fact? If the answer is "No," what does it mean to make an "error" with respect to a finding of fault? What contribution will a personal hearing make to avoiding such errors?

5. Perhaps cases like *Yamasaki* should be analyzed in entirely different terms. In *Administrative Due Process: The Quest for a Dignitary Theory*, 61 B. U. L. Rev. 885, 902–03 (1981), Professor Mashaw concludes that reasonable accuracy is but one of several instrumental, process values tending to protect individual autonomy and self-respect. More fundamentally, the so-called "dignitary" approach argues that it is these latter, more basic, human rights that due process affirms. On this premise the procedural value at stake in *Yamasaki* might more realistically be characterized in the following terms:

'Participation' is an obvious candidate for our set of dignitary process values. One constantly confronts the claim that the dignity and self-respect of the individual can be protected only through processes of government in which there is 'meaningful participation' by affected interests. * * *

The basis for a connection between participation and self-respect may, however, be variously explained. * * * [I]t has become traditional in the due process jurisprudence to make the connection only in circumstances in which the individual is attempting to defend some previously recognized "right." That is arguably a dignitary approach, but with a substantive entitlements trigger. Yet, others would assert that participation is equally important in proceedings that function to develop the *content* of rights, rather than merely to enforce rights previously specified. The latter claim—and it seems a persuasive one—may be said to be that our self-respect is called in question not only when our rights are dealt with in proceedings to which we are not admitted, but also when we are excluded from a process of social decisionmaking in which the set of rights we all hold are defined or elaborated.

This point is extended by those who argue that the true relationship between participation and self-respect is that participation increases self-respect to the degree that participation gives the participant *control* over the process of decisionmaking. And loss of control, it is argued, is particularly damaging to self-respect precisely in those circumstances in which rights are amorphous and decisionmaking depends importantly on "contextualizing" the events or norms that appear to be relevant to the issue to be decided. It is in these situations that we are especially conscious of the need to explain and justify our actions and in which the loss of the opportunity to do so denies our self-worth. Indeed, the argument is pressed further still to urge the necessity of employing broad principles and contextualizing processes if we are to avoid inducing perceptions of injustice and loss of individual status.

For further elaboration of similar ideas, see Mashaw, *Conflict and Compromise Among Models of Administrative Justice*, 1981 Duke L.J. 181; Michelman, *Formal and Associated Aims in Procedural Due Process* in DUE PROCESS, NOMOS XVIII 126 (J. Pennock & J. Chapman, eds. 1977); Thibaut & Walker, *A Theory of Procedure*, 66 Calif. L. Rev. 541 (1978); Tribe, *Perspectives on Bakke: Equal Protection, Procedural Fairness, or Structural Justice?*, 92 Harv. L. Rev. 864 (1979); Tribe, *Structural Due Process*, 10 Harv. C.R.-C.L. L. Rev. 269 (1975).

O'BANNON v. TOWN COURT NURSING CENTER

Supreme Court of the United States, 1980.
447 U.S. 773, 100 S.Ct. 2467, 65 L. Ed.2d 506.

Mr. JUSTICE STEVENS delivered the opinion of the Court.

The question presented is whether approximately 180 elderly residents of a nursing home operated by Town Court Nursing Center, Inc., have a constitutional right to a hearing before a state or federal agency may revoke the home's authority to provide them with nursing care at government expense. Although we recognize that such a revocation may be harmful to some patients, we hold that they have no constitutional right to participate in the revocation proceedings.

Town Court Nursing Center, Inc. (Town Court), operates a 198-bed nursing home in Philadelphia, Pa. In April 1976 it was certified by the Department of Health, Education, and Welfare (HEW) as a "skilled nursing facility," thereby becoming eligible to receive payments from HEW and from the Pennsylvania Department of Public Welfare (DPW), for providing nursing care services to aged, disabled, and poor persons in need of medical care. After receiving its certification, Town Court entered into formal "provider agreements" with both HEW and DPW. In those agreements HEW and DPW agreed to reimburse Town Court for a period of one year for care provided to persons eligible for Medicare or Medicaid benefits under the Social Security Act, on the condition that Town Court continue to qualify as a skilled nursing facility.

On May 17, 1977, HEW notified Town Court that it no longer met the statutory and regulatory standards for skilled nursing facilities and that, consequently, its Medicare provider agreement would not be renewed.[3] The HEW notice stated that no payments would be made for services

---

3. HEW based its determination on a survey conducted by DPW, which recommended that the home be decertified. In its notice to Town Court HEW stated in part:

* * *

"On May 8-11, 1977, the Pennsylvania Department of Health performed a survey of your facility. That survey found that your facility does not comply with seven of the eighteen conditions of partici-

rendered after July 17, 1977, explained how Town Court might request reconsideration of the decertification decision, and directed it to notify Medicare beneficiaries that payments were being discontinued.   Three days later DPW notified Town Court that its Medicaid provider agreement would also not be renewed.[4]

[Town Court and a group of its residents filed suit in federal district court claiming a right to an evidentiary hearing prior to decertification of the nursing home.   Town Court's claim was rejected by both the district court and the court of appeals on the ground that the statutory post-termination hearing guaranteed providers under the federal medical assistance programs was sufficient to satisfy the *Eldridge* formulation of due process.   The residents, who had no statutory right to hearing, nevertheless prevailed before the Third Circuit, sitting *en banc*.   *Town Court Nursing Center, Inc. v. Beal*, 586 F.2d 280 (3rd Cir. 1978).]

At the outset, it is important to remember that this case does not involve the question whether HEW or DPW should, as a matter of administrative efficiency, consult the residents of a nursing home before making a final decision to decertify it.   Rather, the question is whether the patients have an interest in receiving benefits for care in a particular facility that entitles them, as a matter of constitutional law, to a hearing before the Government can decertify that facility.   The patients have identified two possible sources of such a right.   First, they contend that the Medicaid provisions * * * give them a property right to remain in the home of their choice absent good cause for transfer and therefore entitle them to a hearing on whether such cause exists.   Second, they argue that a transfer may have such severe physical or emotional side effects that it is tantamount to a deprivation of life or liberty, which must be preceded by a due process hearing.[16]   We find both arguments unpersuasive.

---

pation.   The seven conditions not being complied with are:

"II.   Governing Body and
          Management   (405.1121)
"III.   Medical Direction   (405.1122)
"IV.   Physical Services   (405.1123)
"V.   Nursing Services   (405.1124)
"VIII. Pharmaceutical Services (405.1127)
"XIII. Medical Records   (405.1132)
"XV.   Physical Environment (405.1134)

"Your facility's failure to comply with these conditions of participation precludes renewal of your agreement.   * * *

4.   The state agency's letter read in part: "Because the Medicare Program has terminated your participation, the Department of Public Welfare has no alternative but to likewise terminate your participation under the Medical Assistance Program.   The Federal regulations, 45 C.F.R. § 249.33(a)(9), require that a State medical assistance plan must:

" 'Provide that * * * *upon notification that an agreement with a facility under title XVIII of the Act has been terminated or cancelled, the single State agency will take appropriate action to terminate the facility's participation under the plan.* * * *   (emphasis supplied)

16.   The patients cite a number of studies indicating that removal to another home may cause "transfer trauma," increasing the possibility of death or serious illness for elderly, infirm patients.   They also argue that associational interests, such as friendship among patients and staff and family ties, may be disrupted if the patients are scattered to other nursing homes, perhaps in other areas of the country.   In denying the motion for a preliminary injunction, the District Court did not take evidence or make any findings on the harm that might result from a transfer.   Nevertheless, we assume for purposes of this decision that there is a risk that some residents may encounter severe emotional and physical hardship as a result of a transfer.

Whether viewed singly or in combination, the Medicaid provisions relied upon by the Court of Appeals do not confer a right to continued residence in the home of one's choice. Title 42 U.S.C.A. § 1396a(a)(23) (1976 ed., Supp. II) gives recipients the right to choose among a range of *qualified* providers, without government interference. By implication, it also confers an absolute right to be free from government interference with the choice to remain in a home that continues to be qualified. But it clearly does not confer a right on a recipient to enter an unqualified home and demand a hearing to certify it, nor does it confer a right on a recipient to continue to receive benefits for care in a home that has been decertified. Second, although the regulations do protect patients by limiting the circumstances under which a *home* may transfer or discharge a Medicaid recipient, they do not purport to limit the Government's right to make a transfer necessary by decertifying a facility. Finally, since decertification does not reduce or terminate a patient's financial assistance, but merely requires him to use it for care at a different facility, regulations granting recipients the right to a hearing prior to a reduction in financial benefits are irrelevant.

* * *

Medicaid patients who are forced to move because their nursing home has been decertified are in no different position for purposes of due process analysis than financially independent residents of a nursing home who are forced to move because the home's state license has been revoked. Both groups of patients are indirect beneficiaries of government programs designed to guarantee a minimum standard of care for patients as a class. Both may be injured by the closing of a home due to revocation of its state license or its decertification as a Medicaid provider. Thus, whether they are private patients or Medicaid patients, some may have difficulty locating other homes they consider suitable or may suffer both emotional and physical harm as a result of the disruption associated with their move. Yet none of these patients would lose the ability to finance his or her continued care in a properly licensed or certified institution. And, while they might have a claim against the nursing home for damages, none would have any claim against the responsible governmental authorities for the deprivation of an interest in life, liberty, or property. Their position under these circumstances would be comparable to that of members of a family who have been dependent on an errant father; they may suffer serious trauma if he is deprived of his liberty or property as a consequence of criminal proceedings, but surely they have no constitutional right to participate in his trial or sentencing procedures. * * *

Whatever legal rights these patients may have against Town Court for failing to maintain its status as a qualified skilled nursing home—and we express no opinion on that subject—we hold that the enforcement by HEW and DPW of their valid regulations did not directly affect the patients' legal rights or deprive them of any constitutionally protected interest in life, liberty, or property.

The judgment of the Court of Appeals is reversed, and the case is remanded for further proceedings consistent with this opinion.

It is so ordered.

Mr. JUSTICE MARSHALL took no part in the consideration or decision of this case.

Mr. JUSTICE BLACKMUN, concurring in the judgment.

In my view, the Court deals far too casually with § 1902(a)(23) of the Social Security Act, 42 U.S.C.A. § 1396(a)(23) (1976 ed., Supp. II), in rejecting the patients' "property" claim. That provision guarantees that a patient may receive nursing home care "from any institution * * * qualified to perform the * * * services * * * who undertakes to provide him such services." The statute thus vests each patient with a broad right to resist governmental removal, which can be disrupted only when the Government establishes the home's noncompliance with program participation requirements. Given this fact and our precedents, one can easily understand why seven judges of the Court of Appeals adopted the patients' argument. It would seem that, because the Government has generated a "justifiable expectation that [the patients] would not be transferred except for misbehavior or upon the occurrence of other specified events," *Vitek v. Jones,* 445 U.S. 480, 489 (1980), they are "entitled * * * to the benefits of appropriate procedures in connection with determining the conditions that warranted [their] transfer." Especially since the patients assert an interest in a home,[2] I believe their claim to property has substantial force.

* * * [I]t "begs the question" to counter this argument with the observation that § 1396(a)(23) expressly gives the patients only a right to stay in *qualified* facilities. We have repeatedly rejected as too facile an approach that looks no further than the face of the statute to define the scope of protected expectancies. * * *

Perhaps aware that its treatment of § 1396(a)(23) is in some tension with our precedents, the Court * * * reasons that "decertification * * * is not the same for purposes of due process analysis as a decision to transfer a particular patient." I am left wondering why. Certainly, the "real world" effect of the two actions is the same. Thus the Court's assertion will come as cold comfort to patients forced to relocate because of this decision.

I have no quarrel with the Court's observation that the Due Process Clause generally is unconcerned with "indirect" losses. I fear, however,

---

2. It is well recognized that the Due Process Clauses of the United States Constitution grew out of the "law of the land" provision of Magna Carta and its later manifestations in English statutory law. That the home was at the center of those property interests historically sought to be protected by due process is underscored by the fact the phrase "due process of law" first appeared in the following codification: "No man of what state or condition he be, shall be *put out of his lands or tenements* or taken, nor disinherited, nor put to death, without he be brought to answer by due process of law." 28 Edw. III, ch. 3 (1354) (emphasis added), as quoted in The Constitution of the United States of America, Analysis and Interpretation 1138 (Cong. Research Serv. 1973).

that such platitudes often submerge analytical complexities in particular cases. * * * To say that the decertification decision directly affects the home is not to say that it "indirectly" affects the patients. Transfer is not only the "inevitabl[e]," clearly foreseeable consequences of decertification; a basic *purpose* of decertification is to force patients to relocate. To be sure, decertification-induced transfers are designed to benefit patients. But so are a wide range of other governmental acts that invoke due process protections for the intended beneficiary. See, e.g., *Vitek v. Jones,* supra; *Parham v. J. R.,* 442 U.S. 584 (1979). See also *In re Gault,* 387 U.S. 1 (1967). Indeed a basic purpose of affording a hearing in such cases is to test the Government's judgment that its actions will in fact prove to be beneficial.

In my view, there exists a more principled and sensible analysis of the patients' "property" claim. Given § 1396(a)(23), I am forced to concede that the patients have some form of property interest in continued residence at Town Court. And past decisions compel me to observe that where, as here, a substantial restriction inhibits governmental removal of a presently enjoyed benefit, a property interest normally will be recognized.[5] To state a general rule, however, is not to decide a specific case. The Court never has held that *any* substantive restriction upon removal of *any* governmental benefit gives rise to a generalized property interest in its continued enjoyment. Indeed, a majority of the Justices of this Court are already on record as concluding that the term "property" sometimes incorporates limiting characterizations of statutorily bestowed interests. See *Arnett v. Kennedy,* 416 U.S. 134 (1974) (plurality opinion); *Goss v. Lopez,* 419 U.S. 565, 586-587, and n.4 (1975) (dissenting opinion). Common sense and sound policy support this recognition of some measure of flexibility in defining "new property" expectancies. Public benefits are not held in fee simple. And even if we analogize the patients' claim to "continued residence" to holdings more familiar to the law of private property—even to interests in homes, such as life tenancies—we would find that those interests are regularly subject to easements, conditions subsequent, possibilities of reverter, and other similar limitations. In short, it does not suffice to say that a litigant holds property. The inquiry also must focus on the dimensions of that interest. See *Board of Regents v. Roth,* 408 U.S. 564, 577 (1972).

---

5. See *Memphis Light, Gas & Water Div. v. Craft,* 436 U.S. 1, 11 (1978) (receipt of services from public utility not terminable except for "good and sufficient cause"); *Bishop v. Wood,* 426 U.S., at 345, n.8 (finding determinative that public employment was terminable "at will," rather than for cause); *Goss v. Lopez,* 419 U.S. 565, 573-574 (1975) (public education must be continued absent "misconduct"); *Board of Regents v. Roth,* 408 U.S., at 578 (distinguishing situation where nonrenewal of state college professor's employment authorized only for "sufficient cause"); *Goldberg v. Kelly,* 397 U.S. 254, 262 (1970) (public support payments to be continued unless recipient not qualified). See also *Vitek v. Jones,* 445 U.S. 480, 488-491 (1980); *Greenholz v. Nebraska Penal Inmates,* 442 U.S. 1, 9-11 (1979); *Montanye v. Haymes,* 427 U.S. 236, 242 (1976); *Meachum v. Fano,* 427 U.S. 215, 226-227 (1976); *Wolff v. McDonnell,* 418 U.S. 539, 558 (1974); *Gagnon v. Scarpelli,* 411 U.S. 778 (1973); *Morrissey v. Brewer,* 408 U.S. 471 (1972). See generally *Murray's Lessee v. Hoboken Land & Improvement Co.,* 18 How. 272, 276 (1856) (Fifth Amendment "cannot be so construed as to leave congress free to make any process 'due process of law,' by its mere will").

The determinative question is whether the litigant holds such a legitimate "claim of entitlement" that the Constitution, rather than the political branches, must define the procedures attending its removal. Claims of entitlement spring from expectations that are "justifiable," *Vitek v. Jones*, 445 U.S., at 489; "protectible," *Greenholtz v. Nebraska Penal Inmates*, 442 U.S. 1, 7 (1979); "sufficient," *Bishop v. Wood*, 426 U.S. 341, 344 (1976); or "proper," id., at 362 (dissenting opinion). In contrast, the Constitution does not recognize expectancies that are "unilateral," *Board of Regents v. Roth*, 408 U.S., at 577, or "too ephemeral and insubstantial." *Meachum v. Fano*, 427 U.S. 215, 228 (1976).

To mouth these labels does not advance analysis far. We must look further to determine which set of labels applies to particular constellations of fact. Whether protected entitlements exist and how far they extend, although dependent on subconstitutional rules, are ultimately questions of constitutional law. See *Memphis Light, Gas & Water Div. v. Craft*, 436 U.S., at 9. Application of that law will seldom pose difficulties when the Government has exercised its option to bestow a benefit wholly at will, or the litigant has identified a "for cause" condition resembling those held to be property-creating in past cases. Cases, however, will not always fit neatly into these categories. And when such cases arise, some new analysis is needed. In my view, that inquiry should be broad-gauged. Reason and shared perceptions should be consulted to define the scope of the claimant's "justifiable" expectations. Nor should constitutional policy be ignored in deciding whether constitutional protections attach. This approach not only permits sensible application of due process protections; it reflects the unremarkable reality that reasonable legal rules themselves comport with reasonable expectations.

In applying this analysis to this case, four distinct considerations convince me that—even though the statutes place a significant substantive restriction on transferring patients—their expectancy in remaining in their home is conditioned upon its status as a qualified provider.

(1) The lengthy process of deciding the disqualification question has intimately involved Town Court. The home has been afforded substantial procedural protections, and, throughout the process, has shared with the patients who wish to stay there an intense interest in keeping the facility certified. * * *

(2) Town Court is more than a *de facto* representative of the patients' interests; it is the underlying source of the benefit they seek to retain. * * * The Constitution would not have entitled John Kelly to a fair hearing if New York had chosen to disband its public assistance programs rather than to cut off his particular award. See *Goldberg v. Kelly*, 397 U.S. 254 (1970). * * *

(3) That the asserted deprivation of property extends in a nondiscriminatory fashion to some 180 patients also figures in my calculus. * * * *BiMetallic Investment Co. v. State Board*, 239 U.S. 441, 445 (1915). When governmental action affects more than a few individuals, concerns beyond economy, efficiency, and expedition tip the balance against finding that due process attaches. We may expect that as the sweep of govern-

mental action broadens, so too does the power of the affected group to protect its interests outside rigid constitutionally imposed procedures. * * *

(4) Finally, I find it important that the patients' interest has been jeopardized not at all because of alleged shortcomings on their part. Frequently, significant interests are subjected to adverse action upon a contested finding of fault, impropriety, or incompetence. In these contexts the Court has seldom hesitated to require that a hearing be afforded the "accused." This tendency reflects due process values extending beyond the need for accurate determinations. Affording procedural protections also aims at "generating the feeling, so important to a popular government, that justice has been done." It may be that patients' participation in the decertification decision would vaguely heighten their and others' sense of the decision's legitimacy, even though the decision follows extensive government inspections undertaken with the very object of protecting the patients' interests. Even so, that interest is far less discernible in this context than when a stigmatizing determination of wrongdoing or fault supplements removal of a presently enjoyed benefit.

For these reasons, I am willing to recognize in this case that "the very legislation which 'defines' the 'dimension' of the [patient's] entitlement, while providing a right to [remain in a home] generally, does not establish this right free of [disqualification of the home] in accord with [federal statutory] law."

Citing articles and empirical studies, the patients argue that the trauma of transfer so substantially exacerbates mortality rates, disease, and psychological decline that decertification deprives them of life and liberty. Although the Court assumes that "transfer trauma" exists, it goes on to reject this argument. By focusing solely on the "indirectness" of resulting physical and psychological trauma, the Court implies that regardless of the degree of the demonstrated risk that widespread illness or even death attends decertification-induced transfers, it is of no moment. I cannot join such a heartless holding. Earlier this Term, the Court recognized that a liberty interest emanates even from the likelihood that added stigma or harmful treatment might attend transfer from a prison to a mental hospital. *Vitek v. Jones*, supra; see also *Parham v. J. R.*, 442 U.S., at 601. For me it follows easily that a governmental decision that imposes a high risk of death or serious illness on identifiable patients must be deemed to have an impact on their liberty. * * *

The fact of the matter, however, is that the patients cannot establish that transfer trauma is so substantial a danger as to justify the conclusion that transfers deprive them of life or liberty. Substantial evidence suggests that "transfer trauma" does not exist, and many informed researchers have concluded at least that this danger is unproved. Recognition of a constitutional right plainly cannot rest on such an inconclusive body of research and opinion. It is for this reason, and not for that stated by the Court, that I would reject the patients' claim of a deprivation of life and liberty. * * *

Mr. JUSTICE BRENNAN, dissenting.

The statutory and regulatory scheme gives a patient the right to choose any qualified nursing home.   Once a patient has chosen a facility, the scheme carefully protects against undesired transfers by limiting the circumstances under which a home may transfer patients.   And a qualified nursing home, which must have met detailed federal requirements to gain certification, cannot be decertified unless the Government can show good cause.   Thus, the scheme is designed to enable a patient to stay in the chosen home unless there is a specific reason to justify a transfer.

Respondent patients chose a home which was, at the time, qualified.   They moved into the home reasonably expecting that they would not be forced to move unless, for some sufficient reason, the home became unsuitable for them.   The Government's disqualification of the home is, of course, one such reason.   Respondents have no right to receive benefits if they choose to live in an unqualified home.   That does not mean, however, that they have no right to be heard on the question whether the home is qualified—the answer to which will determine whether they must move to another home and suffer the allegedly great ills encompassed by the term "transfer trauma."   The Government's action in withdrawing the home's certification deprives them of the expectation of continued residency created by the statutes and regulations.   Under our precedents, they are certainly "entitled * * * to the benefits of appropriate procedures" in connection with the decertification.*

The requirements of due process, to be sure, are flexible and are meant to be practical.   Here, the provider is entitled to formal proceedings in connection with the disqualification of the home.   To the extent that patients want to remain in a home, their interests very nearly coincide with the home's own interests.   The patients can count on the home to argue that it should not be disqualified.   Nevertheless, the patients have some interests which are separate from the interests of the provider, and they could contribute some information relevant to the decertification decision if they were given an opportunity.   There is no indication that the patients have been accorded any opportunity to present their views on decertification.   Because they were accorded no procedural protection, I dissent.

"Life, Liberty or Property"

As Justice Blackmun's extensive citation of prior jurisprudence in *O'Bannon* suggests, the characterization of the "private interest * * * affected by the official action," *Eldridge*'s first factor, has generated sustained controversy.   Indeed, the qualitative facet of this inquiry—deciding whether a private interest falls within the "life, liberty or property"

---

* It is no answer to say that respondents' only right is to stay in a *qualified* home because whether the home is qualified is precisely the issue to be determined.   Nor is it an answer to say that respondents are third parties not "directly" affected by the governmental action.   As the Court admits, the regulatory scheme operates for the direct benefit of the patients, and it generates expectations and reliance just as deserving of protection as other statutory entitlements.

language of the Fifth or Fourteenth Amendment—has had a long and checkered career.

For example, at one time one might confidently have asserted that because there was no "right" to government employment or to contract with the government beyond the terms of a particular statute, regulation, or agreement, there was no right to a hearing should the government decide to terminate or modify an advantageous relationship. Such advantageous relationships were often denominated mere "privileges," and were treated as constitutionally insignificant. See, e.g., *Bailey v. Richardson*, supra; *Perkins v. Lukens Steel Co.*, 310 U.S. 113 (1940). But the period of the 1960's and early 1970's witnessed major erosion and apparently, in *Goldberg*, outright rejection of the "right-privilege" dichotomy as the litmus test of interests entitled to protection under the due process clause. See generally Van Alstyne, *The Demise of The Right-Privilege Distinction in Constitutional Law*, 81 Harv. L. Rev. 1439 (1968). As the *Goldberg* Court notes, this shift in the focus of due process concern seems to follow almost inexorably from the recognition that in modern society much wealth is held in the fragile currency of a government license, contract, or grant.

Yet the celebrants at the burial of the right-privilege distinction may discover that the reports of its death are exaggerated. Two years after *Goldberg*, for example, some surprising language appeared in another welfare case, *Wyman v. James*, 400 U.S. 309 (1971). The claim in *Wyman* raised not due process, but Fourth Amendment search and seizure issues. In upholding a New York provision which conditioned eligibility for public assistance on consent to home visits by welfare workers, the Court per Mr. Justice Blackmun said, "We note, too, that the visitation * * * is not * * * compelled. * * * If consent to the visitation is withheld, no visitation takes place. The aid then never begins or merely ceases, as the case may be." The opinion went on to analogize public welfare to private charity in which the donor "naturally has an interest in and expects to know how his funds are utilized. * * * *" The majority opinion provoked only one dissent and one special concurrence.

Board of Regents of State Colleges v. Roth, 408 U.S. 564 (1972), was another straw in the wind. There a teacher on a one-year contract had been notified that he would not be rehired for the following year. No reason was given and the college refused to state one or to provide a hearing, although the teacher claimed that absent some reason for declining to renew his contract, he had every expectation of renewal. The court said, in part (408 U.S. at 578):

> Just as the welfare recipients' "property" interest in welfare payments was created and defined by statutory terms, so the respondent's "property" interest in employment at Wisconsin State University-Oshkosh was created and defined by the terms of his appointment. Those terms secured his interest in employment up to June 30, 1969. But the important fact in this case is that they specifically provided that the respondent's employment was to terminate on June 30. They did not provide for contract renewal absent "sufficient cause." Indeed, they made no provision for renewal whatsoever.

Thus, the terms of the respondent's appointment secured absolutely no interest in re-employment for the next year. They supported absolutely no possible claim of entitlement to re-employment. Nor, significantly, was there any state statute or University rule or policy that secured his interest in re-employment or that created any legitimate claim to it. In these circumstances, the respondent surely had an abstract concern in being rehired, but he did not have a *property* interest sufficient to require the University authorities to give him a hearing when they declined to renew his contract of employment.

Only Justices Douglas and Marshall dissented, the former on a free speech issue that other members of the Court treated as not properly raised by the record.

The Court's holding in *Roth* was amplified by the decision in a companion case, *Perry v. Sindermann,* 408 U.S. 593, 599-600 (1972), involving another teacher serving on a year-to-year basis, but with ten years' service. In an opinion, again written by Justice Stewart, the Court said:

> [T]he respondent's allegations—which we must construe most favorably to the respondent at this stage of the litigation—do raise a genuine issue as to his interest in continued employment at Odessa Junior College. He alleged that this interest, though not secured by a formal contractual tenure provision, was secured by a no less binding understanding fostered by the college administration. In particular, the respondent alleged that the college had a *de facto* tenure program, and that he had tenure under that program. He claimed that he and others legitimately relied upon an unusual provision that had been in the college's official Faculty Guide for many years:
>
> > "*Teacher Tenure:* Odessa College has no tenure system. The Administration of the College wishes the faculty member to feel that he has permanent tenure as long as his teaching services are satisfactory and as long as he displays a cooperative attitude toward his co-workers and his superiors, and as long as he is happy in his work."
>
> Moreover, the respondent claimed legitimate reliance upon guidelines promulgated by the Coordinating Board of the Texas College and University System that provided that a person, like himself, who had been employed as a teacher in the state college and university system for seven years or more has some form of job tenure. Thus, the respondent offered to prove that a teacher with his long period of service at this particular State College had no less a "property" interest in continued employment than a formally tenured teacher at other colleges, and had no less a procedural due process right to a statement of reasons and a hearing before college officials upon their decision not to retain him. * * *
>
> * * * We disagree with the Court of Appeals insofar as it held that a mere subjective "expectancy" is protected by procedural due process, but we agree that the respondent must be given an opportunity to prove the legitimacy of his claim of such entitlement in light of "the policies and practices of the institution."

While *Roth* and *Sinderman* had suggested a close connection between legal rights as defined by the positive law and property interests, as protected—and defined—by the Constitution, Justice Rehnquist's plurality opinion (joined by Justice Stewart and the Chief Justice) in *Arnett v. Ken-*

nedy, 416 U.S. 134 (1974), seemed to make the former the full measure of the latter. Kennedy had been removed from his federal employment at OEO's Chicago Regional Office by his supervisor, Mr. Verduin, for possibly alleging that Verduin had made an offer of a $100,000 community action grant as a "bribe" to a local community action representative. As a non-probationary civil servant protected by the Lloyd-LaFollette Act, Kennedy could only be removed for "such cause as will promote the efficiency of the service." That same statute provided only an informal appeal to the employer's supervisor prior to taking any "adverse action," but it assured a formal post-removal hearing before either the employing agency or the Civil Service Commission. Kennedy challenged the limited pre-removal procedures as a denial of due process. In denying that claim Justice Rehnquist had this to say about that interrelationship of Kennedy's substantive and procedural rights (416 U.S. at 152, 154):

> * * * But the very section of the statute which granted him that right, * * * expressly provided also for the procedure by which "cause" was to be determined, and expressly omitted the procedural guarantees which appellee insists are mandated by the Constitution. Only by bifurcating the very sentence of the Act of Congress which conferred upon appellee the right not to be removed save for cause could it be said that he had an expectancy of that substantive right without the procedural limitations which Congress attached to it. * * * Congress was obviously intent on according a measure of statutory job security to governmental employees which they had not previously enjoyed, but was likewise intent on excluding more elaborate procedural requirements which it felt would make the operation of the new scheme unnecessarily burdensome in practice. Where the focus of legislation was this strongly on the procedural mechanism for enforcing the substantive right which was simultaneously conferred, we decline to conclude that the substantive right may be viewed wholly apart from the procedure provided for its enforcement. The employee's statutorily defined right is not a guarantee against removal without cause in the abstract, but such a guarantee as enforced by the procedures which Congress has designated for the determination of cause. * * *

Rehnquist's opinion went on to remind Kennedy that he had to "take the [statutory] bitter with the sweet."

Justice Powell and Justice Blackmun concurred in the result but objected strongly to the plurality's analysis, as did the four dissenters. In Powell's words (416 U.S. at 166–67):

> The plurality opinion evidently reasons that the nature of appellee's interest in continued federal employment is necessarily defined and limited by the statutory procedures for discharge and that the constitutional guarantee of procedural due process accords to appellee no procedural protections against arbitrary or erroneous discharge other than those expressly provided in the statute. * * * This view misconceives the origin of the right to procedural due process. That right is conferred not by legislative grace, but by constitutional guarantee. While the legislature may elect not to confer a property interest in federal employment, it may not constitutionally authorize the de-

privation of such an interest, once conferred, without appropriate procedural safeguards. * * *

By 1976, in another state public employee case, Justice Stevens could write for five members of the Court:

> A property interest in employment can, of course, be created by ordinance, or by an implied contract.   In either case, however, the sufficiency of the claim of entitlement must be decided by reference to state law. * * *
>
> On its face the ordinance on which petitioner relies may fairly be read as conferring such a guarantee.   However, such a reading is not the only possible interpretation; the ordinance may also be construed as granting no right to continued employment but merely conditioning an employee's removal on compliance with certain specified procedures. * * *
>
> In this case, as the District Court construed the ordinance, the City Manager's determination of the adequacy of the grounds for discharge is not subject to judicial review; the employee is merely given certain procedural rights which the District Court found not to have been violated in this case.   The District Court's reading of the ordinance is tenable; it derives some support from a decision of the North Carolina Supreme Court; and it was accepted by the Court of Appeals for the Fourth Circuit.   These reasons are sufficient to foreclose our independent examination of the state law issue.
>
> Under that view of the law, petitioner's discharge did not deprive him of a property interest protected by the Fourteenth Amendment.

Bishop v. Wood, 426 U.S. 341, 344-47 (1976).

Writing for himself and for Justices Brennan, Marshall, and Blackmun, Justice White responded (id. at 355):

> I dissent because the decision of the majority rests upon a proposition which was squarely addressed and in my view correctly rejected by six Members of this Court in *Arnett v. Kennedy.*"

The post-*Bishop* history of "legal interest" analysis fails to reveal any settled principle or approach for determining when substantive interests amount to "life, liberty or property."   The constellation of Justices *apparently* subscribing to the Rehnquist "bittersweet" theory, or to some other view, has constantly shifted.   "Life" interests are rarely asserted or discussed, and traditional liberty interests in freedom from incarceration do not *seem* to require support in the positive law to gain judicial recognition.   See, e.g., *Parham v. J. R.,* 442 U.S. 584 (1979).   Beyond this, however, consensus ends.   Indeed, most Justices can be found on several sides of the issue.   Compare, e.g., Justice Blackmun's *O'Bannon* concurrence with his concurrence in *New Motor Vehicle Board v. Orrin W. Fox Co.,* 439 U.S. 96, 113 (1978).

The Justices' ambivalence about how to proceed is, perhaps, understandable.   Rehnquist's approach, pursued to its logical limits, would apparently confine the Due Process Clause to assuring the uniform application of existing statutory and common law procedures.   This vision of due process was rejected as early as *Hurtado v. California,* 110 U.S. 516 (1884).   Yet, Rehnquist's apparent repudiation of this constitutional history has some allure, for the alternative seems to be unconstrained judicial evaluation of the importance of human interests and the procedural requisites for their protection. For additional discussion of this quandary, see Mashaw, *Administrative Due Process: The Quest for a Dignitary Theory*, 61 B.U.L. Rev. 885 (1981); Michelman, *Formal and Associational Aims in Procedural Due Process* in DUE PROCESS, NOMOS XVIII 126 (J. R. Pennock & J. Chapman, eds. 1977); Monaghan, *Of "Liberty" and "Property"*, 62 Corn. L. Rev. 405 (1976); Tushnet, *The Newer Property: Suggestions for the Revival of Substantive Due Process*, 1975 Sup. Ct. Rev. 261; Van Alstyne, *Cracks in "The New Property": Adjudicative Due Process in the Administrative State*, 62 Corn. L. Rev. 445 (1977).

B.   BUREAUCRATIC DECISIONMAKING AND FORMAL ADJUDICATION

1. GENERAL CONCERNS

The "minimum safeguards" of adjudicatory process recognized in *Goldberg v. Kelly* included: an impartial decisionmaker, timely and adequate notice of issues, personal appearance, oral presentation of evidence, confrontation and cross-examination of adverse witnesses, participation of counsel, a decision based on the record, and a written statement of reasons. These are, of course, familiar features of civil trials, whose contours and significance shift with the substantive issues and decisional contexts that emerge from the myriad activities of administrative adjudicators. Two peculiarities of administration, however, present special problems for the structure of formal adjudicative processes.

The first is the bureaucratic character of modern government. One of the great strengths of administrative organization is its capacity—through the combination of specialization and coordination—to utilize the talent, knowledge, and energy of many persons to achieve a common goal. The customary routines of bureaucratic decisionmaking thus emphasize particularized expertise and dispersed responsibility, unified ultimately through hierarchical control.

Second, most bureaucracies exist primarily to pursue positive programs, not to resolve individualized disputes. The role of the bureaucratic enterprise is, in Weber's words, "to exercise power on the basis of knowledge." Adjudication in such a context is a means of implementation, a device for achieving general goals in particular cases. Moreover, implementation of a continuing national program extends across space and through time. Each adjudicatory decision, therefore, is but a part of an overall scheme whose ultimate, aggregate success provides the agency's *raison d'etre*.

The superimposition of trial-type procedures on the process of bureaucratic implementation produces some discordant notes, for the techniques of trial are borrowed from a different institutional context. Courts have no institutional responsibility to seek out crimes, torts, or breaches of contract or to "implement" bodies of law governing these categories of activity; nor do they possess armies of specialists who can pursue the technical facts germane to legal disputes.   Courts decide disputes within a particularistic microcosm of fact and law, developed and presented by outsiders, shaped to suit those parties' particular purposes, and related primarily to their past conduct.   Many of the key features of conventional trial process—party initiative, exclusionary rules, pleading requirements, confinement to "record" evidence—may do more to preserve the privacy of litigants than to inform the decisionmaker.

In his study of the administration of the social security disability program Professor Mashaw suggests that "administration" and "adjudication"—in his terms "bureaucratic rationality" and "moral judgment"—have distinct goals, decisional techniques, legitimating values, and organizational presuppositions.   The core of these two different approaches or "models" of legal decisionmaking may be captured in the following terms.

J. MASHAW, BUREAUCRATIC JUSTICE

(Yale 1983)

BUREAUCRATIC RATIONALITY

Given the democratically (legislatively) approved task—to pay disability benefits to eligible persons—the administrative goal in the ideal conception of bureaucratic rationality is to develop, at the least possible cost, a system for distinguishing between true and false claims.   Adjudication should be both accurate (the legislatively specified goal) and cost-effective. This approach can be stated more broadly by introducing trade-offs between error, administrative, and other "process" costs such that the goal becomes "minimize the sum of error and other associated costs."

A system focused on correctness defines the questions presented to it by implementing decisions in essentially factual and technocratic terms. Individual adjudicators must be concerned about the facts in the real world that relate to the truth or falsity of the claimed disability.   At a managerial level the question becomes technocratic: What is the least-cost methodology for collecting and combining those facts about claims that will reveal the proper decision?   To illustrate by contrast, this model would exclude questions of value or preference as obviously irrelevant to the administrative task, and it would view reliance on nonreplicable, nonreviewable *judgment* or *intuition* as a singularly unattractive methodology for decision.   The legislature should have previously decided the value questions; and decision on the basis of intuition would cause authority to devolve from the bureau to individuals, thereby preventing a supervisory determination of whether any adjudicative action taken corresponded to a true state of the world.

The general decisional technique, then, is information retrieval and processing. * * * And, of course, this application of knowledge must in any large-scale program be structured through the usual bureaucratic routines: selection and training of personnel, detailed specification of administrative tasks, specialization and division of labor, coordination via rules and hierarchical lines of authority, and hierarchical review of the accuracy and efficiency of decisionmaking. In the disability program, for example, decisionmaking goes on not in one head but, initially, in the heads of thousands of state agency examiners.

From the perspective of bureaucratic rationality, administrative justice is accurate decisionmaking carried on through processes appropriately rationalized to take account of costs. The legitimating force of this conception flows both from its claim to correct implementation of otherwise legitimate social decisions and from its attempt to realize society's preestablished goals in some particular substantive domain while conserving social resources for the pursuit of other valuable ends. No program, after all, exhausts our conception of good government, much less of a good society or a good life. * * *

MORAL JUDGMENT

The traditional goal of the adjudicatory process is to resolve disputes about rights, about the allocation of benefits and burdens. The paradigm adjudicatory situations are those of civil and criminal trial. In the former, the contest generally concerns competing claims to property or the mutual responsibilities of the litigants. Property claims of "It has been in my family for generations" confront counterclaims of "I bought it from a dealer" or "I have made productive use of it"; "The smell of your turkey farm is driving me mad" confronts "I was here first." In the latter, accused murderers claim self-defense or diminished responsibility. The goal in individual adjudications is to decide who deserves what.

To some degree these traditional notions of justice in adjudicatory process imply merely getting the facts right in order to apply existing legal rules. So conceived, the goal of a moral judgment model of justice is the same as that of a bureaucratic rationality model—factually correct realization of previously validated legal norms. If this conception exhausted the notion of adjudicatory fairness, moral judgment's competition with bureaucratic rationality would entail merely a technical dispute about the most efficient way to find facts. But there is more to the competition than that.

The moral judgment model views decisionmaking as value defining. The turkey farmer's neighbor makes a valid appeal not to be burdened by "noisome" smells, *provided* his conduct in locating nearby is "reasonable" and he is not being "overly sensitive." The turkey farmer also has a valid claim to carry on a legitimate business, *provided* he does so in ways that will not unreasonably burden his neighbors. The question is not just who did what, but who is to be preferred, all things considered, when interests and the values to which they can be relevantly connected conflict. Similarly, the criminal trial seeks to establish not just whether a harmful and proscribed act took place but also whether or to what extent the actor is culpable.

This entitlement-awarding goal of the moral judgment model gives an obvious and distinctive cast to the basic issue for adjudicatory resolution.   The issue is the deservingness of some or all of the parties in the context of certain events, transactions, or relationships that give rise to a claim.   This issue, in turn, seems to imply certain things about a just process of proof and decision.   For example, fair disposition of charges of culpability or lack of desert requires that claims be specifically stated and that any affected party be given an opportunity to rebut or explain allegations.   And in order for this contextualized exploration of individual deservingness to be meaningful the decisionmaker must be neutral—that is, not previously connected with the relevant parties or events in ways that would impair the exercise of independent judgment on the evidence and arguments presented.

Moreover, given the generally threatening nature of an inquiry into moral desert, parties should be able to exclude from the decisional context information not directly related to the entitlements issue that gives rise to the disputed claim.   This power of exclusion may take the form of pleading rules, of notions of standing or proper parties, and, more importantly, may permit total exclusion of directive judgment where claims are abandoned or disputants come to some mutually satisfactory agreement concerning the relevant allocation.   [See generally, Damaska, *Structure of Authority and Comparative Criminal Procedure*, 84 Yale L.J. 480 (1975).]   The goal is limited: to resolve particular claims of entitlement in a way that fairly allocates certain benefits and burdens, not to allocate benefits and burdens in general in accordance with the relative deservingness of individuals or groups.   The decider is to a degree passive. The parties control how much of their lives or relationships is put at issue and what factual and normative arguments are brought to bear on the resolution of the dispute.

While the traditional examples of entitlements-oriented individualized adjudication involve adversary process, this feature is not critical. Claims to publicly provided benefits via nonadversary hearing processes may also conform to the model.   Indeed, the Supreme Court has come very close to saying that such processes must involve a traditional oral hearing where substantive standards are so open-textured that each decision both defines the nature of the entitlement and awards or denies it to a particular party.   [See *Califano v. Yamasaki*, 442 U.S. 682 (1979).]

The goals of this most traditional model of justice may suggest additional decisional techniques and routines designed to preserve party equality and control, promote agreed allocations, and protect the authority of the decider.   But these are details that need not detain us.   The important point is that the "justice" of this model inheres in its promise of a full and equal opportunity to obtain one's entitlements.   Its authority rests on the neutral development and application of common moral principles within the contexts giving rise to entitlement claims.

COMPARISON

As we have described them, each justice model is composed of distinctive goals, specific approaches to framing the questions for administrative determination, basic techniques for resolving those questions, **and** subsidiary decision processes and routines that functionally describe the model.   The distinctive features of the * * * models are outlined in the accompanying chart.   These features are, of course, meant to indicate the central tendencies, not to suggest that features, and whole models, do not shade one into another at the margins.

Dimension/ Model	Legitimating Values	Primary Goal	Structure or Organization	Cognitive Technique
Bureaucratic Rationality	Accuracy & Efficiency	Program Imple- mentation	Hierarchical	Information Processing
Moral Judgment	Fairness	Conflict Resolution	Independent	Contextual Interpretation

2. TENSIONS BETWEEN ADMINISTRATION AND ADJUDICATION

These contrasts cannot be pressed too far.   Some "agencies" might as easily be viewed as courts, and modern public law litigation has thrust federal trial courts into managerial and political tasks that are tradition-ally the domain of administration.   See, e.g., Chayes, *The Role of the Judge in Public Law Litigation*, 89 Harv. L. Rev. 1281 (1976); *Forward: Public Law Litigation and the Burger Court*, 96 Harv. L. Rev. 4 (1982); Diver, *Judge as Political Power Broker: Superintending Change in Pub-lic Institutions*, 65 Va. L. Rev. 43 (1979); Fiss, *Forward: The Forms of Justice*, 93 Harv. L. Rev. 1 (1979).   Compare Eisenberg and Yeazell, *The Ordinary and Extraordinary in Institutional Litigation, 93 Harv. L. Rev. 465 (1980);* Yeazell, *From Group Litigation to Class Action—Part I: The Industrialization of Group Litigation*, 27 U.C.L.A. L. Rev. 514 (1980); *Part II: Interest, Class, and Representation*, 27 U.C.L.A. L. Rev. 1067 (1980).   Yet the central tendencies of judicial and administrative functions are sufficiently distinct to provide a basis for predicting that the use of trial process in administrative contexts will often render certain features of that process problematic.   This recognition, of course, in-forms the Supreme Court's obvious reluctance to impose trial-type pro-cess on many administrative functions *via* the Due Process Clause.   But the difficulties of accommodating bureaucratic organization and adjudica-tory formality do not disappear when the right to formal adjudicatory process is expressly secured by statute.

Hierarchy Versus Personal Judgment

A classic illustration is provided by the famous *Morgan cases*.   There the complaining parties alleged that the Secretary of Agriculture had is-sued a commodity rate order, which was required to be made on the rec-ord after formal hearing, without personally reviewing the evidence pre-sented or having read the briefs or heard oral argument.   They further alleged that the Secretary's decision was based solely on *ex parte* consultations with employees of the Department of Agriculture who were familiar with the case.   The Supreme Court held that proof of these allegations would establish a denial of an adequate hearing, *Morgan v. United States*, 298 U.S. 468 (1936), and, in oft-quoted language, it said, "The one who decides must hear."   Id. at 481.

Yet, in the same opinion the Court also said, "Evidence may be taken by an examiner.   Evidence thus taken may be sifted and analyzed by competent subordinates."   Id.   Obviously, the Court was not using "hear" literally.   Indeed, the second time the case came before it, the Court specifically approved the manner in which the Secretary proceeded, that is, by reading the briefs of the parties and the transcript of oral argument and by discussing the issues with several subordinates. The Secretary did not read the bulky record, but "dipped into it * * * to get its drift"; and he described the decision as his "independent reactions to the findings of the men in the Bureau of Animal Industry."   On this basis the Court was convinced that the Secretary had "considered the evidence before signing the order."   *Morgan v. United States*, 304 U.S. 1, 17-18 (1938).   Yet the Court simultaneously decided that the parties had not received a full and fair hearing because they had not been given notice of the proposed findings and conclusions submitted to the Secretary by subordinates and ultimately adopted by him virtually verbatim.   This practice was said to have deprived the complainants of a reasonable opportunity "to know the claims thus presented and to meet them."

The complainants managed to return to the Supreme Court two more times.   And in its fourth *Morgan* opinion the Court, perhaps perceiving the implications of the process of review on which it had embarked, stated categorically that once the Secretary had been shown to have considered the evidence, the extent to which he considered it and how he went about arriving at a decision could not be inquired into any more than one could attack a judicial decision on the ground that the judge had not thought about it hard or long enough.   *United States v. Morgan*, 313 U.S. 409 (1941).   In the end the Court in the *Morgan* cases seems to have given a very wide latitude to an ultimate decision-maker, who has *some* exposure to evidence and argument, to use the assistance of subordinates in arriving at a decision and to hear or read the raw evidentiary record developed by others, if at all, only to the extent that he believes necessary for conscientious decision-making.   The Court thus placed its imprimatur on what has come to be called the "institutional decision"—that is, a decision that is the product of many hands and minds but that is the final responsibility of those at the top of the agency hierarchy.   Yet, and crucially, it did so in litigation that repeatedly reversed the Secretary of Agriculture's decisions in the interest of providing a personal hearing that was meaningful to the ultimate exercise of judgment.

Factual Context versus Policy Implementation

This ambivalence about the linkage between hearing rights and bureaucratic decisionmaking is also implicit in two provisions of the APA. Section 557(b) provides that an agency reviewing an examiner's initial decision has "all the powers it would have had in making the initial decision." But section 557(c) provides that all decisions, including recommended, tentative or initial decisions, are a part of the record of an agency proceeding. The problem thus posed is this: Suppose a reviewing court is convinced that there is not substantial evidence in the whole record for an agency decision because the hearing examiner (whose initial decision is a part of the record) made convincing findings of fact that are contrary to those made by the agency. But assume further that, absent the hearing officer's initial decision, the court would be willing to find that the agency decision was based on substantial evidence. Should the court reverse, thereby denying to the agency the power it would have had had it made the initial decision; or should it affirm on the basis of evidence which it considers insubstantial in the light of the hearing officer's evaluation?

This was precisely the situation presented to the Court in *Universal Camera Corp. v. NLRB*, 340 U.S. 474, 493, 496-97 (1951). The hearing examiner in that case had found that a particular employee had been discharged because of insubordination, not, as charged in an unfair labor practices complaint, because he had been a witness in a previous NLRB proceeding. The testimony at the hearing had been sharply conflicting and the decision may have turned in the final analysis on who was to be believed. The Board independently examined the record and reversed the hearing examiner's ruling. The Board's decision was upheld by the court of appeals on the ground that it could not say that the Board had committed a clear error of law in reversing the examiner, and that therefore it was constrained to treat the fact that the examiner had made a contrary finding as irrelevant. *NLRB v. Universal Camera Corp.*, 179 F.2d 749 (2d Cir. 1950). The Supreme Court rejected the court of appeals' approach:

> We are aware that to give the examiner's findings less finality than a master's and yet entitled them to consideration in striking the account, is to introduce another and an unruly factor into the judgmatical process of review. But we ought not to fashion an exclusionary rule merely to reduce the number of imponderables to be considered by reviewing courts. * * *
>
> We do not require that the examiner's findings be given more weight than in reason and in the light of judicial experience they deserve. The "substantial evidence" standard is not modified in any way when the Board and its examiner disagree. We intend only to recognize that evidence supporting a conclusion may be less substantial when an impartial, experienced examiner who has observed the witnesses and lived with the case has drawn conclusions different from the Board's than when he has reached the same conclusion. The findings of the examiner are to be considered along with the consistency and inherent probability of testimony. The significance of his report, of course, depends largely on the importance of credibility in the particular case. To give it this significance does not seem to us materially more difficult than to heed the other factors which in sum determine whether evidence is "substantial."

This approach seems sensible, but the Court correctly anticipated the unruliness of the consideration introduced into judicial review by *Universal Camera*. Certainly, in the next case that raised a similar issue, *NLRB v. James Thompson & Co.*, 208 F.2d 743, 746 (2d Cir. 1953). Judge Hand stated the principle much too broadly when he said:

> We do not see any rational escape from accepting a finding [of the examiner] unless we can say that the corroboration of this lost [demeanor] evidence could not have been enough to satisfy any doubts raised by the words; and it must be owned that few findings will not survive such a test.

The issue upon which the Board and its examiner had disagreed in *James Thompson & Co.* was whether an employer had unlawfully refused to deal with a union. The examiner believed the employer when he said that he was justifiably uncertain about whether the union had obtained enough employees' authorizations to act as their representative. The Board thought that the undisputed acts of the employer, both before and after the principal instance of his refusal to deal, indicated a pattern of hostility toward the formation of a union which was unlawful under the Act. The court of appeals thus seemed to be saying that the Board could not rely on circumstantial evidence in the record as a whole to rebut a fact found by the examiner on the basis of direct testimony.

The Supreme Court in *FCC v. Allentown Broadcasting Corp.*, 349 U.S. 358, 364 (1955), sought to redress the balance between agencies and their hearing officers. Although the case was resolvable, and perhaps resolved, on other grounds, the Court had this to say about the court of appeals' emphasis on the conflict between the FCC's findings and its examiner's:

> The Court of Appeals' conclusion of error as to evasiveness relies largely on its understanding that the Examiner's findings based on demeanor of a witness are not to be overruled by a Board without a "very substantial preponderance in the testimony as recorded," citing *National Labor Relations Board v. Universal Camera Corp.* We think this attitude goes too far. It seems to adopt for examiners of administrative agencies the "clearly erroneous" rule of the Fed. Rules Civ. Proc., 52(a), applicable to courts. In *Universal Camera Corp. v. Labor Board*, we said, as to the Labor Management Relations Act hearings:
>
>> "Section 10(c) of the Labor Management Relations Act provides that 'If upon the preponderence of the testimony taken the Board shall be of the opinion that any person named in the complaint has engaged in or is engaging in any such unfair labor practice, then the Board shall state its findings of fact * * * .' The responsibility for decision thus placed on the Board is wholly inconsistent with the notion that it has power to reverse an examiner's findings only when they are 'clearly erroneous.' Such a limitation would make so drastic a departure from prior administrative practice that explicitness would be required."
>
> That comment is here applicable.

The conflict between adjudicatory fairness and effective decisionmaking appears most sharply in agencies that develop policy primarily through formal adjudication. (On the related issue of policy bias in courts, see Justice Rehnquist's memorandum declining to recuse himself in *Laird v. Tatum*, 409 U.S. 824 (1972).) The tension is evident in *Universal Camera*. Justice in the individual case seems to demand broad discretion for the hearing examiner (now ALJ) to allocate fault in accordance with his or her contextualized judgment of what actually occurred. Protection of the Board's regulatory functions, on the other hand, may argue for resolving doubts in a way that provides the most complete possible protection to witnesses in Board proceedings. While in *Universal Camera* the conflict emerges in a debate about the substantial evidence test, similar differences concerning the appropriate perspective from which to view adjudication have often also been imbedded in arguments concerning the separation or combination of functions within agencies.

Neutrality versus Institutional Intelligence

That the persons who comprise an agency—FTC Commissioners, NLRB Board Members, the FDA Commissioner—may be ultimately responsible for investigation, prosecution, and final decision in the same case without impairing fundamental fairness is now a well-entrenched feature of American administrative law. Such "combination of functions," however, provided a basis for intense opposition to administrative regulation in the New Deal era and in the years leading up to the adoption of the APA in 1946. Administrative agencies were chastised as "that hybrid thing beloved by tyrants and abhorred by free men," and the ABA Special Committee on Administrative Law in 1934 strongly argued that the adjudicatory functions of agencies be transferred to an administrative court or courts. Partisans on the other side inflamed the debate by advocating that independent regulatory commissions be absorbed into the Executive Branch to make them more responsive to governmental policy. See generally C. WOLTZ, ed., ADMINISTRATIVE PROCEDURE IN GOVERNMENT AGENCIES vi (1968). While some of the heat has gone out of the fight, the debate still rages. On February 11, 1971, President Nixon released the ASH COUNCIL REPORT ON SELECTED INDEPENDENT REGULATORY AGENCIES, which in substance recommended that the independent regulatory agencies be abolished, their judicial functions transferred to a special administrative court, and their administrative functions performed by agencies responsible directly to the President. See generally Symposium, *Federal Regulatory Agencies: A Response to the Ash Report*, 57 Va. L. Rev. 923 (1971).

The general approach to separation of functions that has prevailed at the federal level, however, is that recommended by the Attorney General's Committee on Administrative Procedure and embodied in the APA—an internal separation of personnel within agencies for purposes of formal adjudication, which results in clear divisions of responsibility at the lower levels of adjudication and an insulation of even top administrators from investigative and prosecutorial staff, save on the public record.

ATTORNEY GENERAL'S COMMITTEE ON ADMINISTRATIVE PROCEDURE, ADMINISTRATIVE PROCEDURE IN GOVERNMENT AGENCIES

Senate Document No. 8, 77th Cong., 1st Sess. 55-59 (1941).

The recommendations made in the preceding sections of this report looking toward the creation of the office of hearing commissioners [subsequently called "hearing examiners" in the APA and now "administrative law judges"] to hear and initially to decide cases which go to formal proceedings, together with the recommendations looking toward a greater delegation of administrative functions within the agencies, would insure internal but nevertheless real and actual separation of the adjudicating and the prosecuting or investigating functions. The person who heard and weighed the evidence, who made the initial findings of fact and the initial order in each case, would be entirely different from those persons who had investigated the case and presented it in formal proceedings. He would have had no connection with the initiation or prosecution of the case. * * *

But current discussions of the administrative process raise the question whether separation of function ought not to go further than this. Specifically, it has been urged that possession of the deciding functions of a "judge" is inconsistent with possession of the "prosecutor's" functions of investigation, initiation of action, and advocacy. The proposal is accordingly made that the deciding powers of Federal administrative agencies should be vested in separate tribunals which are independent of the bodies charged with the functions of prosecution and perhaps other functions of administration.

Two points are important to put the problem in a just perspective. The first is that * * * an administrative agency is not one man or a few men but many. It is important, the Committee believes, not to make the mistake of conceiving of an agency as a collective person and concluding that, because the agency initiates action and renders decision thereafter, the same person is doing both. In an agency's organization there are varied possibilities of internal separation of function to the end that the same individuals who do the judging do not do the "prosecuting." Such internal separation by no means eliminates the problem of combination of functions; but it alters, or if wisely done may alter, its entire set and cast. The second major point is that the functions of so-called prosecution belonging to administrative agencies are actually of varying types. It is important to distinguish among these types not only because agencies differ in the functions which they possess but because different questions, in relation to the function of judging, arise with respect to different types of functions.

Two characteristic tasks of a prosecutor are those of investigation and advocacy. It is clear that when a controversy reaches the stage of hearing and formal adjudication the persons who did the actual work of investigating and building up the case should play no part in the decision.

* * * [Likewise] the advocate—the agency's attorney who upheld a definite position adverse to the private parties at the hearing—cannot be permitted to participate after the hearing in the making of the decision. * * *

These types of commingling of functions of investigation or advocacy with the function of deciding are thus plainly undesirable. But they are also avoidable and should be avoided by appropriate internal division of labor. For the disqualifications produced by investigation or advocacy are personal psychological ones which result from engaging in those types of activity; and the problem is simply one of isolating those who engage in the activity. Creation of independent hearing commissioners insulated from all phases of a case other than hearing and deciding will, the Committee believes, go far toward solving this problem at the level of the initial hearing provided the proper safeguards are established to assure the insulation. A similar result can be achieved at the level of final decision on review by the agency heads by permitting the views of the investigators and advocates to be presented only in open hearing where they can be known and met by those who may be adversely affected by them.

A distinctive function, which may be regarded as one of prosecution, is that of making preliminary decisions to issue a complaint or to proceed to formal hearing in cases which later the agency heads will decide. Before a complaint is issued * * * or before an application raising doubtful questions is set down for formal hearing, a determination must be made that the action is proper. The Committee has heretofore recommended * * * that authority to make such preliminary determinations should be delegated as far as possible to appropriate officers. Where this is done, no question can arise that the ultimate deciding officers have been biased through having made, ex parte, a preliminary determination in a case which they have later to decide. Yet such delegation, of course, cannot be complete; novel and difficult questions must from time to time be presented to the heads of the agency. The question must be faced, therefore, whether the making of such a preliminary determination in itself works unfairness in the final decision. Assuming that the agency heads simply pass on the sufficiency of material developed and presented to them by others, the Committee is satisfied that no such unfairness results. * * * The ultimate judgment of the agency heads need be no more influenced by the preliminary authorization to proceed than is the ultimate judgment of a court by the issuance of a temporary restraining order pending a formal hearing for a permanent injunction.

What remains to be discussed is the heart of the problem. * * * [S]o far as the agency is empowered to initiate action at all, the agency heads do have the responsibility of determining the general policy according to which action is taken. They have at least residual powers to control, supervise, and direct all the activities of the agency, including the various preliminary and deciding phases of the process of disposing of particular cases. The question is whether there are dangers in the possession of these powers such as to make advisable a total separation.

An answer to this question requires first of all a counting of the costs which such a separation would entail. These costs include substantial dangers both to private and to public interests. Most obvious are the disadvantages of sheer multiplication of separate governmental organizations. If the proposal were rigorously carried out, two agencies would grow in each case where one grew before.

Particularly in cases where adjudicatory functions are not a principal part of the agency's work or are closely interrelated with other activities, whatever gains might result from separation would be plainly outweighed by the loss in consistency of action as a whole. * * * The Civil Aeronautics Board, the Securities and Exchange Commission, and other agencies * * * act through exercise of a number of interrelated powers. These powers must be exercised consistently and, therefore, by the same body, not only to realize the public purposes which the statutes are designed to further but also to avoid confusion of private interests.

There are, however, some agencies such as the Federal Trade Commission and the National Labor Relations Board whose principal duty is the enforcement, by decision of cases, of certain statutory prohibitions. In the case of such agencies, the practical objection which has just been noted to isolating the adjudicatory function and handing it over to some independent body would not exist to the same extent. It would be theoretically possible to assign to one agency the task of investigating charges and filing complaints of statutory violations, and to another agency the task of deciding the controversies thus arising. * * *

Further practical objections, however, have to be taken into account in relation to these as well as other agencies. Of prime importance among these objections is the danger of friction and of a break-down of responsibility as between the two complementary agencies. * * * At present the added responsibility of deciding exercises a restraining influence which limits the activities of the agency as a whole. If only to save itself time and expense an agency will not prosecute cases which it knows are defective on the facts or on the law—which it knows, in short, it will dismiss after hearing. The situation is likely to be different where the function of prosecuting is separated out. First, a body devoted solely to prosecuting often is intent upon "making a record." It has no responsibility for deciding and its express job is simply to prosecute as often and successfully as possible. Second, it must guess what the deciding branch will think. It can explore the periphery; it can try everything; and meanwhile the individual citizen must spend time and money before some curb can be exercised by the deciding branch. And, it should be noted, a separation of functions would seriously militate against what this Committee has already noted as being, numerically and otherwise, the lifeblood of the administrative process—negotiations and informal settlements. * * *

These factors are thrown into clear relief if it is recalled that the statutory prohibitions which administrative agencies are commonly called upon to enforce are not and cannot be as clear and precise as a promissory note or bill of sale. * * * It is and must be left to the administrative agencies to apply these general prohibitions to a great variety of conduct. As this is done, it is expected that the general terms will take on concreteness and that subsidiary principles may be worked out by which certain types of conduct will be known as improper and others as permissible. To do this involves the investigation of many informal complaints and the settlement by agreement of many situations where the practices may have been innocently or inadvertently or not consistently engaged in. To divorce entirely the investigating and enforcing arm from the deciding arm may well impart additional confusion to this process. * * *

Moreover, when one examines the specific criticisms of specific agencies, one is struck by the fact that a mere splitting up of functions would not itself cure the criticisms which appear most common. Insofar as predispositions may exist in the more highly charged fields in which administrative agencies operate, they are mainly the product of many factors of mind and experience, and have comparatively little relation to the administrative machinery. There is no simple way of eliminating them by mere change in the administrative structure. They can only be exercised by wise and self-controlled men.

Notes

1. The Supreme Court has addressed the issue under the Due Process Clause. *Withrow v. Larkin,* 421 U.S. 35, 39, 51-52 (1975), involved investigation and decertification by a state professional licensing board. In this instance the focus of investigation by the Wisconsin Medical Examining Board was a Michigan physician who also had obtained licensure in Wisconsin through a reciprocity agreement between the states. His practice in Wisconsin consisted of performing abortions in a Milwaukee office. He sought to enjoin the board's proceedings after it initiated an investigation and hearing to determine whether he had "engaged in practices that are inimical to the public health, whether he ha[d] engaged in conduct unbecoming a person licensed to practice medicine, and whether he ha[d] engaged in conduct detrimental to the best interests of the public."

In vacating a lower court injunction premised on a general antipathy to such "combinations of functions" the Court, through Justice White, said:

> * * * The issue is substantial, it is not new, and legislators and others concerned with the operations of administrative agencies have given much attention to whether and to what extent distinctive administrative functions should be performed by the same persons. No single answer has been reached. Indeed, the growth, variety, and complexity of the administrative process have made any one solution highly unlikely. Within the Federal Government itself, Congress has addressed the issue in several different ways, providing for varying degrees of separation from complete separation of functions to virtually none at all. * * *
>
> * * * Similarly, our cases, although they reflect the substance of the problem, offer no support for the bald proposition applied in this case by the District Court that agency members who participate in an investigation are disqualified from adjudicating * * * .

See also *Friedman v. Rogers,* 440 U.S. 1 (1979); *Gibson v. Berryhill,* 411 U.S. 564 (1973); *FTC v. Cement Institute,* 333 U.S. 683 (1948).

On the other hand, the failure of agencies that combine prosecutorial and adjudicatory function to exercise the self-control thought necessary by the Attorney General's Committee may result in judicial intervention.

2. In *American Cyanamid v. FTC*, 363 F.2d 757, 767-78 (6th Cir. 1966), for example, the Commission had found that American Cyanamid and others had entered into a complex series of agreements by which they monopolized the market in the sale of the "wonder drug" tetracycline. The company sought judicial review of the decision on the ground that Chairman Dixon had prejudged the case while serving as Chief Counsel and Staff Director of the Senate Subcommittee on Antitrust and Monopoly. Undisputed evidence revealed that prior to his appointment to the Commission, but during the pendency of the *Cyanamid* complaint, Dixon had directed an intensive inquiry into the pharmaceutical industry and particularly into the marketing of tetracycline. At the conclusion of that inquiry the subcommittee issued a report, of which Dixon was reputedly primary author, that detailed the machinations of the companies producing tetracycline and concluded that, "With the consummation of these arrangements, the *orderly and controlled* marketing of tetracycline was an inevitable and expected result."

The court of appeals reversed the Commission's order, stating in part:

It is to be emphasized that the Commission is a factfinding body. As Chairman, Mr. Dixon sat with the other members as triers of the facts and joined in making the factual determination upon which the order of the Commission is based. As counsel for the Senate Subcommittee, he had investigated and developed many of these same facts.

The result of the participation of Chairman Dixon in the decision of the Commission is not altered by the fact that his vote was not necessary for a majority. "Litigants are entitled to an impartial tribunal whether it consists of one man or twenty and there is no way which we may know of whereby the influence of one upon the others can be quantitatively measured."

We therefore must vacate the order and decision of the Federal Trade Commission and remand the case for a de novo consideration of the record without the participation of Chairman Dixon. We reject the argument of the Commission that such a holding "would create an unworkable concept of administrative bias." Our decision on this issue goes no further than to hold that disqualification is required when, as in the present case, the legislative committee investigation involved the same facts and issues concerning the same parties named as respondents before the administrative agency, and to the extent here presented. We do not hold that the service of Mr. Dixon as counsel for the subcommittee, standing alone, necessarily would require disqualification. Our decision is based upon the depth of the investigation and the questions and comments by Mr. Dixon as counsel. * * *

3. On March 15, 1968, the ubiquitous Chairman Dixon made a speech before the Government Relations Workshop of the National Newspaper Association concerning press responsibility for policing consumer frauds. In it he said:

How about ethics on the business side of running a paper? What standards are maintained on advertising acceptance? * * * What about carrying ads that offer college educations in five weeks, fortunes by raising mushrooms in the basement, getting rid of pimples with a magic lotion, or becoming an airline's hostess by attending a charm school? * * * Without

belaboring the point I'm sure you're aware that advertising acceptance standards could stand more tightening by many newspapers. Granted that
newspapers are not in the advertising policing business, their advertising
managers are savvy enough to smell deception when the odor is strong
enough. * * *

At the time Dixon spoke the Commission had pending before it a case charging
false advertising by the Cinderella Career and Finishing Schools, Inc. The
Commission's complaint charged that Cinderella's advertisements had deceptive-
ly promised the equivalent of a college course in five weeks and that its graduates
might be qualified for jobs as airline hostesses. The company subsequently appealed an adverse Commission ruling on the ground, *inter alia*, that Chairman
Dixon's statements prejudged the case and denied it due process. The court of
appeals agreed, waxing indignant in the process:

> It requires no superior olfactory powers to recognize that the danger of
> unfairness through prejudgment is not diminished by a cloak of self-
> righteousness. * * *

> We indicated in our earlier opinion in this case that "there is in fact and
> law authority in the Commission, acting in the public interest, to alert the
> public to *suspected violations* of the law by *factual press releases* whenever
> the Commission shall have reason to believe that a respondent is engaged in
> activities made unlawful by the Act. * * * " This does not give individual
> Commissioners license to prejudge cases or to make speeches which give the
> appearance that the case has been prejudged. Conduct such as this may
> have the effect of entrenching a Commissioner in a position which he has pub-
> licly stated, making it difficult, if not impossible, for him to reach a different
> conclusion in the event he deems it necessary to do so after consideration of
> the record. There is a marked difference between the issuance of a press re-
> lease which states that the Commission has filed a complaint because it has
> "reason to believe" that there have been violations, and statements by a Com-
> missioner after an appeal has been filed which gave the appearance that he
> has already prejudged the case and that the ultimate determination of the
> merits will move in predestined grooves. * * *

> Chairman Dixon, sensitive to theory but insensitive to reality, made the
> following statement in declining to recuse himself from this case after peti-
> tioners requested that he withdraw:

>> As * * * I have stated * * * this principle "is not a rigid command
>> of the law, compelling disqualification for trifling causes, but a consider-
>> ation addressed to the discretion and sound judgment of the administrator
>> himself in determining whether, irrespective of the law's requirement, he
>> should disqualify himself." * * *

> We find it hard to believe that former Chairman Dixon is so indifferent to
> the dictates of the Courts of Appeals that he has chosen once again to put his
> personal determination of what the law requires ahead of what the courts
> have time and again told him the law requires. If this is a question of "dis-
> cretion and judgment," Commissioner Dixon has exercised questionable dis-
> cretion and very poor judgment indeed, in directing his shafts and squibs at a
> case awaiting his official action. We can use his own words in telling Com-
> missioner Dixon that he has acted "irrespective of the law's requirements";
> we will spell out for him once again, avoiding tired cliche and weary general-

ization, in no uncertain terms, exactly what those requirements are, in the fervent hope that this will be the last time we have to travel this wearisome road.

The test for disqualification * * * [is] whether "a disinterested observer may conclude that [the agency] has in some measure adjudged the facts as well as the law of a particular case in advance of hearing it." * * *

Cinderella Career and Finishing Schools, Inc. v. FTC, 425 F.2d 583, 590-91 (D.C. Cir. 1970).

3. THE SOCIAL SECURITY ADMINISTRATION AND ITS ADMINISTRATIVE LAW JUDGES

The need to harness formal adjudicatory activity to administrative policy presents different issues for an agency like the Social Security Administration, which does not attempt to make policy in the course of adjudication. Rather, it seeks to prevent the disposition of individual cases from altering its policies or (which is much the same thing) from implicitly generating policies that agency managers view as undesirable. Both of these latter activities involve attempts to control or direct the decisions made by the SSA staff of over 600 Administrative Law Judges. This administrative "control" or "direction" may, of course, impair the ALJs' independence. It, therefore, raises questions concerning the adequacy of the formal hearings prescribed by the Social Security Act and governed by the requirements of sections 554, and 556-57 of the APA.

The "ALJ-independence problem" at the SSA chiefly involves the disability program, which we encountered earlier in *Mathews v. Eldridge.* Pursuant to that program persons insured under the Social Security Act are entitled to early retirement if they are unable "to engage in any substantial gainful activity by reason of any medically determinable physical or mental impairment" which may last for at least one year or result in death. Benefits are also available to needy persons under Title XVI of the Social Security Act, but in both cases

> * * * an individual shall be determined to be under a disability only if his physical or mental impairment or impairments are of such severity that he is not only unable to do his previous work but cannot, considering his age, education and work experience, engage in any other kind of substantial gainful work which exists in the national economy, regardless of whether such work exists in the immediate area in which he lives, or whether a specific job vacancy exists for him, or whether he would be hired if he applied for work. For purposes of the preceding sentences (with respect to any individual), "work which exists in the national economy" means work which exists in significant numbers either in the region where such individual lives or in several regions of the country.

In 1982 the SSA disability program supported 4.3 million Americans at an annual cost of over $20 billion. SSA receives approximately 1.5 million applications per year for disability benefits. Disappointed applicants, or, as in *Eldridge*, terminated recipients, request nearly 250,000 hearings per year before the agency's Administrative Law Judges. As the Court in *Eldridge* noted, one problem with this process is its "torpidity." Applicants receive a judgment from the initial, informal level of adjudication within 30 to 45 days of application. But ALJ hearing decisions generally require something like nine months from request to disposition. This is, of course, extremely swift by comparison with civil court trials involving similar amounts (on average in excess of $30,000) but nonetheless distressingly slow for persons who are ill, lack alternative means of support, and may be able to obtain benefits only if eligible for disability benefits.

There is also concern that the hearing process is both profligate and arbitrary. Over time the ALJs have accounted for an increasing share of disability awards. In 1964, 97.5% of all recipients received these awards at the pre-hearing levels of decision; ALJ awards thus accounted for a negligible 2.5%. By 1980, however, 21% of all recipients were receiving benefits pursuant to an administrative law judge's award. Moreover, ALJ generosity is far from uniform. Indeed, the histogram that follows (adapted from J. MASHAW, *et. al.* SOCIAL SECURITY HEARINGS AND APPEALS 21 (1978)) suggests that the likelihood of an award is largely a function of which ALJ hears a particular case. No systematic differences have been discovered in the disability caseloads of SSA ALJs that might explain this variance.

```
10 |                        *        *  *
 9 |                        *        *  *
 8 |                        *     *  *  *  *
 7 |                     *  *  *  *  *  *  *
 6 |               *  *  *  *  *  *  *  *  *
 5 |            *  *  *  *  *  *  *  *  *  *  *
 4 |            *  *  *  *  *  *  *  *  *  *  *  *        *
 3 |         *  *  *  *  *  *  *  *  *  *  *  *  *        *
 2 |   *     *  *  *  *  *  *  *  *  *  *  *  *  *  *  *  *
 1 | *    *  *  *  *  *  *  *  *  *  *  *  *  *  *  *  *  *  *  *
   |_____
     8-12%  16-20%  24-28%  32-36%  40-44%  48-52%  56-60%  64-68%  72-76%  80-84%
        12-16%  20-24%  28-32%  36-40%  44-48%  52-56%  60-64%  68-72%  76-80%  84-88%
```

PERCENT HEARINGS RESULTING IN AN AWARD

Each asterisk represents approximately 1% of observations. Data are from 1976.

The SSA has addressed the problems of timeliness, generosity, and inconsistency in a variety of ways. Hierarchical control through the enunciation of precedents has been largely unsuccessful. Although SSA has a centralized Appeals Council, that body decides nearly 40,000 cases per year. Claimants, their attorneys (should they be represented), and ALJs can hardly be expected to retrieve and follow a decisional output of this magnitude—even if the Appeals Council were capable of unifying its own jurisprudence through carefully crafted opinions. Indeed, the fact-based, highly contextual decisionmaking involved in the disability program simply cannot be structured through precedent. Variation among ALJs is something like the variance that one would expect from one-person juries applying the "reasonable man" standard. And, of course, precedential decisions would do nothing about the problem of delay.

The inaccessibility or irrelevance of precedent as a corrective leaves the SSA with two other techniques: managerial supervision and attempts to constrain ALJ discretion through substantive rulemaking. It has used both; and both have been challenged as incompatible with the independence of SSA ALJs and with the rights of claimants to an individualized hearing on eligibility.

NASH v. CALIFANO

United States Court of Appeals, Second Circuit, 1980.
613 F.2d 10.

IRVING R. KAUFMAN, CHIEF JUDGE.

* * *

The appellant, Simon Nash, is an Administrative Law Judge (ALJ) of 22 years' experience in the Social Security Administration's Bureau of Hearings and Appeals. * * *

The Bureau's corps of approximately 650 ALJs is divided among 145 field offices, each on headed by an Administrative Law Judge in Charge (ALJIC), who has managerial and administrative authority over all personnel assigned to his or her field office, in addition to responsibility for the same caseload as other ALJs. ALJICs receive the same salaries as other ALJs. Each ALJIC reports to one of the ten Regional Chief Administrative Law Judges who, in turn, are under the managerial authority of the Director of the Bureau of Hearings and Appeals and his chief assistant, the Chief Administrative Law Judge. While Administrative Law Judges are civil service employees, the Director of the Bureau is appointed by, and serves at the pleasure of, the Commissioner of the Social Security Administration.

In December of 1967, Judge Nash became ALJIC for the Buffalo field office. During his tenure in that position, he, along with numerous other ALJICs, urged adoption of a number of administrative reforms—including the hiring of staff attorneys and the use of summary opinions in appropriate cases—to cope with the mounting backlog of cases before the Bureau of Hearings and Appeals. Those pleas for reform went unheeded until 1975, when appellee Robert Trachtenberg was appointed Director fo the Bureau. Facing a record backlog of 113,000 cases,[6] Director Trachtenberg instituted many of the reforms long advocated by Nash and his colleagues.

Trachtenberg's goal of eliminating unconscionable delays in processing appeals is, of course, commendable. Appellant, however, alleges

---

6. Several courts have found that the long delays in processing appeals from denials of Social Security benefits have denied claimants the right to a hearing within the reasonable time called for by 42 U.S.C.A. § 405(b). In *White v. Mathews*, 559 F.2d 852 (2d Cir. 1977), *cert. denied*, 435 U.S. 908 (1978), this court affirmed an order granting prospective benefits to claimants who had not received administrative adjudication of their claims within specified time periods. * * *

that appellees and their staff employees have interfered with the decisional independence of the administrative law judges in violation of the Administrative Procedure Act, the Social Security Act and the due process clause of the Fifth Amendment. * * *

The first practice challenged in the complaint is the Bureau's "Regional Office Peer Review Program." According to Nash, Trachtenberg, Brown and Tannenbaum, as well as non-ALJ members of their staffs, known as "Development Center Analysts" and "Program Operation Officers," review the work of ALJs outside the normal appellate process. In conjunction with this ongoing review, the appellees or their staffs give plaintiff and all other ALJs detailed, purportedly mandatory instructions concerning the proper length of hearings and opinions, the amount of evidence required in specific cases, and the proper use of expert witnesses. Through the Peer Review Program, the Bureau has allegedly arrogated to itself the power to control the conduct of hearings vested in ALJs by the Administrative Procedure Act, 5 U.S.C.A. § 556.

Nash also avers that an arbitrary monthly production quota has been established for him and all his colleagues. Unless an ALJ renders a specified number of decisions per month, the agency, appellant claims, threatens to file incompetence charges against him with the Civil Service Commission. In his view, the agency's production quota constitutes a performance rating forbidden by the Administrative Procedure Act, 5 U.S.C.A. § 4301 (2) (E) and 5 C.F.R. § 930.211.

An additional threat to the ALJs statutory independence is allegedly posed by the so-called "Quality Assurance Program," which attempts to control the number of decisions denying Social Security Benefits. The agency has "let it be known" that the average 50% "reversal rate" for all ALJs is an "acceptable" one. Appellant further claims in his amended complaint that the reversal rates of all ALJs are monitored, and those who deviate from the mean are counseled and admonished to bring their rates in line with the national average. This attempt to influence the ALJs' decisionmaking process, it is urged, violates 5 U.S.C.A. §§ 556 & 3105 and the Fifth Amendment to the Constitution.

Nash's fourth claim centers upon plans that call for the national implementation (in whole or in part) of an "Employee Pool System" developed at the White Plains, New York field office with the knowledge and approval of the Director. Under this program, many of the ALJs' judicial responsibilities—including the writing of decisions—are vested in clerical and managerial personnel. The use of such "mass production" techniques, it is charged, violates 5 U.S.C.A. § § 556(c) & 3105.

The amended complaint goes on to contest the authority of the Secretary of HEW to delegate the power to hold hearings to members of the Appeals Council. Although no members of the Council are alleged to have held hearings in that capacity, Nash asserts that such power may be vested only in an ALJ. Finally, he contends, the Chief ALJ and the 10 Regional Chief ALJs improperly combine judicial and managerial duties in violation of 5 U.S.C.A. § 3105.

Procedure

D

* * * Without addressing Nash's claims separately, but after considering affidavits and submitted documents, Judge Elfvin, apparently treating the motion as one for summary judgment, dismissed the amended complaint for lack of standing in a colloquial statement delivered after argument, since he found "nothing right here and now that lands on * * * Judge Nash." No written opinion was filed by the district judge. Judgment dismissing the complaint was entered on July 10, 1979 and this appeal, *pro se*, followed.

Article III limits federal judicial power to the adjudication of "cases or controversies." Thus, a threshold question in every suit is whether plaintiff has alleged that he has in fact suffered (or is imminently subject to suffering) a cognizable injury. * * * The gravamen of appellant's complaint is that rights conferred upon him and all other ALJs by statute, regulation and prior agency practice are being continuously infringed by the appellees' actions. Accordingly, we must turn to the sources of the right asserted to assess appellant's claim of injury.

* * *

As originally enacted in 1946, the Administrative Procedure Act (APA) vested hearing examiners (as ALJs were then called) with a limited independence from the agencies they served. The hearing examiners had previously been on a par with other agency employees, their compensation and promotion dependent upon agency ratings. The expanding scope of agency activity during the 1930s and early 1940s led to increasingly heavy criticism,[10] however, because the hearing examiners came to be perceived as "mere tools of the agency concerned." *Ramspeck v. Trial Examiners Conference*, 345 U.S. 128, 131 (1953). In response, Congress enacted § 11 of the APA, removing control over the hearing examiners' tenure and compensation from the agencies and vesting it, to a large degree, in the Civil Service Commission.

The APA provides that ALJs "are entitled to pay prescribed by the Office of Personnel Management independently of agency recommendations or ratings." 5 U.S.C.A. § 5372. In addition, section 4301 and its implementing regulation (5 C.F.R. § 930.211) exempts ALJs from the performance ratings prescribed for other civil service employees. ALJ tenure, moreover, is specially safeguarded by 5 U.S.C.A. § 554, which provides that ALJs, unlike other civil servants, may not be removed without a formal adjudication.

* * *

It is clear that these provisions confer a qualified right of decisional independence upon ALJs. First recognized by the Supreme Court in *Ramspeck v. Trial Examiners Conference*, this special status is a creation of statute, rather than the Constitution. And as their role has ex-

10. See, e.g., Administrative Procedure Act-Legislative History, S. Doc. No. 248, 79th Cong. 2d Sess. (1946); Thomas, *The Selection* *of Federal Hearing Examiners: Pressure Groups and the Administrative Process*, 59 Yale L. J. 431 (1950).

panded, the ALJs' functional comparability to judges has gained recognition. For example, in *Butz v. Economou,* 438 U.S. 478 (1978), the Supreme Court held that ALJs enjoy absolute immunity from liability in damages for actions taken in their quasi-judicial capacity.

The Social Security Administration has, moreover, recognized the limitations upon its power over the ALJs' decisionmaking process. The position description for ALJs issued by the Administration's Bureau of Hearings and Appeals states that ALJs possess "full and complete individual independence of action and decision * * * without review [and] full responsibility and authority" for the conduct of hearings and the disposition of cases. "The Social Security and Administrative Procedure Acts," the description continues, "prohibit substantive review and supervision of the [ALJ] in the performance of his quasi-judicial functions. His decisions may not be reviewed before publication, and after publication only by the Appeals Council in certain prescribed circumstances. He is subject only to such administrative supervision as may be required in the course of general office management."

It is not insignificant that when Director Trachtenberg instituted the extraordinary review and counseling practices challenged in Nash's complaint, he recognized their potential dangers. In a memorandum dated February 7, 1977 to the Regional Chief ALJs setting forth the Regional Office Peer Review Program, he wrote:

> "You can readily discern from this memorandum my concern and, indeed, my resolve that none of these programs, including this new regional technical review effort, should denigrate or undermine the ALJs' substantive independence. While these programs can serve a needed, valued public service, in the wrong hands, with the wrong attitude, and without constant vigilance, they could cause a serious setback to the system of administrative justice of which we all rightly should be proud. * * * *"

Director Trachtenberg apparently entertained similar doubts as to the propriety of instituting special programs for low-producing and high- and low-reversing ALJs. In a letter dated November 1, 1977, he solicited the comments of the Executive Director of the U.S. Civil Service Commission on possible conflicts between the Quality Assurance System and the Administrative Procedure Act or Civil Service Commission regulations. The Executive Director was of the opinion that the system, as outlined to him, would not violate the APA but qualified his statement appropriately: "Agency programs which seek to enhance the efficiency and quality of an adjudicatory program are in the public interest *so long as they do not impinge upon the decisional independence of Administrative Law Judges.*" (emphasis supplied).

The APA creates a comprehensive bulwark to protect ALJs from agency interference. The independence granted to ALJs is designed to maintain public confidence in the essential fairness of the process through which Social Security benefits are allocated by ensuring impartial decisionmaking. Since that independence is expressed in terms of such personal rights as compensation, tenure and freedom from performance evaluations and extraordinary review, we cannot say that ALJs are so disinterested as to lack even standing to safeguard their own independence.

The scrutiny and affirmative direction alleged by Nash reaches virtually every aspect of an ALJ's daily role.   Under the Quality Assurance System and the Peer Review Program, the number of reversals, the number of dispositions, and the manner of trying and deciding each case are recorded and measured against prescribed standards.   ALJ Nash and his colleagues allegedly receive mandatory, unlawful instructions regarding every detail of their judicial role.   Nash, therefore, has "the personal stake and interest that impart the concrete adverseness required by Article III." * * *

* * *

Finally, we reiterate that our discussion of Nash's standing to sue in no way reflects upon the merits of his claims.   We merely note that premature dismissal for want of standing may deprive litigants of the "focused and careful decision on the merits to which they are clearly entitled." The current explosion of claims and appeals within the Social Security system has posed an awesome challenge to effective administration, and our holding is not intended to undermine the Bureau's good faith attempts to meet this challenge.   By providing an authoritative delineation of the respective rights and powers of the parties to this litigation, and by recognizing that good administration must not encroach upon adjudicative independence, the district court on remand will have the opportunity to advance the principal goal of judicial and quasi-judicial administration: reduction of delay without compromise to the demands of due process, of which judicial independence is but one, important part.

Notes

1. Which, if any, of the complaints made by Nash and his colleagues seem to you to involve an infringement of ALJ decisional independence, as defined by the Administrative Procedure Act?

2. To what extent would Director Trachtenberg's initiatives benefit or harm claimants to disability benefits?

3. Would a "quota" or "target" of 50% grants be unconstitutional? Would you view an institutionally prescribed grading curve, designed to unify the grading practices of professors, as unfair to students?

4. Do any of the other allegations of SSA's managerial interference suggest due process problems?   For additional insight into these questions see J. MASHAW, *et. al.*, SOCIAL SECURITY HEARINGS AND APPEALS 101–24 (1978); Chassman and Rolston, *Social Security Disability Hearings: A Case Study in Quality Assurance and Due Process*, 65 Cornell L. Rev. 801 (1980); Mashaw, *How Much of What Quality: A Comment on Conscientious Procedural Design*, 65 Cornell L. Rev. 823 (1980); Scalia, *the ALJ Fiasco—A Reprise*, 47 U. Chi. L. Rev. 56 (1979).   For a detailed history of the controversy over the position of the Administrative Law Judge, see Rosenblum, *The Administrative Law Judge in the Administrative Process: Interrelations of the Case Law with Statutory and Pragmatic Factors in Determining ALJ Roles*, in Subcommittee on Social

Security, Committee on Ways and Means, U.S. House of Representatives, *Recent Studies Relevant to the Disability Hearings and Appeals Crisis*, 94th Cong., 1st Sess. (1975).

HECKLER v. CAMPBELL

Supreme Court of the United States, 1983
461 U.S. 458, 103 S.Ct. 1952, 76 L.Ed.2d 66

JUSTICE POWELL delivered the opinion of the court.

The issue is whether the Secretary of Health and Human Services may rely on published medical-vocational guidelines to determine a claimant's right to Social Security disability benefits. * * *

In 1978, the Secretary of Health and Human Services promulgated regulations implementing [the statutory definition of disability]. See 43 Fed. Reg. 55349 (1978). The regulations recognize that certain impairments are so severe that they prevent a person from pursuing any gainful work. A claimant who establishes that he suffers from one of these impariments will be considered disabled without further inquiry. If a claimant suffers from a less severe impairment, the Secretary must determine whether the claimant retains the ability to perform either his former work or some less demanding employment. If a claimant can pursue his former occupation, he is not entitled to disability benefits. If he cannot, the Secretary must determine whether the claimant retains the capacity to pursue less demanding work.

The regulations divide this last inquiry into two stages. First, the Secretary must assess each claimant's present job qualifications. The regulations direct the Secretary to consider the factors Congress has identified as relevant: physical ability, age, education and work experience. * * *

Prior to 1978, the Secretary relied on vocational experts to establish the existence of suitable jobs in the national economy. After a claimant's limitations and abilities had been determined at a hearing, a vocational expert ordinarily would testify whether work existed that the claimant could perform. Although this testimony often was based on standardized guides, see 43 Fed. Reg. 9286 (1978), vocational experts frequently were criticized for their inconsistent treatment of similarly situated claimants. To improve both the uniformity and efficiency of this determination, the Secretary promulgated medical-vocational guidelines as part of the 1978 regulations.

These guidelines relieve the Secretary of the need to rely on vocational experts by establishing through rulemaking the types and numbers of jobs that exist in the national economy. They consist of a matrix of the four factors identified by Congress—physical ability, age, education, and work experience[3]—and set forth rules that identify whether jobs requir-

---

3. Each of these four factors is divided into defined categories. A person's ability to perform physical tasks, for example, is categorized according to the physical exertion requirements necessary to perform varying classes of jobs—i. e., whether a claimant can perform sedentary, light, medium, heavy, or very heavy work. 20 CFR § 404.1567.

ing specific combinations of these factors exist in significant numbers in the national economy. Where a claimant's qualifications correspond to the job requirements identified by a rule,[5] the guidelines direct a conclusion as to whether work exists that the claimant could perform. If such work exists, the claimant is not considered disabled.

In 1979, Carmen Campbell applied for disability benefits because a back condition and hypertension prevented her from continuing her work as a hotel maid. After her application was denied, she requested a hearing *de novo* before an Administrative Law Judge. He determined that her back problem was not severe enough to find her disabled without further inquiry, and accordingly considered whether she retained the ability to perform either her past work or some less strenuous job. He concluded that even though Campbell's back condition prevented her from returning to her work as a maid, she retained the physical capacity to do light work. In accordance with the regulations, he found that Campbell was 52-years old, that her previous employment consisted of unskilled jobs and that she had a limited education. He noted that Campbell, who had been born in Panama, experienced difficulty in speaking and writing English. She was able, however, to understand and read English fairly well. Relying on the medical-vocational guidelines, the Administrative Law Judge found that a significant number of jobs existed that a person of Campbell's qualifications could perform. Accordingly, he concluded that she was not disabled.

This determination was upheld by both the Social Security Appeals Council, and the District Court for the Eastern District of New York. The Court of Appeals for the Second Circuit reversed. *Campbell v. Secretary of HHS*, 665 F.2d 48 (CA2 1982). It accepted the Administrative Law Judge's determination that Campbell retained the ability to do light work. And it did not suggest that he had classified Campbell's age, education, or work experience incorrectly. The court noted, however, that it

> "has consistently required that 'the Secretary identify specific alternative occupations available in the national economy that would be suitable for the claimant' and that 'these jobs be supported by "a job description clarifying the nature of the job, [and] demonstrating that the job does not require" exertion or skills not possessed by the claimant.' " Id., at 53 (quoting *Decker v. Harris*, 647 F.2d 291, 298 (CA2 1981)).

The court found that the medical-vocational guidelines did not provide the specific evidence that it previously had required. It explained that

Each of these work categories is defined in terms of the physical demands it places on a worker, such as the weight of objects he must lift and whether extensive movement or use of arm and leg controls is required.

5. The regulations recognize that the rules only describe "major functional and vocational patterns." 20 CFR pt. 404, subpt. P, app. 2, § 200.00(a). If an individual's capabilities are not described accurately by a rule, the regulations make clear that the individual's

particular limitations must be considered. See app. 2, § § 200.00(a), (d). Additionally, the regulations declare that the Administrative Law Judge will not apply the age categories "mechanically in a borderline situation," 20 CFR § 404.1563(a), and recognize that some claimants may possess limitations that are not factored into the guidelines, see app. 2, § 200.00(e). Thus, the regulations provide that the rules will be applied only when they describe a claimant's abilities and limitations accurately.

in the absence of such a showing, "the claimant is deprived of any real chance to present evidence showing that she cannot in fact perform the types of jobs that are administratively noticed by the guidelines." The court concluded that because the Secretary had failed to introduce evidence that specific alternative jobs existed, the determination that Campbell was not disabled was not supported by substantial evidence. * * *

The Secretary argues that the Court of Appeals' holding effectively prevents the use of the medical-vocational guidelines. By requiring her to identify specific alternative jobs in every disability hearing, the court has rendered the guidelines useless. * * *

The Social Security Act directs the Secretary to "adopt reasonable and proper rules and regulations to regulate and provide for the nature and extent of the proofs and evidence and the method of taking and furnishing the same" in disability cases. * * * Where, as here, the statute expressly entrusts the Secretary with the responsibility for implementing a provision by regulation, our review is limited to determining whether the regulations promulgated exceeded the Secretary's statutory authority and whether they are arbitrary and capricious.

We do not think that the Secretary's reliance on medical-vocational guidelines is inconsistent with the Social Security Act. It is true that the statutory scheme contemplates that disability hearings will be individualized determinations based on evidence adduced at a hearing. But this does not bar the Secretary from relying on rulemaking to resolve certain classes of issues. The Court has recognized that even where an agency's enabling statute expressly requires it to hold a hearing, the agency may rely on its rulemaking authority to determine issues that do not require case-by-case consideration. See *FPC v. Texaco, Inc.*, 377 U.S. 33, 41–44 (1964); *United States v. Storer Broadcasting Co.*, 351 U.S. 192, 205 (1956). A contrary holding would require the agency continually to relitigate issues that may be established fairly and efficiently in a single rulemaking proceeding.

The Secretary's decision to rely on medical-vocational guidelines is consistent with *Texaco* and *Storer*. As noted above, in determining whether a claimant can perform less strenuous work, the Secretary must make two determinations. She must assess each claimant's individual abilities and then determine whether jobs exist that a person having the claimant's qualifications could perform. The first inquiry involves a determination of historic facts, and the regulations properly require the Secretary to make these findings on the basis of evidence adduced at a hearing. We note that the regulations afford claimants ample opportunity both to present evidence, relating to their own abilities and to offer evidence that the guidelines do not apply to them.[11] The second inquiry re-

---

11. Both *FPC v. Texaco, Inc.* and *United States v. Storer Broadcasting Co.* were careful to note that the statutory scheme at issue allowed an individual applicant to show that the rule promulgated should not be applied to him. The regulations here provide a claimant with equal or greater protection since they state that an Administrative Law Judge will not apply the rules contained in the guidelines when they fail to describe a claimant's particular limitations.

quires the Secretary to determine an issue that is not unique to each claimant—the types and numbers of jobs that exist in the national economy. This type of general factual issue may be resolved as fairly through rule-making as by introducing the testimony of vocational experts at each disability hearing.

As the Secretary has argued, the use of published guidelines brings with it a uniformity that previously had been perceived as lacking. To require the Secretary to relitigate the existence of jobs in the national economy at each hearing would hinder needlessly an already over-burdened agency. We conclude that the Secretary's use of medical-vocational guidelines does not conflict with the statute, nor can we say on the record before us that they are arbitrary and capricious.

We now consider Campbell's argument that the Court of Appeals properly required the Secretary to specify alternative available jobs. Campbell contends that such a showing informs claimants of the type of issues to be established at the hearing and is required by both the Secretary's regulation, 20 CFR § 404.944 (1980), and the Due Process Clause.

By referring to notice and an opportunity to respond, the decision below invites the interpretation given it by respondent. But we do not think that the decision fairly can be said to present the issues she raises. * * * Rather the court's reference to notice and an opportunity to respond appears to be based on a principle of administrative law—that when an agency takes official or administrative notice of facts, a litigant must be given an adequate opportunity to respond.

This principle is inapplicable, however, when the agency has promulgated valid regulations. Its purpose is to provide a procedural safeguard: to ensure the accuracy of the facts of which an agency takes notice. But when the accuracy of those facts already has been tested fairly during rulemaking, the rulemaking proceeding itself provides sufficient procedural protection.

The Court of Appeals' decision would require the Secretary to introduce evidence of specific available jobs that respondent could perform. It would limit severely her ability to rely on the medical-vocational guidelines. We think the Secretary reasonably could choose to rely on these guidelines in appropriate cases rather than on the testimony of avocational expert in each case. Accordingly, the judgment of the Court of Appeals is

Reversed.

[Justice Brennan concurred, while pointing out that the record contained very little evidence concerning Campbell's capacity to do "light work." Justice Marshall dissented essentially on the same ground.]

Notes

1. The so-called "grid regulations" at issue in *Heckler* are set out in the form of four tables—one for each classification of work—sedentary, light, medium, and heavy work. Each table then breaks down into a series of age classifications (55

and over, 50–54, 45–49, 18–44), educational qualifications (high school or more, limited high school or less, illiterate or unable to communicate in English), and skill categories (skilled or semi-skilled, skills transferable; skilled or semi-skilled, skills non-transferable; unskilled or none). Having found that a claimant, such as Ms. Campbell, can do light work, is between 50–54, has a limited education, and has previously done unskilled work, the ALJ can go to the line in the "light work" table presenting these characteristics and read out the appropriate conclusion—"not disabled." The tabular conclusion is based upon a determination by the Secretary that there are substantial members of jobs in the national economy that can be performed by persons fitting this categorical description. The Secretary's determination, in the rulemaking proceeding that produced the grid regulations, was again premised largely on Labor Department descriptions of job classifications and their requirements in the *Dictionary of Occupational Titles*, a compendium of thousands of job descriptions assembled over many years of collecting data on the national labor market.

Given this background, how does the Supreme Court answer Ms. Campbell's complaints (1) that her hearing fails to consider her individual circumstances, (2) that this process permits the ALJ to base his or her decision on matters that have not been adduced by evidence in the record, and (3) that it fails to give the claimant notice of precisely what she must prove to prevent a finding that she can perform jobs available in substantial numbers in the national economy? Are the Court's answers responsive? Convincing?

2. Would the Second Circuit's approach have undermined the Secretary's attempt to regulate ALJ handling of disability cases by prescribing uniform and appropriate policy?

C. JUDICIAL REVIEW OF AGENCY ADJUDICATION

Virtually all statutes that prescribe formal adjudicatory process for administrative decisionmaking also provide for judicial review of the resulting decisions. Review is usually placed in the courts of appeals, confined to the record of the administrative hearing, and limited to questions of law. Those questions include issues of procedural regularity, jurisdiction, statutory interpretation and the question whether there is "substantial evidence" in the record to support the agency decision.

There are many variations on this basic scheme. For example, the approximately ten thousand annual appeals from SSA disability hearings are lodged, for obvious practical reasons, in the federal district courts. Statutory review provisions also use different language to describe the degree of evidentiary support necessary to support an agency's finding. Nevertheless, the dominant approach is that articulated by section 706 of the APA: "substantial evidence review," extending to all relevant questions of law, is available for the formal adjudicatory decisions of federal agencies.

This generalization, however, does not begin to capture the essence of judicial review of agency adjudication. Indeed, no generalization can do so. As the preceding materials attest, agencies make law and policy in the course of adjudication, as well as determine facts. Issues of law, policy, and fact shade together at the margins.   Their resolution in any particular adjudication is related to the whole course of an agency's adjudicatory and regulatory activity in complex and subtle ways—perceptible perhaps only to those immersed in the administrative routine.   And yet protection from the skewed perceptions and bureaucratic imperatives produced by total immersion in program tasks is a basic justification for judicial review by generalist judges.   The question of what evidence amounts to "substantial evidence"—or, more broadly, how a court's appropriate "scope of review" is to be defined—is not a question of finding the right verbal formula, but rather of striking the right balance between generalized legal ideals and the particularized objectives of administration.

To put the question in this way is to suggest that many considerations are likely to be relevant to the scope of review actually exercised by a reviewing court—the type of issue presented (constitutional, statutory, evidentiary), the impact of a decision either way on the agency's effectiveness, the social importance of the agency's function, the political history of the agency and its governing statutes, the consistency of the judgment under review with past actions, general public and judicial confidence in the agency's performance, the "equities" of the particular case, and a host of other factors.   Not surprisingly, this contextual approach to defining the scope of review to be exercised in a specific case—including, in thousands of cases, the meaning of "substantial evidence"—constantly fuels the fires of litigation and provides multitudinous occasions for judicial eloquence as well as despair.   Perhaps no one has done better than the late Judge Harold Leventhal in *Greater Boston Television Corp. v. FCC*, 444 F.2d 841, 851–52 (D.C. Cir. 1970), *cert. denied* 403 U.S. 923 (1971), when he described the court as looking for some "combination of danger signals" that would justify close scrutiny and perhaps a reversal or remand. Judge Leventhal further suggested that the relationship between court and agency has a dynamic, almost an organic character.   In his view, the review function

> combines judicial supervision with a salutary principle of judicial restraint, an awareness that agencies and courts together constitute a 'partnership' in the furtherance of the public interest and are 'collaborative instrumentalities of justice.'   The court is in a real sense part of the total administrative process, and not a hostile stranger to the office of first instance.

In *Greater Boston* Judge Leventhal was hardly writing on a clean slate. Thirty years earlier the Attorney General's Committee had observed:

> Judicial review of administrative action has developed even as the common law itself, gradually, from case to case, in response to the pressures of particular situations, the teachings of experience, the guidance of ideal and general principle, and the influence of legislation—with the courts playing a chief role in the development.   As an incident of the administrative process, it shares many features of that process.   * * *   Like the agencies, judicial review is a complex of old and new, of historical survivals and purposive innovations.

Attorney General's Committee On Administrative Procedure, Administrative Procedure In Government Agencies, Sen. Doc. No. 8, 77th Cong., 1st Sess. 75–76 (1941).

A feel for this evolving common law can be gained only by exposure to hundreds of cases, not a handful. Every case in this book contributes to the process of acculturation. In this section, where we focus on the issue of scope of review, we can provide only a snapshot of the interactions among analytic distinctions, history, functional concerns, and equity, in determining the relationship between adjudication agencies and reviewing courts. We have chosen to feature judicial review of decisions of the National Labor Relations Board, an agency that has produced some of the most-often-cited, if not most important, judicial pronouncements on the scope of judicial review of agency adjudication.

NLRB v. HEARST PUBLICATIONS

Supreme Court of the United States, 1944.
322 U.S. 111, 64 S. Ct.851, 88 L.Ed. 1170.

MR. JUSTICE RUTLEDGE delivered the opinion of the Court.

These cases arise from the refusal of respondents, publishers of four Los Angeles daily newspapers, to bargain collectively with a union representing newsboys who distribute their papers on the streets of that city. Respondents' contention that they were not required to bargain because the newsboys are not their "employees" within the meaning of that term in the National Labor Relations Act, 49 Stat. 450, 29 U.S.C.A. § 152,[1] presents the important question which we granted certiorari to resolve.

The proceedings before the National Labor Relations Board were begun with the filing of four petitions for investigation and certification by Los Angeles Newsboys Local Industrial Union No. 75. Hearings were held in a consolidated proceeding after which the Board made findings of fact and concluded that the regular full-time newsboys selling each paper were employees within the Act and that questions affecting commerce concerning the representation of employees had arisen. It designated appropriate units and ordered elections. At these the union was selected as their representative by majorities of the eligible newsboys. After the union was appropriately certified, the respondents refused to bargain with it. Thereupon proceedings under § 10 were instituted, a hearing was held and respondents were found to have violated § § 8(1) and 8(5) of the Act. They were ordered to cease and desist from such violations and to bargain collectively with the union upon request.

Upon respondents' petitions for review and the Board's petitions for enforcement, the Circuit Court of Appeals, one judge dissenting, set

---

1. Section 2(3) of the Act provides that "The term 'employee' shall include any employee, and shall not be limited to the employees of a particular employer, unless the Act explicitly states otherwise, and shall include any individual whose work has ceased as a consequence of, or in connection with, any current labor dispute or because of any unfair labor practice, and who has not obtained any other regular and substantially equivalent employment, but shall not include any individual employed as an agricultural laborer, or in the domestic service of any family or person at his home, or any individual employed by his parent or spouse."

aside the board's orders.   Rejecting the Board's analysis, the Court independently examined the question whether the newsboys are employees within the Act, decided that the statute imports common-law standards to determine that question, and held the newsboys are not employees. * * *

The papers are distributed to the ultimate consumer through a variety of channels, including independent dealers and newsstands often attached to drug, grocery or confectionery stores, carriers who make home deliveries, and newsboys who sell on the streets of the city and its suburbs. Only the last of these are involved in this case.

The newsboys work under varying terms and conditions.   They may be "bootjackers," selling to the general public at places other than established corners, or they may sell at fixed "spots."   They may sell only casually or part-time, or full-time; and they may be employed regularly and continuously or only temporarily.   The units which the Board determined to be appropriate are composed of those who sell full-time at established spots.   Those vendors, misnamed boys, are generally mature men, dependent upon the proceeds of their sales for their sustenance, and frequently supporters of families.   Working thus as news vendors on a regular basis, often for a number of years, they form a stable group with relatively little turnover, in contrast to schoolboys and others who sell as bootjackers, temporary and casual distributors.

* * *

The newsboys' compensation consists in the difference between the prices at which they sell the papers and the prices they pay for them.   The former are fixed by the publishers and the latter are fixed either by the publishers or, in the case of the News, by the district manager.   In practice the newsboys receive their papers on credit.   They pay for those sold either sometime during or after the close of their selling day, returning for credit all unsold papers.   Lost or otherwise unreturned papers, however, must be paid for as though sold.   Not only is the "profit" per paper thus effectively fixed by the publisher, but substantial control of the newsboys' total "take home" can be effected through the ability to designate their sales areas and the power to determine the number of papers allocated to each.   While as a practical matter this power is not exercised fully, the newsboys' "right" to decide how many papers they will take is also not absolute.   In practice, the Board found, they cannot determine the size of their established order without the cooperation of the district manager.   And often the number of papers they must take is determined unilaterally by the district managers.

In addition to effectively fixing the compensation, respondents in a variety of ways prescribe, if not the minutiae of daily activities, at least the broad terms and conditions of work.   This is accomplished largely through the supervisory efforts of the district managers, who serve as the nexus between the publishers and the newsboys.   The district managers assign "spots" or corners to which the newsboys are expected to confine their selling activities. Transfers from one "spot" to another may be ordered by the district manager for reasons of discipline or efficiency or other cause. Transportation to the spots from the newspaper building is offered by each of respondents. Hours of work on the spots are determined not simply by the impersonal pressures of the market, but to a real extent by explicit instructions from the district managers. Adherence to the prescribed hours is observed closely by the district managers or other supervisory agents of the publishers. Sanctions, varying in severity from reprimand to dismissal, are visited on the tardy and the delinquent. By similar supervisory controls minimum standards of diligence and good conduct while at work are sought to be enforced. However wide may be the latitude for individual initiative beyond those standards, district managers' instructions in what the publishers apparently regard as helpful sales techniques are expected to be followed. Such varied items as the manner of displaying the paper, of emphasizing current features and headlines, and of placing advertising placards, or the advantages of soliciting customers at specific stores or in the traffic lanes are among the subjects of this instruction. Moreover, newsboys are furnished with sales equipment, such as racks, boxes and change aprons, and advertising placards by the publishers. In this pattern of employment the Board found that the newsboys are an integral part of the publishers' distribution system and circulation organization. * * *

[After concluding that "employee" in the NLRA was not intended to vary with state common law, the Court addressed the issue of statutory interpretation.]

The mischief at which the Act is aimed and the remedies it offers are not confined exclusively to "employees" within the traditional legal distinctions separating them from "independent contractors." Myriad forms of service relationship, with infinite and subtle variations in the terms of employment, blanket the nation's economy. Some are within this Act, others beyond its coverage. Large numbers will fall clearly on one side or on the other, by whatever test may be applied. But intermediate there will be many, the incidents of whose employment partake in part of the one group, in part of the other, in varying proportions of weight. And consequently the legal pendulum, for purposes of applying the statute, may swing one way or the other, depending upon the weight of this balance and its relation to the special purpose at hand.

* * *

Interruption of commerce through strikes and unrest may stem as well from labor disputes between some who, for other purposes, are technically "independent contractors" and their employers as from disputes between persons who, for those purposes, are "employees" and their employers. Inequality to bargaining power in controversies over wages, hours and working conditions may as well characterize the status of the one group as of the other. The former, when acting alone, may be as "helpless in dealing with an employer," as "dependent * * * on his daily wage" and as "unable to leave the employ and to resist arbitrary and unfair treatment" as the latter. For each, "union * * * [may be] essential to give * * * opportunity to deal on equality with their employer." And for each, collective bargaining may be appropriate and effective for the "friendly adjustment of industrial disputes arising out of differences as to wages, hours, or other working conditions." In short, when the particular situation of employment combines these characteristics, so that the economic facts of the relation make it more nearly one of employment than of independent business enterprise with respect to the ends sought to be accomplished by the legislation, those characteristics may outweigh technical legal classification for purposes unrelated to the statute's objectives and bring the relation within its protections.

* * *

It is not necessary in this case to make a completely definitive limitation around the term "employee." That task has been assigned primarily to the agency created by Congress to administer the Act. Determination of "where all the conditions of the relation require protection" involves inquiries for the Board charged with this duty. Everyday experience in the administration of the statute gives it familiarity with the circumstances and backgrounds of employment relationships in various industries, with the abilities and needs of the workers for self-organization and collective action, and with the adaptability of collective bargaining for the peaceful settlement of their disputes with their employers. The experience thus acquired must be brought frequently to bear on the question who is an employee under the Act. Resolving that question, like determing whether unfair labor practices have been committed, "belongs to the usual administrative routine" of the Board.

In making that body's determinations as to the facts in these matters conclusive, if supported by evidence, Congress entrusted to it primarily the decision whether the evidence establishes the material facts. Hence in reviewing the Board's ultimate conclusions, it is not the court's function to substitute its own inferences of fact for the Board's, when the latter have support in the record. Undoubtedly questions of statutory interpretation, especially when arising in the first instance in judicial proceedings, are for the courts to resolve, giving appropriate weight to the judgment of those whose special duty is to administer the questioned statute. *Norwegian Nitrogen Products Co. v. United States*, 288 U.S. 294; *United States v. American Trucking Associations*, 310 U.S. 534. But where the question is one of specific application of a broad statutory term in a proceeding in which the agency administering the statute must determine it initially, the reviewing court's function is limited. Like the commissioner's determination under the Longshoremen's & Harbor Workers' Act, that a man is not a "member of a crew' (*South Chicago Coal & Dock Co. v. Bassett*, 309 U.S. 251) or that he was injured "in the course of employment" (*Parker v. Motor Boat Sales, Inc.*, 314 U.S. 244) and the Federal Communications Commission's determination that one company is under the "control" of another (*Rochester Telephone Corp. v. United States*, 307 U.S. 125), the Board's determination that specified persons are "employees" under this Act is to be accepted if it has "warrant in the record" and a reasonable basis in law.

In this case the Board found that the designated newsboys work continuously and regularly, rely upon their earnings for the support of themselves and their families, and have their total wages influenced in large measure by the publishers, who dictate their buying and selling prices, fix their markets and control their supply of papers. Their hours of work and their efforts on the job are supervised and to some extent prescribed by the publishers or their agents. Much of their sales equipment and advertising materials is furnished by the publishers with the intention that it be used for the publisher's benefit. Stating that "the primary consideration in the determination of the applicability of the statutory definition is whether effectuation of the declared policy and purposes of the Act comprehend securing to the individual the rights guaranteed and protection afforded by the Act," the Board concluded that the newsboys are employees. The record sustains the Board's findings and there is ample basis in the law for its conclusion

* * *

MR. JUSTICE ROBERTS.

* * *

I think it plain that newsboys are not "employees" of the respondents within the meaning and intent of the National Labor Relations Act. When Congress, in § 2(3), said "The term 'employee' shall include any employee, * * * " it stated as clearly as language could do it that the provisions of the Act were to extend to those who, as a result of decades of tradition which had become part of the common understanding of our people, bear the named relationship. Clearly also Congress did not delegate to the National Labor Relations Board the function of defining the relationship of employment so as to promote what the Board understood to be the underlying purpose of the statute. The question who is an employee, so as to make the statute applicable to him, is a question of the meaning of the Act and, therefore, is a judicial and not an administrative question. * * *

The "warrant in the record and a reasonable basis in law" formulation in *Hearst* signals a judicial deference that was replicated in many other early Labor Board cases. Although the Wagner Act, which established the NLRB, provided that "the findings of the Board as to facts, if supported by evidence, shall be conclusive," the Supreme Court read the Act to require Board determinations to be supported by "substantial evidence." *Washington, Virginia & Maryland Coach Co. v. NLRB*, 301 U.S. 142, 147 (1937). However, this requirement imposed only modest demands on agency fact-finding. "Substantial evidence" was defined to mean something "more than a mere scintilla * * * or such relevant evidence as a reasonable mind might accept as adequate to support a conclusion." *Consolidated Edison Co. v. NLRB*, 305 U.S. 197, 229 (1938). The

Board's findings of fact would not be disturbed unless the record was "wholly barren of evidence." Id. See also *NLRB v. Columbian Enameling and Stamping Co.*, 306 U. S. 292 (1939). These judicial glosses on the text of the Wagner Act were translated into reflexive deference in practice. Board determinations were aproved whenever the Court could find record evidence which, when viewed in isolation, substantiated its findings. Indeed, congressional critics charged that the Court made a practice of sustaining Board decisions based on little more than "hearsay, opinion, and emotional speculation in place of factual evidence." *Intermediate Report of the House Special Committee to Investigate the National Labor Relations Board*, 76th Cong., 3rd Sess. 76 (1940).

Influential members of the judiciary also found the Supreme Court's performance unsatisfactory. In *NLRB v. Standard Oil Co.*, 138 F.2d 885, 887 (2d Cir. 1943), Judge Learned Hand characterized the Supreme Court's interpretation of the "substantial evidence" test as "momentous" judicial "abdication." Other judges begrudgingly accepted the Supreme Court's definition of the scope of review, but with undeferential cynicism:

> We have recognized (or tried to) that findings must be sustained, even when they are contrary to the great weight of the evidence, and we have ignored, or at least endeavored to ignore, the shocking injustices which such findings, opposed to the overwhelming weight of the evidence, produce. We must confess that at times we have apparently failed to recognize that evidence which would not appeal to any rational appraiser of the truth, may yet fall within the field of "some evidence." On the asumption that such evidence would not be sufficient to sustain a finding in an ordinary civil suit, we have rejected it. We have at times set aside the findings of the Board, but only * * * when the findings were so overwhelmingly opposed by the evidence as to require it. Our conclusions have not met with the approval of the Supreme Court to whose superior judgment we bow."

Wilson & Co. v. NLRB, 126 F.2d 114, 117 (7th Cir. 1942) (citations omitted).

Congress reacted, first, with oversight hearings and, ultimately, legislation. In condemnatory tones, House Resolution 258 created a Special Committee of the House of Representatives to investigate the NLRB. The Senate Judiciary Committee held similar hearings. Appearing before the Senate committee, Dean Blythe Stason echoed the prevailing dissatisfaction with the Supreme Court's interpretation of the substantial evidence test in reviewing Labor Board decisions,

> Construed gramatically, the term "substantial evidence" might conceivably— although not reasonably—mean little more than a sort of modified "scintilla" rule—the rule formerly regarded as sufficient to block a motion for directed verdict in jury cases. So defined, the requirement simply calls for a searching of the record to find some relevant testimony which can be regarded as substantial to support the order, ignoring all countervailing testimony introduced by the opposing party. There are decisions apparently adopting this modified scintilla method of applying the substantial evidence rule. In fact, in two recent Supreme Court decisions in Labor Board cases, the *NLRB v. Waterman Steamship Corporation*, 309 U.S. 206 (1940), and *NLRB v. Brad-*

ford Dyeing Association, 310 U.S. 318 (1940), this scintilla technique seems to have been followed, at least so far as the method is revealed by the written opinion of the Court. * * *

Hearings on S.672 Before a Subcomm. of the Senate Judiciary Committee, 77th Cong., 1st Sess. 1355 6 (1941)

Such testimony intensified pressure for legislative action, and in 1940 both Houses of Congress passed the Walter-Logan amendments to the APA, calling generally for stricter review of agency determinations of fact. H.R. 6324, S. 915, 76th Cong., 1st Sess. This legislation was vetoed by President Roosevelt, who believed that it imposed other unduly rigid limitations on the administrative process, and threatened to preempt the separate investigation of administrative agencies then being conducted by the Attorney General's Committee.

The Final Report of the Attorney General's Committee, released in January 1941, noted the wide-spread dissatisfaction with the prevailing scope of review of agency adjudications. The majority concluded, however, that Congress should not attempt to correct the problem by legislation. Changing the prevailing statutory standard, the majority thought, would not eliminate the discretionary aspect of judicial review and might encourage involvement by the federal courts in inefficient reconsideration of evidentiary questions. *Attorney General's Committee on Administrative Procedure in Government Agencies*, S. Doc. No. 8, 77th Cong., 1st Sess. 75–76 (1941).

The dissenting members of the Attorney General's Committee favored a general reform of the scope of review standard and in particular criticized the Supreme Court's treatment of NLRB findings of fact as "unsatisfactory" and "unfair." Under the prevailing interpretation of the scope of review, they argued, "if what is called 'substantial evidence' is found anywhere in the record to support conclusions of fact, the courts are said to be obliged to sustain the decision without reference to how heavily the countervailing evidence may preponderate. * * * Under this interpretation, the courts need to read only one side of the case and, if they find any evidence there, the administrative action is to be sustained and the record to the contrary is to be ignored." Id. at 210–211. They recommended that the courts be allowed to "set aside decisions *clearly* contrary to the *manifest* weight of the evidence." Id. at 211 (emphasis in original). This led them to advocate a formula for judicial review that would extend to "findings of fact, including inferences and conclusions of fact," "unsupported, upon the *whole* record, by substantial evidence." Ibid.

The substance of the minority position found its way into the statute books, both as section 10(e) [now section 706] of the APA and as part of the 1947 amendments to the National Labor Relations Act. The stage was thus set for *Universal Camera Corp. v. NLRB*, 340 U.S. 474 (1951), which involved the effect of a hearing examiner's initial decision on the substantiality of the record evidence supporting a contrary Board decision.

Narrowly construed, the question was whether the examiner's decision was a part of the whole record, and if so, what weight it should have. But the Court recognized that broader questions were involved. After recounting the movement to enlarge judicial review of NLRB decisions, the Court concluded that the addition of the requirement that its findings of fact be supported "by substantial evidence on the record considered as a whole," 61 Stat. 136, 29 U.S.C.A. § 141(e), legislated a much more demanding standard of review, and "expressed a mood" of dissatisfaction with the excessive deference previously afforded Board decisions (340 U.S. at 487–91):

> From the legislative story we have summarized, two concrete conclusions do emerge. One is the identity of aim of the Administrative Procedure Act and the Taft-Hartley Act regarding the proof with which the Labor Board must support a decision. The other is that now Congress has left no room for doubt as to the kind of scrutiny which a Court of Appeals must give the record before the Board to satisfy itself that the Board's order rests on adequate proof. * * *

> Whether or not it was ever permissible for courts to determine the substantiality of evidence supporting a Labor Board decision merely on the basis of evidence which in and of itself justified it, without taking into account contradictory evidence or evidence from which conflicting inferences could be drawn, the new legislation definitively precludes such a theory of review and bars its practice. The substantiality of evidence must take into account whatever in the record fairly detracts from its weight. This is clearly the significance of the requirement in both statutes that courts consider the whole record. Committee reports and the adoption in the Administrative Procedure Act of the minority views of the Attorney General's Committee demonstrate that to enjoin such a duty on the reviewing court was one of the important purposes of the movement which eventuated in that enactment.

> To be sure, the requirement for canvassing "the whole record" in order to ascertain substantiality does not furnish a calculus of value by which a reviewing court can assess the evidence. Nor was it intended to negative the function of the Labor Board as one of those agencies presumably equipped or informed by experience to deal with a specialized field of knowledge, whose findings within that field carry the authority of an expertness which courts do not possess and therefore must respect. Nor does it mean that even as to matters not requiring expertise a court may displace the Board's choice between two fairly conflicting views, even though the court would justifiably have made a different choice had the matter been before it *de novo*. Congress has merely made it clear that a reviewing court is not barred from setting aside a Board decision when it cannot conscientiously find that the evidence supporting that decision is substantial, when viewed in the light that the record in its entirety furnishes, including the body of evidence opposed to the Board's view.

> There remains, then, the question whether enactment of these two statutes has altered the scope of review other than to require that substantiality be determined in the light of all that the record relevantly presents.

* * * We should fail in our duty to effectuate the will of Congress if we denied recognition to expressed Congressional disapproval of the finality accorded to Labor Board findings by some decisions of this and lower courts, or even of the atmosphere which may have favored those decisions.

We conclude, therefore, that the Administrative Procedure Act and the Taft-Hartley Act direct that courts must now assume more responsibility for the reasonableness and fairness of Labor Board decisions than some courts have in the past.   Reviewing courts must be influenced by a feeling that they are not to abdicate the conventional judicial function.   Congress has imposed on them responsibility for assuring that the Board keeps within reasonable bounds. * * * The Board's findings are entitled to respect; but they must nonetheless be set aside when the record before a Court of Appeals clearly precludes the Board's decision from being justified by a fair estimate of the worth of the testimony of witnesses or its informed judgment on matters within its special competence or both. * * * Whether on the record as a whole there is substantial evidence to support agency findings is a question which Congress has placed in the keeping of the Courts of Appeals.

Whether the "new mood" ushered in by the APA, the Wagner Act, and *Universal Camera* has persisted is difficult to determine.   In one of the few general studies of the subject, *Judicial Review of Agency Decisions: The Labor Board and the Court*, 1968 Sup. Ct. Rev. 53, 71–73, 74–75, Professor (now Judge) Winter suggested that the dual aspects of the judicial stance enunciated in *Universal Camera* may produce a peculiar dynamic—a retreat by the Board into the facts of cases in ways that both elude serious judicial review and avoid the agency's responsibilities to develop reasoned and politically responsive labor relations policy.

The Supreme Court is of course responsible for establishing the proper doctrine and attitudes concerning the scope of review of Labor Board decisions involving questions of law or mixed fact and law.   The opinions of the Court, however, do not establish a coherent view of the scope of that review.   In some cases they seem to show great deference to Board discretion and experience both in establishing doctrine and in changing it.   In others, deference is expressed but not in fact shown.   In yet others, the Court talks and acts as though it is merely reviewing the decisions of another court.

If the verbiage of the Court has not articulated a meaningful role for judicial review, however, there is a clear trend apparent.   The Supreme Court has in fact shown little deference to Board discretion in exercising the power delegated to it and has demonstrated little interest in the Board's views of its experience or in seeing that the Board acts as a specialized agency.   And more frequently than not, the Court has employed a broad scope of review that has permitted it to substitute its own judgment. * * *

Nor is it only in reversing the Board that the Court impinges on the functions of the agency.   If the Board is affirmed by an opinion that approves the decision below as being the only one possible, rather than as a correct one within the realm of agency discretion, a future Board will be precluded from changing the rule because the doctrine of *stare decisis* will lead to judicial reversal of its decision.   Thus, the rigid distinction between mandatory and nonmandatory subjects of bargaining has become embedded in the law as the result of a Supreme Court decision and no longer seems subject to Board reversal.   The Board's ability to experiment and to be politically responsive has thus been unduly narrowed.

The Court in short has failed to permit the Board sufficient discretion in statutory interpretation and in doctrinal change over time.   It has behaved as though the board's only function is to "flesh out" the statute and has focused almost entirely on the coherence of the body law developed through judicial review.   Over time the Court has permitted less and less discretion to the Board and has adopted the policy-making functions for itself.

So much for the portion of *Universal Camera* that holds Congress intended the courts to "assume more responsibility for the reasonableness and fairness of Labor Board decisions."   But Winter went on to question *Universal Camera's* approach to findings of fact in a fashion that very nearly turns the conventional wisdom about scope of review on its head:

> The discussion to this point has focused almost entirely on the scope of judicial review of Board decisions on matters of law or mixed fact and law and has not encompassed Board findings of adjudicative facts.   The present test, based on the Administrative Procedure and Taft-Hartley Acts, requires courts merely to determine whether such findings are supported by substantial evidence viewing the record as a whole.   And, as elaborated by Justice Frankfurter in the *Universal Camera* decision, the report of a trial examiner is entitled only to "such probative force as it intrinsically commands."   The Board, therefore, has greater power to reverse a trial examiner on issues of adjudicative fact than a court has to reverse the Board.

> I have doubts regarding the propriety of this scope of review of Board findings.   The conduct of the Board, because it is a politically responsive agency, must be carefully scrutinized to insure that this responsiveness affects only principles of general application and that the board otherwise behaves in an even-handed fashion.   In the absence of such controls, the agency might decide cases on an ad hoc basis.   There is, however, an evident danger in entrusting the Board with substantial control of findings of adjudicative fact because whatever controls are exercised through judicial review of questions of law can easily be circumvented by carefully contrived findings of fact. And whatever expertness the Board may bring to questions of fact seems to me outweighed by the dangers created by its political responsiveness.   I would, therefore, tentatively suggest a statutory amendment limiting the substantial evidence test to cases in which the Board affirms the factual findings of trial examiners—assuming they can be made truly independent—and compelling the Board to apply the same test to those findings when it reviews them initially.   Or, if the trial examiners are thought in some way to be infected by the agency, the courts might be permitted to apply a "weighing the evidence" test that would increase the scope of their review of Board decisions and not vary the Board's control of the examiners.

> To be sure, these are only partially formulated proposals, and then only tentatively suggested.   But it seems to me that the reasons for permitting the Board greater leeway in establishing legal principles imply a need for greater restrictions on its power to find facts.   And, paradoxically, therefore, the scope of judicial review of matters of law ought to be narrower than that of matters of fact.

Consider Winter's views as you examine the next case.

NATIONAL LABOR RELATIONS BOARD v. BELL AEROSPACE CO., DIVISION OF TEXTRON, INC.

Supreme Court of the United States, 1974,
416 U.S. 267, 94 S. Ct. 1757, 40 L. Ed. 2d 134.

MR. JUSTICE POWELL delivered the opinion of the Court.

This case presents two questions: first, whether the National Labor Relations Board properly determined that all "managerial employees," except those whose participation in a labor organization would create a conflict of interest with their job responsibilities, are covered by the National Labor Relations Act; and second, whether the Board must proceed by rulemaking rather than by adjudication in determining whether certain buyers are "managerial employees." We answer both questions in the negative.

I

Facts

Respondent Bell Aerospace Co., Division of Textron, Inc. (company), operates a plant in Wheatfield, New York, where it is engaged in research and development in the design and fabrication of aerospace products. On July 30, 1970, Amalgamated Local No. 1286 of the United Automobile, Aerospace and Agricultural Implement Workers of America (union) petitioned the National Labor Relations Board (Board) for a representation election to determine whether the union would be certified as the bargaining representative of the 25 buyers in the purchasing and procurement department at the company's plant. The company opposed the petition on the ground that the buyers were "managerial employees" and thus were not covered by the Act.

The relevant facts adduced at the representation hearing are as follows. The purchasing and procurement department receives requisition orders from other departments at the plant and is responsible for purchasing all of the company's needs from outside suppliers. Some items are standardized and may be purchased "off the shelf" from various distributors and suppliers. Other items must be made to the company's specifications, and the requisition orders may be accompanied by detailed blueprints and other technical plans. Requisitions often designate a particular vendor, and in some instances the buyer must obtain approval before selecting a different one. Where no vendor is specified, the buyer is free to choose one.

Absent specific instructions to the contrary, buyers have full discretion, without any dollar limit, to select prospective vendors, draft invitations to bid, evaluate submitted bids, negotiate price and terms, and prepare purchase orders. Buyers execute all purchase orders up to $50,000. They may place or cancel orders of less than $5,000 on their own signature. On commitments in excess of $5,000, buyers must obtain the approval of a superior, with higher levels of approval required as the purchase cost increases. For the Minute Man missile project, which represents 70% of the company's sales, purchase decisions are made by a team of personnel from the engineering, quality assurance, finance, and manufacturing departments. The buyer serves as team chairman and signs the purchase order, but a representative from the pricing and negotiation department participates in working out the terms.

After the representation hearing, the Regional Director transferred the case to the Board. On May 20, 1971, the board issued its decision holding that the company's buyers constituted an appropriate unit for purposes of collective bargaining and directing an election. Relying on its recent decision in *North Arkansas Electric Cooperative, Inc.*, 185 N.L.R.B. 550 (1970), the board first stated that even though the company's buyers might be "managerial employees," they were nevertheless covered by the Act and entitled to its protections. The Board then rejected the company's alternative contention that representation should be denied because the buyers' authority to commit the company's credit, select vendors, and negotiate purchase prices would create a potential conflict of interests between the buyers as union members and the company. In essence, the company argued that buyers would be more receptive to bids from union contractors and would also influence "make or buy" decisions in favor of "make," thus creating additional work for sister unions in the plant. The Board thought, however, that any possible conflict was "unsupported conjecture" since the buyers' "discretion and latitude for independent action must take place within the confines of the general directions which the Employer has established" and that "any possible temptation to allow sympathy for sister unions to influence such decisions could effectively be controlled by the Employer."

On June 16, 1971, a representation election was conducted in which 15 of the buyers voted for the union and nine against. On August 12, the Board certified the union as the exclusive bargaining representative for the company's buyers. That same day, however, the Court of Appeals for the Eighth Circuit denied enforcement of another Board order in *NLRB v. North Arkansas Electric Cooperative, Inc.*, 446 F.2d 602, and held that "managerial employees" were not covered by the Act and were therefore not entitled to its protections.

Encouraged by the Eighth Circuit's decision, the company moved the Board for reconsideration of its earlier order. The Board denied the motion, stating that it disagreed with the Eighth Circuit and would adhere to its own decision in *North Arkansas*. In the Board's view, Congress intended to exclude from the Act only those "managerial employees" associated with the "formulation and implementation of labor relations policies." In each case, the fundamental touchstone" was "whether the duties and responsibilities of any managerial employee or group of managerial employees do or do not include determinations which should be made free of any conflict of interest which could arise if the person involved was a participating member of a labor organization." Ibid. Turning to the present case, the Board reiterated its prior finding that the company had not shown that union organization of its buyers would create a conflict of interest in labor relations.

The company stood by its contention that the buyers, as "managerial employees," were not covered by the Act and refused to bargain with the union. An unfair labor practice complaint resulted in a Board finding that the company had violated § § 8(a) (5) and (1) of the Act, 29 U.S.C.A. § § 158(a) (5) and (1), and an order compelling the company to bargain with the union. Subsequently, the company petitioned the United States Court of Appeals for the Second Circuit for review of the order and the Board cross-petitioned for enforcement.

The Court of Appeals denied enforcement. 475 F.2d 485 (1973). * * *

II

We begin with the question whether all "managerial employees," rather than just those in positions susceptible to conflicts of interest in labor relations, are excluded from the protections of the Act.[4] The Board's early decisions, the legislative history of the Taft-Hartley Act of 1947, 61 Stat. 136, and subsequent board and court decisions provide the necessary guidance for our inquiry. * * *

The Wagner Act did not expressly mention the term "managerial employee." After the Act's passage, however, the Board developed the concept of "managerial employee" in a series of cases involving the appropriateness of bargaining units. * * * The Board summarized its policy on "managerial employees" in *Ford Motor Co.*, 66 N.L.R.B. 1317, 1322 (1946):

"We have customarily excluded from bargaining units of rank and file workers executive employees who are in a position to formulate, determine and effectuate management policies. These employees we have considered and still deem to be 'managerial,' in that they express and make operative the decisions of management."

Whether the Board regarded all "managerial employees" as entirely outside the protection of the Act, as well as inappropriate for inclusion in a rank-and-file bargaining unit, is less certain. To be sure, at no time did

---

4. Section 2(3) of the Act defines the term "employee" as follows:

"The term 'employee' shall include any employee, and shall not be limited to the employees of a particular employer, unless this chapter explicitly states otherwise, and shall include any individual whose work has ceased as a consequence of, or in connection with, any current labor dispute or because of any unfair labor practice, and who has not obtained any other regular and substantially equivalent employment, but shall not include any individual employed as an agricultural laborer, or in the domestic service of any family or person at his home, or any individual employed by his parent or spouse, or any individual having the status of an independent contractor, or any individual employed as a supervisor, or

any individual employed by an employer subject to the Railway Labor Act, as amended from time to time, or by any other person who is not an employer as herein defined."

Supervisory employees are expressly excluded from the protections of the Act. That term is defined in § 2(11):

"The term 'supervisor' means any individual having authority, in the interest of the employer, to hire, transfer, suspend, lay off, recall, promote, discharge, assign, reward, or discipline other employees, or responsibility to direct them, or to adjust their grievances, or effectively to recommend such action, if in connection with the foregoing the exercise of such authority is not of a merely routine or clerical nature but requires the use of independent judgment."

the Board certify even a separate unit of "managerial employees" or state that such was possible.   The Board was cautious, however, in determining which employees were "managerial."   For example, in *Dravo Corp.*, 54 N.L.R.B. 1174, 1177 (1944), the Board excluded buyers and expediters from a unit of office and clerical employees, but reserved the question whether all such employees were to be considered "managerial":

> "This is not to say, however, that buyers and expediters are to be denied the right to self-organization and to collective bargaining under the Act.   The precise relationship of the buyers and expediters to management here is not now being determined by us."

During this period the Board's policy with respect to the related but narrower category of "supervisory employees" manifested a progressive uncertainty.   The board first excluded supervisors from units of rank-and-file employees but in *Union Collieries Coal Co.*, 41 N.L.R.B. 961, 44 N.L.R.B. 165 (1942), it certified a separate unit composed of supervisors who were to be represented by an independent union.   Shortly thereafter, in *Godchaux Sugars, Inc.*, 44 N.L.R.B. 874 (1942), the Board approved a unit of supervisors whose union was affiliated with a union of rank-and-file employees.   This trend was soon halted, however, by *Maryland Drydock Co.*, 49 N.L.R.B. 733 (1943), where the Board held that supervisors, although literally "employees" under the Act, could not be organized in any unit.   And in *Yale & Towne Mfg. Co.*, 60 N.L.R.B. 626, 628–629 (1945), the Board further held that timestudy men, whose " 'interests and functions' " were " 'sufficiently akin to those of management,' " should neither be included in a unit with other employees, nor be established as a separate unit."

Maryland Drydock was subsequently overruled in *Packard Motor Car Co.*, where the Board held that foremen could constitute an appropriate unit for collective bargaining.   The Board's position was upheld 5–4 by this Court in *Packard Co. v. NLRB*, 330 U.S. 485 (1947). * * *

Significantly, both the House Report and the Senate Report voiced concern over the board's broad reading of the term "employee" to include those clearly within the managerial hierarchy. * * * [T]he Senate Report specifically mentioned that even vice presidents might be unionized under the Board's decision.   It also noted that unionization of supervisors had hurt productivity, increased the accident rate, upset the balance of power in collective bargaining, and tended to blur the line between management and labor.* * *

The legislative history of the Taft-Hartley Act of 1947 may be summarized as follows.   The House wanted to include certain persons within the definition of "supervisors," such as straw bosses, whom the Senate believed should be protected by the Act.   As to these persons, the Senate's view prevailed.   There were other persons, however who both the House and the Senate believed were plainly outside the Act.   The House wanted to make the exclusion of certain of these persons explicit.   In the conference agreement representatives from both the House and the Senate agreed that a specific provision was unnecessary since the Board had

long regarded such persons as outside the Act.   Among those mentioned
as impliedly excluded were persons working in "labor relations, personnel and employment departments," and "confidential employees."   But
assuredly this did not exhaust the universe of such excluded persons. * * *

Following the passage of the Taft-Hartley Act, the Board itself adhered to the view that "managerial employees" were outside the Act.   In
Denver Dry Goods, 74 N.L.R.B. 1167, 1175 (1947), assistant buyers, who
were required to set good sales records as examples to sales employees,
to assist buyers in the selection of merchandise, and to assume the buyer's duties when the latter was not present, were excluded by the Board
on the ground that "the interests of these employees are more closely
identified with those of management." * * *

* * * Until its decision in *North Arkansas* in 1970, the Board consistently followed this reading of the Act.   It never certified any unit of
"managerial employees," separate or otherwise, and repeatedly stated
that it was Congress' intent that such employees not be accorded bargaining rights under the Act.   And it was this reading which was permitted
to stand when Congress again amended the Act in 1959. * * *

In sum, the Board's early decisions, the purpose and legislative history of the Taft-Hartley Act of 1947, the Board's subsequent and consistent
construction of the Act for more than two decades and the decisions of the
courts of appeals all point unmistakably to the conclusion that "managerial
employees" are not covered by the Act.   We agree with the Court of Appeals below that the Board "is not now free" to read a new and more restrictive meaning into the Act.

In view of our conclusion, the case must be remanded to permit the
Board to apply the proper legal standard in determining the status of
these buyers. * * *

[Part III of the Court's opinion considers whether the NLRB was obligated to engage in rulemaking before determining whether specific employees were entitled to the protections of the Act or fell within the "managerial" category.   Justice Powell held that the Board could make such
decisions in the course of individual adjudications.]

MR. JUSTICE WHITE, with whom MR. JUSTICE BRENNAN, MR. JUS-
TICE STEWART, and MR. JUSTICE MARSHALL join, dissenting in part.

[The dissent rejected Justice Powell's conclusion that no "managerial"
employees could be considered "employees" within the meaning of the
Act.   After reviewing the legislative and judicial history canvassed by
the majority, Justice White's opinion concluded:]

The Board's decisions in this area have not established a cohesive and
precise pattern of rulings.   It is often difficult to tell whether an individual decision is based on the propriety of excluding certain employees from
a particular bargaining unit or whether the worker under consideration is
thought to be outside the scope of the Act.   But this Court has consistently said that it will accept the Board's determination of whether a particular individual is an "employee" under the Act if that determination

"has 'warrant in the record' and a reasonable basis in law," *NLRB v. Hearst Publications, Inc.*, 322 U.S. 111 (1944); *NLRB v. United Insurance Co.*, 390 U.S. 254, 260 (1968). There is no reason here to hamstring the Board and deny a broad category of employees those protections of the Act which neither the statutory language nor its legislative history requires simply because the Board at one time interpreted the Act—erroneously it seems to me—to exclude all managerial as well as supervisory employees.

I respectfully dissent.

The Impact of Judicial Review of Agency Adjudication

Federal administrative agencies conduct hundreds of thousands of formal adjudications each year, each theoretically subject to judicial review. The Social Security Administration is the source of a majority of these decisions, but other agencies, like the NLRB, also decide several thousand contested cases annually. And, by one count, S. KRISLOV & L. MUSOLF, eds., THE POLITICS OF REGULATION 2 (1964), 120 different federal agencies are engaged in formal adjudication of rights and duties under various federal statutory regimes. Of this vast caseload only a small percentage are pressed to judicial review. While 10,000 SSA cases per year filed in the federal district courts hardly can be called a light caseload, these appeals represent only 4% of ALJ decisions after hearing and less than 1% of initial disability decisions. Similarly, of 2000 formal orders issued by Securities Exchange Commission in its first 10 years of operation, only 100 were apealed to the courts. W. GELLHORN & C. BYSE, ADMINISTRATIVE LAW 213–14 (1960).

The exposure of courts to something less than the tip of the iceberg of agency adjudications raises two fundamental questions: ① What effect can intermittent judicial scrutiny have on the general course of administrative adjudication? ② Are the perceptible effects of judicial review, on the whole, beneficial? Both questions are complex and the evidence available to answer them incomplete.

The materials that we have already explored are, however, suggestive. The impact of review will obviously depend to some degree on the basis for the judicial judgment and on the capacity of the agency to respond to judicial direction. A decision such as *Goldberg v. Kelly*, which finds particular procedures unconstitutional and prescribes minimums for the future, should have a much greater impact than a remand for lack of substantial evidence, even if that remand is by the Supreme Court. But as the administrative response to *Goldberg* also demonstrates, the uneven capacity of agencies to implement judicial direction may make the ultimate effects of judicial review quite unpredictable at the time of decision. Moreover, the very uncertainty of consequences raises substantial questions about the desirability of "effective" judicial intervention. See also J. MASHAW, BUREAUCRATIC JUSTICE 187-88 (1983) (describing similar dynamic problems in response to the hearing delay cases cited in *Heckler v. Campbell*).

Justice White's remarks about the interaction of the NLRB and the Supreme Court further suggest that agency recalcitrance can affect the efficacy of judicial review. For whatever impact the Court might anticipate when it interprets the Board's statutory authority could be undermined by findings of fact in particular adjudications. Notice that following the remand in *Bell Aerospace* the board retains the power to find as a "fact" that the company's buyers are not managerial employees. The NLRB's previous non-compliance with court of appeals opinions suggests a strong predisposition to do so.

Agency non-compliance with court decisions need not necessarily entail the subterfuge of masking policy judgments in factual findings. Federal administrative agencies generally exercise national jurisdiction; the territorial powers of reviewing courts end at the district or circuit boundary. Opinions in one district or circuit need not be followed elsewhere—indeed, where circuit rules conflict, could not be. Moreover, having lost one "case," the agency may not acquiesce even in that local jurisdiction. SSA policy concerning the treatment of judicial precedent, for example, is set out in the Office of Hearings and Appeals Handbook, § 1–161, which states in part:

> While the ALJs are bound by decisions of the United States Supreme Court, they should also make every reasonable effort to follow the district or circuit court's views regarding procedural or evidentiary matters when handling similar cases in that particular district or court.
>
> However, where a district or circuit court's decision contains interpretations of the law, regulations, or rulings which are inconsistent with the Secretary's interpretations, the ALJs should not consider such decisions binding on future cases simply because the case is not appealed. In certain cases SSA will not appeal a court decision it disagrees with, in view of special circumstances of the particular case (e.g., the limited effect of the decision).
>
> When SSA decides to acquiesce in a district court decision, or a circuit court decision, which is inconsistent with our previous interpretation of the law, regulations, or rulings, SSA will take appropriate action to implement changes by means of regulations, rulings, etc. ALJs will be promptly advised of such action.

As the SSA's General Counsel once tersely put the point, "the federal courts do not run SSA's programs * * * ." Associate Commissioner, Office of Hearings and Appeals Memorandum, "ALJ Policy Council Meeting" p. 2 (Jan. 7, 1982) (unpublished mimeo). Indeed, the single occasion on which the SSA acquiesced nationally in a court of appeals decision has been rendered almost meaningless by the grid regulations approved in *Heckler v. Campbell.*

Agencies may not display substantially greater fidelity to the dictates of Supreme Court decisions. In THE SUPREME COURT AND ADMINISTRATIVE AGENCIES (1968), Martin Shapiro made a careful study of the U.S. Patent Office. Although the Patent Office rules on patentability and issues patents, the ultimate authority to determine patentability presumably lies with the federal courts in cases challenging a patent or involving claims of infringement. Beginning in the 1930's a sharp divergence emerged between the Patent Office's and the Supreme Court's conceptions of patentability. In the base period 1920–29 the Court invalidated about 50% of the patents challenged before it. The percentage invalidated increased dramatically thereafter; between 1934 and 1966 the Court sustained only two patents on the merits.

The differences between the Supreme Court and the Patent Office were recognized by the courts of appeals, which generally followed the former, often not only reversing the Patent Office but lecturing it for re-calcitrance:

> * * * Over the years the courts of the United States, and particularly the Supreme Court, have found meaning implicit in the scheme and purpose of the patent laws which aids in the construction of their general language.   In this process, rules and standards have been developed for use as guides to the systematic and orderly definition and application of such a conception as invention in accordance with what the courts understand to be the true meaning of the Constitution and the patent laws. * * *

> This patent of the obviously unpatentable and indications that the category of patented unpatentables is a large one, cause us to express a final word of regret that the Patent Office in analyzing and disposing of patent applications does not more consistently use that expertise with which courts credit it along with other specialized administrative agencies. * * *

Packwood v. Briggs & Stratton Corp., 195 F.2d 971, 973–74 (3d Cir. 1952).   The Patent Office remained unrepentant, however, presumably convinced that it *was* exercising its expertise, harrassed by the judiciary.

One should not conclude from an examination of two or three examples that judicial review of agency adjudication is generally ineffectual because agencies are recalcitrant.   Others have suggested that the more common judicial agency interaction is accommodation, not conflict.   See Fiorio, *Judicial-Administrative Interaction in Regulatory Policy Making: The Case of the Federal Power Commission*, 28 Ad. L. Rev. 41 (1976).   See also M. SHAPIRO, *op. cit.* supra.   Yet these findings, combined with the tiny percentage of agency decisions that reach the courts for review, make one wonder about the value of judicial review of administrative adjudication.

The central value of judicial review may be its residual guarantee of *justice in individual cases.*   From this perspective judicial review protects the citizen from the extremes of bureaucratic tunnel-vision or incompetence—extremes revealed, one hopes, by the lack of substantial evidence in the record or by some other "danger signal" that can be converted into a legal claim.   Somewhat more broadly, judicial review is a *protection against official illegality.*   Agencies zealously pursuing particular programs on the basis of specialized knowledge should not be expected simultaneously to maintain a detached perspective about the impact of their actions on tangential statutory, constitutional, or common-law rights—or to display modesty in interpreting the extent of their own jurisdiction.   Judicial review thus polices the boundaries of agency power and sustains general substantive and procedural norms where the latter compete with the implementation of particular programs.

That judicial review should help assure justice and protect the rule of law is as conventional as it is plausible.   Indeed, it is its common-sensical character that gives judicial review power to *legitimate administrative action*.   The assurance that the courts remain open to check administrative lawlessness is surely one of the major means by which the administrative apparatus of the modern welfare state has been accommodated to an historically liberal-individualist political ideology.   See, e.g., *Amalgamated Meatcutters v. Connally*, 337 F. Supp. 737 (D.D.C. 1971), supra p. 6.

More recently, it has become common to think of judicial review as more than a mere check at the boundaries of agency power or a case-by-case oversight for inequity.   Whether or not one is attracted by Judge Leventhal's "partnership" analogy, it is difficult not to imagine that reviewing courts are in some sense co-inhabitants of a legislatively-created arena for the formulation and implementation of policy.   To believe otherwise is to believe in sharper boundaries among fact, law, and policy than most contemporary lawyers can discern.   Moreover, because the judicial process of review is now accessible to many individuals and groups affected by agency action, judicial review may play a *democratizing role*.   See, e.g., Stewart, *The Reformation of American Administrative Law*, 88 Harv. L. Rev. 1667 (1975).   This is true partly because parties who can invoke judicial review, by virtue of that power alone, necessarily gain some leverage in negotiations with the agency over protection of their interests. In this way political pluralism, as Professor Lowi has lamented, *op. cit.* supra, can be maintained all the way to the stage of concrete implementation.   Moreover, a judiciary constantly compelled to resolve disputes concerning administrative action cannot be expected continuously to maintain a neat division between agency and judicial discretion.   Judicial conceptions of appropriate policy are insinuated into the administrative process even as the judiciary struggles to understand and maintain a proper respect for agency action.   In the view of many commentators, the judiciary has a special claim to represent social or public values in our particular brand of constitutional democracy.   See, e.g., P. BOBBITT, CONSTITUTIONAL FATE (1982); Fiss, *Forward: The Forms of Justice*, 93 Harv. L. Rev. 1 (1979); Wellington, *The Nature of Judicial Review*, 91 Yale L.J. 486 (1982).

That these functional hypotheses concerning the role of judicial review—ensuring individualized justice, maintaining the rule of law, legitimating the administrative state, and democratizing bureaucratic choices among competing values—may be plausible, however, does not make them true.   And, if true, their pursuit within the current structure of judicial review of agency adjudication may nevertheless be sub-optimal or even deleterious.   Such a conclusion might be applicable generally or, as Judge Winter's critique suggests, one reached about particular agencies or functions.

Nor is Winter alone in his criticism.   In their study of the SSA disability program, SOCIAL SECURITY HEARINGS AND APPEALS 125–

150 (1978), Mashaw and his colleagues found little evidence that judicial review either produced justice in individual cases or maintained the appropriate norms of the program.   They concluded that judicial review should be retained on the sole ground that to remove it might impair the perceived legitimacy of SSA administration.   But surely that conclusion, too, is suspect.   Others have concluded that judicial oversight has pressed SSA toward defensive administrative actions that are widely considered dysfunctional.   See Symposium, *Judicial Review of Social Security Disability Decisions: A Proposal for Change*, 11 Tex. Tech L. Rev. 215 (1980).   Does the possible "legitimation" value of review outweigh the potential costs of dysfunctional administrative adaptation?   And if legitimacy flows from functional assumptions about justice and the rule of law that are either demonstrably false or problematic, how much weight should the former have?   Is judicial review merely a prop supporting what Murray Edelman has termed the "expressive function" of administrative agencies: "to create and sustain an impression that ensures acquiescence in the public in the face of private tactics that might otherwise be expected to produce resentment, protest and resistance." M. EDELMAN, THE SYMBOLIC USES OF POLITICS 56 (1964). See also T. ARNOLD, THE SYMBOLS OF GOVERNMENT 34 (1935).

Students of other programs question the capacity of reviewing courts to understand the subtle interconnections of the discrete decisions they are called upon to review with the broader programs and policies that those decisions seek to implement.   These misunderstandings produce "a multitude of unintended and undesirable consequences."   S. MELNICK, REGULATION AND THE COURTS 351–52 (1983).

One of Melnick's case studies is instructive.   The Clean Air Act gave the EPA responsibility, in effect, to "license" state enforcement of federal air quality standards by approving state implementation plans (SIPs). Because of federal statutory deadlines the SIP approval process was hurried.   Many states had limited information about prevailing air quality. They therefore adopted draconian control requirements with escape clauses in the form of "variance" provisions that could be used to tailor enforcement to the facts as they become known.   EPA approved these SIPs recognizing the critical role that variances would play in both the state and the federal enforcement efforts.

This enforcement calculus was upset by judicial intervention.   In 1973, the National Resources Defense Council (NRDC) filed suit in six federal courts of appeals to force the EPA to disapprove the variance provisions in most state plans.   The ensuing interaction between the federal courts and the federal and state pollution control agencies over the variance issue is summarized by Melnick:

> Fearing that administrative leniency would undermine the Clean Air Act's rigid deadlines, several circuit courts prohibited the EPA from allowing states to grant polluters variances after 1975.   The EPA first ignored these decisions and then announced ambiguous guidelines designed to appease the courts.   These guidelines angered state enforcement officials, many of whom

either cut back on their activities or stopped talking with the federal agency. The EPA responded by issuing new guidelines that reassured the states but flew in the face of the court orders.   While the Supreme Court eventually reversed the decisions that had caused the EPA so much trouble, it could not repair the damage already done.   * * *

Why was judicial review of EPA's actions under the state implementation plans so misinformed?   Why was it that no court—not even the Supreme Court, which sided with the EPA—recognized that variances formed the linchpin of state and federal enforcement efforts?   The reasons Melnick offers rehearse some of the institutional explanations advanced by others:

> The adjudicatory process failed to probe the inadequacies of the original SIPs, the weakness of state and federal enforcement programs, or the different ways in which the EPA and the states used variances.   The original cases were argued and decided well before the EPA had had any experience enforcing the act.   Neither the EPA's lawyers nor the NRDC anticipated what was to come.   More disturbing still was the failure of the government's attorneys to explain the problem candidly to the Supreme Court in 1975.   The EPA's Office of General Counsel and the Department of Justice, themselves far removed from the centers of enforcement, insisted upon arguing "the law" and declined to complicate their argument with a discussion of the fact of widespread noncompliance.   Public admission that SIPs were vague, confused, and unreasonable or that the EPA lacked credible enforcement sanctions might further weaken enforcement.   Neither the NRDC nor the business groups that intervened in the case saw any advantage in explaining these bleak facts to the Court.

See also B. ACKERMAN & W. HASSLER, CLEAN COAL/DIRTY AIR 25 (1981).   Melnick also comments on the democratizing effects of the SIP episode:

> Once again court decisions gave environmental groups greater access to EPA decisionmaking.   The EPA's 1974 variance guidelines were the direct result of negotiations with the NRDC.   But in the long run these guidelines served only to diminish the influence of environmentalists.   Rather than granting fewer concessions to polluters, state officials merely made their concessions in a less formal manner.   Consequently, their actions were less subject to scrutiny by environmentalists—and by the EPA.   It is interesting to note that the NRDC at first approved of the EPA's rules on variances and only later chose to bring suit.   They chose wrong.

At a broader level, Melnick questions whether the contribution of the courts to the development of policy reveals a "partnership" in good working order:

> Taken as a whole, the consequences of court action under the Clean Air Act are neither random nor beneficial.   * * * Court action has encouraged legislators and administrators to establish goals without considering how they can be achieved, exacerbating the tendency of these institutions to promise far more than they can deliver.   The policymaking system of which the federal courts are now an integral part has produced serious inefficiency

and inequities, has made rational debate and conscious political choice difficult, and has added to frustration and cynicism among participants of all stripes.

Op. cit., supra at 345. Here, Melnick is speaking not just of judicial review of adjudication, but of judicial review of all forms of agency action under the Clean Air Act. The extent and character of the effects of judicial review are, thus, subjects to which we shall return in other contexts.

D. AVOIDING FORMAL ADJUDICATION BY MAKING RULES

In Parts A and B of this chapter we have examined the circumstances under which administrators may be obliged to provide trial-type safeguards in resolving individual claims and disputes, and discovered tensions between adjudicatory fairness and the development of general administrative policy. The formulation of general policies obviously affects the kinds of issues that require resolution in specific cases. Thus, Congress' determination that physical capacity, and not economic circumstance shall largely determine eligibility for disability insurance inevitably focuses the SSA's attention on the first of these theoretically plausible criteria for public support. But even this narrowing of the inquiry leaves broad scope for dispute in individual cases, and *Heckler v. Campbell* depicts one effort by administrators to narrow further the adjudicator's field of vision—by fashioning general standards that embody, and presumably implement, the agency's long-term policies.

This section explores further the interplay between the formulation of general agency policy, i.e., the making of rules, and the adjudication of individual disputes. We examine specifically the incentives and opportunities agencies have to frame general rules in order to limit the scope of statutorily or constitutionally demanded trial-type hearings.

1. THE EFFECT OF AGENCY RULES

As judges do in the common law system, administrators often enunciate policy in the course of deciding individual disputes. For example, the Federal Communications Commission's determination that an applicant for a broadcast license possesses the requisite qualifications implies, and may even be explained in terms of, some general policies that the agency believes should govern the allocation of such operating authority. But the adjudicatory model has obvious limitations as a method for developing general policy. Ordinarily the participants include only the agency and a single private party, e.g., the applicant, or beneficiary, or respondent. The issues that demand resolution typically concern the activities or qualifications of the private party rather than the characteristics of the universe of which he is a part. And the procedures designed to assure a fair and accurate resolution of such focused issues may be poorly suited, or simply too expensive, for eliciting the kind of information a decisionmaker might want before formulating general criteria for action. (In Chapter 4 we explore in depth the types of procedures agencies do or should follow in establishing such general standards, i.e., in rulemaking.)

Administrative agencies vary in their functions. Whatever its primary mission, however, virtually every agency on occasion finds it useful to adopt some general principles governing the performance of its functions—specifying the content of license applications, or the criteria of eligibility for benefits, or the legality of specific business practices. It is well accepted that administrators possess inherent authority to announce formally how they intend to exercise their powers and offer interpretations of their statutory authority. Indeed, such inherent power would appear to be indispensable if effect is to be given to Professor Kenneth Davis's suggestion, adopted by some reviewing courts, that agencies solve the "nondelegation problem" by formulating and following their own "standards."

Our purpose here is to consider the effects of clearly established general standards for resolving individual disputes. Specifically, we are interested in the impact on an agency's adjudicatory functions of its ability to influence, if not dictate, the content of the standards it is empowered to implement. Responsibility for both case deciding and policy-making may be necessary ingredients of effective regulation, but the combination also affords opportunities for powerful agency leverage.

NATIONAL PETROLEUM REFINERS ASSOCIATION v. FEDERAL TRADE COMMISSION

United States Court of Appeals, District of Columbia Circuit, 1973.
482 F.2d 672, cert. denied 415 U.S. 951, 94 S. Ct. 1475, 39 L.Ed. 2d 567 (1974).

J. SKELLY WRIGHT, CIRCUIT JUDGE.

This case presents an important question concerning the powers and procedures of the Federal Trade Commission. We are asked to determine whether the Commission, under its governing statute, the Trade Commission Act and specifically 15 U.S.C.A. § 46(g), is empowered to promulgate substantive rules of business conduct or, as it terms them, "Trade Regulation Rules." The effect of these rules would be to give greater specificity and clarity to the broad standard of illegality—"unfair methods of competition in commerce, and unfair or deceptive acts or practices in commerce"—which the agency is empowered to prevent. Once promulgated, the rules would be used by the agency in adjudicatory proceedings aimed at producing cease and desist orders against violations of the statutory standard. The central question in such adjudicatory proceedings would be whether the particular defendant's conduct violated the rule in question.

The case is here on appeal from a District Court ruling that the Commission lacks authority under its governing statute to issue rules of this sort. * * * Specifically at issue in the District Court was the Commission's rule declaring that failure to post octane rating numbers on gasoline pumps at service stations was an unfair method of competition and an unfair or deceptive act or practice.[1]   The plaintiffs in the District Court, appellees here, are two trade associations and 34 gasoline refining companies.   Plaintiffs attacked the rule on several grounds, but the District Court disposed of the case solely on the question of the Commission's statutory authority to issue such rules.   That is the only question presented for our consideration on appeal.   We reverse and remand to the District Court for further consideration of appellee's challenge to the validity of the procedure before the Commission which resulted in the rule.

I

* * *

As always, we must begin with the words of the statute creating the Commission and delineating its powers.   Section 5 directs the Commission to "prevent persons, partnerships, or corporations * * * from using unfair methods of competition in commerce and unfair or deceptive acts or practices in commerce."   Section 5(b) of the Trade Commission Act specifies that the Commission is to accomplish this goal by means of issuance of a complaint, a hearing, findings as to the facts, and issuance of a cease and desist order.   * * *

Appellees argue that since Section 5 mentions only adjudication as the means of enforcing the statutory standard, any supplemental means of putting flesh on that standard such as rule-making, is contrary to the overt legislative design.   But Section 5(b) does not use limiting language suggesting that adjudication alone is the only proper means of elaborating the statutory standard.   * * * Nor are we persuaded by appellees' argument that, despite the absence of limiting language in Section 5 regarding the role of adjudication in defining the meaning of the statutory standard, we should apply the maxim of statutory construction *expressio unius est exclusio alterius* * * * .   * * * For the Trade Commission Act includes a provision which specifically provides for rule-making * * * .   Section 6(g) of the Act, 15 U.S.C.A. § 46(g), states that the Commission may "[f]rom time to time * * * classify corporations and

---

1. The rule provides:
"In connection with the sale or consignment of motor gasoline for general automotive use, in commerce as 'commerce' is defined in the Federal Trade Commission Act, it constitutes an unfair method of competition and an unfair or deceptive act or practice for refiners or others who sell to retailers, when such refiners or other distributors own or lease the pumps through which motor gasoline is dispensed to the consuming public, to fail to disclose clearly and conspicuously in a permanent manner on the pumps the minimum octane number or numbers of the motor gasoline being dispensed. In the case of those refiners or other distributors who lease pumps, the disclosure required by this section should be made as soon as it is legally practical; for example, not later than the end of the current lease period.   Nothing in this section should be construed as applying to gasoline sold for aviation purposes.

"NOTE: For the purposes of this section, 'octane number' shall mean the octane number derived from the sum of research (R) and motor (M) octane numbers divided by 2; (R + M)/2.   The research octane (R) and motor octane number (M) shall be as described in the American Society for Testing and Materials (ASTM) 'Standard Specifications for Gasoline' D 439–70, and subsequent revisions, and ASTM Test Methods D 2699 nd D 2600."
36 Fed. Reg. 23871 (1971).

* * * make rules and regulations for the purpose of carrying out the provisions of sections 41 to 46 and 47 to 58 of this title."[7]

* * *

Of course, it is at least arguable that * * * [Section 6(g) only empowers the Commission] to promulgate procedural, as opposed to substantive, rules for administration of the Section 5 adjudication and enforcement powers. But we see no reason to import such a restriction on the "rules and regulations" permitted by Section 6(g). * * * The substantive rule here unquestionably implements the statutory plan. Section 5 adjudications—trial type proceedings—will still be necessary to obtain cease and desist orders against offenders, but Section 5 enforcement through adjudication will be expedited, simplified, and thus "carried out" by use of this substantive rule. And the overt language of both Section 5 and Section 6, read together, supports its use in Section 5 proceedings.

II

Our belief that "rules and regulations" in Section 6(g) should be construed to permit the Commission to promulgate binding substantive rules as well as rules of procedure is reinforced by the construction courts have given similar provisions in the authorizing statutes of other administrative agencies. * * * In *National Broadcasting Co. v. United States*, 319 U.S. 190 (1943), for example, the Supreme Court upheld the Federal Communications Commission's chain broadcasting rules regulating programming arrangements between networks and affiliates, in part on the basis of the FCC's generalized rule-making authority in 47 U.S.C.A. § 303(r) (1962). It rejected arguments similar to those made here, ruling that this authority extended beyond specification technical and financial qualifications to be used as guides in the administration of the Commission's license-granting power. It permitted the FCC to use rule-making to elaborate the terms of its mandate to pursue the "public convenience, interest, or necessity," by framing rules carrying out public policy objectives like affiliate independence and avoidance of undue network control over programming in the hope that listeners would be ensured a diversity of program offerings.

United States v. Storer Broadcasting Co., 351 U.S. 192 (1956), took the FCC's rule-making power a step further, holding that applicants for licenses could be rejected before receiving a hearing specified by statute in the event they did not comply with the Commission's rule limiting networks' power to own stock in affiliates and did not give sufficient reasons why the rule should be waived. * * *

Storer and its successors are, of course, closely related to the question we face here. For a major component of appellees' complaint is the abridgement of their interest in having the Trade Commission Act's stan-

7. 15 U.S.C.A. § 45 is § 5 of the Trade Commission Act.

dard of illegality elaborated only in an adjudicatory context. In our view, this argument was adequately answered in *Storer*, at least to the extent the FTC's rule serves the "purpose of shortening and simplifying the adjudicative process and of clarifying the law in advance," and thus, in *Storer's* language, aids the Commission in the "orderly conduct of its business."

* * *

Just as there has been little question of allowing substantive rule-making to intrude on asserted rights to a full hearing before an agency for a determination of a party's rights and liabilities, there has been a similar lack of hesitation in construing broad grants of rule-making power to permit promulgation of rules with the force of law as a means of agency regulation of otherwise private conduct. * * * Indeed, the general rule courts have adopted toward agencies' use of rule-making power to define standards of conduct by regulated parties, where a general rule-making provision is in the agency statute, was stated succinctly and definitively for this court by Judge Fahy in *Public Service Comm'n of State of New York v. FPC*, 327 F.2d 893, 897 (1964):

> "All authority of the Commission need not be found in explicit language. Section 16 [the general rule-making provision] demonstrates a realization by Congress that the Commission would be confronted with unforeseen problems of administration in regulating this huge industry and should have a basis for coping with such confrontation. While the action of the Commission must conform with the terms, policies and purposes of the Act, it may use means which are not in all respects spelled out in detail. * * * * "

* * *

Thus there is little question that the availability of substantive rule-making gives any agency an invaluable resource-saving flexibility in carrying out its task of regulating parties subject to its statutory mandate. More than merely expediting the agency's job, use of substantive rule-making is increasingly felt to yield significant benefits to those the agency regulates. Increasingly, courts are recognizing that use of rule-making to make innovations in agency policy may actually be fairer to regulated parties than total reliance on case-by-case adjudication.

* * *

* * * [U]tilizing rule-making procedures opens up the process of agency innovation to a broad range of criticism, advice and data that is ordinarily less likely to be forthcoming in adjudication. Moreover, the availability of notice before promulgation and wide public participation in rule-making avoids the problem of singling out a single defendant among a group of competitors for initial imposition of a new and inevitably costly legal obligation.

* * *

III

Appellees contend, however, that these cases and the general practice of agencies and courts in underwriting the broad use of rule-making are irrelevant to the FTC. They argue that the Trade Commission is somehow *Sui generis*, that it is best characterized as a prosecuting rather than a regulatory agency, and that substantive rule-making power should be less readily implied from a general grant of rule-making authority where the agency does not stand astride an industry with pervasive license-granting, rate-setting, or clearance functions. * * *

Given the expanse of the Commission's power to define proper business practices, we believe it is but a quibble to differentiate between the potential pervasiveness of the FTC's power and that of the other regulatory agencies merely on the basis of its prosecutorial and adjudicatory mode of proceeding. Like other agencies, wholly apart from the question of rule-making power it exerts a powerfully regulatory effect on those business practices subject to its supervision. * * *

IV

* * * The opinion of the District Court argues forcefully that, in spite of the clear and unlimited language of Section 6 (g) granting rule-making authority to the Commission, the Congress that enacted Section 5 and Section 6 (g) gave clear indications of its intent to reject substantive rule-making, that the FTC's own behavior in the years since that time supports a narrow interpretation of its mandate to promulgate "rules and regulations," and that where Congress desired to give the FTC substantive rule-making authority in discrete areas it did so in subsequent years in unambiguous terms. Our own conclusion, based on an independent review of this history, is different. We believe that, while the legislative history of Section 5 and Section 6 (g) is ambiguous, it certainly does not compel the conclusion that the Commission was not meant to exercise the power to make substantive rules with binding effect in Section 5 (a) adjudications. * * *

Moreover, while we believe the historical evidence is indecisive of the question before us, we are convinced that the broad, undisputed policies which clearly motivated the framers of the Federal Trade Commission Act of 1914 would indeed be furthered by our view as to the proper scope of the Commission's rule-making authority. * * *

* * * Without the rule, the Commission might well be obliged to prove and argue that the absence of the rating markers in each particular case was likely to have injurious and unfair effects on consumers or competition. Since this laborious process might well have to be repeated every time the Commission chose to proceed subsequently against another defendant on the same ground, the difference in administrative efficiency between the two kinds of proceedings is obvious. Furthermore, rules, as contrasted with the holdings reached by case-by-case adjudication, are more specific as to their scope, and industry compliance is more likely

simply because each company is on clearer notice whether or not specific rules apply to it.

Moreover, when delay in agency proceedings is minimized by using rules, those violating the statutory standard lose an opportunity to turn litigation into a profitable and lengthy game of postponing the effect of the rule on their current practice. As a result, substantive rules will protect the companies which willingly comply with the law against what amounts to the unfair competition of those who would profit from delayed enforcement as to them. This, too, will minimize useless litigation and is likely to assist the Commission in more effectively allocating its resources. * * *

V

Despite the import of Section 6 (g)'s plain language, the overwhelming judicial support given to expansive agency readings of statutory rule-making authorizations that are not flatly inconsistent with other statutory provisions, and the incontestable relationship between the broad policies behind the 1914 Act and the utility of substantive rule-making power, appellee's argue that substantive rule-making represents a sufficiently important innovation in Commission practice for us to balk at authorizing its use on the basis of an arguably ambiguous statute in the absence of very firm indications of affirmative and specific legislative intent. * * *

* * *

Any fears that the agency could successfully use rule-making power as a means of oppressive or unreasonable regulation seem exaggerated in view of courts' general practice in reviewing rules to scrutinize their statement of basis and purpose to see whether the major issues of policy pro and con raised in the submissions to the agency were given sufficient consideration. *Automotive Parts & Accessories Ass'n v. Boyd*, 407 F.2d 330 (1968). The Commission is hardly free to write its own law of consumer protection and antitrust since the statutory standard which the rules may define with greater particularity is a legal standard. Although the Commission's conclusions as to the standard's reach are ordinarily shown deference, the standard must "get [its] final meaning from judicial construction." * * *

VI

Our conclusion as to the scope of Section 6 (g) is not disturbed by the fact that the agency itself did not assert the power to promulgate substantive rules until 1962 and indeed indicated intermittently before that time that it lacked such power. * * * The various statements made by Commission representatives questioning its authority to promulgate rules which are to be used with binding effect on subsequent adjudications are not determinative of the question before us. True, the accustomed judicial practice is to give "great weight" to an agency's construction of its own enabling legislation, particularly when such a construction stretches back, as here, to a time close to the agency's origin.   The argument for judicial deference is not so strong where, as here, the question does not require special agency competence or expertise, requiring the agency, for example, to make a complex judgment involving its areas of expertise, competition and impact of business practices on consumer behavior. Here, the question is simply one of statutory interpretation concerning the procedures and setting in which the Commission may elaborate its statutory standard.   Since this sort of question calls largely for the exercise of historical analysis and logical and analogical reasoning, it is the everyday staple of judges as well as agencies.   Thus we feel confident in making our own judgment as to the proper construction of Section 6 (g). We are, of course, reassured by the fact that the Commission itself, as distinguished from its former spokesman, has come to the same conclusion.

* * *

A more troubling obstacle to the Commission's position here is the argument that Congress was made fully aware of the formerly restrictive view of the Commission's power and passed a series of laws granting limited substantive rule-making authority to the Commission in discrete areas allegedly on the premise that the 1914 debate withheld such authority. * * *

* * * The view that the Commission lacked substantive rule-making power has been clearly brought to the attention of Congress and, rather than simply failing to act on the question, Congress, in expanding the agency's powers in several discrete areas of marketing regulation, affirmatively enacted limited grants of substantive rule-making authority in the Wool Products Act of 1939, the Fur Products Labeling Act of 1951, the Flammable Fabrics Act of 1953, as amended in 1967, the Textile Fiber Products Identification Act of 1958 and the Fair Packaging and Labeling Act of 1967.   Thus it is argued that Congress would not have granted the agency such powers unless it had felt that otherwise the agency lacked rule-making authority.

Conceding the greater force of this argument than one premised on congressional inaction, we believe it must not be accepted blindly.   In such circumstances, it is equally possible that Congress granted the power out of uncertainty, understandable caution, and a desire to avoid litigation. * * * For there is ample evidence that, while some of the limited rule-making legislation may well have been influenced by the belief that the 1914 Act did not grant the Commission substantive rule-making power, at least during the passage of the Packaging and Labeling Act of 1967, this assumption was not accepted and was thought by many congressmen to be an open question, despite the protestations of the Commission's chairman that the agency was powerless under the 1914 Act.   The report of the House Committee on Interstate and Foreign Commerce, while pointing out that the agency lacked "*specific* authority" (emphasis added) to issue regulations prescribing standards for package labeling, suggested that the question of the agency's general authority under Section 6 (g) to do so was open.   The report noted that the "authority of the Commission to issue trade regulation rules * * * has never been passed on in the courts."   H.R. Rep. No. 2076, 89th Cong., 2d Sess., 22 (1966). * * * Where there is solid reason, as there plainly is here, to believe that Congress, in fact, has not wholeheartedly accepted the agency's viewpoint and instead enacted legislation out of caution and to eliminate the kind of disputes that invariably attend statutory ambiguity, we believe that relying on the *de facto* ratification argument is unwise.   In such circumstances, we must perform our customary task of coming to an independent judgment as to the statute's meaning, confident that if Congress believes that its creature, the Commission, thus exercises too much power, it will repeal the grant.[40]

VII

In sum, we must respectfully register our disagreement with the District Court's painstaking opinion.   Its result would render the Commission ineffective to do the job assigned it by Congress.   Such a result is not required by the legislative history of the Act.   We rely, therefore, on the plain language of Section 6 (g) which gives the Commission the authority to "make rules and regulations for the purpose of carrying out the provisions of [Section 5]."   We hold that under the terms of its governing statute, and under Section 6 (g) in particular, the Federal Trade Commission is authorized to promulgate rules defining the meaning of the statutory standards of the illegality the Commission is empowered to prevent.   Thus we must reverse the District Court's judgment and remand this case for further proceedings.

It is so ordered.

Notes

1. Is the power of the FTC to "legislate" codes of "fair" and "non-deceptive" conduct for all businesses in interstate commerce comparable to the power of the FCC or the FPC to issue rules governing the licensing of broadcasters or pipelines?   Should the magnitude of the power claimed by the FTC, combined with the generality of section 5's prohibitions, have raised the specter of the nondelegation doctrine?   The majority opinion in *Schecter* distinguished the power granted to the FTC by section 5 from the power to issue industry codes of "fair competition" that it there struck down precisely on the ground that the Commission was required to exercise its power in quasi-judicial proceedings.   295 U.S. at 532, 533.

2. Judge Wright's opinion portrays rulemaking in much the same way that courts concerned about delegation have viewed it—as a means for cabining agency discretion and ultimately for protecting individual interests.   The petroleum companies, on the other hand, viewed the FTC's claimed authority as hostile to their interests.   This suggests that the exercise of rulemaking authority may operate both as a means of agency self-limitation and as a means of enhancing agency power.

---

40. We are aware, of course, that in both the just concluded 92nd Congress and the current 93rd Congress legislation granting the FTC limited substantive rule-making power in the area of "unfair and deceptive practices" has been under consideration * * * .

Obviously, the FTC was free, without adopting a formal rule, to bring individual proceedings against distributors who failed to post octane ratings, relying on precisely the same legal theory as embodied in its rule, viz., that the failure to provide this information was "unfair" or "deceptive" under section 5 (a).   And it unquestionably could have announced publicly its policy to institute such proceedings.   Moreover, as Judge Wright's opinion makes clear, confirmation of the FTC's power to adopt the rule did not relieve the agency of the burden of enforcing it through individual cease-and-desist proceedings: A gasoline dealer who ignored the rule could suffer no legal penalty until a cease-and-desist order was entered against him, for the FTC Act did not in 1974 provide any penalty for past violations.

Assuming all of the foregoing is true, why were the petroleum refiners so strenuously opposed to recognition of the FTC's power to make legislative rules? By the same token, why was the Commission so concerned to have its rediscovered rulemaking authority upheld?

Any attempt to answer these questions requires a more thorough understanding of the FTC's traditional mode of enforcing section 5.   Traditionally, when the FTC encountered a business practice it considered deceptive, it issued a complaint against the responsible party.   If the respondent was not prepared to change its practices, the matter was sent for a trial-type hearing at which the Commission bore the burden of showing that the respondent's practices had deceived, or were likely to deceive, a substantial number of purchasers.   Counsel assigned to prosecute the complaint customarily had to introduce evidence sufficient to support the Commission's theory of deception.   In the *Petroleum Refiners* context, this would have meant that they would attempt to show the wide range of octane levels among marketed gasolines, general consumer ignorance of the ratings of specific brands, the waste of purchasing more octane than one's car engine requires, and, probably, the tendency of consumers, in the absence of information, to purchase more octane than their cars required.   On each of these issues the respondent would be entitled to present evidence and cross-examine the agency's witnesses.   Following the evidentiary hearing an administrative law judge, and ultimately the Commission, would have had to decide whether the facts found demonstrated a violation of the Act.   If the Commission concluded that they did, its decision would have been subject to judicial review, in the same fashion as the decisions of the NLRB.   The most important features of this process, from the respondent's viewpoint, were probably the assurance of an opportunity to present his own evidence and the right to cross-examine adverse witnesses on the central factual issues in the case.

What procedure could the Commission follow after adopting the octane-posting rule?   The basic procedural steps would remain unchanged, but the issues to be litigated would be narrowed significantly.   If any gasoline distributors failed to comply with the rule, the Commission would have to initiate the complaint, hearing, decision, and judicial review process previously outlined against each one. However, assuming the validity of its rule, the Commission would have only to show that the respondent had failed to comply—not that his omission of octane ratings was deceptive under section 5; the Commission would have established the necessary factual predicate for its judgment that such omission was deceptive in the original rule-making proceeding.   The respondent could of course present evidence and cross-examine on the issue of whether the required postings were made, but he would not be able to relitigate the factual premises of the rule.

Suppose that the FTC lacked authority to adopt binding rules but decided nonetheless to announce its intention to enforcement proceedings against every gasoline distributor who failed to post octane ratings?   This "interpretation" of section 5 by the expert agency responsible for its enforcement would undoubtedly elicit deference from the courts and probably engender voluntary compliance from *some* gasoline distributors, but in litigated cases the Commission could not rely on its "policy" to sustain its burden of proof or foreclose the introduction of contrary evidence by respondents.

Other interests may also have been at stake in *Petroleum Refiners*.   The very fact that the octane-posting rule would ease the Commission's burden of proof and narrow the issues to be litigated might reduce litigation.   Probably few gasoline distributors would be prepared to expend the resources necessary to defend a proceeding in which the central issue was the easily resolved: "Did you or did you not display the octane ratings required by the Commission's rule?" And though the FTC Act did not in 1974 provide penalties for past failure to comply with a Commission rule—by contrast with failure to comply with a cease-and-desist order—blatant defiance of a specific regulatory policy would have little appeal for many companies.   Furthermore, the opportunities for broad participation afforded by informal agency rulemaking, which Judge Wright applauds, may have been viewed skeptically by firms potentially subject to the FTC's requirements.

3. The Magnuson-Moss Warranty—Federal Trade Commission Improvement Act, 88 Stat. 2183, Pub. L. No. 93–637 (1975), made several important changes in the FTC's powers:

a. The amendments confirmed the agency's authority to adopt legislative rules implementing section 5's broad prohibition of unfair or deceptive acts or practices, and permitted it to sue to recover civil penalties for violations of such rules.

b. The amendments subjected FTC rulemaking to procedural requirements that include some trial-type features.   The agency was required, for example, to permit oral submissions, receive rebuttal testimony, and allow cross-examination on "disputed material facts" when "necessary for fair determination * * * of the rulemaking proceeding."

c. Finally, the 1975 amendments accorded FTC orders in adjudicatory proceedings enforcing section 5 a status akin to that of legislative rules, at least for some purposes.   Amended section 5 (m) (B) permits the FTC to enforce a final cease and desist order determining that a practice is unfair or deceptive against persons not parties to the original proceeding who thereafter engage in the practice "with actual knowledge that [it] * * * is unfair or deceptive and is unlawful. * * * "

4. The FTC's experience under the Magnuson-Moss amendments at least raises questions about Judge Wright's predictions of the advantages of rulemaking for implementation of Commission policy—though it casts no doubt on his understanding of the effects of adopted rules in adjudication.

It was 1977 before the Commission sought to use its congressionally-confirmed authority to adopt trade regulation rules defining and proscribing unfair practices.   By the end of the decade the agency had begun twenty rulemaking proceedings addressed to practices in a wide range of industries, including vocational schools, funeral services, used car sales, and the merchandising of prescription drugs, hearing aids, and home insulation.　However, only three of these proceedings had then been completed—one by the agency's withdrawal of its proposed rule.　See B. BOYER, REPORT ON THE TRADE REGULATION RULEMAKING PROCEDURES OF THE FTC (Executive Summary) (1979), in U.S. ADMINISTRATIVE CONFERENCE: RECOMMENDATIONS AND REPORTS 41 (1980).　Professor Boyer's report documents many of the problems that the Commission encountered in attempting to use this "new" authority, including lack of technical personnel, experience, and information.　A major impediment to completion of the rulemaking proceedings that the agency began was the statutory requirement for trial-type hearings on critical factual issues, a topic to which we shall return in Chapter 4, p. 422 infra.　The latter difficulties prompted the Administrative Conference to adopt a series of recommendations for the conduct of FTC rulemaking proceedings.　See *Recommendation 79–1: Hybrid Rulemaking Procedures of the Federal Trade Commission* (Adopted June 7–8, 1979), in U.S. ADMINISTRATIVE CONFERENCE: RECOMMENDATIONS AND REPORTS 3, 10 (1980).

The Commission encountered greater difficulties in the courts and, ultimately, in Congress.　Its first trade regulation rule to be reviewed was set aside in *Katherine Gibbs School v. FTC*, 612 F.2d 658 (2d Cir. 1979), *cert. denied* 628 F.2d 755 (1979), where the court concluded that the agency had failed to document that each of the practices its rule proscribed was "unfair" or "deceptive."　The Commission's next encounter with judicial review was also a disappointment, though less threatening to its basic authority.　See *American Optometric Association v. Federal Trade Commission*, 626 F.2d 896 (D.C. Cir. 1980).　As of 1984, no court of appeals had sustained a trade regulation rule adopted pursuant to the 1975 Magnuson-Moss amendments to the 1914 FTC Act.

Congress, however, had amended the Act to limit the impact of the FTC's quasi-legislative powers, and it had come close to enacting others that would exclude entire areas of business activity from the Commission's jurisdiction.　The Federal Trade Commission Improvements Act of 1980, Pub. L. No. 96–252, was the product of mounting congressional exasperation with the agency's attempts to regulate business practices in several sensitive areas—used car sales, funeral services, and sales of hearing aids, among others.　These were sensitive precisely because they involved so many locally-owned and managed enterprises located in every congressional district and effectively represented by national organizations.　The primary source materials for a study of the legislative reaction to what, by 1980, was perceived in Congress as bureaucratic overreaching are the trade journals circulated in Washington and *The Washington Post*.　One illustrative account of the lobbying effort is *Doctors, Dairymen Join in Effort to Clip the Talons of the FTC*, National Journal, August 18, 1982, at 1589.

In addition to curtailing the FTC's appropriations, limiting its reauthorization to two years, and demanding that it demonstrate that any trade practice to be proscribed by rule be "prevalent" within the industry, the 1980 Amendments' major change was to subject Commission rules to a one-house Congressional veto. This provision was, of course, later imperiled by the Supreme Court's decision in *Chadha*, and then expressly invalidated in *Consumers Union v. Federal Trade Commission*, 691 F.2d 575 (D.C. Cir. 1982), *affirmed* ___U.S.___, 103 S.Ct. 3556 (1983).

The FTC has never made extensive use of what might have been an even more controversial authority conferred by the Magnuson-Moss Amendments—

the authority to enforce as "rules," against respondents with actual notice, the principles embodied in cease and desist orders issued in earlier adjudications. See Comment, *Federal Trade Commission Improvements Act Section 5(m)(1)(B): Minimum Alterations to Preserve Constitutionality*, 1981 Ariz. St. L. J. 1029.

2. FDA IMPLEMENTATION OF THE 1962 DRUG AMENDMENTS

The *Petroleum Refiners* case illustrates how an agency can use rulemaking both to establish uniform policy and to narrow the scope of adjudications when that policy is implemented.   In this section we examine, through a case study, one agency's efforts to apply this learning to solve the special problems confronting it.   The case study features the U.S. Food and Drug Administration, an executive agency within the Department of Health and Human Services (at the time the Department of Health, Education, and Welfare).   In 1962 Congress enacted legislation requiring that all "new drugs" be proved effective as well as safe before marketing.   The FDA's efforts over more than two decades to implement that requirement illuminate the interaction between an agency's power to make general rules and its obligation to dispose of individual disputes on the basis of a hearing record.

The Regulatory Scheme for Therapeutic Drugs

The statutory authority for the FDA regulation of therapeutic drugs is the much-amended 1938 Food, Drug, and Cosmetic Act, 21 U.S.C.A. § § 321 *et seq*.   Since the original Pure Food and Drugs Act of 1906, federal legislation in this area has followed a standard framework: Congress has prohibited the distribution in interstate commerce of products that are "adulterated" or "misbranded," and then set out a series of detailed definitions of adulteration and misbranding.   The 1906 Act was exclusively a policing statute; it prohibited the marketing of adulterated or misbranded products and authorized court enforcement proceedings against either the offending products or against the persons responsible for their distribution.   The Act contained no requirements for premarketing review of the safety, effectiveness, or labeling of any product.

The current statute retains many features of the original 1906 law.   It provides three types of judicial sanctions: seizure of the offending product, injunction against its manufacture or shipment, and criminal prosecution.   The FDA does not, however, have independent authority to initiate court proceedings; it must proceed through local U.S. Attorneys who are agents of the Department of Justice.   For a general treatment of the dynamics of this typical bifurcation of federal enforcement authority, see discussion pp. 163–72 supra.   While the 1938 Act did not change the penal character of the original law for most products within FDA jurisdiction, it fundamentally altered federal regulation of therapeutic drugs by imposing a system of premarketing administrative review of their safety, i.e., a form of licensing.

* * * The crux of the premarketing review scheme was the designation of certain drugs as "new drugs."   A new drug was defined as one not generally recognized by experts "as safe for use under the conditions prescribed, recommended, or suggested in the labeling thereof" or one which had become generally recognized as safe but "which [had] not * * * been used to a material extent or for a material time."   In order for a new drug to be marketed, it had to be the subject of an "effective" (not disapproved) new drug application (NDA) * * * .   Such an application was required to include a list of components, a report of investigations verifying the drug's safety, specimens of the proposed labeling, and a description of the methods of manufacture.

An NDA would become "effective" automatically after 60 days unless positive steps were taken to refuse approval. * * * Approval could be refused if, after notice and opportunity for hearing, the [FDA] determined that the application contained inadequate data to establish that the drug was safe, failed to establish that the drug was safe, or established that the drug was unsafe. * * *

Note, *Drug Efficacy and the 1962 Drug Amendments*, 60 Geo, L. J. 185, 187–89 (1971).   The 1938 Act required premarketing proof only of the safety of new drugs; the fact that a drug had not been shown to be effective for any condition could not be a basis for FDA disapproval.   (If the manufacturer later made false claims for the drug, the FDA could proceed in court by seizure, injunction, or prosecution.)   Because all drugs are biologically active, few could ever be considered wholly benign, and therefore the FDA often took note of a drug's efficacy when evaluating its safety.   For, if a drug's pharmacological effects did not have some therapeutic value the agency could hardly find that it was "safe" for its intended use.   The agency did not officially rule on effectiveness, however, nor did it prescribe the kinds of clinical studies a drug's sponsor might or should conduct to confirm its utility.   Thus many pre-1962 drugs came on the market without thorough examination of their effectiveness.

The 1962 Amendments grew out of Senator Estes Kefauver's lengthy investigation of the pricing and promotion practices of the pharmaceutical industry.   Kefauver's own bill, which was aimed at reducing the high prices of prescription drugs, was stalled in Congress when Americans first heard about Thalidomide.   This tranquilizer was reported to be responsible for grotesque deformities in babies born to many European women who had taken it during pregnancy.   Though Thalidomide never received marketing approval in this country, the alarming reports from Europe revived Congressional interest in prescription drugs.   The resulting statutory amendments dealt primarily with the testing and approval of new drugs, and clearly subordinated Kefauver's original objective of reducing prices.

The principal change made by Congress in 1962 was to require premarketing proof of the effectiveness as well as the safety of new drugs. The "new drug" definition was expanded to comprise drugs not generally recognized as safe *and effective*.   In addition, the amendments required the FDA's affirmative approval before a drug could be marketed.   The FDA was directed to refuse approval of an NDA if, after notice and opportunity for hearing, it determined that "there is a lack of substantial evidence that the drug will have the effect it purports or is represented to have * * * ."   And the agency was similarly directed to withdraw approval of any drug after notice and opportunity for hearing if it found that, "on the basis of new information," substantial evidence of its efficacy was lacking.   The history of the 1962 Drug Amendments is vividly depicted in R. HARRIS, THE REAL VOICE (1964); P. TEMIN, TAKING YOUR MEDICINE: DRUG REGULATION IN THE UNITED STATES (1980).

The major problems that confronted FDA following passage of the 1962 Amendments stemmed from the new effectiveness standard and the procedures for withdrawal of approval of previously approved NDA's. An understanding of FDA's problems requires familiarity with the statutory provision that contains both of these requirements, section 505 of the Act, 21 U.S.C.A. § 355, which reads in pertinent part as follows:

(a) No person shall introduce or deliver for introduction into interstate commerce any new drug, unless an approval of an application * * * is effective with respect to such drug.   * * *

(c) Within one hundred and eighty days after the filing of an application under this subsection, or such additional period as may be agreed upon by the Secretary and the applicant, the Secretary shall either—

(1) approve the application if he then finds that none of the grounds for denying approval specified in subsection (d) applies, or

(2) give the applicant notice of an opportunity for a hearing before the Secretary under subsection (d) on the question whether such application is approvable.

(d) If the Secretary finds, after due notice to the applicant in accordance with subsection (c) * * * and giving him an opportunity for a hearing, in accordance with said subsection, that (1) the investigations * * * do not include adequate tests by all methods reasonably applicable to show whether or not such drug is safe for use under the conditions prescribed, recommended, or suggested in the proposed labeling thereof; (2) the results of such tests show that such drug is unsafe for use * * * or do not show that such drug is safe for use; * * * or (5) evaluated on the basis of the information submitted to him as part of the application and any other information before him with respect to such drug, there is lack of substantial evidence that the drug will have the effect it purports or is represented to have under the conditions of use prescribed, recommended, or suggested in the proposed labeling thereof * * * he shall issue an order refusing to approve the application. * * * As used in this subsection and subsection (e) * * * the term "substantial evidence" means evidence consisting of adequate and well-controlled investigations, including clinical investigations, by experts qualified by scientific training and experience to evaluate the effectiveness of the drug involved, on the basis of which it could fairly and responsibly be concluded by such experts that the drug will have the effect it purports or is represented to have under the conditions of use prescribed, recommended, or suggested in the labeling or proposed labeling thereof.

(e) The Secretary shall, after due notice and opportunity for hearing to the applicant, withdraw approval of an application with respect to any drug under this section if the Secretary finds (1) that clinical or other experience, tests, or other scientific data show that such drug is unsafe for use * * * ; (2) that new evidence * * * shows that such drug is not shown to be safe for use * * * ; or (3) on the basis of new information before him with respect to such drug, evaluated together with the evidence available to him when the application was approved, that there is a lack of substantial evidence that the drug will have the effect it purports or is represented to have under the conditions of use prescribed, recommended, or suggested in the labeling thereof. * * *

These arcane statutory provisions convey little of the true nature of the process the FDA follows or the judgment it makes when it decides whether to approve or withdraw approval of a new drug. In essence, the agency attempts to determine whether a drug's therapeutic benefits outweigh its potential risks. Though the system relies heavily on scientific evidence, the FDA's decision is necessarily judgmental; neither benefits nor risks can be forecast precisely on the basis of the sorts of clinical tests that are conducted prior to marketing. The process is further complicated by the necessity of devising labeling that will permit physicians to use a drug in conditions for which it is effective and enable them to avoid administering it for uses that involve the greatest risks. See generally Merrill, *Compensation for Prescription Drug Injuries*, 59 Va. L. Rev. 1, 9–12 (1973).

Section 505 likewise provides little insight into the FDA's procedures for handling NDA's. The new drug approval process is essentially consensual and, because much of the information involved is proprietary, largely closed to public scrutiny. Typically, it involves many exchanges of correspondence and several meetings between FDA staff and the manufacturer in which agency officials demand additional information, the manufacturer attempts to respond to questions, and both sides bargain over the language of final labeling. No public announcement is made of the filing of applications, nor may any third party participate in the process or examine the data that a manufacturer submits. Notably, since 1962 the FDA has held only three hearings on a refusal to approve a drug, one in response to a court order, *Edison Pharmaceutical Co. v. Food and Drug Administration*, 513 F.2d 1063 (D.C. Cir. 1975), and only Edison challenged the agency's post-hearing ruling in court. The agency and the applicant generally reach agreement on conditions for the release of a drug for which a formal NDA has been filed; when the agency appears unlikely to be persuaded, the applicant typically never submits a completed NDA.

The NAS-NRC Efficacy Review

In section 505(e) Congress not only instructed the FDA to demand proof of efficacy for drugs subsequently developed but also directed it, after a two-year grace period (§ 107(c)(3), 76 Stat. 7880–89 (1962)), to withdraw approved NDA's for which "substantial evidence" was lacking. Those directives confronted the FDA with an enormous task. The agency's resources were fully extended in evaluating the more than 100 NDA's submitted annually; a retrospective review of all drugs marketed prior to

1962 was beyond its capacity.   Between 1938 and 1962 some 7,000 drug formulations had acquired NDA's, and approximately 4,000 of these remained on the market.   Furthermore, tens of thousands of products which essentially copied the formulas of NDA'd drugs, so-called "me too" products, had entered the market without FDA review of any kind.   Accordingly, the agency went outside for assistance.   In June 1966 it signed a contract with the National Academy of Sciences-National Research Council (NAS-NRC) to undertake the retrospective review of all previously licensed drugs.   The review was performed by thirty panels of experts appointed by the Academy, most of them physicians affiliated with academic institutions.   Technically, their assessments were to be only advisory.

At the outset, the NAS-NRC defined six categories in which the panels were to place each claim of effectiveness made for a drug: (1) effective; (2) probably effective; (3) possibly effective; (4) ineffective; (5) "effective, but"—a rating devised for drugs for which better, safer, or more convenient substitutes existed; and (6) "ineffective as a fixed combination." The panels varied in their use of the ratings, but most of them interpreted the statutory standard of substantial evidence as exceedingly exacting. For many drug indications they found no evidence based on "adequate and well-controlled investigations."   For many drugs recognized as effective by physicians but for which supporting clinical investigations were lacking, the panels liberally assigned ratings as "probably" or "possibly effective."

The NAS-NRC transmitted the panels' ratings to the FDA from October 1967 through midsummer 1968.   Including multiple dosage forms and sizes, the panels reviewed almost 4,000 drug formulations and more than 16,000 claims, rating them as follows:

Rating	Number of claims	Percent of claims
Ineffective	2,442	14.7
Possibly effective	5,778	34.9
Probably effective	1,204	7.3
Effective	3,159	19.1
Effective, but	3,990	24.0
	16,573	100.0

Since only the FDA could rule definitively on the sufficiency of the evidence for a drug's efficacy, it undertook to review the NAS-NRC findings for each drug, and only then released its own findings along with a synopsis of the panel's evaluations.   As it received the panels' reports, however, the agency began to realize that implementation of their ratings would present major difficulties.   The FDA's initial attempt to withdraw an approved NDA based on the NAS-NRC findings was delayed by litigation. See *USV Pharmaceutical Corp. v. Richardson*, 461 F.2d 223 (4th Cir. 1972).   It then turned its attention to the Upjohn Company's drug, Panalba, a fixed dosage combination of two antibiotics whose annual sales in 1968 exceeded $20 million.   The Panalba case became a test of the agency's ability to discharge its responsibility to apply the effectiveness standard to pre-1962 drugs.

The FDA concurred in the NAS-NRC panel's finding that Panalba was ineffective as a fixed combination and gave notice of its intent to withdraw the drug's approval after affording Upjohn thirty days to submit additional data. Testimonial letters supporting Panalba, some inspired by the company, poured into the agency from doctors all around the country. Concluding that these testimonials did not qualify as "substantial evidence," the FDA in May, 1969, published an order declaring its intention to withdraw approval of the drug and providing that anyone adversely affected could submit objections which, if supported by reasonable grounds, could require a hearing. But the order stipulated that any demand for a hearing had to identify the adequate and well-controlled studies that supported Panalba's efficacy.

Upjohn promptly requested a hearing and proferred some fifty studies. When the FDA delayed ruling on its request, Upjohn brought suit contending that it was entitled to a hearing as a matter of right and that, in any case, the FDA should rule on the adequacy of its objections before taking final action. In a confusing opinion, *Upjohn Co. v. Finch*, 303 F. Supp. 241 (W. D. Mich. 1969), the district court found in the company's favor. The court was obviously influenced by the FDA's refusal to release the names of the members of the NAS-NRC panel that had evaluated Panbalba and by the drug's enormous popularity among practicing physicians. Almost simultaneously, the FDA lost a similar suit brought by the manufacturer of another fixed combination antibiotic drug. *American Home Products Corp. v. Finch*, 303 F. Supp. 448 (D. Del. 1969).

Thus, in mid-summer of 1969, the FDA saw its efforts to implement the NAS-NRC efficacy review stalled. Manufacturers had shown little inclination to cease marketing commercially successful drugs that the panels had rated less than effective. One court had intimated that a showing of the kind made for Panalba—consisting of favorable endorsements in the medical literature and a record of long use among practicing physicians—ought to suffice to obtain a hearing. And in such a hearing the agency would likely be unable to avoid protracted inquiry into the reliability and import of all the data submitted by manufacturers, which had strong incentives for delay. At the same time, Congressional pressure was building on the agency to speed up its long-delayed implementation of the NAS-NRC evaluations.

Following the *Upjohn* decision, the FDA ruled that the company's objections did not demonstrate the "reasonable grounds" expressly required by the Act for an evidentiary hearing on the withdrawal of an antibiotic. See 21 U.S.C.A. § 357(c). And on September 19, 1969, it issued a final order denying an evidentiary hearing and ordering Panalba withdrawn. Simultaneously, the agency published new regulations, effective immediately, requiring a showing of "reasonable grounds" to obtain a hearing on the withdrawal of any NDA and specifying in detail the "adequate and well-controlled investigations" that would have to be presented to establish such grounds. The agency believed that these regulations would help it avoid lengthy formal hearings on the withdrawal of drugs whose effectiveness was supported solely by the subjective endorsements of practicing physicians.

21 C.F.R. § 130.12(a)(5)

34 Fed. Reg. 14596–97 (1969).

(ii) The following principles have been developed over a period of years and are recognized by the scientific community as the essentials of adequate and well-controlled clinical investigations. They provide the basis for the determination whether there is "substantial evidence" to support the claims of effectiveness for "new drugs" and antibiotic drugs.

(a) The plan or protocol for the study must include the following:

(1) A clear statement of the objectives of the study.

(2) A method of selection of the subjects that provides for:
(i) Adequate confirmation of the disease state present, including criteria of diagnosis and appropriate confirmatory laboratory tests.
(ii) Assignment of the patients to test groups without bias.

(3) An outline of the methods of quantitation and observation of the parameters studied in the subjects.

(4) A description of the steps taken to document comparability of variables, such as age, sex, duration of disease and use of drugs other than those being studied.

(5) A description of the methods of recording and analyzing the patient response variables studied and the means of excluding or minimizing bias from the observations.

(6) A precise statement of the nature of the control group against which the effects of the new treatment modality can be compared. Three types of controlled comparisons are possible:

(i) Placebo control: The new drug entity may be compared quantitatively with an inactive placebo control. This type of study requires at the minimum that the patient not be able to distinguish between the active product and the placebo. Double binding, to include the clinical observer, may or may not be desirable, depending on the measurement system used to evaluate the results.

(ii) Active drug control: The new drug entity may be compared quantitatively with another drug known to be effective in situations where it is not ethical to deprive the subject of therapy. The same considerations to the level of "blinding" apply as with a placebo control study.

(iii) Historical control: In some circumstances, involving diseases with high and predictable mortality (acute leukemia of childhood) or with signs and symptoms of predictable duration or severity (fever in certain infections), the results of use of a new drug entity may be compared qualitatively with prior experience historically derived from the adequately documented natural history of the disease in comparable patients with no treatment or with treatment with an established **effective** therapeutic regimen.

(7) A summary of statistical methods used in analysis of the data derived from the subjects.

(b) For such an investigation to be considered adequate for consideration for approval of a new drug, it is required that the test drug be standardized as to identity, strength, quality, purity, and dosage form to give significance to the results of the investigation.

(iii) Uncontrolled studies or partially controlled studies are not acceptable evidence to support claims of effectiveness. A study is uncontrolled when there is no comparison study against which to evaluate the treatment results, or when such experimental factors as disease identity are not controlled.

(iv) A study is inadequately controlled when the criteria for patient selection are not adequately defined, investigator bias is not minimized, or an inadequately sensitive method of observation and evaluation of results is employed.

––––––

FDA's new regulations were promptly challenged by the Pharmaceutical Manufacturers Association, makers of more than 90 percent of all prescription drugs marketed in the U.S. In *Pharmaceutical Manufacturers Association v. Finch*, 307 F. Supp. 858 (D. Del. 1970), the court ruled that FDA had promulgated its criteria for clinical studies without notice and opportunity for public comment in violation of section 553 of the Administrative Procedure Act:

> The September regulations, which prescribe in specific detail, for the first time, the kinds of clinical investigations that will be deemed necessary to establish the effectiveness of existing and future drug products and which require that such evidence be submitted as a condition to avoiding summary removal from the market, are pervasive in their scope and have an immediate and substantial impact on the way PMA's members subject to FDA regulation, conduct their everyday business. * * *

> * * * [T]he Commissioner does not deny that compliance with the testing requirements of the September regulations will have a substantial and pervasive effect on the drug industry. Rather, the Commissioner argues that the testing standards of the September regulations are not new and that any burden imposed by them is the direct result of the "substantial evidence" of effectiveness requirements embodied in the 1962 amendments to the Act. * * *

> Despite this argument, the record is clear that the administrative practice applying the statutory standard to drugs marketed before 1962 has not uniformly insisted on evidence produced in accordance with the carefully controlled testing requirements of the September regulations. * * *

> * * * Many of the important issues now raised by PMA in this Court are matters which require thorough and expert consideration by the Commissioner. For example, PMA asserts that it would be difficult, if not impossible, to employ sufficient research investigators to perform the extensive testing required by the September regulations for all drug products currently marketed, especially because many trained clinicians are not interested in testing drugs which have been marketed for a long period of time and accepted by the medical profession as effective. Claims concerning the scarcity of

testing resourses, and their proper allocation among competing uses are, of course, matters requiring the special expertise and judgment of the Secretary and the Commissioner. * * * Determinations of such sensitivity and importance of course are for the Commissioner and not the Court. The existence of such important questions, however, certainly suggests that the Commissioner has the responsibility to fully inform himself concerning these and other important implications of the September regulations. * * *

307 F. Supp. at 864–66. Within a few weeks after this ruling the FDA republished its "adequate and well-controlled studies" regulations as a proposal for public comment. And in May 1970, following the receipt of public comments, the agency promulgated final regulations which closely resembled the original version. 35 Fed. Reg. 7251 (1970). The May 1970 regulations included the following language, as part of a new 21 C.F.R. § 130.14:

(a) The notice to the applicant of opportunity for a hearing on a proposal by the Commissioner to refuse to approve an application or to withdraw the approval of an application will specify the grounds upon which he proposes to issue his order. * * *

(b) If the applicant elects to avail himself of the opportunity for a hearing, he is required to file a written appearance requesting the hearing within 30 days after the publication of the notice and giving the reason why the application should not be refused or should not be withdrawn, together with a well-organized and full-factual analysis of the clinical and other investigational data he is prepared to prove in support of his opposition to the notice of opportunity for a hearing. A request for a hearing may not rest upon mere allegations or denials, but must set forth specific facts showing that there is a genuine and substantial issue of fact that requires a hearing. When it clearly appears from the data in the application and from the reasons and factual analysis in the request for the hearing that there is no genuine and substantial issue of fact which precludes the refusal to approve the application or the withdrawal of approval of the application, e.g., no adequate and well-controlled clinical investigations to support the claims of effectiveness have been identified, the Commissioner will enter an order on this data, making findings and conclusions on such data. * * *

FDA's repromulgated regulations were then upheld against substantive challenge in *Pharmaceutical Manufacturers Association v. Richardson*, 318 F. Supp. 301 (D. Del. 1970).

Even before this later ruling, the Sixth Circuit had rejected Upjohn's appeal from the FDA's September 1969 order withdrawing approval of Panalba. *Upjohn Co. v. Finch*, 422 F.2d 944 (6th Cir. 1970). The court upheld the criteria the agency had used in evaluating Upjohn's evidence in support of its request for a hearing. The court concluded that, at least as applied to Upjohn, the September regulations were not procedurally defective, for the company had ample warning of the FDA's position and opportunity to provide the evidence called for.

Having thus established the validity of its criteria for "adequate and well-controlled clinical investigations," the FDA systematically commenced proceedings to withdraw approval of many of the drugs rated "ineffective" by the NAS-NRC review panels. When an NDA holder sought an evidentiary hearing, the agency invariably found that its supporting evidence failed to satisfy the regulations and summarily withdrew marketing approval. This approach was upheld by the Second Circuit. See *Pfizer, Inc. v. Richardson*, 434 F.2d 536 (2d Cir. 1970); *Ciba-Geigy Corp. v. Richardson*, 446 F.2d 466 (2d Cir. 1971).

By the end of 1971 the FDA had disposed of several dozen requests for hearings on drugs evaluated by the NAS-NRC as "ineffective." In no instance had it found a manufacturer's objections and supporting data sufficient to require a hearing. One explanation, of course, is that the agency's substantial evidence regulations embodied requirements for clinical investigations that few, if any, pre-1962 studies could meet. But it was also obvious that a manufacturer would have to make a very strong showing to persuade the FDA to expend the time and resources even one hearing would require.

Legal Impediments to FDA Implementation

HYNSON, WESTCOTT AND DUNNING, INC. v. RICHARDSON

United States Court of Appeals, Fourth Circuit, 1972.
461 F.2d 215.

DONALD RUSSELL, CIRCUIT JUDGE.

The appellant * * * seeks review of a final order withdrawing marketing approval (NDA) of the drug Lutrexin. * * * The appellant alleges error * * * (1) for failure to sustain its claim of exemption from withdrawal * * * and, if this claim of exemption is overruled, (2) for denial of a hearing, as required under the applicable statute, on its showing of effectiveness. We reverse.

* * *

* * * [T]he appellant did * * * submit a considerable amount of clinical medical studies and investigations * * * for its product by way of compliance with the new regulations. The Commissioner, however, dismissed the appellant's request for a hearing on the basis of such showing, finding * * * that its showing of effectiveness was insufficient to demonstrate a "genuine and material issue of fact" under the test of "substantial evidence" as defined in the Amendments. On [that] basis * * * it withdrew the approved NDA for Lutrexin. It is from this order that appeal has been taken. * * *

The crucial issue in this case * * * revolves about the requirement in the Act that, before the entry of a final order of withdrawal, the applicant be given an "opportunity for hearing." At such a hearing, the procedure adopted by the Commissioner allows the applicant to "produce evidence and arguments to show why approvals of (its drugs) * * * should not be withdrawn." Of course, the Commissioner might, as he did by his regulations issue in 1970, provide for the denial of a hearing where it clearly appeared from the applicant's own showing there was no "genuine and substantial issue of fact" on which the claim of the applicant might be sustained. * * * But, in applying this regulation and in making his determination thereunder, the Commissioner's discretion is not absolute. Neither due process nor the Administrative Practice Act permits an arbitrary denial in any case where it can be fairly said there are "genuine and substantial issues of fact" in dispute. Such a denial would, in addition, be violative of the Congressional purpose expressed in the provision for a hearing. * * * Accordingly, only if it can be fairly said that the clinical tests and medical studies and investigations submitted by the applicant, if credited and accepted, will not support a finding that they provide "substantial evidence" of effectiveness was it proper for the Commissioner to deny the appellant a hearing before entering a final order of withdrawal. The judicial test is somewhat the converse of that to be applied in a review of a decision of the Commissioner entered *after* a hearing. In that instance, his decision is to be upheld if sustained by any substantial evidence. But in determining whether the Commissioner acted within the limits of his discretion on the procedural question of whether a hearing is to be allowed, the test is whether there is any "genuine and substantial" evidence that supports the position of the applicant. * * *

Applying the foregoing principles, we are of opinion the showing of the appellant was such that, under a reasonable construction of the Commissioner's own regulations, as well as under familiar principles of due process, and the requirements of the Administrative Procedure Act, it was entitled to an impartial hearing before its NDA was withdrawn. It must be noted that no qualified expert has given an opinion that Lutrexin is ineffective for the uses intended. The NAS-NRC review concluded it was "possibly effective." Neither is there any contention that it is unsafe when used for the purposes intended. The real basis for the determination by the Commissioner that the appellant had failed to make a showing of any genuine issue of fact on the effectiveness of its drug was the conclusion that the various scientific articles and tests submitted by the appellant were not "adequate and well-controlled clinical investigations" within the statutory definition of "substantial evidence." * * * In making that statement, he disregards the categorical opinion of his former Director of the Bureau of Medicine and Medical Director that the clinical tests and investigations submitted by the appellant represented " 'well-controlled' clinical studies." He proceeds to fault two investigations published in an authoritative medical journal, submitted by the appellant, because, "There is no way to determine the percentage of patients on concurrent medication or whether the results of the study were thereby influenced," and "There is no summary or explanation of the statistical methods used in analysis of the data to show that results were not biased or due to chance." Another unpublished investigation is dismissed because, "Substantiating documentation to establish an historical control and percentage of patients with medical or surgical complications of pregnancy is not provided." Two published studies by a clinical professor of Obstetrics at the University of Illinois are criticized, in one instance, because "The report does not state the method of patient selection" and "Concomitant medication is not excluded" and, in the other, because "The method of selection of the patients does not show progressive dilation of the cervix, which is necessary to accurately diagnose premature labor." Assuming that all the objections by the Commissioner to these clinical studies, conducted as they were by competent medical authorities, may have some validity, they do not justify a final conclusion, made *ex parte*, without a hearing, that it "clearly appears" that there is no genuine issue of fact on the effectiveness of Lutrexin, which is the test under the Commissioner's own regulation for denial of a hearing; at most, they merely create a genuine question of fact to be resolved at a hearing upon proper evidence. Whether the studies were as controlled as they might have been and whether there was a failure in these studies as published to fill in all the details the Commissioner might think appropriate are matters that could be developed at a hearing, after the authors were examined and the reliability of the investigations further inquired into.

The order of the Commissioner, from which this appeal is taken, is set aside. * * *

Notes

1. *USV Pharmaceutical Corp. v. Secretary of HEW*, 466 F.2d 455, 460–61 (D. C. Cir. 1972), took an even dimmer view of the FDA's power to award itself summary judgment. While reversing the agency's summary withdrawal of USV's line of citrus bioflavonoid drugs (CVP) the court said:

> The Commissioner acted pursuant to 21 C.F.R. § 130.14, the regulation establishing a summary judgment procedure for the Food and Drug Administration. This regulation is modeled after Rule 56 of the Federal Rules of Civil Procedure, the summary judgment rule of the federal district courts. As counsel for the government stated at oral argument, the agency's procedure is analogous to the procedure under Rule 56. A vital distinction, however, is that the Commissioner here was not an impartial arbiter of the contentions of opposing parties, but was himself the moving party undertaking to support his own proposed order. * * * In this situation we think it was incumbent upon the Commissioner, before calling upon the petitioner for additional evidence establishing a right to a hearing, to state facts and reasons showing at least prima facie that the evidence before him raised no material issue of fact which would justify a hearing. This view of the Commissioner's burden is consistent with the practice under Rule 56 of the Federal Rules of Civil Procedure. Under that rule the moving party has the burden of presenting evidence that establishes his right to summary judgment as a matter of law; and he may not, by the bare assertion that he is entitled to summary judgment, shift to his opponent the burden of establishing the contrary.

> At no stage of this proceeding did the Commissioner present anything approaching a prima facie showing that there was no genuine and substantial issue of fact requiring a hearing. The reports of the NAS-NRC panels which we have quoted, and upon which the Commissioner relied in his notice of January 23, 1968, were cryptic and conclusory, without any statement of supporting facts. The Commissioner's notice of January 23, 1968 and his notice of July 10, 1968 parroted the language of the statute without reference to any evidence. In short, at no time did the Commissioner set forth the facts and reasons upon which he relied in reaching his conclusion that no material issue of fact existed. We think that such an application of the Commissioner's

summary judgment rule is not in harmony with the principle of the rule and is fundamentally unsound and unfair. * * *

2. At least equally disconcerting to the FDA was the decision in *Bentex Pharmaceuticals, Inc. v. Richardson*, 463 F.2d 363 (4th Cir. 1972). There, instead of waiting for the FDA to withdraw approval, the manufacturer had sought a declaratory judgment, in a district court that its product was not a "new drug." The agency moved to dismiss claiming that it had "primary jurisdiction" to determine both new drug status and the applicability of "grandfather clause" exemption. As the court of appeals explained:

> The District Court sustained the right of the plaintiffs to maintain a suit for a declaratory judgment and the jurisdiction of the Court in such action to determine judicially whether the products of the plaintiffs were "new drugs," on the effective date of the Amendments, and whether they were or were not entitled to the benefits of the "grandfather clause." However,—and this is the nub of the controversy between the parties on this appeal—it concluded that the Secretary had concurrent jurisdiction to determine whether plaintiffs' products were "new drugs," requiring pre-marketing clearance, and that, because of the greater expertise of the Secretary in the field, it deferred to the Secretary's assumed jurisdiction to determine whether the drugs of the plaintiffs came within the exemption provided by the "grandfather clause." * * *

> * * * Contrary to the conclusion of the District Court, we conclude that the Act confers no such jurisdiction on the Secretary, and, therefore, is no basis for any deference by that Court to the concurrent jurisdiction of the Secretary.

> The FDA has neither primary jurisdiction, as the defendants argue, nor concurrent jurisdiction, as the District Court concluded, to adjudicate whether a product is an old or a new drug. It may, in its prosecutorial role, reach a conclusion that a product being marketed is a "new drug" requiring pre-marketing approval; but that opinion is not adjudicatory, it is only the basis on which the FDA, as the prosecutor or initiator of either a seizure or injunctive action in the District Court, may invoke the jurisdiction of that Court to determine, among other issues, whether the drug challenged is a "new drug." There is manifestly no provision in the Act for an administrative proceeding before the Secretary to compel the filing of a "new drug" application or to halt the marketing of a drug for which there is no approval by the Secretary. It is not without significance that so far as the official reports reflect, the Secretary has never attempted directly to exercise such jurisdiction. * * * [T]he halting of the marketing of a drug, for which there is no NDA, may not be by administrative action but must be by an injunction or an *in rem* seizure proceeding, in which the Secretary appears, not in a judicial but in a prosecutorial role. Those are the procedures prescribed and available to the Government under the Act. The Secretary, it is true, has offered to provide "advice" on whether a product meets the qualification of an old drug but he categorizes his action in such instances as merely "advice" and makes no claim of finality therefor. Nor is there, as we have already observed, any provision for judicial review of such "advice." The only adjudicatory right vested by the Act in the Secretary relates to approval, or withdrawal of an approval, of a "new drug" application. * * *

The District Court, in finding concurrent jurisdiction, held that "This grant of authority to approve or withhold approval of new drug application, * * * necessarily implies authority for F.D.A. to determine the threshold question of whether the article involved is a drug which required an approved new drug application for lawful interstate shipment." This reasoning assumes that an application for approval by the Secretary under the Act poses as its initial issue whether the product is a new drug. No such issue is posed by the application. The very filing of the application is a concession and recognition by the applicant-manufacturer that the article is a "new drug"; otherwise, there would be no reason to file the application. * * * The applicant makes the determination whether his product is a "new drug" and whether he must file for pre-marketing clearance by the Secretary. And when filed, the application puts in issue only one question: Is the article safe and effective? That and that alone is the issue to be considered by the Secretary in connection with an application for approval filed by a manufacturer under Section 355(d). That issue is quite different from that presented when there is an issue whether a drug fits the statutory definition of "new drug" in the Act. The criterion for ascertaining whether a product is within the statutory definition of "new drug" under the Act is not safety and effectiveness *per se* * * * but "whether the government has shown by a preponderance of the evidence that the 'drug is not generally recognized, among experts qualified by scientific training and experience to evaluate the safety and effectiveness of drugs, as safe and effective for use under the conditions prescribed, recommended or suggested in the labeling thereof.' " That is an issue that must be and is resolved, sometimes with, and at other times without a jury, in practically every injunctive, seizure, or criminal proceeding under the Act. * * *

463 F.2d at 369–72.

The Attempt to Accelerate FDA Action

Not all suits sought to retard the FDA's implementation of the efficacy requirement. In *American Public Health Association v. Veneman*, 349 F. Supp. 1311, 1315–16 (D.D.C. 1972), the plaintiffs challenged (1) the FDA's failure to release the panel reports, (2) its delays in "noticing" drugs for NDA withdrawal after its preliminary determination that substantial evidence of efficacy was lacking, and (3) long delays in holding hearings and removing drugs from the market after a notice of proposed withdrawal. The district court rejected the agency's claim that these functions were "unreviewable," relying on language in section 505(e) which it interpreted as constraining the agency's discretion:

The statute states unequivocally that

The Secretary *shall* * * * withdraw approval of any application with respect to any drug under this section if the Secretary finds * * * that there is a lack of substantial evidence. * * *

Thus it could not be clearer that the Secretary *must* begin the procedures to withdraw a drug when he concludes that there is no substantial evidence of efficacy. The defendants contend that the many announcements which have been published in the Federal Register regarding FDA conclusions about the efficacy of various drugs are not findings by the agency and that the FDA is "not required by law to notice the cases [where a drug has been found less than effective] or press them to hearing immediately upon its announcement of the NAS-NRC findings and its concurrence. * * * It has discretion in the selection of cases to notice for hearing." This argument is unpersuasive in view of the clear language of the statute and regulations and the Congressional intent to rid the marketplace of ineffective drugs.

* * * Plaintiffs assert, and the defendants do not refute it, that for many drugs the FDA has published in the Federal Register the required notice of an opportunity for a hearing and that the manufacturers have failed to avail themselves of the opportunity for the hearing within the required 30 days; nevertheless the FDA has failed to withdraw these drugs from the market. In these circumstances, the withdrawal is both required by the statute and purely a ministerial duty, and failure to withdraw constitutes agency action unlawfully withheld.

In addition, plaintiffs contend that where drug manufacturers have requested a hearing, such hearings have been a long time in coming. * * * As the court reads 21 C.F.R. § 130.14(b), a hearing on withdrawal of a new drug application is to be scheduled as soon as practicable, and while such a provision confers some agency discretion in scheduling the hearing, interminable delay obviously is not contemplated. * * *

* * * The Congress * * * allowed a two-year grace period before the 1962 amendments were to become effective. * * * [I]t seems inappropriate for an agency to adopt procedures which extend the grace period far beyond that envisioned by the statute, and which effectively stay implementation of the Congressional mandate that drugs in the marketplace be both safe and effective.

The district court thereafter entered an order prescribing a detailed timetable for the FDA's implementation of the review of pre-1962 drugs. The order read in part:

II. Defendant shall proceed expeditiously, using available resources and personnel to the maximum extent feasible consistent with its other obligations under the law, to complete implementation of the drug effectiveness review with respect to human drugs as soon as possible.

III. Within 120 days from the date of this Order, defendants shall evaluate all NAS-NRC reports for drugs not previously evaluated, and publish in the Federal Register an evaluation of each product as "effective," or "less than effective." * * *

IV. Defendants shall, beginning immediately, proceed to implementation of the drug effectiveness review with respect to human prescription drugs classified as "ineffective," in accordance with the following procedures, priorities and time limitations:

A. For each drug * * * which is classified as "ineffective" a Notice of Opportunity for Hearing on a proposal to withdraw approval of the new drug application * * * for such drug shall be published in the Federal Register concurrently with the publication on that evaluation.

B. Within 60 days from the date of this Order, a Notice of Opportunity for Hearing shall be published for all drugs previously classified in an evaluation published in the Federal Register as "ineffective" but for which such a Notice has not yet been published, unless a review of new data or information results in reclassification of the drug. * * *

C. With respect to each drug previously classified as "ineffective" and for which a Notice of Opportunity for Hearing has already been published in the Federal Register, a final order shall be published in the Federal Register ruling on such Notice as follows:

(1) Within 60 days from the date of this Order, where no request for hearing has been filed in response to the Notice of Opportunity for Hearing within the statutory time limit or where a request for hearing is supported by no data or information whatever; and

(2) within 150 days from the date of this Order, where a request for hearing supported by data and information has been filed in response to such proposal.

D. Within 12 months of this Order, for a drug determined to be "ineffective" and for which a Notice of Opportunity for Hearing has been published * * * a final order shall be published in the Federal Register ruling upon such request for hearing. * * *

X. Defendants shall not grant an extension of time for any request for a hearing or other response to a Notice of Opportunity for Hearing. * * *

XIV. A limited number of drugs may remain on the market pending completion of scientific studies to determine effectiveness where there is a compelling justification of the medical need for the drug.   Such justification shall be made by Defendants in writing, shall be filed with the Court, and shall be available for public inspection. * * *

XVII. Six months after the date of this Order, and every six months thereafter until completion of the implementation of the drug effectiveness review, a report on the actions implementing this Order shall be submitted to this Court and shall be available for public inspection.

The *Veneman* court's demand that the FDA expedite implementation of the NAS-NRC review, coupled with the Fourth Circuit's refusal to uphold its primary jurisdiction in *Bentex* or its denial of a hearing in *Hynson*, prompted the FDA to pursue review in the Supreme Court.

WEINBERGER v. HYNSON, WESTCOTT AND DUNNING, INC.

Supreme Court of the United States, 1973.
412 U.S. 609, 93 S.Ct. 2469, 37 L.Ed.2d 207.

MR. JUSTICE DOUGLAS delivered the opinion of the Court.

* * *

Section 505(e) directs the FDA to withdraw approval of an NDA if the manufacturer fails to carry the burden of showing there is "substantial evidence" respecting the *efficacy* of the drug.   The Act and the Regulations, in their reduction of that standard to detailed guidelines, make the FDA's so-called administrative summary judgment procedure appropriate.

The general contours of "substantial evidence" are defined by § 505(d) of the Act to include "evidence consisting of adequate and well-controlled investigations, including clinical investigations, by experts qualified by scientific training and experience to evaluate the effectiveness of the drug involved, on the basis of which it could fairly and responsibly be concluded by such experts that the drug will have the effect it purports or is represented to have under the conditions of use prescribed, recommended, or suggested in the labeling or proposed labeling thereof."   Acting pursuant to his "authority to promulgate regulations for the efficient enforcement" of the Act, § 701(a), the Commissioner has detailed the "principles * * * recognized by the scientific community as the essentials of adequate and well-controlled clinical investigations.   They provide the basis for the determination whether there is 'substantial evidence' to support the claims of effectiveness for 'new drugs' * * * " * * *

Lower courts have upheld the validity of these regulations, and it is not disputed here that they express well-established principles of scientific investigation.   Moreover, their strict and demanding standards, barring anecdotal evidence indicating that doctors "believe" in the efficacy of a drug, are amply justified by the legislative history.   The hearings underlying the 1962 Act show a marked concern that impressions or beliefs of physicians, no matter how fervently held, are treacherous.   Congress in its definition of "substantial evidence" in § 505(d) wrote the requirement of "evidence consisting of adequate and well-controlled investigations."   The Senate Report makes clear that an abrupt departure was being taken from old norms for marketing drugs.   There had been mounting concern over *efficacy* of drugs as well as their safety.   The Report stated:

> "[A] claim could be rejected if it were found (a) that the investigations were not 'adequate'; (b) that they were not 'well controlled'; (c) that they had been conducted by experts not qualified to evaluate the effectiveness of the drug for which the application is made; or (d) that the conclusions drawn by such experts could not fairly and responsibly be derived from their investigations."

To be sure, the Act required the FDA to give "due notice and opportunity for hearing to the applicant" before it can withdraw its approval of an NDA.   FDA, however, by regulation, requires any applicant who desires a hearing to submit reasons "why the application * * * should not be withdrawn, together with a well-organized and full-factual analysis of the clinical and other investigational data he is prepared to prove in support of his opposition to the notice of opportunity for a hearing. * * * When it clearly appears from the data in the application and from the reasons and factual analysis in the request for the hearing that there is no genuine and substantial issue of fact * * * , e.g., no adequate and well-controlled clinical investigations to support the claims of effectiveness," the Commissioner may deny a hearing and enter an order withdrawing the application based solely on these data.   21 CFR § 130.14(b).   What the agency has said, then, is that it will not provide a formal hearing where it is apparent at the threshold that the applicant has not tendered *any* evidence which *on its face* meets the statutory standards as particularized by the regulations.

The propriety of such a procedure was decided in *United States v. Storer Broadcasting Co.*, 351 U.S. 192, 205, and *FPC v. Texaco*, 377 U.S. 33, 39. We said in *Texaco*:

> "[T]he statutory requirement for a hearing under § 7 [of the Natural Gas Act] does not preclude the Commission from particularizing statutory standards through the rulemaking process and barring at the threshold those who neither measure up to them nor show reasons why in the public interest the rule should be waived."

There can be no question that to prevail at a hearing an applicant must furnish evidence stemming from "adequate and well-controlled investigations." We cannot impute to Congress the design of requiring, nor does due process demand, a hearing when it appears conclusively from the applicant's "pleadings" that the application cannot succeed.[17]

The NAS-NRC panels evaluated approximately 16,500 claims made on behalf of the 4,000 drugs marketed pursuant to effective NDA's in 1962. Seventy percent of these claims were found not to be supported by substantial evidence of effectiveness, and only 434 drugs were found effective for all their claimed uses. If the FDA were required automatically to hold a hearing for each product whose efficacy was questioned by the NAS-NRC study, even though many hearings would be an exercise in futility, we have no doubt that it could not fulfill its statutory mandate to remove from the market all those drugs which do not meet the effectiveness requirements of the Act.

If this were a case involving trial by jury as provided in the Seventh Amendment, there would be sharper limitations on the use of summary judgment,[18] as our decisions reveal. But Congress surely has great leeway in setting standards for releasing on the public, drugs which may well be miracles or, on the other hand, merely easy money-making schemes through use of fraudulent articles labeled in mysterious scientific dress. The standard of "well-controlled investigations" particularized by the regulations is a protective measure designed to ferret out those drugs for which there is no affirmative, reliable evidence of effectiveness. The drug manufacturers have full and precise notice of the evi-

---

17. This applies, of course, only to those regulations that are precise. For example, the plan or protocol for a study must include "[a] summary of the methods of analysis and an evaluation of data derived from the study, including any appropriate statistical methods." A mere reading of the study submitted will indicate whether the study is totally deficient in this regard. Some of the regulations, however, are not precise, as they call for the exercise of discretion or subjective judgment in determining whether a study is adequae and well controlled. For example, § 130.12(a)(5)(ii)(a)(2)(i) requires that the plan or protocol for the study include a method of

selection of the subjects that provide "*adequate* assurance that they are suitable for the purposes of the study." (Emphasis added.) The qualitative standards "adequate" and "suitable" do not lend themselves to clear-cut definition, and it may not be possible to tell from the face of a study whether the standards have been met. Thus, it might not be proper to deny a hearing on the ground that the study did not comply with this regulation.

18. Under the Rules of Civil Procedure the party moving for summary judgment has the burden of showing the absence of a genuine issue as to any material fact.

dence they must present to sustain their NDA's, and under these circumstances we find the FDA hearing regulations unexceptionable on any statutory or constitutional ground.

Our conclusion that the summary judgment procedure of the FDA is valid does not end the matter, for Hynson argues that its submission to the FDA satisfied its threshold burden. In reviewing an order of the Commissioner denying a hearing, a court of appeals must determine whether the Commissioner's findings accurately reflect the study in question and if they do, whether the deficiencies he finds conclusively render the study inadequate or uncontrolled in light of the pertinent regulations.[19] There is a contrariety of opinion within the Court concerning the adequacy of Hynson's submission. Since a majority are of the view that the submission was sufficient to warrant a hearing, we affirm the Court of Appeals on that phase of the case.

* * *

* * * The Court of Appeals suggested that only a district court has authority to determine whether Lutrexin is a "new drug." The Government contends that the Commissioner has authority to determine new drug status in proceedings to withdraw approval of the product's new drug application (NDA) under § 505(e). Although Hynson agrees, some of the manufacturers, parties to other suits in this group of cases, advance the contrary view.

* * *

It is clear to us that the FDA has power to determine whether particular drugs require an approved NDA in order to be sold to the public. The FDA is indeed the administrative agency selected by Congress to administer the Act, and it cannot administer the Act intelligently and rationally unless it has authority to determine what drugs are "new drugs" under § 201(p) and whether they are exempt from the efficacy requirements of the 1962 amendments by the grandfather clause of § 107(c)(4).

* * *

Judgment affirmed.

MR. JUSTICE POWELL, concurring in part, and concurring in the result in part.

* * *

Insofar as the Court today sustains the holding below that Hynson's submission to the FDA raised "a genuine and substantial issue of fact" requiring a hearing on the ultimate issue of efficacy, I am in accord. Hyn-

---

19. Under the Administrative Procedure Act, a court reviews agency findings to determine whether they are supported by substantial evidence only in a case subject to the hearing provisions of 5 U.S.C.A. §§556 and 557 or "otherwise reviewed on the record of an agency hearing provided by statute * * * ." 5 U.S.C.A. § 706(2)(E). This is not such a case. The question with which we are concerned involves the initial agency determination whether a hearing is required by statute.

son's presentation in support of the efficacy of Lutrexin clearly justified a hearing as to whether the drug was supported by "adequate and well-controlled investigations," even as that term is defined in the Commission's regulations. For this reason I concur in the result reached in this case. I cannot agree on this record, however, with any implications or conclusions in the Court's opinion to the effect that the regulations—as construed and applied by the Commissioner in this case—are either compatible with the statutory scheme or constitutional under the Due Process Clause.[1] Such questions have not been squarely presented here and, in light of the Court's conclusion that Hynson has complied with the regulations, their resolution is unnecessary to the Court's decision.

Were we required to reach these issues, there might well be serious doubt whether the Commissioner's rigorous threshold specifications as to proof of "adequate and well-controlled investigations," coupled with his restrictive summary judgment regulation, go beyond the statutory requirements and in effect frustrate the congressional mandate for a pre-withdrawal "opportunity for hearing." There is also a genuine issue of procedural due process where, as in this case, the Commissioner construes his regulations to deny a hearing as to the efficacy of a drug established and used by the medical profession for two decades, and where its effectiveness is supported by a significant volume of clinical data and the informed opinions of experts whose qualifications are not questioned.

These important and complex questions should await decision in future cases in which the issues are briefed fully and are necessary to the Court's decision.

WEINBERGER v. BENTEX PHARMACEUTICALS, INC.

Supreme Court of the United States, 1973.
412 U.S. 645, 93 S.Ct. 2448, 37 L.Ed.2d 235.

MR. JUSTICE DOUGLAS delivered the opinion of the Court.

* * *

* * * [The Circuit] court in holding that FDA has no jurisdiction to determine the "new drug" status of a drug, stated that the question of "new drug" status is never presented when an application of a manufacturer for approval is filed. Parties, of course, cannot confer jurisdiction; only Congress can do so. The line sought to be drawn by the Court of Appeals is FDA action on NDAs pursuant to § 505(e) on the one hand and the question of "new drug" determination on the other. We can discern no such jurisdictional line under the Act. The FDA, as already stated, may deny an NDA where there is a lack of "substantial evidence" of the

---

1. Cf. *Fuentes v. Shevin*, 407 U.S. 67, 80, (1972), and cases cited therein. I do not question, of course, the authority of the Commissioner to adopt reasonable regulations consistent with the statute and which do not, as applied, deprive persons of their property without the elementary due process of a fair opportunity for a hearing.

drug's effectiveness, based as we have outlined on clinical investigation by experts. But the "new drug" definition under § 201(p) encompasses a drug "not generally recognized, among experts qualified by scientific training and experience to evaluate the safety and effectiveness of drugs, as safe and effective for use." Whether a particular drug is a "new drug," depends in part on the expert knowledge and experience of scientists based on controlled clinical experimentation and backed by substantial support in scientific literature. One function is not peculiar to judicial expertise, the other to administrative expertise. The two types of cases overlap and strongly suggest that Congress desired that the administrative agency make both kinds of determinations. Even where no such administrative determination has been made and the issue arises in a district court in enforcement proceedings, it would be commonplace for the court to await an appropriate administrative declaration before it acted. It may, of course, be true that in some cases general recognition that a drug is efficacious might be made without the kind of scientific support necessary to obtain approval of an NDA. But as we indicate in the *Hynson* cases, the reach of scientific inquiry under both § 505(d) and under § 201 (p) is precisely the same.

We think that it is implicit in the regulatory scheme, not spelled out *in haec verba*, that FDA has jurisdiction to decide with administrative finality, subject to the types of judicial review provided, the "new drug" status of individual drugs or classes of drugs. The deluge of litigation that would follow if "me-too" drugs and OTC drugs had to receive *de novo* hearings in the courts would enure to the interests of manufacturers and merchants in drugs, but not to the interests of the public that Congress was anxious to protect by the 1962 amendments. * * * We are told that FDA is incapable of handling a caseload of more than perhaps 10 or 15 *de novo* judicial proceedings in a year. Clearly, if FDA were required to litigate, on a case-by-case basis, the "new drug" status of each drug now marketed, the regulatory scheme of the Act would be severely undermined, if not totally destroyed. Moreover, a case-by-case approach is inherently unfair because it requires compliance by one manufacturer while his competitors marketing similar drugs remain free to violate the Act. * * *

We conclude that the District Court's referral of the "new drug" and the "grandfather" issues to FDA was appropriate, as these are the kinds of issues peculiarly suited to initial determination by the FDA. As the District Court said: "Evaluation of conflicting reports as to the reputation of drugs among experts in the field is not a matter well left to a court without chemical or medical background." The determination whether a drug is generally recognized as safe and effective within the meaning of § 201 (p) (1) necessarily implicates complex chemical and pharmacological considerations. Threshold questions within the peculiar expertise of an administrative agency are appropriately routed to the agency, while the court holds its hand. * * *

Reversed.

Notes

1. Justice Douglas relies on *United States v. Storer Broadcasting Co.*, 351 U.S. 192, 205 (1956), and *FPC v. Texaco, Inc.*, 377 U.S. 33, 39 (1964), as supporting the FDA's "summary judgment" procedure. In *Storer* (also relied upon by Judge Wright in *Petroleum Refiners*) the Court upheld an FCC rule limiting the number of FM radio and television stations one person could own. Section 309 of the Communications Act of 1934 requires the Commission to grant a broadcast license if it finds that the "public interest, convenience, and necessity would be served" and entitles a license applicant to a "full hearing" before an application may be denied. The FCC proposed to reject, without a hearing, applications from persons who already owned the maximum number of stations authorized by its station ownership regulation. The regulation thus amounted to a ruling that the agency could not find that the "public interest, convenience, and necessity" would be served by the granting of additional broadcast authority to any such person. In sustaining this approach as consistent with the Act and Constitution, the Supreme Court observed:

> We agree with the contention of the Commission that a full hearing, such as is required by [§ 309], would not be necessary on all such applications. As the Commission has promulgated its Rules after extensive administrative hearings, it is necessary for the accompanying papers to set forth reasons, sufficient if true, to justify a change or waiver of the Rules. We do not think Congress intended the Commission to waste time on applications that do not state a valid basis for a hearing. * * *

In *Texaco*, the Court upheld a FPC regulation similarly restricting the opportunity for a hearing on applications by natural gas companies for certificates approving the sale of gas to interstate pipelines. The agency's regulation provided for summary rejection of contracts containing pricing provisions other than those it specifically identified as "permissible." Like the Communications Act, the Natural Gas Act required the FPC to set "for hearing" all producer applications for permission to supply natural gas.

The Court concluded, on the authority of *Storer*, that the FPC's approach was permissible:

> [T]he statutory requirement for a hearing under § 7 does not preclude the Commission from particularizing statutory standards through the rule making process and barring at the threshold those who neither measure up to them nor show reasons why in the public interest the rule should be waived.

2. In *Heckler v. Campbell*, supra p. 246, Justice Powell finds support in *Storer* and *Texaco* for the SSA's so-called grid regulations. Does Powell's embrace of these precedents suggest he has abandoned the views stated in his *Hynson* dissent? Or do the FDA's "adequate and well-controlled studies" regulations operate differently than the SSA guidelines?

3. In both *Storer* and *Texaco* the Supreme Court called attention to language in the agencies' regulations permitting an applicant to seek a waiver from their terms, and implied that such restrictions on the availability of statutorily-mandated hearings might present a more difficult issue if they purported to prevent the agency from changing its mind when confronted by special circumstances. Judge Wright suggested in *Petroleum Refiners* that some opportunity had to be given respondents to show "special circumstances" justifying waiver of the

FTC's rule.   These judicial suggestions have prompted many agencies to include some form of waiver process or "escape clause" in their so-called "bright line" rules, and courts occasionally find that these waiver provisions have been applied arbitrarily.   See, e.g., *Matlovich v. Secretary of the Air Force*, 591, F.2d 852, 857 (D.C. Cir. 1978); *WAIT Radio v. FCC*, 418 F.2d 1153, 1157–59 (D.C. Cir. 1969). See generally Aman, *Administrative Equity: An Analysis of Exceptions to Administrative Rules*, 1982 Duke L. J. 277.

Yet by no means all rules permit waivers.   The FAA, for example, has for many years held that, "no person may serve as a pilot on an airplane engaged in [commercial] operations * * * if that person has reached his 60th birthday."   14 C.F.R. § 121.383 (c).   The Airline Pilots Association initially challenged the rule as depriving its members of property without due process.   The Second Circuit rejected this attack in *Air Line Pilots Association, Intl. v. Quesada*, 276 F.2d 892, 896 (2nd Cir. 1960).   For the court it was enough that the rule had been validly promulgated under the FAA's general rulemaking power and in conformity with the APA, and that the rule served a legitimate regulatory purpose.

Three more recent cases consider challenges to the FAA's refusal to recognize exceptions to the age 60 rule.   *Starr v. FAA*, 589 F.2d 307 (7th Cir. 1978); *Rombough v. FAA*, 594 F.2d 893 (2d Cir. 1979); *Gray v. FAA*, 594 F.2d 793 (10th Cir. 1979).   In each case the petitioner sought a waiver of the rule on the ground that he was completely healthy and posed no safety risk.   The FAA denied each request without considering any medical evidence proffered.   The court in *Starr*, relying on the same rationale that sustained the original rule, concluded that the Administrator could legitimately establish a "no exemption" policy.   589 F.2d at 312.   It agreed that the burden of evaluating waiver requests from each pilot as he turned sixty would undermine the agency's efficiency.   The court suggested, however, that the FAA might abuse its discretion if it failed to keep abreast of advances in methods for assessing pilot performance that could render the rule obsolete.   The courts in *Rombough* and *Gray* similarly refused to overturn the FAA's unwaivering adherence to its age 60 rule, as has the Congress.   See, e. g., *To Eliminate Age Limitations Presently Imposed on Certain Pilots of Aircraft*, Hearings Before the Subcomm. on Aviation of the House Comm. on Public Works and Transportation, 96th Cong., 1st Sess. (1979).   See also Comment, *Mandatory Retirement of Airline Pilots: An Analysis of the FAA's Age 60 Retirement Rule*, 33 Hastings L. J. 241 (1981); cf. Diver, *The Optimal Precision of Administrative Rules*, 93 Yale L. J. 65 (1983).

FDA's Subsequent Experience with Summary Judgment

The Supreme Court's ruling in *Hynson* that the FDA could, in appropriate cases, withdraw NDA's without a formal evidentiary hearing represented an important legal victory for the agency and appeared to promise major efficiencies in its effort to implement the 1962 effectiveness requirement.   The FDA has since withdrawn approval, without a hearing, for dozens of pre-1962 drugs that the NAS/NRC panels rated ineffective.   In most cases the NDA holders did not seek judicial review of the agency's "summary judgment."   When manufacturers did challenge its rulings that their evidence was not sufficient even to justify a hearing, however, the FDA began to discern some practical limits of the *Hynson* doctrine.

The *Hynson* case itself represented only a partial victory for the FDA, for a majority of the Court concluded that the studies submitted by the manufacturer were sufficient to require a hearing. Not surprisingly, the subsequent hearing resulted in a finding by the FDA Commissioner that Lutrexin had not been shown to be effective and the drug was ultimately withdrawn from the market in 1976—14 years after the enactment of the 1962 Drug Amendments. 41 Fed. Reg. 14406 (1976).

The FDA did not seek review of the *USV* decision because it had previously altered the practice to which the court had objected. The agency's subsequent notices of opportunity for a hearing continued merely to recite its concurrence with the NAS-NRC panel's rating and call attention to its "adequate and well-controlled studies" regulations. But in each final order denying a hearing the agency has provided a detailed critique of each of the studies relied on by the NDA holder. This exercise became increasingly onerous as the agency reached drugs for which there is extensive clinical evidence. The chore of explaining why studies fail to satisfy its regulations contributed to the delays that plagued FDA's drug effectiveness study implementation.

The first major test of the FDA's use of administrative summary judgment following *Hynson* came in *Cooper Laboratories, Inc. v. Commissioner,* 501 F.2d 772 (D.C. Cir. 1974), where the manufacturer challenged the agency's refusal to hold a hearing on the withdrawal of the NDA for the drug Protamide. Cooper argued that most of the FDA's objections to its clinical studies rested on the "judgmental" rather than the "precise" requirements of the May 1970 regulations and that, therefore, in accordance with footnote 17 of Justice Douglas' *Hynson* opinion, it should have been permitted to demonstrate the adequacy of those studies at a hearing.

A majority of the court of appeals upheld the FDA's action. Judge Wright acknowledged the difficulty of classifying particular requirements as "precise" and commented that, in any case, "[t]the [Supreme] Court did not say that FDA reliance on a less than 'precise' regulatory provision is necessarily improper, but only that it 'might' be so." He then undertook "a searching examination" of Cooper's evidence, finally concluding "that the [FDA] has located for each item of evidence at least one deficiency (and usually many such) which conclusively disqualifies the item 'in light of the pertinent regulations.' " Among the "deficiencies" Judge Wright attributed to the FDA was the judgment—divined from the agency's use of quotation marks around the word "control"—that Vitamin B-12 was not a proper control in a test of Protamide for the treatment of shingles because, though it was not a recognized treatment for the disease, it might have unknown therapeutic qualities.

Judge Leventhal, dissenting, questioned the fairness of the FDA's procedure because it afforded Cooper no opportunity to respond to the Commissioner's analysis of its evidence, which appeared in the agency's final order. He offered the following recommendations:

The first move toward untying the tangle could be taken if the FDA allowed the petitioners an opportunity for at least a written response to the determination that is now issued as the FDA's final order, but which, under a change in procedure to cope with the problem, would become a proposed disposition. At that time, NDA holders would, for the first time, have the FDA's declared approach for rejection of the study, and have a genuine opportunity to respond to that approach. * * * Perhaps petitioners could supplement the studies, say, by provision of raw data, if that were identified as a need. Or perhaps they could point out flaws in the FDA's approach.

It may be that such a response by the applicant would lead FDA to schedule a hearing. This is not an unthinkable calamity. * * * [W]hen we come to what purport on their face to be studies with a control element, conducted by persons who have at least a prima facie claim to expertise, then we have a matter that calls for resolution after hearing.

Judge Leventhal then provided this provocative advice on the character of the hearing the FDA might conduct if one were required:

The "hearing" appropriate for such cases need not borrow the characteristics of conventional courtroom controversy. * * *

* * * [E]ven when statutes contemplate an adjudicatory hearing baseline, a particular case may involve the kind of issue that calls for an oral argument rather than an evidentiary hearing or for a legislative rather than an adjudicative hearing. These comments are highly pertinent when what is at issue are technical questions of methodology. Indeed, in such a case the reality of technical dialogue and interchange of views can perhaps best be provided by an on the record conference-hearing procedure, modeled on conference discussions between lawyers and experts. The law does not require a bog-down at the agency level; it seeks only an opportunity for reasonable give and take. * * *

Id. at 792–93. Following the decision in *Hess & Clark v. Food and Drug Administration*, 495 F.2d 975 (D.C. Cir. 1974), infra, the FDA revised its summary judgment regulations to *permit* the kind of three-stage exchange that Judge Leventhal recommended. See 39 Fed. Reg. 9750 (1974). This procedure obviously prolongs the time required to achieve summary judgment when that is appropriate, and it may be perceived as redundant when a hearing must be held. For these reasons, the three-stage procedure authorized by the FDA's revised regulations has never become routine.

Nor was a variant suggested later by a different panel of the D.C. Circuit when it handed the FDA another rebuff. In *Smithkline Corp. v. FDA*, 587 F.2d 1107, 1118–19, 1126, 1127–28 (D.C. Cir. 1978), the court refused to sustain the FDA's denial of a hearing for Dexamyl, a combination drug used in the treatment of obesity. Yet the majority also declined to hold that a full evidentiary hearing was required. The history of the case varied from the traditional pattern. Dexamyl had first been marketed in 1949 without an NDA on the premise, with which FDA then agreed, that it was "generally recognized as safe." When the NAS-NRC rated the combination of ingredients only "possibly effective," however,

Smithkline submitted NDA's for its various dosages forms, and undertook five new clinical trials.   Three years later the FDA, in a lengthy Federal Register order, found conclusive deficiencies in each study.   The court again faulted the agency's approach:

> The issues entail complicated questions of scientific methodology, an area in which courts have little institutional competence.   These questions must be confronted, moreover, in the absence of an evidentiary record. FDA's interpretation of its summary judgment regulations does not require it to provide an applicant the opportunity to respond to the agency's determination that the applicant's submission is conclusively inadequate in light of regulations defining "substantial evidence."   The record will thus normally contain only FDA's unchallenged characterizations of an applicant's submissions.   * * *

> The instant case amply illustrates these difficulties.   SKF strenuously urges that FDA's criticisms of its multi-investigator clinical trials are based upon "imprecise" regulations and are scientifically fallacious. Since FDA refused to consider these contentions, however, the record before us consists chiefly of SKF's NDA, together with its multi-investigator clinical trials, and FDA's August 24, 1976, order.   We are thus confronted on one side by the arguments of lawyers, and on the other by the untested conclusions of FDA.   To decide the scientific merit of these disputes, on the basis of the record now before us, would certainly be to risk the dangerous unreliability likely to occur when "technically illiterate judges" attempt substantively to review mathematical and scientific questions.

> * * * If we were to follow our usual practice under Rule 56 of accepting as true petitioner's version of the facts, petitioner might be entitled, despite the present abortive state of the record, to a full adjudicatory hearing, even though such a hearing might well be "an exercise in futility." Full adjudicatory hearings represent a serious drain on FDA's limited resources.   * * * Therefore, we will, if possible, avoid ordering an adjudicatory hearing until we are asured, with some basis in a record, that a genuine issue of fact exists there to be resolved.   * * *

> Since we cannot sustain FDA's summary judgment order and since, at the same time, we have no assurance that there is presently a genuine issue of fact to be aired at an adjudicatory hearing, this record should be remanded to FDA for a proceeding to determine whether such a genuine issue of fact exists.   The extent of this proceeding should be as limited as its circumscribed purpose.   Were this proceeding to become too lengthy or elaborate, it would create precisely the drain on FDA's resources FDA's summary judgment regulations were designed to prevent.   * * *   FDA itself must submit on the record and for the comments of petitioner evidence for FDA's conclusions.   Confident, however, that "court and agency [are] 'collaborative instrumentalities of justice,' " we decline to specify any particular procedures to be used on remand.   * * *   We require only that the proceeding on remand provide assurance that FDA has given reasoned consideration to all material facts and issues.

Judge McGowan, concurring and dissenting, found the approach of his colleagues unsatisfactory:

> * * * I suspect the parties will have substantial difficulties in accommodating their views on the precise nature of the hearing to be held on remand;

and I can foresee this court once more required to wrestle with conflicting contentions on this score. * * *

On the one hand, if the applicant's burden on remand—having been charged by FDA with failing to meet one of the agency's "imprecise" testing requirements—is simply to put in the record some factual or logical "support for [its] view" that the requirement is indeed met, it is hard to imagine that an applicant, whose submissions to FDA do not appear to us at this stage to be conclusively insufficient on their face, could not almost automatically comply on remand.   Hence, the result of remand and review in this court almost inevitably would be to require a statutory hearing anyway, with only further delay on the road to the merits.   On the other hand, if the applicant's burden of production is more stringent—and thus is inconsistent with any recognizable notion of "summary judgment"—it is difficult to see how the more or less informal remand proceeding contemplated will place FDA or us in a better position than we now are in to resolve the "complicated questions in scientific methodology" referred to by the majority.   In either case, considerations of expedition cannot be overlooked, especially in a proceeding which has been going on as long as this one has; and it may well be—indeed, it seems probable to me—that, in light of the problems raised by the majority opinion, abandonment of this point of summary judgment is the shorter—rather than the longer—route to final termination of the matter.

587 F.2d at 1127–28.   The FDA heeded Judge McGowan' advice, for it subsequently announced a hearing on the approvability of the NDA's for Dexamyl.   Just before this hearing was scheduled to commence, however, Smithkline agreed to discontinue marketing the drug on the condition that the agency would not seize stocks already in commerce.

The FDA's application of summary judgment in implementing the NAS-NRC findings was also challenged in *Brandenfels v. Heckler*, 716 F.2d 553 (9th Cir. 1983); *Sterling Drug, Inc. v. Weinberger*, 503 F.2d 675 (2d Cir. 1974); *North American Pharmacal, Inc. v. Department of HEW*, 491 F.2d 546 (8th Cir. 1973); and *E. R. Squibb & Sons, Inc. v. Weinberger*, 483 F.2d 1382 (3d Cir. 1973).   See also *Edison Pharmaceutical Co. v. Food and Drug Administration*, 513 F.2d 1063 (D.C. Cir. 1975), *rehearing en banc denied* 517 F.2d 164 (D.C. Cir. 1975).   For further analysis of FDA's efforts to utilize "summary judgment" in its implementation of the NAS-NRC efficacy review, see R. MERRILL & P. HUTT, FOOD AND DRUG LAW 376–77 (1980); Ames and McCracken, *Framing Regulatory Standards to Avoid Formal Adjudication: The FDA as a Case Study*, 64 Calif. L. Rev. 14 (1976).

Status of the NAS-NRC Review

The FDA's innovative use of summary judgment was the most notable of several administrative techniques the agency adopted as it attempted to discharge Congress' 1962 mandate to assure that pre-1962 drugs were eventually proved effective as well as safe.   It is therefore appropriate to assess the agency's approach at least partly in terms of its contribution to its ultimate achievement of that goal—a goal finally within sight at the end of 1984. See *FDA Wraps Up 22-Year Study on Merit of Prescription Drugs*.   The Washington Post, Sept. 17, 1984, A3.

The reader will recall that in 1972 the American Public Health Association successfully sued to force the FDA to expedite its efforts to implement the NAS-NRC panel evaluations. *American Public Health Association v. Veneman*, 349 F. Supp. 1311 (D.D.C. 1972). The resulting judicially-approved schedule for completing the process, formulated, it should be noted, by the FDA's own attorneys, contemplated completion of the process in approximately four years. Yet, despite the threat of judicial oversight, the FDA's task remained unfinished as this edition went to press. Some of the original *Veneman* plaintiffs returned to court in 1980 and, after failing to secure a ruling that the Commissioner was in contempt, entered into a court-sanctioned agreement outlining a new schedule for final implementation of the NAS-NRC evaluations. See *American Public Health Association v. Harris*, Civ. No. 70–1847 (D.D.C. Sept. 17, 1982). By that date, however, most of the parties to the original litigation had departed the scene. The incumbent Commissioner, Dr. Jere Goyan, was the fourth to serve since the APHA first filed its suit, and Veneman, an Assistant Secretary for Health, had left office a full decade earlier.

The picture may be depressing but it is hardly surprising. It should be recalled that the FDA was seeking to assure that pre-1962 drugs were proved effective; they had already been found safe, and thus the prospect of imminent injury that often galvanizes administrators into action was missing. In addition, most of the drugs in question either experienced declining sales—because physicians found that they were not effective—or they enjoyed considerable popularity among prescribers—suggesting that they might be shown to work if subjected to appropriate tests. Equally important, the FDA's interest in the efficacy program began to decline about the time it achieved its victories in *Hynson* and companion cases. New problems attracted the attention of agency managers. The names saccharin, cyclamate, nitrite, Red No. 2, DES, and estrogens only recall the headlines of the agency's ensuing agenda, but they help explain the inevitable redirection of attention, and resulting reallocation of resources, that characterize the life of any government organization. Within the FDA's Bureau of Drugs—the component responsible for administering the drug efficacy review—other projects soon assumed higher priority. Changes in the prescription drug market also diminished the FDA's original fervor. The agency's initial targets were drugs whose effectiveness was most in doubt and for which published clinical trials were most elusive. In short, the FDA attacked the easiest cases first. Many drugs rated less than effective for one claim earned higher ratings for others, and large numbers were relabeled to bring their indications more nearly in line with the evidence—and the statute. As time passed, older products were supplanted by safer and more effective approved new drugs. Some pre-1962 drugs simply ceased to command sufficient patronage to make continued marketing profitable.

There are, therefore, many reasons why an agency short on human resources and long on problems might lose interest in an assignment now more than two decades' old. But it is also worth observing that the administrative law doctrines that the FDA exploited in pursuing its efforts—notably, the principle that an agency may, through rulemaking, narrow the scope of material issues in individual adjudicatory proceedings and the doctrine of primary jurisdiction—could not eliminate the larger problems the FDA confronted: an enormous workload; a recalcitrant industry whose members remain internally divided and pursue legal claims with an eye primarily on their competitive effect; and standards of clinical effectiveness and professional prescribing habits that were continually changing.

A final dimension of the FDA's efforts to implement the drug efficacy standard merits comment here.   The agency's May 1970 regulations applied to new drugs then still in development, as well as to pre-1962 drugs. With respect to the former universe, obviously, the regulations' impact was sure to appear less draconian if only because drug sponsors had some opportunity to tailor their tests to the new requirements.   Indeed, the agency argued, with some plausibility, that its requirements merely codified what had become accepted practice in the clinical testing of drugs. The FDA's adherence to the regulations in evaluating applications submitted after 1970 never generated the sort of legal controversy that attended their application to pre-1962 drugs, such as Panalba.

This does not mean, however, that the law's standards for proving effectiveness have not been challenged on a different level.   Several serious scholars hold that the 1962 effectiveness standard has retarded the introduction of new drugs in the United States.   The earliest proponent of this view, Sam Peltzman, purported to demonstrate that 1962 Amendments had exacted a cost higher, in treatments delayed or precluded, than any benefits yielded in the form of side effects prevented and dollars saved on ineffective drugs.   See, e.g., S. PELTZMAN, REGULATION OF PHARMACEUTICAL INNOVATION: THE 1962 AMENDMENTS (1974).   Peltzman's provocative study triggered a continuing stream of scholarship addressing the so-called "drug lag" controversy.   Some writings purport to demonstrate that improved drugs are available sooner in other industrialized countries; others claim that FDA controls have not deprived Americans of any important therapies.   A balanced assessment of the literature would conclude that the critics have not been adequately answered and that the 1962 Amendments have surely slowed the introduction of new drugs into the U.S. markets.   Debate has increasingly focused on the delays associated with sophisticated drug testing and with the sometimes byzantine FDA review process, rather than on the effectiveness standard itself.   For reviews of the pertinent literature, see R. MERRILL & P. HUTT, FOOD AND DRUG LAW 432–33 (1980); P. TEMIN, TAKING YOUR MEDICINE 141 *et seq.* (1982).

Administrative Summary Judgment Without Rules

The decisions in *Storer*, *Hynson*, and *Petroleum Refiners* confirm the legitimacy of an agency's use of legislative rules to limit the scope of adjudicatory proceedings.   The analogy to summary judgment in civil litigation raises the possibility that an agency can avoid statutorily-mandated formal hearings even when it has not adopted—"bright line" rules narrowing a general statutory standard. Yet two FDA cases, both from the D.C. Circuit, suggest that, absent clarifying regulations, the usual presumptions against a party seeking summary judgment are likely to preclude effective use of the device.

Hess & Clark v. Food and Drug Administration, 495 F.2d 975 (D.C. Cir. 1974), grew out of FDA's efforts to regulate human exposure to the animal drug diethystilbestrol, or DES, one of several compounds developed to promote growth in livestock. Because such drugs may leave residues in meat, milk, or eggs, Congress has imposed dual requirements for their approval: A veterinary drug must be shown to be safe and effective for animals and if it is to be used in food-producing animals, it must also meet the standards for human food additives. The best known of these standards is a version of the Delaney Clause, 21 U.S.C.A. § 360b(d)(1)(H), which prohibits FDA from approving any animal drug that is shown to cause cancer unless the agency determines that "no residue" will be found in edible tissue using an analytic method it prescribes. The Act additionally specifies that the FDA shall not approve, or shall withdraw approval for, an animal drug capable of leaving residues that have not been shown to be "safe" for human consumption.

DES was first used as a growth promotant for cattle and sheep in the early 1950's. When in 1958 Congress mandated pre-market approval for food additives and added the Delaney Clause, the FDA continued its approval of DES on the assumption that, when the drug was properly administered (in feed or by implantation), no residues were likely to be found by the agency's prescribed method of analysis, the so-called mouse uterine method. By the early 1970's much more sensitive chemical analyses had been developed, and USDA inspectors using these newer methods began to detect DES residues in many slaughtered carcasses. Because DES had long been recognized as a carcinogen, the FDA soon faced pressure to respond.

The agency ultimately withdrew approvals (new animal drug applications or NADA's) for DES implants and refused to accord the manufacturers a hearing on the ground that, in light of USDA's discovery of residues, no material facts remained in dispute. The agency's alternative theories were that the finding of DES residues triggered the Delaney Clause's automatic ban and, in any case, that the residues could not be considered "safe." The agency thus claimed that it could particularize the statutory safety standard as forbidding *any* residues of a carcinogenic drug and deny a hearing if the manufacturers failed to demonstrate that material factual issues were in dispute. The manufacturers challenged this ruling in the D.C. Circuit.

Writing for the court, Judge Leventhal agreed in principle that an agency could issue summary judgment, even in the absence of narrowing regulations, if its uncontested evidence demonstrated that the statutory standard for action was met. But he found the FDA's procedure fatally flawed: The agency had failed to provide the DES manufacturers notice of the USDA assay findings so that they could respond to them in a timely fashion.   Moreover, Leventhal concluded, assuming that the manufacturers had been apprised of the bases for the FDA's proposed withdrawal, their responses had raised factual issues that required an evidentiary hearing.   As he explained:

> * * * When the FDA issues a Notice of Opportunity for Hearing, its summary judgment procedures are available if the requesting party fails to raise material issues of fact.   For that reason, the contents of the response are of critical importance, and the need for and importance of the response in turn enhances the significance of the notice given by the adverse party.   In order to be adequate, such notice given by the agency to an adverse party must contain enough information to provide the respondent a genuine opportunity to identify material issues of fact.   * * *

> * * * If the Commissioner of FDA is relying on his Notice as a device for invoking a summary judgment procedure that avoids the statute's general requirement of a hearing, he must include in such notice references to the "facts" that he deems to be established in order that there may be meaningful opportunity to controvert the alleged facts and present a material issue for hearing.   * * *

Judge Leventhal proceeded to evaluate the alternative legal theories on which the FDA relied to discern what material factual issues had to be resolved in the agency's favor:

> The statute provides that the FDA may withdraw its approval of an NADA when new evidence * * * together with the evidence available to the Secretary when the application was approved, shows that such drug is not shown to be safe for use under the conditions for use upon the basis of which the application was approved or that [the Delaney Clause] applies to such drug;   * * *

Summary disposition could not be sustained on the basis of the Delaney Clause because the residues that USDA found in cattle that had received implants were not detected by the assay method "prescribed or approved" by the FDA.   In other words, the FDA had summoned no legally relevant evidence that this condition of approval had been violated.   Leventhal then turned to the agency's second ground:

> The Commissioner relies on the alternative theory of the "general safety" clause * * * contending that the new evidence from the USDA tests "shows that [DES] is not shown to be safe."   More precisely, the Commissioner asserts that nothing in petitioners' responses raises any material issues of fact about his conclusion that DES is no longer shown to be safe.   * * *

> The statute plainly places on the FDA an initial burden to adduce the "new evidence" and what that new evidence "shows."   Only when the FDA has met this initial burden of coming forward with the new evidence is there a burden on the manufacturer to show that the drug is safe.   * * *

> Because he is not using the Delaney Clause, it is not enough for the Commissioner merely to show that animal carcasses contain residues and that DES is a carcinogen.   Instead, the FDA must show that two different issues are resolved in its favor before it can shift to petitioners the burden of show-

ing safety: (1) whether the detected residues are related to the use of DES implants; (2) if so, whether the residues, because of their composition, and in the amounts present in the tissues, present some potential hazard to the public health.

Petitioners have submitted material supporting the assertion that the testing method itself produced the detected residues. The thrust of these submissions is that the residues resulted from the presence of impurities in the specially made "tagged" implants. * * *

* * * This issue is quite material: if the residues are caused by the test, then the Commissioner could hardly maintain that their presence shows that commercial use of DES implants is not shown to be safe. Accordingly, we conclude that petitioners' submissions raised substantial and material issues of fact about the very premise of the FDA action, i.e. that commercial use of DES implants had caused harmful residues in human food. * * *

* * * The * * * statute [further] requires the FDA to consider the relationship between a drug's safety and residues left in food because of use of the drug. The statute does not say that because a drug leaves residues, it is unsafe *per se*. We think it implicit in the statute that when the FDA proposes to withdraw an approval because new evidence shows the drug leaves residues, it has an initial burden of coming forward with some evidence of the relationship between the residue and safety to warrant shifting to the manufacturer the burden of showing safety. This is at least the case where, as here, the residues are of unknown composition. * * *

The FDA's second experiment with summary judgment unaided by clarifying regulations was successfully challenged in *American Cyanamid Co. v. FDA*, 606 F.2d 1307 (D.C. Cir. 1979).

Chapter 4

ADMINISTRATIVE RULEMAKING

Lawmaking by administrators who are not subject directly to the constraints of electoral politics raises a host of perennial issues in American administrative law. Among these are (1) the scope of administrative power and the ability of reviewing courts to confine administrators within the range of choices contemplated by the legislature; (2) the adequacy of notice to affected persons of the legal standards administrators intend to enforce; and (3) the availability of opportunities for such persons to participate in the formulation of those standards and to protect themselves from inconsistent, unfair, or incompetent administration. Judicial insistence that the legislature provide "adequate standards" for the exercise of delegated power is one answer to these questions, but this answer is at once inadequate—because legislators often cannot or will not anticipate the entire range of considerations they wish administrators to weigh—and destructive—because it impedes the assignment of lawmaking responsibility to institutions better equipped to devise sensible rules of behavior. For example, Congress can identify only in general terms the criteria it wishes pollution control officials to consider in licensing industrial dischargers, and thus leaves to administrators crucial value judgments concerning the relative strengths of health, aesthetic, and economic interests in particular contexts. To require Congress to do more is to require it to make specific rules of conduct covering a host of only imperfectly anticipated contingencies (rules which if faulty would, like the Delaney Clause, be difficult to alter) or to issue licenses itself. The first approach is undesirable and the second unworkable. Moreover, while procedural regularity and judicial review, see *Amalgamated Meatcutters v. Connally*, p. 6 supra, provide only partial answers to the problems created by loose legislative delegations, the "adequate standards" requirement is only partially responsive to the other concerns implicit in the nondelegation doctrine. Thus courts, as well as Congress, have generally attempted to fashion more limited, and more sensitive, solutions to the problem of ensuring the rule of law in the administrative state.

This chapter explores judicial and legislative attempts to resolve these issues of administrative accountability and individual fairness in contexts in which administrators are called upon to make law through the formal adoption of general rules of conduct, i.e., by legislating. In the federal arena this process is termed "rulemaking." Broadly speaking,

317

the central legal problems associated with the adoption of such general administrative rules are the development of appropriate substantive checks on the exercise of agency discretion and the construction of processes through which agency judgments can be informed by the perspectives and interests of affected persons.

The suggestion of substantive and procedural checks on agency discretion implies that the courts play a larger role in reviewing administrative legislation than they customarily assume when rules adopted by legislators themselves are challenged. This implication is intended. There is no administrative counterpart to the enrolled bill rule, see *Field v. Clark*, 143 U.S. 649 (1892), that forestalls judicial examination of the processes an agency followed in formulating general rules of conduct. By contrast, too, with their customary deference to the substantive policy choices of elected legislators, e.g., *Williamson v. Lee Optical Co.*, 348 U.S. 483 (1955), courts purport to demand evidentiary support for and rational explanation of rules adopted by administrators. This different judicial attitude is in part the product of the Administrative Procedure Act, which prescribes both generally applicable minimum procedures for agency rulemaking and limited judicial review of agency substantive decisions. But more fundamentally, the judicial posture toward administrative "quasi-legislation" reflects a continuing lack of assurance concerning the political legitimacy of administrative policy choices. In studying the materials that follow, the reader should, therefore, be more than usually attentive to the manner in which courts justify their supervision of the processes of administrative agencies and, to a considerable extent, the formulation of agency policies.

A. JUDICIAL REVIEW OF THE SUBSTANCE OF AGENCY RULES

Although Judge Leventhal asserts in *Amalgamated Meatcutters*, that judicial review is a legitimizing condition of Congressional delegations of lawmaking power to administrative officers, he does not reveal criteria by which such rules are to be evaluated. And if Congress uses imprecise or open-ended language to delegate authority, the exhortation that courts must insist on obedience to Congressional policy choices is itself an empty guarantee of the rule of law.

The question, then, is what judicially enforceable constraints are there on the substance of administrative policies? In exploring possible answers to this question we look, first, to determine what constraints the Constitution imposes on the substance of agency rules. We then examine the impact of the APA and agency organic statutes on substantive judicial review. In this context, study of decisions of the past decade suggests that courts are playing an increasingly active role in reviewing the content of federal agency rules. We will consider whether their role can be explained in terms of instructions provided by Congress, or whether there is an emerging "common law" of administrative rationality anchored in neither statute nor the Constitution. Finally, we explore the problems presented to reviewing courts by administrative efforts to formulate policy in highly complex technical fields.

1. CONSTITUTIONAL LIMITS ON THE RATIONALITY OF AGENCY RULES

PACIFIC STATES BOX & BASKET CO. v. WHITE

Supreme Court of the United States, 1935.
296 U.S. 176, 56 S.Ct. 159, 82 L. Ed. 138.

MR. JUSTICE BRANDEIS delivered the opinion of the Court.

[The plaintiff, a California manufacturer of fruit and vegetable containers, challenged an order of the Chief of the Oregon Division of Plant Industry prescribing the type, size, and shape of containers for the sale of strawberries and raspberries. The defendant had acted, after investigation, notice, and a public hearing, pursuant to an Oregon statute empowering him to promulgate "official standards for containers of horticultural products * * * in order to promote, protect, further and develop the horticultural interests" of the state. The box company claimed that the new standard had the effect of preventing use of its containers by growers in Oregon. It charged, *inter alia*, that the standard thus violated its rights under the due process clause of the Fourteenth Amendment because it "is arbitrary, capricious, and not reasonably necessary for the accomplishment of any legitimate purpose of the police power." The district court dismissed the company's complaint on the ground that it did not allege facts that would entitle it to relief.]

Plaintiff does not question the reasonableness of the standard so far as it prescribes the capacity of the box or basket. Its challenge is directed solely to the fixing of the dimensions and the form of the container. But to fix both the dimensions and the form may be deemed necessary in order to assure observance of the prescribed capacity and to effect other purposes of the regulation. It may be that in Oregon, where hallocks* have long been in general use, buyers at retail are less likely to be deceived by dealers as to the condition and quantity of these berries if they are sold in containers of the prescribed form and dimensions. It is said that there are 34 other styles or shapes of berry basket in use somewhere in the United States. Obviously, a multitude of shapes and sizes of packages tends to confuse the buyer. Furthermore, the character of the container may be an important factor in preserving the condition of raspberries and strawberries, which are not only perishable but tender. * * *

Different types of commodities require different types of containers; and as to each commodity there may be reasonable difference of opinion as to the type best adapted to the protection of the public. Whether it

*[A hallock is described by the Court as "a type of rectangular till box with perpendicular sides and a raised bottom." The plaintiff manufactured a cup-shaped container known as a "tin-top" or "metal rim." Eds.]

was necessary in Oregon to provide a standard container for raspberries and strawberries; and, if so, whether that adopted should have been made mandatory, involve questions of fact and of policy, the determination of which rests in the legislative branch of the state government. The determination may be made, if the constitution of the State permits, by a subordinate administrative body. With the wisdom of such a regulation we have, of course, no concern. We may enquire only whether it is arbitrary or capricious. That the requirement is not arbitrary or capricious seems clear. That the type of container prescribed by Oregon is an appropriate means for attaining permissible ends cannot be doubted.

* * *

* * * Plaintiff contends that since the case was heard on motion to dismiss the bill, all allegations therein made must be accepted as true; and, among others, the charge that "there is no necessity for the particular orders relating to strawberries or raspberries" "based on considerations of public health, or to prevent fraud or deception, or any other legitimate use of the police power, and the particular container described * * * does not of necessity promote, protect, further or develop the horticultural interests of the State"; and that its necessary effect is "to grant a monopoly to manufacturers of the so-called hallocks." The order here in question deals with a subject clearly within the scope of the police power. When such legislative action "is called in question, if any state of facts reasonably can be conceived that would sustain it, there is a presumption of the existence of that state of facts, and one who assails the classification must carry the burden of showing by a resort to common knowledge or other matters which may be judicially noticed, or to other legitimate proof, that the action is arbitrary." * * *

* * * It is urged that this rebuttable presumption of the existence of a state of facts sufficient to justify the exertion of the police power attaches only to acts of legislature; and that where the regulation is the act of an administrative body, no such presumption exists, so that the burden of proving the justifying facts is upon him who seeks to sustain the validity of the regulation. The contention is without support in authority or reason, and rests upon misconception. Every exertion of the police power, either by the legislature or by an administrative body, is an exercise of delegated power. Where it is by a statute, the legislature has acted under power delegated to it through the Constitution. Where the regulation is by an order of an administrative body, that body acts under a delegation from the legislature. The question of law may, of course, always be raised whether the legislature had power to delegate the authority exercised. But where the regulation is within the scope of authority legally delegated, the presumption of the existence of facts justifying its specific exercise attaches alike to statutes, to municipal ordinances, and to orders of administrative bodies. Here there is added reason for applying the presumption of validity; for the regulation now challenged was adopted after notice and public hearing as the statute required. It is contended that the order is void because the administrative body made no special findings of fact. But the statute did not require special findings;

doubtless because the regulation authorized was general legislation, not an administrative order in the nature of a judgment directed against an individual concern. * * *

Notes

1. The box company's challenge to the Oregon container rule relied mainly on the Due Process Clause of the Fourteenth Amendment.   Students of Constitutional Law will recall the history of the Supreme Court's treatment of similar challenges to state legislation during the first half of this century. After initially embracing the notion that "due process" imposes substantive limits on state (and federal) legislation in the economic arena, see *Lochner v. New York*, 198 U.S. 45 (1905), the Court during the New Deal quickly retreated to a posture of substantial indifference to legislative motives or rationality.   Compare *Williamson v. Lee Optical Co.*, 348 U.S. 483 (1955): "The day is gone when this Court uses the Due Process Clause of the Fourteenth Amendment to strike down state laws, regulatory of business and industrial conditions, because they may be unwise, improvident, or out of harmony with a particular school of thought."   On an initial reading, therefore, Justice Brandeis' deference to Oregon's rule seems unsurprising.

The box company, undoubtedly aware of the unlikelihood of successfully challenging actions of state legislators, contended that administrative rules should not be accorded the same presumption of regularity.   Should the Court have given that contention more serious consideration?   Can a persuasive argument be made that courts should more carefully scrutinize rules adopted by institutions that are not electorally accountable?   Can they realistically expect that legislative oversight of the policies and decisions of administrative officials will provide adequate assurance of political legitimacy?

2. Can the Court's decision be read as implying that the presumption of regularity that will be accorded agency rules may depend on the procedures followed by the rulemakers?   Did the public hearing conducted in adopting the Oregon container rule afford sufficient protection for the out-of-state plaintiff?   Is there any evidence the box company knew about or participated in the hearing?

3. As most readers will appreciate, the Supreme Court has not been consistently indifferent to the substantive content of all state laws challenged as unconstitutional.   Challenges invoking guarantees of the Bill of Rights have continued to elicit more searching review of legislative judgments, as have claims based on the Equal Protection Clause of the Fourteenth Amendment.   The Court has found intense due process scrutiny justified for laws encroaching on numerous personal rights and interests, e.g., *Roe v. Wade*, 410 U.S. 113 (1973), and sometimes for essentially economic legislation.   See Jackson and Jeffries, *Commercial Speech: Economic Due Process and the First Amendment*, 65 Va. L. Rev. 1 (1979).   Predictably, the Court's willingness to scrutinize the substance of legislative policies that are perceived to affect important personal rights has extended to administrative rules as well.   See, e.g. *Bob Jones University v. United States*, 461 U.S. 574 (1983) (reviewing IRS regulations for conformity with the First Amendment's guarantee of freedom of religion); *Red Lion Broadcasting Co. v. FCC*, 395 U.S. 367 (1969) (reviewing FCC rules for conformity with the First Amendment's guarantee of free speech).

It should be stressed, however, that the Supreme Court has never disavowed or, indeed, obviously departed from its posture in *Pacific States Box* on the intensity of constitutional review of administrative rules that deal with the traditional subjects of government regulation. The more intrusive judicial oversight of administrative rulemaking evident during the past three decades has other origins.

2. SUBSTANTIVE REVIEW OF AGENCY RULES UNDER THE APA

The Administrative Procedure Act contemplates the possibility of judicial review of most federal administrative actions. According to the Supreme Court, the APA embodies a "presumption" that review shall be available in some court at some time. *Abbott Laboratories v. Gardner*, 387 U.S. 136, 140 (1967). The APA is, however, peculiarly delphic in its instructions to courts called on to review administrative rules. Section 706 (part of section 10 of the original statute) provides:

> To the extent necessary to decision and when presented, the reviewing court shall decide all relevant questions of law, interpret constitutional and statutory provisions, and determine the meaning or applicability of the terms of an agency action. The reviewing court shall—
>
> (1) Compel agency action unlawfully withheld or unreasonably delayed; and
>
> (2) hold unlawful and set aside agency action, findings, and conclusions found to be—
>
> > (A) arbitrary, capricious, an abuse of discretion, or otherwise not in accordance with law;
> >
> > (B) contrary to constitutional right, power, privilege, or immunity;
> >
> > (C) in excess of statutory jurisdiction, authority, or limitations, or short of statutory right;
> >
> > (D) without observance of procedure required by law;
> >
> > (E) unsupported by substantial evidence in a case subject to sections 556 and 557 of this title or otherwise reviewed on the record of an agency hearing provided by statute; or
> >
> > (F) unwarranted by the facts to the extent that the facts are subject to trial de novo by the reviewing court.
>
> In making the foregoing determinations, the court shall review the whole record or those parts of it cited by a party, and due account shall be taken of the rule of prejudicial error.

Note that this language does not specifically mention agency rules or purport to recognize, for the purposes of review, any difference between rulemaking and adjudication. It does, however, recognize different types of claims of administrative impropriety and intimates different roles for a reviewing court depending on the type of claim that is asserted.

The APA is by no means the only source of Congressional guidance to courts called on to review rules or other administrative actions. Often, and in recent years routinely, Congress has specified in the agency's organic statute the terms upon which court review of its actions may be obtained. As we will see, however, the language Congress employs in the narrower, and thus ostensibly more focused, context of specific legislation sometimes leaves reviewing courts in doubt about the extent of their responsibility to reexamine the substance of agency rules—and thus with some freedom to follow their best judgment. The materials that follow explore the sources of judicial authority to reexamine administrative "legislation," and seek to depict the competing influences of statutory language, functional context, political circumstance, and contemporaneous perceptions of appropriate institutional roles on the intensity of judicial review of agency rules.

Our first principal case, *Automotive Parts & Accessories Association v. Boyd*, involves a typical challenge to agency rules promulgated under a modern regulatory statute. Indeed, that case set the tone for much that was to follow in the developing common law of judicial review of rulemaking. The petitioners in *Auto Parts* contended that the respondent, the Secretary of Transportation, failed to follow mandated procedures for the adoption of regulations and also failed to justify the regulations' substantive requirements. Our immediate concern is with the latter claim—and the court's response to it—but the reader should recall the conjunction of these claims and be attentive, as Judge McGowan surely was, to the interplay between the procedures an agency may follow in making rules and the character of the evidence and reasons that will suffice to sustain their content.

AUTOMOTIVE PARTS & ACCESSORIES ASSOCIATION v. BOYD

United States Court of Appeals, District of Columbia Circuit, 1968.
407 F.2d 330.

MCGOWAN, CIRCUIT JUDGE.

These consolidated review proceedings are among the first to be initiated under the National Traffic and Motor Vehicle Safety Act of 1966 (Safety Act), 15 U.S.C.A. § § 1381–1409. The object of this challenge is Motor Vehicle Safety Standard No. 202, which requires that, effective January 1, 1969, all new passenger cars manufactured for sale in this country must be factory-equipped with front seat head restraints which meet specific federal standards. Petitioners are not motor car manufacturers but, rather, a manufacturer of auto accessories including head restraints (Sterling Products Co., Inc.), and two trade associations representing persons engaged in the auto accessory business (Automotive Parts & Accessories Association, Inc. (APAA), and Automotive Service Industry Association (ASIA)). Their common grievance appears to flow not from the recognition and establishment of the head restraint as an essential safety device but from the adverse impact upon their business inherent in a vehicle standard which necessarily requires that the head restraints be factory installed.[1] Their attack upon the Standard takes two major forms. One is procedural in nature, raising a number of issues as

---

1. The Safety Act provides that the Secretary of Transportation can issue (1) safety standards *for motor vehicles* which require that no automobile can be manufactured for sale without meeting the standard (vehicle standard), or (2) safety standards for motor vehicle *equipment* (equipment standard) which require that all such equipment manufactured for sale must meet that standard.

to the manner in which the legislative grant of authority was exercised. The other goes to the merits of the Standard, including, interestingly enough, contentions—made here for the first time—that head restraints endanger, rather than promote, passenger safety. We deal with them separately hereinafter, although the conclusion we reach in each instance is the same, namely, that the Standard is to be left undisturbed.

In the procedural area, petitioners claim that respondents misconceived their authority under the Act with respect to the kind of rule making proceeding they could hold. This issue can be posed simply as whether the rule making procedures provided by Section 4(b) [§ 553(c)] (informal rule making) of the Administrative Procedure Act (APA) were appropriate for the promulgation of this safety standard, or whether the Safety Act requires the more stringent procedures of Sections 7 and 8 [§ §556 and 557] of the APA (formal rule making). * * *

There is no issue between the parties as to which procedure was employed in the promulgation of the Standard, since respondents do not purport to have engaged in anything other than informal rule making. * * *

It was on November 30, 1966, that the respondent Boyd first issued a notice of proposed rule making under the Act. That notice related to twenty-three suggested safety standards, only one of which involved head restraints. Written comments were invited to be submitted by January 3, 1967. On the following January 31, respondent Bridwell issued rules as to twenty of the proposed subjects; he did not act with respect to head restraints because he thought it desirable to seek further information. Accordingly, on the same day, he issued a new notice of proposed rule making with respect to head restraints, and he invited written comments to be submitted by the following May. As a part of the consideration process, a meeting was held by respondents on November 14, 1967, with both car and accessory manufacturers, and other interested persons. On December 22, 1967, a notice was issued embodying the proposed Standard, and written comments about it were invited by January 26, 1968. The Standard was promulgated on February 12 thereafter.

The Standard as issued reflected certain alterations responsive to comments received, but the announcement accompanying it noted that the changes proposed by those interested in accessory equipment had been rejected for the reasons indicated. Various participants in the proceedings, including petitioners, filed petitions for reconsideration. On May 20, 1968, petitioners were sent a letter by respondents denying their request for the reasons stated therein.

Petitioners' central claim is that the Standard is invalid because this manner of proceeding was unauthorized from the beginning since it did not comport with the requirements of Sections 7 and 8 of the APA. This is not a complaint which petitioners appear to have directed to respondents during the course of the proceeding itself, nor in their request for reconsideration.[5]   There is, thus, a serious question as to whether they should now be permitted to press the matter for the first time here.   Respondents have, however, chosen to deal with it on the merits, and the public interest in the effective administration of the new Safety Act argues for our doing the same.

The question, as we have said, turns upon whether Congress, under the Safety Act, required the rule "to be made on the record after opportunity for agency hearing."*   The Safety Act contents itself with what is, in this context, the somewhat Delphic pronouncement that "[t]he Administrative Procedure Act shall apply to all orders establishing, amending, or revoking a Federal motor vehicle safety standard under this subchapter." Since the APA contains both Section 4(b), on the one hand, and Sections 7 and 8, on the other, this treatment falls somewhat short of the apogee of the legislative draftsman's art.   In any event, the classic conditions are present for recourse to legislative history for illumination of the Congressional purposes vis-a-vis formal and informal rule making.

What emerges from this quest is reasonably explicit, and it points away from where petitioners would have us go.   The Senate version of the Safety Act expressly stated that rules would be prescribed in accordance with Sections 3, 4, and 5 of the APA, and that "[n]othing in this title or in the Administrative Procedure Act shall be construed to make Sections 7 and 8   * * *   applicable."   The House bill, on the other hand, simply stated that the APA would apply, without discriminating among its parts.   In explaining this provision, however, the accompanying committee report stated that "The Secretary may utilize either the informal rule making procedure of section 4 of the APA or the more formal and extensive procedures of the act   * * * ."   In conference the language of the House version was adopted.   In explaining the Conference Bill on the floor of the Senate, Senator Magnuson, the sponsor of the Act and a conferee, pointed out that the change in no way threatened the legitimacy of informal rule making procedures, but instead was only to allow the Sec-

---

5. The one procedural issue which the petitioners did raise at the administrative level, and again press here, is that the National Motor Vehicle Safety Advisory Council does not contain "adequate representation of the automobile aftermarket equipment industry." Under the Act, the Secretary is, before issuing safety standards, required to consult with this Council, and with the Vehicle Equipment Safety Commission.   Petitioners also claim that the Secretary failed to consult with either the Commission or the Council.   The record clearly indicates, however, that both the Council and Commission were consulted before the issuance of the Standard.   It further appears that the only mandatory membership requirement on the Council imposed by Section 1393 of the Act is that the Secretary appoint a majority as "representatives of the general public."   Although the remainder of the Council is to be composed of representatives of various enumerated automotive interests, we think that the statute, when read in light of its legislative history, does not *compel* the Secretary to appoint representatives from each of those interest groups.

*[Judge McGowan's reference here is to the final sentence of section 553(c) of the APA. Subsection (b) and (c) set forth the basic requirements for informal rulemaking.   See Appendix C for full text.   Subsection (c) concludes with: "When rules are required by statute to be made on the record after opportunity for an agency hearing, sections 556 and 557 of this title apply instead of this subsection."   Eds.]

retary to adopt formal procedures should he wish to do so in a particular instance:

> With respect to sections 7 and 8 of the Administrative Procedure Act, which apply to formal hearings, the Senate bill had expressly provided that these sections would not apply to standard-setting procedures under the act. *It was the clear understanding of the conferees, however, that under the language of the House bill, the Secretary will utilize the informal rulemaking procedures of section 4 of the Administrative Procedure Act; and that he need hold a formal hearing under sections 7 and 8 only if he determines that such hearing is desirable.* (Emphasis added).

Quite apart from this concrete evidence of Congressional intent, an examination of other provisions of the Act, as well as the particular function which the Secretary is to perform, serves to reinforce the view that informal rule making was appropriate. First, the Act provides for the Secretary to consult informally with the National Motor Vehicle Safety Advisory Council, as well as various state, interstate and legislative committees. Also, the Act contemplates that, within the Department, experimentation and research will be used to generate data useful in formulating safety standards. Both of these approaches are far more consistent with informal than with formal rule making. More importantly, they only further emphasize the inherently legislative nature of the task which the Act delegates to the Secretary and his subordinates. In this context, where the Department is concerned with the issuance of rules requiring basic policy determinations rather than the resolution of particular factual controversies, the informal procedures provided by Section 4(b) of the APA are appropriate.

In the face of this formidable threat to their position from both the legislative history and the general structure of the Act itself, petitioners refer to the judicial review provisions of the Safety Act, and argue that they make manifest a Congressional intent that the "rules are required by statute to be made on the record after opportunity for an agency hearing," and therefore are to be the product of formal rule making. This is said to be implicit in (1) the requirement that, where review is sought of an order establishing a standard, there shall be filed in court "the record of the proceedings on which the Secretary based his order," (2) the jurisdiction given the court to review safety standards "in accordance with" Section 10 of the APA, and (3) the provision made for a remand by the court, at the request of a petitioner for the taking of additional evidence. Petitioners argue that all these aspects of the judicial review contemplated and authorized by the Safety Act are instinct with the idea of a record compiled in formal evidentiary hearings, from which record the agency makes findings and conclusions required to be supported, in the familiar adjudicatory sense, by substantial evidence in the record. Otherwise, so it is said, the judicial review provisions would be meaningless.

We are not persuaded that this is so, at least when the matter is weighed against the backdrop of legislative history set forth above. As to petitioners' first contention, there *is* a record compiled in a Section 4 proceeding, and available for filing in court. It consists of the submissions made in response to the invitations issued for written comments. And, as to the third, a court *could*, at the instance of a petitioner dissatisfied with the state of such a record, remand it to the agency for the receipt of further expressions of views and related information. Thus, there is nothing in these two provisions from the Safety Act's judicial review section which renders them completely inapt in relation to judicial scrutiny of the product of a Section 4 proceeding; and Congress can, accordingly, be rationally taken as having fashioned them with such a proceeding in view.

Petitioners press closely upon us the reference in the judicial review provisions of the Safety Act[9] to Section 10 of the Administrative Procedure Act. They point to paragraph (e) of Section 10 [§ 706] which, as its title indicates, is generally concerned with the scope of the review by a court of agency action, and, in particular, to subparagraph (B)(5) which directs that the court shall set aside agency action "unsupported by substantial evidence in a case subject to [Sections 7 and 8 of the APA] or otherwise reviewed on the record of an agency hearing provided by statute." We think that this language of Section 10, although not free from ambiguity, suggests that this "substantial evidence" standard for judicial review is addressed to the review of formal hearings, either under Sections 7 and 8 or other special statutory provision. Since we have found that a formal hearing is not required by the Safety Act, Subsection (B)(5) by its own terms appears to have no application to this case. This is not to say, however, that Congress has given no guidance as to the proper standards for judicial review of informal proceedings. Section 10(e) [§ 706(e)] e)] is, as noted above, addressed in the large to scope of review, and subsection (B)(5) is only one of its components. The other standards set out in that section, all of which would apply to informal rule making, allow an appellate court to apply 10(e) quite apart from subsection (B)(5).

In any event, although the judicial review provisions of the Safety Act and the APA contain some terms which are normally associated with formal evidentiary hearings, we refuse to infer that Congress, in this unnecessarily oblique way, intended to require the procedures of formal rule making for the issuance of safety standards. To do so would be to negate the specific legislative history and general Congressional purpose which in our view clearly demonstrate that issuance of standards by informal rule making was to be permissible.

* * * Section 4(b) of the APA [§ 533(c)] says in terms that the agency, after considering the relevant matter received by it in response to its invitation of comments, "shall incorporate in the rules adopted a concise general statement of their basis and purpose."

We think * * * that the statement in the text of the promulgation of the Standard, when considered in the light of the reasons stated by the Administrator's denial of rehearing, is "a concise general statement"

9. 15 U.S.C.A. § 1394 (a)(3) provides:

Upon the filing of the petition referred to in paragraph (1) of this subsection, the court shall have jurisdiction to review the order in accordance with [APA § 10], and to grant appropriate relief as provided in such section.

which passes muster under Section 4 of the APA.[12]   However, on the occasion of this first challenge to the implementation of the new statute it is appropriate for us to remind the Administrator of the ever present possibility of judicial review, and to caution against an overly literal reading of the statutory terms "concise" and "general."   These adjectives must be accommodated to the realities of judicial scrutiny, which do not contemplate that the court itself will, by a laborious examination of the record, formulate in the first instance the significant issues faced by the agency and articulate the rationale of their resolution.   We do not expect the agency to discuss every item of fact or opinion included in the submissions made to it in informal rule making.   We do expect that, if the judicial review which Congress has thought it important to provide is to be meaningful, the "concise general statement of   * * *   basis and purpose" mandated by Section 4 will enable us to see what major issues of policy were ventilated by the informal proceedings and why the agency reacted to them as it did.

Because the "concise general statement" envisaged by Congress is something different from the detailed "findings and conclusions" on all "material issues of fact, law, or discretion" referred to in Section 8, there will inevitably be differences of emphasis and approach in the application of the judicial review standards prescribed in APA § 10.   An adversary lawsuit, which most closely resembles the formal hearing of Sections 7 and 8, throws up issues of law and fact in a form quite unlike those which take shape in informal rule making, which has many analogies to a legislative committee hearing.   When the issue on appeal is whether a rule made in informal proceedings meets the criteria of Section 10, the court must necessarily go about the application of that standard in a manner unlike its review of findings of fact and conclusions of law compiled in a formal proceeding.

This exercise need be no less searching and strict in its weighing of whether the agency has performed in accordance with the Congressional purposes, but, because it is addressed to different materials, it inevitably varies from the adjudicatory model.   The paramount objective is to see whether the agency, given an essentially legislative task to perform, has carried it out in a manner calculated to negate the dangers of arbitrariness and irrationality in the formulation of rules for general application in the future.   With this concept of the scope of review enjoined upon us by the interaction of the Safety Act and Section 10 of the APA, we turn to petitioners' attack upon the merits of the Standard.

Petitioner APAA, by letters dated November 20, 1967 and January 22, 1968, responded to the invitation to comment extended in the notices of proposed rule making.   It also, jointly with petitioner Sterling, filed a

---

12. The statement in the text of the standard simply stated:

This standard specifies requirements for head restraints to reduce the frequency and severity of neck injury in rear-end and other collisions.

33 Fed. Reg. 2916 (1968).   The reasoning of the Administrator's denial of rehearing is discussed at length in the second part of this opinion.   That a court may consider the statement of an agency in denying a request for rehearing in deciding whether the requirements of APA § 4(b) have been met is shown by *Logansport Broadcasting Corp. v. United States,* 210 F.2d 24, 27–28 (1954).

petition for reconsideration after the Standard had been promulgated. * * * In all three documents, objection was made to any standard which would require factory implemented head restraints because, quite apart from depriving petitioners of sales, it would result, so it was said, in:

   a. higher costs for the consumer;

   b. an aggravation of monopolistic conditions in the auto industry;

   c. longer delays and lead times in implementing the original standard, as well as subsequent improvements;

   d. encouragement of minimum standards; and

   e. deprivation of consumers' choice.

It was further argued that, if the standard were to apply to the equipment and not to the vehicles themselves (in other words, if all head restraints had to meet the Federal standards but there was no requirement that they be in place as the cars leave the factory), there would be:

   a. continual improvement and innovation through competition;

   b. consumer choice (allowing each consumer to buy a head restraint which was best for a person of his size); and

   c. faster implementation of the standard.

It was also urged that there were no technical reasons why head restraints had to be factory installed, that the independent manufacturers had already produced millions of head restraints, and that installation was simple and inexpensive; and that "any possible ease in enforcement * * * cannot and should not be the sole criteria" for preferring factory implementation.

The alternative suggested by petitioners to factory implementation was to permit consumers to select the particular head restraint which best suited their needs from among competing brands certified to be in compliance with Federal standards. In short, consumers would choose head restraints as they might choose the color of their car. And, if it were felt that head restraints should be mandatory, then the regulation should simply require installation before delivery.

In the order promulgating Standard No. 202, the Administrator responded to several comments received from different parties. The following was directed toward petitioner's submissions:

> A comment from an equipment manufacturer and an equipment manufacturer's association asserted that the Standard should not require that motor vehicle manufacturers provide head restraints at the time of vehicle manufacture, but that each customer should be free to equip his vehicle with head restraints of his own choice, maintaining that the installation of head restraints is a relatively simple matter and that there appears to be virtually no technological advantage in requiring factory installation. The Administration has determined that safety dictates that head restraints be provided on all passenger cars manufactured on or after January 1, 1969, and that a head restraint standard that merely specified performance requirements for head restraint equipment would not insure that all passenger cars would be so

equipped, and would not, therefore, meet the need for safety. Furthermore, the Administration has determined that the performance of a head restraint is dependent upon the strength of the structure of the seat to which it is attached, as well as the compatibility of the head restraint with its anchorage to the seat structure.

In response to the petitioners' petition for reconsideration, the Administrator further elaborated his reasons for rejection in a three page letter, dated May 20, 1968. The Administrator first noted that "Your submissions concede, and indeed strongly champion the safety protection and benefit to the public provided by head restraint devices in vehicles. * * * [but] you would have us make the matter of affording this kind of protection optional with the purchaser of the vehicle in order to preserve a part of your business." The Administrator stated that he did not have the authority under the Act to require purchasers of vehicles to install equipment, and said that petitioners misconstrued the law if they thought the Act allows the Administrator to establish equipment standards applicable to equipment rather than to vehicles and then "to require purchasers of vehicles to install such equipment."

* * *

After noting that most of the arguments in the petition for reconsideration had been made earlier, the Administrator stated that:

> Among the reasons for not adopting the recommendations made in the comments and denying the Petition for Reconsideration are:
> (1) a head restraint standard promulgated as an equipment standard would not result in all passenger cars being equipped with head restraints on or after the effective date of the standard, but instead would make available head restraints that meet a standard which could be installed in vehicles if vehicle owners, at their option, so desired. This would therefore not meet the need for safety.
> (2) The performance of a head restraint system is dependent upon the interrelation between the head restraint, the structure of the seat and the seat anchorage.
> (3) An equipment standard in lieu of a vehicle performance standard would result in a restriction of design that would dictate that head restraints be add-on equipment without allowing other design options such as making the head restraint an integral part of the seat.
> In addition it is determined that an earlier effective date of Standard No. 202 would not be reasonable or practicable for Standard No. 202 in its present form; and that revision of Standard 202 to make such an effective date possible, such as your request that head restraints be optional add-on equipment, would result in a substantial reduction in the protection afforded the public.

And, in a paragraph which perhaps best summarizes the Administrator's reasons for rejecting petitioners' position, he wrote:

> In weighing petitioners' contentions with regard to Standard No. 202 the public interest was clearly on the side of a vehicle performance requirement which would require the vehicle manufacturer to install the device using any design he might choose to provide a requisite level of protection against whip-

lash injuries. In issuing the standard this consideration far outweighed the possible economic disadvantage that such a decision might impose on the petitioners and best accomplished the stated purpose and policy of the National Traffic and Highway Safety Act of 1966 "To reduce traffic accidents and deaths and injuries to persons resulting from traffic accidents. (15 U.S.C. 1381.)"

The question before us is whether these responses to the objections raised by petitioners adequately reflect, in the language of Section 4, a rational "consideration of the relevant matter presented" as embodied in "a concise general statement of [the] basis and purpose" of the Standard under view. We think they do, and that the picture they present is one of conscientious attention to the objections raised to the proposed rule, and their reasoned disposition on the basis of technical information and other relevant considerations which we have no basis for rejecting. The principal elements in the decision to require factory installation appear to have been (1) greater ease of enforcement and consequent assurance of the extension of protection to consumers and (2) the enhancement of protection due to the relationship between the head restraint and the structure of which it is a part. The one seems evident to us as a matter of common experience, while the other is amply supported by expert opinion in the record. The record also supports the reasonableness of the effective date of January 1, 1969, as against petitioners' insistence upon greater haste.

ALTERNATIVE ARGUMENT

For the first time in this court, petitioners change gears and question the contributions of head restraints to the cause of safety. They assert in their brief that:

> "A considerable amount of evidence and material was submitted in the course of the Administrative proceedings suggesting that a head restraint standard was not needed to protect the public against 'unreasonable risk' of injury, that head restraints could increase safety hazards for individual drivers and passengers, that any standard with regard to head restraints should continue to make their use optional, and that there was a lack of reliable information with regard to the entire subject matter."

This "evidence and material" was not, of course, forthcoming from petitioners, since at that time they were busily applauding the Administrator's apparent purpose to impose the blessings of head restraints upon the motoring public, albeit chiding him at the same time for being so slow about it. The sources of this "evidence and material" were, of course, mainly the motor car manufacturers who tended to greet the proposed rule with controlled rapture and who generally argued that the restraints should be optional and not mandatory.

Petitioners now tell us that the Administrator did not, by appropriate findings, deal adequately with these objections, and that, although those who propounded them are not here attacking the Standard, the Standard should be set aside for this reason. This is, to say the least, a soaringly expansive concept of the scope to be afforded on judicial review to a participant in a rule making proceeding. Having urged upon the Administrator the adoption of a mandatory requirement of head restraints because of their contribution to safety, petitioners now tell us to set the order aside because it did not answer the arguments of those who said that the safety aspects were so dubious as to justify, at most, an optional system. We find it hard to take petitioners seriously on this score, despite their effort to analogize themselves to private attorneys general with an unlimited right to expose all dangers to the public interest.

In any event, we find substantial support in the record for a conclusion that the contribution of head restraints to consumer safety is such as to warrant their inclusion in all newly-manufactured motor cars. There can be no question but that the Administrator, on the basis of the submission made to him, could reasonably determine that the benefits from mandatory head restraints far outweighed any disadvantages from such restraints due to decreased visibility, or other possible adverse effects upon safety. On the one hand, the benefits from the reduction of neck injuries in rear-end crashes were clearly identifiable from information and specific data contained in submissions from such independent sources as the Office of Biomechanics Research Center of Wayne State University, and the American Association for Automotive Medicine, as well as a substantial statistical compilation within the Department. The evidence that head restraints might lead to significant safety disadvantages, on the other hand, seems rather speculative. The Administrator must of necessity consider many variables, and make "trade-offs" between various desiderata in deciding upon a particular standard for auto safety. On the record before us, we think it clear that Standard No. 202 meets the substantive requirements of the Safety Act.[18]

Thus, having appraised all of petitioners' claims against the Standard, we find no occasion to interfere with its operation. Rule makers, as the delegatees of legislative power, are no more likely than their delegators to make everybody happy with a particular exercise of that power. Our function is to see only that the result is reasonable and within the range of authority conveyed, that it has been formulated in the manner prescribed, and that the disappointed have had the opportunity provided by Congress to try to make their views prevail. On all these counts we are satisfied by the record before us. The petitions for review are

Denied.

---

18. Section 103 of the Vehicle Safety Act provides:

(a) * * * Each such Federal motor vehicle safety standard shall be practicable, shall meet the need for motor vehicle safety, and shall be stated in objective terms.

* * *

(f) In prescribing standards under this section, the Secretary shall

(1) consider relevant available motor vehicle safety data, including the results of research, development, testing and evaluation activities conducted pursuant to this chapter;

(2) consult with the Vehicle Equipment Safety Commission, and such other state or interstate agencies (including legislative committees) as he deems appropriate;

(3) consider whether any such proposed standard is reasonable, practicable and appropriate for the particular type of motor vehicle or item of motor vehicle equipment for which it is prescribed; and

(4) consider the extent to which such standards will contribute to carrying out the purposes of this chapter.

Notes

1. The procedural requirements and judicial review standards of the APA have historically been viewed as symmetrical: When a statute requires an agency's action to be based "on the record after opportunity for an agency hearing," the substantial evidence standard applies; when an agency may proceed informally—in making rules or reaching other decisions—its actions are reviewable under the "arbitrary and capricious" standard. A corollary is the belief that review under the latter standard is less exacting than under the "substantial evidence" test. But the relationship between agency procedure and the scope of substantive review goes beyond the explicit linkages of the APA. If, as Judge McGowan acknowledges, the Secretary had followed sections 556 and 557, he would necessarily have generated an extensive formal record—including direct testimony or written statements of witnesses, cross-examination, exhibits, findings of fact, and conclusions of law—resembling the record in a civil trial. The "record" yielded by the typical informal rulemaking during the late 1960's looked very different. Indeed, probably few agencies saw the process as producing a recognizable "record"—either for internal decision or court review.

To be sure, informal rulemaking has always generated a good deal of paper. Even in 1967, a conscientious agency might have assembled voluminous views, data, and reports in developing a proposed rule. But these sources might or might not be public, and they probably would not have been assembled into an organized record even when presented to agency decisionmakers. The agency's notice of proposed rulemaking probably set forth the text of its contemplated rule, usually accompanied by a few paragraphs describing what the rule was supposed to accomplish. Rarely did a proposal analyze the data on which the agency relied or explain its tentative choices among competing approaches.

A proposed rule might elicit numerous written comments, which would be collected as they were submitted, usually at the end of the comment period. Comments followed no standard form; they ranged from brief expostulatory letters to lengthy briefs of law and fact. Comments are not required to address issues in a particular order, so agency analysts had to array submissions around some predetermined matrix of issues. If comments were later arranged in other than chronological sequence, this would have been done to meet the needs of the agency—not to satisfy any requirement of the APA. Sometimes comments remained unassembled, unindexed, and possibly even unread long after a rulemaking concluded.

An agency's final regulation would be published in the Federal Register, generally accompanied by assurances that the comments had been considered. Changes in the rule's text might reveal such consideration, and specific references to comments that had prompted changes were common. But few agencies made a serious effort to canvass all of the issues raised or to explain how they had resolved them. (In this respect, the Secretary of Transportation may have been more conscientious than many federal rulemakers of the era.) An agency's Federal Register publication typically consisted of the final text of the rule and a brief explanation of its rationale, a so-called "preamble." The NHTSA's head restraint rule occupied slightly more than one three-column page in the Federal Register, of which roughly half was introductory discussion or "preamble."

Federal agency practice in informal rulemaking has changed dramatically since the late 1960's, in part in response to judicial review. For discussions of this development, see DeLong, *Informal Rulemaking and the Integration of Law and Policy*, 65 Va. L. Rev. 257 (1979); Diver, *Policymaking Paradigms in Administrative Law*, 95 Harv. L. Rev. 393 (1981); and Pedersen, *Formal Records and Informal Rulemaking*, 85 Yale L.J. 38 (1975).

2. In *Auto Parts* Judge McGowan focuses on the requirement in section 553(c) of the APA that an agency "shall incorporate in the rules adopted a concise general statement of their basis and purpose." Since the court purports to be reviewing only for arbitrariness, conventional doctrine would suggest that any colorable explanation could sustain the agency's rule. And the court's apparent acceptance of the Secretary's obvious statement—that the "standard specifies requirements for head restraints to reduce the frequency and severity of head injury in rear-end and other collisions"—might suggest this is all that was required. Yet Judge McGowan's scrutiny of the Secretary's justification for the head restraint rule is far more searching than would be the case if "arbitrary or capricious" were taken in its constitutional sense. He quotes liberally from portions of the Federal Register publication in which the Secretary explains his choices and also cites passages from the Secretary's denial of reconsideration. These sources together comprise an explanation for the head restraint rule that, while by no means prolix, is more expansive and detailed than the APA language (or the court's footnote 12) might suggest. In surveying these materials, Judge McGowan seems to demand, first, that the agency provide reasons for its choices—not merely summarize the purpose of its rule. Further, he implies that the reasons offered must be plausible—the enhanced enforcibility of requiring manufacturer-installed headrests—or supported by data in the rulemaking record—the strength advantages of manufacturer-installation. Finally, McGowan looks to see that the agency considered key arguments put forward in comments from members of the public, in this case from the petitioners themselves.

The APA legislative history contains the following explanation of section 553(c)'s "concise general statement" requirement: "The agency must analyze and consider all relevant matter presented. The required statement * * * should not only relate to the data so presented but with reasonable fullness explain the actual basis and objectives of the rule." Sen. Doc. No. 248, 79th Cong., 2d Sess. 201, 259 (1946). The Attorney General's Manual on the Administrative Procedure Act (1947) expressed the opinion that these statements would be important as an aid to interpretation, but that "findings of fact and conclusions of law are not necessary. Nor is there required an elaborate analysis of the rules or of the considerations upon which the rules were issued. Rather, the statement is intended *to advise the public* of the general basis and purpose of the rules." Id. at 32 (emphasis supplied).

3. The APA's demand for an adequate, contemporaneous, statement of a regulation's "basis and purpose" has not been enforced literally. Rarely has an agency rule been overturned because the required explanation failed to appear in the Federal Register text. Reviewing courts have discerned an agency's rationale in other documents prepared contemporaneously by agency decisionmakers and sometimes inferred it from the content of the rule itself. See, e.g., *Alabama Association of Insurance Agents v. Board of Governors*, 533 F.2d 224 (5th Cir. 1976), cert. denied 435 U.S. 904 (1978) (employing amicus briefs and the records of adjudicatory hearings applying the rule to discern the agency's "basis and purpose"). Yet the jurisprudence is hardly uniform. Many cases reject the use of any agency generated explanations or data put forward in support of a rule, but subsequent

to its issuance, as *"post hoc rationalizations,"* see *Tabor v. Joint Board for Enrollment of Actuaries,* 566 F.2d 705 (D.C. Cir. 1977); *Rodway v. United States Department of Agriculture,* 514 F.2d 809 (D.C. Cir. 1975), and refuse to parse the record for supporting data not relied upon in the agency's contemporaneous rationale. E. g., *Kennecott Copper Corp. v. EPA,* 462 F.2d 846 (D.C. Cir. 1972). The concerns reflected in this less generous jurisprudence seem to include (1) a desire to provide information to potential litigants who, if well-informed, might pursue further administrative procedures (such as a request for rehearing) rather than judicial review; (2) a desire to force agencies to be more explicitly rational in justifying their choices, thereby (presumably) guarding against unknown influences that might have corrupted the administrative process; and (3) a desire to force reconsideration of superficially implausible decisions.

Petitioner

NATIONAL TIRE DEALERS & RETREADERS ASSOCIATION v. BRINEGAR

United States Court of Appeals, District of Columbia Circuit, 1974.
491 F.2d 31.

WILKEY, CIRCUIT JUDGE.

Petitioner National Tire Dealers and Retreaders Association, Inc. (NTDRA) seeks review of Federal Motor Vehicle Safety Standard No. 117. * * *

Petitioner focuses its challenge on paragraph S6.3.2 of Standard No. 117, which requires that all pneumatic passenger tires retreaded on or after 1 February 1974 have the following information *permanently* molded into or on one sidewall of the tire: size, maximum inflation pressure and load; actual number of plies or ply rating; the words "tubeless" or "tube-type," as applicable; and the words "bias/belted" or "radial," as applicable.[3] The administrative record does not adequately demonstrate that these requirements are practicable, nor does it establish any more than a remote relation between the requirements and motor vehicle safety. The Act mandates that motor vehicle safety standards promulgated thereunder be "practicable" and "meet the need for motor vehicle safety." Therefore, we vacate that portion of the Order establishing Motor Vehicle Safety Standard No. 117 which relates to permanent labeling of tire size, maximum inflation pressure, ply rating, tubeless or tube-type, and

---

3. 49 C.F.R. § 571.117a (1972) reads in pertinent part:

S6.3.2 Each retreaded pneumatic tire produced on or after [February 1, 1974] shall be permanently labeled in at least one location on the completed retreaded tire, in letters and numerals not less than three thirty-seconds of an inch that are molded into or onto the tire sidewall, with the following information:

(a) The tire's size designation;

(b) The tire's maximum permissible inflation pressure, either as it appears on the casing or as set forth in Table I;

(c) The tire's maximum load, either as it appears on the casing or as set forth in Table I;

(d) The actual number of plies, ply rating, or both;

(e) The word "tubeless' if the tire is a tubeless tire, or the words "tube-type" if the tire is a tube-type tire;

(f) The word "bias/belted" if the tire is of bias-belted construction;

(g) The word "radial" if the tire is of radial construction.

bias/belted or radial construction. However, since section 201 of the Act commands that the Secretary promulgate permanent labeling standards with respect to actual number of plies and maximum permissible load,[5] the portion of Standard No. 117 relating to those characteristics must remain in effect.[6]

* * *

The stated purpose of the National Traffic and Motor Vehicle Safety Act of 1966 is "to reduce traffic accidents and deaths and injuries to persons resulting from traffic accidents." Thus, "each * * * Federal motor vehicle safety standard * * * shall meet the need for motor vehicle safety." The Act defines "motor vehicle safety" as "the performance of motor vehicles or motor vehicle equipment in such a manner that the public is protected against *unreasonable risk* of accidents occurring as a result of the design, construction or performance of motor vehicles and is also protected against *unreasonable risk* of death or injury to persons in the event accidents do occur. * * * "

The general requirement that retreaded tires be labeled with the items of information specified in paragraph S6.3.2 of Standard No. 117 clearly bears a substantial relation to the Act's purpose of achieving motor vehicle safety. * * *

* * *

But the issue here is what relation *permanent* labeling has to avoidance of those hazards. Petitioner recognizes the importance of labeling retreaded tires with the information required by Standard No. 117, and states:

> The retreading industry can and will record such information as is available on a label affixed to the retreaded tire so that the information will be known to the consumer at the time of purchase.

5. 15 U.S.C.A. § 1421 (1970):

In all standards for pneumatic tires established under subchapter I of this chapter, the Secretary shall require that tires subject thereto be permanently and conspicuously labeled with such safety information as he determines to be necessary to carry out the purposes of this chapter. Such labeling shall include—
* * *

(3) the actual number of plies in the tire.

(4) the maximum permissible load for the tire. * * *

The Secretary may require that additional safety related information be disclosed to the purchaser of a tire at the time of sale of the tire.

6. We would note further that section 201 mandates permanent labeling of retreaded tires with information about "the composition of the material used in the ply of the tire." 15 U.S.C.A. § 1421(2) (1970). Standard No. 117, however, contains no requirement relating to ply composition. The reason for this omission is set forth in the preamble to Standard No. 117:

> The proposed requirement that the tire be labeled with the generic name of its cord material is not retained. The comments have argued, and NHTSA agrees, that in the case of retreaded tires this information is not substantially related to safety. This, combined with the fact that it appears only on certain casings, where it must if it is to be relabeled, has convinced the NHTSA that at present the requirement should not be included in the standard.

37 Fed. Reg. 5952 (1972). Since Congress apparently concluded that permanent labeling of ply material is safety-related, the Secretary was powerless to conclude otherwise and thus erred in omitting a ply material requirement from Standard No. 117.

However, petitioner asserts that *the Secretary "has not found* that the information required by S6.3.2 can meet the need for motor vehicle safety *only if it is permanently labeled into the retreaded tire."*

A permanent labeling requirement is clearly unnecessary to protect original purchasers of retreaded tires. A non-permanent, affixed label can supply such purchasers with all the information specified in Standard No. 117 and thus permit them to select tires of proper size and construction. Therefore, lack of permanent labeling could become a factor affecting safety only in the event that a retreaded tire is resold or put to some different use after the affixed label has worn off. The Secretary raised this possibility in the preamble to Standard No. 117:

> Tires * * * may be subject to many applications during their useful life. They are transferred from wheel to wheel and from vehicle to vehicle, and each time this takes place the information on the tire sidewall becomes important. Permanent labeling is therefore required if the information is to perform its function, as it can be readily assumed that affixed labels will last little longer than the first time the tire is mounted.

The Secretary has supplied no illustrations or references to the record to amplify these observations. We can hypothesize two situations in which lack of permanent labeling could conceivably affect safety:

1. An original purchaser of retreaded tires wishes to replace one or more of those tires, and he needs to match up his new tire or tires with the remaining retreads.

2. Someone wishes to purchase retreaded tires from the original purchaser or from some other second-hand source.

There is no suggestion in the record or briefs of how frequently these hypothetical situations arise. They might occur so rarely that a costly and burdensome permanent labeling requirement geared to ensure safety in such situations is unreasonable. Furthermore, it is not clear that a second-hand purchaser of retreads or an original owner who seeks replacements is dependent on the tires' labeling for information necessary to proper match-ups, inflation, and loading. The Secretary's brief observes that an expert can determine many of the critical characteristics of a tire by mere inspection. Therefore, even in the hypothetical situations posed above, a permanent labeling requirement may not make a significant contribution to the Act's goal of enhancing the safety of motor vehicles. If there is a significant nexus between the permanent labeling requirement of Standard No. 117 and the goal of safety, it does not appear in the briefs or in the record of the rule-making proceedings.

As noted above, however, section 201 of the Act mandates that new and retreaded pneumatic tires be "permanently and conspicuously labeled" with safety information which the Secretary "determines to be necessary to carry out the purposes" of the Act. The section further provides, "Such labeling shall include * * * (3) the actual number of plies in the tire. (4) the maximum permissible load for the tire. * * * * " Thus, Congress has determined that permanent labeling of ply and load information on retreaded tires bears a significant relation to safety. Although our discussion of the relation of Standard No. 117 to safety applies with equal logic to permanent labeling of ply and load information, we must faithfully carry out the express mandate of Congress. No administrative procedure test applies to an act of Congress. Consequently, that portion of Standard No. 117 relating to permanent labeling of ply and load information must stand.

The apparently remote relationship between the permanent labeling requirements of Standard No. 117 and the goal of motor vehicle safety might be tolerable if those standards imposed no significant burden on the tire retreading industry. However, there are numerous indications in the record that permanent labeling of retreaded tires with the information required by Standard No. 117 would be economically unfeasible. In the face of these indications, the Secretary offers mere assertions, unsupported by any citations to the record, that the requirements are practicable. Therefore, the Secretary's Order establishing the permanent labeling requirements of Standard No. 117 is an "arbitrary" agency action that must be set aside under section 10(e) of the APA.

Section 103(a) of the Act provides that each "Federal motor vehicle safety standard shall be practicable. * * * " Section 103(f) further provides, "In prescribing standards under this section, the Secretary shall * * * (3) consider whether any such proposed standard is reasonable, practicable and appropriate for the particular type of motor vehicle or item of motor vehicle equipment for which it is prescribed." * * *

The record in the case at bar contains considerable comment to the effect that the permanent labeling required by Standard No. 117 would be unreasonably costly and economically unfeasible. The basic problem is that most tire casings received by retreaders either do not bear permanent labeling or the information required by Standard No. 117 or are labeled in a location where the markings are subject to obliteration during the retreading process. While permanent labeling of new tires has been required for several years by Motor Vehicle Safety Standard No. 109, the *location* of the labeling was not specified until the Department of Transportation promulgated an amendment, effective 1 July 1973, which requires that one sidewall bear the requisite information between the "maximum section width and bead." This belated recognition of the practicalities of the retreading process will ensure that the markings are not buffed off during retreading so that, eventually, as the Department explained, "retreaders need not relabel tires in meeting the requirements of Standard No. 117."

The amended requirements for new tire labeling have little impact on the current inventories of new tire casings maintained by the retreading industry. It has been estimated that only about one third of the casings presently in supply bear the requisite labeling in a location where it is not subject to buffing off during the retreading process. Therefore, Standard No. 117 would force the retreading industry to choose between two equally undesirable alternatives. First, retreaders might use only those new tire casings that bear the requisite information in a permanent location. This course of action would necessarily result in a two-thirds reduction in the volume of retreaded tire production and inevitably cause severe economic dislocation in the industry. Second, retreaders could mold the required information into the tire sidewalls during the retreading process. However, the comments of retreaders in the administrative record indicate that this, too, is far from an economically feasible alternative.

Apparently the retreading process cannot be economically adapted to labeling each tire permanently with the seven items of information required by Standard No. 117. * * * In order to label tires permanently with the requisite information during this process "it would be necessary for an employee to work with handtools on a mold that would have a temperature somewhere between 250 and 300 degrees F. exposing him to the danger of burns in an effort to change the varied plates with this information on it as each tire is changed in the mold." Altering the mold plates in this fashion would be necessary for almost every tire run through the production lines, since the size, number of plies, construction, maximum pressure, and other characteristics vary from tire to tire. * * *

One retreader has summarized the economic unfeasibility of the permanent labeling requirements specified in Standard No. 117:

> As an experiment, we ran a series of casings that had labeling in the shoulder area that would be removed in the retreading process. Our experience has indicated that the best we can do with a relabeling program is to be 80% effective, and our additional cost is more than $2.50 per retread. This is an increase of 30%.

Of course, the court need not accept at face value the self-serving comments of interested members of the retreading industry. However, such comments raise serious doubts about the practicability of Standard No. 117. In the face of these doubts, the Secretary offers only unsupported and unconvincing assertions that the permanent labeling requirements are practicable and economically feasible, and, in so doing, attempts to equate the data required for safety with that already required for record-keeping.[40] However, the information required by the Identification and Record Keeping Regulations is significantly different. It consists of such items as the name of the manufacturer and week in which the tire was retreaded. With the exception of the latter, these items do not vary from tire to tire as do the items specified in Standard No. 117; the week of retreading can easily be changed at the start of each week while the retreading molds are cool. The Administration's further suggestion that

---

40. In the preamble to Standard No. 117, the National Highway Traffic Safety Administration stated:

The NHTSA disagrees with industry claims that permanent labeling presents unreasonable technical problems. *Methods for permanent labeling developed for compliance with the Tire Identification and Recordkeeping Regulations (49 CFR Part 574) can be readily adapted to meet these requirements.* In fact, of all the information required in today's amendment, only the "size" and "maximum load rating" will vary to a significant amount from casing to casing. Each of the other items of required information can be applied uniformly to large groups of casings and need not be changed from tire to tire if proper sorting is done before retreading occurs.

37 Fed. Reg. 5952 (1972) (emphasis supplied.) * * *

casings could be sorted into uniform groups before retreading to minimize the frequency of alterations in the retreading mold appears reasonable, but there is nothing in the record to indicate whether such a sorting process would be practicable and not unreasonably costly.

Ultimately the Secretary's position rests on the following statement that appears in the Administration's Denial of Petitions for Reconsideration:

> Many of the petitions request the NHTSA to furnish data supporting specific decisions and determinations reflected in the standard. The decisions and determinations embodied in this standard are based on all the information at the agency's disposal, together with the informed judgment and expertise of agency personnel. Documentary materials relating to NHTSA decisions regarding the standard are part of the public docket. The agency is not obliged by law, nor does it consider it appropriate, to categorize or interpret those records as supporting particular statements or decisions made on rulemaking issuances.

While it is true that an agency may act after informal rule-making procedures "upon the basis of information available in its own files, and upon the knowledge and expertise of the agency," in the case at bar the Secretary's allusions to information and knowledge outside the record are unpersuasive in light of the powerful doubts raised by the on-the-record comments of petitioner and others about the practicability of the permanent labeling requirements. The Secretary's statement of the reasons for his conclusion that the requirements are practicable is not so inherently plausible that the court can accept it on the agency's mere *ipse dixit*. We are compelled to conclude that the Secretary's practicability determination was arbitrary and thus requires us to set aside Standard No. 117 under section 10(e) of the APA.[45]

* * *

Vacated in part.

Notes

1. There can be no mistaking the intensity of court review in *Brinegar*. What is Judge Wilkey's basis for rejecting NHTSA'S rule: The Secretary's failure to marshall evidence that permanent labeling of retreaded tires would be "practicable"? Or his failure to meet the retreaders' claims that permanent labeling would not be "practicable"?

2. What explains the different outcomes in *Auto Parts* and *Brinegar*? The Secretary of Transportation followed similar rulemaking procedures in the two

---

45. It must be noted that by enacting section 201 of the Motor Vehicle Safety Act. * * * Congress apparently concluded that permanent labeling of retreads with the actual number of plies and maximum permissible load would be practicable. Therefore, we are powerless to overturn the corresponding portions of Safety Standard No. 117 on the ground of impracticability. Consequently, retreaders will be compelled permanently to label their tires with the actual number of plies, maximum permissible load and, pursuant to section 201(2) of the Act, "the composition of the material used in the ply of the tire." While permanent labeling of these three items will likely be difficult and costly for retreaders, it should not be as burdensome as the labeling of all seven items specified in Standard No. 117 would be.

cases and, according to Judge Wilkey, the court applied the same standard of review. Does the Secretary have a heavier burden of justifying the practicability of standards than their relationship to safety?

Judge Robinson was the only member of the court of appeals who participated in both cases; and in a separate opinion he explained his concurrence in *Brinegar* as follows (491 F.2d at 41–43):

> The problem * * * is that the Secretary's standard calls for permanent labeling on each retreaded tire of six individual characteristics of that tire. The methodology of permanent labeling on which the industry settled is insertion into the retread matrix of a slug that accomplishes the labeling. The number of combinations of characteristics is vast; a change of slugs becomes necessary each time a change of a single characteristic occurs, and the standard would currently intercept an estimated 20 million of the tires now retreaded annually. The administrative record echoes the many complaints that operational and economic havoc in the retreading industry will be the inevitable result.

> In this milieu, I agree that the Secretary was summoned to focus on these realities. The Act directs the Secretary to consider, among other things, whether standards he proposes are "practicable," and as the legislative history denotes, it does not suffice to view merely the "technological ability to achieve the goal of a particular standard." "[E]conomic factors" as well must be scrutinized, and these include "reasonableness of cost" and "feasibility." * * *

> * * * One may search the record before us for acceptable support for the Secretary's conclusion that the test of practicality was met, but the search will be in vain. That, in my view, is the fatal flaw in the Secretary's case.

3. The inference is strong that the retreaders' primary objections were to the size and maximum load requirements which, as the Secretary acknowledged, may preclude pre-sorting of casings into large groups. What accounts for the court's contrasting treatment of these requirements? Did Congress make a more convincing factual case for its maximum load requirement than the Secretary made for permanent size labeling? Since Congress, in the court's words, "apparently concluded" that permanent labeling of maximum load rating was "practicable," why wasn't the Secretary entitled to rely on that legislative judgment as dispositive of the practicability of imprinting tire size—and the other characteristics prescribed in the rule?

4. The *Brinegar* case is only one of numerous decisions that appear to undermine the traditional theory that review for arbitrariness is less demanding than review for substantial evidence. See, e.g., *Bunny Bear, Inc. v. Peterson*, 473 F.2d 1002 (1st Cir. 1973). Though often reiterated, this traditional assumption has been characterized as mistaken:

> The essential constraint of the "substantial evidence" test is not that it requires a higher degree of support for an agency determination (the arbitrary and capricious standard itself would probably be violated by a determination made on the basis of insubstantial evidence) but rather, that it requires this support to be contained within the confines of the public record made pursuant to the provisions of sections 556 and 557 of the Administrative Procedure Act.

Scalia and Goodman, *Procedural Aspects of the Consumer Product Safety Act,* 20 U.C.L.A. L. Rev. 899, 934 (1973).

Several statutes passed by Congress during the 1970's eroded the APA's original symmetry between the procedures required for rulemaking and the applicable standard for review. But far from accepting the proposition that the "arbitrary or capricious" standard can be as demanding as the "substantial evidence" test, Congress has assumed that the latter *is* more rigorous—and specifically incorporated it in many statutes that authorize rules to be made through informal rulemaking.   One example is the Consumer Product Safety Act, 15 U.S.C.A. § § 2051 *et seq.*, which empowers the Consumer Product Safety Commission to adopt product safety rules through notice and comment procedures, with the added requirement that interested parties be allowed to make oral representations, but specifies that such rules must be "supported by substantial evidence on the record as a whole."   The Occupational Safety and Health Act, 29 U.S.C.A. § 651 *et seq.*, similarly authorizes essentially informal rulemaking while prescribing substantial evidence review.   This hybrid was the product of a compromise between those members of Congress who wanted informal rulemaking with review under the arbitrary or capricious standard and those, many of whom opposed the basic legislation, who held out for formal procedures with substantial evidence review.   See *Industrial Union Department AFL-CIO v. Hodgson,* 499 F.2d 467, 469 (D.C. Cir. 1974), where Judge McGowan lamented that "the federal courts * * * surely have some claim to be spared additional burdens deriving from the illogic of legislative compromise."

5. The trend, discernible in *Auto Parts* and *Brinegar,* toward more exacting judicial scrutiny of the substantive basis for administrative rules, has continued. See K. DAVIS, ADMINISTRATIVE LAW OF THE SEVENTIES § 29.01-2 (Cum. Supp. 1977).   Regardless of the standard of review prescribed by Congress, reviewing courts now are accustomed to insist that the agency have taken a "hard look" at the agency's resolution of all material issues.   See *Greater Boston Television Corp. v. FCC,* 444 F.2d 841, 850-53 (D.C. Cir. 1970), cert. denied 403 U.S. 923 (1971).

Several factors have stimulated the trend toward more exacting review.   It stems, in part, from language in Justice Marshall's opinion for the Supreme Court in *Citizens to Preserve Overton Park, Inc. v. Volpe,* 401 U.S. 402 (1971), p. 629 infra.   Though that case did not involve rulemaking, Marshall wrote that a reviewing court charged with determining whether agency action was arbitrary or capricious must conduct a "searching and careful" factual inquiry into whether the action "was based on a consideration of the relevant factors and whether there has been a clear error of judgment."   Id. at 416.   Lower courts have relied upon this language to justify painstaking scrutiny of the evidentiary basis for many varieties of administrative action, including regulations adopted through informal rulemaking.   The trend also is attributable to the conviction among reviewing courts that they play an integral role in the administrative process.   See generally Gardner, *Federal Courts and Agencies: An Audit of the Partnership Books,* 75 Colum. L. Rev. 800 (1975); Leventhal, *Environmental Decision Making and the Role of the Courts,* 122 U. Pa. L. Rev. 509 (1974); Verkuil, *Judicial Review of Informal Rulemaking,* 60 Va. L. Rev. 185 (1974); Wright, *The Courts and the Rulemaking Process: The Limits of Judicial Review,* 59 Cornell L. Rev. 375 (1974).

MOTOR VEHICLE MANUFACTURERS ASSOCIATION v.
STATE FARM MUTUAL INSURANCE CO.

Supreme Court of the United States, 1983.
463 U.S. 29, 103 S. Ct. 2856, 77 L. Ed. 2d 443.

JUSTICE WHITE delivered the opinion of the Court.

* * * While a consensus exists that the current loss of life on our highways is unacceptably high, improving safety does not admit to easy solution. * * * Before changes in automobile design could be mandated, the effectiveness of these changes had to be studied, their costs examined, and public acceptance considered. This task called for considerable expertise and Congress responded by enacting the National Traffic and Motor Vehicle Safety Act of 1966, (Act), 15 U.S.C.A § § 1381 *et seq*. The Act * * * directs the Secretary of Transportation or his delegate to issue motor vehicle safety standards that "shall be practicable, shall meet the need for motor vehicle safety, and shall be stated in objective terms." * * *

The Act also authorizes judicial review under the provisions of the Administrative Procedure Act (APA) of all "orders establishing, amending, or revoking a Federal motor vehicle safety standard." Under this authority, we review today whether NHTSA acted arbitrarily and capriciously in revoking the requirement in Motor Vehicle Safety Standard 208 that new motor vehicles produced after September 1982 be equipped with passive restraints to protect the safety of the occupants of the vehicle in the event of a collision. Briefly summarized, we hold that the agency failed to present an adequate basis and explanation for rescinding the passive restraint requirement * * * .

Holding

As originally issued by the Department of Transportation in 1967, Standard 208 simply required the installation of seatbelts in all automobiles. It soon became apparent that the level of seatbelt use was too low to reduce traffic injuries to an acceptable level. The Department therefore began consideration of "passive occupant restraint systems"— devices that do not depend for their effectiveness upon any action taken by the occupant except that necessary to operate the vehicle. Two types of automatic crash protection emerged: automatic seatbelts and airbags.

* * * The life-saving potential of these devices was immediately recognized, and in 1977, after substantial on-the-road experience with both devices, it was estimated by NHTSA that passive restraints could prevent approximately 12,000 deaths and over 100,000 serious injuries annually.

In 1969, the Department formally proposed a standard requiring the installation of passive restraints, thereby commencing a lengthy series of proceedings. In 1970, the agency revised Standard 208 to include passive protection requirements, and in 1972, the agency amended the standard to require full passive protection for all front seat occupants of vehicles manufactured after August 15, 1975. In the interim, vehicles built between August 1973 and August 1975 were to carry either passive restraints or lap and shoulder belts coupled with an "ignition interlock" that would prevent starting the vehicle if the belts were not connected.   On review, the agency's decision to require passive restraints was found to be supported by "substantial evidence" and upheld.   *Chrysler Corp. v. Dep't of Transportation,* 472 F.2d 659 (CA6 1972).

In preparing for the upcoming model year, most car makers chose the "ignition interlock" option, a decision which was highly unpopular, and led Congress to amend the Act to prohibit a motor vehicle safety standard from requiring or permitting compliance by means of an ignition interlock or a continuous buzzer designed to indicate that safety belts were not in use.   The 1974 Amendments also provided that any safety standard that could be satisfied by a system other than seatbelts would have to be submitted to Congress where it could be vetoed by concurrent resolution of both houses.   15 U.S.C.A. § 1410b(b)(2).[6]

The effective date for mandatory passive restraint systems was extended for a year until August 31, 1976.   But in June 1976, Secretary of Transportation William Coleman initiated a new rulemaking on the issue. After hearing testimony and reviewing written comments, Coleman extended the optional alternatives indefinitely and suspended the passive restraint requirement.   Although he found passive restraints technologically and economically feasible, the Secretary based his decision on the expectation that there would be widespread public resistance to the new systems.   He instead proposed a demonstration project involving up to 500,000 cars installed with passive restraints, in order to smooth the way for public acceptance of mandatory passive restraints at a later date.

Coleman's successor as Secretary of Transportation disagreed. Within months of assuming office, Secretary Brock Adams decided that the demonstration project was unnecessary.   He issued a new mandatory passive restraint regulation, known as Modified Standard 208.   The Modified Standard mandated the phasing in of passive restraints beginning with large cars in model year 1982 and extending to all cars by model year 1984.   The two principal systems that would satisfy the Standard were airbags and passive belts; the choice of which system to install was left to the manufacturers.   In *Pacific Legal Foundation v. Dep't of Transportation,* 593 F.2d 1338 (CADC), cert. denied, 444 U.S. 830 (1979), the Court of Appeals upheld Modified Standard 208 as a rational, nonarbitrary regulation consistent with the agency's mandate under the Act. The standard also survived scrutiny by Congress, which did not exercise its authority under the legislative veto provision of the 1974 Amendments.

Over the next several years, the automobile industry geared up to comply with Modified Standard 208.   * * *   In February 1981, however, Secretary of Transportation Andrew Lewis reopened the rulemaking due to changed economic circumstances and, in particular, the difficulties of

---

6.   * * *   [T]he issue was not submitted to Congress until a passive restraint requirement was reimposed by Secretary Adams in 1977.   To comply with the Amendments, NHTSA proposed new warning systems to replace the prohibited continuous buzzers.   More significantly, NHTSA was forced to rethink an earlier decision which contemplated use of the interlocks in tandem with detachable belts.

the automobile industry. Two months later, the agency ordered a one-year delay in the application of the standard to large cars, extending the deadline to September 1982, and at the same time, proposed the possible rescission of the entire standard. After receiving written comments and holding public hearings, NHTSA issued a final rule that rescinded the passive restraint requirement contained in Modified Standard 208.

In a statement explaining the rescission, NHTSA maintained that it was no longer able to find, as it had in 1977, that the automatic restraint requirement would produce significant safety benefits. This judgment reflected not a change of opinion on the effectiveness of the technology, but a change in plans by the automobile industry. In 1977, the agency had assumed that airbags would be installed in 60% of all new cars and automatic seatbelts in 40%. By 1981 it became apparent that automobile manufacturers planned to install the automatic seatbelts in approximately 99% of the new cars. For this reason, the life-saving potential of airbags would not be realized. Moreover, it now appeared that the overwhelming majority of passive belts planned to be installed by manufacturers could be detached easily and left that way permanently. Passive belts, once detached, then required "the same type of affirmative action that is the stumbling block to obtaining high usage levels of manual belts." For this reason, the agency concluded that there was no longer a basis for reliably predicting that the standard would lead to any significant increased usage of restraints at all.

In view of the possibly minimal safety benefits, the automatic restraint requirement no longer was reasonable or practicable in the agency's view. The requirement would require approximately $1 billion to implement and the agency did not believe it would be reasonable to impose such substantial costs on manufacturers and consumers without more adequate assurance that sufficient safety benefits would accrue. In addition, NHTSA concluded that automatic restraints might have an adverse effect on the public's attitude toward safety. Given the high expense and limited benefits of detachable belts, NHTSA feared that many consumers would regard the standard as an instance of ineffective regulation, adversely affecting the public's view of safety regulation and, in particular, "poisoning popular sentiment toward efforts to improve occupant restraint systems in the future."

State Farm Mutual Automobile Insurance Co. and the National Association of Independent Insurers filed petitions for review of NHTSA's rescission of the passive restraint standard. The United States Court of Appeals for the District of Columbia Circuit held that the agency's rescission of the passive restraint requirement was arbitrary and capricious. 680 F.2d 206 (1982). While observing that rescission is not unrelated to an agency's refusal to take action in the first instance, the court concluded that, in this case, NHTSA's discretion to rescind the passive restraint requirement had been restricted by various forms of congressional "reaction" to the passive restraint issue. It then proceeded to find that the rescission of Standard 208 was arbitrary and capricious for three reasons. First, the court found insufficient as a basis for rescission

NHTSA's conclusion that it could not reliably predict an increase in belt usage under the Standard.   The court held that there was insufficient evidence in the record to sustain NHTSA's position on this issue, and that, "only a well-justified refusal to seek more evidence could render rescission non-arbitrary."   Second, a majority of the panel concluded that NHTSA inadequately considered the possibility of requiring manufacturers to install nondetachable rather than detachable passive belts.   Third, the majority found that the agency acted arbitrarily and capriciously by failing to give any consideration whatever to requiring compliance with Modified Standard 208 by the installation of airbags.

* * *

* * * Both the Motor Vehicle Safety Act and the 1974 Amendments concerning occupant crash protection standards indicate that motor vehicle safety standards are to be promulgated under the informal rulemaking procedures of § 553 of the Administrative Procedure Act.   The agency's action in promulgating such standards therefore may be set aside if found to be "arbitrary, capricious, an abuse of discretion, or otherwise not in accordance with law."   We believe that the rescission or modification of an occupant protection standard is subject to the same test. * * *

Petitioner Motor Vehicle Manufacturers Association (MVMA) disagrees, contending that the rescission of an agency rule should be judged by the same standard a court would use to judge an agency's refusal to promulgate a rule in the first place—a standard Petitioner believes considerably narrower than the traditional arbitrary and capricious test and "close to the borderline of nonreviewability."   We reject this view.   The Motor Vehicle Safety Act expressly equates orders "revoking" and "establishing" safety standards; neither that Act nor the APA suggests that revocations are to be treated as refusals to promulgate standards.   Petitioner's view would render meaningless Congress' authorization for judicial review of orders revoking safety rules.   Moreover, the revocation of an extant regulation is substantially different than a failure to act.   Revocation constitutes a reversal of the agency's former views as to the proper course.   A "settled course of behavior embodies the agency's informed judgment that, by pursuing that course, it will carry out the policies committed to it by Congress.   There is, then, at least a presumption that those policies will be carried out best if the settled rule is adhered to."   Accordingly, an agency changing its course by rescinding a rule is obligated to supply a reasoned analysis for the change beyond that which may be required when an agency does not act in the first instance.

In so holding, we fully recognize that "regulatory agencies do not establish rules of conduct to last forever," and that an agency must be given ample latitude to "adapt their rules and policies to the demands of changing circumstances."   But the forces of change do not always or necessarily point in the direction of deregulation.   In the abstract, there is no more reason to presume that changing circumstances require the rescission of prior action, instead of a revision in or even the extension of current regulation.   If Congress established a presumption from which judicial review should start, that presumption—contrary to petitioners' views—is not *against* safety regulation, but *against* changes in current policy that are not justified by the rulemaking record. While the removal of a regulation may not entail the monetary expenditures and other costs of enacting a new standard, and accordingly, it may be easier for an agency to justify a deregulatory action, the direction in which an agency chooses to move does not alter the standard of judicial review established by law.

The Department of Transportation accepts the applicability of the "arbitrary and capricious" standard. It argues that under this standard, a reviewing court may not set aside an agency rule that is rational, based on consideration of the relevant factors and within the scope of the authority delegated to the agency by the statute. We do not disagree with this formulation.[9] * * *

The Court of Appeals * * * erred in intensifying the scope of its review based upon its reading of legislative events. * * * [T]he Court of Appeals found significance in three legislative occurrences:

> "In 1974, Congress banned the ignition interlock but did not foreclose NHTSA's pursuit of a passive restraint standard. In 1977, Congress allowed the standard to take effect when neither of the concurrent resolutions needed for disapproval was passed. In 1980, a majority of each house indicated support for the concept of mandatory passive restraints and a majority of each house supported the unprecedented attempt to require some installation of airbags."

From these legislative acts and non-acts the Court of Appeals derived a "congressional commitment to the concept of automatic crash protection devices for vehicle occupants."

This path of analysis was misguided and the inferences it produced are questionable. * * * [T]his Court has never suggested that the *standard* of review is enlarged or diminished by subsequent congressional action. While an agency's interpretation of a statute may be confirmed or ratified by subsequent congressional failure to change that interpretation, in the case before us, even an unequivocal ratification—short of statutory incorporation—of the passive restraint standard would not connote approval or disapproval of an agency's later decision to rescind the regulation. * * *

* * *

The ultimate question before us is whether NHTSA's rescission of the passive restraint requirement of Standard 208 was arbitrary and capricious. We conclude, as did the Court of Appeals, that it was. We also conclude, but for somewhat different reasons, that further consideration of the issue by the agency is therefore required. * * *

---

9. The Department of Transportation suggests that the arbitrary and capricious standard requires no more than the minimum rationality a statute must bear in order to withstand analysis under the Due Process Clause. We do not view as equivalent the presumption of constitutionality afforded legislation drafted by Congress and the presumption of regularity afforded an agency in fulfilling its statutory mandate.

The first and most obvious reason for finding the rescission arbitrary and capricious is that NHTSA apparently gave no consideration whatever to modifying the Standard to require that airbag technology be utilized. Standard 208 sought to achieve automatic crash protection by requiring automobile manufactuers to install either of two passive restraint devices: airbags or automatic seatbelts. There was no suggestion in the long rulemaking process that led to Standard 208 that if only one of these options were feasible, no passive restraint standard should be promulgated. Indeed, the agency's original proposed standard contemplated the installation of inflatable restraints in all cars. Automatic belts were added as a means of complying with the standard because they were believed to be as effective as airbags in achieving the goal of occupant crash protection. At that time, the passive belt approved by the agency could not be detached. Only later, at a manufacturer's behest, did the agency approve of the detachability feature—and only after assurances that the feature would not compromise the safety benefits of the restraint. Although it was then foreseen that 60% of the new cars would contain airbags and 40% would have automatic seatbelts, the ratio between the two was not significant as long as the passive belt would also assure greater passenger safety.

The agency has now determined that the detachable automatic belts will not attain anticipated safety benefits because so many individuals will detach the mechanism. Even if this conclusion were acceptable in its entirety, standing alone it would not justify any more than an amendment of Standard 208 to disallow compliance by means of the one technology which will not provide effective passenger protection. It does not cast doubt on the need for a passive restraint standard or upon the efficacy of airbag technology. * * * Given the effectiveness ascribed to airbag technology by the agency, the mandate of the Safety Act to achieve traffic safety would suggest that the logical response to the faults of detachable seatbelts would be to require the installation of airbags. At the very least this alternative way of achieving the objectives of the Act should have been addressed and adequate reasons given for its abandonment. But the agency not only did not require compliance through airbags, it did not even consider the possibility in its 1981 rulemaking. Not one sentence of its rulemaking statement discusses the airbags-only option. * * *

The automobile industry has opted for the passive belt over the airbag, but surely it is not enough that the regulated industry has eschewed a given safety device. * * *

Although the agency did not address the mandatory airbags option the Court of Appeals noted that "airbags seem to have none of the problems that NHTSA identified in passive seatbelts," petitioners recite a number of difficulties that they believe would be posed by a mandatory airbag standard. * * * But these are not the agency's reasons for rejecting a mandatory airbag standard. Not having discussed the possibility, the agency submitted no reasons at all. The short—and sufficient—

answer to petitioners' submission is that the courts may not accept appellate counsel's *post hoc* rationalizations for agency action. * * *

* * * It is true that a rulemaking "cannot be found wanting simply because the agency failed to include every alternative device and thought conceivable by the mind of man * * * regardless of how uncommon or unknown that alternative may have been. * * * But the airbag is more than a policy alternative to the passive restraint standard; it is a technological alternative within the ambit of the existing standard. We hold only that given the judgment made in 1977 that airbags are an effective and cost-beneficial life-saving technology, the mandatory passive-restraint rule may not be abandoned without any consideration whatsoever of an airbags-only requirement.

Although the issue is closer, we also find that the agency was too quick to dismiss the safety benefits of automatic seatbelts. NHTSA's critical finding was that, in light of the industry's plans to install readily detachable passive belts, it could not reliably predict "even a 5 percentage point increase as the minimum level of expected usage increase." * * *

* * * We agree with petitioners that just as an agency reasonably may decline to issue a safety standard if it is uncertain about its efficacy, an agency may also revoke a standard on the basis of serious uncertainties if supported by the record and reasonably explained. Rescission of the passive restraint requirement would not be arbitrary and capricious simply because there was no evidence in direct support of the agency's conclusion. It is not infrequent that the available data does not settle a regulatory issue and the agency must then exercise its judgment in moving from the facts and probabilities on the record to a policy conclusion. Recognizing that policymaking in a complex society must account for uncertainty, however, does not imply that it is sufficient for an agency to merely recite the terms "substantial uncertainty" as a justification for its actions. The agency must explain the evidence which is available, and must offer a "rational connection between the facts found and the choice made." * * *

In this case, the agency's explanation for rescission of the passive restraint requirement is *not* sufficient to enable us to conclude that the rescission was the product of reasoned decisionmaking. To reach this conclusion, we do not upset the agency's view of the facts, but we do appreciate the limitations of this record in supporting the agency's decision. We start with the accepted ground that if used, seatbelts unquestionably would save many thousands of lives and would prevent tens of thousands of crippling injuries. Unlike recent regulatory decisions we have reviewed, *Industrial Union Department v. American Petroleum Institute*, 448 U.S. 607 (1980); *American Textile Manufacturers Inst., Inc. v. Donovan*, 452 U.S. 490 (1981) [infra p. 354 *et seq.*], the safety benefits of wearing seatbelts are not in doubt and it is not challenged that were those benefits to accrue, the monetary costs of implementing the standard would be easily justified. We move next to the fact that there is no direct evidence in support of the agency's finding that detachable automatic belts cannot be predicted to yield a substantial increase in usage. The empirical evidence on the record, consisting of surveys of drivers of automobiles equipped with passive belts, reveals more than a doubling of the usage rate experienced with manual belts. Much of the agency's rulemaking statement—and much of the controversy in this case—centers on the conclusions that should be drawn from these studies. The agency maintained that the doubling of seatbelt usage in these studies could not be extrapolated to an across-the-board mandatory standard because the passive seatbelts were guarded by ignition interlocks and purchasers of the tested cars are somewhat atypical. Respondents insist these studies demonstrate that Modified Standard 208 will substantially increase seatbelt usage. We believe that it is within the agency's discretion to pass upon the generalizability of these field studies. This is precisely the type of issue which rests within the expertise of NHTSA, and upon which a reviewing court must be most hesitant to intrude.

But accepting the agency's view of the field tests on passive restraints indicates only that there is no reliable real-world experience that usage rates will substantially increase. * * * [S]tatements that passive belts will not yield substantial increases in seatbelt usage apparently take no account of the critical difference between detachable automatic belts and current manual belts. A detached passive belt does require an affirmative act to reconnect it, but—unlike a manual seat belt—the passive belt, once reattached, will continue to function automatically unless again disconnected. Thus, inertia—a factor which the agency's own studies have found significant in explaining the current low usage rates for seatbelts—works in *favor* of, not *against*, use of the protective device. Since 20 to 50% of motorists currently wear seatbelts on some occasions, there would seen to be grounds to believe that seatbelt use by occasional users will be substantially increased by the detachable passive belts. Whether this is in fact the case is a matter for the agency to decide, but it must bring its expertise to bear on the question.

The agency is correct to look at the costs as well as the benefits of Standard 208. * * * When the agency reexamines its findings as to the likely increase in seatbelt usage, it must also reconsider its judgment of the reasonableness of the monetary and other costs associated with the Standard. In reaching its judgment, NHTSA should bear in mind that Congress intended safety to be the preeminent factor under the Motor Vehicle Safety Act. * * *

The agency also failed to articulate a basis for not requiring nondetachable belts under Standard 208. It is argued that the concern of the agency with the easy detachability of the currently favored design would be readily solved by a continuous passive belt, which allows the occupant to "spool out" the belt and create the necessary slack for easy extrication from the vehicle. * * *

By failing to analyze the continuous seatbelts in its own right, the agency has failed to offer the rational connection between facts and judgment required to pass muster under the arbitrary and capricious standard. We agree with the Court of Appeals that NHTSA did not suggest that the emergency release mechanisms used in nondetachable belts are any less effective for emergency egress than the buckle release system used in detachable belts. In 1978, when General Motors obtained the agency's approval to install a continuous passive belt, it assured the agency that nondetachable belts with spool releases were as safe as detachable belts with buckle releases. NHTSA was satisfied that this belt design assured easy extricability: "the agency does not believe that the use of [such] release mechanisms will cause serious occupant egress problems * * * ." While the agency is entitled to change its view on the acceptability of continuous passive belts, it is obligated to explain its reasons for doing so.

The agency also failed to offer any explanation why a continuous passive belt would engender the same adverse public reaction as the ignition interlock, and, as the Court of Appeals concluded, "every indication in the record points the other way." We see no basis for equating the two devices: the continuous belt, unlike the ignition interlock, does not interfere with the operation of the vehicle. More importantly, it is the agency's responsibility, not this Court's, to explain its decision.

"An agency's view of what is in the public interest may change, either with or without a change in circumstances. But an agency changing its course must supply a reasoned analysis. * * * " We do not accept all of the reasoning of the Court of Appeals but we do conclude that the agency has failed to supply the requisite "reasoned analysis" in this case. Accordingly, we vacate the judgment of the Court of Appeals and remand the case to that court with directions to remand the matter to the NHTSA for further consideration consistent with this opinion.

So ordered.

JUSTICE REHNQUIST, with whom THE CHIEF JUSTICE, JUSTICE POWELL, and JUSTICE O'CONNOR join, concurring in part and dissenting in part.

* * * I agree that, since the airbag and continuous spool automatic seatbelt were explicitly approved in the standard the agency was rescinding, the agency should explain why it declined to leave those requirements intact. In this case, the agency gave no explanation at all. Of course, if the agency can provide a rational explanation, it may adhere to its decision to rescind the entire standard.

I do not believe, however, that NHTSA's view of detachable automatic seatbelts was arbitrary and capricious. * * *

* * * It seems to me that the agency's explanation, while by no means a model, is adequate. The agency acknowledged that there would probably be some increase in belt usage, but concluded that the increase would be small and not worth the cost of mandatory detachable automatic belts. The agency's obligation is to articulate a "rational connection between the facts found and the choice made." I believe it has met this standard. * * *

The agency's changed view of the standard seems to be related to the election of a new President of a different political party. It is readily apparent that the responsible members of one administration may consider public resistance and uncertainties to be more important than do their counterparts in a previous administration. A change in administration brought about by the people casting their votes is a perfectly reasonable basis for an executive agency's reappraisal of the costs and benefits of its programs and regulations. As long as the agency remains within the bounds established by Congress,* it is entitled to assess administrative records and evaluate priorities in light of the philosophy of the administration.

Notes

1. As Justice Rehnquist's opinion intimates, rescission of the passive restraint standard was proposed by the Reagan administration as part of a larger package of "regulatory relief" for the automobile industry. See G. EADS & M. FIX, RELIEF OR REFORM?: REAGAN'S REGULATORY DILEMMA 125–33 (1984). This reason for the action was only hinted at in NHTSA's statement of basis and purpose accompanying rescission of the passive restraints rule. Apparently, the Administrator did not believe that he could simply say: "There has been an election since this rule was promulgated. The Carter administration thought passive restraints were a good idea; we do not. This disagreement reflects a fundamental difference in ideology. When in doubt the Carter administration chose to pursue protection of the public safety, notwithstanding the substantial economic costs and the intrusions on individual choice that such a posture entailed. Faced with these competing considerations, we make the contrary choice." Why should not such an explanation suffice?

2. In Secretary of Transportation Coleman's 1976 notice of proposed rulemaking (NPRM) he listed several "issues to be addressed" in the passive restraint proceedings. One issue was described in the following terms:

Appropriate Role of the Federal Government in Prescribing Motor Vehicle Safety Standards

The goal of motor vehicle safety expressed in the statute is clear and unequivocal. The question arises, however, as to the precise nature of the government's duty in this area and how to achieve the important end of motor vehicle safety while preserving, to the extent possible, both individual freedom of choice and the role of the marketplace in making economic decisions. In the democratic society in which we live, I believe it is my responsibility as a Federal official to consider these important concerns when prescribing safety standards.

Under the terms of the Safety Act, the Federal government's duty in prescribing safety standards is to protect the public "against unreasonable risk of death or injury to persons in the event accidents do occur." I believe that

---

*Of course, a new administration may not choose not to enforce laws of which it does not approve, or to ignore statutory standards in carrying out its regulatory functions. But in this case, as the Court correctly concludes, Congress has not required the agency to require passive restraints.

what constitutes an "unreasonable" risk of death or injury is a difficult but critical issue. * * *

In considering a mandate of any particular crash protection system, such as passive restraints, we are talking about government regulations which restrict individuals' freedom to choose the degree of safety protection they want and how much they are willing to pay for it. Individuals should be able to exercise some freedom of choice about how much they are willing to pay for safety protection in private transportation systems. Those who put a premium on freedom of choice contend that is not the role of the Federal government to protect citizens absolutely from deaths and injuries in automotive accidents. Rather, government should only ensure that adequate protection is provided which individuals can avail themselves of if they so choose. On the other hand, the stated purpose of the Safety Act is unequivocally "to reduce deaths and injuries to persons resulting from traffic accidents." While safety standards must be "reasonable," according to the statute, individual freedom of choice is not one of the statutorily explicit prescribed considerations and, arguably, should not be allowed to interfere arbitrarily with the basic purposes of the Act.

Mandating passive restraints in motor vehicles might create, additionally, a problem of equity. The issuance of a passive restraint standard will result in the manufacture of vehicles equipped with air bags or passive belts rather than lap and shoulder seat belts. These passive restraint-equipped vehicles will cost more, but, in tests to date, have been found to provide no materially greater protection to those individuals who already use lap and shoulder seat belts. Nevertheless, these individuals will have to pay more for their automobiles, without any measurable benefit, to help provide passive restraints to those who choose not to wear seat belts. Thus, those who currently wear seat belts would be forced to subsidize those who do not. How public policy should deal with such a subsidy is an issue upon which I would welcome comment.

Personal convenience is another aspect of individual freedom of choice. The Federal government's experiences with ignition interlock systems demonstrate that, despite reasonable cost and demonstrable safety benefits, personal convenience can be of overwhelming importance. In this regard, passive restraint systems appear to be very attractive; they probably are more convenient than safety belts in that they do not require any action by the automobile occupant to be effective.

Government regulation in the safety area, as elsewhere, tends to limit the role of the marketplace in making economic decisions, and thereby also to inhibit innovation. Certainly, mandating passive restraints does not comport with the ideal of a free enterprise economy. On the other hand, there are limitations to the benefits that the free market can provide. Some people supported the original passage of the Safety Act because they concluded that the traditional marketplace mechanism was not effective in satisfying our society's need for automotive safety. It is difficult to believe, for instance, that there would be seat belts in every car today if their installation had had to rely on the demands of the marketplace. The extent to which Federal regulations governing occupant crash protection should strive to preserve the role of the marketplace is an issue upon which I invite discussion.

41 Fed. Reg. 24,071 (June 14, 1976).

Suppose NHTSA Administrator Peck had wanted to rely on lack of "unreasonable risk," "individual freedom of choice," "equity" or the encouragement of "innovation" as a basis for rescinding standard 208. Could you have written him a reversal-proof statement of basis and purpose? What "facts" would be relevant to a decision premised on any of these grounds?

3. Given that the auto companies were indeed tooling-up to comply with standard 208 there may have been good reason to act immediately once it was decided that the rule should not be implemented in its then-promulgated form. Suppose the Administrator had published the rescission and, simultaneously, a new NPRM inviting comments on "where to go from here" concerning passive restraints. Presume further that there was language in the statement of basis and purpose to the effect that, while current data were incomplete, the prudent course seemed to be to prevent wasteful expenditures by manufacturers while the agency reconsidered its position. Is that essentially the posture the Administrator was in after the Supreme Court's decision? Would the Court have sustained the rescission under those circumstances? If it had, what would then be the agency's burden of justification were it to decide not to go forward with any of the proposed alternatives?

4. For a provocative analysis of the Court's *State Farm* opinion, see Sunstein, *Deregulation and the Hard-Look Doctrine*, 1983 Sup. Ct. Rev. 177.

INDUSTRIAL UNION DEPARTMENT v. AMERICAN PETROLEUM INSTITUTE

Supreme Court of the United States, 1980.
448 U.S. 607, 100 S. Ct. 2844, 65 L. Ed. 2d 1010.

MR. JUSTICE STEVENS announced the judgment of the Court and delivered an opinion, in which THE CHIEF JUSTICE and MR. JUSTICE STEWART joined and in Parts I, II, III–A–C and E of which MR. JUSTICE POWELL joined.

The Occupational Safety and Health Act of 1970, 29 U.S.C.A. § 651 *et seq.* (the Act), was enacted for the purpose of ensuring safe and healthful working conditions for every working man and woman in the Nation. This litigation concerns a standard promulgated by the Secretary of Labor to regulate occupational exposure to benzene, a substance which has been shown to cause cancer at high exposure levels. The principal question is whether such a showing is a sufficient basis for a standard that places the most stringent limitation on exposure to benzene that is technologically and economically possible.

The Act delegates broad authority to the Secretary to promulgate different kinds of standards. The basic definition of an "occupational safety and health standard" is found in § 3(8), which provides:

> "The term 'occupational safety and health standard' means a standard which requires conditions, or the adoption or use of one or more practices, means, methods, operations, or processes, reasonably necessary or appropriate to provide safe or healthful employment and places of employment."

Where toxic materials or harmful physical agents are concerned, a standard must also comply with § 6(b)(5), which provides:

High Std. for Toxic materials

"The secretary, in promulgating standards dealing with toxic materials or harmful physical agents under this subsection, shall set the standard which most adequately assures, to the extent feasible, on the basis of the best available evidence, that no employee will suffer material impairment of health or functional capacity even if such employee has regular exposure to the hazard dealt with by such standard for the period of his working life. Development of standards under this subsection shall be based upon research, demonstrations, experiments, and such other information as may be appropriate. In addition to the attainment of the highest degree of health and safety protection for the employee, other considerations shall be the latest available scientific data in the field, the feasibility of the standards, and experience gained under this and other health and safety laws."

Wherever the toxic material to be regulated is a carcinogen, the Secretary has taken the position that no safe exposure level can be determined and that § 6(b)(5) requires him to set an exposure limit at the lowest technologically feasible level that will not impair the viability of the industries regulated. * * *

On pre-enforcement review * * * the United States Court of Appeals for the Fifth Circuit held the regulation invalid. 581 F.2d 493 (1978). The court concluded that OSHA had exceeded its standard-setting authority because it had not shown that the new benzene exposure limit was "reasonably necessary or appropriate to provide safe or healthful employment" as required by § 3(8), and because § 6(b)(5) does "not give OSHA the unbridled discretion to adopt standards designed to create absolutely risk-free workplaces regardless of costs." Reading the two provisions together, the Fifth Circuit held that the Secretary was under a duty to determine whether the benefits expected from the new standard bore a reasonable relationship to the costs that it imposed. The court noted that OSHA had made an estimate of the costs of compliance, but that the record lacked substantial evidence of any discernible benefits.

Procedure

Balancing

We agree with the Fifth Circuit's holding that § 3(8) requires the Secretary to find, as a threshold matter, that the toxic substance in question poses a significant health risk in the workplace and that a new, lower standard is therefore "reasonably necessary or appropriate to provide safe or healthful employment and places of employment." Unless and until such a finding is made, it is not necessary to address the further question whether the Court of Appeals correctly held that there must be a reasonable correlation between costs and benefits, or whether, as the federal parties argue, the Secretary is then required by § 6(b)(5) to promulgate a standard that goes as far as technologically and economically possible to eliminate the risk. * * *

I.

Benzene is a familiar and important commodity. It is a colorless, aromatic liquid that evaporates rapidly under ordinary atmospheric conditions. Approximately 11 billion pounds of benzene were produced in the United States in 1976. Ninety-four percent of that total was produced by the petroleum and petrochemical industries, with the remainder produced by the steel industry as a byproduct of coking operations. Benzene is used in manufacturing a variety of products including motor fuels (which may contain as much as 2% benzene), solvents, detergents, pesticides, and other organic chemicals.

* * *

Industrial health experts have long been aware that exposure to benzene may lead to various types of nonmalignant diseases. * * * In 1969 the American National Standards Institute (ANSI) adopted a national consensus standard of 10 ppm averaged over an 8-hour period with a ceiling concentration of 25 ppm for 10-minute periods or a maximum peak concentration of 50 ppm. In 1971, after the Occupational Safety and Health Act was passed, the Secretary adopted this consensus standard as the federal standard, pursuant to 29 U.S.C.A. § 655(a).

* * * In the late 1960's and early 1970's a number of epidemiological studies were published indicating that workers exposed to high concentrations of benzene were subject to a significantly increased risk of leukemia. In a 1974 report recommending a permanent standard for benzene, the National Institute for Occupational Safety and Health (NIOSH), OSHA's research arm, noted that these studies raised the "distinct possibility" that benzene caused leukemia. But, in light of the fact that all known cases had occurred at very high exposure levels, NIOSH declined to recommend a change in the 10 ppm standard, which it considered sufficient to protect against nonmalignant diseases. NIOSH suggested that further studies were necessary to determine conclusively whether there was a link between benzene and leukemia and, if so, what exposure levels were dangerous.

Between 1974 and 1976 additional studies were published which tended to confirm the view that benzene can cause leukemia, at least when exposure levels are high. In an August 1976 revision of its earlier recommendation, NIOSH stated that these studies provided "conclusive" proof of a causal connection between benzene and leukemia. Although it acknowledged that none of the intervening studies had provided the dose-response data it had found lacking two years earlier, NIOSH nevertheless recommended that the exposure limit be set as low as possible. * * *

* * *

In the spring of 1976, NIOSH had selected two Pliofilm plants in St. Mary's and Akron, Ohio, for an epidemiological study of the link between leukemia and benzene exposure. In April 1977, NIOSH forwarded an interim report to OSHA indicating at least a five-fold increase in the expected incidence of leukemia for workers who had been exposed to benzene at the two plants from 1940 to 1949. The report submitted to OSHA erroneously suggested that exposures in the two plants had generally been between zero and 15 ppm during the period in question.[16] * * *

In its published statement giving notice of the proposed permanent standard, OSHA did not ask for comments as to whether or not benzene presented a significant health risk at exposures of 10 ppm or less. Rather, it asked for comments as to whether 1 ppm was the minimum feasible exposure limit. * * * [T]his formulation of the issue to be considered by the Agency was consistent with OSHA's general policy with respect to carcinogens. Whenever a carcinogen is involved, OSHA will presume that no safe level of exposure exists in the absence of clear proof establishing such a level and will accordingly set the exposure limit at the lowest level feasible. The proposed 1 ppm exposure limit in this case thus was established not on the basis of a proven hazard at 10 ppm, but rather on the basis of "OSHA's best judgment at the time of the proposal of the feasibility of compliance with the proposed standard by the [a]ffected industries." Given OSHA's cancer policy, it was in fact irrelevant whether there was any evidence at all of a leukemia risk at 10 ppm. The important point was that there was no evidence that there was not some risk, however small, at that level. The fact that OSHA did not ask for comments on whether there was a safe level of exposure for benzene was indicative of its further view that a demonstration of such absolute safety simply could not be made.

* * *

As presently formulated, the benzene standard is an expensive way of providing some additional protection for a relatively small number of employees. According to OSHA's figures, the standard will require capital investments in engineering controls of approximately $266 million, first-year operating costs (for monitoring, medical testing, employee training, and respirators) of $187 million to $205 million and recurring annual costs of approximately $34 million. The figures outlined in OSHA's explanation of the costs of compliance to various industries indicate that only 35,000 employees would gain any benefit from the regulation in terms of a reduction in their exposure to benzene. Over two-thirds of these workers (24,450) are employed in the rubber-manufacturing industry. Compliance costs in that industry are estimated to be rather low with no capital costs and initial operating expenses estimated at only $34 million ($1,390 per employee); recurring annual costs would also be rather low, totaling less than $1 million. By contrast, the segment of the petroleum refining industry that produces benzene would be required to incur $24 million in capital costs and $600,000 in first-year operating expenses to

[handwritten: INTEREST BALANCING]

16. * * * Industry representatives argued at the hearing that this evidence indicated that the exposure levels had been very high, as they had been in the other epidemiological studies conducted in the past. NIOSH witnesses, however, simply stated that actual exposure levels for the years in question could not be determined; they did agree, however, that their study should *not* be taken as proof of a fivefold increase in leukemia risk at 10–15 ppm. In its explanation of the permanent standard, OSHA agreed with the NIOSH witnesses that no dose-response relationship could be inferred from the study. * * *

provide additional protection for 300 workers ($82,000 per employee), while the petrochemical industry would be required to incur $20.9 million in capital costs and $1 million in initial operating expenses for the benefit of 552 employees ($39,675 per employee).[29]

Although OSHA did not quantify the benefits to each category of worker in terms of decreased exposure to benzene, it appears from the economic impact study done at OSHA's direction that those benefits may be relatively small.   Thus, although the current exposure limit is 10 ppm, the actual exposures outlined in that study are often considerably lower. For example, for the period 1970–1975 the petrochemical industry reported that, out of a total of 496 employees exposed to benzene, only 53 were exposed to levels between 1 and 5 ppm and only 7 (all at the same plant) were exposed to between 5 and 10 ppm.

II.

The critical issue at this point in the litigation is whether the Court of Appeals was correct in refusing to enforce the 1 ppm exposure limit on the ground that it was not supported by appropriate findings.

Any discussion of the 1 ppm exposure limit must, of course, begin with the agency's rationale for imposing that limit.   The written explanation of the standard fills 184 pages of the printed appendix.   Much of it is devoted to a discussion of the voluminous evidence of the adverse effects of exposure to benzene at levels of concentration well above 10 ppm.   This discussion demonstrates that there is ample justification for regulating occupational exposure to benzene and that the prior limit of 10 ppm, with a ceiling of 25 ppm (or a peak of 50 ppm), was reasonable.   It does not, however, provide direct support for the Agency's conclusion that the limit should be reduced from 10 ppm to 1 ppm.

The evidence in the administrative record of adverse effects of benzene exposure at 10 ppm is sketchy at best.   OSHA noted that there was "no dispute" that certain nonmalignant blood disorders, evidenced by a reduction in the level of red or white cells or platelets in the blood, could result from exposures of 25–40 ppm.   It then stated that several studies had indicated that relatively slight changes in normal blood values could result from exposures below 25 ppm and perhaps below 10 ppm.   OSHA did not attempt to make any estimate based on these studies of how significant the risk of nonmalignant disease would be at exposures of 10 ppm or less.   Rather, it stated that because of the lack of data concerning the linkage between low-level exposures and blood abnormalities, it was impossible to construct a dose-response curve at this time.[33]   OSHA did

---

29. The high cost per employee in the latter two industries is attributable to OSHA's policy of requiring engineering controls rather than allowing respirators to be used to reduce exposures to the permissible limit.   The relatively low estimated cost per employee in the rubber industry is based on OSHA's assumption that other solvents and adhesives can be substituted for those that contain benzene and that capital costs will therefore not be required.

33. OSHA's comments with respect to the insufficiency of the data were addressed primarily to the lack of data at low exposure levels.   OSHA did not discuss whether it was possible to make a rough estimate, based on the more complete epidemiological and animal studies done at higher exposure levels, of the significance of the risks attributable to those levels, nor did it discuss whether it was possible to extrapolate from such estimates to derive a risk estimate for low-level exposures.

conclude, however, that the studies demonstrated that the current 10 ppm exposure limit was inadequate to ensure that no single worker would suffer a nonmalignant blood disorder as a result of benzene exposure. Noting that it is "customary" to set a permissible exposure limit by applying a safety factor of 10–100 to the lowest level at which adverse effects had been observed, the Agency stated that the evidence supported the conclusion that the limit should be set at a point "substantially less than 10 ppm" even if benzene's leukemic effects were not considered. OSHA did not state, however, that the nonmalignant effects of benzene exposure justified a reduction in the permissible exposure limit to 1 ppm. * * *

With respect to leukemia, evidence of an increased risk (i. e., a risk greater than that borne by the general population) due to benzene exposures at or below 10 ppm was even sketchier. Once OSHA acknowledged that the NIOSH study it had relied upon in promulgating the emergency standard did not support its earlier view that benzene had been shown to cause leukemia at concentrations below 25 ppm, there was only one study that provided any evidence of such an increased risk. That study, conducted by the Dow Chemical Co., uncovered three leukemia deaths, versus 0.2 expected deaths, out of a population of 594 workers; it appeared that the three workers had never been exposed to more than 2 to 9 ppm of benzene. The authors of the study, however, concluded that it could not be viewed as proof of a relationship between low-level benzene exposure and leukemia because all three workers had probably been occupationally exposed to a number of other potentially carcinogenic chemicals at other points in their careers and because no leukemia deaths had been uncovered among workers who had been exposed to much higher levels of benzene. In its explanation of the permanent standard, OSHA stated that the possibility that these three leukemias had been caused by benzene exposure could not be ruled out and that the study, although not evidence of an increased risk of leukemia at 10 ppm, was therefore "consistent with the findings of many studies that there is an excess leukemia risk among benzene exposed employees." The Agency made no finding that the Dow study, any other empirical evidence, or any opinion testimony demonstrated that exposure to benzene at or below the 10 ppm level had ever in fact caused leukemia. * * *

In the end OSHA's rationale for lowering the permissible exposure limit to 1 ppm was based, not on any finding that leukemia has ever been caused by exposure to 10 ppm of benzene and that it will *not* be caused by exposure to 1 ppm, but rather on a series of assumptions indicating that some leukemias might result from exposure to 10 ppm and that the number of cases might be reduced by reducing the exposure level to 1 ppm. In reaching that result, the Agency first unequivocally concluded that benzene is a human carcinogen. Second, it concluded that industry had failed to prove that there is a safe threshold level of exposure to benzene below which no excess leukemia cases would occur. In reaching this conclusion OSHA rejected industry contentions that certain epidemiological studies indicating no excess risk of leukemia among workers exposed to levels below 10 ppm were sufficient to establish that the threshold level of safe exposure was at or above 10 ppm. It also rejected an industry witness' testimony that a dose-response curve could be constructed on the basis of the reported epidemiological studies and that this curve indicated that reducing the permissible exposure limit from 10 to 1 ppm would prevent at most one leukemia and one other cancer death every six years.[38]

Third, the Agency applied its standard policy with respect to carcinogens, concluding that, in the absence of definitive proof of a safe level, it must be assumed that *any* level above zero presents *some* increased risk of cancer. As the federal parties point out in their brief, there are a number of scientists and public health specialists who subscribe to this view, theorizing that a susceptible person may contract cancer from the absorption of even one molecule of a carcinogen like benzene.[41]

Fourth, the Agency reiterated its view of the Act, stating that it was required by § 6(b)(5) to set the standard either at the level that has been demonstrated to be safe or at the lowest level feasible, whichever is higher. If no safe level is established, as in this case, the Secretary's interpretation of the statute automatically leads to the selection of an exposure limit that is the lowest feasible. Because of benzene's importance to the economy, no one has ever suggested that it would be feasible to eliminate its use entirely, or to try to limit exposures to the small amounts that are omnipresent. Rather, the Agency selected 1 ppm as a workable exposure level and then determined that compliance with that level was technologically feasible and that "the economic impact of * * * [compliance] will not be such as to threaten the financial welfare of the affected firms or the general economy." It therefore held that 1 ppm was the minimum feasible exposure level within the meaning of § 6(b)(5) of the Act.

5 Finally, although the agency did not refer in its discussion of the pertinent legal authority to any duty to identify the anticipated benefits of the new standard, it did conclude that some benefits were likely to result from reducing the exposure limit from 10 ppm to 1 ppm. This conclusion was based, again, not on evidence, but rather on the assumption that the risk of leukemia will decrease as exposure levels decrease. Although the Agency had found it impossible to construct a dose-response curve that would predict with any accuracy the number of leukemias that could be expected to result from exposures at 10 ppm, or 1 ppm, or at any intermediate level, it nevertheless "determined that the benefits of the proposed standard are likely to be appreciable." * * *

38. OSHA rejected this testimony in part because it believed the exposure data in the epidemiological studies to be inadequate to formulate a dose-response curve. It also indicated that even if the testimony was accepted—indeed as long as there was any increase in the risk of cancer—the Agency was under an obligation to "select the level of exposure which is most protective of exposed employees."

41. * * * [A] number of the scientists testifying on both sides of the issue agreed that every individual probably does have a threshold exposure limit below which he or she will not contract cancer. The problem, however, is that individual susceptibility appears to vary greatly and there is at present no way to calculate each and every person's threshold. Thus, even industry witnesses agreed that if the standard must ensure with absolute certainty that every single worker is protected from any risk of leukemia, only a zero exposure limit would suffice.

III.

Our resolution of the issues in these cases turns, to a large extent, on the meaning of and the relationship between § 3(8), which defines a health and safety standard as a standard that is "reasonably necessary and appropriate to provide safe or healthful employment," and § 6(b)(5), which directs the Secretary in promulgating a health and safety standard for toxic materials to "set the standard which most adequately assures, to the extent feasible, on the basis of the best available evidence, that no employee will suffer material impairment of health or functional capacity * * * ."

In the Government's view, § 3(8)'s definition of the term "standard" has no legal significance or at best merely requires that a standard not be totally irrational. It takes the position that § 6(b)(5) is controlling and that it requires OSHA to promulgate a standard that either gives an absolute assurance of safety for each and every worker or reduces exposures to the lowest level feasible. The Government interprets "feasible" as meaning technologically achievable at a cost that would not impair the viability of the industries subject to the regulation. The respondent industry representatives, on the other hand, argue that the Court of Appeals was correct in holding that the "reasonably necessary and appropriate" language of § 3(8), along with the feasibility requirement of § 6(b)(5), requires the Agency to quantify both the costs and the benefits of a proposed rule and to conclude that they are roughly commensurate.

In our view, it is not necessary to decide whether either the Government or industry is entirely correct. For we think it is clear that § 3(8) does apply to all permanent standards promulgated under the Act and that it requires the Secretary, before issuing any standard, to determine that it is reasonably necessary and appropriate to remedy a significant risk of material health impairment. * * *

* * *

By empowering the Secretary to promulgate standards that are "reasonably necessary or appropriate to provide safe or healthful employment and places of employment," the Act implies that, before promulgating any standard, the Secretary must make a finding that the workplaces in question are not safe. But "safe" is not the equivalent of "risk-free." There are many activities that we engage in every day—such as driving a car or even breathing city air—that entail some risk of accident or material health impairment; nevertheless, few people would consider these activities "unsafe." Similarly, a workplace can hardly be considered "unsafe" unless it threatens the workers with a significant risk of harm.

Therefore, before he can promulgate *any* permanent health or safety standard, the Secretary is required to make a threshold finding that a place of employment is unsafe—in the sense that significant risks are present and can be eliminated or lessened by a change in practices. This requirement applies to permanent standards promulgated pursuant to § 6(b)(5), as well as to other types of permanent standards. * * *

* * *

In the absence of a clear mandate in the Act, it is unreasonable to assume that Congress intended to give the Secretary the unprecedented power over American industry that would result from the Government's view of § § 3(8) and 6(b)(5), coupled with OSHA's cancer policy. Expert testimony that a substance is probably a human carcinogen—either because it has caused cancer in animals or because individuals have contracted cancer following extremely high exposures—would justify the conclusion that the substance poses some risk of serious harm no matter how minute the exposure and no matter how many experts testified that they regarded the risk as insignificant. That conclusion would in turn justify pervasive regulation limited only by the constraint of feasibility. In light of the fact that there are literally thousands of substances used in the workplace that have been identified as carcinogens or suspect carcinogens, the Government's theory would give OSHA power to impose enormous costs that might produce little, if any, discernible benefit.

If the Government were correct in arguing that neither § 3(8) nor § 6(b)(5) requires that the risk from a toxic substance be quantified sufficiently to enable the Secretary to characterize it as significant in an understandable way, the statute would make such a "sweeping delegation of legislative power" that it might be unconstitutional under the Court's reasoning in *A. L. A. Schechter Poultry Corp. v. United States* and *Panama Refining Co. v. Ryan.* A construction of the statute that avoids this kind of open-ended grant should certainly be favored.

The legislative history also supports the conclusion that Congress was concerned, not with absolute safety, but with the elimination of significant harm. The examples of industrial hazards referred to in the Committee hearings and debates all involved situations in which the risk was unquestionably significant. * * *

Moreover, Congress specifically amended § 6(b)(5) to make it perfectly clear that it does not require the Secretary to promulgate standards that would assure an absolutely risk-free workplace. Section 6(b)(5) of the initial Committee bill provided that

> "[t]he Secretary, in promulgating standards under this subsection, shall set the standard which most adequately and feasibly assures, on the basis of the best available evidence, that no employee will suffer *any* impairment of health or functional capacity, or diminished life expectancy even if such employee has regular exposure to the hazard dealt with by such standard for the period of his working life." (Emphasis supplied.)

On the floor of the Senate, Senator Dominick questioned the wisdom of this provision, stating:

> "How in the world are we ever going to live up to that? What are we going to do about a place in Florida where mosquitoes are getting at the employee—perish the thought that there may be mosquitoes in Florida? But there are black flies in Minnesota and Wisconsin. Are we going to say that if employees get bitten by those for the rest of their lives they will not have been done any harm at all? Probably they will not be, but do we know?"

He then offered an amendment deleting the entire subsection. After discussions with the sponsors of the Committee bill, Senator Dominick revised his amendment. Instead of deleting the first sentence of § 6(b)(5) entirely, his new amendment limited the application of that subsection to toxic materials and harmful physical agents and changed "any" impairment of health to "material" impairment. * * *

In their reply brief the federal parties argue that the Dominick amendment simply means that the Secretary is not required to eliminate threats of insignificant harm; they argue that § 6(b)(5) still requires the Secretary to set standards that ensure that not even one employee will be subject to any risk of serious harm—no matter how small that risk may be. This interpretation is at odds with Congress' express recognition of the futility of trying to make all workplaces totally risk-free. Moreover, not even OSHA follows this interpretation of § 6(b)(5) to its logical conclusion. Thus, if OSHA is correct that the only no-risk level for leukemia due to benzene exposure is zero and if its interpretation of § 6(b)(5) is correct, OSHA should have set the exposure limit as close to zero as feasible. But OSHA did not go about its task in that way. Rather, it began with a 1 ppm level, selected at least in part to ensure that employers would not be required to eliminate benzene concentrations that were little greater than the so-called "background" exposures experienced by the population at large. Then, despite suggestions by some labor unions that it was feasible for at least some industries to reduce exposures to well below 1 ppm, OSHA decided to apply the same limit to all, largely as a matter of administrative convenience.

* * *

Given the conclusion that the Act empowers the Secretary to promulgate health and safety standards only where a significant risk of harm exists, the critical issue becomes how to define and allocate the burden of proving the significance of the risk in a case such as this, where scientific knowledge is imperfect and the precise quantification of risks is therefore impossible. The Agency's position is that there is substantial evidence in the record to support its conclusion that there is no absolutely safe level for a carcinogen and that, therefore, the burden is properly on industry to prove, apparently beyond a shadow of a doubt, that there *is* a safe level for benzene exposure. The Agency argues that, because of the uncertainties in this area, any other approach would render it helpless, forcing it to wait for the leukemia deaths that it believes are likely to occur before taking any regulatory action.

We disagree. As we read the statute, the burden was on the Agency to show, on the basis of substantial evidence, that it is at least more likely than not that long-term exposure to 10 ppm of benzene presents a significant risk of material health impairment. Ordinarily, it is the proponent of a rule or order who has the burden of proof in administrative proceedings. * * *

In this case OSHA did not even attempt to carry its burden of proof. The closest it came to making a finding that benzene presented a significant risk of harm in the workplace was its statement that the benefits to be derived from lowering the permissible exposure level from 10 to 1 ppm were "likely" to be "appreciable." The Court of Appeals held that this finding was not supported by substantial evidence. Of greater importance, even if it were supported by substantial evidence, such a finding would not be sufficient to satisfy the Agency's obligations under the act.

* * *

Contrary to the Government's contentions, imposing a burden on the Agency of demonstrating a significant risk of harm will not strip it of its ability to regulate carcinogens, nor will it require the Agency to wait for deaths to occur before taking any action. First, the requirement that a "significant" risk be identified is not a mathematical straitjacket. It is the Agency's responsibility to determine, in the first instance, what it considers to be a "significant" risk. Some risks are plainly acceptable and others are plainly unacceptable. If, for example, the odds are one in a billion that a person will die from cancer by taking a drink of chlorinated water, the risk clearly could not be considered significant. On the other hand, if the odds are one in a thousand that regular inhalation of gasoline vapors that are 2% benzene will be fatal, a reasonable person might well consider the risk significant and take appropriate steps to decrease or eliminate it. Although the Agency has no duty to calculate the exact probability of harm, it does have an obligation to find that a significant risk is present before it can characterize a place of employment as "unsafe."

Second, OSHA is not required to support its finding that a significant risk exists with anything approaching scientific certainty. Although the Agency's findings must be supported by substantial evidence, § 6(b)(5) specifically allows the Secretary to regulate on the basis of the "best available evidence." * * * Thus, so long as they are supported by a body of reputable scientific thought, the Agency is free to use conservative assumptions in interpreting the data with respect to carcinogens, risking error on the side of overprotection rather than underprotection.

Finally, the record in this case and OSHA's own rulings on other carcinogens indicate that there are a number of ways in which the Agency can make a rational judgment about the relative significance of the risks associated with exposure to a particular carcinogen.[64]

* * *

64. For example, in the coke-oven emissions standard, OSHA had calculated that 21,000 exposed coke-oven workers had an annual excess mortality of over 200 and that the proposed standard might well eliminate the risk entirely. 41 Fed. Reg. 46742, 46750 (1976), upheld in *American Iron & Steel Inst. v. OSHA*, 577 F.2d 825 (CA3 1978), *cert. granted* [448 U.S. at 909]. In hearings on the coke-oven emissions standard, the Council on Wage and Price Stability estimated that 8 to 35 lives would be saved each year, out of an estimated population of 14,000 workers, as a result of the proposed standard. Although noting that the range of benefits would vary depending on the assumptions used, OSHA did not make a

Because our review of these cases has involved a more detailed examination of the record than is customary, it must be emphasized that we have neither made any factual determinations of our own, nor have we rejected any factual findings made by the Secretary. We express no opinion on what factual findings this record might support, either on the basis of empirical evidence or on the basis of expert testimony; nor do we express any opinion on the more difficult question of what factual determinations would warrant a conclusion that significant risks are present which make promulgation of a new standard reasonably necessary or appropriate. The standard must, of course, be supported by the findings actually made by the Secretary, not merely by findings that we believe he might have made.

In this case the record makes it perfectly clear that the Secretary relied squarely on a special policy for carcinogens that imposed the burden on industry of proving the existence of a safe level of exposure, thereby avoiding the Secretary's threshold responsibility of establishing the need for more stringent standards. In so interpreting his statutory authority, the Secretary exceeded his power.

* * *

The judgment of the Court of Appeals remanding the petition for review to the Secretary for further proceedings is affirmed.

It is so ordered.

MR. CHIEF JUSTICE BURGER, concurring.

* * *

The Congress is the ultimate regulator, and the narrow function of the courts is to discern the meaning of the statute and the implementing regulations with the objective of ensuring that in promulgating health and safety standards the Secretary "has given reasoned consideration to each of the pertinent factors" and has complied with statutory commands. Our holding that the Secretary must retrace his steps with greater care and consideration is not to be taken in derogation of the scope of legitimate agency discretion. When the facts and arguments have been presented and duly considered, the Secretary must make a

finding as to whether its own staff estimate or CWPS's was correct, on the ground that it was not required to quantify the expected benefits of the standard or to weigh those benefits against the projected costs.

In other proceedings, the Agency has had a good deal of data from animal experiments on which it could base a conclusion on the significance of the risk. For example, the record on the vinyl chloride standard indicated that a significant number of animals had developed tumors of the liver, lung, and skin when they were exposed to 50 ppm of vinyl chloride over a period of 11 months. One hundred out of 200 animals died during that period. * * *

In this case the Agency did not have the benefit of the animal studies, because scientists have been unable as yet to induce leukemia in experimental animals as a result of benzene exposure. It did, however, have a fair amount of epidemiological evidence, including both positive and negative studies. Although the Agency stated that this evidence was insufficient to construct a precise correlation between exposure levels and cancer risks, it would at least be helpful in determining whether it is more likely than not that there is a significant risk at 10 ppm.

policy judgment as to whether a specific risk of health impairment is significant in terms of the policy objectives of the statute. When he acts in this capacity, pursuant to the legislative authority delegated by Congress, he exercises the prerogatives of the legislature—to focus on only one aspect of a larger problem, or to promulgate regulations that, to some, may appear as imprudent policy or inefficient allocation of resources. The judicial function does not extend to substantive revision of regulatory policy. That function lies elsewhere—in Congressional and Executive oversight or amendatory legislation—although to be sure the boundaries are often ill-defined and indistinct.

Nevertheless, when discharging his duties under the statute, the Secretary is well admonished to remember that a heavy responsibility burdens his authority. Inherent in this statutory scheme is authority to refrain from regulation of insignificant or *de minimis* risks. When the administrative record reveals only scant or minimal risk of material health impairment, responsible administration calls for avoidance of extravagant, comprehensive regulation. Perfect safety is a chimera; regulation must not strangle human activity in the search for the impossible.

MR. JUSTICE POWELL, concurring in part and concurring in the judgment.

* * * For the reasons stated by the plurality, I agree that § § 6(b)(5) and 3(8) of the Occupational Safety and Health Act of 1970 must be read together. * * * When OSHA acts to reduce existing national consensus standards, therefore, it must find that (i) currently permissible exposure levels create a significant risk of material health impairment; and (ii) a reduction of those levels would significantly reduce the hazard.

Although I would not rule out the possibility that the necessary findings could rest in part on generic policies properly adopted by OSHA, no properly supported agency policies are before us in these cases. I therefore agree with the plurality that the regulation is invalid to the extent it rests upon the assumption that exposure to known carcinogens always should be reduced to a level proved to be safe, or if no such level is found, to the lowest level that the affected industry can achieve with available technology.

*   *   *

Although I regard the question as close, I do not disagree with the plurality's view that OSHA has failed, on this record, to carry its burden of proof on the threshold issues summarized above. But even if one assumes that OSHA properly met this burden, I conclude that the statute also requires the agency to determine that the economic effects of its standard bear a reasonable relationship to the expected benefits. An occupational health standard is neither "reasonably necessary" nor "feasible," as required by statute, if it calls for expenditures wholly disproportionate to the expected health and safety benefits.

OSHA contends that § 6(b)(5) not only permits but actually requires it to promulgate standards that reduce health risks without regard to economic effects, unless those effects would cause widespread dislocation throughout an entire industry. Under the threshold test adopted by the plurality today, this authority will exist only with respect to "significant" risks. But the plurality does not reject OSHA's claim that it must reduce such risks without considering economic consequences less serious than massive dislocation. In my view, that claim is untenable.

Although one might wish that Congress had spoken with greater clarity, the legislative history and purposes of the statute do not support OSHA's interpretation of the Act. It is simply unreasonable to believe that Congress intended OSHA to pursue the desirable goal of risk-free workplaces to the extent that the economic viability of particular industries—or significant segments thereof—is threatened. As the plurality observes, OSHA itself has not chosen to carry out such a self-defeating policy in all instances. If it did, OSHA regulations would impair the ability of American industries to compete effectively with foreign businesses and to provide employment for American workers.

* * * Perhaps more significantly, however, OSHA's interpretation of § 6(b)(5) would force it to regulate in a manner inconsistent with the important health and safety purposes of the legislation we construe today. Thousands of toxic substances present risks that fairly could be characterized as "significant." Even if OSHA succeeded in selecting the gravest risks for earlier regulation, a standard-setting process that ignored economic considerations would result in a serious misallocation of resources and a lower effective level of safety than could be achieved under standards set with reference to the comparative benefits available at a lower cost. I would not attribute such an irrational intention to Congress.

In these cases, OSHA did find that the "substantial costs" of the benzene regulations are justified. But the record before us contains neither adequate documentation of this conclusion, nor any evidence that OSHA weighed the relevant considerations. The agency simply announced its finding of cost-justification without explaining the method by which it determines that the benefits justify the costs and their economic effects. No rational system of regulation can permit its administrators to make policy judgments without explaining how their decisions effectuate the purposes of the governing law, and nothing in the statute authorizes such laxity in these cases. * * *

MR. JUSTICE REHNQUIST, concurring in the judgment.

* * * According to the Secretary * * * § 6(b)(5) imposes upon him an absolute duty, in regulating harmful substances like benzene for which no safe level is known, to set the standard for permissible exposure at the lowest level that "can be achieved at bearable cost with available technology." * * *

* * * According to respondents, § 6(b)(5), as tempered by § 3(8), requires the Secretary to demonstrate that any particular health standard is justifiable on the basis of a rough balancing of costs and benefits.

In considering these alternative interpretations, my colleagues manifest a good deal of uncertainty, and ultimately divide over whether the Secretary produced sufficient evidence that the proposed standard for benzene will result in any appreciable benefits at all. This uncertainty, I would suggest, is eminently justified, since I believe that this litigation presents the Court with what has to be one of the most difficult issues that could confront a decisionmaker: whether the statistical possibility of future deaths should ever be disregarded in light of the economic costs of preventing those deaths. I would also suggest that the widely varying positions advanced in the briefs of the parties and in the opinions of Mr. Justice Stevens, The Chief Justice, Mr. Justice Powell, and Mr. Justice Marshall demonstrate, perhaps better than any other fact, that Congress, the governmental body best suited and most obligated to make the choice confronting us in this litigation, has improperly delegated that choice to the Secretary of Labor and, derivatively, to this Court.

*   *   *

* * * Read literally, the relevant portion of § 6(b)(5) is completely precatory, admonishing the Secretary to adopt the most protective standard if he can, but excusing him from that duty if he cannot. In the case of a hazardous substance for which a "safe" level is either unknown or impractical, the language of § 6(b)(5) gives the Secretary absolutely no indication where on the continuum of relative safety he should draw his line. Especially in light of the importance of the interests at stake, I have no doubt that the provision at issue, standing alone, would violate the doctrine against uncanalized delegations of legislative power. For me the remaining question, then, is whether additional standards are ascertainable from the legislative history of statutory context of § 6(b)(5) or, if not, whether such a standardless delegation was justifiable in light of the "inherent necessities" of the situation.

* * * [T]he legislative history of that section, far from shedding light on what important policy choices Congress was making in the statute, gives one the feeling of viewing the congressional purpose "by the dawn's early light." * * *

To my mind, there are several lessons to be gleaned from this somewhat cryptic legislative history. First, as pointed out by Mr. Justice Marshall, to the extent that Senator Javits, Senator Dominick, and other Members were worried about imposing upon the Secretary the impossible burden of assuring absolute safety, they did not view § 3(8) of the Act as a limitation on that duty. I therefore find it difficult to accept the conclusion of the lower court, as embellished by respondents, that § 3(8) acts as a general check upon the Secretary's duty under § 6(b)(5) to adopt the most protective standard feasible.

Second, and more importantly, I believe that the legislative history demonstrates that the feasibility requirement, as employed in § 6(b)(5), is a legislative mirage, appearing to some Members but not to others, and assuming any form desired by the beholder. * * *

In sum, the legislative history contains nothing to indicate that the language "to the extent feasible" does anything other than render what had been a clear, if somewhat unrealistic, standard largely, if not entirely, precatory. There is certainly nothing to indicate that these words, as used in § 6(b)(5), are limited to technological and economic feasibility. When Congress has wanted to limit the concept of feasibility in this fashion, it has said so, as is evidenced in a statute enacted the same week as the provision at issue here. I also question whether the Secretary wants to assume the duties such an interpretation would impose upon him. In these cases, for example, the Secretary actually declined to adopt a standard lower than 1 ppm for some industries, not because it was economically or technologically infeasible, but rather because "different levels for different industries would result in serious administrative difficulties." If § 6(b)(5) authorizes the Secretary to reject a more protective standard in the interest of administrative feasibility, I have little doubt that he could reject such standards for any reason whatsoever, including even political feasibility.

* * *

* * * [I]n some cases this Court has abided by a rule of necessity, upholding broad delegations of authority where it would be "unreasonable and impracticable to compel Congress to prescribe detailed rules" regarding a particular policy or situation. But no need for such an evasive standard as "feasibility" is apparent in the present cases. In drafting § 6(b)(5), Congress was faced with a clear, if difficult, choice between balancing statistical lives and industrial resources or authorizing the Secretary to elevate human life above all concerns save massive dislocation in an affected industry. * * * That Congress chose, intentionally or unintentionally, to pass this difficult choice on to the Secretary is evident from the spectral quality of the standard it selected. * * *

As formulated and enforced by this Court, the nondelegation doctrine serves three important functions. First, and most abstractly, it ensures to the extent consistent with orderly governmental administration that important choices of social policy are made by Congress, the branch of our Government most responsive to the popular will. * * * Second, the doctrine guarantees that, to the extent Congress finds it necessary to delegate authority, it provides the recipient of that authority with an "intelligible principle" to guide the exercise of the delegated discretion. * * * Third, and derivative of the second, the doctrine ensures that courts charged with reviewing the exercise of delegated legislative discretion will be able to test that exercise against ascertainable standards. * * *

I believe the legislation at issue here fails on all three counts. The decision whether the law of diminishing returns should have any place in the regulation of toxic substances is quintessentially one of legislative policy. For Congress to pass that decision on to the Secretary in the manner it did violates, in my mind, John Locke's caveat—reflected in the cases cited earlier in this opinion—that legislatures are to make laws, not legislators. Nor, as I think the prior discussion amply demonstrates, do the provisions at issue or their legislative history provide the Secretary with any guidance that might lead him to his somewhat tentative conclusion that he must eliminate exposure to benzene as far as technologically and economically possible. Finally, I would suggest that the standard of "feasibility" renders meaningful judicial review impossible.

* * *

I would invalidate the first sentence of § 6(b)(5) of the Occupational Safety and Health Act of 1970 as it applies to any toxic substance or harmful physical agent for which a safe level, that is, a level at which "no employee will suffer material impairment of health or functional capacity even if such employee has regular exposure to [that hazard] for the period of his working life," is, according to the Secretary, unknown or otherwise "infeasible." Absent further congressional action, the Secretary would then have to choose, when acting pursuant to § 6(b)(5), between setting a safe standard or setting no standard at all. * * *

MR. JUSTICE MARSHALL, with whom MR. JUSTICE BRENNAN, MR. JUSTICE WHITE, and MR. JUSTICE BLACKMUN join, dissenting.

In cases of statutory construction, this Court's authority is limited. If the statutory language and legislative intent are plain, the judicial inquiry is at an end. Under our jurisprudence, it is presumed that ill-considered or unwise legislation will be corrected through the democratic process; a court is not permitted to distort a statute's meaning in order to make it conform with the Justices' own views of sound social policy.

Today's decision flagrantly disregards these restrictions on judicial authority. The plurality ignores the plain meaning of the Occupational Safety and Health Act of 1970 in order to bring the authority of the Secretary of Labor in line with the plurality's own views of proper regulatory policy. * * *

The plurality's discussion of the record in this case is both extraordinarily arrogant and extraordinarily unfair. It is arrogant because the plurality presumes to make its own factual findings with respect to a variety of disputed issues relating to carcinogen regulation. * * * And the plurality's discussion is unfair because its characterization of the Secretary's report bears practically no resemblance to what the Secretary actually did in this case. Contrary to the plurality's suggestion, the Secretary did not rely blindly on some Draconian carcinogen "policy." If he had, it would have been sufficient for him to have observed that benzene is a carcinogen, a proposition that respondents do not dispute. Instead, the Secretary gathered over 50 volumes of exhibits and testimony and offered a detailed and evenhanded discussion of the relationship between exposure to benzene at all recorded exposure levels and chromosomal damage, aplastic anemia, and leukemia. In that discussion he evaluated, and took seriously, respondents' evidence of a safe exposure level.

The hearings on the proposed standard were extensive, encompassing 17 days from July 19 through August 10, 1977. The 95 witnesses included epidemiologists, toxicologists, physicians, political economists, industry representatives, and members of the affected work force. Witnesses were subjected to exhaustive questioning by representatives from a variety of interested groups and organizations.

* * *

Areas of uncertainty. The Secretary examined three areas of uncertainty that had particular relevance to his decision. First, he pointed to evidence that the latency period for benzene-induced leukemia could range from 2 to over 20 years. Since lower exposure levels lead to an increase in the latency period, it would be extremely difficult to obtain evidence showing the dose-response relationship between leukemia and exposure to low levels of benzene. Because there has been no adequate monitoring in the past, it would be practically impossible to determine what the exposure levels were at a time sufficiently distant so that the latency period would have elapsed. The problem was compounded by the difficulty of conducting a suitable study. Because exposure levels approaching 10 ppm had been required only recently, direct evidence showing the relationship between leukemia and exposure levels between 1 and 10 ppm would be unavailable in the foreseeable future.

Second, the Secretary observed that individuals have differences in their susceptibility to leukemia. Among those exposed to benzene was a group of unknown but possibly substantial size having various "predisposing factors" whose members were especially vulnerable to the disease. The permanent standard was designed to minimize the effects of exposure for these susceptible individuals as well as for the relatively insensitive and also to facilitate early diagnosis and treatment.

The Secretary discussed the contention that a safe level of exposure to benzene had been demonstrated. From the testimony of numerous scientists, he concluded that it had not. He also found that although no dose-response curve could be plotted, the extent of the risk would decline with the exposure level. Exposure at a level of 1 ppm would therefore be less dangerous than exposure at one of 10 ppm. * * *

* * *

This not a case in which the Secretary found, or respondents established, that no benefits would be derived from a permanent standard, or that the likelihood of benefits was insignificant. Nor was it shown that a quantitative estimate of benefits could be made on the basis of "the best available evidence." Instead, the Secretary concluded that benefits will result, that those benefits "may" be appreciable, but that the dose-response relationship of low levels of benzene exposure and leukemia, nonmalignant blood disorders, and chromosomal damage was impossible to determine. The question presented is whether, in these circumstances, the Act permits the Secretary to take regulatory action, or whether he must allow continued exposure until more definitive information becomes available.

As noted above, the Secretary's determinations must be upheld if supported by "substantial evidence in the record considered as a whole." 29 U.S.C.A. § 655(f). This standard represents a legislative judgment that regulatory action should be subject to review more stringent than the traditional "arbitrary and capricious" standard for informal rulemaking. * * * As we have emphasized, however, judicial review under the substantial evidence test is ultimately deferential. The agency's decision is entitled to the traditional presumption of validity, and the court is not authorized to substitute its judgment for that of the Secretary. If the Secretary has considered the decisional factors and acted in conformance with the statute, his ultimate decision must be given a large measure of respect.

The plurality is insensitive to three factors which, in my view, make judicial review of occupational safety and health standards under the substantial evidence test particularly difficult. First, the issues often reach a high level of technical complexity. In such circumstances the courts are required to immerse themselves in matters to which they are unaccustomed by training or experience. Second, the factual issues with which the Secretary must deal are frequently not subject to any definitive resolution. * * * Causal connections and theoretical extrapolations may be uncertain. Third, when the question involves determination of the acceptable level of risk, the ultimate decision must necessarily be based on considerations of policy as well as empirically verifiable facts. Factual determinations can at most define the risk in some statistical way; the judgment whether that risk is tolerable cannot be based solely on a resolution of the facts.

* * *

* * * On this record, the Secretary could conclude that regular exposure above the 1 ppm level would pose a definite risk resulting in material impairment to some indeterminate but possibly substantial number of employees. Studies revealed hundreds of deaths attributable to benzene exposure. Expert after expert testified that no safe level of exposure had been shown and that the extent of the risk declined with the exposure level. There was some direct evidence of incidence of leukemia, nonmalignant blood disorders, and chromosomal damage at exposure levels of 10 ppm and below. Moreover, numerous experts testified that existing evidence required an inference that an exposure level above 1 ppm was hazardous. * * * Nothing in the Act purports to prevent the Secretary from acting when definitive information as to the quantity of a standard's benefits is unavailable. Where, as here, the deficiency in knowledge relates to the extent of the benefits rather than their existence, I see no reason to hold that the Secretary has exceeded his statutory authority.

The plurality avoids this conclusion through reasoning that may charitably be described as obscure. * * *

At the outset, it is important to observe that "reasonably necessary or appropriate" clauses are routinely inserted in regulatory legislation, and in the past such clauses have uniformly been interpreted as general provisos that regulatory actions must bear a reasonable relation to those statutory purposes set forth in the statute's substantive provisions. * * *

The plurality suggests that under the "reasonably necessary" clause, a workplace is not "unsafe" unless the Secretary is able to convince a reviewing court that a "significant" risk is at issue. That approach is particularly embarrassing in this case, for it is contradicted by the plain language of the Act. The plurality's interpretation renders utterly superfluous the first sentence of § 655(b)(5) * * * . By so doing, the plurality makes the test for standards regulating toxic substances and harmful physical agents substantially identical to the test for standards generally—plainly the opposite of what Congress intended. * * *

The plurality is obviously more interested in the consequences of its decision than in discerning the intention of Congress. But since the language and legislative history of the Act are plain, there is no need for conjecture about the effects of today's decision. * * * I do not pretend to know whether the test the plurality erects today is, as a matter of policy, preferable to that created by Congress and its delegates: the area is too fraught with scientific uncertainty, and too dependent on considerations of policy, for a court to be able to determine whether it is desirable to require identification of a "significant" risk before allowing an administrative agency to take regulatory action. But in light of the tenor of the plurality opinion, it is necessary to point out that the question is not one-sided, and that Congress' decision to authorize the Secretary to promulgate the regulation at issue here was a reasonable one.

* * *

* * * If the plurality means to require the Secretary realistically to "quantify" the risk in order to satisfy a court that it is "significant," the record shows that the plurality means to require him to do the impossible. But regulatory inaction has very significant costs of its own. The adoption of such a test would subject American workers to a continuing risk of cancer and other serious diseases; it would disable the Secretary from regulating a wide variety of carcinogens for which quantification simply cannot be undertaken at the present time.

There are encouraging signs that today's decision does not extend that far. My Brother POWELL concludes that the Secretary is not prevented from taking regulatory action "when reasonable quantification cannot be accomplished by any known methods." The plurality also indicates that it would not prohibit the Secretary from promulgating safety standards when quantification of the benefits is impossible. The Court might thus allow the Secretary to attempt to make a very rough quantification of the risk imposed by a carcinogenic substance, and give considerable deference to his finding that the risk was significant. If so, the Court would permit the Secretary to promulgate precisely the same regulation involved in these cases if he had not relied on a carcinogen "policy," but undertaken a review of the evidence and the expert testimony and concluded, on the basis of conservative assumptions, that the risk addressed is a significant one. Any other interpretation of the plurality's approach would allow a court to displace the agency's judgment with its own subjective conception of "significance," a duty to be performed without statutory guidance.

*   *   *

Notes

1. The benzene case illustrates the difficulties of reviewing agency decisions that rest on resolution of complex issues, where the limitations of contemporary knowledge leave substantial uncertainties. Judge McGowan discussed this problem in *Industrial Union Department, AFL-CIO v. Hodgson*, 499 F.2d 467, 473–76 (D.C. Cir. 1974), a challenge to OSHA's first health standard, for asbestos. The court attempted to apply the Congressionally mandated substantial evidence test to a rule that was the product of informal rulemaking and rested in part on unverifiable estimates of potential health effects.

One question generated by this anomalous combination [of standard and procedure] is whether the determinations in question here are of the kind to which substantial evidence review can appropriately be applied. * * *

From extensive and often conflicting evidence, the Secretary in this case made numerous factual determinations. With respect to some of those questions, the evidence was such that the task consisted primarily of evaluating the data and drawing conclusions from it. The court can review that data in the record and determine whether it reflects substantial support for the Secretary's findings. But some of the questions involved in the promulgation of these standards are on the frontiers of scientific knowledge, and consequently as to them insufficient data is presently available to make a fully informed factual determination. Decision making must in that circumstance depend to a greater extent upon policy judgments and less upon purely factual analysis. Thus, in addition to currently unresolved factual issues, the formulation of standards involves choices that by their nature require basic policy determinations rather than resolution of factual controversies. Judicial review of inherently legislative decisions of this sort is obviously an undertaking of different dimensions.

*   *   *

Regardless of the manner in which the task of judicial review is articulated, policy choices of this sort are not susceptible to the same type of verification or refutation by reference to the record as are some factual questions. Consequently, the court's approach must necessarily be different no matter how the standards of review are labeled. * * *

*   *   *

What we are entitled to at all events is a careful identification by the Secretary, when his proposed standards are challenged, of the reasons why he chooses to follow one course rather than another. Where that choice purports to be based on the existence of certain determinable facts, the Secretary must, in form as well as substance, find those facts from evidence in the record. By the same token, when the Secretary is obliged to make policy judgments where no factual certainties exist or where facts alone do not provide the answer, he should so state and go on to identify the considerations he found persuasive.

In the light of Judge McGowan's analysis, was OSHA's mistake in the benzene case not explicitly acknowledging that its decision embodied a social policy judgment—one that Congress had directed it to make?

2. *Ethyl Corp. v. EPA*, 541 F.2d 1 (D.C. Cir.), cert. denied 426 U. S. 941 (1976), involved a challenge to EPA regulations requiring a step-wise reduction in the lead content of gasoline. The pertinent language of the Clean Air Act authorized the EPA Administrator to promulgate regulations controlling or prohibiting the manufacture, distribution, or sale of "any fuel or fuel additive for use in a motor vehicle engine * * * any emission products of such fuel additive will endanger the public health or welfare." 42 U.S.C.A. § 1857f–6c(c)(1)(A), now incorporated and revised in 42 U.S.C.A. § 7545(c). In an unpublished opinion, a divided panel of the D.C. Circuit overturned the regulations on the ground that the Administrator had not adequately demonstrated that lead particulates in auto emissions endanger the public health. On rehearing *en banc*, a bare majority of the full court upheld the regulations. In interpreting the statutory phrase "will endanger," Judge Wright endorsed Judge McGowan's *Hodgson* approach to the requisite factual support for an agency's disposition of unresolvable scientific questions (541 F.2d at 28):

> Where a statute is precautionary in nature, the evidence difficult to come by, uncertain, or conflicting because it is on the frontiers of scientific knowledge, the regulations designed to protect the public health, and the decision that of an expert administrator, we will not demand rigorous step-by-step proof of cause and effect. Such proof may be impossible to obtain if the precautionary purpose of the statute is to be served. Of course, we are not suggesting that the Administrator has the power to act on hunches or wild guesses. * * * He must take account of available facts, of course, but his inquiry does not end there. The Administrator may apply his expertise to draw conclusions from suspected, but not completely substantiated, relationships between facts, from trends among facts, from theoretical projections from imperfect data, from probative preliminary data not yet certifiable as "fact," and the like. * * *

The majority opinion in *Ethyl*, however, goes one step beyond *Hodgson* by explicitly freeing the agency, in areas on the frontiers of scientific knowledge, from "the procedural [as well as] the substantive rigor proper for questions of fact." Id. at 24. Yet Judge Wright made clear that his approach still contemplated a substantial role for reviewing courts. His majority opinion and Judge Wilkey's dissent filled more than thirty-eight pages of the Federal Reporter with conflicting analyses of the scientific evidence bearing on the health hazards of lead additives to gasoline. "The more technical the case," Judge Wright observed, "the more intensive must be the court's effort to understand the evidence, for without an appropriate understanding of the case before it the court cannot properly perform its appellate function." 541 F.2d at 36.

In a concurring opinion, however, Judge Bazelon took issue with the latter suggestion, and offered an alternative approach:

> I agree with the court's construction of the statute that the Administrator is called upon to make "essentially legislative policy judgments" in assessing risks to public health. But I cannot agree that this automatically relieves

the Administrator's decision from the "procedural * * * rigor proper for questions of fact."   Quite the contrary, this case strengthens my view that

> * * * in cases of great technological complexity, the best way for courts to guard against unreasonable or erroneous administrative decisions is not for the judges themselves to scrutinize the technical merits of each decision.   Rather, it is to establish a decision-making process that assures a reasoned decision that can be held up to the scrutiny of the scientific community and the public.   [*International Harvester Co. v. Ruckelshaus*, 478 F.2d 615, 652 (D.C. Cir. 1973) (Bazelon, C. J., concurring).]

This record provides vivid demonstration of the dangers implicit in the contrary view, ably espoused by Judge Leventhal, which would have judges "steeping" themselves "in technical matters to determine whether the agency 'has exercised a reasoned discretion.' "   It is one thing for judges to scrutinize FCC judgments concerning diversification of media ownership to determine if they are rational.   But I doubt judges contribute much to improving the quality of the difficult decisions which must be made in highly technical areas when they take it upon themselves to decide, as did the panel in this case, that "in assessing the scientific and medical data the Administrator made clear errors of judgment."   The process of making a de novo evaluation of the scientific evidence inevitably invites judges of opposing views to make plausible-sounding, but simplistic, judgments of the relative weight to be afforded various pieces of technical data. * * *

Because substantive review of mathematical and scientific evidence by technically illiterate judges is dangerously unreliable, I continue to believe we will do more to improve administrative decision-making by concentrating our efforts on strengthening administrative procedures. * * *

541 F.2d at 66–67.   In a separate statement, Judge Leventhal responded:

> * * * Judge Bazelon has * * * over-reacted.   His opinion—if I read it right—advocates engaging in no substantive review at all, whenever the substantive issues at stake involve technical matters that the judges involved consider beyond their individual technical competence. * * *
>
> * * * [W]hile giving up is the easier course, it is not legitimately open to us at present.   In the case of legislative enactments, the sole responsibility of the courts is constitutional due process review.   In the case of agency decision-making, the courts have an additional responsibility set by Congress.   Congress has been willing to delegate its legislative powers broadly—and courts have upheld such delegation—because there is court review to assure that the agency exercises the delegated power within statutory limits, and that it fleshes out objectives within those limits by an administration that is not irrational or discriminatory. * * *
>
> Our present system of review assumes judges will acquire whatever technical knowledge is necessary as background for decision of the legal questions.   It may be that some judges are not initially equipped for this role, just as they may not be technically equipped initially to decide issues of obviousness and infringement in patent cases.   If technical difficulties loom large, Congress may push to establish specialized courts.   Thus far, it has proceeded on the assumption that we can both have the important values secured by generalist judges and rely on them to acquire whatever technical background is necessary. * * *

* * * Once the presumption of regularity in agency action is challenged with a factual submission, and even to determine whether such a challenge has been made, the agency's record and reasoning has to be looked at. If there is some factual support for the challenge, there must either be evidence or judicial notice available explicating the agency's result, or a remand to supply the gap.

Mistakes may mar the exercise of any judicial function. While in this case the panel made such a mistake, it did not stem from judicial incompetence to deal with technical issues, but from confusion about the proper stance for substantive review of agency action in an area where the state of current knowledge does not generate customary definitiveness and certainty. * * *

3. For other illustrations of intensive judicial review of agency scientific decisions, see, e.g., *Weyerhaeuser Co. v. Costle*, 590 F.2d 1011 (D.C. Cir. 1978); *Amoco Oil Co. v. EPA*, 501 F.2d 722 (D.C. Cir. 1974); *Portland Cement Association v. Ruckelshaus*, 486 F.2d 375 (D.C. Cir. 1973), cert. denied 417 U.S. 921 (1974); *International Harvester Co. v. Ruckelshaus*, 478 F.2d 615 (D.C. Cir. 1973).

4. While Judge Leventhal may be correct in suggesting that candid abdication of substantive review cannot be reconciled with the APA, one may question whether federal judges are equipped to reexamine the resolution of complex scientific questions. The difficulty of combining the deference and skepticism that seems called for by the foregoing cases is captured by Judge Brown in *American Petroleum Institute v. EPA*, 661 F.2d 340, 349 (5th Cir. 1981):

> In summary, we must accord the agency considerable, but not too much deference; it is entitled to exercise its discretion, but only so far and no further; and its decision need not be ideal or even, perhaps, correct so long as not "arbitrary" or "capricious" and so long as the agency gave at least minimal consideration to the relevant facts as contained in the record.

5. "Deferential skepticism" is indeed a difficult attitude to maintain. Several proposals have sought to retain the inherent skepticism of judicial process, without the necessity for deference, by creating a "science court," empowered to resolve scientific issues confronting administrative policymakers. See generally Martin, *The Proposed "Science Court,"* 75 Mich. L. Rev. 1058 (1977). Can you imagine how such a court would have helped in resolving the underlying uncertainties in the benzene case?

6. The central issue left open in the benzene case—whether OSHA is obligated to balance costs and benefits in setting exposure limits for substances that pose "significant" risks—reached the Court two terms later. *American Textile Manufacturers Institute v. Donovan*, 452 U.S. 490 (1981), was a challenge to OSHA's standard for cotton dust, ambient particles generated in the production of cotton fabric which have long been known to cause the congestive pulmonary disease byssinosis, or "brown lung." After a protracted rulemaking which, like the benzene standard, produced an enormous administrative record containing information on both health effects and the costs of achieving alternative exposure limits, OSHA promulgated different limits for each segment of the cotton fabric industry, ranging from 200 to 750 micrograms per cubic meter of air, to be achieved primarily through engineering controls.

In the Supreme Court the industry petitioners did not take issue with OSHA's express finding that prevailing worker exposure to cotton dust posed a "significant" risk to their health. Indeed, it was conceded that many workers would continue to experience serious and potentially disabling byssinosis even under the new standard. The petitioners' central claims were, first, that sections 3(8) and 6(b)(5) of the statute required OSHA to "demonstrate that the reduction in risk of material health impairment is significant in light of the costs of attaining that reduction," i.e., that the benefits justify the costs, and second, that OSHA's estimate of the costs of meeting the new standard was not supported by substantial evidence. The D.C. Circuit had ruled in OSHA's favor on both issues. 617 F.2d 636 (D.C. Cir. 1979).

Writing for a majority that included Justice Stevens, Justice Brennan upheld the cotton dust standard in all but one respect. Concerning the industry's cost-benefit argument, Justice Brennan focused on the "to the extent feasible" language of section 6(b)(5), which all parties conceded to be the "critical language" (452 U.S. at 508–14, 521–22):

> The plain meaning of the word "feasible" supports respondents' interpretation of the statute. According to Webster's Third New International Dictionary of the English Language 831 (1976), "feasible" means "capable of being done, executed, or effected." Accord, the Oxford English Dictionary 116 (1933) ("Capable of being done, accomplished or carried out"); Funk & Wagnalls New "Standard" Dictionary of the English Language 903 (1957) ("That may be done, performed or effected"). Thus, § 6(b)(5) directs the Secretary to issue the standard that "most adequately assures * * * that no employee will suffer material impairment of health," limited only by the extent to which this is "capable of being done." In effect then, as the Court of Appeals held, Congress itself defined the basic relationship between costs and benefits, by placing the "benefit" or worker health above all other considerations save those making attainment of this "benefit" unachievable. Any standard based on a balancing of costs and benefits by the Secretary that strikes a different balance than that struck by Congress would be inconsistent with the command set forth in § 6(b)(5). Thus, cost-benefit analysis by OSHA is not required by the statute because feasibility analysis is.

*   *   *

> Agreement with petitioners' argument that § 3(8) imposes an additional and overriding requirement of cost-benefit analysis on the issuance of § 6(b)(5) standards would eviscerate the "to the extent feasible" requirement. Standards would inevitably be set at the level indicated by cost-benefit analysis, and not at the level specified by § 6(b)(5). For example, if cost-benefit analysis indicated a protective standard of 1,000 $\mu g/m^3$ PEL, while feasibility analysis indicated a 500 $\mu g/m^3$ PEL, the agency would be forced by the cost-benefit requirement to choose the less stringent point. We cannot believe that Congress intended the general terms of § 3(8) to countermand the specific feasibility requirement of § 6(b)(5). * * *

> The legislative history of the Act, while concededly not crystal clear, provides general support for respondents' interpretation of the Act. * * *

> * * * Nowhere is there any indication that Congress contemplated a different balancing by OSHA of the benefits of worker health and safety against the costs of achieving them. Indeed Congress thought that the *financial costs* of health and safety problems in the workplace were as large as or larger than the *financial costs* of eliminating these problems. In its statement of findings and declaration of purpose encompassed in the Act itself,

Congress announced that "personal injuries and illnesses arising out of work situations impose a substantial burden upon, and are a hindrance to, interstate commerce in terms of lost production, wage loss, medical expenses, and disability compensation payments." * * *

Justice Brennan's treatment of OSHA's estimate of the costs of complying with the cotton dust standard displayed considerable deference to the agency's fact-finding and analysis, at least when previously sustained by the court of appeals (id. at 522–29, 530–32, 535–36):

* * * Petitioners contend that the Secretary's determination that the Cotton Dust Standard is "economically feasible" is not supported by substantial evidence in the record considered as a whole. * * *

* * * Since the Act places responsibility for determining substantial evidence questions in the courts of appeals, we apply the familiar rule that "[t]his Court will intervene only in what ought to be the rare instance when the [substantial evidence] standard appears to have been misapprehended or grossly misapplied" by the court below. Therefore, our inquiry is not to determine whether we, in the first instance, would find OSHA's findings supported by substantial evidence. Instead we turn to OSHA's findings and the record upon which they were based to decide whether the Court of Appeals "misapprehended or grossly misapplied" the substantial evidence test.

OSHA derived its costs estimate for industry compliance with the Cotton Dust Standard after reviewing two financial analyses, one prepared by the Research Triangle Institute (RTI), an OSHA-contracted group, the other by industry representatives (Hocutt-Thomas). * * *

OSHA rejected RTI's cost estimate of $1.1 billion for textile industry engineering controls for three principal reasons. First, OSHA believed that RTI's estimate should be discounted by 30%, because that estimate was based on the assumption that engineering controls would be applied to all equipment in mills, including those processing pure synthetic fibers, even though cotton dust is not generated by such equipment. * * * Since the Standard did not require controls on synthetics-only equipment, OSHA rejected RTI's assumption about application of controls to synthetics-only machines. Second, OSHA concluded that RTI "may have over-estimated compliance costs since some operations are already in compliance with the permissible exposure limit of the new standard." * * * OSHA disagreed with RTI's assumption that the industry had not reduced cotton dust exposure below the existing standard's 1,000 $\mu g/m^3$ total dust PEL. Third, OSHA found that the RTI study suffered from lack of recent accurate industry data.

In light of these deficiencies in the RTI study, OSHA adopted the Hocutt-Thomas estimate for textile industry engineering controls of $543 million, emphasizing that, because it was based on the most recent industry data, it was more realistic than RTI's estimate. Nevertheless OSHA concluded that the Hocutt-Thomas estimate was overstated for four principal reasons. First, Hocutt-Thomas included costs of achieving the existing PEL of 1,000 $\mu g/m^3$, while OSHA thought it likely that compliance was more widespread and that some mills had in fact achieved the final standard's PEL. Second, Hocutt-Thomas declined to make any allowance for the trend toward replacement of existing production machines with newer more productive equipment. Relying on this "[n]atural production tren[d]," OSHA concluded that fewer machines than estimated by Hocutt-Thomas would require retrofitting or other

controls.   Third, OSHA thought that Hocutt-Thomas failed to take into account development of new technologies likely to occur during the 4-year compliance period.   Fourth, OSHA believed that Hocutt-Thomas might have improperly included control costs for synthetics-only machines, an inclusion
which could result in a 30% cost overestimate.

Petitioners criticize OSHA's adoption of the Hocutt-Thomas estimate,
since that estimate was based on achievement of somewhat less stringent
PEL's than those ultimately promulgated in the final Standard.   Thus, even
if the Hocutt-Thomas estimate was exaggerated, they assert that "only by
the most remarkable coincidence would the amount of that overestimate be
equal to the additional costs required to attain the far more stringent limits of
the Standard OSHA actually adopted."   The agency itself recognized the
problem cited by petitioners, but found itself limited in the precision of its estimates by the industry's refusal to make more of its own data available.
OSHA explained that, "in the absence of the [industry] survey data [of textile
mills], OSHA cannot develop more accurate estimates of compliance costs."
Since § 6(b)(5) of the Act requires that the Secretary promulgate toxic material and harmful physical agent standards "on the basis of the best available
evidence," and since OSHA could not obtain the more detailed confidential industry data it thought essential to further precision, we conclude that the
agency acted reasonably in adopting the Hocutt-Thomas estimate.   While a
cost estimate based on the standard actually promulgated surely would be
preferable, we decline to hold as a matter of law that its absence under the circumstances required the Court of Appeals to find that OSHA's determination
was unsupported by substantial evidence. * * *

After estimating the cost of compliance with the Cotton Dust Standard,
OSHA analyzed whether it was "economically feasible" for the cotton industry to bear this cost.   OSHA concluded that it was, finding that "although
some marginal employers may shut down rather than comply, the industry as
a whole will not be threatened by the capital requirements of the regulation."   In reaching this conclusion on the Standard's economic impact,
OSHA made specific findings with respect to employment, energy consumption, capital financing availability, and profitability.   To support its findings,
the agency relied primarily on RTI's comprehensive investigation of the Standard's economic impact.

* * *

The Court of Appeals found that the agency "explained the economic impact it projected for the textile industry," and that OSHA has "substantial
support in the record for its * * * findings of economic feasibility for the
textile industry."   On the basis of the whole record, we cannot conclude that
the Court of Appeals "misapprehended or grossly misapplied" the substantial
evidence test.

The majority's acquiescence in OSHA's economic analysis provoked this response from Justice Stewart in dissent (id. at 542–43):

The simple truth about OSHA's assessment of the cost of the Cotton Dust
Standard is that the agency never relied on any study or report purporting to
predict the cost to industry of the Standard finally adopted by the agency.
* * * I am willing to defer to OSHA's determination that the Hocutt-Thomas

study was such an overestimate, conceding that such subtle financial and technical matters lie within the discretion and skill of the agency. But in a remarkable non sequitur, the agency decided that because the Hocutt-Thomas study was an overestimate of the cost of a less stringent standard, it could be treated as a reliable estimate for the more costly final Standard actually promulgated, never rationally explaining how it came to this happy conclusion. This is not substantial evidence. It is unsupported speculation.

* * * I think this is one of those rare instances where an agency has categorically misconceived the nature of the evidence necessary to support a regulation, and where the Court of Appeals has failed to correct the agency's error. * * *

Justice Rehnquist, joined by the Chief Justice, also dissented, reviving his contention that section 6(b)(5) of the OSH Act violated the non-delegation doctrine. Justice Powell took no part in the Court's decision.

The Supreme Court's benzene decision spawned a large body of commentary, much of it focused on the historical accuracy of the majority's interpretation of the OSH Act and the unresolved cost-benefit issue or on the availability of methods of quantifying the risks of low-level exposure to environmental carcinogens. Like Colin Diver, *Policymaking Paradigms in Administrative Law*, 95 Harv. L. Rev. 393 (1980), William Rodgers saw in the case some broader lessons about the relationship between courts and agencies.

ROGERS, JUDICIAL REVIEW OF RISK ASSESSMENTS: THE ROLE OF DECISION THEORY IN UNSCRAMBLING THE BENZENE DECISION

11 Environ. L. 301 (1981).

There are three prominent contenders for the most suitable descriptive theory of contemporary administrative decisionmaking. * * * The first is what may be called the classical theory, which views the administrator as a surrogate for the legislative policymaker. Rulemaking, under this view, is a free-wheeling and many-splendored process in which the administrator reaches out for information from any source—hearings, libraries, whispers in the hall. Decisionmaking is perceived to be intuitive, involving as it does horsetrading among the interests and the deft balancing of value choices. Experience, stability, and expertise are valued decisionmaking traits, as lawmakers are expected to know the players, know the industry, and know the history of prior arrangements. Negotiated settlements are expected to achieve decision by compromise, adjustment, and even the logrolling so familiar to the legislative process. * * *

A second model, in many ways the converse of the first, could be called the rational or formal model of administrative decisionmaking. * * * These [various] decision methods to a large degree depend upon the identification of alternatives, the projection of consequences, and the conscious selection of a "best" decision. Decisionmaking is perceived to be less political than under the classical theory and more scientific. Information from any old source will not do; scientific reliability is required and for some reason this often is associated with quantification. There is a heavy reliance upon outside technical consultants. Modeling, decision trees, and risk analyses are much in vogue, and data needs are compelling. * * *

* * * Administrative expertise, under this theory, means not so much a sophisticated savvy about the business of the agency as it does a knowledge of pertinent technologies, requiring a stable of professionals skilled in a variety of disciplines. A decision is not a negotiated bill of accord, with a little bit here and there for the prominent interests and bearing the stamp of consensus; it is perceived as correct and definitive, carefully developed and imposed. * * *

A third, and now eminently popular, theory of administrative decision-making is the theory of successive limited comparisons, known less elegantly as the science of muddling through. This is my own nominee, in essential particulars, for the theory best capturing the realities of how agencies decide. This is a hybrid theory, combining the classical and formal approaches. * * * Like the classicists, the muddlers reach out to the interest groups and engage them in negotiation and searches for common criteria, or at least agreed-upon processes. They are similarly familiar, however, with the techniques and methods of formal decisionmaking, although the data which is received is altered and shaped to take into account financial, informational, administrative, and political limits. * * * Decisionmaking is marked by long delays, repeated hearings, erratic shifts as one or another faction gains temporary ascendancy. Decisions reflect combinations of truncated formality (considering alternatives within perceived limits), and intuitive policy and political judgments. * * *

The choice of administrative decisionmaking models and their legislative counterparts strongly influences one's normative perceptions of appropriate judicial review. Acceptance of the classical free-wheeling agency model begets a mild regime of review. Administrative know-how, and ergo judicial deference, extends even to the reading of the legislative charter and the interpretation to be accorded legal terms. The agencies, like the legislative body for which they speak, are accorded wide freedom in selecting the procedural techniques used to reach their policy conclusions. * * *

By contrast, the assumption that agency decisionmakers are supposed to be rational in the strictest sense of the term encourages a regime of close judicial scrutiny. If the goal is an ideal "best" decision, departures from standards of perfection are viewed with intolerance. Interpretation of the legislative charter should be closely supervised as this charter sets the ultimate bounds of the formal inquiry undertaken. Procedures, too, are in for a close reading, both because Congress has made process an important ingredient of substantive result and because procedural exactitude has long been associated with correct outcomes. * * * There is little judicial tolerance for political balancing or policy guesswork from the agencies, for the results are supposed to be scientifically derived, and whatever the meaning of the scientific method, it is thought to yield results supportable by evidence and to differ sharply from political tradeoff.

* * * [P]artial, erratic, and fragmented decisionmaking calls for highly skeptical oversight as pragmatic and *ad hoc* action proceeds by no set patterns. * * * Procedural oversight and interest representation are also important because of the strong process orientation of strategic decisionmaking. Explanations of what was done and why must be demanded by the courts to protect against the dangers of subjectivity associated with incremental decisions under uncertain criteria. The essence of the contemporary hard look doctrine of judicial review is to compel explanations of methodology and identification of the criteria for judgment. An important distinction between review under the formal model and review under the muddling model is that the latter must leave room for the resolution of uncertainty, and for policy and value choice. * * *

* * * Justice Stevens' plurality opinion [in the benzene case] comes close to adopting the rational decisionmaking model, and demonstrates the vulnerability of that model to judicial nitpicking over evidentiary gaps in the record supporting the supposedly ideal decision. Mr. Justice Burger's concurring opinion is classicist in tone, prepared to defer broadly to the policy and procedural choices of the agency. * * * Mr. Justice Powell comes down somewhere between the muddling and the rational decisionmaking model, honoring the agency's ability to make predictive judgments but finding insubstantial evidence to support the conclusion that the risk perceived was a significant one. The dissenters are probably believers in muddling, and the analysis adopted is consistent with that theory. Mr. Justice Marshall's opinion, however, together with the Stevens and Powell opinions, makes clear that the choice of theory does not automatically dictate results. Courts overseeing administrative muddlers must distinguish between explanations, which are sharply scrutinized, and predictive judgments to which deference is owed. And courts are obliged also to face up to the questions of who has the burden of predictive judgment and what investigations are necessary to support it, subjects upon which Congress rarely speaks with clarity and judges often disagree. * * *

Congressional Proposals to Intensify Judicial Review of Agency Decisions

Over the past decade, many members of Congress have supported legislation authored by Arkansas Senator Dale Bumpers that would harness judicial inquisitiveness to the objective of greater administrative fidelity to Congressional policy choices. In every session of Congress since 1975, Senator Bumpers has introduced bills to amend section 706 of the APA to intensify judicial review of agency decisions generally, and of rules specifically. The original version, S. 86, 95th Cong., 1st Sess., 123 Cong. Rec. 639 (1977), read as follows:

> To the extent necessary to decision and when presented, the reviewing court shall decide de novo all relevant questions of law, interpret constitutional and statutory provisions, and determine the meaning or applicability of

the terms of the agency action.   There shall be no presumption that any rule or regulation of any agency is valid, and whenever the validity of any such rule or regulation is drawn in question in any court of the United States or of any State, the court shall not uphold the validity of such challenged rule or regulation unless such validity is clearly and convincingly shown; *Provided, however,* That if any rule or regulation is set up as a defense to any criminal prosecution or action for civil penalty, such rule or regulation shall be presumed valid until the party initiating the criminal prosecution or action for civil penalty shall have sustained the burden of proof normally applicable in such actions.

On September 7, 1979, the Senate adopted a modified version this amendment to the APA as a rider to legislation restructuring the federal judicial system.   S. 1477, 96th Cong., 1st Sess., 125 Cong. Rec. 23478 *et seq.*   The amendment did not survive the House-Senate conference on the judiciary bill.

According to Senator Bumpers, the objective of his amendment was to place "the American citizen seeking to challenge an agency action * * * on an even level with the bureaucracy."   Light, *Senate Approves Proposal Making It Easier to Contest Federal Regulations in Court,* 37 Cong. Q. Weekly Rep. 2014 (1979).   Proponents of the original amendment were distressed by the apparent propensity of courts to defer to agency statutory interpretations, in particular their determination of their own jurisdiction.   Senator Bumpers cited *NLRB v. Hearst Publications, Inc.,* 322 U.S. 111 (1944), supra p. 252, as a particularly egregious illustration of this approach.

Despite its success in the Senate, the Bumpers amendment has been criticized in several quarters.   Some critics argued that its author has misgauged the prevailing attitude of reviewing courts, which are increasingly willing to "second guess" agency determinations of legal authority, administrative procedure, and even regulatory policy.   See, e.g., Letters from Professor Clark Byse and Professor Nathaniel L. Nathanson to Francis M. Gregory (September 8, 1976), *reprinted in* 123 Cong. Rec. 639–40 (1977) (statement of Sen. Bumpers).   At the same time, they argue that mandatory "de novo" review and explicit rejection of the presumption of validity will introduce unpredictability as different courts try to decide for themselves what an agency's statute means and further undermine the values of agency expertise.   The critics' difficulty stemmed in part from the language of the original Bumpers bill, which in their view invited judicial retrial of agency cases and wholesale rejection of administrative policy judgments.   The demand for "de novo" decision of "all relevant questions of law," it was suggested could be construed as embracing the question of whether an agency's determination of facts was supported by substantial evidence.

Senator Bumpers subsequently attempted to meet some of these objections.   Later versions of the amendment have omitted the "de novo review" language and, instead, directed courts to "independently" determine questions of law.   The latest version expressly retains the "arbitrary and capricious" standard for policy determinations and devises a "substantial support in the record" standard for agency factual determinations in other than formal rulemaking—a formulation designed to "negate any implication that the intent of these amendments is to require indirectly the use of trial-type procedures in informal rulemaking." S. 1766, 98th Cong., 1st Sess., 129 Cong. Rec. S11583–84 (daily ed., August 4, 1983).

In 1982, Bumpers introduced a version of his bill that was a product of negotiations with the White House, which had opposed the amendment but apparently concurred that some compromise was needed to secure Senate passage of President Reagan's regulatory reform legislation, S. 1080, 97th Cong., 2d Sess. The principal change was a "clarification" to permit a reviewing court to give an agency's determination on a question of law "such weight as it warrants." S. 1080 § 5, 97th Cong., 2nd Sess., 128 Cong. Rec. S2406 (daily ed. March 18, 1982). S. 1080 was passed overwhelmingly by the Senate on March 24, 1982, but it expired in the House. In the next session of Congress, Senator Bumpers retreated to the earlier formulation that purports to accord no weight to agency determinations of their own legal authority.

For discussions of successive versions of the Bumpers amendment and its rationale, see, e.g., McGowan, *Congress, Court, and Control of Delegated Power*, 77 Colum. L. Rev. 1119, 1162–68 (1977); O'Reilly, *Deference Makes a Difference: A Study of Impacts of the Bumpers Judicial Review Amendment*, 49 U. Cinn. L. Rev. 739 (1980); Woodward and Levin, *In Defense of Deference: Judicial Review of Agency Action*, 31 Ad. L. Rev. 329 (1979).

B. THE CHOICE BETWEEN RULEMAKING AND ADJUDICATION

As the *Petroleum Refiners* and *Hynson* cases illustrate, an agency may develop regulatory policy either through rulemaking or as it disposes of individual cases. These cases further suggest that rulemaking may offer an agency strategic advantages in developing and implementing policy, such as the avoidance of formal hearings and court litigation, immediate broader application, and a clarity and prospectivity that invites widespread compliance. But despite these apparent advantages, some agencies routinely, and all agencies frequently, spurn rulemaking. The questions of immediate concern, therefore, are why administrators may prefer adjudication to rulemaking and whether there are enforceable constraints on that preference.

1. THE NLRB'S PROCLIVITY FOR ADJUDICATION

Though often referred to as the "National Labor Relations Act," the "Act" administered by the National Labor Relations Board is really a combination of three statutes: the Wagner Act (1935), the Taft-Hartley Act (1947), and the Landrum-Griffin Act (1959). The Wagner Act was designed to protect the right of workers to organize and to bargain collectively with employers while the Taft-Hartley Act was designed to protect both employees and employers from union excesses in the exercise of these rights. The Landrum-Griffin Act, to the extent it dealt with the employer-union relationship, was a tidying-up statute dealing with particular problems that had arisen in the application of the other two statutes. The heart of the statutory scheme is section 7 of the Wagner Act, 29 U.S.C.A. § 157, which provides:

> Employees shall have the right to self-organization, to form, join, or assist labor organizations, to bargain collectively through representatives of their own choosing, and to engage in other concerted activities for the purpose of collective bargaining or other mutual aid or protection. * * *

Section 8 then prohibits both employers and unions from engaging in any action which would "interfere with, restrain, or coerce employees" in the exercise of those rights. This broad prohibition, along with more specific proscriptions, defines what are referred to as "unfair labor practices."

The NLRB, a five-member independent agency appointed by the President, subject to Senate confirmation, has basically two functions: (1) to enforce the Act's prohibition against unfair labor practices by issuing cease and desist orders and orders for the reinstatement of workers or for the payment of wages wrongfully withheld; and (2) to supervise elections in which employees choose representatives to deal with management. Both functions may result in contested adjudicatory proceedings before the Board. Representation cases raise such questions as the authenticity of petitions for an election, the appropriateness of bargaining units for which certification is sought (as in the *Hearst* and *Bell Aerospace* cases), whether a previously certified union still represents a majority of employees, and the timing of elections in the light of existing labor contracts. Indeed, although representation petitions are filed at one third the rate of unfair labor practice complaints (13,318 to 44,063 in 1980), almost three times as many representation cases result in the issuance of a decision by the Board itself or by NLRB Regional Directors (3,109 to 1,181).

Petitions and complaints are filed by interested parties with NLRB Regional Directors. The regional staff investigates each matter and, if the petition or complaint is not withdrawn or dismissed (at the discretion of the Board's General Counsel) or a settlement reached, the NLRB staff takes the case to hearing. Initial or recommended decisions after hearing are made by the Regional Directors or Administrative Law Judges. Cases reach the Board itself almost exclusively on appeal.

Even so, the Board carries a very substantial caseload, roughly one case per working day for each member. The Board historically has had difficulty keeping its docket current. Delay has significant implications for representation cases in particular. For if an employer, by appealing to the Board and then to the courts, can forestall certification of a union, its support will often slip away through employee turnover and frustration.

NATIONAL LABOR RELATIONS BOARD
v. WYMAN-GORDON CO.

Supreme Court of the United States, 1969
394 U.S. 759, 895. Ct. 1426, 22 L. Ed.2d 709.

MR. JUSTICE FORTAS announced the judgment of the Court and delivered an opinion in which THE CHIEF JUSTICE, MR. JUSTICE STEWART, and MR. JUSTICE WHITE join.

On the petition of the International Brotherhood of Boilermakers * * * the National Labor Relations Board ordered an election among the production and maintenance employees of the respondent company. At the election, the employees were to select one of two labor unions as their exclusive bargaining representative, or to choose not to be represented by a union at all. In connection with the election, the Board ordered the respondent to furnish a list of the names and addresses of its employees who could vote in the election, so that the unions could use the list for election purposes. The respondent refused to comply with the order, and the election was held without the list. Both unions were defeated in the election.

The Board upheld the union's objections to the election because the respondent had not furnished the list, and the Board ordered a new election. The respondent again refused to obey a Board order to supply a list of employees, and the Board issued a subpoena ordering the respondent to provide the list or else produce its personnel and payroll records showing the employees' names and addresses. The Board filed an action in the United States District Court for the District of Massachusetts seeking to have its subpoena enforced or to have a mandatory injunction issued to compel the respondent to comply with its order.

The District Court held the Board's order valid and directed the respondent to comply. The United States Court of Appeals for the First Circuit reversed. The Court of Appeals thought that the order in this case was invalid because it was based on a rule laid down in an earlier decision by the Board, *Excelsior Underwear, Inc.*, 156 N.L.R.B. 1236 (1966), and the *Excelsior* rule had not been promulgated in accordance with the requirements that the Administrative Procedure Act prescribes for rule making * * * .

The *Excelsior* case involved union objections to the certification of the results of elections that the unions had lost at two companies. The companies had denied the unions a list of the names and addresses of employees eligible to vote. In the course of the proceedings, the Board "invited certain interested parties" to file briefs and to participate in oral argument of the issue whether the Board should require the employer to furnish lists of employees. Various employer groups and trade unions did so, as *amici curiae*. After these proceedings, the Board issued its decision in *Excelsior*. It purported to establish the general rule that such a list must be provided, but it declined to apply its new rule to the companies involved in the *Excelsior* case.   Instead, it held that the rule would apply "only in those elections that are directed, or consented to, subsequent to 30 days from the date of [the] Decision."

Specifically, the Board purported to establish "a requirement that will be applied in all election cases.   That is, within 7 days after the Regional Director has approved a consent-election agreement entered into by the parties * * * , or after the Regional director or the Board has directed an election * * * , the employer must file with the Regional Director an election eligibility list, containing the names and addresses of all the eligible voters.   The Regional Director, in turn, shall make this information available to all parties in the case.   Failure to comply with this requirement shall be grounds for setting aside the election whenever proper objections are filed."

Section 6 of the National Labor Relations Act empowers the Board "to make * * * , in the manner prescribed by the Administrative Procedure Act, such rules and regulations as may be necessary to carry out the provisions of this Act." * * * The Board asks us to hold that it has discretion to promulgate new rules in adjudicatory proceedings, without complying with the requirements of the Administrative Procedure Act.

The rule-making provisions of that Act, which the Board would avoid, were designed to assure fairness and mature consideration of rules of general application.   They may not be avoided by the process of making rules in the course of adjudicatory proceedings.   There is no warrant in law for the Board to replace the statutory scheme with a rule-making procedure of its own invention.   Apart from the fact that the device fashioned by the Board does not comply with statutory command, it obviously falls short of the substance of the requirements of the Administrative Procedure Act.   The "rule" created in *Excelsior* was not published in the Federal Register, which is the statutory and accepted means of giving notice of a rule as adopted; only selected organizations were given notice of the "hearing," whereas notice in the Federal Register would have been general in character; under the Administrative Procedure Act, the terms or substance of the rule would have to be stated in the notice of hearing, and all interested parties would have an opportunity to participate in the rule making.

The Solicitor General does not deny that the Board ignored the rule-making provisions of the Administrative Procedure Act.[3]   But he appears to argue that *Excelsior's* command is a valid substantive regulation, binding upon this respondent as such, because the Board promulgated it in the *Excesior* proceeding, in which the requirements for valid adjudication had been met.   This argument misses the point.   There is no question that, in an adjudicatory hearing, the Board could validly decide the issue whether the employer must furnish a list of employees to

---

3. The Board has never utilized the Act's rule-making procedures.   It has been criticized for contravening the Act in this manner.   See, e.g., 1 K. Davis, Administrative Law Treatise § 6.13 (Supp. 1965); Peck, the Atrophied Rule Making Powers of the National Labor Relations Board, 70 Yale L. J. 729 (1961).

the union. But that is not what the Board did in *Excelsior*. The Board did not even apply the rule it made to the parties in the adjudicatory proceeding, the only entities that could properly be subject to the order in that case. Instead, the Board purported to make a rule: i.e., to exercise its quasi-legislative power.

Adjudicated cases may and do, of course, serve as vehicles for the formulation of agency policies, which are applied and announced therein. They generally provide a guide to action that the agency may be expected to take in future cases. Subject to the qualified role of *stare decisis* in the administrative process, they may serve as precedents. But this is far from saying, as the Solicitor General suggests, that commands, decisions, or policies announced in adjudication are "rules" in the sense that they must, without more, be obeyed by the affected public.

In the present case, however, the respondent itself was specifically directed by the Board to submit a list of the names and addresses of its employees for use by the unions in connection with the election. This direction, which was part of the order directing that an election be held, is unquestionably valid. Even though the direction to furnish the list was followed by citation to *"Excelsior Underwear Inc.,"* it is an order in the present case that the respondent was required to obey. Absent this direction by the Board, the respondent was under no compulsion to furnish the list because no statute and no validly adopted rule required it to do so.

Because the Board in an adjudicatory proceeding directed the respondent itself to furnish the list, the decision of the Court of Appeals for the First Circuit must be reversed.

The respondent also argues that it need not obey the board's order because the requirement of disclosure of employees' names and addresses is substantively invalid. This argument lacks merit. The objections that the respondent raises to the requirement of disclosure were clearly and correctly answered by the Board in its *Excelsior* decision. All of the United States Courts of Appeals that have passed on the question have upheld the substantive validity of the disclosure requirement, and the court below strongly intimated a view that the requirement was substantively a proper one.

* * *

MR. JUSTICE BLACK, with whom MR. JUSTICE BRENNAN and MR. JUSTICE MARSHALL join, concurring in the result.

I agree with [the portions] of the prevailing opinion * * * holding that the *Excelsior* requirement * * * is valid on its merits and can be enforced by subpoena. But I cannot subscribe to the criticism * * * of the procedure followed by the Board. * * * Nor can I accept the novel theory by which the opinion manages to uphold enforcement of the *Excelsior* practice in spite of what it considers to be statutory violations present in the procedure by which the requirement was adopted. Although the opinion is apparently intended to rebuke the Board and encourage it to follow the plurality's conception of proper administrative practice, the result instead is to free the Board from all judicial control whatsoever regarding compliance with procedures specifically required by applicable federal statutes.   * * *   Apparently, under the prevailing opinion, courts must enforce any requirement announced in a purported "adjudication" even if it clearly was not adopted as an incident to the decision of a case before the agency, and must enforce "rules" adopted in a purported "rule making" even if the agency materially violated the specific requirements that Congress has directed for such proceedings in the Administrative Procedure Act.   I for one would not give judicial sanction to any such illegal agency action.

In the present case, however, I am convinced that the *Excelsior* practice was adopted by the Board as a legitimate incident to the adjudication of a specific case before it, and for that reason I would hold that the Board properly followed the procedures applicable to "adjudication" rather than "rule making."   * * *

Most administrative agencies, like the Labor Board here, are granted two functions by the legislation creating them: (1) the power under certain conditions to make rules having the effect of laws, that is, generally speaking, quasi-legislative power; and (2) the power to hear and adjudicate particular controversies, that is quasi-judicial power.   The line between these two functions is not always a clear one and in fact the two functions merge at many points.   For example, in exercising its quasi-judicial function an agency must frequently decide controversies on the basis of new doctrines, not theretofore applied to a specific problem, though drawn to be sure from broader principles reflecting the purposes of the statutes involved and from the rules invoked in dealing with related problems.   If the agency decision reached under the adjudicatory power becomes a precedent, it guides future conduct in much the same way as though it were a new rule promulgated under the rule-making power, and both an adjudicatory order and a formal "rule" are alike subject to judicial review.   Congress gave the Labor Board both of these separate but almost inseparably related powers.   No language in the National Labor Relations Act requires that the grant or the exercise of one power was intended to exclude the Board's use of the other.

Nor does any language in the Administrative Procedure Act require such a conclusion.   * * * [S]o long as the matter involved can be dealt with in a way satisfying the definition of either "rule making" or "adjudication" under the Administrative Procedure Act, that Act, along with the Labor Relations Act, should be read as conferring upon the Board the authority to decide, within its informed discretion, whether to proceed by rule making or adjudication.   * * *

In the present case there is no dispute that all the procedural safeguards required for "adjudication" were fully satisfied in connection with the Board's *Excelsior* decision, and it seems plain to me that that decision did constitute "adjudication" within the meaning of the Administrative Procedure Act, even though the requirement was to be prospectively applied.   The Board did not abstractly decide out of the blue to announce a brand new rule of law to govern labor activities in the future, but rather established the procedure as a direct consequence of the proper exercise of its adjudicatory powers. * * *

* * * [T]he *Excelsior* order was * * * an inseparable part of the adjudicatory process. The principal issue before the Board in the *Excelsior* case was whether the election should be set aside on the ground, urged by the unions, that the employer had refused to make the employee lists available to them. The Board decided that the election involved there should not be set aside and thus rejected the contention of the unions. In doing so, the Board chose to explain the reasons for its rejection of their claim, and it is this explanation, the Board's written opinion, which is the source of the *Excelsior* requirement. The Board's opinion should not be regarded as any less an appropriate part of the adjudicatory process merely because the reason it gave for rejecting the unions' position was not that the Board disagreed with them as to the merits of the disclosure procedure but rather, that while fully agreeing that disclosure should be required, the Board did not feel that it should upset the Excelsior Company's justified reliance on previous refusals to compel disclosure by setting aside this particular election.

Apart from the fact that the decisions whether to accept a "new" requirement urged by one party and, if so, whether to apply it retroactively to the other party are inherent parts of the adjudicatory process, I think the opposing theory accepted by the Court of Appeals and by the prevailing opinion today is a highly impractical one. In effect, it would require an agency like the Labor Board to proceed by adjudication only when it could decide, *prior* to adjudicating a particular case, that any new practice to be adopted would be applied retroactively. Obviously, this decision cannot properly be made until all the issues relevant to adoption of the practice are fully considered in connection with the final decision of that case. If the Board were to decide, after careful evaluation of all the arguments presented to it in the adjudicatory proceeding, that it might be fairer to apply the practice only prospectively, it would be faced with the unpleasant choice of either starting all over again to evaluate the merits of the question, this time in a "rule-making" proceeding, or overriding the considerations of fairness and applying its order retroactively anyway, in order to preserve the validity of the new practice and avoid duplication of effort. I see no good reason to impose any such inflexible requirement on the administrative agencies.

* * *

MR. JUSTICE DOUGLAS, dissenting.

* * *

I am willing to assume that, if the Board decided to treat each case on its special facts and perform its adjudicatory function in the conventional way, we should have no difficulty in affirming its action. The difficulty is that it chose a different course in the *Excelsior* case and, having done so, it should be bound to follow the procedures prescribed in the [Administrative Procedure] Act as my Brother HARLAN has outlined them. When we hold otherwise, we let the Board "have its cake and eat it too."

* * *

* * * [I]t is no answer to say that the order under review was "adjudicatory." For as my Brother HARLAN says, an agency is not adjudicating when it is making a rule to fit future cases. A rule like the one in *Excelsior* is designed to fit all cases at all times. It is not particularized to special facts. It is a statement of far-reaching policy covering all future representation elections.

It should therefore have been put down for the public hearing prescribed by the Act.

The rule-making procedure performs important functions. It gives notice to an entire segment of society of those controls or regimentation that is forthcoming. It gives an opportunity for persons affected to be heard. * * *

* * * Agencies discover that they are not always repositories of ultimate wisdom; they learn from the suggestions of outsiders and often benefit from that advice. * * *

It has been stated that "the survival of a questionable rule seems somewhat more likely when it is submerged in the facts of a given case" than when rule making is used. See Shapiro, The Choice of Rulemaking or Adjudication in the Development of Administrative Policy, 78 Harv. L. Rev. 921 (1965). Moreover, "agencies appear to be freer to disregard their own prior decisions than they are to depart from their regulations." Failure to make full use of rule-making power is attributable at least in part "to administrative inertia and reluctance to take a clear stand."

Rule making is no cure-all; but it does force important issues into full public display and in that sense makes for more responsible administrative action. * * *

MR. JUSTICE HARLAN, dissenting.

The language of the Administrative Procedure Act does not support the Government's claim that an agency is "adjudicating" when it announces a rule which it refuses to apply in the dispute before it. The Act makes it clear that an agency "adjudicates" only when its procedures result in the "formulation of an *order*." An "order" is defined to include "the whole or a *part* of a final disposition * * * of an agency *in a matter other than rule making.* * * * 5 U.S.C.A. § 551(6). (Emphasis supplied.) This definition makes it apparent that an agency is not adjudicating when it is making a rule, which the Act defines as "an agency statement of general or particular applicability and *future effect.* * * * " 5 U.S.C.A. § 551(4). (Emphasis supplied.) Since the Labor Board's *Excelsior* rule was to be effective only 30 days after its promulgation, it clearly falls within the rule-making requirements of the Act.

Nor can I agree that the natural interpretation of the statute should be rejected because it requires the agency to choose between giving its rules immediate effect or initiating a separate rule-making proceeding. An agency chooses to apply a rule prospectively only because it represents such a departure from pre-existing understandings that it would be unfair to impose the rule upon the parties in pending matters. But it is precisely in these situations, in which established patterns of conduct are revolutionized, that rule-making procedures perform the vital functions that my Brother DOUGLAS describes so well in a dissenting opinion with which I basically agree.

* * *

Notes

1.   From the perspective of a reviewing court, asked to determine whether a novel agency policy is justifiable and consistent with the governing statute, does it make a difference whether the policy is the product of rulemaking or of adjudication?   From the vantage point of parties subject to the policy, what difference might its origin make?   Is there any indication that Wyman-Gordon had an opportunity to participate in the *Excelsior Underwear* proceeding where the Board fashioned its "list disclosure" requirement?   Did it have, or did it seek, an opportunity in the proceeding to which it was a party to persuade the Board that the requirement was unsound generally or inappropriate on context?   Did the company suggest arguments it might have advanced that were not considered by the Board in *Excelsior?*

2.   Justice Black's opinion in *Wyman-Gordon* relied heavily on an earlier decision of the Court, *SEC v. Chenery Corp.*, 332 U.S. 194, 202–03 (1947), a case widely cited for the proposition that agencies enjoy broad discretion to choose between rulemaking and adjudication.   In *Chenery*, the Court upheld the SEC's policy, announced for the first time in that case, that it would refuse to approve the reorganization of a public utility holding company when the reorganization plan failed to prohibit managers of the company from continuing to trade in its stock during reorganization.   Justice Murphy's opinion dismissed the petitioners' contention that the SEC could only make failure to prohibit management trading a disqualification by adopting a general, prospective rule:

Since the Commission, unlike a court, does have the ability to make new law prospectively through the exercise of its rule-making powers, it has less reason to rely upon *ad hoc* adjudication to formulate new standards of conduct within the framework of the Holding Company Act.   The function of filling in the interstices of the Act should be performed, as much as possible, through this quasi-legislative promulgation of rules to be applied in the future.   But any rigid requirement to that effect would make the administrative process inflexible and incapable of dealing with many of the specialized problems which arise.   Not every principle essential to the effective administration of a statute can or should be cast immediately into the mold of a general rule.   Some principles must await their own development, while others must be adjusted to meet particular, unforeseeable situations.   * * *

* * * [P]roblems may arise in a case which the administrative agency could not reasonably foresee, problems which must be solved despite the absence of a relevant general rule.   Or the agency may not have had sufficient experience with a particular problem to warrant rigidifying its tentative judgment into a hard and fast rule.   Or the problem may be so specialized and varying in nature as to be impossible to capture within the boundaries of a general rule.   In those situations, the agency must retain power to deal with the problems on a case-to-case basis if the administrative process is to be effective.   There is thus a very definite place for the case-by-case evolution of statutory standards. And the choice made between proceeding by general rule or by individual, *ad hoc* litigation is one that lies primarily in the informed discretion of the administrative agency.

* * * That such action might have a retroactive effect was not necessarily fatal to its validity. Every case of first impression has a retroactive effect, whether the new principle is announced by a court or by an administrative agency. But such retroactivity must be balanced against the mischief of producing a result which is contrary to a statutory design or to legal and equitable principles. * * *

3. The Labor Board's attempt in *Excelsior* to avoid retroactive changes in established policy was responsive to a continuing problem in its operations. As it grapples with a continuous, if changing caseload, the Board inevitably discovers that some of its prior policies are dysfunctional or require adaptation to fit new economic circumstances of industrial practices. On several occasions its shifts in policy have been challenged on essentially due process grounds.

NLRB v. Guy F. Atkinson Co., 195 F.2d 141 (9th Cir. 1952), for example, involved the Board's long-standing policy of declining to exercise jurisdiction over the construction industry. In a complaint by a discharged employee of the respondent, the Board reversed field, found an unfair labor practice, and ordered the employee reinstated with back pay. The Court of Appeals refused to enforce the Board's order because the change of policy worked "hardship upon [the] respondent altogether out of proportion to the public ends to be accomplished." In the court's view the inequity of this type of retroactive law making was "manifest. It is the sort of thing our system of law abhors. * * * * " Id. at 149.

The dictates of fairness must, however, be balanced against the exigencies of effective regulation. In 1953 the Board announced a "contract bar rule," *General Motors Corp.*, 102 N.L.R.B. 1140 (1953), under which it would not authorize a representation election during the life of a collective bargaining agreement, provided the agreement had a term of no more than five years. But in 1958 it revised this policy, *Pacific Coast Ass'n of Pulp & Paper Mfrs.*, 121 N.L.R.B. 990 (1958), announcing that it would entertain an election petition after a contract had run two years, and it applied this new policy to contracts entered into while the five-year "rule" was in effect. This "retroactive" application was upheld in *Leedom v. International Bhd. of Electrical Workers, Local 108*, 278 F.2d 237, 243 (D.C. Cir. 1960). Judge Bazelon, writing for the court, distinguished *Guy v. Atkinson* on the ground that the Board had not purported to disapprove or punish conduct previously considered proper. Moreover, it was simply unacceptable to require the Board to make its change of policy wholly prospective because it would have "to wait up to five years to put its new policies into full effect. This drag on the administrative process would tend to destroy its flexibility."

NLRB v. Majestic Weaving Co., 355 F.2d 854, 861 (2d Cir. 1966), involved, *inter alia*, a Board finding that the company had unlawfully negotiated an exclusive bargaining agreement with a union prior to the time that the latter had attained majority status. In so deciding, the Board reversed its longstanding position that such negotiations were proper so long as the agreement was, as in this case, conditional upon the union's obtaining the support of a majority of the employees. The court, per Judge Friendly, denied enforcement of the order, ultimately on the narrow procedural ground that the Board had not given the company adequate notice of the issue on which it decided the case. The court made clear, however, that it thought the retroactive application of the new policy (the company was ordered to reimburse initiation fees and dues withheld from employee paychecks and paid to the unlawfully assisted union) had an ill effect that "so far outweighs any demonstrated need for immediate application to past conduct as to render the action 'arbitrary'" within the meaning of the APA.

4.   The Labor Board's power, through adjudication, to announce new principles of law and repudiate old ones was challenged again in *NLRB v. Bell Aerospace Co.*, 416 U.S. 267 (1974), supra p. 262.   In that case the Board had appeared to depart from prior law by holding that certain buyers for the company, though recognized as "managerial employees"—a class long considered outside the protection of the Labor Act—had the right to organize and bargain because their unionization would not create a conflict of interest on labor-management relations questions—the agency's new touchstone of statutory coverage.   The Second Circuit, in an opinion by Judge Friendly, invalidated the change in policy on the ground, among others, that the Board's failure to use rulemaking was contrary to the considered dictum of six Justices in *Wyman-Gordon*.

The Supreme court reversed.   Justice Powell began his opinion for the court by rejecting the Board's reinterpretation of the Labor Act, holding that Congress had indeed intended that all "managerial employees" were to be excluded from its protections.   But Powell went on to hold that the agency could, in adjudicatory proceedings on remand, find that Bell's buyers were not truly "managerial employees."   His opinion contained the following reaffirmation of *Chenery:*

> The views expressed in *Chenery II* and *Wyman-Gordon* make plain that the Board is not precluded from announcing new principles in an adjudicative proceeding and that the choice between rulemaking and adjudication lies in the first instance within the Board's discretion.   Although there may be situations where the Board's reliance on adjudication would amount to an abuse of discretion or a violation of the Act, nothing in the present case would justify such a conclusion.   Indeed, there is ample indication that adjudication is especially appropriate in the instant context.   As the Court of Appeals noted, "[t]here must be tens of thousands of manufacturing, wholesale and retail units which employ buyers, and hundreds of thousands of the latter."   Moreover, duties of buyers vary widely depending on the company or industry.   It is doubtful whether any generalized standard could be framed which would have more than marginal utility.   The Board thus has reason to proceed with caution, developing its standards in a case-by-case manner with attention to the specific character of the buyers' authority and duties in each company. The Board's judgment that adjudication best serves this purpose is entitled to great weight.

> The possible reliance of industry on the Board's past decisions with respect to buyers does not require a different result.   It has not been shown that the adverse consequences ensuing from such reliance are so substantial that the Board should be precluded from reconsidering the issue in an adjudicative proceeding.   Furthermore, this is not a case in which some new liability is sought to be imposed on individuals for past actions which were taken in good-faith reliance on Board pronouncements.   Nor are fines or damages involved here.   In any event, concern about such consequences is largely speculative, for the Board has not yet finally determined whether these buyers are "managerial."

> It is true, of course, that rulemaking would provide the Board with a forum for soliciting the informed views of those affected in industry and labor

before embarking on a new course.   But surely the Board has discretion to decide that the adjudicative procedures in this case may also produce the relevant information necessary to mature and fair consideration of the issues. Those most immediately affected, the buyers and the company in the particular case, are accorded a full opportunity to be heard before the Board makes its determination.

5.   Several "fairness" values seem to be at stake in the choice between formulating general policy by rule and making policy in the course of adjudication. One is the availability of prior warning about the consequences of primary conduct.   Another is the availability of an opportunity for all affected parties to participate in developing policy.   A third is agency adherence to consistent policies, that is, assurance that like cases are resolved under the same standards or criteria.   Rulemaking may support all of these values because rules are generally (1) published and prospective, (2) made through procedures in which all interested persons may participate, and (3) available to parties in particular proceedings and to reviewing courts as a standard against which to measure the legality of particular agency action.

6.   But more that fairness is at stake in the debate over the Labor Board's preference for adjudication over rulemaking.   There is also the question of whether an agency that concentrates largely on deciding cases is in a position to develop sound policy.)   In its brief in *Wyman-Gordon*, the Board observed:

> Unlike some other administrative agencies, the Board itself cannot initiate its own processes.   * * *   Lacking independent authority to investigate or oversee the industrial scene generally, the Board frequently becomes aware of a problem   * * *   only when it is raised in the context of a particular case. Thus, the bulk of the Board's experience has been accumulated through the adjudication of issues brought to it by outside parties.

Using this statement as a point of departure, Merton Bernstein, *The NLRB's Adjudication-Rule Making Dilemma under the Administrative Procedure Act*, 79 Yale L.J. 571, 577–92 (1970), critiqued the NLRB's preference for adjudication:

> * * *   Litigation occurs where labor-management relations have been disrupted, if they ever existed.   Seeing only diseased conditions   * * *   is a dubious way of becoming acquainted with healthy labor relationships.   Nor do Board members experience extensive exposure to industrial relations outside of litigation.   * * *

> I suggest that an enormous number of Board doctrines are based upon untested suppositions.   For example, we have had more than twenty-five years of litigation about organizing activities on and off company property but little data on how employees actually react to various organizing devices.   We simply do not know what makes an employee feel fear in election situations.   We do not even know whether substantial groups of employees regard Board elections as truly secret.   If many do not, the whole Board election process is askew.

> What the Board needs is a body of information it has not been getting. Whenever the Board is able to obtain such information, however, the data and conclusions should be subject to critical commentary by the affected public and interested critics *before* the Board acts upon it.   For that task, formal rule making on notice seems indispensable.   * * *

> We have been conditioned to the view that case-by-case development guards against premature generalization, but there is at least an equal and op-

posite danger of excessive particularization.   A distorted emphasis upon the dominant factors in particular cases which have been decided tends to stunt the growth of balanced and flexible doctrine.   It is a fact of legal life that when confronted by a problem in which the law is uncertain, counsel will attempt to bring his case * * * within the confines of what little doctrine there is. This tactical approach means that instead of confronting an expanding panorama of industrial experience * * * the Board often confronts a steady stream of lawyers who seek to persuade it that what has happened is governed by the Board's smidgen of doctrine. * * *

How Board members allocate their time and talents is a major problem. * * * Rulemaking would require them to focus upon a comparatively few major policy issues rather than spread their attention thinly over hundreds of litigated cases.   * * *   The synthesizing talents of the Board members and their staffs * * * would seem best concentrated upon major policy— explicitly considered as such and from which they cannot hide in the thicket of case peculiarities.

For a corroborating assessment of the Board's development of policy governing representation elections, see J. GETMAN, S. GOLDBERG & J. HERMAN, UNION REPRESENTATION ELECTIONS: LAW & REALITY (1976).

7.   The NLRB is perhaps the most conspicuous illustration of disinclination to use rulemaking to formulate administrative policy, but it is by no means unique.   Peter Strauss, on a leave from academia, found similar behavior in the Department of the Interior, the agency responsible for implementating federal law governing mining on public lands:

The failure to use rulemaking is far less a product of conscious departmental choice than a result of impediments to the making of rules created by the Department's internal procedures.   The channels which lead to rulemaking, and to a lesser extent other forms of legislative policy statement such as production of the Manual, are so clogged with obstacles, and the flow through them so sluggish, that staff members hesitate to use them. * * * And like an adult game of "Telephone," Department personnel complain, what is suggested at the outset for possible rulemaking is often unrecognizable when and if a formal proposal ultimately emerges.   Absent commitment at the highest levels, the process is one that is easily blocked at almost any stage by determined opposition.   As a result, rulemaking may be consciously avoided by an individual with an idea for policy change when other means for achieving the same policy ends appear to be available.

* * * [C]onversations with departmental and Bureau staff invariably reflected awareness of those obstacles and, indeed, a resulting distaste for rulemaking.[59]

59. Thus, an official in one office stated: "We are not a pioneering agency * * * we want to try to stick to the good old steady tried and proven ways. * * * [We tried rule making on one occasion and] it never got anyplace * * * We at this level, this lower level here, we just don't pioneer things other than making suggestions, and we have made suggestions—we have made suggestions on changing our regulations that haven't been promulgated."

An official in another office similarly complained: "We have made proposals from time to time.   Frequently we get the argument, on specific proposals, that the problem should be approached overall; then we do that, with encouragement, and it seems there is always some reason that radical changes aren't made. We are given more freedom and there is less control in handling litigation.   The Department is so damn busy with day-to-day emergencies that it can't handle, that no one can pay attention to what we are doing in litigation."

Strauss, *Rules, Adjudications, and Other Sources of Law in an Executive Department: Reflections on the Interior Department's Administration of the Mining Law,* 74 Colum. L. Rev. 1231, 1245–47 (1974).

8.   Professor Strauss's study of the Interior Department suggests that institutional impediments to the development of policy through rulemaking are likely to be increased by requirements for additional levels of administrative review, such as those imposed by Executive Order No. 12,291.   See discussion at pp. 143–55, supra.   The significant delays imposed on agency rulemaking by the OMB review process may prove more burdensome to regulators than the substantive requirements of the executive order. See, e.g., G. EADS & M. FIX, RELIEF OR REFORM: REAGAN'S REGULATORY DILEMMA 118–25 (1984); Olson, *The Quiet Shift of Power: Office of Management & Budget Oversight of EPA Rulemaking Under E.O. 12291,* 4 Va. J. Nat'l Res. L. 1 (1984).

9.   The implications of the splintered opinions in *Wyman-Gordon* still beguile litigants and puzzle courts.   In *Cities of Anaheim, Riverside, Banning, Colton and Azusa v. FERC,* 723 F.2d 656 (9th Cir. 1984), the petitioners challenged the Commission's decision allowing implementation of an increase in utility rates after a suspension of only one day.   The agency had purported to follow an earlier decision *(West Texas)* announcing that it would routinely issue only one-day suspensions when its preliminary analysis suggested that new rates were not excessive even though the increases were subject to a hearing.   The court of appeals rejected the petitioners' argument that this policy should have been adopted by rulemaking, declaring (id. at 659):

> [A]dministrative agencies are free to announce new principles during adjudication.   Two exceptions qualify this general proposition.   First, agencies may not impose undue hardship by suddenly changing direction, to the detriment of those who have relied on past policy.   * * *   The cities have not taken any particular action in reliance on FERC's pre-*West Texas* suspension policy.   Also, *West Texas* did not abruptly change but rather strengthened and clarified a previously recognized exception to the rule of five-month suspensions.   * * *
>
> The second limiting doctrine is that agencies may not use adjudication to circumvent the Administrative Procedure Act's rulemaking procedures.   * * * This exception is inapplicable to the present case.   FERC has not used *West Texas* to amend a recently adopted rule, * * * or to supplant a pending rule-making proceeding.   * * *

See also *Independent U.S. Tanker Owners Committee v. Lewis,* 690 F.2d 908 (D.C. Cir. 1982), a shipowner's challenge to a Maritime Administration approval of competitors' application to operate in the domestic trade.   Judge Wilkey agreed that a rule on which the agency purported to rely had been improperly promulgated, and he believed Justice Harlan's reasoning in *Wyman-Gordon,* would have required a remand had the the invalid rule in fact dictated the agency's disposition of the application.   But he found the cases distinguishable: "In Wyman-Gordon the challenged order followed automatically from the invalid [*Excelsior*] rule.   * * *   The NLRB did not reconsider the factors pro and con requiring employers to furnish addresses when it issued the order."   In the present case, however, the Maritime Administration's invalid rule merely outlined the procedures it would follow in passing on applications to enter the domestic trade; it did not in any sense direct the outcome of such proceedings.   And the agency had in fact entertained all evidence and every argument that the ship-owners wished to make.   Judge Wilkey then proceeded to set aside the agency's order on the basis of errors made in evaluating the application.

2. REQUIRED RULEMAKING .

Petitioner

MORTON v. RUIZ *Respondent*

Supreme Court of the United States, 1974.
415 U.S. 199, 945. Ct. 1055, 39 L.Ed. 2d 270.

MR. JUSTICE BLACKMUN delivered the opinion of the Court.

This case presents a narrow but important issue in the administration of the federal general assistance program for needy Indians:

Are general assistance benefits available only to those Indians living *on* res-ervations in the United States (or in areas regulated by the Bureau of Indian Affairs in Alaska and Oklahoma), and are they thus unavailable to Indians (outside Alaska and Oklahoma) living *off*, although near, a reservation?

The United States District Court for the District of Arizona answered this question favorably to petitioner, the Secretary of the Interior, when, without opinion and on cross-motions for summary judgment, it dis-missed the respondent's complaint.   The Court of Appeals, one judge dissenting, reversed. * * *

* * * The respondents, Ramon Ruiz and wife, Anita, are Papago In-dians and United States citizens.   In 1940 they left the Papago Reserva- *Facts* tion in Arizona to seek employment 15 miles away at the Phelps-Dodge copper mines at Ajo.   Mr. Ruiz found work there, and they settled in a community at Ajo called the "Indian Village" and populated almost en-tirely by Papagos.   Practically all the land and most of the homes in the Village are owned or rented by Phelps-Dodge.   The Ruizes have lived in Ajo continuously since 1940 and have been in their present residence since 1947.   A minor daughter lives with them.   They speak and under-stand the Papago language but only limited English.   Apart from Mr. Ruiz' employment with Phelps-Dodge, they have not been assimilated into the dominant culture, and they appear to have maintained a close tie with the nearby reservation.

In July 1967, 27 years after the Ruizes moved to Ajo, the mine where he worked was shut down by a strike.   It remained closed until the fol-lowing March. * * *

On December 11, 1967, Mr. Ruiz applied for general assistance bene-fits from the Bureau of Indian Affairs (BIA).   He was immediately noti-fied by letter that he was ineligible for general assistance because of the provision (in effect since 1952) in 66 Indian Affairs Manual 3.1.4 (1965) that eligibility is limited to Indians living "on reservations" and in jurisdic-tions under the BIA in Alaska and Oklahoma.   An appeal to the Superin-tendent of the Papago Indian Agency was unsuccessful.   A further ap-peal to the Phoenix Area Director of the BIA led to a hearing, but this, too, proved unsuccessful.   The sole ground for the denial of general assistance benefits was that the Ruizes resided outside the boundaries of the Papago Reservation.

*   *   *

[After extensive discussion of BIA practice and congressional understanding, as ventilated in numerous appropriations hearings, the Court concluded that Congress had not knowingly restricted relief funds to Indians who resided on reservations. The legislation authorizing the payment of benefits to needy Indians did not contain any express locational criteria of eligibility.]

Having found that the congressional appropriation was intended to cover welfare services at least to those Indians residing "on or near" the reservation, it does not necessarily follow that the Secretary is without power to create reasonable classifications and eligibility requirements in order to allocate the limited funds available to him for this purpose. * * * But in such a case the agency must, at a minimum, let the standard be generally known so as to assure that it is being applied consistently and so as to avoid both the reality and the appearance of arbitrary denial of benefits to potential beneficiaries.

Assuming, *arguendo*, that the Secretary rationally could limit the "on or near" appropriation to include only the smaller class of Indians who lived directly "on" the reservation plus those in Alaska and Oklahoma, the question that remains is whether this has been validly accomplished. The power of an administrative agency to administer a congressionally created and funded program necessarily requires the formulation of policy and the making of rules to fill any gap left, implicitly or explicitly, by Congress. In the area of Indian affairs, the Executive has long been empowered to promulgate rules and policies, and the power has been given explicitly to the secretary and his delegates at the BIA. This agency power to make rules that affect substantial individual rights and obligations carries with it the responsibility not only to remain consistent with the governing legislation, but also to employ procedures that conform to the law. No matter how rational or consistent with congressional intent a particular decision might be, the determination of eligibility cannot be made on an *ad hoc* basis by the dispenser of the funds.

The Administrative Procedure Act was adopted to provide, *inter alia*, that administrative policies affecting individual rights and obligations be promulgated pursuant to certain stated procedures so as to avoid the inherently arbitrary nature of unpublished *ad hoc* determinations. * * *

*   *   *

* * * [T]he BIA has chosen not to publish its eligibility requirements for general assistance in the Federal Register or in the CFR. This continues to the present time. The only official manifestation of this alleged policy of restricting general assistance to those directly on the reservations is the material in the Manual which is, by BIA's own admission, solely an internal-operations brochure intended to cover policies that "do not relate to the public." Indeed, at oral argument the Government conceded that for this to be a "real legislative rule," itself endowed with the force of law, it should be published in the Federal Register.

Where the rights of individuals are affected, it is incumbent upon agencies to follow their own procedures. This is so even where the internal procedures are possibly more rigorous than otherwise would be required. The BIA, by its Manual, has declared that all directives that "inform the public of privileges and benefits available" and of "eligibility requirements" are among those to be published. The requirement that, in order to receive general assistance, an Indian must reside directly "on" a reservation is clearly an important substantive policy that fits within this class of directives. Before the BIA may extinguish the entitlement of these otherwise eligible beneficiaries, it must comply, at a minimum, with its own internal procedures.

The Secretary has presented no reason why the requirements of the Administrative Procedure Act could not or should not have been met. The BIA itself has not attempted to defend its rule as a valid exercise of its "legislative power," but rather depends on the argument that Congress itself has not appropriated funds for Indians not directly on the reservations. The conscious choice of the Secretary not to treat this extremely significant eligibility requirement, affecting rights of needy Indians, as a legislative-type rule, renders it ineffective so far as extinguishing rights of those otherwise within the class of beneficiaries contemplated by Congress is concerned.

The overriding duty of our Federal Government to deal fairly with Indians wherever located has been recognized by this Court on many occasions. Particularly here, where the BIA has continually represented to Congress, when seeking funds, that Indians living near reservations are within the service area, it is essential that the legitimate expectation of these needy Indians not be extinguished by what amounts to an unpublished *ad hoc* determination of the agency that was not promulgated in accordance with its own procedures, to say nothing of those of the Administrative Procedure Act. The denial of benefits to these respondents under such circumstances is inconsistent with "the distinctive obligation of trust incumbent upon the Government in its dealings with these dependent and sometimes exploited people." * * *

Even assuming the lack of binding effect of the BIA policy, the Secretary argues that the residential restriction in the Manual is a longstanding interpretation of the Snyder Act by the agency best suited to do this, and that deference is due its interpretation. * * *

* * * In order for an agency interpretation to be granted deference, it must be consistent with the congressional purpose. It is evident to us that Congress did not itself intend to limit its authorization to only those Indians directly on, in contrast to those "near," the reservation, and that, therefore, the BIA's interpretation must fail. * * *

The judgment of the Court of Appeals is affirmed and the case is remanded for further proceedings consistent with this opinion.

Notes

1. See Fuchs, *Development and Diversification in Administrative Rule Making*, 72 Nw. U.L.Rev. 83, 102 (1977):

> The Court's exclusion of case-by-case development of eligibility standards, without advance notice of the standards, arose at least in part because they affected "substantial individual rights and obligations. * * * " The principle underlying the decision on this point probably does not extend beyond similar situations involving the interests of individual human beings. It would be a mistake to conclude on the basis of the *Ruiz* holding that the use of agency adjudication to develop policy generally is newly restricted by the decision. The Court's reaffirmation in *NLRB v. Bell Aerospace Co.*, decided two months later, of the Board's authority to develop new policies by adjudication, emphasizes the point. In *Bell Aerospace*, the *Ruiz* decision was neither cited nor distinguished and seemingly was not regarded as relevant to the regulation of collective labor relations.

2. The opinion in *Sun Ray Drive-In Dairy, Inc. v. Oregon Liquor Control Comm.*, 16 Or. App. 63, 517 P.2d 289 (1973), supra p. 19, is probably the most notable state court ruling directing an agency to adopt rules setting forth its policies for disposing of individual cases or claims. However, the fundamental issue in *Sun Ray* was not whether the liquor control agency had properly chosen another process for making policy, but whether it had any discernible policy at all. Compare, e.g., *Holmes v. New York City Housing Auth.*, 398 F.2d 262 (2d Cir. 1968); *Hornsby v. Allen*, 326 F.2d 605 (5th Cir. 1964). In *Hornsby*, the district court was instructed to enjoin the denial of liquor licenses by the City of Atlanta unless and until "ascertainable standards" for such denials had been established by the Board of Aldermen. The *Holmes* court held that a complaint alleging that the Housing Authority had established no standards governing the selection of non-preference applicants for public housing in New York City stated a cause of action under the due process clause.

While the result in *Sun-Ray* has been influential in the development of state administrative law, see Bonfield, *State Law in the Teaching of Administrative Law: A Critical Analysis of the Status Quo*, 61 Tex. L. Rev. 95 (1982), the case had relatively few federal parallels until recently.

3. *Patel v. Immigration and Naturalization Service*, 638 F.2d 1199 (9th Cir. 1980), grew out of an attempt to invoke the Attorney General's discretionary authority to admit a deportable alien for permanent residence in the United States, the same authority whose affirmative exercise was, until *Chadha*, supra p. 31, subject to veto by either house of Congress. Under 8 U.S.C.A. § 1182(a)(14), the Secretary of Labor must certify that the presence of such an alien will not be detrimental to the domestic labor force. The INS has long recognized an exception to this requirement for aliens who intend to enter a business in which they have made a substantial investment. Patel sought to take advantage of this exception, but the INS turned him down, insisting that an alien's investment also "must tend to expand job opportunities" in this country. The Service relied on two previous decisions which had engrafted this job-creation condition onto the "investor exemption" as set forth in its regulations. When the agency later revised the regulation, however, it did not mention this additional condition.

The court of appeals held that the INS had committed the same error as the Labor Board in *Excelsior Underwear*, i.e., it had fashioned a "broad requirement of prospective application" in an adjudicatory proceeding. According to the court, it "was an abuse of discretion to thus circumvent the rulemaking procedures of the APA." Furthermore, the Service abused its discretion by applying the job-creation criterion in evaluating Patel's application:

> Although Patel invested money and applied for the investor exemption well after *Heitland* [one of the two previous cases] was decided, we doubt that he could have clearly determined what he must do to qualify for the exemption. The INS had been sending aliens confusing signals. In promulgating the 1973 regulation, the INS had expressly eliminated language similar to the job-creation criterion of *Heitland*. When the Board decided in *Heitland* that the criterion applied to the out-of-date, pre-1973 regulation, it only obscurely stated in dictim that it would also be applied to the 1973 regulation. It was not until 1976 that the regulation was amended to include clearly the job-creation criterion.
>
> The hardship Patel has experienced as a result of his failure to comply with the job-creation criterion is great. * * *

The court went on to hold, however, that the INS correctly found that Patel failed to show that his deportation would impose "extreme hardship," an additional necessary condition for exercise of the Attorney General's discretion, and it therefore upheld his exclusion.

4. In *Ford Motor v. FTC*, 673 F.2d 1008 (9th Cir. 1981), *cert. denied* 459 U.S. 999 (1982), the Ninth Circuit vacated an order of the Federal Trade Commission addressed to the respondent's practice in giving credit to purchasers of cars that it later repossessed. Frances Ford's practice conformed to that of car dealers nationwide and the Commission brought parallel section 5 proceedings against Ford Motor Company, Chrysler, and General Motors, their finance companies, and one other dealer. All of the respondents eventually consented to decrees against their practice, except for Frances Ford, which unsuccessfully resisted the charge in formal hearings before the agency. On appeal, Ford contended that the Commission should have proceeded by rulemaking. Citing the dictum in *Bell Aerospace* that "there may be situations where the [agency's] reliance on adjudication would amount to an abuse of discretion," the court of appeals accepted Frances Ford's contention:

> * * * [T]he precise issue therefore is whether this adjudication changes existing law, and has widespread application. It does, and the matter should be addressed by rulemaking.
>
> The F.T.C. admits that industry practice has been to do what Francis Ford does—credit the debtor with the wholesale value and charge the debtor for indirect expenses. But the F.T.C. contends that Francis Ford's particular practice violates state law (ORS 79.5040); that the violation will not be reached by the [Commission's] proposed trade rule on credit practices; and that this adjudication will have only local application. The arguments are not persuasive.
>
> By all accounts this adjudication is the first agency action against a dealer for violating ORS 79.5040 by doing what Francis Ford does. Although the U.C.C. counterpart of ORS 79.5040 is enacted in 49 states, nearly word for word, we have been cited to no case which has interpreted the provision to require a secured creditor to credit the debtor for the "best possible price" and not charge him for overhead and lost profits. It may well be that Oregon

courts will interpret U.C.C. § 9-504 in the manner advocated by the F.T.C. if the question is put to them. But it is speculation to contend, as does the F.T.C. here, that Francis Ford is in violation of *existing* Oregon law. * * *

Ultimately, however, we are persuaded to set aside this order because the rule of the case made below will have general application. It will not apply just to Francis Ford. Credit practices similar to those of Francis Ford are widespread in the car dealership industry; and the U.C.C. section the F.T.C. wishes us to interpret exists in 49 states. The F.T.C. is aware of this. It has already appended a "Synopsis of Determination" to the order, apparently for the purpose of advising other automobile dealerships of the results of this adjudication. To allow the order to stand as presently written would do far more than remedy a discrete violation of a singular Oregon law as the F.T.C. contends; it would create a national interpretation of U.C.C. § 9-504 and in effect enact the precise rule the F.T.C. has proposed, but not yet promulgated.

5. The cases on agency choice between rulemaking and adjudication, together with those on agency rulemaking to avoid adjudication, raise issues that are analogous of the vagueness versus rigidity problems encountered by legislative draftsmen, which we considered in Chapter One.

In either context, the specificity of legal rules substantially determines the ratio between discretion exercised at the stage of rule enunciation and that exercised at the stage of rule application. And the Supreme Court has come to essentially the same practical conclusion concerning the role of judicial review in both contexts—the lawmaker's choice will be respected save in exceptional circumstances.

Yet the concerns in the two contexts are hardly identical. Separation of powers generally is not an issue in the case of administrative choice of legal form. The allocation of discretion implicated by the choice will be an allocation confined to different stages of the agency's own processes. And while vague legislative delegations are sometimes thought to have rather serious implications for judicial review, a hard look at an agency's choice of substantive policy seems equally feasible when reviewing adjudicatory decisions (e.g., *Bell Aerospace*) and when reviewing rules (e.g., *State Farm*). Moreover, statutory rigidity is particularly difficult to soften at the stage of application without implying an administrative discretion similar to prosecutorial discretion that almost entirely escapes judicial review.

While these distinctions might suggest the appropriateness of greater judicial vigilance when reviewing legislative choices concerning the specificity of legal rules than when reviewing similar choices by administrators, there are countervailing considerations. Legislators lack the procedural options, contextual flexibility, and unified leadership of administrative agencies. Second-guessing legislative judgments concerning the tradeoffs between overgeneralization and underspecification thus would be particularly disruptive. Intensive review would have a greater propensity to disable than to improve legislative policy choice. Moreover, by long constitutional tradition judicial reexamination itself raises graver separation of powers problems when legislative rather than administrative action is at issue.

Bracketed by these competing considerations, judicial consideration of "appropriate specificity" problems has made little doctrinal headway in either context. The "non-delegation" and "irrebuttable presumption" doctrines are, respectively, ineffectual and dislocating restraints on legislative choices.

"Arbitrariness" perhaps captures, but hardly renders transparent or general, the basis for invalidation of analogous administrative decisions.   In a heroic and rewarding attempt to give some structure to the multiple concerns that inhabit this policy space, Colin Diver concludes:

> * * * [C]ourts are repeatedly drawn into controversies about the appropriate precision of administrative rules as they review the legality of actions predicated upon them.   What they need to discharge that function is neither philosophizing nor modelmaking, but hardheaded guidelines for adjudicating disputes between the government and the public.   When is a rule so opaque that its application denies a person "due process of law"?   When is it an "abuse of discretion" to ground actions on an accretion of ad hoc rationales rather than on a more comprehensive directive?   When does the application of a rule become so mechanistic that it denies an individualized hearing guaranteed by statute?   At what point does its application to borderline cases become arbitrary and capricious or deny equal protection of the law?

> To a large degree, answers to these questions depend on the peculiar statutory or doctrinal context in which they arise.   Regulatory incongruities that impair speech or disadvantage suspect minorities will receive far less tolerance, for instance, than those that burden economic interests.   Some statutory schemes will display greater legislative concern for individualized treatment or clarity of regulatory exposition than others.

> But even after allowing for such doctrinal or statutory peculiarities, there still remains an irreducible core of legal controversy about rule precision that yields only to an indwelling jurisprudential principle of fairness or propriety.   * * * Courts, as much as politicians, must throw competing values on the scales and somehow total the score.   * * *

> The difficulty of the task counsels broad deference to administrators' choice of rule formulations.   Not only are administrators better equipped for "social-cost accounting," but * * * the political "marketplace" can often be relied upon to restrain administrative excesses.   Courts, however, cannot wholly escape their editorial responsibility, precisely because the formal dimensions of a rule are so intertwined with its substantive and procedural legality.   * * * Courts should, first of all, reserve their closest scrutiny for rules least likely to be subject to effective political discipline.   As organization-cost disparities progressively skew the "reinternalization" of "external" effects, the need for judicial oversight grows.   Our earlier discussion suggests that courts should be most sensitive to the plaint of the unorganized beneficiary of regulatory protection and the adversarially disadvantaged public assistance recipient.

> When courts are drawn into disputes about regulatory precision, they should be sensitive to the inevitable tradeoffs among transparency, accessibility, and congruence.   They should look for evidence of the factors that drive rules toward one extreme or the other—for example, the high social costs of misspecification error associated with rules of reason, the large rule application costs and quality control problems associated with per se rules.   Prohibitory rules should presumptively be more transparent that licensure rules, liability rules more transparent than remedial rules, external rules more transparent than internal rules.   Incongruent outcomes should be more tolerable when they appear to cluster near the boundary than at the extremes. In many ways, of course, homilies like this misrepresent the complexity of the

subject.   But they serve to remind us that "social-cost accounting," for all its intimidating connotations, is really the sophisticated and sensitive application of common sense. * * *

Diver, *The Optimal Precision of Administrative Rules*, 93 Yale L.J. 65, 106–09 (1983).

Implementing Policy Without Making Rules

The foregoing materials examine case-by-case adjudication as an alternative to the development of policy through rules.   Yet federal agencies possess, and regularly exercise, other powers that can also be viewed as alternatives to rulemaking—and often have similar effects.

Indeed, *Morton v. Ruiz* is an illustration.   The case did not, after all, challenge the use of case-by-case decisionmaking to develop agency policy. To be sure, the BIA policy of not providing benefits to Indians living off reservations is presented for judicial review in the context of a specific case, but the policy itself had been formulated long before and was reflected in a document, the agency's manual, that has many of the effects of a rule. It guides, indeed dictates, the exercise of judgment on individual claims by BIA officials throughout the country.   While not published in the Federal Register, the policy was hardly a secret.   And it probably contributed to even-handedness in the administration of the BIA benefits: all off-reservation Indians were treated similarly.   Thus, it is reasonable to assume that the BIA had for many years followed a uniform policy it had formulated by neither rulemaking nor adjudication.

An agency's ability to formulate clear policy without involving formal procedures is a function, in part, of its organizational coherence.   Agencies with a stable workforce, well-recognized responsibilities, and broadly accepted program objectives are likely to be more successful in obtaining internal agreement on, and adherence to, policies than agencies whose pathways are less well worn.   The more volatile the issues requiring resolution, the less likely any large organization will be able to develop a coherent policy that will command the consistent support of all of the officials involved in its implementation.

An agency's success in implementing its policies, once agreed upon, is subject to other variables.   In programs that function through the granting of approval or largesse, government administrators typically exercise greater leverage than do those in programs that depend on agency initiative.   Thus one would not be surprised to learn that the FDA's criteria for testing of food additives, most of which are not codified in regulations, elicit substantial adherence by petitioners who need the agency's agreement before they can market a new product.   Administrators of government benefit programs possess similar leverage.

Successful implementation of policy, however, is not solely a function of agency leverage over those whose compliance is sought.   The FDA is responsible for regulating the safety of all food products, most of which do not require premarket approval.   Its authority over food sanitation, for example, must be exercised in the same fashion that the police officer "regulates" traffic offenders, i.e., by observation and prosecution. When it seizes a food as "adulterated," the FDA theoretically appears in court in the same posture as a public prosecutor, whose views about the defendant's guilt are not oficially entitled to any deference. The FDA's judgment that the bacteria level in food renders it "unfit," however, does command deference from courts precisely because the agency is considered Congress's expert on the subject. And the agency has published many of its enforcement criteria, or "action levels," which have come to enjoy a status comparable to that of rules even though they are not established through public rulemaking. Food distributors understand this and rarely resist the FDA's efforts to enforce its policies and generally lose when they do. The agency's success in court is translated into considerable extra-statutory influence during the investigation process, where an inspector's statement that a food *appears* adulterated may be sufficient to precipitate its withdrawal from commerce.

The field inspection context illustrates the power of many agencies to elicit compliance with administrative policies that are nowhere embodied in rules but possess many of their characteristics, e.g., generality, prospectivity, and specificity. But it is also a setting that permits the exercise of unguided and perhaps arbitrary individual authority. The threat implicit in an FDA or OSHA inspector's report of observed deficiencies may be enough to elicit compliance with *ad hoc* demands that may or may not enjoy the endorsement of agency management. Professor Davis has been a penetrating critic of this phenomenon and vigorous advocate of the importance of rulemaking as a device for controlling decentralized enforcement discretion. See e.g., K. DAVIS, DISCRETIONARY JUSTICE (1969).

It is obviously impossible for any agency, in published rules or any other format, to formulate policies with respect to all of the issues it is likely to confront. Even when a problem is anticipated, e.g., the need for railings at hazardous locations, the appropriate response may require the exercise of judgment on the premises. For the view that many administrative rules stifle precisely this necessary form of discretion, see E. BARDACH & R. KAGAN, GOING BY THE BOOK (1982). Formal adjudication is one mode for resolving disputes over what response is appropriate, but more often individual disputes are resolved—and "policy" made—without any kind of hearing or published decision.

Many disagreements between regulatory agencies and those they regulate are settled through informal negotiation. The results may be evident from the behavior of the parties but the principles on which they rest may only be inferred. More than 99 percent of all FDA seizure actions result in default or consent judgments. See Hutt, *Philosophy of Regulation under the Federal Food, Drug and Cosmetic Act*, 28 Food Drug Cosm. L.J. 177, 186 (1973). A majority of complaints issued by the FTC charging violations of section 5 of the Federal Trade Commission Act are voluntarily dismissed or result in consent settlements. G. ROBINSON, E. GELLHORN, & H. BRUFF, THE ADMINISTRATIVE PROCESS 544 (2d ed. 1980). Recalls of substandard consumer products are generally the result of intensive negotiation between regulatory and private entre-preneurs. See, e.g., Madden, *Consumer Products Safety Act Section 15 and Substantial Product Hazards*, 30 Cath. U.L. Rev. 195 (1981); T. Schwartz and R. Adler, Product Recalls: A Remedy in Need of Repair (1983) (Report for the Administrative Conference of the United States).

Negotiation can also serve as an alternative to rulemaking for the de-velopment of general policy. Almost any statutory grant of authority to adopt rules implicitly accords the agency power to achieve comparable compliance through voluntary agreement. Whether negotiation will supplant public rulemaking depends on several circumstances, including the procedures prescribed for making rules, the scope of the agency's re-sponsibilities, and the desire of private parties to minimize public atten-tion.

A contemporary example involves EPA's implementation of section 4 of the Toxic Substances Control Act (TSCA), 15 U.S.C. § 2603. Under this provision, EPA is directed to promulgate rules requiring the toxico-logical testing of chemicals nominated by an interagency committee of scientists. The Act prescribes hybrid rulemaking as the procedure for adopting test rules. In the first seven years following TSCA's passage in 1976, EPA did not adopt a single test rule under section 4—but it has been able to secure private testing of several chemicals. The method the agency has preferred is negotiation with producers of the chemicals whose testing it desires. The negotiated testing agreements afford EPA the considerable advantage of speed; rulemaking to order testing of any of the more than fifty chemicals already nominated would require at least one year. The manufacturers believe that negotiation has resulted in less onerous testing requirements than rules might impose because EPA is less concerned about "precedent" and, frankly, less vulnerable to claims from environmental groups that its proposed requirements are not tough enough. Environmental groups, for their part, have claimed that the EPA is flaunting Congress's intention in passing TSCA, and very re-cently persuaded one court to agree. See *Natural Resources Defense Council v. Ruckelshaus*, ___ F.Supp. ___, No. 83-8844, (S.D.N.Y. 1984). See also General Accounting Office, EPA Implementation of Se-lected Aspects of the Toxic Substances Control Act (December 7, 1982).

Agencies' Obligations to Comply With Their Own Rules

Many cases purport to hold that an agency is obligated to follow its own procedural rules even though it might not have been obligated to adopt those rules in the first place. For example, *Morton v. Ruiz*, supra p. 399, turned in part on the BIA's failure to comply with its manual's mandate that it publish all of its eligibility criteria. Justice Blackmun stressed that, "where the rights of individuals are affected, it is incum-bent upon agencies to follow their own procedures." 415 U.S. at 235.

The line of authority supporting the proposition that an agency must comply with its own rules stems from three cases decided during the 1950's. The petitioner in the first of these cases, *United States ex rel. Accardi v. Shaughnessy*, 347 U.S. 260 (1954), sought habeas corpus after denial of his application for suspension of deportation.   He alleged that the deliberations of the Board of Immigration Appeals, which had affirmed a finding of deportability, was not the product of deliberations on the merits but a response to the Attorney General's public announcement that he planned to deport certain "unsavory characters" and his subsequent circulation throughout the INS of a confidential list that included Accardi's name. The Court found that the Attorney General's actions, if proved, deprived the petitioner of the Board's independent consideration contemplated by Justice Department regulations.   While it conceded that the Board was appointed by the Attorney General and served at his pleasure, the Court held that, having accorded the Board "discretionary authority as broad as the statute confers," the Attorney General could not thereafter dictate its decision.

Service v. Dulles, 354 U.S. 363 (1957), was a challenge to the Secretary of State's termination of a Foreign Service Officer whose loyalty had been reviewed through departmental procedures.   The Secretary purported to rely solely on the Loyalty Review Board's finding that there was reasonable doubt as to Service's loyalty; he expressly disclaimed having read any of the birefs in the case or having reached an independent determination on the evidence.   This omission, according to the Court, violated the State Department regulations governing removal of Foreign Service Offices, which prescribed that "the decision shall be reached after consideration of the complete file, arguments, briefs, and testimony presented." "While it is of course true that under the [statute] the Secretary was not obligated to impose upon himself these more rigorous substantive and procedural standards, neither was he prohibited from doing so * * * and having done so he could not, so long as the Regulations remained unchanged, proceed without regard to them."   354 U.S. at 388.   The Court read *Accardi* as announcing the principle "that regulations validly prescribed by a government administrator are binding upon him as well as the citizen * * * even when the administrative action is discretionary in nature."   Id. at 372.

Vitarelli v. Seaton, 359 U.S. 535 (1959), also involved the dismissal of a federal employee on loyalty grounds.   Vitarelli was removed from the Department of the Interior following a hearing at which the Department adduced no evidence and presented no witnesses; the hearing board relied exclusively on reported prior activities and friendships, whose significance Vitarelli sought vigorously to contest.   When Vitarelli sued, the Department expunged his record, eliminated all reference to doubts about his loyalty, and relied simply on the ground that, as a Schedule A employee, he could be dismissed at any time for any procedural safeguards prescribed by its own regulations for such cases: (1) it failed to afford Vitarelli specific notice of the charges against him; (2) it failed to limit questioning of witnesses to the relevant issues; and (3) it failed to afford him an opportunity to confront and cross-examine witnesses whose confidentiality was not protected.   "Having chosen to proceed against petitioner on security grounds, the Secretary here, as in *Service*, was bound by the regluations which he himself had promulgated for dealing with such cases, even though without such regulations he could have discharged petitioner summarily. * * * [I]n matters of this kind * * * scrupulous observance of departmental procedural safeguards is clearly of particular importance." 359 U.S. at 539–40.

It is hard to doubt that the charged political context of these cases—particularly *Service* and *Vitarelli*—influenced their outcome. In an era when the "right-privilege" dichotomy still claimed support, the Court's insistence on scrupulous adherence to self-imposed procedural safeguards provided a useful middle ground between outright rejection of the accompanying constitutional claims and judicial restructuring of agency procedures. It should also be observed that the Court's rulings in *Accardi*, *Service*, and *Vitarelli* did not prevent the agencies from resuming their proceedings—in compliance with applicable regulations—to pursue the results they had originally sought. Compare *Nader v. Bork*, 366 F. Supp. 104 (D.D.C. 1973) (holding that the Acting Attorney General had violated Departmental regulations in firing Watergate Special Prosecutor Archibald Cox).

Accardi, *Service*, and *Vitarelli* do not purport to be grounded in the Due Process Clause. What, then, is the legal basis for the Court's insistence that agencies follow their own regulations? One possibility, of course, is that the Due Process Clause *is* operative, and obligates an agency to follow whatever procedures it prescribes for itself. See, e.g., *Courts v. Economic Opportunity Authority*, 451 F. Supp. 587 (D. Ga. 1978). Such an interpretation could also be thought to promote the equality of treatment of like-situated individuals (and, presumably, firms) that is a recognized counterpart of the Equal Protection Clause of the Fourteenth Amendment. See, e.g., *Bolling v. Sharpe*, 347 U.S. 497 (1954). See also Note, *Violations by Agencies of Their Own Regulations*, 87 Harv. L. Rev. 629 (1974). However, there is hardly a hint of such reasoning in any of these holdings. And in *Board of Curators of the University of Missouri v. Howowitz*, 435 U.S. 78 (1978), the Court—albeit in a footnote—dismissed the proposition that the *Accardi-Service-Vitarelli* doctrine is grounded in the Constitution, claiming instead that they "enunciate principles of federal administrative law rather of constitutional law binding on the states." 435 U.S. at 92 n.8.

Perhaps the source of the doctrine is APA § 706 which directs a reviewing court to set aside "arbitrary" or "capricious" agency action. It would not be far-fetched to argue that an agency's unexplained failure to comply with its own regulations amounts to "arbitrary" action. But the APA was relied on by petitioners in only two of the three cases and is not mentioned in any of the opinions.

The Supreme Court has not been unwaivering in its insistence that agencies must comply with their own regulations. In *American Farm Lines v. Black Ball Freight Service*, 397 U.S. 532 (1970), the Court sustained the ICC award of temporary operating authority to American Farm Lines (AFL). Pursuant to statute, AFL had sought such authority in order to serve the Department of Defense. AFL's application included a statement from the DOD outlining the need for the service but it failed to describe efforts to obtain it from other carriers—as ICC regulations appeared to require.   Writing for the Court, Justice Douglas found that the Commission was entitled to treat the application as adequate, explaining (id. at 538–39):

> The failure of the Caputo statement to provide these particular specifics did not prejudice the carriers in making precise and informed objections to AFL's application.   The briefest perusal of the objecting carriers' replies, which cover some 156 pages in the printed record of these appeals, belies any such contention.   Neither was the statement so devoid of information that it, along with the replies of the protesting carriers, could not support a finding that AFL's service was required to meet DOD's immediate and urgent transportation needs.   In our view, the District Court exacted a standard of compliance with procedural rules that was wholly unnecessary to provide an adequate record to review the Commission's decision.
>
> The Commission is entitled to a measure of discretion in administering its own procedural rules in such a manner as it deems necessary to resolve quickly and correctly urgent transportation problems. * * *
>
> We agree with the Commission that the rules were promulgated for the purpose of providing the "necessary information" for the Commission "to reach an informed and equitable decision" on temporary authority applications. * * * The rules were not intended primarily to confer important procedural benefits upon individuals in the face of otherwise unfettered discretion as in *Vitarelli v. Seaton*, 359 U.S. 535; nor is this a case in which an agency required by rule to exercise independent discretion has failed to do so. *Accardi v. Shaughnessy*, 347 U.S. 260; *Yellin v. United States*, 374 U.S. 109.   Thus there is no reason to exempt this case from the general principle that "[i]t is always within the discretion of a court or an administrative agency to relax or modify its procedural rules adopted for the orderly transaction of business before it when in a given case the ends of justice require it.   The action of either in such a case is not reviewable except upon a showing of substantial prejudice to the complaining party."

In *United States v. Caceres*, 440 U.S. 741 (1979), the Court refused to overturn the conviction for attempted bribery of a taxpayer against whom evidence was obtained by electronic surveillance carried out without the Department of Justice approval required by IRS regulations. Writing for the majority, Justice Stevens observed (id. at 749):

> A court's duty to enforce an agency regulation is most evident when compliance with the regulation is mandated by the Constitution or federal law. * * *
>
> Our decisions * * * demonstrate that the IRS was not required by the Constitution to adopt these regulations.   It is equally clear that the violations of agency regulations disclosed by this record do not raise any constitutional questions.
>
> It is true, of course, that respondent's conversations were monitored without the approval of the Department of Justice, whereas the conversations of others in a similar position would, assuming the IRS generally follows its regulations, be recorded only with Justice Department approval.   But this difference does not even arguably amount to a denial of equal protection.   No claim is, or reasonably could be, made that if the IRS had more

promptly addressed this request to the Department of Justice, it would have been denied. * * *

Moreover, the failure to secure Justice Department authorization, while conceded here to be a violation of the IRS regulations, was attributable to the fact that the IRS officials responsible for administration of the relevant regulations, both in San Francisco and Washington, construed the situation as an emergency within the meaning of those regulations. Their construction of their own regulations, even if erroneous, was not obviously so. That kind of error by an executive agency in interpreting its own regulations surely does not raise any constitutional questions.

Nor is this a case in which the Due Process Clause is implicated because an individual has reasonably relied on agency regulations promulgated for his guidance or benefit and has suffered substantially because of their violation by the agency. * * *

Finally, the Administrative Procedure Act provides no grounds for judicial enforcement of the regulation violated in this case. * * * Agency violations of their own regulations, whether or not also in violation of the Constitution, may well be inconsistent with the standards of agency action which the APA directs the courts to enforce. * * *

But this is not an APA case, and the remedy sought is not invalidation of the agency actions. Rather, we are dealing with a criminal prosecution in which respondent; seeks judicial enforcement of the agency regulations by means of the exclusionary rule. That rule has primarily rested on the judgment that the importance of deterring police conduct that may invade the constitutional rights of individuals throughout the community outweighs the importance of securing the conviction of the specific defendant on trial. In view of our conclusion that none of respondent's constitutional rights has been violated here, either by the actual recording or by the agency violation of its own regulations, our procedents enforcing the exclusionary rule to deter constitutional violations provide no support for the rule's application in this case.

The decision triggered a dissent by Justices Marshall and Brennan, who viewed the *Accardi-Service-Vitarelli* line of cases as "resting on due process foundations." In their view, therefore, the courts were obligated to exclude evidence obtained in violation of agency regulations.

A few cases have held agencies obligated to follow long-established administrative practice not codified in regulations. In *Gardner v. FCC*, 530 F.2d 1086 (D.C. Cir. 1976), the Commission sought dismissal of a late-filed petition to review its decision. The petitioner claimed, without dispute, that the agency had long made it a practice of sending copies of decisions to parties in the proceedings and that its failure to do so in this case had caused it to assume that no decision had been issued—until the time for challenge had passed. The court found the agency's unexplained deviation from its routine practice a sufficient basis for rejecting the motion to dismiss.

An analogy to the issues dealt with in the foregoing cases can be found in judicial discussions of the role of *stare decisis* in administrative decisionmaking. Most courts acknowledge that the doctrine has less force in the administrative than in the judicial context, e.g., *International Business Machines v. United States*, 170 Ct. Cl. 357, 343 F.2d 914 (1965), cert. denied 382 U.S. 1028 (1966), but many decisions make clear that an agency's departure from prior law must be explained, expressly invoking APA § 706. K. DAVIS, ADMINISTRATIVE LAW TEXT § 17.07, at 352 (1972). Illustrative is *FTC v. Crowther*, 430 F.2d 510 (D.C. Cir. 1970), in which Judge McGowan refused to enforce a FTC subpoena of records from the respondent's competitors. They had objected to providing sales and marketing data directly to the respondent's counsel, arguing instead that the data should be massaged by an independent intermediary to protect confidentiality—a safeguard that the Commission itself had forcefully imposed in a similar proceeding only a few months before. Judge McGowan held that the agency's failure to explain its departure from that recent precedent made its present posture untenable. See also *Secretary of Agriculture v. United States*, 347 U.S. 645 (1954); *Public Interest Research Group v. FCC*, 522 F.2d 1060 (1st Cir. 1975), cert. denied 424 U.S. 965 (1976); cf. *Motor Vehicle Manufacturers Association v. State Farm Mutual Insurance Co.*, p. 343 supra.

C. PROCEDURES FOR AGENCY RULEMAKING

1. INTRODUCTION

In *Ethyl Corp. v. EPA*, p. 375 supra, Judge Bazelon expressed skepticism about the ability of judges to evaluate the rationality of agency rules, particularly those addressed to highly technical subjects; he argued instead that "the best way for courts to guard against unreasonable or erroneous administrative decisions is * * * to establish a decision-making process that assures a reasoned decision that can be held up to the scrutiny of the scientific community and the public." 541 F.2d at 66. Judicial oversight of agency rulemaking procedures is thus offered as an alternative—or perhaps a surrogate—for substantive review of agency judgments.

Our previous examination of the role of courts in reviewing administrative rules reveals the close relationship between scrutiny of the rationality of agency judgments and review of the adequacy of their procedures. The claim that a rule is "arbitrary or capricious" can be construed as an attack on the adequacy of the record compiled by the agency or of its explanation for the choices made. In some sense, both claims can be viewed as procedural in character, for either normally implies that the agency's rule cannot be sustained on the basis of the record it has offered—not necessarily that a similar rule cannot be supported by *any* record that might be produced. And the usual judicial response to a deficient rule is to declare that it is unsupported by the record, not to hold that such rule can never be adopted. Thus, Justice Stevens' opinion in the benzene case leaves open the possibility that OSHA may be able to demonstrate, with new evidence or perhaps even with the evidence in hand, that the risk at prevailing levels of exposure is "significant," and that a l ppm standard is "feasible."

The requirement of APA § 553(c) that an agency provide "a concise statement of basis and purpose" similarly possesses procedural as well as substantive connotations.   Viewed as an essential step in the rulemaking process, the "basis and purpose" statement can be analogized to procedural obligations imposed on other tribunals authorized to decide questions of fact and law.   As we have seen, this formal step has sometimes been omitted, but the courts have not been willing to relieve agencies of the obligation to explain, somewhere, the factual and policy bases for their rules.   What might appear to be a procedural requirement, therefore, has been transformed into a substantive demand.

Judge Bazelon's opinion in *Ethyl* advocates the opposite approach, i.e., judicial enforcement, and perhaps creation, of procedural safeguards as an alternative means of assuring the legitimacy of agency decisions. His argument raises an obvious question: What are the appropriate sources of procedures for agencies to follow in rulemaking?   One possible answer is the Constitution, but case law suggests that this rich source of procedural safeguards in the criminal justice system and in administrative adjudication speaks with only a whisper in the rulemaking context. One can burrow through judicial opinions construing the requirements of "due process" and encounter relatively few cases dealing with administrative rulemaking.   Some of these precedents even suggest that when an agency is formulating prospective rules of general applicability— regardless of the potential impact of those rules—the Constitution may impose no procedural requirements whatever.   E.g., *Curlott v. Campbell*, 598 F.2d 1175 (9th Cir. 1979); *Love v. United States Department of HUD*, 704 F. 2d 100 (3d Cir. 1983); *Nolan v. Ramsey*, 597 F.2d 577 (5th Cir. 1979); cf. *Minnesota State Board for Community Colleges v. Knight*, ___ U.S. ___, 104 S.Ct. 1058 (1984).   Only a few cases have held that due process sometimes demands at least notice of and an opportunity to comment on proposed agency rules.   E.g., *Burr v. New Rochelle Municipal Housing Authority*, 479 F.2d 1165 (2d Cir. 1973); *Williams v. Barry*, 708 F.2d 789 (D.C. Cir. 1983).   And the dominant view is that the procedural requirements of section 553 of the APA meet whatever minimum standards for rulemaking procedure the Constitution imposes.   See *Vermont Yankee Nuclear Power Corp. v. Natural Resources Defense Council*, 435 U.S. 519 (1978), infra p. 461.   See also Sinaiko, *Due Process Rights of Participation in Administrative Rulemaking*, 63 Calif. L. Rev. 886 (1975).

The troubling implications of this constitutional jurisprudence are perhaps muted by the realization that there *are* other important sources of procedures that agencies must follow in making rules.   They include, most prominently, the APA and, of increasing importance, the organic statutes that establish agency programs and convey the authority to promulgate rules.   Since the mid 1960's Congress has rarely enacted new regulatory legislation without explicitly incorporating procedural requirements for rulemaking.   Even now, however, many federal statutes that authorize the adoption of rules are silent on the subject of rulemaking procedures or, like the Motor Vehicle Safety Act, broadly incorporate requirements of the APA.

2. THE APA'S DICHOTOMOUS RULEMAKING MODELS

The APA visualizes two basic, and ostensibly quite different, procedural models for the making of rules—as for many years did most judicial decisions and commentators. The more extensive procedure, so-called "formal rulemaking," embodies many features of the judicial trial. In its most elaborate version, formal rulemaking includes what is essentially a pleading stage, in which the agency announces a proposed rule and entertains written responses from all interested parties; a trial stage, in which the agency seeks to assemble through live and documentary evidence, subject to cross-examination and rebuttal, facts supporting its rule; and a decision stage, in which the agency announces its final rule, which must be based exclusively upon the facts marshalled in the hearing record. With some differences, this is the same process that the APA prescribes, where it applies, for the adjudication of individual disputes.

The APA's second model, known as "informal rulemaking," is described in section 553, whose entire text reads as follows:

§ 553. Rule Making

(a) This section applies, according to the provisions thereof, except to the extent that there is involved—

(1) a military or foreign affairs function of the United States; or

(2) a matter relating to agency management or personnel or to public property, loans, grants, benefits or contracts.

(b) General notice of proposed rule making shall be published in the Federal Register, unless persons subject thereto are named and either personally served or otherwise have actual notice thereof in accordance with law. The notice shall include—

(1) a statement of the time, place, and nature of public rule making proceedings;

(2) reference to the legal authority under which the rule is proposed; and

(3) either the terms or substance of the proposed rule or a description of the subjects and issues involved.

Except when notice or hearing is required by statute, this subsection does not apply—

(A) to interpretative rules, general statements of policy, or rules of agency organization, procedure, or practice; or

(B) when the agency for good cause finds (and incorporates the finding and a brief statement of reasons therefor in the rules issued) that notice and public procedure thereon are impracticable, unnecessary, or contrary to the public interest.

(c) After notice required by this section, the agency shall give interested persons an opportunity to participate in the rule making through submission of written data, views, or arguments with or without opportunity for oral presentation. After consideration of the relevant matter presented, the agency shall incorporate in the rules adopted a concise general statement of their basis and purpose. When rules are required by statute to be made on the record after opportunity for an agency hearing, sections 556 and 557 of this title apply instead of this subsection.

(d) The required publication or service of a substantive rule shall be made not less than 30 days before its effective date, except—

(1) a substantive rule which grants or recognizes an exemption or relieves a restriction;

(2) interpretative rules and statements of policy; or

(3) as otherwise provided by the agency for good cause found and published with the rule.

(e) Each agency shall give an interested person the right to petition for the issuance, amendment, or repeal of a rule.

Even a cursory reading of this language reveals that Congress' procedural directions—except when "rules are required by statute to be made on the record after opportunity for an agency hearing"—are sparse. Section 553(b) and (c) appear to require merely that an agency publish in the Federal Register its proposed rule, allow time for the submission at least of written comments, and, "after consideration of the relevant" comments, publish its final rule accompanied by "a concise general statement of * * * basis and purpose." The sharp differences between such a procedure and the quasi-judicial trappings of formal rulemaking under sections 556 and 557 have been a perennial provocation for litigation over agency rulemaking procedures and for debate in the context of new legislation.

Before turning to the case law and to attempts to reform rulemaking by statute, we might reflect briefly on the state of agency rulemaking prior to the adoption of the APA in 1946. Without some appreciation of agency practice in the pre-APA era, it is difficult to fathom how Congress could fashion such dramatically different models for rulemaking without, apparently, making any contemporaneous effort to specify which model should be followed in particular cases.

Any attempt to describe the "general" practice of federal agencies prior to the APA immediately invites qualification, for it was precisely the lack of uniformity among federal agencies that occasioned the appointment of the Attorney General's Committee on Administrative Procedure and, later, prompted adoption of the APA. The final report of the Committee did, however, discern some interesting historical trends. While statutory delegations of rulemaking authority to administrators can be found in the early days of the Republic, with very few exceptions Congress said nothing about the procedures its delegates were to follow in promulgating rules. Initially, private parties probably were given no opportunity to participate in rulemaking, though presumably they were free to express their views in correspondence with an agency if they knew it was considering a rule. By 1900, some agencies had begun consulting regularly with affected parties about contemplated rules, a practice that had become common by 1940, and had led to the establishment of standing "advisory committees" in many agencies.

The Interstate Commerce Commission, to which Congress had delegated substantial rulemaking authority, was among the first agencies required by statute to hold legislative-type hearings before promulgating rules. This practice spread as Congress wrote similar requirements into other laws, and several agencies provided informal oral hearings even though they were not required to do so.   By 1941 oral "hearings [were] generally held in connection with the fixing of prices and wages, the prescription of rules for the construction of vessels and other instruments of transportation, the regulation of ingredients and physical properties of food, the prescription of commodity standards, and the regulation of competitive practices."   Final Report of the Attorney General's Committee on Administrative Procedure, S. Doc. No. 8, 77th Cong., 1st Sess. 107 (1941).   The usual form of these hearings was legislative in character; formal hearings in rulemaking were relatively uncommon.   However, a few agencies, such as the FDA and the Labor Department's Wage and Hour Division, operated under statutes that required adversary hearings which emulated many features of the judicial trial.   Other agencies occasionally followed such procedures by choice.   The Attorney General's Committee does not mention "notice-and-comment" rulemaking in its historical review, perhaps revealing that this now-common practice had not yet become an important procedural device.

In assessing the procedural developments of the past two decades, one should be sensitive to other changes in the character and scope of federal administrative government.   One is that rulemaking of the kind we encountered in Part A—administrative attempts to prescribe future conduct for an entire industry (e.g., *Petroleum Refiners*) or a group of industries (e.g., benzene)—was uncommon before World War II.   Most federal agencies studied by the Attorney General's Committee dealt with one industry, e.g., airlines, broadcasting, or a single activity, e.g., agricultural marketing.   With the exception of the FTC, which had not then "discovered" its rulemaking power, and the NLRB, which was uninterested in using its, few agencies had been granted jurisdiction as vast as that later accorded the EPA or OSHA.   In exercising their responsibilities, these agencies relied heavily on case-by-case enforcement or implemented policy through the issuance of licenses or establishment of rates.   Neither the FTC nor (as we have seen) the NLRB resorted to rulemaking to formulate general policy or to limit the scope of individual enforcement proceedings.   And in the licensing and ratemaking that were the modus operandi of such agencies as the FCC, ICC, and CAB, the ability simply to withhold approval apparently provided all the leverage administrators believed they needed.

In the pre-APA era, judicial review of agency rules was by no means routine.   And when courts evaluated agency policies—whether or not crystallized in rules—it was usually in the context of a challenge to a license denial or rate order or a defense to a finding of statutory violation, all of which followed formal agency adjudications.   It was rare for courts to confront a challenge to an agency rule based solely on the record compiled in the rulemaking proceeding, except for those few rules that were the product of formal hearings and for which Congress specifically authorized preenforcement review in the courts of appeals.

The passage of the APA did not immediately, or indeed fundamentally, alter this landscape; rather, it established a procedural framework that became consequential with the occurrence of other changes in federal administration.   The most obvious of these changes was the enormous expansion of administrative jurisdiction with the enactment of new federal programs to regulate the economy, protect health and safety, and provide social services.   More enterprises and more individuals have fallen under federal regulation or been affected by federal agency decisions. Policymaking by rule has simultaneously become popular among federal administrators.   In some programs, e.g., OSHA's program for protecting workers' health, rulemaking is indispensable to accomplishemnt of the agency's mission.   While it was obvious prior to *Storer Broadcasting* that an agency rule could have the effect of limiting factual inquiry in specific cases, *Petroleum Refiners* and *Hynson* not only exposed the potential efficiencies of policymaking by rule but confirmed that administrators were justified in seeking to exploit them.   Finally, one perceived changes in the typical context in which agency policies were exposed to judicial review.   Instead of review of the application of agency rules in specific cases, i.e., in adjudications before the agency itself or following trial in a district court, both statutes and case law sanctioned judicial review of agency regulations upon their promulgation—review that, unless courts were to retry the issues decided by the agency, presumably had to focus on the administrative record.

These shifts in administrative practice during the 1950's and 1960's were individually important and collectively transforming.   For many if not most agencies, rulemaking proceedings became the primary context for formulating official policy, i.e., for filling in the interstices of broad statutory standards.   Furthermore, it became obvious that issues resolved in making rules would not be open for reexamination when the rules were applied or enforced.   These changes caused administrators, reviewing courts, private citizens, and finally Congress to focus on the procedures agencies were required to use in developing and promulgating rules.

3.   RULEMAKING ON A RECORD

WIRTZ v. BALDOR ELECTRIC CO.

United States Court of Appeals, District of Columbia Circuit, 1964.
337 F.2d 518.

WASHINGTON, CIRCUIT JUDGE.

The Secretary of Labor appeals from a District Court order setting aside his determination, under the Walsh-Healey Public Contracts Act, of the prevailing minimum wage in the electrical motors and generators industry.[1]   The chief questions presented are whether the Secretary of La-

---

1. The purpose of the Walsh-Healey Act was of course to make certain that the United States, in contracting for materials for its own use, did not patronize firms which paid wages lower than those being generally paid in the industry.   Under Section 1(b) of the Act every contract made by a Government agency must contain a stipulation that the manufacturer will pay to his employees engaged in the manufacture or furnishing of the contract goods minimum wages which are not less than—

"the minimum wages as determined by the Secretary of Labor to be the prevailing minimum wages for persons employed on similar work or in the particular or similar industries or groups of industries currently operating in the locality in which the materials, supplies, articles, or equipment are to be manufactured or furnished under said contract * * * ."

bor properly based his determination of the prevailing minimum wages in the industry on a broad survey conducted under his auspices, where at the same time (a) he declined to disclose at the hearing the underlying data on which the wage conclusions in the survey were based, and (b) uncontradicted evidence was submitted by the industry which cast serious doubt on the accuracy and reliability of the survey's results.)

* * *

Section 10 of the Walsh-Healey Act * * * provides in pertinent part: * * *

"(b) All wage determinations under section 1(b) of this Act shall be made on the record after opportunity for a hearing. * * *

The relevant portion of Section 7(c) of the Administrative Procedure Act states:

> "Except as statutes otherwise provide, the proponent of a rule or order shall have the burden of proof. * * * no sanction shall be imposed or rule or order be issued except upon consideration of the whole record or such portions thereof as may be cited by any party and as supported by and in accordance with the reliable, probative, and substantial evidence. Every party shall have the right to present his case or defense by oral or documentary evidence, to submit rebuttal evidence, and to conduct such cross-examination as may be required for a full and true disclosure of the facts."

* * *

The suit presently under review was brought on the theory that under Section 10(e)(B) of the Administrative Procedure Act the District Court should set aside the Secretary's minimum wage determination for the industry because the administrative hearing did not provide the procedural safeguards conferred by Section 7(c) of the Act and the determination was not supported by reliable and substantial evidence. * * *

* * * [T]he Department of Labor instituted an administrative proceeding for the purpose of determining minimum wages which prevail in two branches of the electric motors and generators industry. * * * In connection with this proceeding, the Bureau of Labor Statistics ("BLS") of the Department of Labor undertook a survey by means of a questionnaire, designed to ascertain the number of establishments in the industry, the number of covered workers in each establishment, and the wages paid by each establishment.

The BLS questionnaire, which contained a pledge of confidentiality, was circulated to 775 establishments. The names of these establishments were primarily obtained from unemployment compensation insurance listings furnished in confidence by the several States to the Department of Labor. Establishments within the scope of the survey were asked to report data respecting total employment, total covered workers, and hourly earnings of covered workers for the payroll period ending nearest October 15, 1960.

After the answers had been received, BLS compiled six tables summarizing the wage data of 216 firms determined by it to be within the scope of the survey but not identified in the tables. Of these firms, 212 had answered the questionnaire circulated by BLS and the data as to the other 4 firms (which had declined to answer) was estimated.

After the tables had been compiled, a hearing to determine the prevailing minimum wages in the industry, pursuant to Section 10(b) of the Walsh-Healey Act, was scheduled before a Hearing Examiner. Copies of the BLS wage tables were furnished to the National Electrical Manufacturers Association ("NEMA," appellees' trade association) about five weeks before the hearing date.

Eight days before the hearing NEMA informed the Bureau that it had obtained from 61 companies, which had received the BLS questionnaire, copies of their answers and also independent data as to the wages paid by the companies; and that it (NEMA) had found discrepancies between the wage data given to it and the data reported to the Bureau. The Bureau examined the discrepancies cited and found that only two would affect the result. These lowered to some extent the original estimates in the tables as to prevailing minimum wages.

The day before the hearing NEMA applied to the Hearing Examiner for a *subpoena duces tecum* requiring the Commissioner of Labor Statistics to produce for inspection:

(1) The completed questionnaire forms.

(2) A list of all establishments to which the BLS questionnaire was sent.

(3) A list of all establishments from which answers to the questionnaire were received.

(4) All the correspondence relating to the questionnaire.

In support of its application NEMA pointed out that on the basis of its own limited investigations there was a substantial possibility that the BLS questionnaire had been widely misunderstood, that the answers given contained significant errors, and that the documents requested were necessary to evaluate the BLS wage tabulations and to assist in cross-examination relating to their accuracy and reliability. Department counsel argued that disclosure would violate the pledge of confidence given to business firms and to States which had furnished their unemployment compensation lists, and would seriously impede the Bureau's efforts to obtain economic data in the future. The Hearing Examiner denied the subpoena application.

At the hearing, the Government introduced without objection the six wage tables. Mr. Samuels, the BLS witness who had supervised the survey, testified that without examining the answers tabulated he could not answer questions relating to names and specific types of company included. When counsel for NEMA asked Mr. Samuels to refresh his recollection by examining the answered questionnaires, the Secretary's counsel successfully objected. Counsel for NEMA thereupon unsuccessfully attempted to introduce affidavits by officials of several establishments stating that data had been erroneously reported to BLS by their companies. NEMA then moved to strike the testimony of Mr.

Samuels and the BLS wage tables, on the ground that Mr. Samuel's testimony "was based on a perusal of records which have not been made available to us and on the further ground that we are not being allowed to impeach his testimony with respect to the wage tables by offering these affidavits." This motion was denied. The affidavits were however admitted by agreement. On the basis of the affidavits BLS agreed to further revisions in the wage tables.

* * * Secretary Goldberg, the predecessor of the appellant, upon review of the record upheld the Hearing Examiner's rulings refusing to issue the subpoena, and denying NEMA's motion to strike the BLS wage tables and the testimony of Mr. Samuels. * * *

* * * The wage determinations made by the Secretary were based solely on the summary tabulations; at no time did he (or the Hearing Examiner) consult the underlying survey data.

We are faced with two separate, but related, issues: whether—in the face of the receipt in evidence of the summary wage tabulations with the refusal to produce or to permit inspection of the answered questionnaires or to disclose the names of the 216 establishments tabulated—the administrative hearing afforded the appellees the opportunity "to submit rebuttal evidence, and to conduct such cross-examination as may be required for a full and true disclosure of the facts," within the meaning of Section 7(c) of the Administrative Procedure Act; and whether, in light of the evidence offered by appellees in an effort to impeach the survey, the determination was "supported by and in accordance with the reliable, probative, and substantial evidence." * * *

There is of course no question as to the admissibility of the summary tabulations compiled by the Bureau. But it is also the general requirement that where tables of this kind are received in evidence, the documents supporting the tables and on which they are based must also be introduced or at last be made available to the opposing party to the extent that they are necessary for purposes of rebuttal and cross-examination. We think that the statute which placed the burden on the Secretary and gave appellees a right to rebut and cross-examine with a view to a full and true disclosure of the facts clearly would require that the general rule be applied here, unless the fact that the questionnaire answers were obtained under a pledge of confidentiality compels a different rule. * * *

Much has been argued to us about the confidential nature of the BLS survey, and the damage that disclosure of the data received would cause to the procurement of information in the future for minimum wage determinations and for important economic investigations in other areas. * * * All of this may be quite true. We are not without sympathy for the problems faced by the Secretary, but we have found nothing in the Walsh-Healey Act, the Fulbright Amendment, the Administrative Procedure Act or any other legislation that has been called to our attention which would empower us to release the Secretary from conforming to the procedural commands of the controlling statutes because of such considerations. * * *

We must necessarily conclude that the admission of the wage tabulations compiled from undisclosed confidential data, as to which we will not compel disclosure, failed to accord to appellees the adequate opportunity for rebuttal and cross-examination that the Congress prescribed. But this does not entirely dispose of the matter.

On the record before us, we could sustain the minimum wage determination only if the wage tabulations, used as the sole basis for the determination, themselves meet the requirements of "reliable, probative and substantial evidence." Where impeaching evidence of probative worth is introduced, however, the precarious structure upon which the Bureau's tabulations rest must topple, unless it is reinforced. Although there may be cases where this is not so, here we are obliged to conclude that sufficient impeaching evidence has been adduced as to require that the wage tables received in evidence be bolstered by some reliable supporting evidence.

In the instant case, the appellees mounted a strong attack on the reliability of the survey. As we have seen, after receiving the Bureau's tabulations, appellees made a limited survey in the short time remaining before the hearing and discovered alleged errors in the tabulations. Two of these were accepted by the Bureau and caused changes in the wage conclusions reached in the tables. During the hearing appellees submitted evidence, in the form of affidavits and testimony of company officials, which resulted in additional downward modifications of the Bureau's minimum wage estimates. The total effect of the eight reductions accepted by the Bureau was by no means *de minimis*.

We need not try to review or evaluate the evidence as to other alleged errors in the answers given to BLS and presumably included in its tabulations, or as to answers resulting from an alleged misunderstanding of the questions asked by BLS. Suffice it to say that the evidence in this case, which we have not detailed, leads to an inescapable inference that the definition of "covered worker" in the BLS questionnaire could have been widely, if not universally, misunderstood, and that the answers given, apart from the errors found by the appellants in their limited survey, could have been erroneous in several respects. In view of the evidence casting serious doubt on the validity of the Bureau's survey results, it was certainly incumbent upon the Bureau, if it meant to rely on the survey, to offer some evidence in rebuttal of the attack. The Secretary, however, offered nothing tending to substantiate the accuracy and reliability of the underlying data. For these reasons the Secretary's determination must be set aside for the further reason that it is not supported by "reliable, probative, and substantial evidence." * * *

Notes

1. Following, and largely because of, the decision in *Baldor Electric*, the Department of Labor abandoned its wage determination program under the Walsh-Healey Act. Does this seem too high a price to pay for the procedural safeguards required by formal rulemaking? Other agencies subject to formal

rulemaking have similarly abandoned specific programs or adopted alternative approaches to regulation.   See, e.g., Merrill and Collier, *"Like Mother Used to Make": An Analysis of FDA Food Standards of Identity,* 74 Colum. L. Rev. 561, 583–84 (1974).

2. Formal rulemaking requirements appear in several regulatory statutes enacted prior to the APA, including the Walsh-Healey Act, some laws administered by the Department of Agriculture, and the Federal Food, Drug, and Cosmetic Act of 1938.   In addition, a smattering of post-1946 laws, such as the Fair Packaging and Labeling Act, Pub. L. No. 89–755 (now codified at 15 U.S.C.A. § § 1451 et seq., and the Federal Coal Mine Safety and Health Act of 1969, Pub. L. No. 91–173 (originally codified at 30 U.S.C.A. § § 801 et seq., § 811, now amended), require trial-type procedures for the adoption of rules.   These requirements have been defended on several grounds.   Formal procedures are said to facilitate the full development of information necessary to the formulation of reasonable regulatory policies.   They produce a closed evidentiary record that permits meaningful judicial review of an agency's factual premises as well as its policy judgments.   Moreover, it is argued, only a trial-type hearing affords affected persons a genuine opportunity to question the agency's factual premises. "[H]e who regulates ought to appear publicly if there is a challenge, and put on the table, subject to cross-examination, the facts on which he grounds his proposal."   Austern, *Food Standards: The Balance Between Certainty and Innovation,* 24 Food Drug Cosm. L.J. 440, 451 (1969).   Implicit in many defenses of formal rulemaking are the trial lawyer's abiding faith in proceedings that place primary emphasis on oral rather than written presentation and that expose witnesses to the rigors of cross-examination.

3. Critics of formal rulemaking have been unconvinced.   In a study for the U.S. Administrative Conference, Professor Hamilton found that requiring rulemaking to be conducted on the record imposes substantial disadvantages in terms of cost, delay, and agency effectiveness.   *Procedures for the Adoption of Rules of General Applicability: The Need for Procedural Innovation in Administrative Rulemaking,* 60 Calif. L. Rev. 1276, 1312–13 (1972):

> The actual agency experience with these procedural requirements raises serious doubts about their desirability.   At best, some agencies have learned to live with them, even though preferable procedures are probably available.   At worst, these procedures have warped regulatory programs or resulted in virtual abandonment of them.   It is surprising to discover that most agencies required to conduct formal hearings in connection with rulemaking in fact did not do so during the previous five years.   * * *   Thus, the primary impact of these procedural requirements is often not as one might otherwise have expected, the testing of agency assumptions by cross-examination or the testing of agency conclusions by courts on the basis of substantial evidence of record.   Rather these procedures either cause the abandonment of the program * * * , the development of techniques to reach the same regulatory goal but without a hearing   * * * , or the promulgation of noncontroversial regulations by a process of negotiation and compromise.   * * * [172]   In practice, therefore, the principal effect of imposing rulemaking on a record

172. It probably does not need pointing out that valid and non-arbitrary regulations may be controversial.   Rulemaking on a record is favored by industry attorneys, I suspect, precisely because it may help to impede or prevent the adoption of quite valid and reasonable regulations which are objectionable to their clients.

has often been the dilution of the regulatory process rather than the protection of persons from arbitrary action.

4. One of Professor Hamilton's prominent illustrations was the FDA, whose unhappy experience with formal rulemaking has caused it largely to abandon those regulatory initiatives that are subject to formal procedures. See, e.g., Hamilton, *Rulemaking on a Record by the Food and Drug Administration*, 50 Tex. L. Rev. 1132 (1972). For discussions of the alternative approaches to regulation that FDA has devised in order to avoid formal rulemaking, see Merrill and Collier, supra; Merrill and Schewel, *FDA Regulation of Environmental Contaminants of Food*, 66 Va. L. Rev. 1357, 1382–91 (1980).

Perhaps the quintessential illustration of the worst of formal rulemaking is a proceeding that the FDA undertook to prescribe labeling and compositional requirements for nutritional supplements and fortified foods, a proceeding governed by section 701(e) of the Federal Food, Drug, and Cosmetic Act. The proceeding began in 1962 with the publication of a proposal. Four years elapsed before the agency published a "final order" subject to objections and requests for a hearing which, after a legal skirmish over differences between the proposal and final order, see *Pharmaceutical Manufacturers Association v. Gardner*, 381 F.2d 271 (D.C. Cir. 1967), engulfed the agency. The hearing commenced in 1968; it involved over 100 parties and lasted nearly two years. A court challenge to the first installment of final regulations issued by the agency was successful, *National Nutritional Foods Association v. FDA*, 540 F.2d 761 (2d Cir. 1974), partly on the ground that the agency's hearing officer had abridged rights of some parties to cross-examine a key witness. By the time the hearing was reopened on remand, that witness had long since departed his position as chairman of the NAS-NRC committee (whose recommendations the FDA was seeking to implement), so a substitute had to be found. In the meantime, Congress intervened to amend provisions of the agency's statute which authorized certain of the proposed regulations. The FDA's attempt to reissue revised regulations, based on the amended hearing record but without additional opportunity to comment on the impact of Congress' action, was set aside in part, *National Nutritional Foods Association v. Kennedy*, 572 F.2d 377 (2d Cir. 1978). For discussion of this exercise, see R. MERRILL & P. HUTT, FOOD AND DRUG LAW 229–46, 895–96 (1980).

5. Professor Boyer has argued that use of formal trial-type procedures for making general regulatory policy may introduce, or reinforce, an agency bias in favor of inaction:

> [T]rial procedures with their heavy emphasis on intensive and searching cross-examination as a method of finding truth may be more effective in exposing the negative features of a proposed action than in illuminating its positive virtues. If so, it would be possible to say that trial procedures are more "accurate" when implementing a policy that large-scale development projects should be restrained in the face of uncertain environmental consequences, than they would be in implementing a policy that economic growth should go forward despite uncertainty.

Boyer, *Alternatives to Administrative Trial-Type Hearings for Resolving Complex Scientific, Economic and Social Issues*, 71 Mich. L. Rev. 111, 138 (1972).

Consider, by contrast, the views of Robinson, *The Making of Administrative Policy: Another Look at Rulemaking and Adjudication and Administrative Procedure Reform*, 118 U. Pa. L. Rev. 485, 521–24 (1970):

Challenges to the suitability of adjudicative methods (particularly the reliance on testimonial evidence and cross-examination) where the issues involve policy planning, appear to rest in large part on the notion that "policy" * * * is something pure, uncontaminated by particular data and questions, assumptions, opinions and biases which have been regarded as properly the subject of such methods in other contexts. * * *

First, it is doubtful that predictive judgment is radically different from determinations of historical fact. In both cases the determination must almost invariably rest on general conclusions that are inferred from particular factual data and an evaluation of probabilities that may be as appropriate for testimonial proof and cross-examination in one case as in the other.

Second, in some cases testimonial proof and cross-examination can serve a more valuable function in testing forecasts and generalized conclusions underlying future policy planning than in making findings concerning specific past events. * * * Even if there is no dispute about specific identifiable "facts," * * * and even if the [agency's] judgment cannot be proved or disproved * * * it may still be desirable to force [it] through cross-examination of its experts, to disclose the particular premises, including facts, opinions, and reasoning, which underlie its "policy" conclusions. * * * At the very least it puts some burden on the agency to explain and articulate the assumptions and the foundations on which its policy rests. * * *

Naturally, some price is paid for these methods: they entail additional hearing time, which aggravates the problem of delay, and they increase the size of the record in a case, which aggravates the difficulty of defining the relevant issues and distilling the material facts. * * * While delay is unquestionably present in administrative regulation, the problem tends to be exaggerated by reference to extraordinary cases which are not fairly representative of the process as a whole. Even accepting the time honored view that delay is a major problem, it is still questionable how much of it is attributable to reliance on formal procedures. * * * A recent congressional survey of the major federal agencies indicates, for example, that testimonial procedures, and cross-examination in particular, were regarded by agency personnel and practitioners before the agencies as only a minor cause of significant delay. * * *

See also Pierce, *The Choice Between Adjudicating and Rulemaking for Formulating and Implementing Energy Policy*, 31 Hastings L.J. 1 (1979).

Appellees

UNITED STATES v. FLORIDA EAST COAST RAILWAY CO.

Supreme Court of the United States, 1973.
410 U.S. 224, 93 S.Ct. 810, 35 L.Ed.2d 223.

MR. JUSTICE REHNQUIST delivered the opinion of the Court.

Appellees, two railroad companies, brought this action in the District *Procedure* Court for the Middle District of Florida to set aside the incentive per diem rates established by appellant Interstate Commerce Commission in a rulemaking proceeding. The District Court sustained appellees' position that the Commission had failed to comply with the applicable provisions of the Administrative Procedure Act, and therefore set aside the or- *RR* der. * * * The District Court held that the language of § 1(14)(a)[1] of the Interstate Commerce Act required the Commission in a proceeding such as this to act in accordance with the Administrative Procedure Act, 5 U.S.C.A. § 556(d) and that the Commision's determination to receive submissions from the appellees only in written form was a violation of that section because the appellees were "prejudiced" by that determination within the meaning of that section. * * *

I.

This case arises from the factual background of a chronic freight-car shortage on the Nation's railroads. * * * Congressional concern for the problem was manifested in the enactment in 1966 of an amendment to § 1(14)(a) of the Interstate Commerce Act, enlarging the Commission's authority to prescribe per diem charges for the use by one railroad of freight cars owned by another. * * *

The Commission in 1966 commenced an investigation "to determine whether information presently available warranted the establishment of an incentive element increase, on an interim basis, to apply pending futher study and investigation." * * *

In December 1967, the Commission initiated the rulemaking procedure giving rise to the order that appellees here challenge. It directed Class I and Class II line-haul railroads to compile and report detailed information with respect to freight-car demand and supply at numerous sample stations for selected days of the week during 12 four-week periods, beginning January 29, 1968.

Some of the affected railroads voiced questions about the proposed study or requested modification in the study procedures outlined by the Commission in its notice of proposed rulemaking. In response to petitions setting forth these carriers' views, the Commission staff held an informal conference in April 1968, at which the objections and proposed modifications were discussed. Twenty railroads, including appellee Sea-

---

1. Section 1(14)(a) provides:

"The Commission may, after hearing, on a complaint or upon its own initiative without complaint, establish reasonable rules, regulations, and practices with respect to car service by common carriers by railroad subject to this chapter, including the compensation to be paid and other terms of contract, agreement, or arrangement for the use of any locomotive, car, or other vehicle not owned by the carrier using it (and whether or not owned by another carrier), and the penalties or other sanctions for nonobservance of such rules, regulations, or practices. In fixing such compensation to be paid for the use of any type of freight car, the Commission shall give consideration to the national level of ownership of such type of freight car and to other factors affecting the adequacy of the national freight car supply, and shall, on the basis of such consideration, determine whether compensation should be computed solely on the basis of elements of ownership expense involved in owning and maintaining such type of freight car, including a fair return on value, or whether such compensation should be increased by such incentive element or elements of compensation as in the Commission's judgment will provide just and reasonable compensation to freight car owners, contribute to sound car service practices (including efficient utilization and distribution of cars), and encourage the acquisition and maintenance of a car supply adequate to meet the needs of commerce and the national defense. * * * "

board, were represented at this conference, at which the Commission's staff sought to answer questions about reporting methods to accommodate individual circumstances of particular railroads. The conference adjourned on a note that undoubtedly left the impression that hearings would be held at some future date. A detailed report of the conference was sent to all parties to the proceeding before the Commission.

The results of the information thus collected were analyzed and presented to Congress by the Commission during a hearing before the Subcommittee on Surface Transportation of the Senate Committee on Commerce in May 1969. Members of the Subcommittee expressed dissatisfaction with the Commission's slow pace in exercising the authority that had been conferred upon it by the 1966 Amendments to the Interstate Commerce Act. * * *

The Commission, now apparently imbued with a new sense of mission, issued in December 1969 an interim report announcing its tentative decision to adopt incentive per diem charges on standard boxcars based on the information compiled by the railroads. * * * Embodied in the report was a proposed rule adopting the Commission's tentative conclusions and a notice to the railroads to file statements of position within 60 days, couched in the following language:

> "That verified statements of facts, briefs, and statements of position respecting the tentative conclusions reached in the said interim report, the rules and regulations proposed in the appendix to this order, and any other pertinent matter, are hereby invited to be submitted pursuant to the filing schedule set forth below by an interested person whether or not such person is already a party to this proceeding.

> * * *

> "That any party requesting oral hearing shall set forth with specificity the need therefor and the evidence to be adduced." *Proof*

Both appellee railroads filed statements objecting to the Commission's proposal and requesting an oral hearing, as did numerous other railroads. In April 1970, the Commission, without having held further "hearings," issued a supplemental report making some modifications in the tentative conclusions earlier reached, but overruling *in toto* the requests of appellees. * * *

II.

In *United States v. Allegheny-Ludlum Steel Corp.*, [406 U.S. 742 (1972)] we held that the language of § 1(14)(a) * * * authorizing the Commission to act "after hearing" was not the equivalent of a requirement that a rule be made "on the record after opportunity for an agency hearing" as the latter term is used in § 553(c) of the Administrative Procedure Act. Since the 1966 amendment to § 1(14)(a), under which the Commission was here proceeding, does not by its terms add to the hearing requirement contained in the earlier language, the same result should obtain here unless that amendment contains language that is tantamount to such a requirement. Appellees contend that such language is found in the provisions of that Act requiring that:

> "[T]he Commission shall give consideration to the national level of ownership of such type of freight car and to other factors affecting the adequacy of the national freight car supply, and shall, on the basis of such consideration, determine whether compensation should be computed. * * * "

While this language is undoubtedly a mandate to the Commission to consider the factors there set forth in reaching any conclusion as to imposition of per diem incentive charges, it adds to the hearing requirements of the section neither expressly nor by implication. We know of no reason to think that an administrative agency in reaching a decision cannot accord consideration to factors such as those set forth in the 1966 amendment by means other than a trial-type hearing or the presentation of oral argument by the affected parties. Congress by that amendment specified necessary components of the ultimate decision, but it did not specify the method by which the Commission should acquire information about those components.

* * *

* * * The District Court observed that it was "rather hard to believe that the last sentence of § 553(c) was directed only to the few legislative sports where the words 'on the record' or their equivalent had found their way into the statute book." This is, however, the language which Congress used, and since there are statutes on the books that do use these very words, see, e.g., the Fulbright Amendment to the Walsh-Healey Act, 41 U.S.C.A. § 43a, and 21 U.S.C.A. § 371(e)(3), the regulations provision of the Food and Drug Act, adherence to that language connot be said to render the provision nugatory or ineffectual. We recognized in *Allegheny-Ludlum* that the actual words "on the record" and "after * * * hearing" used in § 553 were not words of art, and that other statutory language having the same meaning could trigger the provisions of § §556 and 557 in rulemaking proceedings. But we adhere to our conclusion, expressed in that case, that the phrase "after hearing" in § 1(14)(a) * * * does not have such an effect.

III.

Inextricably intertwined with the hearing requirement of the Administrative Procedure Act in this case is the meaning to be given to the language "after hearing" in § 1(14)(a) * * * . Appellees, both here and in the court below, contend that the Commission procedure here fell short of that mandated by the "hearing" requirement of § 1(14)(a), even though it may have satisfied § 553 of the Administrative Procedure Act. * * *

The term "hearing" in its legal context undoubtedly has a host of meanings. Its meaning undoubtedly will vary depending on whether it is used in the context of a rulemaking-type proceeding or in the context of a proceeding devoted to the adjudication of particular disputed facts. It is by no means apparent what the drafters of the Esch Car Service Act of

1917, which became the first part of § 1(14)(a), * * * meant by the term. * * * What is apparent, though, is that the term was used in granting authority to the Commission to make rules and regulations of a prospective nature.

* * *

Under these circustances, confronted with a grant of substantive authority made after the Administrative Procedure Act was enacted, we think that reference to that Act, in which Congress devoted itself exclusively to questions such as the nature and scope of hearings, is a satisfactory basis for determining what is meant by the term "hearing" used in another statute. Turning to that Act, we are convinced that the term "hearing" as used therein does not necessarily embrace either the right to present evidence orally and to cross-examine opposing witnesses, or the right to present oral argument to the agency's decisionmaker.

Section 553 excepts from its requirements rulemaking devoted to "interpretative rules, general statements of policy, or rules of agency organization, procedure, or practice," and rulemaking "when the agency for good cause finds * * * that notice and public procedure thereon are impracticable, unnecessary, or contrary to the public interest." This exception does not apply, however, "when notice or hearing is required by statute"; in those cases, even though interpretative rulemaking be involved, the requirements of § 553 apply. But since these requirements themselves do not mandate any oral presentation, it cannot be doubted that a statute that requires a "hearing" prior to rulemaking may in some circumstances be satisfied by procedures that meet only the standards of § 553. * * *

Similarly, even where the statute requires that the rulemaking procedure take place "on the record after opportunity for an agency hearing," thus triggering the applicability of § 556, subsection (d) provides that the agency may proceed by the submission of all or part of the evidence in written form if a party will not be "prejudiced thereby." Again, the Act makes it plain that a specific statutory mandate that the proceedings take place on the record after hearing may be satisfied in some circumstances by evidentiary submission in written form only.

We think this treatment of the term "hearing" in the Administrative Procedure Act affords a sufficient basis for concluding that the requirement of a "hearing" contained in § 1(14)(a) * * * did not by its own force require the Commission either to hear oral testimony, to permit cross-examination of Commission witnesses, or to hear oral argument. Here, the Commission promulgated a tentative draft of an order, and accorded all interested parties 60 days in which to file statements of position, submissions of evidence, and other relevant observations. The parties had fair notice of exactly what the Commission proposed to do, and were given an opportunity to comment, to object, or to make some other form of written submission. The final order of the Commission indicates that it gave consideration to the statements of the two appellees here. Given the "open-ended" nature of the proceedings, and the Commission's announced willingness to consider proposals for modification after operating experience had been acquired, we think the hearing requirement of § 1(14)(a) of the Act was met.

Appellee railroads cite a number of our previous decisions dealing in some manner with the right to a hearing in an administrative proceeding. Although appellees have asserted no claim of constitutional deprivation in this proceeding, some of the cases they rely upon expressly speak in constitutional terms, while others are less than clear as to whether they depend upon the Due Process Clause of the Fifth and Fourteenth Amendments to the Constitution or upon generalized principles of administrative law formulated prior to the adoption of the Administrative Procedure Act. * * *

The basic distinction between rulemaking and adjudication is illustrated by this Court's treatment of two related cases under the Due Process Clause of the Fourteenth Amendment. In *Londoner v. Denver*, cited in oral argument by appellees, 210 U.S. 373 (1908), the Court held that due process had not been accorded a landowner who objected to the amount assessed against his land as its share of the benefit resulting from the paving of a street. Local procedure had accorded him the right to file a written complaint and objection, but not to be heard orally. This Court held that due process of law required that he "have the right to support his allegations by argument however brief, and if need be, by proof, however informal." But in the later case of *Bi-Metallic Investment Co. v. State Board of Equalization*, 239 U.S. 441 (1915), the Court held that no hearing at all was constitutionally required prior to a decision by state tax officers in Colorado to increase the valuation of all taxable property in Denver by a substantial percentage. The Court distinguished *Londoner* by stating that there a small number of persons "were exceptionally affected, in each case upon individual grounds."

Later decisions have continued to observe the distinction adverted to in *Bi-Metallic Investment Co.* * * * While the line dividing them may not always be a bright one, these decisions represent a recognized distinction in administrative law between proceedings for the purpose of promulgating policy-type rules or standards, on the one hand, and proceedings designed to adjudicate disputed facts in particular cases on the other.

Here, the incentive payments proposed by the Commission in its tentative order, and later adopted in its final order, were applicable across the board to all of the common carriers by railroad subject to the Interstate Commerce Act. No effort was made to single out any particular railroad for special consideration based on its own peculiar circumstances. Indeed, one of the objections of appellee Florida East Coast was that it and other terminating carriers should have been treated differently from the generality of the railroads. But the fact that the order may in its effects have been thought more disadvantageous by some railroads than by others does not change its generalized nature. Though the Commission obviously relied on factual inferences as a basis for its order, the source of these factual inferences was apparent to anyone who read the order of December 1969. The factual inferences were used in the formulation of a basically legislative-type judgment, for prospective application only, rather than in adjudicating a particular set of disputed facts.

* * *

MR. JUSTICE DOUGLAS, with whom MR. JUSTICE STEWART concurs, dissenting.

* * * Seaboard argued that it had been damaged by what it alleged to be the Commission's sudden change in emphasis from specialty to unequipped boxcars and that it would lose some $1.8 million as the result of the Commission's allegedly hasty and experimental action. Florida East Coast raised significant challenges to the statistical validity of the Commission's data, and also contended that its status as a terminating railroad left it with a surfeit of standard boxcars which should exempt it from the requirement to pay incentive charges. * * *

Section 1(14)(a) of the Interstate Commerce Act bestows upon the Commission broad discretionary power to determine incentive rates. These rates may have devastating effects on a particular line. According to the brief of one of the appellees, the amount of incentive compensation paid by debtor lines amounts to millions of dollars each six-month period. Nevertheless, the courts must defer to the Commission as long as its findings are supported by substantial evidence and it has not abused its discretion. "All the more insistent is the need, when power has been bestowed so freely, that the 'inexorable safeguard' * * * of a fair and open hearing be maintained in its integrity."

Accordingly, I would hold that appellees were not afforded the hearing guaranteed by § 1(14)(a) of the Interstate Commerce Act and 5 U.S.C.A. § § 553, 556 and 557, and would affirm the decision of the District Court.

Note

Justice Rehnquist's *Florida East Coast* opinion was surprising and, according to some commentators, e.g. Nathanson, *Probing the Mind of the Administrator: Hearing Variations and Standards of Judicial Review Under the Administrative Procedure Act and Other Federal Statutes*, 75 Colum. L. Rev. 721 (1975), wrong in its narrow interpretation of the reach of the APA's procedures for formal rulemaking. His ruling did not entirely nullify the triggering language of section 554(d). A few statutes in so many words specify that rules shall be made "on the record after opportunity for an agency hearing." E.g., Walsh-Healey Act, 41 U.S.C.A. § 43a (1982). A number of others spell out procedures for rulemaking that are at least as formal as those mandated by sections 556 and 557 of the APA. See, e.g., Federal Food, Drug, and Cosmetic Act § 701(e), 21 U.S.C.A. § 371(e). Without question, however, *Florida East Coast* confined the obligation to follow the APA's formal rulemaking procedures to a small universe of federal programs. See also Auerbach, *Informal Rule Making: A Proposed Relationship Between Administrative Procedures and Judicial Review*, 72 Nw. U.L. Rev. 15 (1977).

4. EVOLUTION OF INFORMAL RULEMAKING UNDER SECTION 553

Florida East Coast did not sharply curtail the practice of formal rulemaking because relatively few statutes prescribed on-the-record rulemaking, and few agencies had interpreted general "hearing" language in their laws as requiring the full-blown procedures of sections 556–57. But the decision did shatter understandings of what a statutory "hearing" might entail, and it refocused attention on the procedural requirements of section 553.

Those requirements, as we have observed, appear sparse. By its terms, section 553 makes an oral hearing optional. It says nothing about the form or time for the submission of "data, views, or argument," nor does it mention the materials that the agency consulted in developing its proposal. It is not obvious that the agency is obligated to make those materials public, to confine its decision to any particular "record," or to refrain from consultation with any individual, group, or other governmental body. From the bare language of section 553, the agency apparently need only publish its proposed rule, allow some reasonable (but unspecified) period for written comments, and then promulgate a final regulation accompanied by a brief statement of reasons.

From the materials in Part A, however, we know that agencies now *do* more, indeed that they *must* do more in explaining the judgments embodied in final rules. But this was not always the case. Current "informal rulemaking" by federal agencies differs sharply from the customs of the late 1960's and early 1970's. The prevailing norms are the product of several forces: judicial decisions interpreting section 553—or perhaps announcing general principles of an administrative "common law"; other Congressional directives; scholarly and professional criticism; pressure from individuals and groups interested in government policies; and, by no means least important, agency self-interest. An objective of these materials is to convey an understanding of current practice, but we are primarily interested in its philosophical and pragmatic underpinnings, i.e., in the competing concerns for fairness, efficiency, and rationality that have influenced its evolution.

Coverage of Section 553

Before exploring the basic elements of section 553 rulemaking, we should recognize there are circumstances in which these requirements do not apply. Section 553 contains three kinds of exemptions from all or some of its requriements:

Subsection 553(a) exempts categorically rules relating to military or foreign affairs functions, agency management and personnel, and "public property, loans, grants, benefits, or contracts." At face value, these exemptions exclude a substantial slice of the contemporary activities of the federal government.

Subsection 553(b) contains two other types of exemptions from the obligation to provide notice and permit comment on proposed rules. The first of these—for "interpretative rules, general statements of policy, or rules of agency organization, procedure, or practice"—focuses on the legal character of the agency pronouncement rather than its subject matter. The second exemption ostensibly is available for any rule otherwise subject to section 553 when circumstances lead the agency "for good cause" to find, and document, "that notice and public procedure thereon are impracticable, unnecessary, or contrary to the public interest."

We shall not attempt a thorough review of the judicial treatment of these various exemptions from the public rulemaking requirements of section 553, for the case law is voluminous. But it is useful to illustrate the circumstances in which agencies invoke these exemptions, as they frequently do, and to convey the courts' customarily skeptical response.

The definitive treatment of the exemption for rules relating to public property, loans, grants, benefits, or contracts is still Bonfield, *Public Participation in Federal Rulemaking Relating to Public Property, Loans, Grants, Benefits, or Contracts*, 118 U. Pa. L. Rev. 540 (1970). As Professor Bonfield points out, the exclusion of these fields may reflect Congressional, and perhaps judicial, attitudes toward claims to do business with or obtain financial support from the government, attitudes reflected in the now-discredited distinction between "rights" and "privileges." Congress clearly believed that the government should be able to transact its own business without unnecessary procedural impediments, perhaps underestimating the extent to which that "business" affected members of the public.

Unhappiness with subsection (a)'s broad exclusions led the U.S. Administrative Conference to recommend that, notwithstanding the APA, agencies responsible for government grants, benefits, and contracts should, whenever feasible, follow the rulemaking requirements of section 533. Recommendation No. 16, U.S. ADMINISTRATIVE CONFERENCE, RECOMMENDATIONS AND REPORTS 29–30 (1970). Many agencies, such as the Department of Health and Human Services, did precisely this, in effect committing themselves to provide notice of and permit comment on proposed rules to which the exclusion might otherwise apply. See, e.g., 36 Fed. Reg. 2532 (1971). Recently, however, the Department has proposed to alter this commitment to public rulemaking on otherwise exempt rules because of the additional costs and associated delays. 47 Fed. Reg. 26860 (1982).

There remain important areas of government activity, such as the contracts and procurement area, where statutory rulemaking requirements do not apply. The combination of voluntary compliance with section 553 and grudging judicial interpretation of the exclusions, however, have narrowed their impact. Illustrative of the judicial posture is *Vigil v. Andrus*, 667 F.2d 931 (10th Cir. 1982), in which the plaintiffs challenged a decision by the Bureau of Indian Affairs to discontinue a program providing free lunches to Indian children attending New Mexico public schools. The Bureau's decision, made effective in 1976, implemented a 1970 understanding with the U. S. Department of Agriculture, which undertook responsibility for providing free meals to school children, including Indians, but limited eligibility to those demonstrating economic need. In New Mexico and other states, however, all Indians enrolled in the public school for several years thereafter continued to receive free meals which were apparently charged to the federal government. The discovery of this practice led the federal defendants to attempt immediately to implement the 1970 understanding by promulgating the challenged rules. The plaintiffs charged that they could not do so without first allowing public comment.

The court of appeals rejected the defendants' claim that their policy of not providing free lunches for Indians who could not show need, embodied in the 1970 understanding and formulated in the 1976 rule, fell within the pA "grants" or "benefits" exclusion. The decision relied heavily on *Morton v. Ruiz*, 415 U. S. 199 (1974), p. 399 infra. The court observed that the BIA in 1971 had voluntarily undertaken to follow section 553, and concluded that this commitment applied here—because the policy agreed to in 1970 was not to be effective until 1974 and because the Bureau had not announced the policy change until after its procedural commitment became effective.

Subsection (b)'s exemption for "interpretative rules, general statements of policy, or rules of agency * * * procedure" has provoked a good deal of litigation. Reviewing courts have generally been skeptical of agency efforts to invoke these exceptions. It is clear that the APA's language cannot be taken literally. *Pharmaceutical Manufacturers Association v. Finch*, 307 F. Supp. 858 (D. Del. 1970), is typical. There the district court displayed impatience with the FDA's efforts to characterize its new standards for clinical drug trials as "interpretative," stressing that agencies were obligated to comply with section 553 whenever their rules, regardless of their technical legal status, were likely to have substantial impact on members of the public.

The FDA was again unsuccessful when it attempted to defend publication, without prior opportunity for comment, of comprehensive new procedures for rulemaking, adjudication, and other less formal regulatory proceedings. Without doubt the regulations were in form "rules of agency * * * procedure," but they were without precedent in their ambition and scope. The district court refused to accept that regulations occupying more than 150 pages in the Federal Register could legitimately be exempt from the rulemaking requirements of section 553. See *American College of Neuropsychopharmacology v. Weinberger*, 1975 Developments, Food, Drug, Cosm. L. Rep. (CCH) ¶ 38,025 (D.D.C. July 31, 1975).

The exclusion that has occasioned the most debate and demanded greatest judicial understanding of the relations between the promulgating agency and persons affected by its actions is that for "interpretative" rules. Perhaps the best synthesis of judicial attitude appears in *American Bus Association v. United States*, 627 F.2d 525 (D.C. Cir. 1980), in which petitioners challenged an ICC announcement of relaxed criteria for evaluating applications to provide bus service between the U.S. and Canada. The Commission claimed that its announcement was merely a statement of policy, and thus, exempt from public rulemaking under section 553. The court, per Judge McGowan, disagreed:

> We do not, of course, doubt that agencies may bypass section 533's requirements when genuinely acting within the scope of the few specified exceptions to it. However, Congress was alert to the possibility that these exceptions might, if broadly defined and indiscriminately used, defeat the section's purpose. Thus the legislative history of the section is scattered with warnings that various of the exceptions are not to be used to escape the requirements of section 553. * * *

> Because the term "general statement of policy" is defined neither in the Act nor its legislative history, we turn to the definition proffered in the *Attorney General's Manual on the Administrative Procedure Act* (1947). * * * That document's only discussion of our problem occurs in a footnote which defines general statements of policy as "statements issued by an agency to advise the public prospectively of the manner in which the agency proposes to exercise a discretionary power." While this definition is not free form ambiguity, it does convey what this court has identified as a basic, defining characteristic of a policy statement:

>> A general statement of policy * * * does not establish a "binding norm." It is not finally determinative of the issues or rights to which it is addressed. The agency cannot apply or rely upon a general statement of policy as law because a general statement of policy only announces what the agency seeks to establish as policy. A policy statement announces the agency's tentative intentions for the future.

Pacific Gas & Electric Co. v. FPC, 506 F.2d 33, 38 (D.C. Cir. 1974).

> In deciding whether an agency's pronouncement is a policy statement or is in fact a "binding norm," courts have employed two criteria. First, courts have said that, unless a pronouncement acts prospectively, it is a binding norm. * * *

> The second criterion is whether a purported policy statement genuinely leaves the agency and its decisionmakers free to exercise discretion. A purported policy statement which did not do so could not be an "announce[ment of] the general policy which the Commission hopes to establish in subsequent proceedings," but would, impermissibly, be a "binding norm." * * *

> The second criterion cannot, of course, be applied mechanically. * * * "A matter of judgment is involved in distinguishing between rules, however discretionary in form, that effectively circumscribe administrative choice, and rules that contemplate that the administrator will exercise an informed discretion in the various cases that arise." * * *

> In applying the second criterion in *Pickus v. U.S. Board of Parole*, 507 F.2d 1107 (D.C. Cir. 1974), we took into account the language, structure, and calculable effect of the statement. The Parole Board claimed that guidelines specifying many of the factors it used in deciding whether to parole prisoners were "general statements of policy." The court disagreed, on the grounds that those guidelines

>> were of a kind calculated to have a substantive effect on ultimate parole decisions. * * * Although they provide no formula for parole determination, they cannot help but focus the decisionmaker's attention on the

Board-approved criteria. They thus narrow his field of vision, minimizing the influence of other factors and encouraging decisive reliance upon factors whose significance might have been differently articulated had Section 4 [now section 553 of the APA] been followed.

In sum, the court held, the guidelines "are substantive agency action, for they define a fairly tight framework to circumscribe the Board's statutorily broad power." * * *

Measuring the ICC's announcement by these criteria, Judge McGowan concluded that it went well beyond a "statement of policy." First, it purported to relieve holders of previously issued licenses of outdated restrictions on their service to Canada. Second, it contained no hint that Commission officials responsible for passing on new applications had any discretion to deviate from the criteria set forth.

In addition to its self-executing categorical exclusions, subsection 553(b) contemplates that circumstances surrounding promulgation of a concededly legislative rule may sometimes justify omission of notice and opportunity for comment. Here again, however, courts have been reluctant to permit agencies to escape the obligation to expose new policies to public debate. They have insisted that the agency invoke the "good cause" exception at the time its rule is issued, rather than when it is challenged, and they have rigorously scrutinized the reasons offered to support the claim that public rulemaking is "impractical, unnecessary, or contrary to the public interest." See, e.g., *National Nutritional Foods Association v. Kennedy*, 572 F.2d 377, 384 (2d Cir. 1978).

Statutory and judicial deadlines for the promulgation of regulations have frequently been the stimulus for agency efforts to avoid the inevitable delays accompanying compliance with section 553. These efforts have usually been unsuccessful. EPA's implementation of 1977 amendments to the Clean Air Act produced challenges in five circuits and a split of authority over what circumstances justify departure from section 553. The amendments, embellishing an already complicated structure for controlling air quality, called on the states to designate areas within their borders that had attained, could attain, or should be exempt from attaining national standards. EPA had first to approve these designations and then approve individual state plans for achieving the forecast objectives. Congress had set a tight time schedule for completing the entire process, including a fixed date for EPA's approval of the state goals. The agency concluded that it could not meet the statutory deadline if it invited public comment on the state submissions, and on this ground it invoked the "good cause" exemption in section 553 (b). By the time challenges to this action reached the D.C. Circuit, the Third and the Fifth Circuits had ruled against EPA, while the Sixth and Seventh had found its failure to allow public comment justified under the circumstances. With the direct authority thus in equipoise, the D.C. Circuit examined the statutory exemption:

* * * [It] should be clear beyond contradiction or cavil that Congress expected, and the courts have held, that the various exceptions to the notice-

and comment provisions of section 553 will be narrowly construed and only reluctantly countenanced.   Nowhere did Congress make its intention in this respect plainer than in its deliberations over the very exception respondent cites.   The Senate Committee responsible for the APA warned:

> The exemption of situations of *emergency* or *necessity* is not an "escape clause" in the sense that any agency has discretion to disregard its terms of the facts.   A true and supported or supportable finding of necessity or emergency must be made and published.   "Impracticable" means a situation in which the due and required execution of the agency functions would be *unavoidably prevented* by its undertaking public rule-making proceedings.

S. Doc. No. 248, 79th Cong., 2d Sess. 200 (1946) (emphasis added).   * * *

* * * The Sixth and Seventh Circuits assume that the goals of the Clean Air Act and the Administrative Procedure Act irreconcilably conflict, and no doubt the * * * rules of the latter Act may be employed to thwart the goals of the former.   But this assumption fundamentally misconceives the purpose and shrugs off the wisdom of the APA.   Both the case at bar and our explication of the APA show that the APA may be deployed to insure that the Administrator fulfills his obligations under the Clean Air Act: Here petitioner is challenging the Administrator's decision that a large expanse of the country need not be designated "nonattainment" and hence need not be required to establish special programs to reduce pollution.   * * * If the agency scanted its duty under the Clean Air Act when it subsequently cut back the regions to be designated nonattainment, the protests of affected parties such as New Jersey are the congressionally mandated and perhaps the only systematic means of identifying the error and urging its reformation.   Furthermore, the case at bar points up the lesson that, in the implementation of the Clean Air Act, where the heaviest responsibilities rest upon state governments and where federalism concerns are implicated, the usefulness and desirability of the APA's notice-and-comment provision may be magnified.

* * * [W]hatever one's conclusions about the general compatibility of the APA and the Clean Air Act, * * * under the facts of this case, the Administrator could have reconciled the commands of the two acts by publishing the designations submitted to him by the states as proposed rules.   Neither the Seventh and Sixth Circuits nor respondents have shown us how that reconciliation might be unsatisfactory.   If the admonition to construe the good-cause exception of section 553(b)(B) narrowly means anything, it means that we cannot condone its invocation where, as here, such a reconciliation is possible.   * * *

* * * [We] cannot accept in any absolute form the * * * argument that the Administrator cannot be reversed here because to do so would delay implementation of the Clean Air Act.   An agency's functions will be impaired any time it is reversed on procedural grounds, and such occasional impairments are the price we pay to preserve the integrity of the APA.   Of course, cases under the "tight schedule" version of good cause are sure to be particularly troublesome in this respect, since if an agency's allegations as to the need for expedition are remotely true, the elapse of time necessary to secure judicial review will assure that a court cannot easily reverse the agency.   But a court serves neither the law nor, ultimately, the parties before it by succumbing, without a cautious examination of a case's facts, to whatever *fait ac-*

compli an agency may choose to present.   Fortunately, such an examination of this case indicates that   *   *   *   our reversal of the Administrator should not noticeably interfere with, and may actually promote, the ends of the Clean Air Act.   *   *   *

It will be recalled that, after promulgating a "final rule" which was to be effective "immediately," the Administrator stated the Agency would accept public comments received within sixty days of the promulgation of the rule. The Administrator now argues that his provision for *post hoc* comment "cures" his failure to follow section 553's procedures.   We cannot agree.

Once again, we accept the reasoning of the Fifth Circuit in its *U.S. Steel* [595 F.2d 207 (1979)]:

> Section 553 is designed to ensure that affected parties have an opportunity to participate in and influence agency decision making at an early stage, when the agency is more likely to give real consideration to alternative ideas.   *   *   *

We are convinced that the Fifth Circuit accurately assessed the psychological and bureaucratic realities of *post hoc* comments in rule-making.   It was in recognition of those realities that Congress specified that notice and an opportunity for comment are to *precede* rule-making.   *   *   *

*   *   *   [P]etitioner challenges only designations of "attainment" or "unclassifiable" as to oxidant pollution.   We therefore set aside only those challenged designations and remand the record for reconsideration of them.

That reconsideration must, certainly, be preceded by notice of the designations proposed and by opportunity for public comment, as section 553 prescribes.   Reconsideration, and any consequent alterations of state implementation plans, shall proceed as expeditiously as possible.   In no case shall a stage of the reconsideration process extend beyond the time allotted for such stage by 42 U.S.C.A. § 7407.   In view of the need for expedition, we retain jurisdiction over the case so that parties will be able to submit motions to us where necessary to secure the prompt and proper accomplishment of the mandate of the Clean Air Act.

State of New Jersey v. United States Environmental Protection Agency, 626 F.2d 1038, 1049–50 (D.C. Cir. 1980).

In interpreting section 553(b), however, the courts have not been wholly oblivious to the pressures under which agencies often operate.   See *Council of the Southern Mountains, Inc. v. Donovan*, 653 F.2d 573 (D.C. Cir. 1981).   *American Federation of Government Employees, AFL–CIO v. Block*, 655 F.2d 1153 (D.C. Cir. 1981), for example, countenanced the Secretary of Agriculture's failure to comply with public rulemaking requirements.   In response to a court order that it "forthwith" eliminate regional differences in the rate at which USDA inspectors examined slaughtered poultry, the Secretary had promulgated and made immediately effective new regulations governing the inspection process.   The court concluded that "the promulgation of emergency regulations   *   *   * was a reasonable and perhaps inevitable response to the injunctive court order," but it chastized the Secretary for making the regulations permanent and ordered him to entertain and respond to post-promulgation comments.

Shortly after President Reagan's inauguration in 1981, the new administration launched its efforts, which we have already examined in Chapter 2, to change the character and direction of federal regulation. Executive Order No. 12,291 directed agencies to postpone implementation of regulations promulgated prior to January 20, but not yet effective, so that the new managers could reevaluate them. Several agency actions summarily postponing or suspending promulgated rules for further review provoked suits alleging violations of the APA. The most notable of these, *Natural Resources Defense Council, Inc. v. EPA*, 683 F.2d 752 (3d Cir. 1982), held that the EPA's postponement of the effective date of regulations governing the discharge of toxic water pollutants was itself a "rule" to which section 553 of the APA applied, and that the agency's obligations under the executive order did not constitute "good cause" to dispense with rulemaking. The court specifically rejected the agency's alternative of inviting comments *after* announcing the postponement. See also *Public Citizen v. Department of Health and Human Services*, 671 F.2d 518 (D.C. Cir. 1981).

For a thorough discussion of the issues raised by this third exception to section 553, see Jordan, *The Administrative Procedure Act's "Good Cause" Exemption*, 36 Admin. L. Rev. 113 (1984). The exception for interpretative rules and statements of policy is examined in Koch, *Public Procedures for the Promulgation of Interpretative Rules and General Statements of Policy*, 64 Geo. L.J. 1047 (1976); Note, 43 Chi. L. Rev. 430 (1976).

The Evolving Judicial Understanding of Section 553

Section 553's sparse language has allowed agencies considerable freedom to fashion their own approaches to compliance, but has also provided numerous opportunities for judicial elaboration of its requirements. Several features of traditional agency practice have proved controversial. For example, section 553(c) does not require an agency to entertain oral communications and the typical informal rulemaking proceeding does not include a hearing of any kind. Some observers have been critical of the lack of opportunity for oral exchange generally, and of the foreclosure of cross-examination specifically. The comments of Professor Robinson, p. 424 supra, capture some of the flavor of this criticism. See also Dixon, *Rulemaking and the Myth of Cross-Examination*, 34 Admin. L. Rev. 389 (1982).

William Pedersen described another deficiency of the traditional informal model:

> The central loss in discarding the adjudicatory model in favor of notice and comment rulemaking was not cross-examination or oral testimony in particular; rather it was the focused and defined record which all the procedures used in adjudication were intended to produce. This record served as the basis for decision both at the agency level and on review. There is at present in informal rulemaking no parallel requirement that the record certified to the court be the fruit of special procedures designed to produce it. As a re-

sult the courts are confronted with huge unwieldy records, and are forced to spend undue effort in weighting the parts of each record and extracting underlying reasons from the documents—jobs which the agencies should have done themselves. * * *

Formal Records and Informal Rulemaking, 85 Yale L. J. 38, 61 (1975).

UNITED STATES v. NOVA SCOTIA FOOD PRODUCTS CORP.

United States Court of Appeals, Second Circuit, 1977.
568 F.2d 240.

GURFEIN, CIRCUIT JUDGE.

This appeal involving a regulation of the Food and Drug Administration is not here upon a direct review of agency action. It is an appeal from a judgment of the District Court * * * enjoining the appellants, after a hearing, from processing hot smoked whitefish except in accordance with time-temperature-salinity (T-T-S) regulations contained in 21 C.F.R. Part 122 (1977). * * *

* * *

The regulations cited above require that hot-process smoked fish be heated by a controlled heat process that provides a monitoring system positioned in as many strategic locations in the oven as necessary to assure a continuous temperature through each fish of not less that 180° F. for a minimum of 30 minutes for fish which have been brined to contain 3.5% water phase salt or at 150° F. for a minimum of 30 minutes if the salinity was at 5% water phase. * * *

Government inspection of appellants' plant established without question that the minimum T-T-S requirements were not being met. There is no substantial claim that the plant was processing whitefish under "insanitary conditions" in any other material respect. Appellants, on their part, do not defend on the ground that they were in compliance, but rather that the requirements could not be met if a marketable whitefish was to be produced. They defend upon the grounds that the regulation is invalid (1) because it is beyond the authority delegated by the statute; (2) because the FDA improperly relied upon undisclosed evidence in promulgating the regulation and because it is not supported by the administrative record; and (3) because there was no adequate statement setting forth the basis of the regulation. We reject the contention that the regulation is beyond the authority delegated by the statute, but we find serious inadequacies in the procedure followed in the promulgation of the regulation and hold it to be invalid as applied to the appellants herein.

The hazard which the FDA sought to minimize was the outgrowth and toxin formation of Clostridium botulinum Type E spores of the bacteria which sometimes inhabit fish. There had been an occurrence of several cases of botulism traced to consumption of fish from inland waters in 1960 and 1963 which stimulated considerable bacteriological research. These bacteria can be present in the soil and water of various regions. They can invade fish in their natural habitat and can be further disseminated in the course of evisceration and preparation of the fish for cooking.   A failure to destroy such spores through an adequate brining, thermal, and refrigeration process was found to be dangerous to public health.

The Commissioner of Food and Drugs ("Commissioner"), employing informal "notice-and-comment" procedures under 21 U.S.C.A. § 371(a), issued a proposal for the control of C. botulinum bacteria Type E in fish. * * *

* * * Responding to the Commissioner's invitation in the notice of proposed rulemaking, members of the industry, including appellants and the intervenor-appellant, submitted comments on the proposed regulation.

The Commissioner thereafter issued the final regulations in which he adopted certain suggestions made in the comments, including a suggestion by the National Fisheries Institute, Inc. ("the Institute"), the intervenor herein.   The original proposal provided that the fish would have to be cooked to a temperature of 180°F. for at least 30 minutes, if the fish have been brined to contain 3.5% water phase salt, with no alternative. In the final regulation, an alternative suggested by the intervenor "that the parameter of 150°F. for 30 minutes and 5% salt in the water phase be established as an alternate procedure to that stated in the proposed regulation for an interim period until specific parameters can be established" was accepted, but as a permanent part of the regulation rather than for an interim period.

The intervenor suggested that "specific parameters" be established. This referred to particular processing parameters for different species of fish on a "species by species" basis.   Such "species by species" determination was proposed not only by the intervenor but also by the Bureau of Commercial Fisheries of the Department of the Interior.   That Bureau objected to the general application of the T-T-S requirement proposed by the FDA on the ground that application of the regulation to all species of fish being smoked was not commercially feasible, and that the regulation should therefore specify time-temperature-salinity requirements, as developed by research and study, on a species-by-species basis.   The Bureau suggested that "wholesomeness considerations could be more practically and adequately realized by reducing processing temperature and using suitable concentrations of nitrite and salt."   The commissioner took cognizance of the suggestion, but decided, nevertheless, to impose the T-T-S requirement on *all* species of fish (except chub * * *).

He did acknowledge, however, in his "basis and purpose" statement * * * that "adequate times, temperatures and salt concentrations have not been demonstrated for each individual species of fish presently smoked."   The Commissioner concluded, nevertheless, that "the processing requirements of the proposed regulations are the safest now known to prevent the outgrowth and toxin formation of *C. botulinum* Type E."   He determined that "the conditions of current good manufacturing practice for this industry should be established without further delay."

The Commissioner did not answer the suggestion by the Bureau of Fisheries that nitrite and salt as additives could safely lower the high temperature otherwise required, a solution which the FDA had accepted in the case of chub. Nor did the Commissioner respond to the claim of Nova Scotia through its trade association the Association of Smoked Fish Processors, Inc., Technical Center that "[t]he proposed process requirements suggested by the FDA for hot processed smoked fish are neither commercially feasible nor based on sound scientific evidence obtained with the variety of smoked fish products to be included under this regulation."

Nova Scotia, in its own comment, wrote to the Commissioner that "the heating of certian types of fish to high temperatures will completely destroy the product." * * * We have noted above that the response given by the Commissioner was in general terms. He did not specifically aver that the T-T-S requirements as applied to whitefish were, in fact, commercially feasible. * * *

Appellants contend that there is an inadequate administrative record upon which to predicate judicial review, and that the failure to disclose to interested persons the factual material upon which the agency was relying vitiates the element of fairness which is essential to any kind of administrative action. Moreover, they argue that the "concise general statement of * * * basis and purpose" by the Commissioner was inadequate.

The question of what is an adequate "record" in informal rulemaking has engaged the attention of commentators for several years. The extent of the administrative record required for judicial review of informal rulemaking is largely a function of the scope of judicial review. Even when the standard of review is whether the promulgation of the rule was "arbitrary, capricious, an abuse of discretion, or otherwise not in accordance with law," as specified in 5 U.S.C.A. § 706(2)(A), judicial review must, nevertheless, be based on the "whole record" (id.). Adequate review of a determination requires an adequate record, if the review is to be meaningful. What will constitute an adequate record for meaningful review may vary with the nature of the administrative action to be reviewed. Review must be based on the whole record even when the judgment is one of policy, except that findings of fact such as would be required in an adjudicatory proceeding or in a formal "on the record" hearing for rulemaking need not be made. Though the action was informal, without an evidentiary record, the review must be "thorough, probing, [and] in depth." * * *

With respect to the content of the administrative "record," the Supreme Court has told us that in informal rulemaking, "the focal point for judicial review should be the administrative record already in existence, not some new record made initially in the reviewing court." See *Camp v. Pitts*, 411 U.S. 138 (1973).

No contemporaneous record was made or certified.[13] When, during the enforcement action, the basis for the regulation was sought through

---

13. A practice developed in the early years of the APA of not making a formal contemporaneous record, but rather, when challenged, to put together a historical record of what had been available for agency consideration at the time the regulation was promulgated.

pretrial discovery, the record was created by searching the files of the FDA and the memories of those who participated in the process of rule-making.   This resulted in what became Exhibit D at the trial of the injunction action.   Exhibit D consists of (1) Tab A containing the comments received from outside parties during the administrative "notice-and-comment" proceeding and (2) Tabs B through L consisting of scientific data and the like upon which the Commissioner now says he relied but which was not made known to the interested parties.

Appellants object to the exclusion of evidence in the District Court "aimed directly at showing that the scientific evidence relied upon by the FDA was inaccurate and not based upon a realistic appraisal of the true facts.   Appellants attempted to introduce scientific evidence to demonstrate that in fixing the processing parameters FDA relied upon tests in which ground fish were injected with many millions of botulism [sic] spores and then tested for outgrowth at various processing levels whereas the spore levels in nature are far less and outgrowth would have been prevented by far less stringent processing parameters." The District Court properly excluded the evidence.

In an enforcement action, we must rely exclusively on the record made before the agency to determine the validity of the regulation.   The exception to the exclusivity of that record is that "there may be independent judicial fact-finding when issues that were not before the agency are raised in a proceeding to *enforce* non-adjudicatory agency action." *Overton Park*, 401 U.S. at 415 (1971).   (Emphasis added.)

Though this is an enforcement proceeding and the question is close, we think that the "issues" *were* fairly before the agency and hence that *de novo* evidence was properly excluded by Judge Dooling.   Our concern is, rather, with the manner in which the agency treated the issues tendered.

The key issues were (1) whether, in the light of the rather scant history of botulism in whitefish, that species should have been considered separately rather than included in a general regulation which failed to distinguish species from species; (2) whether the application of the proposed T-T-S requirements to smoked whitefish made the whitefish commercially unsaleable; and (3) whether the agency recognized that prospect, but nevertheless decided that the public health needs should prevail even if that meant commercial death for the whitefish industry.   The procedural issues were whether, in the light of these key questions, the agency procedure was inadequate because (i) it failed to disclose to interested parties the scientific data and the methodology upon which it relied; and (ii) because it failed utterly to address itself to the pertinent question of commercial feasibility.

ISSUES

The history of botulism occurrence in whitefish, as established in the trial record, which we must assume was available to the FDA in 1970, is as follows.   Between 1899 and 1964 there were only eight cases of botulism reported as attributable to hot-smoked whitefish.   In all eight instances, vacuum-packed whitefish was involved.   All of the eight cases occurred in 1960 and 1963.   The industry has abandoned vacuum-packing, and there has not been a single case of botulism associated with commercially prepared whitefish since 1963, though 2,750,000 pounds of whitefish are processed annually. Thus, in the seven-year period from 1964 through 1970, 17.25 million pounds of whitefish have been commercially processed in the United States without a single reported case of botulism.   The evidence also disclosed that defendant Nova Scotia has been in business some 56 years, and that there has never been a case of botulism illness from the whitefish processed by it.

Interested parties were not informed of the scientific data, or at least of a selection of such data deemed important by the agency, so that comments could be addressed to the data.   Appellants argue that unless the scientific data relied upon by the agency are spread upon the public records, criticism of the methodology used or the meaning to be inferred from the data is rendered impossible.

We agree with appellants in this case, for although we recognize that an agency may resort to its own expertise outside the record in an informal rulemaking procedure, we do not believe that when the pertinent research material is readily available and the agency has no special expertise on the precise parameters involved, there is any reason to conceal the scientific data relied upon from the interested parties. * * * This is not a case where the agency methodology was based on material supplied by the interested parties themselves.   Here all the scientific research was collected by the agency, and none of it was disclosed to interested parties as the material upon which the proposed rule would be fashioned.[15]   Nor was an articulate effort made to connect the scientific requirements to available technology that would make commercial survival possible, though the burden of proof was on the agency.   This required it to "bear a burden of adducing a reasoned presentation supporting the reliability of its methodology."

Though a reviewing court will not match submission against counter-submission to decide whether the agency was correct in its conclusion on scientific matters (unless that conclusion is arbitrary), it will consider whether the agency has taken account of all "relevant factors and whether there has been a clear error of judgment." * * *

If the failure to notify interested persons of the scientific research upon which the agency was relying actually prevented the presentation of relevant comment, the agency may be held not to have considered all "the relevant factors."   We can think of no sound reasons for secrecy or reluctance to expose to public view (with an exception for trade secrets or national security) the ingredients of the deliberative process.   Indeed, the FDA's own regulations now specifically require that every notice of proposed rulemaking contain "references to all data and information on which the Commissioner relies for the proposal (copies or a full list of which shall be a part of the administrative file on the matter * * *)."   21 C.F.R. § 10.40(b)(1) (1977).   And this is, undoubtedly, the trend.

---

15. We recognize the problem posed by Judge Leventhal in *International Harvester,* 478 F.2d 615 (D.C. Cir. 1973), that a proceeding might never end if such submission required a reply *ad infinitum.*   Here the exposure of the scientific research relied on simply would have required a single round of comment addressed thereto.

We think that the scientific data should have been disclosed to focus on the proper interpretation of "insanitary conditions." When the basis for a proposed rule is a scientific decision, the scientific material which is be-~Rule lieved to support the rule should be exposed to the view of interested parties for their comment. One cannot ask for comment on a scientific paper without allowing the participants to read the paper. Scientific research is sometimes rejected for diverse inadequacies of methodology; and statistical results are sometimes rebutted because of a lack of adequate gathering technique or of supportable extrapolation. Such is the stuff of scientific debate. To suppress meaningful comment by failure to disclose the basic data relied upon is akin to rejecting comment altogether. For unless there is common ground, the comments are unlikely to be of a quality that might impress a careful agency. The inadequacy of comment in turn leads in the direction of arbitrary decision-making. We do not speak of findings of fact, for such are not technically required in the informal rulemaking procedures. We speak rather of what the agency should make known so as to elicit comments that probe the fundamentals. Informal rulemaking does not lend itself to a rigid pattern. Especially, in the circumstance of our broad reading of statutory authority in support of the agency, we conclude that the failure to disclose to interested persons the scientific data upon which the FDA relied was procedurally erroneous. Moreover the burden was upon the agency to articulate rationally why the rule should apply to a large and diverse class, with the same T-T-S parameters made applicable to all species. |APPlicATion

Appellants additionally attack the "concise general statement" required by APA, 5 U.S.C.A. § 553, as inadequate. We think that, in the circumstances, it was less than adequate. It is not in keeping with the rational process to leave vital questions, raised by comments which are of cogent materiality, completely unanswered. The agencies certainly have a good deal of discretion in expressing the basis of a rule, but the agencies do not have quite the prerogative of obscurantism reserved to legislatures.

* * *

The Secretary was squarely faced with the question whether it was necessary to formulate a rule with specific parameters that applied to all species of fish, and particularly whether lower temperatures with the addition of nitrite and salt would not be sufficient. Though this alternative was suggested by an agency of the federal government, its suggestion, though acknowledged, was never answered.

Moreover, the comment that to apply the proposed T-T-S requirements to whitefish would destroy the commercial product was neither discussed nor answered. We think that to sanction silence in the face of such vital questions would be to make the statutory requirement of a "concise general statement" less than an adequate safeguard against arbitrary decision-making.

* * *

One may recognize that even commercial infeasibility cannot stand in the way of an overwhelming public interest.   Yet the administrative process should disclose, at least, whether the proposed regulation is considered to be commercially feasible, or whether other considerations prevail even if commercial infeasibility is acknowledged.   This kind of forthright disclosure and basic statement was lacking in the formulation of the T-T-S standard made applicable to whitefish.   It is easy enough for an administrator to ban everything.   In the regulation of food processing, the worldwide need for food also must be taken into account in formulating measures taken for the protection of health.   In the light of the history of smoked whitefish to which we have referred, we find no articulate balancing here sufficient to make the procedure followed less than arbitrary.

*   *   *

We cannot, on this appeal, remand to the agency to allow further comments by interested parties, addressed to the scientific data now disclosed at the trial below.   We hold in this enforcement proceeding, therefore, that the regulation, as it affects non-vacuum-packed not-smoked whitefish, was promulgated in an arbitrary manner and is invalid.

Notes

1.   Judge Gurfein's opinion provides another illustration of the close linkage between review of agency rulemaking procedures and review of the substance of the rules they adopt.   His criticisms of the FDA's failure to respond to the suggestion that nitrite be permitted as an alternative preservative and its silence on the matter of commercial infeasibility are redolent of judicial treatment of the tire retread rule in *Brinegar* and of OSHA's benzene standard.

2.   Because FDA was operating under section 553 of the APA, Judge Gurfein's criticisms of the procedures it followed in promulgating the "smoked fish" regulations presumably have general import.   He chastizes the FDA for failing—when it proposed the regulations—to disclose scientific studies concerning the risk of botulism and methods of preventing it in fish.   He observes that the agency's practice in 1977—mandated by its own regulations—was to do so and notes that "this is undoubtedly the trend."   One can perhaps understand how the FDA in 1969 neglected to mention these studies—all of them, incidentally, available in the published literature—when one recalls that the agency was not then maintaining a contemporaneous record in rulemakings.   The studies emerged as part of the "record" for review that FDA lawyers compiled by scouring the agency's files and collecting all of the materials they thought *might have been* consulted when the regulations were adopted.   It is thus hardly surprising that the reconstructed record contained materials the defendants had not seen, or at least not had their attention drawn to, when the regulations were proposed.

The court's reaction to this omission, by no means trivial in principle, reflects two concerns.   Judge Gurfein comments on the special importance of the need for adversarial review of scientific evidence—"the stuff of scientific debate."   But his objection goes further: the FDA's failure to invite comment on the data was "akin to rejecting comment altogether."   The suggestion is that even in informal rulemaking there must be opportunity for critique and rebuttal of the facts that the agency accepts as justifying its rules.   But would not an even more effective way of meeting an adversary's case involve cross-examination and submission of rebuttal evidence once the effects of that examination are revealed, i.e., trial-type procedures? Could the court mandate such procedures under section 553?

3. Judge Gurfein's second procedural concern relates to the exclusiveness of the rulemaking "record." His ruling effectively forced agencies generally to adopt what by 1977 had become FDA practice, i.e., disclosing the sources on which it relied when publishing a proposed rule and collecting them with all of the comments in a package that comprises the "record" for possible judicial review. (The reader will recall that in *Auto Parts* Judge McGowan similarly suggested that such materials could comprise the "record" of informal rulemaking.) Judge Gurfein then accepts the FDA's claim that the court's review of its regulations should be confined to the (in this case reconstructed) "administrative record," a ruling supported by Supreme Court precedent. But is the agency likewise limited to the "record" it assembles during the rulemaking? Presumably it cannot present new evidence in court, but may it consider any materials that have not been made public in time for comment? And, if so, what kinds of materials?

Persistent Issues in Informal Agency Rulemaking

Section 553 of the APA speaks mainly—to the extent it speaks at all—to an agency's procedural obligations once it has decided to initiate regulation and publishes a notice of proposed rulemaking. And, as the *Nova Scotia* case and the materials later in this chapter reveal, the debate about the character of those obligations focuses primarily on the post-proposal period. But, from the perspective of persons who may be affected by an agency's rules, meaningful participation and influence also depend on what happens before a proposal is published. Such persons will want to discover possible subjects for rulemaking and, perhaps, consider how to direct an agency's attention away from their activities or to problems they want addressed. They will be concerned about the sources of information on which the agency relies, and desire opportunities to contribute information themselves. They will want to know, in advance if possible, all of the alternatives the agency is considering, and be able to communicate their views before the agency has made up its mind, even tentatively. All of these concerns, at some time, are likely to be reflected in claims for procedural protection based on statute or case law.

Choice of subjects for rulemaking. During the Carter presidency, executive officials became convinced that agency policymaking was too haphazard, that the targets selected often did not reflect a careful consideration of priorities, and that affected groups were too often surprised—and thus frequently annoyed—by new rulemaking initiatives. Accordingly, the administration, through a body called the Regulatory Council—a sort of "trade association" of regulatory agencies—required all executive branch agencies to prepare and, semiannually, to publish in the Federal Register an agenda of new and pending rules. As time went on, agency agendas became more elaborate; entries typically included a statement of the subject of the rule, a description of the problem to which it was addressed, a summary of alternatives considered, and a predicted time-table for completing rulemaking. It was hoped that the exercise of preparing an agenda would induce agency officials to consider which of the problems facing them most deserved their attention. Publication of the calendar theoretically also permitted members of the public to argue with an agency over the priorities it had chosen.

President Reagan disbanded the Regulatory Council and created the Task Force of Regulatory Relief, which coordinated the administration's initial efforts to curtail regulation and make decisions more cost-conscious. The practice of preparing and publishing agendas of pending and contemplated regulations has continued, however, and is now coordinated by OMB pursuant to the requirements of E.O. No. 12, 498, 50 Fed. Reg. 1036 (1985).

The APA provides that "each agency shall give an interested person the right to petition for the issuance, amendment, or repeal of a rule." 5 U.S.C.A. § 553(e). It is common for groups interested in an agency's activities to invoke this provision, often relying as well on language in the agency's own statute obligating it to accept and, often respond to public petitions. See, e.g., Toxic Substances Control Act § 21, 15 U.S.C.A. § 2620. The APA does not expressly mandate a response or set any time limit for consideration, but an agency's failure to respond within some reasonable period may be challengable in court as an abuse of discretion. See, e.g., *Telecommunications Research and Action Center v. FCC*, 750 F.2d 70 (D.C. Cir. 1984). The petition process is used most by "beneficiary" groups and public interest organizations, but industry associations—whose members are generally the targets of regulation—also frequently exercise their right to petition an agency, seeking relaxation of controls or, as often, changes in existing rules to permit the exploitation of new technologies.

Statutes that require a response within a fixed period can significantly affect an agency's behavior. Petitions may occasionally identify a serious problem that deserves higher rank in the agency's priorities. As often, however, they address problems to which the agency is already giving attention, and many are filed on the eve of an expected decision so that the petitioner can claim credit with constituents for precipitating the agency's action. Preparing a formal response to a petition requires substantial staff time and sometimes costly tests or investigations, potentially diverting resources from higher priority problems. Experiences such as these prompted the Consumer Product Safety Commission, whose original statute obligated it to respond to petitions within 120 days, to seek an amendment eliminating this mandatory response requirement. See Merrill, *CPSC Regulation of Cancer Risks in Consumer Products: 1972–1981*, 67 Va. L. Rev. 1261, 1363–64, 1374-75 (1981).

The argument in favor of statutory provisions that mandate a response to petitions for rulemaking is, of course, that they help assure that the agency will perform its job aggressively. The evidence of bureaucratic inertia across the federal government is a matter of debate, but some examples are notorious. During the first six years of operations, the CPSC issued product safety rules for only three products. OSHA has been severely criticized for not promulgating more standards for workplace carcinogens, critics observing that it has regulated fewer than 20 of the more than 200 carcinogenic chemicals known to be present in U.S. workplaces. See McGarity, *OSHA's Generic Carcinogen Policy: Rule Making under Scientific and Legal Uncertainty*, in J. NYHART & M. CARROW, eds. LAW AND SCIENCE IN COLLABORATION 55 (1983). OSHA has also been engaged for more than a decade in litigation over its failure to promulgate a so-called "field situation" standard for farm-workers—a standard petitioned for in 1974. See, e.g., *National Congress of Hispanic American Citizens v. Marshall*, 626 F.2d 882 (D.C. Cir. 1979).

There has been no comprehensive study of the many ways in which problems become subjects of agency rulemaking, but casual empiricism allows at least an anecdotal accounting. Often the initial subjects of an agency's attention will have been identified during Congressional consideration of its authorizing legislation. Thus, there was little doubt that OSHA would give early attention to asbestos, or that the CPSC would concern itself with lawnmowers. Such familiar problems often provide the publicity needed to precipitate passage of new laws. Occasionally, Congress will go further and specify in the statute itself a problem it expects the agency to address. The 1976 Toxic Substances Control Act, for example, directs EPA to regulate PCB's in accordance with a specific timetable. 15 U.S.C.A. § 2605(e). It is not uncommon—indeed it is routine—for members of congress to communicate *their* candidates for regulation to an agency. A powerful committee chairman can have major impact on an agency's agenda. A series of hearings in 1975 and 1976 on industry testing of drugs and food additives spearheaded by Senator Edward Kennedy, then chairman of two oversight subcommittees, led to a major enhancement of FDA's budget for the designated purpose of promulgating and enforcing new federal rules governing toxicological testing laboratories.

Congress has other ways of influencing the agendas of administrative agencies. Many environmental and safety laws of the 1970's create structures or procedures designed to affect the implementing agency's choice of targets. For example, the Occupational Safety and Health Act created the National Institute of Occupational Safety and Health (NIOSH) as an entity separate from OSHA, located in another department, HHS. NIOSH was created to provide expertise in identifying and evaluating workplace hazards, and its production of health assessments provides a continuing source of candidates for OSHA workplace standards—a source whose ostensible independence lends credibility to its recommendations. See T. GREENBERG, KNOWLEDGE AND DISCRETION IN GOVERNMENT REGULATION 20–21 (1984). The Toxic Substances Control Act reflects unusual Congressional self-consciousness about the systematic priority-setting. The Act creates an interagency testing committee, which is to consider and recommend to EPA chemicals for priority testing. EPA in turn is obligated, within one year, to promulgate rules mandating such testing by industry or publish in the Federal Register its reasons for concluding that testing is not necessary.   15 U.S.C.A. § 2603(e).

Perhaps the most powerful—but the most unpredictable and difficult to control—influences in an administrator's choice of rulemaking candidates fall under the heading of "public crises."   Top agency officials operate in a glare of publicity and pay attention to problems that are perceived as demanding immediate attention.   Of course, the press plays a major role in informing and influencing public attitudes, which members of Congress both respond to and help nurture.   Every era is marked by episodes of apparent public hazard, official wrong-doing, or marketplace abuse that elicit new rulemaking initiatives by administrators, if not new legislation.   Any attempt to provide examples would soon be outdated, but our point can be captured in a few names or phrases: Acid Rain, Welfare Fraud, EDB, Saccharin, Formaldehyde, Love Canal, and Three Mile Island.   Even this brief listing is a reminder of the substantial extent to which regulatory agendas are unplanned and uncontrollable.

Identification of options.   Unlike formal rulemaking or civil court proceedings, the procedures outlined in section 553 do not provide obvious opportunities for identifying disputable issues of fact or policy that an agency must resolve in framing final regulations.   The practice among federal agencies has changed dramatically since the 1960's.   Then notices of proposed rulemaking (NPRM) were often uninformative except to cognoscenti.   Proposals now typically describe the problem proposed rules are intended to address, set forth a contemplated regulatory text, and often specify issues on which comment is particularly invited.   Even so, NPRMs sometimes treat the agency's premises only briefly and may fail to discuss alternative approaches.   Additional reflection may surface new issues within the agency, or a thoughtful comment may uncover chinks in its analysis or advance new solutions.   When the agency is persuaded to depart from its proposed solution, it may confront claims that its original notice did not adequately describe the options it was considering.

In *Wagner Electric Corp. v. Volpe*, 466 F.2d 1013 (3d Cir. 1972), one of the first such challenges, the court set aside changes in the Department of Transportation's safety standard for automobile turn signals on the ground that the Secretary's proposal had not afforded interested persons adequate notice of the criteria he ultimately adopted.   The proposal had recited that the Secretary was considering the elimination of sampling and permissible failure rates for turn signals, thereby requiring all signals produced to meet existing performance criteria.   A number of manufacturers filed comments objecting to the proposed change unless the performance criteria were downgraded, but none submitted data directed to specific modifications in those criteria.   Without inviting additional comments, the Secretary adopted a final rule that eliminated the sampling and failure rate specifications *and* relaxed performance criteria. The Third Circuit concluded that the Secretary's procedure had deprived manufacturers, state agencies, and consumer groups of an effective opportunity to submit their views on what, if any, changes should be made in the performance criteria for turn signals.

Contrast *South Terminal Corp. v. EPA*, 504 F.2d 646, 658–59 (1st Cir. 1974), in which the petitioners challenged EPA's plan to reduce automobile pollution around Boston. EPA had proposed an on-street parking ban during certain hours, a $5 surcharge for off-street parking, and a one-day-a-week ban on automobile travel on Boston's circumferential highway which relied on a windshield sticker system. EPA's notice specifically requested comments on the sticker system and assured the public that the agency would be influenced by what it heard. The final plan deleted the sticker system and the parking surcharge, which was also heavily criticized, and substituted reductions in parking spaces, preferential treatment for car pools, special review of new parking facilities, and semi-annual for annual inspection of automobiles. The petitioners contended that the final regulations departed so "radically" from the proposal as to have denied them an effective opportunity for comment. Judge Campbell rejected this claim:

> Although the changes were substantial, they were in character with the original scheme and were additionally foreshadowed in proposals and comments advanced during the rulemaking. Parties had been warned that strategies might be modified in light of their suggestions. * * *

> We conclude that interested persons were sufficiently alerted to likely alternatives to have known what was at stake. In the published notice, mention had been made of alternative measures for "effective reductions" in the number of parking spaces in downtown Boston, Logan Airport and "other trip attraction centers throughout the metropolitan area." EPA made plain its intention to adopt "stringent controls." * * *

> A hearing is intended to educate an agency to approaches different from its own; in shaping the final rule it may and should draw on the comments tendered. The plan seems a logical outgrowth of the hearing and related procedures. * * * As the Court of Appeals for the District of Columbia Circuit recently said:

> > "The requirement of submission of a proposed rule for comment does not automatically generate a new opportunity for comment merely because the rule promulgated by the agency differs from the rule it proposed, partly at least in response to submissions.[51]

> *International Harvester Co. v. Ruckelshaus*, 478 F.2d 615, 632 (D.C. Cir. 1973).

> Cases cited by petitioners in which there was no notice or opportunity to comment or submit evidence are not in point, nor is their reliance on *Wagner Electric Corp. v. Volpe*. A circumscribed announcement, as in the latter case, that standards for testing an automotive product would be revised, is not to be compared to EPA's comprehensive notice. The former did not

51. "A contrary rule would lead to the absurdity that in rule-making under the APA the agency can learn from the comments on its proposals only at the peril of starting a new procedural round of commentary."

make it clear that interrelated aspects, such as performance criteria, would also be considered.   The instant notice left no doubt that EPA would consider all reasonable alternatives for cutting down vehicle use.

See also *United Steelworkers v. Marshall*, 647 F.2d 1189 (D.C. Cir. 1980), *cert. denied* 453 U.S. 913 (1981), upholding OSHA's standard for occupational exposure to lead, which embodied an ambient standard of 50 micrograms per cubic meter of air after the agency had originally proposed a reduction only to 100.   Judge Wright concluded that the agency's notice had clearly alerted all participants to the possibility that it might find a lower limit was necessary to protect worker health.   But see *Animal Health Institute v. FDA*, 1977-1978 Developments, Food Drug Cosm L. Rep. (CCH) ¶ 38,154 (D.D.C. February 8, 1978), which reversed the FDA for relying upon (and arguably misinterpreting) a post-proposal revision in the sophisticated quantitative risk formula it had put forward as the basis for regulating animal drugs residues in food.

Willingness to consider comments.   Participants in the administrative process often contend that notice-and-comment rule-making fails to allow meaningful participation in the formulation of policy because an agency is unwilling seriously to consider changes in its proposed rule. Compare *Nova Scotia Food Products Corp. v. United States*, supra p. 440.   But it is too cynical to conclude that comments responding to a NPRM have no prospect of altering an agency's contemplated policy. Prior to the *Petroleum Refiners* court challenge, for example, the FTC, in response to comments from refiners, made several significant changes in its definition of "octane rating."

The problem here is the converse of that in *Wagner Electric*.   Indeed, these two problems frame a dilemma: if an agency engages in extensive consultations with third parties before publishing its notice and weighs all conceivable alternatives to the proposed rule on which it invites comments, any objections voiced or information submitted are far less likely to have an impact on the final rule.   Yet if an agency wants to obtain outside views before it has made up its own mind, how does it frame a proposal that is sufficiently detailed to afford adequate notice?

Agencies have many ways of soliciting information before developing proposed regulations.   Several make it a practice of holding public meetings when a problem emerges in order to elicit ideas about how it should respond.   This is one means of avoiding the dilemma posed by the *Wagner Electric* case on the one hand and claims of unresponsiveness on the other.   Holding a public meeting on a controversial problem has one additional advantage for the agency, though it also entails some risk.   The very announcement of such a meeting can sometimes be depicted for the press as the prompt response of a concerned administrator.   But it may be difficult to predict, much less control, the tenor of the meeting itself. An agency head may find himself sitting through vituperative or theatrical criticisms of his performance, recorded by eager media, with no effective opportunity to respond.   In the 1970's the Secretary of Transportation devised a procedure for developing vehicle safety standards that represents one workable response to the dilemma.   The Secretary would first convene a public meeting or conference to canvass ways of dealing with a particular safety issue. Following the meeting, in which any interested person could participate, he weighed the options and developed a proposed standard, which was then published for further comment prior to final adoption.

Another technique available to agencies, often mandated by statute, is to discuss contemplated rules at a preliminary stage with a permanent advisory committee which includes experts in the field or representatives of affected interests. The agency then develops a formal proposal for submission to the usual notice-and-comment procedure of the APA. See Federal Insecticide, Fungicide, and Rodenticide Act, 7 U.S.C.A. § 136w(d); Occupational Safety and Health Act, 29 U.S.C.A. § 656. Still another approach is the practice of publishing an advance notice of proposed rule-making as a first public stage of the process. The objectives of this device are several. Primarily it is intended to meet objections that agency decisionmakers have made up their minds about desired policy when they publish a proposed rule. An ANPR, published before agency officials have selected an option—conceivably even before they have identified alternative options—can provide a genuine opportunity for the public to influence the content of agency policy. It can also permit the agency to identify pockets of resistance to, or arguments against, new policies before committing its full energies and prestige to an unpopular initiative.

Publication of an ANPR has become a common, though not universal, practice among federal agencies. The Occupational Safety and Health Administration has committed itself to publish an advance notice as the first step in establishment standards for cancer hazards. 29 C.F.R. § 1990.141, 45 Fed. Reg. 5001, 5285 (1980). Amendments to the Consumer Product Safety Act in 1981 obligate the CPSC to proceed in this fashion when it contemplates setting a standard for, or banning, a consumer product. Consumer Product Safety Amendments of 1981, Pub. L. No. 97–35, § 1206, amending 15 U.S.C.A. § 2077.

The frequency with which agencies now utilize one or more of these means suggests that *Wagner Electric*-type claims, while common, are not often well founded. More troublesome are the situations where an agency receives new information late in or after the comment period, which it believes supports its proposal but on which, by hypothesis, there has been no opportunity for comment. See *Animal Health Institute v. FDA*, supra.

Sources of information. Agencies are also criticized for relying on information supplied by the potential targets of regulation. But in many circumstances, persons outside an agency may be in a better position to supply the information on which rules should be based and perhaps in some cases even better equipped to make judgments about what rules should contain. It is arguable, for example, that the tire retreaders in *Brinegar* were better able than the Secretary of Transportation to assess the technological feasibility of permanent imprinting of various types of information. The FDA's relative lack of expertise in smoking of fish was exposed, or at least effectively put in issue, in *Nova Scotia*, supra p. 440.

The original Consumer Product Safety Act, 15 U.S.C.A. § 2051, et seq., embodied an explicit Congressional judgment that agencies sometimes would rely on those they regulate. The Act required the CPSC initially to publish a "determination that a consumer product safety standard is necessary," accompanied by an invitation for any person to offer to develop a proposal. Id. at § 2056(b). Congress clearly contemplated that offerors often would include manufacturers, distributors, or retailers of products for which standards were to be developed. See generally Scalia and Goodman, *Procedural Aspects of the Consumer Product Safety Act*, 20 U.C.L.A. L. Rev. 899 (1973). This experiment was abandoned in 1981, however, when Congress was persuaded that the "invitation for proposal" procedure was in major part responsible for embarrassing delays in the Commission's issuance of product safety standards. See generally Schwartz, *The Consumer Product Safety Commission: A Flawed Product of the Consumer Decade*, 51 G.W.U. L. Rev. 35 (1982).

An agency's dependence on private information and expertise creates the risk that it will hear or listen to only one side of an issue. This risk is particularly acute when an agency's rules have immediate impact on groups whose interests sharply diverge. The original Consumer Product Safety Act anticipated this problem by requiring the Commission to prescribe regulations assuring that "interested persons (including representatives of consumers and consumer organizations)" have an opportunity to participate in the development of a product safety standard by any outside offeror and requiring offerors to maintain public records disclosing the course of development and any comments received from third parties. The FDA, lacking such statutory guidance, in 1975 sought a middle course, displaying perhaps greater concern for possible charges of preferential access than its need for information. The agency announced that it generally would no longer make available to or discuss with any outsiders preliminary drafts of proposed regulations. In cases where it depended on industry data or expertise, the FDA said it would publish in the Federal Register an announcement of the availability of its preliminary draft to any interested person.

During the 1970's, several agencies experimented with a novel means of broadening their sources of information in rulemaking by providing financial support for organizations or individuals whose viewpoints might not otherwise be expressed on the public record. The Magnuson-Moss Amendments to the FTC Act specifically authorized the Federal Trade Commission to provide support for "public participation" in trade regulation rule proceedings. Other agencies asserted authority to fund "public interest" participants based on their organic laws or inherent authority, several successfully. The FDA's five-year effort to implement such a program, however, was nullified in *Pacific Legal Foundation v. Goyan*, 664 F.2d 1221 (4th Cir. 1981), which contains language that casts doubt on the authority of other agencies, save for those like the FTC that have been expressly empowered to fund public participation. For an assessment of the FTC experience, see Boyer, *Funding Public Participation in Agency Proceedings: The Federal Trade Commission Experience*, 70

Geo. L.J. 51 (1981).   Agency funding of public participation is viewed from a broader perspective in Tobias, *Of Public Funds and Public Participation: Resolving The Issue of Agency Authority to Reimburse Public Participations in Administrative Proceedings*, 82 Colum. L. Rev. 906 (1982).

Agency expertise has in many areas not kept pace with official responsibility.   Furthermore, government personnel ceilings have encouraged agencies to rely on contract services for many of the studies and investigations needed for regulatory decisionmaking.   The reader will recall that in adopting its standard for cotton dust, OSHA placed substantial weight on a consultant's study of economic effects.   *American Textile Manufacturers Institute v. Donovan*, 452 U.S. 490 (1981), supra, p. 377.   Reliance on consultant-generated studies and analyses has become routine in many agencies, but occasionally it has led to court challenges to the agency's underlying rule.   A recent illustration is *United Steelworkers of America v. Marshall*, 647 F.2d 1189 (D.C. Cir. 1980), *cert. denied* 453 U.S. 913 (1981), a challenge to OSHA's lead standard.   The agency had relied on contract consultants for most of its information on economic feasibility and for analysis of the relevant portions of the rulemaking record.   This conduct was challenged as improper, but the court of appeals disagreed:

> * * * [Lead Industry Association] contends that the Assistant Secretary hired so many consultants and relied on them so heavily for so many tasks that she essentially abdicated her responsibility for setting the lead standard to outsiders.   OSHA itself admits it lacked sufficient staff expertise to deal with all the important issues without outside help, thus perhaps earning LIA's ironic observation that the agency requests deference to its expertise while pleading it does not have enough of that commodity.   But the question is whether the use of consultants here violated the law.
>
> The record shows that OSHA did make rather broad requests for help from the consultants.   * * *   OSHA relied heavily on David Burton Associates (DBA) and Nicholas Ashford and his Center for Policy Alternatives (CPA) in examining the data on feasibility and developing a "technology-forcing" rationale for the standard.   The agency hired a number of other expert consultants, giving them fairly broad mandates to summarize and evaluate data in the record, prepare record data for computer processing, and help draft portions of the Preamble and the final standard.   LIA argues that such reliance on outsiders invites abuse, even if one assumes the honesty of the ones in this case, since hired hands have a financial incentive to tell the agency what it wants to hear, and have no civil service protection against retaliation for telling uncomfortable truths.
>
> LIA asserts that no case has considered and upheld the legality of such reliance.   But neither can LIA locate a case or statute forbidding such a practice * * * .   If anything, the law generally bearing on the issue supports OSHA here.   The OSH Act empowers the agency to employ expert consultants, and OSHA might have possessed that power even without express statutory authority.   * * *
>
> LIA's position thus comes down to the challenge that OSHA has violated the principle of *Morgan v. United States*, 298 U.S. 468, 480–81 (1936) (*Morgan*

I): "The one who decides must hear," and an agency denies the parties a true hearing if the official who acts for the agency has not personally confronted the evidence and the arguments. Though *Morgan I* expressly allowed agency officials to rely on their subordinates in reviewing the record, it did not, of course, address the question of outside consultants. Nevertheless, applying the general principle of *Morgan I*, we see that LIA cannot buttress its general allegation of excessive reliance with any specific proof that the Assistant Secretary failed to confront personally the essential evidence and arguments in setting the final standard. Without at this point addressing the substantive validity of the lead standard, we note that in the lengthy Preamble and Attachments to the final standard the decisionmaker reviewed the evidence and explained the evidentiary bases for each part of the standard. Moreover, the Assistant Secretary demonstrated her independence from the consultants by strongly criticizing some of their conclusions on the key issue of feasibility.

To inquire further would be to probe impermissibly into the mental processes by which the Assistant Secretary made her decision. The unsupported allegation that hired consultants might have an incentive to act dishonestly cannot overcome the presumption that agency officials and those who assist them have acted properly. Thus we generally see no reason to force agencies to hire enormous regular staffs versed in all conceivable technological issues, rather than use their appropriations to hire specific consultants for specific problems.

LIA's second attack goes to *specific* uses of consultants, and alleges damage to the state of the rulemaking record, rather than to the Assistant Secretary's fulfillment of her personal responsibility. After closing the record, OSHA sought help from outside consultants in reviewing the record and preparing the Preamble. Two consultants were primary. The agency asked David Burton and DBA to help review the record to determine the feasibility of a permissible air-lead standard of 50 μug/m^3, as opposed to the 100 μg/m^3 standard the agency had proposed in the original notice of rulemaking, and on which most of the public commentary had focused. And OSHA asked Nicholas Ashford and CPA to analyze, in light of the record, the possibility of making a correlation between air-lead levels and blood-lead levels. Both these consultants had previously aided OSHA by supplying on-the-record reports and testifying as expert witnesses at the public hearings. Both fulfilled the new requests by submitting written reports, of 117 and 192 pages respectively, neither of which the agency has released or placed in the rulemaking record. LIA contends that the reports are illegal *ex parte* communications which * * * constitute "secret briefs" and off-the-record evidence which LIA was deprived of a chance to rebut and the court a chance to review.

* * * [T]he documents show that the communications between the agency and the consultants were simply part of the deliberative process of drawing conclusions from the public record. The consultants acted after the record was closed as the functional equivalent of agency staff, so the question of the legal propriety of OSHA's reliance on DBA and CPA is foreclosed by our earlier conclusion that neither the APA nor the *Home Box Office* doctrine imposes a separation-of-functions requirement on the agencies. Thus, even though we readily assume that OSHA used the consultants' reports—and even incorporated parts of them verbatim in the Preamble—LIA has suffered no legal prejudice from such use. * * *

When performed by agency *staff*, this sort of sophisticated review of evidence has always been recognized as legitimate participation in the deliberative process. And the circuit courts, in applying the intra-agency exemption to the Freedom of Information Act, 5 U.S.C.A. § 552(b)(5), have recognized that where outside consultants so engage in the deliberative process there is no *functional* difference between staff and consultants, and so there should be no *legal* difference. * * *

Recognizing that the principle of Exemption 5 of the FOIA bears generally on the question of post-hearing contacts with consultants, we find ourselves fortunate in having before us Judge Friendly's recent opinion holding that Exemption 5 applies directly to the very reports at issue in this case. After petitioning for review of this rulemaking, LIA went to federal court in New York to seek disclosure of various consultants' reports under the FOIA. In *Lead Industries Association, Inc. v. OSHA*, 610 F.2d 70 (2d Cir. 1979), Judge Friendly examined the same affidavits, agreements, and indices that we have examined, and concluded that both the DBA report and the CPA report contributed to the process by which the Assistant Secretary made her final decision. He conceded that the reports might contain some factual matter, but asserted that in a vast rule-making like this one such information was necessarily incident to and not severable from the process of summary and analysis. He suggested, moreover, that to the extent the reports drew inferences from and weighed the evidence they were more truly "deliberative" and thus better candidates for exemption than mere summaries of the record.

Finally, responding to LIA's argument that CPA's off-the-record response to criticisms of its earlier report and testimony was improper, Judge Friendly found that the response contained no new evidentiary material, and that "the answers are of the same sort that could have been made by a knowledgeable member of OSHA's staff defending his expert witness' credibility before the decisionmaker." Thus, the earlier participation of these consultants as expert witnesses in no way disqualifies them as aides in the final decision. Indeed, their participation is even less suspect than that of the staff advocates we discussed earlier, since any predisposition they held was not a result of their factual research and not, as in the case of staff, an incident of serving as legal advocates for an institutional position. * * *

Many federal agencies, by statute or choice, use committees of outside advisers to assist in the development of regulations. Typically, an advisory committee is composed of experts, some of whom may hold jobs in industries directly concerned with the actions of the agency it is supposed to advise. The federal government includes—for they are counted as separate entities in the OMB organization chart—more than 500 advisory committees. In 1972 Congress responded to concerns about industry influence on regulatory policy conveyed through advisory committees, concerns heightened by the secrecy that often surrounded advisory committee deliberations. It enacted the Federal Advisory Committee Act of 1972, 5 U.S.C.A. App. I, whose basic requirements are summarized in Chapter 1, supra p. 54. Some of the most troublesome issues under the Advisory Committee Act have related to the circumstances under which a committee's deliberations may be closed to the public. The 1972 Act simply incorporated the FOIA exemptions, allowing closing when a meeting dealt with a subject that would not have to be disclosed if in record form.   This approach was workable with some exemptions, such as (b)(6) (privacy) and (b)(4) (trade secrets), but proved more difficult with others, notably (b)(5), which exempts inter- and intra-agency memoranda. Some agencies took the view that any committee discussion which, if reduced to memorandum form, would be exempt from disclosure under (b)(5) could be closed, a view that encountered stormy weather in court. E.g., *Wolfe v. Weinberger*, 403 F. Supp. 238 (D.D.C. 1975).   In the Government in the Sunshine Act, Congress, recognizing the incompatibility between exemptions devised for documentary material and "access" requirements designed for meetings, made the same standards for closing applicable to federal advisory committees as it was applying to multi-member agencies.   See 5 U.S.C.A. App. I, § 10(d).

Advisory committees can perform a variety of functions in the regulatory process, including the review or development of proposed regulations.   In highly technical areas they provide a means of enlisting in temporary government service expertise that the government probably could not attract in full-time employees.   During the early 1970's, when the FACA was enacted, many members of Congress were suspicious that advisory committees had become vehicles for private interest group influence in government decisionmaking.   By the latter part of the decade, however, Congress was again mandating agency consultation with advisory committees as a prelude to rulemaking under several statutes, including the Toxic Substances Control Act, 15 U.S.C.A. § § 2601, 2629 and the Medical Device Amendments to the Food, Drug, and Cosmetic Act, 21 U.S.C.A. § § 351-60.   Amendments in 1981 to the Consumer Product Safety Act obligate the CPSC to establish a panel of outside scientists to review its staff's findings whenever the agency contemplates regulation of a product believed to pose a risk of cancer, mutagenic damage, or birth defects.   See Merrill, *CPSC Regulation of Cancer Risks in Consumer Products: 1972-1981*, 67 Va. L. Rev. 1261, 1375 (1981).

Judicial Demands for Oral Hearings

In a series of decisions in the early 1970's the D.C. Circuit Court of Appeals, and in one case the Fourth Circuit, purported to require agencies making rules in complex fields to provide participants at least limited opportunity for a trial-type hearing.

In *International Harvester Co. v. Ruckelshaus*, 478 F.2d 615 (D.C. Cir. 1973), the court set aside the EPA's refusal to extend a 1975 deadline for achieving limits on automotive emissions.   Judge Leventhal found fatal deficiencies in the agency's response to manufacturer criticisms of its methods for determining the feasibility of the deadline. The court directed the EPA, on remand, to permit "some opportunity for cross-examination" on technical issues, and provide the participants "an opportunity to address themselves to matters not previously put before them * * * "   Judge Leventhal did not suggest that EPA was subject to the APA's formal rulemaking requirements, nor did he hold that section 553 required oral hearings.   Rather, he relied on the Clean Air Act's requirement that EPA provide a "public hearing" before reaching a decision and on the court's inability to engage in meaningful review if the agency's factual predicate had not been thus tested.

Appalachian Power Co. v. EPA, 477 F.2d 495 (4th Cir. 1973), set aside the EPA's approval, under section 10 of the Clean Air Act, of state plans for achieving ambient air standards. The Act required each state to hold a "hearing" before adopting its plan. The Fourth Circuit held that the EPA could itself dispense with a hearing only if the state hearing had been adequate, which, according to the court, meant the "opportunity to submit an effective presentation" and, if proper "in the context of the issues involved, 'cross-examination on the crucial issues.'" The court relied not on section 553 or the Clean Air Act, but on its need for a record that would permit meaningful judicial review of EPA's decision.

The *Appalachian Power* court quoted liberally from an earlier D.C. Circuit opinion, *Walter Holm & Co. v. Hardin*, 449 F.2d 1009 (D.C. Cir. 1971), a challenge to a USDA marketing order issued pursuant to the Agricultural Marketing Agreement Act of 1937. The statute required orders to be issued after "due notice of an opportunity for a hearing," but the Secretary of Agriculture had long followed a practice of issuing, without formal proceedings, "regulations" interpreting and adopting existing marketing orders. The Secretary's 1955 Tomato Marketing Order authorized the issuance of future regulations establishing, "in terms of grades, sizes, or both, minimum standards of quality and maturity." Subsequent USDA "regulations" were challenged by importers of Mexican tomatoes, who claimed that they gave "mature green" tomatoes an unjustified competitive advantage over "vine ripe" tomatoes. The court of appeals held that the plaintiffs were entitled to a hearing, including limited cross-examination, on the crucial commercial issues involved in tomato marketing control. While alluding to the "due notice of an opportunity for a hearing" language of the Marketing Act, Judge Leventhal justified the court's demand for cross-examination in terms of the factual issues before the Secretary and fairness to the plaintiffs.

Perhaps the most notable case in this sequence is *Mobil Oil Corp. v. FPC*, 483 F.2d 1238 (D.C. Cir. 1973), a suit to review an order setting minimum rates to be charged by natural gas pipelines for transporting liquid hydrocarbons. The petitioners raised a host of objections to the Commission's order, but a key claim was that the agency had improperly denied them the opportunity to cross-examine the evidence on which it relied on allocating pipeline costs between gaseous and liquid products. Though the Natural Gas Act specified that the Commission could act only "after a hearing," the agency contended that, under *Florida East Coast*, it could proceed in accordance with section 553.

Judge Wilkey's opinion agreed that the FPC was not statutorily required to engage in formal rulemaking, but held the Commission was still obligated to accord the petitioners a broader opportunity to contest its factual premises than informal procedures could assure:

> Flexibility in fitting administrative procedures to particular functions is critically important in evaluating the APA and has been a dominant theme in a number of opinions by this court. No court, to our knowledge, has ever

treated the explicit language of section 553 on the one hand and sections 556 and 557 on the other as expressing every type of procedure that might be called for in a particular situation. * . * *

* * * [A]n examination of the purposes and provisions of the substantive statute being administered may require that more than the comparatively feeble protections of section 553 of the APA may be called for. * * *

The degree of fact dispute resolution necessary in a particular proceeding is directly related to the degree of evidentiary support required by Congress in establishing a factual basis for a proposed rate. If a relatively high degree of evidentiary support is required in establishing a factual predicate, the rule-making procedures must be designed to create this. * * *

The Natural Gas Act explicitly states that factual determinations must be supported by "substantial evidence." Unlike many other forms of rule-making, rate-making necessarily rests upon findings of facts. The phrase "substantial evidence" is a term of art well recognized in administrative law. This requirement imposes a considerable burden on the agency and limits its discretion in arriving at a factual predicate. * * *

* * * Clearly some evidence supporting the FPC's finding must be in the record. *More importantly for our purposes, the rule that the "whole record" be considered—both evidence for and against—means that the procedures must provide some mechanism for interested parties to introduce adverse evidence and criticize evidence introduced by others.* This process of introduction and criticism helps assure that the factual basis of the FPC rates will be accurate and provides the reviewing court with a record from which it can determine if the agency has properly exercised its discretion. * * *

Informal comments simply cannot create a record that satisfies the substantial evidence test. Even if controverting *information* is submitted in the form of comments by adverse parties, the procedure employed cannot be relied upon as adequate. A "whole record," as that phrase is used in this context, does not consist merely of the raw data introduced by the parties. It includes the process of testing and illumination ordinarily associated with adversary, adjudicative procedures. Without this critical element, informal comments, even by adverse parties, are two halves that do not make a whole. Thus, it is adversary procedural devices which permit testing and elucidation that raise information from the level of mere inconsistent data to evidence "substantial" enough to support rates. * * *

For other cases mandating "hybrid rulemaking," see *Public Service Commission v. FPC*, 487 F.2d 1043 (D.C. Cir. 1973), *vacated and remanded* 417 U.S. 964 (1974); *Portland Cement Association v. Ruckelshaus*, 486 F.2d 375 (D.C. Cir. 1973), *cert. denied* 417 U.S. 921 (1974). Compare Wright, *The Courts and the Rulemaking Process: The Limits of Judicial Review*, 59 Cornell L. Rev. 375 (1974).

The effects of these rulings were problematic. Only the Department of Agriculture, following *Walter Holm*, ever held an evidentiary hearing with opportunity for cross-examination. In each of the other cases the agency was able, usually with the agreement of the parties involved, to resolve the disputed issues without resorting to formal proceedings.

For example, following *International Harvester,* the EPA modified its position on the 1975 deadline, but it did so without affording an opportunity for cross-examination. According to one account "Chrysler, which had vociferously insisted on the need to cross-examine, never once requested an opportunity to do so. And although Ford requested an opportunity to cross-examine the EPA staff members * * * it accepted the EPA's alternative offer of an off-the-record conference with those staff members." Williams, *"Hybrid Rulemaking" Under the Administrative Procedure Act: A Legal and Empirical Analysis,* 42 U. Chi. L. Rev. 401, 434 (1975); see also Stewart, *The Development of Administrative and Quasi-Constitutional Law in Judicial Review of Environmental Decisionmaking: Lessons from the Clean Air Act,* 62 Iowa L. Rev. 713 (1977).

VERMONT YANKEE NUCLEAR POWER CORP. v. NATURAL RESOURCES DEFENSE COUNCIL, INC.

Supreme Court of the United States, 1978.
435 U.S. 519, 98 S.Ct. 1197, 55 L.Ed.2d 460.

MR. JUSTICE REHNQUIST delivered the opinion of the Court.

* * * [I]n *United States v. Allegheny-Ludlum Steel Corp.,* 406 U. S. 742 (1972), and *United States v. Florida East Coast R. Co.,* we held that generally speaking * * * section [553] of the [Administrative Procedure] Act established the maximum procedural requirements which Congress was willing to have the courts impose upon agencies in conducting rulemaking procedures.[1] * * * This is not to say necessarily that there are no circumstances which would ever justify a court in overturning agency action because of a failure to employ procedures beyond those required by the statute. But such circumstances, if they exist, are extremely rare.

Even apart from the Administrative Procedure Act this Court has for more than four decades emphasized that the formulation of procedures was basically to be left within the discretion of the agencies to which Congress had confided the responsibility for substantive judgments. * * *

* * * [T]he Court of Appeals for the District of Columbia Circuit * * * seriously misread or misapplied this statutory and decisional law. * * *

Under the Atomic Energy Act of 1954, 42 U.S.C.A. § 2011 *et seq.,* the Atomic Energy Commission[2] was given broad regulatory authority over

---

1. While there was division in this Court in *United States v. Florida East Coast R. Co.,* with respect to the constitutionality of such an interpretation in a case involving ratemaking, which MR. JUSTICE DOUGLAS and MR. JUSTICE STEWART felt was "adjudicatory" within the terms of the Act, the cases in the Court of Appeals for the District of Columbia Circuit which we review here involve rule-making procedures in their most pristine sense.

2. The licensing and regulatory functions of the Atomic Energy Commission (AEC) were transferred to the Nuclear Regulatory Commission (NRC) by the Energy Reorganization Act of 1974. Hereinafter both the AEC and NRC will be referred to as the Commission.

STATUTE

the development of nuclear energy.   Under the terms of the Act, a utility seeking to construct and operate a nuclear power plant must obtain a separate permit or license at both the construction and the operation stage of the project.   In order to obtain the construction permit, the utility must file a preliminary safety analysis report, an environmental report, and certain information regarding the antitrust implications of the proposed project.   This application then undergoes exhaustive review by the Commission's staff and by the Advisory Committee on Reactor Safeguards (ACRS), a group of distinguished experts in the field of atomic energy. Both groups submit to the Commission their own evaluations, which then become part of the record of the utility's application.   The Commission staff also undertakes the review required by the National Environmental Policy Act of 1969 (NEPA), and prepares a draft environmental impact statement, which, after being circulated for comment, is revised and becomes a final environmental impact statement.   Thereupon a three-member Atomic Safety and Licensing Board conducts a public adjudicatory hearing, and reaches a decision which can be appealed to the Atomic Safety and Licensing Appeal Board, and currently, in the Commission's discretion, to the Commission itself.   The final agency decision may be appealed to the courts of appeals.   The same sort of process occurs when the utility applies for a license to operate the plant, except that a hearing need only be held in contested cases and may be limited to the matters in controversy.

*   *   *

FACTS   In December 1967, after the mandatory adjudicatory hearing and necessary review, the Commission granted petitioner Vermont Yankee a permit to build a nuclear power plant in Vernon, Vt.   Thereafter, Vermont Yankee applied for an operating license.   Respondent Natural Resources Defense Council (NRDC) objected to the granting of a license, however, and therefore a hearing on the application commenced on August 10, 1971.   Excluded from consideration at the hearings, over NRDC's objection, was the issue of the environmental effects of operations to reprocess fuel or dispose of wastes resulting from the reprocessing operations.   This ruling was affirmed by the Appeal Board in June 1972.

In November 1972, however, the Commission, making specific reference to the Appeal Board's decision with respect to the Vermont Yankee license, instituted rulemaking proceedings that would specifically deal with the question of consideration of environmental effects associated with the uranium fuel cycle in the individual cost-benefit analyses for light water cooled nuclear power reactors.   The notice of proposed rulemaking offered two alternatives, both predicated on a report prepared by the Commission's staff entitled "Environmental Survey of the Nuclear Fuel Cycle."   The first would have required no quantitative evaluation of the environmental hazards of fuel reprocessing or disposal because the Environmental Survey had found them to be slight.   The second would have specified numerical values for the environmental impact of this part of the fuel cycle, which values would then be incorporated into a table, along with the other relevant factors, to determine the overall cost-benefit balance for each operating license.

Much of the controversy in this case revolves around the procedures used in the rulemaking hearing which commenced in February 1973. In a supplemental notice of hearing the Commission indicated that while discovery or cross-examination would not be utilized, the Environmental Survey would be available to the public before the hearing along with the extensive background documents cited therein. All participants would be given a reasonable opportunity to present their position and could be represented by counsel if they so desired. Written and, time permitting, oral statements would be received and incorporated into the record. All persons giving oral statements would be subject to questioning by the Commission. At the conclusion of the hearing, a transcript would be made available to the public and the record would remain open for 30 days to allow the filing of supplemental written statements. More than 40 individuals and organizations representing a wide variety of interests submitted written comments. * * * The hearing was held on February 1 and 2, with participation by a number of groups, including the Commission's staff, the United States Environmental Protection Agency, a manufacturer of reactor equipment, a trade association from the nuclear industry, a group of electric utility companies, and a group called Consolidated National Intervenors who represented 79 groups and individuals including responding NRDC.

After the hearing, the Commission's staff filed a supplemental document for the purpose of clarifying and revising the Environmental Survey. Then the Licensing Board forwarded its report to the Commission without rendering any decision. The Licensing Board identified as the principal procedural question the propriety of declining to use full formal adjudicatory procedures. The major substantive issue was the technical adequacy of the Environmental Survey.

In April 1974, the Commission issued a rule which adopted the second of the two proposed alternatives described above. The Commission also approved the procedures used at the hearing,[7] and indicated that the record, including the Environmental Survey, provided an "adequate data base for the regulation adopted." Finally, the Commission ruled that to the extent the rule differed from the Appeal Board decisions in Vermont Yankee "those decisions have no further precedential significance," but

---

7. The Commission stated:

"In our view, the procedures adopted provide a more than adequate basis for formulation of the rule we adopted. All parties were fully heard. Nothing offered was excluded. The record does not indicate that any evidentiary material would have been received under different procedures. Nor did the proponent of the strict 'adjudicatory' approach make an offer of proof—or even remotely suggest—what substantive matters it would develop under different procedures. In addition, we note that 11 documents including the Survey were available to the parties several weeks before the hearing, and the Regulatory staff, though not requested to do so, made available various drafts and handwritten notes. Under all of the circumstances, we conclude that adjudicatory type procedures were not warranted here."

that since "the environmental effects of the uranium fuel cycle have been shown to be relatively insignificant, * * * it is unnecessary to apply the amendment to applicant's environmental reports submitted prior to its effective date or to Final Environmental Statements for which Draft Environmental Statements have been circulated for comment prior to the effective date."

Respondents appealed from both the Commission's adoption of the rule and its decision to grant Vermont Yankee's license to the Court of Appeals for the District of Columbia Circuit.

Procedure

* * *

With respect to the challenge of Vermont Yankee's license, the court first ruled that in the absence of effective rulemaking proceedings,[13] the Commission must deal with the environmental impact of fuel reprocessing and disposal in individual licensing proceedings. The court then examined the rulemaking proceedings and, despite the fact that it appeared the agency employed all the procedures required by § 553 and more, the court determined the proceedings to be inadequate and overturned the rule. Accordingly, the Commission's determination with respect to Vermont Yankee's license was also remanded for further proceedings.

* * *

* * * The court conceded that absent extraordinary circumstances it is improper for a reviewing court to prescribe the procedural format an agency must follow, but it likewise clearly thought it entirely appropriate to "scrutinize the record as a whole to insure that genuine opportunities to participate in a meaningful way were provided. * * * " The court also refrained from actually ordering the agency to follow any specific procedures, but there is little doubt in our minds that the ineluctable mandate of the court's decision is that the procedures afforded during the hearings were inadquate. * * *

In prior opinions [e.g., *Londoner v. Denver*, 210 U. S. 373 (1908)] we have intimated that even in a rulemaking proceeding when an agency is making a " 'quasi-judicial' " determination by which a very small number of persons are " 'exceptionally affected, in each case upon individual grounds,' " in some circumstances additional procedures may be required in order to afford the aggrieved individuals due process.[16] It might also be true, although we do not think the issue is presented in this case and accordingly do not decide it, that a totally unjustified departure from well-settled agency procedures of long standing might require judicial correction.

---

13. In the Court of Appeals no one questioned the Commission's authority to deal with fuel cycle issues by informal rulemaking as opposed to adjudication. Neither does anyone seriously question before this Court the Commission's authority in this respect.

16. Respondent NRDC does not now argue that additional procedural devices were required under the Constitution. Since this was clearly a rulemaking proceeding in its purest form, we see nothing to support such a view.

But this much is absolutely clear.   Absent constitutional constraints or extremely compelling circumstances the "administrative agencies 'should be free to fashion their own rules of procedure and to pursue methods of inquiry capable of permitting them to discharge their multitudinous duties.'" * * *

* * *

Respondent NRDC argues that § 553 of the Administrative Procedure Act merely establlishes lower procedural bounds and that a court may routinely require more than the minimum when an agency's proposed rule addresses complex or technical factual issues or "Issues of Great Public Import."   We have, however, previously shown that our decisions reject this view.   We also think the legislative history, even the part which it cites, does not bear out its contention.   * * *

There are compelling reasons for construing [§ 553] in this manner.   In the first place, if courts continually review agency proceedings to determine whether the agency employed procedures which were, in the court's opinion, perfectly tailored to reach what the court perceives to be the "best" or "correct" result, judicial review would be totally unpredictable.   And the agencies, operating under this vague injunction to employ the "best" procedures and facing the threat of reversal if they did not, would undoubtedly adopt full adjudicatory procedures in every instance.   Not only would this totally disrupt the statutory scheme, through which Congress enacted "a formula upon which opposing social and political forces have come to rest," but all the inherent advantages of informal rulemaking would be totally lost.

Secondly, it is obvious that the court in these cases reviewed the agency's choice of procedures on the basis of the record actually produced at the hearing, and not on the basis of the information available to the agency when it made the decision to structure the proceedings in a certain way.   This sort of Monday morning quarterbacking not only encourages but almost compels the agency to conduct all rulemaking proceedings with the full panoply of procedural devices normally associated only with adjudicatory hearings.

Finally, and perhaps most importantly, this sort of review fundamentally misconceives the nature of the standard for judicial review of an agency rule.   The court below uncritically assumed that additional procedures will automatically result in a more adequate record because it will give interested parties more of an opportunity to participate in and contribute to the proceedings.   But informal rulemaking need not be based solely on the transcript of a hearing held before an agency.   Indeed, the agency need not even hold a formal hearing.   Thus, the adequacy of the "record" in this type of proceeding is not correlated directly to the type of procedural devices employed, but rather turns on whether the agency has followed the statutory mandate of the Administrative Procedure Act or other relevant statutes.   If the agency is compelled to support the rule which it ultimately adopts with the type of record produced only after a full adjudicatory hearing, it simply will have no choice but to conduct a full adjudicatory hearing prior to promulgating every rule. In sum, this sort of unwarranted judicial examination of perceived procedural short-comings of a rulemaking proceeding can do nothing but seriously interfere with that process prescribed by Congress.

* * *

There remains, of course, the question of whether the challenged rule finds sufficient justification in the administrative proceedings that it should be upheld by the reviewing court. Judge Tamm, concurring in the result reached by the majority of the Court of Appeals, thought that it did not. There are also intimations in the majority opinion which suggest that the judges who joined it likewise may have thought the administrative proceedings an insufficient basis upon which to predicate the rule in question. We accordingly remand so that the Court of Appeals may review the rule as the Administrative Procedure Act provides. We have made it abundantly clear before that when there is a contemporaneous explanation of the agency decision, the validity of that action must "stand or fall on the propriety of that finding, judged, of course, by the appropriate standard of review. * * * "

MR. JUSTICE BLACKMUN and MR. JUSTICE POWELL took no part in the consideration or decision of these cases.

Notes

1. The D.C. Circuit's original decision in *Vermont Yankee* was in some sense a reprise of the debate in the *Ethyl* case, supra p. 375, where Judge Bazelon favored careful scrutiny of agency procedures while Judge Leventhal defended the necessity for intensive substantive review. But Judge Bazelon's opinion in *Vermont Yankee* had found problems with the NRC's substantive conclusion that the environmental effects of the nuclear fuel cycle were likely to be minimal, and the Supreme Court may have stretched to interpret his ruling as a demand that the NRC provide more than the minimum procedures guaranteed by section 553.

2. What difference is there between a remand to an agency premised on the inadequacy of the agency's procedure for testing evidence in informal rulemaking and a remand premised on the inadequacy of the factual support for a rule because the record fails to illuminate adequately issues that some participants considered critical to the agency's decision and on which they are prepared to offer rebuttal evidence?

3. Justice Rehnquist's invitation to the court of appeals to focus on the factual bases for the NRC's conclusion did not end the *Vermont Yankee* litigation. Even before the Court's decision, the NRC had begun proceedings to reformulate its "generic rule" assessing the environmental effects of the nuclear fuel cycle. Its final rule, promulgated before the case was reheard in the D.C. Circuit, forecast that long-term isolation of waste fuel would have no adverse environmental effects, that permanent waste storage facilities could be developed, and that these facilities would perform as expected. The rule was accompanied by a table of numerical values that purported to quantify the environmental effects of nuclear power generation, which were to be drawn on in evaluating any nuclear

power facility.   The NRC declined to factor acknowledged uncertainties into the tabular values, and went on to state that "no further discussion of such environmental effects [in individual licensing proceedings] shall be required."   A year later, the Commission amended the rule to permit licensing boards to consider environmental effects not addressed by the table.   44 Fed. Reg. 45362 (1979). The NRC's revised rule and accompanying table became the focus of the D.C. Circuit's next encounter with the case, *NRDC v. NRC*, 685 F.2d 459 (D.C. Cir. 1982).   Judge Bazelon again wrote for the court of appeals, which once more set aside the NRC's action, this time on substantive grounds.   Noting that the APA required the court to set aside agency action that is "arbitrary and capricious" or "not in accordance with law," Judge Bazelon pointed out that section 102(2)(C) of NEPA demands that federal agencies fully consider and disclose the environmental impact of their actions.   " '[T]he thrust of § 102(2)(C) is * * * ' that environmental concerns be integrated into the very process of agency decisionmaking. * * * We conclude that the Table S-3 rules are arbitrary and in violation of NEPA because they fail to allow for consideration of uncertainties underlying the assumption that no radiological effluents will be released into the biosphere once wastes are sealed in a permanent repository."   685 F.2d at 476-77.   The court invalidated two other parts of the NRC's rule because of their "failure to allow consideration of health, socioeconomic, and cumulative effects of fuel-cycle activities."   Id. at 477-78.

Judge Bazelon's chief concern was that the NRC had excluded a critical issue at the heart of the debate over nuclear power—the problem of permanent disposal of spent fuel—from consideration by those who have the authority to issue or deny licenses.   Analyzed either as a factual finding or as a decisionmaking device by which the Commission retained exclusive responsibility for considering the uncertainties concerning long-term waste disposal, the rule was invalid: "NEPA requires an agency to consider the environmental risks of a proposed action in a manner that allows the existence of such risks to influence the agency's decision to take the action."   Id. at 486.   The court also found that the original and interim rules which accompanied Table S-3 violated NEPA because they could be interpreted as cutting off any inquiry by the licensing board into the health, socioeconomic, and cumulative environmental impacts of waste disposal. However, it upheld the NRC's final rule, which specifically allowed the boards to explore these issues in individual licensing proceedings.

Judge Bazelon was not content to rest his decision solely on the special requirements of NEPA (and the APA's command to set aside action "not in accordance with law") (id. at 485):

　　　　* * * [T]he same result can be reached under the arbitrary and capricious standard.   Under that standard, as stated above, our inquiry focuses upon whether the zero-release assumption is based on "consideration of the relevant factors."   Under NEPA, significant uncertainty surrounding the environmental effect of a proposed action is relevant to an agency's decision to rule generically that the effect will not occur.   For an agency to go forward in the face of significant uncertainty and issue such a rule indicates either a failure to consider a relevant factor or a clear error in judgment.   Because that is precisely what the Commission did in promulgating the Table S-3 Rule, we could also conclude that its action was arbitrary and capricious.

Judge Wilkey's dissenting opinion espoused a narrower view of the court's role. He found that the NRC had taken the requisite "hard look" at waste storage and supported its rule with "reasoned decisionmaking." At bottom, Wilkey believed that the Commission had reached a policy judgment on the nuclear waste issue that was entitled to deference, and he accused Judge Bazelon of manufacturing a NEPA standard to defeat the broad authority granted the Commission by the Atomic Energy Act.

Predictably, the case returned to the Supreme Court, which again reversed the circuit court. *Baltimore Gas & Electric Co. v. NRDC*, 462 U. S. 1 (1983). Writing for a unanimous court, Justice O'Connor held that the circuit court exceeded its proper role in reviewing the NRC's informed resolution of difficult and controversial issues, and discouraged the courts from becoming embroiled in the debate over the wisdom of nuclear energy. "Resolution of these fundamental policy questions lies * * * with Congress and the agencies to which Congress has delegated authority, as well as with state legislatures and, ultimately, the populace as a whole." Id. at 2252. Justice O'Connor found that the NRC's extensive hearings on the uncertainties of waste disposal were sufficient to satisfy NEPA's requirements. "As a general proposition," she agreed with the court of appeals' statement that "an agency must allow all significant environmental risks to be factored into the decision whether to undertake a proposed action." Id. at 2254. But the NRC's decision to evaluate the impact generically and use Table S-3 to inform individual licensing boards of its conclusions was

> clearly an appropriate method of conducting the hard look required by NEPA. * * * Administrative efficiency and consistency of decision are both furthered by a generic determination of these effects without needless repetition of the litigation in individual proceedings, which are subject to review by the [NRC] in any event.

The Court went on to rule that the NRC's use of a zero value to represent the environmental impact of long term storage of nuclear waste was not arbitrary because it was but one figure in a larger table of reasonably conservative values. Moreover, it recognized the NRC was making predictions "at the frontiers of science," not findings of fact, and stressed that in such situations " * * * a reviewing court must generally be at its most deferential." Id. at 2256.

4. The Court's original *Vermont Yankee* decision provoked a large secondary literature. Among the most insightful analyses is Nathanson, *The Vermont Yankee Nuclear Power Opinion: A Masterpiece of Statutory Misinterpretation,* 16 San Diego L. Rev. 183 (1979), whose title betrays the author's viewpoint. The late Professor Nathanson argued persuasively that the Court misinterpreted the governing statutes in *Vermont Yankee*—the Hobbs Act and the Atomic Energy Act—which together with their legislative history reveal that Congress expected that NRC regulations would be adopted in on-the-record proceedings meeting the requirements of sections 556 and 557 of the APA. But he went on to suggest that the agency's procedures in fact probably met those requirements.

Nathanson also challenged Justice Rehnquist's earlier holding in *Florida East Coast Railway* that formal rulemaking is required only when an agency's governing statute specifies that rules are "to be made on the record after opportunity for an agency hearing." Nathanson contended that the framers of the APA expected that rules destined for review on the record in the courts of appeals would be the product of formal proceedings. By contrast, rules adopted pursuant to the procedures of section 553 were to be evaluated on the basis of the factual record compiled in enforcement suits (and preenforcement challenges?) in district courts.   Professor Nathanson's analysis thus casts doubt on the many decisions, like *Nova Scotia Food Products Corp.*, that assume judicial review of rules promulgated in section 553 rulemaking will be based on, and confined to, the administrative record.

5. Professor, now Judge, Scalia assessed *Vermont Yankee* more sympathetically, but offered a historical explanation for the insistence of reviewing courts that agencies provide procedural safeguards beyond the bare essentials historically associated with section 553:

> Consider two categories of massive post-APA change in the particular area of informal rulemaking:
>
> 1. Not until 1956 [*Storer Broadcasting*] was it established that an agency charged with issuing and denying licenses in adjudicatory hearings could establish generic disqualifying factors in informal rulemaking, thereby avoiding adversarial procedures on those issues.   Not until 1968 was it established that a major rate-making agency (the FPC) had implicit authority to fix rates on an areawide basis rather than company by company, enabling the avoidance of constitutional and statutory requirements for an adjudicatory hearing. And not until 1973 [*Petroleum Refiners*] was it judicially determined that the FTC, one of the oldest of the regulatory agencies, had authority to prohibit unfair trade practices by rule, as opposed to operating exclusively through individual "cease-and-desist" proceedings.
>
> Decisions such as these have facilitated what is perhaps the most notable development in federal government administration during the past two decades: "The contrivance of more expeditious administrative methods"— that is, the constant and accelerating flight away from individualized, adjudicatory proceedings to generalized disposition through rulemaking. * * *
>
> 2. Another post-APA development of monumental importance was the establishment in 1967 [*Abbott Laboratories*, infra p. 753] of the principle that rules could be challenged in court directly rather than merely in the context of an adjudicatory enforcement proceeding against a particular individual, combined with the doctrine (clearly enunciated in 1973) that "the focal point for judicial review should be the administrative record already in existence, not some new record made initially in the reviewing court." * * *
>
> The cumulative effect of these developments was that by the mid-1970s vast numbers of issues of the sort which in 1946 would have been resolved in a formal adjudicatory context before the agency, or even in an adjudicatory judicial proceeding, were being resolved in informal rulemaking and informal adjudication; that the courts were expected to provide, in the words of one of the Supreme Court's more expansive descriptions (which it probably now regrets), "a thorough, probing, in-depth review" of that agency action, but taking the agency record as it was and without conducting any additional evidentiary proceedings. * * *

Scalia, *Vermont Yankee: The APA, The D.C. Circuit, and the Supreme Court,* 1978 Sup. Ct. Rev. 345 (1979).   For other useful discussions of the *Vermont Yankee* decision, see Breyer, *Vermont Yankee and the Courts' Role in the Nuclear Energy Controversy* 91 Harv. L. Rev. 1833 (1978); Byse, *Vermont Yankee and the Evolution of Administrative Procedure: A Somewhat Different View,* 91 Harv. L. Rev. 1823 (1978); Stewart, *Vermont Yankee and the Evolution of Administrative Procedure,* 91 Harv. L. Rev. 1805 (1978).   See also Gifford, *Administrative Rule-*

making and Judicial Review: Some Conceptual Models, 65 Minn. L. Rev. 63 (1980).

Ex Parte Contacts and Adversarial Comment

The courts' increasing emphasis on an exclusive rulemaking record encouraged by *Nova Scotia Food Prods.*, has blurred the distinction between informal and formal procedures. A 1977 decision of the District of Columbia Circuit touched off a flurry of debate and led to a series of sequels.

Home Box Office, Inc. v. F.C.C. 567 F.2d 9 (1977), *cert. denied* 434 U.S. 829 (1978), grew out of a petition to review regulations that restricted the program fare cablecasters and subscription broadcast television stations could offer. Judge Wright's lengthy per curiam opinion, after accepting some and rejecting other substantive challenges to the regulations, centered on a procedural attack on the FCC's conduct during the rulemaking proceedings (567 F.2d at 51-57):

> It is apparently uncontested that a number of participants before the Commission sought out individual commissioners or Commission employees for the purpose of discussing *ex parte* and in confidence the merits of the rules under review here. * * *
>
> Although it is impossible to draw any firm conclusions about the effect of *ex parte* presentations upon the ultimate shape of the pay cable rules, the evidence is certainly consistent with often-voiced claims of undue industry influence over Commission proceedings, and we are particularly concerned that the final shaping of the rules we are reviewing here may have been by compromise among the contending industry forces, rather than by exercise of the independent discretion in the public interest the Communications Act vests in individual commissioners. * * *
>
> Even the possibility that there is here one administrative record for the public and this court and another for the Commission and those "in the know" is intolerable. * * * [I]t is the obligation of this court to test the actions of the Commission for arbitrariness or inconsistency with delegated authority. Yet here agency secrecy stands between us and fulfillment of our obligation. Moreover, where, as here, an agency justifies its actions by reference only to information in the public file while failing to disclose the substance of other relevant information that has been represented to it, a reviewing court cannot presume that the agency has acted properly, but must treat the agency's justifications as a fictional account of the actual decisionmaking process and must perforce find its actions arbitrary.
>
> * * * Even if the Commission had disclosed to this court the substance of what was said to it *ex parte*, it would still be difficult to judge the truth of what the Commission asserted it knew about the television industry because we would not have the benefit of an adversarial discussion among the parties. The importance of such discussion to the proper functioning of the agency decisionmaking and judicial review processes is evident in our cases. * * *
>
> Equally important is the inconsistency of secrecy with fundamental notions of fairness implicit in due process and with the ideal of reasoned deci-

sionmaking on the merits which undergirds all of our administrative law. * * *

From what has been said above, it should be clear that information gathered *ex parte* from the public which becomes relevant to a rulemaking will have to be disclosed at some time.   On the other hand, we recognize that informal contacts between agencies and the public are the "bread and butter" of the process of administration and are completely appropriate so long as they do not frustrate judicial review or raise serious questions of fairness.   Reconciliation of these considerations in a manner which will reduce procedural uncertainty leads us to conclude that communications which are received prior to issuance of a formal notice of rulemaking do not, in general, have to be put in a public file.   Of course, if the information contained in such a communication forms the basis for agency action, then, under well established principles, that information must be disclosed to the public in some form.   Once a notice of proposed rulemaking has been issued, however, any agency official or employee who is or may reasonably be expected to be involved in the decisional process of the rulemaking proceeding, should "refus[e] to discuss matters relating to the disposition of a [rulemaking proceeding] with any interested private party, or an attorney or agent for any such party, prior to the [agency's] decision * * *," * * * .   If *ex parte* contacts nonetheless occur, we think that any written document or a summary of any oral communication must be placed in the public file established for each rulemaking docket immediately after the communication is received so that interested parties may comment thereon.

Within a few months another panel of the D.C. Circuit, which included Judge MacKinnon who had dissented from the treatment of the *ex parte* contacts issue in *Home Box Office*, limited the earlier ruling.   *Action for Children's Television v. F.C.C.*, 564 F.2d 458 (D.C. Cir. 1977), involved a challenge to the FCC's failure to adopt proposed regulations for improving children's programming.   The primary reason offered by the Commission for its decision to terminate the rulemaking was its belief that proposals developed by the broadcast industry for self-regulation could adequately serve the objectives of the contemplated rules.   The proposals had been discussed by various broadcaster representatives with members of the Commission in meetings that were not announced or open to the public, and the agency afforded no opportunity for public comment on the proposals before it terminated its proceeding.   Predictably, the petitioners challenged the agency's decision not to regulate based in part on its undeniable "violation" of *Home Box Office*.   Responding to this argument, the *Action for Children's Television* panel refused to apply that ruling retroactively, and then proceeded to narrow its prospective application (564 F.2d at 474, 477–78):

> If we go as far as *Home Box Office* does in its ex parte ruling in ensuring a "whole record" for our review, why not go further to require the decisionmaker to summarize and make available for public comment every status inquiry from a Congressman or any germane material—say a newspaper editorial—that he or she reads or their evening-hour ruminations?   In the end, why not administer a lie-detector test to ascertain whether the required summary is an accurate and complete one?   The problem is obviously a matter of

degree, and the appropriate line must be drawn somewhere. In light of
what must be presumed to be Congress' intent to not to prohibit or require
disclosure of all ex parte contacts during or after the public comment stage,
we would draw that line at the point where the rulemaking proceedings involve "competing claims to a valuable privilege."   It is at that point where
the potential for unfair advantage outweighs the practical burdens, which we
imagine would not be insubstantial, that such a judicially conceived rule
would place upon administrators. * * *

    * * * Private groups were not competing for a specific valuable privilege.
Furthermore, this case does not raise serious questions of fairness.
Chairman Wiley met with representatives of NAB, as Chairman Burch had
met with representatives of ACT, and there is no indication that he "gave to
any interested party advantages not shared by all." * * * Not only were no
rules adopted for the time being in our case, but the Commission's *Children's
Television Report* demonstrates that the agency in good faith examined all
the relevant factors raised during the comment stage, and comprehensively
and rationally justified its decision to proceed cautiously by giving industry
self-regulation a chance to prove that it could be effective.

The debate within the D.C. Circuit over the legitimacy of, and appropriate limitations on, ex parte contacts in agency decisionmaking has continued.   In *United States Lines, Inc. v. Federal Maritime Commission*,
584 F.2d 519 (D.C. Cir. 1978), the petitioner challenged a FMC order approving an agreement among its competitors, an approval that was necessary to exempt the agreement from the antitrust laws.   The court overturned the FMC's order for failure to consider the antitrust implications
and because the agency had improperly relied on unspecified materials
outside the record and on recorded ex parte contacts.   Judge Wright
stated that the Commission's reliance on undisclosed "data then available" effectively precluded a reviewing court from assessing the basis for
its agency's decision.   Furthermore, he observed, even if disclosed in the
agency's final ruling, the information would not have been subjected to
"adversarial comment among the parties."   In concluding that these defects were fatal, Judge Wright relied on language in the Shipping Act
which requires a "hearing" prior to approval of agreements among competitors.

Hercules, Inc. v. EPA, 598 F.2d 91 (D.C. Cir. 1978), reviewed a proceeding to establish limits on the discharge of two toxic water pollutants,
toxaphene and endrin.   Although Congress amended the pertinent provisions of the Federal Water Pollution Control Act to permit informal rulemaking before EPA had completed its rulemaking, the agency nonetheless conducted a formal evidentiary hearing before promulgating the
limits.   An approaching statutory deadline, however, forced the Administrator to digest a large hearing record in a very short period of time and
he therefore relied heavily on the agency's judicial officer, who in turn
consulted with certain other EPA officials for help in locating materials in
the record.   Among those she talked with were two agency attorneys
who had helped present the case in support of the proposed limits.

In an opinion hedged with qualifications, the court of appeals sanctioned the judicial officer's conduct in this case, but expressed serious doubts about the practice generally:

* * * For two reasons, we have determined that EPA's standards must be upheld in this particular context; the broader questions posed by the parties are reserved for another day.

First, both the adoption by EPA of its procedural rules and the issuance of the final decision preceded *Home Box Office.*

Second, the administrative history under section 307(a) created a peculiar context wherein the necessity for staff contacts existed with unusual and compelling force.   As we have noted, section 307(a) sets forth rigid and compressed timetables.   Previous EPA failures to meet these timetables resulted in a judicial decree fixing the time for rulemaking.   These congressional and judicial time restraints were imposed to minimize the period during which the public and the environment would be exposed to toxic substances.   The administrative delay would not only have been contrary to law, but would also have increased exposure to hazardous substances.   In view of the extraordinary bulk and complexity of the administrative record, a judicial officer attempting to digest the record and prepare a decision in a matter of weeks would face, at the least, great difficulty in proceeding without staff assistance.   Thus, this context invokes the rule of ancient origin that expedition in protecting the public health justifies less elaborate procedure than may be required in other contexts. * * *

Notwithstanding our decision, however, we feel compelled to record our uneasiness with one aspect of this case—the communication between Ms. Marple and EPA staff legal advocates (Mr. Hall and Ms. Chang).   The fact that the attorneys who represented the staff's position at the administrative hearing were later consulted by the judicial officer who prepared the final decision possibly gives rise to an appearance of unfairness, even though the consultations did not involve factual or policy issues. * * *

Amendatory legislation may be justified if agencies do not themselves proscribe post-hearing contacts between staff *advocates* and decisionmakers in formal rulemaking proceedings, lest there be an erosion of public trust and confidence in the administrative process. * * *

Other courts of appeals have appeared less concerned about the *ex parte* contacts problem.   Compare the foregoing language, for example, with the Second Circuit's curt dismissal of a complaint about *ex parte* communications in rulemaking between members of the Federal Trade Commission "and an allegedly biased staff" as "more properly addressed to Congress."   *Katharine Gibbs School v. FTC*, 612 F.2d 658 (2d Cir. 1979).   For a provocative exchange, see Gellhorn and Robinson, *Rulemaking "Due Process": An Inconclusive Dialogue*, 48 U. Chi. L. Rev. 201 (1981).

Notes

Professor Robinson, a former member of the FCC, perceives a collision between quasi-judicial procedural requirements designed to protect the integrity of administrative decisionmaking and the practical necessities of information gathering in a quasi-political environment.   *The Federal Communications Commission: An Essay on Regulatory Watchdogs*, 64 Va. L. Rev. 169, 228-30 (1978):

Militating against a ban on ex parte communications is the loss of flexibility, speed, and efficiency (in the narrow sense of minimized procedural costs) that would arise if all contacts with agency decisionmakers were restricted to on-the-record communications.   Indeed, such a ban would cause more than a loss of efficiency, because the additional procedural burdens almost certainly would reduce the amount of available information.   Despite my earlier comments about the FCC's "information overload," it is not clear that cutting off the flow of informal information is the best way to handle the overload problem.   In many cases, informal outside consultation is a useful means to cut through a mass of formal documentary material buried in elephantine dockets and to cull out the essential information.

Ex parte contacts also are an important check on the reliability of staff information.   Students of bureaucracy have noted that large organizations rarely exhibit a free flow of information from lower to higher echelons due to obstacles such as conflicting self-interests among members of the different echelons.   Because staff information and interpretation is not always reliable, ex parte contacts outside the agency are an important means of avoiding "staff capture."   To be sure, one does not want to rely entirely on outside informants, but neither does one want to be the prisoner of agency staff.

In support of some restraint on ex parte communications, it must be acknowledged that a totally laissez-faire rulemaking process provides a fertile bed for arbitrary administrative action.   For example, when interested persons—without providing notice to others—are able to present their facts and arguments to individual agency members and staff, the rulemaking process imposes no check on the reliability of information presented to the decisionmakers.   This raises obvious concerns of fairness and substantial problems of effectiveness and efficiency.   Allowing unfettered ex parte communications also undermines the incentive for interested persons to submit carefully prepared studies and briefs because their work is lost so easily in the shuffle of off-the-record encounters.   Most FCC Commissioners place great reliance on oral briefing and discussion with staff and, where permitted, with outside persons.   Because of this heavy reliance, even the most careful written commentary of one party may be negated by the offhand, ex parte criticism of another.   These factors encourage regular participants in FCC proceedings to emphasize ex parte communication at the expense of more painstaking, careful written analysis.

The arguments for and against ex parte communications are balanced sufficiently to commend a solution somewhere between the extremes of laissez-faire and flat prohibition.   I believe that most of the desired goals of a ban could be achieved by a system requiring all decisionmakers to record both the fact and the essential content of all communications with interested persons regarding any substantive issue within the Commission's concern.   Such a record would be available to the public—including, of course, all persons interested in particular proceedings, to which such discussions pertain.   This system would not altogether meet the objections to such communications; it would not necessarily improve the low quality of the dialogue that ex parte communication encourages.   However, by making the discussion a matter of public record, it would impose some measure of discipline that is now wanting.

The position advocated by Professor Robinson is essentially that adopted in 1977 by the FDA in comprehensive regulations governing agency rulemaking.   See 21 C.F.R. § § 10.65, 10.70, and 10.80, published at 42 Fed. Reg. 4680 (1977).

White House Oversight and Ex Parte Contacts

Presidential attempts to induce regulatory agencies to pay greater attention to the economic impact of their regulations have raised novel issues of administrative procedure as well as of institutional authority. The efforts of OMB or White House staff to persuade agencies to change proposed regulations obviously involve contacts in the form of meetings and telephone calls as well as the exchange of written memos.   Accusations that such intra-executive consultations are improper have been levied by consumer and environmental groups.

Such complaints, coupled with uncertainty about the reach of *Home Box Office,* brought the matter to the Department of Justice in 1978. The specific context was Secretary of the Interior's consideration of proposed regulations under the Surface Mining Control and Reclamation Act of 1977, 30 U.S.C.A. § § 1201 et seq.   The Office of Legal Counsel of the Department of Justice was asked for advice on the procedures the Secretary should follow in discussing the regulations with representatives of the Council of Economic Advisers (CEA), and responded in part as follows:

> * * * [I]t is our conclusion that there is no prohibition against communications within the Executive Branch after the close of the comment period on these proposed rules.   Nothing in the relevant statutes or in the decisions of the D.C. Circuit suggest the existence of a bar against full and detailed consultations between those charged with promulgating the rules and the President's advisers.   The rulings of the D.C. Circuit, however, do suggest that it might be inappropriate for interested persons outside the Executive Branch to have so-called *ex parte* communications with you and your staff.   If that is so, we think it logical to conclude that the D.C. Circuit would disapprove of CEA or other advisers to the President serving as a conduit for those same *ex parte* communications.   In order to prevent CEA from serving as such a conduit, we recommended a procedure which is outlined in detail in the letter from this Office to CEA dated December 29, 1978. * * *

The OLC's letter went on to describe the procedure that it recommended, which had been followed by the Department:

> (1) The CEA staff compiled a record of all of the oral and written communications they may have had with private persons interested in the proposed regulations.   This catalog sets forth the content of all of these communications as accurately and fully as is possible.   For the sake of completeness, it also includes recollections of CEA conversations with other Executive branch offices.
>
> (2) Following receipt and review of this material, OSM [Office of Surface Mining] made it available to the public in the document room at the Department of Interior.   At the same time OSM published in the *Federal Register* for Thursday, January 4, 1979, a statement acknowledging, and explaining the reason for, this addition to the administrative record.   The statement also announced the reopening of the record to allow comments on factual material

contained in the submission. * * * As an additional precaution to assure the widest public availability of these CEA documents, we understand that copies of the complete packet have been delivered to every Regional Office of your Department and that an effort was made to contact directly State governments that were likely to have an interest in reviewing this material.

(3) Once the compilation was made publicly available and the notice was transmitted to the *Federal Register* for publication, the Chairman [of the CEA] and/or his staff conferred with OSM on particular portions of the proposed rules. * * *

(4) Although we have been advised that no changes were made in the proposed rules as a result of these consultations, we did counsel that if any communications made during this consultation process did become in part the basis for the Secretary's final decision concerning the rulemaking, their relationship to that decision would be fully spelled out with the promulgation of the final rule.   There would, however, be no need to reopen the record again prior to the final decision unless you propose to rely on other information that was not included in the record at some stage and subjected to reasonable public comment in advance of your final decision.

(5) During the period of consultation, the participants were instructed to refrain from having any communications with other persons interested in the rulemaking, including other Executive branch officials, if those officials have either directly or indirectly had contacts with non-Government persons having an interest in this rulemaking.

SIERRA CLUB v. COSTLE

United States Court of Appeals, District of Columbia Circuit, 1981.
657 F.2d 298.

WALD, CIRCUIT JUDGE.

This case concerns the extent to which new coal-fired steam generators that produce electricity must control their emissions of sulfur dioxide and particulate matter into the air.   In June of 1979 EPA revised the regulations called "new source performance standards" ("NSPS" or "standards") governing emission control by coal burning power plants. On this appeal we consider challenges to the revised NSPS brought by environmental groups which contend that the standards are too lax and by electric utilities which contend that the standards are too rigorous. * * *

* * *

The Clean Air Act provides for direct federal regulation of emissions from new stationary sources of air pollution by authorizing EPA to set performance standards for significant sources of air pollution which may be reasonably anticipated to endanger public health or welfare.   In June 1979 EPA promulgated the NSPS involved in this case.   The new standards increase pollution controls for new coal-fired electric power plants by tightening restrictions on emissions of sulfur dioxide and particulate matter.   Sulfur dioxide emissions are limited to a maximum of 1.2 lbs./MBtu (or 520 ng/j) and a 90 percent reduction of potential uncontrolled sulfur dioxide emissions is required except when emissions to the atmosphere are less than 0.60 lbs./MBtu (or 260 ng/j). When sulfur dioxide emissions are less than 0.60 lbs./MBtu potential emissions must be reduced by no less than 70 percent.   In addition, emissions of particulate matter are limited to 0.03 lbs./MBtu (or 13 ng/j).

Petitioners in this case are Sierra Club and the State of California Air Resources Board ("CARB"), which oppose the variable 70 to 90 percent reduction requirement of the NSPS; Appalachian Power Co. ("APCO"), *et al.*, a group comprised of APCO, the Edison Electric Institute, the National Rural Electric Cooperative Association, and 86 individual utilities ("Electric Utilities"), which challenge both the maximum 90 percent reduction requirement and the 0.03 lbs./MBtu limit on emissions of particulate matter; and, the Environmental Defense Fund ("EDF"), which challenges the 1.2 lbs./MBtu ceiling imposed by the NSPS.

* * *

Coal is the dominant fuel used for generating electricity in the United States.   When coal is burned, it releases sulfur dioxide and particulate matter into the atmosphere.   At the very least these pollutants are known to cause or contribute to respiratory illnesses.   In 1975 alone electric power plants emitted 18.6 million tons of sulfur dioxide.   If the former NSPS had not been changed the total annual national sulfur dioxide emissions could have exceeded 23 million tons by 1995: a 27 percent increase. * * *   In 1976 power plant emissions accounted for 64 percent of the total estimated sulfur dioxide emissions and 24 percent of the total estimated particulate matter emissions in the entire country.

EPA's revised NSPS are designed to curtail these emissions.   EPA predicts that the new standards would reduce national sulfur dioxide emissions from new plants by 50 percent and national particulate matter emissions by 70 percent by 1995.   The cost of the new controls, however, is substantial.   EPA estimates that utilities will have to spend tens of billions of dollars by 1995 on pollution control under the new NSPS.   Consumers will ultimately bear these costs, both directly in the form of residential utility bills, and indirectly in the form of higher consumer prices due to increased energy costs.   Coinciding with these trends the utility industry is expected to have continued and significant growth. * * * Not surprisingly, coal burning power plants' already preeminent share of electric power produced in the United States will grow over the remainder of this century.

* * *

While EPA's decision was pending the Clean Air Act Amendments of 1977 were signed into law.   Section 111 of the amendments * * * required EPA to revise the standards of performance for electric power plants within one year after the August 1977 enactment date.   When it appeared that EPA would not meet this deadline, the Sierra Club filed a complaint in the District Court for the District of Columbia.   The court approved a stipulation requiring the proposed regulations to issue in September 1978, and promulgation of final regulations within six months after the proposal. Eventually, after further delay, the final NSPS were promulgated in June 1979.

* * *

V. THE 1.2 LBS./MBTU EMISSION CEILING

EPA proposed and ultimately adopted a 1.2 lbs./MBtu ceiling for total sulfur dioxide emissions which is applicable regardless of the percentage of sulfur dioxide reduction attained. The 1.2 lbs./MBtu standard is identical to the emission ceiling required by the former standard. The achievability of the standard is undisputed.

EDF challenges this part of the final NSPS on procedural grounds, contending that although there may be evidence supporting the 1.2 lbs./MBtu standard, EPA should have and would have adopted a stricter standard if it had not engaged in post-comment period irregularities and succumbed to political pressures. * * *

A. EPA's RATIONALE FOR THE EMISSION CEILING

EPA explained in the preamble to the proposed rule that two primary factors were considered in selecting the 1.2 lbs./MBtu ceiling: FGD performance, and the impact of the ceiling on high sulfur coal reserves. * * *

Following the September 1978 proposal the joint interagency working group investigated options lower than the 1.2 lbs./MBtu ceiling, according to EPA, in order "to take full advantage of the cost effectiveness benefits of a joint coal washing/scrubbing strategy on high-sulfur coal." The joint working group reasoned that since coal washing is relatively inexpensive, an emission ceiling which would require 90 percent scrubbing in addition to coal washing "could substantially reduce emissions in the East and Midwest at a relatively low cost." Since coal washing is a widespread practice, it was thought that the 1.2 lbs./MBtu proposal would not have a seriously detrimental impact upon Eastern coal production. During phase two EPA analyzed 10 different full control and partial control options with its econometric model. These various options included emission ceilings at the 1.2 lbs./MBtu, 0.80 lbs./MBtu and the 0.55 lbs./MBtu levels. The modeling results, published before the close of the public comment period in December 1978, confirmed the joint working group's conclusion that the 1.2 lbs./MBtu standard should be lowered. The results of the phase two modeling exercise were cited by internal EPA memoranda in January and March 1979 as a basis for lowering the 1.2 lbs./MBtu standard. After the phase two modeling, however, EPA undertook "a more detailed analysis of regional coal producing impacts," using BOM seam by seam data on the sulfur content of the reserves and the coal washing potential for those reserves. This analysis identified the amount of reserves that would require more than 90 percent scrubbing of *washed* coal to meet alternative ceilings.

As a result of concerns expressed on the record by NCA and others about the impacts of more rigorous emission ceilings, EPA called a meeting of principal participants in the rulemaking for April 15, 1979. At the meeting EPA presented its new analysis which showed that a 0.55 lbs./MBtu limit would require more than 90 percent scrubbing on 5 to 10 percent of Northern Appalachian reserves and 12 to 25 percent of Eastern Midwest reserves. A 0.80 ceiling would require more than 90 percent scrubbing on less than 5 percent of the reserves in each of these regions. * * *

* * * The agency's analysis, according to EPA, showed that up to 22 percent of high sulfur coal reserves in the Eastern Midwest and parts of the Northern Appalachian coal regions would require more than 90 percent reduction if emissions were held to a 1.0 lbs./MBtu standard. Thus, although acknowledging that stricter controls were technically feasible, EPA chose to retain the 1.2 lbs./MBtu standard because "conservatism in utility perceptions of scrubber performance could create a significant disincentive against the use of these coals and disrupt the coal markets in these regions." EPA concluded that "[a] more stringent emission limit would be counter to one of the basic purposes of the 1977 Amendments, that is, encouraging the use of higher sulfur coals."

B. EDF's PROCEDURAL ATTACK

EDF alleges that as a result of an "ex parte blitz" by coal industry advocates conducted after the close of the comment period, EPA backed away from adopting the .55 lbs./MBtu limit, and instead adopted the higher 1.2 lbs./MBtu restriction. EDF asserts that even before the comment period had ended EPA had already narrowed its focus to include only options which provided for the .55 lbs./MBtu ceiling. EDF also claims that as of March 9, 1979, the three proposals which EPA had under active consideration all included the more stringent .55 lbs./MBtu ceiling, and the earlier 1.2 lbs./MBtu ceiling had been discarded. Whether or not EDF's scenario is credible, it is true that EPA did circulate a draft NSPS with an emissions ceiling below the 1.2 lbs./MBtu level for interagency comment during February, 1978. Following a "leak" of this proposal, EDF says, the so-called "ex parte blitz" began. "Scores" of pro-industry "ex parte" comments were received by EPA in the post-comment period, states EDF, and various meetings with coal industry advocates—including Senator Robert Byrd of West Virginia—took place during that period. These communications, EDF asserts, were unlawful and prejudicial to its position.

* * *

The comment period for the NSPS began on September 19, 1978, and closed on January 15, 1979. After January 15, EPA received almost 300 written submissions on the proposed rule from a broad range of interests. EPA accepted these comments and entered them all on its administrative docket. EPA did not, however, officially reopen the comment period, nor did it notify the public through the Federal Register or by other means that it had received and was entering the "late" comments. According to EDF, most of the approximately 300 late comments were received after the "leak" of the new .55 lbs./MBtu proposal. EDF claims that of the 138 late comments from non-government sources, at least 30 were from "representatives of the coal or utility industries," and of the 53 comments from members of Congress, 22 were either forwarded by the Congressmen from industry interests, or else were prepared and submitted by Congressmen as advocates of those interests.

EDF objects to nine different meetings. A chronological list and synopsis of the challenged meetings follows:

1. *March 14, 1979*—This was a one and a half hour briefing at the White House for high-level officials from the Department of Energy (DOE), the Council of Economic Advisors (CEA), the White House staff, the Department of Interior, the Council on Environmental Quality (CEQ), the Office of Management and Budget (OMB), and the National Park Service. The meeting was reported in a May 9, 1979 memorandum from EPA to Senator Muskie's staff, responding to the Senator's request for a monthly report of contacts between EPA staff and other federal officials concerning the NSPS. A summary of the meeting and the materials distributed were docketed on May 30, 1979. EDF also obtained, after promulgation of the final rule, a copy of the memorandum to Senator Muskie in response to its Freedom of Information Act ("FOIA") request.

2. *April 5, 1979*—This * * * meeting was attended by representatives of EPA, DOE, NCA, EDF, Congressman Paul Simon's office, ICF, Inc. (who performed the microanalysis), and Hunton & Williams (who represented the Electric Utilities). The participants were notified in advance of the agenda for the meeting. Materials relating to EPA's and NCA's presentations during the meeting were distributed and copies were later put into the docket along with detailed minutes of the meeting. Followup calls and letters between NCA and EPA came on April 20, 23, and 29, commenting or elaborating upon the April 5 data. All of these followup contacts were recorded in the docket.

3. *April 23, 1979*—This was a 30-45 minute meeting held at then Senate Majority Leader Robert Byrd's request, in his office, attended by EPA Administrator Douglas Costle, Chief Presidential Assistant Stuart Eizenstat, and NCA officials. A summary of this meeting was put in the docket on May 1, 1979, and copies of the summary were sent to EDF and to other parties. In its denial of the petition for reconsideration, EPA was adamant that no new information was transmitted to EPA at this meeting.

4. *April 27, 1979*—This was a briefing on dry scrubbing technology conducted by EPA for representatives of the Office of Science and Technology Policy, the Council on Wage and Price Stability, DOE, the President's domestic policy staff, OMB, and various offices within EPA. A description of this briefing and copies of the material distributed were docketed on May 1, 1979.

5. *April 30, 1979*—At 10:00 a.m., a one hour White House briefing was held for the President, the White House staff, and high ranking members of the Executive Branch "concerning the issues and options presented by the rulemaking." This meeting was noted on an EPA official's personal calendar which EDF obtained after promulgation in response to its FOIA request, but was never noted in the rulemaking docket.

6. *April 30, 1979*—At 2:30 p.m., a technical briefing on dry scrubbing technology at the White House was conducted by EPA for the White House staff. A short memorandum describing this briefing was docketed on May 30, 1979.

7. *May 1, 1979*—Another White House briefing was held on the subject of FGD technology. A description of the meeting and materials distributed were docketed on May 30, 1979.

8. *May 1, 1979*—EPA conducted a one hour briefing of staff members of the Senate Committee on Environmental and Public Works concerning EPA's analysis of the effect of alternative emission ceilings on coal reserves. The briefing was "substantially the same as the briefing given to Senator Byrd on May 2, 1980." No persons other than Committee staff members and EPA officials attended the briefing. This meeting, like the one at 10:00 a.m. on April 30, was never entered on the rulemaking docket but was listed on an EPA official's calendar obtained by EDF in response to its FOIA request. This EPA official has since stated that it was an oversight not to have a memorandum of this briefing prepared for the docket.

9. *May 2, 1979*—This was a brief meeting between Senator Byrd, EPA, DOE and NCA officials held ostensibly for Senator Byrd to hear EPA's comments on the NCA data. A 49 word, not very informative, memorandum describing the meeting was entered on the docket on June 1, 1979. * * *

C. STANDARD FOR JUDICIAL REVIEW OF EPA PROCEDURES

This court's scope of review is delimited by the special procedural provisions of the Clean Air Act, which declare that we may reverse the Administrator's decision for procedural error only if (i) his failure to observe procedural requirements was arbitrary and capricious, (ii) an objection was raised during the comment period, or the grounds for such objection arose only after the comment period and the objection is "of central relevance to the outcome of the rule," and (iii) "the errors were so serious and related to matters of such central relevance to the rule that there is a substantial likelihood that the rule would have been significantly changed if such errors had not been made." The essential message of so rigorous a standard is that Congress was concerned that EPA's rulemaking not be casually overturned for procedural reasons, and we of course must respect that judgment.

Our authority to reverse informal administrative rulemaking for procedural reasons is also informed by *Vermont Yankee Nuclear Power Corp. v. Natural Resources Defense Council, Inc.* * * *

D. STATUTORY PROVISIONS CONCERNING PROCEDURE

The procedural provisions of the Clean Air Act specifying the creation and content of the administrative rulemaking record are contained in section 307. * * *

* * * [T]he 1977 Amendments required the agency to establish a "rulemaking docket" for each proposed rule which would form the basis of the record for judicial review.   The docket must contain, *inter alia* (1) "notice of the proposed rulemaking * * * accompanied by a statement of its basis and purpose," and a specification of the public comment period; (2) "all written comments and documentary information on the proposed rule received from any person * * * during the comment period[;] [t]he transcript of public hearings, if any[;] and [a]ll documents * * * which become available after the proposed rule has been published and which the Administrator determines are of central relevance to the rulemaking. * * * "; (3) drafts of proposed rules submitted for interagency review, and all documents accompanying them and responding to them; and (4) the promulgated rule and the various accompanying agency documents which explain and justify it.

In contrast to other recent statutes, there is no mention of any restrictions upon "ex parte" contacts.   However, the statute apparently did envision that participants would normally submit comments, documentary material, and oral presentations during a prescribed comment period.   Only two provisions in the statute touch upon the post-comment period, one of which, as noted immediately supra, states that "[a]ll documents which become available after the proposed rule has been published and which the Administrator determines are of central relevance to the rulemaking shall be placed in the docket as soon as possible after their availability."   But since all the post-comment period written submissions which EDF complains of were in fact entered upon the docket, EDF cannot complain that this provision has been violated.

* * *

E. VALIDITY OF EPA'S PROCEDURES DURING THE POST-COMMENT PERIOD

The post-comment period communications about which EDF complains vary widely in their content and mode; some are written documents or letters, others are oral conversations and briefings, while still others are meetings where alleged political arm-twisting took place. For analytical purposes we have grouped the communications into categories and shall discuss each of them separately. * * *

Although no express authority to admit post-comment documents exist, the statute does provide that:

> All documents which become available after the proposed rule has been published and which the Administrator determines are of central relevance to the rulemaking shall be placed in the docket as soon as possible after their availability.

This provision, in contrast to others in the same subparagraph, is not limited to the comment period. Apparently it allows EPA not only to put documents into the record after the comment period is over, but also to define which documents are of "central relevance" so as to require that they be placed in the docket. The principal purpose of the drafters was to define in advance, for the benefit of reviewing courts, the record upon which EPA would rely in defending the rule it finally adopted; it was not their purpose to guarantee that every piece of paper or phone call related to the rule which was received by EPA during the post-comment period be included in the docket. EPA thus has authority to place post-comment documents into the docket, but it need not do so in all instances.

Such a reading of the statute accords well with the realities of Washington administrative policymaking, where rumors, leaks, and overreactions by concerned groups abound, particularly as the time for promulgation draws near. In a proceeding such as this, one of vital concern to so many interests—industry, environmental groups, as well as Congress and the Administration—it would be unrealistic to think there would not naturally be attempts on all sides to stay in contact with EPA right up to the moment the final rule is promulgated. The drafters of the 1977 Amendments were practical people, well versed in such activity, and we decline now to infer from their silence that they intended to prohibit the lodging of documents with the agency at any time prior to promulgation. Common sense, after all, must play a part in our interpretation of these statutory procedures.

EPA of course could have extended, or reopened, the comment period after January 15 in order formally to accommodate the flood of new documents; it has done so in other cases. But under the circumstances of this case, we do not find that it was necessary for EPA to reopen the formal comment period. In the first place, the comment period lasted over four months, and although the length of the comment period was not specified in the 1977 Amendments, the statute did put a premium on speedy decisionmaking by setting a one year deadline from the Amendments' enactment to the rules' promulgation. EPA failed to meet that deadline, and subsequently entered into a consent decree where it promised to adopt the final rules by March 19, 1979, over seven months late. EPA also failed to meet that deadline, and it was once more extended until June 1, 1979 upon agreement of the parties pursuant to court order. Reopening the formal comment period in the late spring of 1979 would have confronted the agency with a possible violation of the court order, and would further have frustrated the Congressional intent that these rules be promulgated expeditiously.

If, however, documents of central importance upon which EPA intended to rely had been entered on the docket too late for any meaningful public comment prior to promulgation, then both the structure and spirit of section 307 would have been violated. * * *

The case before us, however, does not present an instance where documents vital to EPA's support for its rule were submitted so late as to preclude any effective public comment. The vast majority of the written comments referred to earlier * * * were submitted in ample time to afford an opportunity for response. Regarding those documents submitted closer to the promulgation date, our review does not reveal that they played any significant role in the agency's support for the rule. The decisive point, however, is that EDF itself has failed to show us any particular document or documents to which it lacked an opportunity to respond, and which also were vital to EPA's support for the rule.

*   *   *

The statute does not explicitly treat the issue of post-comment period meetings with individuals outside EPA. Oral face-to-face discussions are not prohibited anywhere, anytime, in the Act. The absence of such prohibition may have arisen from the nature of the informal rulemaking procedures Congress had in mind. Where agency action resembles judicial action, where it involves formal rulemaking, adjudication, or quasi-adjudication among "conflicting private claims to a valuable privilege," the insulation of the decisionmaker from ex parte contacts is justified by basic notions of due process to the parties involved. But where agency action involves informal rulemaking of a policymaking sort, the concept of ex parte contacts is of more questionable utility.

Under our system of government, the very legitimacy of general policymaking performed by unelected administrators depends in no small part upon the openness, accessibility, and amenability of these officials to the needs and ideas of the public from whom their ultimate authority derives, and upon whom their commands must fall. As judges we are insulated from these pressures because of the nature of the judicial process in which we participate; but we must refrain from the easy temptation to look askance at all face-to-face lobbying efforts, regardless of the forum in which they occur, merely because we see them as inappropriate in the judicial context.[503] Furthermore, the importance to effective regulation of continuing contact with a regulated industry, other affected groups, and the public cannot be underestimated. Informal contacts may enable the agency to win needed support for its program, reduce future enforcement requirements by helping those regulated to anticipate and shape their plans for the future, and spur the provision of information which the agency needs. The possibility of course exists that in permitting ex parte communications with rulemakers we create the danger of "one administrative record for the public and this court and another for the Com-

---

503. *See* remarks of Carl McGowan (Chief Judge, U.S. Court of Appeals, D.C. Circuit), Ass'n of Amer. Law Schools, Section on Admin. Law (San Antonio, Texas, Jan. 4, 1981):

I think it likely that ambivalence will continue to pervade the *ex parte* contact problem until we face up to the question of whether legislation by informal rulemaking under delegated authority is, in terms of process, to be assimilated to lawmaking by the Congress itself, or to the adversary trial carried on in the sanitized and insulated atmosphere of the courthouse. Anyone with experience of both knows that a courtroom differs markedly in style and tone from a legislative chamber. The customs, the traditions, the mores, if you please, of the processes of persuasion, are emphatically not the same. What is acceptable in the one is alien to the other.

mission."   Under the Clean Air Act procedures, however, "[t]he promulgated rule may not be based (in part or whole) on any information or data which has not been placed in the docket. * * * Thus EPA must justify its rulemaking solely on the basis of the record it compiles and makes public. * * *

Lacking a statutory basis for its position, EDF would have us extend our decision in *Home Box Office, Inc. v. FCC* to cover all meetings with individuals outside EPA during the post-comment period.   Later decisions of this court, however, have declined to apply *Home Box Office* to informal rulemaking of the general policymaking sort involved here, and there is no precedent for applying it to the procedures found in the Clean Air Act Amendments of 1977.

It still can be argued, however, that if oral communications are to be freely permitted after the close of the comment period, then at least some adequate summary of them must be made in order to preserve the integrity of the rulemaking docket, which under the statute must be the sole repository of material upon which EPA intends to rely.   The statute does not require the docketing of all post-comment period conversations and meetings,[512] but we believe that a fair inference can be drawn that in some instances such docketing may be needed in order to give practical effect to section 307(d)(4)(B)(i), which provides that all *documents* "of central relevance to the rulemaking" shall be placed in the docket as soon as possible after their availability.   This is so because unless oral communications of central relevance to the rulemaking are also docketed in some fashion or other, information central to the justification of the rule could be obtained without ever appearing on the docket, simply by communicating it by voice rather than by pen, thereby frustrating the command of section 307 that the final rule not be "based (in part or whole) on any information or data which has not been placed in the docket. * * * [513]

---

512. EDF believes that the statute, 42 U.S.C.A. § 760 (4)(B), (d)(5), requires a transcript of any oral presentation in the course of the rulemaking.   In context, however, we think the transcript requirement refers to formal presentations made on request during the comment period, and is designed to insure that both oral and written presentations made during that time are included in the record.   It does not mean that a party can demand an opportunity for an oral presentation or insist upon a full transcript of such presentation being inserted in the record after the comment period has closed.   We believe the Administrator may receive oral contacts thereafter without making a complete transcript of such contacts, however useful such recording might be to ward off criticism.   All oral contacts, in other words, are not "oral presentation[s]" within the meaning of the statute.

persons" in the period between proposal and promulgation but "[i]n all cases, however, a written summary of the significant points made at the meetings must be placed in the comment file."   Memorandum from the Administrator, Ex Parte Contacts in EPA Rulemaking, App. of Lodged Documents, Schedule C-1 (Aug. 4, 1977).   This requirement applies "to every form of discussion with outside interested persons," in meetings or over the telephone, "as long as the discussion is significant."   All new data or significant arguments presented at the meeting should be reflected in the memorandum."   Id.

Many commentators agree that ex parte comments during informal rulemaking should not be restricted; but there is also agreement that at least those communications which produce *significant new information* should be noted on a public record.   *See,* e.g., K. Davis, at § 6:18; 1 C.F.R. § 205.77-3 (Admin. Conf. of the United States, Ex Parte Communications in Informal Rulemaking Proceedings, Rec. No. 77-3). * * *

513. EPA's own internal procedures are consistent with this interpretation of the statute.   EPA allows meetings with "interested

Turning to the particular oral communications in this case, we find that only two of the nine contested meetings were undocketed by EPA. The agency has maintained that, as to the May 1 meeting where Senate staff people were briefed on EPA's analysis concerning the impact of alternative emissions ceilings upon coal reserves, its failure to place a summary of the briefing in the docket was an oversight. We find no evidence that this oversight was anything but an honest inadvertence; furthermore, a briefing of this sort by EPA which simply provides background information about an upcoming rule is not the type of oral communication which would require a docket entry under the statute.

The other undocketed meeting occurred at the White House and involved the President and his White House staff. * * *

We have already held that a blanket prohibition against meetings during the post-comment period with individuals outside EPA is unwarranted, and this perforce applies to meetings with White House officials. We have not yet addressed, however, the issue whether such oral communications with White House staff, or the President himself, must be docketed on the rulemaking record, and we now turn to that issue. * * *

We note initially that section 307 makes specific provision for including in the rulemaking docket the "written comments" of other executive agencies along with accompanying documents on any proposed draft rules circulated in advance of the rulemaking proceeding. Drafts of the final rule submitted to an executive review process prior to promulgation, as well as all "written comments," "documents," and "written responses" resulting from such interagency review process, are also to be put in the docket prior to promulgation. This specific requirement does not mention informal meetings or conversations concerning the rule which are not part of the initial or final review processes, nor does it refer to oral comments of any sort. Yet it is hard to believe Congress was unaware that intra-executive meetings and oral comments would occur throughout the rulemaking process. We assume, therefore, that unless expressly forbidden by Congress, such intra-executive contacts[520] may take place, both during and after the public comment period; the only real issue is whether they must be noted and summarized in the docket.

The court recognizes the basic need of the President and his White House staff to monitor the consistency of executive agency regulations with Administration policy. He and his White House advisors surely

---

520. In this case we need not decide the effect upon rulemaking proceedings of a failure to disclose so-called "conduit" communications, in which administration or inter-agency contacts serve as mere conduits for private parties in order to get the latter's off-the-record views into the proceeding. EDF alleges that many of the executive comments here fell into that category. We note that the Department of Justice Office of Legal Counsel has taken the position that it may be improper for White House advisers to act as conduits for outsiders. It has therefore recommended that Council of Economic Advisers officials summarize and place in rulemaking records a compilation of all written or oral comments they receive relevant to particular proceedings. * * * EDF has given us no reason to believe that a policy similar to this was not followed here, or that unrecorded conduit communications exist in this case; we therefore decline to authorize further discovery simply on the unsubstantiated hypothesis that some such communications may be unearthed thereby.

must be briefed fully and frequently about rules in the making, and their contributions to policymaking considered.   The executive power under our Constitution, after all, is not shared—it rests exclusively with the President.   The idea of a "plural executive," or a President with a council of state, was considered and rejected by the Constitutional Convention. Instead the Founders chose to risk the potential for tyranny inherent in placing power in one person, in order to gain the advantages of accountability fixed on a single source.   To ensure the President's control and supervision over the Executive Branch, the Constitution—and its judicial gloss—vests him with the powers of appointment and removal, the power to demand written opinions from executive officers, and the right to invoke executive privilege to protect consultative privacy.   In the particular case of EPA, Presidential authority is clear since it has never been considered an "independent agency," but always part of the Executive Branch.

The authority of the President to control and supervise executive policymaking is derived from the Constitution; the desirability of such control is demonstrable from the practical realities of administrative rulemaking.   Regulations such as those involved here demand a careful weighing of cost, environmental, and energy considerations.   They also have broad implications for national economic policy.   Our form of government simply could not function effectively or rationally if key executive policymakers were isolated from each other and from the Chief Executive.   Single mission agencies do not always have the answers to complex regulatory problems.   An overworked administrator exposed on a 24-hour basis to a dedicated but zealous staff needs to know the arguments and ideas of policymakers in other agencies as well as in the White House.

We recognize, however, that there may be instances where the docketing of conversations between the President or his staff and other Executive Branch officers or rulemakers may be necessary to ensure due process.   This may be true, for example, where such conversations directly concern the outcome of adjudications or quasi-adjudicatory proceedings; there is no inherent executive power to control the rights of individuals in such settings.   Docketing may also be necessary in some circumstances where a statute like this one *specifically requires* that essential "information or data" upon which a rule is based be docketed.   But in the absence of any further Congressional requirements, we hold that it was not unlawful in this case for EPA not to docket a face-to-face policy session involving the President and EPA officials during the post-comment period, since EPA makes no effort to base the rule on any "information or data" arising from that meeting.   Where the President himself is directly involved in oral communications with Executive Branch officials, Article II considerations—combined with the strictures of *Vermont Yankee*—require that courts tread with extraordinary caution in mandating disclosure beyond that already required by statute.

The purposes of full-record review which underlie the need for disclosing ex parte conversations in some settings do not require that courts know the details of every White House contact, including a Presidential one, in this informal rulemaking setting. After all, any rule issued here with or without White House assistance must have the requisite factual support in the rulemaking record, and under this particular statute the Administrator may not base the rule in whole or in part on any *"information or data"* which is not in the record, no matter what the source. The courts will monitor all this, but they need not be omniscient to perform their role efffectively. Of course, it is always possible that undisclosed Presidential prodding may direct an outcome that is factually based on the record, but different from the outcome that would have obtained in the absence of Presidential involvement. In such a case, it would be true that the political process did affect the outcome in a way the courts could not police. But we do not believe that Congress intended that the courts convert informal rulemaking into a rarified technocratic process, unaffected by political considerations or the presence of Presidential power. In sum, we find that the existence of intra-Executive Branch meetings during the post-comment period, and the failure to docket one such meeting involving the President, violated neither the procedures mandated by the Clean Air Act nor due process.

Finally, EDF challenges the rulemaking on the basis of alleged Congressional pressure, citing principally two meetings with Senator Byrd. EDF asserts that under the controlling case law the political interference demonstrated in this case represents a separate and independent ground for invalidating this rulemaking. But among the cases EDF cites in support of its position, only *D.C. Federation of Civic Associations v. Volpe* [459 F.2d 1231 (D.C. Cir. 1971), *cert. denied* 405 U.S. 1030 (1972)] seems relevant to the facts here.

* * *

D.C. Federation * * * requires that two conditions be met before an administrative rulemaking may be overturned simply on the grounds of Congressional pressure. First, the content of the pressure upon the Secretary is designed to force him to decide upon factors not made relevant by Congress in the applicable statute. Representative Natcher's threats were of precisely that character, since deciding to approve the bridge in order to free the "hostage" mass transit appropriation was not among the decisionmaking factors Congress had in mind when it enacted the highway approval provisions of Title 23 of the United States Code. Second, the Secretary's determination must be affected by those extraneous considerations.

In the case before us, there is no persuasive evidence that either criterion is satisfied. Senator Byrd requested a meeting in order to express "strongly" his already well-known views that the SO_2 standards' impact on coal reserves was a matter of concern to him. EPA initiated a second responsive meeting to report its reaction to the reserve data submitted by the NCA. In neither meeting is there any allegation that EPA made any commitments to Senator Byrd. The meetings did underscore Senator Byrd's deep concerns for EPA, but there is no evidence he attempted actively to use "extraneous" pressures to further his position.   Americans rightly expect their elected representatives to voice their grievances and preferences concerning the administration of our laws.   We believe it entirely proper for Congressional representatives vigorously to represent the interests of their constituents before administrative agencies engaged in informal, general policy rulemaking, so long as individual Congressmen do not frustrate the intent of Congress as a whole as expressed in statute, nor undermine applicable rules of procedure.   Where Congressmen keep their comments focused on the substance of the proposed rule—and we have no substantial evidence to cause us to believe Senator Byrd did not do so here—administrative agencies are expected to balance Congressional pressure with the pressures emanating from all other sources.   To hold otherwise would deprive the agencies of legitimate sources of information and call into question the validity of nearly every controversial rulemaking. * * *

In sum, we conclude that EPA's adoption of the 1.2 lbs./MBtu emissions ceiling was free from procedural error. * * *

Notes

For additional discussion of the substantive as well as procedural implications of Presidential involvement in agency rulemaking, see *Symposium: Presidential Intervention in Administrative Rulemaking*, 56 Tul. L. Rev. 811–902 (1982).

Official Bias and Prejudgment

In judicial proceedings the trier of fact is expected to have no connection with, or knowledge of, the parties or the issues that could conceivably affect his judgment.   In administrative adjudication, even though cases may be initiated by officials who will ultimately decide them, evidence of prejudgment of the facts is disqualifying.   See, e.g., *Withrow v. Larkin*, 421 U.S. 35 (1975); *Gibson v. Berryhill*, 411 U.S. 564 (1973); see also supra p. 236.   As agency rulemaking has become more formal and record-confined, demands for neutrality and objectivity have been advanced in proceedings whose ostensible purpose is to establish future administrative policy.   See Strauss, *Disqualification of Decisional Officials in Rulemaking*, 80 Colum. L. Rev. 990 (1980).

ASSOCIATION OF NATIONAL ADVERTISERS, INC. v. FTC

United States Court of Appeals, District of Columbia Circuit, 1979.
627 F.2d 1151, cert. denied 447 U.S. 921, 100 S.Ct. 3011, 65 L.Ed.2d 1113 (1980).

TAMM, CIRCUIT JUDGE.

Plaintiffs, appellees here, brought an action in the United States District Court for the District of Columbia to prohibit Michael Pertschuk, Chairman of the Federal Trade Commission (Commission), from participating in a pending rulemaking proceeding concerning children's advertising.   The district court, citing this court's decision in *Cinderella Career & Finishing Schools, Inc. v. FTC*, 425 F.2d 583 (D.C. Cir. 1970), found that Chairman Pertschuk had prejudged issues involved in the rulemaking and ordered him disqualified. * * *

On April 27, 1978, the Commission issued a Notice of Proposed Rulemaking that suggested restrictions regarding television advertising directed toward children. * * * The Commission explained that it had decided to propose a rule limiting children's advertising after consideration of a staff report that discussed

> facts which suggest that the televised advertising of any product directed to young children who are too young to understand the selling purpose of, or otherwise comprehend or evaluate, commercials may be unfair and deceptive within the meaning of Section 5 of the Federal Trade Commission Act, requiring appropriate remedy.   The Report also discloses facts which suggest that the current televised advertising of sugared products directed to older children may be unfair and deceptive, again requiring appropriate remedy.

The Commission invited interested persons to comment upon any issue raised by the staff proposal.

On May 8, 1978, the Association of National Advertisers, Inc. (ANA), the American Association of Advertising Agencies (AAAA), the American Advertising Federation (AAF), and the Toy Manufacturers of America, Inc. (TMA) petitioned Chairman Pertschuk to recuse himself from participation in the children's advertising inquiry. The petition charged that Pertschuk had made public statements concerning regulation of children's advertising that demonstrated prejudgment of specific factual issues sufficient to preclude his ability to serve as an impartial arbiter. The charges were based on a speech Pertschuk delivered to the Action for Children's Television (ACT) Research Conference in November 1977, on several newspaper and magazine articles quoting Chairman Pertschuk's views on children's television, on the transcript of a televised interview, and on a press release issued by the Commission during the summer of 1977.

On July 13, 1978, Chairman Pertschuk declined to recuse himself from the proceeding. * * * Five days later, the Commission, without Pertschuk participating, also determined that Pertschuk need not be disqualified.

In August 1978, ANA, AAAA, AAF, and TMA petitioned the district court to declare that Chairman Pertschuk should be disqualified from participating in the children's television proceeding. * * * The plaintiffs introduced copies of three letters, sent by Chairman Pertschuk on the day after he delivered the ACT speech, as additional evidence of his alleged prejudgment. * * *

On November 3, 1978, the district court ruled on cross-motions for summary judgment.   The court, relying on *Cinderella*, found that Chairman Pertschuk "has prejudged and has given the appearance of having prejudged issues of fact involved in a fair determination of the Children's Advertising rulemaking proceeding."   Accordingly, the court granted the plaintiffs' motion for summary judgment and ordered Pertschuk enjoined from further participation.   This appeal followed.

* * *

The district court * * * held that "the standard of conduct delineated in *Cinderella*" governs agency decisionmakers participating in a section 18 proceeding.   Section 18 authorizes the Commission to promulgate rules designed to "define with specificity acts or practices which are unfair or deceptive."   The district court ruled that a section 18 proceeding, notwithstanding the appellation rulemaking, "is neither wholly legislative nor wholly adjudicative."   According to the district court, the "adjudicative aspects" of the proceeding render *Cinderella* applicable.

* * *

Because legislative facts combine empirical observation with application of administrative expertise to reach generalized conclusions, they need not be developed through evidentiary hearings.   To the contrary, however, "[w]here adjudicative, rather than legislative, facts are involved, the parties must be afforded a hearing to allow them an opportunity to meet and to present evidence."   This distinction has been established in judicial, as well as administrative, processes.

Evidentiary hearings, although not necessary to determine legislative facts, nevertheless may be helpful in certain circumstances.   For example, Congress, when it enacted the Magnuson-Moss Act, recognized that special circumstances might warrant the use of evidentiary proceedings in determining legislative facts.   Under section 18(c)(1)(B) and section 18(c)(2)(B), the Commission must conduct a hearing, with a limited right of cross-examination, when it resolves disputed issues of material fact.   The legislative history of the Magnuson-Moss Act states that "[t]he only disputed issues of material fact to be determined for resolution by the Commission are those issues characterized as issues of specific fact in contrast to legislative fact."

Although neither the Conference Report nor subsequent congressional debate amplify the term "specific fact," its genesis can be traced to a recommendation of the Administrative Conference of the United States (ACUS).   Prior to congressional action on the Magnuson-Moss Act, ACUS promulgated Recommendation No. 72-5, which suggested that Congress should not require trial-type procedures "for making rules of general applicability, except that it may sometimes appropriately require such procedures for resolving issues of specific fact."   1 C.F.R. § 305.72-5.   In a letter dated July 27, 1973, then-ACUS Chairman Antonin Scalia answered Congressman Moss's request for a definition of the term "specific fact":

Conference Recommendation 72-5 is addressed exclusively to agency rulemaking of *general* applicability.   In such a proceeding, almost by definition, adjudicative facts are not at issue, and the agency should ordinarily be free to, and ordinarily would, proceed by the route of written comments, supplemented, perhaps, by a legislative-type hearing. Yet there may arise occasionally in such rulemaking proceedings factual issues which, though not adjudicative, nevertheless justify exploration in a trial-type format—because they are sufficiently narrow in focus and sufficiently material to the outcome of the proceeding to make it reasonable and useful for the agency to resort to trial-type procedure to resolve them. These are what the Recommendation refers to as issues of specific fact.

A review of this and subsequent ACUS correspondence demonstrates that the term "specific fact" refers to a category of legislative fact, the resolution of which may be aided by the type of adversarial procedures inherent in an evidentiary proceeding with limited cross-examination. Nothing in the legislative history or background of section 18 suggests, however, that Congress believed that the use of evidentiary hearings transformed the nature of the proceedings from rulemaking to adjudication or altered the factual predicate of rulemaking from legislative to adjudicative fact. Accordingly, the appellees' contention that the *Cinderella* standard must be applied to section 18 rulemaking because it invokes the same type of factual judgments as Commission adjudication is simply incorrect. * * *

Had Congress amended section 5 of the FTC Act to declare certain types of children's advertising unfair or deceptive, we would barely pause to consider a due process challenge. No court to our knowledge has imposed procedural requirements upon a legislature before it may act. Indeed, any suggestion that congressmen may not prejudge factual and policy issues is fanciful. A legislature must have the ability to exchange views with constituents and to suggest public policy that is dependent upon factual assumptions. Individual interests impinged upon by the legislative process are protected, as Justice Holmes wrote, "in the only way that they can be in a complex society, by [the individual's] power, immediate or remote, over those who make the rule." *Bi-Metallic Investment Co. v. State Board of Equalization,* 239 U.S. 441, 445 (1915).

Congress chose, however, to delegate its power to proscribe unfair or deceptive acts or practices to the Commission because "there were too many unfair practices for it to define." In determining the due process standards applicable in a section 18 proceeding, we are guided by its nature as rulemaking. When a proceeding is classified as rulemaking, due process ordinarily does not demand procedures more rigorous than those provided by Congress. *See Vermont Yankee Nuclear Power Corp. v. NRDC,* 435 U.S. 519. Congress is under no requirement to hold an evidentiary hearing prior to its adoption of legislation, and "Congress need not make that requirement when it delegates the task to an administrative agency." Accordingly, we must apply a disqualification standard that is consistent with the structure and purposes of section 18.

* * *

The legitimate functions of a policymaker, unlike an adjudicator, demand interchange and discussion about important issues. We must not impose judicial roles upon administrators when they perform functions very different from those of judges. * * *

* * *

Accordingly, a Commissioner should be disqualified only when there has been a clear and convincing showing that the agency member has an unalterably closed mind on matters critical to the disposition of the proceeding. The "clear and convincing" test is necessary to rebut the presumption of administrative regularity. The "unalterably closed mind" test is necessary to permit rulemakers to carry out their proper policy-based functions while disqualifying those unable to consider meaningfully a section 18 hearing.

HOLDING

We view the statements offered as grounds for disqualification as a whole to discern whether they evidence a clear and convincing showing that Chairman Pertschuk has an unalterably closed mind on matters critical to the children's television proceeding. * * *

Chairman Pertschuk's remarks, considered as a whole, represent discussion, and perhaps advocacy, of the legal theory that might support exercise of the Commission's jurisdiction over children's advertising. The mere discussion of policy or advocacy on a legal question, however, is not sufficient to disqualify an administrator. To present legal and policy arguments, Pertschuk not unnaturally employed the factual assumptions that underlie the rationale for Commission action. The simple fact that the Chairman explored issues based on legal and factual assumptions, however, did not necessarily bind him to them forever. Rather, he remained free, both in theory and in reality, to change his mind upon consideration of the presentations made by those who would be affected. * * *

Indeed, section 18 in effect requires the Commission to formulate tentative judgments on suggested rules. Before the Commission initiates rulemaking proceedings, it must "publish a notice of proposed rulemaking stating with particularity the reason for the proposed rule prior to the comment stage of the proceeding." The Conference Committee on the Magnuson-Moss Act referred to the period following this notice as one during which affected parties could "challenge the factual assumptions on which the Commission is proceeding and to show in what respect these assumptions are erroneous." Congress intended for the Commission to develop proposals that subsequently would be published and discussed openly. To perform this task intelligently necessarily involves making tentative conclusions of fact, even if they later are open to public challenge.

In sum, we hold that the materials adduced by the appellees are insufficient to rebut the strong presumption of administrative regularity. * * * The statements do not demonstrate that Chairman Pertschuk is unwilling or unable to consider rationally argument that a final rule is unnecessary because children are either unharmed by sugared products or are able to understand advertising. The appellees have failed to make a clear and convincing showing that Chairman Pertschuk has an unalterably closed mind on matters critical to the children's television proceedings.

The appellees have a right to a fair and open proceeding; that right includes access to an impartial decisionmaker. Impartial, however, does not mean uninformed, unthinking, or inarticulate. The requirements of due process clearly recognize the necessity for rulemakers to formulate policy in a manner similar to legislative action. The standard enunciated today will protect the purposes of a section 18 proceeding, and, in so doing, will guarantee the appellees a fair hearing.

We would eviscerate the proper evolution of policymaking were we to disqualify every administrator who has opinions on the correct course of his agency's future action. Administrators, and even judges, may hold policy views on questions of law prior to participating in a proceeding. The factual basis for a rulemaking is so closely intertwined with policy judgments that we would obliterate rulemaking were we to equate a statement on an issue of legislative fact with unconstitutional prejudgment. The importance and legitimacy of rulemaking procedures are too well established to deny administrators such a fundamental tool.

Finally, we eschew formulation of a disqualification standard that impinges upon the political process. An administrator's presence within an agency reflects the political judgment of the President and Senate. As Judge Prettyman of this court aptly noted, a "Commission's view of what is best in the public interest may change from time to time. Commissions themselves change, underlying philosophies differ, and experience often dictates changes." *Pinellas Broadcasting Co. v. FCC*, 230 F.2d 204, 206 (D.C. Cir. 1956), *cert. denied* 350 U.S. 1007 (1956). We are concerned that implementation of the *Cinderella* standard in the rulemaking context would plunge courts into the midst of political battles concerning the proper formulation of administrative policy. We serve as quarantors of statutory and constitutional rights, but not as arbiters of the political process. Accordingly, we will not order the disqualification of a rulemaker absent the most compelling proof that he is unable to carry out his duties in a constitutionally permissible manner.

Reversed.

LEVENTHAL, CIRCUIT JUDGE, concurring.

The ultimate test announced by Judge Tamm * * * is that disqualification from a rulemaking proceeding results "only when there has been a clear and convincing showing that [the agency member] has an unalterably closed mind on matters critical to the disposition of the [proceeding]." * * *

The application of this test to agencies must take into account important differences in function and functioning between the agencies and court systems. In fulfilling the functions of applying or considering the validity of a statute, or a government program, the judge endeavors to put aside personal views as to the desirability of the law or program, and he is not disqualified because he personally deems the program laudable or objectionable.   In the case of agency rulemaking, however, the decisionmaking officials are appointed precisely to implement statutory programs, and with the expectation that they have a personal disposition to enforce them vigilantly and effectively.   They work with a combination rather than a separation of functions, in legislative modes, and take action on the basis of information coming from many sources, even though that provides a mindset before a proceeding is begun, subject to reconsideration in the light of the proceeding.

* * *

* * * Of course, there remains a requirement of fairness for those with authority to act by rulemaking but the standards are not identical with those pertinent for judicial-type decisionmaking in adjudicatory actions. * * *

MacKINNON, CIRCUIT JUDGE (dissenting in part and concurring in part).

* * *

The majority opinion holds, and I agree with such holding, that "The appellees have a right to a fair and open proceeding; that right includes access to an *impartial decisionmaker.*"   However, the majority considers that one qualifies as an "impartial decisionmaker" unless he is shown by clear and convincing evidence to have an *unalterably closed mind* on matters critical to the children's television proceeding.   This rule would establish a legal principle that evidence of bias and prejudice would not be disqualifying unless it could surmount a fence that is horse high, pig tight and bull strong.   In my view that is too much protection for a biased decisionmaker.   In a great many instances it would deprive the public of decisionmakers that are actually "impartial."

The current case * * * illustrates how strong evidence of prejudgment can be played down to almost sanitize the attitudes expressed. * * *

* * * On TV's Today Show on October 31, 1977 [Chairman Pertschuk] admitted that "the implicit indication of [his] personal opinions in these replies are [sic] self-evident."   By this statement he recognized that it is the *implicit indications* of his personal opinions that should be evaluated.   He next stated: "I have some serious doubt as to whether any television advertising should be directed at a 3 or 4 or 5 year old, a pre-schooler * * * we have never treated children as commercial objects in our society."   This expresses a very firm opinion that, by its advertising, television *was* treating such children as "commercial objects"— presumably trigger words in his vocabulary.

Next, in response to the question whether he would like to see the Federal Trade Commission ban children's advertising *altogether* he replied "not necessarily.   But we've not excluded the possibility of bans on certain advertising of certain products to children."   In the next paragraph, in an apparent attempt to save the Commission from the taint of any bias that his personal statements indicate, he attempts to spread the responsibility by stating that there are 4 other Commissioners and consequently his views do not bind the others.   However, a Commission is prohibited from acting with even *one* biased Commissioner.   Then the Chairman stated that the Commission has "not as a body yet approached the question of a remedy for the *evils we see* in children's advertising."   So the Commission (we) had already determined that the advertising was "evil."   Apparently, the only issue was what remedy to apply.

Next, in his speech to the Action for Children's Television Research Conference at Boston on November 8, 1977, he referred to the "*moral myopia* of children's television advertising." (Emphasis added.)   He also stated that "advertisers *seize* on the child's trust and *exploit* it as a weakness for their gain." (Emphasis added.)   These remarks evidence definite conclusions, definite opinions and a biased slant.   Later he stated: "using sophisticated techniques like fantasy and animation, they [TV advertisers] *manipulate* children's attitudes." (Emphasis added.) This also indicates a prejudgment of the purpose and intent of TV advertisers.

He then argued:

> Why isn't [the] * * * principle [that those responsible for children's well being are entitled to the support of laws designed to aid discharge of that responsibility] applicable to television advertising directed at young children?   Why shouldn't established legal precedents embodying this public policy be applied to protect children from this *form of exploitation*?   In short, why isn't such advertising unfair within the meaning of the Federal Trade Commission Act and, hence, unlawful?   (Emphasis added.)

Can any reasonable person contend that such remarks do not indicate that he has prejudged TV Advertising and decided that it *exploits* children? * * *

Finally, we come to several letters written by the Chairman. * * *

November 9, 1977

MEMORANDUM
TO: Coleman McCarthy
FROM: Mike Pertschuk

Coleman, I know you share my concern in raising public consciousness to the part we play as a society for permitting children to be made commercial objects.   I thought you'd want to see this statement in which I've tried to establish underpinnings [*sic*] for a *fundamental assault* on television advertising directed toward young children.
(Emphasis added.)

*   *   *

November 17, 1977

Honorable Donald Kennedy
Food and Drug Administration
Parklawn Building
5600 Fishers Lane
Rockville, Maryland 20852

Dear Don:

Setting legal theory aside, the truth is that we've been drawn into this issue because of the *conviction*, which I know you share, that one of the *evils* flowing from the *unfairness* of children's advertising is the resulting distortion of children's perceptions of nutritional values.   I see, at this point, our logical process as follows: children's advertising is inherently unfair.   As a policy planning agency we have to make judgments as to our priorities.   The first area in which we choose to act is an area in which a substantial controversy exists as to the health consequences of encouraging consumption of sugared products (not just cereals).   With this formulation we do not have to prove the health consequences of sugared cereals.   What we do have to prove is that there is a substantial health controversy regarding the health consequences of sugar—a much lower burden of proof.

I'm convinced that the convergence of public policies regarding the commercial exploitation of children with the health controversy over sugared products give us a stronger base and frankly deal directly with the underlying concerns which prompt our action.

Sincerely yours,
Michael Pertschuk

(Emphasis added.)

* * *

Thus, if the Notice of Rulemaking were truthful, so far as Chairman Pertschuk's views were concerned, it would have stated in substance:

The Commission has decided to make a fundamental assault upon Children's Advertising on TV because we are convinced that it is *evil*, unfair and allowed solely because of the moral myopia of the public and the industry.   We solicit comments as to whether it should be prohibited entirely or to some lesser degree.

Notwithstanding that the majority opinion holds that a "fair decision-maker" is to be guaranteed for this rulemaking, the opinion seeks to obviate such guarantee, if I read the opinion correctly, by holding that Commissioners in their Magnuson-Moss rulemaking are to be considered the same as Congressmen, and the fairness with which they approach their rulemaking cannot be attacked because Congressmen are not subject to similar constraints in enacting legislation. * * *

It is true that legislators are not required to make findings of fact to support their legislation and that they cannot be disqualified by any court for bias, but there are other safeguards in the legislative process that compensate for the absence of such safeguards as are expressly imposed or implicit in the administrative process. First of all, legislators are *elected* by the voters of their district, and those in the House are elected for a relatively short term—only two years. They can be turned out very quickly if any bias they disclose offends their constituents. Secondly, there is a protection in the sheer size of Congress—535 members of the House and Senate—that implicitly diffuses bias and guarantees that impermissible bias of individual members will not control. There is safety in numbers and a biased Congressman soon loses influence among the other members, if he ever acquired any. Also, the two house system and the Presidential veto are tremendous guarantees that legislation will not be the result of individual bias or even the impermissible bias of one house. * * *

Reforms of Federal Agency Rulemaking

During the 1970's, dissatisfaction with "hybridized" rulemaking under the APA emerged from many quarters. See, e. g., Hamilton, *Procedures for the Adoption of Rules of General Applicability: The Need for Procedural Innovation in Administrative Rulemaking*, 60 Calif. L. Rev. 1276 (1972). Suggestions for procedural reform came from almost as many sources, including Congress, the academic community, the White House, and agencies themselves.

1. In several regulatory statutes enacted since the early 1970's, Congress has not been content with the minimum requirements of section 553, and instead has attempted to prescribe procedures that meet objections to bare notice-and-comment rulemaking. The textual variations are almost as numerous as the laws themselves. One example is the Consumer Product Safety Act, 15 U.S.C.A. § § 2051 *et seq.*, which empowers the CPSC to adopt safety standards for hazardous consumer products. Rulemaking commences with the publication of a notice identifying the product and the hazard, stating the Commission's determination that to a safety standard is necessary, and inviting interested persons propose an existing standard or to offer to develop a proposed standard. The second stage is publication of a proposed standard, which may be an existing standard, a proposal developed by an outside offeror, or the Commission's own work. 15 U.S.C.A. § § 2051 *et seq.* Section 2058 describes the final steps in the process:

(d)(1) Within 60 days after the publication * * * of a proposed consumer product safety rule * * * the Commission shall—

(A) promulgate a consumer product safety rule respecting the risk of injury associated with such product if it makes the findings required under subsection (f). * * *

(2) Consumer product safety rules shall be promulgated in accordance with section 553 of title 5, except that the Commission shall give interested persons an opportunity for the oral presentation of data, views, or arguments, in addition to an opportunity to make written submissions. A transcript shall be kept of any oral presentation. * * *

(f)(1)   Prior to promulgating a consumer product safety rule, the Commission shall consider, and shall make appropriate findings for inclusion in such rule with respect to—

(A)   the degree and nature of the risk of injury the rule is designed to eliminate or reduce;

(B)   the approximate number of consumer products, or types or classes thereof, subject to such rule;

(C)   the need of the public for the consumer products subject to such rule, and the probable effect of such rule upon the utility, cost, or availability of such products to meet such need; and

(D)   any means of achieving the objective of the order while minimizing adverse effects on competition or disruption or dislocation of manufacturing and other commercial practices consistent with the public health and safety.

(2)   The Commission shall not promulgate a consumer product safety rule unless it has prepared, on the basis of the findings of the Commission under paragraph (1) and on other information before the Commission, a final regulatory analysis of the rule containing the following information:

(A)   A description of the potential benefits and potential costs of the rule, including costs and benefits that cannot be quantified in monetary terms, and the identification of those likely to receive the benefits and bear the costs.

(B)   A description of any alternatives to the final rule which were considered by the Commission, together with a summary description of their potential benefits and costs and a brief explanation of the reasons why these alternatives were not chosen.

(C)   A summary of any significant issues raised by the comments submitted during the public comment period in response to the preliminary regulatory analysis, and a summary of the assessment by the Commission of such issues.

The Commission shall publish its final regulatory analysis with the rule.

(3)   The Commission shall not promulgate a consumer product safety rule unless it finds (and includes such finding in the rule)—

(A)   that the rule (including its effective date) is reasonably necessary to eliminate or reduce an unreasonable risk of injury associated with such product;

(B)   that the promulgation of the rule is in the public interest;

(C)   in the case of a rule declaring the product a banned hazardous product, that no feasible consumer product safety standard under this chapter would adequately protect the public from the unreasonable risk of injury associated with such product.

For two skeptical accounts of the CPSC's experience under this legislation, see Hamilton, *The Role of Nongovernmental Standards in the Development of Mandatory Federal Standards Affecting Safety or Health*, 56 Tex. L. Rev. 1329 (1978); Schwartz, *The Consumer Product Safety*

Commission: A Flawed Product of the Consumer Decade, 51 G.W.U. L. Rev. 32 (1982).

2. In this section we have been concerned primarily with procedural obligations that are imposed by statute or judicial decree. Enlarged procedural protections impose costs, among them delay, which administrators may consider excessive. But agency heads, in addition to being administrators of large bureaucracies are also political appointees and some are public personalities who recognize the importance of "consensus building" and the desirability of maintaining good communication with groups affected by their decisions. In addition, tough-minded agency heads are usually eager to embrace procedures that contribute to their ability to obtain and analyze relevant information. They thus may pursue divergent paths to improving rulemaking, as OSHA's experience illustrates.

The Occupational Safety and Health Act, 29 U.S.C.A. § 651 *et seq.*, permits informal rulemaking for the adoption of workplace safety standards, except that it requires OSHA, in addition to receiving written comments, to hold a "public hearing" on objections to any proposed standard. The Act's legislative history suggests that Congress contemplated a legislative-style hearing, but it also authorized preenforcement judicial review of final standards under the substantial evidence test. To implement these statutory requirements, the Secretary of Labor at an early date adopted the following procedures for the mandated hearing (29 C.F.R. § 1911.15):

> (a)(2)   * * * Although these sections are not read as requiring   * * * the application of the formal requirements of 5 U.S.C.A. 556 and 557, they do suggest a Congressional expectation that the rulemaking would be on the basis of a record to which a substantial evidence test, where pertinent, may be applied in the event an informal hearing is held.   * * *
>
> (b) Although any hearing shall be informal and legislative in type, this part is intended to provide more than the bare essentials of informal rulemaking under 5 U.S.C.A. 553. The additional requirements are the following:
>
> > (1) The presiding officer shall be a hearing examiner appointed under 5 U.S.C.A. 3105.
> >
> > (2) The presiding officer shall provide an opportunity for cross-examination on crucial issues.
> >
> > (3) The hearing shall be reported verbatim   * * *

OSHA soon came under criticism for its apparently slow pace in promulgating occupational standards, particularly standards for chemicals suspected of causing cancer. See, *e.g.*, McGarity, *OSHA's Generic Carcinogen Policy: Rule Making under Scientific and Legal Uncertainty* in J. NYHART & M. CARROW, eds., LAW AND SCIENCE IN COLLABORATION 55 (1983), and sources cited therein. According to some critics, one cause of delay was the enormous records generated by OSHA's rulemaking—such as those for benzene and cotton dust—which reflected both the controversy of its proposals and the scope of the issues on which it entertained comment. Agency officials became convinced that the rulemaking process had to be expedited. Taking a leaf from the FDA's experience with administrative summary judgment in adjudication, OSHA in 1977 proposed general criteria and procedures for setting standards for potential carcinogens. 42 Fed. Reg. 54147 (1977). The proposed criteria would determine, as matters of scientific act or administrative policy, the principles by which OSHA would identify, classify, and regulate chemicals that posed a cancer risk for humans.

Development of OSHA's "generic carcinogen policy" proved more difficult than any of its rulemakings for specific chemicals. The mandated informal hearing lasted from May 16, 1978 until June 25, 1978 and generated a transcript of over 8,500 pages. The full rulemaking record eventually exceeded 250,000 pages. The agency itself offered more than forty-five witnesses, and a larger number of witnesses appeared on behalf of other participants. The final policy occupied more than 280 Federal Register pages of preamble and a dozen pages of regulatory text. *Identification, Classification and Regulation of Potential Occupational Carcinogens*, 45 Fed. Reg. 5001 (1980).

OSHA's regulations set forth the criteria it will use in evaluating different types of evidence concerning a chemical's carcinogenicity. The regulations state, for example, that the agency will accept positive results in well-designed epidemiological studies as establishing "the qualitative inference of carcinogenic hazards to workers." By contrast, negative human evidence, "will be considered" only if

> (i) The epidemiological study involved at least 20 years' exposure of a group of subjects to the substance and at least 30 years' observation of the subjects after initial exposure; [and] * * *

> (iii) The group of exposed subjects was large enough for an increase in cancer incidence of 50% above that in unexposed controls to have been detected at any of the predicted sites. * * *

OSHA's regulations also purport to resolve issues of regulatory policy. They assert, as a binding rule, that the Act requires the agency to reduce employee exposure to substances posing a significant cancer risk to the lowest level compatible with industry survival and achievable by foreseeable technology. The regulations rule out cost-benefit analysis to establish such exposure limits and establish a decisive preference for engineering controls and work practices to achieve compliance.

These ambitious regulations differ from other agency rules previously upheld as the basis for summary judgment. The regulations address the full range of scientific policy issues encountered in previous rulemakings; they describe the process by which OSHA will evaluate chemicals before commencing rulemaking; and they speak to remedial issues, such as the content of standards and the desired means of compliance with them. On the other hand, the regulations purport only to narrow the issues the agency will consider in subsequent rulemakings, not to foreclose hearings altogether.

OSHA's regulations were almost immediately derailed. Soon after President Reagan's inauguration the agency announced that extensive revisions would soon be proposed and it purported to stay implementation of those provisions that had become operative. 46 Fed. Reg. 11253, 19000 (1981).

Even before these events, observers questioned whether the regulations would improve OSHA's efficiency. The agency cannot avoid rulemaking to set a standard for any chemical and many issues were expressly left open for individual proceedings. More important, the regulations are studiously ambiguous about the fate of arguments or evidence that challenge the agency's general conclusions but do not meet its criteria for "consideration." Notably, they do not state that such submissions will be excluded from the rulemaking record or ignored by the Assistant Secretary. Rigid notions of admissibility are probably incompatible with informal rulemaking, and the obligation to respond to pertinent comments will lead OSHA to devote time to submissions that it might technically be entitled to ignore. Professor McGarity questioned the very premise of OSHA's regulations:

> Even if hearings were eliminated entirely, the pace at which OSHA proposes and finalizes regulations would probably not accelerate appreciably.
> * * * [T]he time consumed in actual hearings is a miniscule proportion of the time consumed between the moment the agency is asked to promulgate a standard and the time it issues a final standard. The glacial pace at which the agency has issued health standards has deeper reasons, including White House pressure to delay issuance of standards, inadequate and/or poor management, rapid turnover in leadership, poor interaction between managers in OSHA and scientists in the National Institute for Occupational Safety and Health, poor interaction between OSHA and its lawyers in the Office of the Solicitor of Labor, and the requirement that OSHA perform lengthy regulatory analyses before it issues standards.

McGarity, *op. cit.* supra, at 77.

3. One of the most provocative proposals for reform carries the label "negotiated rulemaking," a concept that accepts the premise that federal rulemaking is fundamentally a political exercise rather than an effort at rational analysis aimed at identifying cost-effective solutions. A leading proponent of the concept is Philip Harter, who critiqued the rulemaking process in *Negotiating Regulations: A Cure for Malaise*, 71 Geo. L. J. 1 (1982), an article based on a study for the U.S. Administrative Conference:

> Hybrid rulemaking has become a surrogate for direct participation in the political decision because parties have no means of direct participation in the policy choice. Parties can limit the agency's range of choices only by influencing the record. As a result, the process of developing the record has become bitterly adversarial. Such adversity may be an inevitable concomitant of the regulatory state in which massive costs and benefits are at stake; it may even be the best way of reaching many decisions. This adversarial system, however, fails to provide a mechanism for deciding the inherently political issues in a politically legitimate way. * * *
>
> * * * [T]he adversarial process has many drawbacks. The agencies and the private parties tend to take extreme positions, expecting that they may be pushed toward the middle. * * *

* * * Because the parties advocate the extreme, they may be reluctant to provide data to the agency and to each other because they fear the data may be misused or reveal weaknesses in the extreme position. Thus, it is frequently difficult for parties to join forces, and frontally address the factual and policy questions. Instead, the parties dig in and defend their extreme positions.

In addition, the adversarial process affects the presentation of proposals when people deal with each other as adversaries. A party is likely to encounter difficulty in expressing its true concerns because it may fear losing on issues of minor interest without gaining concessions on those it cares about a great deal. Moreover, a party may feel compelled to advocate a position it may not actually favor at the time to preserve the option of advocating that position in the future. Thus, the parties' presentations appear flat: they raise every issue to nearly equal prominence and place far more issues in contention than may be necessary.

The parties in an adversarial process do not deal directly with one another; rather, each makes its presentation to the decisionmaker. Because of this presentation, the issues in controversy may be limited to those within the jurisdiction of the forum. These issues, however, may not be the ones actually separating the parties. * * *

The adversarial process also causes parties to engage in defensive research to bolster the factual record for a proposed rule. An agency and other affected parties may feel compelled to compile a great amount of factual material to counter other positions and to build affirmative cases, although such information may be of only marginal value in making the ultimate decision. This research, which may take the form of data gathering, new laboratory work, or the employment of recognized leaders in a field, is both time consuming and expensive. Moreover, the adversarial process tends to warp the quality of the scientific and technical information submitted. Because the parties must develop the best arguments for the positions they advocate, qualifications, limitations, and expressions of doubt are lost. We have grown accustomed to rulemaking procedures that take several years to complete at the agency level and, in the event judicial review is sought, another year or two in the courts. The cost of participating in such a proceeding for both the agency and the private parties can be staggeringly high. * * *

* * * Negotiations among directly affected groups conducted within both the existing policies of the statute authorizing the regulation and the existing policies of the agency, would enable the parties to participate directly in the establishment of the rule. The significant concerns of each could be considered frontally. Direct participation in rulemaking through negotiations is preferable to entrusting the decision to the wisdom and judgment of the agency, which is essential under the basic provisions of the APA, or to relying on the more formal, structured method of hybrid rulemaking in which it is difficult for anyone to make the careful trade offs necessary for an enlightened regulation. A regulation that is developed by and has the support of the respective interests would have a political legitimacy that regulations developed under any other process arguably lack. * * *

74 Geo. L.J. at 7, 16-21.

The process envisaged by Harter (and others, *e.g.*, Note, *Rethinking Regulation: Negotiation as an Alternative to Traditional Rulemaking,*

94 Harv. L. Rev. 1871 (1981)), is designed to produce agreement among the principal interested parties on a text that becomes the responsible agency's notice of proposed rulemaking. Harter visualizes a series of carefully structured meetings among principals to identify points of dispute, areas of agreement, and avenues of accommodation—all off the record and outside the glare of public attention that assertedly generates overstatement and rigidity. Some versions contemplate that the agency will become actively involved in the negotiations to develop a proposed rule; others confine the agency to the role of "meeting arranger" until a proposal is developed.

Harter concedes that his approach faces many obstacles, not the least its novelty, and he accordingly recommends that negotiation be used only when circumstances suggest it is likely to succeed. To be successful, the parties who would be likely to contest the content of the agency's rule if it employed customary rulemaking procedures must believe they are "more likely to achieve [their] overall goals by" negotiation. Harter goes on to identify several conditions that might sustain such a belief: (1) the power of the contesting parties should be sufficiently well-balanced to make the outcome of rulemaking uncertain; (2) the number of significantly affected parties should be small; (3) the disputable issues should be sufficiently crystalized to permit resolution or compromise; (4) the need for resolution should be apparent, i.e., it should be clear that the agency will make *some* rule; (5) the dispute should be one whose resolution can potentially benefit most or all parties; (6) the dispute should not involve what Harter terms "fundamental values"; (7) the legal standards governing the agency should permit trade-offs and the dispute should contain enough elements that most parties can prevail on some; (8) the outcome should not depend on additional research; (9) the agency should be willing to adopt the negotiated text as its proposal, and be capable of implementing that result if it emerges intact from public rulemaking.

It is unclear whether these conditions will coexist in many contexts or whether, even if they do, negotiation will in fact yield proposals that elicit broad support among affected groups and can withstand judicial review. Nonetheless the negotiation concept has sufficient appeal that several agencies have begun to experiment with it. OSHA attempted to elicit a negotiated resolution of the dispute over its benzene standard following the Supreme Court's reversal, and went so far as to engage Mr. Harter as the "covenor" of contesting parties. EPA has created a new office to experiment with negotiated rulemaking, and selected two problems—penalties for nonconformance under the Clean Air Act and emergency exemption from restrictions on pesticide use—as candidates. 49 Fed. Reg. 31145 (1984). See Mosher, *EPA, Looking for Better Way to Settle Rules Disputes, Tries Some Mediation*, National Journal, March 5, 1983, at 504.

Proponents of negotiation have recognized that its success may require judicial sympathy and perhaps even modification of prevailing legal doctrine. They express concern that an agency's apparent relinquishment of its role as the author of rules to interested private parties will invite claims of invalid delegation of legislative power—a mere spectre, they believe, so long as the agency retains authority to determine the content of the final rule and acts within its governing statute. The proponents also acknowledge that court interpretations of the APA may impede use of negotiation. For example, the requirement that an agency's rule be sustainable solely on the basis of the "record" may be difficult to satisfy if the agency does not participate in the negotiations. Similarly, the agency might have difficulty supplying a statement of basis and purpose that revealed all of the adjustments embodied in a privately negotiated rule. Yet, if the agency becomes a participant, excluded parties may contend that it was exposed to unlawful ex parte contacts. See Note, 94 Harv. L. Rev., supra, at 1885-90.

4. While regulatory negotiation is in its infancy, privately-negotiated rules of conduct have long been influential in many governmental programs. This influence flows from standard-setting activities in the private sector—among commercial organizations, trade associations, and professional groups. A study for the U. S. Administrative Conference, Hamilton, *The Role of Nongovernmental Standards in the Development of Mandatory Federal Standards Affecting Safety or Health*, 56 Tex. L. Rev. 1329 (1978), documents the extent of such private standard-setting. It ranges from the familiar testing of electrical equipment by Underwriters Laboratory—whose certification has been made a legal requirement by most local building codes—to the work of non-profit organizations, such as the American Society for Testing and Materials, The National Fire Protection Association, and the American National Standards Institute (ANSI), the latter a trade association of standard-setting organizations.

The impact of these activities on government regulation is broad-ranging. Official reliance on private voluntary standards can be grouped under three headings. Existence of a generally observed private standard for a product or process may cause an agency to turn its attention to other problems; private standards may thus avert or supplant regulation. An example is the FDA's 1982 announcement that it will consider the adequacy of private standards for Class II medical devices in deciding whether to initiate or defer proceedings to establish mandatory standards, and will seek actively to encourage private standard-setting activities to avoid the need for regulation. 45 Fed. Reg. 7474 (1980).

A second model is the use of private standards as the starting point for the development of mandatory government requirements. The so-called "offeror" provisions of the original Consumer Product Safety Act, 15 U.S.C.A. § 2058, and the 1976 Medical Device Amendments to the Food, Drug, and Cosmetic Act, 21 U.S.C.A. § 360d, represent variants of this approach. In both laws Congress sought to encourage private sector groups to submit proposals for mandatory standards, including specifically proposals based on, or incorporating, existing voluntary standards. This model can be viewed as a variety of negotiated rulemaking, for a government agency is encouraged or directed to rely on agreements previously reached by private parties to serve as proposals with which it then commences traditional rulemaking.

At the extreme, an agency may simply adopt private standards as its own. Incorporation of U.L. certification as a measure of eligibility for government procurement or compliance with local building codes is an illustration of this model. A more dramatic example is the 1970 Occupational Safety and Health Act, which authorized OSHA, within two years of passage, to adopt—without public rulemaking but as binding workplace standards—existing "national consensus standards" for workplace hazards. 29 U.S.C.A. § 655(2). Pursuant to this authority, OSHA adopted wholesale several thousand published standards, almost all addressed to safety rather than health. The agency's lack of discrimination, according to some observers, was a major cause of its subsequent unpopularity within the business community; many of these "carried-over" standards were obsolete, their coverage was incomplete, and their focus, e.g., the color of ladders or the height of toilets, often invited ridicule. Kelman, *Occupational Safety and Health Administration*, in J. Q. WILSON, ed., THE POLITICS OF REGULATION 236 (1980); Nichols and Zeckhauser, *Government Comes to the Workplace: An Assessment of OSHA*, Pub. Int. No. 49, p. 39 (1977).

Professor Hamilton began his study of private standard-setting with profound skepticism, believing that the agreed-upon practice of industry groups would hardly correspond with the needs and objectives of regulatory programs. He emerged with a revised view:

> [My starting] assumptions for the most part were oversimplified, at least with regard to the standards developed by the best procedures followed by the private sector. Such procedures develop standards that deserve serious consideration for regulatory use and certainly much greater respect than they have been accorded in the past.

Prospects for the Nongovernmental Development of Regulatory Standards, 32 Am. U. L. Rev. 455, 459 (1983). Hamilton nonetheless identified several featurs of private standard-setting that ought to engender caution before the results are incorporated into governmental mandate. First, private standards may undesirably constrain innovation and competition. Second, private procedures for standards development rarely afford affected interests equivalent opportunities for participation. Among those interests most frequently excluded, or underrepresented, are labor organizations, consumer groups, and small businesses. Hamilton further points out that the criteria embodied in private standards will often either ignore or subordinate values that the agency or Congress wants given prominence. Still, he offers constructive recommendations for regulatory use of private standards in the development of mandatory rules to protect health and safety. See 56 Tex. L. Rev. at 1447-65.

Recent administrations, concerned about the economic and the political effects of aggressive command-and-control regulation, have also seen voluntary, private-sector standards as an underexploited resource. In 1980, OMB issued Circular No. A-119, which promoted use of private standards in government procurement and encouraged federal agency support for the activities of standard-setting bodies. But the circular also conditioned federal involvement on certification by the standard-setting body that it adhered to procedures that provided opportunities for participation by underrepresented interests. The Reagan administration found the latter requirement repugnant, and proposed revisions to Circular No. A-119 that would eliminate it and, further, would encourage federal agency use of voluntary standards "for regulatory purposes." See OMB Memorandum for the Heads of Executive Departments and Establishments, April 12, 1982.

Chapter 5

GOVERNMENT INFORMATION
ACQUISITION AND DISCLOSURE

The federal government acquires and stores more information than any other institution in our society. Some of this information is obtained specifically for the purposes of developing and enforcing regulatory policy, much is compiled in implementing public benefits programs, and of course a good deal is the byproduct of the government's activities as purchaser—of weapons systems, space shuttles, and office supplies—and owner/manager of buildings and real estate. Indeed, one can hardly conceive of a governmental function for which administrators do not require, or unavoidably receive, information from private citizens. In this chapter we explore, first, the principles applicable to the government's authority to demand the production of information or access to private premises and, second, the competing obligations imposed on federal administrators to provide access to government records and to protect confidential and sensitive information in government files.

A. INVESTIGATION AND DISCOVERY

Sound decisionmaking obviously requires good information. Federal administrative agencies accordingly devote substantial effort to data collection and analysis. Indeed, a primary activity of some bodies, like the Department of Commerce, consists of acquiring and disseminating information to assist either other governmental activities or private firms and individuals. In some cases an agency may be its own best source of needed information. The Social Security Administration's own personnel are probably in a better position than anyone outside the government to supply data about its caseload of disability claims, about the costs of processing these claims, and perhaps even about the aggregate effects of government disability benefits on the economy and/or the health and well-being of claimants. Often, however, beneficiaries or subjects of regulation are closer to the facts than any official body. The retreaders of tires whom we encountered in Chapter 4, for example, seemed better equipped to supply information about prevailing industry practices and available technology than employees of the National Highway Traffic Safety Administration.

Agencies obtain needed information from private parties in a variety of ways. Perhaps surprisingly, most of it is provided voluntarily, or at least without formal objection. Individuals or businesses often desire to supply information to administrators in order to obtain some benefit—such as welfare assistance, a government loan, a license to market a product, a larger allocation of publicly controlled resources, or protective regulation. While in such cases the submission of information may be initiated by the party seeking governmental favor, the responsible agency usually has made known generally the type of information it requires in order to act favorably. Frequently, the agency's needs are made known more specifically as when information is supplied in response to an agency's request, as in *Baldor Electric*, supra p. 418, or its invitation, as in rulemaking.

Nevertheless, some information that government officials require to develop policy, adjudicate cases, or initiate enforcement action is not willingly disclosed. The difficult questions, and most of the law in this area, relate to the power of governmental bodies to compel the production of information. Our attention will focus on three techniques for obtaining compulsory access to information: (1) the power to subpoena or otherwise order testimony or the production of documents; (2) the power to require the maintenance of records and the submission of reports; and (3) the power physically to enter and explore private premises to obtain information. This preoccupation with the compulsory production of information is justified not only by the difficulty and interest of the questions presented, but by the fact that the extent of voluntary disclosure of information is likely to depend significantly on the scope of official power to compel production.

Several issues recur in our examination of government power to compel disclosure. One is the existence of statutory or inherent authority to order disclosure in a particular context. A second is the scope of legally recognized "privileges" to withhold information, or at least to insist upon its confidential treatment, even in the face of a lawful demand for production. Central to this latter inquiry are the constitutional limits on forced production of information, grounded in the Fourth Amendment's guarantee of security for homes and personal effects and in the Fifth Amendment's protection against forced self-incrimination. Resistance to disclosure may also be supported by the textually inchoate "right of privacy" recognized in *Griswold v. Connecticut*, 381 U.S. 479 (1965).

1. AUTHORITY TO SUBPOENA WITNESSES AND DOCUMENTS

While the courts have liberally interpreted express grants of information-gathering authority to administrators, Congress must have conferred such power; no administrator possesses inherent authority to conduct inspections, require reports, or issue subpoenas. The original provisions of the Federal Trade Commission Act are typical. Section 6(a) of the Act expansively empowered the FTC "[t]o gather and compile information concerning, and to investigate from time to time the organization, business, conduct, practices and management of any corporation engaged in commerce. * * * and its relation to other corporations and to individuals, associations, and partnerships." 15 U.S.C.A. § 46(a) (1970). Section 9, 15 U.S.C.A. § 49, authorized the use of compulsory process in support of the Commission's investigatory and enforcement activities:

> For the purposes of sections [1–6] * * * the Commission, or its duly authorized agent or agents, shall at all reasonable times have access to, for the purpose of examination, and the right to copy any documentary evidence of any corporation being investigated or proceeded against; and the Commission shall have power to require by subpoena the attendance and testimony of witnesses and the production of all such documentary evidence relating to any matter under investigation. * * *

> * * * And in case of disobedience to a subpoena the Commission may invoke the aid of any court of the United States in requiring the attendance and testimony of witnesses and the production of documentary evidence.

> Any of the district courts of the United States within the jurisdiction of which such inquiry is carried on may, in case of contumacy or refusal to obey a subpoena issued to any corporation or other person, issue an order requiring such corporation or other person to appear before the Commission, or to produce documentary evidence if so ordered, or to give evidence touching the matter in question; and any failure to obey such order of the court may be punished by such court as a contempt thereof.*

Despite this broad language, judicial reaction to the FTC's initial attempts to compel the production of evidence was hostile. In 1923, spurred by a Senate resolution, the Commission undertook an investigation of charges that two tobacco manufacturers, American and P. Lorillard, had unlawfully controlled the prices at which jobbers resold their products. Before issuing a formal complaint the agency ordered each company to produce "all letters and telegrams received by the Company from, or sent by it to all of its jobber customers, between January 1, 1921, to December 31, 1921, inclusive." The companies resisted this demand, essentially on constitutional grounds, and were upheld by the district court in which the Commission sought enforcement of its order. In *FTC v. American Tobacco Co.*, 264 U.S. 298, 305–07 (1924), the Supreme Court, through Justice Holmes, affirmed:

> [T]he Commission claims an unlimited right of access to the respondents' papers with reference to the possible existence of practices in violation of § 5.

> The mere facts of carrying on a commerce not confined within state lines and of being organized as a corporation do not make men's affairs public, as those of a railroad company now may be. Anyone who respects the spirit as well as the letter of the Fourth Amendment would be loath to believe that Congress intended to authorize one of its subordinate agencies to sweep all our traditions into the fire and to direct fishing expeditions into private pa-

---

*The 1975 Magnuson-Moss Warranty—Federal Trade Commission Improvement Act, 88 Stat. 2183, Pub. L. No. 93-637, broadens the FTC's investigatory jurisdiction to include individuals and partnerships, as well as corporations. That an investigation is directed at an entity other than a corporation is probably not significant under modern decisions concerning the permissible reach of agency subpoena power, save in circumstances that implicate the Fifth Amendment. Eds.

pers on the possibility that they may disclose evidence of crime.   We do not discuss the question whether it could do so if it tried, as nothing short of the most explicit language would induce us to attribute to Congress that intent. * * *   It is contrary to the first principles of justice to allow a search through all the respondents' records, relevant or irrelevant, in the hope that something will turn up.   * * *

The right of access given by the statute is to documentary evidence—not to all documents, but to such documents as are evidence.   The analogies of the law do not allow the party wanting evidence to call for all documents in order to see if they do not contain it.   Some ground must be shown for supposing that the documents called for do contain it.   Formerly in equity the ground must be found in admissions in the answer.   We assume that the rule to be applied here is more liberal, but still a ground must be laid and the ground and the demand must be reasonable.   A general subpoena in the form of these petitions would be bad.   Some evidence of the materiality of the papers demanded must be produced.   * * *

We have considered this case on the general claim of authority put forward by the Commission.   The argument for the Government attaches some force to the investigations and proceedings upon which the Commission had entered.   The investigations and complaints seem to have been only on hearsay or suspicion—but, even if they were induced by substantial evidence under oath, the rudimentary principles of justice that we have laid down would apply.   We cannot attribute to Congress an intent to defy the Fourth Amendment or even to come so near to doing so as to raise a serious question of constitutional law.

Holmes' opinion assumed, almost without discussion, that the Fourth Amendment guarantee against "unreasonable searches and seizures" imposes limits on the government's power to obtain evidence through administrative subpoenas.   His reading seriously threatened the FTC's authority to investigate activities prior to issuing a complaint charging actual violations of the Act.   For the agency might often have no secure basis for determining whether violations had been committed before it had an opportunity to examine the very information Holmes seemed to put out of reach.

Holmes' ruling inhibited administrative investigations for almost two decades, but by World War II the Court was displaying greater sympathy toward agency demands for information.   In *Endicott Johnson Corp. v. Perkins*, 317 U.S. 501, 508-10 (1943), the Secretary of Labor sought enforcement of a subpoena issued in connection with an investigation of compliance with the Walsh-Healey Act.   The subpoena sought information concerning the contractors' payrolls at plants that arguably were not covered by the Act.   The district court held that it first had to determine whether the Act applied to the plants and contracts about which the Secretary sought information, asserting that if it did not, the subpoena was not in aid of an authorized function.   This time, the Supreme Court reversed, beginning a retreat from *American Tobacco*:

The matter which the Secretary was investigating and was authorized to investigate was an alleged violation of this Act and these contracts.   Her scope would include determining what employees these contracts and the Act covered.   It would also include whether the payments to them were lower than the scale fixed pursuant to the Act.   She could not perform her full statutory duty until she examined underpayments wherever the coverage extended. * * *

Nor was the District Court authorized to decide the question of coverage itself.   The evidence sought by the subpoena was not plainly incompetent or irrelevant to any lawful purpose of the Secretary in the discharge of her duties under the Act, and it was the duty of the District Court to order its production for the Secretary's consideration. * * * The consequence of the action of the District Court was to disable the Secretary from rendering a complete decision on the alleged violation as Congress had directed her to do, and that decision was stated by the Act to be conclusive as to matters of fact for purposes of the award of government contracts. * * *

The subpoena power delegated by the statute as here exercised is so clearly within the limits of Congressional authority that it is not necessary to discuss the constitutional questions urged by the petitioner. * * *

Oklahoma Press Publishing Co. v. Walling, 327 U.S. 186, 201-14 (1946), marked a decisive step in the evolution of modern doctrine governing the exercise of administrative subpoena powers.   There the Department of Labor, in an investigation to determine compliance with the Fair Labor Standards Act, subpoenaed extensive records of the respondent newspaper company before charging any violation.   The Court rejected the newspaper's arguments that such extensive inquiry, prior to any formal complaint, was not authorized by the FLSA (which expressly incorporated the investigatory provisions of the FTC Act) or, if authorized, was barred by the Fourth Amendment.

[T]his case presents an instance of "the most explicit language" which leaves no room for questioning Congress' intent.   The very purpose of the subpoena and of the order, as of the authorized investigation, is to discover and procure evidence, not to prove a pending charge or complaint, but upon which to make one if, in the Administrator's judgment, the facts thus discovered should justify doing so.

Accordingly, if § § 9 and 11(a) are not to be construed as authorizing enforcement of the orders, it must be, as petitioners say, because this construction would make them so dubious constitutionally as to compel resort to an interpretation which saves rather than to one which destroys or is likely to do so. * * * The Court has adopted this course at least once in this type of case [citing *American Tobacco*].

The primary source of misconception concerning the Fourth Amendment's function lies perhaps in the identification of cases involving so-called "figurative" or "constructive" search with cases of actual search and seizure. Only in this analogical sense can any question related to search and seizure be thought to arise in situations which, like the present ones, involve only the validity of authorized judicial orders. * * *

The confusion obscuring the basic distinction between actual and so-called "constructive" search has been accentuated where the records and papers sought are of corporate character, as in these cases.   Historically private corporations have been subject to broad visitorial power, both in England and in this country.   And it long has been established that Congress may exercise wide investigative power over them, analogous to the visitorial power of the incorporating state, when their activities take place within or affect interstate commerce.   Correspondingly it has been settled that corporations are not entitled to all of the constitutional protections which private individuals have in these and related matters. * * *

Without attempt to summarize or accurately distinguish all of the cases, the fair distillation, in so far as they apply merely to the production of corporate records and papers in response to a subpoena or order authorized by law and safeguarded by judicial sanction, seems to be that the Fifth Amendment affords no protection by virtue of the self-incrimination provision, whether for the corporation or for its officers; and the Fourth, if applicable, at the most guards against abuse only by way of too much indefiniteness or breadth in the things required to be "particularly described," if also the inquiry is one the demanding agency is authorized by law to make and the materials specified are relevant.   The gist of the protection is in the requirement, expressed in terms, that the disclosure sought shall not be unreasonable.

* * * It is not necessary, as in the case of a warrant, that a specific charge or complaint of violation of law be pending or that the order be made pursuant to one.   It is enough that the investigation be for a lawfully authorized purpose, within the power of Congress to command.   This has been ruled most often perhaps in relation to grand jury investigations, but also frequently in respect to general or statistical investigations authorized by Congress.   The requirement of "probable cause, supported by oath or affirmation," literally applicable in the case of a warrant, is satisfied in that of an order for production by the court's determination that the investigation is authorized by Congress, is for a purpose Congress can order, and the documents sought are relevant to the inquiry.   Beyond this the requirement of reasonableness, including particularity in "describing the place to be searched, and the persons or things to be seized," also literally applicable to warrants, comes down to specification of the documents to be produced adequate, but not excessive, for the purposes of the relevant inquiry.   Necessarily, as has been said, this cannot be reduced to formula; for relevancy and adequacy or excess in the breadth of the subpoena are matters variable in relation to the nature, purposes and scope of the inquiry.

When these principles are applied to the facts of the present cases, it is impossible to conceive how a violation of petitioners' rights could have been involved.   Both were corporations.   The only records or documents sought were corporate ones.   No possible element of self-incrimination was therefore presented or in fact claimed.   All the records sought were relevant to the authorized inquiry,[46] the purpose of which was to determine two issues, whether petitioners were subject to the Act and, if so, whether they were vio-

---

46. The subpoena in No. 61 called for production of:

"All of your books, papers, and documents showing the hours worked by and wages paid to each of your employees between October 28, 1938, and the date hereof, including all payroll ledgers, time sheets, time cards and time clock records, and all your books, papers and documents showing the distribution of papers outside the State of Oklahoma, the dissemination of news outside the State of Oklahoma, the source and receipt of news from outside the State of Oklahoma, and the source and receipt of advertisements of nationally advertised goods."

The specification in No. 63 was substantially identical except for the period of time covered by the demand.

lating it.   These were subjects of investigation authorized by § 11(a), the latter expressly, the former by necessary implication.   It is not to be doubted that Congress could authorize investigation of these matters.   In all these respects,[48] the specifications more than meet the requirements long established by many precedents. * * *

We think * * * that the courts of appeals were correct in the view that Congress has authorized the Administrator, rather than the district courts in the first instance, to determine the question of coverage in the preliminary investigation of possibly existing violations; in doing so to exercise his subpoena power for securing evidence upon that question, by seeking the production of petitioners' relevant books, records, and papers; and, in case of refusal to obey his subpoena, issued according to the statute's authorization, to have the aid of the district court in enforcing it.   No constitutional provision forbids Congress to do this. * * *

In *Oklahoma Press*, as in *Endicott Johnson*, the Court held that the issue of the agency's jurisdiction—at least where resolution depends on a factual determination such as whether employees are engaged in the production of goods for the government—is for the agency to decide in the first instance.   The Court's vindication of agency power to compel disclosure thus closely parallels contemporaneous judicial affirmations of agency authority to conduct enforcement proceedings without judicial interruption to resolve challenges to its jurisdiction prior to completion of the administrative process.   See *Myers v. Bethlehem Shipbuilding Corp.*, 303 U.S. 41 (1938); cf. *Federal Trade Commission v. Standard Oil Co.*, 449 U.S. 232 (1980).

Oklahoma Press was recently reaffirmed in *Donovan v. Lone Steer, Inc.*, ___ U.S. ___, 104 S.Ct. 769 (1984), a case arising out of investigations of compliance with the Fair Labor Standards Act.   The respondents refused to comply with the Secretary of Labor's subpoena duces tecum, claiming that the Act violated the Fourth Amendment insofar as it authorized issuance of a subpoena without a prior judicial warrant.   The district court concluded that this result was demanded by *Marshall v. Barlow's, Inc.*, 436 U.S. 307 (1978), infra p. 546.   The Court dismissed the suggestion that the Secretary's entry into a public motel and restaurant lobby to serve the subpoena was a "search" covered by the Fourth Amendment, and that judicial supervision of enforcement of the subpoena under *Oklahoma Press* fully protected the respondent's rights.

The Judicial Role in Enforcement of Agency Subpoenas

Endicott Johnson and *Oklahoma Press* appear to recognize only three basic limitations on agency subpoena powers: (1) any demand for information must fall within the authority conferred on an agency by statute;

---

48. The description was made with all of the particularity the nature of the inquiry and the Administrator's situation would permit. See note 46.   The specifications more than meet the requirements long established by many   precedents. * * * The subpoenas were limited to the books, papers and documents of the respective corporations, to which alone they were addressed.   They required production at specified times and places in the cities of publication and stated the purpose of the investigation to be one affecting the respondent, pursuant to the provisions of §§ 9 and 11(c), "regarding complaints of violations by said company of Sections 6, 7, 11(c), 15(a)(1), 15(a)(2) and 15(a)(5) of the Act."

(2) any information demanded must be relevant to a proper subject of agency inquiry; and (3) a demand for information must not be unreasonable. If the recipient of a subpoena wishes to contest the agency's demand on any of these grounds, it may either seek a judicial order to quash or simply fail to comply. In the latter case the agency must obtain a judicial order directing compliance, disobedience of which may entail punishment for contempt. This two-step procedure thus affords an opportunity for judicial scrutiny of an agency's authority to compel the production of information and of the propriety of its exercise in particular cases before there can be any penalty for non-compliance. It should also be noted that an order enforcing an agency's subpoena ordinarily does not preclude later objection to the admissibility of evidence produced in formal agency proceedings.

Within Statutory Authorization. An agency generally must find authority to issue subpoenas (or other formal demands for information) in the language of its governing statute. Thus, for example, *Serr v. Sullivan*, 390 F.2d 619 (3d Cir. 1968), upheld a refusal to respond to a demand for information issued by the Treasury Department's Alcohol and Tobacco Tax Division to permit holders. Although the ATTD had been given broad authority to grant and withhold permits, its statute did not expressly authorize the agency to issue subpoenas or to conduct special investigations of permittees. This general principle is reiterated in APA § 555(c): "Process, requirement of a report, inspection, or other investigative act or demand may not be issued, made, or enforced except as authorized by law."

Compare *United States v. Exxon Corp.*, 628 F.2d 70 (D.C. Cir.), *cert. denied* 446 U.S. 964 (1980), in which the Secretary of Energy's authority to subpoena information for use in studies under the Petroleum Marketing Practices Act (PMPA) was challenged. The court of appeals held that the subpoena power conferred by the Department of Energy Organization Act, the department's chartering statute, could support the Secretary's demand despite the absence of subpoena power in the PMPA. The court reasoned that the latter act merely confirmed the department's authority to conduct a study that it could have undertaken under its organic law. Circuit Judge Wilkey dissented, pointing out that neither the PMPA nor its legislative history contained a single word about use of subpoenas to obtain information for authorized studies. See Comment, *Department of Energy Needs No Express Grant of Subpoena Power to Study Oil Company Fuel Sales Subsidization*, 56 Notre Dame Law. 515 (1981).

While an agency's demand for information must relate to a subject within its investigatory authority, the party upon whom demand is made need not be within the agency's regulatory jurisdiction. Thus, *Freeman v. Brown Brothers Harriman & Co.*, 357 F.2d 741 (2d Cir.), *cert. denied* 384 U.S. 933 (1966), sustained the Secretary of Agriculture's attempt to compel a bank to disclose information about the account of a depositor over whom the Secretary lacked jurisdiction. The information was relevant to determining whether a company concededly subject to regulation had paid illegal rebates to the bank's customer—a permissible subject of inquiry. See *Crafts v. FTC*, 244 F.2d 882 (9th Cir.), *reversed per curiam* 355 U.S. 9 (1957).

United States v. Minker, 350 U.S. 179 (1956), represents a departure from the general judicial willingness to construe grants of subpoena authority generously. In a denaturalization proceeding the INS sought to compel the appearance and testimony of Minker, the person whose citizenship was threatened, pursuant to a statute authorizing the issuance of subpoenas for "witnesses." Weighing the serious consequences of denaturalization and impressed by arguments that drew analogies to the Fifth Amendment's protection against self-incrimination, a majority of the Supreme Court concluded that the statutory term "witness" should not be read to include the persons under investigation.

Statutes sometimes specify the purposes for which the power to issue subpoenas is conferred. This may give rise to claims that the "real" objective of an agency in demanding documents or testimony is inconsistent with the limited purposes for which the power was given. See *United States v. O'Connor*, 118 F. Supp. 248 (D. Mass. 1953), refusing to enforce a facially legitimate subpoena demanding information from a taxpayer when the issuing IRS official admitted he had sometimes used his subpoena power to aid Justice Department prosecution of criminal tax fraud cases. But the Supreme Court has made clear that the burden in such circumstances rests on the taxpayer (or, presumably, any other recipient of a subpoena) to show that the agency's demand represents an abuse of its power. *United States v. Powell*, 379 U.S. 48 (1964). See also *United States v. Litton Industries, Inc.*, 462 F.2d 14 (9th Cir. 1972) (court will not assume FTC might misuse information otherwise properly demanded from subject of merger investigation). Some recipients of subpoenas have met this burden. In *Shasta Minerals & Chemical Co. v. SEC*, 328 F.2d 285 (10th Cir. 1964), the Commission, having subpoenaed the company's list of shareholders, failed to respond to affidavits alleging systematic persecution and harassment of the company and its president. The court of appeals ruled that the district judge, before ordering enforcement, should have explored the accuracy of the corporation's allegations which presented material questions of "whether or not the Commission acted arbitrarily or outside of its statutory authority." See also *SEC v. Wheeling-Pittsburgh Steel Corp.*, 648 F.2d 118 (3d Cir. 1981); Comment, *Bad Faith and the Abuse-of-Process Defense to Administrative Subpoenas*, 82 Colum. L. Rev. 811 (1981).

In *United States v. LaSalle National Bank*, 437 U.S. 298 (1978), the Supreme Court explored the scope of the "bad faith" defense to enforcement of an IRS administrative summons. The Court there overturned the Seventh Circuit's refusal to enforce a summons issued under 26 U.S.C.A. § 7602 to a bank that had custody of the taxpayer's records. The district court had found as a fact that the investigating agent sought the records "solely" for purposes of obtaining evidence of criminal conduct by the taxpayer—an objective the appellate court believed beyond the authority conferred by section 7602. In reversing, the Court observed that *Donaldson v. United States*, 400 U.S. 517 (1971), had sustained the IRS' use of the summons where criminal prosecution was a potential outcome of its investigation, and it confirmed that section 7602 authorizes use of a summons "in aid of a tax investigation that could have both civil and criminal consequences" until the Service formally recommends prosecution to the Department of Justice—so long as it acts in "good faith." The Court then quoted its summary of the components of good faith from *United States v. Powell*, supra:

> [The Service] must show that the investigation will be conducted pursuant to a legitimate purpose, that the inquiry may be relevant to the purpose, that the information sought is not already within the Commissioner's possession, and that the administrative steps required by the Code have been followed. * * * [A] court may not permit its process to be abused. Such an abuse would take place if the summons had been issued for an improper purpose, such as to harrass the taxpayer or to put pressure on him to settle a collateral dispute, or for any other purpose reflecting on the good faith of the particular investigation.

The Court proceeded to hold that the summons should have been enforced in this case. Conceding that the investigating agent's purpose may have been to develop evidence for prosecution, it stressed that the Service as a whole retained responsibility to "calculate and to collect civil fraud penalties and fraudulently reported or unreported taxes." The institutional channels for review of the agent's findings, moreover, assured that the Service retained ability to explore these options as well. To show that a summons was issued in "bad faith," the opponent of enforcement had the heavy burden of disproving "the actual existence of a valid civil tax determination or collection purpose *by the Service.* * * * " 437 U.S. at 316.

In an opinion joined by three other members of the Court, Justice Stewart would have reversed on a more objective ground: He believed that a section 602 summons was lawful even when the Service's sole interest was in criminal prosecution, so long as it had not yet referred the case to the Department of Justice.

Germane to a Lawful Subject of Inquiry. Courts may insist that information whose production is demanded be potentially relevant to a proper subject of investigation. This requirement has occasionally led to refusal to enforce demands for information that failed adequately to disclose the purpose for which it was sought. As Circuit Judge Bazelon wrote in *Montship Lines Ltd. v. Federal Maritime Board*, 295 F.2d 147, 154-55 (D.C. Cir. 1961), "[w]hat is 'reasonably relevant' depends on the purpose and nature of the investigation undertaken by the agency." There, the Board's failure to state its purpose "precluded a determination of relevancy." See *Hellenic Lines Ltd. v. Federal Maritime Board*, 295 F.2d 138, 140 (D.C. Cir. 1961) (recitation that Board was acting " * * * pursuant to the responsibilities vested * * * by the interest of the Board's regulatory duties under that Act" held inadequate statement of purpose). The courts will hardly demand the specificity of code pleading, however, particularly when the precise direction of investigation has yet to be determined. In *Pacific Westbound Conference v. United*

States, 332 F.2d 49, 52-53 (9th Cir. 1964), the court sustained a Federal Maritime Commission demand for information that was challenged on the authority of *Montship* and *Hellenic Lines*:

> The statement of purpose set forth in the order here under review * * * is far more comprehensive than that which was found inadequate in Hellenic Lines, Ltd. That statement of purpose appears to us to be about as complete and specific as it could possibly be, considering the fact that, as the Commission had a right to do, it had not yet determined that any agreements, rates or fares were unlawful but was seeking information to ascertain the measure of compliance with the named regulatory statutes and the need of future Commission action in fulfillment of its statutory duties.

When an agency's investigation has acquired a focus that focus must be disclosed and the demand for relevance may become more demanding. Thus, in *United States v. Associated Merchandising Corp.*, 261 F. Supp. 553 (S.D.N.Y. 1966), the FTC, in connection with a proceeding charging violations of the Robinson-Patman Act, demanded the disclosure of documents by respondents that embraced some two million invoices and went well beyond any transactions charged in its complaint. Relying in part on a Commission rule requiring a showing of "good cause" for the production of documents, the court refused enforcement as to several items it concluded were not germane to the agency's specific charges.

The cases make clear that an agency need not conclusively demonstrate the legal relevance of information in advance of obtaining it. The test appears to be one of "possible relevance" to matters properly subject to investigation. And according to the D.C. Circuit, *FTC v. Texaco, Inc.*, 555 F.2d 862 (D.C. Cir.), *cert. denied* 431 U.S. 974 (1977), the courts have only a limited role in assuring adherence to this standard. For a suggestion that courts should demand more, see Note, *Reasonable Relation Reassessed: The Examination of Private Documents by Federal Regulatory Agencies*, 56 N.Y.U.L. Rev. 742 (1981).

Specific and Not Unreasonably Burdensome. Closely related to the requirement that an agency explain the purpose of its demand for information in sufficient detail to demonstrate relevance is the requirement that the material sought be identified with reasonable precision. A subpoena may be so general in describing the information sought as to defy assessment of compliance. For example, a demand for "all documents bearing upon * * * " specific events or activities may not afford guidance as to whether particular papers must be produced. Yet it is rarely possible for an agency to identify with specificity everything it desires when it has not yet had an opportunity to examine the documents it is demanding. In such situations, the agency will usually attempt to identify the types of documents that might be useful and, often, specify the period of time in which it is interested. The resulting demand for, e.g., "all bank statements and cancelled checks for 1961 and 1962" cannot really be faulted for imprecision—the recipient knows what is demanded—but it may be overbroad or burdensome.

In this area, the decisions do not provide clear guidance for either agencies or those from whom information is sought. In *Kerr Steamship*

Co. v. United States, 284 F.2d 61 (2d Cir. 1960), *appeal dismissed as moot* 369 U.S. 422 (1962), the court sustained a demand that carriers produce "a list identifying every contract * * * involving the water-borne commerce of the United States" made between it and any other carrier or "any freight forwarder, terminal operator, stevedore, or ship's agent" pertaining to seven specified types of activities. The court concluded that this demand was as definite as the subject-matter under investigation permitted. It promised that no carrier that attempted to comply in good faith would risk imposition of any penalties for non-compliance. Contrast *United States v. Theodore*, 479 F.2d 749 (4th Cir. 1973), which held too "vague" and "burdensome" an IRS demand on a preparer of tax returns to produce all returns prepared and all work records compiled for all of its clients between 1969 and 1971. The objection to generality, in addition to reflecting a concern for relevance, also often reflects a suspicion that an agency has demanded more information than it needs, given the burden on the respondent of assembling it or functioning without it.

The federal courts generally take seriously their responsibility to restrain indiscriminate demands for disclosure. In *CAB v. Hermann*, 353 U.S. 322 (1957), the Supreme Court upheld a district court order enforcing a subpoena for records whose production would require examination of more than a million documents, but it also sustained that part of the court's order that staggered compliance with the Board's demand so that the respondent would not be deprived of all of its records at once. According to *FTC v. Texaco, Inc.*, 555 F.2d 862 (D.C. Cir.), *cert. denied* 431 U.S. 974 (1977), the primary responsibility for assuring that an agency's demand is not unreasonably burdensome lies with the district courts, whose determinations should be reversed only for abuse of discretion.

Issued by Proper Authority. Occasionally, an agency's demand for information will be resisted on the ground that it has not been issued by the proper official. The FTC Act, for example, authorizes only the Commission members to issue subpoenas. Obviously, it would be tremendously burdensome if a Commissioner personally had to evaluate and authorize each of the many thousand demands for information the FTC issues each year. Thus, it is common in the FTC, the NLRB, and other agencies operating under similar statutory grants of power for members to sign subpoenas in blank, leaving to subordinates the job of filling in the details when a specific demand for information is issued. The courts have approved this practice. *NLRB v. Lewis*, 249 F.2d 832 (9th Cir. 1957), *affirmed* 357 U.S. 10 (1958). Similarly, the courts will sustain a formal subdelegation of authority to sign and issue subpoenas, unless that statutory language or history clearly precludes such a result. In *Fleming v. Mohawk Wrecking & Lumber Co.*, 331 U.S. 111 (1947), the Supreme Court upheld such a subdelegation by the OPA administrator, based on a general grant of authority to delegate his powers to subordinates and his general rulemaking powers. Compare *Cudahy Packing Co. v. Holland*, 315 U.S. 357 (1942). In *Fleming*, as in so many other contexts, the Court's willingness to accord flexibility at the administrative level seems tied to its awareness that a recipient of a subpoena could obtain a judicial hearing before facing the risk of contempt.

Notice of Investigation

Sometimes the custodians of subpoenaed material will have little, or at least comparatively less, interest in assuring that investigative demands comply with the foregoing limitations if they are not themselves the focus of the agency's investigations. In *SEC v. Jerry T. O'Brien, Inc.*, ___ U.S. ___, 104 S.Ct. 2720 (1984), the Supreme Court overturned a Ninth Circuit ruling that the SEC was obligated to notify the "target" of its investigation when it demanded records from third parties. The Court found no support for such an obligation in the Due Process Clause of the Fifth Amendment or in the statutes administered by the Commission. It then preceeded to consider—and to dismiss—the argument that such notice was essential to protect the "right" of a target to have any investigation of his affairs carried out in compliance with the authority, relevance, propriety, and reasonableness standards set forth in *United States v. Powell*, 379 U.S. 48 (1964), supra:

> There are several tenuous links in respondents' argument. Especially debatable are the proposition that a target has a substantive right to be investigated in a manner consistent with the *Powell* standards and the assertion that a target may obtain a restraining order preventing voluntary compliance by a third party with an administrative subpoena. Certainly we have never before expressly so held. For the present, however, we may assume, *arguendo*, that a target enjoys each of the substantive and procedural rights identified by respondents. Nevertheless, we conclude that it would be inappropriate to elaborate upon those entitlements by mandating notification of targets whenever the Commission issues subpoenas.
>
> Two considerations underlie our decision on this issue. First, administration of the notice requirement advocated by respondents would be highly burdensome for both the Commission and the courts. The most obvious difficulty would involve identification of the persons and organizations that should be considered "targets" of investigation. The SEC often undertakes investigations into suspicious securities transactions without any knowledge of which of the parties involved may have violated the law. * * * Even in cases in which the Commission could identify with reasonable ease the principal targets of its inquiry, another problem would arise. In such circumstances, a person not considered a target by the Commission could contend that he deserved that status and therefore should be given notice of subpoenas issued to others. To assess a claim of this sort, a district court would be obliged to conduct some kind of hearing to determine the scope and thrust of the ongoing investigation. Implementation of this new remedy would drain the resources of the judiciary as well as the Commission.
>
> Second, the imposition of a notice requirement on the SEC would substantially increase the ability of persons who have something to hide to impede legitimate investigations by the Commission. A target given notice of every subpoena issued to third parties would be able to discourage the recipients from complying, and then further delay disclosure of damaging information by seeking intervention in all enforcement actions brought by the Commission. More seriously, the understanding of the progress of an SEC inquiry that would flow from knowledge of which persons had received subpoenas would enable an unscrupulous target to destroy or alter documents, intimi-

date witnesses, or transfer securities or funds so that they could not be reached by the Government.   Especially in the context of securities regulation, where speed in locating and halting violations of the law is so important, we would be loathe to place such potent weapons in the hands of persons with a desire to keep the Commission at bay.

We acknowledge that our ruling may have the effect in practice of preventing some persons under investigation by the SEC from asserting objections to subpoenas issued by the Commission to third parties for improper reasons.   However, to accept respondents' proposal "would unwarrantedly cast doubt upon and stultify the [Commission's] every investigatory move." * * *

Recognition of Constitutional and Other Privileges

American courts recognize numerous "privileges" to withhold information or testimony otherwise properly demanded in judicial proceedings.   The most notable of these, of course, is the privilege guaranteed by the Fifth Amendment (and, as against the states, by the Fourteenth) to refuse to provide self-incriminating evidence.   It is well accepted that this privilege attaches in administrative proceedings.   Because efforts to compel testimony in administrative proceedings are uncommon, the privilege here focuses principally on the right to withhold documentary materials.

The privilege against self-incrimination is subject to several important limitations.   First, it justifies the withholding only of information that may expose one to criminal prosecution; other damaging consequences of disclosure, ranging from embarrassment to loss of employment to potential civil liability, may not be the basis for resisting an agency's demand.   The distinction between potential criminal liability and other legal consequences can pose difficulties when the recipient of a subpoena simultaneously is exposed to criminal and civil investigations, as happens with some frequency.   In such circumstances, a court may defer the civil proceedings (and any accompanying demand for information) until the criminal proceedings have concluded, but it is not obligated to do so.   For discussion of the circumstances that are to be considered in making this judgment, see *SEC v. Dresser Industries, Inc.*, 628 F.2d 1368 (D.C. Cir.) *(en banc)*, *cert. denied* 449 U.S. 993 (1980).

Second, and more important in the administrative context, the privilege is not available to corporations, or other non-natural persons, such as associations, nor may the custodian of a corporation's records refuse to produce them because they contain matter that may incriminate him. He can claim the privilege only for evidence that belongs to him.   See generally Note, *The Constitutional Rights of Associations to Assert the Privilege Against Self-Incrimination*, 112 U. Pa. L. Rev. 394 (1964).

Third, one who is custodian for another individual's records may not refuse to produce them, for the privilege is personal.   In *Fisher v. United States*, 425 U.S. 391 (1976), the Court sustained enforcement of an IRS summons seeking documents that the taxpayers had retrieved from their accountants and delivered to attorneys who were representing them in the investigation. The attorneys could claim no Fifth Amendment privilege in the documents, which belonged either to the taxpayers or their accountants. Nor did forced production of documents in the attorneys' hands violate the taxpayers' Fifth Amendment rights even though they might contain incriminating material; "the privilege protects a person only against being incriminated by his own compelled testimonial communications," 425 U.S. at 409, and the summons imposed no compulsion on them. See also *United States v. Rylander*, 460 U.S. 752 (1983), where the Court upheld the petitioner's conviction for civil contempt of an order enforcing an IRS summons. The petitioner had, by affidavit, denied that he still possessed the demanded documents but refused to testify at the contempt hearing on the ground that he might incriminate himself. The Court concluded that he had thus failed to sustain his burden of showing that the documents were not in his possession.

Statutory grants of immunity from prosecution constitute another important limitation on the Fifth Amendment privilege. In *Ullmann v. United States*, 350 U.S. 422 (1956), the Supreme Court upheld the Federal Immunity Act, which accorded witnesses immunity from prosecution under federal or state law for any activities revealed during compelled testimony. In *Kastigar v. United States*, 406 U.S. 441 (1972), and *Zicarelli v. New Jersey State Commission of Investigation*, 406 U.S. 472 (1972), the Court reaffirmed *Ullmann* and held, moreover, that statutory immunity need only protect the compelled witness against the *use* of his testimony in a subsequent prosecution; the unwilling witness may still be prosecuted if the authorities can demonstrate that the evidence they intend to use was "derived from a legitimate source wholly independent of the compelled testimony." Thus, the Court sanctioned statutes according only "use," as contrasted with "transactional," immunity, such as the law invoked in *Ullman*. But in *Lefkowitz v. Turley*, 414 U.S. 70 (1973), the Court struck down a New York statute that required public contractors to waive their immunity when called upon to provide information to investigational authorities about their dealings with the State or face cancellation of their contracts and disqualification. The Court, however, acknowledged that New York could constitutionally compel a contractor's testimony in return for a grant of use immunity.

The extent to which other testimonial privileges limit agency demands for information is a matter of uncertainty. Statutes conferring power on agencies to obtain information habitually ignore the issue, so guidance must be found exclusively in judicial decisions. In *McMann v. SEC*, 87 F.2d 377, 378 (2d Cir.), *cert. denied* 301 U.S. 684 (1937), Judge Learned Hand rejected a claim of customer-broker privilege but at the same time observed: "[W]e assume * * * that the conduct of investigations under these statutes is subject to the same testimonial privileges as judicial proceedings. * * * " No later case has embraced so broad and formulation, although several have considered the availability of specific privileges to withhold information. The attorney-client privilege has received a sympathetic hearing, as in *CAB v. Air Transport Association*,

201 F. Supp. 318 (D.D.C. 1961), where the court observed: "The attorney-client privilege is deeply imbedded and is part of the warp and woof of the common law." The leading case on this point is now *Upjohn Co. v. United States*, 449 U.S. 383 (1981), which held that the attorney-client privilege extended to communications from the company's employees to its general counsel. The Court also held that an IRS summons may not demand production of attorneys' "work product," even in the face of claims of necessity or inability to obtain the information in other ways.

Courts have also sometimes recognized the privilege of patients to prevent disclosure of information in the possession of their physicians and the like privilege of one spouse to prevent the compelled testimony of the other, but they have consistently rejected claims based on the relation between client and accountant. For a general discussion of the area, see Note, *Privileged Communications Before Federal Administrative Agencies: The Law Applied in the District Courts*, 31 U. Chi. L. Rev. 395 (1964).

Responsibility for Enforcement

A practical problem that confronts federal agencies when the recipient of a subpoena resists compliance is the need to persuade the Department of Justice to seek enforcement. In addition to rendering the process more cumbersome, the need to apply to the Justice Department to initiate enforcement may inhibit an agency's investigations to the extent that it must anticipate the Department's attitudes when deciding to issue or seek enforcement of subpoenas. This does not mean that the Department of Justice is uncooperative or that its views are antithetical to agency policies, but its enthusiasm for their programs is rarely likely to match their own. Moreover, the Department of Justice may be inclined to weigh administrative, law enforcement, or budgetary considerations in responding to agency requests that would never occur to most agencies. The result of this external scrutiny of agency investigative activities ordinarily may be benign, but the possibilities for conflict and misunderstanding are obvious. See generally *S & E Contractors, Inc. v. United States*, 406 U.S. 1 (1972). See also Chapter 2, supra at 163–72.

2. REPORTING AND RECORD-KEEPING REQUIREMENTS

From the agency perspective, an efficient method of obtaining information for policy formulation, license approval, or enforcement action is to require persons subject to regulation to compile it. This device not only shifts the burden and cost of acquiring information to private parties, but recognizes that they are often in a better position to obtain the facts. It makes good sense, for example, to require that an applicant for approval to market a new drug supply information about its composition, method and place of manufacture, and proposed labeling, rather than force the FDA to discover these facts for itself. It is also common practice to require applicants to provide the results of tests to determine a product's compliance with legal standards, e.g., a drug's safety and effectiveness, but requirements of this kind have been questioned by persons who are skeptical of the objectivity—and even the integrity—of applicants for governmental approval.

Requirements to collect, maintain, and report information pervade both federal and the state licensing programs. Similarly, income tax laws rely primarily on taxpayers to supply needed information about their liability for tax. Even in areas where administrative responsibilities are primarily of a policing type—aimed at preventing or punishing prohibited conduct—record-keeping and reporting requirements are common.

Basic Doctrine

An agency's demand for the production of or access to required records may raise many legal questions similar to those that surround the exercise of agency subpoena power. A principal difference is that here the agency has ordered the assembly and retention of information, as well as its production for regulatory use. The Supreme Court has generally endorsed such demands when authorized by Congress, subject to conditions of relevance and reasonableness that pertain to subpoenas as well.

The mainspring case is *United States v. Morton Salt Co.*, 338 U.S. 632 (1950). The FTC had previously found several salt producers and their trade association guilty of violating section 5 of the FTC Act. The Seventh Circuit affirmed, with modifications, a cease and desist order which directed the respondents to file reports of compliance within 90 days and reserved jurisdiction to enter further orders to enforce compliance. Later, under section 6 of the Act, the Commission ordered Morton and others to file additional special reports demonstrating compliance with the original decree. The court of appeals affirmed a lower court refusal to enforce this order, on the grounds, *inter alia*, that the Commission lacked authority to require such additional reports and that its order violated the Fourth and Fifth Amendments.

The Supreme Court reversed. Mr. Justice Jackson's opinion began by recognizing differences between the Commission's role and that of a court following the conclusion of litigation:

> The court in this case advisedly left it to the Commission to receive the report of compliance and to institute any contempt proceedings. This was in harmony with our system. When the process of adjudication is complete, all judgments are handed over to the litigant or executive officers, such as the sheriff or marshal, to execute. Steps which the litigant or executive department lawfully takes for their enforcement are a vindication rather than a usurpation of the court's power. * * *

> This case illustrates the difference between the judicial function and the function the Commission is attempting to perform. The respondents argue that since the Commission made no charge of violation either of the decree or the statute, it is engaged in a mere "fishing expedition" to see if it can turn up evidence of guilt. We will assume for the argument that this is so. * * *

We must not disguise the fact that sometimes, especially early in the history of the federal administrative tribunal, the courts were persuaded to engraft judicial limitations upon the administrative process. The courts could not go fishing, and so it followed neither could anyone else. * * * More recent views have been more tolerant of it than those which underlay many older decisions.

The only power that is involved here is the power to get information from those who best can give it and who are most interested in not doing so. Because judicial power is reluctant if not unable to summon evidence until it is shown to be relevant to issues in litigation, it does not follow that an administrative agency charged with seeing that the laws are enforced may not have and exercise powers of original injury. * * * When investigative and accusatory duties are delegated by statute to an administrative body, it, too, may take steps to inform itself as to whether there is probable violation of the law.

Jackson concluded that the FTC's order infringed neither the court of appeals' jurisdiction nor sections 552 and 555 of the APA, and that it was within the agency's statutory authority. He then proceeded to consider the company's constitutional claims:

While they may and should have protection from unlawful demands made in the name of public investigation, corporations can claim no equality with individuals in the enjoyment of a right to privacy. They are endowed with public attributes. They have a collective impact upon society, from which they derive the privilege of acting as artificial entities. The Federal Government allows them the privilege of engaging in interstate commerce. Favors from government often carry with them an enhanced measure of regulation. Even if one were to regard the request for information in this case as caused by nothing more than official curiosity, nevertheless law-enforcing agencies have a legitimate right to satisfy themselves that corporate behavior is consistent with the law and the public interest.

Of course a governmental investigation into corporate matters may be of such a sweeping nature and so unrelated to the matter properly under inquiry as to exceed the investigatory power. But it is sufficient if the inquiry is within the authority of the agency, the demand is not too indefinite and the information sought is reasonably relevant. "The gist of the protection is in the requirement, expressed in terms, that the disclosure sought shall not be unreasonable." Nothing on the face of the Commission's order transgressed these bounds.

* * * Before the courts will hold an order seeking information reports to be arbitrarily excessive, they may expect the supplicant to have made reasonable efforts before the Commission itself to obtain reasonable conditions. Neither respondent raised objection to the order's sweep, nor asked any modification, clarification or interpretation of it. Both challenged, instead, power to issue it. * * *

If respondents had objected to the terms of the order, they would have presented or at least offered to present evidence concerning any records required and the cost of their books, matters which now rest on mere assertions in their briefs. The Commission would have had opportunity to disclaim any inadvertent excesses or to justify their demands in the record. We think these respondents could have obtained any reasonable modifications necessary, but, if not, at least could have made a record that would convince us of the measure of their grievance rather than ask us to assume it.

An agency's demand that records be kept or reports submitted, of course, must be authorized by statute and properly adopted. A general rule requiring periodic reports from persons within its regulatory jurisdiction can be successfully resisted if the agency failed to observe proper rulemaking procedures. The procedures required, however, may vary with context. For example, in *Morton Salt*, the FTC's order did not purport to apply generally, and rulemaking procedures would thus not have been appropriate, but the agency must have afforded Morton the opportunities for objection and argument that any respondent would have in any cease-and-desist proceeding.

While *Morton Salt* appears to confirm the FTC's authority to adopt general reporting requirements, as well as to require reports of particular respondents by order, these powers are distinct and each arguably must be supported by law. However, an agency that possesses clear authority to enjoin individual violations may have some inherent power to demand compliance information from a respondent, even though Congress has accorded it no general authority to require records and reports. E.g., *In re: FTC Line of Business Report Litigation*, 595 F.2d 685 (D.C. Cir. 1978).

Fifth Amendment Limits

The issue that has most often arisen in disputes over an individual's failure to produce required information is whether the agency's demand violates the Fifth Amendment privilege against self-incrimination.

In *Shapiro v. United States*, 335 U.S. 1 (1948), the petitioner was convicted of violating regulations issued under the Emergency Price Control Act, a wartime economic measure. Evidence supporting the conviction was obtained from records that OPA rules required but that were of the sort that persons in the same business (selling fruits and vegetables) would maintain in the ordinary course. The petitioner, after first resisting production of the records in response to a subpoena, yielded them; but he claimed that he was entitled to immunity from prosecution under section 202(g) of the Act, which incorporated the Compulsory Testimony Act of 1983, a law according transactional immunity to persons required to testify or produce evidence before the ICC. The court of appeals held that, because they were required to be kept by valid regulations, the records "thereby became public documents, as to which no constitutional privilege against self-incrimination attaches" and to which "accordingly the [statutory] immunity did not extend."

Writing for the Court, Chief Justice Vinson agreed that Congress had not intended to extend immunity so far "as to confer a bonus for the production of information otherwise obtainable." He proceeded to consider whether this construction of the statute raised constitutional doubts:

It may be assumed at the outset that there are limits which the Government cannot constitutionally exceed in requiring the keeping of records which may be inspected by an administrative agency and may be used in prosecuting statutory violations committed by the record-keeper himself.   But no serious misgiving that those bounds have been overstepped would appear to be evoked when there is a sufficient relation between the activity sought to be regulated and the public concern so that the Government can constitutionally regulate or forbid the basic activity concerned, and can constitutionally require the keeping of particular records, subject to inspection by the Administrator.   It is not questioned here that Congress has constitutional authority to prescribe commodity prices as a war emergency measure, and that the licensing and recordkeeping requirements of the Price Control Act represent a legitimate exercise of that power.   Accordingly, the principle enunciated in the *Wilson* case [*Wilson v. United States*, 221 U.S. 361 (1911)] is clearly applicable here: namely, that the privilege which exists as to private papers cannot be maintained in relation to "records required by law to be kept in order that there may be suitable information of transactions which are the appropriate subjects of governmental regulation and the enforcement of restrictions validly established."   [*Davis v. United States*, 328 U.S. 582 (1946).]

* * *   In the case at bar, it cannot be doubted that the sales record which petitioner was required to keep as a licensee under the Price Control Act has "public aspects."   Nor can there be any doubt that when it was obtained by the Administrator through the use of a subpoena, as authorized specifically by § 202(b) of the statute, it was "legally obtained" and hence "available as evidence."   The record involved in the case at bar was a sales record required to be maintained under an appropriate regulation, its relevance to the lawful purpose of the Administrator is unquestioned, and the transaction which it recorded was one in which the petitioner could lawfully engage solely by virtue of the license granted to him under the statute.

This discussion provoked the following dissenting comments from Justice Frankfurter:

If records merely because required to be kept by law *ipso facto* became public records, we are indeed living in glass houses.   Virtually every major public law enactment—to say nothing of State and local legislation—has record-keeping provisions.   In addition to record-keeping requirements, is the network of provisions for filing reports. * * *

* * *   [T]he authorities give no support to the broad proposition that because records are required to be kept by law they are public records and, hence, non-privileged.   Private records do not thus become "public" in any critical or legally significant sense; they are merely the records of an industry or business regulated by law.   Nor does the fact that the Government either may make, or has made, a license a prerequisite for the doing of business make them public in any ordinary use of the term.   While Congress may in time of war, or perhaps in circumstances of economic crisis, provide for the licensing of every individual business, surely such licensing requirements do not remove the records of a man's private business from the protection afforded by the Fifth Amendment.   Just as the licensing of private motor vehicles does not make them public carriers, the licensing of a man's private business,

for tax or other purposes, does not under our system, at least so I had supposed, make him a public officer.

Different considerations control where the business of an enterprise is, as it were, the public's. Clearly the records of a business licensed to sell state-owned property are public records. And the records of a public utility, apart from the considerations relevant to corporate enterprise, may similarly be treated as public records. This has been extended to the records of "occupations which are *malum in se*, or so closely allied thereto, as to endanger the public health, morals or safety."

Here the subject matter of petitioner's business was not such as to render it public. Surely, there is nothing inherently dangerous, immoral, or unhealthy about the sale of fruits and vegetables. Nor was there anything in his possession or control of the records to cast a cloud on his title to them. They were the records that he customarily kept. I find nothing in the Act, or in the Court's construction of the Act, that made him a public officer. He was being administered, not administering. Nor was he in any legitimate sense of the word a "custodian" of the records. * * *

The phrase "required to be kept by law," then, is not a magic phrase by which the legislature opens the door to inroads upon the Fifth Amendment. Statutory provisions * * * , requiring the keeping of records and making them available for official inspection, are constitutional means for effective administration and enforcement. It follows that those charged with the responsibility for such administration and enforcement may compel the disclosure of such records in conformity with the Fourth Amendment. But it does not follow that such disclosures are beyond the scope of the protection afforded by the Fifth Amendment. For the compulsory disclosure of a man's "private books and papers, to convict him of crime or to forfeit his property, is contrary to the principles of a free government. It is abhorrent to the instincts of an Englishman; it is abhorrent to the instincts of an American. It may suit the purposes of despotic power; but it cannot abide the pure atmosphere of political liberty and personal freedom."

Notes

1. The decision in *Shapiro* left unanswered many questions concerning the limits on administrative record-keeping and reporting requirements. For example, does anything in the Court's opinion indicate that Congress could not constitutionally require records to be kept by participants in any activity it had prohibited? See Miltzer, *Required Records, the McCarran Act, and the Privilege Against Self-Incrimination*, 18 U. Chi. L. Rev. 687 (1951).

2. Should it make a difference that the records the government requires are records an individual would ordinarily maintain anyway? See *California Bankers Association v. Shultz*, 416 U.S. 21 (1974). What characteristics—beyond the fact that Congress has by statute required their maintenance—give records "public aspects" that justify official access?

3. In *Albertson v. Subversive Activities Control Board*, 382 U.S. 70, 79 (1965), the Court overturned, on Fifth Amendment grounds, SACB orders instructing named individuals to register with the Attorney General as members of the Communist Party. Those named in the orders faced substantial penalties in the form of fines or imprisonment for failure to register, while proof of their party mem-

bership would support conviction under both the Smith Act and the Subversive Activities Control Act. Writing for a unanimous Court, Justice Brennan declared:

> Petitioners' claims are not asserted in an essentially noncriminal and regulatory area of inquiry, but against an inquiry in an area permeated with criminal statutes, where response to any of the [registration] form's questions in context might involve the petitioners in the admission of a crucial element of a crime.

His opinion made no reference to *Shapiro*, perhaps because the case involved a requirement to report, and not the maintenance of required records.

Albertson grew out of a protracted controversy between federal security officials and the American Communist party. In *Communist Party of the United States v. Subversive Activities Control Board*, 367 U.S. 1 (1961), the Supreme Court avoided the Fifth Amendment issue presented by the Subversive Activities Control Act's registration requirements by ruling that, since individual members might not invoke the Fifth Amendment when ordered to register and since, in any case, the Attorney General might accept their claims, their attack was premature. But as *Albertson* indicates, this subterfuge was short-lived. Following the ruling on the merits, the D.C. Circuit struck down the whole registration procedure as "hopelessly at odds with the protections afforded by the Fifth Amendment." *Communist Party of the United States v. United States*, 384 F.2d 957 (D.C. Cir. 1967).

Required Records of Unlawful Activity

Albertson betrayed deep judicial suspicion of statutory reporting requirements designed to force persons to disclose information on which to base enforcement action against them. In 1968 the Supreme Court again addressed the Fifth Amendment's limitations on compulsory record-keeping and reporting. The petitioner in *Marchetti v. United States*, 390 U.S. 39 (1968), a professional gambler, was convicted for wilfully failing to register with the IRS and to pay an occupation tax for engaging in the business of accepting wagers, as required by 26 U.S.C.A. § § 4411 and 4412, and for conspiring to evade payment of the occupational tax. Following the verdict, Marchetti moved unsuccessfully to arrest judgment, claiming that the statutory obligations to register and to pay the occupational tax violated his constitutional privilege against self-incrimination. The Second Circuit affirmed his convictions.

Justice Harlan, who wrote for the Court, began by observing that "every aspect of petitioner's wagering activities thus subjected him to possible state or federal prosecution." He went on to describe the consequences of compliance with the Code's licensing and reporting requirements:

> Information obtained as a consequence of the federal wagering tax laws is readily available to assist the efforts of state and federal authorities to enforce these penalties. Section 6107 of Title 26 requires the principal internal revenue offices to provide to prosecuting officers a listing of those who have paid the occupational tax. Section 6806(c) obliges taxpayers either to post the revenue stamp "conspicuously" in their principal places of business, or to

keep it on their persons, and to produce it on the demand of Treasury officers. Evidence of the possession of a federal wagering tax stamp, or of payment of the wagering taxes, has often been admitted at trial in state and federal prosecutions for gambling offenses; such evidence has doubtless proved useful even more frequently to lead prosecuting authorities to other evidence upon which convictions have subsequently been obtained. * * *

In these circumstances, it can scarcely be denied that the obligations to register and to pay the occupational tax created for petitioner "real and appreciable," and not merely "imaginary and unsubstantial," hazards of self-incrimination. Petitioner was confronted by a comprehensive system of federal and state prohibitions against wagering activities; he was required, on pain of criminal prosecution, to provide information which might reasonably suppose would be available to prosecuting authorities, and which would surely prove a significant "link in a chain" of evidence tending to establish his guilt. * * * It would appear to follow that petitioner's assertion of the privilege as a defense to this prosecution was entirely proper, and accordingly should have sufficed to prevent his conviction.

Nonetheless, this Court has twice concluded that the privilege against self-incrimination may not appropriately be asserted by those in petitioner's circumstances. * * *

The Court then proceeded to overrule two of its prior decisions, *United States v. Kahriger*, 345 U.S. 22 (1953), and *Lewis v. United States*, 348 U.S. 419 (1955), both of which had held that registration and occupational tax requirements did not infringe the Fifth Amendment privilege against self-incrimination. The Court rejected the basic premises of those decisions, viz., that a person who engaged in activities subject to registration and taxation voluntarily "waived" the privilege, and that the privilege did not protect against disclosure of future activities. It then turned to *Shapiro*:

We think that neither *Shapiro* nor the cases upon which it relied are applicable here.[14] * * *

* * * First, petitioner Marchetti was not, by the provisons now at issue, obliged to keep and preserve records "of the same kind as he has customarily kept"; he was required simply to provide information, unrelated to any records which he may have maintained, about his wagering activities.

* * * Second, whatever "public aspects" there were to the records at issue in *Shapiro*, there are none to the information demanded from Marchetti. The Government's anxiety to obtain information known to a private individual does not without more render that information public; if it did, no room would remain for the application of the constitutional privilege. Nor does it stamp information with a public character that the Government has formalized its demands in the attire of a statute; if this alone were sufficient, the con-

---

14. The United States has urged that this case is not reached by *Shapiro* simply because petitioner was required to submit reports, and not to maintain records. Insofar as this is intended to suggest that the crucial issue respecting the aplicability of *Shapiro* is the method by which information reaches the Government, we are unable to accept the distinction. We perceive no meaningful difference between an obligation to maintain records for inspection, and such an obligation supplemented by a requirement that those records be filed periodically with officers of the United States. * * *

stitutional privilege could be entirely abrogated by any Act of Congress. Third, the requirements at issue in *Shapiro* were imposed in "an essentially noncriminal and regulatory area of inquiry" while those here are directed at a "selective group inherently suspect of criminal activities."　Cf. *Albertson v. SACB.*　The United States' principal interest is evidently the collection of revenue, and not the punishment of gamblers, but the characteristics of the activities about which information is sought, and the composition of the groups to which inquiries are made, readily distinguish this situation from that in *Shapiro.*　*　*　*

　　*　*　* We emphasize that we do not hold that these wagering tax provisions are as such constitutionally impermissible; we hold only that those who properly assert the constitutional privilege as to these provisions may not be ciriminally punished for failure to comply with the requirements.　*　*　*

Notes

　　1. In two companion cases, the Court invalidated other federal revenue and registration requirements.　*Grosso v. United States,* 390 U.S. 62 (1968), involved a conviction for willful failure to pay the federal excise tax on wagers. Again writing for the majority, Justice Harlan distinguished *Shapiro* on the grounds that the excise tax provisions were not primarily "regulatory" in purpose, that the information required to be disclosed by the taxpayer had not acquired any "public records" character, and that it was by no means clear that the information was of a kind persons engaged in wagering could customarily keep. In *Haynes v. United States,* 390 U.S. 85 (1968), the same majority overturned a conviction for knowing possession of a sawed-off shotgun which the petitioner had not registered with the Secretary of the Treasury as required by 26 U.S.C.A. § 5841.　See also *Leary v. United States,* 395 U.S. 6 (1969), where the Court struck down, as violative of the Fifth Amendment, a provision of the Internal Revenue Code requiring persons dealing in marijuana to register and file tax returns covering all transfers of marijuana.　*Mackey v. United States,* 401 U.S. 667 (1971), held that *Marchetti* did not apply retroactively to invalidate a prior conviction for income tax evasion based on wagering tax returns.　But cf. *United States v. United States Coin and Currency,* 401 U.S. 715 (1971).　See *United States v. Freed,* 401 U.S. 601 (1971) (upholding amended record-keeping requirements of National Firearms Act).

　　2. *Marchetti* does not prevent prosecution of one who responds falsely to an invalid reporting requirement.　In *United States v. Knox,* 396 U.S. 77 (1969), the Court reversed the dismissal of an indictment charging the defendants with furnishing false information on wagering tax forms.　Justice Harlan's majority opinion held that *Marchetti* would have protected the defendants if they had filed no forms at all, but did not apply where they had "voluntarily" supplied false information.

　　3. Several lower courts have attempted to discern the line between reporting and recordkeeping requirements whose purpose is "regulatory" and those whose purpose is penal.　In *Application of Nadelson,* 353 F. Supp. 971 (S.D.N.Y. 1973), the court ordered production of records by a process server under grand jury investigation for engaging in "sewer service."　The records were required to be kept by a regulation of the New York City Department of Consumer Affairs. The district judge distinguished *Marchetti, et al,* emphasizing that here the activ-

ity for which records were required was not one that the government had sought to prohibit altogether. Instead, required recordkeeping was simply one feature of a general regulatory program designed to protect the public interest. The fact that the applicant's records might disclose evidence of crime did not, without more, bring them within the protection of the Fifth Amendment. Similarly, in *United States v. Warren*, 453 F.2d 738 (2d Cir.), *cert. denied* 406 U.S. 944 (1972), records required to be maintained by persons engaged in dispensing controlled drugs were held to fall within the *Shapiro* rationale as "part of a regulatory scheme with public purposes." See also *United States v. Reiff*, 435 F.2d 257 (7th Cir. 1970), *cert. denied* 401 U.S. 938 (1971); *United States v. Silverman*, 449 F.2d 1341 (2d Cir. 1971), *cert. denied* 405 U.S. 918 (1972) (affirming attorney's conviction for income tax evasion based in part on reports of contingent fees required by state law to be filed in court).

4. May records properly required under *Shapiro* be examined by agency officials on the maker's premises without a warrant? The issue has arisen infrequently in litigation. In *United States ex rel. Terraciano v. Montanye*, 493 F.2d 682 (2d Cir.), *cert. denied* 419 U.S. 875 (1974), the court of appeals upheld the warrantless examination of the required records of a pharmacist, but implied that if a statutorily authorized warrantless search were not sufficiently limited in the nature of the material sought and the manner of access, the Fourth Amendment might require an intruding official to obtain a warrant.

5. Other cases that have grappled with the elusive relationship between the Fourth and Fifth Amendments in the context of required records have achieved no consensus. In a curious opinion a three-judge court in *Stark v. Connally*, 347 F. Supp. 1242 (N.D. Cal. 1972), *modified sub nom. California Bankers Association v. Schultz*, 416 U.S. 21 (1974), struck down certain reporting provisions of the Bank Secrecy Act and implementing Treasury regulations on the ground that they authorized unreasonable searches and seizures within the meaning of the Fourth Amendment. The provisions required banks automatically to report the details of virtually all domestic transactions in order to facilitate discovery of wrongdoing by bank customers. In reversing this portion of the lower court's decision, Justice Rehnquist's plurality opinion discerned a rational relationship between the recordkeeping and reporting requirements and the congressional objective of scrutinizing the business operations of organized crime. Rehnquist interpreted the legislative history and implementing regulations as indicating that access to records of domestic transactions could be obtained only by proper legal process, *e.g.*, by subpoena. Despite estimates that the Act would require banks each year to photocopy between 20 and 30 billion checks, weighing some 166 million pounds, the plurality opinion suggested that banks may have been keeping similar records for their own purposes in the past. Although the opinion characterized the bank petitioners as parties to the financial transactions of their customers, it can be read as sustaining recordkeeping requirements imposed on third parties having information about activities or persons who are the targets of regulation.

6. In another controversial case, *Hill v. Philpott*, 445 F.2d 144 (7th Cir.), *cert. denied* 404 U.S. 991 (1971), the Seventh Circuit reversed a lower court decision approving the introduction in evidence of a taxpayer's personal records, which had been seized pursuant to a search warrant. Ignoring *Shapiro*, the government had claimed that once a search is shown to be valid under the Fourth Amendment, an individual can no longer assert his Fifth Amendment privilege

with respect to any materials lawfully seized. The court of appeals in *United States v. Warren*, supra p. 532, distinguished *Hill v. Philpott* as involving personal tax records not specifically required to be kept by the Internal Revenue Code, which provides simply that taxpayers shall maintain records adequate to substantiate their returns.

7. Another line of cases holds that if the demanded records are not in the defendant's possession, the privilege is lost. *E.g., Andresen v. Maryland*, 427 U.S. 463 (1976); *Couch v. United States*, 409 U.S. 322 (1973); cf. *United States v. LaSalle National Bank*, 437 U.S. 298 (1978). See generally Note, *Formalism, Legal Realism, and Constitutionally Protected Privacy Under the Fourth and Fifth Amendments*, 90 Harv. L. Rev. 945 (1977).

Costs of Government-Mandated Records and Reports

Record-keeping and reporting requirements can impose substantial burdens on those subject to them. For example, a requirement that every industrial enterprise continuously monitor the contents of its liquid waste or smoke emissions could necessitate the employment of additional personnel, the maintenance of testing and sample storage facilities, and enormous amounts of paper work. The cost of assembling the data necessary to obtain FDA approval of a new drug may amount to several million dollars—for animal tests, clinical studies, chemical analyses, and for reproducing the several hundred volumes that comprise a New Drug Application. It has been estimated that the premarket notification requirement for new chemicals, prescribed by the 1976 Toxic Substances Control Act, imposes on average a cost of between $9,000 and $41,000 for each compound introduced—a cost that exceeds the expected return on most new chemicals, though it is dwarfed by the yield of the relatively few significant innovations. According to the same estimate, this "reporting charge" has diminished the rate of introduction of new chemicals in this country by 250 to 700 a year. Such costs may be easily absorbed by large business, but not all drug or chemical manufacturers are large, and many dischargers of industrial waste are small enterprises. Moreover, it is to be expected that so far as possible the expense of record-keeping and reporting will be passed on to customers, as a cost of doing business. See generally EPA, IMPACT OF TSCA PREMANUFACTURING NOTIFICATION REQUIREMENTS (December 1978).

Although judicial control of administrative reporting requirements obviously permits agencies wide latitude in demanding information, other supervising institutions may exercise stricter oversight. Until 1980, all new information requirements had to be approved for most executive agencies by OMB, while independent regulatory commissions had to submit their proposals to the Government Accounting Office, an agency of Congress. 44 U.S.C.A. § § 3501-512. Congress established this division of authority between OMB and the GAO in 1973, *inter alia*, to protect the "independence" of regulatory commissions.

The potentially significant differences between OMB and GAO oversight were recognized in *In re: FTC Line of Business Report Litigation*, 595 F.2d 685 (D.C. Cir. 1978). The case involved the FTC's demand that information concerning sales, profits and other indicators of business activity levels and market structure be reported by product or "line of business." The purpose of the requirements was to create a data base on the activities of "conglomerates," which normally produce accounting and other data on some basis other than by product line. Affected businesses found the new requirements onerous and challenged their validity on varied grounds.

While upholding the Commission's order to produce the reports on all counts, the court had this to say concerning GAO "review" of the proposal:

> The Comptroller construes Section 3512 of the Federal Reports Act as establishing two criteria for review of data-collection plans. * * *
>
> (1) avoiding duplication of effort by independent regulatory agencies, and
>
> (2) minimizing the compliance burden on business enterprises and other persons.
>
> * * *
>
> Appellants argue that the Comptroller was obliged to determine additionally that the data sought was "appropriate" to the FTC's expressed need. * * *
>
> Prior to the 1973 amendment, the OMB possessed authority to undertake a substantive appraisal of the data that a regulatory agency sought and to bar collection upon a finding that the data were not necessary for effectuation of the agency's function or the particular program's purpose. Congress regarded the evaluation of the regulatory agency's need for data as essentially a policy determination and considered the reviewing agency's veto power as a source of interference with the independence of the regulatory agencies. So in creating a separate clearance procedure for these agencies, Congress specifically provided in Section 3512(d) that the independent regulatory agency shall make the final determination as to the necessity of the information in carrying out its statutory responsibilities and whether to collect such information. Appellants' construction of "appropriateness" as a requirement that the Comptroller evaluate the data sought in terms of the agency's needs is untenable in light of this provision reserving for the agency the determination as to the necessity of the information in carrying out its statutory responsibilities.

In 1980, at the urging of the Carter Administration, Congress substantially overhauled the regime for administrative oversight of agency reporting and record-keeping requirements by enacting the Paperwork Reduction Act, Pub. L. No. 96-511, now codified at 44 U.S.C.A. § § 3501 *et seq.* While the new law made modest changes in the criteria for review and approval of proposed agency requirements, its major changes were the restoration and invigoration of OMB's oversight role for all agencies, both executive and independent and the elimination of most categorical and agency-specific exemptions to centralized review. The Act reflected broad concerns about the impact of federal regulation generally on the nation's economic vitality. See OMB, PAPERWORK AND RED TAPE (Sept. 1979).

The Paperwork Act is nominally administered by the Director of OMB, but contemplates that his duties will be performed by the Administrator of an Office of Information and Regulatory Affairs (OIRA), who is to have no other competing duties. The Act amends the Federal Reports Act of 1942, which had been construed as inapplicable to three-quarters of all federal information demands on the private sector. See S. Rep. No. 96-930, 96th Cong., 2d Sess. 75 (1980). In addition to creating a central office in OMB to formulate government information management policies and to oversee agency demands the Act requires that each agency head designate a senior official to oversee the agency's compliance with the Act and, with OMB's concurrence, exercise that body's final approval authority.

Before imposing a new demand for information on the private sector, an agency must first convince the OIRA that the information sought "is necessary for the proper performance of the functions of the agency, including whether the information will have practical utility." OIRA's refusal to approve a request is final, unless the request comes from an independent agency and a majority of its members vote to override the "veto." OIRA may not veto a proposal to obtain information that is demanded by an agency's organic legislation, but the Act requires that it have an opportunity to review such proposals.

The Paperwork Reduction Act also directs OMB to establish general policies and procedures for controlling the government's collection of information. Further, the Act itself enunciated a specific goal of reducing the burden of federally-mandated paperwork by 25 percent by the end of Fiscal Year 1983, and directed that OMB annually provide Congress a report estimating the hours required to comply with each agency's reporting obligations. The Reagan Administration has pursued these directives with some vigor. In 1981 OMB issued a regulation, Controlling Paperwork Burdens on the Public, 5 C.F.R. § 1320, which creates a so-called "information collection budget" as a mechanism for accomplishing the Act's directives. OMB, INFORMATION COLLECTION BUDGET OF THE UNITED STATES GOVERNMENT: FISCAL YEAR 1984, describes the budgeting process and its, from OMB's perspective, healthy impact:

> The Information Collection Budget (ICB) is a process for measuring and controlling the costs of Federal information collections to individuals, businesses, and State and local governments. * * *

> The Information Collection Budget attempts to balance the costs of supplying this information against its practical utility to the government and the public. First instituted as a prototype of Fiscal Year 1981 and on a government-wide basis in Fiscal Year 1982, it is the first effort to employ budgeting procedures—long familiar in connection with direct employment expenditures—to the *private* costs of public policies. * * *

> The ICB is prepared each Fall through a procedure similar to the preparation of the President's fiscal budget. Based upon the prior year's experience and the best current estimates of the "burden hours" imposed by each form,

survey, and other information collection, each agency submits to OMB a proposed budget of total burden hours for the new fiscal year, together with a description of changes in existing paperwork requirements that will meet this budget.   Agency submissions are followed by OMB reviews, passbacks, and meetings between agency and OMB officials, until final budgets are settled upon that will minimize paperwork burden consistent with program needs and actual use of collected information.   Changes to meet the budgeted burden hours are made during the fiscal year through review and revision of individual paperwork requirements. * * *

Following the close of Fiscal Year 1983, Federal agencies prepared a final accounting of actual reductions obtained against the Federal paperwork known to exist in 1980 (the "1980 Base").   Last year's ICB projected a 29 percent reduction from the 1980 base by the end of FY 1983.   However, reductions actually achieved during FY 1983, combined with those achieved in earlier years, amount to a 32 percent reduction from the 1980 base, far surpassing the 25-percent reduction goal established by the Paperwork Reduction Act.   Total paperwork reduction since the Reagan Administration took office in January 1981 is over 400 million hours. * * *

The OMB report outlined the primary sources of record-keeping and reporting requirements and went on to detail the areas of major impact of the budgeting process:

Of the total paperwork burden to be imposed in FY 1984, almost two thirds will be levied by two agencies, the Department of Defense (31%) and the Department of the Treasury (29%). * * *

Over 99 percent of Defense Department paperwork burden consists of reporting and recordkeeping associated with procurement.   Treasury's burden continues to be primarily reporting and recordkeeping required by the Internal Revenue Service.   The next largest agency share of the total burden results from information collections from the Department of Health and Human Services (8%), which are primarily associated with the Social Security and Medicare programs.   The Department of Agriculture (5%), Transportation (5%), Energy (4%), and Labor (4%) are the other agencies that each impose annual paperwork burdens in excess of 85 million hours. * * *

[An] effect of the incorporation of procurement paperwork is shown in the analysis of entities providing the government with information.   Reporting provided by businesses and institutions such as schools and hospitals (73%) has shown a substantial increase; in previous years, this group had provided slightly less than half of the reporting.   There have been corresponding decreases in the burden now being imposed on individuals or households (22%, down from 35% in FY 1981) and State and local governments (4%, down from 10% in FY 1981), while reporting provided by farms (1%) has remained constant.

* * * Most Federal paperwork (56%) is associated with obtaining Federal benefits such as Medicare payments; procurement and other contracts; and program and research grants.   Mandatory information collections—collections for which penalties may be assessed against the respondent for failure to comply, such as census and tax reporting—constitute 42% of the total Federal reporting burden.   Voluntary information collections not associated with government benefits or contracts constitute only 2% of total paperwork. * * *

During FY 1983, Federal agencies reduced paperwork burdens imposed on the American public by 144 million hours—an 11 percent reduction from the approximately 1.3 billion hours in the measured paperwork inventory at the close of FY 1982.

The OMB report's summary of "major paperwork reductions in FY 1983" provides some insights into the potential implications of this effort for the ultimate performance of regulatory programs:

Major paperwork reductions achieved during FY 1983 include:

— Elimination of the Department of Transportation's (DOT) recordkeeping requirements associated with the Highway Safety Program (– 62 million hours).   DOT has required States to maintain records in 18 highway safety-related areas, including accident investigation, motor vehicle registration, and motor vehicle inspection.   During FY 1983 a significant portion of these requirements was discontinued.

— Reduction in the Department of Agriculture's cost accounting recordkeeping requirements associated with the National School Lunch and School Breakfast Programs and elimination of the Annual Report of Revenue and Cost (– 21 million hours).   These changes were made possible through legislative changes, and provided significant paperwork relief to State and local school authorities.

— Reduction in the DOT Driver's Log (– 11 million hours).   At the close of FY 1982 DOT issued a final rule modifying requirements for daily records of working hours that must be kept by truck drivers.   Over half of the data elements were deleted from the log, and industry was provided added flexibility in the recordkeeping process.

— Reduction in the Internal Revenue Service's (IRS) Employers Quarterly Tax Return (– 8 million hours).   IRS reduced the burden associated with its Form 941 during FY 1983 by eliminating a number of data elements.   This reduced the burden imposed by this form during FY 1982 by about 33 percent.

— Reductions in the Internal Revenue Service's Corporate Income Tax and Partnership Returns (– 6 million hours).   IRS eliminated certain date elements, and filings of certain parts of the forms were eliminated for many small corporations and firms.   This resulted in a reduction in burden of approximately 15 percent from that imposed in FY 1982.

OMB, INFORMATION COLLECTION BUDGET OF THE UNITED STATES GOVERNMENT: FISCAL YEAR 1984, at 1-3, 8-9, 13.

3. PHYSICAL INSPECTIONS

Many statutes authorize administrative inspections as a means of policing compliance with regulatory requirements.   Such provisions are common in laws whose focus is the protection of the public health or the collection of revenue.   Probably the most pervasive government inspection program exists in the meat and poultry industries, where resident federal inspectors supervise slaughtering and packing operations from beginning to end, throughout the work day.   On-site inspection or visitation also has obvious utility in the enforcement of pollution controls, housing ordinances, and health and fire regulations.   But government intrusions into private premises, however benign their purpose or peaceful their execution, raise constitutional issues. Indeed, the clash between the requirements of efficient enforcement and the values protected by the Fourth Amendment is more obvious here than in the subpoena context, for agency subpoenas customarily threaten no violation of the physical integrity of a citizen's home or business. While our attention will be focused on the constitutional issues, this focus should not obscure other issues that may be raised by an agency's attempt to conduct physical inspections. For example, here too clear statutory authority is surely a prerequisite to the conduct of any administrative search or inspection.

Basic Premises

Notwithstanding the prevalence of state and federal laws authorizing physical inspections, it was not until 1959 that the Supreme Court squarely faced the question whether administrative searches are subject to the same constitutional restrictions as those conducted by police officers engaged in enforcing the criminal law. Repeated visits to this question since *Frank v. Maryland*, 359 U.S. 360 (1959), however, have yet to produce a coherent set of governing principles. In *Frank* the Court upheld, by a five-to-four vote, a state conviction of a homeowner who refused to permit a municipal health inspector to enter his premises without a search warrant—in substance recognizing warrantless administrative inspections as "reasonable" under the Fourth Amendment. Within eight years, however, the Court had revised its view of the Fourth Amendment's applicability in this context.

Camara v. Municipal Court, 387 U.S. 523 (1967), and *See v. Seattle*, 387 U.S. 541 (1967), mark the beginnings of contemporary doctrine. The Court overturned convictions for refusing legislatively authorized peaceful inspections of an apartment and a warehouse, upholding each defendant's claim that he was entitled to insist on a search warrant. Writing for the majority in both cases, Justice White rejected attempts to distinguish these contexts from customary police searches for evidence of crime and from one another (387 U.S. at 530-33):

> We may agree that a routine inspection of the physical condition of private property is a less hostile intrusion than the typical policeman's search for the fruits and instrumentalities of crime. * * * But we cannot agree that the Fourth Amendment interests at stake in these inspection cases are merely "peripheral." It is surely anomalous to say that the individual and his private property are fully protected by the Fourth Amendment only when the individual is suspected of criminal behavior. For instance, even the most law-abiding citizen has a very tangible interest in limiting the circumstances under which the sanctity of his home may be broken by official authority, for the possibility of criminal entry under the guise of official sanction is a serious threat to personal and family security. * * * Like most regulatory laws, fire, health, and housing codes are enforced by criminal processes. In some cities, discovery of a violation by the inspector leads to a criminal complaint. Even in cities where discovery of a violation produces only an administrative compliance order, refusal to comply is a criminal offense, and the fact of com-

pliance is verified by a second inspection, again without a warrant. Finally, as this case demonstrates, refusal to permit an inspection is itself a crime, punishable by fine or even by jail sentence.

The *Frank* majority suggested, and appellee reasserts, two other justifications for permitting administrative health and safety inspections without a warrant. First, it is argued that these inspections are "designed to make the least possible demand on the individual occupant." The ordinances authorizing inspections are hedged with safeguards, and at any rate the inspector's particular decision to enter must comply with the constitutional standard of reasonableness even if he may enter without a warrant. In addition, the argument proceeds, the warrant process could not function effectively in this field. The decision to inspect an entire municipal area is based upon legislative or administrative assessment of broad factors such as the area's age and condition. Unless the magistrate is to review such policy matters, he must issue a "rubber stamp" warrant which provides no protection at all to the property owner.

In our opinion, these arguments unduly discount the purposes behind the warrant machinery contemplated by the Fourth Amendment. Under the present system, when the inspector demands entry, the occupant has no way of knowing whether enforcement of the municipal code involved requires inspection of his premises, no way of knowing the lawful limits of the inspector's power to search, and no way of knowing whether the inspector himself is acting under proper authorization. These are questions which may be reviewed by a neutral magistrate without any reassessment of the basic agency decision to canvass an area. Yet, only by refusing entry and risking a criminal conviction can the occupant at present challenge the inspector's decision to search. And even if the occupant possesses sufficient fortitude to take this risk, as appellant did here, he may never learn any more about the reason for the inspection than that the law generally allows housing inspectors to gain entry. The practical effect of this system is to leave the occupant subject to the discretion of the official in the field. This is precisely the discretion to invade private property which we have consistently circumscribed by a requirement that a disinterested party warrant the need to search. We simply cannot say that the protections provided by the warrant procedure are not needed in this context; broad statutory safeguards are no substitute for individualized review, particularly when those safeguards may only be invoked at the risk of a criminal penalty.

The final justification for warrantless administrative searches is that the public interest demands such a rule: it is vigorously argued that the health and safety of entire urban populations is dependent upon enforcement of minimum fire, housing, and sanitation standards, and that the only effective means of enforcing such codes is by routine systematized inspection of all physical structures. * * * [W]e think this argument misses the mark. The question is not, at this stage at least, whether these inspections may be made, but whether they may be made without a warrant. * * * It has nowhere been urged that fire, health, and housing code inspection programs could not achieve their goals within their confines of a reasonable search warrant requirement. * * *

In *See*, Justice White asserted: "The businessman, like the occupant of a residence, has a constitutional right to go about his business free from unreasonable official entries upon his private commercial property." Accordingly, "the basic component of a reasonable search under the Fourth Amendment—that it not be enforced without a suitable warrant procedure—is applicable in this context, as in others, to business premises as well as to residential premises." 387 U.S. at 543, 546.

Having concluded that the occupant of private residential or business premises is entitled to demand a warrant to inspect, Justice White considered the kind of showing an inspector must make to obtain a magistrate's approval for an unconsented-to inspection (Id. at 534-40):

> * * * "[P]robable cause" is the standard by which a particular decision to search is tested against the constitutional mandate of reasonableness. To apply this standard, it is obviously necessary first to focus upon the governmental interest which allegedly justifies official intrusion upon the constitutionally protected interests of the private citizen. * * *
>
> There is unanimous agreement among those most familiar with this field that the only effective way to seek universal compliance with the minimum standards required by municipal codes is through routine periodic inspections of all structures. It is here that the probable cause debate is focused, for the agency's decision to conduct an area inspection is unavoidably based on its appraisal of conditions in the area as a whole, not on its knowledge of conditions in each particular building. * * *
>
> * * * [T]here can be no ready test for determining reasonableness other than by balancing the need to search against the invasion which the search entails. But we think that a number of persuasive factors combine to support the reasonableness of area code-enforcement inspections. First, such programs have a long history of judicial and public acceptance. Second, the public interest demands that all dangerous conditions be prevented or abated, yet it is doubtful that any other canvassing technique would achieve acceptable results. Many such conditions—faulty wiring is an obvious example—are not observable from outside the building and indeed may not be apparent to the inexpert occupant himself. Finally, because the inspections are neither personal in nature nor aimed at the discovery of evidence of crime, they involve a relatively limited invasion of the urban citizen's privacy. * * *
>
> Having concluded that the area inspection is a "reasonable" search of private property within the meaning of the Fourth Amendment, it is obvious that "probable cause" to issue a warrant to inspect must exist if reasonable legislative or administrative standards for conducting an area inspection are satisfied with respect to a particular dwelling. Such standards, which will vary with the municipal program being enforced, may be based upon the passage of time, the nature of the building (e.g., a multi-family apartment house), or the condition of the entire area, but they will not necessarily depend upon specific knowledge of the condition of the particular dwelling. It has been suggested that so to vary the probable cause test from the standard applied in criminal cases would be to authorize a "synthetic search warrant" and thereby to lessen the overall protections of the Fourth Amendment. But we do not agree. The warrant procedure is designed to guarantee that a decision to search private property is justified by a reasonable governmental interest. But reasonableness is still the ultimate standard. * * *

Since our holding emphasizes the controlling standard of reasonableness, nothing we say today is intended to foreclose prompt inspections, even without a warrant, that the law has traditionally upheld in emergency situations. On the other hand, in the case of most routine area inspections, there is no compelling urgency to inspect at a particular time or on a particular day. Moreover, most citizens allow inspections of their property without a warrant. Thus, as a practical matter and in light of the Fourth Amendment's requirement that a warrant specify the property to be searched, it seems likely that warrants should normally be sought only after entry is refused unless there has been a citizen complaint or there is other satisfactory reason for securing immediate entry. * * *

A familiarity with the procedure for the issuance of search warrants is helpful in understanding the debate in *Camara* and *See* and later cases. The principal safeguard afforded by a warrant requirement is that it forces law enforcement officers to establish a factual basis for the search of private premises before any entry is made, and thus forestalls *post hoc* attempts to justify conduct that could not have been justified at the time. Typically, an officer seeking a warrant must appear before a magistrate—a judge or other judicial officer—and persuade the magistrate that "probable cause" exists to support two conclusions: (1) that the items the officer hopes to find in the search are in some way connected with unlawful, usually criminal, activity; and (2) that the items are likely to be found on the premises to be searched. Most often, the officer presents what supporting information he has in the form of a sworn affidavit. Very occasionally this will be supplemented by affidavits of other witnesses. Frequently, but by no means always, the officer seeking the warrant will himself testify before the magistrate. No one is present to represent the person whose premises are to be searched.

Theoretically, the requirement of "probable cause" demands information that, if true, would make it more probable than not that the items sought are indeed connected with unlawful activity and will be found on the premises. But it is clear that a magistrate's decisions can follow no mathematical formula. Furthermore, decisions often must be made hastily and, in situations where warrant applications tend to be duplicative, are probably made casually. Moreover, the information offered to establish "probable cause" need not be admissible in a criminal trial or administrative proceeding likely to grow out of the search.

Notes

1. What householder interest is protected by the Court's criteria for the issuance of inspection warrants? Does the requirement do more than assure equality of random vulnerability to government intrusions not based upon probable cause? For a suggestion that in *Camara* and *See* the Supreme Court was attempting to impose on administrative inspections essentially the same controls as apply to agency subpoenas, see Note, *Inspections by Administrative Agencies: Clarification of the Warrant Requirement*, 49 Notre Dame Law. 879 (1974).

2. The ground rules laid down by the Supreme Court in *Camara* and *See* for the conduct of administrative inspections are similar to those prescribed by many, though not all, English inspection statutes. Apparently these ground rules have not created serious problems for regulatory agencies there, although not all English inspection laws embody them. See Waters, *Rights of Entry in Administrative Officers*, 27 U. Chi. L. Rev. 79 (1959).

Exceptions and Elaborations

The Supreme Court continued to wrestle after *Camara* and *See* with the Fourth Amendment's applicability to administrative searches and inspections and with the adequacy of procedures for the issuance of warrants. Three years later, the Court recognized an exception to the warrant requirement for businesses with a history of regulation—embracing a distinction that Justice Brennan had suggested in his concurring opinion in the latter case.

In *Colonnade Catering Corp. v. United States*, 397 U.S. 72 (1970), a licensed liquor dealer challenged the legality of a forced and warrantless entry of a locked storeroom which led to his conviction for violating an Internal Revenue Code prohibition against refilling bottles used for the sale of alcoholic beverages. The Court overturned the conviction on the ground that the statutory authorization to inspect licensees could not be read as affording IRS agents the option to break in if access were denied. But in dictum the majority validated the statutory penalty for refusal to permit inspection without a warrant, on the ground that alcoholic beverage licensees had historically been subject to broader administrative scrutiny and control.

In *United States v. Biswell*, 406 U.S. 311 (1972), this "exception" to *Camara* and *See* appeared to expand. The 1968 Federal Gun Control Act, 18 U.S.C.A. § 923(g), authorizes the premises of registered gun dealers to be entered and inspected by Treasury Department agents during business hours. When agents arrived to inspect Biswell's pawn shop they acknowledged they did not have a warrant, but he acquiesced in their search of his premises after being shown a copy of the statutory provision authorizing entry. Convicted of unauthorized dealing in firearms based on evidence found during the inspection, Biswell claimed that the agents' conduct was unlawful under *See* and that he could not be understood as having waived his constitutional right to demand a warrant. A majority of the Court upheld his conviction (406 U.S. at 314-17):

> Here, the search was not accompanied by any unauthorized force, and if the target of the inspection had been a federally licensed liquor dealer, it is clear under *Colonnade* that the Fourth Amendment would not bar a seizure of illicit liquor. * * *
>
> * * * Federal regulation of the interstate traffic in firearms is not as deeply rooted in history as is governmental control of the liquor industry, but close scrutiny of this traffic is undeniably of central importance to federal efforts to prevent violent crime and to assist the States in regulating the firearms traffic within their borders. Large interests are at stake, and inspection is a crucial part of the regulatory scheme, since it assures that weapons

are distributed through regular channels and in a traceable manner and makes possible the prevention of sales to undesirable customers and the detection of the origin of particular firearms.

It is also apparent that if the law is to be properly enforced and inspection made effective, inspections without warrant must be deemed reasonable official conduct under the Fourth Amendment. In *See v. City of Seattle* the mission of the inspection system was to discover and correct violations of the building code, conditions that were relatively difficult to conceal or to correct in a short time. Periodic inspection sufficed, and inspection warrants could be required and privacy given a measure of protection with little if any threat to the effectiveness of the inspection system there at issue. * * * Here, if inspection is to be effective and serve as a credible deterrent, unannounced, even frequent, inspections are essential. In this context, the prerequisite of a warrant could easily frustrate inspection; and if the necessary flexibility as to time, scope, and frequency is to be preserved, the protections afforded by a warrant would be negligible.

It is also plain that inspections for compliance with the Gun Control Act pose only limited threats to the dealer's justifiable expectations of privacy. When a dealer chooses to engage in this pervasively regulated business and to accept a federal license, he does so with the knowledge that his business records, firearms and ammunition will be subject to effective inspection. Each licensee is annually furnished with a revised compilation of ordinances that describe his obligations and define the inspector's authority. * * *

We have little difficulty in concluding that where, as here, regulatory inspections further urgent federal interest, and the possibilities of abuse and the threat to privacy are not of impressive dimensions, the inspection may proceed without a warrant where specifically authorized by statute.

The Court in *Biswell* conspicuously avoided resting on the government's contention that the petitioner had given his consent to the particular search of his premises, thereby "waiving" any constitutional objections. But clearly acquiescence in an officer's request for entry may under some circumstances obviate the need for a warrant. The traditional rubric is that, to be valid, any waiver of constitutional safeguards must be knowing and voluntary. In the regulatory context, however, the standard appears to be less strict. For example, in *United States v. Thriftimart, Inc.*, 429 F.2d 1006 (9th Cir.), *cert. denied* 400 U.S. 926 (1970), the court upheld the convictions of a corporation and responsible officers for violating federal food sanitation requirements. Evidence of the offenses was obtained during a plant inspection by FDA agents, who obtained entry without a warrant. The inspectors had presented a formal notice of inspection and request for permission to enter the defendants' premises, reciting their general inspection authority under the Federal Food, Drug and Cosmetic Act. The inspectors did not advise the defendants that they were entitled to insist that a warrant be obtained. The Ninth Circuit found the inspection valid and sustained the convictions. The court noted that in *Camara* and *See* the Supreme Court had acknowledged that it was not necessary for inspectors to seek a warrant before being denied permission to inspect, and suggested that a different measure of "consent" should apply to administrative inspections. Emphasizing that the record was barren of evidence that the defendants were uninformed of their rights, surprised by the inspectors' visit, or coerced into admitting them, the court found it entirely plausible that a businessman might consciously adopt a policy of full cooperation with regulatory officials.   See also *United States v. J. B. Kramer Grocery Co.*, 418 F.2d 987 (8th Cir. 1969) (voluntary consent to inspection obviates need for warrant, but whether consent was given is issue for trier of fact); *Stephenson Enterprises, Inc. v. Marshall*, 578 F.2d 1021 (5th Cir. 1978).   In *Weyerhaeuser Co. v. Marshall*, 592 F.2d 373 (7th Cir. 1979), the court of appeals held that an employer who had consented "under protest" to an OSHA inspection conducted pursuant to a warrant had preserved his right later to challenge the warrant's validity.

In *Wyman v. James*, 400 U.S. 309 (1971), the notion of "consent" to inspections that are an integral part of a governmental regulatory scheme took root in a different context.   Mrs. James, who received welfare payments on behalf of her son under the Aid to Families with Dependent Children program, was stricken from New York's list of eligible recipients after she declined to allow her caseworker to conduct a home visit without a warrant.   In a curious opinion by Justice Blackmun, the Court paid homage to *Camara*'s interpretation of the Fourth Amendment but found its teachings inapplicable to this case (400 U.S. at 317–18):

> This natural and quite proper protective attitude, however, is not a factor in this case, for the seemingly obvious and simple reason that we are not concerned here with any search by the New York social service agency in the Fourth Amendment meaning of that term.   It is true that the governing statute and regulations appear to make mandatory the initial home visit and the subsequent periodic "contacts" (which may include home visits) for the inception and continuance of aid.   It is also true that the caseworker's posture in the home visit is perhaps, in a sense, both rehabilitative and investigative.   But this latter aspect, we think is given too broad a character and far more emphasis than it deserves if it is equated with a search in the traditional criminal law context.   We note, too, that the visitation in itself is not forced or compelled, and that the beneficiary's denial of permission is not a criminal act.   If consent to the visitation is withheld, no visitation takes place.   The aid then never begins or merely ceases, as the case may be.   There is no entry of the home and there is no search.

Assuming, *arguendo*, that the home visit, "despite its interview nature, does possess some of the characteristics of a search," Justice Blackmun held that it "does not descend to the level of unreasonableness." 400 U.S. at 318.   Its objective was to protect the interests of the child and assure proper expenditure of aid provided by the state which, as a donor of charity, was entitled to a "gentle means, of limited extent and of practical and considerate application, of achieving that assurance."   Furthermore, Mrs. James had advance notice of the visit, could adjust its timing, and offered "no specific complaint of any unreasonable intrusion of her home.   * * * " Id. at 319, 321.

Justice Douglas, dissenting, viewed the case as one in which the state had attempted to "buy up" the constitutional rights of persons dependent on public largesse.   While the home visit had benevolent as well as investigatory objectives, it clearly represented governmental invasion of the "sanctity of the sanctuary of the *home*" and should not escape the requirements of the Fourth Amendment.

Notes

1. Professor Burt was not persuaded by the Court's reasons for refusing to require a warrant for welfare home visitations:

> The beneficent purposes of this compulsory visit—either on behalf of the resisting parent or her child—do not necessarily establish the inapplicability of the fourth amendment search warrant requirement. * * * As Justice Marshall stated in his *Wyman* dissent, the housing code program in *Camara* was potentially beneficial for the inspected homeowner as well as for his neighbors, who were necessarily affected by the condition of his house.   *Camara* cannot be distinguished on this ground from the welfare home visit. Nor can *Camara* be convincingly distinguished from *Wyman* on the ground that the sanction available for refusal to permit housing inspector access, though formally labeled a "criminal" penalty, was more onerous than the total loss of support threatened in *Wyman*. * * *

Forcing Protection on Children and Their Parents: The Impact of Wyman v. James, 69 Mich. L. Rev. 1259, 1302, (1971).

2. Would a warrant requirement more seriously interfere with the functioning of welfare agencies than the activities of building or fire or health inspectors? If the Court had concluded that a warrant was required in *Wyman v. James,* what standard of "probable cause" could it reasonably have applied?   If the primary purpose of such visits were to discover the misuse of public funds, would it be reasonable to issue a warrant simply on a showing that a household was receiving public assistance?   If the primary purpose were to protect children against abuse and deprivation, on what basis could authorities justify visits of some welfare households and not others?   Indeed, on what basis could they justify limiting visits to households receiving public assistance?

3. If the Court were to require a warrant in this context, could it countenance warrantless visits if the householder consented?   Is a recipient's "consent" to a welfare agency's visit ever likely to be knowing and voluntary?   Or is this also an area in which the subjects of administrative intrusion are likely to feel compelled to cooperate fully with officials on whom their well-being depends?   See generally Handler, *Controlling Official Behavior in Welfare Administration,* 54 Calif. L. Rev. 479 (1966).

4. Some post-*Wyman* cases have upheld other welfare regulations eliciting production of information by recipients.   *Doe v. Norton,* 365 F.Supp. 65 (D.Conn. 1973), *vacated Roe. v. Norton,* 422 U.S. 391 (1975), for example, validated a Connecticut statute that required an unwed mother receiving AFDC benefits to disclose the identity of the putative father, observing: "There is no intrusion into the home nor any participation in interpersonal decisions among its occupants, even to the extent held permissible in *Wyman v. James.*"   By contrast, *Rosen v. Hursh,* 464 F.2d 731 (8th Cir. 1972), overturned a state practice of terminating AFDC payments to children if their non-adoptive step-father refused to disclose his income to welfare officials.   The court found the practice inconsistent with the Social Security Act, but it pointedly limited *Wyman* to its facts, refusing to read it as supporting broader regulation of AFDC recipients.

5. *United States v. Cogwell*, 486 F.2d 823, 835-36 (7th Cir. 1973), *cert. denied* 416 U.S. 959 (1974), contains echoes of *Colonnade Catering* and *Biswell*. The defendants were convicted of conspiring to make false statements to obtain OEO funds under a job training program for street gang members. Their conviction was in part based on testimony of local police officers who, without a warrant, visited and observed the job training centers. The court upheld the convictions, relying heavily on *Wyman v. James*:

> Defendants were voluntary participants in an educational program subject to continual monitoring by United States government officials. * * * They cannot, therefore, reasonably claim the same expectancy of privacy which might shroud their purely personal activities. * * *

> * * * As in *Wyman*, there was no snooping, no visitation outside working hours, and no entry under false pretenses.

Contemporary Doctrine

MARSHALL v. BARLOW'S, INC.

Supreme Court of the United States, 1978.
436 U.S. 307, 98 S.Ct. 1816, 56 L. Ed.2d 305.

MR. JUSTICE WHITE delivered the opinion of the Court.

Section 8(a) of the Occupational Safety and Health Act of 1970 (OSHA or Act)[1] empowers agents of the Secretary of Labor (Secretary) to search the work area of any employment facility within the Act's jurisdiction. The purpose of the search is to inspect for safety hazards and violations of OSHA regulations. No search warrant or other process is expressly required under the Act.

On the morning of September 11, 1975, an OSHA inspector entered the customer service area of Barlow's, Inc., an electrical and plumbing installation business located in Pocatello, Idaho. The president and general manager, Ferrol G. "Bill" Barlow, was on hand; and the OSHA inspector, after showing his credentials, informed Mr. Barlow that he wished to conduct a search of the working areas of the business. Mr. Barlow inquired whether any complaint had been received about his company. The inspector answered no, but that Barlow's, Inc., had simply turned up in the agency's selection process. The inspector again asked to enter the nonpublic area of the business; Mr. Barlow's response was to inquire whether the inspector had a search warrant. The inspector had none. Thereupon, Mr. Barlow refused the inspector admission to the employee area of his business. He said he was relying on his rights as guaranteed by the Fourth Amendment of the United States Constitution.

---

1. "In order to carry out the purposes of this chapter, the Secretary, upon presenting appropriate credentials to the owner, operator, or agent in charge, is authorized—

"(1) to enter without delay and at reasonable times any factory, plant, establishment, construction site, or other area, workplace or environment where work is performed by an employee of an employer; and

"(2) to inspect and investigate during regular working hours and at other reasonable times, and within reasonable limits and in a reasonable manner, any such place of employment and all pertinent conditions, structures, machines, apparatus, devices, equipment, and materials therein, and to question privately any such employer, owner, operator, agent, or employee." 29 U.S.C.A. § 657(a).

Three months later, the Secretary petitioned the United States District Court for the District of Idaho to issue an order compelling Mr. Barlow to admit the inspector.[3] The requested order was issued on December 30, 1975, and was presented to Mr. Barlow on January 5, 1976. Mr. Barlow again refused admission, and he sought his own injunctive relief against the warrantless searches assertedly permitted by OSHA. A three-judge court was convened. On December 30, 1976, it ruled in Mr. Barlow's favor. Concluding that *Camara v. Municipal Court*, and *See v. Seattle*, controlled this case, the court held that the Fourth Amendment required a warrant for the type of search involved here and that the statutory authorization for warrantless inspections was unconstitutional. * * * The Secretary appealed, challenging the judgment, and we noted probable jurisdiction. * * *

This court has already held that warrantless searches are generally unreasonable, and that this rule applies to commercial premises as well as homes. * * *

These same cases [*Camara* and *See*] also held that the Fourth Amendment prohibition against unreasonable searches protects against warrantless intrusions during civil as well as criminal investigations. * * * It therefore appears that unless some recognized exception to the warrant requirement applies, *See v. Seattle* would require a warrant to conduct the inspection sought in this case.

The Secretary urges that an exception from the search warrant requirement has been recognized for "pervasively regulated business[es]," *United States v. Biswell*, and for "closely regulated" industries "long subject to close supervision and inspection." *Colonnade Catering Corp. v. United States*. These cases are indeed exceptions, but they represent responses to relatively unique circumstances. Certain industries have such a history of government oversight that no reasonable expectation of privacy could exist for a proprietor over the stock of such an enterprise. Liquor (*Colonnade*) and firearms (*Biswell*) are industries of this type; when an entrepreneur embarks upon such a business, he has voluntarily chosen to subject himself to a full arsenal of governmental regulation. * * *

The clear import of our cases is that the closely regulated industry of the type involved in *Colonnade* and *Biswell* is the exception. The Secretary would make it the rule. Invoking the Walsh-Healey Act of 1936, the Secretary attempts to support a conclusion that all businesses involved in interstate commerce have long been subjected to close supervision of employee safety and health conditions. But the degree of federal involvement in employee working circumstances has never been of the order of specificity and pervasiveness that OSHA mandates. It is quite unconvincing to argue that the imposition of minimum wages and maximum hours on employers who contracted with the Government under the Walsh-Healey Act prepared the entirety of American interstate com-

---

3. A regulation of the Secretary, 29 CFR § 1903.4 (1977), requires an inspector to seek compulsory process if an employer refuses a requested search.

merce for regulation of working conditions to the minutest detail. Nor can any but the most fictional sense of voluntary consent to later searches be found in the single fact that one conducts a business affecting interstate commerce; under current practice and law, few businesses can be conducted without having some effect on interstate commerce.

* * *

The Secretary nevertheless stoutly argues that the enforcement scheme of the Act requires warrantless searches, and that the restrictions on search discretion contained in the Act and its regulations already protect as much privacy as a warrant would. The Secretary thereby asserts the actual reasonableness of OSHA searches, whatever the general rule against warrantless searches might be. * * *

The Secretary submits that warrantless inspections are essential to the proper enforcement of OSHA because they afford the opportunity to inspect without prior notice and hence to preserve the advantages of surprise. While the dangerous conditions outlawed by the Act include structural defects that cannot be quickly hidden or remedied, the Act also regulates a myriad of safety details that may be amenable to speedy alteration or disguise. The risk is that during the interval between an inspector's initial request to search a plant and his procuring a warrant following the owner's refusal of permission, violations of this latter type could be corrected and thus escape the inspector's notice. To the suggestion that warrants may be issued *ex parte* and executed without delay and without prior notice, thereby preserving the element of surprise, the Secretary expresses concern for the administrative strain that would be experienced by the inspection system, and by the courts, should *ex parte* warrants issued in advance become standard practice.

We are unconvinced, however, that requiring warrants to inspect will impose serious burdens on the inspection system or the courts, will prevent inspections necessary to enforce the statute, or will make them less effective. In the first place, the great majority of businessmen can be expected in normal course to consent to inspection without warrant; the Secretary has not brought to this Court's attention any widespread pattern of refusal.[11] In those cases where an owner does insist on a warrant, the Secretary argues that inspection efficiency will be impeded by the advance notice and delay. The Act's penalty provisions for giving advance notice of a search and the Secretary's own regulations indicate that surprise searches are indeed contemplated. However, the Secretary has also promulgated a regulation providing that upon refusal to permit an inspector to enter the property or to complete his inspection, the inspector shall attempt to ascertain the reasons for the refusal and report to his superior, who shall "promptly take appropriate action, including compulsory process, if necessary." 29 CFR § 1903.4 (1977). The regulation

---

11. We recognize that today's holding itself might have an impact on whether owners choose to resist requested searches; we can only await the development of evidence not present on this record to determine how serious an impediment to effective enforcement this might be.

represents a choice to proceed by process where entry is refused; and on the basis of evidence available from present practice, the Act's effectiveness has not been crippled by providing those owners who wish to refuse an initial requested entry with a time lapse while the inspector obtains the necessary process.[13]   Indeed, the kind of process sought in this case and apparently anticipated by the regulation provides notice to the business operator.   If this safeguard endangers the efficient administration of OSHA, the Secretary should never have adopted it, particularly when the Act does not require it.   Nor is it immediately apparent why the advantages of surprise would be lost if, after being refused entry, procedures were available for the Secretary to seek an *ex parte* warrant and to reappear at the premises without further notice to the establishment being inspected.[15]

Whether the Secretary proceeds to secure a warrant or other process, with or without prior notice, his entitlement to inspect will not depend on his demonstrating probable cause to believe that conditions in violation of OSHA exist on the premises.   Probable cause in the criminal law sense is not required.   For purposes of an administrative search such as this, probable cause justifying the issuance of a warrant may be based not only on specific evidence of an existing violation but also on a showing that "reasonable legislative or administrative standards for conducting an * * * inspection are satisfied with respect to a particular [establishment]."   *Camara v. Municipal Court.*   A warrant showing that a specific business has been chosen for an OSHA search on the basis of a general administrative plan for the enforcement of the Act derived from neutral sources such as, for example, dispersion of employees in various types of industries across a given area, and the desired frequency of searches in any of the lesser divisions of the area, would protect an employer's Fourth Amendment rights.   We doubt that the consumption of

---

13. A change in the language of the Compliance Operations Manual for OSHA inspectors supports the inference that, whatever the Act's administrators might have thought at the start, it was eventually concluded that enforcement efficiency would not be jeopardized by permitting employers to refuse entry, at least until the inspector obtained compulsory process. The 1972 Manual included a section specifically directed to obtaining "warrants," and one provision of that section dealt with *ex parte* warrants:

> "In cases where a refusal of entry is to be expected from the past performance of the employer, or where the employer has given some indication prior to the commencement of the investigation of his intention to bar entry or limit or interfere with the investigation, a warrant should be obtained before the inspection is attempted.   Cases of this nature should also be referred through the Area Director to the appropriate Regional Solicitor and the Regional Administrator alerted."

The latest available manual, incorporating changes as of November 1977, deletes this provision, leaving only the details for obtaining "compulsory process" *after* an employer has refused entry.   In its present form, the Secretary's regulation appears to permit establishment owners to insist on "process"; and hence their refusal to permit entry would fall short of criminal conduct within the meaning of 18 U.S.C.A. § § 111 and 1114 (1976 ed.), which make it a crime forcibly to impede, intimidate, or interfere with federal officials, including OSHA inspectors, while engaged in or on account of the performance of their official duties.

15. Insofar as the Secretary's statutory authority is concerned, a regulation expressly providing that the Secretary could proceed *ex parte* to seek a warrant or its equivalent would appear to be as much within the Secretary's power as the regulation currently in force and calling for "compulsory process."

enforcement energies in the obtaining of such warrants will exceed manageable proportions.

Finally, the Secretary urges that requiring a warrant for OSHA inspectors will mean that, as a practical matter, warrantless-search provisions in other regulatory statutes are also constitutionally infirm. The reasonableness of a warrantless search, however, will depend upon the specific enforcement needs and privacy guarantees of each statute. Some of the statutes cited apply only to a single industry, where regulations might already be so pervasive that a *Colonnade-Biswell* exception to the warrant requirement could apply. Some statutes already envision resort to federal-court enforcement when entry is refused, employing specific language in some cases[18] and general language in others. In short, we base today's opinion on the facts and law concerned with OSHA and do not retreat from a holding appropriate to that statute because of its real or imagined effect on other, different administrative schemes.

Nor do we agree that the incremental protections afforded the employer's privacy by a warrant are so marginal that they fail to justify the administrative burdens that may be entailed. The authority to make warrantless searches devolves almost unbridled discretion upon executive and administrative officers, particularly those in the field, as to when to search and whom to search. A warrant, by contrast, would provide assurances from a neutral officer that the inspection is reasonable under the Constitution, is authorized by statute, and is pursuant to an administrative plan containing specific neutral criteria.[20] Also, a warrant would then and there advise the owner of the scope and objects of the search, beyond which limits the inspector is not expected to proceed. These are important functions for a warrant to perform, functions which underlie the Court's prior decisions that the Warrant Clause applies to inspections for compliance with regulatory statutes.[22] We conclude that the con-

---

18. The Federal Metal and Nonmetallic Mine Safety Act provides: "Whenever an operator * * * refuses to permit the inspection or investigation of any mine which is subject to this chapter * * * a civil action for preventive relief, including an application for a permanent or temporary injunction, restraining order, or other order, may be instituted by the Secretary in the district court of the United States for the district * * * ." 30 U.S.C.A. § 733(a). "The secretary may institute a civil action for relief, including a permanent or temporary injunction, restraining order, or any other appropriate order in the district court * * * whenever such operator or his agent * * * refuses to permit the inspection of the mine * * * . Each court shall have jurisdiction to provide such relief as may be appropriate." 30 U.S.C.A. § 818. * * *

20. The application for the inspection order filed by the Secretary in this case represented that "the desired inspection and inves-

tigation are contemplated as a part of an inspection program designed to assure compliance with the Act and are authorized by Section 8(a) of the Act." The program was not described, however, or any facts presented that would indicate why an inspection of Barlow's establishment was within the program. The order that issued concluded generally that the inspection authorized was "part of an inspection program designed to assure compliance with the Act."

22. Delineating the scope of a search with some care is particularly important where documents are involved. Section 8(c) of the Act provides that an employer must "make, keep and preserve, and make available to the Secretary [of Labor] or to the Secretary of Health, Education and Welfare" such records regarding his activities relating to OSHA as the Secretary of Labor may prescribe by regulation as necessary or appropriate for enforcement of the statute or for developing information regarding the causes and prevention of occupa-

cerns expressed by the Secretary do not suffice to justify warrantless inspections under OSHA or vitiate the general constitutional requirement that for a search to be reasonable a warrant must be obtained.

We hold that Barlow's was entitled to a declaratory judgment that the Act is unconstitutional insofar as it purports to authorize inspections without warrant or its equivalent and to an injunction enjoining the Act's enforcement to that extent.   The judgment of the District Court is therefore affirmed.

So Ordered.

MR. JUSTICE STEVENS, with whom MR. JUSTICE BLACKMUN and MR. JUSTICE REHNQUIST join, dissenting.

The Fourth Amendment contains two separate Clauses, each flatly prohibiting a category of governmental conduct.   The first Clause states that the right to be free from unreasonable searches "shall not be violated"; the second unequivocally prohibits the issuance of warrants except "upon probable cause."   In this case the ultimate question is whether the category of warrantless searches authorized by the statute is "unreasonable" within the meaning of the first Clause.

* * *

The warrant requirement is linked "textually * * * to the probable-cause concept" in the Warrant Clause.   The routine OSHA inspections are, by definition, not based on cause to believe there is a violation on the premises to be inspected.   Hence, if the inspections were measured against the requirements of the Warrant Clause, they would be automatically and unequivocally unreasonable.

Because of the acknowledged importance and reasonableness of routine inspections in the enforcement of federal regulatory statutes such as OSHA, the Court recognizes that requiring full compliance with the Warrant Clause would invalidate all such inspection programs.   Yet, rather than simply analyzing such programs under the "Reasonableness" Clause of the Fourth Amendment, the Court holds the OSHA program invalid under the Warrant Clause and then avoids a blanket prohibition on all routine, regulatory inspections by relying on the notion that the "prob-

tional accidents and illnesses.   Regulations requiring employers to maintain records of and to make periodic reports on "work-related deaths, injuries and illnesses" are also contemplated, as are rules requiring accurate records of employee exposures to potential toxic materials and harmful physical agents.

In describing the scope of the warrantless inspection authorized by the statute, § 8(a) does not expressly include any *records* among those items or things that may be examined, and § 8(c) merely provides that the employer is to "make available" his pertinent records and to make periodic reports.

The Secretary's regulation, 29 CFR § 1903.3 (1977), however, expressly includes among the inspector's powers the authority "to review records required by the Act and regulations published in this chapter, and other records which are directly related to the purpose of the inspection."   Further, § 1903.7 requires inspectors to indicate generally "the records specified in § 1903.3 which they wish to review" but "such designations of records shall not preclude access to additional records specified in § 1903.3."   It is the Secretary's position, which we reject, that an inspection of documents of this scope may be effected without a warrant. * * *

able cause" requirement in the Warrant Clause may be relaxed whenever the Court believes that the governmental need to conduct a category of "searches" outweighs the intrusion on interests protected by the Fourth Amendment.

The Court's approach disregards the plain language of the Warrant Clause and is unfaithful to the balance struck by the Framers of the Fourth Amendment—"the one procedural safeguard in the Constitution that grew directly out of the events which immediately preceded the revolutionary struggle with England." * * *

Since the general warrant, not the warrantless search, was the immediate evil at which the Fourth Amendment was directed, it is not surprising that the Framers placed precise limits on its issuance. The requirement that a warrant only issue on a showing of particularized probable cause was the means adopted to circumscribe the warrant power. While the subsequent course of Fourth Amendment jurisprudence in this Court emphasizes the dangers posed by warrantless searches conducted without probable cause, it is the general reasonableness standard in the first Clause, not the Warrant Clause, that the Framers adopted to limit this category of searches. It is, of course, true that the existence of a valid warrant normally satisfies the reasonableness requirement under the Fourth Amendment. But we should not dilute the requirements of the Warrant Clause in an effort to force every kind of governmental intrusion which satisfies the Fourth Amendment definition of a "search" into a judicially developed, warrant-preference scheme.

Fidelity to the original understanding of the Fourth Amendment, therefore, leads to the conclusion that the Warrant Clause has no application to routine, regulatory inspections of commercial premises. If such inspections are valid, it is because they comport with the ultimate reasonableness standard of the Fourth Amendment. * * *

Even if a warrant issued without probable cause were faithful to the Warrant Clause, I could not accept the Court's holding that the Government's inspection program is constitutionally unreasonable because it fails to require such a warrant procedure. * * *

Congress has determined that regulation and supervision of safety in the workplace furthers an important public interest and that the power to conduct warrantless searches is necessary to accomplish the safety goals of the legislation. In assessing the public interest side of the Fourth Amendment balance, however, the Court today substitutes its judgment for that of Congress on the question of what inspection authority is needed to effectuate the purposes of the Act. * * *

The Court's analysis does not persuade me that Congress' determination that the warrantless-inspection power as a necessary adjunct of the exercise of the regulatory power is unreasonable. It was surely not unreasonable to conclude that the rate at which employers deny entry to inspectors would increase if covered businesses, which may have safety violations on their premises, have a right to deny warrantless entry to a compliance inspector. The Court is correct that this problem could be avoided by requiring inspectors to obtain a warrant prior to every inspection visit. But the adoption of such a practice undercuts the Court's explanation of why a warrant requirement would not create undue enforcement problems. For, even if it were true that many employers would not exercise their right to demand a warrant, it would provide little solace to those charged with administration of OSHA; faced with an increase in the rate of refusals and the added costs generated by futile trips to inspection sites where entry is denied, officials may be compelled to adopt a general practice of obtaining warrants in advance. While the Court's prediction of the effect a warrant requirement would have on the behavior of covered employers may turn out to be accurate, its judgment is essentially empirical. On such an issue, I would defer to Congress' judgment regarding the importance of a warrantless-search power to the OSHA enforcement scheme.

* * *

* * * The essential function of the traditional warrant requirement is the interposition of a neutral magistrate between the citizen and the presumably zealous law enforcement officer so that there might be an objective determination of probable cause. But this purpose is not served by the newfangled inspection warrant. * * * To obtain a warrant, the inspector need only show that "a specific business has been chosen for an OSHA search on the basis of a general administrative plan for the enforcement of the Act derived from neutral sources. * * * " Thus, the only question for the magistrate's consideration is whether the contemplated inspection deviates from an inspection schedule drawn up by higher level agency officials.

* * *

The inspection warrant is supposed to assure the employer that the inspection is in fact routine, and that the inspector has not improperly departed from the program of representative inspections established by responsible officials. But to the extent that harassment inspections would be reduced by the necessity of obtaining a warrant, the Secretary's present enforcement scheme would have precisely the same effect. The representative inspections are conducted " 'in accordance with criteria based upon accident experience and the number of employees exposed in particular industries.' " If, under the present scheme, entry to covered premises is denied, the inspector can gain entry only by informing his administrative superiors of the refusal and seeking a court order requiring the employer to submit to the inspection. The inspector who would like to conduct a nonroutine search is just as likely to be deterred by the prospect of informing his superiors of his intention and of making false representations to the court when he seeks compulsory process as by the prospect of having to make bad-faith representations in an *ex parte* warrant proceeding.

The other two asserted purposes of the administrative warrant are also adequately achieved under the existing scheme. If the employer has doubts about the official status of the inspector, he is given adequate opportunity to reassure himself in this regard before permitting entry. The OSHA inspector's statutory right to enter the premises is conditioned upon the presentation of appropriate credentials. * * *

The warrant is not needed to inform the employer of the lawful limits of an OSHA inspection. * * * While it is true that the inspection power granted by Congress is broad, the warrant procedure required by the Court does not purport to restrict this power but simply to ensure that the employer is apprised of its scope. Since both the statute and the pertinent regulations perform this informational function, a warrant is superfluous.

* * *

The Court * * * concludes that the deference accorded Congress in *Biswell* and *Colonnade* should be limited to situations where the evils addressed by the regulatory statute are peculiar to a specific industry and that industry is one which has long been subject to Government regulation. The Court reasons that only in those situations can it be said that a person who engages in business will be aware of and consent to routine, regulatory inspections. I cannot agree that the respect due the congressional judgment should be so narrowly confined.

In the first place, the longevity of a regulatory program does not, in my judgment, have any bearing on the reasonableness of routine inspections necessary to achieve adequate enforcement of that program. Congress' conception of what constitute urgent federal interests need not remain static. The recent vintage of public and congressional awareness of the dangers posed by health and safety hazards in the workplace is not a basis for according less respect to the considered judgment of Congress. Indeed, in *Biswell*, the Court upheld an inspection program authorized by a regulatory statute enacted in 1968. The Court there noted that "[f]ederal regulation of the interstate traffic in firearms is not as deeply rooted in history as is governmental control of the liquor industry, but close scrutiny of this traffic is undeniably" an urgent federal interest. Thus, the critical fact is the congressional determination that federal regulation would further significant public interests, not the date that determination was made.

In the second place, I see no basis for the Court's conclusion that a congressional determination that a category of regulatory inspections is reasonable need only be respected when Congress is legislating on an industry-by-industry basis. The pertinent inquiry is not whether the inspection program is authorized by a regulatory statute directed at a single industry, but whether Congress has limited the exercise of the inspection power to those commercial premises where the evils at which the statute is directed are to be found. * * *

Finally, the Court would distinguish the respect accorded Congress' judgment in *Colonnade* and *Biswell* on the ground that businesses engaged in the liquor and firearms industry " 'accept the burdens as well as the benefits of their trade. * * * .'" In the Court's view, such businesses consent to the restrictions placed upon them, while it would be fiction to conclude that a businessman subject to OSHA consented to routine safety inspections. In fact, however, consent is fictional in both contexts. Here, as well as in *Biswell*, businesses are required to be aware of and comply with regulations governing their business activities. In both situations, the validity of the regulations depends not upon the consent of those regulated, but on the existence of a federal statute embodying a congressional determination that the public interest in the health of the Nation's work force or the limitation of illegal firearms traffic outweighs the businessman's interest in preventing a Government inspector from viewing those areas of his premises which relate to the subject matter of the regulation. * * * [11]

I respectfully dissent.

Notes

1. Justice White speculates that the obligation to obtain a warrant when inspection is refused will not prove a serious burden for OSHA because most employers will in fact consent. And one commentator later observed: "Although a final judgment cannot be made at this time, it appears that the Court's decision will *not* have a significant adverse impact on OSHA enforcement." Rothstein, *OSHA Inspections After Marshall v. Barlow's, Inc.*, 1979 Duke L.J. 63, 84. Rothstein pointed out that in the three to four months immediately after the ruling, "approximately 11,000 inspections were attempted by OSHA, and employers demanded warrants in fewer than 500 cases." Id. at 132 n.84. However, it is unclear whether the passage of time will make employers more familiar with, and thus more inclined to insist upon, the agency's warrant obligation, or diminish resistance as the decision fades from memory. There appear to be no studies of the systemic effects of the Court's ruling, which in any case would be difficult to conduct because of shifts in the agency's enforcement emphasis prompted by independent concerns.

2. Whether or not the demand on OSHA inspectors to obtain warrants has increased significantly or has impeded their work, the reports are full of cases grappling with the companion issues of the content of *Barlow's* probable cause standard and the appropriate scope of OSHA warrants. The issues are not unrelated.

Showing necessary to obtain a warrant. The first part of *Barlow's* two-part standard—"specific evidence of an existing violation," is usually satisfied by evidence of employee complaints. Note, *FDA, EPA, and OSHA Inspections— Practical Considerations in Light of Marshall v. Barlow's, Inc.*, 39 Md. L. Rev. 715, 732 (1980). In *In re Establishment Inspection of Gilbert & Bennett Manufacturing Co.*, 589 F.2d 1335 (7th Cir.), *cert. denied Chromalloy American Corp.*

---

11. The decision today renders presumptively invalid numerous inspection provisions in federal regulatory statutes. E.g., 30 U.S.C.A. § 813 (Federal Coal Mine Health and Safety Act of 1969); 30 U.S.C.A. § § 723, 724 (Federal Metal and Nonmetallic Mine Safety Act); 21 U.S.C.A. § 603 (inspection of meat and food products). That some of these provisions apply only to a single industry, as noted above, does not alter this fact. And the fact that some "envision resort to federal-court enforcement when entry is refused" is also irrelevant since the OSHA inspection program invalidated here requires compulsory process when a compliance inspector has been denied entry.

v. Marshall, 444 U.S. 884 (1979), the court of appeals held that an OSHA warrant application did not have to identify the employee mailing the complaint nor establish the complainant's credibility, *id.* at 1339; however, it must do more than recite that a complaint has been received.   Some information concerning the nature of the alleged violation must be provided to establish the presence of probable cause.

Barlow's also allows issuance of a warrant based on "a general administrative plan derived from neutral sources."   Thus the Court contemplated that OSHA could obtain warrants on the basis of some showing that the generic characteristics of the employer's establishment made it a logical target for inspection.   The agency may not, however, conflate the two parts of the probable cause standard. In *In re Establishment Inspection of Northwest Airlines, Inc.*, 587 F.2d 12 (7th Cir. 1978), the court separated OSHA's claim of a reasonable investigation program from the claim involving an employee complaint, and held that the agency had not provided sufficient information about its inspection program to justify a warrant.   *In re Establishment Inspection of Urick Property*, 472 F.Supp. 1193 (W.D. Pa. 1979), denied OSHA's warrant application on grounds that it had not described or demonstrated the neurtality of its inspection plan.   See also *Marshall v. Weyerhauser Co.*, 456 F.Supp. 474 (D.N.J. 1978).   Verified allegations that an employer operates in an industry with a high risk of accident, that the establishment fits criteria for selection within the industry (e.g., size, time since last inspection, accident record), and that these criteria are regularly followed will usually suffice.   See generally Rader, *OSHA Warrants and Administrative Probable Cause*, 33 Baylor L. Rev. 97, 101 (1981).

Scope of authorized inspection.   The courts will generally allow broader scope for routine inspections than inspections based on employee complaints. See, e.g., *In re Establishment Inspection of Gilbert & Bennett Manufacturing Co.*, 589 F.2d 1335, 1343 (7th Cir.), *cert. denied Chromalloy American Corp. v. Marshall*, 444 U.S. 884 (1979).   ("The scope of an OSHA inspection warrant must be as broad as the subject matter regulated by the statute and restricted only by the limitations imposed by Congress and the reasonableness requirement of the Fourth Amendment.")   The courts have divided over the propriety of so-called "wall-to-wall" warrants often sought by OSHA inspectors, with most inclined to confine inspections to the area cited in the complaint that initially supplies the justification for the warrant.   For an argument that both these polar approaches are wrong, see Note, *Permissible Scope of OSHA Inspection Warrants*, 66 Corn. L. Rev. 1254 (1981).

In *Marshall v. Pool Offshore Co.*, 467 F.Supp. 978 (W.D. La. 1979), the court held that the OSHA warrants were too broad since they permitted the agency to inspect all records pursuant to an investigation of employee accidents caused by offshore drilling rigs.   Under this reasoning, a warrant that fails to specify which records may be inspected may be overly broad. The court in *Pool Offshore* also held that the warrants were invalid because they gave OSHA inspectors the power to question *any* employee found on the rigs.   In *Marshall v. Wollaston Alloys, Inc.*, 479 F.Supp. 1102 (D. Mass. 1979), the court found that general language in a warrant could not be used to permit private employee interviews. Id. at 1104.   Thus courts generally seem "unwilling to accept 'boilerplate' recitations of statutory authority when the agency is capable of specifying the extent of its search."   Note, *FDA, EPA and OSHA Inspections—Practical Considerations in Light of Marshall v. Barlow's Inc.*, 39 Md. L. Rev. 715, 740 (1980).

3. Under OSHA's practice at the time of the decision in *Barlow's*, an inspector could not seek compulsory process until he had first been denied entry. An agency regulation specified that such a refusal would be reported to the regional director, who would then determine what further steps to take, as a practical matter assuring that an employer would have notice of any effort to obtain a warrant. Early rulings conceded that OSHA could constitutionally seek *ex parte* warrants prior to attempting inspection, but enjoined the agency from doing so, so long as its regulation remained unchanged. E.g., *Cerro Metal Products v. Marshall*, 467 F.Supp. 869 (E.D. Pa. 1979). OSHA promptly published an amended regulation, which it made effective immediately as an "interpretative rule" under APA § 553(b). The Third Circuit has held that the amendment was not an interpretative rule and was subject to notice and comment. *Cerro Metal Products v. Marshall*, 620 F.2d 964 (3d Cir. 1980), but the Ninth and Tenth Circuits upheld the agency. *Marshall v. W&W Steel Co.*, 604 F.2d 1322 (10th Cir. 1979); *Stoddard Lumber Co., Inc. v. Marshall*, 627 F.2d 984 (9th Cir. 1980). The agency ultimately republished the amended regulation authorizing pre-inspection requests for warrants, but its general practice remains as before, i.e., to seek entry before resorting to compulsory process. See generally Note, *Administrative Agency Searches Since Marshall v. Barlow's, Inc.: Probable Cause Requirements for Nonroutine Administrative Searches*, 70 Geo. L.J. 1183 (1982).

Just three years after *Barlow's*, *Donovan v. Dewey*, 452 U.S. 594 (1981), confronted the Court with the challenge to section 103(a) of the Federal Mine Safety and Health Act, the inspection provision that the dissenters had forecast the majority's approach would jeopardize. But *Dewey* confounded the prediction that *Barlow's* would necessitate its invalidation. Section 103(a) resembles the provision of the OSH Act struck down in *Barlow's*, expressly authorizing unannounced, warrantless inspections of "any coal or other mine" and permitting imposition of civil penalties for denial or entry. Douglas Dewey had refused entry to a federal mine inspector who sought to inspect his stone quarry without a search warrant. The Secretary of Labor proposed a civil penalty of $1000, upheld by an administrative law judge, and brought suit to enjoin Dewey from refusing to permit warrantless inspections of the quarry. The district court granted summary judgment against the government, holding that section 103(a) clashed with the Fourth Amendment.

Writing for the Court, Justice Marshall read *Barlow's* narrowly and found that the Mine Safety Act's authorization of warrantless inspections fell within the *Biswell-Colonnade* line of authority (452 U.S. at 602-06):

> * * * As an intitial matter, it is undisputed that there is a substantial federal interest in improving the health and safety conditions in the Nation's underground and surface mines. In enacting the statute, Congress was plainly aware that the mining industry is among the most hazardous in the country and that the poor health and safety record of this industry has significant deleterious effects on interstate commerce. Nor is it seriously contested that congress in this case could reasonably determine, as it did with respect to the Gun Control Act in *Biswell*, that a system of warrantless inspections was necessary "if the law is to be properly enforced and inspection made effec-

tive." In designing an inspection program, Congress expressly recognized that a warrant requirement could significantly frustrate effective enforcement of the Act. * * * We see no reason not to defer to this legislative determination. * * *

Because a warrant requirement clearly might impede the "specific enforcement needs" of the Act, the only real issue before us is whether the statute's inspection program, in terms of the certainty and regularity of its application, provides a constitutionally adequate substitute for a warrant. We believe that it does. Unlike the statute at issue in *Barlow's*, the Mine Safety and Health Act applies to industrial activity with a notorious history of serious accidents and unhealthful working conditions. The Act is specifically tailored to address those concerns, and the regulation of mines it imposes is sufficiently pervasive and defined that the owner of such a facility cannot help but be aware that he "will be subject to effective inspection." First, the act requires inspection of *all* mines and specifically defines the frequency of inspection. Representatives of the Secretary must inspect all surface mines at least four times annually. Similarly, all mining operations that generate explosive gases must be inspected at irregular 5-, 10-, or 15-day intervals. Moreover, the Secretary must conduct followup inspections of mines where violations of the Act have previously been discovered, and must inspect a mine immediately if notified by a miner or a miner's representative that a violation of the Act or an imminently dangerous condition exists. Second, the standards with which a mine operator is required to comply are all specifically set forth in the Act or in Title 30 of the Code of Federal Regulations. Indeed, the Act requires that the Secretary inform mine operators of all standards proposed pursuant to the Act. Thus, rather than leaving the frequency and purpose of inspections to the unchecked discretion of Government officers, the Act establishes a predictable and guided federal regulatory presence. * * *

Finally, the Act provides a specific mechanism for accommodating any special privacy concerns that a specific mine operator might have. The Act prohibits forcible entries, and instead requires the Secretary, when refused entry into a mining facility, to file a civil action in federal court to obtain an injunction against future refusals. This proceeding provides an adequate forum for the mineowner to show that a specific search is outside the federal regulatory authority, or to seek from the district court an order accommodating any unusual privacy interests that the mineowner might have. * * *

Appellees contend, however, that even if § 103(a) is constitutional as applied to most segments of the mining industry, it nonetheless violates the Fourth Amendment as applied to authorize warrantless inspections of stone quarries. Appellees' argument essentially tracks the reasoning of the court below. That court, while expressly acknowledging our decisions in *Colonnade* and *Biswell*, found the exception to the warrant requirement defined in those cases to be inapplicable solely because surface quarries, which came under federal regulation in 1966, do "not have a long tradition of government regulation." * * * [I]t is the pervasiveness and regularity of the federal regulation that ultimately determines whether a warrant is necessary to render an inspection program reasonable under the Fourth Amendment. * * * Of course, the duration of a particular regulatory scheme will often be an important factor in determining whether it is sufficiently prevasive to make the imposition of a warrant requirement unnecessary. But if the length of regulation were the only criterion, absurd results would occur. Under appellees' view, new or emerging industries, including ones such as the nuclear power industry that pose enormous potential safety and health problems, could never be subject to warrantless searches even under the most carefully structured inspection program simply because of the recent vintage of regulation.

The Fourth Amendment's central concept of reasonableness will not tolerate such arbitrary results, and we therefore conclude that warrantless inspection of stone quarries, like similar inspections of other mines covered by the Act, are constitutionally permissible. * * *

A bemused Justice Stevens agreed with the majority that the present case was distinguishable from *Barlow's* and thus found it unnecessary to "confront the more difficult question whether *Camara* represented such a fundamental misreading of the Fourth Amendment that it should be overruled." Justice Stewart, a member of the majority in *Frank* and of the minority in *Camara*, felt compelled to dissent:

I must * * * accept the law as it is, and the law is now established that administrative inspections are searches within the meaning of the Fourth Amendment. As such, warrantless administrative inspections of private property without consent, are, like other searches, constitutionally invalid except in a few precisely defined circumstances. * * *

* * * [A]s explained in *Barlow's*, the *Colonnade-Biswell* exception is a single and narrow one: the exception applies to businesses that are both pervasively regulated *and* have a long history of regulation. Today the Court conveniently discards the latter portion of the exception. Yet the very rationale for the exception—that the "businessman * * * in effect consents to the restrictions placed upon him"—disappears without it. It can hardly be said that a businessman consents to restrictions on his business when those restrictions are not imposed until *after* he has entered the business. * * *

As I read today's opinion, Congress is left free to avoid the Fourth Amendment industry by industry even though the Court held in *Barlow's* that Congress could not avoid that Amendment all at once.[6] Congress after today can define any industry as dangerous, regulate it substantially, and provide for warrantless inspections of its members. But, because I do not be-

---

6. Factually, *Barlow's* and this case are nearly identical. Both cases arose when a business proprietor refused entry to a federal inspector who had come to conduct a warrantless health and safety inspection of business premises. In both cases, warrantless inspections were authorized by statute, § 8(a) of the Occupational Health and Safety Act in *Barlow's* and § 103(a) of the Federal Mine Safety and Health Act of 1977 in this case. Both statutes were similarly intended to improve health the safety standards in the Nation's workplaces, and their language is unmistakably parallel.

Moreover, *Barlow's* cannot be distinguished from this case because MSHA relates to a specific industry, whereas the Occupational Safety and Health Act sought to regulate a far broader range of workplaces. MSHA, like the Occupational Safety and Health Act, relates to many different industries with widely disparat characteristics and occupational injury rates. Limestone quarries, sand and gravel operations, surface operations, and various noncoal underground mines are all quite distinct, and cannot be equivalent for constitutional purposes to underground coal mines. The Court today does not so much as mention the voluminous materials submitted by appellees and *amici* that show this to be true.

lieve that Congress can, by legislative fiat, rob the members of any industry of their constitutional protection, I dissent from the opinion and judgment of the Court.

Notes

1. The varied contexts of administrative searches and inspections may make development of a coherent jurisprudence impossible—or at least unlikely.   In contexts other than those we have already encountered the Court has followed a wavering line between demands for warrant protection and claims of administrative necessity.

Several cases have upheld the validity of warrantless searches of airplane passengers and visitors to federal office buildings.   See, e.g., *United States v. Davis*, 482 F.2d 893, 908 (9th Cir. 1973): "The essence of these decisions [of the Supreme Court] is that searches conducted as part of a general regulatory scheme in furtherance of an administrative purpose, rather than as part of a criminal investigation to secure evidence of crime, may be permissible under the Fourth Amendment though not supported by a showing of probable cause directed to a particular place or person to be searched."   See also *Barrett v. Kunzig*, 331 F. Supp. 266 (M.D. Tenn. 1971), *cert. denied* 409 U.S. 914 (1972).

By contrast, in *Almeida-Sanchez v. United States*, 413 U.S. 266 (1973), the Supreme Court invalidated a warrantless Border Patrol search conducted under the authority of a federal statute and regulations permitting warrentless automobile stops and searches within 100 air miles of the border.   Yet in *United States v. Martinez-Fuente*, 428 U.S. 543 (1976), the Court upheld the INS practice of routinely stopping vehicles at fixed checkpoints in California and Texas near the Mexican border.   The Court stressed the limited discretion accorded to the inspecting officers, which justified confidence in the control exercised by INS headquarters officials as a safeguard against abuse.

In *GM Leasing Corp. v. United States*, 429 U.S. 338 (1977), the Court invoked *Camara* in holding that the government's interest in revenue collection does not justify a broad exception to the warrant requirement when IRS agents seize property pursuant to jeopardy assessments.

2.   There is a reasonably well-established exception from the warrant requirement for observations that are made without intrusion onto private property or into work or business areas that have some plausible claim to privacy.   In *Air Pollution Variance Board v. Western Alfalfa Corp.*, 416 U.S. 861, 864-65 (1974), the Court sustained the warrantless visual inspection of the smoke being emitted from the respondent's chimneys.   To make his visual reading of the respondent's emissions a Colorado health inspector came onto the respondent's property without its knowledge or consent.   His findings later supported the board's conclusion that the respondent was violating applicable air quality standards.   Justice Douglas' opinion held that *Camara* and *See* were not applicable:

> The field inspector did not enter the plant or offices.   He was not inspecting stakes, boilers, scrubbers, flues, grates, or furnaces; nor was his inspection related to respondent's files or papers.   He had sighted what anyone in the city who was near the plant could see in the sky—plumes of smoke.   * * *   The field inspector was on respondent's property but we are not advised that he was on premises from which the public was excluded.   * * *   The invasion of privacy * * * , if it can be said to exist, is abstract and theoretical.

See also *Stephenson Enterprises, Inc. v. Marshall*, 578 F.2d 1021, 1024 n.2 (5th Cir. 1978).

3. Yet another "exception" was recognized only eight days after the decision in *Barlow's*. In *Michigan v. Tyler*, 436 U.S. 499 (1978), the court sustained the right of firemen engaged in fighting a fire to conduct contemporaneous searches of the smoldering premises to determine the cause of the blaze. Except in such "emergencies," however, a warrant would be required for either routine inspections to monitor fire hazards or after-the-event investigations into the causes of fires already extinguished.

B. ACCESS TO INFORMATION HELD BY THE FEDERAL GOVERNMENT

The extent of its demands on private individuals and organizations to keep records and submit reports has made the federal government a vast depository of information that is potentially of interest to third parties. Furthermore, the government itself creates information—through its own numerous investigatory activities and by manipulating data obtained from private parties—that also excites curiosity. Perhaps of greatest general interest is information about the activities and plans of government administrators themselves: What issues are before them? What arguments are they hearing and from whom? What staff advice are they receiving? What small part of the files assembled by subordinates are they exposed to? When are they planning to act? Access to information about the deliberations of government officials has value for individuals and businesses whose affairs will be affected by the decisions to be made. For organs of the press, it is key to their functioning, both in the competitive world of the commercial media and in the world of politics, where their performance is believed important to our system of self-government.

But public access to information in government hands, even information about what officials are planning, may not always be desirable. We all would probably acknowledge that there is a core of facts about the operations of the military that should be secret, though we might differ about its dimensions. Most would concede that law enforcement authorities should be entitled, at least for a time, to conduct investigations in confidence. And recalling that much—indeed perhaps the majority— of the information in government hands comes from private individuals and organizations, we would stipulate that some of it ought not be routinely available to third parties, either at all or at least without notice to the provider. The protections accorded by the Fourth and Fifth Amendments for interests in privacy and autonomy suggest that government should not become the automatic transfer agent for all information that it obtains from private sources.

In this section, we shall explore the legal doctrines governing private access to information that the government obtains or creates, including the limitations on such access that are intended to protect interests in commercial secrecy and personal privacy.

1. CLAIMS TO ACCESS TO GOVERNMENT INFORMATION

The circumstances under which, and purposes for which, a person may wish to obtain information in the possession of the government are virtually limitless. Nevertheless, it is instructive to categorize the circumstances and purposes which have predominated in claims of right to government information. First are claims asserted for the purpose of preparing for or engaging in contested legal proceedings. A second category consists of attempts to gain access to the deliberations of public agencies and officials for the purpose of overseeing public decisionmaking. A final, residual group of claims to access might be characterized as "proprietary"—claims inspired by the desire to obtain for commercial, academic, or other purposes generally useful information in the government's possession. While not prominent in litigation, this final group of claims makes up the bulk of the requests to agencies for information. A particular demand for information may, and often does, fit into more than one category, but the legal principles traditionally applicable to each category are quite distinct.

Claims of access for purposes of contested legal proceedings have traditionally been governed by the procedural rules regulating discovery and by limitations on the government's ability to enforce regulatory requirements without adequate disclosure of their factual and judgmental bases. Thus, the ability of a litigant to obtain official material, whether for purposes of litigation with the government, e.g., *United States v. Reynolds*, 345 U.S. 1 (1953), or with a third party, e.g., *Carl Zeiss Stiftung v. V.E.B. Carl Zeiss, Jena*, 40 F.R.D. 318 (D.D.C. 1966), *affirmed per curiam* 384 F.2d 979 (D.C. Cir.), *cert. denied* 389 U.S. 952 (1967), has depended upon general federal rules governing discovery in civil or criminal litigation. These rules customarily require the courts to balance the claimant's need for the information against the consequences of disclosure for the government and are enforced through the traditional modes of subpoenas and interlocutory orders. Similarly, discovery in administrative adjudication has been governed by agency rules of procedure. See generally Tomlinson, *Discovery in Agency Adjudication*, 1971 Duke L.J. 89. Although under common discovery practices not all potentially relevant factual material need be made available at trial, when it is a party to formal proceedings the government will be required to choose between exposing its evidence to rebuttal and cross-examination and risking a failure to prove its case. *Wirtz v. Baldor Electric Co.*, supra, p. 418. Moreover, the government may not enforce or rely upon secret law—regulatory requirements that are not published or filed as required by law.

Claims for access to government information for purposes of contested legal proceedings thus have two dominant characteristics: (1) a relatively limited set of circumstances gives rise to requests for disclosure, and (2) reasonably well-developed procedural rules govern the degree to which disclosure may be required and determine the legal consequences of non-disclosure.

The second category of claims embraces a somewhat less cohesive set of what we term "oversight" demands and is subject to an evolving set of legal principles. In terms of applicable legal doctrine, a major subset of these claims involves requirements for disclosure of the factual basis and rationale for official decisions in order to facilitate judicial review. These claims invoke the familiar "findings" requirement applicable to formal administrative proceedings or the requirement that the complete administrative record be disclosed to a court called upon to determine whether there is adequate support for an administrative determination. Such claims are, of course, subject to limitations on court review, such as the judicial reluctance to inquire into the internal decision processes of an agency or official. See supra p. 228.

Another type of oversight claim is represented by legislative demands for information from executive officers relating to the latter's areas of administrative responsibility. Here the applicable legal principles include only the negligible limitations on the legislative power of investigation, see, e.g., E. J. EBERLING, CONGRESSIONAL INVESTIGATIONS: A STUDY OF THE DEVELOPMENT OF THE POWER OF CONGRESS TO INVESTIGATE AND PUNISH FOR CONTEMPT (1928, reprinted 1973), and the amorphous doctrine of "executive privilege"—that is, the asserted right of the executive branch to treat as confidential information relating to state secrets, disclosures of informers, and internal processes of policy formation. See discussion infra p. 585. Finally, there are claims by private persons for access either to the decision process itself or to the documents that support and explain formulated policy. To the extent that such claims do not relate to contested proceedings and are not asserted in aid of judicial review, they are premised on statutes requiring that certain decision processes be carried on in "public," see Government on the Sunshine Act, 5 U.S.C.A. § 552b; 26; Note, *Open Meeting Statutes: The Press Fights For The "Right to Know"*, 75 Harv. L. Rev. 1199 (1962), or that agency records be available to persons requesting access to them.

The unifying feature of oversight claims is that they relate to fundamental aspects of the American constitutional system—judicial review of administrative action, separation of powers, mutual checks and balances in the institutional order—and to the democratic ideal of an informed and vigilant electorate.

"Proprietary claims," our catch-all third category, have no strong public policy foundation. The individual citizen has no distinct property interest in government information, nor do First Amendment freedoms to disseminate or to receive information voluntarily transmitted imply a right to obtain information from the government over its protest. See generally BeVier, *An Informed Public, an Informing Press: The Search for a Constitutional Principle*, 68 Calif. L. Rev. 482 (1980); Note, *The Rights of the Public and the Press to Gather Information*, 87 Harv. L. Rev. 1505 (1974). That information in the government's possession might be useful to private parties for myriad social, economic, and intellectual purposes is no doubt true, but we would not ordinarily expect the mere desire to obtain information in another's possession to be translated into a legal right of access without some firm policy basis for honoring the claim. Nevertheless, the Freedom of Information Act (hereafter sometimes "FOIA"), 5 U.S.C.A. § 552, by eliminating any requirement that a person requesting government information show why it should be made available to him, seems to place proprietary claims on the same footing as claims growing out of formal legal proceedings and claims relating to oversight activities.

The apparent anomaly of the FOIA's treatment of strong and weak claims as legal equivalents is readily explicable: It is often difficult to determine the true or primary purpose of requests for government information. Moreover, Congress was convinced that the existing disclosure provisions of the APA were used by bureaucrats to shield most of their activities from effective citizen oversight. To avoid abusive non-disclosure, therefore, Congress provided a means of access to government information which cut across analytically distinct categories of requests and which, by its very breadth, has become the standard against which any claim for information (with the possible exception of requests from Congress, see 5 U.S.C.A. § 552(c)) may ultimately be judged.

2. THE FEDERAL FREEDOM OF INFORMATION ACT

The FOIA, 5 U.S.C.A. § 552, deals both with "secret law" and with the much larger universe of government documents or records that lack legal force. In section 552(a) the FOIA restates the Federal Register Act's requirements for agency publication of organization, procedures, and general rules or policies, and it further requires that decisions, statements of policy and interpretation, and staff manuals containing instructions affecting the public shall be indexed and made available for public inspection and copying. Failure to comply with these subsections precludes agency reliance on the unpublished or unavailable materials save with respect to a person who otherwise has actual and timely notice of them. Subsection (3) then provides that agencies shall, on request by any person in accordance with agency rules governing such requests, make available all other "identifiable records." This obligation is enforceable by expedited suit in a federal district court, in which the recalcitrant agency has the burden of justifying its refusal. Paragraph (b) of section 552 exempts nine categories of records from the reach of paragraph (a), and paragraph (c) limits agency authority to withhold information to those exemptions "specifically stated."

Passage of the FOIA gave rise to two contrasting fears. Critics argued that the elimination of any necessity for showing "good cause" or even a "lawful purpose" for a request, combined with an exhaustive listing of exemptions, would prevent courts and agencies from making sound equitable judgments in particular cases concerning the balance of benefits over costs of disclosure. They predicted that the FOIA would result in burdensome fishing expeditions that would fail to promote—and perhaps hinder—sensible public policy objectives. The contrasting fear was that the potential breadth of some of the exemptions, the grant of agency power to prescribe the form of requests and to set fees for disclosure, and the necessity of bringing suit to force disclosure would make the Act a paper tiger. For an interim assessment of these competing forecasts, see generally Note, *The Freedom of Information Act: A Seven-Year Assessment*, 74 Colum. L. Rev. 895 (1974).

In amendments to the Act in 1974 Congress displayed a preoccupation with strengthening the requirements for disclosure. For example, the amended Act (1) stipulates that a request need only "reasonably describe" desired documents, thus eliminating the requirement that a request be for "identifiable documents," (2) directs that agencies, except in "unusual circumstances," respond to requests for documents within ten days by stating whether they intend to comply with the request, (3) authorizes the award of attorneys' fees to successful private litigants, and (4) requires disciplinary investigation of any employee found by a court to have acted arbitrarily and capriciously in withholding information. See Pub. L. No. 93-502, 88 Stat. 1561 (1974).

G. ROBINSON, ACCESS TO GOVERNMENT INFORMATION: THE AMERICAN EXPERIENCE

14 Federal L. Rev. 35 (1983).

A. THE ANCIEN REGIME.

*   *   *

Section 3 [of the original APA] mandated publication of a variety of information about agency decision-making, except in a situation "requiring secrecy in the public interest". This provision for "secrecy in the public interest" permitted agency evasion of publication requirements. Secondly, s[ection] 3(b) required agencies to make available "all final opinions or orders in the adjudication of cases". But this requirement did not extend to opinions or orders "required for good cause to be held confidential". The vagueness with which this exception was phrased made it susceptible to inappropriate application. This same "good cause" language was repeated in s[ection] 3(c), which provided access to public records generally. These records were to be available to "persons properly and directly concerned except information held confidential for good cause found". In addition to the invitation to evasion presented by a "good cause" exception, this sub-section also provided another route to nondisclosure by allowing agencies to determine the standing of persons wishing access to information. A fourth weakness of s[ection] 3 was that it supplied no remedy to a citizen wrongfully denied access to information. The lack of any remedy made possible a too heavy reliance on the vague language of the section to withhold government records. * * *

* * * Eventually the Freedom of Information Bill passed through Congress virtually unopposed despite universal departmental hostility to its broad disclosure principles and its new remedy for requesters of information. Two groups allied to support passage of this law allowing public access to government information. Bar groups and other administrative reformers pressed for the Bill in order to secure publication of agency rules and opinions. These groups were joined by the press which pushed even harder for the FOI Act to gain access to more newsworthy documents disclosing agency activities. * * *

B. The Revolution

The new Act was revolutionary in its basic approach to the question of government disclosure and public access. The FOI Act established a broad norm of disclosure and access with relatively narrow exceptions. It removed all restrictions on who was entitled to information or the purpose for which it may be obtained. * * *

The coverage of the FOI Act is co-extensive with the Administrative Procedure Act itself and extends to virtually every executive department, bureau, agency or official, the Office of the President being a notable exception.[22] Congress and the courts are not agencies within the meaning of the APA and hence are not within the Act.

In general terms the Act imposes three distinct obligations with respect to disclosure of, or access to, agency records and information:

The first is to publish in the Federal Register descriptions of its organization; methods of operation; general substantive rules and policies; and rules of procedure.

The second is to make available for public inspection and copying, agency opinions and orders, statements of general policy and interpretation not published in the Federal Register, administrative staff manuals and staff instructions that affect a member of the public.

The third is to disclose agency records to any person who requests and reasonably describes such records. Agencies may charge reasonable fees for document search and duplication but are admonished to waive or reduce fees where disclosure benefits the general public. * * * Judicial enforcement of the disclosure requirement is provided in the form of immediate *de novo* review of agency denials of disclosure requests; including *in camera* review of the documents requested where the court deems it necessary to determine their exempt status. * * *

C. Interpretive Issues and Controversies. * * *

(2) Exemptions.

Most of the attention and most of the controversy over the FOI Act has centered on the disclosure of agency records. Interpretive problems can be conveniently aggregated into two general categories: those specifically concerned with the scope of the nine exemptions, and those involving general issues of definition, implementation and enforcement. * * *

Exemption one embraces what is sometimes called "state secrets", in its narrowest sense: information required to be kept secret in the interest

---

22. In *Kissinger v. Reporters Committee for Freedom of the Press*, 445 U.S. 136 (1980), the Court distinguished between the "Executive Office of the President" and the "Office of the President", the latter being limited to the President, his immediate personal staff and other executive office staff whose *sole* function is to advise the President. * * *

of national defense or foreign policy.   As amended in 1974 the exemption is limited to information that is *properly* classified pursuant to Executive Order, which has been interpreted to permit judicial review of the substantive reasonableness as well as the procedural regularity of individual classifications.[39]   For this purpose *in camera* examination of specific documents is authorised, but discretionary in the district court.   Given the indefinite constitutional dimensions of executive privilege it remains uncertain how far courts may go in ordering disclosure of classified information.   A similar ambiguity arises in connection with exemptions five (inter/intra agency memoranda) and seven (investigatory files) which also involve aspects of the executive privilege. * * *

Exemption three, covering all information which Congress in other statutes has required or permitted to be held confidential, also requires little attention.   As amended in 1976 the exemption embraces only those statutes that are directed at the particular type of information in question or that specify particular criteria by which confidentiality shall be determined.[46] * * *

Exemption four, covering trade secrets and confidential commercial or financial information, has been among the most controversial of the nine exemptions.   Unlike exemption three the number and variety of cases calling for interpretation is essentially open-ended. * * *

Exemption five, covering intra-agency and inter-agency memoranda and letters, was intended to incorporate the broad common law executive privilege for confidential internal communications.   Unfortunately, the contours of that privilege have never been well defined, presenting substantial interpretive problems as to the scope of the exemption. * * *

Exemption six, protecting personnel and medical files whose disclosure would cause unwarranted invasion of personal privacy, is similar to exemption four in several respects.   As with exemption four, the *primary* thrust of the exemption is to protect the interests of persons outside the agency about whom the information is pertinent (though in both cases the agency may have an interest in maintaining confidentiality as a means of protecting its ability to obtain information) and the exemption is essentially open-ended in requiring evaluation of the harm of disclosure to the individual in each case.   Exemption six has been interpreted to require

---

39.   * * * As originally drafted, exemption one of the U.S. FOI Act was interpreted to preclude judicial review of the reasonableness of the classification. See *Environmental Protection Agency v. Mink*, 410 U.S. 73 (1973).   The 1974 amendments overruled *Mink* and provided for *de novo* review of classifications and *in camera* scrutiny of documents themselves where necessary to determine the reasonableness of the classifications.   See Attorney General's Memorandum on the 1974 Amendments to The Freedom of Information Act (1975) 1-4 ("Attorney General's Memorandum").   However, legis-

lative history indicates that "*de novo* review" in this context requires courts to give "substantial weight to an agency's affidavit concerning the details of the classified status of the disputed record".

46. The 1976 amendment, enacted as a rider to the Sunshine Act * * * was intended to overrule *Federal Aviation Administration v. Robertson*, 422 U. S. 255 (1975), where the Supreme Court construed the exemption to cover statutes that gave broad discretion to agencies to withhold documents. * * *

an explicit balancing of the interest in privacy against the interest in disclosure.[60] Thus, predictability is sacrificed for greater refinement in measuring the competing interests. * * *

Exemption seven protects investigatory records compiled for law enforcement purposes where disclosure would harm any of several specified interests: enforcement proceedings generally, impartial adjudication, personal privacy, confidentiality of investigative sources, or techniques and safety of enforcement personnel. * * * Responding to what it perceived as an overly expansive judicial interpretation of the scope of the exemption Congress narrowed its scope in 1974 by specifying particular interests to be protected. * * * The greater specificity added in 1974 did not, needless to say, resolve all interpretive problems. * * *

(3) DISCLOSURE: IMPLEMENTATION AND ENFORCEMENT

As might be expected, substantive issues concerning the scope of disclosure (or, equivalently, the scope of the exemptions) have been the paramount concern over the years. * * * [This has tended] to obscure procedural problems of implementation and enforcement, problems that are in a sense more fundamental to the actual working of the disclosure system.

* * * [P]rovision for direct and immediate judicial enforcement was among the most important, if not the most important, reforms wrought by the 1966 Act. Faithful to the active role of the judiciary throughout American public law, the courts have been more than mere enforcement agents of Congress assuring compliance with statutory directives, they have been "creative" interpreters of public policy—indeed virtual lawmakers in their own right. * * *

———

As Professor Robinson notes, judicial decisions under the FOIA have also emphasized the dominant goal of disclosure of covered records. But in mediating the conflicting claims of litigants, the courts have had to deal more particularly than has Congress with the interplay of dominant and subsidiary legislative purposes in the Act and with its integration into the pre-existing structure of common law, statutory, and constitutional principles. We cannot here pursue the judicial approaches to enforcement of the Act down the many by-ways that crisscross the jurisprudential terrain. Instead, we focus on two recurrent issues: (1) the extent to which the investigatory and decision-making processes of government agencies should be exposed to public examination, and on what conditions; and (2) the accommodation of competing claims of access to information in the government's possession, on the one hand, and protection of the interests of businesses and individuals who provided that information, on the other. At the conclusion of this section we briefly examine the debate over the systemic effects of the FOIA.

---

60. See, e.g., Department of Air Force v. Rose, 425 U.S. 352 (1976). * * *

3. BALANCING GOVERNMENT INTERESTS IN CONFIDENTIALITY

NLRB v. SEARS, ROEBUCK & CO.

Supreme Court of the United States, 1975.
421 U.S. 132, 95 S. Ct. 1504, 44 L.Ed.2d 29

MR. JUSTICE WHITE delivered the opinion of the Court.

The National Labor Relations Board (the Board) and its General Counsel seek to set aside an order of the United States District Court directing disclosure to respondent, Sears, Roebuck & Co. (Sears), pursuant to the Freedom of Information Act, of certain memoranda, known as "Advice Memoranda" and "Appeals Memoranda," and related documents generated by the Office of the General Counsel in the course of deciding whether or not to permit the filing with the Board of unfair labor practice complaints.

* * *

Sears claims, and the courts below ruled, that the memoranda sought are expressions of legal and policy decisions already adopted by the agency and constitute "final opinions" and "instructions to staff that affect a member of the public," both categories being expressly disclosable under § 552(a)(2) of the Act, pursuant to its purposes to prevent the creation of "secret law." In any event, Sears claims, the memoranda are nonexempt "identifiable records" which must be disclosed under § 552(a)(3). The General Counsel, on the other hand, claims that the memoranda sought here are not final opinions under § 552(a)(2) and that even if they are "identifiable records" otherwise disclosable under § 552(a)(3), they are exempt under § 552(b), principally as "intra-agency" communications under § 552(b)(b)(5) (Exemption 5), made in the course of formulating agency decisions on legal and policy matters.

I

Crucial to the decision of this case is an understanding of the function of the documents in issue in the context of the administrative process which generated them. We deal with this matter first. Under § 1 *et seq.* of the National Labor Relations Act, the process of adjudicating unfair labor practice cases begins with the filing by a private party of a "charge." Although Congress has designated the Board as the principal body which adjudicates the unfair labor practice case based on such charge, the Board may adjudicate only upon the filing of a "complaint"; and Congress has delegated to the Office of General Counsel "on behalf of the Board" the unreviewable authority to determine whether a complaint shall be filed. In those cases in which he decides that a complaint shall issue, the General Counsel becomes an advocate before the Board in support of the complaint. In those cases in which he decides not to issue a complaint, no proceeding before the Board occurs at all. The practical effect of this administrative scheme is that a party believing himself the victim of an unfair labor practice can obtain neither adjudication nor remedy under the labor statute without first persuading the Office of General Counsel that his claim is sufficiently meritorious to warrant Board consideration.

In order to structure the considerable power which the administrative scheme gives him, the General Counsel has adopted certain procedures for processing unfair labor practice charges. Charges are filed in the first instance with one of the Board's 31 Regional Directors, to whom the General Counsel has delegated the initial power to decide whether or not to issue a complaint. A member of the staff of the Regional Office then conducts an investigation of the charge, which may include interviewing witnesses and reviewing documents. If, on the basis of the investigation, the Regional Director believes the charge has merit, a settlement will be attempted, or a complaint issued. If the charge has no merit in the Regional Director's judgment, the charging party will be so informed by letter with a brief explanation of the reasons. In such a case, the charging party will also be informed of his right to appeal within 10 days to the Office of the General Counsel in Washington, D.C.

If the charging party exercises this right, the entire file in the possession of the Regional Director will be sent to the Office of Appeals in the General Counsel's Office in Washington, D. C. * * * The charging party may make a written presentation of his case as of right and an oral presentation in the discretion of the General Counsel. If an oral presentation is allowed, the subject of the unfair labor practice charge is notified and allowed a similar but separate opportunity to make an oral presentation. In any event, a decision is reached by the Appeals Committee; and the decision and the reasons for it are set forth in a memorandum called the "General Counsel's Minute" or the "Appeals Memorandum." This document is then cleared through the General Counsel himself. If the case is unusually complex or important, the General Counsel will have been brought into the process at an earlier stage and will have had a hand in the decision and the expression of its basis in the Appeals Memorandum. In either event, the Appeals Memorandum is then sent to the Regional Director who follows its instructions. If the appeal is rejected and the Regional Director's decision not to issue a complaint is sustained, a separate document is prepared and sent by the General Counsel in letter form to the charging party, more briefly setting forth the reasons for the denial of his appeal.[6] The Appeals Memoranda, whether sustaining or overruling the Regional Directors, constitute one class of documents at issue in this case.

The appeals process affords the General Counsel's Office in Washington some opportunity to formulate a coherent policy, and to achieve some measure of uniformity, in enforcing the labor laws. The appeals process

---

6. In April 1971, the General Counsel ceased preparing a separate Appeals Memorandum in every case, and ceased preparing one in any case in which the Regional Director's decision not to issue a complaint was sustained. In this latter class of cases, the General Counsel adopted the policy of expanding the letter sent to the charging party and sending the Regional Director a copy of the letter.

alone, however, is not wholly adequate for this purpose: when the Regional Director initially decides to file a complaint, no appeal is available and when the Regional Director decides not to file a complaint, the charging party may neglect to appeal. Accordingly * * * the General Counsel requires the Regional Directors, before reaching an initial decision in connection with charges raising certain issues specified by the General Counsel, to submit the matter to the General Counsel's "Advice Branch," also located in Washington, D.C. In yet other kinds of cases, the Regional Directors are permitted to seek the counsel of the Advice Branch.

When a Regional Director seeks "advice" from the Advice Branch, he does so through a memorandum which sets forth the facts of the case, a statement of the issues on which advice is sought, and a recommendation. * * * The General Counsel will decide the issue submitted, and his "final determination" will be communicated to the Regional Director by way of an Advice Memorandum. The memorandum will briefly summarize the facts, against the background of which the legal or policy issue is to be decided, set forth the General Counsel's answer to the legal or policy issue submitted together with a "detailed legal rationale," and contain "instructions for the final processing of the case." Depending upon the conclusion reached in the memorandum, the Regional Director will either file a complaint or send a letter to the complaining party advising him of the Regional Director's decision not to proceed and informing him of his right to appeal. It is these Advice Memoranda which constitute the other class of documents of which Sears seeks disclosure in this case.

II

This case arose in the following context. By letter dated July 14, 1971, Sears requested that the General Counsel disclose to it pursuant to the Act all Advice and Appeals Memoranda issued within the previous five years on the subjects of "the propriety of withdrawals by employers or unions from multi-employer bargaining, disputes as to commencement date of negotiations, or conflicting interpretations in any other context of the Board's *Retail Associates* (120 NLRB 388) rule." The letter also sought the subject-matter index or digest of Advice and Appeals Memoranda.[10] The letter urged disclosure on the theory that the Advice and Appeals Memoranda are the only source of agency "law" on some issues. By letter dated July 23, 1971, the General Counsel declined Sears' disclosure request in full. The letter stated that Advice Memoranda are simply "guides for a Regional Director" and are not final; that they are exempt from disclosure under 5 U.S.C.A. § 552(b)(5) as "intra-agency

10. Sears was then in the process of preparing an appeal to the General Counsel in Washington from a refusal by the Regional Director to file a complaint with the Board in response to an unfair labor practice charge earlier filed by Sears with the Regional Director in Seattle, Wash. * * *

Sears' rights under the Act are neither increased nor decreased by reason of the fact that it claims an interest in the Advice and Appeals Memoranda greater than that shared by the average member of the public. The Act is fundamentally designed to inform the public about agency action and not to benefit private litigants. Accordingly, we will not refer again to Sears' underlying unfair labor practice charge.

memoranda" which reflect the thought processes of the General Counsel's staff; and that they are exempt pursuant to 5 U.S.C.A. § 552(b)(7) as part of the "investigative process."   The letter said that Appeals Memoranda were not indexed by subject matter and, therefore, the General Counsel was "unable" to comply with Sears' request.   In further explanation of his decision, with respect to Appeals Memoranda, the General Counsel wrote to Sears on August 4, 1971, and stated that Appeals Memoranda which ordered the filing of a complaint were not "final opinions." The letter further stated that those Appeals Memoranda which *were* "final opinions, i.e., those in which an appeal was denied" and which directed that no complaint be filed, numbered several thousand, and that in the General Counsel's view they had no precedential significance.   Accordingly, if disclosable at all, they were disclosable under 5 U.S.C.A. § 552(a)(3) relating to "identifiable records."   The General Counsel then said that Sears had failed adequately to identify the material sought and that he could not justify the expenditure of time necessary for the agency to identify them.

On August 4, 1971, Sears filed a complaint pursuant to the Act seeking a declaration that the General Counsel's refusal to disclose the Advice and Appeals Memoranda and indices thereof requested by Sears violated the Act, and an injunction enjoining continued violations of the Act. * * * The answer denied that the Act required disclosure of any of the documents sought but referred to a letter of the same date in which the General Counsel informed Sears that he would make available the index to Advice Memoranda and also all Advice and Appeals Memoranda in cases which had been closed—either because litigation before the Board had been completed or because a decision not to file a complaint had become final.   He stated, however, that he would not disclose the memoranda in open cases; that he would, in any event, delete names of witnesses and "security sensitive" matter from the memoranda he did disclose; and that he did not consider the General Counsel's Office bound to pursue this new policy "in all instances" in the future.

Not wholly satisfied with the voluntary disclosures offered and made by the General Counsel, Sears moved for summary judgment and the General Counsel did likewise.   Sears thus continued to seek memoranda in open cases.   Moreover, Sears objected to the deletions in the memoranda in closed cases and asserted that many Appeals Memoranda were unintelligible because they incorporated by reference documents which were not themselves disclosed and also referred to "the 'circumstances of the case' " which were not set out and about which Sears was ignorant.   The General Counsel contended that all of the documents were exempt from disclosure as "intra-agency" memoranda within the coverage of 5 U.S.C.A. § (b)(5); and that the documents incorporated by reference were exempt from disclosure as "investigatory files" pursuant to 5 U.S.C.A. § 552(b)(7).   * * *

III

It is clear, and the General Counsel concedes, that Appeals and Advice Memoranda are at the least "identifiable records" which must be disclosed on demand, unless they fall within one of the Act's exempt categories. It is also clear that, if the memoranda do fall within one of the Act's exempt categories, our inquiry is at an end, for the Act "does not apply" to such documents. Thus our inquiry, strictly speaking, must be into the scope of the exemptions which the General Counsel claims to be applicable—principally Exemption 5 relating to "intra-agency memorandums." * * * The General Counsel argues * * * that no Advice or Appeals Memorandum is a final opinion made in the adjudication of a case and that all are "intra-agency" memoranda within the coverage of Exemption 5. He bases this argument in large measure on what he claims to be his lack of adjudicative authority. It is true that the General Counsel lacks any authority finally to adjudicate an unfair labor practice claim in favor of the claimant; but he does possess the authority to adjudicate such a claim against the claimant through his power to decline to file a complaint with the Board. We hold for reasons more fully set forth below that those Advice and Appeals Memoranda which explain decisions by the General Counsel not to file a complaint are "final opinions" made in the adjudication of a case and fall outside the scope of Exemption 5; but that those Advice and Appeals Memoranda which explain decisions by the General Counsel to file a complaint and commence litigation before the Board are not "final opinions" made in the adjudication of a case and do fall within the scope of Exemption 5.

The parties are in apparent agreement that Exemption 5 withholds from a member of the public documents which a private party could not discover in litigation with the agency. Since virtually any document not privileged may be discovered by the appropriate litigant, if it is relevant to his litigation, and since the Act clearly intended to give any member of the public as much right to disclosure as one with a special interest therein, it is reasonable to construe Exemption 5 to exempt those documents, and only those documents, normally privileged in the civil discovery context. The privileges claimed by petitioners to be relevant to his case are (i) the "generally * * * recognized" privilege for "confidential intra-agency advisory opinions * * * ," disclosure of which "would be 'injurious to the consultative functions of government * * * ' (sometimes referred to as "executive privilege"), and (ii) the attorney-client and attorney work-product privileges generally available to all litigants.

That Congress had the Government's executive privilege specifically in mind in adopting Exemption 5 is clear. The precise contours of the privilege in the context of this case are less clear, but may be gleaned from expressions of legislative purpose and the prior case law. The cases uniformly rest the privilege on the policy of protecting the "decision making processes of government agencies"; and focus on documents "reflecting advisory opinions, recommendations and deliberations comprising part of a process by which governmental decisions and policies are formulated." The point, plainly made in the Senate Report, is that the "frank discussion of legal or policy matters" in writing might be inhibited if the discussion were made public; and that the "decisions" and "policies formulated" would be the poorer as a result. * * * [A]s we have said in an analogous context, "[h]uman experience teaches that those who expect public dissemination of their remarks may well temper candor with a concern for appearances * * * to the *detriment of the decision-making process.*" *United States v. Nixon,* 418 U.S. 683, 705 (1974) (emphasis added).[17]

Manifestly, the ultimate purpose of this long-recognized privilege is to prevent injury to the quality of agency decisions. The quality of a particular agency decision will clearly be affected by the communications received by the decisionmaker on the subject of the decision prior to the time the decision is made. However, it is difficult to see how the quality of a decision will be affected by communications with respect to the decision occurring after the decision is finally reached; and therefore equally difficult to see how the quality of the decision will be affected by forced disclosure of such communications, as long as prior communications and the ingredients of the decisionmaking process are not disclosed. Accordingly, the lower courts have uniformly drawn a distinction between predecisional communications, which are privileged,[18] and communications made after the decision and designed to explain it, which are not.[19] This distinction is supported not only by the lesser injury to the decisionmaking process flowing from disclosure of postdecisional communications, but also, in the case of those communications which explain the decision, by the increased public interest in knowing the basis for agency policy already adopted. The public is only marginally concerned with reasons supporting a policy which an agency has rejected, or with reasons which might have supplied, but did not supply, the basis for a policy which was actually adopted on a different ground. In contrast, the public is vitally concerned with the reasons which did supply the basis for an agency policy actually adopted. These reasons, if expressed within the agency, constitute the "working law" of the agency and have been held by the lower courts to be outside the protection of Exemption 5. Exemption 5, properly construed, calls for "disclosure of all 'opinions and interpreta-

---

17. Our remarks in *United States v. Nixon* were made in the context of a claim of "executive privilege" resting solely on the Constitution of the United States. No such claim is made here and we do not mean to intimate that any documents involved here are protected by whatever constitutional content the doctrine of executive privilege might have.

18. Our emphasis on the need to protect pre-*decisional* documents does not mean that the existence of the privilege turns on the ability of an agency to identify a specific decision in connection with which a memorandum is prepared. Agencies are, and properly should be, engaged in a continuing process of examining their policies; this process will generate memoranda containing recommendations which do not ripen into agency decisions; and the lower courts should be wary of interfering with this process.

19. We are aware that the line between predecisional documents and postdecisional documents may not always be a bright one. Indeed, even the prototype of the postdecisional document—the "final opinion"—serves the dual function of explaining the decision just made and providing guides for decisions of similar or analogous cases arising in the future. In its latter function, the opinion is predecisional; and the manner in which it is written may, therefore, affect decisions in later cases. For present purposes it is sufficient to note that final opinions are *primarily* postdecisional—looking back on and explaining, as they do, a decision already reached or a policy already adopted—and that their disclosure poses a negligible risk of denying to agency decisionmakers the uninhibited advice which is so important to agency decisions.

tions' which embody the agency's effective law and policy, and the withholding of all papers which reflect the agency's group thinking in the process of working out its policy and determining what its law shall be."

This conclusion is powerfully supported by the other provisions of the Act. The affirmative portion of the Act, expressly requiring indexing of "final opinions," "statements of policy and interpretations which have been adopted by the agency," and "instructions to staff that affect a member of the public," represents a strong congressional aversion to "secret [agency] law," and represents an affirmative congressional purpose to require disclosure of documents which have "the force and effect of law." We should be reluctant, therefore, to construe Exemption 5 to apply to the documents described in 5 U.S.C.A. § 552(a)(2); and with respect at least to "final opinions," which not only invariably explain agency action already taken or an agency decision already made, but also constitute "final dispositions" of matters by an agency, we hold that Exemption 5 can never apply.

It is equally clear that Congress had the attorney's work-product privilege specifically in mind when it adopted Exemption 5 and that such a privilege had been recognized in the civil discovery context by the prior case law. The Senate Report states that Exemption 5 "would include the working papers of the agency attorney and documents which would come within the attorney-client privilege if applied to private parties," and the case law clearly makes the attorney's work-product rule of *Hickman v. Taylor*, 329 U.S. 495 (1947), applicable to Government attorneys in litigation. Whatever the outer boundaries of the attorney's work-product rule are, the rule clearly applies to memoranda prepared by an attorney in contemplation of litigation which set forth the attorney's theory of the case and his litigation strategy.

Applying these principles to the memoranda sought by Sears, it becomes clear that Exemption 5 does not apply to those Appeals and Advice Memoranda which conclude that no complaint should be filed and which have the effect of finally denying relief to the charging party; but that Exemption 5 does protect from disclosure those Appeals and Advice Memoranda which direct the filing of a complaint and the commencement of litigation before the Board.

Under the procedures employed by the General Counsel, Advice and Appeals Memoranda are communicated to the Regional Director *after* the General Counsel, through his Advice and Appeals Branches, has decided whether or not to issue a complaint; and represent an explanation to the Regional Director of a legal or policy decision already adopted by the General Counsel. In the case of decisions *not* to file a complaint, the memoranda effect as "final" a "disposition" as an administrative decision can—representing, as it does, an unreviewable rejection of the charge filed by the private party. Disclosure of these memoranda would not intrude on predecisional processes, and protecting them would not improve the quality of agency decisions, since when the memoranda are communicated to the Regional Director, the General Counsel has already reached his decision and the Regional Director who receives them has no decision to make—he is bound to dismiss the charge. Moreover, the General Counsel's decisions not to file complaints together with the Advice and Appeals Memoranda explaining them, are precisely the kind of agency law in which the public is so vitally interested and which Congress sought to prevent the agency from keeping secret.[22] * * *

The General Counsel contends, however, that the Appeals Memoranda represent only the first step in litigation and are not final; and that Advice Memoranda are advisory only and not binding on the Regional Director, who has the discretion to file or not to file a complaint. The contentions are without merit. Plainly, an Appeals Memorandum is the first step in litigation only when the appeal is sustained and it directs the filing of a complaint;[23] and the General Counsel's current characterization of an Advice Memorandum is at odds with his own description of the function of an Advice Memorandum in his statement to the House Committee. That statement says that the Advice Branch establishes "*uniform* policies" in those legal areas with respect to which Regional Directors are "required" to seek advice until a "definitive" policy is arrived at. This is so because if Regional Directors were "free" to interpret legal issues "the *law* could, as a practical matter and before Board decision of the issue, be one thing in one Region and conflicting in others." Therefore, the Advice Memorandum is created after consideration of "prior advice determinations in similar or related cases" and contains "instructions for the final processing of the case." In light of this description, we cannot fault the District Court for concluding that the Advice Memorandum achieves a *pro tanto* withdrawal from the Regional Director of his discretion to file or not to file a complaint. Nor can we avoid the conclusion that Advice Memoranda directing dismissal of a charge represent the "law" of the agency. Accordingly, Advice and Appeals Memoranda directing that a charge be dismissed fall outside of Exemption 5 and must be disclosed.

For essentially the same reasons, these memoranda are "final opinions" made in the "adjudication of cases" which must be indexed pursuant to 5 U.S.C.A. § 552(a)(2)(A). * * *

---

22. The General Counsel argues that he makes no law, analogizing his authority to decide whether or not to file a complaint to a public prosecutor's authority to decide whether a criminal case should be brought, and claims that he does not adjudicate anything resembling a civil dispute. Without deciding whether a public prosecutor makes "law" when he decides not to prosecute or whether memoranda explaining such decisions are "final opinions," it is sufficient to note that the General Counsel's analogy is far from perfect. The General Counsel, unlike most prosecutors, may authorize the filing of a complaint with the Board only if a private citizen files a "charge." Unlike the victim of a crime, the charging party will, if a complaint is filed by the General Counsel, become a party to the unfair labor practice proceeding before the Board. And, if an unfair labor practice is found to exist, the ensuing cease-and-desist order will, unlike the punishment of the defendant in a criminal case, coerce conduct by the wrongdoer flowing particularly to the benefit of the charging party. For these reasons, we have declined to characterize the enforcement of the laws against unfair labor practices either as a wholly public or wholly private matter.

23. The General Counsel himself in his letter to Sears of August 4, 1971, referred to the Appeals Memoranda "in which an appeal was denied" as "final opinions."

Advice and Appeals Memoranda which direct the filing of a complaint, on the other hand, fall within the coverage of Exemption 5. The filing of a complaint does not finally dispose even of the General Counsel's responsibility with respect to the case. The case will be litigated before and decided by the Board; and the General Counsel will have the responsibility of advocating the position of the charging party before the Board. The Memoranda will inexorably contain the General Counsel's theory of the case and may communicate to the Regional Director some litigation strategy or settlement advice. Since the Memoranda will also have been prepared in contemplation of the upcoming litigation, they fall squarely within Exemption 5's protection of an attorney's work product. At the same time, the public's interest in disclosure is substantially reduced by the fact * * * that the basis for the General Counsel's legal decision will come out in the course of litigation before the Board; and that the "law" with respect to these cases will ultimately be made not by the General Counsel but by the Board or the courts.

We recognize that an Advice or Appeals Memorandum directing the filing of a complaint—although representing only a decision that a legal issue is sufficiently in doubt to warrant determination by another body— has many of the characteristics of the documents described in 5 U.S.C.A. § 552(a)(2). Although not a "final opinion" in the "adjudication " of a "case" because it does not effect a "final disposition," the memorandum does explain a decision already reached by the General Counsel which has real operative effect—it permits litigation before the Board; and we have indicated a reluctance to construe Exemption 5 to protect such documents. We do so in this case only because the decisionmaker—the General Counsel—must become a litigating party to the case with respect to which he has made his decision. The attorney's work-product policies which Congress clearly incorporated into Exemption 5 thus come into play and lead us to hold that the Advice and Appeals Memoranda directing the filing of a complaint are exempt whether or not they are, as the District Court held, "instructions to staff that affect a member of the public."

Petitioners assert that the District Court erred in holding that documents incorporated by reference in nonexempt Advice and Appeals Memoranda lose any exemption they might previously have held as "intra-agency" memoranda.[27] We disagree.

The probability that an agency employee will be inhibited from freely advising a decisionmaker for fear that his advice, *if adopted,* will become public is slight. First, when adopted, the reasoning becomes that of the agency and becomes *its* responsibility to defend. Second, agency employees will generally be encouraged rather than discouraged by public knowledge that their policy suggestions have been adopted by the agency. Moreover, the public interest in knowing the reasons for a policy actually

27. It should be noted that the documents incorporated by reference are in the main factual documents which are probably not enti- tled to Exemption 5 treatment in the first place.

adopted by an agency supports the District Court's decision below. Thus, we hold that, if an agency chooses *expressly* to adopt or incorporate by reference an intra-agency memorandum previously covered by Exemption 5 in what would otherwise be a final opinion, that memorandum may be withheld only on the ground that it falls within the coverage of some exemption other than Exemption 5.

Petitioners also assert that the District court's order erroneously requires it to produce or create explanatory material in those instances in which an Appeals Memorandum refers to the "circumstances of the case." We agree. The Act does not compel agencies to write opinions in cases in which they would not otherwise be required to do so. It only requires disclosure of certain documents which the law requires the agency to prepare or which the agency has decided for its own reasons to create. * * *

IV

Finally, petitioners argue that the Advice and Appeals Memoranda are exempt, pursuant to 5 U.S.C.A. § § 552(b)(2) and (7) (Exemptions 2 and 7), and that the documents incorporated therein are protected by Exemption 7. With respect to the Advice and Appeals Memoranda, we decline to reach a decision on these claims for the reasons set forth below, and with respect to the documents incorporated therein, we remand for further proceedings.

Exemption 7 provided, at the time of Sears' request for documents and at the time of the decisions of the courts below, that the Act does not apply to "investigatory files compiled for law enforcement purposes except to the extent available by law to a party other than an agency." Noting support in the legislative history for the proposition that this exemption applies to the civil "enforcement" of the labor laws, the General Counsel asserts that the "documentation underlying advice and appeals memoranda are 'investigatory files' " and that he "believes" the memoranda are themselves similarly exempt in light of the "purposes" of Exemption 7. * * *

* * * Congress has amended Exemption 7 since petitioners filed their brief in this case. * * * The legislative history clearly indicates that Congress disapproves of those cases, relied on by the General Counsel, which relieve the Government of the obligation to show that disclosure of a particular investigatory file would contravene the purposes of Exemption 7. The language of the amended Exemption 7 and the legislative history underlying it clearly reveal a congressional intent to limit application of Exemption 7 to agency records so that it would apply only to the extent that "the production of such records would interfere with enforcement proceedings, deprive a person of a right to a fair trial or an impartial adjudication, constitute [an] * * * unwarranted invasion of personal privacy, disclose the identity of an informer, or disclose investigative techniques and procedures."

Any decision of the Exemption 7 issue in this case would have to be under the Act, as amended, and, apart from the General Counsel's failure to raise the issue, the lower courts have had no opportunity to pass on the applicability of the Act, as amended, to Advice and Appeals Memoranda, since the amendment occurred after the decision by the Court of Appeals.

The General Counsel's claim that Advice and Appeals Memoranda are documents "related solely to the internal personnel rules and practices of an agency" and therefore protected by Exemption 2 was raised neither in the District Court nor in the Court of Appeals and we decline to reach it for the reasons set forth above.

*   *   *

THE CHIEF JUSTICE concurs in the judgment.

MR. JUSTICE POWELL took no part in the consideration or decision of this case.

Notes

1. Of the nine exemptions contained in the FOIA, exemption 5 is potentially the most far-reaching. Although this exemption might arguably include almost any agency-authored document, its application has been restricted in two ways, as the *Sears* opinion suggests.

a. It is accepted that exemption 5 does not protect factual material. This limitation is supported both by the legislative history of the FOIA and by the underlying policy of the exemption—protection of the free flow of ideas and opinions in agency policy-making. Because the disclosure of factual information presumably does not hinder that flow, factual material is treated as outside the exemption. See *Soucie v. David*, 448 F.2d 1067 (D.C. Cir. 1971); *Environmental Protection Agency v. Mink*, 410 U.S. 73 (1973).

Montrose Chemical Corp. v. Train, 491 F.2d 63 (D.C. Cir. 1974), refined the factual-deliberative distinction by refusing to order disclosure of factual summaries of public administrative hearings prepared by agency attorneys to aid the EPA Administrator in making a decision concerning the cancellation of registrations for DDT. The court reasoned that such summaries, although largely factual, were prepared as part of the deliberative process which the exemption was designed to protect. Access to the basic facts, as distinguished from the summaries, was available to the plaintiff in a 9200-page public hearing record.

b. A second limitation on exemption 5, confirmed in *Sears*, is that documents containing statements of agency policy or interpretations of law and documents forming the basis for completed decisions must be disclosed even though they contain recommendatory and judgmental materials. In *American Mail Line, Limited v. Gulick*, 411 F.2d 696 (D.C. Cir. 1969), the plaintiffs sued to enjoin the withholding of an advisory memorandum which the agency had quoted in part in its cryptic final decision and had referred to as supplying the justification for its order. The memorandum was found not to be within the intra-agency exemption because its incorporation in the agency's decision made it disclosable as part of a "final decision" under section 552(a)(2)(A). See also *General Services Administration v. Benson*, 415 F.2d 878 (9th Cir. 1969), where the court allowed the party demanding disclosure to prove by extrinsic means that memoranda contained "statements of policy and interpretations * * * adopted by the agency."

2. Effecting the disclosure of secret law while also protecting the free flow of ideas during the process of policy formation may require the drawing of fine

lines. *Sterling Drug, Inc. v. FTC*, 450 F.2d 698 (D.C. Cir. 1971), is exemplary. The appellant, a diversified drug and cosmetic company, was charged with violating Clayton Act § 7 by acquiring Lehn & Fink Products Corp., producers of "Lysol" brand disinfectants and deodorizers. Prior to any formal proceedings on the complaint, Sterling requested documents concerning the Commission's earlier approval of Miles Laboratories' acquisition of the S.O.S. Company from the General Foods Corporation. The FTC had ordered General Foods to divest itself of S.O.S. and, as a part of that divestiture proceeding, had approved Miles as the purchaser. In approving the General Foods plan the agency had stated that it had "entirely relied upon the information submitted by General Foods and its approval [was] conditioned upon this information being accurate and complete."

Sterling hoped to show that its acquisition of Lehn & Fink was so similar to the approved Miles-S.O.S. acquisition that the FTC could not consistently charge Sterling with violating section 7. It unsuccessfully requested disclosure of three groups of informal Commission memoranda relating to that earlier case. The court concluded that the documents were clearly of the type protected by exemption 5, but recognized that this determination did not necessarily dispose of the case. Sterling had argued that under *Gulick* the documents were required to be disclosed "in order to provide access to the basis for the agency decision [approving the Miles-S.O.S. acquisition] and its rationale." The court responded (450 F.2d at 706-08):

   * * * [W]e feel it is necessary to divide the Commission memoranda into three categories—those prepared by the Commission staff, those prepared by individual members of the Commission, and those prepared, or at least issued, by the Commission itself. With regard to the first category, we do not believe *Gulick* supports appellant's position. Here the Commission has not indicated publicly that staff memoranda contained the rationale for this decision, and we do not agree with Sterling's assertion that this must of necessity be the case. To begin with, most of these memoranda were written after the Commission's decision in Miles-S.O.S. and were directed toward the litigation in the Sterling-Lehn & Fink case. * * *

   The staff memoranda submitted to the Commission prior to the Miles-S.O.S. decision undoubtedly contain ideas which affected that decision to some extent. However, our experience with the decision-making process leads us to believe that the material in these memoranda was probably filtered and refined by the Commission, with the result that its ultimate decision was something more than, or at least different from, the sum of its "parts." * * *

   * * * Sterling contends * * * that disclosure is only warranted in this case because the Commission did not issue an opinion giving the reason for its *Miles-S.O.S.* decision and that requiring disclosure in this case and others like it will have the salutary effect of requiring agencies to issue an opinion with every order. Although persuasive in the abstract, this reasoning is unrealistic when applied to the everyday world of overburdened administrative agencies. Agencies are required to issue opinions with many of their orders, but it is completely unreasonable to suppose that every agency order can be accompanied by an opinion. The probable effect of a decision requiring disclosure of the staff memoranda would thus be to inhibit "a full and frank exchange of opinions" at least in that class of cases where opinions are not, and as practical matter cannot be, issued. We decline to make such a decision. * * *

We also feel that *Gulick* does not compel disclosure of the two memoranda written by individual Commissioners.　Although the Commissioners were obviously parties to the *Miles-S.O.S.* decision and probably discussed the grounds for that decision to some extent in their memoranda, these memoranda do not necessarily contain a full and accurate account of the grounds for the decision.　* * *

　* * *　[But we] are primarily motivated by our belief that there is a great need to preserve the free flow of ideas between Commissioners.　* * *　In our opinion any attempt to separate a Commissioner's statements as to the basis for a past decision from his views regarding the disposition of a current case and to disclose the former might well infringe upon these essential communications.　* * *

With regard to the memoranda issued by the Commission, however, we think the philosophy underlying *Gulick* requires a different result.　These memoranda were prepared by the individuals directly responsible for the *Miles-S.O.S.* decision and, as documents emanating from the Commission as a whole, they are presumably neither argumentative in nature nor slanted to reflect a particular Commissioner's view.　Hence, the danger that any explanation they may give of Miles-S.O.S. is not the correct one is greatly reduced.　We also feel the policy of promoting the free flow of ideas within the agency does not apply here, for private transmittals of binding agency opinions and interpretations should not be encouraged.　These are not the ideas and theories which go into the making of the law, they are the law itself, and as such should be made available to the public.

3. Closely related to the problem of distinguishing "decisions" from "deliberations" is the problem of determining what bodies are "agencies" under the APA—whose decisions must be indexed and disclosed.　In *Renegotiation Board v. Grumman Aircraft Engineering Corp.*, 421 U.S. 168 (1975), *rev'g* 482 F.2d 710 (D.C. Cir. 1973), Grumman sought disclosure of the reports of Regional Boards in certain classes of disputes involving competitors and contractors as well as the reports of divisions of the Board itself.　Disclosure was resisted under exemption 5 on the ground that the Regional Boards' reports were merely advisory and that the division reports were not final decisions because they required the concurrence of the entire Board.

The Supreme Court agreed that both types of reports fell within exemption 5. Its opinion describes the roles played by the two entities in the government's elaborate system for recovering excess profits earned by contractors (421 U.S. at 185-90):

It is undisputed that the Regional Boards had no legal authority to decide whether a contractor had received "excessive profits" in Class A cases.　In such cases, the Regional Boards could investigate and recommend, but only the Board could decide.　The reports were prepared long before the board reached its decision.　The Board used the Regional Board Report as a basis for discussion and, even when it agreed with the Regional Board's conclusion, it often did so as a result of an analysis of the flexible statutory factors completely different from that contained in the Regional Board Report.　* * *

The Court of Appeals' attempt to impute decisional authority to Regional Boards by analogizing their final recommendations to the final decisions of United States district courts must fail.　The decision of a United States district court, like the decision of the General Counsel of the NLRB discussed in

NLRB v. Sears, Roebuck & Co. has real operative effect independent of "review" by a court of appeals: absent appeal by one of the parties, the decision has the force of law; and, even if an appeal is filed, the court of appeals will be bound, within limits, by certain of the district court's conclusions. The recommendation of a Regional Board, by contrast, has no operative effect independent of the review: consideration of the case by the Board is not dependent on the decision by a party to "appeal"—such consideration is an inevitable event without which there is no agency decision; and the recommendation of the Regional Board carries no *legal* weight whatever before the Board—review by the latter is, as the Court of Appeals conceded, *de novo.* * * *

It is equally clear that a division of the Board has no legal authority to decide. Once again, it may analyze and recommend, but the power to decide remains with the full Board. The evidence is uncontradicted that the Division Reports were prepared before the Board reached its decision, were used by the full Board as a basis for discussion, and, as the Chairman testified, were "prepared for and designed to assist the members of the Board in their deliberations"; nor is the discussion limited to the material and analysis contained in the Division Report. Following the discussion, *any* Board member may disagree with the report's conclusion or agree with it for reasons other than those contained in the report. * * *

It is true that those who participate in the writing of the Division Report are among those who participate in the Board's decision, and that, human nature being what it is, they may not change their minds after discussion by the full Board. This creates a greater likelihood that the Board's decision will be in accordance with the Division Report than is the case with respect to a Regional Board Report and that, where the Board's decision is different, the Division Report will reflect the final views of at least one of the Board's members. However, this is not necessarily so. The Board obviously considers its discussion following the creation of the Division Report to be of crucial importance to its decision for, notwithstanding the fact that a division is made up of a majority of the Board, it has been delegated no decisional authority. The member of the Board who wrote the report may change his mind as a result of the discussion or, consistent with the philosophy of Exemption 5, he may have included thoughts in the report with which he was not in agreement at the time he wrote it. The point is that the report is created for the purpose of discussion, and we are unwilling to deprive the Board of a thoroughly uninhibited version of this valuable deliberative tool by making Division Reports public on the unsupported assumption that they always disclose the final views of at least some members of the Board.

4. In *Federal Open Market Committee v. Merrill,* 443 U.S. 340 (1979), the Court recognized a different facet of the government's interest in avoiding disclosure of documents articulating administrative policy. Merrill was a Georgetown University law student who sought immediate disclosure of monthly documents, called Domestic Policy Directives, issued by the FOMC, a body composed of the Governors of the Federal Reserve System and representatives of system banks. Each month's Domestic Policy Directive set forth goals to guide the Federal Reserve System's agent in the sale of government securities during the coming month. At the end of each month, the expiring directive was routinely made public as part of the FOMC's approved minutes.

The committee denied Merrill's request on the practical grounds that "immediate release" of the Domestic Policy Directive and tolerance ranges [for growth in the money supply and the interest rate on federal securities]" would make it difficult to implement limited or gradual changes in monetary policy" and "would permit large institutional investors * * * to obtain an unfair advantage over small investors." The committee advanced a battery of legal arguments to legitimize these pragmatic objections to disclosure, but ultimately relied exclusively on exemption 5. In a tortuous opinion, the Supreme Court sustained this claim.

Justice Blackmun agreed that the Domestic Policy Directives were "interagency or intra-agency memorandums or letters," but noted that they were also clearly definitive statements of FOMC policy during the months they were effective. And the Committee could hardly claim an absolute exemption from disclosure in the face of its own practice of publicizing the directives as soon as they expired. For Blackmun, the central question under the language of exemption 5 was whether a civil court would be entitled to recognize a privilege to delay discovery of the directives. In concluding that it would, he had the following comments on the exemption's scope (443 U.S. at 354-57):

> Preliminarily, we note that it is not clear that Exemption 5 was intended to incorporate every privilege known to civil discovery. There are, to be sure, statements in our cases construing Exemption 5 that imply as much. * * * Heretofore, however, this Court has recognized only two privileges in Exemption 5, and, as *NLRB v. Sears, Roebuck & Co.*, emphasized, both these privileges are expressly mentioned in the legislative history of that Exemption. Moreover, material that may be subject to some other discovery privilege may also be exempt from disclosure under one of the other eight exemptions of FOIA, particularly Exemptions 1, 4, 6, and 7. * * *

> The most plausible of the three privileges asserted by the FOMC[17] is based on Fed. Rule Civ. Proc. 26(c)(7), which provides that a district court, "for good cause shown," may order "that a trade secret or other confidential research, development, or commercial information not be disclosed or be disclosed only in a designated way." The Committee argues that the Domestic Policy Directives constitute "confidential * * * commercial information," at least during the month in which they provide guidance to the Account Manager, and that they therefore would be privileged from civil discovery during this period.

> The federal courts have long recognized a qualified evidentiary privilege for trade secrets and other confidential commercial information. The Federal Rules of Civil Procedure provide similar qualified protection for trade secrets and confidential commercial information in the civil discovery context. Federal Rule Civ. Proc. 26(c)(7), which replaced former Rule 30(b) in 1970, was intended in this respect to "reflec[t] existing law." The Federal Rules, of course, are fully applicable to the United States as a party. And we see no reason why the Government could not, in an appropriate case, obtain a protective order under Rule 26(c)(7). * * *

17. The two other privileges advanced by the FOMC are a privilege for "official government information" whose disclosure would be harmful to the public interest, and a privilege based on Fed. Civ. Proc. 26(c)(2), which permits a court to order that discovery "may be had only on specified terms and conditions, including a designation of the time or place." In light of our disposition of this case, we do not consider whether either asserted privilege is incorporated in Exemption 5.

The Court found support in the FOIA's legislative history for recognizing the government's interest in temporarily withholding documents prepared in the course of awarding procurement contracts, whose premature release could prejudice negotiations. It distinguished this interest from the other, ostensibly central, objective of exemption 5 (443 U.S. at 359-60):

> * * * The purpose of the privilege for predecisional deliberations is to insure that a decisionmaker will receive the unimpeded advice of his associates. The theory is that if advice is revealed, associates may be reluctant to be candid and frank. It follows that documents shielded by executive privilege remain privileged even after the decision to which they pertain may have been effected, since disclosure at any time could inhibit the free flow of advice, including analysis, reports, and expression of opinion within the agency. The theory behind a privilege for confidential commercial information generated in the process of awarding a contract, however, is not that the flow of advice may be hampered, but that the Government will be placed at a competitive disadvantage or that the consummation of the contract may be endangered. Consequently, the rationale for protecting such information expires as soon as the contract is awarded or the offer withdrawn.
>
> We are further convinced that recognition of an Exemption 5 privilege for confidential commercial information generated in the process of awarding a contract would not substantially duplicate any other FOIA exemption. The closest possibility is Exemption 4, which applies to "trade secrets and commercial or financial information obtained from a person and privileged or confidential." Exemption 4, however, is limited to information "obtained from a person," that is, to information obtained outside the Government. * * * [23]
>
> * * * We are mindful that "the discovery rules can only be applied under Exemption 5 by way of rough analogies," and, in particular, that the individual FOIA applicant's need for information is not to be taken into account in determining whether materials are exempt under Exemption 5. Nevertheless, the sensitivity of the commercial secrets involved, and the harm that would be inflicted upon the Government by premature disclosure, should continue to serve as relevant criteria in determining the applicability of this Exemption 5 privilege. Accordingly, we think that if the Domestic Policy Directives contain sensitive information not otherwise available, and if immediate release of these Directives would significantly harm the Government's monetary functions or commercial interests, then a slight delay in the publication of the Directives, such as that authorized by 12 CFR § 271.5, would be permitted under Exemption 5. * * *

---

23. Our conclusion that the Domestic Policy Directives are at least potentially eligible for protection under Exemption 5 does not conflict with the District Court's finding that the Directives are "statements of general policy * * * formulated and adopted by the agency," which must be "currently publish[ed]" in the Federal Register pursuant to 5 U.S.C.A. § 552(a)(1). It is true that in *NLRB v. Sears, Roebuck & Co.*, we noted that there is an obvious relationship between Exemption 5 and the affirmative portion of the FOIA which requires the prompt disclosure and indexing of final opinions and statements of policy that have been adopted by the agency. We held that, with respect to final opinions, Exemption 5 can never apply; with respect to other documents covered by 5 U.S.C.A. § 552(a)(2), we said that we would be "reluctant" to hold that the Exemption 5 privilege would ever apply. These observations, however, were made in the course of a discussion of the privilege for predecisional communications. It should be obvious that the kind of mutually exclusive relationship between final opinions and statements of policy, on one hand, and predecisional communications, on the other, does not necessarily exist between final statements of policy and other Exemption 5 privileges. * * *

Because the district court had made no findings respecting the FOMC's claims of adverse impact, the Court declined to "consider whether, or to what extent, the * * * Directives would in fact be afforded protection in civil discovery." It accordingly remanded the case for further proceedings.

Justice Stevens dissented, in an opinion joined by Justice Stewart (443 U.S. at 367):

> * * * [The] Court's temporary exemption is inconsistent with the structure of the Act.   Under FOIA, all information must be released, in the specified manner—i.e., in this case, "currently"—unless it fits into one of nine categories.   As to material in those categories, the Act simply *does not apply*."   Between "current" release and total exemption, therefore, the statute establishes no middle ground.   Accordingly, I cannot agree with the Court's recognition of a third alternative for "exempt" material to which the Act nonetheless applies—albeit on a delayed basis.   If there is to be a new category subject to full disclosure but only after a "slight delay," I believe it should be created by Congress rather than the Court.   * * *

Executive Privilege

Exemption 5 is sometimes described as codifying—or at least incorporating—the executive's "privilege" to limit Congressional or judicial (and thus presumably public) inquiry into its deliberative processes—whether by review of internal documents or examination of participants.   But the elusive doctrine of executive privilege implies more than confidentiality of papers and discussions, for it is sometimes asserted as providing the President immunity from supervision by either the Congress or the courts.   Thus the doctrine, whatever its scope, seems potentially farther reaching than the protection afforded by exemption 5.   Yet the language of exemption 5 surely bears on the scope of any immunity the President's advisors may assert against mandatory disclosure of executive documents.

The modern Presidential view of the reach of "executive privilege" was set forth in a 1958 memorandum by Attorney General William Rogers, which identified five categories of information privileged from disclosure:

1. military and diplomatic secrets and foreign affairs;
2. information made confidential by statute;
3. investigations relating to pending litigation, and investigative files and reports;
4. information relating to internal governmental affairs privileged from disclosure in the public interest; and
5. records incidental to the making of policy including interdepartmental memoranda, advisory opinions, recommendations of subordinates and informal working papers.

Within the boundaries of these five categories, executive privilege to withhold documents in the public interest is sometimes said to be "absolute," that is, not subject to review by the courts.   Not surprisingly this absolute view of the privilege has been urged by the executive branch on various occasions throughout American history, and the debate over executive privilege has focused as much on the issue of whether the President has the unreviewable discretionary authority under the Constitution to withhold some kinds of information from the Congress or the courts as it has on the scope of the privilege. See generally R. BERGER, EXECUTIVE PRIVILEGE: A CONSTITUTIONAL MYTH (1974).

Three principal arguments have been advanced to support the claim of absolute presidential privilege. Proponents maintain that the privilege is inherent in the office of the President as chief of state and the embodiment of executive authority. Secondly, they cite the need for confidentiality between the President and his advisors in order to generate candor. Finally, it is argued that an absolute view of the privilege is necessitated by the constitutional separation of powers—the branches of government are equals and an absolute executive privilege is required to maintain that equality. Although the issue of executive privilege was raised as early as Washington's administration, the historical record is inconclusive concerning the intentions of the Founding Fathers and the views of early presidents regarding the proper exercise of the privilege. (That this record is subject to quite different interpretations may be seen in the majority and dissenting opinions in *Nixon v. Sirica*, 487 F.2d 700, 709, 775-81 (D.C. Cir. 1973)).

For many years, the leading judicial treatment of executive privilege was *United States v. Reynolds*, 345 U.S. 1, 11 (1953). There, the widow of a civilian killed in the crash of an Air Force plane sought copies of the Air Force investigative reports, which the Secretary of the Air Force claimed were privileged documents. In a confusing opinion, the Supreme Court upheld the government's claim of privilege, yet granted the judiciary the power to determine whether the privilege was applicable, while failing to clarify the scope of judicial review of the executive's claim. As a guideline for review, the Court adopted a necessity formula:

> In each case, the showing of necessity [for disclosure] which is made will determine how far the court should probe in satisfying itself that the occasion for invoking the privilege is appropriate. Where there is a strong showing of necessity, the claim of privilege should not be lightly accepted, but even the most compelling necessity cannot overcome the claim of privilege if the court is ultimately satisfied that military secrets are at stake.

Nothing approaching a definitive statement of the constitutional basis for executive privilege and the role of judicial review was forthcoming until the Watergate tapes case, *United States v. Nixon*, 418 U.S. 683 (1974). There the Court considered both whether the privilege was absolute and whether a specific exercise of the privilege was justified. Although the Court recognized a constitutional basis for the privilege—its relation to the effective discharge of presidential powers—it specifically rejected the dual notions that the privilege was absolute and that its exercise in particular cases was immune from judicial scrutiny. Rather, the legitimate needs of the judicial process (and presumably the legislative process also) may outweigh presidential privilege. More specifically, the Court held that although presidential communications are presumptively privileged, a generalized assertion of privilege must yield to a demonstrated specific need of constitutional dimensions, in this case the need (supported by the Sixth Amendment) for evidence in a pending criminal trial.   See generally *Symposium: United States v. Nixon,* 22 U.C.L.A. L. Rev. 1 (1974).

The relationship between the doctrine of executive privilege and the FOIA remains poorly defined.   Certain of the Act's exemptions codify various facets of the common law privilege: exemption 1 embodies at least part of the "state secrets" privilege; exemption 5 covers much, if not all, of the "official information" privilege; and exemption 9 deals with the informant's privilege, albeit obliquely.   However, material relating to military and foreign affairs, but not made confidential by statute, and information which should remain confidential "in the public interest"—two of Attorney General Rogers' claimed categories of privilege—are not mentioned (save as the latter may be covered by one or another of the remaining exemptions in particular instances).   Presumably, if executive privilege is constitutionally based and if the FOIA's stated exemptions do not exhaust the scope of the privilege, the declaration that its exemptions are exhaustive would have to give way.   The constitutional basis of the privilege might also be thought to render inappropriate the FOIA's allocation of the burden of proof in all cases to the executive department claiming exemption.   The *Reynolds* necessity doctrine suggests that the party requesting disclosure bears at least an initial burden of justification, and *Nixon v. Sirica* is not necessarily to the contrary.   But the latter case did not arise in an FOIA context, nor did it involve a specific claim of privilege.   The courts have yet to explore the significance of presidential approval of the precise terms of the Act itself.

In *Environmental Protection Agency v. Mink,* 410 U.S. 73 (1973), the court skirted an opportunity to address the possible collision between statutory directives to release information, such as the FOIA, and the Constitutional dimensions of executive privilege.   In holding that the courts could not review the reasonableness of executive classification of documents under exemption 1, the Court relied expressly on its understanding of the original FOIA.   It acknowledged that Congress could overturn that interpretation (as it soon did), while noting that Congress's power was inhibited by an undefined, yet Constitutionally-based, executive privilege.

Judicial Techniques for Monitoring Agency Compliance With the FOIA

Environmental Protection Agency v. Mink upheld, and Congress later confirmed, the courts' general authority to satisfy themselves personally that all non-exempt records are released.   In that case Congresswoman Patsy Mink and 32 other members of the House sued to obtain the report and recommendations of a high-level interdepartmental committee concerning a planned underground nuclear test at Amchitka Island, Alaska.   EPA, which had possession of the documents, resisted disclosure on the grounds that some were classified "in the interest of the national defense or foreign policy," and the remainder were covered by exemption 5. The Court held that the propriety of executive classification of documents was not subject to judicial review and, further, that the district court was not entitled to conduct an in camera inspection of classified documents to segregate their possible "nonsecret components." With respect to documents withheld under exemption 5, however, the Court made clear that segregable factual portions were subject to mandatory disclosure and that it would be appropriate for the district court to inspect them *in camera*, notwithstanding their top-level origin, if it was not satisfied that the government had justified withholding.

In one respect the debate over *in camera* inspection can be viewed as the procedural counterpart of the dispute over absolute executive privilege. The argument against *in camera* inspection roughly parallels the argument for denying judicial review in toto: The executive branch has a much surer feel for the types of disclosures that might injure the national interest than have district judges who confront these questions only occasionally and who cannot be fully aware of the implications of apparently innocuous data for other sensitive areas of executive branch operations. In *Mink* the Court came very close to accepting this argument for exemption 1 materials. The Congress, however, disagreed. The 1974 Freedom of Information Act Amendments expressly authorized *in camera* inspections with respect to "any" claimed exemption and also modified exemption 1 to make it clear that the exemption applies only to those documents that "are in fact properly classified pursuant to such Executive Order." President Ford vetoed the amendments on the ground that they unconstitutionally infringed the necessary discretion of the Executive to maintain secrecy in the national interest, but the Congress overrode his veto.

Beyond the constitutional issues, questions of judicial efficiency and workload are also at stake in a court's decision whether to engage in *in camera* inspection of withheld documents. In *Vaughan v. Rosen*, 484 F.2d 820 (D.C. Cir. 1973), *cert. denied* 415 U.S. 977 (1974), for example, a law professor sought all Civil Service Commission documents evaluating government personnel management programs. The CSC denied the request and justified its posture in an affidavit merely asserting that all the documents were protected by at least one of several exemptions. Faced with the prospect of reviewing voluminous documents to determine the validity of this claim, the district court accepted the agency's affidavit as sufficient proof of exemption, but the court of appeals reversed. In its view the district court should have required the agency to submit a particularized analysis that correlated the claimed exemptions with the documents or portions of documents purportedly exempted from disclosure. Otherwise broad agency claims of exemption covering voluminous documents would destroy the capacity of the district courts to engage in a serious *de novo* review of claimed exemptions. Should inspection be necessary after receipt of the agency's detailed justification for its refusal to disclose, the district court was advised that it might appoint a special master to assist.

See also *Ash Grove Cement Co. v. FTC*, 371 F. Supp. 370, 373 (D.D.C. 1973), where the courts, after initially refusing to examine the demanded materials until the FTC described with particularity each document for which it claimed an exemption, accepted the agency's affidavit as sufficient to render *in camera* inspection unnecessary. The affidavit listed each document, described its contents, and indicated which division of the agency authorized the document, which received it, and what was discussed in it. The court concluded that "to require a more detailed affidavit * * * would be tantamount to requiring full disclosure of the substance of the documents."

Resistance to *in camera* inspections need not be predicated wholly on separation of powers or judicial efficiency grounds. Such inspections are necessarily *ex parte* and, therefore, may provide less opportunity for a requesting party to know and meet the agency's claims than would a particularized affidavit. Together these considerations suggest that there is much more to the *in camera* inspections issue than simply the need of the judiciary for "the facts" upon which it may base a de novo finding. For a useful discussion, see Comment, *In Camera Inspections Under the Freedom of Information Act*, 41 U. Chi. L. Rev. 557 (1974).

Scope of Judicial Discretion to Refuse to Order Mandatory Disclosures

Cases under the FOIA sometimes present a court with disputes in which the adverse consequences of disclosure seem to dwarf the importance of the requester's interest in the records at issue. In such cases, a court may be tempted to search for a rationale to justify the agency's decision to withhold. The case law, however, generally supports the proposition that such rationales must be found within the Act's nine exemptions; courts apparently retain no discretion to refuse to order disclosure of nonexempt records. In the words of Judge Butzner in *Wellford v. Hardin*, 444 F.2d 21, 25 (4th Cir. 1971): "It is not the province of the courts to restrict that legislative judgment under the guise of judicially balancing the same interests that Congress has considered." But see *Federal Open Market Committee v. Merrill*, supra p. 582.

The court's refusal to balance "the same interests Congress has considered" may be viewed as a renunciation of the traditional discretion of a court of equity to determine whether an available remedy should, under all the circumstances, be granted. This narrow view of the judicial function under the FOIA is supported by the language of section 552(c), but subsection (a)(3) states merely that the district courts have "jurisdiction to enjoin" the withholding of records, not that the courts "shall" enjoin such withholding in every case. Nor does the legislative history speak unmistakably on this issue. The Senate Report accompanying the original Act, for example, states generally that "[i]t is essential that agency personnel, *and the courts as well*, be given definitive guidelines in setting information policies." S. Rep. No. 813, 89th Cong., 1st Sess. 3 (1965) (emphasis added). By contrast, the House Report states: "The Court will have authority *whenever it considers such action equitable and appropriate* to enjoin the agency from withholding its records." H. R. Rep. No. 1497, 89th Cong., 2d Sess. 9 (1966) (emphasis added).

In *Soucie v. David*, 448 F.2d 1067, 1077 (D.C. Cir. 1971), the court opined that "Congress did not intend to confer on district courts a general power to deny relief on equitable grounds apart from the exemptions in the Act itself," language repeated in *Getman v. NLRB*, 450 F.2d 670, 678 (D.C. Cir. 1971), and echoed in *Wellford*. However, in *Consumers Union v. Veterans Administration*, 301 F. Supp. 796, 808 (S.D.N.Y. 1969), the court refused to require release of a VA scoring system and quality index for hearing aids because in the court's view "the danger of the public being misled * * * and the disruption of the VA programs that [disclosure] * * * would cause outweighs any benefits." See also *General Services Administration v. Benson*, 415 F.2d 878, 880 (9th Cir. 1969).

In *Renegotiation Board v. Bannercraft Clothing Co.*, 415 U.S. 1 (1974), three contractors involved in separate renegotiation proceedings obtained a district court injunction barring further proceedings until the Board complied with their FOIA requests for disclosure of pertinent records. Although it acknowledged that the district court had power under the FOIA to issue such an injunction, the Supreme Court, divided five to four, held that the contractors were required to exhaust their administrative remedies (i.e., to complete the renegotiation proceedings) before invoking the equity power of the district court. The FOIA, according to the majority, was not intended "to change the Renegotiation Act's purposeful design of negotiation without interruption for judicial review." 415 U.S. at 22.

The relationship between ongoing agency proceedings and contemporaneous demands for records claimed to be germane to their outcome was also at issue in *Forsham v. Harris*, 445 U.S. 169 (1980). The narrow question was whether data recorded by private clinicians engaged in a federally-funded study of drugs for diabetes constituted "agency records" subject to mandatory disclosure under the FOIA. Investigators from both the sponsoring institute and the FDA were legally entitled to have access to the data to verify the study findings, and the FDA had proposed major changes in the labeling of the drugs based on those findings as reported. The plaintiffs were several prominent diabetologists who sought access to the actual patient records because of suggestions that the reported findings, indicating that the drugs might *increase* patients' risk of heart attack, were erroneous and possibly even fraudulent. The Court held, that notwithstanding the agencies' financial support of the study and their right to obtain access to the data, the records could not be considered "agency records" subject to FOIA because they belonged to and remained in the custody of the investigators and study coordinator. But it did not disagree with the court of appeals' statement that the FDA would have to make public the key portions of the study records if it ultimately decided to issue a rule based on the reported study results. *Forsham v. Califano*, 587 F.2d 1128 (D.C. Cir. 1978); Cf. *United States v. Nova Scotia Food Products*, 568 F.2d 240 (2d Cir. 1977); *Wirtz v. Baldor Elec-*

tric, 337 F.2d 518 (D.C. Cir. 1963). See also *Kissinger v. Reporters Committee for Freedom of the Press,* 445 U.S. 136 (1980) (holding that materials delivered to the Library of Congress were no longer "agency records").

NLRB v. ROBBINS TIRE & RUBBER CO.

Supreme Court of the United States, 1978.
437 U.S. 214, 98 S.Ct. 2311, 57 L. Ed. 2d 159

MR. JUSTICE MARSHALL delivered the opinion of the Court.

The question presented is whether the Freedom of Information Act (FOIA) requires the National Labor Relations Board to disclose, prior to its hearing on an unfair labor practice complaint, statements of witnesses whom the Board intends to call at the hearing. Resolution of this question depends on whether production of the material prior to the hearing would "interfere with enforcement proceedings" within the meaning of Exemption 7(A) of FOIA.

I

Following a contested representation election in a unit of respondent's employees, the Acting Regional Director of the NLRB issued an unfair labor practice complaint charging respondent with having committed numerous violations of § 8(a)(1) of the National Labor Relations Act (NLRA), during the pre-election period. A hearing on the complaint was scheduled for April 27, 1976. On March 31, 1976, respondent wrote to the Acting Regional Director and requested, pursuant to FOIA, that he make available for inspection and copying, at least seven days prior to the hearing, copies of all potential witnesses' statements collected during the Board's investigation. The Acting Regional Director denied this request on April 2, on the ground that this material was exempt from the disclosure requirements of FOIA. * * * He placed particular reliance on Exemption 7(A), which provides that disclosure is not required of "matters that are * * * investigatory records compiled for law enforcement purposes, but only to the extent that the production of such records would * * * interfere with enforcement proceedings."

Respondent appealed to the Board's General Counsel. Before expiration of the 20-day period within which FOIA requires such appeals to be decided, respondent filed this action in the United States District Court for the Northern District of Alabama, pursuant to 5 U.S.C.A. § 552(a)(4)(B). The complaint sought not only disclosure of the statements, but also a preliminary injunction against proceeding with the unfair labor practice hearing pending final adjudication of the FOIA claim and a permanent injunction against holding the hearing until the documents had been disclosed. * * * The District Court held that, since the Board did not claim that release of the documents at issue would pose any unique or unusual danger of interference with this particular enforcement proceeding, Exemption 7(A) did not apply. It therefore directed the Board to provide the statements for copying on or before April 22, 1976, or at least five days before any hearing where the person making the statement would be called as a witness.

On the Board's appeal, the United States Court of Appeals for the Fifth Circuit commenced its discussion by observing that while "[t]his is a [FOIA] case, * * * it takes on the troubling coloration of a dispute about the discovery rights * * * in [NLRB] proceedings." It concluded * * * that the legislative history of certain amendments to FOIA in 1874 demonstrated that Exemption 7(A) was to be available only where there was a specific evidentiary showing of the possibility of actual interference in an individual case.

* * *

The Board filed a petition for a writ of certiorari, seeking review, *inter alia*, of the Exemption 7(A) ruling below, on the ground that the decision was in conflict with the weight of Circuit authority that had followed the lead of the United States Court of Appeals for the Second Circuit in *Title Guarantee Co. v. NLRB*, 534 F.2d 484, cert. denied, 429 U.S. 834 (1976). There, on similar facts, the court held that statements of employees and union representatives obtained in an NLRB investigation leading to an unfair labor practice charge were exempt from disclosure under Exemption 7(A) until the completion of all reasonably foreseeable administrative and judicial proceedings on the charge. Rejecting the employer's contention that the Board must make a particularized showing of likely interference in each individual case, the Second Circuit found that such interference would "necessarily" result from the production of the statements.

We granted certiorari to resolve the conflict among the Circuits on this important question of federal statutory law. We now reverse the judgment of the Fifth Circuit.

II

* * *

Exemption 7 as originally enacted permitted nondisclosure of "investigatory files compiled for law enforcement purposes except to the extent available by law to a private party." In 1974, this exemption was rewritten to permit the nondisclosure of "investigatory records compiled for law enforcement purposes," but only to the extent that producing such records would involve one of six specified dangers. The first of these, with which we are here concerned, is that production of the records would "interfere with enforcement proceedings."

* * *

The starting point of our analysis is with the language and structure of the statute. We can find little support in the language of the statute itself for respondent's view that determinations of "interference" under Exemption 7(A) can be made only on a case-by-case basis. Indeed, the literal language of Exemption 7 as a whole tends to suggest that the contrary is true. The Exemption applies to:

"investigatory records compiled for law enforcement purposes, but only to the extent that the production of such records would (A) interfere with enforcement proceedings, (B) deprive a person of a right to a fair trial or an impartial adjudication, (C) constitute an unwarranted invasion of personal privacy, (D) disclose the identity of a confidential source and, in the case of a record compiled by a criminal law enforcement authority in the course of a criminal investigation, or by an agency conducting a lawful national security intelligence investigation, confidential information furnished only by the confidential source, (E) disclose investigative techniques and procedures, or (F) endanger the life or physical safety of law enforcement personnel."

There is a readily apparent difference between subdivision (A) and subdivisions (B), (C), and (D). The latter subdivisions refer to particular cases—"a person," "an unwarranted invasion," "a confidential source"— and thus seem to require a showing that the factors made relevant by the statute are present in each distinct situation. By contrast, since subdivision (A) speaks in the plural voice about "enforcement proceedings," it appears to contemplate that certain generic determinations might be made.

Respondent points to other provisions of FOIA in support of its interpretation. It suggests that, because FOIA expressly provides for disclosure of segregable portions of records and for *in camera* review of documents, and because the statute places the burden of justifying nondisclosure on the Government, the Act necessarily contemplates that the Board must specifically demonstrate in each case that disclosure of the particular witness' statement would interfere with a pending enforcement proceeding. We cannot agree. The *in camera* review provision is discretionary by its terms, and is designed to be invoked when the issue before the District Court could not be otherwise resolved; it thus does not mandate that the documents be individually examined in every case. Similarly, although the segregability provision requires that nonexempt portions of documents be released, it does not speak to the prior question of what material is exempt. Finally, the mere fact that the burden is on the Government to justify nondisclosure does not, in our view, aid the inquiry as to what kind of burden the Government bears.

* * *

In originally enacting Exemption 7, Congress recognized that law enforcement agencies had legitimate needs to keep certain records confidential, lest the agencies be hindered in their investigations or placed at a disadvantage when it came time to present their cases. Foremost among the purposes of this Exemption was to prevent "harm [to] the Government's case in court," S. Rep. No. 813, 89th Cong., 1st Sess. (1965), by not allowing litigants "earlier or greater access" to agency investigatory files than they would otherwise have. Indeed, in an unusual, post-passage reconsideration vote, the Senate modified the language of this Exemption specifically to meet Senator Humphrey's concern that it might be construed to require disclosure of "statements of agency witnesses" prior to the time they were called on to testify in agency proceedings.

Senator Humphrey was particularly concerned that the initial version of the Exemption passed by the Senate might be "susceptible to the interpretation that once a complaint of unfair labor practice is filed by the General Counsel of the NLRB, access could be had to the statements of all witnesses, whether or not these statements are relied upon to support the complaint." * * *

In light of this history, the Board is clearly correct that the 1966 Act was expressly intended to protect against the mandatory disclosure through FOIA of witnesses' statements prior to an unfair labor practice proceeding. * * *

In 1974 Congress acted to amend FOIA in several respects. The move to amend was prompted largely by congressional disapproval of our decision in *EPA v. Mink*, 410 U.S. 73 (1973), regarding the availability of *in camera* review of classified documents. Congress was also concerned that administrative agencies were being dilatory in complying with the spirit of the Act and with court decisions interpreting FOIA to mandate disclosure of information to the public. As the amending legislation was reported out of the respective Committees, no change in Exemption 7 was recommended. The 1974 amendment of Exemption 7 resulted instead from a proposal on the floor by Senator [Philip] Hart during Senate debate.

* * *

* * * [T]he thrust of congressional concern in its amendment of Exemption 7 was to make clear that the Exemption did not endlessly protect material simply because it was in an investigatory file. * * *

In the face of this history, respondent relies on Senator Hart's floor statement that "it is only relevant" to determine whether an interference would result "in the context of the particular enforcement proceeding." Respondent argues that this statement means that in each case the court must determine whether the material of which disclosure is sought would actually reveal the Government's case prematurely, result in witness intimidation, or otherwise create a demonstrable interference with the particular case.

We believe that respondent's reliance on this statement is misplaced. Although Congress could easily have required in so many words that the Government in each case show a particularized risk to its individual "enforcement proceedin[g]," it did not do so; the statute, if anything, seems to draw a distinction in this respect between subdivision (A) and subdivisions (B), (C), and (D). Senator Hart's words are ambiguous, moreover, and must be read in light of his primary concern: that by extending blanket protection to anything labeled an investigatory file, the D.C. Circuit had ignored Congress' original intent. His remarks plainly do not preclude a court from considering whether "particular" *types* of enforcement proceedings, such as NLRB unfair labor practice proceedings, will be interfered with by particular types of disclosure.

* * *

What Congress clearly did have in mind was that Exemption 7 permit nondisclosure only where the Government "specif[ies]" that one of the six enumerated harms is present, and the court, reviewing the question *de novo*, agrees that one of those six "reasons" for nondisclosure applies. Thus, where an agency fails to "demonstrat[e] that the * * * documents [sought] relate to any ongoing investigation or- * * * would jeopardize any future law enforcement proceedings," Exemption 7(A) would not provide protection to the agency's decision. While the Court of Appeals was correct that the amendment of Exemption 7 was designed to eliminate "blanket exemptions" for Government records simply because they were found in investigatory files compiled for law enforcement purposes, we think it erred in concluding that no generic determinations of likely interference can ever be made. We conclude that Congress did not intend to prevent the federal courts from determining that, with respect to particular kinds of enforcement proceedings, disclosure of particular kinds of investigatory records while a case is pending would generally "interfere with enforcement proceedings."

III

The remaining question is whether the Board has met its burden of demonstrating that disclosure of the potential witnesses' statements at this time "would interfere with enforcement proceedings." A proper resolution of this question requires us to weigh the strong presumption in favor of disclosure under FOIA against the likelihood that disclosure at this time would disturb the existing balance of relations in unfair labor practice proceedings, a delicate balance that Congress has deliberately sought to preserve and that the Board maintains is essential to the effective enforcement of the NLRA. Although reasonable arguments can be made on both sides of this issue, for the reasons that follow we conclude that witness statements in pending unfair labor practice proceedings are exempt from FOIA disclosure at least until completion of the Board's hearing.

Historically, the NLRB has provided little prehearing discovery in unfair labor practice proceedings and has relied principally on statements such as those sought here to prove its case. While the NLRB's discovery policy has been criticized, the Board's position that § 6 of the NLRA, 29 U.S.C. § 156, commits the formulation of discovery practice to its discretion has generally been sustained by the lower courts. A profound alteration in the Board's trial strategy in unfair labor practice cases would thus be effectuated if the Board were required, in every case in which witnesses' statements were sought under FOIA prior to an unfair labor practice proceeding, to make a particularized showing that release of these statements would interfere with the proceeding.[17]

---

17. If the Court of Appeals' ruling below were not reversed, the Board anticipated that prehearing requests for witnesses' statements under FOIA would be made by employer-respondents in virtually all unfair labor practice proceedings.

Not only would this change the substantive discovery rules, but it would do so through mechanisms likely to cause substantial delays in the adjudication of unfair labor practice charges. In addition to having a duty under FOIA to provide public access to its processes, the NLRB is charged with the duty of effectively investigating and prosecuting violations of the labor laws. To meet its latter duty, the Board can be expected to continue to claim exemptions with regard to prehearing FOIA discovery requests, and numerous court contests will thereby ensue. Unlike ordinary discovery contests, where rulings are generally not appealable until the conclusion of the proceedings, an agency's denial of an FOIA request is immediately reviewable in the district court, and the district court's decision can then be reviewed in the court of appeals. The potential for delay and for restructuring of the NLRB's routine adjudications of unfair labor practice charges from requests like respondent's is thus not insubstantial.

* * *

The most obvious risk of "interference" with enforcement proceedings in this context is that employers or, in some cases, unions will coerce or intimidate employees and others who have given statements, in an effort to make them change their testimony or not testify at all. This special danger flowing from prehearing discovery in NLRB proceedings has been recognized by the courts for many years, and formed the basis for Senator Humphrey's particular concern. Indeed, Congress recognized this danger in the NLRA itself, and provided in § 8(a)(4) that it is an unfair labor practice for an employer "to discharge or otherwise discriminate against an employee because he has filed charges or given testimony under this subchapter. Respondent's argument that employers will be deterred from improper intimidation of employees who provide statements to the NLRB by the possibility of a § 8(a)(4) charge misses the point of Exemption 7(A); the possibility of deterrence arising from *post hoc* disciplinary action is no substitute for a prophylactic rule that prevents the harm to a pending enforcement proceeding which flows from a witness' having been intimidated.[19]

The danger of witness intimidation is particularly acute with respect to current employees—whether rank and file, supervisory, or managerial — over whom the employer, by virtue of the employment relationship, may exercise intense leverage. Not only can the employer fire the employee, but job assignments can be switched, hours can be adjusted, wage and salary increases held up, and other more subtle forms of influence exerted. A union can often exercise similar authority over its members and officers. * * * While the risk of intimidation (at least from employers) may be somewhat diminished with regard to statements that are favor-

---

19. Respondent argues that the relatively small percentage of unfair labor practice charges filed under § 8(a)(4) demonstrates that the Board's justifications for its nondisclosure rules are illusory. But the small percentage may reflect the effectiveness of the intimidation, rather than any lack thereof. It may also reflect the success of the Board's current policy.

able to the employer, those known to have already given favorable statements are then subject to pressure to give even more favorable testimony.

Furthermore, both employees and nonemployees may be reluctant to give statements to NLRB investigators at all, absent assurances that unless called to testify in a hearing, their statements will be exempt from disclosure until the unfair labor practice charge has been adjudicated. Such reluctance may flow less from a witness' desire to maintain complete confidentiality—the concern of Exemption 7(D)—than from an all too familiar unwillingness to "get too involved" unless absolutely necessary. Since the vast majority of the Board's unfair labor practice proceedings are resolved short of hearing, without any need to disclose witness statements, those currently giving statements to Board investigators can have some assurance that in most instances their statements will not be made public (at least until after the investigation and any adjudication is complete).[20] The possibility that an FOIA-induced change in the Board's prehearing discovery rules will have a chilling effect on the Board's sources cannot be ignored.[21]

In short, prehearing disclosure of witnesses' statements would involve the kind of harm that Congress believed would constitute an "interference" with NLRB enforcement proceedings: that of giving a party litigant earlier and greater access to the Board's case than he would otherwise have. * * * While those drafting discovery rules for the Board might determine that this "interference" is one that should be tolerated in order to promote a fairer decisionmaking process, that is not our task in construing FOIA.

The basic purpose of FOIA is to ensure an informed citizenry, vital to the functioning of a democratic society, needed to check against corruption and to hold the governors accountable to the governed. Respondent concedes that it seeks those statements solely for litigation discovery purposes, and that FOIA was *not* intended to function as a private discovery tool. Most, if not all, persons who have sought prehearing disclosure of Board witnesses' statements have been in precisely this posture—parties respondent in Board proceedings.[23] Since we are dealing here with the narrow question whether witnesses' statements must be released five days prior to an unfair labor practice hearing, we cannot see how FOIA's

---

20. According to the Board, 94% of all unfair labor practice charges filed are resolved short of hearing; in the remaining 6% that go to hearing, many potential witnesses are not actually called to testify, since their testimony is cumulative.

21. Respondent argues that the Court of Appeals was correct in concluding that this danger is nonexistent with respect to a witness scheduled to testify, since the Board under its own discovery rules will turn over those statements once the witness has actually testified. This argument falters, first, on the fact that only those portions of the witness' statements relating to his direct examination or the issues raised in the pleadings are disclosed under the Board's discovery rules. In addition, to uphold respondent's FOIA request would doubtless require the Board in many cases to turn over statements of persons whom it did not actually call at the adjudicatory hearings.

23. This is not to suggest that respondent's rights are in any way diminished by its being a private litigant, but neither are they enhanced by respondent's particular, litigation-generated need for these materials.

purposes would be defeated by deferring disclosure until after the Government has "presented its case in court." * * *

The judgment of the Court of Appeals is, accordingly,

Reversed.

[The concurring opinion of Justice Stevens, joined by the Chief Justice and Justice Rehnquist, is omitted.]

MR. JUSTICE POWELL, with whom MR. JUSTICE BRENNAN joins, concurring in part and dissenting in part.

* * * I cannot accept the Court's approval of the application of the Board's rule of nondisclosure to *all* witness statements, unless and until a witness gives direct testimony before an administrative law judge.   And I disagree with the Court's apparent interpretation of Exemption 7(A) as providing no "earlier or greater access" to records than that available under the discovery rules that an agency chooses to promulgate.   There is no persuasive evidence that Congress in 1974 intended to authorize federal agencies to withhold all FOIA-requested material in pending proceedings by invoking restrictive rules of discovery promulgated under their "housekeeping" rulemaking authority.

* * *

* * * Exemption 7(A) requires that the Board demonstrate a reasonable possibility that disclosure would "interfere with enforcement proceedings * * * ."   In my view, absent a particularized showing of likely interference, statements of all witnesses—other than current employees in proceedings against employers (or union members in proceedings against unions)—are subject to the statutory presumption in favor of disclosure. In contrast to the situation of current employees or union members, there simply is no basis for presuming a particular likelihood of employer interference with union representatives or others not employed by the charged party, or, in a proceeding against a union, of union interference with employer representatives and other nonmembers of the union or the bargaining unit.   Similarly, I am unwilling to presume interference with respect to disclosure of favorable statements by current employees, and would require the Board to show a reasonable possibility of employer reprisal.

I do not read the Act to authorize agencies to adopt or adhere to nonstatutory rules barring all prehearing disclosure of investigatory records.   The Court reasons that such disclosure—which is deemed "premature" only because it is in advance of the time of release set by the agency—will enable "suspected violators * * * to learn the Board's case in advance and frustrate the proceedings or construct defenses which would permit violations to go unremedied. * * * "   This assumption is not only inconsistent with the congressional judgment expressed in the Federal Rules of Civil Procedure that "trial by ambush," well may disserve the cause of truth, but it also threatens to undermine the Act's overall presumption of disclosure, at least during the pendency of enforcement proceedings.

There may be exceptional cases that would permit the Board to withhold all witness statements for the duration of an unfair labor practice proceeding. Such a situation could arise where prehearing revelation would divulge incompletely developed information which, if prematurely disclosed, may interfere with the proceedings before the Board, or where the facts of a case suggest a strong likelihood that the charged party will attempt to interfere with any and all of the Board's witnesses. The Act requires, however, that the Board convince a federal court that there is a reasonable possibility of this kind of interference. * * *

Notes

1. Although most of the FOIA exemptions are couched in categorical rather than contextual terms—embodying legislative judgments about the appropriate balance between access and confidentiality—a few, like exemption 6 and exemption 7(A) and (D), appear to require some balancing to determine whether or not records are disclosable. The FOIA's directives that courts shall review agency denials *de novo*, and that agencies bear the burden of justifying withholding would seem to accord agencies little, if any, room to strike this balance themselves. But is this not precisely what the NLRB has accomplished through its discovery rules, which the Court upholds in *Robbins Tire?*

Judicial willingness to recognize any "generic" exclusions under an exemption that appears to call for balancing appears destined to accord some deference to the agency's initial striking of the balance. Is it not inevitable that an agency will have a comparative advantage in assessing the likely consequences of disclosure of documents of a particular kind? Surely the agency is likely to have had more experience with the clientele who seek such documents.

On the other hand, the interpretation of exemption 7(A) urged by the respondent—requiring the NLRB to demonstrate that disclosure of specific documents would interfere with a specific pending proceeding—would have significant implications for the courts as well as the Board. Unless the Board were to revise its judgment that disclosure of witness statements would often interfere with its enforcement efforts, it would routinely decline FOIA requests. Many of those denials would be litigated, requiring in each instance a district judge to determine after a hearing whether disclosure of the demanded materials would interfere with a pending unfair labor practice proceeding. Quite apart from the impact on NLRB enforcement, would not such a result significantly "interfere" with the performance of the judiciary?

2. *Robbins Tire* illustrates a context of government information gathering in which the agency has a strong incentive not only to claim exemption from the FOIA, but a strong incentive to assert that claim in all cases where it has plausability. The records at issue are assembled after a complaint for the specific purpose of possible enforcement action, rather than in the course of routine inquiry that yields vast quantities of paper only a small part of which will ever have use. In many circumstances, however, an agency's interest in preserving the confidentiality of materials obtained from third parties is considerably less than in *Robbins Tire*. An agency may have little at stake in disclosure—save as its inability to safeguard providers' interests in confidentiality may undermine their willingness to provide the information voluntarily. See *National Parks and Conservation Association v. Morton*, 498 F.2d 765 (D.C. Cir. 1974).

4. PROTECTING PRIVATE INTERESTS IN INFORMATION IN THE GOVERNMENT'S POSSESSION

The FOIA represents an emphatic statement in favor of general public access to information in the government's possession. But it is not surprising to find that persons who relinquish information to the government, whether voluntarily or under compulsion, are often reluctant to have it seen by anyone else. The kinds of information sought to be protected range from personal records about private individuals to the practices of businesses to scientific studies of new products and technologies. The motives of providers to prevent public access even as they yield information to the government are obvious and, in some instances, compelling.

Exemptions 4 and 6 of the FOIA evidence Congress' recognition that other interests sometimes override the public interest in knowledge of government plans and actions. And numerous federal statutes prescribe confidential treatment for categories of information in government hands. Notable examples are the Privacy Act of 1974 and 18 U.S.C.A. § 1905, which makes it a criminal offense for government officials, without legal authorization, to disclose trade secret information acquired in performing their duties. But the FOIA exemptions merely relieve an agency of the obligation to disclose in response to a request; they do not demand that an agency keep exempt material secret. Moreover, the effectiveness of prohibitions against disclosure found in section 1905 and other statutes depends, in the first instance, on the willingness of other government officials—in the Department of Justice—to enforce them against violators. In these circumstances, it is not surprising that providers of information to the government have sought more effective measures to protect their interests in confidentiality.

CHRYSLER CORP. v. BROWN

Supreme Court of the United States, 1979.
441 U.S. 281, 99 S.Ct. 1705, 60 L. Ed. 2d 208.

MR. JUSTICE REHNQUIST delivered the opinion of the Court.

* * *

This case belongs to a class that has been popularly denominated "reverse-FOIA" suits. The Chrysler Corp. (hereinafter Chrysler) seeks to enjoin agency disclosure on the grounds that it is inconsistent with the FOIA and 18 U.S.C.A. § 1905, a criminal statute with origins in the 19th century that proscribes disclosure of certain classes of business and personal information. We agree with the Court of Appeals for the Third Circuit that the FOIA is purely a disclosure statute and affords Chrysler no private right of action to enjoin agency disclosure. But we cannot agree with that court's conclusion that this disclosure is "authorized by law" within the meaning of § 1905. Therefore, we vacate the Court of Appeals' judgment and remand so that it can consider whether the documents at issue in this case fall within the terms of § 1905.

As a party to numerous Government contracts, Chrysler is required to comply with Executive Orders 11246 and 11375, which charge the Secretary of Labor with ensuring that corporations that benefit from Government contracts provide equal employment opportunity regardless of race or sex. The U.S. Department of Labor's Office of Federal Contract Compliance Programs (OFCCP) has promulgated regulations which require Government contractors to furnish reports and other information about their affirmative-action programs and the general composition of their work forces.

The Defense Logistics Agency (DLA) * * * of the Department of Defense is the designated compliance agency responsible for monitoring Chrysler's employment practices. OFCCP regulations require that Chrysler make available to this agency written affirmative action programs (APP's) and annually submit Employer Information Reports, known as EEO-1 Reports. * * *

Regulations promulgated by the Secretary of Labor provide for public disclosure of information from records of the OFCCP and its compliance agencies. Those regulations state that notwithstanding exemption from mandatory disclosure under the FOIA, 5 U.S.C.A. § 552,

> "records obtained or generated pursuant to Executive Order 11246 (as amended) * * * shall be made available for inspection and copying * * * if it is determined that the requested inspection or copying furthers the public interest and does not impede any of the functions of the OFCC[P] or the Compliance Agencies except in the case of records disclosure of which is prohibited by law."

It is the voluntary disclosure contemplated by this regulation, over and above that by the FOIA, which is the gravamen of Chrysler's complaint in this case.

This controversy began on May 14, 1975, when the DLA informed Chrysler that third parties had made an FOIA request for disclosure of the 1974 AAP for Chrysler's Newark, Del., assembly plant and an October 1974 CIR [Complaint Investigation Report] for the same facility. Nine days later Chrysler objected to release of the requested information, relying on OFCCP's disclosure regulations and on exemptions to the FOIA. Chrysler also requested a copy of the CIR, since it had never seen it. DLA responded the following week that it had determined that the requested material was subject to disclosure under the FOIA and the OFCCP disclosure rules, and that both documents would be released five days later.

On the day the documents were to be released Chrysler filed a complaint in the United States District Court for Delaware seeking to enjoin release of the Newark documents. * * *

Chrysler made three arguments in support of its prayer for an injunction: that disclosure was barred by the FOIA; that it was inconsistent with 18 U.S.C.A. § 1905, 42 U.S.C.A. § 2000e-8(e), and 44 U.S.C.A. § 3508, which for ease of reference will be referred to as the "confidentiality statutes"; and finally that disclosure was an abuse of agency discretion insofar as it conflicted with OFCCP rules. * * *

* * *

In contending that the FOIA bars disclosure of the requested equal employment opportunity information, Chrysler relies on the Act's nine exemptions and argues that they require an agency to withhold exempted material.   In this case it relies specifically on Exemption 4:

"(b) [FOIA] does not apply to matters that are—

* * *

"(4) trade secrets and commercial or financial information obtained from a person and privileged or confidential * * * ."

Chrylser contends that the nine exemptions in general, and Exemption 4 in particular, reflect a sensitivity to the privacy interests of private individuals and nongovernmental entities.   That contention may be conceded without inexorably requiring the conclusion that the exemptions impose affirmative duties on an agency to withhold information sought.   In fact, that conclusion is not supported by the language, logic, or history of the Act.

The organization of the Act is straightforward.   Subsection (a), 5 U.S.C.A. § 552(a), places a general obligation on the agency to make information available to the public and sets out specific modes of disclosure for certain classes of information.   Subsection (b), 5 U.S.C.A. § 552(b), which lists the exemptions, simply states that the specified material is not subject to the disclosure obligations set out in subsection (a).   By its terms, subsection (b) demarcates the agency's obligation to disclose; it does not foreclose disclosure.

That the FOIA is exclusively a disclosure statute is, perhaps, demonstrated most convincingly by examining its provision for judicial relief. Subsection (a)(4)(B) gives federal district courts "jurisdiction to enjoin the agency from withholding agency records and to order the production of any agency records improperly withheld from the complainant." 5 U.S.C.A. § 552 (a)(4)(B).   That provision does not give the authority to bar disclosure * * * .   Congress appreciated that, with the expanding sphere of governmental regulation and enterprise, much of the information within Government files has been submitted by private entities seeking Government contracts or responding to unconditional reporting obligations imposed by law.   There was sentiment that Government agencies should have the latitude, in certain circumstances, to afford the confidentiality desired by these submitters.   But the Congressional concern was the *agency's* need or preference for confidentiality; the FOIA by itself protects the submitters' interest in confidentiality only to the extent that this interest is endorsed by the agency collecting the information.

* * *

This conclusion is further supported by the legislative history. * * *

We therefore conclude that Congress did not limit an agency's discretion to disclose information when it enacted the FOIA. It necessarily follows that the Act does not afford Chrysler any right to enjoin agency disclosure.

Chrysler contends, however, that even if its suit for injunctive relief cannot be based on the FOIA, such an action can be premised on the Trade Secrets Act, 18 U.S.C.A. § 1905. The act provides:

> "Whoever, being an officer or employee of the United States or of any department or agency thereof, publishes, divulges, discloses, or makes known in any manner or to any extent not authorized by law any information coming to him in the course of his employment or official duties or by reason of any examination or investigation made by, or return, report or record made to or filed with, such department or agency or officer or employee thereof, which information concerns or relates to the trade secrets, processes, operations, style of work, or apparatus, or to the identity, confidential statistical data, amount or source of any income, profits, losses, or expenditures of any person, firm, partnership, corporation, or association; or permits any income return or copy thereof or any book containing any abstract or particulars thereof to be seen or examined by any person except as provided by law; shall be fined not more than $1,000, or imprisoned not more than one year, or both; and shall be removed from office or employment."

There are necessarily two parts to Chrysler's argument: that § 1905 is applicable to the type of disclosure threatened in this case, and that it affords Chrysler a private right of action to obtain injunctive relief.

The Court of Appeals held that § 1905 was not applicable to the agency disclosure at issue here because such disclosure was "authorized by law" within the meaing of the Act. The court found the source of that authorization to be the OFCCP regulations that DLA relied on in deciding to disclose information on the Hamtramck and Newark plants. Chrysler contends here that these agency regulations are not "law" within the meaning of § 1905.

* * *

The regulations relied on by the respondents in this case as providing "authoriz[ation] by law" within the meaning of § 1905 certainly affect individual rights and obligations; they govern the public's right to information in records obtained under Executive Order 11246 and the confidentiality rights of those who submit information to OFCCP and its compliance agencies. It is a much closer question, however, whether they are the product of a congressional grant of legislative authority.

* * * Since materials that are exempt from disclosure under the FOIA are * * * outside the ambit of that Act, the Government cannot rely on the FOIA as congressional authorization for disclosure regulations that permit the release of information within the Act's nine exemptions.

* * *

The relationship between any grant of legislative authority and the disclosure regulations becomes more remote when one examines § 201 of the Executive Order. It speaks in terms of rules and regulations "necessary and appropriate" to achieve the purposes of the Executive Order. Those purposes are an end to discrimination in employment by the Federal Government and those who deal with the Federal Government. One cannot readily pull from the logic and purposes of the Executive Order any concern with the public's access to information in Government files or the importance of protecting trade secrets or confidential business statistics.

*   *   *

The respondents argue, however, that even if these regulations do not have the force of law by virtue of Executive Order 11246, an explicit grant of legislative authority for such regulations can be found in 5 U.S.C.A. § 301, commonly referred to as the "housekeeping statute." It provides:

> "The head of an Executive department or military department may prescribe regulations for the government of his department, the conduct of its employees, the distribution and performance of its business, and the custody, use, and preservation of its records, papers, and property. This section does not authorize withholding information from the public or limiting the availability of records to the public."

The antecedents of § 301 go back to the beginning of the Republic, when statutes were enacted to give heads of early Government departments authority to govern internal departmental affairs. * * *

* * * [T]here is nothing in the legislative history of § 301 to indicate it is a substantive grant of legislative power to promulgate rules authorizing the *release* of trade secrets or confidential business information. It is indeed a "housekeeping statute," authorizing what the APA terms "rules of agency organization, procedure or practice" as opposed to "substantive rules."

This would suggest that regulations pursuant to § 301 could not provide the "authoriz[ation] by law" required by § 1905. * * *

*   *   *

We reject [as well] Chrysler's contention that the Trade Secrets Act affords a private right of action to enjoin disclosure in violation of the statute. In *Cort v. Ash*, 422 U.S. 66 (1975) [infra p. 861], we noted that this Court has rarely implied a private right of action under a criminal statute, and where it has done so "there was at least a statutory basis for inferring that a civil cause of action of some sort lay in favor of someone." Nothing in § 1905 prompts such an inference. Nor are other pertinent circumstances outlined in *Cort* present here. As our review of the legislative history of § 1905—or lack of same—might suggest, there is no indication of legislative intent to create a private right of action. Most importantly, a private right of action under § 1905 is not "necessary to make effective the congressional purpose," for we find that review of DLA's decision to disclose Chrysler's employment data is available under the APA.

While Chrysler may not avail itself of any violations of the provisions of § 1905 in a separate cause of action, any such violations may have a dispositive effect on the outcome of judicial review of agency action pursuant to § 10 of the APA. Section 10(a) of the APA provides that "[a] person suffering legal wrong because of agency action, or adversely affected or aggrieved by agency action * * * is entitled to judicial review thereof." * * *

Both Chrysler and the respondents agree that there is APA review of DLA's decision. They disagree on the proper scope of review. Chrysler argues that there should be *de novo* review, while the respondents contend that such review is only available in extraordinary cases and this is not such a case.

* * * For the reasons previously stated, we believe any disclosure that * * * violates § 1905 is "not in accordance with law" within the meaning of 5 U.S.C.A. § 706(2)(A). *De novo* review by the District Court is ordinarily not necessary to decide whether a contemplated disclosure runs afoul of § 1905. The District Court in this case concluded that disclosure of some of Chrysler's documents was barred by § 1905, but the Court of Appeals did not reach the issue. We shall therefore vacate the Court of Appeals' judgment and remand for further proceedings consistent with this opinion in order that the Court of Appeals may consider whether the contemplated disclosures would violate the prohibition of § 1905.[49] Since the decision regarding this substantive issue—the scope of § 1905—will necessarily have some effect on the proper form of judicial review pursuant to § 706(2), we think it unnecessary, and therefore unwise, at the present stage of this case for us to express any additional views on that issue.

Vacated and remanded.

MR. JUSTICE MARSHALL, concurring.

* * *

Our conclusion that disclosure pursuant to OFCCP regulations is not "authorized by law" for purposes of § 1905 * * * does not mean *the regulations themselves* are "in excess of statutory jurisdiction, authority, or limitations, or short of statutory right" for purposes of the Administrative Procedure Act. 5 U.S.C.A. § 706(2)(C). As the Court recognizes, that inquiry involves very different considerations than those presented in the instant case. Accordingly, we do not question the general validity of these OFCCP regulations or any other regulations promulgated un-

---

49. Since the Court of Appeals assumed for purposes of argument that the material in question was within an exemption to the FOIA, that court found it unnecessary expressly to decide that issue and it is open on remand. We, of course, do not here attempt to determine the relative ambits of Exemption 4 and § 1905, or to determine whether § 1905 is an exempting statute within the terms of the amended Exemption 3, 5 U.S.C. § 552(b)(3).

Although there is a theoretical possibility that material might be outside Exemption 4 yet within the substantive provisions of § 1905, and that therefore the FOIA might provide the necessary "authoriz[ation] by law" for purposes of § 1905, that possibility is at most of limited practical significance in view of the similarity of language between Exemption 4 and the substantive provisions of § 1905.

der § 201 of Executive Order No. 11246. Nor do we consider whether such an Executive Order must be founded on a legislative enactment. The Court's holding is only that the OFCCP regulations in issue here do not "authorize" disclosure within the meaning of § 1905.

Notes

1. The Supreme Court's *Chrysler* decision had been awaited as the definitive ruling on issues raised by the growing stream of "reverse FOIA" suits by suppliers of information to the government. The Court's opinion provides relatively clear guidance on the elements of such suits, with the notable exception of the persistent issue of the scope of § 1905. On that issue, the Court has never spoken decisively, and the legislative history of the provision is no more helpful. Because providers of information to the government frequently are as concerned about the timing as about the occurrence of disclosure, e.g., if the information relates to decisions not yet implemented, many "reverse FOIA" suits are brought to delay release and may never yield rulings on the underlying issues of confidentiality.

2. As the *Chrysler* opinion describes, it has been the practice of the Department of Defense, as well as many other agencies, to give notice to suppliers of information before releasing it, thus affording an opportunity for them to protect their "property" by administrative appeal or judicial challenge. But no court has held that such notice is legally required, and the one opinion that has discussed the issue at length holds that it is not. See *Pharmaceutical Manufacturers Association v. Weinberger*, 401 F. Supp. 444 (1975), 411 F. Supp. 576 (D.D.C. 1976). A Congressional investigating committee, on the other hand, has concluded that "It is consistent with basic notions of fairness that a corporate submitter be given some form of notice about the pending release of information it supplied the Government." Committee on Government Operations, Freedom of Information Act Requests for Business Data and Reverse-FOIA Lawsuits, H.R. Rep. No. 1382, 95th Cong., 2d Sess. 2 (1978). See also The Freedom of Information Reform Act, S. 1730, 97th Cong., 1st Sess. (1981), *reprinted in* Freedom of Information Act: Hearings Before the Subcommittee on the Constitution of the Senate Committee on the Judiciary, 97th Cong., 1st Sess. 41 (1982).

3. The useful secondary literature on "reverse FOIA" litigation includes Clement, *The Rights of Submitters to Prevent Agency Disclosure of Confidential Business Information: The Reverse Freedom of Information Act Lawsuit*, 55 Tex. L. Rev. 587. (1977); Comment, *Reverse-Freedom of Information Act Suits: Confidential Information in Search of Protection*, 70 Nw. U.L. Rev. 995 (1976); Note, *Protection from Government Disclosure—The Reverse-FOIA Suit*, 1976 Duke L. J. 330 (1976).

Exemption of Proprietary Information

Exemption 4 has been one of the most frequently invoked, and its coverage and implementation have increasingly generated concern within the business community as the FOIA has become a mechanism for industrial "espionage." A common objective of businesses is to find out what competitors are doing; if one's competitors must share that information with the government, what better way of finding out than an FOIA request?

The most frequently cited statement of the scope of exemption 4, *National Parks and Conservation Association v. Morton*, 498 F.2d 765 (D.C. Cir. 1974), grew out of a request to the National Park Service for financial records submitted by park concessionaires. The Service claimed that the materials were exempt from disclosure as "commercial or financial information obtained from a person and privileged or confidential." Because the parties agreed that the information sought was not privileged, the court focused on its confidentiality.

Judge Tamm identified two justifications for the FOIA's exemption of commercial records: "(1) encouraging cooperation by those who are not obliged to provide information to the government and (2) protecting the rights of those who must." He went on to conclude that information should be considered "confidential" for purposes of exemption 4 if its disclosure would either impair the government's ability to obtain such information in the future, or "cause substantial harm to the competitive position of the person from whom the information was obtained." The finding that a provider of information would not ordinarily have made it public, by itself, would not justify withholding. Because the Park Service was authorized to require the submission of the records in question, disclosure could not imperil its ability to obtain information in the future. But the court could not, on the record before it, determine whether disclosure would harm the concessionaires' competitive position; though in one sense monopolists, the concessionaires could face competition from other applicants for their exclusive franchise to do business in the parks.

The "trade secret" language of exemption 4 has generated fewer disputes than the "confidential commercial interpretation" language at issue in *Morton*, supra, but it is hardly self-defining. Several agencies and many courts have embraced the definition of "trade secret" in the Restatement of Torts § 757, comment b (1939). The D.C. Circuit, in *Public Citizen Health Research Group v. FDA*, 704 F.2d 1280 (D.C. Cir. 1983), embraced a restrictive interpretation of this term, limiting protection to information about the "productive process" as distinct from more general matters of commercial confidentiality.

The issue in *Public Citizen* was the disclosability of safety and efficacy tests conducted on drugs and medical devices to obtain FDA marketing approval. The FDA has treated such information as confidential since the early 1940's, based on a plausible but clearly not mandatory reading of the Federal Food, Drug, and Cosmetic Act. One consequence of this position is that the data that supply the basis for many of the agency's key decisions have not been accessible to the public, and product approvals have accordingly emerged through a process of private negotiation rather than formal, public adjudication, as section 505 of the Act, 21 U.S.C.A. § 355, appears to contemplate. With the passage of time, manufacturers have developed a major stake in the FDA's position on the confidentiality of this information, for if it cannot be released to the public, it arguably cannot be relied upon by manufacturers of competitive products.

Congress has often been invited, but always declined, to reexamine this policy of the FDA. But on several occasions it has grappled with the analogous problem in the context of pesticide registration.   Through a series of statutory amendments beginning in 1972, Congress had created a complex legal structure which essentially provides for (a) public disclosure of all safety data submitted by pesticide registrants; (b) "exclusive use" of that data by the originator for a limited period of time; and (c) permission for the EPA and competing manufacturers to rely on that data after the exclusive use period, subject to the latters' obligation to compensate the originator.   This scheme was challenged by several pesticide manufacturers on the ground that it effects an uncompensated "taking" of private property.   The statute was upheld as interpreted by the Supreme Court in *Ruckelshaus v. Monsanto Co.*, ___ U.S. ___, 104 S.Ct. 2862 (1984).   See McGarity and Shapiro, *The Trade Secret Status of Health and Safety Testing Information: Reforming Agency Disclosure Policies*, 93 Harv. L. Rev. 837 (1980).

Protection of Personal Privacy

Exemption 6 excludes from the FOIA's coverage "personnel and medical files and similar files the disclosure of which would constitute a clearly unwarranted invasion of personal privacy."   In 1974 Congress amended exemption 7 to permit withholding of information in investigatory files where disclosure would result in an "unwarranted" invasion of personal privacy.

Exemptions 6 and 7 are not the Act's only safeguards of personal privacy interests.   Exemption 3's reference to material "specifically exempted from disclosure by statute" reaches scores, if not hundreds (see H.R. Rep. No. 1497, 89th Cong., 2d Sess. 10 (1966)), of existing statutory prohibitions against disclosure of information held by the government, many of which are designed to protect individual privacy.

The language and legislative history of exemption 6 confirm that it alone of the nine original exemptions contemplates case-by-case balancing.   The question is what factors are to be balanced in determining whether disclosure is "clearly unwarranted"?   In *Getman v. NLRB*, 450 F.2d 670 (D.C.Cir. 1971), the court used the approach traditionally followed in resolving discovery issues in civil proceedings: Does the plaintiff's need for the material outweigh the affected party's interest in privacy.   The court concluded that the loss of privacy resulting from disclosure of a list of names and addresses of employees eligible to vote in NLRB supervised elections was relatively minor, while the study to be made with the use of the list had unusual potential for evaluating Board policies.   Disclosure was therefore required.   This broad approach to balancing interests, however, is not uniformly accepted as appropriate. In *Robles v. Environmental Protection Agency*, 484 F.2d 843 (4th Cir. 1973), the court refused to consider the plaintiff's need for the demanded information (EPA surveys of radiation levels in home built on fill composed of uranium tailings).   The only question considered relevant was the impact of disclosure on the privacy of third parties.   Finding that impact not "clearly" unwarranted, the court ordered disclosure.   A consideration of the plaintiff's need for the information would, in the view of the

Robles court have required the exercise of the "equitable discretion" that the FOIA withdrew.

The plaintiffs in *Department of the Air Force v. Rose,* 425 U.S. 352, 369-70, 371-72 (1976), were student editors of a law review who requested access to case summaries, with names and identifying information deleted, of honor and ethics hearings at the Air Force Academy.   The Air Force denied their request even though such summaries were routinely posted on bulletin boards at the Academy.   The Court rejected the contention that the summaries were covered by exemptions 2 and 6 and affirmed a ruling ordering the Air Force to submit the summaries to the district court for an in camera inspection and to cooperate in redacting the records to delete all names and identifying information.   Noting that "the general thrust of the exemption [2] is simply to relieve agencies of the burden of assembling and maintaining for public inspection matter in which the public could not reasonably be expected to have an interest," the majority found it inapplicable to the case summaries because they were not routine matters of internal significance, but rather were matters of significant public interest.   The majority held that the phrase in exemption 6 "the disclosure of which would constitute a clearly unwarranted invasion of personal privacy" modified "personnel and medical files" as well as "similar files."   Thus limited to "clearly unwarranted" invasions of privacy, the exemption required balancing "the individual's right of privacy against the preservation of the basic purpose of the * * * Act 'to open agency action to the light of public scrutiny.' "   This balance would be achieved by the district court's in camera inspection and expurgation of the case summaries.

In the Privacy Act of 1974, Pub. L. No. 93-579, 5 U.S.C.A. § 552a, Congress enlarged the legal protections for individual privacy.   The basic objectives of that law are to restrict dissemination of information about individuals within the government, to assure that such information is not released to third parties without the knowledge and consent of the individuals, and to afford individuals a procedure for challenging the accuracy of information about them in government files.   A decade later, the relationship between the Privacy Act and the FOIA remains elusive.

That relationship can be an issue in a variety of contexts.   Most of the reported cases deal with the question whether information that can be withheld from an individual under the Privacy Act, e.g., information in open investigatory files, can be obtained under the FOIA.   Presumably, in such cases exemption 6 would not afford a basis for withholding, for its purpose is to protect the privacy of individuals about whom records are maintained by the government.   The question, then, is whether in such cases the Privacy Act qualifies as a statute "specifically exempting" material from disclosure under exemption 3 of the FOIA.   The D.C. and the Third Circuits hold that it is not, see, e.g., *Greentree v. United States Customs Service,* 674 F.2d 74 (D.C. Cir. 1982); *Porter v. United States Department of Justice,* 717 F.2d 787 (3d Cir. 1983), while the Seventh and Fifth Circuits hold that it is, see *Shapiro v. Drug Enforcement Administration,* 721 F.2d 215 (7th Cir. 1983); *Painter v. FBI,* 615 F.2d 689 (5th Cir. 1980).

The secondary literature contains support for both views. See, e.g., Note, 56 Temp. L.Q. 127 (1983); Comment, 63 B.U.L. Rev. 507 (1983).

A second question is whether material that exemption 6 of the FOIA exempts from disclosure—because its release would constitute an "unwarranted invasion of personal privacy"—is automatically barred by the Privacy Act from disclosure to third parties. An affirmative answer to this question, see *Florida Medical Association v. Department of Health, Education and Welfare*, 479 F. Supp. 1291 (M.D. Fla. 1979), means that the Privacy act nullifies pro tanto an agency's discretion to release records that are exempt under the FOIA.

For further discussion of the relationship between these two laws, see Note, *The Freedom of Information Act's Privacy Exemption and the Privacy Act of 1974*, 11 Harv. C.R.-C.L. L. Rev. 596 (1976); Project, *Government Information and the Rights of Citizens*, 73 Mich. L. Rev. 971 (1975).

5. IMPACT AND REFORM OF THE FOIA

For legislation that is ostensibly ancillary to the central functions of government agencies, the FOIA has stimulated not only an extraordinary volume of litigation but also continuous, often strident debate over its effects, its costs, and its value. During the latter years of the Carter Administration and throughout President Reagan's first term, some Congressional critics of the Act, encouraged by the Department of Justice, have pressed for further amendments designed mainly to reduce the cost of administering the law and broaden certain of the exemptions. But other informed observers, including spokespersons for public interest organizations, have claimed that the agencies responsible for compliance with FOIA have been persistently recalcitrant in fulfilling their obligations.

In this part, we examine a trio of excerpts that expose some points of the debate and display—as some titles betray—a range of views on the merits. In an acerbic commentary, *The Freedom of Information Act Has No Clothes*, Regulation, March/April 1982, at 15, Professor (now Judge) Scalia dramatizes two of the most often cited defects of the FOIA: its expense and its indiscriminate exposure of information about the internal workings, not of government, but of private organizations who must provide it information:

> The Freedom of Information Act (FOIA) is part of the basic weaponry of modern regulatory war, deployable against regulators and regulated alike. It differs, however, from other weaponry in the conflict, in that it is largely immune from arms limitation debate. * * * It is the Taj Mahal of the Doctrine of Unanticipated Consequences, the Sistine Chapel of Cost-Benefit Analysis Ignored. * * *
>
> * * * [T]he 1974 amendments were estimated by Congress to cost $100,000 a year. They have in fact cost many millions of dollars—no one knows precisely how much. The main reason is that the amendments forbid the government from charging the requester for the so-called processing costs. Responding to a request generally requires three steps: (1) searching for the requested documents; (2) reviewing or "processing" them to deter-

mine whether any of the material they contain is exempt from disclosure, to decide whether the exemption should be asserted, and, if so, to make the line-by-line deletions; and (3) duplicating them. Before 1974, the cost for all of this work was chargeable to the requester; since 1974, step two has been at the government's expense. In many cases, it is the most costly part of the process, often requiring the personal attention of high-level personnel for long periods of time. If, for example, material in an investigative file is requested, someone familiar with the investigation must go through the material line by line to delete those portions, and only those portions, that would disclose a confidential source or come within one of the other specific exceptions to the requirement of disclosure. Moreover, even steps one and three are at the government's expense "where the agency determines that waiver or reduction of the fee is in the public interest because furnishing the information can be considered as primarily benefiting the general public." Even where the agency parsimoniously refuses to grant this waiver, the more generous judiciary sometimes mandates it—which happened for example, in the case of the FOIA request by the Rosenberg children. * * *

Other features of the amendments reflect the same unthinking extravagance and disregard of competing priorities. Although federal agencies carry out a great many important activities, rarely does the law impose a specific deadline for agency action. Yet the FOIA requester is entitled by law to get an answer to his request within ten working days—and, if it is denied, to get a ruling on his appeal within another twenty. * * * So the investigative agent who is needed to review a file must lay aside his other work and undertake that task as his top priority. * * *

In the courts, the statute provides that FOIA appeals shall "take precedence on the docket over all cases and shall be assigned for hearing and trial or for argument at the earliest practicable date and expedited in every way. * * *

But the most ironic absolute defect of the '74 amendments was perhaps unintended at the time and seems to have gone virtually unnoticed since. The amendments have significantly reduced the privacy, and hence the autonomy, of all our nongovernmental institutions—corporations, labor unions, universities, churches, political and social clubs—all those private associations that form, as Tocqueville observed, diverse centers of power apart from what would otherwise be the all-powerful democratic state. * * * [V]irtually all activities of private institutions may be subjected to *governmental investigation*—and increasingly are, to ensure compliance with the innumerable requirements of federal laws and regulations. * * *

* * * The way things now work, the government may obtain almost anything in the course of an investigation; and once the investigation is completed the public (or, more specifically, the opponents or competitors of the investigated institution) may obtain all that the investigative file contains, unless one of a few narrow exemptions applies. There is an exemption (though the agency has discretion not to invoke it) for confidential commercial information. But there is none that protects an institution's consultative and deliberative processes—the minutes of a university's faculty meetings, for example. It is noteworthy that internal consultation and advice within the government itself is exempted from disclosure since, as the 1966 House Committee Report explained, "a full and frank exchange of opinions would be im-

possible if all internal communications were made public." But no such exemption exists for the internal communications of private organizations that come into the government's hands. * * *

The defects of the Freedom of Information Act cannot be cured as long as we are dominated by the obsession that gave them birth—that the first line of defense against an arbitrary executive is do-it-yourself oversight by the public and its surrogate, the press. On that assumption, the FOIA's excesses are not defects at all, but merely the necessary price for our freedoms. It is a romantic notion, but the facts simply do not bear it out. The major exposes of recent times, from CIA mail openings to Watergate to the FBI COINTEL-PRO operations, owe virtually nothing to the FOIA but are primarily the product of the institutionalized checks and balances within our system of representative democracy. This is not to say that public access to government information has no useful role—only that it is not the ultimate guarantee of responsible government, justifying the sweeping aside of all other public and private interests at the mere invocation of the magical words "freedom of information." * * *

A contrasting viewpoint, though equally critical of experience under the FOIA, is provided by Professor Vaughan, himself sometimes a patron of the Act, see *Vaughan v. Rosen*, 484 F.2d 820 (D.C. Cir. 1973), *cert. denied* 415 U.S. 977 (1974), who in *Our Government Stymies Open Government*, Washington Post, July 1, 1984 at C1, inveighs against the propensity of government agencies to impede its operation:

The Founding Fathers would be proud of the act—unless they could see how the peoples' government often frustrates its purpose. * * *

* * * [D]ozens of [judicial opinions] issued since 1979 * * * indict the federal government for subverting the spirit and intent of the Freedom of Information Act by delay, intransigence, evasion and even open hostility toward those attempting to avail themselves of their legal rights.

So costly and difficult has the government made it for the public to gain speedy access to information that the Freedom of Information Act may become useless for all but the most-patient and the best-financed citizens. * * *

No doubt some of the problems, including the huge backlog of cases, often result from circumstances beyond the control of agencies, such as the heavy volume of requests and inadequate resources to cope with it. But * * * delays are sometimes motivated by hostility and are used by the government to its own tactical advantage. * * *

The act's current deadlines for response to requests have limited practical significance. The volume of requests and inadequate resources devoted to processing them guarantee large backlogs.

Courts have recognized the practical problems faced by the government by deferring judicial review if an agency is processing its backlog in good faith. The backlog itself has become an issue for the courts. * * *

The courts understandably prefer that cases be resolved without judicial intervention, given that the process of judicial review can be as lengthy as the delay at the agency level. (The administrative office of the United States Courts found that the median time between the filing of an FOIA suit and its disposition in district courts was eight months for the year ending June 30, 1981. And 10 percent of the cases took more than 23 months.)

As things now stand, courts have limited ability to evaluate the reasons for a backlog—and little power to modify the practices of government agencies. One federal court expressed the limitations of judicial enforcement this way: "To be sure, the court deplores the 10-month delay between plaintiffs' request and the agency's action on their appeal, but the staggering practicalities of the 'FOIA explosion' render [other judicial action] both unrealistic and probably unenforceable."

Confronted with delays by government departments, the costs of seeking judicial review and the courts' inability to deal with delay, requesters are left to bargain with the same bureaucracy from which they are seeking information. This procedure discourages individuals and journalists, in particular, from using the act and undoubtedly helps explain why the main users are large organizations, corporations and well-funded interest groups.

One modification made by Congress in 1974 was the establishment of a complicated procedure under which a federal court could initiate an investigation by the executive branch leading to possible disciplining of federal officials who arbitrarily or capriciously withhold information. * * *

But in the 10 years since that provision was passed, the courts have referred only a handful of cases to the agency authorized to investigate: the Office of Special Counsel in the Merit Systems Protection Board, and no federal official has *ever* been disciplined under the provision.

ROBINSON, ACCESS TO GOVERNMENT INFORMATION: THE AMERICAN EXPERIENCE

14 Federal L. Rev. 35 (1983).

The real issues of enforcement are more homely than the Watergate problem would suggest. They relate to such matters as administrative costs of disclosure, and benefits of confidentiality of private and governmental information versus the benefits of openness—these are the important elements to be weighed. * * *

(1) ADMINISTRATIVE COSTS

The concern over administrative costs is not new; the agencies have for some time complained of the burdens imposed by the heavy volume of requests generated by the liberal disclosure policies and the strict compliance requirements imposed by Congress and the courts. * * *

* * * [T]he common complaint that the fiscal burden is unacceptably high seems to me somewhat overdrawn. We do not have sufficiently detailed cost accounts for FOI Act related activity, but a recent estimate puts the aggregate annual administrative costs at more than $50 million. It is not clear what functions the estimate covers, but it is probably an underestimate; for example, the above estimate does not include judicial enforcement *or* other "indirect" costs. Suppose to allow for all unaccounted costs we estimate the costs at $100 million. To those who balance their cheque books each month, this will seem a royal sum, but in the

mega-dimensional budgetary world in which the United States Government operates, $100 million is a trifle.   It is indeed far less then the United States Government spends annually in support of programmes to disseminate information abroad.   If one supposes that the information needs of United States citizens are entitled to the same respect as those of foreigners, one would have to imagine a large adjustment to the present estimate before costs would warrant serious concern in terms of budgetary impact.

Moreover, one would still not be in a position to declare the budgetary burden to be an important problem without some attention to the benefits of public access to information.   To date no one has devised any method for measuring these intangible benefits in quantitative terms. * * *

The real case for increasing the fee level—or for other cost-related administrative reforms—is not a macroeconomic budgetary argument. * * *   The real case for cost recovery is more in the nature of a microeconomic rationale of forcing a cost discipline on particular kinds of requests.   In this context, the proposal to recoup some of the profits earned by the sale of commercially valuable information by FOI Act requesters is especially noteworthy.

Part of the FOI Act-spawned cottage industry * * * is the thriving business in merchandising FOI Act services or information obtained through the FOI Act, particularly trade secrets or other confidential business information about competitors.[85]   While commercialisation is in the best tradition of Yankee entrepreneurship, it is also a minor embarrassment to the public interest objectives that supposedly guided Congress. * * *

The real point is that whatever Congress contemplated about the public or private uses to which information would be put, it surely did not intend, through the FOI Act, to put its processes of information gathering at the *free* disposal of private interests except where the information had public benefits over and above those reflected in commercial information markets. * * * I do not suggest that disclosure requirements themselves be redefined in terms of public versus private purpose—that disclosure be restricted to those who seek to use it "in the public interest".   In the abstract such a distinction would be hard to observe if not wholly meaningless.   There is no necessary *conflict* between public and private welfare.   The conflict arises when, in the name of public welfare, one group is able to secure *special, distinctive* private benefits at the public expense.

---

85. See "Government, Business and the People's Right to Know" (1978) 3 Media Law Reporter 20-21 (discussing FOI Act service bureaus).   See also Montgomery, Peters & Weinburg, "The Freedom of Information Act: Strategic Opportunities and Threats" (1978) Sloan Management Review 1-2 (use of FOI Act to obtain trade secrets and other information about competitors).

The merchandising of FOI Act services and information is not, of course, confined to obtaining business secrets.   One enterprising company promotes its "Freedom of Information Kit" with an advertisement that promises: "Here's How to Find Out Which 'Enemies List' You're On—Within 10 Working Days".   Weinstein, "Open Season on 'Open Government'" (19 June 1979) New York Times Magazine, 32, 85-86. * * *

(2) CONFIDENTIAL COMMERCIAL INFORMATION

The existence of a private market for commercially valuable information obtained from the government highlights a more basic complaint about the FOI Act than the *free* access to commercially valuable information. The more basic complaint is that the FOI Act has been used to obtain confidential commercial information the disclosure of which is harmful to legitimate business interests. * * *

Exemption four has not, however, * * * prevented some "leakage" of legitimately privileged business information. We do not have reliable evidence as to the magnitude of the problem. The very existence of an apparently successful business devoted to selling commercially valuable information is some evidence that the problem is not imaginary, but as with other claims of FOI Act abuse, the evidence of serious injury from disclosure of confidential commercial information is a bit thin—certainly it is less robust than the expressions of concern by businessmen.

Some of the "leakage" of legitimately confidential information is unintended—the product of careless treatment by agency personnel. But the more significant problem appears to be deliberate disclosure by agencies. * * * The larger problem here is defining the scope of agency discretion. Agency discretion in "reverse FOI Act" cases [see *Chrysler v. Brown,* supra p. 600] is subject to judicial review, but the review standards are not as demanding as for judicial determination of the scope of the exemption itself. The asymmetry between judicial review of agency action in FOI Act and reverse-FOI Act cases thus favours disclosure. * * *

(3) EXECUTIVE SECRETS: NATIONAL SECURITY AND LAW ENFORCEMENT

* * * A parallel concern over disclosure of confidential information sources underlies proposals to restrict access to investigatory files of law enforcement agencies—most notably the Federal Bureau of Investigation. The concern, again, is twofold: first, a fear that criminals (particularly organized crime) are gaining access to investigative files for the purpose of thwarting law enforcement—*inter alia,* by retaliating against informers—and, secondly, that the very perception that such files will be disclosed is deterring informers. * * * [S. 1730, 97th Cong.] proposed a relatively minor expansion of the scope of exemption seven, a prohibition of the use of FOI Act information for civil or criminal discovery, and an authorization of regulations to restrict access to FOI Act information by felons and to exempt information related to organized crime, terrorism and foreign counter-intelligence.

I am sympathetic to the notion that the FOI Act was not intended as a discovery tool for felons. * * * But it is hard to see the efficacy, and hence the justification, of these proposed changes. A relaxation of some of the restrictions on exemption seven might be a useful corrective to the overly strict limitations that Congress imposed on that exemption in 1974. But the proposals affect disclosure only in the marginal case. As for restrictions on FOI Act use by felons, it would be all but impossible to enforce.   Requiring requesters to file affidavits that the information is not for unauthorized persons, and will not be made available to them, seems as unlikely to prevent access by felons as it is to prevent access by the KGB.

* * *

* * * At least in terms of a simple increase in the *quantitative* flow of information from government agency files to the public I do not think there can be much question about the effectiveness of the FOI Act.

As to whether the public has significantly benefitted from that information, this is more problematical. * * *

Absent a calculus for quantitative measurement we must resort to general "principles"—faith informed by intuition.   It has always been a professed article of faith that an informed public is vital to democratic society. * * * [G]iven our social, political commitment to open, even relatively indiscriminate dissemination of information generally, it is hard to make government disclosure of information dependent on some *specified* positive benefit to the individual or to the society.   We simply take that as an axiom of our political and social system that information is good and more information is better.

To be sure, in neither the private nor the public sector are we so committed to the free flow of information as to be indifferent to the costs of unrestrained dissemination.   In the private sector we have a complex set of laws designed to limit various kinds of information in order to protect a variety of interests from being injured (suffering costs).   Protection of trademarks and copyrights, business "secrets", personal privacy; protection against various forms of misleading or otherwise injurious information (defamation) are illustrative of efforts to prevent certain costs caused by free flow of information.   To the extent that these restrictions on information are recognized in the private sector they are properly protected in the public sector.   The government should not allow itself to be the vehicle for undermining protected interests in the name of promoting "open government".

This much seems plain.   Less plain is the recognition to be given to secrets about the government processes themselves.   To what extent should democratic government be forced to operate in a fishbowl? * * *

* * * [G]overnment politicians and bureaucrats are close kin to ordinary people; their personal preferences are very similar to those of people outside government, as are the motives that drive their behaviour.   In particular, they probably have about the same mixture of self-interest and "public interest" motivation as others.   Of course, politicians and bureaucrats operate in a different environment, with different kinds of freedoms and constraints than those that others confront.   Bureaucrats in particular are not subject directly or indirectly to market discipline.

Their behaviour is subject to the control of official superiors, or public constituents, but performance standards lack objective measures.[111]

In any environment individuals have a natural self-interest incentive to control information about themselves in order favourably to influence other persons' perceptions of them and of their behaviour. If there is anything distinctive about the public sector environment in this respect, it is the degree to which bureaucrats or politicians are able to control information about their activities and the extent to which evaluations of them and their performance depends on information within their control.

In the private sector, consumer evaluation of the firm's product does not typically depend on public perusal of intracorporate records. Direct experience of the product, measured against competitive substitutes, is normally considered a better measure of the firm's "output". Evaluation of the "output" of the "public firm" of bureaucrats and politicians is not so easily measured by external criteria. Indeed, we need some internal information from the "public firm" even to determine what the relevant output is. It follows that a degree of access to government information, concerning its activities in particular, is essential in order to make the political "marketplace" work.

The above argument merely restates in the somewhat stilted style of academic theory the homely common sense of elementary civics: there are no better guarantees that entrusted power will be well used than an *informed* and critical public *attitude*. The FOI Act makes a positive, if modest, contribution to that guarantee.

---

111. See Aranson, Gellhorn & Robinson, "A Theory of Legislative Delegation" (1983) 68 Corn. L. Rev. 1, for an elaboration of this point. On the absence of market discipline particularly in the case of bureaucrats see, e.g. A. Downs, *Inside Bureaucracy* (1967) 29-

30. See also W. Niskanen, *Bureaucracy and Representative Government* (1971), advancing the thesis that bureaucrats seek to maximize their budgets as a means of enhancing their characteristic preferences (utility functions).

Part III

PUBLIC LAW REMEDIES

The discussion in the previous three chapters has proceeded on the general assumption that judicial remedies were available to protect private rights and to test the legality of administrative action. That discussion repeatedly raised questions, however, concerning the limits of this "judicial review" function—often drawing attention to the inevitable tension between judicial control and administrative efficacy. Occasionally, we encountered questions not just of limits, but of whether *any* judicial relief should be available. Yet, these remedial concerns have been secondary to our interest in observing the means through which agencies accomplish their public purposes within whatever procedural or substantive constraints are enforced through judicial review.

In the three chapters that follow we focus explicitly on the structure of the public law remedial system. Here our interests will be in the public law analogues of familiar private law remedial issues: questions of judicial jurisdiction; of the necessary elements of a "claim" or "cause of action"; of the types of relief available; and of the scope of peremptory defenses that preclude judicial decision on the merits of claims. This is not to say that the questions addressed are all of a technical nature. While legal doctrine and lore abound, clearly discernible beneath the surface of the technical legal rules are broader concerns about the appropriate legal structure of the administrative state.

Remedial issues in the public law system can be conceptualized in several ways. By our chapter divisions we reflect our choice to address them as emerging from three broad and interrelated categories of claims. The first type of remedial claim, considered in Chapter 6, we call simply "Review of the Legality of Official Action." Here we deal with the most conventional remedies in federal public law—injunctions either prohibitory or mandatory in form, often accompanied by a formal declaration of legal rights and obligations. And it is here that the public law system of remedies differs most sharply from the private law system. For in federal public law, the injunction is the least problematic remedy a litigant can pursue.

Often judicial review in this injunctive mode is expressly authorized by a statutory provision that establishes judicial jurisdiction, specifies the form and timing of review proceedings, indicates who can seek review, and empowers the reviewing court to affirm, reverse, or remand particular agency decisions. In other cases, plaintiffs proceed under more general grants of federal jurisdiction, and the questions of *who* may seek review, *when*, and *how* it is to be effected are more obviously determined by administrative common law. Whatever the form of proceeding and the specific doctrinal issues raised, such review actions are recognized as oriented broadly to public law concerns. The social function of "judicial review" as we conceptualize it here is the maintenance of the rule of law, given the constraints on judicial authority inherent in a system committed also to a separation of governmental powers.

In Chapter 7 we consider a category of claims that we denominate claims for "Relief From Officially Inflicted Injuries." As in the more common form of "review" proceedings, examined in Chapter 6, plaintiffs who seek damages or specific performance from the government, or from government officials, also invariably question the legality of administrative conduct. To that degree actions sounding essentially in tort, contract, or property against the government and its officials invite judicial review of administrative action. Yet, both the doctrinal categories relevant to these actions and their broader orientation differ from the so-called review proceedings. Whereas review proceedings revolve around issues of "standing," "ripeness," "exhaustion of administrative remedies," and "reviewability," the linguistic conventions of our second category of remedies emphasize doctrinal questions of "sovereign" and "official immunity." This shift in the language of judicial discourse is not merely cosmetic. Suits for "relief" rather than "review" tend to emphasize concerns that are more like those encountered in the private law context—questions such as the appropriateness of spreading risks of loss, or the potential for damage actions to provide incentives for the regulation of primary conduct. More than "maintaining the rule of law," courts operating in this remedial mode seem to be concerned with "corrective justice."

A final category of claims, explored in Chapter 8, we term suits for "Beneficiary Enforcement." Here, rather than suing federal officials, either to review or to remedy the effects of their behavior, plaintiffs seek to enforce duties owed to them under federal statutes or constitutional provisions by private persons or federal, state, and local officials. In this mode the remedial system directly implements federal public law. Or, perhaps we should say, raises questions of whether it *should* be directly implemented by private lawsuits. Here the characteristic doctrinal concerns have to do with the existence or non-existence of "implied rights of action" and with the potentially "primary jurisdiction" of federal administrators to enforce public law.

This third category of remedial actions has a decidedly hybrid character. Beneficiary suits invoke statutes or the Constitution in a fashion reminiscent of a petition for review. Yet the claims also have a flavor of actions in tort or contract: the plaintiff often seeks damages or an injunctive order that looks rather like specific performance of a duty to a third-party beneficiary. Moreover, the policy questions that surround these actions implicate both the essentially public law concerns of separation of powers and the more characteristically private law concerns of spreading risks and influencing primary conduct.

Figure 1 attempts to fix these ideas somewhat more concretely by noting the divergent characteristics of the three types of claims we shall be discussing.

FIGURE 1

Claim Type	Social Function	Broad Issue Orientation	Forms of Action	Doctrinal Categories
Review of Legality of Official Action	Maintain Rule of Law	Public law concerns, particularly separation of powers	General or specific statutory proceeding	Standing, Ripeness, Exhaustion of Administrative Remedies, Reviewability
Relief from Officially Inflicted Injuries	Corrective Justice	Private Law Concerns —Risk Spreading —Incentives	Tort or contract action (damages or specific performance)	Sovereign and Official Immunity
Beneficiary Enforcement of Public Law	Implementation	Hybrid	Suit on a statute or contract (including 42 U.S.C.A. § 1983)	Implied rights of action, Primary jurisdiction

But we should note immediately that this apparent divergence of remedial prototypes masks many similarities and cross-cutting doctrinal concerns. Each category of claims raises issues that may be framed in terms of the existence of federal court jurisdiction. Questions of the effect on administrative power or discretion of recognizing a particular judicial remedy on administrative power or discretion—broadly speaking, separation of powers issues—are likewise pervasive. And, obviously, the existence or non-existence of a particular type of judicial remedy in part defines what it means to be a citizen or "rights holder" in our liberal-democratic, but increasingly administrative, state.

Indeed, given the numerous overlaps among the categories our treatment of rights of action under 42 U.S.C.A. § 1983 as suits for beneficiary enforcement may be viewed by some as "arbitrary" if not "capricious." This categorization reflects our belief that the remedial conceptualization of section 1983 actions should mirror the implementation concerns that attend the allocation to non-federal officials of the power to effectuate federal policies. Hence, we see private suits against state officials under section 1983 as attempts to implement federal rights where "cooperative federalism" has left the concrete realization of those rights in local hands.

One can obviously view section 1983 actions differently.   In one sense they may be "review proceedings" that subject state and local implementors of federal norms to the same sort of judicial supervision available against federal implementors.   In this guise, for example, section 1983 becomes the means by which a beneficiary of Title IV of the Social Security Act (the program of Aid to Families with Dependent Children) obtains review opportunities similar to those available to a beneficiary of Title II (Disability Insurance), in which final determinations are made directly by federal employees (ALJs).   And, in yet another incarnation, section 1983 actions raise critical issues of public tort law.   Indeed such suits have generated much of the modern law of official immunity.

The conceptualization that we offer in these pages is, therefore, but one of many possible visions.   Yet, together these three categories of claims canvass the principle remedial interests of most citizens of the American administrative state.   The oysterman whom the FDA prevents from marketing his allegedly contaminated catch will want to know the possibilities for "review" *vis a vis* the FDA.   He may have a similar, if not livelier, interest in the prospects for recovering damages from either the U.S. Government or from an errant FDA official, should the agency's allegations prove incorrect.   And this same oysterman also may want to consider suit against the upstream chemical company whose violation of the Federal Water Pollution Control Act produced the contamination and/or against the state officials charged with administering that statute.   These are the three interrelated sets of remedial possibilities—claims for "review," for "relief," and for "enforcement"—that we pursue in the chapters that follow.

Chapter 6

SUITS TO REVIEW ADMINISTRATIVE ACTION

A. INTRODUCTION

In suits to obtain judicial review of the legality of official conduct, the familiar "right-duty" dichotomies of private law are attenuated by considerations peculiar to the public law context. Government officers have duties, but they derive from legislative prescriptions of official functions and, in form at least, are owed to the public at large. The role of the government officer, i.e., of one charged with public functions and ultimately, if remotely, responsible politically to the general citizenry, raises difficult questions concerning how official compliance with statutory directives should be policed and who should do the policing.

For example, should any citizen's general interest in the proper administration of law confer "standing" to seek a remedy against an officer who performs same function improperly? Or should a citizen be required to show that the official has invaded some personal interest or "right" belonging to the citizen? If the former premise is accepted, the federal courts may exceed their historic function of deciding concrete controversies and, simultaneously, their Article III jurisdiction. If they adopt the latter posture, however, legal control of the conduct of government officials might be confined to the boundaries of legal redress for private wrongs. Yet, in a liberal-democratic state the merger of private and public law remedies is not obviously appropriate. A basic presupposition of such a polity is that private conduct should be restricted only by specific legal proscription and by the duty to avoid unnecessary injury to one's neighbors. Limitations on judicial remedies in the private and criminal law thus embody a general policy of non-interference with private autonomy. Actions by government officials, on the other hand, are presumptively lawful only if within the boundaries of some empowering statute. Recognition of broad judicial jurisdiction to confine officials within statutory limits would therefore support both individual autonomy and democratic control. Yet, the very notion of representative democracy suggests that every disagreement about policy should not be resolved or resolvable by lawsuit. Where is the balance to be struck?

623

Similar problems are encountered on the duty side of the equation. The breadth of the officer's duty, that is, to the citizenry as a whole, may imply the exercise of political judgment not subject to the rational elaboration of coherent principles associated with court enforcement of legal rights. Does the political nature of administration thus defy judicial scrutiny? And, if not generally, in what contexts? What if the official appeals to administrative necessity rather than political discretion? To what extent should the potential for interference with efficient execution of public business be considered in defining remedies against public officers? Should such considerations influence the existence as well as the extent of such remedies? Their timing?

Such basic questions—who can obtain review, what official actions are subject to review, to what extent, and when—are recurrent themes in the jurisprudence of judicial review of administrative action. Instead of the "right-duty-remedy" language encountered in the discussion of private law remedies, however, these issues are generally discussed in terms of such conceptual headings as "standing," "reviewability," "ripeness," and, as we have seen in prior chapters, "scope of judicial review." Moreover, were we writing as late as 1975, these questions (of who, what, and when) would also be affected critically by concerns about "sovereign immunity" and by limitations on the jurisdiction of the federal courts to decide cases challenging the conduct of federal officials. In the context of "judicial review," as we use the term, those issues are no longer of great moment. Yet old legal doctrine is remarkably sturdy in the face of both piecemeal and general efforts at reform. Even if wholly "abolished," ancient lore may nonetheless influence the application and elaboration of newer doctrinal categories. To understand the extent to which earlier approaches to jurisdiction and governmental immunity may retain some capacity to render judicial review problematic we need to review briefly the history of those issues and how they relate to the *mode* of judicial review that is being sought. For, as we shall see, this last notion—the mode of review—is still influential with respect to contemporary remedial questions. One mode of review—the damage action, which we consider in Chapter 7—reintroduces jurisdictional and immunity questions, and in Chapter 8 we encounter state sovereign immunity under the Eleventh Amendment in a jurisprudence that draws explicitly on doctrine developed in defining the immunity of the United States government.

1. SOVEREIGN IMMUNITY, JURISDICTION, AND MODES OF JUDICIAL REVIEW

Judicial review of the actions of federal officials may be obtained in a number of ways: in an action for damages against an officer or his employer; by way of defense in an enforcement proceeding initiated by a public officer; in a proceeding created by a specific statutory review provision; or, in a proceeding initiated under one of the general heads of federal court jurisdiction, or by prerogative writ. Review in enforcement proceedings obviously presents few problems of jurisdiction or sovereign immunity. The person challenging the legality of agency action is doing so by way of defense in a proceeding initiated by the government, presumably in a proper court. This is not to say that there are never problems in obtaining review in enforcement proceedings. It is only to say that, assuming the enforcing agency has brought an appropriate action, judicial jurisdiction and the government's possible immunity from suit should not be relevant concerns.

Nor do these issues pose difficulty where Congress has specifically authorized review; statutes that specifically provide for judicial review typically confer jurisdiction *and* waive sovereign immunity. Indeed, it is only because the set of available specific review provisions remains incomplete that the governmental defenses of sovereign immunity or lack of judicial jurisdiction ever arise. Thus, while Congress, when enacting regulatory legislation, has generally and increasingly been alert to provide judicial review of final administrative orders, it has not been equally alert to provide for judicial review when an agency fails to perform. Furthermore, many governmental functions, such as the construction activities of the Corps of Engineers, were originally conceived not to require or be susceptible of judicial review. The statutes authorizing such activities contained few criteria beyond "need" or "desirability," often determined by Congress in the appropriations process, coupled with some exercise of engineering or other technical judgment. In recent years, however, social or environmental criteria have been specifically incorporated in many statutes and are appended to all federal functions by certain general statutes, such as the National Environmental Policy Act. But the addition of new substantive criteria has not always been accompanied by revision of specific statutory review provisions. In such circumstances, among others, litigants must search for routes of review outside specific statutory review provisions—routes sometimes collectively termed "non-statutory" review.

In the federal system suits for injunction or declaratory judgment conventionally serve as the primary vehicles for these more general remedies. The "great writ," habeus corpus, has a venerable role in the federal courts, but other prerogative writs have had inauspicious histories. One explanation is the generally flexible use of injunction by federal courts, coupled with the generous authorization of specific statutory review. In addition, writs commonly pursued in the state courts, certiorari and mandamus, have been narrowly confined by the federal courts. See *Degge v. Hitchcock*, 229 U.S. 162 (1913); *United States ex rel. McLennan v. Wilbur*, 283 U.S. 414, 420 (1931). Moreover, until 1962 federal courts outside of the District of Columbia lacked jurisdiction to issue either writ. See generally Byse and Fiocca, *Section 1361 of the Mandamus and Venue Act of 1962 and "Nonstatutory" Judicial Review of Federal Administrative Action*, 81 Harv. L. Rev. 308 (1967).

The perplexities of federal jurisdiction and sovereign immunity have thus affected a confined, but nevertheless important, class of non-statutory review proceedings, i.e., suits seeking injunctive or declaratory relief against allegedly illegal government conduct that do not fall within a specific statutory review provision. One jurisdictional impediment was posed by 28 U.S.C.A. § 1331's historic requirement that a claim "arising under federal law" involve an amount in controversy of at least $10,000. Many paths around the amount in controversy requirement have been explored, including other grants of jurisdiction. The district courts have jurisdiction as well over claims, without regard to value, arising under any act of Congress "regulating commerce," 28 U.S.C.A. § 1337, a provision potentially applicable to actions of many federal officials. Claims under acts for the protection of civil rights, 28 U.S.C.A. § 1343(4), and for mandamus, 28 U.S.C.A. §§ 1361, 1391(e), similarly escape the $10,000 requirement. There is also the possibility that once a litigant presents a colorable claim over which jurisdiction clearly exists, the court will treat other claims, not independently within its jurisdiction, as "pendent." See, e.g., *Hagans v. Lavine*, 415 U.S. 528 (1974). But note that an action for declaratory relief cannot be used as an independent basis for "apending" other claims because the Declaratory Judgments Act authorizes that form of relief only where the claim is otherwise within the court's jurisdiction. 28 U.S.C.A. § 2201.

Even with these multiple grants of federal court jurisdiction, some litigants seeking judicial review have had difficulty raising issues within a federal court's subject matter competence. The complex interaction among such questions as the type of claim asserted, the sort of remedy sought, and the statutory basis for jurisdiction pushed federal judges into any number of technical distinctions and creative legal fictions to allow review of potentially meritorious claims. To eliminate confusion and provide a sounder basis for review, Congress in 1976 amended 28 U.S.C.A. § 1331(a), Pub. L. No. 94–574, 90 Stat. 2721, to provide that "no such sum or value shall be required in any such action brought against the United States, any agency thereof, or any officer or employee thereof in his official capacity." In the same statute Congress revised the venue provisions of 28 U.S.C.A. § 1391(e) to eliminate other troublesome technical impediments. Finally, in 1980, Pub. L. No. 96–486, 94 Stat. 2369, amended 28 U.S.C.A. § 1331 to eliminate the $10,000 requirement for all "civil actions arising under the Constitution, laws, or treaties of the United States."

Yet, ironically, satisfaction of the general "federal question" jurisdictional provision does not necessarily assure that the court will reach the merits. For the government might still claim sovereign immunity, a "jurisdictional" bar to review that prior to 1976 described a not insubstantial number of challenges to agency actions. See Cramton, *Nonstatutory Review of Federal Administrative Action: The Need for Statutory Reform of Sovereign Immunity, Subject Matter Jurisdiction, and Parties Defendant*, 68 Mich. L. Rev. 387, 392 (1970).

Simply stated, sovereign immunity means that the sovereign (read "the government") cannot be sued without its consent. But as a doctrine, sovereign immunity is anything but simple. Its history is cloudy and its rationale obscure. In *United States v. Lee*, 106 U.S. 196, 207 (1882), Justice Miller observed that "the principle has never been discussed or the reasons for it given, but it has always been treated as an established doctrine." Moreover, despite the vitrolic criticism of sovereign immunity by academics and others, the Supreme Court has never been willing to "disestablish" the doctrine. As the Court put it in the leading modern case on sovereign immunity, *Larson v. Domestic and Foreign Commerce Corp.*, 337 U.S. 682, 704 (1949), the government should not be "stopped in its tracks by any plaintiff who presents a disputed question." At that level of generality, the *Larson* case almost suggests a general presumption against judicial review.

But this was hardly the reality of judicial review, even in the era when *Larson* was decided in 1949. As Kenneth Culp Davis noted:

> The plain, clear, visible reality is, as no one knows better than the Supreme Court Justices, that courts including the Supreme Court are constantly interfering with the public administration and constantly stopping the government in its tracks. Many of the great constitutional decisions throughout our history have stopped the government in its tracks and have interfered in public administration.

K. DAVIS, ADMINISTRATIVE LAW TREATISE, § 27.00–7 at 915 (1970 Supp.). That "reality" was made possible by the legal fiction that a suit against the *official* was not a suit against the *government* subject to the bar of sovereign immunity. Yet, as the *Larson* case itself noted, the fiction could be exposed. Suit could be entertained only to the extent that it was not "really against the government" or where the challenged action could be described as either "unconstitutional" or completely outside the official's authority or jurisdiction (*ultra vires*).

The efforts to determine whether suits were "really against the government" and the interpretive conundra that resulted from attempts to distinguish between *ultra vires* and merely illegal action produced a chaotic jurisprudence. As the court conceded in *Littell v. Morton*, 445 F.2d 1207, 1211–12 (4th Cir. 1971):

> * * * [A]n effort to establish logical consistency in the decisions dealing with sovereign immunity is bound to be frustrating. The authorities are not reconcilable, and there are conceptual conflicts in the various holdings with which an intermediate appellate court must grapple. Our task is magnified because we have been unable to find any case in which the Supreme Court has sought to reconcile the notion of sovereign immunity with the fundamental concept of the APA that a person adversely affected by administrative action is presumptively entitled to judicial review of its correctness.
>
> Two Courts of Appeals have sought to resolve the problem by holding that the APA, where applicable, constitutes a waiver by the government of sovereign immunity. * * *
>
> Despite the attractiveness of the waiver theory, we do not consider ourselves free to adopt it. The judicial review provisions of the APA were adopted in 1946 in substantially the same form as exists today. Yet between 1946 and 1963 the Supreme Court decided at least five cases dealing with at-

tempts to review administrative decisions in which sovereign immunity was applied.   In none of these cases was mention made of the judicial review provisions of the APA, although, because they dealt with final administrative decisions, some discussion of the APA would have seemed to have been appropriate. * * * As a source of further confusion, the Supreme Court has recently decided a number of cases dealing with final administrative decisions in which judicial review was permitted under the APA without any mention of the doctrine of "sovereign immunity."

Congress came to the rescue in 1976, Pub. L. No. 94–574, 90 Stat. 2721, by amending APA § 702 to include the following language:

> An action in a court of the United States seeking relief other than money damages and stating a claim that an agency or an officer or employee thereof acted or failed to act in an official capacity or under color of legal authority shall not be dismissed nor relief therein be denied on the ground that it is against the United States or that the United States is an indispensable party.   The United States may be named as a defendant in any such action, and a judgment or decree may be entered against the United States.

This clear waiver for claims, other than those for "money damages," virtually eliminates the barrier of sovereign immunity where a plaintiff seeks the standard public law remedies of injunction or declaratory judgment.   Yet, as with any statute, not all of the problems have been solved. See, e.g., *Jaffee v. United States*, 592 F.2d 712 (3rd Cir.), *on remand* 468 F. Supp. 632 (D.N.J.), *cert. denied* 441 U. S. 961 (1979); *Estate of Watson v. Blumenthal*, 586 F.2d 925 (2d Cir. 1978).

Congressional action has thus finally redeemed the promise of presumptive judicial review by broadly removing both technical barriers to jurisdiction and venue and the anachronistic barrier of sovereign immunity in non-damage actions.   Litigants may thus proceed under specific statutory review provisions, through "non-statutory" review proceedings, and by way of defense in enforcement actions, without confronting those initial and theoretically absolute barriers to review.   The remaining barriers are largely those functional and prudential limits thought necessary to maintain appropriate separation of powers, to promote administrative efficiency, and to limit multiplicity of judicial proceedings. Yet, even in a contemporary jurisprudence whose intellectual style is purposive and policy-oriented, we shall encounter limitations on or barriers to judicial review that are reminiscent of the jurisprudence of sovereign immunity and limited federal question jurisdiction.

2. PRESUMPTIVE REVIEW

The persistent criticism of sovereign immunity as a barrier to review of federal administrative action, punctuated by judicial decisions narrowing its scope and Congressional action to eliminate jurisdictional limitations, have combined to produce a legal environment in which it can be presumed that most final decisions of federal administrators are subject to judicial review in some court, at some time.   The following ubiquitously-cited case is the cornerstone of the prevailing judicial posture.

Petitioners

CITIZENS TO PRESERVE OVERTON
PARK, INC. v. VOLPE

Supreme Court of the United States, 1971.
401 U.S. 402, 91 S.Ct. 814, 28 L. Ed.2d 136,.

Opinion of the Court by MR. JUSTICE MARSHALL, announced by MR. JUSTICE STEWART.

* * * We are concerned in this case with § 4(f) of the Department of Transportation Act of 1966, as amended, and § 18(a) of the Federal-Aid Highway Act of 1968, 23 U.S.C.A. § 138.[3] These statutes prohibit the Secretary of Transportation from authorizing the use of federal funds to finance the construction of highways through public parks if a "feasible and prudent" alternative route exists. If no such route is available, the statutes allow him to approve construction through parks only if there has been "all possible planning to minimize harm" to the park.

Statute →

Petitioners, private citizens as well as local and national conservation organizations, contend that the Secretary has violated these statutes by authorizing the expenditure of federal funds for the construction of a six-lane interstate highway through a public park in Memphis, Tennessee. * * *

P|c

* * *

Petitioners contend that the Secretary's action is invalid without * * * formal findings and that the Secretary did not make an independent determination but merely relied on the judgment of the Memphis City Council. They also contend that it would be "feasible and prudent" to route I–40 around Overton Park either to the north or to the south. And they argue that if these alternative routes are not "feasible and prudent," the present plan does not include "all possible" methods for reducing harm to the park. * * *

2)c

Respondents argue that it was unnecessary for the Secretary to make formal findings, and that he did, in fact, exercise his own independent judgment which was supported by the facts. In the District Court, respondents introduced affidavits, prepared specifically for this litigation, which indicated that the Secretary had made the decision and that the decision was supportable. These affidavits were contradicted by affidavits introduced by petitioners, who also sought to take the deposition of a for-

---

3. "It is hereby declared to be the national policy that special effort should be made to preserve the natural beauty of the countryside and public park and recreation lands, wildlife and waterfowl refuges, and historic sites. * * * After the effective date of the Federal-Aid Highway Act of 1968, the Secretary shall not approve any program or project which requires the use of any publicly owned land from a public park, recreation area, or wildlife and waterfowl refuge of national, State, or local significance as determined by the Federal, State, or local officials having jurisdiction thereof, or any land from an historic site of national, State, or local significance as so determined by such officials unless (1) there is no feasible and prudent alternative to the use of such land, and (2) such program includes all possible planning to minimize harm to such park, recreational area, wildlife and waterfowl refuge, or historic site resulting from such use." 23 U.S.C.A. § 138 (1964 ed., Supp. V).

[The language of section 4(f) of the Transportation Act is virtually identical.]

mer Federal Highway Administrator who had participated in the decision to route I–40 through Overton Park.

The District Court and the Court of Appeals found that formal findings by the Secretary were not necessary and refused to order the deposition of the former Federal Highway Administrator because those courts believed that probing of the mental processes of an administrative decisionmaker was prohibited. And, believing that the Secretary's authority was wide and reviewing courts' authority narrow in the approval of highway routes, the lower courts held that the affidavits contained no basis for a determination that the Secretary had exceeded his authority.

We agree that formal findings were not required. But we do not believe that in this case judicial review based solely on litigation affidavits was adequate.

A threshold question—whether petitioners are entitled to any judicial review—is easily answered. Section 701 of the Administrative Procedure Act provides that the action of "each authority of the Government of the United States," which includes the Department of Transportation, is subject to judicial review except where there is a statutory prohibition on review or where "agency action is committed to agency discretion by law." In this case, there is no indication that Congress sought to prohibit judicial review and there is most certainly no "showing of 'clear and convincing evidence' of a * * * legislative intent" to restrict access to judicial review. *Abbott Laboratories v. Gardner*, 387 U.S. 136, 141 (1967).

Similarly, the Secretary's decision here does not fall within the exception for action "committed to agency discretion." This is a very narrow exception.[23] Berger, Administrative Arbitrariness and Judicial Review, 65 Col. L. Rev. 55 (1965). The legislative history of the Administrative Procedure Act indicates that it is applicable in those rare instances where "statutes are drawn in such broad terms that in a given case there is no law to apply." S. Rep. No. 752, 79th Cong., 1st Sess. 26 (1945).

* * *

Despite the clarity of the statutory language, respondents argue that the Secretary has wide discretion. They recognize that the requirement that there be no "feasible" alternative route admits of little administrative discretion. For this exemption to apply the Secretary must find that as a matter of sound engineering it would not be feasible to build the highway along any other route. Respondents argue, however, that the requirement that there be no other "prudent" route requires the Secretary to engage in a wide-ranging balancing of competing interests. They contend that the Secretary should weigh the detriment resulting from the destruction of parkland against the cost of other routes, safety consid-

---

23. The scope of this exception has been the subject of extensive commentary. See, e.g., Berger, Administrative Arbitrariness: A Synthesis, 78 Yale L.J. 965 (1969); Saferstein, Nonreviewability: A Functional Analysis of "Committed to Agency Discretion," 82 Harv. L. Rev. 367 (1968); Davis, Administrative Arbitrariness is Not Always Reviewable, 51 Minn. L. Rev. 643 (1967); Berger, Administrative Arbitrariness: A Sequel, 51 Minn. L. Rev. 601 (1967).

erations, and other factors, and determine on the basis of the importance that he attaches to these other factors whether, on balance, alternative feasible routes would be "prudent."

But no such wide-ranging endeavor was intended. It is obvious that in most cases considerations of cost, directness of route, and community disruption will indicate that parkland should be used for highway construction whenever possible. Although it may be necessary to transfer funds from one jurisdiction to another, there will always be a smaller outlay required from the public purse when parkland is used since the public already owns the land and there will be no need to pay for right-of-way. And since people do not live or work in parks, if a highway is built on parkland no one will have to leave his home or give up his business. Such factors are common to substantially all highway construction. Thus, if Congress intended these factors to be on an equal footing with preservation of parkland there would have been no need for the statutes.

Congress clearly did not intend that cost and disruption of the community were to be ignored by the Secretary. But the very existence of the statutes indicates that protection of parkland was to be given paramount importance. * * * If the statutes are to have any meaning, the Secretary cannot approve the destruction of parkland unless he finds that alternative routes present <u>unique</u> problems.

Plainly, there is "law to apply" and thus the exemption for action "committed to agency discretion" is inapplicable. But the existence of judicial review is only the start: the standard for review must also be determined. For that we must look to § 706 of the Administrative Procedure Act, which provides that a "reviewing court shall * * * hold unlawful and set aside agency action, findings, and conclusions found" not to meet six separate standards. In all cases agency action must be set aside if the action was "arbitrary, capricious, an abuse of discretion, or otherwise not in accordance with law" or if the action failed to meet statutory, procedural, or constitutional requirements. In certain narrow, specifically limited situations, the agency action is to be set aside if the action was not supported by "substantial evidence." And in other equally narrow circumstances the reviewing court is to engage in a *de novo* review of the action and set it aside if it was "unwarranted by the facts."

Petitioners * * * contend that the "substantial evidence" standard of § 706(2)(E) must be applied. In the alternative, they claim that § 706(2)(F) applies and that there must be a *de novo* review to determine if the Secretary's action was "unwarranted by the facts." Neither of these standards is, however, applicable.

Review under the substantial-evidence test is authorized only when the agency action is taken pursuant to a rulemaking provision of the Administrative Procedure Act itself, or when the agency action is based on a public adjudicatory hearing. The Secretary's decision to allow the expenditure of federal funds to build I–40 through Overton Park was plainly not an exercise of a rulemaking function. And the only hearing that is required by either the Administrative Procedure Act or the statutes regulating the distribution of federal funds for highway construction is a public hearing conducted by local officials for the purpose of informing the community about the proposed project and eliciting community views on the design and route.   23 U.S.C.A. § 128 (1964 ed., Supp. V).   The hearing is nonadjudicatory, quasi-legislative in nature.   It is not designed to produce a record that is to be the basis of agency action—the basic requirement for substantial-evidence review.

Petitioners' alternative argument also fails.   *De novo* review of whether the Secretary's decision was "unwarranted by the facts" is authorized by § 706(2)(F) in only two circumstances.   First, such *de novo* review is authorized when the action is adjudicatory in nature and the agency factfinding procedures are inadequate.   And, there may be independent judicial factfinding when issues that were not before the agency are raised in a proceeding to enforce nonadjudicatory agency action.   Neither situation exists here.

Even though there is no *de novo* review in this case and the Secretary's approval of the route of I–40 does not have ultimately to meet the substantial-evidence test, the generally applicable standards of § 706 require the reviewing court to engage in a substantial inquiry.   Certainly, the Secretary's decision is entitled to a presumption of regularity.   But that presumption is not to shield his action from a thorough, probing, in-depth review.

The court is first required to decide whether the Secretary acted within the scope of his authority.   This determination naturally begins with a delineation of the scope of the Secretary's authority and discretion.   * * *   Also involved in this initial inquiry is a determination of whether on the facts the Secretary's decision can reasonably be said to be within that range.   * * *

Scrutiny of the facts does not end, however, with the determination that the Secretary has acted within the scope of his statutory authority.   Section 706(2)(A) requires a finding that the actual choice made was not "arbitrary, capricious, an abuse of discretion, or otherwise not in accordance with law."   To make this finding the court must consider whether the decision was based on a consideration of the relevant factors and whether there has been a clear error of judgment.   Although this inquiry into the facts is to be searching and careful, the ultimate standard of review is a narrow one.   The court is not empowered to substitute its judgment for that of the agency.

The final inquiry is whether the Secretary's action followed the necessary procedural requirements.   Here the only procedural error alleged is the failure of the Secretary to make formal findings and state his reason for allowing the highway to be built through the park.

Undoubtedly, review of the Secretary's action is hampered by his failure to make such findings, but the absence of formal findings does not necessarily require that the case be remanded to the Secretary.   Neither the Department of Transportation Act nor the Federal-Aid Highway Act requires such formal findings.   Moreover, the Administrative Procedural Act requirements that there be formal findings in certain rulemaking and adjudicatory proceedings do not apply to the Secretary's action here. * * *

* * * The lower courts based their review on the litigation affidavits that were presented. These affidavits were merely *"post hoc"* rationalizations which have traditionally been found to be an inadequate basis for review. And they clearly do not constitute the "whole record" compiled by the agency: the basis for review required by § 706 of the Administrative Procedure Act.

Thus it is necessary to remand this case to the District Court for plenary review of the Secretary's decision. That review is to be based on the full administrative record that was before the Secretary at the time he made his decision. But since the bare record may not disclose the factors that were considered or the Secretary's construction of the evidence it may be necessary for the District Court to require some explanation in order to determine if the Secretary acted within the scope of his authority and if the Secretary's action was justifiable under the applicable standard.

The court may require the administrative officials who participated in the decision to give testimony explaining their action. Of course, such inquiry into the mental processes of administrative decisionmakers is usually to be avoided. *United States v. Morgan,* 313 U.S. 409, 422 (1941). And where there are administrative findings that were made at the same time as the decision, as was the case in *Morgan,* there must be a strong showing of bad faith or improper behavior before such inquiry may be made. But here there are no such formal findings and it may be that the only way there can be effective judicial review is by examining the decisionmakers themselves.

The District Court is not, however, required to make such an inquiry. It may be that the Secretary can prepare formal findings * * * that will provide an adequate explanation for his action. Such an explanation will, to some extent, be a *"post hoc* rationalization" and thus must be viewed critically. If the District Court decides that additional explanation is necessary, that court should consider which method will prove the most expeditious so that full review may be had as soon as possible.

Reversed and remanded.

[The separate opinion of Justice Black is omitted.]

Notes

1. Justice Marshall cites *Abbott Laboratories v. Gardner,* 387 U.S. 136 (1967), infra p. 753, for the proposition that administrative actions are presumed to be judicially reviewable. And surely *Overton Park* is convincing support for this proposition. The Court entertains a challenge by a group of citizens who apparently have slight individual stake in the routing of the highway to an administrative determination for which Congress has prescribed no procedures and which, as a matter of custom, results in no formal documentation or written explanation. Nor has Congress anywhere specifically authorized review. This is not to say that the circumstances surrounding the Secretary of Transportation's decision

cannot be fitted into the shape of a lawsuit; it is to suggest that the prevailing judicial willingness to engage in review of administrative actions extends well beyond those situations in which clashes between private and official interests appear close analogs of disputes in the private law system.

2. The federal aid highway program involved in *Overton Park* is a quintessential example of the progressive legal formalization of federal developmental and managerial functions that have substantial social, economic, and political impacts. One of the principal techniques for managing the "externalities" of public as well as private activities is to subject those activities to consideration of a broader range of values. Statutory requirements for broadened consideration of federal activities inhabit both the framework statutes discussed in Chapter 1 and many amendments to the basic laws that authorize these so-called "proprietary" programs. As *Overton Park* demonstrates, these criteria provide a "law to apply" that is sufficient to trigger judicial review.

The conclusion that judicial review is appropriate has its own progressive logic. The court cannot review the activities of highway officials stretching over many years except on the basis of some sort of "record." If the Federal Highway Administration were simply to dump on the District Court all of the paperwork relating to the planning, design, approval and construction of I–40 through Memphis, the judge would be buried. Hence, the Supreme Court requires an explanation with some "findings" by the Secretary of Transportation in order to structure judicial evaluation of the underlying record. The Secretary's decision and its "rationale" will then be tested against the material in the record.

The implications of "record" review for the administrative process are predictable. Any official who knows that his/her action will be tested by reference to a record must somehow build one that will support the decision that is made. This requires the development of administrative routines which can be followed by subordinates—in this case the federal district engineers and the Federal Highway Administration—to assure that appropriate information is assembled on the crucial questions of feasibility and prudence. Judicial review thus reinforces the inexorable bureaucratization of those agency functions that it touches.

3. That such a bureaucratic process did not exist at the time of *Overton Park* is evident from the subsequent history of the case. Given the Supreme Court's remarkably narrow conception of "prudent" and its broad conception of "all possible planning," Secretary Volpe was certainly unlikely to have developed (or had developed for him) a record that would justify the decision to use park land. And, after numerous days of trial in the District Court on remand, it became clear that neither the contemporaneous record nor the recollections of the various persons involved in the project would provide a sufficient record upon which to uphold the Secretary's decision. The matter was therefore remanded to the Secretary. In the face of the Supreme Court's interpretation of 23 U.S.C.A. § 138, the Secretary declined to approve the parkland route. But this decision too was overturned. *Citizens to Preserve Overton Park, Inc. v. Volpe*, 357 F.Supp. 846 (W.D. Tenn. 1973). The second reversal came on petition by the State of Tennessee, which objected to the Secretary's refusal to approve the Overton Park route on the ground that he had specified no other route that would be either feasible or prudent. The State's argument, with which the district court agreed, was that without such a finding the Secretary, in rejecting the park route, had not complied with the findings requirement of the Supreme Court's *Overton Park* opinion.

This turn of events is not surprising. The Secretary had before him a record on the basis of which both the Tennessee Highway Department, in consultation with the Memphis City Council, and the Federal Highway Administrator had concluded that there was no feasible or prudent alternative to the Overton Park route. It seems unlikely that the same record would support a finding that a particular alternative route was both feasible and prudent. In the end, however, the Secretary's (then Brinegar) remand decision was upheld. The Sixth Circuit held that the district court was wrong to interpret section 4(f) as demanding the specification of an alternative route as a necessary element in justifying a refusal to find that there was "no feasible or prudent alternative." *Citizens to Preserve Overton Park v. Brinegar,* 494 F.2d 1212 (1974), *cert. denied* 421 U.S. 991 (1975).

4. More important, perhaps, than the law made by the *Overton Park* cases, that litigation illustrates the difficulty of inserting a rationalistic model of decisionmaking—records, formal findings, and judicial review—into the highly flexible, dynamic, and inherently political process of highway construction. But to understand this point, some history is necessary. Until the Federal Aid Road Act of 1916, roads were normally built and maintained by localities and turnpike companies. See generally Netherton, *Intergovernmental Relations Under the Federal Aid Highway Program,* 1 Urb. L. Ann. 15, 16–17 (1968). The federal government's participation in road building was premised on the notion that there was a national interest in providing a linked system of toll free roads for the movement of persons and goods in interstate commerce. Thus, in providing aid, the federal government required that monies be spent pursuant to an overall design or long-range plan for the development of highway networks. This system's conception entailed some coordination of local activity if not outright displacement of local authority. The federal legislation therefore required that states have highway departments with sufficient authority and responsibility to approve all projects and to certify their compliance with any requirements of federal law.

The interests of localities were, however, not forgotten in the federal highway program. Congress over the years strengthened the role of local governing bodies by requirements for local public hearings; for state certification that projects were consistent with the goals and objectives of local urban planning; for cooperative planning between localities and state highway departments; and for consideration of the views of local governing bodies on highway projects within standard metropolitan statistical areas.

At the time of the *Overton Park* decision the involvement of localities in highway planning was reinforced by the Intergovernmental Cooperation Act (ICA) of 1968, 42 U.S.C.A. § § 4201–4244. As implemented by circulars and directives from the Office of Management and Budget, compliance with the ICA was integrated with other federal policies as well. Thus, for example, section 102(2)(C) of the NEPA, 42 U.S.C.A. § 4332(2)(C), was synthesized with the ICA by the requirement that localities make, or be given the opportunity to make, comments on environmental quality questions arising in the planning and construction of highways. See DOT Order 5610.1A (Oct. 4, 1971). Section 128 of Title 23 also required that state highway departments certify that their projects were consistent with area planning objectives, and section 134(a) required that all projects be based on "a continuing comprehensive transportation planning process carried on cooperatively by States and local communities. * * * 23 U.S.C.A. § 134(a).

In short, the Federal Aid Highways Act, combined with other structural requirements of federal legislation, created a complex intergovernmental relationship.   And as in all such relationships there were cross currents, conflicts, and constituent pressures that required continuous negotiation and accommodation among the three levels of actors in the process.   See generally M. DERTHICK, THE INFLUENCE OF FEDERAL GRANTS (1970).

This is not to say that all was "blooming, buzzing confusion" in the administration of the Federal Aid Highways program.   As in all bureaucracies, the administration of the program is surrounded and in part structured by highly detailed statements of the various standards that must be satisfied, as well as the procedural steps through which satisfaction is to be demonstrated.   See generally FEDERAL HIGHWAY ADMINISTRATION, REVIEW OF FEDERAL-AID HIGHWAY PROGRAMS (1970).   But this was not a grant process that functioned like the applications process for graduate fellowships or research grants. State highway departments did not engage separately in something called "highway planning" and then apply for federal aid which was approved on the basis of a review of documentary evidence demonstrating compliance with federal standards.   Instead, the FHA delegated virtually all of its grant approval authority to its division engineer in each state.   That engineer worked constantly with each state highway department to improve the state's planning and engineering capabilities in connection with ongoing projects.   The federal objective was not to "build a record" which demonstrated compliance with all federal standards, but to get the best possible job out of quite diverse state highway departments in relation to those standards.   Moreover, the federal engineer had to remember at all times that the state department was embedded in state politics and was therefore also required to negotiate with, and take account of, local interests and local officials.

In this connection, one should note that 23 U.S.C.A. § 138's protection for park lands at issue in *Overton Park* demanded that the Secretary make certain findings only to the extent that the project involved a park having local significance as determined by elected local representatives.   And while there was no claim in the *Overton Park* case that the Memphis City Council had determined Overton Park to be insignificant, it is equally clear that the Tennessee State Department of Highways, in consultation with those same elected officials, had determined and certified that the planned route through Overton Park was consistent with the Memphis transportation planning process.   In short, the Secretary's initial determination that there was no feasible or prudent alternative had been made within the context of an ongoing process of intergovernmental consultation.

From this perspective one might question the Supreme Court's approach to the interpretation of the Federal Aid Highways Act.   For that interpretation suggests that the Congress intended that a Washington-based administrative official determine, on the basis of narrow federal criteria, the appropriate utilization of local public property.   Moreover, that decision was to be made in a "rational" fashion, presumably giving little weight to the political accommodations and trade-offs built into the general structure, or to the dynamics of the intergovernmental system from which the decision emerged.

Judicial review thus tends to push administrative action into a conceptual mold that employs clear divisions of function, sharp criteria for judgment, and detailed explanation for decisions.   Questions of administrative discretion or judgment are sharply formulated by the well drawn complaints of anti-highway plaintiffs. Or, as the second district court remand in *Overton Park* suggests, by pro highway plaintiffs as well. The influences of history, intergovernmental politics, and of the non-scientific or non-rational side of planning, tend to be ignored.

At the very least the influence of these factors on decisionmaking is difficult to reproduce in a "record" that is accessible for judicial review. Such factors appear, therefore, in the mouths of administrative defendants to be lame explanations for apparent incompetence or for the evasion of legislative mandates. The Administrator, thus, seems trapped between a Congress, which found comprehensive rationalization of his program impossible, and a reviewing court, which insisted that all exercises of judgment be explicable in terms of some cogently articulated policy. For a more extended discussion of the Federal Aid Highways Program, see Mashaw, *The Legal Structure of Frustration: Alternative Strategies for Public Choice Concerning Federally Aided Highway Construction*, 122 U. Pa. L. Rev. 1 (1973).

5. The Supreme Court in *Overton Park* says that the reasons offered by the Secretary for his decision cannot provide a basis for determining its legality because those reasons appear in litigation affidavits. They are, in the Court's terms, "post-hoc rationalizations." The Court then remands to the District Court, anticipating that it will, in turn, have to remand the case to the Secretary for a new "explanation" which, as the Court recognizes, will itself be "to some extent, * * * a post-hoc rationalization." In countless cases after *Overton Park*, courts have rejected administrators' explanations on the ground that they were post-hoc rationalizations. Yet it is not obvious why post-hoc rationalizations are offensive—at least in the case of informal actions that are not required by the APA, or by an agency's organic statute, to be accompanied by contemporaneous reasons.

Why are after-the-fact rationalizations any more suspect than contemporaneous reason-giving? To be sure, the ordinary meaning of *rationalize* is "to provide plausible but untrue reasons or motives for a course of conduct." WEBSTER'S THIRD NEW INTERNATIONAL DICTIONARY (Unabridged) 1885 (1971). Presumably this is to be distinguished from *explain*, which is "to make manifest: present in detail * * * to make plain or understandable * * * to give the meaning or significance of." Id. at 801. Is there any reason to believe that reasons given after a decision has been made are more likely to be disingenuous than reasons provided contemporaneously? Are the latter more likely to be genuine?

To pose such a question is to raise another. Is it not always the case that reason-giving follows decisionmaking? *"Post hocness"* seems to be merely a matter of degree. Moreover, few psychologists or psychoanalysts since J.H. ROBINSON, THE MIND IN THE MAKING (1921), have believed that articulated reasons capture much of the truth about human motivation. Although he disagreed strongly with the baleful line of reading, thinking, and teaching about judicial opinions that Robinson's position supported, Karl Llewellyn nevertheless said:

> I do not think that, save on occasions normally impossible to spot, an opinion reflects with any accuracy a third of the variegated great and petty motivating stimuli that have somehow combined to produce the particular decision, or that it shows the weight of such factors as it may happen to mention expressly, nor yet the manner of their interaction.

K. LLEWELLYN, THE COMMON LAW TRADITION: DECIDING APPEALS 131 (1960).   If this is true, the Supreme Court would have been equally justified in suggesting to the District Court in *Overton Park* that it view *all* reason-giving by administrators skeptically.

But perhaps there are other grounds for doubting the sort of post-hoc rationalization that confronted the Court in the *Overton Park* case.   Statements made in litigation affidavits may not reflect the administrator's thinking, but rather his lawyer's.   Again, however, this is hardly a decisive objection.   As we noted in Chapter 3, the Court has accepted "collegial" or "organizational" decisions as a fact of life in bureaucracy.   And presumably an administrator has access to the agency's legal staff in informal proceedings as in other settings. Moreover, having once been reversed, it seems highly unlikely that any prudent administrator would formulate a new rationale for decision without relying heavily on legal counsel.

This observation prompts one to wonder what might be going on in a case like *Local 814, International Brotherhood of Teamsters v. NLRB.*, 546 F.2d 989 (D.C. Cir. 1976), *cert. denied* 434 U.S. 818 (1977).   There the court had remanded to the Board a decision which was apparently inconsistent with another NLRB case that had been decided almost simultaneously.   In upholding the Board's re-rationalization on review in *Local 814* following remand, the court suggested that the *Overton Park* proscription against post-hoc rationalization did not preclude the Board from rendering a valid decision based on an "amplified articulation".   This, the court reasoned, was not a "post-hoc rationalization," because it did not violate the purpose of the Supreme Court's prohibition in *Overton Park*, to wit, upholding "agency action on the basis of rationales offered by anyone other than the proper decisionmakers."   Id. at 992.   Apparently the court convinced itself that the people who draft "amplified articulations" are different from those who prepare litigation affidavits.

Other cases suggest different rationalizations for the prohibition against post-hoc rationalizations.   They include the difficulty for reviewing courts in parsing the agency record without the assistance of a contemporaneous rationale and the similar difficulty for petitioners who wish to seek reconsideration within the agency.   However, since briefs can focus a court on the relevant portions of the record, it is hard to see why judges cannot accept the same advice from agency post-hoc rationalizations, however provided.   And any litigant who can petition for reconsideration can also request clarification of the agency's rationale.

A more plausible explanation of the Court's reaction in *Overton Park* is that it was searching for some device to force administrators to reason *within* applicable statutory criteria *at the time* they are making decisions.   For surely it is only through such a reasoning process that statutory criteria take on life and force. That the prohibition against post-hoc rationalizations is likely to have only modest impact is perhaps not a decisive argument against it, given the Court's modest arsenal of weapons to induce administrative fidelity to statutory commands. Moreover, in *Overton Park* it was clear that, under the Court's interpretation, the Secretary had misconstrued his authority.   On the other hand, where an agency is acting within its authority and offers, *post hoc*, a rationale that, if contemporaneously made, would have justified its action, a remand for a rearticulation of reasons in a "decisional context" may be pointless.

B. STANDING TO OBTAIN REVIEW

The standing doctrine, narrowly characterized, is the federal court's answer to the question: Can any citizen who encounters what appears to be unlawful conduct by a government agency obtain review of its actions? In blunt words, the answer is "No." The issues that concern us in this section are thus "Why not?" And, if not any citizen, then which citizens?

The concept of standing is analytically separable from ripeness and reviewability, which are considered in succeeding sections, but the student will soon discover many areas of overlap among these doctrines as they are applied by the courts. According to Justice Brennan's opinion in *Association of Data Processing Servicing Organizations, Inc. v. Camp* and *Barlow v. Collins*, infra pp. 645 *et seq.*, each of these doctrines is a facet of the broader concept of justiciability, "a concept of uncertain meaning and scope" embodying a "blend of constitutional requirements and policy considerations" that bear on the central question: Should judicial power be employed to entertain *this* challenge to official conduct at the instigation of *this* litigant at *this* time? Because each new decision on standing may reformulate and recombine the elements of analysis, an essentially chronological, rather conceptual, organization of the materials is appropriate. We begin with some baseline jurisprudence from the New Deal and immediate post-New Deal era and then canvass in more detail the Supreme Court rulings since 1970.

1. STANDING PRIOR TO THE APA

The Supreme Court decisions on standing prior to the enactment of the Administrative Procedure Act—though perhaps not a wholly coherent jurisprudence—followed two main doctrinal axes. The first is illustrated by *Alexander Sprunt & Son v. United States*, 281 U.S. 249 (1930), a suit challenging an order of the Interstate Commerce Commission establishing railroad rates for the shipment of cotton. At the time of the *Sprunt* decision, ICC orders were reviewable in the district courts pursuant to the Urgent Deficiencies Act, which provided:

> Except as otherwise provided by Act of Congress, the district courts shall have jurisdiction of any civil action to enforce, enjoin, set aside, annul or suspend, in whole or in part, any order of the [Interstate Commerce Commission].

Sprunt owned a wharfside warehouse on the Texas gulf coast, which compressed and stored cotton preparatory to shipment to other U.S. ports. Like other similarly located shippers, Sprunt had for several years been the beneficiary of a rate structure that charged it the same rate as warehouses located away from the wharfs, which had to pay extra to deliver their cotton to vessels for shipment to customers elsewhere in the U.S. Export shipments bore an additional charge of 3.5 cents/100 pounds to reflect supposed costs of unloading for compressing and reloading. The apparent inequities of this structure led the ICC, on its own initiative, to investigate the legality of the rates for cotton. After extended hearings, the Commission found that the existing rate structure was "unduly preferential" and it directed that the rates be equalized in any fashion "which would preserve but not increase the carriers' revenues." When the railroads were unable to agree on new rates, the Commission reopened the proceeding and issued an order prescribing adjustments that eliminated Sprunt's competitive advantage.

Sprunt and other shippers, along with the railroads, brought suit challenging the ICC's order under the statutory procedure described above, but the railroads did not pursue their objections beyond the district court. The shippers contended, first, that the Commission's finding of "undue prejudice and preference" was without basis and, second, that its order increasing their rates, without a hearing and specific findings that the new rates were reasonable, was unlawful. The Commission challenged their standing to sue, and the Supreme Court, in an opinion by Justice Brandeis, agreed:

> *First.* The appellants contend that there is no basis for the Commission's finding of undue prejudice and preference. We are of opinion that appellants have no standing, in their own right, to make this attack. * * *
>
> * * * The appellants' position is legally no different from what it would have been if the carriers had filed the rates freely, pursuant to an informal suggestion of the Commission or one of its members; or if the filing had been made by carriers voluntarily after complaint filed before the Commission, which had never reached a hearing, because the rate structure complained of was thus superseded. * * * Since the appellants' economic advantage as shippers was an incident of the supposed right exercised by the carriers, the appellants cannot complain after the carriers are satisfied or prefer not to press their right, if any. * * *
>
> * * * A judgment in appellants' favor would be futile. It would not restore the appellants to the advantage previously enjoyed. If the Commission's order is set aside, the carriers would still be free to continue to equalize the rates; and for aught that appears would continue to do so.
>
> *Second.* Appellants complain of the order also on the ground that it authorized an increase in the local or domestic delivery rates without a hearing and findings as to the reasonableness of the level of either the old or the new rates. It is urged that § 15 of the Act does not authorize the Commission to fix the rates necessary to remove undue prejudice without such hearing and findings. But plainly appellants cannot, in their own right, be heard to complain in this suit of this part of the order. * * * In prescribing the rate, the Commission in no way prejudiced any preexisting rights or remedies of the appellants. Any question as to the reasonableness of the level of the rate was expressly left open by the Commission. It did not prescribe any rate as the minimum. If appellants are aggrieved by the level of the new rates, they still have their remedy before the Commission under § § 13 and 15 of the Act.

Alexander Sprunt is the last of a trilogy of Transportation Act standing cases decided by the Court between 1923 and 1930 in opinions also authorized by Justice Brandeis. The first case, *Edward Hines Yellow Pine*

Trustees v. United States, 263 U.S. 143 (1923), involved an ICC order requiring that railroads discontinue charges for storage of lumber left in railroad cars after arrival at their destination. These charges were imposed during the First World War to combat a shortage of rolling stock, and the ICC order was premised on a finding that shortage conditions no longer existed. A shipper who did not use car storage for its products, and was therefore advantaged by charges against competitors who did, sought review of the order. The Court found that the plaintiff had sustained no legal injury under the act because his statutory interest was limited to protection against "unjust discrimination." It therefore refused to rule on the legality of the ICC's order. By contrast, in *The Chicago Junction Case*, 264 U.S. 258 (1924), competitors who opposed the acquisition of terminal railroads by the New York Central were permitted to obtain review of an ICC order that approved the acquisitions. The Court found that the plaintiffs, who had lost business because of the Central's control of terminals, had a protected interest under a 1920 amendment to the Act, which required ICC approval of terminal acquisitions and, specifically, consideration of the interests of other carriers.

old rule

Later decisions followed the Transportation Act cases in insisting that a plaintiff seeking review demonstrate a "legal right" or "protected interest." In *Tennessee Electric Power Co. v. TVA*, 306 U.S. 118, 137–39 (1939), for example, the Court held that private power companies lacked standing to challenge the constitutionality of the act creating the Tennessee Valley Authority since they had no legal right derived from common law, statute, or franchise to be free from governmentally-sponsored competition. But when Congress, actuated by concern for private utility companies, amended the Tennessee Valley Authority Act in 1959 to restrict the TVA's area of operations, the Court entertained suit by an injured competitor challenging the TVA's interpretation of the new area limitations. *Hardin v. Kentucky Utilities Co.*, 390 U.S. 1 (1968).

Professor Davis, a fierce critic of the "legal right" test, see generally 3 K. DAVIS, ADMINISTRATIVE LAW TREATISE § 22.04 (1958), offered two sources of authority for rejecting it. One was the APA, which he viewed as granting standing to any party "aggrieved in fact"—a reading of section 702 that is certainly not self-evident and has never been fully accepted by the Supreme Court. Davis also suggested an analogy to the common law.

> The natural system is that of the common law: If A and B are private parties and A hurts B, B has standing to get a determination of the legality of A's action. Why should not the law be the same, whether A is the government, an agency, an officer, or a private party, and whether the injury is to B's person, his physical property or his intangible interests? Is not the natural system the simple one that injury in fact is enough for standing?

Davis, *The Liberalized Law of Standing*, 37 U.Chi. L. Rev. 450, 468 (1970).

Professor Jaffe rejected Davis' analogy: "[T]*hat is not the common law.* Rather, * * * if A alleges that B is violating a statute and the court concludes that the statute was not designed to protect A's interest the court will not determine the validity of A's claim." Jaffe, *Standing Again*, 84 Harv. L. Rev. 633, 636 (1971). On that point, Professor Jaffe was clearly correct.

A functional criticism of the "legal right" rule was that courts found it difficult to apply. The search for a "legal right" to determine standing suggested that the court was to resolve that issue as a preliminary matter without reaching the merits. But whether a plaintiff's interest is within statutory, common-law, or constitutional protections is clearly a merits question. *Perkins v. Lukens Steel Co.*, 310 U.S. 113 (1940), is a decision whose errors may well have been the product of confusion between standing and the merits of the claim. The steel company sought to review an order of the Secretary of Labor under the Walsh-Healy Act establishing minimum rates of pay in the steel industry. Lukens claimed that the Secretary had, in establishing six different steel production regions in the country, misinterpreted what the Congress meant by "locality." But the Court never reached the question of statutory construction; it ruled that the company had no legally protected interest in the proper construction of the Walsh-Healy Act and dismissed the suit. In the Court's view, the Act merely constituted instructions to the government's purchasing agents, and, as in the case of a private agent, the common law affords no remedy against an agent who misinterprets his principal's instructions.

Had the Court carefully considered the purpose of the Walsh-Healy Act's requirement that the Secretary's wage determinations be made in terms of "localities," it would have recognized that provision was designed specifically to protect employers from general standard setting that did not take into account differences in local economic situations. (*Perkins* was overturned by the Fulbright Amendment, Act of June 30, 1952, Pub. L. No. 82–430, which also introduced the formal hearing requirements discussed in the *Baldor Electric Case*, supra p. 418.) Similarly one might argue that in *Sprunt* the Court's focus on the Transportation Act shut out the potentially analogous common law tort of interference with advantageous business relationships which might have supported recognition of a legal wrong to the dockside warehouses.

Perkins and *Sprunt* might be explained on other grounds—the former on the Court's reticence to review non-regulatory functions of the government; the latter on Brandeis's interest in protecting fledgling regulatory agencies from disruptive judicial interference. Nevertheless, they suggest that there is some danger that a search for "legal rights," framed as a question of standing, confuses analysis of the merits of claims.

The "legal right" debate raises a broader question: To what degree should a claim for review be required to track the general requirements of a private law claim, i.e., that the plaintiff has been damaged by the wrongful action or inaction of the defendant (or more succinctly "act," "cause," "damage," "fault")? Some approximation of these elements seems sensible, but close adherence to the content of these concepts in private law might narrowly confine review of administrative action. For example, the wrongfulness of a private defendant's conduct often depends upon owing a duty to the plaintiff that is distinct from any duty owed the public generally. Vigorously applied, this notion would suggest that private parties claiming to be damaged by unlawful official conduct would generally fail to state a cause of action, for official duties are generally owed to the public at large. Similarly, many types of "damage" caused by public officials, such as the denial of a license or other public benefit, would not constitute an actionable "injury" under private law. Nor is an agency's failure properly to exercise its regulatory responsibilities readily characterized as the "proximate cause" of harm resulting from unregulated conduct. Consider here the Court's treatment of "causation" in *Sprunt*.

Does judicial review of official action serve the same purposes as a private law suit? Or do review proceedings have public aspects that warrant a different approach to the question of whether a cognizable claim has been stated? See generally J. VINING, LEGAL IDENTITY: THE COMING OF AGE IN PUBLIC LAW (1978); Chayes, *The Supreme Court, 1981 Term—Foreword: Public Law Litigation and the Burger Court*, 96 Harv. L. Rev. 4 (1982); Mashaw, *"Rights" in the Federal Administrative State*, 92 Yale L.J. 1129 (1983).

The second line of pre–1946 standing cases is epitomized by *Federal Communications Commission v. Sanders Brothers*, 309 U.S. 470 (1940). In that case the holder of a broadcast license in East Dubuque, Illinois, challenged the FCC's award of a license to a new station in Dubuque, Iowa, just across the Mississippi River. The challenger claimed, inter alia, that the Commission had improperly failed to take into account that the advertising market that the two stations would share was not adequate to support more than one. The Solicitor General responded that the Communications Act of 1934 did not confer on licensees a legal right to be protected from competition and that, on the authority of *Sprunt* and similar cases, Sanders Bros. lacked standing to challenge the Commission's award of a license to a competitor.

The Supreme Court found the case distinguishable from *Sprunt* in light of the language Congress had used in authorizing judicial review of FCC orders:

> * * * [R]espondent appealed to the Court of Appeals for the District of Columbia. That court entertained the appeal and held that one of the issues which the Commission should have tried was that of alleged economic injury to the respondent's station by the establishment of an additional station and that the Commission had erred in failing to make findings on that issue. * * *

> The petitioner's contentions are that under the Communications Act economic injury to a competitor is not a ground for refusing a broadcast license and that since this is so, the respondent was not a person aggrieved or whose interests were adversely affected by the Commission's action, within the meaning of § 402(b) of the Act which authorizes appeals from the Commission's orders.

* * *

First. We hold that resulting economic injury to a rival station is not, in and of itself, and apart from considerations of public convenience, interest, or necessity, an element the petitioner must weigh, and as to which it must make findings, in passing on an application for a broadcasting license. * * *

This is not to say that the question of competition between a proposed station and one operating under an existing license is to be entirely disregarded by the Commission, and, indeed, the Commission's practice shows that it does not disregard that question.   It may have a vital and important bearing upon the ability of the applicant adequately to serve his public; it may indicate that both stations—the existing and the proposed—will go under, with the result that a portion of the listening public will be left without adequate service; it may indicate that, by a division of the field, both stations will be compelled to render inadequate service.   These matters, however, are distinct from the consideration that, if a license be granted, competition between the licensee and any other existing station may cause economic loss to the latter.   If such economic loss were a valid reason for refusing a license this would mean that the Commission's function is to grant a monopoly in the field of broadcasting, a result which the Act itself expressly negatives. * * *

Second. It does not follow that, because the licensee of a station cannot resist the grant of a license to another, on the ground that the resulting competition may work economic injury to him, he has no standing to appeal from an order of the Commission granting the application.

Section 402(b) of the Act provides for an appeal to the Court of Appeals of the District of Columbia (1) by an applicant for a license or permit, or (2) "by any other person aggrieved or whose interests are adversely affected by any decision of the Commission granting or refusing any such application."

The petitioner insists that as economic injury to the respondent was not a proper issue before the Commission it is impossible that § 402(b) was intended to give the respondent standing to appeal, since absence of right implies absence of remedy.   This view would deprive subsection (2) of any substantial effect.

Congress had some purpose in enacting § 402(b)(2).   It may have been of opinion that one likely to be financially injured by the issue of a license would be the only person having a sufficient interest to bring to the attention of the appellate court errors of law in the action of the Commission in granting the license.   It is within the power of Congress to confer such standing to prosecute an appeal. * * *

Notes

1. Although the *Sanders Brothers* Court states that "it is within the power of Congress to confer such standing," the constitutional issue raised by section 402(b) of the Communications Act was not frivolous.   If "legal right" cases like *Sprunt* rested on the constitutional requirement of a "case or controversy" and if section 402(b) authorized review where the plaintiff's interest was not otherwise "legally protected," the Act attempted to confer jurisdiction that was not a part of the judicial power of the federal courts.   In a famous opinion, *Associated Industries of New York State, Inc. v. Ickes*, 134 F.2d 694 (2d Cir.), *reversed per curiam on other grounds* 320 U.S. 707 (1943), Judge Jerome Frank reconciled the *Sanders'* approach to standing with the "cases or controversies" requirement by

denominating the "person aggrieved" within the meaning of various federal provisions for specific statutory review a "private attorney general." In Frank's view, Congress had the power to direct the Attorney General to bring suit to protect the public interest in federal agency actions and could therefore alternatively direct that such public interest suits be pursued by "persons aggrieved."

Judge Frank's opinion, while later influential, is little more than a play on words. The "private attorney general" rationale proves too much, for it fails to place any limit on the congressional power to expand judicial jurisdiction. Under Judge Frank's theory Congress might just as easily provide for suit by "all green-eyed persons" or, indeed, "all persons." Yet presumably Congress cannot write the case or controversy requirement out of the Constitution. At the same time Frank's opinion reveals too little about the contours of standing under the "any person aggrieved" language of section 402(b) and other specific review provisions; leaving "legal right" behind, the opinion fails to provide any criteria for identifying those "grievances" that confer standing.

2. Constitutional considerations aside, what difference should it make to a court that a litigant is seeking to invoke an express statutory review provision rather than one or more general grants of federal court jurisdiction? Consider the following comment by Professor Scott, *Standing in the Supreme Court—A Functional Analysis*, 86 Harv. L. Rev. 645, 656 (1973):

> The difference, and it is a vital one, is that Congress has weighed the need for and value of judicial review of a given category of administrative decisions, and has decided it is warranted. Congress having explicitly made that decision, the Court has before it only the implementing, secondary decision as to whether there is reason not to allow the particular plaintiff in question to be one of those who may invoke the review—and the standing rules tend to become much more liberal.

Thus, prior to 1970 most lower courts had held that section 702 of the APA merely codified the pre-1946 law of standing: A plaintiff had standing to seek review of agency action only if he could show either that he had suffered a "legal wrong" or that he was "aggrieved or adversely affected" within the meaning of an express review provision of the statute the agency was purporting to implement (the *Sanders Brothers* doctrine). See Comment *Judicial Review of Agency Action: The Unsettled Law of Standing*, 69 Mich. L. Rev. 540, 545–46 (1971).

2. STANDING UNDER THE APA

ASSOCIATION OF DATA PROCESSING SERVICE ORGANIZATIONS, INC. v. CAMP

Supreme Court of the United States, 1970.
397 U.S. 150, 90 S.Ct. 827, 25 L.Ed.2d 184.

MR. JUSTICE DOUGLAS delivered the opinion of the Court.

Petitioners sell data processing services to businesses generally. In this suit they seek to challenge a ruling by respondent Comptroller of the Currency that, as an incident to their banking services, national banks, including respondent American National Bank & Trust Company, may make data processing services available to other banks and to bank customers. The District Court dismissed the complaint for lack of standing of petitioners to bring the suit. * * *

Generalizations about standing to sue are largely worthless as such. One generalization is, however, necessary and that is that the question of standing in the federal courts is to be considered in the framework of Article III which restricts judicial power to "cases" and "controversies." As we recently stated in *Flast v. Cohen*, 392 U.S. 83 (1968), "[I]n terms of Article III limitations on federal court jurisdiction, the question of standing is related only to whether the dispute sought to be adjudicated will be presented in an adversary context and in a form historically viewed as capable of judicial resolution." *Flast* was a *taxpayer's* suit. The present is a *competitor's* suit. And while the two have the same Article III starting point, they do not necessarily track one another.

The first question is whether the plaintiff alleges that the challenged action has caused him injury in fact, economic or otherwise. There can be no doubt but that petitioners have satisfied this test. The petitioners not only allege that competition by national banks in the business of providing data processing services might entail some future loss of profits for the petitioners, they also allege that respondent American National Bank & Trust Company was performing or preparing to perform such services for two customers on whom petitioner Data Systems, Inc., had previously agreed or negotiated to perform such services. The petitioners' suit was brought not only against the American National Bank & Trust Company, but also against the Comptroller of the Currency. The Comptroller was alleged to have caused petitioners injury in fact by his 1966 ruling which stated:

> "Incidental to its banking services, a national bank may make available its data processing equipment or perform data processing services on such equipment for other banks and bank customers." Comptroller's Manual for National Banks ¶ 3500 (October 15, 1966).

The Court of Appeals viewed the matter differently, stating:

> "[A] plaintiff may challenge alleged illegal competition when as complainant it pursues (1) a legal interest by reason of public charter or contract, * * * (2) a legal interest by reason of statutory protection, * * * or (3) a 'public interest' in which Congress has recognized the need for review of administrative action and plaintiff is significantly involved to have standing to represent the public. * * * "[1]

The "legal interest" test goes to the merits. The question of standing is different. It concerns, apart from the "case" or "controversy" test, the question whether the interest sought to be protected by the complainant is arguably within the zone of interests to be protected or regulated by the statute or constitutional guarantee in question. Thus the Administrative Procedure Act grants standing to a person "aggrieved by agency action within the meaning of a relevant statute." That interest, at times,

---

[1]. The first two tests applied by the Court of Appeals required a showing of a "legal interest." * * * The third test mentioned by the Court of Appeals, which rests on an explicit provision in a regulatory statute conferring standing and is commonly referred to in terms of allowing suits by "private attorneys general," is inapplicable to the present case. See *FCC v. Sanders Bros. Radio Station*, 309 U.S. 470; *Associated Industries v. Ickes*, 134 F.2d 694, vacated on suggestion of mootness, 320 U.S. 707.

may reflect "aesthetic, conservational, and recreational" as well as economic values.   A person or a family may have a spiritual stake in First Amendment values sufficient to give standing to raise issues concerning the Establishment Clause and the Free Exercise Clause.   We mention these noneconomic values to emphasize that standing may stem from them as well as from the economic injury on which petitioners rely here. Certainly he who is "likely to be financially" injured may be a reliable private attorney general to litigate the issues of the public interest in the present case.

Apart from Article III jurisdictional questions, problems of standing, as resolved by this Court for its own governance, have involved a "rule of self-restraint."   Congress can, of course, resolve the question one way or another, save as the requirements of Article III dictate otherwise. *Muskrat v. United States*, 219 U.S. 346.

Where statutes are concerned, the trend is toward enlargement of the class of people who may protest administrative action.   The whole drive for enlarging the category of aggrieved "persons" is symptomatic of that trend.   In a closely analogous case we held that an existing entrepreneur had standing to challenge the legality of the entrance of a newcomer into the business, because the established business was allegedly protected by a valid city ordinance that protected it from unlawful competition. *Chicago v. Atchison, T. & S.F. R. Co.*, 357 U.S. 77.   In that tradition was *Hardin v. Kentucky Utilities Co.*, 390 U.S. 1. * * *

It is argued that the *Chicago* case and the *Hardin* case are relevant here because of § 4 of the Bank Service Corporation Act of 1962, which provides:

> "No bank service corporation may engage in any activity other than the performance of bank services for banks."

The Court of Appeals for the First Circuit held in *Arnold Tours, Inc. v. Camp*, 408 F.2d 1147, 1153, that by reason of § 4 a data processing company has standing to contest the legality of a national bank performing data processing services for other banks and bank customers:

> "Section 4 had a broader purpose than regulating only the service corporations.   It was also a response to the fears expressed by a few senators, that without such a prohibition, the bill would have enabled 'banks to engage in a nonbanking activity,' S. Rep. No. 2105 [87th Cong., 2d Sess., 7–12] (Supplemental views of Senators Proxmire, Douglas, and Neuberger), and thus constitute 'a serious exception to the accepted public policy which strictly limits banks to banking.' (Supplemental views of Senators Muskie and Clark).   We think Congress has provided the sufficient statutory aid to standing even though the competition may not be the precise kind Congress legislated against."

We do not put the issue in those words, for they implicate the merits.   We do think, however, that § 4 arguably brings a competitor within the zone of interests protected by it.   * * *

* * * Both [the Bank Service Corporation and the National Bank] Acts are clearly "relevant" statutes within the meaning of § 702.   The

Acts do not in terms protect a specified group. But their general policy is apparent; and those whose interests are directly affected by a broad or narrow interpretation of the Acts are easily identifiable. It is clear that petitioners, as competitors of national banks which are engaging in data processing services, are within the class of "aggrieved" persons who, under § 702, are entitled to judicial review of "agency action."

BARLOW v. COLLINS

Supreme Court of the United States, 1970.
397 U.S. 159, 90 S.Ct. 832, 25 L.Ed.2d 192.

MR. JUSTICE DOUGLAS delivered the opinion of the Court.

The question to be decided in this case is whether tenant farmers eligible for payments under the upland cotton program enacted as part of the Food and Agriculture Act of 1965 have standing to challenge the validity of a certain amended regulation promulgated by the respondent Secretary of Agriculture in 1966.

The upland cotton program incorporates a 1938 statute, § 8(g) of the Soil Conservation and Domestic Allotment Act, thereby permitting participants in the program to assign payments only "as security for cash or advances to finance making a crop."[1] The regulation of the respondent Secretary of Agriculture in effect until 1966 defined "making a crop" to exclude assignments to secure "the payment of the whole or any part of a cash * * * rent for a farm." Following passage of the 1965 Act, however, and before any payments were made under it, the Secretary deleted the exclusion and amended the regulation expressly to define "making a crop" to include assignments to secure "the payment of cash rent for land used [for planting, cultivating, or harvesting]." 31 Fed. Reg. 815 (1966).[3]

Petitioners, cash-rent tenant farmers suing on behalf of themselves and other farmers similarly situated, filed this action in the District Court for the Middle District of Alabama. They sought a declaratory judgment that the amended regulation is invalid and unauthorized by statute, and an injunction prohibiting the respondent federal officials from permitting assignments pursuant to the amended regulation. Their com-

---

1. The Secretary of Agriculture is authorized by 7 U.S.C.A. § 1444(d)(5) to pay a farmer in advance of the growing season up to 50% of the estimated benefits due him. Section 1444(d)(13) authorizes the farmer to assign such benefits subject to the limitations of § 8(g).

3. 32 Fed. Reg. 14921 (1967), 7 CFR § 709.3 (1969) now provides:

"*Purposes for which a payment may be assigned.*

"(a) A payment which may be made to a producer under any program to which this part is applicable may be assigned only as security for cash or advances to finance making a crop, handling or marketing an agricultural commodity, or performing a conservation practice, for the current crop year. No assignment may be made to secure or pay any preexisting indebtedness of any nature whatsoever.

"(b) To finance making a crop means (1) to finance the planting, cultivating, or harvesting a crop, including the purchase of equipment required therefor and the payment of cash rent for land used therefor, or (2) to provide food, clothing, and other necessities required by the producer or persons dependent upon him."

plaint alleged that the petitioners are suffering irreparable injury under the amended regulation because it provides their landlord "with the opportunity to demand that [they] and all those similarly situated assign the [upland cotton program] benefits in advance as a condition to obtaining a lease to work the land."[5]   As a result, the complaint stated, the tenants are required to obtain financing of all their other farm needs—groceries, clothing, tools, and the like—from the landlord as well, since prior to harvesting the crop they lack cash and any source of credit other than the landlord.   He, in turn, the complaint alleges, levies such high prices and rates of interest on these supplies that the tenants' crop profits are consumed each year in debt payments.   Petitioners contend that they can attain a "modest measure of economic independence" if they are able to use their "advance subsidy payments * * * [to] form cooperatives to buy [supplies] at wholesale and reasonable prices in lieu of the excessive prices demanded by [the landlord] of * * * captive consumers with no funds to purchase elsewhere."   Thus, petitioners allege that they suffer injury in fact from the operation of the amended regulation.

The District Court, in an unreported opinion, held that the petitioners "lack standing to maintain this action against these [respondent] government officials," because the latter "have not taken any action which directly invades any legally protected interest of the plaintiffs."   The Court of Appeals for the Fifth Circuit affirmed, one judge dissenting.   It held that petitioners lacked standing not only because they alleged no invasion of a legally protected interest but also because petitioners "have not shown us, nor have we found, any provision of the Food and Agriculture Act of 1965 which either expressly or impliedly gives [petitioners] standing to challenge this administrative regulation or gives the Courts authority to review such administration action." * * *

Our decision in *Data Processing Service v. Camp, ante,* leads us to reverse here.

First, there is no doubt that in the context of this litigation the tenant farmers, petitioners here, have the personal stake and interest that impart the concrete adverseness required by Article III.

Second, the tenant farmers are clearly within the zone of interests protected by the Act.

Implicit in the statutory provisions and their legislative history is a congressional intent that the Secretary protect the interests of tenant farmers.   Both of the relevant statutes expressly enjoin the Secretary to do so.   The Food and Agriculture Act of 1965 states that "[t]he Secretary shall provide adequate safeguards to protect the interests of tenants. * * * Section 8(b) * * * in turn, provides that "the Secretary shall, as far as practicable, protect the interests of tenants. * * * "   The legislative history of the "making a crop" provision, though sparse, similarly in-

5. The complaint stated that some of the petitioners "were denied the right to work the land" when they refused to execute assignments to their landlord.   The complaint also alleged that "[p]laintiffs have been tenant farmers on this land from eleven to sixty-one years * * * and [two of them] have been on this land all their lives."

dicates a congressional intent to benefit the tenants.[7] They are persons "aggrieved by agency action within the meaning of a relevant statute" as those words are used in 5 U.S.C.A. § 702.

Third, judicial review of the Secretary's action is not precluded. * * *

* * * The right of judicial review is ordinarily inferred where congressional intent to protect the interests of the class of which the plaintiff is a member can be found; in such cases, unless members of the protected class may have judicial review the statutory objectives might not be realized.

We hold that the statutory scheme at issue here is to be read as evincing a congressional intent that petitioners may have judicial review of the Secretary's action.

The judgments of the Court of Appeals and of the District Court are vacated and the case is remanded to the District Court for a hearing on the merits.

MR. JUSTICE BRENNAN, with whom MR. JUSTICE WHITE joins, concurring in the result and dissenting.

I concur in the result in both cases but dissent from the Court's treatment of the question of standing to challenge agency action. * * *

Although *Flast v. Cohen* was not a case challenging agency action, its determination of the basis for standing should resolve that question for all cases. We there confirmed what we said in *Baker v. Carr*, 369 U.S. 186 (1962), that the "gist of the question of standing" is whether the party seeking relief has "alleged such a personal stake in the outcome of the controversy as to assure that concrete adverseness which sharpens the presentation of issues upon which the court so largely depends for illumination of difficult * * * questions." "In other words," we said in *Flast*, "when standing is placed in issue in a case, the question is whether the person whose standing is challenged is a proper party to request an adjudication of a particular issue" and not whether the controversy is otherwise justiciable[3] or whether, on the merits, the plaintiff has a legally pro-

---

7. See the remarks of Representative Fulmer, 82 Cong.Rec. 844 (1937), and of Senator Adams, id., at 1756. The fact that assignments could be made at all indicated a congressional concern for the farmers' welfare, in light of the general statutory prohibition on assignment of federal claims embodied in the Anti-Assignment Act, 31 U.S.C.A. § 203. This concern was noted in a letter from the Secretary of Agriculture to the President of the Senate in January 1952, in which the Secretary stated that § 8(g) "was enacted for the purpose of creating additional credit to farmers to assist them in financing farming operations." S.Rep. No. 1305, 82d Cong., 2d Sess., 3.

3. Other elements of justiciability are, for instance, ripeness, and the policy against friendly or collusive suits. "Justiciability" is also the term of art used to refer to the constitutional necessity that courts not deal with certain issues lest they "intrude into areas committed to the other branches of government." The political-question doctrine has its analogue in the sphere of administrative law in the concept of nonreviewability. And, of course, federal courts may not decide questions over which they lack jurisdiction. Thus, on many grounds other than an absence of standing, a court may dismiss a lawsuit without proceeding to the merits to determine whether the plaintiff presents a claim upon which relief may be granted, and, if so, whether he has borne his burden of proof.

tected interest that the defendant's action invaded. The objectives of the Article III standing requirement are simple: the avoidance of any use of a "federal court as a forum [for the airing of] generalized grievances about the conduct of government," and the creation of a judicial context in which "the questions will be framed with the necessary specificity, * * * the issues * * * contested with the necessary adverseness and * * * litigation * * * pursued with the necessary vigor to assure that the * * * challenge will be made in a form traditionally thought to be capable of judicial resolution." Thus, as we held in *Flast*, "the question of standing is related only to whether the dispute sought to be adjudicated will be presented in an adversary context and in a form historically viewed as capable of judicial resolution."

In light of *Flast*, standing exists when the plaintiff alleges, as the plaintiffs in each of these cases alleged, that the challenged action has caused him injury in fact, economic or otherwise. He thus shows that he has the requisite "personal stake in the outcome" of his suit. * * *

When the legality of administrative action is at issue, standing alone will not entitle the plaintiff to a decision on the merits. Pertinent statutory language, legislative history, and public policy considerations must be examined to determine whether Congress precluded all judicial review, and, if not, whether Congress nevertheless foreclosed review to the class to which the plaintiff belongs. Under the Administrative Procedure Act, "statutes [may] preclude judicial review" or "agency action [may be] committed to agency discretion by law." In either case, the plaintiff is out of court, not because he had no standing to enter, but because Congress has stripped the judiciary of authority to review agency action. Review may be totally foreclosed, or, if permitted, it may nonetheless be denied to the plaintiff's case. * * *

* * * Congressional intent that a particular plaintiff have review may be found either in express statutory language granting it to the plaintiff's class, or, in the absence of such express language, in statutory indicia from which a right to review may be inferred. Where, as in the instant case, there is no express grant of review, reviewability has ordinarily been inferred from evidence that Congress intended the plaintiff's class to be a beneficiary of the statute under which the plaintiff raises his claim. In light of *Abbott Laboratories*, slight indicia that the plaintiff's class is a beneficiary will suffice to support the inference.[9]

If it is determined that a plaintiff who alleged injury in fact is entitled to judicial review, inquiry proceeds to the merits—to whether the specific legal interest claimed by the plaintiff is protected by the statute and to whether the protested agency action invaded that interest. It is true, of course, that matters relevant to the merits will already have been touched tangentially in the determination of standing and, in some cases, in the determination of reviewability. The aspect of the merits touched

---

9. This is particularly the case when the plaintiff is the only party likely to challenge the action. Refusal to allow him review would, in effect, commit the action wholly to agency discretion, thus risking frustration of the statutory objectives.

in establishing standing is the identification of injury in fact, the existence of which the plaintiff must prove. The merits are also touched in establishing reviewability in cases where the plaintiff's right to review must be inferred from evidence that his class is a statutory beneficiary. The same statutory indicia that afford the plaintiff a right to review also bear on the merits, because they provide evidence that the statute protects his class, and thus that he is entitled to relief if he can show that the challenged agency action violated the statute. Evidence that the plaintiff's class is a statutory beneficiary, however, need not be as strong for the purpose of obtaining review as for the purpose of establishing the plaintiff's claim on the merits.

*   *   *

To reiterate, in my view, alleged injury in fact, reviewability, and the merits pose questions that are largely distinct from one another, each governed by its own considerations. To fail to isolate and treat each inquiry independently of the other two, so far as possible, is to risk obscuring what is at issue in a given case, and thus to risk uninformed, poorly reasoned decisions that may result in injustice. *   *   *

Notes

1. Does Justice Douglas in *Data Processing* identify the minimum constitutional test for standing? Is that test less demanding than the full requirements for standing articulated in the *Data Processing* opinion? If so, why are any extra-constitutional requirements thought necessary?

2. What does Justice Douglas mean when he says that "the tenant farmers are clearly within the zone of interests protected by the Act?" Is any "legal interest" of the farmers invaded by the Secretary's new regulation? If not, does this mean that any contemplated beneficiary of federal legislation can obtain review of any action by officials responsible for its implementation? Professor Scott observes:

> According to Professor Davis, the Court meant, or should have meant, to say that not the plaintiffs but the "particular interest" they were asserting was within the zone protected by the statutes. This highlights the convenient vagueness of the concept of "interest." In part it has been used to refer to the injury being inflicted on plaintiff, which causes him to seek relief. The injury may be economic and measurable in terms of loss of property or income, or it may be an impairment of other values which he holds; in either case, he sees government action as affecting him in ways he would pay to avoid. On the other hand, "interest" is also used to refer to the constitutional or statutory limitation which he claims the defendant government official is not observing. The greater the particularity with which plaintiff's interest is defined, the more it involves the precise legal issues which he is raising. A determination of whether plaintiff's interest is protected by the statute then comes to turn on a determination of the merits of his legal argument, and we are back to the problem of circularity. On the other hand, a definition of the plaintiff's interest in the most general terms tends to make the search for a protective legislative intent a fiction.

Scott, *Standing in the Supreme Court—A Functional Analysis*, 86 Harv.L.Rev. 645, 664 n.88 (1973).

SIERRA CLUB v. MORTON

Supreme Court of the United States, 1972.
405 U.S. 727, 92 S.Ct. 1361, 31 L.Ed.2d 636.

MR. JUSTICE STEWART delivered the opinion of the Court.

The Mineral King Valley is an area of great natural beauty nestled in the Sierra Nevada Mountains in Tulare County, California, adjacent to Sequoia National Park. It has been part of the Sequoia National Forest since 1926, and is designated as a national game refuge by special Act of Congress. * * *

The United States Forest Service, which is entrusted with the maintenance and administration of national forests, began in the late 1940's to give consideration to Mineral King as a potential site for recreational development. Prodded by a rapidly increasing demand for skiing facilities, the Forest Service published a prospectus in 1965, inviting bids from private developers for the construction and operation of a ski resort that would also serve as a summer recreation area. The proposal of Walt Disney Enterprises, Inc., was chosen from those of six bidders, and Disney received a three-year permit to conduct surveys and explorations in the valley in connection with its preparation of a complete master plan for the resort.

The final Disney plan, approved by the Forest Service in January 1969, outlines a $35 million complex of motels, restaurants, swimming pools, parking lots, and other structures designed to accommodate 14,000 visitors daily. * * * To provide access to the resort, the State of California proposes to construct a highway 20 miles in length. A section of this road would traverse Sequoia National Park, as would a proposed high-voltage power line needed to provide electricity for the resort. Both the highway and the power line require the approval of the Department of the Interior which is entrusted with the preservation and maintenance of the national parks.

Representatives of the Sierra Club, who favor maintaining Mineral King largely in its present state, followed the progress of recreational planning for the valley with close attention and increasing dismay. In June 1969 the Club filed the present suit in the United States District Court for the Northern District of California, seeking a declaratory judgment that various aspects of the proposed development contravene federal laws and regulations governing the preservation of national parks, forests, and game refuges,[2] and also seeking preliminary and permanent

---

2. As analyzed by the District Court, the complaint alleged violations of law falling into four categories. First, it claimed that the special-use permit for construction of the resort exceeded the maximum-acreage limitation placed upon such permits by 16 U.S.C.A. § 497, and that issuance of a "revocable" use permit was beyond the authority of the Forest Service. Second, it challenged the proposed permit for the highway through Sequoia National Park on the grounds that the highway would not serve any of the purposes of the park, in alleged violation of 16 U.S.C.A. § 1, and that it would destroy timber and other natural resources protected by 16 U.S.C.A. §§ 41 and 43. Third, it claimed that the Forest Service and the Department of the Interior had violated their own regulations by failing to hold adequate public hearings on the proposed project. Finally, the complaint asserted that 16 U.S.C.A. § 45c required specific congressional authorization of a permit for construction of a power transmission line within the limits of a national park.

injunctions restraining the federal officials involved from granting their approval or issuing permits in connection with the Mineral King project. The petitioner Sierra Club sued as a membership corporation with "a special interest in the conservation and the sound maintenance of the national parks, game refuges and forests of the country," and invoked the judicial-review provisions of the Administrative Procedure Act.

After two days of hearings, the District Court granted the requested preliminary injunction. * * * The respondents appealed, and the Court of Appeals for the Ninth Circuit reversed. With respect to the petitioner's standing, the court noted that there was "no allegation in the complaint that members of the Sierra Club would be affected by the actions of [the respondents] other than the fact that the actions are personally displeasing or distasteful to them," * * *

* * *

The injury alleged by the Sierra Club will be incurred entirely by reason of the change in the uses to which Mineral King will be put, and the attendant change in the aesthetics and ecology of the area. Thus, in referring to the road to be built through Sequoia National Park, the complaint alleged that the development "would destroy or otherwise adversely affect the scenery, natural and historic objects and wildlife of the park and would impair the enjoyment of the park for future generations." We do not question that this type of harm may amount to an "injury in fact" sufficient to lay the basis for standing under § 10 of the APA. Aesthetic and environmental well-being, like economic well-being, are important ingredients of the quality of life in our society, and the fact that particular environmental interests are shared by the many rather than the few does not make them less deserving of legal protection through the judicial process. But the "injury in fact" test requires more than an injury to a cognizable interest. It requires that the party seeking review be himself among the injured.

The impact of the proposed changes in the environment of Mineral King will not fall indiscriminately upon every citizen. The alleged injury will be felt directly only by those who use Mineral King and Sequoia National Park, and for whom the aesthetic and recreational values of the area will be lessened by the highway and ski resort. The Sierra Club failed to allege that it or its members would be affected in any of their activities or pastimes by the Disney development. Nowhere in the pleadings or affidavits did the Club state that its members use Mineral King for any purpose, much less that they use it in any way that would be significantly affected by the proposed actions of the respondents.[8]

---

8. * * * In an *amici curiae* brief filed in this Court by the Wilderness Society and others, it is asserted that the Sierra Club has conducted regular camping trips into the Mineral King area, and that various members of the Club have used and continue to use the area for recreational purposes. These allegations were not contained in the pleadings, nor were they brought to the attention of the Court of Appeals. Moreover, the Sierra Club in its reply brief specifically declines to rely on its individualized interest, as a basis for standing. Our decision does not, of course, bar the Sierra Club from seeking in the District Court to amend its complaint by a motion under Rule 15, Federal Rules of Civil Procedure.

The Club apparently regarded any allegations of individualized injury as superfluous, on the theory that this was a "public" action involving questions as to the use of natural resources, and that the Club's long-standing concern with and expertise in such matters were sufficient to give it standing as a "representative of the public." This theory reflects a misunderstanding of our cases involving so-called "public actions" in the area of administrative law.

* * *

The trend of cases arising under the APA and other statutes authorizing judicial review of federal agency action has been toward recognizing that injuries other than economic harm are sufficient to bring a person within the meaning of the statutory language, and toward discarding the notion that an injury that is widely shared is *ipso facto* not an injury sufficient to provide the basis for judicial review. We noted this development with approval in *Data Processing*, in saying that the interest alleged to have been injured "may reflect 'aesthetic, conservational, and recreational' as well as economic values." But broadening the categories of injury that may be alleged in support of standing is a different matter from abandoning the requirement that the party seeking review must himself have suffered an injury.

* * * It is clear that an organization whose members are injured may represent those members in a proceeding for judicial review. But a mere "interest in a problem," no matter how longstanding the interest and no matter how qualified the organization is in evaluating the problem, is not sufficient by itself to render the organization "adversely affected" or "aggrieved" within the meaning of the APA. The Sierra Club is a large and long-established organization, with a historic commitment to the cause of protecting our Nation's natural heritage from man's depradations. But if a "special interest" in this subject were enough to entitle the Sierra Club to commence this litigation, there would appear to be no objective basis upon which to disallow a suit by any other bona fide "special interest" organization, however small or short-lived. And if any group with a bona fide "special interest" could initiate such litigation, it is difficult to perceive why any individual citizen with the same bona fide special interest would not also be entitled to do so.

The requirement that a party seeking review must allege facts showing that he is himself adversely affected does not insulate executive action from judicial review, nor does it prevent any public interests from being protected through the judicial process.[15] It does serve as at least a

15. In its reply brief, after noting the fact that it might have chosen to assert individualized injury to itself or to its members as a basis for standing, the Sierra Club states:

"The Government seeks to create a 'heads I win, tails you lose' situation in which either the courthouse door is barred for lack of assertion of a private, unique injury or a preliminary injunction is denied on the ground that the litigant has advanced private injury which does not warrant an injunction adverse to a competing public interest. Counsel have shaped their cases to avoid this trap."

The short answer to this contention is that the "trap" does not exist. The test of injury in fact goes only to the question of standing to obtain judicial review. Once this standing is established, the party may assert the interests of the general public in support of his claims for equitable relief.

rough attempt to put the decision as to whether review will be sought in the hands of those who have a direct stake in the outcome. That goal would be undermined were we to construe the APA to authorize judicial review at the behest of organizations or individuals who seek to do no more than vindicate their own value preferences through the judicial process. The principle that the Sierra Club would have us establish in this case would do just that.

* * *

MR. JUSTICE DOUGLAS, dissenting.

The critical question of "standing" would be simplified and also put neatly in focus if we fashioned a federal rule that allowed environmental issues to be litigated before federal agencies or federal courts in the name of the inanimate object about to be despoiled, defaced, or invaded by roads and bulldozers and where injury is the subject of public outrage. Contemporary public concern for protecting nature's ecological equilibrium should lead to the conferral of standing upon environmental objects to sue for their own preservation. See Stone, *Should Trees Have Standing?—Toward Legal Rights for Natural Objects*, 45 S. Cal. L. Rev. 450 (1972). This suit would therefore be more properly labeled as *Mineral King. v. Morton*.

* * *

The Solicitor General * * * considers the problem in terms of "government by the Judiciary." With all respect, the problem is to make certain that the inanimate objects, which are the very core of America's beauty, have spokesmen before they are destroyed. It is, of course, true that most of them are under the control of a federal or state agency. * * *

Yet the pressures on agencies for favorable action one way or the other are enormous. The suggestion that Congress can stop action which is undesirable is true in theory; yet Congress is too remote to give meaningful direction and its machinery is too ponderous to use very often. The federal agencies of which I speak are not venal or corrupt. But they are notoriously under the control of powerful interests who manipulate them through advisory committees, or friendly working relations, or who have that natural affinity with the agency which in time develops between the regulator and the regulated. * * *

The voice of the inanimate object, therefore, should not be stilled. That does not mean that the judiciary takes over the managerial functions from the federal agency. It merely means that before these priceless bits of Americana (such as a valley, an alpine meadow, a river, or a lake) are forever lost or are so transformed as to be reduced to the eventual rubble of our urban environment, the voice of the existing beneficiaries of these environmental wonders should be heard.

[The dissenting opinion of Justice Blackmun is omitted.]

Notes

1. An article title, composed prior to the decision in *Sierra Club*, may be an appropriate commentary on the law of standing as developed in that case: Chou-

los, *Go Back—You Forgot to Say "May I!" or Standing in Environmental Litigation*, 6 Lincoln L. Rev. 127 (1971). Indeed some found *Sierra Club* significant largely for its broad holding that harm to non-economic interests would support a finding of "injury-in-fact." Scott, *Standing in the Supreme Court—A Functional Analysis*, 86 Harv. L. Rev. 645, 667 (1973).

2. Why is not the sheer expense of litigation in the federal courts—witness fees, attorneys' fees, printing costs, costs of gathering evidence—adequate assurance that any litigant who seeks to challenge administrative action has a sufficient interest that the case "will be presented in an adversary context and in a form historically viewed as capable of judicial resolution"? Professor Scott suggests that the doctrine of standing may serve as a device, albeit imprecise, for allocating what amounts to a public subsidy for litigation—the almost free use of the court system—among competing users of that resource. But he concludes that, to the extent the standing doctrine has become a method of "access screening," it saddles the courts with a job for which the legislature is much better suited. Id. at 682–83. A second possible justification for imposing requirements on standing higher than Article III would independently require, Scott suggests, is to limit judicial involvement in the resolution of disputes that should more appropriately be left to the elected branches of government. Again, Scott agrees that this function is better served by the doctrine of reviewability. Id. at 683–90.

3. *Sierra Club v. Morton* clearly barred the claim that alleges no injury in fact. But what of the claim that alleges injury in fact but does not connect that injury to interests sought to be protected by the statutory provisions alleged to have been violated? Examine the allegations of illegality made in *Sierra Club* (note 2 of the Court's opinion). Did any of those allegations relate to statutory provisions directed toward the protection of the recreational interests asserted by the Club? Might the Sierra Club members have been able to allege both injury in fact and illegal governmental action, but have no standing because their interests were not protected by the relevant statutory sections? What if the plaintiff were a competitive recreational enterprise whose business would be injured by the Disney development? Would economic injury in fact be a sufficient basis for the business firm to attempt to vindicate the wilderness management values that Congress arguably intended to protect? Did the *Data Processing Sierra Club* line of cases do more than recognize that the "legal right" test extends under modern regulatory legislation to noneconomic interests?

A partial answer to this last question was provided by *United States v. Students Challenging Regulatory Agency Procedures (SCRAP)*, 412 U.S. 669, 686–90 (1973). The plaintiffs, a group of law students, challenged an ICC ruling allowing railroads to exact a surcharge on existing freight rates pending the adoption of selective rate increases. They claimed that the rate surcharge would discourage shipment and use of recyclable goods and thereby contribute to the degradation of the environment in the Washington, D.C. area—an area in which they use the forests, streams, mountains, and other resources for recreation and sight-seeing. Over the objections of the railroads and the ICC, the Court, through Justice Stewart, found these allegations of injury sufficient to withstand a motion to dismiss:

> In interpreting "injury in fact" we made it clear [in *Sierra Club*] that standing was not confined to those who could show "economic harm" * * *

Unlike the specific and geographically limited federal action of which the petitioner complained in *Sierra Club*, the challenged agency action in this case is applicable to substantially all of the Nation's railroads, and thus allegedly has an adverse environmental impact on all the natural resources of the country. Rather than a limited group of persons who used a picturesque valley in California, all persons who utilize the scenic resources of the country, and indeed all who breathe its air, could claim harm similar to that alleged by the environmental groups here. But we have already made it clear that standing is not to be denied simply because many people suffer the same injury. * * * To deny standing to persons who are in fact injured simply because many others are also injured, would mean that the most injurious and widespread Government actions could be questioned by nobody. We cannot accept that conclusion.

But the injury alleged here is also very different from that at issue in *Sierra Club* because here the alleged injury to the environment is far less direct and perceptible. * * * Here, the Court was asked to follow a far more attentuated line of causation to the eventual injury of which the appellees complained—a general rate increase would allegedly cause increased use of nonrecyclable commodities as compared to recyclable goods, thus resulting in the need to use more natural resources to produce such goods, some of which resources might be taken from the Washington area, and resulting in more refuse that might be discarded in national parks in the Washington area. The railroads protest that the appellees could never prove that a general increase in rates would have this effect, and they contend that these allegations were a ploy to avoid the need to show some injury in fact.

Of course, pleadings must be something more than an ingenious academic exercise in the conceivable. A plaintiff must allege that he has been or will in fact be perceptibly harmed by the challenged agency action, not that he can imagine circumstances in which he could be affected by the agency's action. And it is equally clear that the allegations must be true and capable of proof at trial. * * * We cannot say on these pleadings that the appellees could not prove their allegations which, if proved, would place them squarely among those persons injured in fact by the Commission's action, and entitled under the clear impact of *Sierra Club* to seek review.

The Transportation Act says nothing about the protection of interests which are neither shipper, nor carrier, nor even consumer, interests. The *SCRAP* decision could therefore be read as administering the *coup de grace* to the "legal right" analysis of the Transportation Act trilogy. However, *SCRAP*'s answer may not be so clear cut, for that case involved a claim under the National Environmental Policy Act (NEPA), which may have created a "zone of interests" for environmentalists' claims quite separate from the Transportation Act. And because NEPA modifies the mandate of all federal agencies, the lesson of *SCRAP* may be that standing should never be an issue in environmental litigation provided the plaintiff has properly plead a NEPA count.

3. CAUSALITY, NEXUS, AND REDRESSABILITY

The attenuated effects of the ICC rate order in *SCRAP* on the plaintiffs' interests troubled the Court but did not prevent review. But during the same term the Court decided, with four justices dissenting, that an unwed mother lacked standing to challenge the failure of Texas officials to enforce the state's criminal child support statute against the father of her illegitimate children.   *Linda R. S. v. Richard D.*, 410 U.S. 614, 617–18 (1973).   Writing for the Court, Justice Marshall concluded that the plaintiff had failed the "injury in fact" requirement of *Sierra Club*:

> [W]e hold that, in the unique context of a challenge to a criminal statute, appellant has failed to allege sufficient nexus between her injury and the government action which she attacks to justify judicial intervention.   To be sure, appellant no doubt suffered an injury stemming from the failure of her child's father to contribute support payments.   But the bare existence of an abstract injury meets only the first half of the standing requirement.   * * *

> Here, appellant has made no showing that her failure to secure support payments results from the nonenforcement, as to her child's father, of Art. 602.   * * *   [T]he statute creates a completed offense with a fixed penalty as soon as a parent fails to support his child.   Thus, if appellant were granted the requested relief, it would result only in the jailing of the child's father.   The prospect that prosecution will, at least in the future, result in payment of support can, at best, be termed only speculative.   Certainly the "direct" relationship between the alleged injury and the claims ought to be adjudicated, which previous decisions of this Court suggest is a prerequisite of standing, is absent in this case.

Two cases decided the following term looked in the same direction. *United States v. Richardson*, 418 U.S. 166 (1974), involved a challenge to the section of the Central Intelligence Agency Act that permits the agency to account for its funds solely by the certificate of its Director that they have been properly spent.   The plaintiff, Richardson, filed suit as a federal taxpayer alleging that the CIA Act violated Article I, section 9, of the Constitution which provides in part that "a regular Statement of Account of the Receipts and Expenditures of all public money shall be published from time to time."   A majority of the Court concluded that Richardson did not have standing because he was not challenging the expenditure of public funds, which might cause him injury as a taxpayer, but only the lack of an accounting.   He had thus failed to demonstrate a sufficient nexus between taxpayer status and the constitutional claim urged. Similarly, in *Schlesinger v. Reservists Committee to Stop the War*, 418 U.S. 208 (1974), the Court found insufficient nexus between the injury to the plaintiffs' interest, as citizens and taxpayers, in the faithful discharge by congressmen of their legislative duties, and the plaintiffs' legal claim that retention by congressmen of military status as reserve officers violated Article I, section 6, which provides that "no person holding any office under the United States, shall be a Member of either House during his continuance in office."

In *Richardson* and *Schlesinger* the Court purported to apply the requirements of *Flast v. Cohen* that in a "taxpayer's suit" the complaint (1) challenge an exercise of Congress' taxing and spending power; (2) that it urge, as grounds of illegality, limitations on the power to tax and spend; and (3) that the claim relate directly to the legality of extracting the citizen's tax dollars for the support of the activity challenged.   The plaintiff in *Flast* satisfied these requirements by claiming that federal aid to religious and sectarian schools violated the Establishment and Free Exercise Clauses of the First Amendment. In *Schlesinger* and *Richardson*, however, the Court concluded that the plaintiffs' success on the merits would not necessarily affect the taxpayer or citizen interests they alleged.

These cases are susceptible of several analyses. One is that the Court was rethinking the "nexus" question and had determined that, contrary to lenient approach of *SCRAP*, the courts should screen out doubtful claims on the basis of a preliminary objection to standing. A second analysis might suggest that these cases are classic examples of the confusion of standing with other aspects of "justiciability." *Linda R. S.* raised a claim related to "prosecutorial discretion"; *Richardson* challenged activity in the perennially sensitive area of national security; and *Schlesinger* involved a collateral attack on the qualifications of members of the legislative branch. A third explanation, suggested by Justice Powell's concurring opinion in *Richardson*, 418 U.S. at 180, was that the Court was becoming generally concerned about the appropriateness of entertaining lawsuits in which the public interest aspects of the litigation predominate. The Court described *Richardson* as a case in which the taxpayer was "seeking 'to employ a federal court as a forum in which to air his generalized grievances about the conduct of the government.'" And the majority in *Schlesinger* said, "[S]tanding to sue may not be predicated upon an interest of the kind alleged here which is held by all members of the public, because of the necessarily abstract nature of the injury all citizens share."

Justice Stewart, dissenting in *Richardson*, read the Court's decision as based on Article III and expressed alarm about what it might foreshadow. As an example, Stewart posed the question of the constitutionality of Congress' creation in the Freedom of Information Act of a right of action by any citizen to force the disclosure of government documents. "If the Court is correct in this case in holding that Richardson lacks standing under Art. III to litigate his claim," he wrote, "it would follow that a person whose request under 5 U.S.C.A. § 552 has been denied would similarly lack standing under Art. III despite the clear intent of Congress to confer a right of action to compel production of the information."

SIMON v. EASTERN KENTUCKY WELFARE RIGHTS ORGANIZATION

Supreme Court of the United States, 1976
426 U.S. 26, 96 S.Ct. 1917, 48 L.Ed.2d 450.

MR. JUSTICE POWELL delivered the opinion of the Court.

Several indigents and organizations composed of indigents brought this suit against the Secretary of the Treasury and the Commissioner of Internal Revenue. They asserted that the Internal Revenue Service (IRS) violated the Internal Revenue Code (the Code) and the Administrative Procedure Act (APA) by issuing a Revenue Ruling allowing favorable tax treatment to a nonprofit hospital that offered only emergency room services to indigents. We conclude that these plaintiffs lack standing to bring this suit.

The Code * * * accords advantageous treatment to several types of nonprofit corporations, including exemption of their income from taxation and deductibility by benefactors of the amounts of their donations. Nonprofit hospitals have never received these benefits as a favored general category, but an individual nonprofit hospital has been able to claim them if it could qualify as a corporation "organized and operated exclusively for * * * charitable * * * purposes" within the meaning of § 501(c)(3) of the Code. As the Code does not define the term *charitable*, the status of each nonprofit hospital is determined on a case-by-case basis by the IRS.

In recognition of the need of nonprofit hospitals for some guidelines on qualification as "charitable" corporations, the IRS in 1956 issued Revenue Ruling 56–185. * * * [T]he Ruling set out four "general requirements" that a hospital had to meet, "among other things," to be considered a charitable organization by the IRS. Only one of those requirements is important here, and it reads as follows:

> "It must be operated to the extent of its financial ability for those not able to pay for the services rendered and not exclusively for those who are able and expected to pay. * * * [I]f it operates with the expectation of full payment from all those to whom it renders services, it does not dispense charity merely because some of its patients fail to pay for the services rendered."

Revenue Ruling 56–185 remained the announced policy with respect to a nonprofit hospital's "charitable" status for 13 years, until the IRS issued Revenue Ruling 69–545 on November 3, 1969. This new Ruling described two unidentified hospitals, referred to simply as Hospital A and Hospital B. * * * The description of Hospital A included the following paragraph:

> "The hospital operates a full time emergency room and no one requiring emergency care is denied treatment. The hospital otherwise ordinarily limits its admissions to those who can pay the cost of their hospitalization, either themselves, or through private health insurance, or with the aid of public programs such as Medicare. Patients who cannot meet the financial requirements for admission are ordinarily referred to another hospital in the community that does serve indigent patients."

Despite Hospital A's apparent failure to operate "to the extent of its financial ability for those not able to pay for the services rendered," as required by Revenue Ruling 56–185, the IRS in this new Ruling held Hospital A exempt as a charitable corporation under § 501(c)(3). * * * [T]he IRS stated that "Revenue Ruling 56–185 is hereby modified to remove therefrom the requirements relating to caring for patients without charge or at rates below cost."

* * * The plaintiff organizations described themselves as an unincorporated association and several nonprofit corporations each of which included low-income persons among its members and represented the inter-

ests of all such persons in obtaining hospital care and services. The 12 individual plaintiffs described themselves as subsisting below the poverty income levels established by the Federal Government and suffering from medical conditions requiring hospital services. * * *

Each of the individuals described an occasion on which he or a member of his family had been disadvantaged in seeking needed hospital services because of his indigency. Most involved the refusal of a hospital to admit the person because of his inability to pay a deposit or an advance fee, even though in some instances the person was enrolled in the Medicare program. At least one plaintiff was denied emergency-room treatment because of his inability to pay immediately. And another was treated in the emergency room but then billed and threatened with suit although his indigency had been known at the time of treatment.

According to the complaint, each of the hospitals involved in these incidents had been determined by the Secretary and the Commissioner to be a tax-exempt charitable corporation, and each received substantial private contributions. The Secretary and the Commissioner were the only defendants. The complaint alleged that by extending tax benefits to such hospitals despite their refusals fully to serve the indigent, the defendants were "encouraging" the hospitals to deny services to the individual plaintiffs and to the members and clients of the plaintiff organizations. Those persons were alleged to be suffering "injury in their opportunity and ability to receive hospital services in nonprofit hospitals which receive * * * benefits * * * as 'charitable' organizations" under the Code. They also were alleged to be among the intended beneficiaries of the Code sections that grant favorable tax treatment to "charitable" organizations.

Plaintiffs made two principal claims. The first was that in issuing Revenue Ruling 69–545 the defendants had violated the Code, and that in granting charitable-corporation treatment to nonprofit hospitals that refused fully to serve indigents the defendants continued the violation. Their theory was that legislative history of the Code, regulations of the IRS and judicial precedent had established the term "charitable" in the Code to mean "relief of the poor," and that the challenged Ruling and current practice of the IRS departed from that interpretation. Plaintiffs' second claim was that the issuance of Revenue Ruling 69–545 without a public hearing and an opportunity for submission of views had violated the rulemaking procedures of the APA * * * .

In this Court petitioners have argued that a policy of the IRS to tax or not to tax certain individuals or organizations, whether embodied in a Revenue Ruling or otherwise developed, cannot be challenged by third parties whose own tax liabilities are not affected. Their theory is that the entire history of this country's revenue system * * * manifests a consistent congressional intent to vest exclusive authority for the administration of the tax laws in the Secretary and his duly authorized delegates, subject to oversight by the appropriate committees of Congress itself. * * *

In addition, petitioners analogize the discretion vested in the IRS with respect to administration of the tax laws to the discretion of a public prosecutor as to when and whom to prosecute.   They thus invoke the settled doctrine that the exercise of prosecutorial discretion cannot be challenged by one who is himself neither prosecuted or threatened with prosecution.   See *Linda R. S. v. Richard D.* * * *

We do not reach either the question of whether a third party ever may challenge IRS treatment of another, or the question of whether there is a statutory or immunity bar to this suit.   We conclude that the District Court should have granted petitioners' motion to dismiss on the ground that respondents' complaint failed to establish their standing to sue.

* * * [W]hen a plaintiff's standing is brought into issue the relevant inquiry is whether, assuming justiciability of the claim, the plaintiff has shown an injury to himself that is likely to be redressed by a favorable decision.   Absent such a showing, exercise of its power by a federal court would be gratuitous and thus inconsistent with the Art. III limitation. * * *

The obvious interest of all respondents, to which they claim actual injury, is that of access to hospital services.   In one sense, of course, they have suffered injury to that interest.   The complaint alleges specific occasions on which each of the individual respondents sought but was denied hospital services solely due to his indigency, and in at least some of the cases it is clear that the needed treatment was unavailable, as a practical matter, anywhere else.   The complaint also alleges that members of the respondent organizations need hospital services but live in communities in which the private hospitals do not serve indigents.   We thus assume, for purpose of analysis, that some members have been denied service.   But injury at the hands of a hospital is insufficient by itself to establish a case or controversy in the context of this suit, for no hospital is a defendant.   The only defendants are officials of the Department of the Treasury, and the only claims of illegal action respondents desire the courts to adjudicate are charged to those officials. * * * [T]he "case or controversy" limitation of Art. III still requires that a federal court act only to redress injury that fairly can be traced to the challenged action of the defendant, and not injury that results from the independent action of some third party not before the court.

The complaint here alleged only that petitioners, by the adoption of Revenue Ruling 69–545, had "encouraged" hospitals to deny services to indigents.   The implicit corollary of this allegation is that a grant of the respondents' requested relief, resulting in a requirement that all hospitals serve indigents as a condition to favorable tax treatment, would "discourage" hospitals from denying their services to respondents.   But it does not follow from the allegation and its corollary that the denial of access to hospital services in fact results from petitioners' new Ruling, or that a court-ordered return by petitioners to their previous policy would result in these respondents' receiving the hospital services they desire. * * *

It is equally speculative whether the desired exercise of the court's remedial powers in this suit would result in the availability to respondents of such services.   So far as the complaint sheds light, it is just as plausible that the hospitals to which respondents may apply for service would elect to forego favorable tax treatment to avoid the undetermined financial drain of an increase in the level of uncompensated services. * * *

The principle of *Linda R. S.* and *Warth* [*v. Seldin*, infra p. 665] controls this case. As stated in *Warth*, that principle is that indirectness of injury, while not necessarily fatal to standing, "may make it substantially more difficult to meet the minimum requirement of Art. III: to establish that, in fact, the asserted injury was the consequence of the defendants' actions, or that prospective relief will remove the harm." Respondents have failed to carry this burden. Speculative inferences are necessary to connect their injury to the challenged actions of petitioners.[25] Moreover, the complaint suggests no substantial likelihood that victory in this suit would result in respondents' receiving the hospital treatment they desire. A federal court, properly cognizant of the Art. III limitation upon its jurisdiction, must require more than respondents have shown before proceeding to the merits. * * *

MR. JUSTICE STEWART, concurring.

I join the opinion of the Court holding that the plaintiffs in this case did not have standing to sue. I add only that I cannot now imagine a case, at least outside the First Amendment area, where a person whose own tax liability was not affected ever could have standing to litigate the federal tax liability of someone else.

[Justices Marshall and Brennan concurred with the judgment on the "ripeness" grounds that (1) the respondents had failed to allege that they had been denied treatment by hospitals that would fall within the IRS' more relaxed definition of "charitable" in the Hospital A example, and (2) the effects of the new ruling on other nonprofit hospitals were unclear. However, they dissented strenuously from the majority's opinion on standing, concluding: "We may properly wonder where the Court, armed with its 'fatally speculative pleadings' tool, will strike next. * * * The Court's treatment of injury in fact without any 'particularization' in light of either the policies properly implicated or our relevant precedents

---

25. The courts below erroneously believed that *United States v. SCRAP* supported respondents' standing. In *SCRAP*, although the injury was indirect and "the Court was asked to follow [an] attenuated line of causation," the complaint nevertheless "alleged a specific and perceptible harm" flowing from the agency action. Such a complaint withstood a motion to dismiss, although it might not have survived challenge on a motion for summary judgment. But in this case the complaint is insufficient even to survive a motion to dismiss, for it fails to allege an injury that fairly can be traced to petitioners' challenged action. Nor did the affidavits before the District Court at the summary judgment stage supply the missing link.

Our decision is also consistent with *Data Processing Service v. Camp*. The Court there stated that "[t]he first question is whether the plaintiff alleges that the challenged action has caused him injury in fact, economic or otherwise." The complaint in *Data Processing* alleged injury that was directly traceable to the action of the defendant federal official, for it complained of injurious competition that would have been illegal without that action. Similarly the complaint in *Data Processing's* companion case of *Barlow v. Collins*, was sufficient because it alleged extortionate demands by plaintiffs' landlord made possible only by the challenged action of the defendant federal official. In the instant case respondent's injuries might have occurred even in the absence of the IRS Ruling that they challenge; whether the injuries fairly can be traced to that Ruling depends upon unalleged and unknown facts about the relevant hospitals.

threatens that it shall 'become a catchall' for an unarticulated discretion on the part of this Court to insist that the federal courts 'decline to adjudicate' claims that it prefers they not hear."   426 U.S. at 63, 66.]

Notes

1. The "causal nexus" issue loomed large in *Warth v. Seldin*, 422 U.S. 490, 504–06 (1975).   There low-income and minority group plaintiffs sought an injunction against restrictive zoning practices in the town of Penfield, N. Y., alleged to deny them the equal protection of the laws.   According to their complaint they all desired and had sought accommodation in Penfield, but could find no housing in a price range that closely approximated their ability to pay.   The complaint further alleged that the high price of housing in Penfield resulted from a zoning ordinance and pattern of enforcement that excluded virtually all high density uses.   In denying the plaintiff's standing the Court concluded:

> We may assume, as petitioners allege, that respondents' actions have contributed, perhaps substantially, to the cost of housing in Penfield.   But there remains the question whether petitioners' inability to locate suitable housing in Penfield reasonably can be said to have resulted, in any concretely demonstrable way, from respondents' alleged constitutional and statutory infractions.   * * *
>
> We find the record devoid of the necessary allegations.   * * *   [P]etitioners claim that respondents' enforcement of the ordinance against third parties—developers, builders, and the like—has had the consequence of precluding the construction of housing suitable to their needs at prices they might be able to afford.   * * *
>
> Here, by their own admission, realization of petitioners' desire to live in Penfield always has depended on the efforts and willingness of third parties to build low- and moderate-cost housing.   The record specifically refers to only two such efforts: that of Penfield Better Homes Corp., in late 1969, to obtain the rezoning of certain land in Penfield to allow the construction of subsidized cooperative townhouses that could be purchased by persons of moderate income and a similar effort by O'Brien Homes, Inc., in late 1971.   But the record is devoid of any indication that these projects, or other like projects, would have satisfied petitioners' needs at prices they could afford, or that were the court to remove the obstructions attributable to respondents, such relief would benefit petitioners.   Indeed, petitioners' descriptions of their individual financial situations and housing needs suggest precisely the contrary—that their inability to reside in Penfield is the consequence of the economics of the area housing market, rather than of respondents' assertedly illegal acts.

The low-income plaintiffs in *Warth* were joined by several groups who supported their position: (1) associations of home builders, some of whose members had been refused variances for high density housing; (2) a non-profit corporation, the purpose of which is "to alert citizens to problems of social concern," representing certain Penfield residents who desired to alleviate the critical shortage of low and moderate income housing; and (3) taxpayers in nearby Rochester who claimed that their tax rates were adversely affected by Penfield's refusal to bear its share of the low an moderate income housing burden.   The homebuilders were denied "standing" on the essentially "ripeness" ground that they had no current proposals for projects in Penfield. The socially concerned corporation was found to be asserting no constitutional rights of its own or of its members—in short, it had no standing because it had no cause of action. And the Rochester taxpayers, as might be expected, failed the "causal nexus" test, not to mention the requirement of stating a claim.

Nor was the Court willing to allow any of these parties to assert the constitutional claim urged by the low-income plaintiffs. The Court's treatment of the *jus tertii* issue in the context of the claim by the Rochester taxpayers is instructive (422 U.S. at 509–10):

> In several cases, this Court has allowed standing to litigate the rights of third parties when enforcement of the challenged restriction against the litigant would result indirectly in the violation of third parties' rights. But the tax-payer-petitioners are not subject to Penfield's zoning practices. Nor do they allege that the challenged zoning ordinance and practices preclude or otherwise adversely affect a relationship existing between them and the persons whose rights assertedly are violated. No relationship, other than an incidental congruity of interest, is alleged to exist between the Rochester taxpayers and persons who have been precluded from living in Penfield. Nor do the taxpayer-petitioners show that their prosecution of the suit is necessary to insure protection of the rights asserted, as there is no indication that persons who in fact have been excluded from Penfield are disabled from asserting their own right in a proper case.

Justices Douglas, Brennan, White, and Marshall dissented. In an opinion joined by Justices White and Marshall, Justice Brennan commented on the majority's treatment of the standing requirement (id. at 521, 522):

> [O]ne glaring defect of the Court's opinion is that it views each set of plaintiffs as if it were prosecuting a separate lawsuit, refusing to recognize that the interests are intertwined, and that the standing of any one group must take into account its position vis-a-vis the others. * * *
>
> * * * [T]he portrait which emerges from the allegations and affidavits is one of total, purposeful, intransigent exclusion of certain classes of people from the town, pursuant to a conscious scheme never deviated from. Because of this scheme, those interested in building homes for the excluded groups were faced with insurmountable difficulties, and those of the excluded groups seeking homes in the locality quickly learned that their attempts were futile. Yet, the Court turns the very success of the allegedly unconstitutional scheme into a barrier to a lawsuit seeking its invalidation. In effect, the Court tells the low-income minority and building company plaintiffs they will not be permitted to prove what they have alleged—that they could and would build and live in the town if changes were made in the zoning ordinance and its application—because they have not succeeded in breaching, before the suit was filed, the very barriers which are the subject of the suit.

2. Whatever its import, *Warth v. Seldin* did not signal a more restrictive approach to *jus tertii* claims. In *Singleton v. Wulff*, 428 U.S. 106, 117–18 (1976), the Court permitted a *physicians'* challenge to the exclusion of abortion services from a state medicaid scheme on grounds of unconstitutional interference with the rights of *patients*. Writing for a plurality Justice Blackmun explained:

> A woman cannot safely secure an abortion without the aid of a physician, and an impecunious woman cannot easily secure an abortion without the physi-

cian's being paid by the State. The woman's exercise of her right to an abortion, whatever its dimension, is therefore necessarily at stake here. Moreover, the constitutionally protected abortion decision is one in which the physician is intimately involved. Aside from the woman herself, therefore, the physician is uniquely qualified to litigate the constitutionality of the State's interference with, or discrimination against, that decision.

As to the woman's assertion of her own rights, there are several obstacles. For one thing, she may be chilled from such assertion by a desire to protect the very privacy of her decision from the publicity of a court suit. A second obstacle is the imminent mootness, at least in the technical sense, of any individual woman's claim. * * * It is true that these obstacles are not insurmountable. Suit may be brought under a pseudonym, as so frequently has been done. A woman who is no longer pregnant may nonetheless retain the right to litigate the point because it is "capable of repetition yet evading review." And it may be that a class could be assembled, whose fluid membership always included some women with live claims. But if the assertion of the right is to be "representative" to such an extent anyway, there seems little loss in terms of effective advocacy from allowing its assertion by a physician.

This section of the opinion garnered the votes of only Justices Brennan, Marshall, and White. Justice Stevens agreed with the statement so long as it applied to a party who had an independent interest—here the physician's interest in a fee. The Chief Justice, joined by Justices Powell, Stewart, and Rehnquist, argued only that a physician had a sufficient monetary interest to assert his or her own personal claim—if any.

Assuming that the woman wished to assert her own rights against the state Medicare scheme, and considering the causality analyses of *Warth* and *Simon*, under what circumstances would she have standing?

———

The Supreme Court's next encounter with the standing issue was *Duke Power Co. v. Carolina Environmental Study Group, Inc.*, 438 U.S. 59 (1978), a suit challenging the Nuclear Regulatory Commission's approval of construction permits for two nuclear power plants in North and South Carolina. The plaintiffs, two environmental organizations and forty residents of the vicinity of the plants, alleged a variety of injuries resulting from their construction and operation. Their central legal claim was that the limitations on utility liability for a nuclear accident imposed by the Price-Anderson Act, a federal statute enacted early in the development of commercial nuclear power, infringed the Fifth Amendment. Under the Act, liability in the event of a nuclear accident is limited to $560 million, of which $315 million would be paid by licensees of nuclear power plants collectively, $140 million by private insurance, and the balance of $105 million by the federal government.

The plaintiffs alleged and, after four days of hearings, the district court found that they would suffer two types of injury from the operation of the power plants (438 U.S. at 73):

The immediate effects included: (a) the production of small quantities of non-natural radiation which would invade the air and water; (b) a "sharp increase" in the temperature of two lakes presently used for recreational purposes resulting from the use of the lake waters to produce steam and to cool the reactor; (c) interference with the normal use of the waters of the Catawba River; (d) threatened reduction in property values of land neighboring the power plants; (e) "objectively reasonable" present fear and apprehension regarding the "effect of the increased radioactivity in the air, land and water upon [appellees] and their property, and the genetic effects upon their descendants"; and (f) the continual threat of "an accident resulting in uncontrolled release of large or even small quantities of radioactive material" with no assurance of adequate compensation for the resultant damage.   Into a second category of potential effects were placed the damages "which may result from a core melt or other major accident in the operation of a reactor. * * * "

Apparently anticipating objections to their standing to press their constitutional claim, the plaintiffs persuaded the district court to find a " 'but for' causal connection between the Price-Anderson Act * * * 'and the construction of the nuclear plants.' "   This purported factual determination was based both on testimony of a Duke Power vice president and the Act's legislative history, which suggested that limited liability was a key to commercial development of nuclear power.

Having reached the merits of the plaintiffs' constitutional claim, the district court held the Price-Anderson Act unconstitutional because, *inter alia* the Act effected a "taking" of the resident plaintiffs' property by restricting their right to be fully compensated in the event of an accident.   The Supreme Court granted certiorari and promptly reversed.

In his majority opinion, Chief Justice Burger took pains to lay to rest objections to the Court's jurisdiction—objections both to the applicability of the judicial code provision, 28 U.S.C.A. § 1331, on which the plaintiffs had relied, and to their standing (438 U.S. at 68–70, 71–74, 77–79, 81–82):

> As a threshold matter, we must address the question of whether the District Court had subject matter jurisdiction over appellees' claims, despite the fact that none of the parties raised this issue and the District Court did not consider it. Appellees' complaint alleges jurisdiction under 28 U.S.C.A. § 1337, which provides for original jurisdiction in the district courts over "any civil action or proceedings arising under any Act of Congress regulating commerce or protecting trade and commerce against restraints and monopolies." Our reading of the pleadings, however, indicates that appellees, claims do not "arise under" the Price-Anderson Act as that statutory language has been interpreted in prior decisions.
>
> Specifically, as we read the complaint, appellees are making two basic challenges to the Act—both of which find their moorings in the Fifth Amendment.   First, appellees contend that the Due Process Clause protects them against arbitrary governmental action adversely affecting their property rights and that the Price-Anderson Act—which both creates the source of the underlying injury and limits the recovery therefor—constitutes such arbitrary action.   And second, they are contending that in the event of a nuclear accident their property would be "taken" without any assurance of just compensation.   The Price-Anderson Act is the instrument of the taking since on this record, without it, there would be no power plants and no possibility of an accident.   Implicit in the complaint is also the assumption that there exists a cause of action directly under the Constitution to vindicate appellees' federal

rights through a suit against the NRC, the executive agency charged with enforcement and administration of the allegedly unconstitutional statute. Appellees' right to relief thus depends not on the interpretation or construction of the Price-Anderson Act itself but instead "upon the construction or application of the Constitution." Hence, if there exists jurisdiction to hear appellees' claims at all, it must be derived from 28 U.S.C.A. § 1331(a), the general federal question statute, rather than from § 1337—the jurisdictional base pleaded. * * *

* * * It is enough for present purposes that the claimed cause of action to vindicate appellees' constitutional rights is sufficiently substantial and colorable to sustain jurisdiction under § 1331(a). * * *

For purposes of the present inquiry, we need not determine whether all the putative injuries identified by the District Court, particularly those based on the possibility of a nuclear accident and the present apprehension generated by this future uncertainty, are sufficiently concrete to satisfy constitutional requirements. It is enough that several of the "immediate" adverse effects were found to harm appellees. Certainly the environmental and aesthetic consequences of the thermal pollution of the two lakes in the vicinity of the disputed power plants is the type of harmful effect which has been deemed adequate in prior cases to satisfy the "injury in fact" standard. And the emission of non-natural radiation into appellees' environment would also seem a direct and present injury given our generalized concern about exposure to radiation and the apprehension flowing from the uncertainty about the health and genetic consequences of even small emissions like those concededly emitted by nuclear power plants.

* * * Considering the documentary evidence and the testimony in the record, we cannot say we are left with "the definite and firm conviction that" the finding by the trial court of a substantial likelihood that the McGuire and Catawba Nuclear Power Plants would be neither completed nor operated absent the Price-Anderson Act is clearly erroneous and hence we are bound to accept it.

* * *

It is further contended that in addition to proof of injury and of a causal link between such injury and the challenged conduct, appellees must demonstrate a connection between the injuries they claim and the constitutional rights being asserted. * * * Since the environmental and health injuries claimed by appellees are not directly related to the constitutional attack on the Price-Anderson Act, such injuries, the argument continues, cannot supply a predicate for standing. We decline to accept this argument.

* * * No cases have been cited outside the context of taxpayer suits where we have demanded this type of subject matter nexus between the right asserted and the injury alleged and we are aware of none. Instead, in *Schlesinger v. Reservists to Stop the War*, we explicitly rejected such a broad compass for the *Flast* nexus requirement:

"Looking 'to the substantive issues' *Flast* stated to be both 'appropriate and necessary' in relation to taxpayer standing was for the express purpose of determining 'whether there is a logical nexus between the [taxpayer] status asserted and the claim sought to be adjudicated.' This step is not appropriate on a claim of citizen standing since the *Flast* nexus test is not applicable where the taxing and spending power is not challenged. * * * "

We continue to be of the same view and cannot accept the contention that, outside the context of taxpayers' suits, a litigant must demonstrate anything more than injury in fact and a substantial likelihood that the judicial relief requested will prevent or redress the claimed injury to satisfy the "case and controversy" requirement of Art. III. * * *

Satisfied that the case was thus properly before the Court, the Chief Justice overturned the district court's holding that the Price-Anderson Act was unconstitutional. Justices Stewart, Stevens, and Rehnquist all filed special concurrences in the result. Each of the former questioned the Chief Justice's treatment of the standing issue. Justice Stewart took issue with the majority's dismissal of the "nexus" argument (438 U.S. at 95):

Apart from a but-for connection in the loosest sense of that concept, there is no relationship at all between the injury alleged for standing purposes and the injury alleged for federal subject matter jurisdiction.

Surely a plaintiff does not have standing simply because his challenge, if successful, will remove the injury relied on for standing purposes *only* because it will put the defendant out of existence. Surely there must be *some* direct relationship between the plaintiff's federal claim and the injury relied on for standing. An interest in the local water temperature does not, in short, give these appellees standing to bring a suit under 28 U.S.C.A. § 1331 to challenge the constitutionality of a law limiting liability in an unrelated and as-yet-to-occur major nuclear accident. * * *

Justice Stevens was likewise unpersuaded that the Court should reach the merits of the plaintiffs' attack on the Price-Anderson Act (id. at 102–03):

The string of contingencies that supposedly holds this case together is too delicate for me. * * * It is remarkable that such a series of speculation is considered sufficient either to make this case ripe for decision or to establish appellees' standing; it is even more remarkable that this occurs in a case in which, as MR. JUSTICE REHNQUIST demonstrates, there is no federal jurisdiction in the first place.

The Court's opinion will serve the national interest in removing doubts concerning the constitutionality of the Price-Anderson Act. I cannot, therefore, criticize the statesmanship of the Court's decision to provide the country with an advisory opinion on an important subject. Nevertheless, my view of the proper function of this Court, or of any other federal court, in the structure of our government is more limited. We are not statesmen; we are judges. When it is necessary to resolve a constitutional issue in the adjudication of an actual case or controversy, it is our duty to do so. But whenever we are persuaded by reasons of expediency to engage in the business of giving legal advice, we chip away a part of the foundation of our independence and our strength. * * *

Justice Rehnquist's argument concerning jurisdiction was fairly straightforward. The plaintiffs had relied on 28 U.S.C.A. § 1337 which provides district court jurisdiction for "any civil action or proceeding arising under any act of Congress regulating commerce. * * * " It seems clear, however, that any cause of action that these plaintiffs might have had against the Duke Power Company would arise under the (tort?) law of North Carolina. The Price-Anderson Act would come into play only if the company raised its limitation of liability provision as a defense in that state, common law action. And it is settled doctrine that the anticipation of a defense based upon federal law does not convert a suit into one "arising under" federal law.

Although Justice Rehnquist conceded that the district court had jurisdiction to hear a suit against the Nuclear Regulatory Commission (NRC), it was equally clear to him that no case or controversy existed between the plaintiff and the Commission. The Commission's only acts were to grant construction permits to the Duke Power Company. The NRC was also authorized under the governing statutes, including Price-Anderson, to enter into an indemnity agreement with Duke Power respecting any nuclear incident causing damage exceeding the amount $125 million dollars, subject to a maximum governmental liability of $560 million dollars. However, this indemnity agreement did not effect the limitation of liability granted Duke Power by the Price-Anderson Act, which would be enforced by any court before which the company raised the limitation as a defense. In short, the Commission had done nothing that the plaintiffs claimed was unconstitutional.

Viewed in terms of Justice Rehnquist's approach to the case, the question of *"nexus"* between the injury suffered and the legal claim asserted takes on a somewhat different aspect. In most "nexus" cases the problem that troubles the Court is the lack of a close linkage between the ground of illegality asserted and the interest that the plaintiff seeks to protect. But, since *Data Processing*, it has been reasonably clear that the question whether the plaintiffs "interest" is legally protected is a merits question. All that need be alleged for standing purposes is that the plaintiff is "arguably within the zone of interests protected or regulated" by the legal norm to which he appeals. And surely the *Duke Power* plaintiffs are within the class of persons protected by the Fifth Amendment. The problem there, however, was that the defendants had not done anything that even arguably violated the Fifth Amendment. The Duke Power Company, as a private company, could not deprive plaintiffs of their Fifth Amendment rights. And the NRC does not administer the statute—or more specifically that section of the statute—claimed to violate the amendment.

VALLEY FORGE CHRISTIAN COLLEGE v. AMERICANS UNITED FOR SEPARATION OF CHURCH AND STATE

Supreme Court of the United States, 1982.
454 U.S. 464, 102 S.Ct. 752, 70 L.Ed.2d 700

JUSTICE REHNQUIST delivered the opinion of the Court.

[Pursuant to the Federal Property and Administrative Services Act of 1949, 40 U.S.C.A. § 471 *et seq.* (1976 ed. & Supp. III), the Secretary of

Health, Education, and Welfare transferred certain real property to the petitioner for use in its education programs, whose purpose is to train men and women for Christian service. Because the Act authorizes reduction of the price of surplus property by the amount of "any benefit which has accrued or may accrue to the U. S." from the transferee's use of the land, the Secretary determined that the price should be zero. Respondent is a non-profit corporation having 90,000 taxpayer members. It and four of its employees objected to the transfer on the grounds it deprived them of "fair and constitutional" use of their tax dollars under the First Amendment. The Supreme Court was asked to review a decision of the Third Circuit, 619 F.2d 252 (1980), which denied respondents' standing as taxpayers but found them to have standing as citizens pursuing protection of their "shared individuated" right to a government that "shall make no law respecting the establishment of religion."]

* * * [O]ur discussion must begin with *Frothingham v. Mellon*, 262 U.S. 447 (1923). In that action a taxpayer brought suit challenging the constitutionality of the Maternity Act of 1921, which provided federal funding to the States for the purpose of improving maternal and infant health. The injury she alleged consisted of the burden of taxation in support of an unconstitutional regime, which she characterized as a deprivation of property without due process. "Looking through forms of words to the substance of [the] complaint," "the Court concluded that the only "injury" was the fact "that officials of the executive branch of the government are executing and will execute an act of Congress asserted to be unconstitutional." Any tangible effect of the challenged statute on the plaintiff's tax burden was "remote, fluctuating, and uncertain." * * *

Following the decision in *Frothingham*, the Court confirmed that the expenditure of public funds in an allegedly unconstitutional manner is not an injury sufficient to confer standing, even though the plaintiff contributes to the public coffers as a taxpayer. In *Doremus v. Board of Education*, 342 U.S. 429 (1952), plaintiffs brought suit as citizens and taxpayers, claiming that a New Jersey law which authorized public school teachers in the classroom to read passages from the Bible violated the Establishment Clause of the First Amendment. * * *

The Court found that plaintiffs' grievance was "not a direct dollars-and-cents injury but is a religious difference." A case or controversy did not exist, even though the "clash of interests [was] real and * * * strong." (Douglas, J., dissenting.)

The Court again visited the problem of taxpayer standing in *Flast v. Cohen*, 392 U.S. 82 (1968). The taxpayer plaintiffs in *Flast* sought to enjoin the expenditure of federal funds under the Elementary and Secondary Education Act of 1965, which they alleged were being used to support religious schools in violation of the Establishment Clause. The Court developed a two-part test to determine whether the plaintiffs had standing to sue. First, because a taxpayer alleges injury only by virtue of his liability for taxes, the Court held that "a taxpayer will be a proper party to allege the unconstitutionality only of exercises of congressional power under the taxing and spending clause of Art. I. § 8, of the Constitution."

Second, the Court required the taxpayer to "show that the challenged enactment exceeds specific constitutional limitations upon the exercise of the taxing and spending power and not simply that the enactment is generally beyond the powers delegated to Congress by Art. I, § 8."

The plaintiffs in *Flast* satisfied this test because "[t]heir constitutional challenge [was] made to an exercise by Congress of its power under Art. I, § 8, to spend for the general welfare," and because the Establishment Clause, on which plaintiffs' complaint rested, "operates as a specific constitutional limitation upon the exercise by Congress of the taxing and spending power conferred by Art. I, § 8." The Court distinguished *Frothingham v. Mellon*, supra, on the ground that Mrs. Flothingham had relied, not on a specific limitation on the power to tax and spend, but on a more general claim based on the Due Process Clause. * * *

Unlike the plaintiffs in *Flast*, respondents fail the first prong of the test for taxpayer standing. Their claim is deficient in two respects. First, the source of their complaint is not a congressional action, but a decision by HEW to transfer a parcel of federal property. * * *

Second, and perhaps redundantly, the property transfer about which respondents complain was not an exercise of authority conferred by the taxing and spending clause of Art. I, § 8. The authorizing legislation, the Federal Property and Administrative Services Act of 1949, was an evident exercise of Congress' power under the Property Clause, Art. IV, § 3, cl. 2. * * * 17

Although the Court of Appeals properly doubted respondents' ability to establish standing solely on the basis of their taxpayer status, it considered their allegations of taxpayer injury to be "essentially an assumed role." * * *

In finding the respondents had alleged something more than "the generalized interest of all citizens in constitutional governance," the Court of Appeals relied on factual differences which we do not think amount to legal distinctions. The court decided that respondents' claim differed

---

17. Although not necessary to our decision, we note that any connection between the challenged property transfer and respondents' tax burden is at best speculative and at worst nonexistent. Although public funds were expended to establish the Valley Forge General Hospital, the land was acquired and the facilities constructed thirty years prior to the challenged transfer. Respondents do not challenge this expenditure, and we do not immediately perceive how such a challenge might now be raised. Nor do respondents dispute the government's conclusion that the property has become useless for federal purposes and ought to be disposed of in some productive manner. In fact, respondents' only objection is that the government did not receive adequate consideration for the transfer, because petitioner's use of the property will not confer a public benefit. Assuming ar- *guendo* that this proposition is true, an assumption by no means clear, there is no basis for believing that a transfer to a different purchaser would have added to government receipts. As the government argues, "the ultimate purchaser would, in all likelihood, have been another non-profit institution or local school district rather than a purchaser for cash." Moreover, each year of delay in disposing of the property *depleted* the Treasury by the amounts necessary to maintain a facility that had lost its value to the government. Even if respondents had brought their claim within the outer limits of *Flast*, therefore, they still would have encountered serious difficulty in establishing that they "personally would benefit in a tangible way from the court's intervention." *Warth v. Seldin*, 422 U.S., at 508.

from those in *Schlesinger* and *Richardson*, which were predicated, respectively, on the Incompatability and Accounts Clauses, because "it is at the very least arguable that the Establishment Clause creates in each citizen a 'personal constitutional right' to a government that does not establish religion."   The court found it unnecessary to determine whether this "arguable" proposition was correct, since it judged the mere allegation of a legal right sufficient to confer standing.

This reasoning process merely disguises, we think with a rather thin veil, the inconsistency of the court's results with our decisions in *Schlesinger* and *Richardson*.   The plaintiffs in those cases plainly asserted a "personal right" to have the government act in accordance with their views of the Constitution; indeed, we see no barrier to the *assertion* of such claims with respect to any constitutional provision.   But assertion of a right to a particular kind of government conduct, which the government has violated by acting differently, cannot alone satisfy the requirements of Art. III without draining those requirements of meaning.

Nor can *Schlesinger* and *Richardson* be distinguished on the ground that the Incompatibility and Accounts Clauses are in some way less "fundamental" than the Establishment Clause.   Each establishes a norm of conduct which the federal government is bound to honor—to no greater or lesser extent than any other inscribed in the Constitution.   To the extent the Court of Appeals relied on a view of standing under which the Art. III burdens diminish as the "importance" of the claim on the merits increases, we reject that notion.   The requirement of standing "focuses on the party seeking to get his complaint before a federal court and not on the issues he wishes to have adjudicated."   * * *

The complaint in this case shares a common deficiency with those in *Schlesinger* and *Richardson*.   Although they claim that the Constitution has been violated, they claim nothing else.   They fail to identify any personal injury suffered by the plaintiffs *as a consequence* of the alleged constitutional error, other than the psychological consequence presumably produced by observation of conduct with which one disagrees.   That is not an injury sufficient to confer standing under Art. III, even though the disagreement is phrased in constitutional terms.   * * *

JUSTICE BRENNAN, with whom JUSTICE MARSHALL and JUSTICE BLACKMUN join, dissenting. * * *

Blind to history, the Court attempts to distinguish this case from *Flast* by wrenching snippets of language from our opinions, and by perfunctorily applying that language under color of the first prong of *Flast's* two-part nexus test.   The tortuous distinctions thus produced are specious, at best: at worst, they are pernicious to our constitutional heritage.

First, the Court finds this case different from *Flast* because here the "source of [plaintiff's] complaint is not a *congressional* action, but a decision by HEW to transfer a parcel of federal property."   This attempt at distinction cannot withstand scrutiny.   *Flast* involved a challenge to the actions of the Commissioner of Education, and other officials of HEW, in disbursing funds under the Elementary and Secondary Education Act of

1965 to "religious and sectarian" schools. Plaintiffs disclaimed "any intention to challenge all programs under * * * the Act." * * *

More fundamentally, no clear division can be drawn in this context between actions of the legislative branch and those of the executive branch.   To be sure, the First Amendment is phrased as a restriction on Congress' legislative authority; this is only natural since the Constitution assigns the authority to legislate and appropriate only to the Congress. But it is difficult to conceive of an expenditure for which the last governmental actor, either implementing directly the legislative will, or acting within the scope of legislatively delegated authority, is not an Executive Branch official.   The First Amendment binds the Government as a whole, regardless of which branch is at work in a particular instance.

The Court's second purported distinction between this case and *Flast* is equally unavailing. * * *

It can make no constitutional difference in the case before us whether the donation to the defendant here was in the form of a cash grant to build a facility, see *Tilton v. Richardson*, 403 U.S. 672 (1971), or in the nature of a gift of property including a facility already built.   That this is a meaningless distinction is illustrated by *Tilton*.   In that case, taxpayers were afforded standing to object to the fact that the Government had not received adequate assurance that if the property that it financed for use as an educational facility was later converted to religious uses, it would receive full value for the property, as the Constitution requires.   The complaint here is precisely that, although the property at issue is actually being used for a sectarian purpose, the government has not received, nor demanded, full value payment.   Whether undertaken pursuant to the Property Clause or the Spending Clause, the breach of the Establishment Clause, and the relationship of the taxpayer to that breach, is precisely the same. * * *

Notes

Justice Rehnquist declines to recognize any hierarchy of constitutional rights for purposes of standing doctrine.   And the Court's decision is consistent with at least this premise.   For surely the generalized, and largely discredited, Fifth Amendment interest in avoiding government regulation of property that underlay the plaintiff's claim in *Duke Power* is conventionally presumed to be a less exigent personal liberty than religious freedom.   Yet the *Duke Power* plaintiffs had standing and the *Valley Forge* plaintiffs did not.

The Court's standing decisions do, however, seem to distinguish between interests founded on statutes and interests founded on the Constitution, but they yield a hierarchy that is the converse of what one would have suspected.   Interests of a "psychological" sort that are recognized in the Constitution, e.g., the interests at stake in *Schlesinger*, *Richardson*, and *Valley Forge*, have had greater difficulty achieving recognition as susceptible to individual injury than have certain statutory interests of similar "psychological" character.   Diminution of aesthetic enjoyment of the Washington, D.C., environment was sufficient in *SCRAP* to confer standing, for example, as was an interest in receiving accurate information about the availability of housing in the next case, *Havens Realty Corp. v.*

Coleman. These latter interests are broadly shared and subjectively appreciated in ways that seem quite analogous to the interests in the next case, constitutional structure that the court has deemed insufficiently "palpable" or "distinct."

The apparent distinction between statutory environmental interests and constitutionally-based religious interests, for example, has produced quite amusing strategic decisions by litigants. In *American Civil Liberties Union v. Rabun County Chamber of Commerce*, 678 F.2d 1379 (11th Cir. 1982), the plaintiffs challenged the private placement of a large illuminated cross in a state park. Apparently because Supreme Court doctrine cast doubt upon the plaintiff's standing as "separationists," the ACLU transformed itself into an organization for the protection of the environment. According to the complaint, the presense of the cross disrupted the camping pleasures of several members. Standing was granted on the environmental theory, although the court was clearly concerned by the complication introduced by the sectarian character of the unwelcome intruder. It is at least ironic that the placement of a cross in a public park complicates, rather than enhances, a claim that would not be problematic were it directed at the discarding of gumwrappers and beer cans. For an excellent attempt to sort out these and other standing conundra, see Nichol, *Rethinking Standing*, 72 Cal. L. Rev. 68 (1984).

HAVENS REALTY CORP. v. COLEMAN

Supreme Court of the United States, 1982.
455 U.S. 363, 102 S.Ct. 1114, 71 L.Ed.2d 214

JUSTICE BRENNAN delivered the opinion of the Court.

This case * * * began as a class action against Havens Realty Corp. (Havens) and one of its employees, Rose Jones. Defendants were alleged to have engaged in "racial steering"[1] violative of § 804 of the Fair Housing Act of 1968, 42 U.S.C.A. § 3604 (Act or Fair Housing Act). The complaint, seeking declaratory, injunctive, and monetary relief, was filed in the United States District Court for the Eastern District of Virginia in January 1979 by three individuals[3]—Paul Coles, Sylvia Coleman, and R. Kent Willis—and an organization—Housing Opportunities Made Equal (HOME).

At the time suit was brought, defendant Havens owned and operated two apartment complexes, Camelot Townhouses and Colonial Court Apartments, in Henrico County, Virginia, a suburb of Richmond. The complaint identified Paul Coles as a black "renter plaintiff" who, attempting to rent an apartment from Havens, inquired on July 13, 1978 about the availability of an apartment at the Camelot complex, and was falsely told

---

1. As defined in the complaint, "racial steering" is a "practice by which real estate brokers and agents preserve and encourage patterns of racial segregation in available housing by steering members of racial and ethnic groups to buildings occupied primarily by members of such racial and ethnic groups and away from buildings and neighborhoods inhabited primarily by members of other races or groups."

3. The individual plaintiffs averred that they were "members of a class composed of all persons who have rented or sought to rent residential property in Henrico County, Virginia, and who have been, or continue to be, adversely affected by the acts, policies and practices of" Havens.

that no apartments were available.   The other two individual plaintiffs, Coleman and Willis, were described in the complaint as "tester plaintiffs" who were employed by HOME to determine whether Havens practiced racial steering.   Coleman, who is black, and Willis, who is white, each assertedly made inquiries of Havens on March 14, March 21, and March 23, 1978 regarding the availability of apartments.   On each occasion, Coleman was told that no apartments were available; Willis was told that there were vacancies.   On July 6, 1978 Coleman made a further inquiry and was told that there were no vacancies in the Camelot Townhouses; a white tester for HOME, who was not a party to the complaint, was given contrary information that same day.

The complaint identified HOME as "a nonprofit corporation organized under the laws of the State of Virginia" whose purpose was "to make equal opportunity in housing a reality in the Richmond Metropolitan Area." * * *   Its activities included the operation of a housing counseling service, and the investigation and referral of complaints concerning housing discrimination.

The three individual plaintiffs, who at the time the complaint was filed were all residents of the City of Richmond or the adjacent Henrico County, averred that they had been injured by the discriminatory acts of petitioners.   Coles, the black renter, claimed that he had been "denied the right to rent real property in Henrico County."   Further, he and the two tester plaintiffs alleged that Havens' practices deprived them of the "important social, professional, business and economic, political and aesthetic benefits of interracial associations that arise from living in integrated communities free from discriminatory housing practices."   And Coleman, the black tester, alleged that the misinformation given her by Havens concerning the availability of apartments in the Colonial Court and Camelot Townhouse complexes had caused her "specific injury."

HOME also alleged injury.   It asserted that the steering practices of Havens had frustrated the organization's counseling and referral services, with a consequent drain on resources.   Additionally, HOME asserted that its members had been deprived of the benefits of interracial association arising from living in an integrated community free of housing discrimination.

Before discovery was begun, and without any evidence being presented, the District Court, on motion of petitioners, dismissed the claims of Coleman, Willis, and HOME. * * *   Each of the dismissed plaintiffs—respondents in this Court—appealed, and the Court of Appeals for the Fourth Circuit reversed and remanded for further proceedings.   *Coles v. Havens Realty Corp.*, 633 F.2d 384 (1980).   The Court of Appeals held that the allegations of injury by Willis and Coleman, both as testers and as individuals who were deprived of the benefits of residing in an integrated community, sufficed to withstand a motion to dismiss.[6]   With re-

---

6. The court noted that the District Court could require respondents to amend their pleadings to make more specific their allegations, and that if their allegations were "not supported by proof at trial, the case [could] be terminated for lack of standing at an appropriate stage of the trial."

spect to HOME, the Court of Appeals held that the organization's allegations of injury to itself and its members were sufficient, at the pleading stage, to afford the organization standing both in its own capacity and as a representative of its members. * * *

Our inquiry with respect to the standing issues raised in this case is guided by our decision in *Gladstone, Realtors v. Village of Bellwood*, 441 U.S. 91 (1979). There we considered whether six individuals and the Village of Bellwood had standing to sue under § 812 of the Fair Housing Act, 42 U.S.C.A. § 3612,[11] to redress injuries allegedly caused by the racial steering practices of two real estate brokerage firms. Based on the complaints, "as illuminated by subsequent discovery," we concluded that the Village and four of the individual plaintiffs did have standing to sue under the Fair Housing Act. In reaching that conclusion, we held that "Congress intended standing under § 812 to extend to the full limits of Art. III" and that the courts accordingly lack the authority to create prudential barriers to standing in suits brought under that section. Thus the sole requirement for standing to sue under § 812 is the Article III minima of injury-in-fact: that the plaintiff allege that as a result of the defendant's actions he has suffered "a distinct and palpable injury," *Warth v. Seldin*. With this understanding, we proceed to determine whether each of the respondents in the present case has the requisite standing.

The Court of Appeals held that Coleman and Willis have standing to sue in two capacities: as "testers" and as individuals deprived of the benefits of interracial association. We first address the question of "tester" standing.

In the present context, "testers" are individuals who, without an intent to rent or purchase a home or apartment, pose as renters or purchasers for the purpose of collecting evidence of unlawful steering practices. Section 804(d) states that it is unlawful for an individual or firm covered by the act "[t]o represent to *any person* because of race, color, religion, sex, or national origin that any dwelling is not available for inspection, sale, or rental when such dwelling is in fact so available," a prohibition made enforceable through the creation of an explicit cause of action in § 812(a) of the Act. Congress has thus conferred on all "persons" a legal right to truthful information about available housing.

This congressional intention cannot be overlooked in determining whether testers have standing to sue. As we have previously recognized, "[t]he actual or threatened injury required by Art. III may exist solely by virtue of 'statutes creating legal rights, the invasion of which creates standing. * * * *Warth v. Seldin*. Section 804(d), which, in terms, establishes an enforceable right to truthful information concerning the availability of housing, is such an enactment. A tester who has been the object of a misrepresentation made unlawful under § 804(d) has

---

11. Section 812 provides in relevant part:

"(a) The rights granted by sections 803, 804, 805, and 806 may be enforced by civil actions in appropriate United States district courts without regard to the amount in controversy and in appropriate State or local courts of general jurisdiction."

suffered injury in precisely the form the statute was intended to guard against, and therefore has standing to maintain a claim for damages under the Act's provisions. That the tester may have approached the real estate agent fully expecting that he would receive false information, and without any intention of buying or renting a home, does not negate the simple fact of injury within the meaning of § 804(d). Whereas Congress, in prohibiting discriminatory refusals to sell or rent in § 804(a) of the Act, 42 U.S.C.A. § 3604(a), required that there be a "bona fide offer" to rent or purchase, Congress plainly omitted any such requirement insofar as it banned discriminatory representations in § 804(d).

In the instant case, respondent Coleman—the black tester—alleged injury to her statutorily created right to truthful housing information. * * * If the facts are as alleged, then * * * the Article III requirement of injury-in-fact is satisfied.

Respondent Willis' situation is different. * * * Willis alleged that on each occasion he inquired he was informed that apartments *were* available. As such, Willis has alleged no injury to his statutory right to accurate information concerning the availability of housing. We thus discern no support for the Court of Appeals' holding that Willis has standing to sue in his capacity as a tester. More to the point, because Willis does not allege that he was a victim of a discriminatory misrepresentation, he had not pleaded a cause of action under § 804(d). * * *

Coleman and Willis argue in this Court, and the Court of Appeals held, that irrespective of their status as testers, they should have been allowed to proceed beyond the pleading stage inasmuch as they have alleged that petitioners' steering practices deprived them of the benefits that result from living in an integrated community. This concept of "neighborhood" standing differs from that of "tester" standing in that the injury asserted is an indirect one: an adverse impact on the neighborhood in which the plaintiff resides resulting from the steering of persons other than the plaintiff. By contrast, the injury underlying tester standing—the denial of the tester's own statutory right to truthful housing information caused by misrepresentations to the tester—is a direct one. The distinction is between "third-party" and "first-party" standing.

This distinction is, however, of little significance in deciding whether a plaintiff has standing to sue under § 812 of the Fair Housing Act. *Bellwood*, as we have already noted, held that the only requirement for standing to use under § 812 is the Article III requirement of injury-in-fact. As long as respondents have alleged distinct and palpable injuries that are "fairly traceable" to petitioners' actions, the Article III requirement of injury-in-fact is satisfied. * * *

Petitioners do not dispute that the loss of social, professional, and economic benefits resulting from steering practices constitutes palpable injury. Instead, they contend that Coleman and Willis, by pleading simply that they were residents of the Richmond metropolitan area, have failed to demonstrate how the asserted steering practices of petitioners in Henrico County may have affected the *particular* neighborhoods in which the individual respondents resided.

It is indeed implausible to argue that petitioners' alleged acts of discrimination could have palpable effects throughout the *entire* Richmond metropolitan area. * * *

Nonetheless, in the absence of further factual development, we cannot say as a matter of law that no injury could be proved. * * *

HOME brought suit against petitioners both as a representative of its members and on its own behalf.   In its representative capacity, HOME sought only injunctive relief.   Under the terms of the letter settlement reached between petitioners and respondents, however, HOME has agreed to abandon its request for injunctive relief. * * * While we therefore will not decide the question involving HOME's representative standing, we do proceed to decide the question whether HOME has standing in its own right; the organization continues to press a right to claim damages in that latter capacity. * * *

If, as broadly alleged, petitioners' steering practices have perceptibly impaired HOME's ability to provide counseling and referral services for low- and moderate-income homeseekers, there can be no question that the organization has suffered injury-in-fact.   Such concrete and demonstrable injury to the organization's activities—with the consequent drain on the organization's resources—constitutes far more than simply a setback to the organization's abstract social interests, see *Sierra Club v. Morton.*   We therefore conclude, as did the Court of Appeals, that in view of HOME's allegations of injury it was improper for the District Court to dismiss for lack of standing the claims of the organization in its own right. * * *

JUSTICE POWELL, concurring.

In claiming standing based on a deprivation of the benefits of an integrated community, the individual respondents alleged generally that they lived in the City of Richmond or in Henrico County. * * * The allegation would have been equally informative if the area assigned had been the Commonwealth of Virginia. * * *

In this case neither the District Court nor apparently counsel for the parties took appropriate action to prevent the case from reaching an appellate court with only meaningless averments concerning the disputed question of standing.   One can well understand the impatience of the District Court that dismissed the complaint.   Yet our cases have established the preconditions to dismissal because of excessive vagueness, e.g., *Gladstone, Realtors*, supra, 441 U.S., at 112–115, with regard to standing, and those conditions were not observed.   The result is more than a little absurd: Both the Court of Appeals and this Court have been called upon to parse pleadings devoid of any hint of support or nonsupport for an allegation essential to jurisdiction.

Liberal pleading rules have both their merit and their price.   This is a textbook case of a high price—in terms of a severe imposition on already overburdened federal courts as well as unjustified expense to the litigants.   This also is a particular disturbing example of lax pleading, for it threatens to trivialize what we repeatedly have recognized as a *constitutional* requirement of Article III standing.

In any event, in the context of this case, as it reaches us after some four years of confusing and profitless litigation, it is not within our province to order a dismissal.   I therefore join the Opinion of the Court.

Notes

1. Note that *Havens Realty*, unlike all the other standing cases in this section, does not involve a suit to "review" the actions of a government official.   Standing analysis is here used to determine whether one private party may invoke federal court jurisdiction to obtain a remedy against another private party.   In the usual legal vernacular (outside of the antitrust field), this question would be considered a question of whether the plaintiffs had stated a claim or a cause of action under the statute.

The utilization of "standing" language in *Havens* seems to have two sources. First, *Havens* is part of a line of "fair housing" cases beginning with *Warth v. Seldin*, and *Warth* was a suit to declare unconstitutional the zoning practices of a municipal government.   Standing language was therefore quite conventional in *Warth* and has been carried over into later fair housing litigation not involving challenges to governmental practices.

Moreover, even prior to *Warth*, cases under Title VIII of the Civil Rights Act of 1968, commonly known as the Fair Housing Act, analyzed the question of what rights of action that statute provided in standing terms.   This approach resulted in no small measure from the language of the Fair Housing Act which, in section 810, provides a right of action to any "person aggrieved" by the various discriminatory practices made illegal elsewhere in the statute.   This "person aggrieved" language is, of course, reminiscent of the judicial review provisions of such statutes as the Federal Communication Act, at issue in the *Sanders Brothers Radio* case.   Thus, in *Trafficante v. Metropolitan Life Insurance Co.*, 409 U.S. 205 (1972), the Supreme Court construed section 810 to extend rights to the broadest class of claimants permitted by Article III.   And it found that residents of a large apartment complex had alleged a sufficient injury when they complained that the defendant's racial steering practices had impaired their opportunity for the "social and professional advantages" of living in an integrated community. The "benefits from interracial associations" were analogized by the *Trafficante* court to the noneconomic injuries said to be sufficient to provide standing in *Sierra Club v. Morton*.

Gladstone v. Realtors, upon which *Havens* principally relies, extended the *Trafficante* analysis to section 812 of the Fair Housing Act—a section which did not include the "person aggrieved" language.   Instead, section 812 merely provides that the rights granted elsewhere in the statute "may be enforced by civil actions."   Nevertheless, the Court, over two dissents, decided that Congress had not, intended to make any distinction between the remedial provisions of sections 810 and 812 of the Fair Housing Act.   Thus, plaintiffs in *Gladstone Realtors* who alleged injuries similar to those found sufficient for standing in *Trafficante* were granted standing to sue.   In addition, the government of the Village of Bellwood was permitted to sue on its claim that the petitioners' racial steering practices effectively manipulated the housing market in the village.

The Court hypothesized that a number of harmful consequences might flow from this manipulation, ranging from the diminution of the village's tax base to impairment of its ability to maintain an integrated school system.   Citing *Linmark Associates, Inc. v. Willingboro*, 431 U.S. 85, 94 (1977), the Court said "there can be no question about the importance to a community of promoting stable, racially integrated housing."

2. *Havens Realty* is notable in other respects as well.   Although the standing of organizations, both in their own right and as representatives for their membership, is now generally accepted, *Havens* seems to be the first case in which the injury to the organization results from a set of practices that, if eliminated, would deprive the organization of its essential purpose.   If causing an organization to expend the resources it was organized to expend constitutes "injury in fact," one is hard pressed to discern why the Sierra Club, for example, was required to plead the interests of its members who used the Mineral King Valley and permitted to challenge the Disney development only in a representative capacity.   For fighting the Disney development would surely impair the Sierra Club's ability to engage in its other organizational activities, such as, the provision of study tours and other outings in wilderness areas.

Equally novel is the notion that someone (here a "tester") who seeks information merely for the purpose of determining whether truthful information will be made available to bona fide applicants is injured by the provision of incorrect information, at least where the Congress has provided a legal right to correct information.   *Havens Realty* should thus put to rest concerns about potential standing problems under statutes like the Freedom of Information Act.   Presumably, anyone seeking government information under the FOIA will actually want to receive it, rather than be merely "testing" whether a particular agency has a forthcoming attitude toward FOIA requests.   The FOIA "requester" should therefore be an *a fortiori* case for statutorily-based standing.

3. After *Havens Realty*, is there any limit to Congress' capacity to legislatively create "injury in fact" sufficient for purposes of Article III? Suppose, for example, Congress passed the following statute: "Every person has a right to the equal, effective, and legitimate implementation of the law of the United States. This right may be enforced by civil action in any court of competent jurisdiction." Would such a statute effectively merge the allegation of injury in fact and illegality on the part of the government?   If so, would it be constitutional?   And if constitutional, does not this suggest that the injury in fact requirement is "prudential," or at least a part of "constitutional common law" subject to Congressional revision?   And if subject to Congressional revision, would it not also be subject to alteration by the Supreme Court?

4. Shortly before this volume went to press, the Supreme Court again dealt with the issue of standing in a suit challenging administration of the Internal Revenue Code.   In *Allen v. Wright*, ___U.S.___, 104 S.Ct. 3315 (1984), the Court denied standing to parents of black public schoolchildren who sought to challenge IRS procedures for assuring that racially discriminatory private schools do not retain tax-exempt status.   The plaintiffs contended that the Service's procedures permitted specific discriminatory schools to enjoy tax-free status through exempt "umbrella" organizations that operated or supported them and, further, that the Service simply accepted certifications of nondiscrimination, without tak-

ing steps to assure that this policy was followed in fact. They claimed the IRS' conduct:

(a) constitutes tangible federal financial aid and other support for racially segregated educational institutions, and

(b) fosters and encourages the organization, operation and expansion of institutions providing racially segregated educational opportunities for white children avoiding attendance in desegregating public school districts and thereby interferes with the efforts of federal courts, HEW and local school authorities to desegregate public school districts which have been operating racially dual school systems.

The plaintiffs did not allege that their children had applied or would apply to, or had been excluded from, any of the schools whose tax exemptions they challenged.

Writing for a majority of the Court, Justice O'Connor began by restating the standing inquiry (104 S.Ct. at 3325):

[T]he law of Art. III standing is built on a single basic idea—the idea of separation of powers. * * *

Determining standing in a particular case may be facilitated by clarifying principles or even clean rules developed in prior cases. Typically, however, the standing inquiry requires careful judicial examination of a complaint's allegations to ascertain whether the particular plaintiff is entitled to an adjudication of the particular claims asserted. Is the injury too abstract, or otherwise not appropriate, to be considered judicially cognizable? Is the line of causation between the illegal conduct and injury too attenuated? Is the prospect of obtaining relief from the injury as a result of a favorable ruling too speculative? These questions and any others relevant to the standing inquiry must be answered by reference to the Art. III notion that federal courts may exercise power only "in the last resort, and as a necessity," and only when adjudication is "consistent with a system of separated powers and [the dispute is one] traditionally thought to be capable of resolution through the judicial process," *Flast v. Cohen.*

Turning to the plaintiffs' first alleged harm, which the court of appeals had characterized as "the denigration they suffer as black parents and schoolchildren when their government graces with tax-exempt status educational institutions in their communities that treat members of their race as persons of lesser worth," Justice O'Connor held that it did not constitute "judicially cognizable injury." She viewed the plaintiff's allegation as a complaint "that their Government is violating the law," and thus as basically indistinguishable from the claims held insufficient in *Schlesinger* and *Richardson,* supra. Her opinion continued (id. at 3326):

The consequences of recognizing respondents' standing on the basis of their first claim of injury illustrate why our cases plainly hold that such injury is not judicially cognizable. If the abstract stigmatic injury were cognizable, standing would extend nationwide to all members of the particular racial groups against which the Government was alleged to be discriminating by its grant of a tax exemption to a racially discriminatory school, regardless of the location of that school. All such persons could claim the same sort of abstract stigmatic injury respondents assert in their first claim of injury. A black person in Hawaii could challenge the grant of a tax exemption to a racially discriminatory school in Maine. Recognition of standing in such circumstances would transform the federal courts into "no more than a vehicle for the vindication of the value interests of concerned bystanders." *United States v. SCRAP.* Constitutional limits on the role of the federal courts preclude such a transformation.

The plaintiffs' second alleged injury—their childrens' diminished ability to receive an education in racially integrated public schools—without question was "not only judicially cognizable but * * * one of the most serious injuries recognized in our legal system." Yet they lacked standing because this injury could not fairly be traced to the government conduct they challenged. For Justice O'Connor, the telling precedents were *Simon* and *Warth* (id. at 3328):

> The chain of causation is even weaker in this case. It involves numerous third parties (officials of racially discriminatory schools receiving tax exemptions and the parents of children attending such schools) who may not even exist in respondents' communities and whose independent decisions may not collectively have a significant effect on the ability of public-school students to receive a desegregated education.

> The idea of separation of powers that underlies standing doctrine explains why our cases preclude the conclusion that respondents' alleged injury "fairly can be traced to the challenged action" of the IRS. That conclusion would pave the way generally for suits challenging, not specifically identifiable Government violations of law, but the particular programs agencies establish to carry out their legal obligations. Such suits, even when premised on allegations of several instances of violations of law, are rarely if ever appropriate for federal-court adjudication.

The majority opinion provoked a discouraged dissent from Justice Brennan who, after quoting liberally from his opinions in *Warth* and *Valley Forge,* found *Simon* "plainly distinguishable" (id. at 3341):

> The respondents in this case do not challenge the denial of any service by a tax-exempt institution; admittedly, they do not seek access to racially discriminatory private schools. Rather, the injury they allege, and the injury that clearly satisfies constitutional requirements, is the deprivation of their children's opportunity and ability to receive an education in a racially integrated school district. This injury * * * is of a kind that is directly traceable to the governmental action being challenged. * * * By interposing its own version of pleading formalities between the respondents and the federal courts, the Court not only has denied access to litigants who properly seek vindication of their constitutional rights, but also has ignored the important historical role that the courts have played in the Nation's efforts to eliminate racial discrimination from our schools.

> More than one commentator has noted that the causation component of the Court's standing inquiry is no more than a poor disguise for the Court's view of the merits of the underlying claims.[10] The Court today does nothing to avoid that criticism.

---

10. See e.g., L. Tribe, American Constitutional Law § 3–21 (1978); Chayes, Foreword: Public Law Litigation and the Burger Court, 96 Harv. L. Rev. 1, 14–22 (1982); Nichol, Causation as a Standing Requirement: The Unprin-cipled Use of Judicial Restraint, 69 Ky. L. J. 185 (1980–81); Tushnet, The New Law of Standing: A Plea for Abandonment, 62 Cornell L. Rev. 663 (1977).

Justice Stevens, in an opinion joined by Justice Blackmun, also dissented. He employed economic theory to support his conclusion that the plaintiff's injury was surely traceable, at least in part, to the governmental conduct they challenged (id. at 3343–48):

We have held that when a subsidy makes a given activity more or less expensive, injury can be fairly traced to the subsidy for purposes of standing analysis because of the resulting increase or decrease in the ability to engage in the activity. Indeed, we have employed exactly this causation analysis in the same context at issue here—subsidies given private schools that practice racial discrimination. Thus, in *Gilmore v. City of Montgomery*, 417 U.S. 556 (1974), we easily recognized the causal connection between official policies [allowing segregated public schools to use public parks] that enhanced the attractiveness of segregated schools and the failure to bring about or maintain a desegregated public school system. Similarly, in *Norwood v. Harrison*, 413 U.S. 455 (1973), we concluded that the provision of textbooks to discriminatory private schools "has a significant tendency to facilitate, reinforce, and support private discrimination."

* * *

This causation analysis is nothing more than a restatement of elementary economics: when something becomes more expensive, less of it will be purchased. Sections 170 and 501(c)(3) [of the Code] are premised on that recognition. If racially discriminatory private schools lose the "cash grants" that flow from the operation of the statutes, the education they provide will become more expensive and hence less of their services will be purchased. Conversely, maintenance of these tax benefits makes an education in segregated private schools relatively more attractive, by decreasing its cost. Accordingly, without tax exempt status, private schools will either not be competitive in terms of cost, or have to change their admissions policies, hence reducing their competitiveness for parents seeking "a racially segregated alternative" to public schools, which is what respondents have alleged many white parents in desegregating school districts seek. In either event the process of desegregation will be advanced in the same way that it was advanced in *Gilmore* and *Norwood*—the withdrawal of the subsidy for segregated schools means the incentive structure facing white parents who seek such schools for their children will be altered. Thus, the laws of economics, not to mention the laws of Congress embodied in § § 170 and 501(c)(3), compel the conclusion that the injury respondents have alleged—the increased segregation of their children's schools because of the ready availability of private schools that admit whites only—will be redressed if these schools' operations are inhibited through the denial of preferential tax treatment.

* * *

* * * The strength of the plaintiff's interest in the outcome has nothing to do with whether the relief it seeks would intrude upon the prerogatives of other branches of government; the possibility that the relief might be inappropriate does not lessen the plaintiff's stake in obtaining that relief. If a plaintiff presents a nonjusticiable issue, or seeks relief that a court may not award, then its complaint should be dismissed for those reasons, and not because the plaintiff lacks a stake in obtaining that relief and hence has no standing. Imposing an undefined but clearly more rigorous standard for redressability for reasons unrelated to the causal nexus between the injury and the challenged conduct can only encourage undisciplined, *ad hoc* litigation, a result that would be avoided if the Court straightforwardly considered the justiciability of the issues respondents seek to raise, rather than using those issues to obfuscate standing analysis.

* * * [T]he Court could be saying that it will not treat as legally cognizable injuries that stem from an administrative decision concerning how enforcement resources will be allocated. This surely is an important point. Respondents do seek to restructure the IRS' mechanisms for enforcing the legal requirement that discriminatory institutions not receive tax-exempt status. Such restructuring would dramatically affect the way in which the IRS exercises its prosecutorial discretion. The Executive requires latitude to decide how best to enforce the law, and in general the Court may well be correct that the exercise of that discretion, especially in the tax context, is unchallengeable.

However, as the Court also recognizes, this principle does not apply when suit is brought "to enforce specific legal obligations whose violation works a direct harm." Here, respondents contend that the IRS is violating a specific constitutional limitation on its enforcement discretion. * * *

* * * It has been clear since *Marbury v. Madison* that "[i]t is emphatically the province and duty of the judicial department to say what the law is." Deciding whether the Treasury has violated a specific legal limitation on its enforcement discretion does not intrude upon the prerogatives of the Executive, for in so deciding we are merely saying "what the law is." Surely the question whether the Constitution or the Code limits enforcement discretion is one within the Judiciary's competence, and I do not believe that the question whether the law * * * imposes such an obligation upon the IRS is so insubstantial that respondents' attempt to raise it should be defeated for lack of subject-matter jurisdiction on the ground that it infringes the Executive's prerogatives. * * *

5. The responsibility for divining and applying standing doctrine falls in the first instance on the lower federal courts. The U.S. Court of Appeals for the District of Columbia Circuit has had to grapple with the Supreme Court's standing jurisprudence more frequently than any other court, and its own jurisprudence displays similar uncertainties and inconsistencies. The appeals court has often lamented the Supreme Court's failure to provide clearer guidance. Its frustration has centered around two issues: (1) the vitality and content of the *Data Processing* "zone of interests" requirement, and (2) the distinction between components of standing analysis that represent Article III requirements and those that are "prudential" limitations fashioned by the judiciary. For illustrations of the court's difficulties, see *Tax Analysts and Advocates v. Blumenthal,* 566 F.2d 130 (D.C. Cir. 1977); *Control Data Corp. v. Baldridge,* 655 F.2d 283 (D.C. Cir.), *cert. denied* 454 U.S. 881 (1981); and *Block v. Community Nutrition Institute,* 698 F.2d 1239 (D.C. Cir. 1983), *reversed* ___ U.S. ___, 104 S.Ct. 2450 (1984).

In the last case, three individual consumers of milk, a non-profit consumer organization (CNI), and a handler of milk products sued to overturn the Agriculture Department's regulation of reconsituted milk under marketing orders issued pursuant to the Agricultural Marketing Agreement Act (AMAA). These marketing orders were designed to ensure that producers received uniform prices for raw milk, regardless of how it was ultimately used. The court found that the plaintiff consumers had alleged sufficient injury by claiming that the existing milk orders precluded them from purchasing a "nutritious dairy beverage at a lower price than fresh drinking milk" and that they were "deprived of a 'stabilizing market influence' since 'reconstituted fluid product could quickly expand the fluid milk supply when (seasonal) changes result in a reduction of the whole fluid milk supply.' " The consumers had also plausibly argued that " 'but for' the regulation, handlers would be able to market reconstituted milk for less than fresh milk and that, as a result, reconstituted milk would be available at a lower retail price than whole milk." They satisfied the redressability requirement by introducing a USDA statement predicting that if the compensatory payment were eliminated, consumers would soon save $186 million per year, and by showing that reconstituted milk was indeed available at lower market prices in unregulated markets.

The court of appeals also found that the consumer plaintiffs satisfied both prudential requirements for standing. By reading the specific provisions of the AMAA in light of Congress' statements of general policy, the court found that the Secretary was obliged to "provide in the interests of producers and consumers, an orderly supply (of milk) * * * to avoid unreasonable fluctuations in supplies and prices." This statutory language created a zone of protected interests within which the consumers' interest "arguably" could fall. Furthermore, the mere fact that their injury was shared by other consumers did not require dismissal of the complaint—a proposition from which Judge Scalia dissented.

The court, however, denied standing to CNI, a non-profit organization specializing in food and nutrition issues. CNI alleged two injuries, one to its interest in "seeing" that consumers have nutritious milk products available at the lowest prices and the other to its ability to inform low-income individuals about sources of low-cost food. While the first was too abstract an injury to fulfill the requirements of organizational standing, the second was sufficient to meet the injury in fact requirement. But CNI had failed to show a causal connection between its injury and the Secretary's actions, for "nothing in the challenged regulation affect[ed] CNI's ability to inform consumers about sources of low-cost food."

The Supreme Court overturned the D.C. Circuit's grant of standing. ___ U.S. ___, 104 S.Ct. 2450 (1984). Instead of focusing on the plaintiff consumers' interests, the Court examined "the statutory scheme 'to determine whether Congress precluded all judicial review, and, if not, whether Congress nevertheless foreclosed review to the class to which the (respondents) belon(g).' " This analysis was dictated, the Court suggested, in suits brought under the APA, which confers a cause of action upon persons " 'adversely affected or aggrieved by agency action within the meaning of a relevant statute * * * but withdraw[s] that cause of action to the extent the relevant statute 'preclude[s] judicial review.' "

The Court concluded that "allowing consumers to sue the Secretary would severely disrupt [the] complex and delicate administrative scheme" of the Agricultural Marketing Agreement Act of 1937. While there was no explicit evidence of congressional intent to preclude suits by consumers, the requisite intent was inferrable from the administrative process Congress designed for issuing milk marketing orders (id. at 2455):

> The Act contemplates a cooperative venture among the Secretary, handlers, and producers the principal purposes of which are to raise the price of agricultural products and to establish an orderly system for marketing them.

Handlers and producers—but not consumers—are entitled to participate in the adoption and retention of market orders. The Act provides for agreements among the Secretary, producers, and handlers, for hearings among them, and for votes by producers and handlers. Nowhere in the Act, however, is there an express provision for participation by consumers in any proceeding. In a complex scheme of this type, the omission of such a provision is sufficient reason to believe that Congress intended to foreclose consumer participation in the regulatory process.

To be sure, the general purpose sections of the Act allude to general consumer interests. But the preclusion issue does not only turn on whether the interests of a particular class like consumers are implicated. Rather, the preclusion issue turns ultimately on whether Congress intended for that class to be relied upon to challenge agency disregard of the law. The structure of this Act indicates that Congress intended only producers and handlers, and not consumers, to ensure that the statutory objectives would be realized.

The Court criticized the D.C. Circuit for overreading "this Court's oft-quoted statement that 'only upon a showing of 'clear and convincing evidence' of a contrary legislative intent should the courts restrict access to judicial review.' " Citing *Morris v. Gressette*, 432 U.S. 491 (1971), infra p. 693, the Court declared that the presumption in favor of judicial review is overcome "whenever the congressional intent to preclude judicial review is 'fairly discernible in the statutory scheme.' " Id. at 2457.

C. REVIEWABILITY

Section 701(a) of the APA declares that the Act's judicial review provisions apply "except to the extent that—(1) statutes preclude judicial review; or (2) agency action is committed to agency discretion by law." The APA thus recognizes that Congress, or perhaps a court, may appropriately decide that some agency actions should not be subject to judicial reexamination. *Overton Park* and *Abbott Laboratories, Inc. v. Gardner*, infra p. 753 would suggest that such circumstances are rare. But they are not unknown, and this part both considers why Congress might wish to foreclose review and explores judicial attitudes toward claims that review should be withheld.

1. STATUTORY PRECLUSION OF REVIEW

Language in federal statutes purporting to *bar* judicial review of final administrative decisions is sparse. Indeed, the prevalent pattern in modern federal regulatory and social legislation is to describe the availability and terms of judicial review in copious detail. See, e.g., Toxic Substances Control Act of 1976, 15 U.S.C.A. § § 2601–2629, which authorizes judicial review of EPA actions under no fewer than seven different provisions. Congressional attempts to *limit* review are not uncommon, however, and every statute that provides for review also raises issues of exclusivity, i.e., of implied "preclusion" of review by other routes. An example of partial preclusion is the Regulatory Flexibility Act, 5 U.S.C.A. § § 601–612 (1982), which purports to bar review of agency compliance with its mandated analysis of alternative regulatory requirements. Verkuil, *A Critical Guide to the Regulatory Flexibility Acts*, 1982 Duke L.J. 213, 259–264. Legislative proposals to require agencies to perform regulatory analyses likewise typically contain language that would in theory prevent courts from policing administrative compliance with that requirement independently of assuring that agency rules are not arbitrary or capricious. E.g., S. 1080, 97th Cong., 2d Sess., 128 Cong. Rec. S2374 (1982).

Such attempts to channel challenges to administrative action or to bar judicial oversight of what might be considered internal decisionmaking requirements do not weaken the general edifice of presumptive review. Occasionally, however, Congress has attempted to bar altogether judicial review of specific types of decisions. And, more often than not, such efforts have met resistance, as a series of decisions under the laws providing benefits to military veterans illustrates.

In *Tracy v. Gleason*, 379 F.2d 469 (D.C. Cir. 1967), the estate of a deceased veteran sought review of a Veterans Administration determination that the decedent was not entitled to disability benefits for the years 1949–1960. The VA had paid Tracy benefits through 1949, before terminating them because of his failure to file an income form. The VA's notice of termination had been sent to St. Elizabeth's Hospital where, as its records showed, Tracy had been confined since 1936 suffering from severe mental illness. No member of Tracy's family knew about his eligibility for benefits until 1960. When the VA refused payment for the intervening eleven years, they brought suit. The district court granted the VA's motion to dismiss for lack of jurisdiction, relying on 38 U.S.C.A. § 211(a), which then provided:

> [T]he decision of the Administrator on any question of law or fact concerning a claim for benefits * * * shall be final and conclusive and no other official or any court of the United States shall have power or jurisdiction to review any such decision.

Relying on its own precedent, *Wellman v. Whittier*, 259 F.2d 163 (D.C.Cir. 1958), the court of appeals avoided this statutory bar to review. It reasoned that the dispute did not grow out of a disposition of a "claim" but rather was the result of an action by the VA Administrator to terminate benefits previously conferred: "[A]fter the claim has been allowed and benefits have been awarded, there is, strictly speaking, no longer a mere claim which the Administrator may unreviewably reject if he chooses. The veteran is then * * * a *beneficiary*, and the Administrator's subsequent termination of his benefits should not be immune from juducial scrutiny * * * . [C]ertainly, [Congress] did not so provide in § 211(a)." 379 F.2d at 473.

Three years later, in Pub. L. No. 91–376, Congress amended 38 U.S.C.A. § 211(a) to read:

> On and after October 17, 1940 * * * the decisions of the Administrator [of Veterans' Affairs] on any question of law or fact under any law administered by the Veterans' Administration providing benefits for veterans and

their dependents or survivors shall be final and conclusive and no other official or any court of the United States shall have power or jurisdiction to review any such decision by an action in the nature of mandamus or otherwise.

JOHNSON v. ROBISON

Supreme Court of the United States, 1974.
415 U.S. 361, 94 S.Ct. 1160, 39 L.Ed.2d 389.

MR. JUSTICE BRENNAN delivered the opinion of the Court.

A draftee accorded Class I-O conscientious objector status and completing performance of required alternative civilian service does not qualify under 38 U.S.C.A. * * * 1652(a)(1) as a "veteran who * * * served on active duty" * * * , and is therefore not an "eligible veteran" entitled under 38 U.S.C.A. § 1661(a) to veterans' educational benefits provided by the Veterans' Readjustments Benefits Act of 1966. Appellants, the Administration and the Administrator of Veterans' Affairs, for that reason, denied the application for educational assistance of appellee Robison, a conscientious objector who filed his application after he satisfactorily completed two years of alternative civilian service at the Peter Bent Brigham Hospital, Boston. Robison thereafter commenced this class action * * * seeking a declaratory judgment that 38 U.S.C.A. §§ 101(21), 1652(a)(1), and 1661(a), read together, violated the First Amendment's guarantee of religious freedom and the Fifth Amendment's guarantee of equal protection of the laws. Appellants moved to dismiss the action on the ground, among others, that the District Court lacked jurisdiction because of 38 U.S.C.A. § § 211(a) which prohibits judicial review of decisions of the Administrator. * * *

We consider first appellants' contention that § 211(a) bars federal courts from deciding the constitutionality of veterans' benefits legislation. Such a construction would, of course, raise serious questions concerning the constitutionality of § 211(a),[8] and in such case "it is a cardinal principle that this Court will first ascertain whether a construction of the statute is fairly possible by which the [constitutional] question[s] may be avoided."

Plainly, no explicit provision of § 211(a) bars judicial consideration of appellee's constitutional claims. * * * The prohibitions would appear to be aimed at review only of those decisions of law or fact that arise in the *administration* by the Veterans' Administration of a *statute* providing benefits for veterans. A decision of law or fact "under" a statute is made by the Administrator in the interpretation or application of a particular provision of the statute to a particular set of facts. Appellee's constitu-

---

8. Compare *Ex parte McCardle*, 7 Wall. 506 (1869); *Sheldon v. Sill*, 8 How. 441 (1850), with *Martin v. Hunter's Lessee*, 1 Wheat. 304 (1816); *St. Joseph Stock Yards Co. v. United States*, 298 U.S. 38, 84 (1936) (Brandeis, J., concurring). See Hart, The Power of Congress to Limit the Jurisdiction of Federal Courts: An Exercise in Dialectic, 66 Harv. L. Rev. 1362 (1953).

tional challenge is not to any such decision of the *Administrator*, but rather to a decision of *Congress* to create a statutory class entitled to benefits that does not include I-O conscientious objectors who performed alternative civilian service.   * * *

* * * No-review clauses similar to § 211(a) have been a part of veterans' benefits legislation since 1933.   While the legislative history accompanying these precursor no-review clauses is almost nonexistent, the Administrator, in a letter written in 1952 in connection with a revision of the clause under consideration by the Subcommittee of the House Committee on Veterans' Affairs, comprehensively explained the policies necessitating the no-review clause and identified two primary purposes: (1) to insure that veterans' benefits claims will not burden the courts and the Veterans' Administration with expensive and time-consuming litigation, and (2) to insure that the technical and complex determinations and applications of Veterans' Administration policy connected with veterans' benefits decisions will be adequately and uniformly made.

RATIONALE FOR NO Review CLAUSES

* * *

Congress perceived * * * [*Tracy v. Gleason*] as a threat to the dual purposes of the no-review clause.   First, the interpretation would lead to an inevitable increase in litigation with consequent burdens upon the courts and the Veterans' Administration.   In its House Report, the Committee on Veterans' Affairs stated that "[s]ince the decision in the *Tracy* case * * * suits in constantly increasing numbers have been filed in the U.S. District Court for the District of Columbia by plaintiffs seeking a resumption of terminated benefits." * * *

Second, Congress was concerned that the judicial interpretation of § 211(a) would involve the courts in day-to-day determination and interpretation of Veterans' Administration policy.   * * *

Thus, the 1970 amendment was enacted to overrule the interpretation of the Court of Appeals for the District of Columbia Circuit, and thereby restore vitality to the two primary purposes to be served by the no-review clause.   Nothing whatever in the legislative history of the 1970 amendment, or predecessor no-review clauses, suggests any congressional intent to preclude judicial cognizance of constitutional challenges to veterans' benefits legislation.   Such challenges obviously do not contravene the purposes of the no-review clause, for they cannot be expected to burden the courts by their volume, nor do they involve technical considerations of Veterans' Administration policy.   We therefore conclude, in agreement with the District Court, that a construction of § 211(a) that does not extend the prohibitions of that section to actions challenging the constitutionality of laws providing benefits for veterans is not only "fairly possible" but is the most reasonable construction, for neither the text nor the scant legislative history of § 211(a) provides the "clear and convincing" evidence of congressional intent required by this Court before a statute will be construed to restrict access to judicial review.   See *Abbott Laboratories v. Gardner*, 387 U.S. 136, 141 (1967).

Notes

1. To characterize the judicial attitude to statutes that preclude review as "uncharitable" may be an overgeneralization. The Supreme Court has routinely acquiesced in statutory language making agency decisions on property claims "final and conclusive." See, e.g., *Schilling v. Rogers*, 363 U.S. 666 (1960); *Work v. United States ex rel. Rives*, 267 U.S. 175 (1925). In cases involving personal liberty, however, the Court has construed preclusion clauses as narrowly as possible. For example, in *Shaughnessy v. Pedreiro*, 349 U.S. 48 (1955), it ruled that a clause making deportation orders of the Immigration and Naturalization Service "final" referred to "administrative finality" and was not meant to limit judicial review. And in a long series of Selective Service cases during the 1960's the Court steadily pushed back the borders of non-reviewability. See generally Note, *Judicial Review of Selective Service Classifications*, 56 Va. L. Rev. 1288 (1970), and the one major case decided after 1970, *Fein v. Selective Service System Local Board No. 7*, 405 U.S. 365 (1972).

Ultimately, the numerous "preclusion" cases are reconcilable only on the most fundamental level—an evaluation of the degree to which the foreclosure of judicial review in a particular case is thought to undermine the sense of the rule of law that obtains only because the courthouse door is open. As Judge Wisdom observed in *Brotherhood of Railroad Trainmen v. Central of Georgia Railway Co.*, 415 F.2d 403, 412–13 (5th Cir. 1969), *cert. denied* 396 U.S. 1008 (1970), " 'Finality' is a mirage if relied upon to preclude *any* judicial review of an * * * administrative agency's decision." And dissenting in *Caulfield v. United States Department of Agriculture*, 293 F.2d 217, 228 (5th Cir. 1961), *petition for cert. dismissed* 369 U.S. 858 (1962), he wrote:

> The only common denominator of the decided cases I am able to discern is the broad principle, loosely applied, that finality language will be whittled down to size—to fit the Court's sense of fundamental fairness, whenever that sense is offended by denial of judicial review. I do not say that the courts decide reviewability cases guided only by their own notions of abstract justice. If courts rationalize fair play in terms of "jurisdiction," "statutory construction," "due process," or some other legal concept it is always, I hope, in proper context, considering the circumstances of the case and the interplay of policy, statute, and regulation; reducing the subjective element by weighing the presence or absence of constitutional safeguards, the reasonableness of the regulatory scheme, the effectiveness of administrative relief, the adequacy of administrative check on initial action, the comparative qualifications of courts on the one hand or administrative tribunals on the other hand to decide the particular question at issue, the nature of the judicial review prayed for, the nature of the administrative action, and many other factors, some at cross-purposes.

2. *Johnson v. Robison* was distinguished in *Weinberger v. Salfi*, 422 U.S. 749 (1975), where the plaintiffs challenged the constitutionality of "duration-of-relationship" eligibility requirements for surviving wives and stepchildren under the Social Security Act. They premised jurisdiction of 28 U.S.C.A. § 1331 in the face of language in section 405(h) of the Act, which provides:

> No action against the United States, the Secretary, or any officer or employee thereof shall be brought under [any provision of] Title 28 to recover on any claim arising under [Title II of the Social Security Act].

The district court, interpreting this language as merely codifying a requirement to exhaust administrative remedies, concluded that it made no sense to insist that the plaintiffs first pursue an administrative claim for benefits when the Secretary lacked authority, under the very requirements they challenged, to grant it.

The Supreme Court, per Justice Rehnquist, disagreed with the district court's interpretation of section 405(h), holding that it flatly precluded any suit seeking Title II benefits, even one challenging the constitutionality of statutory eligibility provisions. Rehnquist contrasted section 405(h)'s language with the provision that the Court had eluded in *Johnson v. Robison* (422 U.S. at 762):

> Its reach is not limited to decisions of the Secretary on issues of law or fact. Rather, it extends to any "action" seeking "to recover on any [Social Security] claim"—irrespective of whether resort to judicial processes is necessitated by discretionary decisions of the Secretary or by his non-discretionary applications of allegedly unconstitutional statutory restrictions.
>
> There is another reason why *Johnson v. Robison* is inapposite. It was expressly based, at least in part, on the fact that if § 211(a) reached constitutional challenges to statutory limitations, then absolutely no judicial consideration of the issue would be available. * * * In the present case * * * [§ 405(g) of] the Social Security Act itself provides jurisdiction for constitutional challenges to its provisions.

Justice Rehnquist then examined the requirements of 405(g), which prescribes a final decision by the Secretary "after a hearing," commencement of suit within 60 days of that decision, and filing in the district where the plaintiff resides or transacts business. He read the latter two of these requirements as waivable by the parties, but the first he considered "central to the requisite grant of subject-matter jurisdiction." At this juncture, he confronted a difficulty, for section 405(g) seems to make a Secretarial decision after an evidentiary hearing a prerequisite to suit—and it was clear that the Secretary would not grant a hearing, much less benefits, to a claimant whose application revealed failure to comply with the challenged duration-of-relationship requirements. Rehnquist escaped this conundrum by holding that jurisdiction under section 405(g) could be sustained if a plaintiff had pursued a claim for benefits far enough to permit the Secretary to conclude that only the allegedly unconstitutional eligibility criteria precluded an award (id. at 765):

> Plainly these purposes [of the statutory limitation] have been served once the Secretary has satisfied himself that the only issue is the constitutionality of a statutory requirement, a matter which is beyond his jurisdiction to determine, and that the claim is neither otherwise invalid nor cognizable under a different section of the Act.

3. *Morris v. Gressette*, 432 U.S. 491 (1977), is a rare illustration of "implied preclusion" of judicial review, again in a context where another route to judicial vindication of rights seems available. Under section 5 of the 1965 Voting Rights Act, no covered state may implement changes in "any voting qualification, or prerequisite to voting, or standard, practice, or procedure with respect to voting" without first pursuing one of two routes of approval. 42 U.S.C.A. § 1973c (1982). A state may initiate declaratory judgment action in the District Court of the District of Columbia to obtain a determination that the proposed change "does not have the purpose and will not have the effect of denying or abridging the right to vote on account of race or color"—an action in which it bears the burden of proof. Alternatively, the state may submit the change to the Attorney

General, who has 60 days in which to object.   If no objection is forthcoming in that period, the change may be implemented.

The facts of *Morris v. Gressette* are complicated.   The State of South Carolina submitted a revised reapportionment plan to the Attorney General while litigation challenging an earlier version was still pending in a South Carolina district court.   Before the Attorney General took any action, the district court held the new plan constitutional.   Soon afterwards the Attorney General announced that he would not interpose any objection because he felt constrained to defer to the court's ruling.   Civil rights groups promptly filed suit in the District of Columbia, seeking review of the Attorney General's failure to exercise his authority to object to the plan; the district court there ordered him to make "a reasoned decision in accordance with his statutory responsibility," and the D.C. Circuit affirmed.   Two of the plaintiffs then filed suit in South Carolina to enjoin implementation of the reapportionment plan, only to be met by a ruling that the Attorney General's determination under section 5—in this case to defer to the South Carolina district court's determination of constitutionality—was not subject to judicial review under either the Voting Rights Act or the APA.

The Supreme Court agreed.   While it conceded that no statutory language barred review of the Attorney General's exercise of his authority under section 5, it found that the legislative history of the Voting Rights Act evidenced a Congressional intent to preclude such challenges.   The alternative route of approval for state election laws was intended to be expeditious.   The Court stressed that this result—according unreviewable discretion to the Attorney General—did not bar direct judicial challenges to such laws once adopted, though it conceded that the plaintiffs in such a case, and not the state, would bear the burden of proof on the issue of constitutionality.   The majority holding of unreviewability provoked a heated dissent from Justices Marshall and Brennan.

Constitutional Restraints on Statutory Preclusion of Review

The *Robison* Court suggests that an interpretation of 38 U.S.C.A. § 211(a) that would preclude judicial review of constitutional claims would itself raise a serious constitutional question.   The question posed goes to the essence of separation of powers, for in general terms the issue is the extent to which the Congress may render the federal courts impotent by controlling their jurisdiction.)   Yet, the latest case the *Robison* court cites as bearing on the matter was decided in 1936—a testament perhaps both to congressional restraint in exercising its authority to regulate the court's jurisdiction and to the Supreme Court's facility at avoiding the issue.   See generally Van Alstyne, *A Critical Guide to Ex Parte McCardle*, 15 Ariz. L. Rev. 229 (1973).

Professor Henry Hart, in the article cited at footnote 8 of the *Robison* opinion, took the position (which is supported by the broad language of the three cases also cited) that the jurisdiction of the federal courts, save the original jurisdiction of the Supreme Court conferred by the Constitution itself, is under Article III subject to the control of the Congress. Hart argued that the vindication of federal rights, including federal constitutional rights, could constitutionally be left to the state courts operating under the Supremacy Clause.   He acknowledged that Congress could not, by restricting court jurisdiction, accomplish what it cannot do by direct substantive prescription. It could not, for example, take property without due process by forbidding any court to hear a claim for compensation. But this caveat would not necessarily constrain Congress' power to remove jurisdiction from the federal courts to hear appeals from administrative bodies, for the Court has never held that there is a due process right to judicial review. See *Ortwein v. Schwab*, 410 U.S. 656 (1973).

The only judicial authority potentially adverse to the Hart view is a series of cases (one of which, *St. Joseph Stock Yards*, is cited in *Robison*) which apparently held that a court cannot be statutorily barred from investigating *de novo* certain "jurisdictional" or "constitutional" facts that determine the agency's power to act. In this respect *St. Joseph Stock Yards* confirmed the prior holding of *Ohio Valley Water Co. v. Ben Avon Borough*, 253 U.S. 287 (1920), that, when a regulatory commission's rate order was challenged as "confiscatory," the utility must have the opportunity for judicial review of the agency's underlying factual determinations. Failing to afford review of these "constitutional" facts, the Supreme Court held, would violate due process.

A parallel doctrine emerged in *Ng Fung Ho. v. White*, 259 U.S. 276 (1922). The petitioner challenged a deportation order of the Secretary of Labor on the ground that he was a citizen and not deportable. The Court held that the petitioner was entitled to a *de novo* judicial determination on the question of citizenship because his allegations went to the Secretary's "jurisdiction" to act. The Court reiterated this "jurisdictional fact" doctrine ten years later in *Crowell v. Benson*, 285 U.S. 22 (1932), holding that employers were entitled to *de novo* judicial review of "fundamental" or "jurisdictional" facts, e.g., the existence of a master-servant relationship and the occurrence of the injury on navigable waters, underlying an award pursuant to the Longshoremen's and Harbor Workers' Compensation Act.

These cases called forth an avalanche of critical commentary, which stressed the possibilities they created for transferring much of administrative fact-finding to the judicial arena. The doctrines they enunciated are now generally considered moribund, although never explicitly rejected by the Supreme Court. See W. GELLHORN, C. BYSE, & P. STRAUSS, ADMINISTRATIVE LAW 293–96 (7th ed. 1979). Professor Jaffe, however, argues that these cases establish at least the limited proposition that a judicial test of the propriety of an administrative order is constitutionally necessary where enforcement ultimately involves execution against person or property through judicial process. L. JAFFE, JUDICIAL CONTROL OF ADMINISTRATIVE ACTION 381–89 (1965). Professor Hart agreed with this analysis because he believed that Congress may not, having provided judicial jurisdiction, instruct the courts to ignore relevant issues of law. 66 Harv. L. Rev. at 1373–74. But he did not think that this negated the power of Congress to remove federal judicial jurisdiction entirely. Id. at 1396–1402. The Hart approach thus implies that the Congress may grant or withhold, but not redefine, the "judicial power" under Article III; or at least may redefine

it only within limits that continue to permit review of constitutional issues, though not necessarily issues of "constitutional fact."

Hart's theory of plenary Congressional power to define and control
the federal courts' jurisdiction is so riddled with exceptions that the exceptions swallow most of the rule.   Once it is admitted that judicial enforcement of administrative orders constitutionally implies judicial review to determine that property and personal liberty are not taken
without due process of law, virtually all regulatory administrative action
becomes reviewable—to some indeterminate degree—as a matter of constitutional necessity.   Moreover, Hart's fundamental thesis is questionable.
For it may be argued that without a federal judicial power sufficient to resolve basic constitutional conflicts, the Constitution's separation and limitation of governmental powers are empty promises.   We should surely
be cautious in concluding that the framers granted Congress an authority
over judicial jurisdiction that could warp the constitutional system.   See,
e.g., Eisenberg, *Congressional Authority to Restrict Lower Federal
Court Jurisdiction*, 83 Yale L.J. 498 (1974); Redish and Woods, *Congressional Power to Control the Jurisdiction of Lower Federal Courts: A
Critical Review and a New Synthesis*, 124 U. Pa. L. Rev. 45 (1975).

Exclusive Routes of Judicial Review

While bald preclusions of review are rare, Congress frequently purports to limit challenges to agency regulations in the context of enforcement proceedings by providing an alternative, time-limited, and sometimes exclusive mode of review elsewhere.   *Yakus v. United States*, 321
U.S. 414 (1944), reveals that such limits are in principle valid, but courts
may strain hard to avoid them where an agency's rule is unlikely to have
come to the defendant's attention during the time allotted for direct review.   *Adamo Wrecking Co. v. United States*, 434 U.S. 275 (1978), is illustrative.   The petitioner was prosecuted for violating the EPA's "National Emission Standard for Asbestos" while demolishing a building.
The EPA's "standard" prescribed procedures designed to limit the disper-
sal of asbestos fibers in old insulation, but it did not, for quite practical
reasons, purport to set a ceiling on fibers discharged by the pollution
sources (as conventional standards do).   Adamo persuaded the district
court to dismiss the charge on the ground that the so-called "standard"
was not authorized by the Clean Air Act of 1970.   On appeal, the court of
appeals held that section 307(b) of the Act, 42 U.S.C.A. § 1857h–5(b), precluded Adamo's claim.   That provision stated:

> (1) A petition for review of action of the Administrator in promulgating
> * * * any emission standard under section 112 * * * may be filed only in
> the United States Court of Appeals for the District of Columbia. * * * Any
> such petition shall be filed within 30 days from the date of such promulgation
> or approval, or after such date if such petition is based solely on grounds aris-
> ing after such 30th day.

(2) Action of the Administrator with respect to which review could have been obtained under paragraph (1) shall not be subject to judicial review in civil or criminal proceedings for enforcement.

No challenge had been made under this provision to the building demolition rule when it was promulgated.

The Supreme Court reversed the lower court, saying, in part (434 U.S. at 285):

We conclude * * * that a federal court in which a criminal prosecution under § 113(c)(1)(C) of the Clean Air Act is brought may determine whether or not the regulation which the defendant is alleged to have violated is an "emission standard" within the meaning of the Act.   We are aware of the possible dangers that flow from this interpretation; district courts will be importuned, under the guise of making a determination as to whether a regulation is an "emission standard," to engage in judicial review in a manner that is precluded by § 307(b)(2) of the Act.   This they may not do.   The narrow inquiry to be addressed by the court in a criminal prosecution is not whether the Administrator has complied with appropriate procedures in promulgating the regulation in question, or whether the particular regulation is arbitrary, capricious, or supported by the administrative record.   Nor is the court to pursue any of the other familiar inquiries which arise in the course of an administrative review proceeding. The question is only whether the regulation which the defendant is alleged to have violated is on its face an "emission standard" within the broad limits of the congressional meaning of that term.

In a concurring opinion, Justice Powell expressed doubts about the constitutionality of the limited review afforded by the Clean Air Act to persons facing criminal prosecution:

If the constitutional validity of § 307(b) of the Clean Air Act had been raised by petitioner, I think it would have merited serious consideration. * * *

Although I express no considered judgment, I think *Yakus* is at least arguably distinguishable.   The statute there came before the Court during World War II, and it can be viewed as a valid exercise of the war powers of Congress under Art. I, § 8, of the Constitution. * * *

The 30-day limitation on judicial review imposed by the Clean Air Act would afford precariously little time for many affected persons even if some adequate method of notice were afforded.   It also is totally unrealistic to assume that more than a fraction of the persons and entities affected by a regulation—especially small contractors scattered across the country—would have knowledge of its promulgation or familiarity with or access to the Federal Register.   Indeed, following *Yakus*, and apparently concerned by Mr. Justice Rutledge's eloquent dissent, Congress amended the most onerous features of the Emergency Price Control Act.

I join the Court's opinion with the understanding that it implies no view as to the constitutional validity of the preclusion provisions of § 307(b) in the context of a criminal prosecution.

Ironically, concern about potential unfairness to parties in subsequent enforcement proceedings may induce a narrow construction of preenforcement review provisions.   *Chrysler Corp. v. EPA*, 600 F.2d 904 (D.C. Cir. 1979), involved review under a provision authorizing exclusive court of appeals review of EPA "action * * * promulgating any standard or regulation under section 6, 17, or 18 of this Act."   Noise Control Act of 1972, 42 U.S.C.A. § § 4901 *et seq.*   The Court held that it lacked jurisdiction under the section to review regulations describing the procedures EPA would use in enforcing noise requirements for trucks, including record-keeping, inspection, and recall requirements.   The EPA and all but one of the petitioners had urged the court to accept jurisdiction in order to avoid bifurcation of suits challenging both substantive standards and enforcement procedures.   The court, however, adopted a reading of the statute that allowed subsequent challenge to the enforcement procedures because "of possible unfairness, particularly to small manufacturers who may lack resources to monitor the Administrator's actions to assure protection of the opportunity to contest regulations affecting their interests."   Id. at 912–13.   See generally McGarity, *Multi-Party Forum Shopping for Appellate Review of Administrative Action*, 129 U. Pa. L. Rev. 302 (1980); Verkuil, *Congressional Limitations on Judicial Review of Rules*, 57 Tul. L. Rev. 733 (1983).   An important recent decision, *Telecommunications Research and Action Center v. FCC*, 750 F.2d 70 (D.C. Cir. 1984), holds that suits challenging an agency's delay in acting must be brought exclusively in the courts of appeals that would have jurisdiction to review it's ultimate action unless Congress specifically directs otherwise.

2. DECISIONS "COMMITTED TO AGENCY DISCRETION" BY LAW

The distinction between the two exceptions to reviewability in APA § 701 is not sharp.   The same statutory language may in one case be described as "precluding review" and in another as "committing decisions to agency discretion."   This latter characterization, however, has broader implications than *statutory* preclusion, for it potentially embraces any legal basis upon which a court might decide that agency's action should be free from judicial review—such as a statute's language, agency function, tradition, or the limitations of the judicial role.

Hahn v. Gottlieb, 430 F.2d 1243 (1st Cir. 1970), and *Langevin v. Chenango Court, Inc.*, 447 F.2d 296 (2d Cir. 1971), illustrate the potential interchangeability of the APA § 701(a)'s twin exceptions to review.   In each case tenants residing in federally subsidized housing sought review of the FHA's approval of rent increases proposed by their landlords.   In *Hahn* Judge Coffin, after first rejecting the tenants' claim that they were entitled to a trial-type hearing on the rent increase, held that the FHA's ultimate decision was "committed to [its] discretion by law" (430 F.2d at 1249–51):

In the absence of a clear declaration of Congressional intent, three factors seem to us determinative: first, the appropriateness of the issues raised for review by the courts; second, the need for judicial supervision to safeguard the interests of the plaintiffs; and third, the impact of review on the effectiveness of the agency in carrying out its assigned role.

* * * [C]ourts are ill-equipped to superintend economic and managerial decisions of the kind involved here. * * * A partial list of the issues raised by plaintiffs either in the FHA hearing or in the court below includes: whether the landlord's increased operating costs were attributable to poor design and construction defects; whether and to what extent costs attributable to such defects should be absorbed by the landlord or passed on to the tenants; whether estimates of the vacancy rate, of commercial occupancy, and of managerial expenses were reasonable; and whether the FHA had properly determined the investment base for computing a reasonable return. Our only guides in answering such questions are the sometimes conflicting statutory goals of increased low-rent housing through private investment and the extremely broad regulatory criteria of maintaining "the economic soundness of the project" while insuring "a reasonable return on the investment consistent with providing reasonable rentals to tenants." Under these circumstances, we willingly confess our incapacity to contribute intelligently to the general course of decisions on rents and charges.

* * * [A]s we have already noted, plaintiffs' interests are not threatened by every rent increase, and other forms of relief, such as rent supplements, are available. We must, in addition, take into account the kind of program which Congress has erected to meet plaintiffs' needs. The National Housing Act does not provide categorical assistance to those in need of housing, nor does it erect detailed statutory safeguards to protect their interests. * * * Instead Congress has attempted to meet plaintiffs' needs indirectly, by stimulating private investors to supply low-rent housing. * * * Given this mechanism, we think plaintiffs' long-run interest may not be well served by a judicially-imposed system of review of all rent increases. Delay, the frictions engendered by the process of litigation, and the possibility—seldom discussed—of landlord appeals from FHA decisions in favor of tenants may lead to higher rentals and ultimately to less participation by private investors.

Turning finally to the impact of review on agency effectiveness, we think that resort to the courts might have a serious adverse impact on the performance of the FHA. Close judicial scrutiny inevitably leads to more formalized decision-making. * * * FHA consideration of rent increases can recur as often as leases expire over the life of a forty-year mortgage. To impose the formalities which attend review on all these essentially managerial decisions seems to us inconsistent with the constant Congressional urgings to simplify procedures and expedite work.

Equally important, such review would discourage the increased involvement of the private sector which is the goal of * * * 221(d)(3). * * *

* * * We therefore hold that the approval of rents and charges is a "matter committed to agency discretion by law", and thus not subject to judicial review. In so holding, we do not reach the question whether courts may intervene in those rare cases where the FHA has ignored a plain statutory duty, exceeded its jurisdiction, or committed constitutional error. The present case, which at best concerns a failure to give proper weight to all the relevant considerations, plainly falls within the area committed to agency discretion.

A year later, in *Langevin*, Judge Friendly confronted the same type of claim and he, too, found that the FHA's approval of rent increases was unreviewable—but he arrived at this result by a different path (447 F.2d at 302–04):

> * * * [U]nder 5 U.S.C.A. § 701(a), reviewability does not exist "to the extent"[11] that "statutes preclude judicial review," or "agency action is committed to agency discretion." * * * [T]he ambiguity in the second exception * * * has created extensive debate among scholars and troubled many courts, including this one. The difficulty is that if the exception were read in its literal breadth, it would swallow a much larger portion of the general rule of reviewability than Congress could have intended, particularly in light of 5 U.S.C.A. § 706(2)(A) which directs a reviewing court to set aside agency actions found to be "arbitrary, capricious, an abuse of discretion, or otherwise not in accordance with law"; yet to read the exception out completely would do violence to an equally plain Congressional purpose. * * * Professor Davis has arrived at the formulation "that administrative action is usually reviewable unless either (a) congressional intent is discernible to make it unreviewable, or (b) the subject matter is for some reason inappropriate for judicial consideration." Administrative Law Treatise, 1970 Supplement, § 28.16 at 965.
>
> * * * [T]he First Circuit [in *Hahn*] relied in part on Professor Davis' second "unless." * * * [W]e fail to see why a court is any worse equipped to pass on the reasonableness of a rent increase approval than it is to consider what was characterized as "an order that readjusts the class rates of the whole country barring only the territory west of the Rockies," an order granting or refusing an increase in liability insurance premiums, or, for that matter, orders made in the administration of local rent control programs. This is especially true when rent increases are limited by the regulatory agreement to those "necessary to compensate for any net increase, occurring since the last approved rent schedule, in taxes * * * and operating and maintenance expenses over which Owners have no effective control." Assessing the reasonableness of an increase which is to be governed by such a standard does not seem beyond judicial competence.
>
> Nevertheless, we reach the same conclusion of nonreviewability as the First Circuit, on the basis of Professor Davis' first "unless." * * * [I]t would be most unusual for Congress to subject to judicial review discretionary action by an agency in administering a contract which Congress authorized it to make. Other factors tending in the direction of nonreviewability are the managerial nature of the responsibilities confided to the FHA, the need for expedition to achieve the Congressional objective, which we have already discussed, and the quantity of appeals that would result if FHA authorizations to increase rents were held reviewable. * * * [W]hatever bounds the due process clause may set upon nonreviewability of agency action, no case goes to the extent of holding that due process mandates judicial review of an order approving—on the basis of an ex parte submission of facts—a rent increase to a landlord who has benefited from a federal aid program.

The significance of the difference in approach reflected in *Hahn* and *Langevin* is a matter of debate. One might assume that a decision

---

11. This is a revision of the former preamble to § 10, which used the words "so far as" rather than "to the extent that." If Congress intended any difference by the latter wording, it did not speak with sufficient clarity to get its message through to us.

couched in terms of legislative preclusion affords the courts less room for maneuver in the future—requiring either a confession of error or new legislation to allow review. But since both paragraphs (1) and (2) of section 701(a) purport to describe categories of cases in which *Congress* has decided that review should not be available, this intuition may be wrong. Yet the sources consulted in determining the applicability of 701(a)(2) often seem so maleable that one has the impression that judicial self-restraint is at work when review is withheld.

In any event, *Hahn* and *Langevin* are relatively unusual in withholding substantive review of the FHA's approval of rent increases—though both acknowledge that the issue might be different if the tenants had alleged an outright violation of the Housing Act or of the Constitution. Judicial refusals to review agency actions under 701(a) are rare enough that the government commonly does not invoke either theory of Congressional withdrawal of jurisdiction, or does so as an afterthought. (The more controversial cases have involved challenges to an agency's failure to take action, e.g., to adopt or enforce rules. We consider the issues implicated by cases of this kind later in this chapter.) But *Hahn* and *Langevin* are not unique, and a sampling of the jurisprudence of nonreviewability of affirmative action reveals some recurrent patterns.

Discretionary Grants and Government Contracts. In *Kletschka v. Driver*, 411 F.2d 436, 443 (2d Cir. 1969), the plaintiff, a Veterans Administration doctor, complained that he had been improperly deprived of a VA research grant and transferred to a less desirable location. The court refused to review either action, even for abuse of discretion:

> In this instance the final decision to withdraw plaintiff's research grant was made by heart research specialists employed at the V.A. facilities in Houston. We do not believe it would be practical for the district court to review such a decision, resting on complex and subtle evaluations of the technical merit of plaintiff's project and the professional competence of the plaintiff himself.
>
> The decision to transfer the plaintiff, while it did not involve any considerations of scientific expertise beyond the competence of a court, did purportedly rest on a judgment that the strained personal relationships between plaintiff and members of the hospital staff were interfering with the work at the hospital. * * * Obviously we cannot review the wisdom of good faith of this transfer without subjecting all such personnel decisions to a similar review. Such a course would encourage a vast quantity of litigation and deprive the V.A. administrator of an element of flexibility which is necessary if he is to operate his department efficiently. Where the challenged personnel decision falls short of discharge we believe that, in general, the courts should seek to discourage arbitrary agency action by enforcing the various procedural rights of affected employees, and not by undertaking a full substantive review of the justification for the decision.

The court went on to hold that, under 38 U.S.C.A. § 4110, Kletschka was entitled to a hearing before a disciplinary board prior to being transferred, and that "since this right to a hearing can be enforced without involving the courts in the wisdom of an agency decision concerning its personnel, in this respect disciplinary action taken by the V.A. is not 'committed to agency discretion by law' * * * " 411 F.2d at 445.

Compare *Gonzalez v. Freman*, 334 F.2d 570 (D.C. Cir. 1964). Gonzalez had been debarred from doing business with the Commodity Credit Corporation, the instrumentality through which the United States purchases and resells surplus agricultural commodities. He claimed that the Secretary of Agriculture could not debar him without first promulgating regulations governing debarment and providing him with notice of the charges against him and a hearing on those charges. The Secretary argued that the following language in 7 U.S.C.A. § 1429 made his decisions unreviewable:

> Determinations made by the Secretary under this Act shall be final and conclusive: *Provided*, That the scope and nature of such determinations shall not be inconsistent with the provisions of the Commodity Credit Corporation Charter Act.

In holding the Secretary's action subject to judicial review, Judge, now Chief Justice, Burger said (334 F.2d at 575):

> Action challenged as a denial of due process—whether substantive in the sense of being arbitrary or by capricious classification, or procedural in the sense of denying minimum safeguards—could be immune from judicial review, if ever, only by the plainest manifestation of congressional intent to that effect. We find no such intent reflected in the statute. * * *
>
> * * * The language, relied upon by appellees, relating to "final and conclusive" determinations of the Secretary has as its primary thrust the removal from judicial scrutiny of the operational policy decisions and programs of the agency, not standards of procedure for debarment. Appellants here do not challenge broad policy decisions * * * but narrowly attack as beyond agency authority a debarment or "blacklisting" which the complaint alleges inflicted a special injury on appellants and was accomplished in a procedurally unfair and unauthorized manner. Nothing in the statute confers unreviewable finality on determinations of the Secretary as to questions of the scope of his congressional authority or of the requisite procedural safeguards.

Compare *Hi-Ridge Lumber Co. v. United States*, 443 F.2d 452 (9th Cir. 1971), with *Scanwell Laboratories v. Shaffer*, 424 F.2d 859, 874–75 (D.C. Cir. 1970). Concerning the remedies of disappointed government contractors, see generally Speidel, *Judicial and Administrative Review of Government Contract Awards*, 37 Law & Contemp. Probs. 63 (1972).

See also *East Oakland-Fruitvale Planning Council v. Rumsfeld*, 471 F.2d 524 (9th Cir. 1972). The plaintiffs, who operated a federally-funded community action program in Oakland, challenged the refusal of the Director of the Office of Economic Opportunity to reconsider and reverse then-Governor Reagan's veto of funding for a second year. The relevant section of the Economic Opportunity Act, 42 U.S.C.A. § 2834, since repealed, specified only that no program shall be funded unless a plan "has been submitted to the Governor of the State, and such plan has not been disapproved by the Governor * * * or, if so disapproved, has been reconsidered by the Director and found by him to be fully consistent with the provisions and in furtherance of the purposes of [the Act]. * * * "

The Ninth Circuit reversed the district court's dismissal of the suit. It found, first, that the Director had no discretion with respect to whether to reconsider the Governor's disapproval; such power would undercut Congress' purpose, when it amended the 1964 Act, of denying state governors the final authority over whether programs should be funded.   The court did, however, acknowledge that the Director's ultimate decision on funding was in general beyond review (471 F.2d at 533–35):

> [T]he standard to be applied by the Director in determining whether to override a governor's veto requires an evaluation of the "wisdom or desirability" of the particular project as a means to further the purposes of the Act, in light of knowledge, information, and insights contributed by the governor.   This standard is extremely general; its application requires the exercise of the Director's expert knowledge regarding the practicality and efficacy of experimental projects.   Its generality and breadth are such that it would not afford a reviewing court a practicable rule for determining the legality of the Director's ultimate decision to override or not to override.   * * *
>
> * * * However, the statute imposes a number of limitations upon the scope of the Director's discretion and the manner in which it is to be exercised that may be effectively enforced through judicial review without undue interference with the administative process.
>
> * * * [T]he courts may hold the Director to his statutory obligation to reconsider a vetoed program even though the merits of the Director's decision upon reconsideration are unreviewable.   Similarly, the Council's claim of entitlement to a specification of issues, a hearing, and formal findings in conjunction with the Director's reconsideration raises procedural issues that are clear, specific, and separable from the merits and that are therefore judicially determinable.
>
> Finally,   * * *   [t]he legislative history of section 242 indicates that Congress intended to confine the Director's review of a vetoed program to a consideration of the merits of the specific program as a means of advancing the purposes and policies of the Act, and to exclude other considerations.   * * *
>
> The Council has failed, however, to plead an infringement of this specific limitation upon the Director's discretion.

The court's opinion then rejects the grounds urged by the plaintiffs for upsetting the Director's decisions: He was not precluded, as the plaintiffs contended, from taking into account a governor's objections to the "philosophy" of underlying projects.   Nor did the Act require him to hold a hearing or afford other procedural safeguards before making his decision.

Public Lands and NEPA.   Decisions governing the sale, lease, or use of public lands involve governmental functions in many ways similar to discretionary grant and procurement functions.   Emphasizing the "permissive" or "discretionary" language of the statutes, e.g., *Ferry v. Udall,* 336 F.2d 706 (9th Cir. 1964), *cert. denied* 381 U.S. 904 (1965); *United States v. Walker,* 409 F.2d 477 (9th Cir. 1969), the courts historically denied review of decisions concerning the disposition of public lands.   However, nonreviewability has eroded under the dual onslaught of NEPA claims and the *East-Oakland Fruitvale* "divisibility" technique, see e.g., *National Forest Preservation Group v. Butz,* 485 F.2d 408 (9th Cir. 1973). Indeed, as *Hanly v. Kleindienst,* 471 F.2d 823 (2d Cir. 1972), *cert. denied* 412 U.S. 908 (1973), suggests, NEPA makes reviewable, at least on environmental grounds, many "managerial" decisions that might otherwise have been considered unreviewable. This "opening-up" of the proprietary functions of government to judicial scrutiny may ultimately be NEPA's major contribution.

Defense and Foreign Affairs. In *Curran v. Laird,* 420 F.2d 122, 131–33 (D.C. Cir. 1969) *(en banc),* the National Maritime Union sought to enforce the requirement of 10 U.S.C.A. § 2631 that supplies for the military forces be shipped *only* in United States vessels. The government admitted using foreign vessels, but only when U.S. ships were not available. Plaintiff conceded that unavailability might justify failure to follow the letter of the statute, but contended that U.S. ships were "unavailable" only because the Secretary had failed to activate portions of the reserve fleet. Judge Leventhal balked at reviewing in any fashion the Secretary's decision:

> The range of executive judgments involved are likely to involve estimates as to when, where, and how much cargo will have to be moved in the future— not only military but also foreign aid cargoes. The decisions also require a judgment of the feasibility of providing sustained employment for a reactivated vessel.
>
> This court cannot sit in judgment to review a determination which involves appraisals like those outlined. The manifest difficulties cannot be obviated by construing the statute as requiring only that the authorities "consider" the feasibility of employing the reserve fleet ships for transporting military cargoes. There is no satisfactory exit once the judiciary crosses the threshold and enters the domain of these matters. * * *
>
> Even restricted review requires probing the surface and going beyond mere conclusory affidavits setting forth the department's reasons. Any other approach belies the notion that these matters before us are not in fact necessarily committed to agency discretion. Settled doctrine does not permit us to accept at face value administrative determinations without at least surveying a record.
>
> We do not deal with officials who are operating under discernible statutory standards, or a mandate to develop standards to assure even-handed justice. They are rather likely to be called on to make and revise judgments freely, perhaps to draw heavily on information from sources abroad or in the domain of the military in making global guesstimates. Not all operations of government are subject to judicial review, even though they may have a profound effect on our lives.

Judges Wright, Bazelon, and Robinson would have reviewed to determine that the Secretary had at least considered activating the reserve fleet and had "reason for passing over it." 420 F.2d at 142.

In *Chicago, & Southern Air Lines v. Waterman Steamship Corp.,* 333 U.S. 103, 111 (1948), Waterman challenged the CAB's award of air routes between the United States and various points in the Caribbean to C. & S. Under the Civil Aeronautics Act, 49 U.S.C.A. § 646, any award of routes to a foreign carrier or any award of overseas routes to a domestic carrier must be approved by the President. Section 1006 of the Act authorizes judicial review of "any order * * * issued by the Board under this Act, except any order in respect of any foreign air carrier subject to the approval of the President * * * ." Waterman contended that, by negative implication, the Act thus contemplated review of awards of overseas routes to domestic carriers. The Supreme Court disagreed, in an opinion emphasizing the President's unusual, authoritative role under the Act:

> [T]he very nature of executive decisions as to foreign policy is political, not judicial. Such decisions are wholly confided by our Constitution to the political departments of the government, Executive and Legislative. They are delicate, complex, and involve large elements of prophecy. They are and should be undertaken only by those directly responsible to the people whose welfare they advance or imperil. They are decisions of a kind for which the Judiciary has neither aptitude, facilities nor responsibility and which has long been held to belong in the domain of political power not subject to judicial intrusion or inquiry.

Nor could review be had of the CAB's recommended order prior to its submission to the President, because in the Court's view that order was not final.

However, in *American Airlines, Inc. v. Civil Aeronautics Board*, 348 F.2d 349 (D.C. Cir. 1965), the Court of Appeals held that *Waterman* did not prevent review of a CAB order authorizing "split charter" fares on overseas flights where the claim was that the CAB was not empowered to approve such a fare structure. The court reasoned that if the initial order was unauthorized there was nothing before the President for him to act on.

Presidential Powers and Political Questions. Cases involving the exercise of presidential powers are sometimes analyzed in terms of the "political question" doctrine rather than the functionally equivalent "non-reviewability" doctrine. See, e.g., *DaCosta v. Laird*, 471 F.2d 1146 (2d Cir. 1973). The controversy over presidential impounding of appropriated or "contract authority" funds in 1972 and 1973, for example, resulted in a rash of lawsuits seeking to have the withholding of particular program funds declared unlawful. In many of these judicial proceedings the government argued that the question of impoundment was a "political question" and therefore non-justiciable. The argument seldom prevailed. See generally Note, *Impoundment of Funds*, 86 Harv. L. Rev. 1505 (1973). See also *Train v. New York*, 420 U.S. 35 (1975).

Certification of Bargaining Units. Agency decisions defining the bargaining status of labor organizations have frequently been held unreviewable. The classic case is *Switchmen's Union v. National Mediation Board*, 320 U.S. 297 (1943), where Justice Douglas held unreviewable the Board's decision to include yardmen in a unit with all other operating railroad employees rather than to permit them to vote for separate representation. Although the Railway Labor Act neither explicitly authorized nor precluded review of such decisions, the Court concluded that Congress intended its certification decisions to be final. In *Brotherhood of Railway and Steamship Clerks v. Association for Benefit of Non-Contract Employees*, 380 U.S. 650 (1965), the Court again held that the

Board's determination of the proper election unit, following an investigation that was procedurally proper, was beyond review. The holding of non-reviewbility in these cases recognizes the necessities of the collective bargaining context. If employers or competing unions could get review of every certification of a bargaining unit prior to contract negotiations, labor-management relations would produce much litigation and little bargaining. Judicial acknowledgement of non-reviewability here reflects a fear that attempts to assure "legality" through judicial review will effectively frustrate congressional policy.

3. REVIEW OF AGENCY INACTION

The traditional law of judicial review of administative action is largely the product of a concern to protect private interests from unlawful *exercises* of governmental authority. In recent years, however, with the rapid development of consumer, environmental, and other "public interest" organizations, more attention has been given to official inaction, that is, to the failure of administrative agencies to enforce existing standards or to develop standards adequate to protect the public interest. With increasing frequency judicial review is sought not to restrain, but to stimulate, administrative activity. See, e.g., *Allen v. Wright*, supra p. 682. See generally Note, *Judicial Review of Agency Inaction*, 83 Colum. L. Rev. 627 (1983).

That such efforts should confront a preliminary objection of non-reviewability is not surprising. The decision to initiate agency enforcement proceedings is closely analogous to the decision to prosecute criminal offenders, and such prosecutorial judgments have traditionally been considered beyond review. E.g., *Smith v. United States*, 411 U.S. 908 (1973). And one searches in vain for any legally enforceable restraints on Congressional decisions to delay, defer, or wholly ignore demands for the enactment of new legislation. One clear analogy to administrative selection of candidates for rulemaking suggests the difficulty of framing a legal challenge to an agency's failure to adopt new rules. The questions raised by the materials in this section thus implicate two central issues: First, should agency enforcement decisions be insulated from judicial review to the same extent as the prosecutorial judgments of general law enforcement officers? Second, does the federal judiciary have any role in overseeing agency priorities for rulemaking?

Enforcement Discretion

DUNN v. RETAIL CLERKS INTERNATIONAL ASSOCIATION

United States Court of Appeals, Sixth Circuit, 1962.
307 F.2d 285.

CECIL, CIRCUIT JUDGE. * * *

The plaintiffs seek damages in the amount of $500,000, an order requiring Regional Director Reynolds to extend equal protection of the laws to them as guaranteed by the Fifth Amendment to the Constitution, and the Labor Management Relations Act, and for injunctive relief against the union and its members, or in the alternative an order requiring the Regional Director to perform the duties of his office. * * *

The plaintiffs * * * operate a grocery business, in the city of Memphis, Tennessee. Retail Clerks International Association, AFL-CIO, Local 1529, hereinafter called Local or Union, is an unincorporated association, chartered, franchised and licensed by Retail Clerks International Association, as its agent and representative, to organize employees of grocery store in Memphis and Shelby County, Tennessee.

Through a petition of the Local and by order of Director Reynolds, an election was held on October 4, 1961, by the employees of the plaintiffs, to determine whether they wanted the Local to represent them as bargaining agent with their employers. Only nineteen valid votes out of a total of ninety cast favored the Union.

On the afternoon and night of the election, both before and during the election, the individual defendant Union members, together with other Union representatives "swarmed" onto the floors of the plaintiffs' stores, mingled and electioneered with the employees, and interfered with them in the performance of their duties. In some stores, they congregated about the door of the voting area and mingled with the employees, as they waited in line to vote. They refused to leave either at the request of the plaintiffs' attorney, or the agent of the N.L.R.B. conducting the election. * * *

The plaintiffs called a commercial photographer to take pictures of the Union representatives, as they roamed about the store mingling with the employees at the time of the election. Two days after the election the Union filed with Reynolds "objections to the conduct affecting the results of the election." It was charged that the employees, at the 1977 South Third Street store, had been intimidated by the presence of the commercial photographer.

On the night of November 6th, at about 9 p.m., the defendant Billy Gibson, an employee of the Board, working under Reynolds, and Amon Hatch, an employee of the Union, approached three schoolboys, part time employees of the 1977 South Third Street store, and asked them to sign affidavits prepared by Gibson. It is alleged that they were threatened with being subpoenaed to some sort of government hearing and otherwise frightened and intimidated, if they refused to sign. They signed and immediately reported to their employer. These affidavits were to the effect that they had been intimidated and that other employees were deterred from voting. There were twenty-four employees in this store all of whom voted. Twenty-one of these voluntarily signed a petition to the Board certifying that they had not been intimidated by the photographers and that they voted their own personal convictions. The three boys above mentioned notified the Director that the affidavits had been procured by threats and were incorrect.

On November 16th, Reynolds issued an order vacating and setting aside the election on the ground that the employees had been intimidated. It is alleged that he knew this to be false and untrue. * * *

It is alleged in the complaint that the unfair labor practices described therein are illegal and unlawful under the laws of the state of Tennessee and the United States, but that they are precluded from seeking injunctive relief by the provisions of the Labor Management Relations Act of 1947, as amended. It is claimed that the Regional Director has power and authority to prevent the wrongs of which complaint is made but that he refuses to act.

We agree with the opinion of the District Judge that this complaint states no cause of action for damages under the civil rights act. (Section 1985(3)). The other phase of the case is essentially an action to require the Regional Director to do his duty. * * *

The National Labor Relations Act provides that the General Counsel of the Board shall exercise general supervision over the officers and employees in the regional offices and "shall have final authority, on behalf of the Board, in respect of the investigation of charges and issuance of complaints under section 160 of this title, and in respect of the prosecution of such complaints before the Board, * * * ." By regulation, the General Counsel has delegated authority to Regional Directors to issue such complaints. A refusal of the Regional Director to issue a complaint may be appealed to the General Counsel. The General Counsel has a wide discretion in determining whether a complaint should issue and the Act provides no appeal from his decision. His position is much the same as that of a United States Attorney in determining whether a criminal charge should be issued. There is no allegation in the complaint that an appeal was made to the General Counsel.

Congress has provided an administrative tribunal, the National Labor Relations Board, to administer the Labor Acts and final orders from it may be reviewed by the United States Courts of Appeal. Otherwise the power of the Board in disputes between labor and management over alleged unfair labor practices is exclusive. * * *

If, aside from their acceptance as the truth for the purposes of the motion to dismiss, the facts alleged in the complaint correctly represent what actually happened, they disclose what the District Judge characterized as "a pretty horrible situation." In such case, we assume that the General Counsel of the N.L.R.B. will take cognizance of the situation and employ his broad powers to make corrections, if they are needed. Congress has invested the N.L.R.B. and its agents with powers which, if withheld or abused, can visit serious and irreparable harm upon those who, under the scheme of the N.L.R.A., cannot obtain the help of judicial intervention. Foreclosed as we are from entrance by judicial writ into such a situation, we must leave an injured party to the assistance of those empowered to apply administrative remedies or executive correction. * * *

Notes

1. The federal courts have consistently followed the *Dunn* approach, although disappointed complainants have relentlessly pursued judicial review of the NLRB General Counsel's exercise of discretion not to initiate unfair labor

practice proceedings. The courts' use of language in many of those cases suggesting that they lacked "jurisdiction" (see the opinion in *Dunn* itself) perhaps has engendered false hopes that review of the General Counsel's actions would be available if only the plaintiff could discover some technical basis for the exercise of judicial power. *Dunn* combined a civil rights action under 42 U.S.C.A. § 1985(3) with a suit in the nature of mandamus. Other cases have run the gamut from suits under the APA and Declaratory Judgment Act, *Balanyi v. Local 1031*, 374 F.2d 723 (7th Cir. 1967), to the inexplicable invocation of the writ of error *coram nobis*. *National Labor Relations Board v. Tennessee Products & Chemical Corp.*, 329 F.2d 873 (6th Cir. 1964). Nor have the courts been bemused by claims seeking to distinguish the General Counsel's refusal to "investigate" from his refusal to prosecute, *Mayer v. Ordman*, 391 F.2d 889 (6th Cir.), *cert. denied* 393 U.S. 925 (1968), or attempting to police his investigation procedures by asserting that they deny due process to the complaining party. *Saez v. Goslee*, 343 F.Supp. 845 (D. Puerto Rico 1971), *affirmed* 463 F.2d 214 (1st Cir.), *cert. denied* 409 U.S. 1024 (1972).

2. The single inroad that has been made on the NLRB General Counsel's discretion to prosecute unfair labor practices has been *Southern California District Council v. Ordman*, 318 F.Supp. 633 (C.D. Cal. 1970). In that case the General Counsel had refused to consider a complaint on the ground that it had been filed more than six months after the alleged unfair labor practice; 29 U.S.C.A. § 160(b) requires that the complaints be filed within six months. The court held that his refusal to consider the complaint on this ground was reviewable to determine whether he had misconstructed the statute. The court found that the General Counsel had indeed mistaken the time at which the alleged unfair labor practice should be held to have occurred and ordered him to consider the complaint as timely filed. See also *Jacobsen v. NLRB*, 120 F.2d 96 (3d Cir. 1941).

3. In making known his reasons for dismissing the complaint in *Southern California District* the NLRB General Counsel acted in accordance with the Board's Rules, Regulations and Statement of Procedures, which in 1968 provided:

> *Sec. 102.19 Appeal to the general counsel from refusal to issue or reissue.*
>
> (a) If, after the charge has been filed, the regional director declines to issue a complaint, or having withdrawn a complaint pursuant to § 102.18, refuses to reissue it, he shall so advise the parties in writing, accompanied by a simple statement of the procedural or other grounds for his action. The person making the charge may obtain a review of such action by filing an appeal with the general counsel in Washington, D.C., and filing a copy of the appeal with the regional director, within 10 days from the service of the notice of such refusal to issue or reissue by the regional director * * * . Consideration of an appeal untimely filed is within the discretion of the general counsel upon goods cause shown. * * *
>
> (c) The general counsel may sustain the regional director's refusal to issue or reissue a complaint, stating the grounds of his affirmance, or may direct the regional director to take further action; the general counsel's decision shall be served on all the parties. * * *

Although *Dunn* may seem very hard law, the exception to review recognized in *Southern California District Council* is not obviously a move in the right direction. There is no requirement that the Board maintain the desirable system of appeals and written reasons prescribed in its regulations. If the courts are willing to review only when reasons are given and if review of decisions not to initiate enforcement is burdensome (which it certainly might be for an agency like the NRLB which rejects thousands of petitions each year), the course the Board should follow seems clear.

4. In a pair of cases the D.C. Circuit seemed to send the same message to the Securities and Exchange Commission concerning its "no-action" letters (letters which indicate to a complaining party that the Commission will take no enforcement action on the complaint). Compare *Medical Committee for Human Rights v. SEC*, 432 F.2d 659 (D.C. Cir. 1970), *cert. granted* 401 U.S. 973 (1971), *vacated as moot* 404 U.S. 403 (1972), with *Kixmiller v. SEC*, 492 F.2d 641 (D.C. Cir. 1974). In the latter opinion the court explained the distinction between the two cases (492 F.2d at 644–45):

> Petitioner relies heavily on *Medical Committee for Human Rights v. Securities and Exchange Commission*, wherein we reviewed on the merits the Commission's approval of a no-action ruling by its staff. We think, however, that very different jurisdictional consequences flow from the antithetical roles which the Commission played in *Medical Committee* and here. There, after the staff announced that it would not recommend action respecting a company's omission of a stockholder's proposal from its proxy materials, the Commission examined the staff's no-action determination and accepted it. As our opinion in *Medical Committee* recounted, the Commission, "after reviewing the petitioner's proxy claim," "exercised its discretion to review [the] controversy," and "approved the recommendation of the [staff] that no objection be raised. * * * In sum, *Medical Committee* involved a no-action ruling by the staff which was sanctioned by the Commission, and that, we held, constituted administrative action subject to judicial review.

> In sharp contrast to that decision is the Commission's refusal here to in any way probe or pass on the staff's no-action position. The distinction is between the Commission's reexamination and affirmance of the staff's conclusion on the one hand, and the Commission's declension of any review or adjudication on the other. We recognized the vitality of that distinction when in *Medical Committee* we admonished that the availability of judicial review of a staff no-action decision respecting proxy proposals "depends upon the Commission's initial determination to review the staff decision." That precondition is not met here.

The court then went on to hold that the full Commission's refusal to review the staff determination in *Kixmiller* was unreviewable:

> The Securities Exchange Act of 1934 provides that "the Commission may, in its discretion, make such investigations as it deems necessary," and that "it may in its discretion bring an action" in court. An agency's decision to refrain from an investigation or an enforcement action is generally unreviewable and, as to the agency before us, the specifications of the Act leave no doubt on that score.

5. An agency's failure to respond to complaints about activities that appear to violate its law is probably the product of a complex set of reasons, usually innocent if not always convincing. These often include conscious allocation of resources to other problems that the agency considers (or has been advised to consider) more serious. No agency has resources adequate to enforce its relevant statutes completely or comprehensively, nor we would wish it to. The Internal

Revenue Service, for example, cannot conceivably audit all income tax returns and, predictably, it has adopted criteria for selecting the relatively few returns that will be carefully reviewed, e.g., those revealing substantial charitable deductions or investments in tax shelters.

Such choices do not always reflect simply a desire to maximize the "impact" of limited enforcement resources. Or perhaps it is more accurate to say that administrative agencies often employ quite catholic measures of "impact." An illustration is the FDA, whose top managers for more than a decade have self-consciously engaged in reevaluating the agency's priorities each year. The effort is to allocate total agency resources, measured both in manpower (e.g., inspector time, laboratory analyst time) and dollars among a huge array of activities that range across several different product lines. The main criterion used is cost-effective health promotion but the agency also considers what has been termed "public interest," which really is a proxy for "press volatility" or "potential public embarrassment." If health protection were the sole criterion, the FDA would allocate its resources differently then it does. Prevention of food borne disease through regular inspection of production and storage establishments and seizure of contaminated lots, in its view, contributes significantly to prolongation of life and prevention of morbidity. Review of food additives, by contrast, has been considered less important as a public health safeguard. But the FDA devotes substantial resources to the latter activity, partly because it realizes—or believes—that consumer groups are anxious about food additive safety and have significant influence with Congress and the press. For one account of the FDA's priority-setting process, see DISCUSSION OF FDA PRIORITIES: FISCAL YEAR 1986 PLANNING PROCESS (March 1984).

The FDA's experience in regulating food sanitation provides a vivid illustration of resource constraints on agency enforcement activities. In the early 1970's, considerable attention was being given in Congress to the adequacy of the FDA's oversight of food production and distribution practices. At Hearings before the Subcommittee on Public Health and Environment of the House Committee on Interstate and Foreign Commerce, 92d Cong., 1st Sess. (1971), the following colloquy occurred:

[FDA Commissioner Dr. Charles] Edwards. * * * Every time an emergency situation or a natural disaster occurs, it is necessary for us to suspend food inspections, suspend planned food analyses and our normal program operations. For example, in the Bon Vivant case, the 125 man-years consumed by this emergency effort to date could have been used to inspect 2,300 food plants. This means that in this fiscal year, FDA will probably not inspect 2,300 plants which might otherwise have been investigated and their products sampled and analyzed. * * *

Congressman Roy. How many food plants are presently subject to your inspection?

Dr. Edwards. We figure there are approximately 60,000 food establishments which come under our jurisdiction. * * *

Mr. Roy. And you presently have 250 inspectors in the field. * * *

Congressman Rogers. Doctor, what is your need for manpower to do an effective job in inspecting the 60,000 food plants coming within your jurisdiction: 1,500 inspectors, is that a sufficient figure?

Dr. Edwards. I think in that order of magnitude; yes. * * *

Mr. Rogers.   That would amount to how much money?

Dr. Edwards. $75 to $85 million.

Mr. Rogers.   About the amount of your total budget now?

Dr. Edwards.   It is getting fairly close; yes.   *   *   *

6. The realization that an agency cannot proceed against all claimed violations obviously invites demands to know what criteria it uses in selecting those it will pursue.   Our concern here is not with the content of such criteria, which differ widely from agency to agency, but with public access to such information. Agencies have been variously successful in resisting disclosure of their internal enforcement criteria under the FOIA.   See generally K. DAVIS, ADMINISTRATIVE LAW TEXT, § 3A.12, at 77–78 (1972).   A desire to retain the *in terrorem* effects of the written law helps explain the unwillingness of most law enforcement officers to reveal their working guides for prosecution.   But every agency has such guides, and some agencies may even find it useful to make them known.

Again the FDA provides an example.   For decades it has maintained so-called "action levels" for filth and other natural contaminants of food—levels that mark the point of regulatory concern and that, if detected, will lead to seizure. In 1972, in response to food distributors, who claimed the knowledge would contribute to voluntary compliance, and to mounting demands for open government, the FDA formally announced that all of its action levels would be disclosed upon request.   37 Fed. Reg. 6497 (Mar. 30, 1972).   The reaction was disconcerting. Citizens wrote the agency and their congressmen, expressing dismay that foods such as bay leaves could have up to or "5% insect infested pieces" or up to "1 milligram rodent excreta per pound" and still be sold!   An FDA official's defensive retort that if food were required to be pure—as the statute theoretically demands—"there would be no food sold in the United States" was hardly reassuring.   See *The Washington Post*, March 29, 1972, § B, at 2.

BACHOWSKI v. BRENNAN

United States Court of Appeals, Third Circuit, 1974.
502 F.2d 79.

Van Dusen, Circuit Judge.

This case is an appeal from the district court's dismissal * * * of a suit to compel the Secretary of Labor (the "Secretary") to bring an action to upset a union election under § 402(b) of the Labor-Management Reporting and Disclosure Act of 1959 ("L-MRDA"), 29 U.S.C.A. § 482(b).[1]   The issue presented is whether the Secretary's decision not to bring such an action is subject to judicial review.

Plaintiff Walter Bachowski was a candidate for the office of District Director of District 20 of the United Steelworkers of America (the "USWA") in an election held on February 13, 1973.   He was defeated in that election by 907 votes out of approximately 24,000 votes cast.   After

---

1. "(b) The Secretary shall investigate such complaint and, if he finds probable cause to believe that a violation of this subchapter has occurred and has not been remedied, he shall, within sixty days after the filing of such complaint, bring a civil action against the labor organization as an entity in the district court of the United States in which such labor organization maintains its principal office to set aside the invalid election.   *   *   *   "

exhausting his administrative remedies within the union, Bachowski filed a complaint with the Department of Labor on June 21, 1973, alleging numerous election irregularities and violations of the union constitution and § 401 of the L-MRDA, 29 U.S.C.A. § 481. Following an investigation of this complaint, the Secretary notified Bachowski and the union that he had decided not to bring an action to set aside the contested election. Bachowski thereupon brought the present lawsuit, naming as defendants the Secretary and the union. The complaint alleges, *inter alia*, that the Secretary's investigation had substantiated the enumerated charges of election irregularities and that these irregularities affected the outcome of the election, but that the Secretary nevertheless refused to file a suit to set aside the election and failed even to inform Bachowski of his reasons for that refusal. The complaint concludes that these actions by the Secretary were arbitrary and capricious and requests that the district court direct the Secretary (1) to make available to the plaintiff all evidence he has obtained concerning his investigation of the contested election, (2) to reach an agreement with the union extending the period of time for filing suit to set aside that election, and (3) to file such suit. * * *

Plaintiff seems to be entitled to judicial review under the APA, 5 U.S.C.A. § 702, unless the Secretary's decision not to bring suit to set aside the election is excluded from the coverage of the APA by § 701(a) * * * The burden of establishing such exclusion, however, is on the defendants. * * *

Defendants contend that Congress' intent to preclude judicial review and to commit to the Secretary's absolute discretion the decision whether to bring suit can be inferred from two features of the L-MRDA: (1) the Secretary has exclusive authority to sue to set aside a union election, and (2) he must exercise that authority within 60 days of the filing of a complaint. After careful consideration of defendants' arguments and the cases cited in supported thereof, we do not find that there exists the necessary "clear and convincing evidence" of a legislative intent to restrict judicial review. * * *

The Secretary contends that his decision whether to bring suit under § 402 of the L-MRDA is an exercise of prosecutorial discretion which is unreviewable and cannot be compelled by a court. Not every refusal by a Government official to take action to enforce a statute, however, is unreviewable. Although the Secretary's decision to bring suit bears some similarity to the decision to commence a criminal prosecution, the principle of absolute prosecutorial discretion is not applicable to the facts of this case.

To begin with, we believe that the doctrine of prosecutorial discretion should be limited to those civil cases which, like criminal prosecutions, involve the vindication of societal or governmental interests, rather than the protection of individual rights. * * * However, the legislative history of the L-MRDA demonstrates a deep concern with the interest of individual union members, as well as the general public, in the integrity of union elections. Thus, in seeking to remedy violations of the Act, the Secretary acts not only for the benefit of the country as a whole, but also on behalf of those individuals whose rights have been infringed.[11] To grant the Secretary absolute discretion in this situation seems particularly inappropriate, for if he wrongfully refuses to file suit, individual union members are left without a remedy.

Furthermore, as Professor Davis has observed, perhaps the most convincing reason for the unreviewability of prosecutorial discretion is that a prosecutor "may be actuated by many considerations that are beyond the judicial capacity to supervise." The factors to be considered by the Secretary, however, are more limited and clearly defined: § 482(b) of the L-MRDA provides that after investigating a complaint, he must determine whether there is probable cause to believe that violations of § 481 have occurred affecting the outcome of the election. Where a complaint is meritorious and no settlement has been reached which would remedy the violations found to exist, the language and purpose of § 402(b) indicate that Congress intended the Secretary to file suit. Thus, apart from the possibility of settlement, the Secretary's decision whether to bring suit depends on a rather straightforward factual determination, and we see nothing in the nature of that task that places the Secretary's decision "beyond the judicial capacity to supervise."

Nevertheless, the question remains as to what the proper scope of such judicial review should be. In *DeVito v. Shultz* [300 F.Supp. 381 (D.D.C. 1969)], the court held that "the Secretary must provide those who petitioned for his intervention with an adequate written statement of his reasons for nonintervention." Since the letter explaining the Secretary's decision not to bring suit conceded that serious irregularities had occurred but failed to mention the Secretary's conclusions as to the effect of those irregularities on the outcome of the election, the court in *DeVito* ordered the Secretary to reconsider his decision, and if after reconsideration he was still determined not to act, the court held that the individual complaint is entitled to a fuller statement of reasons. * * * In addition, "a brief statement of the grounds for denial" is required by the APA, 5 U.S.C.A. § 555(e), and as Professor Davis has pointed out, the practical reasons for requiring findings are as applicable to informal agency action as to action based on formal hearings. Davis, *Administrative Law Treatise* § 16.00 at 559 (1970 Supp.).[14] Thus, judicial review of the Secretary's decision not to bring suit should extend at the very least to an inquiry into his reasons for that decision to ensure that he has not abused the discretion granted him by the L-MRDA.

The relief requested by the complaint in the instant case, however, goes beyond such an inquiry. Anticipating the Secretary's reasons,

11. This case is, therefore, distinguishable from *Vaca v. Sipes*, 386 U.S. 171 (1967), where the Court held that the General Counsel of the National Labor Relations Board has unreviewable discretion to refuse to institute an unfair labor practice complaint because, under § 10(c) of the National Labor Relations Act, "[t]he public interest in effectuating the policies of the federal labor laws, not the wrong done the individual employee, is always the Board's principal concern in fashioning unfair labor practice remedies."

14. Two of these reasons are clearly applicable to the instant case: facilitating judicial review and assuring careful administrative consideration. The latter would be relevant even if the Secretary's decision were unreviewable. * * *

plaintiff seeks an opportunity to challenge the factual basis for his conclusion either that no violations occurred or that they did not affect the outcome of the election. * * * The Secretary may as easily defeat the purpose of the L-MRDA by ignoring overwhelming evidence of violations affecting the outcome of an election as by refusing to file suit for reasons not intended by Congress. In either case, judicial review should be available to ensure that the Secretary's actions are not arbitrary, capricious, or an abuse of discretion. * * *

* * * [R]emanded for further proceedings consistent with this opinion.

DUNLOP v. BACHOWSKI

Supreme Court of the United States, 1975.
421 U.S. 560, 95 S. Ct. 1851, 44 L.Ed.2d 377.

MR. JUSTICE BRENNAN delivered the opinion of the Court.

[The facts are set forth in the Court of Appeals' opinion, supra.] * * *

We agree that 28 U.S.C.A. § 1337 confers jurisdiction upon the District Court to entertain respondent's suit, and that the Secretary's decision not to sue is not excepted from judicial review by 5 U.S.C.A.§ 701(a); rather, § § 702 and 704 subject the Secretary's decision to judicial review under the standard specified in § 706(2)(A). We hold, however, that the Court of Appeals erred insofar as its opinion construes § 706(2)(A) to authorize a trial-type inquiry into the factual bases of the Secretary's conclusion that no violations occurred affecting the outcome of the election. We accordingly reverse the judgment of the Court of Appeals insofar as it directs further proceedings on remand consistent with the opinion of that court, and direct the entry of a new judgment ordering that the proceedings on remand be consistent with this opinion of this Court. * * *

The Secretary urges that the structure of the statutory scheme, its objectives, its legislative history, the nature of the administrative action involved, and the conditions spelled out with respect thereto, combine to evince a congressional meaning to prohibit judicial review of his decision.[7] * * * Our examination of the relevant materials persuades us * * * that although no purpose to prohibit all judicial review is shown, a congressional purpose narrowly to limit the scope of judicial review of the Secretary's decision can, and should, be inferred in order to carry out congressional objectives in enacting the L-MRDA. * * *

Two conclusions follow from [a] * * * survey of our decisions: (1) since the statute relies upon the special knowledge and discretion of the Secretary for the determination of both the probable violation and the probable effect, clearly the reviewing court is not authorized to substitute its judgment for the decision of the Secretary not to bring suit; (2) therefore, to enable the reviewing court intelligently to review the Secretary's

7. We agree with the Court of Appeals, for the reasons stated in its opinion that there is no merit in the Secretary's contention that his decision is an unreviewable exercise of prosecutorial discretion.

determination, the Secretary must provide the court and the complaining witness with copies of a statement of reasons supporting his determination. * * *

Moreover, a statement of reasons serves purposes other than judicial review. Since the Secretary's role as lawyer for the complaining union member does not include the duty to indulge a client's usual prerogative to direct his lawyer to file suit, we may reasonably infer that Congress intended that the Secretary supply the member with a reasoned statement why he determined not to proceed. * * * Finally, a "reasons" requirement promotes thought by the Secretary and compels him to cover the relevant points and eschew irrelevancies, and as noted by the Court of Appeals in this case, the need to assure careful administrative consideration "would be relevant even if the Secretary's decision were unreviewable."

The necessity that the reviewing court refrain from substitution of its judgment for that of the Secretary thus helps define the permissible scope of review. Except in what must be the rare case, the court's review should be confined to examination of the "reasons" statement, and the determination whether the statement, without more, evinces that the Secretary's decision is so irrational as to constitute the decision arbitrary and capricious. Thus, review may not extend to cognizance or trial of a complaining member's challenges to the factual bases for the Secretary's conclusion either that no violations occurred or that they did not affect the outcome of the election. * * * If * * * the Court concludes * * * there is a rational and defensible basis [stated in the reasons statement] for [the Secretary's] determination, then that should be an end of this matter, for it is not the function of the Court to determine whether or not the case should be brought or what its outcome would be. * * *

The District Court, pursuant to the Court of Appeals' order of remand, ordered the Secretary to furnish a statement of reasons. The petitioner did not cross-petition from the order, and petitioner and USWA conceded that the order was proper in this case. The Secretry furnished the statement and it is attached as an Appendix to this opinion. Its adequacy to support a conclusion whether the Secretary's decision was rationally based or was arbitrary and capricious, is a matter of initial determination by the District Court. * * * [12]

MR. CHIEF JUSTICE BURGER, concurring.

I join in the opinion of the Court with the understanding that the Court has fashioned an exceedingly narrow scope of review of the Secretary's determination not to bring an action on behalf of a complainant to

---

12. USWA argues that Arts. II and III of the Constitution "do not countenance a court order requiring the executive branch, against its wishes, to institute a lawsuit in federal court." "[A] judicial direction that such an action be brought would violate the separation of powers * * * [and] because the Secretary agrees with the union that Title IV does not require a new election, the lawsuit would be one lacking the requisite adversity of interests to constitute a 'case' or 'controversy' as required by Article III." Since we do not consider at this time the question of the court's power to order the Secretary to file suit, we need not address those contentions.

set aside an election.   The language and purposes of § 401 of the Labor-Management Reporting and Disclosure Act of 1959 have required the Court to define a scope of review much narrower than applies under 5 U.S.C. § 706(a)(A) in most other administrative areas.   The Court's holding must be read as providing that the determination of the Secretary not to challenge a union election may be held arbitrary and capricious only where the Secretary's investigation, as evidenced by his statement of reasons, shows election irregularities that affected its outcome as to the complainant, and that notwithstanding the illegal conduct so found the Secretary nevertheless refuses to bring an action and advances no rational reason for his decision.

MR. JUSTICE REHNQUIST, concurring in the result in part and dissenting in part.

The parties to this case will have to be excused if they react with surprise to the opinion of the Court.   Instead of deciding the issue presented in the Secretary of Labor's petition for ceritorari, the Court decides an issue about which the parties no longer disagree; to compound the confusion, the reasoning adopted by the Court to resolve the issue it does decide its quite unusual unless it is intended to foreshadow disposition of the issue upon which the Court purports to reserve judgment. * * *

* * * The single question presented by the Secretary's petition for certiorari is:

> "Whether a disappointed union office seeker may invoke the judicial process to compel the Secretary of Labor to bring an action under Title IV of the Labor-Management Reporting and Disclosure Act of 1959 to set aside a union election."

* * * It seems to me that prior decisions of this Court establish that the Secretary's decision to file or not to file a complaint under § 482 is precisely the kind of "agency action * * * committed to agency discretion by law" exempted from the judicial-review provisions of the APA. * * *

The Court recognizes the power of these arguments, if only by understatement, when it acknowledges that any argument for judicial review of the Secretary's determination "obviously presents some difficulty in light of the strong evidence that Congress deliberately gave exclusive enforcement authority to the Secretary."   In my view the parties to this litigation are entitled to adjudication of the issue upon which this Court granted certiorari.   I would accordingly reverse the judgment of the Court of Appeals insofar as it held that the Secretary's refusal to institute an action under 29 U.S.C.A. § 482 is judicially reviewable under the provisions of the APA, 5 U.S.C.A. § § 701–706.

Notes

1. Is *Dunn* distinguishable from *Bachowski* on the ground that the *Dunn* plaintiffs had an alternative remedy under the National Labor Relations Act? On the ground of the L-MRDA's narrower grant of authority to the Secretary of Labor?   On the ground that review would interfere less with the Secretary's allocation of enforcement resources?   On the ground that the employer in *Dunn*

had a weaker interest in protection from unfair labor practices, than a candidate for union office has in protection from rigged elections?

2. Does *Bachowski* solve the problem of discouraging reasoned public explanation posed by the *Dunn-Southern California District Council* and the *Medical Committee-Kixmiller* cases?   From what source can the court derive a requirement of reasoned decisionmaking that is not itself based upon a prior determination that judicial review is available or that an on-the-record hearing is required? Cf. *Goldberg v. Kelly, supra* p. 182.   Does APA § 555(e) support such a requirement?

3. The Eighth Circuit reached a result similar to *Bachowski* in a case construing the duty of the NLRB to seek an injunction against secondary boycotts.   *Terminal Freight Handling Co. v. Solien*, 444 F.2d 699, 708–09 (8th Cir. 1971), *cert. denied* 405 U.S. 996 (1972).   The statutory language defining the Regional Director's duty in *Solien*, 29 U.S.C.A. § 160(l) (1970), was virtually identical to the language of the L-MRDA involved in *Bachowski*.   However, the court's ruling in *Solien* that the Director's failure to bring suit was reviewable was based on the potentially grave and immediate damage to the *public* from secondary boycotts.   The court then went on to describe the standard of review that should apply:

> We * * * conclude the "and that a complaint should issue" phrase reflects Congress' intention that the regional director retain limited prosecutorial discretion once he has made a reasonable cause determination.   We think it is clearly within his discretion to make an initial demand upon the union to cease its unlawful activity.   However, if he is unable to secure cessation upon such summary demand and negotiation, he must then petition for temporary injunctive relief and issue a complaint (or vice-versa) * * * .

> The Director of course may still negotiate settlements in lieu of injunctive relief in cases in which he has petitioned for injunctive relief such as was done here, and undoubtedly such settlements will be approved by the district court in most instances.   If a settlement in lieu of injunctive relief negotiated by the regional director fails to adequately protect the public interest, the district court can override the settlement and grant injunctive relief.

4. The "negotiated settlement" exception to required prosecution outlined in *Solien* may undercut the ruling's value for public interest litigants who doubt an agency's enforcement zeal.   Moreover, an attempt to intervene in negotiations prior to the initiation of enforcement proceedings in order to shape the direction of the informal agency process, may well be rebuffed by the agency.   In *Action on Safety and Health v. FTC*, 498 F.2d 757, 759, 763–63 (D.C. Cir. 1974), the plaintiffs had been denied participation in "pre-complaint" negotiations between the FTC and Volvo concerning the latter's advertising—negotiations which ultimately resulted in a consent decree.   In declining to review the Commission's refusal to allow intervention, the court first described the Commission's consent order procedure:

> Under these rules the Commission may notify a "proposed respondent" of its intention to institute a formal proceeding against him.   Such notification contains a form of the proposed complaint which the Commission will issue, as well as the proposed order which the Commission will seek.   If the proposed respondent elects, within 10 days, to attempt a settlement, negotiations begin between the Commission's staff and the proposed respondent.   If the parties are unable to agree, the Commission may commence formal adjudicative pro-

cedure. If, however, an agreement is reached and accepted by the Commission, the provisionally accepted consent order is placed on the public record for a period of 30 days, during which time any interested party may file comments or views with the Commission. After reviewing any such public comments, the Commission may withdraw its acceptance of the consent order either as originally proposed or as modified in light of comments received.

The Court then had this to say concerning reviewability:

   * * * Congress granted great discretion to the Commission to determine whether a potential respondent has violated the Act and whether a proceeding by the Commission against the violator would be in the public interest. Neither the Federal Trade Commission Act nor the Commission's Rules of Procedure grant appellants any right to intervene in consent negotiations. Rather, the power to prescribe consent negotiation procedure is part of the general enforcement power of the Commission, and such enforcement decisions are generally not subject to judicial review. In this area, concerned as it is with questions of administrative policy and allocation of scarce Commission resources, "the Commission alone is empowered to develop that enforcement policy best calculated to achieve the ends contemplated by Congress and to allocate its available funds and personnel in such a way as to execute its policy efficiently and economically." *Moog Industries, Inc. v. FTC*, 355 U.S. 411, 412 (1958).

   Whether or not the denial of appellants' motion to intervene in the negotiations is agency action committed entirely to agency discretion is a question which must be answered by viewing the *source* of the Commission's power to act. We believe that the whole consent negotiation procedure was promulgated by the Commission pursuant to its broad enforcement discretion. As such, we hold that the decision to grant or deny intervention is an agency action committed to agency discretion and therefore is specifically exempt from judicial review under § 701(a)(2) of the APA.

5. *Local 1219, American Federation of Government Employees v. Donovan*, 683 F.2d 511 (D.C. Cir. 1982), extended judicial review to the Secretary of Labor's enforcement of the provisions of the 1978 Civil Service Reform Act, 5 U.S.C.A. § 7101 et seq., which govern federal employee elections. In that case, the Secretary had reached a settlement with the union on charges of unfair election procedures, one that did not set aside any past election but called for Department supervision of the 1982 election of national union officers. Four union locals and 86 individual members challenged the settlement as inconsistent with 5 U.S.C.A. § 7120, which authorizes settlement agreement "providing for appropriate remedial action" but directs that failing agreement, enforcement proceedings "shall" be instituted. Writing for the court, Judge Wald rejected the government's claim that the Secretary's decision to settle was not subject to review (683 F.2d at 515–56):

   The government argues that there is "no law to apply" in this case because the CSRA, 5 U.S.C.A. § 7120(d), allows the Assistant Secretary of Labor Management Relations ("Assistant Secretary") to provide remedies "as he considers appropriate." Since this langauge does not specify when the Assistant Secretary must provide a remedy, the government concludes that it leaves the Assistant Secretary with unfettered discretion.

   The government's interpretation of section 7120(d) ignores the full language of that section and its implementing regulations. In section 7120 Congress directed that "[a]n agency *shall* only accord recognition to a labor organization that is free from corrupt influences" (emphasis added) and that the Assistant Secretary "*shall* prescribe such regulations as are necessary to carry out the purpose of this section." (Emphasis added). Pursuant to his statutory obligation, the Assistant Secretary promulgated regulations setting forth specific standards for labor organizations and a detailed scheme for enforcing compliance with those standards.[13] These regulations provide that whenever the Director of the Office of Labor Management Standards Enforcement finds probable cause to believe that a violation of election standards has occurred, he must institute an enforcement action unless he has arrived at a settlement that provides "appropriate remedial action." 29 C.F.R. § 208.66. This regulatory scheme does not contemplate that the Director shall have complete discretion to decide whether relief is appropriate for "probable" violations. Instead, it provides the Director with flexibility to pursue remedies for "probabl[y]" illegal elections through either settlement or enforcement proceedings, and to adjust his remedial demands as the circumstances warrant. Having promulgated these regulations pursuant to section 7120(d)'s directive, the Assistant Secretary must abide by them. See generally *Service v. Dulles*, 354 U.S. 363, 373 (1957); *Nader v. NRC*, 513 F.2d 1045, 1051 (D.C. Cir. 1975). See also *United States v. Caceres*, 440 U.S. 741, 753–54 (1979).

The government suggests that judicial review is nonetheless inappropriate because settlement negotiations involve special matters of agency expertise. It suggests that courts are ill-suited to assess the impact of a settlement on a union, its suitability under agency policy or the wisdom of devoting agency resources to an enforcement proceeding. Because the Director has considerable experience in these matters, they conclude, the question of whether, and on what terms, to settle should be left entirely to his discretion.

We do not doubt the experience and expertise of the Director; but we cannot agree that it forecloses judicial review. Far from lacking any experience with reviewing settlement agreements, courts are well acquainted with the task of approving settlements of enormous complexity. Moreover, the judicial review sought in this case would not require courts to probe deeply into the substance of a settlement. Instead, we are asked solely to assess whether the Director's decision was "arbitrary, capricious, an abuse of discretion or otherwise not in accordance with law." This limited determination is one which courts are well-equipped to make. Finally, courts are especially suited to the task of assuring that the interests of those not party to negotiations have been adequately protected. In a case such as this, in which the protesting locals have not been involved in negotiations with the "probabl[y]" abusive union, some judicial oversight is appropriate. * * *

The court went on, however, to hold that the district judge had erred in setting aside the settlement that the Secretary had reached (id. at 518–19):

The Director's Statement of Reasons for settling with the AFGE present ample grounds for upholding his decision. In his statement, the Director

---

13. These regulations set forth virtually the identical enforcement scheme for violations of the CSRA's union democracy provisions as apply to violations of the Labor-Management Reporting and Disclosure Act, 29 U.S.C.A. § 482 ("LMRDA"). This parallel structure is hardly coincidental since section 7120(d) directs the Assistant Secretary to adopt regulations that generally conform to principles applied to private sector labor organizations. * * *

outlined a number of possible impediments to an administrative enforcement action and explained how the relief obtained through settlement—supervision of the next regularly scheduled election—was for all practical purposes the same as that which could be obtained through an enforcement action. Rather than evidencing an abdication of the Director's responsibility to obtain "appropriate remedial action," the Statement of Reasons indicates a careful consideration of the practical consequences of pursuing alternative remedial approaches.

The underlying theme in the Director's Statement of Reasons is that the settlement offered certainty of relief.   In this connection, the Director pointed to four possible weaknesses in his case against the union.   First, some members of organizations affiliated with the AFGE were employed by the private sector.   In the Director's opinion, this fact indicated that the AFGE's elections would be covered by both the LMRDA and the CSRA, and therefore raised the question whether relief under the LMRDA was the exclusive remedy. Were the LMRDA to be the exclusive remedy, he noted, the union would be able to successfully defend any action on the ground that the Director's enforcement actions were not timely.   Second, the Director expressed concern that the original complaints filed against the AFGE were "couched in vague language" raising the possibility that the Director's case would be dismissed for being outside the scope of the complaining member's allegations.   Third, the Director suggested that a factfinder may not be sympathetic to the government's case inasmuch as the violations were not willful or fraudulent.   Finally, the Director noted that he might not be able to prove that the violations affected the election's outcome.

In addition to the certainty provided by the settlement, the major factor counseling against an enforcement action was the practical equivalence of a supervised 1982 election and a supervised re-run of the 1980 election.   The Director explained that supervised elections following an enforcement action probably could not be completed before the regularly scheduled August, 1982 election.   Through the settlement agreement, however, a supervised 1982 election was assured, and supervision of the election of delegates could begin in the fall of 1981.   Thus, while there would not be a re-running of the August, 1980 election, the settlement provided what the Director considered to be a more expeditious route to a supervised national election.

The district court found the Director's reasons inadequate because "the government does nothing to remedy the violations that may have occurred in 1980, nor does it grant plaintiff's any prospective rights other than those to which they are already entitled."   We disagree.   Rather than failing to give aggrieved union members any prospective rights, the settlement provides the essential remedy for an illegal election, namely, a supervised future election.   Indeed, according to the Director's estimates, the settlement provides an earlier supervised election than could have been achieved through an enforcement action.   Under these circumstances, we find the Director's decision to be amply supported.

6. *Investment Co. Institute v. FDIC*, 728 F.2d 518 (D.C. Cir. 1984), is a reminder that, notwithstanding recent inroads on the traditional unreviewability of agency enforcement discretion, statutory language and regulatory context will significantly affect a court's willingness to entertain such challenges.   In that case a majority, over the dissent of Chief Judge Wright, set aside an order to the Federal Deposit Insurance Corporation to "take up and decide the merits of

[ICI's] petition seeking a declaration that" a plan by Boston Five Cents Savings Bank to sell mutual fund shares through subsidiaries violated the federal banking laws and "meanwhile to order the [bank] to halt its allegedly unlawful conduct." The court held, first, that the district court lacked jurisdiction to issue its order under 12 U.S.C.A. § 1818. It then addressed more broadly the FDIC's enforcement rule and concluded that its decision whether to consider the merits of ICI's petition was "committed to agency discretion by law (728 F.2d at 526.27):

> Whether a particular agency decision is committed to agency discretion depends, broadly speaking, on whether there is law to apply in making and reviewing the decision, which in turn depends, we have said, on "pragmatic considerations as to whether an agency determination is the proper subject of judicial review." *Natural Resources Defense Council, Inc. v. SEC*, 606 F.2d 1031, 1043 (D.C. Cir. 1979).[6] Among the important considerations are "the need for judicial supervision to safeguard the interests of the plaintiffs[,] the impact of review on the effectiveness of the agency in carrying out its congressionally assigned role[,] and the appropriateness of the issues raised for judicial review." Each consideration points to nonreviewability of the FDIC's refusal to take up ICI's petition.

In this case, there is no significant need for judicial supervision to safeguard ICI's rights. In *New York Stock Exchange v. Bloom*, 562 F.2d 736 (D.C. Cir. 1977), *cert. denied*, 435 U.S. 942 (1978), this court held that judicial review was not needed to protect the rights of ICI, whose position in that case was virtually identical to its position here. The court gave two reasons for this conclusion. First, since there was no agency decision applicable to ICI, ICI was not exposed to any burden of compliance or risk of penalty for noncompliance. Second, nothing was shown to cast doubt on the ability of ICI to bring an action directly against the bank whose conduct it thought unlawful, an action that, though possibly inconvenient, was an alternative form of relief. Both these reasons apply with full force in this case, and we therefore conclude, as we did in the earlier case, that the hardship to ICI is not substantial enough to justify judicial review.

Regarding the second consideration—whether review would hamper agency effectiveness—we have a less than fully satisfactory basis for making up independent judgment. The FDIC informs us that it supervises some nine thousand state-chartered banks and conducts some twenty thousand bank examinations each year. It informs us, too, that several hundred banks are in danger of failure and therefore require especially close monitoring. It tells us the exercise of its heavy and profound regulatory responsibilities would be severely disrupted if every person seeking FDIC action on a petition seeking enforcement action could invoke judicial review of a simple FDIC refusal to consider the merits of the petition. ICI makes no response to these representations, and we find them quite plausible. * * *

ICI's petition, as noted above, was a request that the FDIC take enforcement action under section 1818. The FDIC's response was a simple refusal

6. The majority members of this panel have, in another case, made plain their discomfort with the test for whether an agency decision is committed to agency discretion articulated by the court in *National Resources Defense Council v. SEC* ("*NRDC*"). See *Chaney v. Heckler*, 718 F.2d 1174 (D.C. Cir. 1983), *reh. denied*, 724 F.2d 1030 (D.C.Cir. 1984). (Statement Dissenting from the Denial of Rehearing En Banc by Scalia, J., joined by Wilkey, Bork, Starr, JJ.). Nonetheless, NRDC remains the law of this circuit and we are bound to apply it as best we can.

to consider the petition on its merits.   For several reasons, that refusal is not an appropriate issue for judicial review.   "An agency's decision to refrain from an investigation or an enforcement action is generally unreviewable. * * * " *Kixmiller v. SEC.*   The FDIC's decision at issue here comes squarely within this general rule and not within any exception to the rule of which we are aware.   Thus, agency action is not the exclusive form of relief for ICI's complaint, as it was for the complaint at issue in *Dunlop v. Bachowski,* 421 U.S. 560 (1975), there being no reason to believe that ICI could not bring an action directly against the bank whose conduct it thinks unlawful.   Nor has the FDIC initiated an action that it subsequently decided to terminate.   * * *   Nor is there the slightest evidence of a consistent policy of abdicating a statutory duty.   * * *   The FDIC decision here was a simple exercise of "prosecutorial" discretion not to invoke a non-exclusive remedy for allegedly unlawful conduct.   That discretion about how to exercise a "general enforcement power," is inappropriate for review where there are no standards to govern the agency exercise of discretion, the statutory language is wholly permissive, the statute itself severely limits the scope of judicial review, and the agency decision involves budgetary constraints and enforcement priorities that we are ill-equipped to evaluate.

Thus, there is "no law to apply" in reviewing a simple refusal to take enforcement action.   There might, of course, be some law to apply in deciding whether the practice challenged by ICI is unlawful; it is even imaginable that there might be law to apply in deciding whether the practice is unsafe or unsound.   But the FDIC has made no such determination.   It has merely decided not to exercise its power under section 1818, and the statute lays down no standards to guide the FDIC in deciding whether to make a finding on the issues of unlawfulness, unsoundness, or unsafeness, let alone in deciding whether to take enforcement action once it has made such a finding.   There is, in short, no basis in the statute for a court to use in reviewing the FDIC decision at issue in this case.

CHANEY v. HECKLER

United States Court of Appeals, District of Columbia Circuit, 1983.
718 F.2d 1174, rehearing en banc denied 724 F.2d 1030 (1984).

WRIGHT, CIRCUIT JUDGE.

In the Food, Drug, and Cosmetic Act (FDCA) Congress has required * * * the Commissioner of the Food and Drug Administration (FDA) to assure that all "new drugs" are "safe and effective" for use under the conditions prescribed, recommended, or suggested on the official labeling.   * * * A drug is "misbranded," and impermissibly available for use by consumers, unless its labeling bears adequate directions for use and such adequate warnings against unapproved uses or methods of administration as are necessary for the protection of its users.   The Commissioner has previously interpreted FDCA's labeling requirements to impose upon FDA the "obligat[ion]" to investigate and take appropriate action against unapproved uses of approved drugs where such unapproved use becomes widespread or endangers the public health.   See *Legal Status of Approved Labeling for Prescription Drugs Prescribing for*

Uses Unapproved by the Food and Drug Administration, 37 Fed. Reg. 16503, 16504 (August 15, 1972) (hereinafter *Policy Statement*). * * *

During the last six years at least five states, including Texas and Oklahoma, have enacted statutes adopting lethal injection as a means of human execution. Prisons in these five states house over 200 of the approximately 1,100 persons sentenced to death in the United States, and at least six other states (with 300 persons on death row) apparently are considering adopting lethal injection as a means of capital punishment. * * *

Because the lethal injection statutes authorize state prison officials to make unapproved use of drugs distributed in interstate commerce, appellants petitioned FDA to enforce the Act against the states. Their December 19, 1980 petition recited the known evidence concerning lethal injection, which strongly indicates that such drugs pose a substantial threat of torturous pain to persons being executed. ROYAL COMMISSION ON CAPITAL PUNISHMENT, 1949–53 REPORT (1953). Appellants appended to their petition affidavits of leading medical and scientific experts which aver that there is no "expert consensus" founded upon "substantial evidence" that these drugs will produce death quickly and without pain and discomfort. * * * With this evidence as grounds, appellants requested that FDA take the following actions:

1. Affix a boxed warning to the labels of the drugs specified for use in a lethal injection by statutes or prison policies in Texas, Oklahoma, Idaho and New Mexico that these drugs are not approved for use as a means of execution, are not considered safe and effective as a means of execution, and should not be used as a means of execution[;]

2. Prepare and send to the manufacturers of the drugs and to prisons and departments of corrections in Texas, Oklahoma, Idaho and New Mexico * * * notices advising that the drugs specified in those states' execution statutes or prison policies for use in an execution as well as any other drug or drugs are not approved for use as a means of execution, are not considered safe and effective as a means of execution, and should not be used as a means of execution;

3. Place in the [FDA] Drug Bulletin an article advising that the drugs specified for use in a lethal injection by statutes or prison policies in Texas, Oklahoma, Idaho and New Mexico are not approved for use as a means of execution, are not considered safe and effective as a means of execution, and should not be used as a means of execution;

4. Adopt a policy and procedure for the seizure and condemnation from prisons or state departments of corrections of drugs which are destined or held for use as a means of execution; [and]

5. Recommend the prosecution of manufacturers, wholesalers, retailers and pharmacists who knowingly sell drugs for the unapproved use of lethal injection and prison officials who knowingly buy, possess or use drugs for the unapproved use of lethal injections.

* * *

On July 7, 1981 the Commissioner of FDA, by letter, refused to take any of the actions requested in appellants' petition.   Rather than investigate appellants' claims, the Commissioner asserted that FDA's jurisdiction did not extend to the regulation of state-sanctioned use of lethal injections.   Indeed, because these were "duly authorized statutory enactments [that furthered] * * * proper State functions," the Commissioner indicated that, even if it had jurisdiction, FDA would not gather any evidence or pursue any enforcement.   He noted two reasons for refusing to investigate or to enforce: (1) the case law on the unapproved use of drugs otherwise approved by FDA was not uniform, and (2) FDA had a policy of not initiating enforcement action against unapproved uses of approved drugs absent "serious danger to the public health."   The Commissioner could find no such "danger" where a state had properly enacted a capital punishment law.

On September 16, 1981 appellants filed suit in the District Court seeking to compel FDA to fulfill its statutory obligation to investigate and to regulate the unapproved use of approved drugs in human execution systems. * * *

On August 30, 1982 the District Court granted summary judgment to FDA.   The court declined to decide the jurisdictional issue, but went on to hold that "decisions of executive departments and agencies to *refrain from instituting investigations and enforcement proceedings are essentially unreviewable by the courts.*" * * *

Neither FDA nor the District Court claims that FDCA precludes judicial review.   Rather, both assert that FDCA gives FDA *absolute* discretion over decisions concerning investigation and enforcement, and thus commits those decisions to agency discretion by law.   Though some courts have traditionally displayed reluctance to review exercises of enforcement discretion, the Supreme Court has consistently instructed us to construe narrowly the "committed to agency discretion" exception, and to find it applicable only in those rare instances where the governing statute is "drawn in such broad terms that in a given case there is no law to apply." *Citizens to Preserve Overton Park, Inc. v. Volpe.* * * *

* * * FDA, in an earlier policy statement, made law to govern and guide its discretion in regulating the unapproved use of approved drugs:

> Where the unapproved use of an approved new drug becomes widespread or endangers the public health, the Food and Drug Administration is obligated to investigate it thoroughly and to take whatever action is warranted to protect the public. * * * When necessary the Food and Drug Administration will not hesitate to take whatever action * * * may be required to bring possible harmful use of an approved drug under control.
>
> * * * Thus, where a manufacturer or his representative, or any person in the chain of distribution, does anything that directly or indirectly suggests to the physician or the patient that an approved drug may properly be used for unapproved uses for which it is neither labeled nor advertised, that action constitutes a direct violation of the Act and is punishable accordingly.

Policy Statement, 37 Fed. Reg. at 16504.   This policy statement * * * comes within the APA's definition of a rule as that term has been consistently interpreted in this circuit. * * * The FDA policy statement * * * also interprets the relevant statute and indicates FDA's policy regarding the exercise of its discretion. * * *

When reviewing informal agency action of this type a court must * * * make a "searching and careful" review of both the administrative record, particularly the uncontroverted evidence submitted by appellant, and the agency's stated reasons for its action. If * * * FDA's inaction in this case was arbitrary, capricious, and without authority of law, and our own analysis of the record leads us to believe it was,[39] we must remand this case for appropriate action. * * *

* * * [T]he Commissioner asserts that the use of drugs in lethal injections does not pose a "serious danger to the public health." But he cites no evidence to support this proposition. Rather, he irrebuttably presumes that "duly authorized statutory enactments * * * [which further] proper State functions" cannot, as a matter of law, pose such a danger to the public. * * * In this case *all* the evidence shows that lethal injection laws *do* endanger users of drugs, and thus the public health.[43] * * * In short, the Commissioner presents no rational basis for concluding that lethal injections do not pose a serious health threat. Thus we must conclude that he has acted arbitrarily, capriciously, and without authority of law. * * *

SCALIA, CIRCUIT JUDGE, dissenting.

The majority converts a law designed to protect consumers against drugs that are unsafe or ineffective for their represented use into a law not only permitting but mandating federal supervision of the manner of state executions. This implausible result is achieved by rewriting the law with regard to enforcement discretion. * * *

* * * [F]ar from there being a "presumption of reviewability" with regard to enforcement determinations, the well known presumption is precisely the contrary. * * *

Proceeding, then, from the premise that an agency's exercise or *(a fortiori)* nonexercise of its enforcement discretion is generally unreviewable, one must consider whether there are any special circumstances justifying departure from that general rule in the present case. * * *

The [majority] opinion places its major reliance upon what it calls the FDA's "Policy Statement." * * * The statement is full of flexible terms, the precise application of which was obviously intended to be, and could properly be, left to the discretion of the agency—for example, whether an unapproved use has become "widespread"; whether it "endangers the public health"; what particular action "is warranted to protect the public"; the meaning of the phrase "when necessary." * * *

---

39. The case was decided below on a motion for summary judgment. Therefore, appellants' factual allegations that lethal injection does not cause a "quick and painless" death and that it "poses a substantial threat of torturous and unnecessary pain to persons being executed" must be assumed to be true.

43. We do not imply that FDA must gather evidence concerning the health effects of all alleged statutory violations to survive judicial scrutiny. We simply hold that FDA cannot irrebutably presume that a particular practice does not pose a "serious danger to the public health" because that practice is sanctioned by state law. * * *

More fundamentally, however, the quoted statement is not an agency rule, and is indeed not even an authoritative policy statement. The majority's opinion gives it the title "Policy Statement" (which it never bore), and uses that conclusory designation throughout. In fact, however, the statement was part of the policy justification set forth in a Notice of Proposed Rulemaking, *with respect to a proposal that was never adopted* * * * .

Thus, there is ultimately no special factor to support the extraordinary assertion of authority to control the agency's enforcement discretion in the present case—nothing, except the majority's disagreement with the agency's determination that no serious danger to the public health exists. * * *

Notes

1. In a part of his dissent not reproduced above, Judge Scalia suggested that the panel majority had mistakenly relied upon *Overton Park* and *Bachowski* when the relevant Supreme Court authority was *Moog Industries, Inc. v. FTC*, 355 U.S. 411 (1958), in which the Court wrote:

In No. 77, petitioner (Moog Industries, Inc.) was found by the Commission to have violated the Act and was ordered to cease and desist from further violation. * * * Upon affirmance of the order, petitioner moved the court to hold the entry of judgment in abeyance on the ground that petitioner would suffer serious financial loss if prohibited from engaging in pricing practices open to its competitors. The court denied the requested relief. * * *

In view of the scope of administrative discretion that Congress has given the Federal Trade Commission, it is ordinarily not for courts to modify ancillary features of a valid Commission order. This is but recognition of the fact that in the shaping of its remedies within the framework of regulatory legislation, an agency is called upon to exercise its specialized, experienced judgment. * * * [T]he Commission alone is empowered to develop that enforcement policy best calculated to achieve the ends contemplated by Congress and to allocate its available funds and personnel in such a way as to execute its policy efficiently and economically.

2. *FTC v. Universal-Rundle Corp.*, 387 U.S. 244, 251 (1967), reaffirmed but arguably narrowed *Moog Industries*. The respondent corporation offered to prove that all of its competitors, five of which had larger market shares, engaged in the practice (truckload discounts) that it was being required to abandon and that losing this ability to meet the competition would cause the company to fail. The respondent's proof was insubstantial, however, and a Commission decision to reject the petition for a stay was held not "patently arbitrary and capricious."

HECKLER v. CHANEY

Supreme Court of the United States, 1985.
____ U.S. ____, 105 S. Ct. 1649, 79 L. Ed. 2d ____.

JUSTICE REHNQUIST delivered the opinion of the Court.

* * *

To this point [following examination of APA § § 701(a)(1) and (2)] our analysis does not differ significantly from that of the Court of Appeals. That court purported to apply the "no law to apply" standard of *Overton Park*. We disagree, however, with that court's insistence that the "narrow construction" of § (a)(2) required application of a presumption of reviewability even to an agency's decision not to undertake certain enforcement actions. Here we think the Court of Appeals broke with tradition, case law, and sound reasoning.

Overton Park did not involve an agency's refusal to take requested enforcement action. It involved an affirmative act of approval under a statute that set clear guidelines for determining when such approval should be given. Refusals to take enforcement steps generally involve precisely the opposite situation, and in that situation we think the presumption is that judicial review is not available. This Court has recognized on several occasions over many years that an agency's decision not to prosecute or enforce, whether through civil or criminal process, is a decision generally committed to an agency's absolute discretion. See *United States v. Batchelder*, 442 U.S. 114, 123–124 (1979); *United States v. Nixon*, 418 U.S. 683, 693 (1974); *Vaca v. Sipes*, 386 U.S. 171, 182 (1967); *Confiscation Cases*, 7 Wall. 454 (1869). This recognition of the existence of discretion is attributable in no small part to the general unsuitability for judicial review of agency decisions to refuse enforcement.

The reasons for this general unsuitability are many. First, an agency decision not to enforce often involves a complicated balancing of a number of factors which are peculiarly within its expertise. Thus, the agency must not only assess whether a violation has occurred, but whether agency resources are best spent on this violation or another, whether the agency is likely to succeed if it acts, whether the particular enforcement action requested best fits the agency's overall policies, and indeed, whether the agency has enough resources to undertake the action at all. An agency generally cannot act against each technical violation of the statute it is charged with enforcing. The agency is far better equipped than the courts to deal with the many variables involved in the proper ordering of its priorities. * * *

In addition to these administrative concerns, we note that when an agency refuses to act it generally does not exercise its *coercive* power over an individual's liberty or property rights, and thus does not infringe upon areas that courts often are called upon to protect. Similarly, when an agency does act to enforce, that action itself provides a focus for judicial review, inasmuch as the agency must have exercised its power in some manner. The action at least can be reviewed to determine whether the agency exceeded its statutory powers. Finally, we recognize that an agency's refusal to institute proceedings shares to some extent the characteristics of the decision of a prosecutor in the Executive Branch not to indict—a decision which has long been regarded as the special province of the Executive Branch, inasmuch as it is the executive who is charged by the Constitution to "take care that the Laws be faithfully executed."

We of course only list the above concerns to facilitate understanding of our conclusion that an agency's decision not to take enforcement action should be presumed immune from judicial review under § 701(a)(2). For good reasons, such a decision has traditionally been "committed to agency discretion," and we believe that the Congress enacting the APA did not intend to alter that tradition. * * * In so stating, we emphasize that the decision is only presumptively unreviewable; the presumption may be rebutted where the substantive statute has provided guidelines for the agency to follow in exercising its enforcement powers. * * *

Dunlop [v. Bachowski] is * * * thus consistent with a general presumption of unreviewability of decisions not to enforce. The statute being administered quite clearly withdrew discretion from the agency and provided guidelines for exercise of its enforcement power. Our decision that review was available was not based on "pragmatic considerations" * * * that amount to an assessment of whether the interests at stake are important enough to justify intervention in the agencies' decisionmaking. The danger that agencies may not carry out their delegated powers with sufficient vigor does not necessarily lead to the conclusion that courts are the most appropriate body to police this aspect of their performance. That decision is in the first instance for Congress, and we therefore turn to the FDCA to determine whether in this case Congress has provided us with "law to apply." * * *

[Justice Rehnquist parsed the language of the FDCA and found no relevant language resembling the articulated criteria or mandatory tone of the statute at issue in *Dunlap v. Bachowski*. Describing the FDA's "policy statement" as "singularly unhelpful," the Court found it both vague and contradicted by a general FDA regulation characterizing its enforcement discretion as unreviewable.]

We therefore conclude that the presumption that agency decisions not to institute proceedings are unreviewable under § 701(a)(2) of the APA is not overcome by the enforcement provisions of the FDCA. The FDA's decision not to take the enforcement actions requested by respondents is therefore not subject to judicial review under the APA. The general exception to reviewability provided by § 701 (a)(2) for action "committed to agency discretion" remains a narrow one, but within that exception are included agency refusals to institute investigative or enforcement proceedings, unless Congress has indicated otherwise. In so holding, we essentially leave to Congress, and not to the courts, the decision as to whether an agency's refusal to institute proceedings should be judicially reviewable. No colorable claim is made in this case that the agency's refusal to institute proceedings violated any constitutional rights of respondents, and we do not address the issue that would be raised in such a case. *Cf. Johnson v. Robinson*, 415 U.S. 361, 366 (1974); *Yick Wo v. Hopkins*, 118 U.S. 356, 372–374 (1886). The fact that the drugs involved in this case are ultimately to be used in imposing the death penalty must not lead this Court or other courts to import profound differences of opinion over the meaning of the Eighth Amendment to the United States Constitution into the domain of administrative law.

The judgment of the Court of Appeals is Reversed.

[The concurring opinion of JUSTICE BRENNAN is omitted.]

JUSTICE MARSHALL, concurring in the judgment.

* * * In my view, the "presumption of unreviewability" announced today is a product of that lack of discipline that easy cases make all too easy. * * * Because this "presumption of unreviewability" is fundamentally at odds with rule-of-law principles firmly embedded in our jurisprudence, because it seeks to truncate an emerging line of judicial authority subjecting enforcement discretion to rational and principled constraint, and because, in the end, the presumption may well be indecipherable, one can only hope that it will come to be understood as a relic of a particular factual setting in which the full implications of such a presumption were neither confronted nor understood.

I write separately to argue for a different basis of decision: that refusals to enforce, like other agency actions, are reviewable in the absence of a "clear and convincing" congressional intent to the contrary, but that such refusals warrant deference when, as in this case, there is nothing to suggest that an agency with enforcement discretion has abused that discretion.

In response to respondents' petition, the FDA Commissioner stated that it would not pursue the complaint

> "under our inherent discretion to decline to pursue certain enforcement matters. The unapproved use of approved drugs is an area in which the case law is far from uniform. Generally, enforcement proceedings in this area are initiated only when there is a serious danger to the public health or a blatant scheme to defraud. We cannot conclude that those dangers are present under State lethal injection laws. * * * [We] decline, as a matter of enforcement discretion, to pursue supplies of drugs under State control that will be used for execution by lethal injection."

The FDA may well have been legally required to provide this statement of basis and purpose for its decision not to take the action requested. Under the Administrative Procedure Act, such a statement is required when an agency denies a "written application, petition, or other request of an interested person made in connection with any agency proceedings." 5 U.S.C.A. § 555(e). Whether this written explanation was legally required or not, however, it does provide a sufficient basis for holding, on the merits, that the FDA's refusal to grant the relief requested was within its discretion.

First, respondents on summary judgment neither offered nor attempted to offer any evidence that the reasons given for the FDA's refusal to act were other than the reasons stated by the agency. Second * * * the FDCA is not a mandatory statute that requires the FDA to prosecute all violations of the Act. Thus, the FDA clearly has significant discretion to choose which alleged violations of the Act to prosecute. Third, the basis on which the agency chose to exercise this discretion—that other problems were viewed as more pressing—generally will be enough to pass muster. Certainly it is enough to do so here, where the number of people currently affected by the alleged misbranding is around 200, and where the drugs are integral elements in a regulatory scheme over which the States exercise pervasive and direct control. * * *

The Court, however, * * * transforms the arguments for deferential review on the merits into the wholly different notion that "enforcement" decisions are presumptively unreviewable altogether. * * *

* * * [T]o support its newfound "presumption of unreviewability," the Court resorts to completely undefined and unsubstantiated references to "tradition," and to citation of four cases.

Yet these cases hardly support such a broad presumption with respect to agency refusal to take enforcement action. The only one of these cases to involve administrative action, *Vaca v. Sipes*, suggests, in dictum, that the General Counsel of the National Labor Relations Board has unreviewable discretion to refuse to initiate an unfair labor practice complaint. To the extent this dictum is sound, later cases indicate that unreviewability results from the particular structure of the National Labor Relations Act and the explicit statutory intent to withdraw review found in 29 U.S.C.A. § 153(d), rather than from some general "presumption of unreviewability" of enforcement decisions. *See NLRB v. Sears, Roebuck & Co.*, 421 U.S. 132, 138 (1975). Neither *Vaca* nor *Sears, Roebuck* discuss the APA. The other three cases—*Batchelder, Nixon*, and the *Confiscation Cases*—all involve prosecutorial discretion to enforce the criminal law. *Batchelder* does not maintain that such discretion is unreviewable, but only that the mere existence of prosecutorial discretion does not violate the Constitution. The *Confiscation Cases*, involving suits to confiscate property used in aid of rebellion, hold that, where the United States brings a criminal action that is "wholly for the benefit of the United States," a person who provides information leading to the action has no "vested" or absolute right to demand, "so far as the interests of the United States are concerned," that the action be maintained. The half-sentence cited from *Nixon*, which states that the Executive has "absolute discretion to decide whether to prosecute a case," is the only apparent support the Court actually offers for even the limited notion that prosecutorial discretion in the criminal area is unreviewable. But that half-sentence is of course misleading, for *Nixon* held it an abuse of that discretion to attempt to exercise it contrary to validly promulgated regulations. Thus, *Nixon* actually stands for a very different proposition than the one for which the Court cites it: faced with a specific claim of abuse of prosecutorial discretion, *Nixon* makes clear that courts are not powerless to intervene. * * *

* * * [A]rguments about prosecutorial discretion do not necessarily translate into the context of agency refusals to act. * * * Criminal prosecutorial decisions vindicate only intangible interests, common to society as a whole, in the enforcement of the criminal law. The conduct at issue has already occurred; all that remains is society's general interest in assuring that the guilty are punished. See *Linda R.S. v. Richard D.* In contrast, requests for administrative enforcement typically seek to pre-

vent concrete and future injuries that Congress has made cognizable—injuries that result, for example, from misbranded drugs, such as alleged in this case, or unsafe nuclear power plants, to obtain palpable benefits that Congress has intended to bestow—such as labor union elections free of corruption, see *Dunlop v. Bachowski*. Entitlements to receive these benefits or to be free of these injuries often run to specific classes of individuals whom Congress has singled out as statutory beneficiaries. The interests at stake in review of administrative enforcement decisions are thus more focused and in many circumstances more pressing than those at stake in criminal prosecutorial decisions. * * *

Perhaps most important, the *sine qua non* of the APA was to alter inherited judicial reluctance to constrain the exercise of discretionary administrative power—to rationalize and make fairer the exercise of such discretion. Since passage of the APA, the sustained effort of administrative law has been to "continuously narro[w] the category of actions considered to be so discretionary as to be exempted from review." Shapiro, Administrative Discretion: The Next Stage, 92 Yale L.J. 1487, 1489, n.11 (1983). * * *

The "tradition" of unreviewability upon which the majority relies is refuted most powerfully by a firmly entrenched body of lower court case law that holds reviewable various agency refusals to act. * * * The lower courts, facing the problem of agency inaction and its concrete effects more regularly than do we, have responded with a variety of solutions to assure administrative fidelity to congressional objectives: a demand that an agency explain its refusal to act, a demand that explanations given be further elaborated, and injunctions that action "unlawfully withheld or unreasonably delayed" be taken. Whatever the merits of any particular solution, one would have hoped the Court would have acted with greater respect for these efforts by responding with a scalpel rather than a blunderbuss.

To be sure, the Court no doubt takes solace in the view that it has created only a "presumption" of unreviewability, and that "this presumption may be rebutted where the substantive statute has provided guidelines for the agency to follow in exercising its enforcement powers." But this statement implies far too narrow a reliance on positive law, either statutory or constitutional, as the sole source of limitations on agency discretion not to enforce. In my view, enforcement discretion is also channelled by traditional background understandings against which the APA was enacted and which Congress hardly could be thought to have intended to displace in the APA. For example, a refusal to enforce that stems from a conflict of interest, that is the result of a bribe, vindictiveness or retaliation, or that traces to personal or other corrupt motives ought to be judicially remediable. Even in the absence of statutory "guidelines" precluding such factors as bases of decision, Congress should not be presumed to have departed from principles of rationality and fair process in enacting the APA. Moreover, the agency may well narrow its own enforcement discretion through historical practice, from which it should arguably not depart in the absence of explanation, or through regulations and informal action. Traditional principles of rationality and fair process do offer "meaningful standards" and "law to apply" to an agency's decision not to act, and no presumption of unreviewability should be allowed to trump these principles. * * *

Discretion to Regulate

NATURAL RESOURCES DEFENSE COUNCIL v. SEC

United States Court of Appeals, District of Columbia Circuit, 1979.
606 F.2d 1031.

McGOWAN, CIRCUIT JUDGE.

This appeal, from a District Court order directing the Securities and Exchange Commission (SEC or Commission) to conduct further proceedings * * * involves * * * a request made of the Commission, and denied by it after seven years of proceedings, to promulgate rules requiring comprehensive disclosures by corporations of their environmental and equal employment policies.

The District Court held that the Commission had acted arbitrarily and capriciously in denying the petition.   Because we find the Commission's action sustainable under the scope of judicial review applicable to this case, we reverse. * * * [1]

On June 7, 1971, appellees petitioned the SEC to promulgate rules requiring corporate disclosure of environmental and equal employment information. * * * In the words of the District Court,

> The petition * * * proposed that companies which file with the SEC be required to describe with respect to each major activity or product, *inter alia:* (1) the nature and extent (quantified to the extent feasible) of the resulting pollution or injury to natural areas and resources, and (2) the feasibility of, and plans for, correcting the same.   The Petition also requested that the SEC require disclosure of whether the registered company has changed company products, projects, production methods, policies, investments or advertising to advance environmental values.
>
> In the equal employment opportunity area, that Petition requested that each company which makes public claims about its employment of minorities or women be required to include in its SEC filings statistical data by which the facts on this subject of major significance could be tested by interested persons.

This employment information would be no more than that information required to be filed by such companies with the Equal Employment Opportunity Commission under existing laws and regulations.   The Petition further requested that the SEC modify the definition of "material litigation", for which disclosure is required in SEC forms, so as to include all proceedings

---

1. The original rulemaking petitioners and plaintiffs in the District Court were the Natural Resources Defense Council, Inc. (NRDC), the Project on Corporate Responsibility, Inc., and the Center on Corporate Responsibility, Inc.   See *NRDC v. SEC*, 389 F.Supp. 689, 693 (D.D.C. 1974) [*NRDC I*].   By order of September 1, 1976, the following additional plaintiffs were joined: the National Organization for Women; the Unitarian Universalist Association; the American Baptist Home Mission Society; and the Province of St. Joseph of the Capuchin Order.   *NRDC v. SEC*, 432 F. Supp. 1190, 1197 n.17 (D.D.C. 1977) [*NRDC II*].   All of the foregoing are appellees here.

against a company under Title VII of the Civil Rights Act of 1964, 42 U.S.C. § 2000e et seq., or under the equal employment regulations covering federal contractors. * * *

The SEC declined to propose the rules they advocated, while proposing other rules requiring more limited forms of corporate disclosure. Securities Act Release No. 5235 (Feb. 16, 1972), 37 Fed. Reg. 4365 (1972). After a preliminary jurisdictional misstep,[2] appellees commenced this suit in District Court on March 2, 1973, as a challenge to the Commission's failure to propose the rules they sought.

After receiving and analyzing written comments on the Commission's rulemaking proposals in Release No. 5235, the SEC adopted part of the proposed rules in Securities Act Release No. 5386 (April 20, 1973), 38 Fed. Reg. 12100 (1973). The adopted rules required disclosure only of the *material* financial effects of corporate compliance with environmental laws.[3] Appellees thereupon supplemented their suit in District Court with challenges to the proceedings leading to Release No. 5386, and moved for summary judgment. The District Court agreed with appellees' position and held that the SEC's proceedings had been inadequate under the APA and NEPA. It remanded with instructions that fuller proceedings be conducted. * * *

> When the SEC reconsiders its rules in accordance with this opinion, it should develop a record and resolve two overriding factual issues. The first is the extent of "ethical investor" interest in the type of information which Plaintiffs have requested. The second issue is what avenues of action are available which ethical investors may pursue and which will tend to eliminate corporate practices that are inimical to the environment and equal employment opportunity.

On remand, the SEC issued Securities Act Release No. 5569 (Feb. 11, 1975), 40 Fed. Reg. 7013 (1975), giving notice of renewed proceedings to fulfill the District Court's instructions. The interest of the public in these proceedings was considerable. In nineteen days of public hearings, fifty-four oral presentations were made and three hundred fifty-three written comments received, creating a record over ten thousand pages long. In large measure, the views expressed were polarized as either in favor of, or in opposition to, appellees' proposal. The comments favoring the proposals generally declared that greater disclosure of information by corporations was essential both to sound voting on corporate policies and to informed consideration of corporate financial positions, in

2. The appellees initially sought review in this court of the SEC's refusal to propose the rules they sought. Their petition for review was dismissed on the ground that the Commission's action was not final agency action subject to judicial review. A later effort to petition this court for review was also dismissed for lack of jurisdiction.

3. Because the SEC did adopt these limited environmental disclosure rules, appellees attempt to characterize their complaint as a challenge to agency action, on the theory that the SEC did not go far enough, rather than as a claim based on the SEC's failure to act in adopting the particular rules they proposed. We find this theory disingenuous. Appellees do not object to the terms of the rules actually adopted, which the District Court has allowed to remain in effect pending further rulemaking action by the SEC. It is clear that their real grievance is with the Commission's nonadoption of the expanded disclosure rules they requested.

light of what the disclosed information would show with respect to environment and equal employment costs, and, generally speaking, the quality of the corporate management.   On the other hand, hundreds of corporations submitted comments opposing the disclosure proposals on the ground that the cost of gathering the required information would be inordinately high, that shareholders were not seriously interested in the information, and that the benefits would be small.

In October, 1975, and May, 1976, the SEC announced that it would not adopt the proposed disclosure rules, and issued lengthy explanatory statements.   Securities Act Releases Nos. 5627 (Oct. 16, 1975), 40 Fed. Reg. 51656 (1975), and 5704 (May 6, 1976), 41 Fed. Reg. 21632 (1976).   It argued, first, that its discretion to adopt particular disclosure requirements was very broad, depending in every case on balancing, in its expert judgment, the incremental value of the proposed disclosure against the potentially confusing effect on investors and the increased costs to registrants.   Despite this broad discretion, however, the Commission contended that its authority was limited to contexts related to the objectives of the federal securities laws.   And these laws, in the Commission's view, were designed generally to require disclosure of financial information in the narrow sense only.   * * *

Turning to its obligations under NEPA, the Commission concluded that * * *

> * * * although the NEPA does not require any specific disclosures, as such, we have been required to explain the alternatives which we considered in meeting our obligations under NEPA and the reasons why we have rejected substantial alternatives, in sufficient detail to permit judicial review.

In determining how best to fulfill these NEPA duties, the Commission considered five alternatives proposed during the proceedings:

> (1) comprehensive disclosures of the environmental effects of corporate activities, (2) disclosure of corporate noncompliance with applicable environmental standards, (3) disclosure of all pending environmental litigation, (4) disclosure of general corporate environmental policy, and (5) disclosure of all capital expenditures and expenses for environmental purposes.

All of these the Commission ultimately rejected.   From the summary of the record prepared by the SEC's staff, it appears that the SEC believed that alternatives (3), (4), and (5) had widespread support among commenters.   However, the record reveals that there was never much organized or documented support for those alternatives.   The appellees and the District Court did not treat them as significant.   Alternative (2) * * * received serious consideration but, after further comments, was rejected in Securities Act Release No. 5704.

Alternative (1) was the proposal of appellees herein.   The Commission rejected it for the following reasons:

> * * * First, the interest among investors that may exist appears to be primarily in whether corporations are acting in an environmentally unacceptable manner, rather than in whether, and to what extent, corporations have gone beyond what is expected of them in this area.   Second * * * [t]here

appears to be no established, uniform method by which the environmental effects of corporate practices may be comprehensively described. * * *

Moreover, there appears to be virtually no direct investor interest in voluminous information of this type. * * *

The Commission determined, finally, not to adopt appellees' equal employment proposals, although it noted that "[w]e will, of course, continue to reevaluate the need for such requirements from time to time." The Commission argued that existing disclosure provisions—which included rules explicitly requiring disclosure of certain economically material equal employment information—were sufficient to satisfy the primarily economic concerns of participants in the rulemaking proceeding. * * *

Following the SEC's rejection of appellees' proposal, the parties cross-moved in the District Court for summary judgment. The District Court granted appellees' motion, finding the SEC's action arbitrary and capricious on three principal grounds. First, and most important, the Court found it arbitrary that

> the Commission failed to consider the possibility of requiring disclosure of environmental information to shareholders (persons presently owning shares of a registrant corporation) solely in connection with proxy solicitations and information statements (provided to shareholders in connection with annual or other meetings) in order to promote "fair opportunity for the operation of corporate suffrage" without requiring identical disclosure in registration statements, prospectuses, and the like.

Second, the District Court found that the SEC's various assessments of costs to corporations and administrative burdens "all merely stand as bald assertions by the Commission," which the SEC had not substantiated, nor shown any serious effort in minimizing, before concluding they were excessive. Third, by refusing to work with the Council on Environmental Quality (CEQ) in developing SEC disclosure guidelines, but instead finding that comprehensive disclosure was the concern of CEQ and the Environmental Protection Agency in their own domain, the Commission violated the requirements of NEPA that it work together with CEQ on its own activity, thus "shunt[ing] aside [NEPA duties] in the bureaucratic shuffle."

The District Court also concluded that the Commission's determinations with respect to equal employment disclosure were arbitrary and capricious. * * *

The Commission * * * urges that the District Court erred because the SEC's decision not to adopt rules was nonreviewable. * * *

We think that judicial review was not precluded by the first section 701(a) exception. Neither the securities acts nor the APA, either expressly or by implication, evidence anything approaching a clear and convincing legislative intent to negate review. * * *

The second exception, that for actions committed to agency discretion by law, applies to those rare instances where " 'statutes are drawn in such broad terms that in a given case there is no law to apply.' " *Citizens to Preserve Overton Park.* In practice, the determination of whether there is "law" to apply necessarily turns on pragmatic considerations as to whether an agency determination is the proper subject of judicial review. In making this determination, we first identify as precisely as possible the aspects of the agency's action against which challenge is brought. We then evaluate the relevance of three particularly important factors: the need for judicial supervision to safeguard the interests of the plaintiffs; the impact of review on the effectiveness of the agency in carrying out its congressionally assigned role; and the appropriateness of the issues raised for judicial review. See *Hahn v. Gottlieb*, 430 F.2d 1243 (1st Cir. 1970). Finally, we inquire whether the considerations in favor of nonreviewability thus identified are sufficiently compelling to rebut the strong presumption of judicial review.

Appellees' challenge, upon analysis, can be seen to rest upon two somewhat different grounds. The first is that the SEC allegedly failed to comply with certain *procedures* mandated by NEPA. * * *

The second ground is purely substantive argument that the Commission's ultimate decision not to adopt the particular rules suggested by appellees was arbitrary and capricious. In this category falls appellees' entire challenge to the SEC's decision not to adopt equal employment rules, as well as their contention that the agency's analysis of the costs and benefits of environmental disclosure was not supported in the administrative record.

We distinguish between these grounds because, in our view, the reviewability analysis is quite different in the two cases. The first ground—appellees' procedural NEPA challenge—presents little difficulty. Congress, in NEPA, has commanded federal agencies, "to the fullest extent possible," 42 U.S.C.A. § 4332, to consider alternatives and consult with CEQ. Congress having imposed these duties on the SEC, appellees can argue with considerable force that their rights as participants in the rulemaking proceeding have been infringed by the SEC's alleged failures.

The SEC's effectiveness in carrying out its mandate will not, in our view, be greatly impaired by judicial review of its procedural compliance with NEPA. * * *

Appellees' challenge to the rationality of the SEC's decision not to adopt their proposed environmental and equal employment rules, however, presents a somewhat different calculus of interests among plaintiffs, agency, and court. This is so largely because the agency, in our view, was under no obligation to adopt rules identical to or even similar to those sought by appellees. * * * [T]he Commission has been vested by Congress with broad discretionary powers to promulgate (or not to promulgate) rules requiring disclosure of information beyond that specifically required by statute. * * *

The interest of plaintiffs in this context will thus rarely present unusual or compelling circumstances calling for judicial review. In the present case, for example, the SEC has not invaded any of appellees' substantive statutory or constitutional rights, nor singled them out for special and seemingly unfair treatment, nor even, indeed, taken any action to alter the *status quo ante*.

Judicial review will, to a limited extent, interfere with an agency's effective performance of its statutory mission. Requiring an agency to defend in court its decision not to adopt proposed rules will divert scarce institutional resources into an area that the agency in its expert judgment has already determined is not even worth the effort already expended. The danger of throwing good money after bad, moreover, also exists in a more subtle form because the very prospect of litigation may cause the agency to give a proposal more elaborate consideration than it might actually merit.

These considerations, however, are more compelling in the context of judicial review of an agency's denial of the initial rulemaking petition than where, as here, the agency has granted the petition and held extensive rulemaking proceedings. Obviously frivolous or unworkable proposals can be weeded out at the outset simply by denying the petition. When an agency agrees to conduct rulemaking proceedings, it evidences its view that the proposals are sufficiently meritorious to warrant further investigation, as well as its willingness to defend in court such rules as may be eventually be adopted. Thus, judicial review in this context would be relatively infrequent, would not be unjustifiable in terms of the merits of the proposals, and would not, in our view, seriously interfere with the agency's budget and personnel planning. * * *

Perhaps the strongest argument against reviewability is the concern that the issues posed will often not be well-suited for judicial resolution. An agency's discretionary decision *not* to regulate a given activity is inevitably based, in large measure, on factors not inherently susceptible to judicial resolution—e.g., internal management considerations as to budget and personnel; evaluations of its own competence; weighing of competing policies within a broad statutory framework. Further, even if an agency considers a particular problem worthy of regulation, it may determine for reasons lying within its special expertise that the time for action has not yet arrived. The area may be one of such rapid technological development that regulations would be outdated by the time they could become effective, or the scientific state of the art may be such that sufficient data are not yet available on which to premise adequate regulations. The circumstances in the regulated industry may be evolving in a way that could vitiate the need for regulation, or the agency may still be developing the expertise necessary for effective regulation.

Moreover, added to the problems already inherent in reviewing the record support for informal rulemaking decisions is the additional concern that, in the context of an agency's non-adoption of a rule, the record and reasons statement will be of little use to a reviewing court unless they are narrowly focused on the particular rule advocated by plaintiff or petitioner. There are an infinite number of rules that an agency could adopt in its discretion; unless the agency has carefully focused its considerations, judicial review will have an undesirably abstract and hypothetical quality. However, in a context like the present one, in which the agency has in fact held extensive rulemaking proceedings narrowly focused on the particular rules at issue, and has explained in detail its reasons for not adopting those rules, we believe that the questions posed will be amenable to at least a minimal level of judicial scrutiny.

Our conclusion is buttressed by two recent cases in which this court reviewed agency decisions not to promulgate rules. *National Black Media Coalition v. FCC*, 589 F.2d 578 (1978), was a challenge to an FCC decision not to adopt certain quantitative program standards for television broadcasters involved in comparative renewal proceedings. The standards had been proposed in detail by the FCC and had been the subject of extensive rulemaking proceedings, lasting six years and involving oral argument and extensive written comments. Although noting that "[t]he decision not to promulgate quantitative standards was a policy judgment traditionally left to agency discretion," the court reviewed the FCC's decision on the merits without explicitly considering the reviewability question.

Action for Children's Television v. FCC [564 F.2d 458 (1977)], was a challenge to an FCC decision not to adopt certain rules proposed by a public interest organization to improve children's television. As in *National Black Media Coalition*, the FCC held extensive rulemaking proceedings focused on the particular rules suggested. Again without explicitly considering the issue of reviewability, the court proceeded to uphold the FCC on the merits.

These cases, in our view, do not support a general rule that discretionary agency decisions not to adopt rules are reviewable *per se*. * * * Rather, *Action for Children's Television* and *National Black Media Coalition* stand for the more limited principle that, in light of the strong presumption of reviewability, discretionary decisions not to adopt rules are reviewable where, as here, the agency has in fact held a rulemaking proceeding and compiled a record narrowly focused on the particular rules suggested but not adopted. * * *

[Noting that "the considerations that counsel against judicial review of a decision not to adopt rules by informal rulemaking also call for us, when we do review, to exercise special deference," Judge McGowan, after many pages of careful analysis, upheld the SEC's actions. With respect to the requested rule on EEO disclosures the court was influenced by the SEC's practice of requiring such disclosures in specific proceedings where the information was deemed "material" under its existing disclosure rules. The court thus concluded that it was dealing not with inaction but with an agency's choice of form of action and that "the SEC may rationally choose to proceed by adjudication."]

Notes

1. Notwithstanding Judge McGowan's careful delineation of the exceptional circumstances that made the SEC's decision not to further regulate corporate disclosure reviewable, the court's subsequent application of the *NRDC* criteria has generally led to review of agency decisions not to regulate. In *WWHT Inc. v. Federal Communications Commission*, 656 F.2d 807 (D.C. Cir. 1981), for example, the court was asked to review the FCC's rejection of a petition for rulemak-

ing. In essence, the producers of subscription television programs had asked the FCC to make paid programming subject to the agency's general requirement that cable companies carry the signals generated by all television stations within their designated localities. The petition was filed pursuant to specific FCC rules governing requests for rulemaking, 47 C.F.R. § 1.401(a) (1979), and supporting and opposing comments were filed by several parties. After reviewing the comments the Commission denied the request for rulemaking and also denied an ancillary request for a declaratory ruling on the scope of the existing mandatory cable carriage rules.

Although noting that the case for reviewability of the FCC's denial of rulemaking was "even less compelling" than in *NRDC*, the court nevertheless thought that limited review could focus on the petition, the comments filed, and the FCC's letter explaining, pursuant to its regulations, its reasons for denying the petition. And, as in *NRDC*, review produced an affirmance of the Commission's determination.

Indeed, the court of appeal's scrutiny was so limited that the distinction between reviewability and nonreviewability now appears elusive. The court said (656 F.2d at 819):

> For us to seriously indulge petitioner's claims in this case would be to ignore the institutional disruption that would be visited on the Commission by our second guessing its expert determination not to pursue a particular program or policy at a given time. It would also require us to ignore the plain fact that the policy determinations made by the Commission in this case—as to the relative merits of a mandatory cable carriage of subscription television signals—raise issues that are not well suited for determination by this court. These considerations lead us to conclude that our review of the Commission's actions should be *extremely narrow,* consistent with the views heretofore expressed. The Commission's substantive determinations are essentially legislative in this case and are thus committed to the discretion of the agency.

Later, in *Center for Auto Safety v. National Highway Traffic Safety Administration,* 710 F.2d 842 (D.C. Cir. 1983), the court was asked to review NHTSA's termination of rulemaking as part of the Reagan Administration's "regulatory relief package" for the auto industry. NHTSA had issued an advance notice of proposed rulemaking seeking public comment on the types of fuel economy standards that should be promulgated for automobile model years 1985 and later. In essence, NHTSA justified its withdrawal of the ANPRM on the ground that market forces were producing a strong demand for fuel efficient cars, to which automobile manufacturers were responding sufficiently to make regulation unnecessary.

The Center sought review under the Motor Vehicle Information and Cost Saving Act, 15 U.S.C.A. § 2004(a) (1976), which authorizes judicial review of "any rule" adopted pursuant to various sections of that statute. The court held that the withdrawal of the ANPRM amounted to a determination, however informal, that manufacturer plans for voluntarily improving fuel economy were sufficient to meet the nation's energy conservation goals as specified in the statute. The court went on (710 F.2d at 846):

> These statements accompanying the withdrawal of the January notice clearly interpret the relevant statute and indicate NHTSA's policy regarding the exercise of discretion granted to it by that legislative enactment. Given our

prior decisions construing the Administrative Procedure Act's broad definition of "rule," we are compelled to conclude that NHTSA has prescribed a rule sufficient to grant this court jurisdiction. * * *

The court in *Center for Auto Safety* did not reach the merits, however, because it determined that NHSTA's action was not "ripe" for judicial review. NHSTA had said that it would continue to monitor the situation and would propose such additional regulations on fuel economy as seemed warranted. Having thus announced its vigilance while withholding regulatory action for the time being, NHSTA convinced the court that it had not yet taken "final agency action." The petitioners protested that, given the lead times necessary for compliance with fuel economy rules, it would never be clear that the agency had finally declined to regulate until it was too late for automobile manufacturers to comply with any rule that might be adopted. The court's refusal to review on ripeness grounds therefore appeared to them the equivalent of a holding of nonreviewability.

Judge MacKinnon, in a separate concurrence, agreed with the petitioners and would have premised the decision squarely on reviewability grounds (id. at 855–56):

> The case for holding the highway administration's decision to withdraw the January notice reviewable is far weaker than the case for finding the agency's decision reviewable in either *NRDC* or *WWHT.* While the Center has failed to identify any significant interest which would be protected by our review of the agency's decision, it is clear that such review would discourage the highway administration from seeking public input into its decision making process, thereby impairing its effectiveness. Furthermore, the record in this case is poorly suited for judicial review because it is not focussed on any particular amendment to the fuel economy standard.

But cf. *Investment Co. Institute v. FDIC*, 728 F.2d 518, 526 n.6 (D.C. Cir. 1984).

2. It should be apparent that the availability of judicial review of agency inaction, may depend on the language that Congress used in conveying and structuring the agency's authority. In the 1970's it became fashionable for regulatory laws, particularly in health, environmental, and energy fields, not only to direct agencies to develop regulations but to "build in" requirements designed to assure that such Congressional directions would be followed. One of the most common devices, and arguably one of the least successful, was to set deadlines for action. In many statutes Congress has specified that the administering agency "shall" promulgate regulations addressed to specific problem or activity within a prescribed period from date of enactment. An illustration is the 1976 Medical Devices Amendments to the Federal Food, Drug, and Cosmetic Act, Pub. L. No. 94–295, 90 Stat. 539 (1976), which included a requirement that the FDA, within 120 days, promulgate regulations governing the use of experimental devices in clinical research. 21 U.S.C.A. § 520 (g) (2) (A). The purpose of this deadline was to minimize disruption of clinical investigations in hospitals throughout the country without having to delay implementation of the entire scheme for regulation of medical experimentation. In the same legislation, however, Congress also specified that the FDA must afford at least 60 days for public comment on all proposed regulations—leaving the agency, in this case, a total of 60 calendar (not working) days to draft a proposal, evaluate comments, and prepare final rules. The FDA was three years late completing this 120-day assignment. See 45 Fed. Reg. 3732 (Jan. 18, 1980).

The FDA's experience with statutory deadlines for issuance of regulations is not unusual. For a treatment of the EPA experience, see R. MERRILL & P. HUTT, FOOD AND DRUG LAW 941–42 (1980). See generally Tomlinson, Report to the U.S. Administrative Conference on the Experience of Various Agencies with Statutory Time Limits Applicable to Licensing or Clearance Functions and to Rulemaking (1978). Courts have taken statutory deadlines seriously by entertaining suits to enforce them, but they rarely demand more than "good faith" efforts at compliance. E.g., *NRDC v. Train*, 510 F.2d 692 (D.C. Cir. 1974). In *Hercules, Inc. v. EPA*, 598 F.2d 91 (D.C. Cir. 1978), supra p. 472, the court approved the agency's omission of a tentative decision as well as compromises of the prohibition against combining functions because of the agency's need to meet deadlines imposed by statute and a previous consent decree.

3. Judicial willingness to review an agency's compliance with Congress's prescriptions for the timing or content of rulemaking may lead to a long and often frustrating relationship. The continuing judicial oversight of the Department of Education's (formerly DHEW's) implementation of desegregation orders in institutions of higher education throughout the southeastern United States, commencing with the famous case of *Adams v. Richardson*, 356 F.Supp. 92 (D.D.C.), *affirmed in part* 480 F.2d 1159 (D.C. Cir. 1973) (*en banc*), illustrates this phenomenon in a context where enforcement really involves a species of rulemaking.

Another example is provided by a series of cases in which representatives of migrant workers have pursued their demand that OSHA adopt a so-called "field sanitation standard," i.e., a rule designed to assure that farm workers have access to drinking water, lavatories, and other health-protective facilities. OSHA initiated investigations in 1973, referring the matter to an advisory committee which conducted hearings and prepared recommendations. When after more than a year OSHA had taken no further action, groups representing migrant workers sued to force the agency to complete the rulemaking process in accordance with 29 U.S.C.A. § 655(b), which sets precise time limits for all steps subsequent to consultation with an advisory committee. *National Congress of Hispanic American Citizens v. Usery*, 554 F.2d 1196 (D.C. Cir. 1977). While acknowledging that the Secretary of Labor had discretion to decide which workplace hazards to address, the plaintiffs contended that once he had commenced the rulemaking process, he was obligated to adhere to the statutory schedule. The court of appeals disagreed (554 F.2d at 1199–1200):

> This makes an absurdity of the Act and a fool out of Congress. We cannot agree. Since the Congress left such open-ended discretion in the Secretary at many key points in the Act * * * we find implicit acknowledgement that traditional agency discretion to alter priorities and defer action due to legitimate statutory considerations was preserved. If the Secretary may rationally order priorities and reallocate his resources at the point when 6(b)(1) through (4) becomes applicable, he should be able to do so at any rulemaking stage, so long as his discretion is honestly and fairly exercised. To hold otherwise would encourage refusals to initiate rulemaking and create incentives to deceive which anyone, including El Congreso, decries. As we see it, there is no sense in proceeding completely through the rulemaking process in accordance with El Congreso's claim that it is mandatory only to end up with the Secretary issuing a notice that the standard is not adopted.

But the court was also unwilling to remit the plaintiffs to the unguided sympathies of the agency, and its order contemplated a continuing role for the judiciary (id. at 1200): * * *

Upon remand the trial court should require the Secretary to file a report as to the present situation on each of these proposed standards, including the time-tables governing each.   If the court is not satisfied as to the sincerity of the effort of the Secretary in the processing of such standards, it should take such action as the circumstances require; if it is satisfied as to the same, it should hold the case on the docket for further report from the Secretary on the issu-ance of the standards.

The dispute was back before the court of appeals two years later. *National Congress of Hispanic American Citizens (El Congreso) v. Marshall*, 626 F.2d 882 (D.C. Cir. 1979), following a district court order directing the Secretary to "com-plete development of a field sanitation standard * * * as soon as possible." This order was a response to a series of agency submissions, which made clear that the field sanitation standard ranked low on its priorities and would not re-ceive serious attention within "the agency's 18-month planning horizon because of both generally limited agency resources" and its "relatively low priority." Before challenging the order, the Secretary had proffered a schedule that could have yielded a final standard by the end of 1979, but he reiterated that unantici-pated problems could cause yet further delays.   Shortly afterwards, the govern-ment moved to withdraw the schedule, explaining it did not reflect the priorities of the OSHA Administrator, who had been out of the country when it was pre-pared, and appealing the district court's order.

Writing for the court, Judge Leventhal reaffirmed OSHA's discretion to allo-cate its resources in accordance with its own assessment of need, the statutory timetable notwithstanding: "So long as his action is rational in the context of the statute, and is taken in good faith, the Secretary has authority to delay develop-ment of a standard at any stage as priorities demand."   The court, however, felt obliged to review the agency's choice under the arbitrary and capricious stan-dard.   In performing this function, Leventhal concluded that the district court had exceeded its role (626 F.2d at 889):

The district court's "own view of appropriate priorities" disregarded, without warrant, material findings made by the agency.   For example, the Secretary specifically concluded that rulemaking concerning the field sanita-tion standard would be quite lengthy, involving the allocation of substantial resources (approximately 3600 man-hours).   The Secretary also concluded that the greatest hazards to agricultural employees had already been reme-died, and that other industries merited allocation of the available resources (the accident rate in the agricultural industry was fifth among eight major groupings).   The district court emphasized almost exclusively the number of employees to be benefited, ignoring numerous other criteria considered by the Secretary such as the nature and the severity of the hazard exposure.

This court is of the view that greater respect is due the Secretary's judg-ment that promulgation of a cancer policy, a lead standard, an anhydrous amonia standard and the like, merited higher priority than a field sanitation standard.   With its broader perspective, and access to a broad range of un-dertakings, and not merely the program before the court, the agency has a better capacity than the court to make the comparative judgments involved in determining priorities and allocating resources.   The district court imper-missibly substituted its judgment for that of the agency.

But Leventhal was not prepared to leave matters as they stood.   He con-cluded with these instructions to the (by now no doubt exasperated) district court (id. at 890–91):

Where the Secretary deems a problem significant enough to warrant initiation of the standard setting process, the Act requires that he have a plan to shepherd through the development of the standard—that he takes pains, regardless of the press of other priorities, to ensure that the standard is not inadvertently lost in the process.

It is not enough for the Secretary merely to state that the standard will not be issued over the next 18 months. If other priorities preclude promulgation of a field sanitation standard within that frame, then the Secretary must provide a timetable—at least for the standard in question—which covers a larger period.

Upon remand to the district court, the Secretary should be granted leeway to reconsider the timetable submitted on January 22, 1979, since it was developed without input from the official charged with responsibility for this area. In constructing the timetable, the Secretary need not be constrained, as he would have been under the district court order, to rearrange priorities that were rationally set. But, the Secretary must give due regard to the principle, presumed in the timetable of 29 U.S.C. § 655(b)(2)–(4) and developed here, that once the process of developing a standard begins, a good faith effort must be made to complete it. It is for the district court to review the timetable submitted—not with regard to the Secretary's setting of priorities, which we have held in this instance to be a rational exercise of his discretionary powers, but with regard to the narrower concerns we have just delineated.

The story does not end here. While Labor Secretary Marshall submitted a new schedule for completing the rulemaking, the 1980 election intervened before any final decision—and the Reagan Administration found new priorities for OSHA. El Congreso was back in court in early 1984, and even as OSHA was promising to produce a final decision, it made clear that a probable outcome was a decision by the Secretary to withdraw the proposed standard on the ground that its costs outweighed its benefits. See *The Washington Post*, March 3, 1984, at A–18.

4. An agency's failure to regulate may not evidence inattention to the problem at hand but rather unhappiness with the tools it has been given. For example, section 4 of the Toxic Substances Control Act, 15 U.S.C.A. § 2603, authorizes the EPA to promulgate rules requiring safety testing of chemicals whose health effects have not been well-studied. The process for issuing such rules is a form of hybrid rulemaking, i.e., section 553 rulemaking accompanied by an oral hearing with opportunity for cross-examination on disputed critical issues of fact. 15 U.S.C.A. § 2603(b)(5). Congress also attempted to structure and accelerate the EPA's use of this power by establishing an interagency testing committee which is to recommend chemicals for testing, and by requiring the agency to act on its recommendations within 12 months. But EPA found that within the time period it could scarcely evaluate the committee's recommendations—with many of which it disagreed—much less complete rulemaking. See *Natural Resources Defense Council v. Costle*, 10 Env. L. Rep. 20274 (S.D.N.Y. 1980). And the prescribed procedure for promulgating rules, in the agency's judgment, assured that mandated studies would not be begun until two or three years after rulemaking commenced. The EPA accordingly sought to escape from these procedures. For their part, chemical manufacturers were prepared to forego the safeguards (and not unwelcome delay) associated with public rulemaking if they could dampen the EPA's expectations about the amount of testing that ought be performed.

What emerged was a process for negotiating testing agreements, in which manufacturers undertake to conduct or commission agreed-upon tests of specific chemicals on a specified timetable. In return, the EPA has declined to initiate rulemaking under section 4, accepting fewer tests than it might be able to mandate, but securing the promised information sooner.

Environmental organizations have been suspicious of this process, initially viewing it as another expression of procrastination in implementing the 1976 law. A suit by NRDC had previously resulted in a consent order under which the agency agreed to accelerate its responses to the testing committee's recommendations. *Natural Resources Defense Council v. Costle*, supra at 20277–78. Demands for access to the negotiation process itself have led EPA to invite public comment on each negotiated testing agreement before approving it. See 47 Fed. Reg. 335 (1982). A Government Accounting Office report concluded that the agency's approach, which has subordinated public rulemaking to establish testing requirements, was compatible with the statute. GAO, EPA Implementation of Selected Aspects of the Toxic Substances Control Act (Dec. 7, 1982). But NRDC has returned to court, successfully claiming that the negotiation process violates the EPA's statutory obligations. *Natural Resources Defense Council v. Ruckelshaus*, 595 F. Supp. 1255 (S.D.N.Y. 1984).

5. Informal dealings between an agency and private groups may entirely supplant public rulemaking. A notable example is an elaborate program for evaluating ingredient safety begun by the U.S. cosmetic industry in 1976. Cosmetics constituted the largest product category whose ingredients the FDA had not scheduled for review. While the agency's statute did not specifically authorize it to mandate safety testing for cosmetics, see *Toilet Goods Association v. Gardner*, 387 U.S. 158 (1967), infra p. 753, it had voiced to Congress concern about this gap in authority and privately toyed with the idea of constructing an ingredient review program through rulemaking.

The Cosmetic, Toiletry, and Fragrance Association (CTFA), seizing the initiative, set in motion an industry-funded program for reviewing the safety of all cosmetic ingredients and testing those on which information was lacking. The association sought frequently to consult with FDA officials to determine, and respond to, their views on the undertaking. These efforts precipitated a legal challenge from persons who found themselves excluded from a process likely to lead to a FDA decision to do nothing about cosmetic ingredient safety. Representatives of Consumers Union sought permission to attend one of the meetings that CTFA had scheduled with the FDA Commissioner; permission was denied on the ground—codified in the FDA's regulations—that any citizen may seek a private meeting with the Commissioner. Consumers Union filed suit, claiming that the meeting from which it was excluded and all subsequent meetings violated the Federal Advisory Committee Act. In *Consumers Union v. Department of HEW*, 409 F.Supp. 473 (D.D.C. 1976), *affirmed without opinion* 551 F.2d 466 (D.C. Cir. 1977), the agency prevailed, but the district court's account of events leaves little doubt that Consumer Union correctly perceived what was occurring (409 F.Supp. at 474–75, 476–77):

> In the area of testing cosmetic ingredients, FDA-CTFA efforts have increased in the past two years. * * * After three exploratory meetings between FDA and CTFA representatives in 1974 and two briefing meetings in early 1975, CTFA requested a meeting with FDA to discuss CTFA's draft proposal. This meeting was held on April 9, 1975, and detailed minutes were

kept for the session. * * * Following the filing of this lawsuit, a second meeting was held on September 17, 1975 to discuss CTFA's revised proposal. * * *

* * * The meetings complained of here were not ad hoc, amorphous or casual group meetings . * * * The FDA-CTFA conferences were the culmination of many months of planning, consulting, and revising. On the other hand * * * the two meetings were not called to consider proposals dealing with impending agency action. They were essentially consultations concerning the *group's own* proposal. * * *

Based on the record, the Court finds that CTFA was not advising the FDA about the cosmetic ingredient testing program. CTFA was presenting a voluntary, industry-sponsored proposal and seeking the FDA's comments and advice. * * * Granting that FDA had frequently expressed its concern for cosmetic ingredient testing, the Court finds that planning had evolved beyond agency control. CTFA in its own discretion was ultimately to decide whether or not to initiate a testing program. Such a relationship of agency and group does not rise to the level of a FACA "advisory" relationship.

Compare *Action for Childrens' Television v. FCC*, 564 F.2d 458 (D.C. Cir. 1977), supra p. 471, sustaining the FCC's decision to defer official action in favor of voluntary private efforts to address a problem.

D. TIMING OF JUDICIAL REVIEW

1. THE "FINAL ORDER" DOCTRINE

ENVIRONMENTAL DEFENSE FUND, INC. v. HARDIN

United States Court of Appeals, District of Columbia Circuit, 1970.
428 F.2d 1093.

BAZELON, CHIEF JUDGE.

This case requires the court to consider under what circumstances there may be a judicial remedy for the failure of an administrative agency to act promptly, and what form that remedy may take.

The shipment of pesticides in interstate commerce is regulated by the Federal Insecticide, Fungicide, and Rodenticide Act (FIFRA), which is administered by the Secretary of the Department of Agriculture. The Act requires pesticides and other "economic poisons" to carry labels bearing certain information, including any warnings necessary to prevent injury to people. A pesticide which fails to comply with the labelling requirement, or which cannot be rendered safe by any labelling, is "misbranded,"[2] and the Secretary must refuse or cancel its registration as an economic poison approved for shipment in interstate commerce.

The statute establishes an elaborate procedure by which a registration may be cancelled, that begins when the Secretary issues a notice of

---

2. The statutory labelling requirement at several points incorporates a substantive standard of product safety. * * * An insecticide is also misbranded if "when used as directed or in accordance with commonly recognized practice it shall be injurious to living man or other vertebrate animals, or vegetation, except weeds, to which it is applied, or to the person applying such economic poison." 7 U.S.C.A. § 135(z)(2)(g) (1964).

EMERGENCY ORDER

cancellation to a registrant.[4] Since the statutory procedures can easily occupy more than a year, the statute also gives the Secretary the power to suspend a registration immediately if he finds such action "necessary to prevent an imminent hazard to the public." Such an interim suspension triggers an expedited version of the procedure that can lead to cancellation.

Petitioners here are five organizations engaged in activities relating to environmental protection. On the basis of extensive evidence of the harmful effects of the pesticide DDT on human, plant, and animal life, they filed a petition with the Secretary of the Department of Agriculture requesting (1) the issuance of notices of cancellation for all economic poisons containing DDT, and (2) the suspension of registration for all such products pending the conclusion of cancellation proceedings. The Secretary issued notices of cancellation with respect to four uses of DDT, solicited comments concerning the remaining uses, and took no action on the request for interim suspension. Petitioners filed this appeal, seeking to compel the Secretary to comply with their request.

The Secretary moved to dismiss for lack of jurisdiction, asserting that petitioners lack standing to complain of his failure to act, that there is no final order ripe for review, that any final order would nevertheless be unreviewable because it involves questions committed by law to agency discretion, and that any available relief can be afforded only by the district court on a writ of mandamus, and not by the court of appeals.* Since we can accept none of those conclusions, the motion to dismiss must be denied, and the case remanded to the Secretary to provide this court with the record necessary for meaningful appellate review. * * *

The main thrust of respondents' argument is that the Secretary has issued no final order reviewable in this court. Petitioners asked the Secretary to take certain actions; he complied in part, and indicated that he was considering further compliance. Since he has neither granted nor denied much of the relief requested, respondents contend that his response to petitioners' request has not yet ripened into a reviewable order.

An order expressly denying the request for suspension or for cancellation would clearly be ripe for review. The doctrines of ripeness and finality are designed to prevent premature judicial intervention in the administrative process, before the administrative action has been fully

---

4. A registrant who receives a notice of cancellation may request the appointment of a special scientific advisory committee to study the matter. After the committee completes its independent study and submits its recommendations, the Secretary must make his determination. The registrant may then file objections and request a public hearing, after which the Secretary must make a new determination. 7 U.S.C.A. § 135b(c).

"Final orders of the Administrator * * * shall be subject to judicial review, in accordance with the provisions of subsection (d) of this section." 7 U.S.C.A. § 135b(c).

"In a case of actual controversy as to the validity of any order * * * any person who will be adversely affected by such order may obtain judicial review by filing in the [appropriate] United States court of appeals. * * * " Id. at § 135b(d).

Paragraph (d) specified that review should be under the substantial evidence standard. Eds.]

*[In 1970 the judicial review provisions of FIFRA provided in part:

considered, and before the legal dispute has been brought into focus.   No subsequent action can sharpen the controversy arising from a decision by the Secretary that the evidence submitted by petitioners does not compel suspension or cancellation of the registration of DDT.   In light of the urgent character of petitioners' claim, and the allegation that delay itself inflicts irreparable injury, the controversy is as ripe for judicial consideration as it can ever be.

Respondents suggest that the district court is the proper forum for any review that may be available, characterizing the petition as one for relief in the nature of mandamus.   We find it unnecessary to decide whether petitioners could have obtained relief from the district court, since the availability of that extraordinary remedy for the failure of an officer to perform his statutory duty need not bar statutory appellate review of the failure to act, when exigent circumstances render it equivalent to a final denial of petitioners' request.   * * *

It remains for us to determine whether, in the circumstances of this case, administrative inaction is the equivalent of an order denying relief.   Clearly relief delayed is not always equivalent to relief denied.   There are many factors that result in delay, and a court is in general ill-suited to review the order in which an agency conducts its business.   But when administrative inaction has precisely the same impact on the rights of the parties as denial of relief, an agency cannot preclude judicial review by casting its decision in the form of inaction rather than in the form of an order denying relief.

With regard to the request for interim suspension of the registration of DDT, we agree that inaction is tantamount to an order denying suspension.   The suspension power is designed to protect the public from an "imminent hazard"; if petitioners are right in their claim that DDT presents a hazard sufficient to warrant suspension, then even a temporary refusal to suspend results in irreparable injury on a massive scale.   The controversy over interim relief is ripe for judicial resolution, because the Secretary's inaction results in a final disposition of such rights as the petitioners and the public may have to interim relief.

Nevertheless, meaningful appellate review of the refusal to suspend DDT's registration is impossible in the absence of any record of administrative action.   The suspension decision is committed by statute to the Secretary; the role of the court is merely to ensure that he exercises his discretion within a reasonable time, and to ensure that his decision is supported by the record.   Therefore, we must remand the case to the Secretary, either for a fresh determination on the question of suspension, or for a statement of reasons for his silent but effective refusal to suspend the registration of DDT.   If he persists in denying suspension in the face of the impressive evidence presented by petitioners, then the basis for that decision should appear clearly on the record, not in conclusory terms but in sufficient detail to permit prompt and effective review.   In view of the emergency nature of the claim, we retain jurisdiction to permit respondents to provide us, within thirty days, with the record necessary for review.

With respect to the request for notices of cancellation, we are more reluctant to equate a tentative and equivocal delay with an outright denial of the request. The Secretary has made a few feeble gestures in the direction of compliance with the request, and further action is apparently under consideration. But the statutory scheme of the FIFRA itself contemplates a lengthy inquiry into the conditions for the safe use of an economic poison before its registration may finally be cancelled. Since the issuance of cancellation notices merely triggers that administrative mechanism, it is questionable whether the Secretary may properly defer the decision to issue notices in order to engage in a preliminary inquiry not contemplated by the statute.

At some point administrative delay amounts to a refusal to act, with sufficient finality and ripeness to permit judicial review. The present record does not permit us to determine whether that point has been reached here. On remand, the Secretary should either decide on the record whether to issue the remaining requested cancellation notices, or explain the reasons for deferring the decision still further. In light of that record, and in view of his disposition of the request for interim relief, the court will be in a better position to evaluate the impact of any further delay and decide whether judicial relief is appropriate.

Remanded for further proceedings in accordance with this opinion.

Notes

1. In *Nor-Am Agricultural Products, Inc. v. Hardin,* 435 F.2d 1151, 1157–58 (7th Cir. 1970) (*en banc*), *cert. dismissed* 402 U.S. 935 (1971), the Seventh Circuit dismissed a suit to enjoin a USDA order suspending registration of certain fungicides. The producers contended that emergency suspension "immediately and drastically affect[ed] their rights and interests as greatly as formally finalized cancellation" and that review following a cancellation hearing would not adequately test the Secretary's determination that the fungicides posed an "imminent hazard to the public." The majority opinion responded that emergency suspension "involves highly discretionary administrative action with deeply rooted antecedents in the realm of public health and safety. * * * The administrative process [would be] interrupted before issues have been crystalized and narrowed and without affording opportunity for application of technical expertise and informed judgment." The majority found *EDF v. Hardin* inapplicable, noting that in that case no further administrative proceedings were available to the plaintiffs. In *Nor-Am,* by contrast, the formal cancellation hearing required by FIFRA to accompany any suspension would sharpen the controversy surrounding the Secretary's suspension decision.

2. Would not the *Nor-Am* rule effectively preclude judicial review of suspension orders under FIFRA? How likely is it that a court would ultimately conclude that the USDA's "imminent hazard" determination was erroneous even though its subsequent order of cancellation was proper? And if, after a hearing, USDA decided that registrations should not be cancelled and thereupon rescinded the suspension order would the registrants be in a position to contest the earlier ruling? What relief would be available to the producers if they should eventually persuade a court that suspension was improper?

ENVIRONMENTAL DEFENSE FUND, INC. v. RUCKELSHAUS

United States Court of Appeals, District of Columbia Circuit, 1971.
439 F.2d 584.

BAZELON, CHIEF JUDGE.

This is a petition for review of an order of the Secretary of Agriculture, refusing to suspend the federal registration of the pesticide DDT or to commence the formal administrative procedures that could terminate that registration. We conclude that the order was based on an incorrect interpretation of the controlling statute, and accordingly remand the case for further proceedings. * * *

We are not persuaded to reach a different result by the recent by the recent opinion of the Seventh Circuit in *Nor-Am Agricultural Products, Inc. v. Hardin.* * * *

* * * In the view of the *Nor-Am* court, a suspension order lacks the finality that is a prerequisite both to statutory review in the court of appeals under the FIFRA, and to review in any court under the Administrative Procedure Act. In the view of the *Nor-Am* court, judicial review under the FIFRA is limited to those orders made after full administrative adjudication on the record. The court acknowledged that an exception might be made for orders denying suspension, like the order involved in this case, because an order denying suspension may terminate the administrative process. But an order granting suspension will always be followed by further administrative proceedings, and therefore it is not ripe for review. * * *

We do not find in the FIFRA any conclusive indication that Congress intended to limit review to those orders made after advisory committee proceedings and a public hearing. * * * Congress contemplated that judicial review would ordinarily occur at the instance of the manufacturer, after advisory committee proceedings and a public hearing. But [the statute does] * * * not make advisory committee proceedings or a public hearing a jurisdictional prerequisite to review. In the first place, statutory review is available to persons other than the manufacturer, who may have no right to call for advisory committee proceedings or a public hearing. In the second place, the manufacturer himself may in some circumstances be entitled to judicial review of an administrative determination that is not subject to further consideration in subsequent administrative proceedings. In either case, the lack of a committee report and a hearing record may limit the scope of review, but it does not preclude review entirely.

Nor can we find in the statutory scheme any support for the *Nor-Am* distinction between orders granting and denying suspension. For the administrative proceedings that follow suspension are equally available after a refusal to suspend. If the Secretary orders suspension, the proceedings are expedited; otherwise they may follow in due course after he issues cancellation notices. In either event, there is a prospect of further administrative action, but that prospect does not resolve for us the question of reviewability. The subsequent proceedings are designed solely to resolve the ultimate question whether cancellation is warranted, and not to shed any further light on the question whether there is a sufficient threat of "imminent hazard" to warrant suspension in the interim. Once the Secretary has made a decision with respect to suspension, whether he decides to grant or to deny that relief, the "imminence" of the hazard is no longer at issue. To determine whether an order relating to suspension is reviewable, therefore, it is necessary to look beyond the mere availability of further administrative proceedings and consider whether the impact of the order is sufficiently "final" to warrant review in the context of the particular case.

     * * * The court emphasized the fact that the *Nor-Am* suspension order threatened harm primarily to plaintiff's private interest in business profits. This case, on the other hand, involves an order denying suspension, which threatens harm to the public interest in health and safety. It might be argued that harm to the public health is more serious and irreparable than private economic injury. * * *

     A threat of economic injury has always been regarded as sufficient, however, for the purpose of finding an order final and reviewable. In our view, a suspension order, like an order denying suspension, is subject to judicial review in a proper case. * * *

     In this case, however, we need not decide in what circumstances an order granting suspension is subject to judicial review. We decide only that an order denying suspension on the ground that there is no threat of "imminent hazard" is sufficiently final in its impact to warrant judicial review under the FIFRA.

     Turning from suspension to the question of cancellation notices, we find substantial merit in the distinction suggested by *Nor-Am*. That is, a decision of the Secretary to issue cancellation notices is not reviewable, because it merely sets in motion the administrative process that terminates in a reviewable final order. An unqualified refusal to issue notices, on the other hand, operates with finality as an administrative rejection of the claim that cancellation is required.

     If the Secretary had simply refused to issue the requested notices of cancellation, we would have no difficulty concluding that his order was a final order, ripe for review in this court in accordance with the FIFRA. Here, however, the Secretary has taken the position that investigations are still in progress, that final determinations have not yet been made concerning the uses for which cancellation notices have not yet issued. Therefore, with respect to the cancellation notices, we treat the petition as a request for relief in the nature of mandamus, to compel the Secretary to issue notices as required by statute. * * *

     Not only the legislative history, but also the statutory scheme itself points to the conclusion that the FIFRA requires the Secretary to issue notices and thereby initiate the administrative process whenever there is a substantial question about the safety of a registered pesticide. * * *

     In this case the Secretary has made a number of findings with respect to DDT. On the basis of the available scientific evidence he has concluded that (1) DDT in large doses has produced cancer in test animals and various injuries in man, but in small doses its effect on man is unknown; (2) DDT is toxic to certain birds, bees, and fish, but there is no evidence of harm to the vast majority of species of nontarget organisms; (3) DDT has important beneficial uses in connection with disease control and protection of various crops.   These and other findings led the Secretary to conclude "[t]hat the use of DDT should continue to be reduced in an orderly, practicable manner which will not deprive mankind of uses which are essential to the public health and welfare.   To this end there should be continuation of the comprehensive study of essentiality of particular uses and evaluations of potential substitutes."

There is no reason, however, for that study to be conducted outside the procedures provided by statute.   The Secretary may, of course, conduct a reasonable preliminary investigation before taking action under the statute. * * * But when, as in this case, he reaches the conclusion that there is a substantial question about the safety of a registered item, he is obliged to initiate the statutory procedure that results in referring the matter first to a scientific advisory committee and then to a public hearing.   We recognize, of course, that one important function of that procedure is to afford the registrant an opportunity to challenge the initial decision of the Secretary.   But the hearing, in particular, serves other functions as well.   Public hearings bring the public into the decision-making process, and create a record that facilitates judicial review.   If hearings are held only after the Secretary is convinced beyond a doubt that cancellation is necessary, then they will be held too seldom and too late in the process to serve either of those functions effectively.

The Secretary's statement in this case makes it plain that he found a substantial question concerning the safety of DDT, which in his view warranted further study.   Since we have concluded that that is the standard for the issuance of cancellation notices under the FIFRA, the case must be remanded to the Secretary with instructions to issue notices with respect administrative process. * * *

Petitioners do not challenge the Secretary's determination of the kinds of harm that may be associated with DDT.   They argue that his estimate of the probability that harm will occur is too low, in light of the available reports of scientific studies.   They also argue that he has set the standard of proof too high, in light of the clear legislative purpose.   On the first point, we think it appropriate in the circumstances of this case to defer to the administrative judgment.   We have neither an evidentiary record, nor the scientific expertise, that would permit us to review the Secretary's findings with respect to the probability of harm.   We have found no error of law that infects the Secretary's inferences from the scientific data.   And we have recognized that it is particularly appropriate to defer to administrative findings of fact in reviewing a decision on a question of interim relief.

The second part of the petitioners' challenge, however, is entirely appropriate for judicial consideration at this time.   The formulation of standards for suspension is entrusted to the Secretary in the first instance, but the court has an obligation to ensure that the administrative standards conform to the legislative purpose, and that they are uniformly applied in individual cases.

The statute provides for suspension in order "to prevent an imminent hazard to the public." Congress clearly intended to protect the public from some risks by summary administrative action pending further procedings. The administrator's problem is to determine which risks fall in that class. The Secretary has made no attempt to deal with that problem, either by issuing regulations relating to suspension, or by explaining his decision in this case. If regulations of general applicability were formulated, it would of course be possible to explain individual decisions by reference to the appropriate regulation. It may well be, however, that standards for suspension can best be developed piecemeal, as the Secretary evaluates the hazards presented by particular products. Even so, he has an obligation to articulate the criteria that he develops in making each individual decision. We cannot assume, in the absence of adequate explanation, that proper standards are implicit in every exercise of administrative discretion.

Since the Secretary has not yet provided an adequate explanation for his decision to deny interim relief in this case, it will be necessary to remand the case once more, for a fresh determination on that issue. On remand, the Secretary should consider whether the information presently available to him calls for suspension of any registrations of products containing DDT, identifying the factors relevant to that determination, and relating the evidence to those factors in a statement of the reasons for his decision.

Notes

In *Dow Chemical Co. Ruckelshaus*, 477 F.2d 1317 (8th Cir. 1973), and *Pax Co. v. United States*, 454 F.2d 93 (10th Cir. 1972), producers sought immediate district court review of notices to cancel registrations for certain pesticides. Both courts declined to review on the ground that a cancellation notice only started the formal administrative process, and did not interrupt continued marketing or use of the pesticides. If the Administrator ultimately cancelled the registrations after hearing, review could be had in a court of appeals. The *Dow* court explained its reasoning in the following terms (477 F.2d at 1325–26):

The reason for the statutory framework is not difficult to comprehend. Without the full record contemplated by the statute for review of final orders a court is not in a position properly to evaluate the basic validity of such asserted facts. * * * All of this may be done in accordance with the statute, at a hearing preceded by the sharpening process of the Administrative prehearing. But this is not yet a final order, thus clearly distinguishable from cases hereinabove cited, such as *EDF v. Hardin*, wherein elaboration of reasons in final orders were required for the purpose of adequate judicial review thereof. * * *

2. PRE-ENFORCEMENT REVIEW

ABBOTT LABORATORIES v. GARDNER

Supreme Court of the United States, 1967.
387 U.S. 136, 87 S.Ct. 1507, 18 L.Ed.2d 681.

MR. JUSTICE HARLAN delivered the opinion of the Court.

In 1962 Congress amended the Federal Food, Drug, and Cosmetic Act to require manufacturers of prescription drugs to print the "established name" of the drug "prominently and in type at least half as large as that used thereon for any proprietary name or designation for such drug," on labels and other printed material. The "established name" is one designated by the Secretary of Health, Education, and Welfare pursuant to § 502(e)(2) of the Act, 21 U.S.C.A. § 352(e)(2); the "proprietary name" is usually a trade name under which a particular drug is marketed. The underlying purpose of the 1962 amendment was to bring to the attention of doctors and patients the fact that many of the drugs sold under familiar trade names are actually identical to drugs sold under their "established" or less familiar trade names at significantly lower prices. The Commissioner of Food and Drugs, exercising authority delegated to him by the Secretary, published proposed regulations designed to implement the statute. After inviting and considering comments submitted by interested parties the Commissioner promulgated the following regulation for the "efficient enforcement" of the Act, § 701(a), 21 U.S.C.A. § 371(a):

> "If the label or labeling of a prescription drug bears a proprietary name or designation for the drug or any ingredient thereof, the established name, if such there be, corresponding to such proprietary name or designation, shall accompany each appearance of such proprietary name or designation."

A similar rule was made applicable to advertisements for prescription drugs.

The present action was brought by a group of 37 individual drug manufacturers and by the Pharmaceutical Manufacturers Association, of which all the petitioner companies are members, and which includes manufacturers of more than 90% of the Nation's supply of prescription drugs. They challenged the regulations on the ground that the Commissioner exceeded his authority under the statute by promulgating an order requiring labels, advertisements, and other printed matter relating to prescription drugs to designate the established name of the particular drug involved every time its trade name is used anywhere in such material.

The District Court, on cross motions for summary judgment, granted the declaratory and injunctive relief sought, finding that the statute did not sweep so broadly as to permit the Commissioner's "every time" interpretation. The Court of Appeals for the Third Circuit reversed without reaching the merits of the case. 352 F.2d 286. It held first that under the statutory scheme provided by the Federal Food, Drug, and Cosmetic Act pre-enforcement[1] review of these regulations was unauthorized and

---

1. That is, a suit brought by one before any attempted enforcement of the statute or regulation against him.

therefore beyond the jurisdiction of the District Court. Second, the Court of Appeals held that no "actual case or controversy" existed and, for that reason, that no relief under the Administrative Procedure Act, or under the Declaratory Judgment Act, was in any event available. * * *

The first question we consider is whether Congress by the Federal Food, Drug, and Cosmetic Act intended to forbid pre-enforcement review of this sort of regulation promulgated by the Commissioner. The question is phrased in terms of "prohibition" rather than "authorization" because a survey of our cases shows that judicial review of a final agency action by an aggrieved person will not be cut off unless there is persuasive reason to believe that such was the purpose of Congress. Early cases in which this type of judicial review was entertained have been reinforced by the enactment of the Administrative Procedure Act, which embodies the basic presumption of judicial review to one "suffering legal wrong because of agency action, or adversely affected or aggrieved by agency action within the meaning of a relevant statute," 5 U.S.C.A. § 702, so long as no statute precludes such relief or the action is not one committed by law to agency discretion, 5 U.S.C.A. § 701(a). The Administrative Procedure Act provides specifically not only for review of "[a]gency action made reviewable by statute" but also for review of "final agency action for which there is no other adequate remedy in a court," 5 U.S.C.A. § 704. The legislative material elucidating that seminal act manifests a congressional intention that it cover a broad spectrum of administrative actions,[2] and this Court has echoed that theme by noting that the Administrative Procedure Act's "generous review provisions" must be given a "hospitable" interpretation. * * *

Given this standard, we are wholly unpersuaded that the statutory scheme in the food and drug area excludes this type of action. The Government relies on no explicit statutory authority for its argument that pre-enforcement review is unavailable, but insists instead that because the statute includes a specific procedure for such review of certain enumerated kinds of regulations, not encompassing those of the kind involved here, other types were necessarily meant to be excluded from any pre-enforcement review. The issue, however, is not so readily resolved; we must go further and inquire whether in the context of the entire legislative scheme the existence of that circumscribed remedy evinces a congressional purpose to bar agency action not within its purview from judicial review. * * *

In this case the Government has not demonstrated such a purpose; indeed, a study of the legislative history shows rather conclusively that the specific review provisions* were designed to give an additional remedy and not to cut down more traditional channels of review. * * *

2. See H. R. Rep. No. 1980, 79th Cong., 2d Sess., 41 (1946): "To preclude judicial review under this bill a statute, if not specific in withholding such review, must upon its face give clear and convincing evidence of an intent to withhold it. The mere failure to provide specially by statute for judicial review is certainly no evidence of intent to withhold review."

*[Section 701(e) of the FD&C Act provides for pre-enforcement court of appeals review of certain types of FDA regulations promulgated following formal rulemaking, but clearly does not provide a basis for review of the regulation challenged in this case. Eds.]

This conclusion is strongly buttressed by the fact that the Act itself, in § 701(f)(6), states, "The remedies provided for in this subsection shall be in addition to and not in substitution for any other remedies provided by law." This saving clause was passed over by the Court of Appeals without discussion. In our view, however, it bears heavily on the issue, for if taken at face value it would foreclose the Government's main argument in this case. The Government deals with the clause by arguing that it should be read as applying only to review of regulations under the sections specifically enumerated in § 701(e). This is a conceivable reading, but it requires a considerable straining both of language and of common understanding. The saving clause itself contains no limitations, and it requires an artificial statutory construction to read a general grant of a right to judicial review begrudgingly, so as to cut out agency actions that a literal reading would cover. * * *

The only other argument of the Government requiring attention on the preclusive effect of the statute is that *Ewing v. Mytinger & Casselberry, Inc.*, 339 U.S. 594, counsels a restrictive view of judicial review in the food and drug area. In that case the Food and Drug Administrator found that there was probable cause that a drug was "adulterated" because it was misbranded in such a way as to be "fraudulent" or "misleading to the injury or damage of the purchaser or consumer." Multiple seizures were ordered through libel actions. The manufacturer of the drug brought an action to challenge directly the Administrator's finding of probable cause. This Court held that the owner could raise his constitutional, statutory, and factual claims in the libel actions themselves, and that the mere finding of probable cause by the Administrator could not be challenged in a separate action. That decision was quite clearly correct, but nothing in its reasoning or holding has any bearing on this declaratory judgment action challenging a promulgated regulation.

The Court in *Ewing* first noted that the "administrative finding of probable cause required by § 304(a) is merely the statutory prerequisite to the bringing of the lawsuit," at which the issues are aired. Such a situation bears no analogy to the promulgation, after formal procedures, of a rule that must be followed by an entire industry. To equate a finding of probable cause for proceeding against a particular drug manufacturer with the promulgation of a self-operative industry-wide regulation, such as we have here, would immunize nearly all agency rulemaking activities from the coverage of the Administrative Procedure Act.

Second, the determination of probably cause in *Ewing* has "no effect in and of itself"; only some action consequent upon such a finding could give it legal life. As the Court there noted, like a determination by a grand jury that there is probable cause to proceed against an accused, it is a finding which only has vitality once a proceeding is commenced, at which time appropriate challenges can be made. The Court also noted that the unique type of relief sought by the drug manufacturer was inconsistent with the policy of the Act favoring speedy action against goods in circulation that are believed on probable cause to be adulterated. Also, such relief was not specifically granted by the Act, which did provide another type of relief in the form of a consolidation of multiple libel actions in a convenient venue.

The drug manufacturer in *Ewing* was quite obviously seeking an unheard-of form of relief which, if allowed, would have permitted interference in the early stages of an administrative determination as to specific facts, and would have prevented the regular operation of the seizure procedures established by the Act. That the Court refused to permit such an action is hardly authority for cutting off the well-established jurisdiction of the federal courts to hear, in appropriate cases, suits under the Declaratory Judgment Act and the Administrative Procedure Act challenging final agency action of the kind present here.

We conclude that nothing in the Food, Drug, and Cosmetic Act itself precludes this action.

A further inquiry must, however, be made. The injunctive and declaratory judgment remedies are discretionary, and courts traditionally have been reluctant to apply them to administrative determinations unless these arise in the context of a controversy "ripe" for judicial resolution. Without undertaking to survey the intricacies of the ripeness doctrine it is fair to say that its basic rationale is to prevent the courts, through avoidance of premature adjudication, from entangling themselves in abstract disagreements over administrative policies, and also to protect the agencies from judicial interference until an administrative decision has been formalized and its effects felt in a concrete way by the challenging parties. The problem is best seen in a twofold aspect, requiring us to evaluate both the fitness of the issues for judicial decision and the hardship to the parties of withholding court consideration.

As to the former factor, we believe the issues presented are appropriate for judicial resolution at this time. First, all parties agree that the issue tendered is a purely legal one: whether the statute was properly construed by the Commissioner to require the established name of the drug to be used *every time* the proprietary name is employed.[16] Both sides moved for summary judgment in the District Court, and no claim is made here that further administrative proceedings are contemplated. It is suggested that the justification for this rule might vary with different circumstances, and that the expertise of the Commissioner is relevant to passing upon the validity of the regulation. This of course is true, but the suggestion overlooks the fact that both sides have approached this case as one purely of congressional intent, and that the Government made no effort to justify the regulation in factual terms.

Second, the regulations in issue we find to be "final agency action" within the meaning of § 10 of the Administrative Procedure Act, 5 U.S.C.A. § 704, as construed in judicial decisions. An "agency action" includes any "rule," defined by the Act as "an agency statement of general or particular applicability and future effect designed to implement, interpret, or

---

16. While the "every time" issue has been framed by the parties in terms of statutory *compulsion*, we think that its essentially legal character would not be different had it been framed in terms of statutory *authorization* for the requirement.

prescribe law or policy." The cases dealing with judicial review of administrative actions have interpreted the "finality" element in a pragmatic way. Thus in *Columbia Broadcasting System v. United States*, 316 U.S. 407, * * * this Court held reviewable a regulation of the Federal Communications Commission setting forth certain proscribed contractual arrangements between chain broadcasters and local stations. The FCC did not have direct authority to regulate these contracts, and its rule asserted only that it would not license stations which maintained such contracts with the networks. Although no license had in fact been denied or revoked, and the FCC regulation could properly be characterized as a statement only of its intentions, the Court held that "Such regulations have the force of law before their sanctions are invoked as well as after. When, as here, they are promulgated by order of the Commission and the expected conformity to them causes injury cognizable by a court of equity, they are appropriately the subject of attack. * * * "

Two more recent cases have taken a similarly flexible view of finality. In *Frozen Food Express v. United States*, 351 U.S. 40, at issue was an Interstate Commerce Commission order specifying commodities that were deemed to fall within the statutory class of "agricultural commodities." Vehicles carrying such commodities were exempt from ICC supervision. An action was brought by a carrier that claimed to be transporting exempt commodities, but which the ICC order had not included in its terms. Although the dissenting opinion noted that this ICC order had no authority except to give notice of how the Commission interpreted the Act and would have effect only if and when a particular action was brought against a particular carrier, and argued that "judicial intervention [should] be withheld until administrative action has reached its complete development," the Court held the order reviewable.

Again, in *United States v. Storer Broadcasting Co.*, 351 U.S. 192, the Court held to be a final agency action within the meaning of the Administrative Procedure Act an FCC regulation announcing a Commission policy that it would not issue a television license to an applicant already owning five such licenses, even though no specific application was before the Commission. The Court stated: "The process of rulemaking was complete. It was final agency action * * * by which Storer claimed to be 'aggrieved.' "

We find decision in the present case following *a fortiori* from these precedents. The regulation challenged here, promulgated in a formal manner after announcement in the Federal Register and consideration of comments by interested parties is quite clearly definitive. There is no hint that this regulation is informal, see *Helco Products Co. v. McNutt*, 78 U.S. App. D.C. 71, 137 F.2d 681 (1943), or only the ruling of a subordinate official, see *Swift & Co. v. Wickham*, D.C., 230 F.Supp. 398, 409, aff'd, 364 F.2d 241 (1966), or tentative. It was made effective upon publication, and the Assistant General Counsel for Food and Drugs stated in the District Court that compliance was expected.

The Government argues, however, that the present case can be distinguished from cases like *Frozen Food Express* on the ground that in those instances the agency involved could implement its policy directly, while here the Attorney General must authorize criminal and seizure actions for violations of the statute.   In the context of this case, we do not find this argument persuasive.   These regulations are not meant to advise the Attorney General, but purport to be directly authorized by the statute.   Thus, if within the Commissioner's authority, they have the status of law and violations of them carry heavy criminal and civil sanctions. Also, there is no representation that the Attorney General and the Commissioner disagree in this area; the Justice Department is defending this very suit.   It would be adherence to a mere technicality to give any credence to this contention.   Moreover, the agency does have direct authority to enforce this regulation in the context of passing upon applications for clearance of new drugs, § 505, 21 U.S.C.A. § 355, or certification of certain antibiotics, § 507, 21 U.S.C.A. § 357.

This is also a case in which the impact of the regulations upon the petitioners is sufficiently direct and immediate as to render the issue appropriate for judicial review at this stage.   These regulations purport to give an authoritative interpretation of a statutory provision that has a direct effect on the day-to-day business of all prescription drug companies; its promulgation puts petitioners in a dilemma that it was the very purpose of the Declaratory Judgment Act to ameliorate.   As the District Court found on the basis of uncontested allegations, "Either they must comply with the every time requirement and incur the costs of changing over their promotional material and labeling or they must follow their present course and risk prosecution."   228 F.Supp. 855, 861.   The regulations are clear-cut, and were made effective immediately upon publication; as noted earlier the agency's counsel represented to the District Court that immediate compliance with their terms was expected.   If petitioners wish to comply they must change all their labels, advertisements, and promotional materials; they must destroy stocks of printed matter; and they must invest heavily in new printing type and new supplies.   The alternative to compliance—continued use of material which they believe in good faith meets the statutory requirements, but which clearly does not meet the regulation of the Commissioner—may be even more costly.   That course would risk serious criminal and civil penalties for the unlawful distribution of "misbranded" drugs.

It is relevant at this juncture to recognize that petitioners deal in a sensitive industry, in which public confidence in their drug products is especially important.   To require them to challenge these regulations only as a defense to an action brought by the Government might harm them severely and unnecessarily.   Where the legal issue presented is fit for judicial resolution, and where a regulation requires an immediate and significant change in the plaintiffs' conduct of their affairs with serious penalties attached to noncompliance, access to the courts under the Administrative Procedure Act and the Declaratory Judgment Act must be permitted, absent a statutory bar or some other unusual circumstance, neither of which appears here.   * * *

The Government further contends that the threat of criminal sanctions for noncompliance with a judicially untested regulation is unrealistic; the Solicitor General has represented that if court enforcement becomes necessary, "the Department of Justice will proceed only civilly for an injunction * * * or by condemnation." We cannot accept this argument as a sufficient answer to petitioners' petition. This action at its inception was properly brought and this subsequent representation of the Department of Justice should not suffice to defeat it.

Finally, the Government urges that to permit resort to the courts in this type of case may delay or impede effective enforcement of the Act. We fully recognize the important public interest served by assuring prompt and unimpeded administration of the Pure Food, Drug, and Cosmetic Act, but we do not find the Government's argument convincing. First, in this particular case, a pre-enforcement challenge by nearly all prescription drug manufacturers is calculated to speed enforcement. If the Government prevails, a large part of the industry is bound by the decree; if the Government loses, it can more quickly revise its regulation.

The Government contends, however, that if the Court allows this consolidated suit, then nothing will prevent a multiplicity of suits in various jurisdictions challenging other regulations. The short answer to this contention is that the courts are well equipped to deal with such eventualities. The venue transfer provision, 28 U.S.C.A. § 1404(a), may be invoked by the Government to consolidate separate actions. Or, actions in all but one jurisdiction might be stayed pending the conclusion of one proceeding. A court may even in its discretion dismiss a declaratory judgment or injunctive suit if the same issue is pending in litigation elsewhere. * * *

Further, the declaratory judgment and injunctive remedies are equitable in nature, and other equitable defenses may be interposed. If a multiplicity of suits are undertaken in order to harass the Government or to delay enforcement, relief can be denied on this ground alone. * * *

In addition to all these safeguards against what the Government fears, it is important to note that the institution of this type of action does not by itself stay the effectiveness of the challenged regulation. There is nothing in the record to indicate that petitioners have sought to stay enforcement of the "every time" regulation pending judicial review. If the agency believes that a suit of this type will significantly impede enforcement or will harm the public interest, it need not postpone enforcement of the regulation and may oppose any motion for a judicial stay on the part of those challenging the regulation. It is scarcely to be doubted that a court would refuse to postpone the effective date of an agency action if the Government could show, as it made no effort to do here, that delay would be detrimental to the public health or safety. * * *

Lastly, although the Government presses us to reach the merits of the challenge to the regulation in the event we find the District Court properly entertained this action, we believe the better practice is to remand the case to the Court of Appeals for the Third Circuit to review the District Court's decision that the regulation was beyond the power of the Commissioner.

Reversed and remanded.

MR. JUSTICE BRENNAN took no part in the consideration or decision of this case.

TOILET GOODS ASSOCIATION v. GARDNER

Supreme Court of the United States, 1967.
387 U.S. 158, 87 S.Ct. 1520, 18 L.Ed.2d 697.

MR. JUSTICE HARLAN delivered the opinion of the Court.

Petitioners in this case are the Toilet Goods Association, an organization of cosmetics manufacturers accounting for some 90% of annual American sales in this field, and 39 individual cosmetics manufacturers and distributors.　They brought this action in the United States District Court for the Southern District of New York seeking declaratory and injunctive relief against the Secretary of Health, Education, and Welfare and the Commissioner of Food and Drugs, on the ground that certain regulations promulgated by the Commissioner exceeded his statutory authority under the Color Additive Amendments to the Federal Food, Drug, and Cosmetic Act. * * *

* * *

* * * The Commissioner of Food and Drugs * * * under statutory authority "to promulgate regulations for the efficient enforcement" of the Act, issued the following regulation after due public notice and consideration of comments submitted by interested parties:

"(a) When it appears to the Commissioner that a person has:

* * *

"(4) Refused to permit duly authorized employees of the Food and Drug Administration free access to all manufacturing facilities, processes, and formulae involved in the manufacture of color additives and intermediates from which such color additives are derived;

"he may immediately suspend certification service to such person and may continue such suspension until adequate corrective action has been taken."[1]

The petitioners maintain that this regulation is an impermissible exercise of authority, that the FDA has long sought congressional authorization for free access to facilities, processes, and formulae, but that Congress has always denied the agency this power except for prescription drugs.　Framed in this way, we agree with petitioners that a "legal" issue is raised, but nevertheless we are not persuaded that the present suit is properly maintainable.

In determining whether a challenge to an administrative regulation is ripe for review a twofold inquiry must be made: first to determine whether the issues tendered are appropriate for judicial resolution, and second

---

1. The Color Additive Amendments provide for listings of color additives by the Secretary "if and to the extent that such additives are suitable and safe. * * * " The Secretary is further authorized to provide "for the certification, with safe diluents or without diluents, of batches of color additives.

* * * "A color additive is "deemed unsafe" unless it is either from a certified batch or exempted from the certification rquirement.　A cosmetic containing such an "unsafe" additive is deemed to be adulterated, and is prohibited from interstate commerce.

to assess the hardship to the parties if judicial relief is denied at that stage.

As to the first of these factors, we agree with the Court of Appeals that the legal issue as presently framed is not appropriate for judicial resolution. This is not because the regulation is not the agency's considered and formalized determination, for we are in agreement with petitioners that under this Court's decisions in *Frozen Food Express v. United States* and *United States v. Storer Broadcasting Co.*, there can be no question that this regulation—promulgated in a formal manner after notice and evaluation of submitted comments—is a "final agency action." * * * Also, we recognize the force of petitioners' contention that the issue as they have framed it presents a purely legal question: whether the regulation is totally beyond the agency's power under the statute, the type of legal issue that courts have occasionally dealt with without requiring a specific attempt at enforcement. * * *

These points which support the appropriateness of judicial resolution are, however, outweighed by other considerations. The regulation serves notice only that the Commissioner *may* under certain circumstances order inspection of certain facilities and data, and that further certification of additives *may* be refused to those who decline to permit a duly authorized inspection until they have complied in that regard. At this juncture we have no idea whether or when such an inspection will be ordered and what reasons the Commissioner will give to justify his order. The statutory authority asserted for the regulation is the power to promulgate regulations "for the efficient enforcement" of the Act, § 701(a). Whether the regulation is justified thus depends not only, as petitioners appear to suggest, on whether Congress refused to include a specific section of the Act authorizing such inspections, although this factor is to be sure a highly relevant one, but also on whether the statutory scheme as a whole justified promulgation of the regulation. This will depend not merely on an inquiry into statutory purpose, but concurrently on an understanding of what types of enforcement problems are encountered by the FDA, the need for various sorts of supervision in order to effectuate the goals of the Act, and the safeguards devised to protect legitimate trade secrets. We believe that judicial appraisal of these factors is likely to stand on a much surer footing in the context of a specific application of this regulation than could be the case in the framework of the generalized challenge made here.

We are also led to this result by considerations of the effect on the petitioners of the regulation, for the test of ripeness, as we have noted, depends not only on how adequately a court can deal with the legal issue presented, but also on the degree and nature of the regulation's present effect on those seeking relief. * * *

This is not a situation in which primary conduct is affected—when contracts must be negotiated, ingredients tested or substituted, or special records compiled. This regulation merely states that the Commissioner may authorize inspectors to examine certain processes or formulae; no advance action is required of cosmetics manufacturers, who since the enactment of the 1938 Act have been under a statutory duty to permit reasonable inspection of a "factory, warehouse, establishment, or vehicle and all pertinent equipment, finished and unfinished materials; containers, and labeling therein." Moreover, no irremediable adverse consequences flow from requiring a later challenge to this regulation by a manufacturer who refuses to allow this type of inspection. Unlike the other regulations challenged in this action, in which seizure of goods, heavy fines, adverse publicity for distributing "adulterated" goods, and possible criminal liability might penalize failure to comply, a refusal to admit an inspector here would at most lead only to a suspension of certification services to the particular party, a determination that can then be promptly challenged through an administrative procedure,[2] which in turn is reviewable by a court. Such review will provide an adequate forum for testing the regulation in a concrete situation.

It is true that the administrative hearing will deal with the "factual basis" of the suspension, from which petitioners infer that the Commissioner will not entertain and consider a challenge to his statutory authority to promulgate the regulation. Whether or not this assumption is correct, given the fact that only minimal, if any, adverse consequences will face petitioners if they challenge the regulation in this manner, we think it wiser to require them to exhaust this administrative process through which the factual basis of the inspection order will certainly be aired and where more light may be thrown on the Commissioner's statutory and practical justifications for the regulation. Judicial review will then be available, and a court at that juncture will be in a better position to deal with the question of statutory authority.

For these reasons the judgment of the Court of Appeals is

Affirmed.

MR. JUSTICE FORTAS [concurring in the portion of the *Toilet Goods* decision set forth above but dissenting in *Abbott Laboratories*], with whom the CHIEF JUSTICE and MR. JUSTICE CLARK join.

* * *

The issues considered by the Court are not constitutional questions. The Court does not rest upon any asserted right to challenge the regulations at this time because the agency lacks authority to promulgate the regulations as to the subject matters involved, or because its procedures have been arbitrary or unreasonable. Its decision is based solely upon the claim of right to challenge these particular regulations at this time on the ground that they are erroneous exercises of the agency's power. It is

---

2. See 21 CFR § § 8.28(b), 130.14–130.26. We recognize that a denial of certification might under certain circumstances cause inconvenience and possibly hardship, depending upon such factors as how large a supply of certified additives the particular manufacturer may have, how rapidly the administrative hearing and judicial review are conducted, and what temporary remedial or protective provisions, such as compliance with a reservation pending litigation, might be available to a manufacturer testing the regulation. In the context of the present case we need only say that such inconvenience is speculative and we have been provided with no information that would support an assumption that much weight should be attached to this possibility.

solely at this point that the Court * * * authorizes threshold or pre-enforcement challenge by action for injunction and declaratory relief to suspend the operation of the regulations in their entirety and without reference to particular factual situations.

With all respect, I submit that established principles of jurisprudence, solidly rooted in the constitutional structure of our Government, require that the courts should not intervene in the administrative process at this stage, under these facts and in this gross, shotgun fashion. * * *

The Administrative Procedure Act and fundamental principles of our jurisprudence insist that there must be some type of effective judicial review of final, substantive agency action which seriously affects personal or property rights. But, "[a]ll constitutional questions aside, it is for Congress to determine how the rights which it creates shall be enforced. * * * In such a case the specification of one remedy normally excludes another." *Switchmen's Union of North America v. National Mediation Board*, 320 U.S. 297, 301 (1943). Where Congress has provided a method of review, the requisite showing to induce the courts otherwise to bring a governmental program to a halt may not be made by a mere showing of the impact of the regulation and the customary hardships of interim compliance. At least in cases where the claim is of erroreous action rather than the lack of jurisdiction or denial of procedural due process, a suit for injunctive or declaratory relief will not lie absent a clear demonstration that the type of review available under the statute would not be "adequate," that the controversies are otherwise "ripe" for judicial decision, and that no public interest exists which offsets the private values which the litigation seeks to vindicate. As I shall discuss, no such showing is or can be made here. * * *

In evaluating the destructive force and effect of the Court's action in these cases, it is necessary to realize that it is arming each of the federal district judges in this Nation with power to enjoin enforcement of regulations and actions under the federal law designed to protect the people of this Nation against dangerous drugs and cosmetics. Restraining orders and temporary injunctions will suspend application of these public safety laws pending years of litigation—a time schedule which these cases illustrate. They are disruptive enough, regardless of the ultimate outcome. The Court's validation of this shotgun attack upon this vital law and its administration is not confined to these suits, these regulations, or these plaintiffs—or even this statute. It is a general hunting license; and I respectfully submit, a license for mischief because it authorizes aggression which is richly rewarded by delay in the subjection of private interests to programs which Congress believes to be required in the public interest. As I read the Court's opinion, it does not seriously contend that Congress authorized or contemplated this type of relief. It does not rest upon the argument that Congress intended that injunctions or threshold relief should be available. The Court seems to announce a doctrine, which is new and startling in administrative law, that the courts, in determining whether to exercise jurisdiction by injunction, will not look to see whether Congress intended that the parties should resort to another avenue of review, but will be governed by whether Congress has "prohibited" injunctive relief. * * *

The regulation in [*Abbott Laboratories*] relates to a 1962 amendment to the Act requiring manufacturers of prescription drugs to print on the labels or other printed material, the "established name" of the drug "prominently and in type at least half as large as that used thereon for any proprietary name or designation for such drug." Obviously, this requires some elucidation, either case-by-case or by general regulation or pronouncement, because the statute does not say that this must be done "every time," or only once on each label or in each pamphlet, or once per panel, etc., or that it must be done differently on labels than on circulars, or doctors' literature than on directions to the patients, etc. This is exactly the traditional purpose and function of an administrative agency. The Commissioner, acting by delegation from the Secretary, took steps to provide for the specification. He invited and considered comments and then issued a regulation requiring that the "established name" appear every time the proprietary name is used. A manufacturer—or other person who violates this regulation—has mislabeled his product. The product may be seized; or injunction may be sought; or the mislabeler may be criminally prosecuted. In any of these actions he may challenge the regulation and obtain a judicial determination.

* * * The Court says that this confronts the manufacturer with a "real dilemma." But the fact of the matter is that the dilemma is no more than citizens face in connection with countless statutes and with the rules of the SEC, FTC, FCC, ICC, and other regulatory agencies. This has not heretofore been regarded as a basis for injunctive relief unless Congress has so provided. The overriding fact here is—or should be—that the public interest in avoiding the delay in implementing Congress' program far outweighs the private interest; and that the private interest which has so impressed the Court is no more than that which exists in respect of most regulatory statutes or agency rules. Somehow, the Court has concluded that the damage to petitioners if they have to engage in the required redesign and reprint of their labels and printed materials without threshold review outweighs the damage to the public of deferring during the tedious months and years of litigation a cure for the possible danger and asserted deceit of peddling plain medicine under fancy trademarks and for fancy prices which, rightly or wrongly, impelled the Congress to enact this legislation. I submit that a much stronger showing is necessary than the expense and trouble of compliance and the risk of defiance. Actually, if the Court refused to permit this shotgun assault, experience and reasonably sophisticated common sense show that there would be orderly compliance without the disaster so dramatically predicted by the industry, reasonable adjustments by the agency in real hardship cases, and where extreme intransigence involving substantial violations occurred, enforcement actions in which legality of the regulation would be tested in specific, concrete situations. I respectfully submit that this would be the correct and appropriate result. Our refusal to respond to the vastly overdrawn cries of distress would reflect not only

healthy skepticism, but our regard for a proper relationship between the courts on the one hand and Congress and the administrative agencies on the other. It would represent a reasonable solicitude for the purposes and programs of the Congress. And it would reflect appropriate modesty as to the competence of the courts. The courts cannot properly—and should not—attempt to judge in the abstract and generally whether this regulation is within the statutory scheme. Judgment as to the "every time" regulation should be made only in light of specific situations, and it may differ depending upon whether the FDA seeks to enforce it as to doctors' circulars, pamphlets for patients, labels, etc. * * *

Notes

1. Does *Abbott* establish the propriety of pre-enforcement review whenever a litigant is torn between the costs of compliance and the risks of prosecution? Or does *Abbott* mean only that pre-enforcement review is appropriate to test administrative policies that apply irrespective of a party's particular circumstances? The drug companies were undoubtedly apprehensive that the FDA would pick out the worse offender among them as a "test case" of the legality of its regulation, thus, presumably, enhancing the chances of a favorable ruling. The companies were also determinedly opposed to the "every time" requirement, because they had been successful in persuading physicians to prescribe drugs by brand, rather than generic name. See generally R. HARRIS, THE REAL VOICE (1964). What harm—apart from the loss of a possible tactical advantage—does the FDA suffer by having its regulation reviewed in advance of enforcement? Is there any good reason why the FDA should be deprived of that advantage?

2. Following the Supreme Court's decision, the *Abbott* case went back to the Third Circuit for resolution on the merits. (The district court, which had found the regulation ripe for review, had also held it invalid.) A few days before scheduled argument, the FDA and the companies agreed to a settlement, on terms that require a manufacturer to disclose the generic name of a drug at least once per page of labeling and advertising, as well as each time the brand name is "featured." The terms of settlement are currently codified at 21 C.F.R. § § 201.6(g)(1), 202.1(b)(1).

3. The Supreme Court's distinction between the rules challenged in *Abbott* and *Toilet Goods* appears to retain significance. In *Alascom, Inc. v. FCC*, 727 F.2d 1212 (D.C. Cir. 1984), the petitioners challenged on FCC rule reallocating a portion of the radio spectrum for a new service, Digital Electronic Message Service (DEMS). In its decision explaining this reallocation, the Commission announced that it intended to preempt state regulation of future DEMS service "that is inconsistent with federal policy and regulations." The petitioners challenged the legality of this announcement, as well as the Commission's failure to address the impact of DEMS service, which would bypass the existing telephone network, on rural telephone service.

The court of appeals held that neither claim was ripe for review. The Commission had not licensed any carriers to provide DEMS service nor had it preempted any state regulations since none existed. The FCC rule imposed no immediate burden on any of the petitioners, and made clear the agency's "intent * * * to conduct further administrative proceedings to determine whether a given state regulation is inconsistent with national DEMS policy."

Moreover, the court found, deciding whether the FCC had authority to preempt a particular regulation would require consideration of its impact on interstate service—consideration better given in the context of a decision to preempt a specific regulation. In sum, "[a] case may lack ripeness * * * even when it involves a final agency action presenting a purely legal question."

4. The D.C. Circuit reached a similar decision in *Air New Zealand Ltd. v. CAB*, 726 F.2d 832, 838 (D.C. Cir. 1984). Air New Zealand (ANZ) had sought CAB approval to carry passengers and freight between Los Angeles and London on flights originating in or terminating in New Zealand. In granting this authority, the Board stipulated that it would terminate automatically if New Zealand regulatory authorities failed to approve requests by authorized U.S. carriers to offer "matching" fares for travel between the same points. ANZ sought review of this condition, claiming that its fulfillment would violate international obligations. The court refused to entertain this challenge on ripeness grounds. It noted that no U.S. carrier had sought approval for matching fares and that ANZ had acknowledged that some fare arrangements could satisfy the Board's condition without violating any international obligation. It further noted that "[t]he condition is not even addressed to conduct of ANZ, but rather to conduct of the New Zealand regulatory authorities." The automatic termination provision, which ANZ also challenged, did not "immediately affect primary conduct and produce adverse consequences irremediable at a later date."

5. In *Abbott* there was no doubt that the drug companies could challenge the FDA's rule in enforcement proceedings; the issue was whether earlier review could be obtained. The uncertainty in this respect stemmed from Congress's failure to make any provision in the FD&C Act for judicial review of regulations adopted pursuant to section 701(a). See Merrill, *FDA and the Effects of Substantive Rules*, 35 Food Drug Cosm. L.J. 270 (1980). In modern regulatory legislation, such an omission would be unusual. Congress usually specifies a procedure by which judicial review of agency rules can be obtained—typically review prior to enforcement. The frequent question then is whether the prescribed route of review is exclusive. In some instances, Congress has addressed this issue as well, as it did in section 307(b) of the Clean Air Act, at issue in *Adamo Wrecking*, supra p. 696. But language purporting to preclude collateral review is likewise unusual, so that a court must balance the values of finality against the contesting party's interest in obtaining some judicial confirmation of the legality of the standard it is accused of violating.

The "exclusivity" issue has arisen frequently in the context of enforcement of OSHA workplace safety standards, which takes place in proceedings before an administrative law judge whose decision is reviewable by the Occupational Safety and Health Review Commission, an independent quasi-judicial tribunal located within the Labor Department. Most courts have declined to read the statutory review provision, 29 U.S.C.A. § 655(f), as exclusive, holding that a respondent in an enforcement proceeding can challenge the underlying OSHA standard(s) on substantive or procedural grounds. E.g., *Marshall v. Union Oil Co.*, 616 F.2d 1113 (9th Cir. 1980); *Deering Milliken, Inc. v. OSHRC*, 630 F.2d 1094 (5th Cir. 1980). Some courts, however, have limited the grounds for collateral attack. *National Industrial Constructors, Inc. v. OSHRC*, 583 F.2d 1048 (8th Cir. 1978), for example, held that a respondent could not object to the procedures OSHA had followed in promulgating a standard. The Fourth Circuit, in *Daniel International Corp. v. OSHRC*, 656 F.2d 925 (4th Cir. 1981), declined to go this far, but held that the respondent had demonstrated that it had been prejudiced by the agen-

procedural errors.   No case has allowed collateral challenge to an OSHA standard on grounds previously rejected in pre-enforcement review proceedings initiated by other parties.

6. *New York Stock Exchange, Inc. v. Bloom,* 562 F.2d 736 (D.C. Cir. 1977), *cert. denied* 435 U.S. 942 (1978), introduced a new dimension into the *Abbott Laboratories* ripeness calculus.   In that case, the court declined to entertain a suit to review the expressed opinion of the Comptroller of the Currency that automatic stock-purchasing services proposed by Security Pacific National Bank would not violate the Glass-Steagall Act.   The Comptroller's opinion was set forth in two letters, the second of which was issued following a request for consideration by investment companies, on which the interested parties had been given opportunity to comment.

Despite the appearance of considered judgment, the court concluded that the Comptroller's opinion was not ripe for review.   Judge McGowan stressed that the Comptroller had "expressly reserved the possibility that his opinion * * * might change if and when he was presented with concrete evidence that AIS [Security Pacific's proposed service] involves the hazards which the Glass-Steagall Act was intended to prevent."   He further concluded that a determination of legality would depend on the precise features and effects of the service actually undertaken by Security Pacific.   Moreover, "appellants' conduct [was] not directly regulated by the agency action at issue and consequently they [were] not facing a 'Hobson's choice' between burdensome compliance and risky noncompliance."   562 F.2d at 741.   Finally, Judge McGowan suggested that the plaintiffs had an alternative means to protect their interest in being free from unlawful competition (id. at 742–43):

> Appellants concede, and the Comptroller agrees, that they could bring a private action for injunctive relief, advancing the same substantive claim they have made here directly against any national bank which offers AIS to its customers.   Although we have been unable to find any case law squarely on point, and in any event are without power to make an authoritative ruling on the issue since it is not currently before us, we have no reason to believe that appellant would not have a private right of action for injunctive relief under the Glass-Steagall Act.   The express language of the statute neither authorizes nor precludes such an action, but under the standards set forth in recent Supreme Court decisions we would suppose, first, that an implied right of action for injunctive relief would exist for appropriate parties and, second, that appellants would qualify as proper plaintiffs.

> Appellants contend that it would be unduly burdensome to bring a multitude of private actions against individual banks offering AIS.   But it is not at all clear, especially in light of the very limited number of banks offering AIS or its equivalent, that a single successful private action would not be just as effective, in convincing the Comptroller to change his position on AIS, as a reversal in the instant case.   And, in any event, we do not consider the inconvenience of having to initiate more than one suit to be a hardship sufficient to justify review in the current circumstances.

> What appellants would have the courts do in this case is to determine the correctness of an informal statement by the Comptroller to the effect that he would not now take any action if Security Pacific goes forward with its proposed AIS, although he might take a different view of its compatibility with the Glass-Steagall Act at some point in the future after there has been some experience with its actual operation.   This is sought to be done at the in-

stance of parties who, although very possibly possessed of standing to litigate the question in some circumstances, are not themselves subject to regulation by the Comptroller and who will be under no compulsion to do, or to refrain from doing, anything by reason of the advisory opinion in question.   Neither is there now before the court any bank currently providing AIS or proposing to do so.

The record made in such a lawsuit would be barren indeed with respect to information highly relevant to, and informative of, the applicability of the statutory provisions in question.   As indicated above, appellants have other avenues open to them for more meaningful and authoritative judicial resolution of the validity of AIS.

7. The *Bloom* court's refusal to review the Comptroller's "tentative" position should not be understood as suggesting that an agency opinion letter can never be "ripe" for review.   In both *National Automatic Laundry and Cleaning Council v. Schultz*, 443 F.2d 689 (D.C. Cir. 1971), and *Continental Air Lines, Inc. v. CAB*, 522 F.2d 107 (D.C. Cir. 1974) *(en banc)*, the court reviewed statements of agency position embodied in correspondence with regulated firms.   In both cases the recipient of the agency's communication faced the choice of immediate compliance or defense against an enforcement proceeding, and in neither case had the agency qualified its statement of applicable legal requirements by reference to as-yet-undetermined factual circumstances.

3. EXHAUSTION OF ADMINISTRATIVE REMEDIES

FEDERAL TRADE COMMISSION v. STANDARD OIL CO.

Supreme Court of the United States, 1980.
449 U.S. 232, 101 S.Ct. 488, 66 L.Ed.2d 416.

MR. JUSTICE POWELL delivered the opinion of the Court.

This case presents the question whether the issuance of a complaint by the Federal Trade Commission is "final agency action" subject to judicial review before administrative adjudication concludes.

On July 18, 1973, the Federal Trade Commission issued and served upon eight major oil companies, including Standard Oil Company of California (Socal), a complaint averring that the Commission had "reason to believe" that the companies were violating § 5 of the Federal Trade Commission Act, 15 U.S.C.A. § 45, and stating the Commission's charges in that respect.[3]   The Commission issued the complaint under authority of § 5(b) of the Act, which provides:

"Whenever the Commission shall have reason to believe that any * * * person, partnership, or corporation has been or is using any unfair method of competition or unfair or deceptive act or practice in or affecting commerce, and if it shall appear to the Commission that a proceeding by it in respect thereof would be to the interest of the public, it shall issue and serve upon

---

3. The Commission charged that the eight companies had "maintained and reinforced a noncompetitive market structure in the refining of crude oil into petroleum products," had "exercised monopoly power in the refining of petroleum products," and had followed "common courses of action in accommodating the needs and goals of each other throughout the petroleum industry."

such person, partnership, or corporation a complaint stating its charges in that respect and containing a notice of a hearing. * * *

An adjudication of the complaint's charges began soon thereafter before an Administrative Law Judge, and is still pending.

On May 1, 1975, Socal filed a complaint against the Commission in the District Court for the Northern District of California, alleging that the Commission had issued its complaint without having "reason to believe" that Socal was violating the Act.   Socal sought an order declaring that the issuance of the complaint was unlawful and requiring that the complaint be withdrawn.   Socal had sought this relief from the Commission and been denied.[5]   In support of its allegation and request, Socal recited a series of events that preceded the issuance of the complaint and several events that followed.   In Socal's estimation, the only inference to be drawn from these events was that the Commission lacked sufficient evidence when it issued the complaint to warrant a belief that Socal was violating the Act.

The gist of Socal's recitation of events preceding the issuance of the complaint is that political pressure for a public explanation of the gasoline shortages of 1973 forced the Commission to issue a complaint against the major oil companies despite insufficient investigation.   The series of events began on May 31, 1973.   As of that day, the Commission had not examined any employees, documents, or books of Socal's, although the Commission had announced in December 1971, that it intended to investigate possible violations of the Federal Trade Commission Act in the petroleum industry.

On May 31, Senator Henry M. Jackson, then Chairman of the Senate Interior and Insular Affairs Committee and of the Permanent Investigation Subcommittee of the Senate Committee of Government Operations, requested the Commission "to prepare a report within thirty days regarding the relationship between the structure of the petroleum industry and related industries and the current and prospective shortages of petroleum products."   Immediately the Commission subpoenaed three Socal officers to testify before it, and they did so in late June.   This examination was the Commission's only inquiry as to Socal's books and records, and the only interview of a Socal officer, prior to the issuance of the complaint.   On July 6, the Commission sent to Senator Jackson a "Preliminary Federal Trade Commission Staff Report on Its Investigation of the Petroleum Industry," requesting that the report not be made public because it had not yet "been evaluated or approved by the Commis-

---

5. The Commission had denied Socal's motion to dismiss the complaint on February 12, 1974.   The Commission also had denied Socal's motion for reconsideration, stating:

"[I]t has long been settled that the adequacy of the Commission's 'reason to believe' a violation of law has occurred and its belief that a proceeding to stop it would be in the 'public interest' are matters that go to the mental processes of the Commissioners and will not be reviewed by the

courts.   Once the Commission has resolved these questions and issued a complaint, the issue to be litigated is not the adequacy of the Commission's pre-complaint information or the diligence of its study of the material in question but whether the alleged violation has in fact occurred.   That is the posture of the instant matter."   *In re Exxon Corp.,* 83 FTC. 1759, 1760 (1974).

sion." On July 9, Senator Jackson informed the Commission by letter that he intended to publish the report as a congressional committee reprint unless the Commission explained by July 13 why public release of the report would be improper. The Commission responded on July 11 that public release of the report, which the Commission characterized as "an internal staff memorandum," would be "inconsistent with [the Commission's] duty to proceed judiciously and responsibly in determining what, if any, action should be taken on the basis of the staff investigation." On July 13, Senator Jackson released the report for publication by the Senate Committee on Interior and Insular Affairs. On July 18, the Commission issued its complaint.

The subsequent events recited by Socal in its complaint were intended to confirm that the Commission lacked sufficient evidence before issuing its complaint to determine that it had reason to believe that Socal was violating the Act. One subsequent event was the issuance on August 27 of a report by the Office of Energy Advisor of the Department of the Treasury, concluding that the Commission's staff report was wrong in implying that the major oil companies had contrived the gasoline shortages. The report recommended that the complaint be withdrawn. A second event was Senator Jackson's statement in January 1974, at the conclusion of congressional hearings about the shortages, that he had found no "hard evidence" that the oil companies had created shortages. In addition to these expressions of doubt about the allegations of the Commission's complaint, Socal recounted the several failures of the Commission's complaint counsel in the adjudication to comply with orders of the Administrative Law Judge to identify the witnesses and documents on which the Commission intended to rely. The complaint counsel admitted that most of the evidence and witnesses the Commission hoped to introduce were yet to be secured through discovery, and he moved to relax the Commission's procedural rules for adjudication in order to allow such extensive discovery. In certifying this motion to the Commission, the Administrative Law Judge recommended "withdrawal of this case from adjudication—that is, dismissal without prejudice—so that it may be more fully investigated." The Commission denied the complaint counsel's motion and declined to follow the Administrative Law Judge's recommendations.

The District Court dismissed Socal's complaint on the ground that "a review of preliminary decisions made by administrative agencies, except under most unusual circumstances, would be productive of nothing more than chaos." The Court of Appeals for the Ninth Circuit reversed. 596 F.2d 1381 (1979). It held the Commission's determination whether evidence before it provided the requisite reason to believe is "committed to agency discretion" and therefore is unreviewable according to 5 U.S.C.A. § 701(a)(2). The Court of Appeals held, however, that the District Court could inquire whether the Commission *in fact* had made the determination that it had reason to believe that Socal was violating the Act. If the District Court were to find upon remand that the Commission had issued the complaint "solely because of outside pressure or with complete absence of a 'reason to believe' determination," then it was to order the

Commission to dismiss the complaint. The Court of Appeals further held that the issuance of the complaint was "final agency action" under 5 U.S.C.A. § 704.

We granted the Commission's petition for a writ of certiorari because of the importance of the questions raised by Socal's request for judicial review of the complaint before the conclusion of the adjudication. We now reverse.

The Commission averred in its complaint that it had reason to believe that Socal was violating the Act. That averment is subject to judicial review before the conclusion of administrative adjudication only if the issuance of the complaint was "final agency action" or otherwise was "directly reviewable" under 5 U.S.C.A. § 704. We conclude that the issuance of the complaint was neither.[7] * * *

By its terms, the Commission's averment of "reason to believe" that Socal was violating the Act is not a definitive statement of position. It represents a threshold determination that further inquiry is warranted and that a complaint should initiate proceedings. To be sure, the issuance of the complaint is definitive on the question whether the Commission avers reason to believe that the respondent to the complaint is violating the Act. But the extent to which the respondent may challenge the complaint and its charges proves that the averment of reason to believe is not "definitive" in a comparable manner to the regulations in *Abbott Laboratories* and the cases it discussed.

Section 5 of the Act, in conjunction with Commission regulations and 5 U.S.C.A. § 554 requires that the complaint contain a notice of hearing at which the respondent may present evidence and testimony before an administrative law judge to refute the Commission's charges. Either party to the adjudication may appeal an adverse decision of the administrative law judge to the full Commission, which then may dismiss the complaint. If instead the Commission enters an order requiring the respondent to cease and desist from engaging in the challenged practice, the respondent still is not bound by the Commission's decision until judicial review is complete or the opportunity to seek review has lapsed. Thus, the averment of reason to believe is a prerequisite to a definitive agency position on the question whether Socal violated the Act, but itself is a determination only that adjudicatory proceedings will commence.

---

7. * * * We agree with Socal and with the Court of Appeals that the issuance of the complaint is "agency action." The language of the APA and its legislative history support this conclusion. According to 5 U.S.C.A. § 701(b)(2), "agency action" has the meaning given to it by 5 U.S.C.A. § 551. That section provides that " 'agency action' includes the whole or a part of an agency rule, order, license, sanction, relief, or the equivalent or denial thereof, or failure to act," 5 U.S.C.A. § 551(13), and also that " 'order' means the whole or a part of a final disposition * * * of an agency in a matter other than rule making. * * * " 5 U.S.C.A. § 551(6). * * * We conclude that the issuance of the complaint by the Commission is "a part of a final disposition" and therefore is "agency action."

In view of our conclusion that the issuance of the complaint was not "*final* agency action," we do not address the question whether the issuance of a complaint is "committed to agency discretion by law."

Serving only to initiate the proceedings, the issuance of the complaint averring reason to believe has no legal force comparable to that of the regulation at issue in *Abbott Laboratories*, nor any comparable effect upon Socal's daily business. * * * Socal does not contend that the issuance of the complaint had any such legal or practical effect, except to impose upon Socal the burden of responding to the charges made against it. Although this burden certainly is substantial, it is different in kind and legal effect from the burdens attending what heretofore has been considered to be final agency action.

In contrast to the complaint's lack of legal or practical effect upon Socal, the effect of the judicial review sought by Socal is likely to be interference with the proper functioning of the agency and a burden for the courts. Judicial intervention into the agency process denies the agency an opportunity to correct its own mistakes and to apply its expertise. Intervention also leads to piecemeal review which at the least is inefficient and upon completion of the agency process might prove to have been unnecessary. Furthermore, unlike the review in *Abbott Laboratories*, judicial review to determine whether the Commission decided that it had the requisite reason to believe would delay resolution of the ultimate question whether the Act was violated. Finally, every respondent to a Commission complaint could make the claim that Socal had made. Judicial review of the averments in the Commission's complaints should not be a means of turning prosecutor into defendant before adjudication concludes.

* * * These pragmatic considerations counsel against the conclusion that the issuance of the complaint was "final agency action."

Socal relies, however, upon different considerations than these in contending that the issuance of the complaint is "final agency action."

Socal first contends that it exhausted its administrative remedies by moving in the adjudicatory proceedings for dismissal of the complaint. By thus affording the Commission an opportunity to decide upon the matter, Socal contends that it has satisfied the interests underlying the doctrine of administrative exhaustion. * * * We think, however, that Socal and the Court of Appeals have mistaken exhaustion for finality. By requesting the Commission to withdraw its complaint and by awaiting the Commission's refusal to do so, Socal may well have exhausted its administrative remedy as to the averment of reason to believe. But the Commission's refusal to reconsider its issuance of the complaint does not render the complaint a "definitive" action. The Commission's refusal does not augment the complaint's legal force or practical effect upon Socal. Nor does the refusal diminish the concerns for efficiency and enforcement of the Act.

Socal also contends that it will be irreparably harmed unless the issuance of the complaint is judicially reviewed immediately. Socal argues that the expense and disruption of defending itself in protracted adjudicatory proceedings constitutes irreparable harm. As indicated above, we do not doubt that the burden of defending this proceeding will be substantial.   But "the expense and annoyance of litigation is 'part of the social burden of living under government.' " * * *

Socal further contends that its challenge to the Commission's averment of reason to believe can never be reviewed unless it is reviewed before the Commission's adjudication concludes.   As stated by the Court of Appeals, the alleged unlawfulness in the issuance of the complaint "is likely to become insulated from any review" if deferred until appellate review of a cease-and-desist order.   Socal also suggests that the unlawfulness will be "insulated" because the reviewing court will lack an adequate record and it will address only the question whether substantial evidence supported the cease-and-desist order.[11]

We are not persuaded by this speculation.   The Act expressly authorizes a court of appeals to order that the Commission take additional evidence.   Thus, a record which would be inadequate for review of alleged unlawfulness in the issuance of a complaint can be made adequate.   We also note that the APA specifically provides that a "preliminary, procedural, or intermediate agency action or ruling not directly reviewable is subject to review on the review of the final agency action," and that the APA also empowers a court of appeals to "hold unlawful and set aside agency action * * * found to be   * * * without observance of procedure required by law."   5 U.S.C.A. § 706.   Thus, assuming that the issuance of the complaint is not "committed to agency discretion by law,"[13] a court of appeals reviewing a cease-and-desist order has the power to review alleged unlawfulness in the issuance of a complaint.   We need not decide what action a court of appeals should take if it finds a cease-and-desist order to be supported by substantial evidence but the complaint to have been issued without the requisite reason to believe.   It suffices to hold that the possibility does not affect the application of the finality rule.

Because the Commission's issuance of a complaint averring reason to believe that Socal violated the Act is not "final agency action" * * * it is not judicially reviewable before administrative adjudication concludes.[14] We therefore reverse the Court of Appeals and remand for the dismissal of the complaint.

---

11. The Court of Appeals additionally suggested that the complaint would be "insulated" from review because the alleged unlawfulness would be moot if Socal prevailed in the adjudication.   These concerns do not support a conclusion that the issuance of a complaint averring reason to believe is "final agency action."   To the contrary, one of the principal reasons to await the termination of agency proceedings is "to obviate all occasion for judicial review."   Thus, the possibility that Socal's challenge may be mooted in adjudication warrants the requirement that Socal pursue adjudication, not shortcut it.

13. Contrary to the suggestion of JUSTICE STEVENS in his concurring opinion, we do not hold that the issuance of the complaint is *reviewable* agency action.   We leave open the question whether the issuance of the complaint is unreviewable because it is "committed to agency discretion by law."

14. By this holding, we do not encourage the issuance of complaints by the Commission without a conscientious compliance with the "reason to believe" obligation in 15 U.S.C.A. § 45(b).   The adjudicatory proceedings which follow the issuance of a complaint may last for months or years.   They result in substantial expense to the respondent and may divert management personnel from their administrative and productive duties to the corportion.   Without a well-grounded reason to believe that unlawful conduct has occurred, the Commission does not serve the public interest by subjecting business enterprises to these burdens.

It is so ordered.

MR. JUSTICE STEVENS, concurring in the judgment.

* * *

In my opinion, Congress did not intend to authorize any judicial review of decisions to initiate administrative proceedings. The definition of "agency action" found in 5 U.S.C.A. § 551 (13) plainly contemplates action that affects legal rights in some way. As the Court points out, the mere issuance of a complaint has no legal effect on the respondent's rights. Although an agency's decision to file a complaint may have a serious impact on private parties who must respond to such complaints, that impact is comparable to that caused by a private litigant's decision to file a lawsuit or a prosecutor's decision to present evidence to a grand jury. A decision to initiate proceedings does not have the same kind of effect on legal rights as "an agency rule, order, license [or other sanction]."[4] I am aware of nothing in the Administrative Procedure Act, or its history, that indicates that Congress intended to authorize judicial review of this type of decision.

The practical consequences of the Court's contrary holding—that the Commission's prelitigation decision, although not reviewable now, will be reviewable later—confirms my opinion that the Court's decision does not reflect the intent of Congress. If the Commission ultimately prevails on the merits of its complaint, Socal surely will not be granted immunity because the Commission did not uncover the evidence of illegality until after the complaint was filed. On the other hand, if Socal prevails, there will be no occasion to review the contention that it now advances, because the only relief it seeks is a dismissal of the Commission's complaint. Socal is surely correct when it argues that unless review is available now, meaningful review can never be had.

The Court's casual reading of the Administrative Procedure Act is unfortunate for another reason. The disposition of a novel and important question of federal jurisdiction in a footnote will lend support to the notion that federal courts have a "carte blanche" authorizing judicial supervision of almost everything that the Executive Branch of Government may do. Because that notion has an inevitable impact on the quantity and quality of judicial service, federal judges should be especially careful to construe their own authority strictly. I therefore respectfully disagree with the Court's perfunctory analysis of the "agency action" is-

---

4. The Court's partial quotation of the definition of the term "order" in § 551(6) implies that the Court regards the initial step in a proceeding as a "part" of the final order terminating the proceeding. In my opinion that is a rather plain misreading of the definition. An ordinary reader would interpret "part" of an order to refer to one of several paragraphs or sections in that document, not to actions that preceded the entry of the order. Under a contrary reading, presumably the Commission's action in filing a brief directed to some preliminary issue in the proceeding would be considered "part" of the agency action terminating the proceedings and therefore subject to judicial review. Section 551(6) reads, in full, as follows:

"'order' means the whole or a part of a final disposition, whether affirmative, negative, injunctive, or declaratory in form, of an agency in a matter other than rule making but including licensing."

sue.   I do, however, concur in its judgment because I am persuaded that
the Commission's decision to initiate a complaint is not "agency action"
within the meaning of 5 U.S.C.A. § 702.

Notes

1. The "exhaustion" doctrine embodies the requirement that one who desires
to challenge agency action must first pursue existing administrative remedies before seeking court review.   The doctrine was articulated in the often-cited decision, *Myers v. Bethlehem Shipbuilding Corp.*, 303 U.S. 41 (1938).   The NLRB
charged the company with unfair labor practices at its Quincy, Massachusetts
plant which, according to the Board's allegations, operated in interstate commerce.   Bethlehem sued the Board members in district court to enjoin the administrative proceeding, contending that the National Labor Relations Act did
not apply because the company did not operate "in interstate or foreign commerce," and that therefore the agency lacked jurisdiction.   Bethlehem further
contended that "hearings would, at best, be futile; and that the holding of them
would result in irreparable damage to the Corporation" through direct costs, loss
of time, and loss of employee good will.

The Supreme Court held that the district court lacked power to enjoin the
Board's proceedings.   Pointing out that the agency's procedures were not under
attack and that under the NLRA no agency order could affect Bethlehem before
it had an opportunity to secure judicial review, the Court concluded that Congress could lawfully vest exclusive jurisdiction in the Board to adjudicate unfair
labor practices, with ultimate review in the courts of appeals.   Its opinion explained (303 U.S. at 49–52):

> It is true that the Board has jurisdiction only if the complaint concerns in-
> terstate or foreign commerce.   Unless the board finds that it does, the com-
> plaint must be dismissed.   And if it finds that interstate or foreign commerce
> is involved, but the Circuit Court of Appeals concludes that such finding was
> without adequate evidence to support it, or otherwise contrary to law, the
> Board's petition to enforce it will be dismissed, or the employer's petition to
> have it set aside will be granted.   Since the procedure before the Board is ap-
> propriate and the judicial review so provided is adequate, Congress had
> power to vest exclusive jurisdiction in the Board and the Circuit Court of Ap-
> peals.

> The Corporation contends that, since it denies that interstate or foreign
> commerce is involved and claims that a hearing would subject it to irreparable
> damage, rights guaranteed by the Federal Constitution will be denied unless
> it be held that the District Court has jurisdiction to enjoin the holding of a
> hearing by the Board.   So to hold would, as the Government insists, in effect
> substitute the District Court for the Board as the tribunal to hear and deter-
> mine what Congress declared the Board exclusively should hear and deter-
> mine in the first instance.   The contention is at war with the long settled rule
> of judicial administration that no one is entitled to judicial relief for a sup-
> posed or threatened injury until the prescribed administrative remedy has
> been exhausted.   That rule has been repeatedly acted on in cases where, as
> here, the contention is made that the administrative body lacked power over
> the subject matter.

> Obviously, the rule requiring exhaustion of the administrative remedy
> cannot be circumvented by asserting that the charge on which the complaint

rests is groundless and that the mere holding of the prescribed administrative hearing would result in irreparable damage. Lawsuits also often prove to have been groundless; but no way has been discovered of relieving a defendant from the necessity of a trial to establish the fact.

2. *Myers* was in many ways the paradigm case for applying the exhaustion doctrine. The injury about which the company complained was one normally attached to an obligation to protect one's interests in a formal legal proceeding—an injury that might be lessened, but not avoided by shifting to the judicial forum. The issue involved was one requiring factual proof, and it would necessarily be canvassed in the agency proceeding that the company sought to avoid. Moreover, the claim of lack of jurisdiction was at least disputable; for if the Bethlehem Shipbuilding Corporation did not operate in "interstate commerce," the Board had indeed been accorded very narrow jurisdiction. One thus should not be surprised to discover that the courts generally have followed a more flexible functional approach to the exhaustion requirement than the *Myers* opinion suggests on its face.

For example, in *AMP, Inc. v. Gardner*, 275 F.Supp. 410 (S.D.N.Y. 1967), *affirmed* 389 F.2d 825 (2d Cir.), *cert. denied* 393 U.S. 825 (1968), a manufacturer sued to review the FDA's letter ruling that its instrument for ligating blood vessels during surgery was a "drug," and therefore required to go through the FDA's premarket approval procedures. AMP succeeded in obtaining an immediate, albeit unfavorable judicial resolution of this essentially "jurisdictional" issue.

A functional analysis could distinguish *AMP* from *Myers* on several grounds: (1) the burden imposed by the available administrative proceeding; (2) the appropriateness of the agency proceeding for resolving the issue raised; and (3) the dependence of the legal issue on the development of a factual record. If AMP were correct that its instrument was not a "drug" but a "device," it would not have had to pursue the FDA's time-consuming pre-marketing approval process. The proceeding was not one in which it would merely have had to defend against agency charges, but one in which it would apparently be required to amass evidence and carry a preliminary burden of proof before the agency would even address the issue it wished to raise. Similarly, while the NLRB was in the habit of entertaining evidence on and resolving the jurisdictional ("interstate commerce") issue in administrative hearings, the FDA has assumed that any product a manufacturer chose to submit for approval was a "drug." Finally, the jurisdictional question in *Myers* turned on specific facts—such as the scope of Bethlehem's operations, its sources of supply, the location of its customers—while the issue in *AMP*— whether the company's product was a "drug" or a "device"—turned largely on construction of the statute.

3. Other labor cases attest to the flexibility of the exhaustion doctrine. Perhaps the most notable is *Leedom v. Kyne*, 358 U.S. 184 (1958). There the Board, without conducting a vote of employees, certified a bargaining unit that contained both professional and non-professional employees. Section 9(b)(1) of the National Labor Relations Act, 29 U.S.C.A. § 159(b)(1), specifically forbids the Board from including professionals in the same unit with non-professionals without obtaining an affirmative vote of the former. But the Act further specifies that Board orders in certification proceedings are not "final" and provides for exclusive review of those orders in the courts of appeals in proceedings to enforce or review an order against an unfair labor practice, such as refusal to bargain with the elected representative of the certified unit. In *Leedom*, representatives of

the professional employees sued in district court to challenge their inclusion in the bargaining unit.   The Supreme Court held that, in the circumstances, the Board's order was immediately reviewable.   When an agency acts in excess of its authority and flaunts a specific statutory prohibition, the Court concluded, an aggrieved party need not await the completion of administrative proceedings before seeking judicial relief.   If the district court were denied jurisdiction, the plaintiffs would be deprived of a "right" conferred by Congress.

4. Litigants have successfully avoided the exhaustion requirement where they challenged the propriety or adequacy of the very administrative procedures to which the doctrine would remit them, see, e.g., *American Federation of Government Employees v. Acree*, 475 F.2d 1289 (D.C. Cir. 1973); *Elmo Division of Drive-X Co. v. Dixon*, 348 F.2d 342 (D.C. Cir. 1965), and where the potentially available administrative procedure could not be invoked as a matter of right by one in the complainant's position. *Rosado v. Wyman*, 397 U.S. 397 (1970).

Mathews v. Eldridge, 424 U.S. 319, 330–32 (1976), supra p. 195, illustrates the prior "exception" to the exhaustion requirement.   You will recall that Eldridge claimed that the Social Security Administrations's failure to accord him an evidentiary hearing before terminating his disability benefits violated due process.   He brought suit in district court immediately after learning that his benefits had been cut off, and never pursued the post-termination hearing to which the SSA's regulations entitled him.   In holding that the Court would entertain his due process claim, Justice Powell wrote:

> As the nonwaivable jurisdictional element was satisfied, we next consider the waivable element.   The question is whether the denial of Eldridge's claim to continued benefits was a sufficiently "final" decision with respect to his constitutional claim to satisfy the statutory exhaustion requirement. Eldridge concedes that he did not exhaust the full set of internal-review procedures provided by the Secretary.   As [*Weinberger v. Salfi*] recognized, the Secretary may waive the exhaustion requirement if he satisfies himself, at any stage of the administrative process, that no further review is warranted either because the internal needs of the agency are fulfilled or because the relief that is sought is beyond his power to confer. * * * [T]he power to determine when finality has occurred ordinarily rests with the Secretary since ultimate responsibility for the integrity of the administrative program is his.   But cases may arise where a claimant's interest in having a particular issue resolved promptly is so great that deference to the agency's judgment is inappropriate.   This is such a case.

> Eldridge's constitutional challenge is entirely collateral to his substantive claim of entitlement.   Moreover, there is a crucial distinction between the nature of the constitutional claim asserted here and that raised in *Salfi*.   A claim to a predeprivation hearing as a matter of constitutional right rests on the proposition that full relief cannot be obtained at a postdeprivation hearing. * * * Eldridge has raised at least a colorable claim that because of his physical condition and dependency upon the disability benefits an erroneous termination would damage him in a way not recompensable through retroactive payments.   Thus * * * denying Eldridge's substantive claim "for other reasons" or upholding it "under other provisions" at the post-termination stage would not answer his constitutional challenge.

As the foregoing excerpt suggests, in cases like *Eldridge*, a court usually will wish to be assured that administrative remedies have been pursued far enough to allow the agency to decide whether there is a non-constitutional basis for resolving the dispute.   In *Eldridge* itself, there was no doubt that the SSA would not provide a pre-termination hearing; its published regulations announced precisely the opposite policy.   Yet the SSA was not statutorily required to adopt those procedures and, in theory, could have changed its mind if it was prepared to do so in all cases.   (In *Weinberger v. Salfi*, 422 U.S. 749 (1975), the Court had enforced what it characterized as a statutory exhaustion requirement for Social Security claims, but it allowed the plaintiff to challenge the constitutionality of eligibility criteria after pursuing a claim far enough through the administrative apparatus to assure that no alternative ground for dispositon existed.)

5. Many opinions suggest that administrative agencies lack capacity to rule on constitutional challenges to their substantive criteria or procedures, and some speak in terms of lack of jurisdiction to consider constitutional issues.   If true, this would suggest that any time a plaintiff challenges an agency's action as unconstitutional, he need not exhaust administrative remedies.   Judicial practice is much less rigid than this analysis suggests.   Surely if the practice challenged as unconstitutional is one that the agency chose to employ, it makes sense for a court to be sure that the agency wishes to defend the practice rather than change it. Even where the plaintiff challenges a criterion or procedure that has been prescribed by Congress—as in *McKart*, infra—the agency proceeding may be a superior, or at least equivalent, forum for eliciting pertinent facts.   And when a plaintiff combines constitutional with other claims, there are usually strong reasons to allow the agency to conclude its proceedings before allowing review.

McKART v. UNITED STATES

Supreme Court of the United States, 1969.
395 U.S. 185, 89 S.Ct. 1657, 23 L.Ed.2d 194.

MR. JUSTICE MARSHALL delivered the opinion of the Court.

[McKart was prosecuted for failure to report for induction into the armed services, and sought to defend on the ground that his local draft board unlawfully reclassified him from IV-A (sole surviving son) to I-A. McKart had failed to appeal his reclassification within the Selective Service System, and the government contended that this failure to exhaust administrative remedies precluded consideration of his defense.   The Supreme Court disagreed.   Having first concluded that McKart clearly was exempt from service as a sole surviving son, the Court responded to the exhaustion claim.]

The doctrine of exhaustion of administrative remedies is well established in the jurisprudence of administrative law. * * * The doctrine is applied in a number of different situations and is, like most judicial doctrines, subject to numerous exceptions.   Application of the doctrine to specific cases requires an understanding of its purposes and of the particular administrative scheme involved.

Perhaps the most common application of the exhaustion doctrine is in cases where the relevant statute provides that certain administrative procedures shall be exclusive.   See *Myers*.   The reasons for making such procedures exclusive, and for the judicial application of the exhaustion doctrine in cases where the statutory requirement of exclusivity is not so explicit, are not difficult to understand. A primary purpose is, of course, the avoidance of premature interruption of the administrative process. The agency, like a trial court, is created for the purpose of applying a statute in the first instance. Accordingly, it is normally desirable to let the agency develop the necessary factual background upon which decisions should be based. And since agency decisions are frequently of a discretionary nature or frequently require expertise, the agency should be given the first chance to exercise that discretion or to apply that expertise. And of course it is generally more efficient for the administrative process to go forward without interruption than it is to permit the parties to seek aid from the courts at various intermediate stages. The very same reasons lie behind judicial rules sharply limiting interlocutory appeals.

Closely related to the above reasons is a notion peculiar to administrative law. The administrative agency is created as a separate entity and invested with certain powers and duties. The courts ordinarily should not interfere with an agency until it has completed its action, or else has clearly exceeded its jurisdiction. As Professor Jaffe puts it, "[t]he exhaustion doctrine is, therefore, an expression of executive and administrative autonomy." This reason is particularly pertinent where the function of the agency and the particular decision sought to be reviewed involve exercise of discretionary powers granted the agency by Congress, or require application of special expertise.

Some of these reasons apply equally to cases like the present one, where the administrative process is at an end and a party seeks judicial review of a decision that was not appealed through the administrative process. Particularly, judicial review may be hindered by the failure of the litigant to allow the agency to make a factual record, or to exercise its discretion or apply its expertise. In addition, other justifications for requiring exhaustion in cases of this sort have nothing to do with the dangers of interruption of the administrative process. Certain very practical notions of judicial efficiency come into play as well. A complaining party may be successful in vindicating his rights in the administrative process. If he is required to pursue his administrative remedies, the courts may never have to intervene. And notions of administrative autonomy require that the agency be given a chance to discover and correct its own errors. Finally, it is possible that frequent and deliberate flouting of administrative processes could weaken the effectiveness of an agency by encouraging people to ignore its procedures.

In Selective Service cases, the exhaustion doctrine must be tailored to fit the peculiarities of the administrative system Congress has created. * * *

* * * We are not here faced with a premature resort to the courts—all administrative remedies are now closed to petitioner. We are asked instead to hold that petitioner's failure to utilize a particular administrative process—an appeal—bars him from defending a criminal prosecution on

grounds which could have been raised on that appeal. We cannot agree that application of the exhaustion doctrine would be proper in the circumstances of the present case.

First of all, it is well to remember that use of the exhaustion doctrine in criminal cases can be exceedingly harsh. The defendant is often stripped of his only defense; he must go to jail without having any judicial review of an assertedly invalid order. This deprivation of judicial review occurs not when the affected person is affirmatively asking for assistance from the courts but when the Government is attempting to impose criminal sanctions on him. Such a result should not be tolerated unless the interests underlying the exhaustion rule clearly outweigh the severe burden impose upon the registrant if he is denied judicial review. The statute as it stood when petitioner was reclassified said nothing which would require registrants to raise all their claims before the appeal boards. We must ask, then, whether there is in this case a governmental interest compelling enough to outweigh the severe burden placed on petitioner. Even if there is no such compelling interest when petitioner's case is viewed in isolation, we must also ask whether allowing all similarly situated registrants to bypass administrative appeal procedures would seriously impair the Selective Service System's ability to perform its functions.

The question of whether petitioner is entitled to exemption as a sole surviving son is, as we have seen, solely one of statutory interpretation. The resolution of that issue does not require any particular expertise on the part of the appeal board; the proper interpretation is certainly not a matter of discretion.[15] In this sense, the issue is different from many Selective Service classification questions which do involve expertise or the exercise of discretion, both by the local boards and the appeal boards.[16] Petitioner's failure to take his claim through all available administrative appeals only deprived the Selective Service System of the opportunity of having its appellate boards resolve a question of statutory interpretation. Since judicial review would not be significantly aided by an additional administrative decision of this sort, we cannot see any compelling reason why petitioner's failure to appeal should bar his only defense to a criminal prosecution. There is simply no overwhelming need

---

15. Of course, it is necessary that the local board, which has the responsibility of classifying registrants in the first instance, be given the information necessary to perform its function. However, the present case does not present an instance where a registrant is trying to challenge a classification on the basis of facts not presented to the local board. In such a case, the smooth functioning of the system may well require that challenges to classifications based upon facts not properly presented to the board be barred. In the case before us, the board was aware of the relevant facts when it made its decision to reclassify pe-

titioner I-A; no further factual inquiry would have been at all useful.

16. Conscientious objector claims, or deferments for those engaged in activities deemed "necessary to the maintenance of the national health, safety, or interest," would appear to be examples of questions requiring the application of expertise or the exercise of discretion. In such cases, the Selective Service System and the courts may have a stronger interest in having the question decided in the first instance by the local board and then by the appeal board, which considers the question anew. * * *

for the court to have the agency finally resolve this question in the first instance, at least not where the administrative process is at an end and the registrant is faced with criminal prosecution.

We are thus left with the Government's argument that failure to require exhaustion in the present case will induce registrants by bypass available administrative remedies. The Government fears an increase in litigation and a consequent danger of thwarting the primary function of the Selective Service System, the rapid mobilization of manpower. This argument is based upon the proposition that the Selective Service System will, through its own processes, correct most errors and thus avoid much litigation. The exhaustion doctrine is assertedly necessary to compel resort to these processes. The Government also speculates that many more registrants will risk criminal prosecution if their claims need not carry into court the stigma of denial not only by their local boards, but also by at least one appeal board.

We do not, however, take such a dire view of the likely consequences to today's decision. At the outset, we doubt whether many registrants will be foolhardy enough to deny the Selective Service System the opportunity to correct its own errors by taking their chances with a criminal prosecution and a possibility of five years in jail. The very presence of the criminal sanction is sufficient to ensure that the great majority of registrants will exhaust all administrative remedies before deciding whether or not to continue the challenge to their classifications. And, today's holding does not apply to every registrant who fails to take advantage of the administrative remedies provided by the Selective Service System. For, as we have said, many classifications require exercise of discretion or application of expertise; in these cases, it may be proper to require a registrant to carry his case through the administrative process before he comes into court. Moreover, we are not convinced that many in this rather small class of registrants will bypass the Selective Service System with the thought that their ultimate chances of success in the courts are enhanced thereby. In short, we simply do not think that the exhaustion doctrine contributes significantly to the fairly low number of registrants who decide to subject themselves to criminal prosecution for failure to submit to induction. Accordingly, in the present case, where there appears no significant interest to be served in having the System decide the issue before it reaches the courts, we do not believe that petitioner's failure to appeal his classification should foreclose all judicial review. * * *

We hold that petitioner's failure to appeal his classification and failure to report for his pre-induction physical do not bar a challenge to the validity of his classification as a defense to his criminal prosecution for refusal to submit to induction. We also hold that petitioner was entitled to exemption from military service as a sole surviving son. Accordingly, we reverse the judgment of the court below and remand the case for entry of a judgment of acquittal.

Chapter 7

DAMAGE ACTIONS AGAINST THE FEDERAL GOVERNMENT AND ITS OFFICERS

A. DAMAGE ACTIONS AGAINST THE GOVERNMENT

Because government, through its millions of employees, engages in most of the activities that regularly give rise to lawsuits between private citizens, the range of potential private claims against the government is at least as broad as the variety of legal disputes between private citizens. Typically, a citizen who sues the government for damages relies on the same body of legal principles that afford protection against similar invasions by other private citizens. If one's tulips have been damaged by a carelessly driven mail delivery truck, any claim for relief must find support in the statutory and common law that generally determines the liability of owners of negligently operated motor vehicles. Even when the government inflicts injuries that are unique, as, for example, when military operations result in the destruction of private property, the property owner may assert a cause of action that is identical or closely analogous to a private law claim.

Beyond these more prosaic damage actions the jurisprudence also reveals that governmental agencies have special capacities to harm. For government not only has unique constitutional duties to refrain from acting, it also undertakes a vast array of protective activities which, if bungled, can produce damages that are peculiar to state action. It is primarily these special duties, and the government's special defenses, that will occupy us in this section.

As noted in Chapter 6, damage actions against the federal government are not included in the sweeping waiver of immunity now found in 5 U.S.C.A. § 706. Claims for damages must therefore proceed pursuant to the more circumscribed provisions of special waiver statutes—the chief examples being the Tucker Act, Act of Mar. 3, 1887, ch. 359, 24 Stat. 505 (codified in scattered sections of 28 U.S.C.A.), and the Federal Tort Claims Act of 1946, 60 Stat. 843 (codified at 28 U.S.C.A. § § 1346(b), 2671 *et seq.*) Both statutes have a long and tortured legislative history, which is paralleled in their subsequent interpretation.

1. THE TUCKER ACT

As early as 1832 John Quincy Adams complained that private bills seeking damage relief consumed half the time of Congress, to the detriment of both that body and the public.   See Hearings on H.R. 5373 and H.R. 6463 before the House Comm. on the Judiciary, Ser. No. 13, 77th Cong. 2d Sess., 49 (1942).   Yet over fifty additional years of experimentation with various modifications of the private bills practice were required to convince Congress to pass the Tucker Act which gave the Court of Claims jurisdiction to render final judgments against the government. Even then actions sounding in tort were excluded.

As currently codified, the Court of Claims' Tucker Act jurisdiction includes claims   " * * * founded either upon the Constitution, or any Act of Congress, or any regulation of an executive department, upon any express or implied contract with the United States, or for liquidated or unliquidated damages in cases not sounding in tort."   28 U.S.C.A. § 1491 (1982).   Yet notwithstanding this rather sweeping language, the Tucker Act has been narrowly, even grudgingly, interpreted.   In 1889, for example, *United States v. Jones*, 131 U.S. 1, established that the Act conferred no jurisdiction to grant specific performance.   Modern cases have extended the bar to include declaratory judgments.   *United States v. King*, 395 U.S. 1 (1969).   A flavor of the jurisprudence can be gleaned from the description of one of the leading contemporary cases, *United States v. Testan*, 424 U.S. 392 (1976), in Orme, *Tucker Act Jurisdiction Over Breach of Trust Claims*, 1979 B.Y.U. L. Rev. 855, 860–62 (1979):

> *Testan* involved a claim by two government attorneys that their positions should have been classified as GS–14 rather than GS–13.   After exhausting their administrative remedies, the attorneys brought suit in the Court of Claims seeking prospective reclassification and an award of backpay.   A divided Court of Claims found the administrative refusal to reclassify plaintiffs arbitrary, but the court concluded that it lacked power to mandate the employees' reclassification.   A monetary award was deemed permissible but premature until an entitlement to the governmental position was created by the proper authority.   Therefore, the case was ordered remanded to the Civil Service Commission.   If on remand the Civil Service Commission should order reclassification, that action "could create a legal right which [could then be enforced] by a money judgment."   The Supreme Court disagreed.
>
> Justice Blackmun, in an opinion that drew no dissent, first quoted from *United States v. King* [395 U.S. 1 (1969)] for the proposition that Tucker Act jurisdiction is limited to money claims against the United States.   He then articulated the Court's general approach to the case:
>
>> The Tucker Act, of course, is itself only a jurisdictional statute; it does not create any substantive right enforceable against the United States for money damages. The Court of Claims has recognized that the Act merely confers jurisdiction upon it whenever the substantive right exists.   * * * We therefore must determine whether the two other federal statutes that are invoked by the respondents confer a substantive right to recover money damages from the United States for the period of their allegedly wrongful civil service classifications.   [424 U.S. at 398.]

The Court first rejected what it deemed the "implicit" conclusion of the lower court that the Classification Act "gives rise to a claim for money damages for pay lost by reason of the allegedly wrongful classifications." The Court stated that, as a sovereignty, the United States cannot be sued without its consent, " 'and the terms of its consent to be sued in any court define that court's jurisdiction to entertain the suit.' " Such consent to suit " 'cannot be implied but must be unequivocally expressed.' " "Thus," wrote Justice Blackmun, "except as Congress has consented to a cause of action against the United States, 'there is no jurisdiction in the Court of Claims more than in any other court to entertain suits against the United States.' "

The Court also rejected the contention that the Tucker Act itself waived sovereign immunity with respect to all claims "invoking a constitutional provision or a federal statute or regulation." Justice Blackmun wrote that since the claim in issue was not based on contract and was not one for the return of money paid the government, "[i]t follows that the asserted entitlement to money damages depends upon whether any federal statute 'can fairly be interpreted as mandating compensation by the Federal Government for the damage sustained.' " He and his brethren declined "to tamper with these established principles," and held that the Court of Claims lacked jurisdiction.

The Court subjected the Back Pay Act to similar scrutiny and found that it granted "a monetary cause of action only to those who were subjected to a reduction in their duly appointed emoluments or position," not to those who contended they were entitled to positions other than the ones they held. The claimants' suit was ordered dismissed.

The Court's language in *Testan* was indeed so stringent that it could be read to suggest that the Tucker Act is, while jurisdictional, not a waiver of sovereign immunity. The necessary waiver would have to be provided by some other statute specifically making the government liable in damages. This narrow view was reinforced by *United States v. Mitchell*, 445 U.S. 535 (1980). In 1983 the *Mitchell* case returned to the Supreme Court.

UNITED STATES v. MITCHELL

Supreme Court of the United States, 1983.
463 U.S. 206, 103 S.Ct. 2961, 77 L.Ed.2d 580.

JUSTICE MARSHALL delivered the opinion of the Court.

The principal question in this case is whether the United States is accountable in money damages for alleged breaches of trust in connection with its management of forest resources on allotted lands of the Quinault Indian Reservation.

In the 1850s, the United States undertook a policy of removing Indian tribes from large areas of the Pacific Northwest in order to facilitate the settlement of non-Indians. Pursuant to this policy, the first Governor and Superintendent of Indian Affairs of the Washington Territory began negotiations in 1855 with various tribes living on the west coast of the Territory. The negotiations culminated in a treaty between the United States and the Quinault and Quileute Tribes (Treaty of Olympia). In the

Treaty the Indians ceded to the United States a vast tract of land on the Olympic Peninsula in the State of Washington, and the United States agreed to set aside a reservation for the Indians.

* * *

In 1905 the Federal Government began to allot the Quinault Reservation in trust to individual Indians under the General Allotment Act of 1887.[5] * * * By 1935 the entire Reservation had been divided into 2,340 trust allotments, most of which were 80 acres of heavily timbered land. * * *

The forest resources on the allotted lands have long been managed by the Department of the Interior, which exercises "comprehensive" control over the harvesting of Indian timber. The Secretary of the Interior has broad statutory authority over the sale of timber on reservations. Sales of timber "must be based upon a consideration of the needs and best interests of the Indian owner and his heirs," and the proceeds from such sales are to be used for the benefit of the Indians or transferred to the Indian owner. Congress has directed the Secretary to adhere to principles of sustained-yield forestry on all Indian forest lands under his supervision. Under these statutes, the Secretary has promulgated detailed regulations governing the management of Indian timber. The Secretary is authorized to deduct an administrative fee for his services from the timber revenues paid to Indian allottees.

The respondents are 1,465 individuals owning interests in allotments on the Quinault Reservation, an unincorporated association of Quinault Reservation allottees, and the Quinault Tribe, which now holds some portions of the allotted lands. In 1971 respondents filed four actions that were consolidated in the Court of Claims. * * * Respondents sought to recover damages from the United States based on allegations of pervasive waste and mismanagement of timber lands on the Quinault Reservation. More specifically, respondents claimed that the Government (1) failed to obtain a fair market value for timber sold; (2) failed to manage timber on a sustained-yield basis; (3) failed to obtain any payment at all for some merchantable timber; (4) failed to develop a proper system of roads and easements for timber operations and exacted improper charges from allottees for maintenance of roads; (5) failed to pay any interest on certain funds from timber sales held by the Government and paid insufficient interest on other funds; and (6) exacted excessive administrative fees from allottees. Respondents assert that the alleged misconduct constitutes a breach of the fiduciary duty owed them by the United States as trustee under various statutes.

* * *

In *United States v. Mitchell*, 445 U.S. 535 (1980), this Court [held] * * * that the General Allotment Act "created only a limited trust

---

5. Section 5 of the Act provided that the United States would hold the allotted land for 25 years "in trust for the sole use and benefit of the Indian to whom such allotment shall have been made." The period during which the United States was to hold the allotted land was extended indefinitely by the Indian Reorganization Act of 1934.

relationship between the United States and the allottees that does not impose any duty upon the Government to manage timber resources." We concluded that "[a]ny right of the respondents to recover money damages for Government mismanagement of timber resources must be found in some source other than [the General Allotment] Act." Since the Court of Claims had not considered respondents' assertion that other statutes render the United States answerable in money damages for the alleged mismanagement in this case, we remanded the case for consideration of these alternative grounds for liability.

On remand, the Court of Claims once again held the United States subject to suit for money damages on most of respondents' claims. 664 F.2d 265 (1981) (*en banc*). The court ruled that the timber management statutes, various federal statutes governing road building and rights of way, statutes governing Indian funds and government fees, and regulations promulgated under these statutes imposed fiduciary duties upon the United States in its management of forested allotted lands. The court concluded that the statutes and regulations implicitly required compensation for damages sustained as a result of the Government's breach of its duties. Thus, the court held that respondents could proceed on their claims. * * *

* * *

It is axiomatic that the United States may not be sued without its consent and that the existence of consent is a prerequisite for jurisdiction. The terminology employed in some of our prior decisions has unfortunately generated some confusion as to whether the Tucker Act constitutes a waiver of sovereign immunity. The time has come to resolve this confusion. For the reasons set forth below, we conclude that by giving the Court of Claims jurisdiction over specified types of claims against the United States, the Tucker Act constitutes a waiver of sovereign immunity with respect to those claims. * * *

For decades this Court consistently interpreted the Tucker Act as having provided the consent of United States to be sued *eo nomine* for the classes of claims described in the Act. * * * These decisions confirm the unambiguous thrust of the history of the Act.

The existence of a waiver is readily apparent in claims founded upon "any express or implied contract with the United States." * * * The source of consent for such suits unmistakably lies in the Tucker Act. Otherwise, it is doubtful that *any* consent would exist, for no contracting officer or other official is empowered to consent to suit against the United States. The same is true for claims founded upon executive regulations. Indeed, the Act makes absolutely no distinction between claims founded upon contracts and claims founded upon other specified sources of law.

In *United States v. Testan*, 424 U.S. 392 (1976), and in *United States v. Mitchell*, this Court employed language suggesting that the Tucker Act does not effect a waiver of sovereign immunity. Such language was not necessary to the decision in either case. Without in any way questioning the result in either case, we conclude that this isolated language should be disregarded.   If a claim falls within the terms of the Tucker Act, the United States has presumptively consented to suit.

It nonetheless remains true that the Tucker Act " 'does not create any substantive right enforceable against the United States for money damages.' "   A substantive right must be found in some other source of law, such as "the Constitution, or any Act of Congress, or any regulation of an executive department." * * * [A]nd the claimant must demonstrate that the source of substantive law he relies upon " 'can fairly be interpreted as mandating compensation by the Federal Government for the damages sustained.' " * * *

* * * The question in this case is thus analytically distinct: whether the statutes or regulations at issue can be interpreted as requiring compensation.   Because the Tucker Act supplies a waiver of immunity for claims of this nature, the separate statutes and regulations need not provide a second waiver of sovereign immunity, nor need they be construed in the manner appropriate to waivers of sovereign immunity.

* * *

Respondents have based their money claims against the United States on various Acts of Congress and executive department regulations. * * *

* * *

The language of these statutory and regulatory provisions directly supports the existence of a fiduciary relationship.   For example, § 8 of the 1910 Act, as amended, expressly mandates that sales of timber from Indian trust lands be based upon the Secretary's consideration of the "the needs and best interests of the Indian owner and his heirs" and that proceeds from such sales be paid to owners "or disposed of for their benefit." Similarly, even in its earliest regulations, the Government recognized its duties in "managing the Indian forests so as to obtain the greatest revenue for the Indians consistent with a proper protection and improvement of the forests."   Office of Indian Affairs, Regulations and Instructions for Officers in Charge of Forests on Indian Reservations 4 (1911).   Thus, the Government has "expressed a firm desire that the Tribe should retain the benefits derived from the harvesting and sale of reservation timber."

Moreover, a fiduciary relationship necessarily arises when the Government assumes such elaborate control over forests and property belonging to Indians.   All of the necessary elements of a common-law trust are present: a trustee (the United States), a beneficiary (the Indian allottees), and a trust corpus (Indian timber, lands, and funds).   "[W]here the Federal government takes on or has control or supervision over tribal monies or properties, the fiduciary relationship normally exists with respect to such monies or properties (unless Congress has provided otherwise) even though nothing is said expressly in the authorizing or underlying statute (or other fundamental document) about a trust fund, or a trust or fiduciary connection."   *Navajo Tribe of Indians v. United States*, 624 F.2d 981, 987 (1980).

Our construction of these statutes and regulations is reinforced by the undisputed existence of a general trust relationship between the United States and the Indian people. This Court has previously emphasized "the distinctive obligation of trust incumbent upon the Government in its dealings with these dependent and sometimes exploited people." * * *

Because the statutes and regulations at issue in this case clearly establish fiduciary obligations of the Government in the management and operation of Indian lands and resources, they can fairly be interpreted as mandating compensation by the Federal Government for damages sustained. Given the existence of a trust relationship, it naturally follows that the Government should be liable in damages for the breach of its fiduciary duties. It is well established that a trustee is accountable in damages for breaches of trust. * * *

The recognition of a damages remedy also furthers the purposes of the statutes and regulations, which clearly require that the Secretary manage Indian resources so as to generate proceeds for the Indians. It would be anomalous to conclude that these enactments create a right to the value of certain resources when the Secretary lives up to his duties, but no right to the value of the resources if the Secretary's duties are not performed. * * *

The Government contends that violations of duties imposed by the various statutes may be cured by actions for declaratory, injunctive or mandamus relief against the Secretary, although it concedes that sovereign immunity might have barred such suits before 1976. In this context, however, prospective equitable remedies are totally inadequate. To begin with, the Indian allottees are in no position to monitor federal management of their lands on a consistent basis. * * *

In addition, by the time government mismanagement becomes apparent, the damage to Indian resources may be so severe that a prospective remedy may be next to worthless. For example, if timber on an allotment has been destroyed through Government mismanagement, it will take many years for nature to restore the timber. * * *

We thus conclude that the statutes and regulations at issue here can fairly be interpreted as mandating compensation by the Federal Government for violations of its fiduciary responsibilities in the management of Indian property. The Court of Claims therefore has jurisdiction over respondents' claims for alleged breaches of trusts.

* * *

JUSTICE POWELL, with whom JUSTICE REHNQUIST and JUSTICE O'CONNOR join, dissenting.

The controlling law in this case is clear. Speaking for the Court in *United States v. Mitchell* (*Mitchell I*), Justice MARSHALL reaffirmed the general principle that a cause of action for damages against the United States " 'cannot be implied but must be unequivocally expressed.' " Where, as here, a claim for money damages is predicated upon an alleged statutory violation, the rule is that the statute does not create a cause of action for damages unless the statute " 'in itself * * * can fairly be interpreted as mandating compensation by the Federal Government for the damage sustained.' "   *United States v. Testan.* * * * In sum, whether the United States has created a cause of action turns upon the intent of Congress, not the inclinations of the courts.

Today, the Court appears disinterested in the intent of Congress. It has effectively reversed the presumption that absent "affirmative statutory authority," the United States has not consented to be sued for damages. * * *

The Court does not—and clearly cannot—contend that any of the statutes standing alone reflects the necessary legislative authorization of a damages remedy. * * * Indeed, nothing in the timber-sales statute,[1] the road and right-of-way statutes, or the interest statute, addresses in any respect the institution of damages actions against the United States. Nor is there any indication in the legislative history of the statutes that Congress intended to consent to damages actions for mismanagement of Indian assets by enacting these provisions. The Court does not suggest otherwise.

* * *

The Court makes little or no pretense that it is following doctrine heretofore established. Without pertinent analysis, it simply concludes: "Because the statutes and regulations at issue in this case clearly establish fiduciary obligations of the Government in the management and operation of Indian lands and resources, they can fairly be interpreted as mandating compensation by the Federal Government for damages sustained." * * *

* * * Some of the statutes involved here, to be sure, create substantive duties that the Secretary must fulfill. But this could equally be said of the Classification Act, considered in *Testan*. It requires that pay classification ratings of federal employees be carried out pursuant to "the principle of equal pay for substantially equal work," 5 U.S.C.A. § 5101(1)(A). Although the federal employee in *Testan* alleged a violation of the Act, the Court concluded that a back-pay remedy was unavailable, rejecting the argument that the substantive right necessarily implies a damages remedy. * * *

It is fair to say that the Court is influenced by its view that an injunctive remedy is inadequate to redress the violations alleged—precisely the inference deemed inadmissible in *Testan*. It is the ordinary result of sovereign immunity that unconsented claims for money damages are barred. The fact that damages cannot be recovered without the sovereign's consent hardly supports the conclusion that consent has been given. Yet this, in substance, is the Court's reasoning. If it is saying that a remedy is necessary to redress every injury sustained, the doctrine of sovereign

---

1. The only monetary obligation imposed upon the Secretary by § 406 or § 407 is to pay the actual "proceeds" of timber sales to the owners of the land. Thus, while it may well be that those sections would permit an action to compel the Secretary to pay over unlawfully retained proceeds, no statutory basis exists for extending that remedy to profits that arguably or ideally should have been, but were not, earned by the Secretary. * * *

immunity will have been drained of all meaning. Moreover, "many of the federal statutes * * * that expressly provide money damages as a remedy against the United States in carefully limited circumstances would be rendered superfluous."

The Court has made no effort to demonstrate that Congress intended to render the United States answerable in damages upon claims of the kind presented here. The mere application by a court of the label "trust" cannot properly justify disregard of an immunity from damages the Government has never waived. I would reverse the judgment of the Court of Claims.

2. THE FEDERAL TORT CLAIMS ACT

As might be imagined the period from 1887 (enactment of the Tucker Act) to the 1946 enactment of the Federal Tort Claims Act was punctuated by a considerable dispute over what cases "sounded in tort." That period also saw enactment of numerous special statutes waiving governmental tort immunity in special circumstances. These statutes ranged from relatively general statutes, such as the Federal Employee's Compensation Act, to statutes waiving governmental immunity for tort suits by oyster growers. See generally W. B. WRIGHT, THE FEDERAL TORT CLAIMS ACT, Chap. 2, ¶¶ 2–18 to 2–50 (1964). Agitation for a general waiver of immunity for torts was also persistent. Finally, in connection with the massive post-war governmental reorganization of 1946, Congress acquiesced.

The Federal Tort Claims Act is codified in numerous sections of Title 28 U.S.C.A., and as originally enacted included the following significant provisions:

§ 1346. United States as Defendant

(b) Subject to [§§ 2674–80] of this title, the district courts * * * shall have exclusive jurisdiction of civil actions on claims against the United States, for money damages * * * for injury or loss of property, or personal injury or death caused by the negligent or wrongful act or omission of any employee of the Government while acting within the scope of his office or employment, under circumstances where the United States, if a private person, would be liable to the claimant in accordance with the law of the place where the act or omission occurred.

§ 2674. Liability of United States

The United States shall be liable, respecting the provisions of this title relating to tort claims, in the same manner and to the same extent as a private individual under like circumstances, but shall not be liable for interest prior to judgment or for punitive damages. * * *

The statute excepted from this broad waiver a number of circumstances, the most important of which, for our purposes, were:

§ 2680. Exceptions

The provisions of [§§ 2674–79] and section 1346(b) of this title shall not apply to—

(a) Any claim based upon an act or omission of an employee of the Government, exercising due care, in the execution of a statute or regulation, whether or not such statute or regulation be valid, or based upon the exercise or performance or the failure to exercise or perform a discretionary function or duty on the part of a federal agency or an employee of the Government, whether or not the discretion involved be abused.

* * *

(h) Any claim arising out of assault, battery, false imprisonment, false arrest, malicious prosecution, abuse of process, libel, slander, misrepresentation, deceit, or interference with contract rights.

Subsection (h) was amended in 1974 to waive immunity for assault, battery, false imprisonment, false arrest, abuse of process or malicious prosecution with regard to the acts of federal "investigative or law enforcement officers." Pub. L. No. 93–253, § 2, 88 Stat. 50.

The critical interest of the subsection (h) exceptions lies in the pressure that the government's narrowed liability has put on litigants and courts to expand the liability of federal officials—a subject to which we shall soon turn. The basic waiver provisions and section 2680(a) shape our current interest. Section 1346(b) not only makes state law the governing norm for tort actions under the act, it reinforces section 2680(a)'s executive and discretionary functions exception to liability by making the government liable only where a "private" party would be. Thus the government may escape liability *either* because its actions as the government have no private counterparts to which liability attaches under state law *or* because the action was "governmental" in the senses specified by section 2680(a).

UNITED STATES v. S.A. EMPRESA DE VIACAO AEREA RIO GRANDENSE (VARIG AIRLINES) ET AL.

Supreme Court of the United States, 1984.
—— U.S. ——, 104 S.Ct. 2755, 81 L.Ed.2d 660.

CHIEF JUSTICE BURGER delivered the opinion of the Court.

We granted certiorari in these two cases to determine whether the United States may be held liable under the Federal Tort Claims Act for the negligence of the Federal Aviation Administration in certificating certain aircraft for use in commercial aviation.

I

A. No. 82–1349

On July 11, 1973, a commercial jet aircraft owned by respondent S. A. Empresa De Viacao Aerea Rio Grandense (Varig Airlines) was flying from Rio de Janeiro to Paris when a fire broke out in one of the aft lavatories. The fire produced a thick black smoke, which quickly filled the cabin and cockpit. Despite the pilots' successful effort to land the plane, 124 of the 135 persons on board died from asphyxiation or the effects of toxic gases produced by the fire. Most of the plane's fuselage was consumed by a postimpact fire.

The aircraft involved in this accident was a Boeing 707, a product of the Boeing Co. In 1958 the Civil Aeronautics Agency, a predecessor of the FAA, had issued a type certificate for the Boeing 707, certifying that its designs, plans, specifications, and performance data had been shown to be in conformity with minimum safety standards. Seaboard Airlines originally purchased this particular plane for domestic use; in 1969 Seaboard sold the plane to respondent Varig Airlines, a Brazilian air carrier, which used the plane commercially from 1969 to 1973.

After the accident respondent Varig Airlines brought an action against the United States under the Federal Tort Claims Act seeking damages for the destroyed aircraft. The families and personal representatives of many of the passengers, also respondents here, brought a separate suit under the Act pressing claims for wrongful death. The two actions were consolidated in the United States District Court for the Central District of California.

Respondents asserted that the fire originated in the towel disposal area located below the sink unit in one of the lavatories and alleged that the towel disposal area was not capable of containing fire. In support of their argument, respondents pointed to an air safety regulation requiring that waste receptacles be made of fire-resistant materials and incorporate covers or other provisions for containing possible fires. 14 CFR § 4b.381(d) (1956). Respondents claimed that the CAA had been negligent when it inspected the Boeing 707 and issued a type certificate to an aircraft that did not comply with CAA fire protection standards. The District Court granted summary judgment for the United States on the ground that California law does not recognize an actionable tort duty for inspection and certification activities. The District Court also found that, even if respondents had stated a cause of action in tort, recovery against the United States was barred by two exceptions to the Act: the discretionary function exception, 28 U.S.C.A. § 2860(a), and the misrepresentation exception, § 2860(h).

The United States Court of Appeals for the Ninth Circuit reversed. 692 F.2d 1205 (1982). The Court of Appeals reasoned that a private person inspecting and certificating aircraft for airworthiness would be liable for negligent inspection under the California "Good Samaritan" rule, see Restatement (Second) of Torts §§ 323 and 324A (1965), and concluded that the United States should be judged by the same rule. * * * Interpreting respondents' claims as arising from the negligence of the CAA inspection rather than from any implicit misrepresentation in the resultant certificate, the Court of Appeals held that the misrepresentation exception did not apply. Finally, the Court of Appeals * * * viewed the inspection of aircraft for compliance with air safety regulations as a function not entailing the sort of policymaking discretion contemplated by the discretionary function exception.

B. No. 82–1350

On October 8, 1968, a DeHavilland Dove aircraft owned by respondent John Dowdle and used in the operation of an air taxi service caught fire in midair, crashed, and burned near Las Vegas, Nev.   The pilot, copilot, and two passengers were killed.   The cause of the crash was an in-flight fire in the forward baggage compartment of the aircraft.   * * *

In the aftermath of the crash, respondent Dowdle filed this action for property damage against the United States under the Federal Tort Claims Act.   * * *   The United States District Court for the Southern District of California found that the crash resulted from defects in the installation of the gasoline line leading to the cabin heater.   The District Court concluded that the installation did not comply with the applicable FAA regulations and held that the Government was negligent in certifying an installation that did not comply with those safety requirements. Accordingly, the District Court entered judgment for respondents.

On appeal, the United States Court of Appeals for the Ninth Circuit reversed and remanded for the District Court to consider whether the California courts would impose a duty of due care upon the Government by applying the "Good Samaritan" doctrine of § § 323 and 324A of the Restatement (Second) of Torts.   * * *   On remand, the District Court again entered judgment for respondents, finding that the California "Good Samaritan" rule would apply in this case and would give rise to liability on these facts.

On the Government's second appeal, the Ninth Circuit affirmed the judgment of the District Court.   692 F.2d 1209 (1982).   * * *

II

In the Federal Aviation Act of 1958, 49 U.S.C.A. § 1421(a)(1), Congress directed the Secretary of Transportation to promote the safety of flight of civil aircraft in air commerce by establishing minimum standards for aircraft design, materials, workmanship, construction, and performance. Congress also granted the Secretary the discretion to prescribe reasonable rules and regulations governing the inspection of aircraft, including the manner in which such inspections should be made.   Congress emphasized, however, that air carriers themselves retained certain responsibilities to promote the public interest in air safety: the duty to perform their services with the highest possible degree of safety, the duty to make or cause to be made every inspection required by the Secretary, and the duty to observe and comply with all other administrative requirements established by the Secretary.

Congress also established a multistep certification process to monitor the aviation industry's compliance with the requirements developed by the Secretary.   Acting as the Secretary's designee, the FAA has promulgated a comprehensive set of regulations delineating the minimum safety standards with which the designers and manufacturers of aircraft must comply before marketing their products.   See 14 CFR pts. 23, 25, 27, 29, 31, 33, and 35 (1983).   At each step in the certification process, FAA employees or their representatives evaluate materials submitted by aircraft manufacturers to determine whether the manufacturer has satisfied these regulatory requirements.   Upon a showing by the manufacturer that the prescribed safety standards have been met, the FAA issues an appropriate certificate permitting the manufacturer to continue with production and marketing.

The first stage of the FAA compliance review is type certification. A manufacturer wishing to introduce a new type of aircraft must first obtain FAA approval of the plane's basic design in the form of a type certificate. After receiving an application for a type certificate, the Secretary must "make, or require the applicant to make, such tests during manufacture and upon completion as the Secretary * * * deems reasonably necessary in the interest of safety. * * * " 49 U.S.C.A. § 1423(a)(2). By regulation, the FAA has made the applicant itself responsible for conducting all inspections and tests necessary to determine that the aircraft comports with FAA airworthiness requirements. The applicant submits to the FAA the designs, drawings, test reports, and computations necessary to show that the aircraft sought to be certificated satisfies FAA regulations. In the course of the type certification process, the manufacturer produces a prototype of the new aircraft and conducts both ground and flight tests. FAA employees or their representatives then review the data submitted by the applicant and make such inspections or tests as they deem necessary to ascertain compliance with the regulations. If the FAA finds that the proposed aircraft design comports with minimum safety standards, it signifies its approval by issuing a type certificate.

Production may not begin, however, until a production certificate authorizing the manufacture of duplicates of the prototype is issued. To obtain a production certificate, the manufacturer must prove to the FAA that it has established and can maintain a quality control system to assure that each aircraft will meet the design provisions of the type certificate. When it is satisfied that duplicate aircraft will conform to the approved type design, the FAA issues a production certificate, and the manufacturer may begin mass production of the approved aircraft.

Before any aircraft may be placed into service, however, its owner must obtain from the FAA an airworthiness certificate, which denotes that the particular aircraft in question conforms to the type certificate and is in condition for safe operation. It is unlawful for any person to operate an aircraft in air commerce without a valid airworthiness certificate.

An additional certificate is required when an aircraft is altered by the introduction of a major change in its type design. * * * The methods used by FAA employees or their representatives to determine an applicant's compliance with minimum safety standards are generally the same as those employed for basic type certification.

With fewer than 400 engineers, the FAA obviously cannot complete this elaborate compliance review process alone. Accordingly, 49 U.S.C.A. § 1355 authorizes the Secretary to delegate certain inspection and certification responsibilities to properly qualified private persons. By regulation, the Secretary has provided for the appointment of private individuals to serve as designated engineering representatives to assist in the

FAA certification process. These representatives are typically employees of aircraft manufacturers who possess detailed knowledge of an aircraft's design based upon their day-to-day involvement in its development. * * * FAA employees may briefly review the reports and other data submitted by representatives before certificating a subject aircraft.

III

* * *

* * * During the years of debate and discussion preceding the passage of the [Tort Claims] Act, Congress considered a number of tort claims bills including exceptions from the waiver of sovereign immunity for claims based upon the activities of specific federal agencies, notably the Federal Trade Commission and the Securities and Exchange Commission. In 1942, however, the Seventy-seventh Congress eliminated the references to these particular agencies and broadened the exception to cover all claims based upon the execution of a statute or regulation or the performance of a discretionary function. The language of the exception as drafted during the Seventy-seventh Congress is identical to that of § 2680(a) as ultimately adopted.

The legislative materials of the Seventy-seventh Congress illustrate most clearly Congress' purpose in fashioning the discretionary function exception. A Government spokesman appearing before the House Committee on the Judiciary described the discretionary function exception as a "highly important exception."

> "[It is] designed to preclude application of the act to a claim based upon an alleged abuse of discretionary authority by a regulatory or licensing agency—for example, the Federal Trade Commission, the Securities and Exchange Commission, the Foreign Funds Control Office of the Treasury, or others. It is neither desirable nor intended that the constitutionality of legislation, the legality of regulations, or the propriety of a discretionary administrative act should be tested through the medium of a damage suit for tort. The same holds true of other administrative action not of a regulatory nature, such as the expenditure of Federal funds, the execution of a Federal project, and the like.
>
> "On the other hand, the common law torts of employees of regulatory agencies, as well as of all other Federal agencies, would be included within the scope of the bill." Hearings on H.R. 5373 and H.R. 6463 before the House Committee on the Judiciary, 77th Cong., 2d Sess., 28, 33 (1942) (statement of Assistant Attorney General Francis M. Shea) * * * .

The nature and scope of § 2680(a) were carefully examined in *Dalehite v. United States*, 346 U.S. 15 (1953). *Dalehite* involved vast claims for damages against the United States arising out of a disastrous explosion of ammonium nitrate fertilizer, which had been produced and distributed under the direction of the United States for export to devastated areas occupied by the Allied Armed Forces after World War II. Numerous acts of the Government were charged as negligent: the cabinet-level decision to institute the fertilizer export program, the failure to experiment with the fertilizer to determine the possibility of explosion, the drafting of the basic plan of manufacture, and the failure properly to police the storage and loading of the fertilizer.

The Court concluded that these allegedly negligent acts were governmental duties protected by the discretionary function exception and held the action barred by § 2680(a). Describing the discretion protected by§ 2680(a) as "the discretion of the executive or the administrator to act according to one's judgment of the best course," the Court stated:

> "It is unnecessary to define, apart from this case, precisely where discretion ends. It is enough to hold, as we do, that the 'discretionary function or duty' that cannot form a basis for suit under the Tort Claims Act includes more than the initiation of programs and activities. It also includes determinations made by executives or administrators in establishing plans, specifications or schedules of operations. Where there is room for policy judgment and decision there is discretion. It necessarily follows that acts of subordinates in carrying out the operations of government in accordance with official directions cannot be actionable."

Respondents here insist that the view of § 2680(a) expressed in *Dalehite* has been eroded, if not overruled, by subsequent cases construing the Act, particularly *Indian Towing Co. v. United States*, 350 U.S. 61 (1955), and *Eastern Air Lines, Inc. v. Union Trust Co.*, 221 F.2d 62, *aff'd per curiam sub nom. United States v. Union Trust Co.*, 350 U.S. 907 (1955). While the Court's reading of the Act admittedly has not followed a straight line, we do not accept the supposition that *Dalehite* no longer represents a valid interpretation of the discretionary function exception.

Indian Towing Co. v. United States involved a claim under the Act for damages to cargo aboard a vessel that ran aground, allegedly owing to the failure of the light in a lighthouse operated by the Coast Guard. The plaintiffs contended that the Coast Guard had been negligent in inspecting, maintaining, and repairing the light. Significantly, the Government *conceded* that the discretionary function exception was not implicated in *Indian Towing*, arguing instead that the Act contained an implied exception from liability for "uniquely governmental functions." The Court rejected the Government's assertion, reasoning that it would "push the courts into the 'non-governmental'-'governmental' quagmire that has long plagued the law of municipal corporations."

In *Eastern Air Lines, Inc. v. Union Trust Co.*, two aircraft collided in midair while both were attempting to land at Washington National Airport. The survivors of the crash victims sued the United States under the Act, asserting the negligence of air traffic controllers as the cause of the collision. The United States Court of Appeals for the District of Columbia Circuit permitted the suit against the Government. In its petition for certiorari, the Government urged the adoption of a "governmental function exclusion" from liability under the Act and pointed to§ 2680(a) as textual support for such an exclusion. The Government stated further that § 2680(a) was "but one aspect of the broader exclusion from the statute of claims based upon the performance of acts of a uniquely governmental nature." This Court summarily affirmed, citing *Indian Towing Co. v. United States.* Given the thrust of the arguments presented in the petition for certiorari and the pointed citation to *Indian Towing*, the summary disposition in *Union Trust Co.* cannot be taken as a wholesale repudiation of the view of § 2680(a) set forth in *Dalehite*.[10]

As in *Dalehite*, it is unnecessary—and indeed impossible—to define with precision every contour of the discretionary function exception. From the legislative and judicial materials, however, it is possible to isolate several factors useful in determining when the acts of a Government employee are protected from liability by § 2680(a). First, it is the nature of the conduct, rather than the status of the actor, that governs whether the discretionary function exception applies in a given case. As the Court pointed out in *Dalehite*, the exception covers "[n]ot only agencies of government * * * but all employees exercising discretion." Thus, the basic inquiry concerning the application of the discretionary function exception is whether the challenged acts of a Government employee—whatever his or her rank—are of the nature and quality that Congress intended to shield from tort liability.

Second, whatever else the discretionary function exception may include, it plainly was intended to encompass the discretionary acts of the Government acting in its role as a regulator of the conduct of private individuals. Time and again the legislative history refers to the acts of regulatory agencies as examples of those covered by the exception, and it is significant that the early tort claims bills considered by Congress specifically exempted two major regulatory agencies by name. This emphasis upon protection for regulatory activities suggests an underlying basis for the inclusion of an exception for discretionary functions in the Act: Congress wished to prevent judicial "second-guessing" of legislative and administrative decisions grounded in social, economic, and political policy through the medium of an action in tort. By fashioning an exception for discretionary governmental functions, including regulatory activities, Congress took "steps to protect the Government from liability that would seriously handicap efficient government operations."

IV

We now consider whether the discretionary function exception immunizes from tort liability the FAA certification process involved in this case. Respondents in No. 82–1349 argue that the CAA was negligent in issuing

---

10. Respondents' reliance upon *Rayonier, Inc. v. United States*, 352 U.S. 315 (1957), is equally misplaced. In *Rayonier* the Court revisited an issue considered briefly in *Dalehite*: whether the United States may be held liable for the alleged negligence of its employees in fighting a fire. In *Dalehite*, the Court held that alleged negligence in firefighting was not actionable under the Act, basing its decision upon "the normal rule that an alleged failure or carelessness of public firemen does not create private actionable rights." In so holding, the *Dalehite* Court did not discuss or rely upon the discretionary function exception. The *Rayonier* Court rejected the reasoning of *Dalehite* on the ground that the liability of the United States under the Act is not restricted to that of a municipal corporation or other public body. While the holding of *Rayonier* obviously overrules one element of the judgment in *Dalehite*, the more fundamental aspects of *Dalehite*, including its construction of § 2680(a), remain undisturbed.

a type certificate for the Boeing 707 aircraft in 1958 because the lavatory trash receptacle did not satisfy applicable safety regulations. Similarly, respondents in No. 82–1350 claim negligence in the FAA's issuance of a supplemental type certificate in 1965 for the DeHavilland Dove aircraft: they assert that the installation of the fuel line leading to the cabin heater violated FAA airworthiness standards. From the records in these cases there is no indication that either the Boeing 707 trash receptacle or the DeHavilland Dove cabin heater was actually inspected or reviewed by an FAA inspector or representative. Respondents thus argue in effect that the negligent failure of the FAA to inspect certain aspects of aircraft type design in the process of certification gives rise to a cause of action against the United States under the Act.

The Government, on the other hand, urges that the basic responsibility for satisfying FAA air safety standards rests with the *manufacturer*, not with the FAA. The role of the FAA, the Government says, is merely to police the conduct of private individuals by monitoring their compliance with FAA regulations. According to the Government, the FAA accomplishes its monitoring function by means of a "spot-check" program designed to encourage manufacturers and operators to comply fully with minimum safety requirements. Such regulatory activity, the Government argues, is the sort of governmental conduct protected by the discretionary function exception to the Act.[12] We agree that the discretionary function exception precludes a tort action based upon the conduct of the FAA in certificating these aircraft for use in commercial aviation.

* * * [T]he Secretary of Transportation has the duty to promote safety in air transportation by promulgating reasonable rules and regulations governing the inspection, servicing, and overhaul of civil aircraft. * * *

In the exercise of this discretion, the FAA, as the Secretary's designee, has devised a system of compliance review that involves certification of aircraft design and manufacture at several stages of production. The FAA certification process is founded upon a relatively simple notion: the duty to ensure that an aircraft conforms to FAA safety regulations lies with the manufacturer and operator, while the FAA retains the responsibility for policing compliance. Thus, the manufacturer is required to develop the plans and specifications and perform the inspections and tests

---

12. The Government presses two additional arguments in support of reversal. First, the Government asserts that the conduct of the FAA in certificating aircraft is a core governmental activity that is not actionable under the Act, because no private individual engages in analogous activity. See 28 U.S.C.A. §§ 1346(b) and 2674. Second, the Government interprets respondents' claims as based upon misrepresentations contained in the certificates and argues that they are barred by the misrepresentation exception to the Act. § 2680(h). Respondents urge that the first argument is precluded by *Indian Towing Co. v. United States* and the second by our decision last Term in *Block v. Neal*, 460

U.S. 289 (1983). Because we rest our decision today upon the discretionary function exception, we find it unnecessary to address these additional issues.

The Government also argues that the Court of Appeals erred in applying California's "Good Samaritan" doctrine to the FAA certification process. But the application of the "Good Samaritan" doctrine is at bottom a question of state law, and we generally accord great deference to the interpretation and application of state law by the Courts of Appeals. We thus decline the Government's invitation to undertake our own examination of this state-law issue.

necessary to establish that an aircraft design comports with the applicable regulations; the FAA then reviews the data for conformity purposes by conducting a "spot check" of the manufacturer's work.

The operation of this "spot-check" system is outlined in detail in the handbooks and manuals developed by the CAA and FAA for the use of their employees. * * *

Respondents' contention that the FAA was negligent in failing to inspect certain elements of aircraft design before certificating the Boeing 707 and DeHavilland Dove necessarily challenges two aspects of the certification procedure: the FAA's decision to implement the "spot-check" system of compliance review, and the application of that "spot-check" system to the particular aircraft involved in these cases. In our view, both components of respondents' claim are barred by the discretionary function exception to the Act.

The FAA's implementation of a mechanism for compliance review is plainly discretionary activity of the "nature and quality" protected by § 2680(a). When an agency determines the extent to which it will supervise the safety procedures of private individuals, it is exercising discretionary regulatory authority of the most basic kind. Decisions as to the manner of enforcing regulations directly affect the feasibility and practicality of the Government's regulatory program; such decisions require the agency to establish priorities for the accomplishment of its policy objectives by balancing the objectives sought to be obtained against such practical considerations as staffing and funding. Here, the FAA has determined that a program of "spot-checking" manufacturers' compliance with minimum safety standards best accommodates the goal of air transportation safety and the reality of finite agency resources. Judicial intervention in such decisionmaking through private tort suits would require the courts to "second-guess" the political, social, and economic judgments of an agency exercising its regulatory function. It was precisely this sort of judicial intervention in policymaking that the discretionary function exception was designed to prevent.

It follows that the acts of FAA employees in executing the "spot-check" program in accordance with agency directives are protected by the discretionary function exception as well. The FAA employees who conducted compliance reviews of the aircraft involved in this case were specifically empowered to make policy judgments regarding the degree of confidence that might reasonably be placed in a given manufacturer, the need to maximize compliance with FAA regulations, and the efficient allocation of agency resources. In administering the "spot-check" program, these FAA engineers and inspectors necessarily took certain calculated risks, but those risks were encountered for the advancement of a governmental purpose and pursuant to the specific grant of authority in the regulations and operating manuals. Under such circumstances, the FAA's alleged negligence in failing to check certain specific items in the course of certificating a particular aircraft falls squarely within the discretionary function exception of § 2680(a).

V

In rendering the United States amenable to some suits in tort, Congress could not have intended to impose liability for the regulatory enforcement activities of the FAA challenged in this case. The FAA has a statutory duty to *promote* safety in air transportation, not to insure it. We hold that these actions against the FAA for its alleged negligence in certificating aircraft for use in commercial aviation are barred by the discretionary function exception of the Federal Tort Claims Act. Accordingly, the judgments of the United States Court of Appeals for the Ninth Circuit are reversed.

It is so ordered.

Notes

1. *Analogous Private Liability*. Although unnecessary to the disposition in *Varig*, the FTCA's reference to state law for its basic notions of "duty owed" can be troublesome in application. The first Supreme Court case to confront the question, *Feres v. United States*, 340 U.S. 135 (1950), held that the government was not liable to servicemen for injuries that were incident to military service, even though such injuries were not within the specific FTCA exception for claims arising out of "combatant activities of the military." The Court reasoned that there simply was no serviceman's recovery for negligence against the government anywhere in American law.

The government pursued this "uniquely governmental" function notion in the *Indian Towing* and *Rayonier* cases discussed in *Varig*. Those cases involved respectively claims of negligence in the operation of a lighthouse and fighting a fire. Taking a broader view of the reference to private law than in *Feres*, however, the Court in those cases analogized the liability asserted to "good Samaritan" liability. The Court interpreted the FTCA to require that claims only be *like* some private claim recognized by state law, not the *same* as some existing private liability. Such a construction seemed essential to avoid remitting both the "waiver" and the "cause of action" issues to state law. For as the government surely recognized, a requirement of *identity* would reintroduce immunity wherever state law provided immunity for "governmental functions." Such a result would be anomalous to say the least.

United States v. Muniz, 374 U.S. 150 (1963), was another step in detaching federal tort liability from state law. There federal prisoners were permitted to maintain a negligence suit against their jailers even though in many states such an action was not recognized. The Court viewed the case as one in which the duty of care was fixed by federal statute (18 U.S.C.A. § 4042) "independent of an inconsistent state rule." Id. at 165.

While the Court ostensibly avoids the issue, does the *Varig* opinion either reconcile—or suggest a choice among—the *Feres, Indian Towing, Rayonier* and *Muniz* approaches?

2. *Negligent or Wrongful*. Section 1346(b) also limits liability to injuries caused by a "negligent or wrongful act." The government's liability for negligence is essentially congruent with that of private persons, subject to the exceptions in section 2680. The actions of a government official can be shown to have been "negligent" not only by proving that the official failed to take the precau-

tions a reasonable person would have taken under the same circumstances, but also by demonstrating that the official deviated from a federal statute or regulation promulgated to assure protection of the plaintiff's interests.   See *Griffin v. United States*, 500 F.2d 1059 (3d Cir. 1974).   The term "wrongful" has been given a narrow construction and expands the government's liability only to the extent of allowing recovery for some trespasses that might not technically be considered negligent.   See *Dalehite v. United States*, 346 U.S. 15, 45 (1953); see also Merrill, *Compensation for Prescription Drug Injuries*, 59 Va.L.Rev. 1, 71 (1973).   An example is *Hatahley v. United States*, 351 U.S. 173 (1956), where the Supreme Court allowed certain Navajo Indians to recover for the destruction of their horses by federal agents purporting to act under federal public lands legislation and the Utah abandoned horse statute.   See also *United States v. Praylou*, 208 F.2d 291 (4th Cir. 1953), *cert. denied* 347 U.S. 934 (1954) (allowing recovery for property damages caused by the crash of government airplane).

In 1972, the Supreme Court laid to rest speculation that the term "wrongful" might permit recovery on a theory of strict or absolute liability.   *Laird v. Nelms*, 406 U.S. 797, 801 (1972), was an action for damages caused by the sonic boom from overflying military aircraft.   The plaintiff relied on North Carolina precedents allowing recovery on a theory of absolute liability for harm caused by an ultrahazardous activity.   A majority held that the Act did not embrace such a theory: "Congress intended to permit liability essentially based on the intentionally wrongful or careless conduct of Government employees, for which the Government was to be made liable according to state law under the doctrine of *respondeat superior*, but to exclude liability based solely on the ultrahazardous nature of an activity undertaken by the Government."   There was a vigorous dissent by Justice Stewart, in which Justice Brennan concurred.

3. *Misrepresentation.*   The statutory exception for injuries arising out of misrepresentation has produced several controversial decisions.   (This is hardly surprising.   At least one torts scholar, Shapo, *A Representational Theory of Consumer Protection*, 60 Va.L.Rev. 1109 (1974), has suggested that much, if not the whole, of tort theory might be unified around a broadly conceived notion of representational harm.)   The troublesome cases under the FTCA have involved negligent or reckless misstatements, rather than deliberate deceptions, which would appear to be covered by "deceit."   For example, in *Jones v. United States*, 207 F.2d 563 (2d Cir. 1953), *cert. denied* 347 U.S. 921 (1954), stockholders in a corporation that obtained oil production rights in certain government land sued to recover damages they sustained when they sold their stock in reliance on an understatement by the U.S. Geological Survey of the land's productive capacity. The court dismissed their action as sounding in misrepresentation.   In a well-known case, *United States v. Neustadt*, 366 U.S. 696 (1961), the Supreme Court held that the government was not liable to the purchaser of a house who had relied on an inspection and appraisal conducted by an FHA inspector.   The "misrepresentation" exception has also twice sheltered the government from liability for injuries resulting from erroneous inspection of food products by FDA officers. *Anglo-American & Overseas Corp. v. United States*, 242 F.2d 236 (2d Cir. 1957); *Mizokami v. United States*, 188 Ct.Cl. 736, 414 F.2d 1375 (1969).

4. *Dalehite and Its Progeny.*   As the *Varig* opinion notes, for thirty years the *Dalehite* case has been the leading authority on the discretionary function exception.   *Dalehite's* test for discretion sought to distinguish "planning" from "oper-

ational" activities.   The former were immune; the latter not.   Yet the Court also said that "[w]here there is room for policy judgment and decision there is discretion," a locution that seems capable of capturing all conscious and voluntary human conduct.   Moreover, the Court found a large number of actions in *Dalehite* that seemed remote from policy judgment—such as selection of the type of bagging to be used and the bagging temperature of the nitrates—embraced in the general "Plan of Activities" concocted by the U.S. Field Director of Ammunition Plants.   Yet the Court soon afterwards took the "liberal" approach to the construction of the FTCA previously described in *Indian Towing* and *Rayonier*.

This Janus-faced posture might suggest that *Dalehite* was explicable almost wholly by its facts.   Indeed, many lower court cases sustain liability where a strict application of *Dalehite* renders such a result problematic at best.   In *Griffin v. United States*, 500 F.2d 1059, 1066–67 (3d Cir. 1974), for example, the court sustained recovery against the government for the severe injuries suffered following administration of a dose of Sabin polio vaccine that the Division of Biological Standards had licensed.   The DBS had formally promulgated a regulation establishing specifications that its employees were to apply in determining nonvirulence of batches of the vaccine—specifications that many outside experts had criticized as unnecessarily stringent.   The DBS had released the batch of vaccine administered to Mrs. Griffin even though it did not meet these specifications.   The court disagreed with the government's contention that the decision whether to release the vaccine was discretionary and that the DBS regulation required a judgmental determination:

> We acknowledge that under DBS' construction of the regulation, the implementation called for a judgmental determination as to the degree to which each of the enumerated criteria indicated neurovirulence. * * * The judgment, however, was that of a professional measuring neurovirulence.   It was not that of a policy-maker promulgating regulations by balancing competing policy considerations in determining the public interest. * * * At issue was a scientific, but not policy-making, determination as to whether each of the criteria listed * * * was met and the extent to which each such factor accurately indicated neurovirulence.   DBS' responsibility was limited to merely executing the policy judgments of the Surgeon General. * * *

> The Government's release of Lot 56 was predicated upon its reliance on a factor called "biological variation."   Reliance on this factor, however, was not authorized by the regulations.   We therefore conclude * * * that DBS' activity was not immunized from judicial review.

See also *Payton v. United States*, 636 F.2d 132 (5th Cir. 1981), *rehearing en banc* 679 F.2d 475 (5th Cir. 1982) (holding certain aspects of a parole board's functions to be "operational" in suit by survivors of persons killed by a prisoner claimed to have been wrongfully released).   But the lower court decisions are hardly uniform or consistently liberal in finding a waiver.   See, e.g., *Federal Tort Claims Act: The Development and Application of the Discretionary Function Exemption*, 13 Cum. L. Rev. 535 (1983).   Some have formulated alternative tests that replicate analyses more commonly associated with questions of "reviewability" or the "political question" doctrine.   See *Smith v. United States*, supra.   Does *Varig* offer an alternative to the *Dalehite* formula?

5. *Constitutional Torts.*   The incorporation of state tort law by the FTCA limits recovery against the government for violations of individual constitutional

rights to situations in which state law recognizes an analogous negligent or intentional tort.   *Birnbaum v. United States*, 436 F. Supp. 967 (E.D.N.Y. 1977), for example, permitted an action under the FTCA when CIA agents opened and copied plaintiff's mail.   But the claim could not be premised on violation of First or Fourth Amendment rights.   The action would lie only for the recognized tort of invasion of privacy under New York law.   And, of course, many official acts may not fit easily, or at all, within the confines of common law tort notions.   See, e.g., *Brown v. United States*, 653 F.2d 196 (5th Cir. 1981), *cert. denied* 456 U.S. 925 (1982) (finding an allegation of false testimony by U.S. official leading to unconstitutional arrest and conviction not actionable under Texas law.)   This anomalous state of affairs has led to numerous proposals for reform of the Federal Tort Claims Act.   Note, *Rejecting Absolute Immunity for Federal Officials*, 71 Calif. L. Rev. 1707, 1708 n.8 (1983).   See generally P. SCHUCK, SUING GOVERNMENT (1983).

Actions founded on the Constitution but seeking recovery for conduct not recognized as tortious by state law might, of course, be thought to fall within the plain language of the Tucker Act.   The generally restrictive approach to Tucker Act claims has, however, prevented relief other than that sought pursuant to the Fifth Amendment's just compensation clause.   See Note, *Rethinking Sovereign Immunity After Bivens*, 57 N.Y.U. L. Rev. 597, 642–47 (1982).   Should *Mitchell (II)*, supra p. 785, be construed as modifying that historic posture?

6. *The Administrative claim requirement.*   In 1966 Congress amended the Tort Claims Act to provide that no action may be instituted under section 1346(b) "unless the claimant shall have first presented the claim to the appropriate Federal agency and his claim shall have been finally denied by the agency in writing * * * " 28 U.S.C.A. § 2675(a).   The failure of the agency to dispose of the claim within six months may be treated by the claimant as a final decision.   If the claimant files suit after obtaining a final agency decision, he may not seek more in damages than the amount he originally claimed, "except where the increased amount is based upon * * * evidence not reasonably discoverable," 28 U.S.C.A. § 2675(b), at the time of the initial claim.   And 28 U.S.C.A. § 2672 gives the head of each Federal agency the power, "in accordance with regulations prescribed by the Attorney General," to "consider, ascertain, adjust, determine, compromise, and settle" any claim that would be cognizable under 1346(b).   Any award exceeding $25,000 must have the prior written approval of the Attorney General.   This authority of individual agencies to dispose of or compromise tort claims makes possible the granting of relief even for injuries for which the United States might not be held liable in court, either because no negligence can be proved or because the action would be held to fall within one of the exceptions to the Act.   The annual volume of claims for administrative relief under this and other provisions is substantial.   See P. KEETON, R. KEETON, L. SARGENTICH & H. STEINER, TORT AND ACCIDENT LAW 304 (1983).   Failure to present a claim within two years of accrual bars relief.   28 U.S.C.A. § 2401(b).

In addition to FTCA suits, relief from governmentally-inflicted harm is frequently available from Congress through a private bill.   According to the Professors Keeton, et al, such petitions for private act relief are so numerous that the Congress has produced and informally adheres to a body of decisional principles in disposing of them.   "The custom of granting relief by private bill in certain types of cases goes far toward doing away with some of the exceptions written into the Tort Claims Act." Id. at 304.

B. SUITS AGAINST FEDERAL OFFICERS

When the local representative of the Small Business Administration runs over your pet poodle, that official's exposure to suit poses no threat to the continued operation of the SBA, and we would expect the case to be disposed of in accordance with the principles that determine the liability of any person who damages the property of another. Should a government employee acting in an official capacity harm the interests of a private citizen, however, the matter becomes more complex. We have already observed that, generally speaking, no action will lie against the U.S. government unless it has consented to be sued. And the exceptions to the coverage of FTCA consent insulate a substantial range of official actions from a suit for damages. This obstacle to relief alone would be sufficient to focus the citizen's attention on the immediate cause of his aggrievement, the official. Moreover, the conduct may have seemed sufficiently independent or so outrageous to make the official, rather than the government, the obvious target for suit. Not surprisingly, therefore, suits against government officers have become common and the principles that govern their disposition are important elements of the American public law system.

Such suits may be based on a variety of legal theories. The aggrieved citizen often can rely on established common law principles governing liability for the infliction of harm to person, property, or reputation. Legislative enactment may afford a basis for suit in addition to any provided by the common law. In particular, the several civil rights acts passed by Congress following the Civil War authorize private suits against state officers for specified types of conduct. (We shall leave consideration of suits against non-federal officials, however, for treatment in the next chapter.) Finally, courts as well as litigants have come to rely on provisions of the Constitution that prohibit specific conduct or protect particular interests as affording an independent basis for private recovery.

1. COMMON LAW ACTIONS AGAINST GOVERNMENT OFFICERS: OFFICIAL IMMUNITY

It requires little imagination to visualize many of the types of suits the wide range of official activities might provoke. Law enforcement officers routinely restrain the freedom of the citizens that they detain or arrest. Often, they use physical force to effect an arrest or carry out a search. Prosecutors devote long hours to achieving the imprisonment, and sometimes even the execution, of persons they believe guilty of crimes. Judges render verdicts and impose sentences that result in deprivation of property and freedom. Agency officers issue public statements describing policies or actions that may seriously damage the reputation of an individual, or business, or product. In short, common law theories would support a wide range of claims for damages for harm sustained by private citizens at the hands of government officers.

In a tort action against a government officer the identity of the defendant should not alter the basic elements of the plaintiff's affirmative case, which will be governed by the common law of the jurisdiction.   The defendant's identity may, however, preclude suit altogether.   For if the plaintiff's claim grows out of activities related to an official function, the defendant certainly will claim "official immunity" from suit.   Typically, official immunity is raised by a motion to dismiss for failure to state a claim; although clearly a defensive doctrine, an assertion of official immunity is the functional equivalent of a demurrer.

The notion that government officers should be shielded from liability for their misconduct is of relatively recent origin.   According to one source, "[e]arly opinions made no distinction between public officers and the ordinary citizen when considering answerability for tortious conduct."   W. GELLHORN & C. BYSE, ADMINISTRATIVE LAW 335 (6th ed. 1974).   Indeed, many early decisions imposed liability for official acts that would not even have been characterized as tortious by private law standards.   A well-known example is *Miller v. Horton*, 152 Mass. 540, 26 N.E. 100 (1891).   The defendant, a state health officer, had ordered the destruction of the plaintiff's horse pursuant to a Massachusetts statute that directed officers to inspect horses believed to be infected with glanders and summarily to destroy and bury diseased animals. Writing for the court, then-state Justice Holmes ruled that the plaintiff could recover damages from the officer personally if the jury found that the horse had not in fact been infected.   The defendant could not escape liability by showing that his action had been undertaken reasonably and in good faith, for he had authority to destroy only diseased horses. Other cases imposed liability for official mistakes based on similarly narrow readings of their authority.   E.g., *Lowe v. Conroy*, 120 Wis. 151, 97 N.W. 942 (1904); *Pearson v. Zehr*, 138 Ill. 48, 29 N.E. 854 (1891).

Nineteenth century decisions thus afforded public officers little protection against liability for actions taken in the performance of their public responsibilities:

> * * * [T]he officer was held personally liable not only for his negligence and omissions and for positive torts which he was not authorized to commit, but even for acts he was authorized-in-fact to do if * * * his authority to do those acts was legally insufficient.   Good faith, mistake, obedience to orders, or even the noblest intentions, were no better defenses to a personal action for damages. * * * These standards of personal official liability were repeatedly reaffirmed and applied during the same decades around the turn of the century when the Supreme Court was enlarging the immunity of the state; indeed it was only for this reason that the expanding state immunity was considered to be consistent with the tradition of effective redress for positive governmental wrongs.

Engdahl, *Immunity and Accountability for Positive Governmental Wrongs*, 44 U. Colo. L. Rev. 1, 47 (1972).

The same draconian rules were not applied to judges, however.   The Supreme Court early recognized the threat to judicial performance that would be posed by allowing a disappointed litigant to sue personally a judge who had assertedly exceeded his jurisdiction or authority.   In

Bradley v. Fisher, 80 U.S. (13 Wall.) 335, 351–54 (1871), Justice Field explained why judges should be accorded immunity from such suits:

> * * * Where there is clearly no jurisdiction over the subject-matter any authority exercised is a usurped authority, and for the exercise of such authority, when the want of jurisdiction is known to the judge, no excuse is permissible.   But where jurisdiction over the subject-matter is invested by law in the judge * * * the manner and extent in which the jurisdiction shall be exercised are generally as much questions for his determination as any other questions involved in the case. * * * [I]f * * * a judge of a criminal court, invested with general criminal jurisdiction over offenses committed within a certain district, should hold a particular act to be a public offense, which is not by the law made an offence, and proceed to the arrest and trial of a party charged with such act, or should sentence a party convicted to a greater punishment than that authorized by the law upon its proper construction, no personal liability to civil action for such acts would attach to the judge. * * *
>
> * * * The allegation of malicious or corrupt motives could always be made, and if the motives could be inquired into judges would be subjected to the same vexatious litigation upon such allegations, whether the motives had or had not any real existence. * * * [F]or malice or corruption in their action whilst exercising their judicial functions within the general scope of their jurisdiction, the judges of these courts can only be reached by public prosecution in the form of impeachment, or in such other form as may be specially prescribed.

This reasoning eventually prompted federal courts to extend similar immunity to officers other than judges who acted for the judicial branch or were engaged in "quasi-judicial" functions. See *Kendall v. Stokes*, 44 U.S. (3 How.) 87 (1845) (Postmaster General).   Still, by the mid-twentieth century the Supreme Court had not recognized any general immunity for administrative officers below Cabinet rank.   Such immunity had, however, been strongly supported by Judge Learned Hand in the following well-known case.

GREGOIRE v. BIDDLE

United States Court of Appeals, Second Circuit, 1949.
177 F.2d 579, cert. denied 339 U.S. 949, 70 S.Ct. 803, 94 L.Ed. 1363 (1950).

L. HAND, CHIEF JUDGE.

The plaintiff has appealed from a judgment, which dismissed a complaint in two counts because of its "failure to state a claim upon which relief can be granted."   The first count alleged that the five defendants were two successive Attorneys-General of the United States, two successive Directors of the Enemy Alien Control Unit of the Department of Justice, and the District Director of Immigration at Ellis Island; and that they arrested the plaintiff on the pretence that he was a German and therefore an enemy alien.   In spite of a ruling of the Enemy Alien Hearing Board after a hearing that he was a Frenchman, they kept him in custody from January 5, 1942, until September 18, 1946, when Judge Knox found that he was a Frenchman and released him by an order, which this court affirmed on November 6, 1947. The count ended by alleging that the arrest and imprisonment was "without any authority of law and without any reasonable or colorable cause," and that the defendants "conspired together and maliciously and wilfully entered into a scheme to deprive the plaintiff * * * of his liberty contrary to law." * * * The judge held that the defendants had an absolute immunity from liability, even though their unlawful acts had been induced only by personal ill-will, and dismissed the complaint for that reason.

We lay aside any extenuating facts * * * not because we should not be free to consider them if need were, but, because we think that the complaint should not stand, even though under Rule 9(b) we read the allegation that the defendants arrested the plaintiff "maliciously and wilfully," as though it had specifically alleged that they had acted altogether from personal spite and had been fully aware that they had no legal warrant for arresting or deporting the plaintiff. True, so stated, that seems at first blush a startling proposition; but we think, not only that it necessarily follows from the decision of the Supreme Court in *Yaselli v. Goff*; but that, as a new question, the result is desirable. * * *

[In *Yaselli v. Goff*, 275 U.S. 503 (1927), the Supreme Court affirmed a lower court's decision extending the absolute immunity previously recognized for judges to a special assistant to the Attorney General sued for malicious prosecution. As Judge Hand noted, in *Yaselli* the Supreme Court relied on *Bradley v. Fisher*, supra; *Alzua v. Johnson*, 231 U.S. 106 (1913) (judicial immunity); and *Spalding v. Vilas*, 161 U.S. 483 (1896) (recognizing immunity of cabinet officers, in that instance the Postmaster General).]

It does indeed go without saying that an official, who is in fact guilty of using his powers to vent his spleen upon others, or for any other personal motive not connected with the public good, should not escape liability for the injuries he may so cause; and, if it were possible in practice to confine such complaints to the guilty, it would be monstrous to deny recovery. The justification for doing so is that it is impossible to know whether the claim is well founded until the case has been tried, and that to submit all officials, the innocent as well as the guilty, to the burden of a trial and to the inevitable danger of its outcome, would dampen the ardor of all but the most resolute, or the most irresponsible, in the unflinching discharge of their duties. Again and again the public interest calls for action which may turn out to be founded on a mistake, in the face of which an official may later find himself hard put to it to satisfy a jury of his good faith. There must indeed be means of punishing public officers who have been truant to their duties; but that is quite another matter from exposing such as have been honestly mistaken to suit by anyone who has suffered from their errors. As is so often the case, the answer must be found in a balance between the evils inevitable in either alternative. In this instance it has been thought in the end better to leave unredressed the wrongs done by dishonest officers than to subject those who try to do their duty to the constant dread of retaliation. Judged as res nova, we should not hesitate to follow the path laid down in the books.

The decisions have, indeed, always imposed as a limitation upon the immunity that the official's act must have been within the scope of his powers; and it can be argued that official powers, since they exist only for the public good, never cover occasions where the public good is not their aim, and hence that to exercise a power dishonestly is necessarily to overstep its bounds. A moment's reflection shows, however, that that cannot be the meaning of the limitation without defeating the whole doctrine. What is meant by saying that the officer must be acting within his power cannot be more than that the occasion must be such as would have justified the act, if he had been using his power for any of the purposes on whose account it was vested in him. For the foregoing reasons it was proper to dismiss the first count. * * *

[The court concluded that the plaintiff's second count—which charged violations of federal civil rights statutes—did not apply to the facts alleged in the complaint.]

Judgment affirmed.

BARR v. MATTEO

Supreme Court of the United States, 1959.
360 U.S. 564, 79 S.Ct. 1335, 3 L.E.2d 1434.

MR. JUSTICE HARLAN announced the judgment of the Court, and delivered an opinion, in which MR. JUSTICE FRANKFURTER, MR. JUSTICE CLARK, and MR. JUSTICE WHITTAKER join.

We are called upon in this case to weigh in a particular context two considerations of high importance which now and again come into sharp conflict—on the one hand, the protection of the individual citizen against pecuniary damage caused by oppressive or malicious action on the part of officials of the Federal Government; and on the other, the protection of the public interest by shielding responsible governmental officers against the harassment and inevitable hazards of vindictive or ill-founded damage suits brought on account of action taken in the exercise of their official responsibilities. * * *

[This was a libel action brought by two officials of the Office of Housing Expediter against the Acting Director of the agency. The alleged libelous statements appeared in a press release, issued by the defendant in response to congressional criticism of an agency plan, devised by the plaintiffs, for making terminal-leave payments to certain employees some two years before. The press release announced that Barr was suspending the plaintiffs as his first official act, asserted that Barr had consistently opposed their plan for terminal-leave payments, and stated that he regarded the payments, even if legal, as violative of the "spirit" of governing legislation. The Court of Claims subsequently upheld the legality of the terminal-leave plan.]

Respondents sued, charging that the press release, in itself and as coupled with the contemporaneous news reports of senatorial reaction to the plan, defamed them to their injury, and alleging that its publication and terms had been actuated by malice on the part of petitioner. Petitioner defended, *inter alia*, on the ground that the issuance of the press release was protected by either a qualified or an absolute privilege. * * *

* * * The judgment of the trial court was affirmed by the Court of Appeals, which held that "in explaining his decision [to suspend respondents] to the general public [petitioner] * * * went entirely outside his line of duty" and that thus the absolute privilege, assumed otherwise to be available, did not attach. We * * * remanded the case "with directions to pass upon petitioner's claim of a qualified privilege."   On remand the Court of Appeals held that the press release was protected by a qualified privilege, but that there was evidence from which a jury could reasonably conclude that petitioner had acted maliciously, or had spoken with lack of reasonable grounds for believing that his statement was true, and that either conclusion would defeat the qualified privilege.

* * * [P]etitioner again sought, and we again granted certiorari to determine whether in the circumstances of this case petitioner's claim of absolute privilege should have stood as a bar to maintenance of the suit despite the allegations of malice made in the complaint.

The law of privilege as a defense by officers of government to civil damage suits for defamation and kindred torts has in large part been of judicial making, although the Constitution itself gives an absolute privilege to members of both Houses of Congress in respect to any speech, debate, vote, report, or action done in session.   This Court early held that judges of courts of superior or general authority are absolutely privileged as respects civil suits to recover for actions taken by them in the exercise of their judicial functions, irrespective of the motives with which those acts are alleged to have been performed, *Bradley v. Fisher*, and that a like immunity extends to other officers of government whose duties are related to the judicial process.   *Yaselli v. Goff*, 275 U.S. 503 (1927), involving a Special Assistant to the Attorney General.   Nor has the privilege been confined to officers of the legislative and judicial branches of the Government and executive officers of the kind involved in *Yaselli*.   In *Spalding v. Vilas*, 161 U.S. 483 (1896), petitioner brought suit against the Postmaster General, alleging that the latter had maliciously circulated widely among postmasters, past and present, information which he knew to be false and which was intended to deceive the postmasters to the detriment of the plaintiff.   This Court sustained a plea by the Postmaster General of absolute privilege. * * * * 8

8. The communication in *Spalding v. Vilas* was not distributed to the general public, but only to a particular segment thereof which had a special interest in the subject matter. Statements issued at the direction of Cabinet officers and disseminated to the press in the form of press releases have also been accorded an absolute privilege, so long as their contents and the occasion for their issuance relate to the duties and functions of the particular department.

The reasons for the recognition of the privilege have been often stated. It has been thought important that officials of government should be free to exercise their duties unembarrassed by the fear of damage suits in respect of acts done in the course of those duties—suits which would consume time and energies which would otherwise be devoted to governmental service and the threat of which might appreciably inhibit the fearless, vigorous, and effective administration of policies of government. * * * [Justice Harlan here quotes at length from *Gregoire v. Biddle*, supra.]

We do not think that the principle announced in *Vilas* can properly be restricted to executive officers of cabinet rank, and in fact it never has been so restricted by the lower federal courts. The privilege is not a badge or emolument of exalted office, but an expression of a policy designed to aid in the effective functioning of government. The complexities and magnitude of governmental activity have become so great that there must of necessity be a delegation and redelegation of authority as to many functions, and we cannot say that these functions become less important simply because they are exercised by officers of lower rank in the executive hierarchy.

To be sure, the occasion upon which the acts of the head of an executive department will be protected by the privilege are doubtless far broader than in the case of an officer with less sweeping functions. But that is because the higher the post, the broader the range of responsibilities and duties, and the wider the scope of discretion, it entails. It is not the title of his office but the duties with which the particular officer sought to be made to respond in damages is entrusted—the relation of the act complained of to "matters committed by law to his control or supervision," which must provide the guide in delineating the scope of the rule which clothes the official acts of the executive officer with immunity from civil defamation suits.

Judged by these standards, we hold that petitioner's plea of absolute privilege in defense of the alleged libel published at his direction must be sustained. The question is a close one, but we cannot say that it was not an appropriate exercise of the discretion with which an executive officer of petitioner's rank is necessarily clothed to publish the press release here at issue in the circumstances disclosed by this record. Petitioner was the Acting Director of an important agency of government, and was clothed by redelegation with "all powers, duties, and functions conferred on the President by Title II of the Housing and Rent Act of 1947. * * * " The integrity of the internal operations of the agency which he headed, and thus his own integrity in his public capacity, had been directly and severely challenged in charges made on the floor of the Senate and given wide publicity; and without his knowledge correspondence which could reasonably be read as impliedly defending a position very different from that which he had from the beginning taken in the matter had been sent to a Senator over his signature and incorporated in the Congressional Record. The issuance of press releases was standard agency practice, as it has become with many governmental agencies in these times. We think that under these circumstances a publicly expressed statement of the position of the agency head, announcing personnel action which he planned to take in reference to the charges so widely disseminated to the public, was an appropriate exercise of the discretion which an officer of that rank must possess if the public service is to function effectively. It would be an unduly restrictive view of the scope of the duties of a policy-making executive official to hold that a public statement of agency policy in respect to matters of wide public interest and concern is not action in the line of duty. That petitioner was not *required* by law or by direction of his superiors to speak out cannot be controlling in the case of an official of policy-making rank, for the same considerations which underlie the recognition of the privilege as to acts done in connection with a mandatory duty apply with equal force to discretionary acts at those levels of government where the concept of duty encompasses the sound exercise of discretionary authority.

The fact that the action here taken was within the outer perimeter of petitioner's line of duty is enough to render the privilege applicable, despite the allegations of malice in the complaint. * * *

We are told that we should forbear from sanctioning any such rule of absolute privilege lest it open the door to wholesale oppression and abuses on the part of unscrupulous government officials. It is perhaps enough to say that fears of this sort have not been realized within the wide area of government where a judicially formulated absolute privilege of broad scope has long existed. It seems to us wholly chimerical to suggest that what hangs in the balance here is the maintenance of high standards of conduct among those in the public service. To be sure, as with any rule of law which attempts to reconcile fundamentally antagonistic social policies, there may be occasional instances of actual injustice which will go unredressed, but we think that price a necessary one to pay for the greater good. And there are of course other sanctions than civil tort suits available to deter the executive official who may be prone to exercise his functions in an unworthy and irresponsible manner. We think that we should not be deterred from establishing the rule which we announce today by any such remote forebodings.

Reversed.

MR. JUSTICE BLACK, concurring.

I concur in the reversal of this judgment but briefly summarize my reasons because they are not altogether the same as those stated in the opinion of MR. JUSTICE HARLAN. * * *

Mr. Barr was peculiarly well qualified to inform Congress and the public about the Rent Stabilization Agency. Subjecting him to libel suits for criticizing the way the Agency or its employees perform their duties would certainly act as a restraint upon him. So far as I am concerned, if federal employees are to be subjected to such restraints in reporting their views about how to run the government better, the restraint will have to be imposed expressly by Congress and not by the general libel laws of the

States or of the District of Columbia. How far the Congress itself could go in barring federal officials and employees from discussing public matters consistently with the First Amendment is a question we need not reach in this case. It is enough for me here that the press release was neither unauthorized nor plainly beyond the scope of Mr. Barr's official business, but instead related more or less to general matters committed by law to his control and supervision.

MR. CHIEF JUSTICE WARREN, with whom MR. JUSTICE DOUGLAS joins, dissenting. * * *

* * * This is not a case where the only interest is in plaintiff's obtaining redress of a wrong. The public interest in limiting libel suits against officers in order that the public might be adequately informed is paralleled by another interest of equal importance: that of preserving the opportunity to criticize the administration of our Government and the action of its officials without being subjected to unfair—and absolutely privileged—retorts. * * *

It is clear that public discussion of the action of the Government and its officials is accorded no more than qualified privilege. * * * Only in a minority of States is a public critic of Government even qualifiedly privileged where his facts are wrong. Thus, at best, a public critic of the Government has a qualified privilege. Yet here the Court has given some amorphous group of officials—who have the most direct and personal contact with the public—an absolute privilege when their agency or their action is criticized. In this situation, it will take a brave person to criticize government officials knowing that in reply they may libel him with immunity in the name of defending the agency and their own position. This extension of *Spalding v. Vilas* can only have the added effect of deterring the desirable public discussion of all aspects of our Government and the conduct of its officials. It will sanctify the powerful and silence debate. This is a much more serious danger than the possibility that a government official might occasionally be called upon to defend his actions and to respond in damages for a malicious defamation. * * *

MR. JUSTICE BRENNAN, dissenting.

* * * In my view, only a qualified privilege is necessary here, and that is all I would afford the officials. A qualified privilege would be the most the law would allow private citizens under comparable circumstances. It would protect the government officer unless it appeared on trial that his communication was (a) defamatory, (b) untrue, and (c) "malicious."[2] We write on almost a clean slate here, and even if *Spalding v. Vilas* allows a Cabinet officer the defense of an absolute privilege in defamation suits, I see no warrant for extending its doctrine to the extent done—apparently to include every official having some color of discretion to utter communications to Congress or the public. * * * MR. JUSTICE HARLAN's approach seems to clothe with immunity the most obscure sub-

---

2. Actual "malice" is required to vitiate a qualified privilege, not simply the "construc- tive" malice that is inferred from the publication.

foreman on an arsenal production line who has been delegated authority to hire and fire and who maliciously defames one he discharges.[4]

* * * The opinion's position is simply that there are certain societal interests in relieving federal officials from judicial inquiry into their motives that outweigh all interest in affording relief. There is adopted Judge Learned Hand's statement of this added factor that is said to make an absolute privilege imperative: "it is impossible to know whether the claim is well founded until the case has been tried, and that to submit all officials, the innocent as well as the guilty, to the burden of a trial and to the inevitable danger of its outcome, would dampen the ardor of all but the most resolute, or the most irresponsible, in the unflinching discharge of their duties." In the first place, Professors Harper and James have, I think, squarely met and refuted that argument on its own terms: "Where the charge is one of honest mistake we exempt the officer because we deem that an *actual holding of liability* would have worse consequences than *the possibility of an actual mistake* (which under the circumstances we are willing to condone). But it is stretching the argument pretty far to say that the *mere inquiry into malice* would have worse consequences than the *possibility of actual malice* (which we would not, for a minute, condone). Since the danger that official power will be abused is greatest where motives are improper, the balance here may well swing the other way." Harper and James, Torts (1956), p. 1645. And in the second place, the courts should be wary of any argument based on the fear that subjecting government officers to the nuisance of litigation and the uncertainties of its outcome may put an undue burden on the conduct of the public business. Such a burden is hardly one peculiar to public officers; citizens generally go through life subject to the risk that they may, though in the right, be subject to litigation and the possibility of a miscarriage of justice. It is one of the goals of a well-operating legal system to keep the burden of litigation and the risks of such miscarriages to a minimum; in this area, which is governed by federal law, proof of malice outside of the bare fact of the making of the statement should be forthcoming, and summary judgment practice offers protection to the defendant; but the way to minimizing the burdens of litigation does not generally lie through the abolition of a right of redress for an admitted wrong. * * *

There is an even more basic objection to the opinion. It deals with large concepts of public policy and purports to balance the societal interests involved in them. It denies the defamed citizen a recovery by characterizing the policy favoring absolute immunity as "an expression of a policy designed to aid in the effective functioning of government." * * * This, I fear, is a gossamer web self-spun without a scintilla of support to which one can point. To come to this conclusion, and to

---

4. The opinion's rationale covers the entire federal bureaucracy, as compared to the numerically much less extensive legislative and judicial privileges. And as to the former, the Constitution speaks, and the resolution of the factors involved in the latter is very obviously within the courts' special competence.

shift the line from the already extensive protection given the public officer by the qualified privilege doctrine, demands the resolution of large imponderables which one might have thought would be better the business of the Legislative Branch.   To what extent is it in the public interest that the Executive Branch carry on publicity campaigns in relation to its activities? * * * To what extent does fear of litigation actually inhibit the conduct of officers in carrying out the public business?   To what extent should it?   Where does healthy administrative frankness and boldness shade into bureaucratic tyranny?   To what extent is supervision by an administrator's superiors effective in assuring that there will be little abuse of a freedom from suit?   To what extent can the referral of constituent complaints by Congressmen to the executive agencies (already myriad in number and quite routinized in processing) take the place of actions in the courts of law in securing the injured citizen redress?   Can it be assumed, as the opinion appears to assume, that an absolute privilege so broadly enjoyed will not be subject to severe abuse?   Does recent history afford instructive parallels in the experience with constitutionally recognized forms of governmental privilege—say the legislative privilege?   I do not purport to know the answers to these questions, and I simply submit that the nature of the questions themselves should lead us to forsake any effort on our own to modify over so wide an area the line the common law generally indicates is to be drawn here. * * *

The courts, it must be remembered, are not the only agency for fashioning policy here.   One would think, in fact, if the solution afforded through a qualified privilege (which would apply between private parties under analogous circumstances) were to be modified on the strength of considerations such as those discussed today, that Congress would provide a more appropriate forum for the determination.   The presence of the imponderables I have discussed, their political flavor, and their intimate relation to the practicalities of government management would support this conclusion.   If the fears expressed materialized and great inconvenience to the workings of the Government arose out of allowing defamation actions subject to a showing of malice, Congress might well be disposed to intervene. * * * We ought not, as I fear we do today, for all practical purposes foreclose such consideration of the problem by expanding on the comparable common-law privilege and wholly immunizing federal officials from defamation suits whenever they can show that their act was incidental to their jobs.

Notes

1. Some writers expressed doubt that Justice Harlan's opinion in *Barr v. Matteo*, which commanded the support of only four Justices, would remain the definitive statement of the immunity of high-ranking federal administrators.   See, e.g., Handler and Klein, *The Defense of Privilege in Defamation Suits Against Government Executive Officials*, 74 Harv. L. Rev. 44 (1960); see also Gray, *Private Wrongs of Public Servants*, 47 Calif. L. Rev. 303 (1959).   Very few would have forecast the expansive reading that the opinion has subsequently received.

2. *Garner v. Rathburn*, 346 F.2d 55, 57–58 (10th Cir. 1965), is an example of this development.   The plaintiff there was an Air Force enlisted man assigned to work with a crew laying asphalt at his base under the supervision of Rathburn, a civilian in the employ of the Air Force who supervised 64 men in all.   Garner claimed he sustained injuries when, as a result of the defendant's negligence, a defective asphalt spreader ran over his leg.   The court sustained Rathburn's claim of immunity:

> * * * [W]e believe that the defendant's duties as supervisor constantly demanded the exercise of judgment and discretion over his men and equipment. * * *

> * * * It appears to us that his functions, in relation to an important military installation, are such that to expose him to damage suits for his acts would likely inhibit the performance of his duties to the public's detriment.

Immunity may protect not only officials who have no policy-making responsibility but also, indeed, individuals who have only loose ties with the government. *Becker v. Philco Corp.*, 372 F.2d 771, 774 (4th Cir.), *cert. denied* 389 U.S. 979 (1967), was an action for defamation brought by two former employees against Philco for false reports made to the government concerning their reported disregard of security controls.   Philco was obligated under the terms of its government contract to report any actions of its employees that deviated from controls designed to maintain the secrecy of information provided by the government.   The logic of *Barr v. Matteo*, the court concluded, sustained Philco's claim of immunity: "[W]e think the company and its trusted personnel were imbued with the official's character, and partake of his immunity to liability, whenever and wherever he would enjoy the absolute privilege."   See also *Heine v. Raus*, 399 F.2d 785 (4th Cir. 1968), *cert denied* 402 U.S. 914 (1971) (paid informant of CIA entitled to immunity).

Courts have occasionally demonstrated unusual concern to protect government officials from harassing litigation.   In *Bailey v. Van Buskirk*, 345 F.2d 298 (9th Cir. 1965), *cert. denied* 383 U.S. 948 (1966), the court ruled that two Army surgeons could not be sued for malpractice by an enlisted man, who underwent a second operation and sustained the loss of a kidney to remove surgical sutures that had been left behind by the defendants.   "It is not yet within the American legal concept that one soldier may sue another for negligent acts performed in the line of duty.   The idea is that an undisciplined army is a mob and he who is in it would weaken discipline if he can civilly litigate with others in the army over the performance of another man's army duty."

3. In all of the foregoing cases the defendant's assertedly tortious acts were committed in the course of activities either directed or clearly contemplated by their employer.   The judicial test thus makes the propriety of the defendant's general activities, rather than the nature of their particular acts, determinative of entitlement to immunity.   And it may fairly be said that the federal courts will accord immunity to almost any administrative officer who can show that harmful conduct fell generally within the scope of assigned responsibilities.   Indeed, it is difficult to find cases since *Barr v. Matteo* in which immunity from common law tort actions was denied.   But see *Kelley v. Dunne*, 344 F.2d 129 (1st Cir. 1965).

2. CONSTITUTIONAL ACTIONS AGAINST FEDERAL OFFICERS

The U.S. Constitution, and more particularly the Bill of Rights, forbids a wide variety of interferences with private rights by agencies or officials of government.   A familiar example is the Fourth Amendment's prohibition against unreasonable searches and seizures, which the Fourteenth Amendment makes applicable to the states.   No provision of the Constitution itself, however, expressly authorizes any remedy, judicial or administrative, for official conduct that violates constitutional rights.   The federal courts, nevertheless, have long been prepared to issue injunctions to protect constitutional rights with no statutory authority for such a remedy beyond the bare grant of jurisdiction, in 28 U.S.C.A. § 1331, over cases "arising under the Constitution, laws, or treaties of the United States."   See generally Hill, *Constitutional Remedies*, 69 Colum. L. Rev. 1109 (1969).   Furthermore the courts have granted what may be termed "defensive" relief for many constitutional violations by invalidating government action taken without observance, or in defiance, of constitutional safeguards.   Thus, for example, the courts have refused to enforce statutes found unconstitutional and have struck down criminal convictions obtained through procedures that violate any of the Bill of Rights.

These several remedies are subject to important limitations.   Injunctive relief may be adequate when a constitutional violation is only incipient or is likely to be repeated, but it is not a satisfactory remedy for the one-time abridgement of rights that occurred in the past.   Moreover, the assurance that a judge will refuse to enforce an unconstitutional statute or will forbid the use of tainted evidence affords scant comfort to the individual who is afraid to resist compliance or to the victim of police brutality who is never brought to trial.   Finally, these essentially defensive remedies may not provide adequate incentives to law enforcement officers to refrain from unconstitutional conduct.   Accordingly, it may be a matter of some importance whether affirmative remedies are available to protect rights guaranteed by the Constitution.

In *Bell v. Hood*, 327 U.S. 678 (1946), the plaintiffs sought damages for alleged unconstitutional arrests, searches, and seizures conducted by agents of the Federal Bureau of Investigation.   The plaintiffs based their claim to damages on the Constitution, not on state law, and they premised federal jurisdiction on the predecessor of 28 U.S.C.A. § 1331. The lower courts held that the case was not one "arising under the Constitution or laws of the United States," and that they therefore lacked jurisdiction.   The Supreme Court reversed, ruling that whether such a cause of action for damages would lie presented an issue sufficiently substantial to support the district court's jurisdiction to decide the case on the merits.   On remand, the district court concluded that an action for damages could not be maintained and distinguished the precedents allowing equitable relief against constitutional violations.   The case did not go further.   Later, in *Wheeldin v. Wheeler*, 373 U.S. 647 (1963), the Supreme

Court in dictum indicated doubt about whether a federal court could award damages for constitutional violations without specific statutory authorization.   As late as 1971, therefore, the availability of such a remedy—in the absence of Congressional authorization remained uncertain. See Katz, *The Jurisprudence of Remedies: Constitutional Legality and Law of Torts in Bell v. Hood*, 117 U. Pa. L. Rev. 1 (1968).

BIVENS v. SIX UNKNOWN NAMED AGENTS OF THE FEDERAL BUREAU OF NARCOTICS

Supreme Court of the United States, 1971.
403 U.S. 388, 91 S.Ct. 1999, 29 L.Ed.2d 619.

MR. JUSTICE BRENNAN delivered the opinion of the Court.

The Fourth Amendment provides that:

"The right of the people to be secure in their persons, houses, papers, and effects, against unreasonable searches and seizures, shall not be violated. * * * "

In *Bell v. Hood*, we reserved the question whether violation of that command by a federal agent acting under color of his authority gives rise to a cause of action for damages consequent upon his unconstitutional conduct.   Today we hold that it does.

This case has its origin in an arrest and search carried out on the morning of November 26, 1965.   Petitioner's complaint alleged that on that day respondents, agents of the Federal Bureau of Narcotics acting under claim of federal authority, entered his apartment and arrested him for alleged narcotics violations.   The agents manacled petitioner in front of his wife and children, and threatened to arrest the entire family.   They searched the apartment from stem to stern.   Thereafter, petitioner was taken to the federal courthouse in Brooklyn, where he was interrogated, booked, and subjected to a visual strip search.

* * * [P]etitioner brought suit in Federal District Court.   In addition to the allegations above, his complaint asserted that the arrest and search were effected without a warrant, and that unreasonable force was employed in making the arrest; fairly read, it alleges as well that the arrest was made without probable cause.   Petitioner claimed to have suffered great humiliation, embarrassment, and mental suffering as a result of the agents' unlawful conduct, and sought $15,000 damages from each of them.   The District Court, on respondents' motion, dismissed the complaint on the ground, *inter alia*, that it failed to state a cause of action.   The Court of Appeals, one judge concurring specially, affirmed on that basis. * * *

Respondents do not argue that petitioner should be entirely without remedy for an unconstitutional invasion of his rights by federal agents. In respondents' view, however, the rights that petitioner asserts—primarily rights of privacy—are creations of state and not of federal law.   Accordingly, they argue, petitioner may obtain money damages to redress invasion of these rights only by an action in tort, under state law, in the state courts. In this scheme the Fourth Amendment would serve merely to limit the extent to which the agents could defend the state law tort suit by asserting that their actions were a valid exercise of federal power: if the agents were shown to have violated the Fourth Amendment, such a defense would be lost to them and they would stand before the state law merely as private individuals. * * *

* * * Respondents seek to treat the relationship between a citizen and a federal agent unconstitutionally exercising his authority as no different from the relationship between two private citizens. In so doing, they ignore the fact that power, once granted, does not disappear like a magic gift when it is wrongfully used. An agent acting—albeit unconstitutionally—in the name of the United States possesses a far greater capacity for harm than an individual trespasser exercising no authority other than his own. Accordingly, as our cases make clear, the Fourth Amendment operates as a limitation upon the exercise of federal power regardless of whether the State in whose jurisdiction that power is exercised would prohibit or penalize the identical act if engaged in by a private citizen. It guarantees to citizens of the United States the absolute right to be free from unreasonable searches and seizures carried out by virture of federal authority. And "where federally protected rights have been invaded, it has been the rule from the beginning that courts will be alert to adjust their remedies so as to grant the necessary relief." *Bell v. Hood.*

First. Our cases have long since rejected the notion that the Fourth Amendment proscribes only such conduct as would, if engaged in by private persons, be condemned by state law. * * *

Second. The interests protected by state laws regulating trespass and the invasion of privacy, and those protected by the Fourth Amendment's guarantee against unreasonable searches and seizures, may be inconsistent or even hostile. Thus, we may bar the door against an unwelcome private intruder, or call the police if he persists in seeking entrance. The availability of such alternative means for the protection of privacy may lead the State to restrict imposition of liability for any consequent trespass. A private citizen, asserting no authority other than his own, will not normally be liable in trespass if he demands, and is granted, admission to another's house. * * * Nor is it adequate to answer that state law may take into account the different status of one clothed with the authority of the Federal Government. For just as state law may not authorize federal agents to violate the Fourth Amendment, neither may state law undertake to limit the extent to which federal authority can be exercised. The inevitable consequence of this dual limitation on state power is that the federal question becomes not merely a possible defense to the state law action, but an independent claim both necessary and sufficient to make out the plaintiff's cause of action.

Third. That damages may be obtained for injuries consequent upon a violation of the Fourth Amendment by federal officials should hardly seem a surprising proposition. Historically, damages have been regarded as the ordinary remedy for an invasion of personal interests in liberty.

Of course, the Fourth Amendment does not in so many words provide for its enforcement by an award of money damages for the consequences of its violation. But "it is * * * well settled that where legal rights have been invaded, and a federal statute provides for a general right to sue for such invasion, federal courts may use any available remedy to make good the wrong done." The present case involves no special factors counselling hesitation in the absence of affirmative action by Congress. We are not dealing with a question of "federal fiscal policy." * * * Nor are we asked in this case to impose liability upon a congressional employee for actions contrary to no constitutional prohibition, but merely said to be in excess of the authority delegated to him by the Congress. Finally, we cannot accept respondents' formulation of the question as whether the availability of money damages is necessary to enforce the Fourth Amendment. For we have here no explicit congressional declaration that persons injured by a federal officer's violation of the Fourth Amendment may not recover money damages from the agents, but must instead be remitted to another remedy, equally effective in the view of Congress. The question is merely whether petitioner, if he can demonstrate an injury consequent upon the violation by federal agents of his Fourth Amendment rights, is entitled to redress his injury through a particular remedial mechanism normally available in the federal courts. Cf. *J. I. Case Co. v. Borak*, 377 U.S. 426, 433 (1964). * * * Having concluded that petitioner's complaint states a cause of action under the Fourth Amendment, we hold that petitioner is entitled to recover money damages for any injuries he has suffered as a result of the agents' violation of the Amendment. * * *

MR. JUSTICE HARLAN, concurring in the judgment.

My initial view of this case was that the Court of Appeals was correct in dismissing the complaint, but for reasons stated in this opinion I am now persuaded to the contrary. Accordingly, I join in the judgment of reversal. * * *

I turn first to the contention that the constitutional power of federal courts to accord Bivens damages for his claim depends on the passage of a statute creating a "federal cause of action." Although the point is not entirely free of ambiguity, I do not understand either the Government or my dissenting Brothers to maintain that Bivens' contention that he is entitled to be free from the type of official conduct prohibited by the Fourth Amendment depends on a decision by the State in which he resides to accord him a remedy. Such a position would be incompatible with the presumed availability of federal equitable relief, if a proper showing can be made in terms of the ordinary principles governing equitable remedies. However broad a federal court's discretion concerning equitable remedies, it is absolutely clear * * * that in a nondiversity suit a federal court's power to grant even equitable relief depends on the presence of a substantive right derived from federal law.

Thus the interest which Bivens claims—to be free from official conduct in contravention of the Fourth Amendment—is a federally protected interest. Therefore, the question of judicial *power* to grant Bivens damages is not a problem of the "source" of the "right"; instead, the question is whether the power to authorize damages as a judicial remedy for the vindication of a federal constitutional right is placed by the Constitution itself exclusively in Congress' hands.

The contention that the federal courts are powerless to accord a litigant damages for a claimed invasion of his federal constitutional rights until Congress explicitly authorizes the remedy cannot rest on the notion that the decision to grant compensatory relief involves a resolution of policy considerations not susceptible of judicial discernment. Thus, in suits for damages based on violations of federal statutes lacking any express authorization of a damage remedy, this Court has authorized such relief where, in its view, damages are necessary to effectuate the congressional policy underpinning the substantive provisions of the statute. *J. I. Case Co. v. Borak* [infra p. 847]. Cf. *Wyandotte Transportation Co. v. United States*, 389 U.S. 191 (1967).[4]

If it is not the nature of the remedy which is thought to render a judgment as to the appropriateness of damages inherently "legislative," then it must be the nature of the legal interest offered as an occasion for invoking otherwise appropriate judicial relief. But I do not think that the fact that the interest is protected by the Constitution rather than statute or common law justifies the assertion that federal courts are powerless to grant damages in the absence of explicit congressional action authorizing the remedy. * * * [I]t would be at least anomalous to conclude that the federal judiciary—while competent to choose among the range of traditional judicial remedies to implement statutory and common-law policies, and even to generate substantive rules governing primary behavior in furtherance of broadly formulated policies articulated by statute or Constitution—is powerless to accord a damages remedy to vindicate social policies which, by virtue of their inclusion in the Constitution, are aimed predominantly at restraining the Government as an instrument of the popular will.

More importantly, the presumed availability of federal equitable relief against threatened invasions of constitutional interests appears entirely to negate the contention that the status of an interest as constitutionally protected divests federal courts of the power to grant damages absent express congressional authorization.

If explicit congressional authorization is an absolute prerequisite to the power of a federal court to accord compensatory relief regardless of

4. The *Borak* case is an especially clear example of the exercise of federal judicial power to accord damages as an appropriate remedy in the absence of any express statutory authorization of a federal cause of action. There we "implied"—from what can only be characterized as an "exclusively procedural provision" affording access to a federal forum—a private cause of action for damages for violation of § 14(a) of the Securities Exchange Act of 1934. We did so in an area where federal regulation has been singularly comprehensive and elaborate administrative enforcement machinery had been provided. The exercise of judicial power involved in *Borak* simply cannot be justified in terms of statutory construction; nor did the *Borak* Court purport to do so. The notion of "implying" a remedy, therefore, as applied to cases like *Borak*, can only refer to a process whereby the federal judiciary exercises a choice among *traditionally available* judicial remedies according to reasons related to the substantive social policy embodied in an act of positive law.

the necessity or appropriateness of damages as a remedy simply because of the status of a legal interest as constitutionally protected, then it seems to me that explicit congressional authorization is similarly prerequisite to the exercise of equitable remedial discretion in favor of constitutionally protected interests.   Conversely, if a general grant of jurisdiction to the federal courts by Congress is thought adequate to empower a federal court to grant equitable relief for all areas of subject-matter jurisdiction enumerated therein, then it seems to me that the same statute is sufficient to empower a federal court to grant a traditional remedy at law.   Of course, the special historical traditions governing the federal equity system might still bear on the comparative appropriateness of granting equitable relief as opposed to money damages.   That possibility, however, relates, not to whether the federal courts have the power to afford one type of remedy as opposed to the other, but rather to the criteria which should govern the exercise of our power. * * *

The major thrust of the Government's position is that, where Congress has not expressly authorized a particular remedy, a federal court should exercise its power to accord a traditional form of judicial relief at the behest of a litigant, who claims a constitutionally protected interest has been invaded, only where the remedy is "essential," or "indispensable for vindicating constitutional rights."   While this "essentiality" test is most clearly articulated with respect to damages remedies, apparently the Government believes the same test explains the exercise of equitable remedial powers.   It is argued that historically the Court has rarely exercised the power to accord such relief in the absence of an express congressional authorization and that "[i]f Congress had thought that federal officers should be subject to a law different than state law, it would have had no difficulty in saying so, as it did with respect to state officers. * * * "   See 42 U.S.C.A. § 1983.   Although conceding that the standard of determining whether a damage remedy should be utilized to effectuate statutory policies is one of "necessity" or "appropriateness," the Government contends that questions concerning congressional discretion to modify judicial remedies relating to constitutionally protected interests warrant a more stringent constraint on the exercise of judicial power with respect to this class of legally protected interests.

These arguments for a more stringent test to govern the grant of damages in constitutional cases seem to be adequately answered by the point that the judiciary has a particular responsibility to assure the vindication of constitutional interests such as those embraced by the Fourth Amendment. * * * [T]he Bill of Rights is particularly intended to vindicate the interests of the individual in the face of the popular will as expressed in legislative majorities; at the very least, it strikes me as no more appropriate to await express congressional authorization of traditional judicial relief with regard to these legal interests than with respect to interests protected by federal statutes.

The question then, is, as I see it, whether compensatory relief is "necessary" or "appropriate" to the vindication of the interest asserted.   In resolving that question, it seems to me that the range of policy considerations we may take into account is at least as broad as the range of those a legislature would consider with respect to an express statutory authorization of a traditional remedy.   In this regard I agree with the Court that the appropriateness of according Bivens compensatory relief does not turn simply on the deterrent effect liability will have on federal official conduct.[8]   Damages as a traditional form of compensation for invasion of a legally protected interest may be entirely appropriate even if no substantial deterrent effects on future official lawlessness might be thought to result.   Bivens, after all, has invoked judicial processes claiming entitlement to compensation for injuries resulting from allegedly lawless official behavior, if those injuries are properly compensable in money damages.   I do not think a court of law—vested with the power to accord a remedy—should deny him his relief simply because he cannot show that future lawless conduct will thereby be deterred.

And I think it is clear that Bivens advances a claim of the sort that, if proved, would be properly compensable in damages.   The personal interests protected by the Fourth Amendment are those we attempt to capture by the notion of "privacy"; while the Court today properly points out that the type of harm which officials can inflict when they invade protected zones of an individual's life are different from the types of harm private citizens inflict on one another, the experience of judges in dealing with private trespass and false imprisonment claims supports the conclusion that courts of law are capable of making the types of judgment concerning causation and magnitude of injury necessary to accord meaningful compensation for invasion of Fourth Amendment rights.[9]

On the other hand, the limitations on state remedies for violation of common-law rights by private citizens argue in favor of a federal damages remedy.   The injuries inflicted by officials acting under color of law, while no less compensable in damages than those inflicted by private parties, are substantially different in kind, as the Court's opinion today discusses in detail.   It seems to me entirely proper that these injuries be compensable according to uniform rules of federal law, especially in light of the very large element of federal law which must in any event control the scope of official defenses to liability. * * *

Putting aside the desirability of leaving the problem of federal official liability to the vagaries of common-law actions, it is apparent that some

8. And I think it follows from this point that today's decision has little, if indeed any, bearing on the question whether a federal court may properly devise remedies—other than traditionally available forms of judicial relief—for the purpose of enforcing substantive social policies embodied in constitutional or statutory policies.   The Court today simply recognizes what has long been implicit in our decisions concerning equitable relief and remedies implied from statutory schemes; that a court of law vested with jurisdiction over the subject matter of a suit has the power—and therefore the duty—to make principled choices among traditional judicial remedies.   Whether so-

cial prophylactic measures—which at least arguably the exclusionary rule exemplifies—are supportable on grounds other than a court's competence to select among traditional judicial remedies to make good the wrong done is a separate question.

9. The same, of course, may not be true with respect to other types of constitutionally protected interests, and therefore the appropriateness of money damages may well vary with the nature of the personal interest asserted.   See *Monroe v. Pape*, 365 U.S. 167, 196 n. 5 (Harlan, J., concurring).

form of damages is the only possible remedy for someone in Bivens' alleged position. It will be a rare case indeed in which an individual in Bivens' position will be able to obviate the harm by securing injunctive relief from any court. However desirable a direct remedy against the Government might be as a substitute for individual official liability, the sovereign still remains immune to suit. Finally, assuming Bivens' innocence of the crime charged, the "exclusionary rule" is simply irrelevant. For people in Bivens' shoes, it is damages or nothing.

The only substantial policy consideration advanced against recognition of a federal cause of action for violation of Fourth Amendment rights by federal officials is the incremental expenditure of judicial resources that will be necessitated by this class of litigation. There is, however, something ultimately self-defeating about this argument. For if, as the Government contends, damages will rarely be realized by plaintiffs in these cases because of jury hostility, the limited resources of the official concerned, etc., then I am not ready to assume that there will be a significant increase in the expenditure of judicial resources on these claims. * * * And I simply cannot agree with my Brother BLACK that the possibility of "frivolous" claims—if defined simply as claims with no legal merit—warrants closing the courthouse doors to people in Bivens' situation. There are other ways, short of that, of coping with frivolous lawsuits.

On the other hand, if—as I believe is the case with respect, at least, to the most flagrant abuses of official power—damages to some degree will be available when the option of litigation is chosen, then the question appears to be how Fourth Amendment interests rank on a scale of social values compared with, for example, the interests of stockholders defrauded by misleading proxies. Judicial resources, I am well aware, are increasingly scarce these days. Nonetheless, when we automatically close the courthouse door solely on this basis, we implicitly express a value judgment on the comparative importance of classes of legally protected interests. And current limitations upon the effective functioning of the courts arising from budgetary inadequacies should not be permitted to stand in the way of the recognition of otherwise sound constitutional principles.

Of course, for a variety of reasons, the remedy may not often be sought. And the countervailing interests in efficient law enforcement of course argue for a protective zone with respect to many types of Fourth Amendment violations. But, while I express no view on the immunity defense offered in the instant case, I deem it proper to venture the thought that at the very least such a remedy would be available for the most flagrant and patently unjustified sorts of police conduct. Although litigants may not often choose to seek relief, it is important, in a civilized society, that the judicial branch of the Nation's government stand ready to afford a remedy in these circumstances. * * *

MR. CHIEF JUSTICE BURGER, dissenting.

I dissent from today's holding which judicially creates a damage remedy not provided for by the Constitution and not enacted by Congress. We would more surely preserve the important values of the doctrine of separation of powers—and perhaps get a better result—by recommending a solution to the Congress as the branch of government in which the Constitution has vested the legislative power. Legislation is the business of the Congress, and it has the facilities and competence for that task—as we do not. * * *

The problems of both error and deliberate misconduct by law enforcement officials call for a workable remedy. Private damage actions against individual police officers concededly have not adequately met this requirement, and it would be fallacious to assume today's work of the Court in creating a remedy will really accomplish its stated objective. There is some validity to the claims that juries will not return verdicts against individual officers except in those unusual cases where the violation has been flagrant or where the error has been complete, as in the arrest of the wrong person or the search of the wrong house. * * *

I conclude, therefore, that an entirely different remedy is necessary but it is one that in my view is as much beyond judicial power as the step the Court takes today. Congress should develop an administrative or quasi-judicial remedy against the government itself to afford compensation and restitution for persons whose Fourth Amendment rights have been violated. The venerable doctrine of *respondeat superior* in our tort law provides an entirely appropriate conceptual basis for this remedy. If, for example, a security guard privately employed by a department store commits an assault or other tort on a customer such as an improper search, the victim has a simple and obvious remedy—an action for money damages against the guard's employer, the department store. Such a statutory scheme would have the added advantage of providing some remedy to the completely innocent persons who are sometimes the victims of illegal police conduct—something that the suppression doctrine, of course, can never accomplish.

A simple structure would suffice. For example, Congress could enact a statute along the following lines:

(a) a waiver of sovereign immunity as to the illegal acts of law enforcement officials committed in the performance of assigned duties;

(b) the creation of a cause of action for damages sustained by any person aggrieved by conduct of governmental agents in violation of the Fourth Amendment or statutes regulating official conduct;

(c) the creation of a tribunal, quasi-judicial in nature or perhaps patterned after the United States Court of Claims, to adjudicate all claims under the statute;

(d) a provision that this statutory remedy is in lieu of the exclusion of evidence secured for use in criminal cases in violation of the Fourth Amendment; and

(e) a provision directing that no evidence, otherwise admissible, shall be excluded from any criminal proceeding because of violation of the Fourth Amendment.

* * *

MR. JUSTICE BLACK, dissenting.

In my opinion for the Court in *Bell v. Hood*, we did as the Court states, reserve the question whether an unreasonable search made by a federal officer in violation of the Fourth Amendment gives the subject of the search a federal cause of action for damages against the officers making the search. There can be no doubt that Congress could create a federal cause of action for damages for an unreasonable search in violation of the Fourth Amendment. Although Congress has created such a federal cause of action against *state* officials acting under color of state law, it has never created such a cause of action against federal officials. If it wanted to do so, Congress could, of course, create a remedy against federal officials who violate the Fourth Amendment in the performance of their duties. But the point of this case and the fatal weakness in the Court's judgment is that neither Congress nor the State of New York has enacted legislation creating such a right of action. For us to do so is, in my judgment, an exercise of power that the Constitution does not give us.

Even if we had the legislative power to create a remedy, there are many reasons why we should decline to create a cause of action where none has existed since the formation of our Government. * * *

We sit at the top of a judicial system accused by some of nearing the point of collapse. Many criminal defendants do not receive speedy trials and neither society nor the accused are assured of justice when inordinate delays occur. Citizens must wait years to litigate their private civil suits. Substantial changes in correctional and parole systems demand the attention of the lawmakers and the judiciary. If I were a legislator I might well find these and other needs so pressing as to make me believe that the resources of lawyers and judges should be devoted to them rather than to civil damage actions against officers who generally strive to perform within constitutional bounds. There is also a real danger that such suits might deter officials from the *proper* and honest performance of their duties.

All of these considerations make imperative careful study and weighing of the arguments both for and against the creation of such a remedy under the Fourth Amendment. I would have great difficulty for myself in resolving the competing policies, goals, and priorities in the use of resources, if I thought it were my job to resolve those questions. But that is not my task. The task of evaluating the pros and cons of creating judicial remedies for particular wrongs is a matter for Congress and the legislatures of the States. Congress has not provided that any federal court can entertain a suit against a federal officer for violations of Fourth Amendment rights occurring in the performance of his duties. A strong inference can be drawn from creation of such actions against state officials that Congress does not desire to permit such suits against federal officials. * * * Cases could be cited to support the legal proposition which I assert, but it seems to me to be a matter of common understanding that the business of the judiciary is to interpret the laws and not to make them.

I dissent.

Notes

1. The Supreme Court has recognized *Bivens*-style actions based on both the Eighth, *Carlson v. Green*, 446 U.S. 14 (1980), and Fifth Amendments, *Davis v. Passman*, 442 U.S. 228 (1979). Lower courts have included at least the First, Sixth, and (against state officers) Fourteenth Amendments as well. See Note, *Rethinking Sovereign Immunity After Bivens*, 57 N.Y.U. L. Rev. 597, 598 n.7 (1982). As of January 1982, over 2,200 *Bivens*-style actions had been filed against federal officials, but only 12 had resulted in damage awards. *The Suits that U.S. Aides Fear*, Nat'l L.J., Jan. 18, 1982, at 1, col. 4.

In an extended argument for shifting liability for constitutional torts to governmental entities, Professor Schuck finds these facts to be doubly perverse: Claimants are undercompensated, while risk averse public officials (who, with some justification, view the mere fact of being sued as a personal calamity) are given strong incentives to refrain from the vigorous execution of their public duties. See generally P. SCHUCK, SUING GOVERNMENT (1983), especially chaps. 3–5.

2. Although *Bivens* recognized a cause of action for damages, it expressly left open the question of possible official immunity from suit. On remand the court of appeals concluded:

> * * * Agents of the Federal Bureau of Narcotics, and other federal police officers such as Agents of the FBI performing similar functions, while in the act of pursuing alleged violators of the narcotics laws or other criminal statutes, have no immunity to protect them from damage suits charging violations of constitutional rights. We further hold, however, that it is a valid defense to such charges to allege and prove that the federal agent or other federal police officer acted in the matter complained of in good faith and with a reasonable belief in the validity of the arrest and search and in the necessity for carrying out the arrest and search in the way the arrest was made and the search was conducted.

456 F.2d 1339, 1341 (2d Cir. 1972). The Supreme Court did not address the immunity issue, however, until seven years after *Bivens*.

BUTZ v. ECONOMOU

Supreme Court of the United States, 1978.
438 U.S. 478, 98 S.Ct. 2894, 57 L.Ed.2d 895.

MR. JUSTICE WHITE delivered the opinion of the Court.

* * *

I

Respondent controls Arthur N. Economou and Co., Inc., which was at one time registered with the Department of Agriculture as a commodity futures commission merchant. Most of respondent's factual allegations in this lawsuit focus on an earlier administrative proceeding in which the Department of Agriculture sought to revoke or suspend the company's registration. On February 19, 1970, following an audit, the Department of Agriculture issued an administrative complaint alleging that respondent, while a registered merchant, had willfully failed to maintain the minimum financial requirements prescribed by the Department. After another audit, an amended complaint was issued on June 22, 1970. A hearing was held before the Chief Hearing Examiner of the Department, who filed a recommendation sustaining the administrative complaint. The Judicial Officer of the Department, to whom the Secretary had delegated his decisional authority in enforcement proceedings, affirmed the Chief Hearing Examiner's decision. On respondent's petition for review, the Court of Appeals for the Second Circuit vacated the order of the Judicial Officer. It reasoned that "the essential finding of willfulness * * * was made in a proceeding instituted without the customary warning letter, which the Judicial Officer conceded might well have resulted in prompt correction of the claimed insufficiencies." 494 F.2d 519 (1974).

While the administrative complaint was pending before the Judicial Officer, respondent filed this lawsuit in Federal District Court. Respondent sought initially to enjoin the progress of the administrative proceeding, but he was unsuccessful in that regard. On March 31, 1975, respondent filed a second amended complaint seeking damages. Named as defendants were the individuals who had served as Secretary and Assistant Secretary of Agriculture during the relevant events; the Judicial Officer and Chief Hearing Examiner; several officials in the Commodity Exchange Authority;[2] the Agriculture Department attorney who had prosecuted the enforcement proceeding; and several of the auditors who had investigated respondent or were witnesses against respondent.

The complaint stated that prior to the issuance of the administrative complaints respondent had been "sharply critical of the staff and operations of Defendants and carried on a vociferous campaign for the reform of Defendant Commodity Exchange Authority to obtain more effective regulation of commodity trading." The complaint also stated that some time prior to the issuance of the February 19 complaint, respondent and his company had ceased to engage in activities regulated by the defendants. The complaint charged that each of the administrative complaints had been issued without the notice or warning required by law; that the defendants had furnished the complaints "to interested persons and others without furnishing respondent's answers as well"; and that following the issuance of the amended complaint, the defendants had issued a "deceptive" press release that "falsely indicated to the public that [respondent's] financial resources had deteriorated, when Defendants knew that their statement was untrue and so acknowledge[d] previously that said assertion was untrue."

The complaint then presented 10 "causes of action," some of which purported to state claims for damages under the United States Constitution. For example, the first "cause of action" alleged that respondent had been denied due process of law because the defendants had instituted unauthorized proceedings against him without proper notice and with the

---

2. These individuals included the Administrator of the Commodity Exchange Authority, the Director of its Compliance Division, the Director of its Compliance Division, the Deputy Director of its Registration and Audit Division, and the Regional Administrator for the New York Region.

knowledge that respondent was no longer subject to their regulatory jurisdiction.   The third "cause of action" stated that by means of such actions "the Defendants discouraged and chilled the campaign of criticism [plaintiff] directed against them, and thereby deprived the [plaintiff] of [his] rights to free expression guaranteed by the First Amendment of the United States Constitution."

The defendants moved to dismiss the complaint on the ground that "as to the individual defendants it is barred by the doctrine of official immunity. * * * *"   The defendants relied on an affidavit submitted earlier in the litigation by the attorney who had prosecuted the original administrative complaint against respondent.   He stated that the Secretary of Agriculture had had no involvement with the case and that each of the other named defendants had acted "within the course of his official duties."

The District Court, apparently relying on the plurality opinion in *Barr v. Matteo,* held that the individual defendants would be entitled to immunity if they could show that "their alleged unconstitutional acts were within the outer perimeter of their authority and discretionary." * * *

The Court of Appeals for the Second Circuit reversed the District Court's judgment of dismissal with respect to the individual defendants.   535 F.2d 688 (1976).   The Court of Appeals reasoned that *Barr v. Matteo* did not "represen[t] the last word in this evolving area," because principles governing the immunity of officials of the Executive Branch had been elucidated in later decisions dealing with constitutional claims against state officials.   E.g., *Pierson v. Ray,* 386 U.S. 547 (1967); *Scheuer v. Rhodes,* 416 U.S. 232 (1974); *Wood v. Strickland,* 420 U.S. 308 (1975). These opinions were understood to establish that officials of the Executive Branch exercising discretionary functions did not need the protection of an absolute immunity from suit, but only a qualified immunity based on good faith and reasonable grounds.   The Court of Appeals rejected a proposed distinction between suits against state officials sued pursuant to § 1983 and suits against federal officials under the Constitution, noting that "[o]ther circuits have also concluded that the Supreme Court's development of official immunity doctrine in § 1983 suits against state officials applies with equal force to federal officers sued on a cause of action derived directly from the Constitution, since both types of suits serve the same function of protecting citizens against violations of their constitutional rights by government officials."   The Court of Appeals recognized that under *Imbler v. Pachtman,* 424 U.S. 409 (1976), state prosecutors were entitled to absolute immunity from § 1983 damages liability but reasoned that Agriculture Department officials performing analogous functions did not require such an immunity because their cases turned more on documentary proof than on the veracity of witnesses and because their work did not generally involve the same constraints of time and information present in criminal cases.   The court concluded that all of the defendants were "adequately protected by permitting them to avail themselves of the defense of qualified 'good faith, reasonable grounds' immunity of the type approved by the Supreme Court in *Scheuer* and *Wood.*"   After noting that summary judgment would be available to the defendants if there were no genuine factual issues for trial, the Court of Appeals remanded the case for further proceedings.

II

The single submission by the United States on behalf of petitioners is that all of the federal officials sued in this case are absolutely immune from any liability for damages even if in the course of enforcing the relevant statutes they infringed respondent's constitutional rights and even if the violation was knowing and deliberate.   Although the position is earnestly and ably presented by the United States, we are quite sure that it is unsound and consequently reject it.

* * *

Bivens established that compensable injury to a constitutionally protected interest could be vindicated by a suit for damages invoking the general federal-question jurisdiction of the federal courts, but we reserved the question whether the agents involved were "immune from liability by virtue of their official position," and remanded the case for that determination.   On remand, the Court of Appeals for the Second Circuit, as has every other Court of Appeals that has faced the question, held that the agents were not absolutely immune and that the public interest would be sufficiently protected by according the agents and their superiors a qualified immunity.

In our view, the Courts of Appeals have reached sound results.   We cannot agree with the United States that our prior cases are to the contrary and support the rule it now urges us to embrace.   Indeed, as we see it, the Government's submission is contrary to the course of decision in this Court from the very early days of the Republic.

The Government places principal reliance on *Barr v. Matteo*.   In that case * * * [t]he Court was divided in reversing the judgment of the Court of Appeals, and there was no opinion for the Court.   The plurality opinion inquired whether the conduct complained of was among those "matters committed by law to [the official's] control" and concluded, after an analysis of the specific circumstances, that the press release was within the "outer perimeter of [his] line of duty" and was "an appropriate exercise of the discretion which an officer of that rank must possess if the public service is to function effectively."   The plurality then held that under *Spalding v. Vilas*, 161 U.S. 483 (1896), the act was privileged and that the officer could not be held liable for the tort of defamation despite the allegations of malice.   *Barr* clearly held that a false and damaging publication, the issuance of which was otherwise within the official's authority, was not itself actionable and would not become so by being issued maliciously.   The Court did not choose to discuss whether the director's privilege would be defeated by showing that he was without reasonable grounds for believing his release was true or that he knew that it was false, although the issue was in the case as it came from the Court of Appeals.

Barr does not control this case. It did not address the liability of the acting director had his conduct not been within the outer limits of his duties, but from the care with which the Court inquired into the scope of his authority, it may be inferred that had the release been unauthorized, and surely if the issuance of press releases had been expressly forbidden by statute, the claim of absolute immunity would not have been upheld. The inference is supported by the fact that MR. JUSTICE STEWART, although agreeing with the principles announced by Mr. Justice Harlan, dissented and would have rejected the immunity claim because the press release, in his view, was not action in the line of duty. It is apparent also that a quite different question would have been presented had the officer ignored an express statutory or constitutional limitation on his authority.

Barr did not, therefore, purport to depart from the general rule, which long prevailed, that a federal official may not with impunity ignore the limitations which the controlling law has placed on his powers. The immunity of federal executive officials began as a means of protecting them in the execution of their federal statutory duties from criminal or civil actions based on state law. A federal official who acted outside of his federal statutory authority would be held strictly liable for his trespassory acts. For example, *Little v. Barreme*, 2 Cranch [6 U.S.] 170 (1840), held the commander of an American warship liable in damages for the seizure of a Danish cargo ship on the high seas. Congress had directed the President to intercept any vessels reasonably suspected of being en route *to* a French port, but the President had authorized the seizure of suspected vessels whether going *to* or *from* French ports, and the Danish vessel seized was en route *from* a forbidden destination. The Court, speaking through Mr. Chief Justice Marshall, held that the President's instructions could not "change the nature of the transaction, or legalize an act which, without those instructions, would have been a plain trespass." Although there was probable cause to believe that the ship was engaged in traffic with the French, the seizure at issue was not among that class of seizures that the Executive had been authorized by statute to effect.

Bates v. Clark, 95 U.S. 204 (1877), was a similar case. The relevant statute directed seizures of alcoholic beverages in Indian country, but the seizure at issue, which was made upon the orders of a superior, was not made in Indian country. The "objection fatal to all this class of defenses is that in that locality [the seizing officers] were utterly without any authority in the premises" and hence were answerable in damages.

As these cases demonstrate, a federal official was protected for action tortious under state law only if his acts were authorized by controlling federal law. "To make out his defence he must show that his authority was sufficient in law to protect him." Since an unconstitutional act, even if authorized by statute, was viewed as not authorized in contemplation of law, there could be no immunity defense.

In both *Barreme* and *Bates*, the officers did not merely mistakenly conclude that the circumstances warranted a particular seizure, but failed to observe the limitations on their authority by making seizures not within the category or type of seizures they were authorized to make. *Kendall v. Stokes*, 3 How. [44 U.S.] 87 (1845), addressed a different situation. The case involved a suit against the Postmaster General for erroneously suspending payments to a creditor of the Post Office. Examining and, if necessary, suspending payments to creditors were among the Postmaster's normal duties, and it appeared that he had simply made a mistake in the exercise of the discretion conferred upon him. He was held not liable in damages since "a public officer, acting to the best of his judgment and from a sense of duty, in a matter of account with an individual [is not] liable in an action for an error of judgment." Having "the right to examine into this account" and the right to suspend it in the proper circumstances, the officer was not liable in damages if he fell into error, provided, however, that he acted "from a sense of public duty and without malice."

Four years later, in a case involving military discipline, the Court issued a similar ruling, exculpating the defendant officer because of the failure to prove that he had exceeded his jurisdiction or had exercised it in a malicious or willfully erroneous manner: "[I]t is not enough to show he committed an error of judgment, but it must have been a malicious and wilful error." *Wilkes v. Dinsman*, 7 How. [48 U.S.] 89, 131 (1849).

In *Spalding v. Vilas*, 161 U.S. 483 (1896), on which the Government relies, the principal issue was whether the malicious motive of an officer would render him liable in damages for injury inflicted by his official act that otherwise was within the scope of his authority. The Postmaster General was sued for circulating among the postmasters a notice that assertedly injured the reputation of the plaintiff and interfered with his contractual relationships. The Court first inquired as to the Postmaster General's authority to issue the notice. In doing so, it "recognize[d] a distinction between action taken by the head of a Department in reference to matters which are manifestly or palpably beyond his authority, and action having more or less connection with the general matters committed by law to his control or supervision." Concluding that the circular issued by the Postmaster General "was not unauthorized by law, nor beyond the scope of his official duties," the Court then addressed the major question in the case—whether the action could be "maintained because of the allegation that what the officer did was done maliciously?" Its holding was that the head of a department could not be "held liable to a civil suit for damages on account of official communications made by him pursuant to an act of Congress, and in respect of matters within his authority," however improper his motives might have been. Because the Postmaster General in issuing the circular in question "did not exceed his authority, nor pass the line of his duty," it was irrelevant that he might have acted maliciously.

Spalding made clear that a malicious intent will not subject a public officer to liability for performing his authorized duties as to which he would otherwise not be subject to damages liability. But *Spalding* did not involve conduct manifestly or otherwise beyond the authority of the official, nor did it involve a mistake of either law or fact in construing or applying the statute.   It did not purport to immunize officials who ignore limitations on their authority imposed by law.   Although the "manifestly or palpably" standard for examining the reach of official power may have been suggested as a gloss on *Barreme, Bates, Kendall,* and *Wilkes,* none of those cases was overruled.   It is also evident that *Spalding* presented no claim that the officer was liable in damages because he had acted in violation of a limitation placed upon his conduct by the United States Constitution.   If any inference is to be drawn from *Spalding* in any of these respects, it is that the official would not be excused from liability if he failed to observe obvious statutory or constitutional limitations on his powers or if his conduct was a manifestly erroneous application of the statute.

Insofar as cases in this Court dealing with the immunity or privilege of federal officers are concerned, this is where the matter stood until *Barr v. Matteo.*   There, as we have set out above, immunity was granted even though the publication contained a factual error, which was not the case in *Spalding.*   The plurality opinion and judgment in *Barr* also appear—although without any discussion of the matter—to have extended absolute immunity to an officer who was authorized to issue press releases, who was assumed to know that the press release he issued was false and who therefore was deliberately misusing his authority.   Accepting this extension of immunity with respect to state tort claims, however, we are confident that *Barr* did not purport to protect an official who has not only committed a wrong under local law, but also violated those fundamental principles of fairness embodied in the Constitution.[22]   Whatever level of protection from state interference is appropriate for federal officials executing their duties under federal law, it cannot be doubted that these officials, even when acting pursuant to congressional authorization, are subject to the restraints imposed by the Federal Constitution.

The liability of officials who have exceeded constitutional limits was not confronted in either *Barr* or *Spalding.*   Neither of those cases supports the Government's position.   Beyond that, however, neither case purported to abolish the liability of federal officers for actions manifestly beyond their line of duty; and if they are accountable when they stray beyond the plain limits of their statutory authority, it would be incongruous to hold that they may nevertheless willfully or knowingly violate constitutional rights without fear of liability.

Although it is true that the Court has not dealt with this issue with respect to federal officers,[23] we have several times addressed the immunity of state officers when sued under 42 U.S.C.A. § 1983 for alleged violations of constitutional rights.   These decisions are instructive for present purposes.

22. We view this case, in its present posture, as concerned only with constitutional issues.   The District Court memorandum focused exclusively on respondent's constitutional claims.   It appears from the language and reasoning of its opinion that the Court of Appeals was also essentially concerned with respondent's constitutional claims.   * * *

23. *Dow v. McMillan,* 412 U.S. 306 (1973), did involve a constitutional claim for invasion of privacy—but in the special context of the Speech or Debate Clause.   The Court held that the executive officials would be immune from suit only to the extent that the legislators at whose behest they printed and distributed the documents could claim the protection of the Speech or Debate Clause.

III

Pierson v. Ray, 386 U.S. 547 (1967), decided that § 1983 was not intended to abrogate the immunity of state judges which existed under the common law and which the Court had held applicable to federal judges in *Bradley v. Fisher*. *Pierson* also presented the issue "whether immunity was available to that segment of the executive branch of a state government that is * * * most frequently exposed to situations which can give rise to claims under § 1983—the local police officer." *Scheuer v. Rhodes*, 416 U.S. 232 (1974). Relying on the common law, we held that police officers were entitled to a defense of "good faith and probable cause," even though an arrest might subsequently be proved to be unconstitutional. We observed, however, that "[t]he common law has never granted police officers an absolute and unqualified immunity, and the officers in this case do not claim that they are entitled to one."

In *Scheuer v. Rhodes*, the issue was whether "higher officers of the executive branch" of state governments were immune from liability under § 1983 for violations of constitutionally protected rights. There, the Governor of a State, the senior and subordinate officers of the state National Guard, and a state university president had been sued on the allegation that they had suppressed a civil disturbance in an unconstitutional manner. We explained that the doctrine of official immunity from § 1983 liability, although not constitutionally grounded and essentially a matter of statutory construction, was based on two mutually dependent rationales:

> "(1) the injustice, particularly in the absence of bad faith, of subjecting to liability an officer who is required, by the legal obligations of his position, to exercise discretion; (2) the danger that the threat of such liability would deter his willingness to execute his office with the decisiveness and the judgment required by the public good."

The opinion also recognized that executive branch officers must often act swiftly and on the basis of factual information supplied by others, constraints which become even more acute in the "atmosphere of confusion, ambiguity, and swiftly moving events" created by a civil disturbance. Although quoting at length from *Barr v. Matteo*, we did not believe that there was a need for absolute immunity from § 1983 liability for these high-ranking state officials. Rather the considerations discussed above indicated:

> "[I]n varying scope, a qualified immunity is available to officers of the executive branch of government, the variation being dependent upon the scope of discretion and responsibilities of the office and all the circumstances as they reasonably appeared at the time of the action on which liability is sought to be based. It is the existence of reasonable grounds for the belief formed at the time and in light of all the circumstances, coupled with good-faith belief, that affords a basis for qualified immunity of executive officers for acts performed in the course of official conduct."

Subsequent decisions have applied the *Scheuer* standard in other contexts. * * *

None of these decisions with respect to state officials furnishes any support for the submission of the United States that federal officials are absolutely immune from liability for their constitutional transgressions. On the contrary, with impressive unanimity, the Federal Courts of Appeals have concluded that federal officials should receive no greater degree of protection from *constitutional* claims than their counterparts in state government. * * *

We agree with the perception of these courts that, in the absence of congressional direction to the contrary, there is no basis for according to federal officials a higher degree of immunity from liability when sued for a constitutional infringement as authorized by *Bivens* than is accorded state officials when sued for the identical violation under § 1983. The constitutional injuries made actionable by § 1983 are of no greater magnitude than those for which federal officials may be responsible. The pressures and uncertainties facing decisionmakers in state government are little if at all different from those affecting federal officials. * * *

The Government argues that the cases involving state officials are distinguishable because they reflect the need to preserve the effectiveness of the right of action authorized by § 1983. But as we discuss more fully below, the cause of action recognized in *Bivens* would similarly be "drained of meaning" if federal officials were entitled to absolute immunity for their constitutional transgressions.

Moreover, the Government's analysis would place undue emphasis on the congressional origins of the cause of action in determining the level of immunity. It has been observed more than once that the law of privilege as a defense to damage actions against officers of Government has "in large part been of judicial making." *Barr v. Matteo*, 360 U.S., at 569. Section 1 of the Civil Rights Act of 1871—the predecessor of § 1983—said nothing about immunity for state officials. It mandated that any person who under color of state law subjected another to the deprivation of his constitutional rights would be liable to the injured party in an action at law. This Court nevertheless ascertained and announced what it deemed to be the appropriate type of immunity from § 1983 liability in a variety of contexts. *Pierson v. Ray; Imbler v. Pachtman; Scheuer v. Rhodes.* The federal courts are equally competent to determine the appropriate level of immunity where the suit is a direct claim under the Federal Constitution against a federal officer.

The presence or absence of congressional authorization for suits against federal officials is of course, relevant to the question whether to infer a right of action for damages for a particular violation of the Constitution. * * *

But once this analysis is completed, there is no reason to return again to the absence of congressional authorization in resolving the question of immunity. Having determined that the plaintiff is entitled to a remedy in damages for a constitutional violation, the court then must address how best to reconcile the plaintiff's right to compensation with the need to protect the decisionmaking processes of an executive department. * * *

IV

* * *

Our system of jurisprudence rests on the assumption that all individuals, whatever their position in government, are subject to federal law:

> "No man in this country is so high that he is above the law.   No officer of the law may set that law at defiance with impunity.   All officers of the government, from the highest to the lowest, are creatures of the law, and are bound to obey it."

United States v. Lee, 106 U.S. 196 (1882).   In light of this principle, federal officials who seek absolute exemption from personal liability for unconstitutional conduct must bear the burden of showing that public policy requires an exemption of that scope.

This is not to say that considerations of public policy fail to support a limited immunity for federal executive officials.   We consider here, as we did in *Scheuer*, the need to protect officials who are required to exercise their discretion and the related public interest in encouraging the vigorous exercise of official authority.   Yet *Scheuer* and other cases have recognized that it is not unfair to hold liable the official who knows or should know he is acting outside the law, and that insisting on an awareness of clearly established constitutional limits will not unduly interfere with the exercise of official judgment.   We therefore hold that, in a suit for damages arising from unconstitutional action, federal executive officials exercising discretion are entitled only to the qualified immunity specified in *Scheuer*, subject to those exceptional situations where it is demonstrated that absolute immunity is essential for the conduct of the public business.[34] * * *

V

Although a qualified immunity from damages liability should be the general rule for executive officials charged with constitutional violations, our decisions recognize that there are some officials whose special functions require a full exemption from liability.   In each case, we have undertaken "a considered inquiry into the immunity historically accorded the relevant official at common law and the interests behind it."

In *Bradley v. Fisher*, the Court analyzed the need for absolute immunity to protect judges from lawsuits claiming that their decisions had been tainted by improper motives.   The Court began by noting that the principle of immunity for acts done by judges "in the exercise of their ju-

---

34. The Government argued in *Bivens* that the plaintiff should be relegated to his traditional remedy at state law.   "In this scheme the Fourth Amendment would serve merely to limit the extent to which the agents could defend the state law tort suit by asserting that their actions were a valid exercise of federal power: if the agents were shown to have violated the Fourth Amendment, such a defense would be lost to them and they would stand before the state law merely as private individuals."   Although, as this passage makes clear, traditional doctrine did not accord immunity to officials who transgressed constitutional limits, we believe that federal officials sued by such traditional means should similarly be entitled to a *Scheuer* immunity.

dicial functions" had been "the settled doctrine of the English courts for many centuries, and has never been denied, that we are aware of, in the courts of this country." The Court explained that the value of this rule was proved by experience. Judges were often called to decide "[c]ontroversies involving not merely great pecuniary interests, but the liberty and character of the parties, and consequently exciting the deepest feelings." Such adjudications invariably produced at least one losing party, who would "accep[t] anything but the soundness of the decision in explanation of the action of the judge." "Just in proportion to the strength of his convictions of the correctness of his own view of the case is he apt to complain of the judgment against him, and from complaints of the judgment to pass to the ascription of improper motives to the judge." Ibid. If a civil action could be maintained against a judge by virtue of an allegation of malice, judges would lose "that independence without which no judiciary can either be respectable or useful." Thus, judges were held to be immune from civil suit "for malice or corruption in their action whilst exercising their judicial functions within the general scope of their jurisdiction."[36]

The principle of *Bradley* was extended to federal prosecutors through the summary affirmance in *Yaselli v. Goff*, 275 U.S. 503 (1927), *aff'g*, 12 F.2d 396 (C.A. 2 1926). * * *

We recently reaffirmed the holding of *Yaselli v. Goff* in *Imbler v. Pachtman* [424 U.S. 409 (1976)], a suit against a state prosecutor under § 1983. The Court's examination of the leading precedents led to the conclusion that "[t]he common-law immunity of a prosecutor is based upon the same considerations that underlie the common-law immunities of judges and grand jurors acting within the scope of their duties." * * *

Despite these precedents, the Court of Appeals concluded that all of the defendants in this case—including the Chief Hearing Examiner, Judicial Officer, and prosecuting attorney—were entitled to only a qualified immunity. The Court of Appeals reasoned that officials within the Executive Branch generally have more circumscribed discretion and pointed out that, unlike a judge, officials of the Executive Branch would face no conflict of interest if their legal representation was provided by the Executive Branch. The Court of Appeals recognized that "some of the Agriculture Department officials may be analogized to criminal prosecutors, in that they initiated the proceedings against [respondent], and presented evidence therein," but found that attorneys in administrative proceedings did not face the same "serious constraints of time and even information" which this Court has found to be present frequently in criminal cases.

We think that the Court of Appeals placed undue emphasis on the fact that the officials sued here are—from an administrative perspective— employees of the Executive Branch. Judges have absolute immunity

---

36. In *Pierson v. Ray*, 386 U.S. 547 (1967), we recognized that state judges sued on constitutional claims pursuant to § 1983 could claim a similar absolute immunity. * * *

not because of their particular location within the Government, but because of the special nature of their responsibilities. * * *

We think that adjudication within a federal administrative agency shares enough of the characteristics of the judicial process that those who participate in such adjudication should also be immune from suits for damages. The conflicts which federal hearing examiners seek to resolve are every bit as fractious as those which come to court. * * * Moreover, federal administrative law requires that agency adjudication contain many of the same safeguards as are available in the judicial process. * * *

* * *

In light of these safeguards, we think that the risk of an unconstitutional act by one presiding at an agency hearing is clearly outweighed by the importance of preserving the independent judgment of these men and women. We therefore hold that persons subject to these restraints and performing adjudicatory functions within a federal agency are entitled to absolute immunity from damages liability for their judicial acts. Those who complain of error in such proceedings must seek agency or judicial review.

We also believe that agency officials performing certain functions analogous to those of a prosecutor should be able to claim absolute immunity with respect to such acts. * * *

The discretion which executive officials exercise with respect to the initiation of administrative proceedings might be distorted if their immunity from damages arising from that decision was less than complete. While there is not likely to be anyone willing and legally able to seek damages from the officials if they do *not* authorize the administrative proceedings, there is a serious danger that the decision to authorize proceedings will provoke a retaliatory response. An individual targeted by an administrative proceeding will react angrily and may seek vengeance in the courts. A corporation will muster all of its financial and legal resources in an effort to prevent administrative sanctions. * * *

* * *

We believe that agency officials must make the decision to move forward with an administrative proceeding free from intimidation or harassment. Because the legal remedies already available to the defendant in such a proceeding provide sufficient checks on agency zeal, we hold that those officials who are responsible for the decision to initiate or continue a proceeding subject to agency adjudication are entitled to absolute immunity from damages liability for their parts in that decision.

We turn finally to the role of an agency attorney in conducting a trial and presenting evidence on the record to the trier of fact. We can see no substantial difference between the function of the agency attorney in presenting evidence in an agency hearing and the function of the prosecutor who brings evidence before a court. * * * Administrative agencies can act in the public interest only if they can adjudicate on the basis of a complete record. We therefore hold that an agency attorney who arranges for the presentation of evidence on the record in the course of an adjudication is absolutely immune from suits based on the introduction of such evidence.

VI

There remains the task of applying the foregoing principles to the claims against the particular petitioner-defendants involved in this case. Rather than attempt this here in the first instance, we vacate the judgment of the Court of Appeals and remand the case to that court with instructions to remand the case to the District Court for further proceedings consistent with this opinion.

So ordered.

MR. JUSTICE REHNQUIST, with whom THE CHIEF JUSTICE, MR. JUSTICE STEWART, and MR. JUSTICE STEVENS join, concurring in part and dissenting in part.

I concur in that part of the Court's judgment which affords absolute immunity to those persons performing adjudicatory functions within a federal agency, those who are responsible for the decision to initiate or continue a proceeding subject to agency adjudication, and those agency personnel who present evidence on the record in the course of an adjudication. I cannot agree, however, with the Court's conclusion that in a suit for damages arising from allegedly unconstitutional action federal executive officials, regardless of their rank or the scope of their responsibilities, are entitled to only qualified immunity even when acting within the outer limits of their authority. The Court's protestations to the contrary notwithstanding, this decision seriously misconstrues our prior decisions, finds little support as a matter of logic or precedent, and perhaps most importantly, will, I fear, seriously "dampen the ardor of all but the most resolute, or the most irresponsible, in the unflinching discharge of their duties," *Gregoire v. Biddle*, 177 F.2d 579, 581 (C.A.2 1949) (Learned Hand, J.). * * * *

History will surely not condemn the Court for its effort to achieve a more finely ground product from the judicial mill, a product which would both retain the necessary ability of public officials to govern and yet assure redress to those who are the victims of official wrongs. But if such a

---

*The ultimate irony of today's decision is that in the area of common-law official immunity, a body of law fashioned and applied by judges, absolute immunity within the federal system is extended only to judges and prosecutors functioning in the judicial system. * * * If one were to hazard an informed guess as to why such a distinction in treatment between judges and prosecutors, on the one hand, and other public officials on the other, obtains, mine would be that those who decide the common law know through personal experience the sort of pressures that might exist for such decisionmakers in the absence of absolute immunity, but may not know or may have forgotten that similar pressures exist in the case of nonjudicial public officials to whom difficult decisions are committed. But the cynical among us might not unreasonably feel that this is simply another unfortunate example of judges treating those who are not part of the judicial machinery as "lesser breeds without the law."

system of redress for official wrongs was indeed capable of being achieved in practice, it surely would not have been rejected by this Court speaking through the first Mr. Justice Harlan in 1896, by this Court speaking through the second Mr. Justice Harlan in 1959, and by Judge Learned Hand speaking for the Court of Appeals for the Second Circuit in 1948. These judges were not inexperienced neophytes who lacked the vision or the ability to define immunity doctrine to accomplish that result had they thought it possible. Nor were they obsequious toadies in their attitude toward high-ranking officials of coordinate branches of the Federal Government. But they did see with more prescience than the Court does today, that there are inevitable trade-offs in connection with any doctrine of official liability and immunity. They forthrightly accepted the possibility that an occasional failure to redress a claim of official wrongdoing would result from the doctrine of absolute immunity which they espoused, viewing it as a lesser evil than the impairment of the ability of responsible public officials to govern.

But while I believe that history will look approvingly on the motives of the Court in reaching the result it does today, I do not believe that history will be charitable in its judgment of the all but inevitable result of the doctrine espoused by the Court in this case. That doctrine seeks to gain and hold a middle ground which, with all deference, I believe the teachings of those who were at least our equals suggest cannot long be held. That part of the Court's present opinion from which I dissent will, I fear, result in one of two evils, either one of which is markedly worse than the effect of according absolute immunity to the Secretary and the Assistant Secretary in this case. The first of these evils would be a significant impairment of the ability of responsible public officials to carry out the duties imposed upon them by law. If that evil is to be avoided after today, it can be avoided only by a necessarily unprincipled and erratic judicial "screening" of claims such as those made in this case, an adherence to the form of the law while departing from its substance. Either one of these evils is far worse than the occasional failure to award damages caused by official wrongdoing, frankly and openly justified by the rule of *Spalding v. Vilas*, *Barr v. Matteo*, and *Gregoire v. Biddle*.

Notes

1. Since *Economou* the Supreme Court has twice returned to the question of the immunity of federal officials. In *Nixon v. Fitzgerald*, 457 U.S. 731 (1982), the Court held that the President, because of his unique constitutional position, was entitled to absolute immunity for all acts within the "outer perimeter of his official responsibility"—hardly a surprising result. *Harlow v. Fitzgerald*, 457 U.S. 800 (1982), presented a more difficult question.

In that case aides to President Nixon asserted absolute immunity from suit for acts taken pursuant to an alleged conspiracy, of which the President was a part, to deprive respondent of his First Amendment rights. The Court rejected this claim with the following explanation (id. at 809–13):

In disputing the controlling authority of *Butz*, petitioners rely on the principles developed in *Gravel v. United States*, 408 U.S. 606 (1972). In *Gravel* we endorsed the view that "it is literally impossible * * * for Members of Congress to perform their legislative tasks without the help of aides and assistants" and that "the day-to-day work of such aides is so critical to the Members' performance that they must be treated as the latter's alter egos. * * * " Having done so, we held the Speech and Debate Clause derivatively applicable to the "legislative acts" of a Senator's aide that would have been privileged if performed by the Senator himself.

Petitioners contend that the rationale of *Gravel* mandates a similar "derivative" immunity for the chief aides of the President of the United States. Emphasizing that the President must delegate a large measure of authority to execute the duties of his office, they argue that recognition of derivative absolute immunity is made essential by all the considerations that support absolute immunity for the President himself.

Petitioners' argument is not without force. Ultimately, however, it sweeps too far. If the President's aides are derivatively immune because they are essential to the functioning of the Presidency, so should the members of the Cabinet—Presidential subordinates some of whose essential roles are acknowledged by the Constitution itself—be absolutely immune. Yet we implicitly rejected such derivative immunity in *Butz*. Moreover, in general our cases have followed a "functional" approach to immunity law. We have recognized that the judicial, prosecutorial, and legislative functions require absolute immunity. But this protection has extended no further than its justification would warrant. In *Gravel*, for example, we emphasized that Senators and their aides were absolutely immune only when performing "acts legislative in nature," and not when taking other acts even "in their official capacity." Our cases involving judges and prosecutors have followed a similar line. The undifferentiated extension of absolute "derivative" immunity to the President's aides therefore could not be reconciled with the "functional" approach that has characterized the immunity decisions of this Court, indeed including *Gravel* itself.

Petitioners also assert an entitlement to immunity based on the "special functions" of White House aides. This form of argument accords with the analytical approach of our cases. For aides entrusted with discretionary authority in such sensitive areas as national security or foreign policy, absolute immunity might well be justified to protect the unhesitating performance of functions vital to the national interest. But a "special functions" rationale does not warrant a blanket recognition of absolute immunity for all Presidential aides in the performance of all their duties. This conclusion too follows from our decision in *Butz*, which establishes that an executive official's claim to absolute immunity must be justified by reference to the public interest in the special functions of his office, not the mere fact of high station.

* * * In order to establish entitlement to absolute immunity a Presidential aide first must show that the responsibilities of his office embraced a function so sensitive as to require a total shield from liability. He then must demonstrate that he was discharging the protected function when performing the act for which liability is asserted.

Applying these standards to the claims advanced by petitioners Harlow and Butterfield, we cannot conclude on the record before us that either has shown that "public policy requires [for any of the functions of his office] an exemption of [absolute] scope."

The Court then went on to analyze the potential qualified immunity available to federal officials, in the process altering the *Butz* formula (id. at 815–18):

Qualified or "good faith" immunity is an affirmative defense that must be pleaded by a defendant official. Decisions of this Court have established that the "good faith" defense has both an "objective" and a "subjective" aspect. The objective element involves a presumptive knowledge of and respect for "basic, unquestioned constitutional rights." The subjective component refers to "permissible intentions." Characteristically the Court has defined these elements by identifying the circumstances in which qualified immunity would *not* be available. Referring both to the objective and subjective elements, we have held that qualified immunity would be defeated if an official *"knew or reasonably should have known* that the action he took within his sphere of official responsibility would violate the constitutional rights of the [plaintiff], *or* if he took the action *with the malicious intention* to cause a deprivation of constitutional rights or other injury. * * * " (emphasis added).

The subjective element of the good-faith defense frequently has proved incompatible with our admonition in *Butz* that insubstantial claims should not proceed to trial. Rule 56 of the Federal Rules of Civil Procedure provides that disputed questions of fact ordinarily may not be decided on motions for summary judgment. And an official's subjective good faith has been considered to be a question of fact that some courts have regarded as inherently requiring resolution by a jury.

In the context of *Butz*'s attempted balancing of competing values, it now is clear that substantial costs attend the litigation of the subjective good faith of government officials. Not only are there the general costs of subjecting officials to the risks of trial—distraction of officials from their governmental duties, inhibition of discretionary action, and deterrence of able people from public service. There are special costs to "subjective" inquiries of this kind. Immunity generally is available only to officials performing discretionary functions. In contrast with the thought processes accompanying "ministerial" tasks, the judgments surrounding discretionary action almost inevitably are influenced by the decisionmaker's experiences, values, and emotions. These variables explain in part why questions of subjective intent so rarely can be decided by summary judgment. Yet they also frame a background in which there often is no clear end to the relevant evidence. Judicial inquiry into subjective motivation therefore may entail broad-ranging discovery and the deposing of numerous persons, including an official's professional colleagues. Inquiries of this kind can be peculiarly disruptive of effective government.

Consistently with the balance at which we aimed in *Butz*, we conclude today that bare allegations of malice should not suffice to subject government officials either to the costs of trial or to the burdens of broadreaching discovery. We therefore hold that government officials performing discretionary functions generally are shielded from liability for civil damages insofar as their conduct does not violate clearly established statutory or constitutional rights of which a reasonable person would have known.

2. Note that in eliminating one element of the *Butz* criterion for "good faith" the Court introduces another—an apparent distinction between "discretionary" and "ministerial" duties. If "discretionary" duties produce only qualified immu-

nity, then presumably officers exercising "ministerial" duties would be entitled to no immunity at all.   The Court, however, provides no guidance concerning this distinction beyond its general allegiance to a "functional" approach based upon the need for protection.

Harlow's vagueness is nevertheless portentious.   How can the *Barr* approach—absolute immunity of federal officials from common law torts—survive the thoroughly functional and fine-grained analysis demanded by *Butz* and *Harlow*?   Surely "ministerial" functions should not be so protected?   And what distinguishes constitutional torts from the common law variety when there is such a large overlap between the two categories (as Justice Rehnquist noted in his *Butz* dissent)?

The continued distinction between immunities available for common law and for constitutional torts has received no greater support among the commentators than the absolute immunity of the government itself for constitutional torts—or at least those that cannot be pressed into a state tort law mold under the Federal Tort Claims Act.   See discussion supra p. 801.   Nevertheless, the lower federal courts since *Butz* generally have continued to view *Barr* as the relevant authority where common law claims are involved.   See, e.g., *Claus v. Gyorkey*, 674 F.2d 427 (5th Cir. 1982); *Queen v. Tennessee Valley Authority*, 689 F.2d 80 (6th Cir. 1982), *cert. denied* 460 U.S. 1082 (1983).   Recent cases have, however, begun to discuss *Harlow*'s discretionary-ministerial distinction and, indeed, to find it implicit in the language of *Barr*.   See, e.g., *Windsor v. The Tennessean*, 719 F.2d 155 (6th Cir. 1983).

Chapter 8

BENEFICIARY ENFORCEMENT OF
PUBLIC LAW

A. EXPLICIT REMEDIES

During the era in which crown courts replaced feudal justice in England and became the primary arenas for litigation, the jurisdictional theory of most actions brought in the royal courts was that the plaintiff represented or stood in the place of the king (*"Qui tam pro domino rege quam pro seipso"*) and that the latter's interests were served by the suit. See generally Note, *The History and Development of Qui Tam*, 1972 Wash. U.L.Q. 81. This historical and purposeful confusion between suits to protect the public interest and suits to protect private interests persists in theory, though not generally in practice, in England. See generally R. JACKSON, THE MACHINERY OF JUSTICE IN ENGLAND (7th ed. 1977).

However, neither the English theory nor the practice of private prosecution was transplanted effectively to American soil. From the earliest days of the Republic there seems to have been a presumption that criminal laws, and other laws designed to protect public interests, would be enforced by public officers. There are historically but three explicit exceptions to the monopoly that American statutes normally give public officers over the enforcement of public law:

(1) In many states a victim is permitted to hire counsel to "assist" the public prosecutor. With the prosecutor's assent, this private collaborator may even handle the case, but the prosecution cannot be initiated without the approval of the public officer. See generally Note, *Private Prosecution: A Remedy for District Attorneys' Unwarranted Inaction*, 65 Yale L.J. 209 (1955).

(2) Numerous early state statutes provided a special *qui tam* or informer's suit to recover a criminal penalty, but most such actions were abolished as state public enforcement capabilities increased. Only one significant federal statute authorizing *qui tam* suits still exists, the Federal Informers Act of 1863, now codified at 31 U.S.C. § 3730. However, because of widespread belief that the statute was being abused by unscrupulous suiters, who brought actions based on evidence already in the hands of the government, the Informers Act was amended in 1943 to

make recovery much more difficult.   Since that time there have been virtually no reported private actions under the statute.   See discussion in *United States v. Burma Oil Co.*, 558 F.2d 43 (2d Cir.), *cert. denied* 434 U.S. 967 (1977).

(3) Several early federal statutes provided a private action for damages, double damages or, as in the antitrust laws, treble damages for violations.   Since private damages were doubled or trebled, obviously Congress must have considered the private action more an enforcement device than a suit to compensate a private party who had been harmed by the violation of the statute.   It is then but a short step to imagine, as does much of the recent law and economics literature, that the principal policy focus of damage actions, of whatever type, is the deterrence of socially costly conduct.

The large conceptual and practical overlap between the functions of public and private enforcement has not often convinced Congress or the courts, however, to abandon the conceptually tidy distinction between public law and private right.   Explicit authorizations of damage actions in modern federal statutes, such as the securities acts of the 1930's or the civil rights laws of the 1960's, tend to be viewed as providing compensation for the infringement of statutorily based private rights, rather than as encouraging private efforts to vindicate the public interest.   The latter function is left securely in the hands of public officials, as some of the materials in Chapter 6 illustrate.   See pp. 706–32, supra.

A significant exception to the customary division between public and private enforcement appears in many environmental statutes.   Beginning with the Clean Air Act of 1970, now codified at 42 U.S.C.A. § § 7401, 7604, Congress has attached a "citizen suit" provision to almost all subsequently enacted environmental laws.   Although these provisions vary in detail, the basic model is that established by the Clean Air Act.   "Any person" may commence an action in federal district court against any other person, including the United States or a state (to the extent permitted by the Eleventh Amendment), to enforce any emission standard or limitation promulgated pursuant to the Act or any order of the EPA or state with respect to such standards or limitations.   A person who contemplates suit must notify the EPA, the state, and the alleged violator sixty days prior to commencing suit and is barred from instituting action if the EPA or state is "diligently prosecuting" a civil action for enforcement.   The Act provides for intervention of right by the EPA in any citizen's suit and by any person in an EPA enforcement action.

The citizen suit provisions obviously attempt to guard against agency inaction by permitting circumvention of the conventional discretion of any agency in the deployment of enforcement resources.   This incursion into the enforcement agency's domain, however, is accomplished ostensibly without interfering with either the agency's allocation of resources or its power to establish environmental quality standards.   The action is one to enforce officially prescribed standards or limitations, and the EPA may intervene or not at its discretion.   Congress thus hoped to add private resources to the campaign to protect the environment without fragmenting authority over substantive requirements or putting agency resources at the disposal of private litigants.

Although citizen suit provisions do not authorize damage awards (see *Middlesex County Sewerage Authority v. National Sea Clammers Association,* infra p. 920), they do permit the award of attorneys' fees and fees for expert witnesses.   Thus these statutory provisions incorporate some private incentives to act in the public interest.   Nevertheless, most commentators agree (without systematic empirical inquiry) that suits under these provisions have been infrequent.   See Feller, *Private Enforcement of Federal Anti-Pollution Laws Through Citizen Suits: A Model,* 60 Den. L.J. 553, 564–65 (1983).   There is, however, some evidence that business is picking up under the Clean Water Act.   See, e.g., *Student Public Interest Research Group of New Jersey v. Fritzsche, Dodge and Olcott, Inc.,* 579 F.Supp. 1528 (D.N.J. 1984).   Requirements in EPA water quality permits that dischargers maintain publicly available records of all of their discharges make proof of violations in suits under the Clean Water Act elementary.   The polluter is convicted out of its own mouth.

The courts seem generally to have been hospitable to citizen suits. The mere pendency of agency efforts to achieve compliance, for example, will not preempt a citizen's suit under the "diligently prosecuting" language of the statutes.   See *Student Public Interest Research of New Jersey, Inc.,* supra.   The courts have also been quite forthcoming with attorney's fees.   See, e.g., *Metropolitan Washington Coalition For Clean Air v. District of Columbia,* 639 F.2d 802 (D.C. Cir. 1981).

While it is difficult to generalize about the use of citizens' suit provisions in environmental statutes, the largest number of cases seem to have been brought by local public authorities (who are "citizens" for purposes of these statutes) in order to stop polluting activity that the local body believes is being inadequately regulated by state and local pollution control authorities.   These local "public citizens" are apparently prepared to pursue the non-degradation desires of their local communities beyond the point at which limited enforcement resources, or a different perspective, convince the EPA and state agencies to adopt a more passive stance toward noncompliance.

The enlistment of citizens, or even local public officials, as enforcers of federal law obviously has some dangers.   Principal among them is the possibility that these parties will zealously pursue matters of great interest to them, but in the process impose burdens on particular defendants much heavier than those that others similarly situated are required to bear.   There is even the possibility of harrassment by private parties who are pursuing objectives only remotely connected to environmental protection.   Thus, while the facts in *Weinberger v. Carlos Romero-Barcelo,* 456 U.S. 305 (1982), appear unusual, that case may not be far from the norm in citizen-suit practice.   The litigation was instituted by the Governor of Puerto Rico against the Defense Department, under the Federal Water Pollution Control Act, to enjoin the Navy from discharging bombs into waters surrounding an island off the coast of Puerto Rico.

Because the Navy had obtained no water quality permit to discharge ordinance into these waters, it clearly was in violation of the Act and of EPA regulations. The underlying dispute, however, had more to do with Puerto Rico's interest in developing tourism in and around the island (which was inhibited to say the least by the Navy's utilization of the vicinity for air to ground weapons training) than it did with any effects of discharged ordinance on water quality. Nevertheless, the court of appeals believed that it had no choice but to issue an injunction against the Navy to cease violating the Federal Water Quality Act until it had obtained a permit. The Supreme Court reversed. The Court reasoned that the citizens' suit provision did not mean to deny to a district court the usual judicial discretion to withhold an injunction based upon the equities of a particular case.

For a review and analysis of the growing technical literature on private enforcement, see Polinsky and Shavell, *The Optimal Tradeoff Between the Probability and Magnitude of Fines*, 69 Am. Econ. Rev. 880 (1979). A recent useful treatment of citizens' suits in the environmental area is Environmental Law Institute, Citizen Suits: An Analysis of Citizen Enforcement Actions under EPA–Administered Statutes, (1984) which documents the increased interest in private enforcement of the Clean Water Act.

B.   IMPLIED RIGHTS OF ACTION

In *Bivens v. Six Unknown Named Agents*, supra p. 818, the Supreme Court held that violations of the Fourth Amendment by federal law enforcement officers may give rise to a private claim for damages. No provision of the Constitution specifically authorized such a remedy, but the Court was not content to remit the victims of unconstitutional conduct to whatever relief state law might afford. It invoked the traditional remedial authority of the federal judiciary to fashion a remedy. Both the majority opinion in *Bivens* and Justice Harlan's concurring opinion referred explicitly to the Court's earlier decision in *J.I. Case Co. v. Borak*.

1. THE BORAK DOCTRINE

J. I. CASE CO. v. BORAK

Supreme Court of the United States, 1964.
377 U.S. 426, 84 S.Ct. 1555, 12 L.Ed.2d 423.

MR. JUSTICE CLARK delivered the opinion of the Court.

This is a civil action brought by respondent, a stockholder of petitioner J.I. Case Company, charging deprivation of the preemptive rights of respondent and other shareholders by reason of a merger between Case and the American Tractor Corporation. It is alleged that the merger was effected through the circulation of a false and misleading proxy statement by those proposing the merger. The complaint was in two counts, the first based on diversity and claiming a breach of the directors' fiduciary duty to the stockholders.   The second count alleged a violation of § 14(a)[1] of the Securities Exchange Act of 1934 with reference to the proxy solicitation material.   The trial court held that as to this count it had no power to redress the alleged violations of the Act but was limited solely to the granting of declaratory relief thereon under § 27 of the Act.[2]   The court held Wis. Stat., 1961, § 180.405(4), which requires posting security for expenses in [stockholder] derivative actions, applicable to both counts, except that portion of Count 2 requesting declaratory relief.   It ordered the respondent to furnish a bond in the amount of $75,000 thereunder and, upon his failure to do so, dismissed the complaint, save that part of Count 2 seeking a declaratory judgment.   On interlocutory appeal the Court of Appeals reversed on both counts, holding that the District Court had the power to grant remedial relief and that the Wisconsin statute was not applicable. * * * We consider only the question of whether § 27 of the Act authorizes a federal cause of action for rescission or damages to a corporate stockholder with respect to a consummated merger which was authorized pursuant to the use of a proxy statement alleged to contain false and misleading statements violative of § 14(a) of the Act. * * *

   * * * The claims pertinent to the asserted violation of the Securities Exchange Act were predicated on diversity jurisdiction as well as on § 27 of the Act.   They alleged: that petitioners, or their predecessors, solicited or permitted their names to be used in the solicitation of proxies of Case stockholders for use at a special stockholders' meeting at which the proposed merger with ATC was to be voted upon; that the proxy solicitation material so circulated was false and misleading in violation of § 14(a) of the Act and Rule 14a–9 which the Commission had promulgated thereunder;[4] that the merger was approved at the meeting by a small margin of

---

1. Section 14(a) of the Securities Exchange Act of 1934, 15 U.S.C.A. § 78n(a), provides: "It shall be unlawful for any person, by the use of the mails or by any means or instrumentality of interstate commerce or of any facility of any national securities exchange or otherwise to solicit or to permit the use of his name to solicit any proxy or consent or authorization in respect of any security (other than an exempted security) registered on any national securities exchange in contravention of such rules and regulations as the [Securities and Exchange] Commission may prescribe as necessary or appropriate in the public interest or for the protection of investors."

2. Section 27 of the Act, 15 U.S.C.A. § 78aa, provides in part: "The district courts of the United States * * * shall have exclusive jurisdiction of violations of this title or the rules and regulations thereunder, and of all suits in equity and actions at law brought to enforce any liability or duty created by this title or the rules and regulations thereunder. Any criminal proceeding may be brought in the district wherein any act or transaction constituting the violation occurred. Any suit or

action to enforce any liability or duty created by this title or rules and regulations thereunder, or to enjoin any violation of such title or rules and regulations, may be brought in any such district or in the district wherein the defendant is found or is an inhabitant or transacts business, and process in such cases may be served in any other district of which the defendant is an inhabitant or wherever the defendant may be found."

4. 17 CFR § 240.14a-9 provides: "*False or misleading statements.* No solicitation subject to § § 240.14a-1 to 240.14a-10 shall be made by means of any proxy statement, form of proxy, notice of meeting, or other communication written or oral containing any statement which at the time and in the light of the circumstances under which it is made, is false or misleading with respect to any material fact, or which omits to state any material fact necessary in order to make the statements therein not false or misleading or necessary to correct any statement in any earlier communication with respect to the solicitation of a proxy for the same meeting or subject matter which has become false or misleading."

votes and was thereafter consummated; that the merger would not have been approved but for the false and misleading statements in the proxy solicitation material; and that Case stockholders were damaged thereby. The respondent sought judgment holding the merger void and damages for himself and all other stockholders similarly situated, as well as such further relief "as equity shall require." The District Court ruled that the Wisconsin security for expenses statute did not apply to Count 2 since it arose under federal law. However, the court found that its jurisdiction was limited to declaratory relief in a private, as opposed to a government, suit alleging violation of § 14(a) of the Act. Since the additional equitable relief and damages prayed for by the respondent would, therefore, be available only under state law, it ruled those claims subject to the security for expenses statute. * * *

It appears clear that private parties have a right under § 27 to bring suit for violation of § 14(a) of the Act. Indeed, this section specifically grants the appropriate District Courts jurisdiction over "all suits in equity and actions at law brought to enforce any liability or duty created" under the Act. The petitioners make no concessions, however, emphasizing that Congress made no specific reference to a private right of action in § 14(a); that, in any event, the right would not extend to derivative suits and should be limited to prospective relief only. * * *

While the respondent contends that his Count 2 claim is not a derivative one, we need not embrace that view, for we believe that a right of action exists as to both derivative and direct causes.

The purpose of § 14(a) is to prevent management or others from obtaining authorization for corporate action by means of deceptive or inadequate disclosure in proxy solicitation. The section stemmed from the congressional belief that "[f]air corporate suffrage is an important right that should attach to every equity security bought on a public exchange." H.R. Rep. No. 1383, 73d Cong., 2d Sess. 13. It was intended to "control the conditions under which proxies may be solicited with a view to preventing the recurrence of abuses which * * * [had] frustrated the free exercise of the voting rights of stockholders." "Too often proxies are solicited without explanation to the stockholder of the real nature of the questions for which authority to cast his vote is sought." S. Rep. No. 792, 73d Cong., 2d Sess. 12. These broad remedial purposes are evidenced in the language of [§ 14(a)] * * * . While this language makes no specific reference to a private right of action, among its chief purposes is "the protection of investors," which certainly implies the availability of judicial relief where necessary to achieve that result.

The injury which a stockholder suffers from corporate action pursuant to a deceptive proxy solicitation ordinarily flows from the damage done the corporation, rather than from the damage inflicted directly upon the stockholder. The damage suffered results not from the deceit practiced on him alone but rather from the deceit practiced on the stockholders as a group. To hold that derivative actions are not within the sweep of the section would therefore be tantamount to a denial of private relief. Private enforcement of the proxy rules provides a necessary supplement to

Commission action. As in antitrust treble damage litigation, the possibility of civil damages or injunctive relief serves as a most effective weapon in the enforcement of the proxy requirements. The Commission advises that it examines over 2,000 proxy statements annually and each of them must necessarily be expedited. Time does not permit an independent examination of the facts set out in the proxy material and this results in the Commission's acceptance of the representations contained therein at their face value, unless contrary to other material on file with it. Indeed, on the allegations of respondent's complaint, the proxy material failed to disclose alleged unlawful market manipulation of the stock of ATC, and this unlawful manipulation would not have been apparent to the Commission until after the merger.

We, therefore, believe that under the circumstances here it is the duty of the courts to be alert to provide such remedies as are necessary to make effective the congressional purpose. As was said in *Sola Electric Co. v. Jefferson Electric Co.*, 317 U.S. 173, 176 (1942):

> "When a federal statute condemns an act as unlawful, the extent and nature of the legal consequences of the condemnation, though left by the statute to judicial determination, are nevertheless federal questions, the answers to which are to be derived from the statute and the federal policy which it has adopted."

It is for the federal courts "to adjust their remedies so as to grant the necessary relief" where federally secured rights are invaded. "And it is also well settled that where legal rights have been invaded, and a federal statute provides for a general right to sue for such invasion, federal courts may use any available remedy to make good the wrong done." *Bell v. Hood*, 327 U.S. 678, 684 (1946). Section 27 grants the District Courts jurisdiction "of all suits in equity and actions at law brought to enforce any liability or duty created by this title. * * * " In passing on almost identical language found in the Securities Act of 1933, the Court found the words entirely sufficient to fashion a remedy to rescind a fraudulent sale, secure restitution and even to enforce the right to restitution against a third party holding assets of the vendor. *Deckert v. Independence Shares Corp.*, 311 U.S. 282 (1940). This significant language was used:

> "The power to *enforce* implies the power to make effective the right of recovery afforded by the Act. And the power to make the right of recovery effective implies the power to utilize any of the procedures or actions normally available to the litigant according to the exigencies of the particular case."

Nor do we find merit in the contention that such remedies are limited to prospective relief. * * * [W]e believe that the overriding federal law applicable here would, where the facts required, control the appropriateness of redress despite the provisions of state corporation law, for it "is not uncommon for federal courts to fashion federal law where federal rights are concerned." In addition, the fact that questions of state law must be decided does not change the character of the right; it remains federal. * * *

Moreover, if federal jurisdiction were limited to the granting of declaratory relief, victims of deceptive proxy statements would be obliged to go into state courts for remedial relief. And if the law of the State happened to attach no responsibility to the use of misleading proxy statements, the whole purpose of the section might be frustrated. Furthermore, the hurdles that the victim might face (such as separate suits, security for expenses statutes, bringing in all parties necessary for complete relief, etc.) might well prove insuperable to effective relief.

Our finding that federal courts have the power to grant all necessary remedial relief is not to be construed as any indication of what we believe to be necessary and appropriate relief in this case. We are concerned here only with a determination that federal jurisdiction for this purpose does exist. Whatever remedy is necessary must await the trial on the merits.

The other contentions of the petitioners are denied.

Affirmed.

Implication Analysis and Federal Common Law

Even though corporate losses cause economic harm to stockholders by diminishing the value of their holdings, stockholders ordinarily have no "direct" right of action for managerial misfeasance. In such a situation, however, an aggrieved stockholder may bring a so-called "derivative" suit against the responsible corporate officer, asserting in effect the right of action the corporation itself has against officers or agents guilty of wrongful conduct that causes corporate losses. While any recovery in a derivative suit goes to the corporation, the fact that the plaintiff's counsel fees, which may be considerable, are payable from the recovery provides a powerful incentive for bringing such suits.

Prior to the *Borak* case derivative suits were governed in almost all particulars by state law. The belief that such suits were subject to abuse by so-called "strike-suitors," holders of a few shares who instigated derivative litigation with the hope of forcing an extortionate settlement from corporate management, had led many states to enact security-for-expenses statutes (like Wisconsin's). These statutes typically required that the plaintiff, as a condition to the filing of a derivative suit, post a bond sufficient to ensure that the defendants would have a fund out of which to recover their legal expenses should they prevail on the merits. Since corporations almost invariably reimburse the legal expenses of successful officer defendants, an unstated objective of these statutes was to discourage the filing of derivative suits altogether. One can readily infer, therefore, that count two of the plaintiff's complaint in *Borak*—the so-called "direct" action based on a violation of section 14(a) of the Securities Act—was calculated to get "review" of the merger decision without posting the $75,000 bond required by the Wisconsin statute. To the extent that the plaintiff was seeking an end-run around the traditional practice of deciding stockholder's suits in accordance with state law, there thus were substantial federalism interests involved in the case.

Indeed, those interests go much beyond the obvious effect on security-for-expenses statutes. *Borak* unleashed a flood of private suits to enforce various sections of the Securities Act of 1933 and the Securities Exchange Act of 1934. This litigation provided alternative federal remedies for many state law causes of action relating to corporate managers' fiduciary duties and created new fiduciary responsibilities to shareholders where none previously existed. Federal securities law has thus become an integral part of the law governing corporations even though the latter is ostensibly a creature wholly of state-law. But see *Burks v. Lasker*, 441 U.S. 471 (1979) (state law practice of allowing disinterested directors to terminate derivative suit could apply to action based on federal statute where practice is consistent with policy of federal legislation.)

This federal law of corporations, however, is not "integrated" into corporation law in the same sense that regulatory statutes are commonly incorporated into other aspects of state common law. Since *Erie Railroad Co. v. Tompkins*, 304 U.S. 64 (1938), there is no federal, general common law. Unlike a state court that adopts a legislative rule of conduct as defining the "duty owed" in a common-law tort action, the federal court that "implies" a private cause of action to effectuate a statute's purpose adds a remedy to the legislative scheme. In so doing the federal court is simultaneously more audacious and more constrained than its state counterpart would be: More audacious because it is assuming a creative remedial role which, since *Erie*, has been problematic outside special fields, such as admiralty law. See, e.g., *Moragne v. United States*, 398 U.S. 375 (1970). And more constrained because, in effectuating the legislature's purposes, the federal court draws upon a potentially narrower range of policies and principles than a state court, which has a general mandate to contribute to the evolution of the whole of a state's common law.

To put the matter somewhat differently, state and federal courts look at legislative intent from different perspectives when assessing the relevance of a statutory norm to a private claim for damages or injunction. State courts, following the famous English precedent of *Gorris v. Scott*, 9 L.R. 125 (Exch. 1874), will be concerned not to extend a statutory duty to situations far beyond those risks of harm that inspired passage of the legislation. See, e.g., *De Haen v. Rockwood Sprinkler Co.*, 258 N.Y. 350, 179 N.E. 764 (1932). But state courts may feel free to treat violations of public regulatory provisions merely as "evidence" of negligence, or as establishing the defendant's fault only "presumptively." Alternatively, they may "borrow" a standard of care from a statute that would be unenforceable by public prosecution because of some technical defect in its adoption. See *Clinkscales v. Carver*, 22 Cal. 2d 72, 136 P.2d 777 (1943). The state courts' search is for an appropriate way to integrate statutes into the fabric of common law claims over which they have general jurisdiction, while likewise giving these general legislative norms an application that is sensible within the context of the facts of a particular case.

Federal court "implication" analysis is inevitably more oriented to statutory language and legislative intent. A private claim for relief in a federal district court based on the defendant's violation of a federal legislative rule of conduct presents a claim founded on the statute itself. It is not a common law claim that asks the court to redefine the defendant's duty in terms of the statutory command while providing a traditional common law remedy. For if the claim is not based on the federal statute (or the Constitution), it does not "arise under" federal law and, in the absence of some other basis for jurisdiction, the court cannot hear the case. Thus, when diversity is lacking, a defendant in federal court can frequently raise the issue of whether the plaintiff has stated a cause of action—whether the federal statute in question affords, or permits the court to afford, relief—through the device of a motion to dismiss for lack of jurisdiction. In recognizing a "claim" or a "cause of action" the court is thus defining its own jurisdiction and simultaneously raising the question whether—in a system of limited and legislatively conferred jurisdiction—the remedy was one that the Congress "intended."

This focus on specific legislative intent can have the curious effect of broadening the reach of implied causes of action once recognized, while limiting the instances in which the courts are prepared to recognize private rights of enforcement in the first instance. For example, the "enforcement" rationale that pervades the *Borak* opinion has had significant effects on the willingness of courts in subsequent cases to allow various affirmative defenses or to otherwise limit the reach of the action. As one court noted:

> This policy of vigorous enforcement through private litigation has been the instrument for forging many salutary developments in the securities fraud area, including a broadening of standing to sue, and a relaxation of the elements of proof in a private action. * * * The scienter requirement * * * appears to have been reduced to a knowledge of falsity or reckless disregard for truth standard. * * * The reliance standard has also been relaxed. * * * These are merely examples of innovations that have been prompted in substantial part by a uniform policy of encouraging vigorous enforcement of the securities laws through private litigation.

Chris-Craft Industries, Inc. v. Piper Aircraft Corp., 480 F.2d 341, 356–57 (2d Cir.), *cert. denied* 414 U.S. 910 (1973).

On the other hand, "jurisdictional" matters that raise both federalism and separation of powers concerns seem likely to induce a caution that *Borak* scarcely reflects. But, the post-*Borak* evolution of implied rights of action in the Supreme Court illustrates both preoccupations and eventually arrives at a position basically consistent with its antecedents in English jurisprudence.

English Antecedants. Implied private action analysis can be traced to the English precedent of *Couch v. Steel*, 118 Eng. Rep. 1193, 1197 (Q.B. 1854). There a seaman was allowed to recover damages from the owner of his ship for neglecting, in violation of a statute, to outfit the vessel with "a sufficient and proper supply of medicines and medicaments suitable to * * * diseases arising on a sea voyage." As a result of the owner's neglect, the seaman "was unable to be cured of * * * sickness on board of the said barque * * * and suffered great pain." The statute provided that any person could institute suit against the ill-equipped shipowner for recovery of a criminal penalty of twenty pounds, a portion of which could be retained by the informer, the balance to be paid to the Seaman's Hospital Society. Responding to the shipowner's contention that the statutory remedy was exclusive, the court declared:

> If the performance of a new duty created by Act of Parliament is enforced by a penalty, recoverable by the party grieved by the nonperformance, there is no other remedy than that given by the Act, either for the public or the private wrong; but, by the penalty given in the Act now in question, compensation for private special damage seems not to have been contemplated. The penalty is recoverable in case of a breach of the public duty; though no damage may actually have been sustained by anybody; and no authority has been cited to us, nor are we aware of any, in which it has been held that, in such a case as the present, the common law right to maintain an action in respect of a special damage resulting from the breach of a public duty (whether such duty exists at common law or is created by statute) is taken away by reason of a penalty, recoverable by a common informer, being annexed as a punishment for the non-performance of the public duty.

Finding no evidence of contrary legislative intent, the court felt free to allow a private remedy consistent with the purposes of the legislation.

Couch v. Steel followed an ancient pattern. As early as the thirteenth century the judges of the King's courts in England began to shape and elaborate the various writs of trespass in order to do justice between the King's subjects and provide personal security. See T. PLUCKNETT, A CONCISE HISTORY OF THE COMMON LAW 366–73 (5th ed. 1956). Indeed, one of the oldest methods of proving a trespass upon the case was to "recite one of the scores of statutes the breach of which caused loss to the plaintiff. * * * " Damages were frequently awarded in such cases, whether or not the statute breached by the defendant specifically provided for special penalties. Katz, *The Jurisprudence of Remedies: Constitutional Legality and the Law of Torts in Bell v. Hood,* 117 U. Pa. L. Rev. 1, 20 (1968).

In these early cases judges were rarely troubled by Parliament's failure to provide explicitly for private relief for statutory violations, nor were they concerned to identify the scope of the legislature's intent before awarding a remedy. But as Parliament's legal dominance became accepted, that body's "will" assumed the same mantle of supremacy as the crown had worn in centuries past. By the nineteenth century, the "intent of the legislature" had become a controlling factor in the development of the common law, and the creation of private remedies under criminal or regulatory legislation which did not provide for such remedies was thought somehow to add to the written law—and therefore to be suspect as judicial "lawmaking." According to this line of thought, legislative silence on the matter of private remedies was to be taken as precluding judicial creativity.

NATIONAL RAILROAD PASSENGER CORP. v. NATIONAL ASSOCIATION OF RAILROAD PASSENGERS

Supreme Court of the United States, 1974.
414 U.S. 453, 94 S.Ct. 690, 38 L.Ed.2d 646.

MR. JUSTICE STEWART delivered the opinion of the Court.

The respondent, the National Association of Railroad Passengers (NARP), brought this action * * * to enjoin the announced discontinuance of certain passenger trains that had previously been operated by the Central of Georgia Railway Company (Central). Named as defendants were Central, its parent, Southern Railway Co. (Southern), and the National Railroad Passenger Corp. (Amtrak) * * * . The question before us is whether this action is maintainable under applicable federal law.

After the enactment of the Rail Passenger Service Act of 1970 (Amtrak Act), 45 U.S.C.A. § 501 et seq., Central contracted with Amtrak for the latter to assume Central's intercity rail passenger service responsibilities.[1] * * * The train discontinuances that precipitated this action were announced by Amtrak pursuant to 45 U.S.C.A. § 564(b)(2).[2] The gravamen of the respondent's complaint was that these discontinuances are not authorized by, and in fact are prohibited by, the Amtrak Act.[3] The District Court concluded that the respondent lacks standing under § 307 of the Amtrak Act, and accordingly dismissed the action. The Court of Appeals reversed and held that the respondent has standing and that § 307 does not otherwise bar such a suit by a private party who is allegedly aggrieved. We granted certiorari to decide whether such a private cause of action can be maintained in light of § 307 (a) of the Amtrak Act.

In this Court and in the Court of Appeals, the parties have approached the question from several perspectives. The issue has been variously stated to be whether the Amtrak Act can be read to create a private right of action to enforce compliance with its provisions; whether a federal district court has jurisdiction under the terms of the Act to entertain such a suit; and whether the respondent has standing to bring such a suit. Because the reference in each instance is to § 307(a) of the Act and the legis-

---

1. Section 401 of the Act, 45 U.S.C.A. § 561, authorizes Amtrak to contract with any railroad to undertake its entire responsibility for intercity rail passenger service. Upon entering such a contract, a railroad can discontinue any intercity passenger train by merely filing a 30-day notice of intent with the Interstate Commerce Commission * * *

2. * * * 45 U.S.C.A. § 564(b)(2) authorizes Amtrak to discontinue any passenger service, other than that contained in a "basic system" designated by the Secretary of Transportation, upon its own initiative.

3. The respondent's position on the merits is based on the fact that the Central of Georgia Railway Co., which entered a contract with Amtrak, is a subsidiary of Southern Railway

Co., which did not enter a contract with Amtrak. The respondent contends that the contract between Amtrak and Central does not comply with § 401(a)(1) of the Amtrak Act because Southern, the parent company, has not contracted with Amtrak. Since § 401(a)(1), authorizes only a contract for Amtrak to undertake a railroad's *entire* responsibility for intercity rail passenger service, the respondent contends that Southern cannot relieve itself of only *part* of this responsibility by allowing a subsidiary to contract with Amtrak while declining itself to do so. Accordingly, the respondent argues that Southern and Central, having entered no statutorily authorized contract with Amtrak, are prohibited by 45 U.S.C.A. § 564(a) from discontinuing any passenger train before January 1, 1975.

lative history behind that provision, these questions overlap in the context of this case even more than they ordinarily would. But, however phrased, the threshold question clearly is whether the Amtrak Act or any other provision of law creates a cause of action whereby a private party such as the respondent can enforce duties and obligations imposed by the Act; for it is only if such a right of action exists that we need consider whether the respondent had standing to bring the action and whether the District Court had jurisdiction to entertain it.

The respondent has pointed to no provision of law outside the Amtrak Act itself that can be read to create or imply the cause of action that it seeks to bring against the petitioners. It follows that support for the bringing of this action must be found, if at all, within the four corners of that Act. The only section of the Act that authorizes any suits to enforce duties and obligations is § 307(a), which provides:

> "If the Corporation or any railroad engages in or adheres to any action, practice, or policy inconsistent with the policies and purposes of this chapter, obstructs or interferes with any activities authorized by this chapter, refuses, fails, or neglects to discharge its duties and responsibilities under this chapter, or threatens any such violation, obstruction, interference, refusal, failure, or neglect, the district court of the United States for any district in which the Corporation or other person resides or may be found shall have jurisdiction, except as otherwise prohibited by law, upon petition of the Attorney General of the United States or, in a case involving a labor agreement, upon petition of any employee affected thereby, including duly authorized employee representatives, to grant such equitable relief as may be necessary or appropriate to prevent or terminate any violation, conduct, or threat."

In terms, § 307(a) purports only to confer jurisdiction, not to create a cause of action. The legislative history, however, makes clear that the congressional purpose was to authorize certain types of suits for the enforcement of the Act's provisions. * * * In light of the language and legislative history of § 307(a), we read it as creating a public cause of action, maintainable by the Attorney General, to enforce the duties and responsibilities imposed by the Act. The only private cause of action created by that provision, however, is explicitly limited to "a case involving a labor agreement." Thus, no authority for the action the respondent has brought can be found in the language of § 307(a). The argument is made, however, that § 307(a) serves only to *authorize* certain suits against Amtrak and that it should not be read to *preclude* other private causes of action for the enforcement of obligations imposed by the Act. The respondent claims that railroad passengers are the intended beneficiaries of the Act and that the courts should therefore imply a private cause of action whereby they can enforce compliance with the Act's provisions. See *J. I. Case Co. v. Borak.* It goes without saying, however, that the inference of such a private cause of action not otherwise authorized by the statute must be consistent with the evident legislative intent and, of course, with the effectuation of the purposes intended to be served by the Act.

* * *

The original draft of § 307(a) differed from its present form in several respects.   It conferred upon federal district courts jurisdiction to entertain suits against Amtrak (but not individual railroads) "upon petition of the Attorney General of the United States or, in a case involving a labor agreement, upon petition of any individual affected thereby * * * ." At the hearings of the House Committee, representatives of organized labor took issue with certain aspects of the draft provision and proposed several changes.   One of these proposals would have authorized suits against the railroads as well as Amtrak.   Another would have authorized private suits by "any person adversely affected or aggrieved thereby, including the representatives of the employees of any railroad or of the Corporation." * * *   The Secretary of Transportation, who was to be the primary administrative officer responsible for the implementation of the Act, sent a letter to the Subcommittee chairman commenting on these proposed changes.   His letter stated that he did not object to allowing suits against railroads as well as Amtrak.   As to the proposal to amend the bill to permit suits by an "aggrieved person," however, he stated:

> "Sanctions are normally imposed by the Government.   Consequently, I would be opposed to permitting 'any person' to seek enforcement of section 307.   I would have no objection, however, if the section were revised to permit employee representatives, as well as employees adversely affected, to seek equitable relief."

Thereafter the committee redrafted § 307(a) in conformity with the Secretary's recommendations.   The Committee's redraft and the bill as finally enacted authorized suits against railroads as well as Amtrak, and permitted suits involving labor agreements by "duly authorized employee representatives" as well as by affected employees, but did *not* authorize suits by "any person adversely affected or aggrieved."

* * *

* * * The Committee's deliberate failure to adopt [organized labor's] proposal, after learning of the Secretary's views, cannot but give weight to the conclusion that the Committee agreed with the Secretary's interpretation of the meaning and effect of the existing language, as well as with his opposition to the proposed change.   These factors are substantial indicia that the legislators understood that § 307(a) as written would preclude private causes of action to enforce compliance with the Act, other than in the limited area of cases "involving a labor agreement." * * *

This construction of § 307(a) is also completely consistent with the Act as a whole and with its more generalized legislative history.   In outlining the purpose of the Amtrak Act, the House Report, refering to a comment by the Secretary of Transportation, noted that "[i]n order to achieve economic viability in a basic rail passenger system, * * * there will have to be a 'paring of uneconomic routes.' "   H.R. Rep. No. 91-1580, p. 3 (1970) * * * .   In § 404 of the Act, Congress provided an efficient means whereby Amtrak could eliminate uneconomic routes (other than a "basic system" designated and from time to time augmented by the Secretary of Transportation) without the necessity of submitting to the time-consuming proceedings of state regulatory bodies or the Interstate Commerce Commission that had been required before the Act's passage. If, however, § 307(a) were to be interpreted as permitting private lawsuits to prevent the discontinuance of passenger trains, then the only effect of the Act in this regard would have been to substitute the federal district courts for the state or federal administrative bodies formerly required to pass upon proposed discontinuances.[9]

If the respondent's view of the Act were to prevail, a private plaintiff could secure injunctive process to prevent the discontinuance of an "uneconomic" passenger train *pendente lite*, which would force Amtrak to continue the train's operation and to incur the resulting deficits and dislocations within its entire system while the court considered the propriety of the proposed discontinuance. Since suits could be brought in any district through which Amtrak trains pass and since there would be a myriad of possible plaintiffs, the potential would exist for a barrage of lawsuits that, either individually or collectively, could frustrate or severely delay any proposed passenger train discontinuance. Even if one court eventually upheld the discontinuance, its judgment would not control a suit brought in another district and would not, in any event, obviate the loss in the interim of substantial sums and the diversion of rolling stock from more heavily travelled routes. This would completely undercut the efficient apparatus that Congress sought to provide for Amtrak to use in the "paring of uneconomic routes." It would also produce the anomalous result of a discontinuance procedure under the Act considerably less efficient than that which existed before, since there would no longer be a single forum that could finally determine the permissibility of a proposed discontinuance. * * *

9. * * * In 1958, in an effort to reduce losses on passenger train operations, Congress enacted § 13a of the Interstate Commerce Act, which gave the railroads the option of bypassing state agencies and petitioning the Interstate Commerce Commission for permission to discontinue passenger trains. Under § 13a after the railroad has filed a notice of discontinuance with the Commission, an aggrieved person may file a complaint. Either upon such complaint or on its own initiative, the Commission may institute an investigation of the proposed discontinuance. If it finds that the discontinuance is contrary to the public interest, the Commission may require the continuance of the route for a period of one year. Orders approving or disapproving proposed discontinuances are subject to judicial review. If, on the other hand, the Commission decides that the discontinuance is clearly permissible under § 13a of the Act, and decides not to conduct an investigation or decides to terminate an investigation already begun, an aggrieved person has no recourse to the courts to review the Commission's decision.

* * * Only if the Commission conducts an investigation and issues an order, a procedure that Congress explicitly eliminated for routes subject to the Amtrak Act but outside the basic system, is judicial review available. It thus appears that the Amtrak Act has in effect substituted, in matters covered by that statute, the scrutiny of the Attorney General for that of the Commission under § 13a. Just as an aggrieved passenger has no access to the courts when the Commission, under § 13a, takes no action on a complaint, so likewise under the Amtrak Act an aggrieved passenger has no access to the courts when the Attorney General has refused to object to a proposed passenger train discontinuance by bringing an action under § 37(a) to enjoin it. There is no reason apparent from the Amtrak Act, its legislative history, or its underlying purposes to think that Congress intended to create a private remedy substantially equivalent to one that had been eliminated under pre-existing federal law.

Congress clearly did not intend to replace the delays often inherent in the administrative proceedings contemplated by § 13a of the Interstate Commerce Act with the probably even greater delays inherent in multiple federal court proceedings. Instead, it clothed the Attorney General with the exclusive (except in cases involving labor agreements) authority to police the Amtrak system and to enforce the various duties and obligations imposed by the Act. In light of the substantial scrutiny to which Amtrak operations are subject by both Congress and the Executive, Congress could quite rationally suppose that this remedy will effectively prevent and correct any Amtrak breaches of obligations under the Act.

For these reasons we hold that § 307(a) provides the exclusive remedies for breaches of any duties or obligations imposed by the Amtrak Act, and that no additional private cause of action to enforce compliance with the Act's provisions can properly be inferred.[13] Accordingly, the judgment of the Court of Appeals is reversed, and the case is remanded to that court for further proceedings consistent with this opinion.

* * *

MR. JUSTICE BRENNAN, concurring in the result.

Although I am in agreement that the legislative history of the Amtrak Act provides a clear and convincing expression of Congress' intent to preclude any except the Attorney General and in certain situations an employee or his duly authorized representative from maintaining an action under the Act against petitioners, I would leave open the question whether a private suit for mandamus under 28 U.S.C.A. § 1361 might be maintained against the Attorney General if his refusal to act under § 307—even though within the letter of his authority—went "beyond any rational exercise of discretion."

MR. JUSTICE DOUGLAS, dissenting.

* * *

The Court phrases the question in terms of whether a "right of action" exists, saying that no question of "standing" or "jurisdiction" is presented. Whatever the merits of the distinction between these three concepts may be in some situations, the difference here is only a matter of semantics. The District Court dismissed the cause for lack of "standing." The Court of Appeals reversed, ruling that there was "standing." The parties argue the case on the basis of "standing." Even the Solicitor General who appears as *amicus curiae* * * * conceives of the issue in terms of "standing." By the Court's own admission this is not a case where all judicial review is foreclosed. For § 307(a) does create a cause of action. May that cause of action be enforced by passengers or only by the Attorney General or by individual employees or railroad un-

---

13. Since we hold that no right of action exists, questions of standing and jurisdiction become immaterial. * * *

ions? Standing of passengers to sue or the existence of a cause of action in passengers is identical in that posture of the case.

*   *   *

* * * Petitioners argue that [§ 307(a)] restricts suits to the Attorney General and to employees. That seems a strained construction. The most I think that can be drawn from the words of [§ 307(a)] and the legislative history is that Congress wanted to make sure that some federal agency had some oversight over this public corporation-for-profit activity. Hence the grant of standing, or cause of action, to the Attorney General. Moreover, it took out of the penumbra of aggrieved persons, employees having rights under collective agreements. Congress left untouched 28 U.S.C.A. § 1337 which provides that "[t]he District Courts shall have original jurisdiction of any civil action or proceeding arising under any Act of Congress regulating commerce * * * ."

Aggrieved passengers are the most obvious complainants when it comes to saving passenger trains from extinction. Certainly passengers of discontinued trains suffer injury in fact and are within the zone of interests protected by the Amtrak Act and thus satisfy two of the three requirements of *Data Processing Service Organizations, Inc. v. Camp*. As to the third—that judicial review has not been precluded—it seems as plain to me as it did to the Court of Appeals. * * *

The Attorney General is a busy person; and it is not credible to believe that a grant of power to him to sue precludes the standing of passengers who are the prime casualties when passenger service is discontinued.

* * * Amtrak is a private-for-profit corporation which is only construing its own enabling Act. If passengers are denied standing to sue, Amtrak is largely on its own. Especially is this so in light of the Attorney General's own view that the grant of power in [§ 307(a)] is limited and does not authorize him to seek correction of all violations of the Act.[4] So far as I can ascertain the Attorney General has not intruded in any case. To leave the complete oversight to employees is to make nonreviewable most of Amtrak's decisions. * * * If * * * there can be no policing of the Act, we have given a corporation, which is private and operating for a profit, an administrative absolutism we seldom have been willing to conclude that Congress has bestowed even on federal agencies. I cannot believe the Congress had any such purpose.

We deal here with a federal cause of action and it is the judicial tradition "for federal courts to fashion federal law where federal rights are concerned." The fact that a private suit to enforce a federal law is not specifically sanctioned by Congress seldom means that standing to sue is

---

4. In refusing to become involved in the case consolidated with this one on the Court of Appeals, the Attorney General's Office expressed the view that "the statutory mandate of section 307(a) does not give the Attorney General the authority to sue for a construction of the Act or to enjoin a purely technical violation." Letter from Assistant Attorney General L. Patrick Gray III to Congressman John Slack, Nov. 19, 1971, in Brief for Respondent 29, 30.

foreclosed. The purpose of the Amtrak Act was to preserve and improve train service. The object was not to protect trains *per se* nor to create an *in rem* action. The purpose, which the Court in its dedication to legalisms overlooks, was to protect the people who ride the trains. The case is very much on all fours with *J. I. Case Co. v. Borak* where Congress made it unlawful to solicit proxies in violation of rules prescribed by the Securities and Exchange Commission. No standing, no cause of action was expressly given stockholders who might suffer from corporate action pursuant to a deceptive proxy solicitation. Yet we held that the Commission was not granted an exclusive role to play in policing the area. * * *

The Court is in the mood to close all possible doors to judicial review so as to let the existing bureaucracies roll on to their goal of administrative absolutism. When the victims of administrative venality or administrative caprice are not allowed even to be heard, the abuses of the monsters we have created will become intolerable. The separation of powers was designed to provide not for judicial supremacy, but for checks and balances. When we turn back this respondent, we turn back passengers who are the victims of the present transportation debacle. Those who complain are not adventurers who seek personal aggrandizement as do jackals who historically have fattened on some economic debacles. The passengers are the victims of the transportation crisis out of which Amtrak seeks to make a fortune. These passengers should be heard. * * *

CORT v. ASH

Supreme Court of the United States, 1975.
422 U.S. 66, 95 S.Ct. 2080, 45 L.Ed.2d 26.

MR. JUSTICE BRENNAN delivered the opinion of the Court.

There are other questions, but the principal issue presented for decision is whether a private cause of action for damages against corporate directors is to be implied in favor of a corporate stockholder under 18 U.S.C.A. § 610, a criminal statute prohibiting corporations from making "a contribution or expenditure in connection with any election at which Presidential and Vice Presidential electors * * * are to be voted for." We conclude that implication of such a federal cause of action is not suggested by the legislative context of § 610 or required to accomplish Congress' purposes in enacting the statute. * * *

*   *   *

We consider first the holding of the Court of Appeals that respondent has "a private cause of action * * * [as] a citizen [or as a stockholder] to secure injunctive relief." The 1972 Presidential election is history, and respondent as citizen or stockholder seeks injunctive relief only as to future elections. In that circumstance, a statute enacted after the decision of the Court of Appeals, the Federal Election Campaign Act Amendments of 1974, requires reversal of the holding of the Court of Appeals.

In terms, § 610 is only a criminal statute, providing a fine or imprisonment for its violation.   At the time this suit was filed, there was no statutory provision for civil enforcement of § 610, whether by private parties or by a Government agency.   But the Amendments created a Federal Election Commission; established an administrative procedure for processing complaints of alleged violations of § 610 after January 1, 1975, and provided that "[a]ny person who believes a violation * * * [of § 610] has occurred may file a complaint with the Commission." * * * The Statute expressly vests the Commission with "primary jurisdiction" over any claimed violation of § 610 within its purview.[9]   Consequently, a complainant seeking as citizen or stockholder to enjoin alleged violations of § 610 in future elections must henceforth pursue the statutory remedy of a complaint to the Commission, and invoke its authority to request the Attorney General to seek the injunctive relief.   Thus, the Amendments constitute an intervening law that relegates to the Commission's cognizance respondent's complaint as citizen or stockholder for injunctive relief against any alleged violations of § 610 in future elections.   In that circumstance the holding of the Court of Appeals must be reversed.   Our duty is to decide this case according to the law existing at the time of our decision.

* * *

* * * There is no "statutory direction or legislative history to the contrary" in or respecting the Amendments, nor is there any possible "manifest injustice" in requiring respondent to pursue with respect to alleged violations which have yet to occur the statutory remedy for injunctive relief created by the Amendments.

* * * [W]e turn next to the holding of the Court of Appeals that "a private cause of action * * * by a stockholder to secure * * * derivative damage relief [is] proper to remedy violation of § 610."   We hold that such relief is not available with regard to a 1972 violation under § 610 itself, but rather is available, if at all, under Delaware law governing corporations.

In determining whether a private remedy is implicit in a statute not expressly providing one, several factors are relevant.   First, is the plaintiff "one of the class for whose especial benefit the statute was enacted,"— that is, does the statute create a federal right in favor of the plaintiff? Second, is there any indication of legislative intent, explicit or implicit, either to create such a remedy or to deny one?   Third, is it consistent with the underlying purposes of the legislative scheme to imply such a

---

9. The parties disagree upon whether this reference to "primary jurisdiction" suggests that a complainant, after filing a complaint with the Commission, may file a civil suit for injunctive relief if the Commission fails to cause one to be filed.   They also dispute whether the exhaustion requirement applies to a suit for damages. * * *

However, these issues are not here relevant; it suffices for the purposes of this case to hold that the statute requires that a private complainant, desiring injunctive relief against alleged future violations of § 610 must at least exhaust his statutory remedy under the Amendments when and if such violations occur.   We note that the question of the availability of a private cause of action by respondent for injunctive relief may not arise at all if the Attorney General seeks and obtains injunctive relief for any claimed violations by Bethlehem.

remedy for the plaintiff?   And finally, is the cause of action one tradition-ally relegated to state law, in an area basically the concern of the States, so that it would be inappropriate to infer a cause of action based solely on federal law? * * *

Clearly, provision of a criminal penalty does not necessarily preclude implication of a private cause of action for damages.   However, in *Wyan-dotte* [*Wyandotte Transportation Co. v. United States*, 389 U.S. 191 (1967)], *Borak,* and *Rigsby* [*Texas & Pacific Railway Co. v. Rigsby*, 241 U.S. 33 (1916)], there was at least a statutory basis for inferring that a civil cause of action of some sort lay in favor of someone.[11]   Here, there was nothing more than a bare criminal statute, with absolutely no indication that civil enforcement of any kind was available to anyone.

We need not, however, go so far as to say that in this circumstance a bare criminal statute can never be deemed sufficiently protective of some special group so as to give rise to a private cause of action by a member of that group.   For the intent to protect corporate shareholders particu-larly was at best a subsidiary purpose of § 610, and the other relevant fac-tors all either are not helpful or militate against implying a private cause of action.

First, § 610 is derived from the Act of January 26, 1907, which "seems to have been motivated by two considerations.   First, the necessity for destroying the influence over elections which corporations exercised through financial contribution.   Second, the feeling that corporate offi-cials had no moral right to use corporate funds for contributions to politi-cal parties without the consent of the stockholders."   Respondent bases the derivative action on the second purpose, claiming that the intent to protect stockholders from use of their invested funds for political pur-poses demonstrates that the statute set up a federal right in shareholders not to have corporate funds used for this purpose.

However, the legislative history of the 1907 Act, * * * demonstrates that the protection of ordinary stockholders was at best a secondary con-cern.   Rather, the primary purpose of the 1907 Act, and of the 1925 Fed-eral Corrupt Practices Act, 43 Stat. 1070, which reenacted the 1907 provi-sion with some changes as § 313 of that Act, was to assure that federal elections are "free from the power of money," to eliminate "the apparent

---

11. In *Wyandotte,* it was conceded that the United States had a civil in rem action against the ship obstructing navigation under § 19 of the Rivers and Harbors Act of 1899, and could retain the proceeds of the sale of the vessel and its cargo.   The only question was whether it also had other judicial remedies for violation of § 51 of the Act, aside from the criminal penalties provided in § 16.

In *Borak*, § 27 of the Securities Exchange Act of 1934 specifically granted jurisdiction to the district courts over civil actions to "en-force any liability or duty created by this title or the rules and regulations thereunder," and there seemed to be no dispute over the fact that at least a private suit for declaratory re-lief was authorized; the question was whether a derivative suit for rescission and damages was also available.   Further it was clear that the Securities and Exchange Commission could sue to enjoy violations of § 41(a) of the Act, the section involved in *Borak*.

Finally, in *Rigsby,* the Court noted that the statutes involved included language perti-nent only to a private right of action for dam-ages, although such a right of action was not expressly provided, thus rendering "[t]he in-ference of a private right of action * * * ir-resistible."

hold on political parties which business interests * * * seek and sometimes obtain by reason of liberal campaign contributions." Thus, the legislation was primarily concerned with corporations as a source of aggregated wealth and therefore of possible corrupting influence, and not directly with the internal relations between the corporations and their stockholders. In contrast, in those situations in which we have inferred a federal private cause of action not expressly provided, there has generally been a clearly articulated federal right in the plaintiff, e.g., *Bivens v. Six Unknown Federal Narcotics Agents*, or a pervasive legislative scheme governing the relationship between the plaintiff class and the defendant class in a particular regard, e.g., *J. I. Case Co. v. Borak.*

Second, there is no indication whatever in the legislative history of § 610 which suggests a congressional intention to vest in corporate shareholders a federal right to damages for violation of § 610. True, in situations in which it is clear that federal law has granted a class of persons certain rights, it is not necessary to show an intention to create a private cause of action, although an explicit purpose to deny such cause of action would be controlling. But where, as here, it is at least dubious whether Congress intended to vest in the plaintiff class rights broader than those provided by state regulation of corporations, the fact that there is no suggestion at all that § 610 may give rise to a suit for damages or, indeed, to any civil cause of action, reinforces the conclusion that the expectation, if any, was that the relationship between corporations and their stockholders would continue to be entrusted entirely to state law.

Third, while "it is the duty of the courts to be alert to provide such remedies as are necessary to make effective the congressional purpose," in this instance the remedy sought would not aid the primary congressional goal. Recovery of derivative damages by the corporation for violation of § 610 would not cure the influence which the use of corporate funds in the first instance may have had on a federal election. Rather, such a remedy would only permit directors in effect to "borrow" corporate funds for a time; the later compelled repayment might well not deter the initial violation and would certainly not decrease the impact of the use of such funds upon an election already past.

Fourth, and finally, for reasons already intimated, it is entirely appropriate in this instance to relegate respondent and others in his situation to whatever remedy is created by state law. In addition to the ultra vires action pressed here, the use of corporate funds in violation of federal law may, under the law of some States, give rise to a cause of action for breach of fiduciary duty. Corporations are creatures of state law, and investors commit their funds to corporate directors on the understanding that, except where federal law expressly requires certain responsibilities of directors with respect to stockholders, state law will govern the internal affairs of the corporation. If, for example, state law permits corporations to use corporate funds as contributions in state elections, shareholders are on notice that their funds may be so used and have no recourse under any federal statute. We are necessarily reluctant to imply a federal right to recover funds used in violation of a federal statute where the laws governing the corporation may put a shareholder on notice that there may be no such recovery.

In *Borak*, we said: "[If] the law of the State happened to attach no responsibility to the use of misleading proxy statements, the whole purpose of [§ 14(a) of the Securities Exchange Act of 1934] might be frustrated." Here, committing respondent to state-provided remedies would have no such effect.   In *Borak*, the statute involved was clearly an intrusion of federal law into the internal affairs of corporations; to the extent that state law differed or impeded suit, the congressional intent could be compromised in state-created causes of action.   In this case, Congress was concerned, not with regulating corporations as such, but with dulling their impact upon federal elections.   As we have seen, the existence or non-existence of a derivative cause of action for damages would not aid or hinder this primary goal.

Because injunctive relief is not presently available in light of the Amendments, and because implication of a federal right of damages on behalf of a corporation under § 610 would intrude into an area traditionally committed to state law without aiding the main purpose of § 610, we reverse. * * *

Notes

1. The four factor test that Justice Brennan enunciated, and to which the whole Court subscribed, in *Cort* is a curious *pastiche* of prior doctrine which combines potentially incompatable concepts.   The "especial benefit" idea is of common law origin and suggests a broad-gauged approach to determining whether the statute creates a "federal right" for which the Court then supplies a remedy.   This factor resonates with Justice Harlan's description in *Bivens* that "The notion of 'implying' a remedy * * * can only refer to a process whereby the federal judiciary exercises a choice among *traditionally available* judicial remedies according to reasons related to the substantive social policy embodied in an act of positive law."   403 U.S. at 402 n.4.

The second factor, by contrast, focuses the Court on specific legislative intent (either express or implied) to create or deny a remedy.   In most contexts where "implication" is necessary this search for intent must be conducted in the materials comprising the statute's legislative history.   And if the statute is silent, the legislative history predictably will be either silent or inconclusive.   The question then will be what to make of legislative intent?   Should silence be construed as negating an intent to allow private suits, as it seems to have been in the *Cort* opinion?   And, if so, what is the Court to do when the general "substantive social policy" of the statute might be furthered by granting the remedy requested?

The third factor then reintroduces a search for purpose, but in an ambiguous form.   The question is apparently "consistency" with "underlying purposes" of the legislation, but it is unclear what a finding of "consistency" would add to the first factor.   This puzzle suggests that the third factor serves primarily as a limitation; it cautions the court to beware of implying remedies even where the first two factors point in that direction without considering the implications of implication for the coherence of the overall statutory scheme.

The fourth factor similarly seems purely cautionary and is, in one sense, non-problematic.   It merely introduces the traditional "federalism" concern.   Yet the suggestion that the question is whether the implication would be "in an area basically the concern of the states" introduces another unruly issue into the calculus.   In most situations the "area" will not define itself, and *how* it is defined will determine whether it is basically of state concern.   For example, is the question in *Cort* one of corporation law or of the law of federal elections?

2. Subsequent developments have confirmed both the intellectual difficulty of applying the *Cort* formula and the message implied by the application in *Cort* itself—the Court was not inclined to carry the *Bivens-Borak* remedial approach over into the wide range of federal "rights" that might be found in the dense growth of statutes and regulations during and since the New Deal.   *Cort's* potential for both restrictive application and conceptual disagreement was soon obvious and is well-illustrated by one of the few post-*Cort* Supreme Court decisions that has "implied" a private federal cause of action under a statute that provides no express remedy.

CANNON v. UNIVERSITY OF CHICAGO

Supreme Court of the United States, 1979.
441 U.S. 677, 99 S.Ct. 1946, 60 L.Ed.2d 560.

MR. JUSTICE STEVENS delivered the opinion of the Court.

* * *

Only two facts alleged in the complaints are relevant to our decision. First, petitioner was excluded from participation in the respondents' medical education programs because of her sex.   Second, these education programs were receiving federal financial assistance at the time of her exclusion.   These facts, admitted *arguendo* by respondents' motion to dismiss the complaints, establish a violation of § 901(a) of Title IX of the Education Amendments of 1972 [20 U.S.C.A. § 1681] (hereinafter Title IX).

That section, in relevant part, provides:

"No person in the United States shall, on the basis of sex, be excluded from participation in, be denied the benefits of, or be subjected to discrimination under any education program or activity receiving Federal financial assistance. * * * "

The statute does not, however, expressly authorize a private right of action by a person injured by a violation of § 901.   For that reason, and because it concluded that no private remedy should be inferred, the District Court granted the respondents' motions to dismiss.

The Court of Appeals agreed * * * .

* * *

The Court of Appeals quite properly devoted careful attention to [the] question of statutory construction.   As our recent cases—particularly *Cort v. Ash*—demonstrate, the fact that a federal statute has been violated and some person harmed does not automatically give rise to a private cause of action in favor of that person.   Instead, before concluding that Congress intended to make a remedy available to a special class of litigants, a court must carefully analyze the four factors that *Cort* identifies as indicative of such an intent. Our review of those factors persuades us, however, that the Court of Appeals reached the wrong conclusion * * * .

First, the threshold question under *Cort* is whether the statute was enacted for the benefit of a special class of which the plaintiff is a member. That question is answered by looking to the language of the statute itself. Thus, the statutory reference to "any employee of any such common carrier" in the 1893 legislation requiring railroads to equip their cars with secure "grab irons or handholds," made "irresistible" the Court's earliest "inference of a private right of action"—in that case in favor of a railway employee who was injured when a grab iron gave way. *Texas & Pacific R. Co. v. Rigsby*, 241 U.S. 33, 40.[10]

Similarly, it was statutory language describing the special class to be benefited by § 5 of the Voting Rights Act of 1965 that persuaded the Court that private parties within that class were implicitly authorized to seek a declaratory judgment against a covered State. *Allen v. State Board of Elections*, 393 U.S. 544. The dispositive language in that statute—"no person shall be denied the right to vote for failure to comply with [a new state enactment covered by, but not approved under, § 5]"—is remarkably similar to the language used by Congress in Title IX.

The language in these statutes—which expressly identifies the class Congress intended to benefit—contrasts sharply with statutory language customarily found in criminal statutes, such as that construed in *Cort*, supra, and other laws enacted for the protection of the general public. There would be far less reason to infer a private remedy in favor of individual persons if Congress, instead of drafting Title IX with an unmistakable focus on the benefited class, had written it simply as a ban on discriminatory conduct by recipients of federal funds or as a prohibition against the disbursement of public funds to educational institutions engaged in discriminatory practices.

Unquestionably, therefore, the first of the four factors identified in *Cort* favors the implication of a private cause of action. * * *

Second, the *Cort* analysis requires consideration of legislative history. We must recognize, however, that the legislative history of a statute that does not expressly create or deny a private remedy will typically be equally silent or ambiguous on the question. * * * But this is not the typical case. Far from evidencing any purpose to *deny* a private cause of

---

10. In that case the Court stated:

"A disregard of the command of the statute is a wrongful act, and where it results in damage to one of the class for whose especial benefit the statute was enacted, the right to recover the damages from the party in default is implied, according to a doctrine of the common law expressed in 1 Com. Dig., *tit.* Action upon Statute (F), in these words: 'So, in every case, where a statute enacts, or prohib-its a thing for the benefit of a person, he shall have a remedy upon the same statute for the thing enacted for his advantage, or for the recompense of a wrong done to him contrary to the said law,' (*Per* Holt, C. J., *Anon.*, 6 Mod. 26, 27.) This is but an application of the maxim, *Ubi jus ibi remedium.* See 3 Black. Com. 51, 123; *Couch v. Steel*, 3 El. & Bl. 402, 411; 23 L. J. Q. B. 121, 125." 241 U.S., at 39–40.

action, the history of the Title IX rather plainly indicates that Congress intended to create such a remedy.

Title IX was patterned after Title VI of the Civil Rights Act of 1964. Except for the substitution of the word "sex" in Title IX to replace the words "race, color, or nation origin" in Title VI, the two statutes use identical language to describe the benefited class. Both statutes provide the same administrative mechanism for terminating federal financial support for institutions engaged in prohibited discrimination. Neither statute expressly mentions a private remedy for the person excluded from participation in a federally funded program. The drafters of Title IX explicitly assumed that it would be interpreted and applied as Title VI had been during the preceding eight years.

In 1972 when Title IX was enacted, the critical language in Title VI had already been construed as creating a private remedy. * * *

* * * Indeed, during the period between the enactment of Title VI in 1964 and the enactment of Title IX in 1972, this Court had consistently found implied remedies—often in cases much less clear than this. It was *after* 1972 that this Court decided *Cort v. Ash* and the other cases cited by the Court of Appeals in support of its strict construction of the remedial aspect of the statute. We, of course, adhere to the strict approach followed in our recent cases, but our evaluation of congressional action in 1972 must take into account its contemporary legal context. In sum, it is not only appropriate but also realistic to presume that Congress was thoroughly familiar with these unusually important precedents from this and other federal courts and that it expected its enactment to be interpreted in conformity with them.

It is not, however, necessary to rely on these presumptions. The package of statutes of which Title IX is one part also contains a provision whose language and history demonstrate that Congress itself understood Title VI, and thus its companion, Title IX, as creating a private remedy. Section 718 of the Education Amendments authorizes federal courts to award attorney's fees to the prevailing parties, other than the United States, in private actions brought against public educational agencies to enforce Title VI in the context of elementary and secondary education. * * *

* * *

Third, under *Cort,* a private remedy should not be implied if it would frustrate the underlying purpose of the legislative scheme. On the other hand, when that remedy is necessary or at least helpful to the accomplishment of the statutory purpose, the Court is decidedly receptive to its implication under the statute.

Title IX, like its model Title VI, sought to accomplish two related, but nevertheless somewhat different, objectives. First, Congress wanted to avoid the use of federal resources to support discriminatory practices; second, it wanted to provide individual citizens effective protection against those practices. * * *

The first purpose is generally served by the statutory procedure for the termination of federal financial support for institutions engaged in discriminatory practices. That remedy is, however, severe and often may not provide an appropriate means of accomplishing the second purpose if merely an isolated violation has occurred. In that situation, the violation might be remedied more efficiently by an order requiring an institution to accept an applicant who had been improperly excluded. Moreover, in that kind of situation it makes little sense to impose on an individual, whose only interest is in obtaining a benefit for herself, or on HEW, the burden of demonstrating that an institution's practices are so pervasively discriminatory that a complete cutoff of federal funding is appropriate. The award of individual relief to a private litigant who has prosecuted her own suit is not only sensible but is also fully consistent with—and in some cases even necessary to—the orderly enforcement of the statute.

The Department of Health, Education, and Welfare, which is charged with the responsibility for administering Title IX, perceives no inconsistency between the private remedy and the public remedy. On the contrary, the agency takes the unequivocal position that the individual remedy will provide effective assistance in achieving the statutory purposes. * * *

Fourth, the final inquiry suggested by *Cort* is whether implying a federal remedy is inappropriate because the subject matter involves an area basically of concern to the States. No such problem is raised by a prohibition against invidious discrimination of any sort, including that on the basis of sex. Since the Civil War, the Federal Government and the federal courts have been the "*primary* and powerful reliances" in protecting citizens against such discrimination. Moreover, it is the expenditure of federal funds that provides the justification for this particular statutory prohibition. There can be no question but that this aspect of the *Cort* analysis supports the implication of a private federal remedy.

In sum, there is no need in this case to weigh the four *Cort* factors; all of them support the same result. Not only the words and history of Title IX, but also its subject matter and underlying purposes, counsel implication of a cause of action in favor of private victims of discrimination.

* * *

When Congress intends private litigants to have a cause of action to support their statutory rights, the far better course is for it to specify as much when it creates those rights. But the Court has long recognized that under certain limited circumstances the failure of Congress to do so is not inconsistent with an intent on its part to have such a remedy available to the persons benefited by its legislation. Title IX presents the atypical situation in which *all* of the circumstances that the Court has previously identified as supportive of an implied remedy are present. We therefore conclude that petitioner may maintain her lawsuit, despite the absence of any express authorization for it in the statute.

The judgment of the Court of Appeals is reversed, and the case is remanded for further proceedings consistent with this opinion.

It is so ordered.

MR. CHIEF JUSTICE BURGER concurs in the judgment.

MR. JUSTICE REHNQUIST, with whom MR. JUSTICE STEWART joins, concurring.

Having joined the Court's opinion in this case, my only purpose in writing separately is to make explicit what seems to me already implicit in that opinion.   I think the approach of the Court, reflected in its analysis of the problem in this case * * * is quite different from the analysis in earlier cases such as *J. I. Case Co. v. Borak*, 377 U.S. 426 (1964).   The question of the existence of a private right of action is basically one of statutory construction.   And while state courts of general jurisdiction still enforcing the common law as well as statutory law may be less constrained than are federal courts enforcing laws enacted by Congress, the latter must surely look to those laws to determine whether there was an intent to create a private right of action under them.

We do not write on an entirely clean slate, however, and the Court's opinion demonstrates that Congress, at least during the period of the enactment of the several Titles of the Civil Rights Act, tended to rely to a large extent on the courts to *decide* whether there should be a private right of action, rather than determining this question for itself.   Cases such as *J. I. Case Co. v. Borak*, supra, and numerous cases from other federal courts, gave Congress good reason to think that the federal judiciary would undertake this task.

I fully agree with the Court's statement that "[w]hen Congress intends private litigants to have a cause of action to support their statutory rights, the far better course is for it to specify as much when it creates those rights."   It seems to me that the factors to which I have here briefly adverted apprise the lawmaking branch of the Federal Government that the ball, so to speak, may well now be in its court.   Not only is it "far better" for Congress to so specify when it intends private litigants to have a cause of action, but for this very reason this Court in the future should be extremely reluctant to imply a cause of action absent such specificity on the part of the Legislative Branch.

MR. JUSTICE WHITE, with whom MR. JUSTICE BLACKMUN joins, dissenting.

In avowedly seeking to provide an additional means to effectuate the broad purpose of § 901 of the Education Amendments of 1972 to end sex discrimination in federally funded educational programs, the Court fails to heed the concomitant legislative purpose not to create a new private remedy to implement this objective. * * *

The Court recognizes that because Title IX was explicitly patterned after Title VI of the Civil Rights Act of 1964, it is difficult to infer a private cause of action in the former but not in the latter. * * * [T]he legislative history, like the terms of Title VI itself, makes it abundantly clear that the Act was and is a mandate to federal agencies to eliminate discrimination in federally funded programs. Although there was no intention to cut back on private remedies existing under 42 U.S.C.A. § 1983 to challenge discrimination occurring under color of state law, there is no basis for concluding that Congress contemplated the creation of private remedies either against private parties who previously had been subject to no constitutional or statutory obligation not to discriminate, or against federal officials or agencies involved in funding allegedly discriminatory programs.

The Court argues that because funding termination, authorized by § 602, is a drastic remedy, Congress must have contemplated private suits in order directly and less intrusively to terminate the discrimination allegedly being practiced by the recipient institutions. But the Court's conclusion does not follow from its premise because funding termination was not contemplated as the only—or even the primary—agency action to end discrimination. Rather, Congress considered termination of financial assistance to be a remedy of last resort, and expressly obligated federal agencies to take measures to terminate discrimination without resorting to termination or funding.

* * *

To be sure, Congress contemplated that there would be litigation brought to enforce Title VI. The "other means" provisions of § 602 include agency suits to enforce contractual antidiscrimination provisions and compliance with agency regulations, as well as suits brought by the Department of Justice under Title IV of the 1964 Act, where the recipient is a public entity. Congress also knew that there would be private suits to enforce § 601; but these suits were not authorized by § 601 itself but by 42 U.S.C.A. § 1983. Every excerpt from the legislative history cited by the Court shows full awareness that private suits could redress discrimination contrary to the Constitution and Title VI, if the discrimination were imposed by public agencies; not one statement suggests contemplation of lawsuits against recipients not acting under color of state law * * * .

The Court further concludes that even if it cannot be persuasively demonstrated that Title VI created a private right of action, nonetheless this remedy should be inferred in Title IX because prior to its enactment several lower courts had entertained private suits to enforce the prohibition on racial discrimination in Title VI. Once again, however, there is confusion between the existing § 1983 right of action to remedy denial of federal rights under color of state law—which, as Congress recognized, would encompass suits to enforce the nondiscrimination mandate of § 601—and the creation of a new right of action against private discrimination. * * *

The legislative intent not to create a new private remedy for enforcement of Title VI or Title IX cannot be ignored simply because in other cases involving analogous language the Court has recognized private remedies. The recent cases inferring a private right of action to enforce various civil rights statutes relied not merely upon the statutory language granting the right sought to be enforced, but also upon the clear compatability, despite the absence of an explicit legislative mandate, between private enforcement and the legislative purpose demonstrated in the statute itself. Having concluded that 42 U.S.C.A. § 1982 prohibited private as well as public racial discrimination in the sale or lease of property, the Court had little choice but to hold that aggrieved individuals could enforce this prohibition, for there existed no other remedy to redress such violations of the statute. The Court's reliance on *Allen v. State Board of Election,* 393 U.S. 544 (1969), is equally unwarranted. The cause of action there recognized—for declaratory relief that a voting change is subject to the authorization requirements of § 5 of the Voting Rights Act of 1965, 42 U.S.C.A. § 1973c—served to trigger the enforcement mechanism provided in the statute itself. The Court pointedly declined to infer a private cause of action to enforce the suspension requirement of § 4 of the Act, 393 U.S., at 552–554; nor may those allegedly discriminated against bring suit to test voting changes in covered units against the substantive standard of § 5, either directly or through judicial review of the Attorney General's preclearance decision, *Morris v. Gressette,* 432 U.S. 491 (1977). The cause of action granted today is of a very different nature. It does not trigger the enforcement scheme provided in §§ 902 and 903, but entirely displaces that scheme in favor of a different approach.

Congress decided in Title IX, as it had in Title VI, to prohibit certain forms of discrimination by recipients of federal funds. Where those recipients were acting under color of state law, individuals could obtain redress in the federal courts for violation of these prohibitions. But, excepting post-Civil War enactments dealing with racial discrimination in specified situations, these forms of discrimination by private entities had not previously been subject to individual redress under federal law, and Congress decided to reach such discrimination not by creating a new remedy for individuals, but by relying on the authority of the Federal Government to enforce the terms under which federal assistance would be provided. Whatever may be the wisdom of this approach to the problem of private discrimination, it was Congress' choice, not to be overridden by this Court.

MR. JUSTICE POWELL, dissenting.

* * * The time has come to reappraise our standards for the judicial implication of private causes of action.

Under Art. III, Congress alone has the responsibility for determining the jurisdiction of the lower federal courts. As the Legislative Branch, Congress also should determine when private parties are to be given causes of action under legislation it adopts. * * * When Congress chooses not to provide a private civil remedy, federal courts should not assume the legislative role of creating such a remedy and thereby enlarge their jurisdiction.

The facts of this case illustrate the undesirability of this assumption by the Judicial Branch of the legislative function. Whether every disappointed applicant for admission to a college or university receiving federal funds has the right to a civil-court remedy under Title IX is likely to be a matter of interest to many of the thousands of rejected applicants. It certainly is a question of vast importance to the entire higher educational community of this country. But quite apart from the interests of the persons and institutions affected, respect for our constitutional system dictates that the issue should have been resolved by the elected representatives in Congress after public hearings, debate, and legislative decision. It is not a question properly to be decided by relatively uninformed federal judges who are isolated from the political process.

In recent history, the Court has tended to stray from the Art. III and separation-of-powers principle of limited jurisdiction. This, I believe, is evident from a review of the more or less haphazard line of cases that led to our decision in *Cort v. Ash,* 422 U.S. 66 (1975). The "four factor" analysis of that case is an open invitation to federal courts to legislate causes of action not authorized by Congress. It is an analysis not faithful to constitutional principles and should be rejected. Absent the most compelling evidence of affirmative congressional intent, a federal court should not infer a private cause of action.

I

The implying of a private action from a federal regulatory statute has been an exceptional occurrence in the past history of this Court. A review of those few decisions where such a step has been taken reveals in almost every case special historical circumstances that explain the result, if not the Court's analysis. These decisions suggest that the doctrine of implication applied by the Court today not only represents judicial assumption of the legislative function, but also lacks a principled precedential basis.

The origin of implied private causes of actions in the federal courts is said to date back to *Texas & Pacific R. Co. v. Rigsby,* 241 U.S. 33 (1916). A close look at the facts of that case and the contemporary state of the law indicates, however, that *Rigsby's* reference to the "inference of a private right of action," carried a far different connotation than the isolated passage quoted by the Court might suggest. The narrow question presented for decision was whether the standards of care defined by the Federal Safety Appliance Act's penal provisions applied to a tort action brought against an interstate railroad by an employee not engaged in interstate commerce at the time of his injury. The jurisdiction of the federal courts was not in dispute, the action having been removed from state court on the ground that the defendant was a federal corporation. Under the regime of *Swift v. Tyson,* 16 Pet. 1 (1842), then in force, the Court was free to create the substantive standards of liability applicable to a common-law negligence claim brought in federal court. The practice of judicial reference to legislatively determined standards of care was a common expedient to establish the existence of negligence. See Thayer, Public Wrong and Private Action, 27 Harv. L. Rev. 317 (1914). *Rigsby* did nothing more than follow this practice, and cannot be taken as authority for the judicial creation of a cause of action not legislated by Congress.

For almost 50 years after *Rigsby*, this Court recognized an implied private cause of action in only one other statutory context. Four decisions held that various provisions of the Railway Labor Act of 1926 could be enforced in a federal court. * * * In each of these cases * * * the implication of some kind of remedial mechanism was necessary to provide the enforcement authority Congress clearly intended.

During this same period, the Court frequently turned back private plaintiffs seeking to imply causes of action from federal statutes. Even in cases where the statute might be said to have been enacted for the benefit of a special class comprising the plaintiff, the factor to which the Court today attaches so much importance, the court refused to create a private action if Congress had provided some other means of enforcing such duties. See, e.g., *Switchmen v. National Mediation Board* [320 U.S. 297 (1943)].

A break in this pattern occurred in *J. I. Case Co. v. Borak*, 377 U.S. 426 (1964). * * * I find this decision both unprecedented and incomprehensible as a matter of public policy. The decision's rationale * * * ignores the fact that Congress, in determining the degree of regulation to be imposed on companies covered by the Securities Exchange Act, already had decided that private enforcement was unnecessary. More significant for present purposes, however, is the fact that *Borak*, rather than signaling the start of a trend in this Court, constitutes a singular and, I believe, aberrant interpretation of a federal regulatory statute.

Since *Borak*, this Court has upheld the implication of private causes of actions derived from federal statutes in only three extremely limited sets of circumstances. First, the Court in *Jones v. Alfred H. Mayer Co.*, 392 U.S. 409 (1968); *Sullivan v. Little Hunting Park, Inc.*, 396 U.S. 229 (1969); and *Johnson v. Railway Express Agency, Inc.*, 421 U.S. 454 (1975), recognized the right of private parties to seek relief for violations of 42 U.S.C.A. § § 1981 and 1982. But to say these cases "implied" rights of action is somewhat misleading, as Congress at the time these statutes were enacted expressly referred to private enforcement actions. * * *

Second, the Court in *Allen v. State Board of Elections*, 393 U.S. 544 (1969), permitted private litigants to sue to enforce the preclearance provisions of § 5 of the Voting Rights Act of 1965. As the Court seems to concede, this decision was reached without substantial analysis, and in my view can be explained only in terms of this Court's special and traditional concern for safeguarding the electoral process. * * *

Finally, the Court in *Superintendent of Insurance v. Bankers Life & Cas. Co.*, 404 U.S. 6 (1971), ratified 25 years of lower-court precedent that had held a private cause of action available under the Securities and Exchange Commission's Rule 10b–5. As the Court concedes, this decision reflects the unique history of Rule 10b–5, and did not articulate any standards of general applicability. * * *

* * *

It was against this background of almost invariable refusal to imply private actions, absent a complete failure of alternative enforcement mechanisms and a clear expression of legislative intent to create such a remedy, that *Cort v. Ash*, 422 U.S. 66 (1975), was decided. * * * [A]s the opinion of the Court today demonstrates, the *Cort* analysis too easily may be used to deflect inquiry away from the intent of Congress, and to permit a court instead to substitute its own views as to the desirability of private enforcement.

* * *

That the *Cort* analysis too readily permits courts to override the decision of Congress not to create a private action is demonstrated conclusively by the flood of lower-court decisions applying it. Although from the time *Cort* was decided until today this Court consistently has turned back attempts to create private actions, other federal courts have tended to proceed in exactly the opposite direction. In the four years since we decided *Cort*, no less than 20 decisions by the Courts of Appeals have implied private actions from federal statutes. It defies reason to believe that in each of these statutes Congress absentmindedly forgot to mention an intended private action. Indeed, the accelerating trend evidenced by these decisions attests to the need to re-examine the *Cort* analysis.

II

In my view, the implication doctrine articulated in *Cort* and applied by the Court today engenders incomparably greater problems than the possibility of occasionally failing to divine an unexpressed congressional intent. If only a matter of statutory construction were involved, our obligation might be to develop more refined criteria which more accurately reflect congressional intent. "But the unconstitutionality of the course pursued has now been made clear" and compels us to abandon the implication doctrine of *Cort*. *Erie R. Co. v. Thompkins*, 304 U.S. 64, 77–78 (1938).

As the * * * decisions of the Courts of Appeals illustrate, *Cort* allows the Judicial Branch to assume policymaking authority vested by the Constitution in the Legislative Branch. It also invites Congress to avoid resolution of the often controversial question whether a new regulatory statute should be enforced through private litigation. Rather than confronting the hard political choice involved, Congress is encouraged to shirk its constitutional obligation and leave the issue to the courts to decide.[14] When this happens, the legislative process with its public scrutiny and participation has been bypassed, with attendant prejudice to

---

14. Mr. Justice Rehnquist, perhaps considering himself temporarily bound by his position in *University of California Regents v. Bakke*, 438 U.S. 265, 418–421 (1978) (opinion of STEVENS, J.), concurs in the Court's decision today. But writing briefly, he correctly observes "that Congress, at least during the period of the enactment of the several Titles of the Civil Rights Act, tended to rely to a large extent on the courts to *decide* whether there should be a private right of action, rather than determining this question for itself." It does not follow, however, that this Court is obliged to indulge Congress in its refusal to confront these hard questions. In my view, the very reasons advanced by Mr. Justice Rehnquist why "this Court in the future should be extremely reluctant to imply a cause of action" absent specific direction by Congress, apply to this case with special force.

everyone concerned.   Because the courts are free to reach a result different from that which the normal play of political forces would have produced, the intended beneficiaries of the legislation are unable to ensure the full measure of protection their needs may warrant.   For the same reason, those subject to the legislative constraints are denied the opportunity to forestall through the political process potentially unnecessary and disruptive litigation.   Moreover, the public generally is denied the benefits that are derived from the making of important societal choices through the open debate of the democratic process.

The Court's implication doctrine encourages, as a corollary to the political default by Congress, an increase in the governmental power exercised by the federal judiciary.   The dangers posed by judicial arrogation of the right to resolve general societal conflicts have been manifest to this Court throughout its history.   * * *

It is true that the federal judiciary necessarily exercises substantial powers to construe legislation, including, when appropriate, the power to prescribe substantive standards of conduct that supplement federal legislation.   But this power normally is exercised with respect to disputes over which a court already has jurisdiction, and in which the existence of the asserted cause of action is established.   Implication of a private cause of action, in contrast, involves a significant additional step.   By creating a private action, a court of limited jurisdiction necessarily extends its authority to embrace a dispute Congress has not assigned it to resolve.   * * *

III

In sum, I believe the need both to restrain courts that too readily have created private causes of action, and to encourage Congress to confront its obligation to resolve crucial policy questions created by the legislation it enacts, has become compelling.   Because the analysis suggested by *Cort* has proved inadequate to meet these problems, I would start afresh. Henceforth, we should not condone the implication of any private action from a federal statute absent the most compelling evidence that Congress in fact intended such an action to exist.   Where a statutory scheme expressly provides for an alternative mechanism for enforcing the rights and duties created, I would be especially reluctant ever to permit a federal court to volunteer its services for enforcement purposes.   Because the Court today is enlisting the federal judiciary in just such an enterprise, I dissent.

Notes

Post-*Cannon* cases have not unified the Court or the jurisprudence.   The Court has refused to overturn or substantially limit established causes of action in the securities area, see *Maclean v. Huddleston*, 459 U.S. 375 (1983), and has even implied remedies under statutory provisions regulating commodities trading that were modelled on the securities laws.   *Merrill Lynch, Pierce, Fenner & Smith v. Curran*, 456 U.S. 353 (1982).   Yet it has refused to extend implied remedies to additional sections of the securities laws.   *Touche Ross & Co. v. Reding-*

ton, 442 U.S. 560 (1979); *Transamerica Mortgage Advisors, Inc. (TAMA) v. Lewis,* 444 U.S. 11 (1979). Indeed, in its flight from judicial creativity the Court unanimously refused to develop a federal rule of contribution among joint tortfeasors when sued under a federal statute that explicitly provided a private remedy. *Northwest Airlines, Inc. v. Transport Workers Union of America, AFL-CIO,* 451 U.S. 77 (1981).

The Court's current approach to implication claims (as distinguished from the results) is hardly more unified than when *Cannon* was decided. Justice Stevens' opinion for the Court in *Northwest Airlines* hardly mentioned *Cort v. Ash* and seemed to emphasize only the "statutory construction" and separation of powers concerns featured by Justices Rehnquist and Powell in *Cannon.* Yet in the same term both he and Justice White described *Cort* as the fountainhead of implication analysis. See *California v. Sierra Club,* 451 U.S. 287, 292 (White, J.), 301 (Stevens, J., concurring) (1981).

The suggestion in *Cannon* that implication analysis might take different paths depending on the background of judge-made law against which Congress has legislated has to some degree been honored in the securities and commodities regulation cases previously mentioned. However, when addressing a pre-*Erie* statute, the 1899 Rivers and Harbors Act, which had previously supported an implied remedy in favor of the United States (see *United States v. Republic Steel Corp.* 362 U.S. 482 (1960)), and which had been enacted in part to overturn a Supreme Court decision denying a federal cause of action to abate navigational nuisances (*Williamette Iron Bridge Co. v. Hatch,* 125 U.S. 1 (1888)), the Court balked at allowing a private remedy. A bemused Justice Stevens concurred in the following *non sequitor* (451 U.S. at 298–301):

> In 1888 this Court reversed a decree enjoining the construction of a bridge over a navigable river. *Williamette Iron Bridge Co. v. Hatch.* The Court's opinion in that case did not question the right of the private parties to seek relief in a federal court; rather, the Court held that no federal rule of law prohibited the obstruction of the navigable waterway. Congress responded to the *Williamette* case in the Rivers and Harbors Act of 1890 by creating a federal prohibition of such obstructions absent a permit from the Secretary of War. At the time the statute was enacted, I believe the lawyers in Congress simply assumed that private parties in a position comparable to that of the litigants in the *Williamette* case would have a remedy for any injury suffered by reason of a violation of the new federal statute. For at that time the implication of private causes of action was a well-known practice at common law and in American courts. Therefore, in my view, the Members of Congress merely assumed that the federal courts would follow the ancient maxim *"ubi jus, ibi remedium"* and imply a private right of action. Accordingly, if I were writing on a clean slate, I would hold that an implied remedy is available to respondents under this statute.

> The slate, however, is not clean. Because the problem of ascertaining legislative intent that is not expressed in legislation is often so difficult, the Court has wisely developed rules to guide judges in deciding whether a federal remedy is implicitly a part of a federal statute. In *Cort v. Ash,* all of my present colleagues subscribed to a unanimous formulation of those rules, and in *Cannon v. University of Chicago,* a majority of the Court joined my attempt to explain the application of those rules in that case. The *Cort v. Ash* analysis is therefore a part of our law.

In these cases, I believe the Court correctly concludes that application of the *Cort v. Ash* analysis indicates that no private cause of action is available. I think it is more important to adhere to the analytical approach the Court has adopted than to base my vote on my own opinion about what Congress probably assumed in 1890. * * *

C. BENEFICIARY ENFORCEMENT UNDER 42 U.S.C.A. § 1983

MAINE v. THIBOUTOT

Supreme Court of the United States, 1979.
448 U.S. 1, 100 S.Ct. 2502, 65 L.Ed.2d 555.

MR. JUSTICE BRENNAN delivered the opinion of the Court.

The case presents two related questions arising under 42 U.S.C.A. § § 1983 and 1988. Respondents brought this suit in the Maine Superior Court alleging that petitioners, the State of Maine and its Commissioner of Human Services, violated § 1983 by depriving respondents of welfare benefits to which they were entitled under the federal Social Security Act, specifically 42 U.S.C.A. § 602(a)(7). The petitioners present two issues: (1) whether § 1983 encompasses claims based on purely statutory violations of federal law, and (2) if so, whether attorney's fees under § 1988 may be awarded to the prevailing party in such an action.

I

Respondents, Lionel and Joline Thiboutot, are married and have eight children, three of whom are Lionel's by a previous marriage. The Maine Department of Human Services notified Lionel that, in computing the Aid to Families with Dependent Children (AFDC) benefits to which he was entitled for the three children exclusively his, it would no longer make allowance for the money spent to support the other five children, even though Lionel is legally obligated to support them. Respondents, challenging the State's interpretation of 42 U.S.C.A. § 602(a)(7), exhausted their state administrative remedies and then sought judicial review of the administrative action in the State Superior Court. By amended complaint, respondents also claimed relief under § 1983 for themselves and others similarly situated. The Superior Court's judgment enjoined petitioners from enforcing the challenged rule and ordered them to adopt new regulations, to notify class members of the new regulations, and to pay the correct amounts retroactively to respondents and prospectively to eligible class members. The court, however, denied respondents' motion for attorney's fees. The Supreme Judicial Court of Maine, 405 A.2d 230 (1979), concluded that respondents had no entitlement to attorney's fees under state law, but were eligible for attorney's fees pursuant to the Civil Rights Attorney's Fees Awards Act of 1976, 42 U.S.C.A. § 1988. * * * We affirm.

II

Section 1983 provides:

> "Every person who, under color of any statute, ordinance, regulation, custom, or usage, of any State or Territory, subjects, or causes to be subjected, any citizen of the United States or other person within the jurisdiction thereof to the deprivation of any rights, privileges, or immunities secured by the Constitution *and laws*, shall be liable to the party injured in an action at law, suit in equity, or other proper proceeding for redress."   (Emphasis added.)

The question before us is whether the phrase "and laws," as used in § 1983, means what it says, or whether it should be limited to some subset of laws.   Given that Congress attached no modifiers to the phrase, the plain language of the statute undoubtedly embraces respondents' claim that petitioners violated the Social Security Act.

Even were the language ambiguous, however, any doubt as to its meaning has been resolved by our several cases suggesting, explicitly or implicitly, that the § 1983 remedy broadly encompasses violations of federal statutory as well as constitutional law.   *Rosado v. Wyman*, 397 U.S. 397 (1970), for example, "held that suits in federal court under § 1983 are proper to secure compliance with the provisions of the Social Security Act on the part of participating States."   *Edelman v. Jordan*, 415 U.S. 651, 675 (1974).   *Monell v. New York City Dept. of Social Services*, 436 U.S. 658 (1978), as support for its conclusion that municipalities are "persons" under § 1983, reasoned that "there can be no doubt that § 1 of the Civil Rights Act [of 1871] was intended to provide a remedy, to be broadly construed, against all forms of official violation of federally protected rights." Similarly, *Owen v. City of Independence*, 445 U.S. 622 (1980), in holding that the common-law immunity for discretionary functions provided no basis for according municipalities a good-faith immunity under § 1983, noted that a court "looks only to whether the municipality has conformed to the requirements of the Federal Constitution and statutes."   *Mitchum v. Foster*, 407 U.S. 225 (1972), and *Lynch v. Household Finance Corp.*, 405 U.S. 538 (1972), noted that § 1983's predecessor "was enlarged to provide protection for rights, privileges, or immunities secured by federal law."   *Greenwood v. Peacock*, 384 U.S. 808 (1966), observed that under § 1983 state "officers may be made to respond in damages not only for violations of rights conferred by federal equal civil rights laws, but for violations of other federal constitutional and statutory rights as well." The availability of this alternative sanction helped support the holding that 28 U.S.C. § 1443(1) did not permit removal to federal court of a state prosecution in which the defense was that the state law conflicted with the defendants' federal rights.   As a final example, Mr. Justice Stone, writing in *Hague v. CIO*, 307 U.S. 496 (1939), expressed the opinion that § 1983 was the product of an "exten[sion] to include rights, privileges and immunities secured by the laws of the United States as well as by the Constitution."

While some might dismiss as dictum the foregoing statements, numerous and specific as they are, our analysis in several § 1983 cases involving Social Security Act (SSA) claims has relied on the availability of a § 1983 cause of action for statutory claims. Constitutional claims were also raised in these cases, providing a jurisdictional base, but the statutory claims were allowed to go forward, and were decided on the merits, under the court's pendent jurisdiction. In each of the following cases § 1983 was necessarily the exclusive statutory cause of action because, as the Court held in *Edelman v. Jordan,* the SSA affords no private right of action against a State. *Miller v. Youakim,* 440 U.S. 125, 132, and n. 13 (1979) (state foster care program inconsistent with SSA); *Ouern v. Mandley,* 436 U.S. 725, 729, and n. 3 (1978) (state emergency assistance program consistent with SSA); *Van Lare v. Hurley,* 421 U.S. 338 (1975) (state shelter allowance provisions inconsistent with SSA); *Townsend v. Swank,* 404 U.S. 282 (1971) (state prohibition against AFDC aid for college students inconsistent with SSA); *King v. Smith,* 392 U.S. 309, 311 (1968) (state cohabitation prohibition inconsistent with SSA).

In the face of the plain language of § 1983 and our consistent treatment of that provision, petitioners nevertheless persist in suggesting that the phrase "and laws" should be read as limited to civil rights or equal protection laws. Petitioners suggest that when § 1 of the Civil Rights Act of 1871, 17 Stat. 13, which accorded jurisdiction and a remedy for deprivations of rights secured by "the Constitution of the United States," was divided by the 1874 statutory revision into a remedial section, Rev. Stat. § 1979, and jurisdictional sections, Rev.Stat. §§ 563(12) and 629(16), Congress intended that the same change made in § 629(16) be made as to each of the new sections as well. Section 629(16), the jurisdictional provision for the circuit courts and the model for the current jurisdictional provision, 28 U.S.C.A. § 1343(3), applied to deprivations of rights secured by "the Constitution of the United States, or of any right secured by any law providing for equal rights." On the other hand, the remedial provision, the predecessor of § 1983, was expanded to apply to deprivations of rights secured by "the Constitution and laws," and § 563(12), the provision granting jurisdiction to the district courts, to deprivations of rights secured by "the Constitution of the United States, or of any right secured by any law of the United States."

We need not repeat at length the detailed debate over the meaning of the scanty legislative history concerning the addition of the phrase "and laws." * * * There is no express explanation offered for the insertion of the phrase "and laws." On the one hand, a principal purpose of the added language was to "ensure that federal legislation providing specifically for equality of rights would be brought within the ambit of the civil action authorized by that statute." On the other hand, there are no indications that that was the only purpose, and Congress' attention was specifically directed to this new language. Representative Lawrence, in a speech to the House of Representatives that began by observing that the revisers had very often changed the meaning of existing statutes, 2 Cong. Rec. 825 (1874), referred to the civil rights statutes as "possibly [showing] verbal modifications bordering on legislation," id., at 827. He went on to read to Congress the original and revised versions.   In short, Congress was aware of what it was doing, and the legislative history does not demonstrate that the plain language was not intended.   Petitioners' arguments amount to the claim that had Congress been more careful, and had it fully thought out the relationship among the various sections, it might have acted differently.   That argument, however, can best be addressed to Congress, which, it is important to note, has remained quiet in the face of our many pronouncements on the scope of § 1983.

III

Petitioners next argue that, even if this claim is within § 1983, Congress did not intend statutory claims to be covered by the Civil Rights Attorney's Fees Awards Act of 1976, which added the following sentence to 42 U.S.C.A. § 1988 (emphasis added):

> "In *any action* or proceeding *to enforce* a provision of sections 1981, 1982, *1983*, 1985, and 1986 of this title, * * * the court, in its discretion, may allow the prevailing party, other than the United States, a reasonable attorney's fee as part of the costs."

Once again, given our holding in Part II, supra, the plain language provides an answer.   The statute states that fees are available in *any* § 1983 action.   Since we hold that this statutory action is properly brought under § 1983, and since § 1988 makes no exception for statutory § 1983 actions, § 1988 plainly applies to this suit.

The legislative history is entirely consistent with the plain language. * * *

* * *

Several States, participating as *amici curiae*, argue that even if § 1988 applies to § 1983 claims alleging deprivations of statutory rights, it does not apply in state courts.   There is no merit to this argument. * * * *Martinez v. California*, 444 U.S. 277 (1980), held that § 1983 actions may be brought in state courts.   Representative Drinan described the purpose of the Civil Rights Attorney's Fees Awards Act as "authoriz[ing] the award of a reasonable attorney's fee in actions brought in State or Federal courts."   122 Cong. Rec. 35122 (1976).   And Congress viewed the fees authorized by § 1988 as "an integral part of the remedies necessary to obtain" compliance with § 1983.   S. Rep. No. 94–1011, p. 5 (1976).   It follows from this history and from the Supremacy Clause that the fee provision is part of the § 1983 remedy whether the action is brought in federal or state court.[12]

Affirmed.

---

12. If fees were not available in state courts, federalism concerns would be raised because most plaintiffs would have no choice but to bring their complaints concerning state actions to federal courts.   Moreover, given that there is a class of cases stating causes of action under § 1983 but not cognizable in federal court absent the $10,000 jurisdictional amount of § 1331(a), some plaintiffs would be forced to go to state courts, but contrary to congressional intent, would still face financial disincentives to asserting their claimed deprivations of federal rights.   [The jurisdictional amount requirement has subsequently been repealed.   Eds.]

MR. JUSTICE POWELL, with whom THE CHIEF JUSTICE and MR. JUS-
TICE REHNQUIST join, dissenting.

The Court holds today, almost casually, that 42 U.S.C.A. § 1983 creates
a cause of action for deprivations under color of state law of any federal
statutory right.   Having transformed purely statutory claims into "civil
rights" actions under § 1983, the Court concludes that 42 U.S.C. § 1988
permits the "prevailing party" to recover his attorney's fees.   These two
holdings dramatically expand the liability of state and local officials and
may virtually eliminate the "American Rule" in suits against those officials.

The Court's opinion reflects little consideration of the consequences of
its judgment.   It relies upon the "plain" meaning of the phrase "and
laws" in § 1983 and upon this Court's assertedly "consistent treatment" of
that statute.   But the reading adopted today is anything but "plain"
when the statutory language is placed in historical context.   * * *

* * *

Section 1983 derives from § 1 of the Civil Rights Act of 1871, which
provided a cause of action for deprivations of constitutional rights only.
"Laws" were not mentioned.   The phrase "and laws" was added in 1874,
when Congress consolidated the laws of the United States into a single
volume under a new subject-matter arrangement.   Consequently, the intent of Congress in 1874 is central to this case.

In addition to creating a cause of action, § 1 of the 1871 Act conferred
concurrent jurisdiction upon "the district or circuit courts of the United
States. * * * "   In the 1874 revision, the remedial portion of § 1 was
codified as § 1979 of the Revised Statutes, which provided for a cause of
action in terms identical to the present § 1983.   The jurisdictional portion
of § 1 was divided into § 563(12), conferring district court jurisdiction, and
§ 629(16), conferring circuit court jurisdiction.   Although §§ 1979, 563(12),
and 629(16) came from the same source, each was worded differently.
Section 1979 referred to deprivations of rights "secured by the Constitution and laws"; § 563(12) described rights secured "by the Constitution of
the United States, or * * * by any law of the United States"; and § 629(16)
encompassed rights secured "by the Constitution of the United States,
or * * * by any law providing for equal rights of citizens of the United
States."   When Congress merged the jurisdiction of circuit and district
courts in 1911, the narrower language of § 629(16) was adopted and ultimately became the present 28 U.S.C.A. § 1343(3).

In my view, the legislative history unmistakably shows that the variations in phrasing introduced in the 1874 revision were inadvertent, and
that each section was intended to have precisely the same scope.   * * *

* * * The Revision Commission, which worked for six years on the
project, submitted to Congress a draft that did contain substantive
changes.   But a Joint Congressional Committee, which was appointed in
early 1873 to transform the draft into a bill, concluded that it would be
"utterly impossible to carry the measure through, if it was understood

that it contained new legislation." Therefore, the Committee employed Thomas Jefferson Durant to "strike out * * * modifications of the existing law" "wherever the meaning of the law had been changed." On December 10, 1873, Durant's completed work was introduced in the House with the solemn assurance that the bill "embodies the law as it is."

The House met in a series of evening sessions to review the bill and to restore original meaning where necessary. During one of these sessions, Representative Lawrence delivered the speech upon which the Court now relies. Lawrence explained that the revisers often had separated existing statutes into substantive, remedial, and criminal sections to accord with the new organization of the statutes by topic. He read both the original and revised versions of the civil rights statutes to illustrate the arrangement, and "possibly [to] show verbal modifications bordering on legislation." 2 Cong. Rec. 827 (Jan. 21, 1874). After reading § 1979 without mentioning the addition of "and laws," Lawrence stated that "[a] comparison of all these will present a fair specimen of the manner in which the work has been done, and from these all can judge of the accuracy of the translation." * * * Nothing in this sequence of remarks supports the decision of the Court today. There was no mention of the addition of "and laws" nor any hint that the reach of § 1983 was to be extended. If Lawrence had any such intention, his statement to the House was a singularly disingenuous way of proposing a major piece of legislation.

In context, it is plain that Representative Lawrence did not mention changes "bordering on legislation" as a way of introducing substantive changes in § 1 of the 1871 Act. Rather, he was emphasizing that the revision was not intended to modify existing statutes, and that his reading might reveal errors that should be eliminated. No doubt Congress "was aware of what it was doing." It was meeting specially in one last attempt to detect and strike out legislative changes that may have remained in the proposed revision despite the best efforts of Durant and the Joint Committee. No Representative challenged those sections of the Revised Statutes that derived from § 1 of the Civil Rights Act of 1871. That silence reflected the understanding of those present that "and laws" did not alter the original meaning of the statute.[6] The Members of Congress who participated in the yearlong effort to expunge all substantive alterations from the Revised Statutes evinced no intent whatever to enact a far-reaching modification of § 1 of the Civil Rights Act of 1871. The relevant evidence, largely ignored by the Court today, shows that Congress painstakingly sought to avoid just such changes.

The legislative history alone refutes the Court's assertion that the 43d Congress intended to alter the meaning of § 1983. But there are other compelling reasons to reject the Court's interpretation of the phrase "and laws." First, by reading those words to encompass every federal enact-

6. The addition of "and laws" did not change the meaning of § 1 because Congress assumed that that phrase referred only to federal equal rights legislation. In 1874, the only such legislation was contained in the 1866 and 1870 Civil Rights Acts, which conferred rights also secured by the recently adopted Fourteenth Amendment.

ment, the Court extends § 1983 beyond the reach of its jurisdictional counterpart. Second, that reading creates a broad program for enforcing federal legislation that departs significantly from the purposes of § 1983. Such unexpected and plainly unintended consequences should be avoided whenever a statute reasonably may be given an interpretation that is consistent with the legislative purpose.

The Court acknowledges that its construction of § 1983 creates federal "civil rights" for which 28 U.S.C.A. § 1343(3) supplies no federal jurisdiction. The Court finds no "inherent illogic" in this view. But the gap in the Court's logic is wide indeed in light of the history and purpose of the civil rights legislation we consider today. Sections 1983 and 1343(3) derive from the same section of the same Act. As originally enacted, the two sections necessarily were coextensive. * * *

* * * Nearly every commentator who has considered the question has concluded that § 1343(3) was intended to supply federal jurisdiction in all § 1983 actions. Since § 1343(3) covers statutory claims only when they arise under laws providing for the equal rights of citizens, the same limitation necessarily is implicit in § 1983. The Court's decision to apply that statute without regard to the scope of its jurisdictional counterpart is at war with the plainly expressed intent of Congress.

The Court's opinion does not consider the nature or scope of the litigation it has authorized. In practical effect, today's decision means that state and local governments, officers, and employees[10] now may face liability whenever a person believes he has been injured by the administration of *any* federal-state cooperative program, whether or not that program is related to equal or civil rights.

Even a cursory survey of the United States Code reveals that literally hundreds of cooperative regulatory and social welfare enactments may be affected.[12] The States now participate in the enforcement of federal laws governing migrant labor, noxious weeds, historic preservation, wildlife conservation, anadromous fisheries, scenic trails, and strip mining. Various statutes authorize federal-state cooperative agreements in most aspects of federal land management. In addition, federal grants administered by state and local governments now are available in virtually every area of public administration. Unemployment, Medicaid, school lunch subsidies, food stamps, and other welfare benefits may provide particularly inviting subjects of litigation. Federal assistance also includes a variety of subsidies for education, housing, health care, transportation,

---

10. Section 1983 actions may be brought against States, municipalities and other subdivisions, officers, and employees. Although I will refer to all such potential defendants as "state defendants" for purposes of this opinion, there may be a notable difference among them. States are protected against retroactive damages awards by the Eleventh Amendment, and individual defendants generally can claim immunity when they act in good faith. Municipalities, however, will be strictly liable for errors in the administration of complex federal statutes. See *Owen v. City of Independence*, 445 U.S. 622 (1980).

12. An incomplete sample of statutes requiring federal-state cooperation is collected in the Appendix to this opinion. * * *

public works, and law enforcement. Those who might benefit from these grants now will be potential § 1983 plaintiffs.

* * *

Moreover, state and local governments will bear the entire burden of liability for violations of statutory "civil rights" even when federal officials are involved equally in the administration of the affected program. Section 1983 grants no right of action against the United States, and few of the foregoing cooperative programs provide expressly for private actions to enforce their terms. Thus, private litigants may sue responsible federal officials only in the relatively rare case in which a cause of action may be implied from the governing substantive statute. It defies reason to believe that Congress intended—without discussion—to impose such a burden only upon state defendants.

Even when a cause of action against federal officials is available, litigants are likely to focus efforts upon state defendants in order to obtain attorney's fees under the liberal standard of 42 U.S.C.A. § 1988. There is some evidence that § 1983 claims already are being appended to complaints solely for the purpose of obtaining fees in actions where "civil rights" of any kind are at best an afterthought. In this case, for example, the respondents added a § 1983 count to their complaint some years after the action was initiated, apparently in response to the enactment of the Civil Rights Attorney's Fees Awards Act of 1976 * * * .

* * *

* * * If any Member of the 43d Congress had suggested legislation embodying these results, the proposal certainly would have been hotly debated. It is simply inconceivable that Congress, while professing a firm intention not to make substantive changes in the law, nevertheless intended to enact a major new remedial program by approving—without discussion—the addition of two words to a statute adopted only three years earlier.

The Court finally insists that its interpretation of § 1983 is foreordained by a line of precedent so strong that further analysis is unnecessary. * * *

* * * Yet, until last Term, neither this Court nor any Justice ever had undertaken—directly and thoroughly—a consideration of the question presented in this case.

Commentators have chronicled the tortuous path of judicial interpretation of the Civil Rights Act enacted after the Civil War. See Gressman, The Unhappy History of Civil Rights Legislation, 50 Mich. L. Rev. 1323 (1952); Note, Developments in the Law—Section 1983 and Federalism, 90 Harv. L. Rev. 1133 (1977); Note, The Proper Scope of the Civil Rights Acts, 66 Harv. L. Rev. 1285 (1953). One writer found only 21 cases decided under § 1983 in the first 50 years of its history. Comment, The Civil Rights Act: Emergence of an Adequate Federal Civil Remedy?, 26 Ind. L.J. 361, 363 (1951). Another lamented, as late as 1952, that the statute could not be given its intended broad effect without a "judicial and constitutional upheaval of the first magnitude." Gressman, supra, at 1357. That upheaval ultimately did take place, and § 1983 actions now constitute a substantial share of the federal caseload.[16] Nevertheless, cases dealing with purely statutory civil rights claims remain nearly as rare as in the early years.

Holt v. Indiana Manufacturing Co., 176 U.S. 68 (1900), appears to be the first reported decision to deal with a statutory claim under § 1983. * * * When the United States Court of Appeals for the Second Circuit considered a statutory claim nearly half a century after *Holt*, it found no case whatever "in which the right or privilege at stake was secured by a 'law' of the United States." *Bomar v. Keyes*, 162 F.2d 136, 139, cert. denied, 332 U.S. 825 (1947). The plaintiff in *Bomar* was a public school teacher who alleged that the school board had discharged her because of absences incurred while exercising her statutory right to serve on a federal jury. The Court of Appeals concluded that the complaint stated a claim under § 1983.

The opinion in *Bomar*, which cited no authority and reviewed no legislative history, provoked widespread commentary. But it appears to have had little practical effect. The issue did not arise with any frequency until the late 1960's, when challenges to state administration of federal social welfare legislation became commonplace. The lower courts responded to these suits with conflicting conclusions. Some found § 1983 applicable to all federal statutory claims. Others refused to apply it to purely statutory rights. Yet others believed that § 1983 covered some but not all rights derived from nonconstitutional sources. Numerous scholarly comments discussed the possible solutions, without reaching a consensus.

The courts and commentators who debated the issue during this period were singularly obtuse if, as the Court now asserts, all doubt as to the meaning of "and laws" had been resolved by a long line of consistent authority going back to 1939. I know of no court or commentator who has thought that all such doubt had been extinguished before today.

The Court quotes the statement in *Edelman v. Jordan*, 415 U.S. 651, 675 (1974), that *Rosado v. Wyman*, 397 U.S. 397 (1970), " 'held that suits in federal court under § 1983 are proper to secure compliance with the provisions of the Social Security Act on the part of participating States.' " If that statement is true, the confusion remaining after *Rosado* is simply inexplicable. In fact, of course, *Rosado* established no such proposition of law. The plaintiffs in that case challenged a state welfare provision on constitutional grounds, premising jurisdiction upon 28 U.S.C.A. § 1343(3), and added a pendent statutory claim. This Court held first

16. Between 1961 and 1977, the number of cases filed in federal court under civil rights statutes increased from 296 to 13,113. New filings have remained relatively constant from 1977 to date. See Director of the Administrative Office of the United States Courts Ann. Rep. 6, Table 6 (1979). These figures do not include the many prisoner petitions filed annually under 42 U.S.C.A. § 1983. If prisoner petitioners are included, the number of civil rights cases filed in 1979 rises to 24,951.

that the District Court retained its power to adjudicate the statutory claim even after the constitutional claim, on which § 1343(3) jurisdiction was based, became moot. The opinion then considered the merits of the plaintiffs' argument that New York law did not comport with the Social Security Act. Although the Court had to assume the existence of a private right of action to enforce that Act, the opinion did not discuss or purport to decide whether § 1983 applies to statutory claims.

Rosado is not the only case to have assumed *sub silentio* that welfare claimants have a cause of action to challenge the adequacy of state programs under the Social Security Act. As the Court observes, many of our recent decisions construing the Act made the same unspoken assumption. It does not necessarily follow that the Court in those cases assumed that the cause of action was provided by § 1983 rather than the Social Security Act itself. But even if it did, these cases provide no support for the Court's ruling today. "[W]hen questions of jurisdiction have been passed on in prior decisions *sub silentio*, this Court has never considered itself bound when a subsequent case finally brings the jurisdictional issue before us." *Hagans v. Lavine*, 415 U.S. 528, 535, n. 5 (1974) * * * .

The Court also relies upon "numerous and specific" dicta in prior decisions. But none of the cited cases contains anything more than a bare assertion of the proposition that is to be proved. Most say much less than that. * * *

To rest a landmark decision of this Court on two statements made in dictum without critical examination would be extraordinary in any case. In the context of § 1983, it is unprecedented. Our decisions construing the civil rights legislation of the Reconstruction era have repudiated "blind adherence to the principle of *stare decisis.* * * * " As Mr. Justice Frankfurter once observed, the issues raised under § 1983 concern "a basic problem of American federalism" that "has significance approximating constitutional dimension." *Monroe v. Pape*, 365 U.S., at 222 (dissenting opinion). Although Mr. Justice Frankfurter's view did not prevail in *Monroe*, we have heeded consistently his admonition that the ordinary concerns of *stare decisis* apply less forcefully in this than in other areas of the law. E.g., *Monell v. New York City Dept. of Social Services, supra*. Against this backdrop, there is no justification for the Court's reliance on unexamined dicta as the principal support for a major extension of liability under § 1983.

* * *

APPENDIX TO OPINION OF POWELL, J., DISSENTING

A small sample of statutes that arguably could give rise to § 1983 actions after today may illustrate the nature of the "civil rights" created by the Court's decision. The relevant enactments typically fall into one of three categories: (A) regulatory programs in which States are encouraged to participate, either by establishing their own plans of regulation that meet conditions set out in federal statutes, or by entering into cooperative agreements with federal officials; (B) resource management programs that may be administered by cooperative agreements between federal and state agencies; and (C) grant programs in which federal agencies either subsidize state and local activities or provide matching funds for state or local welfare plans that meet federal standards.

A. Joint Regulatory Endeavors

1. Federal Insecticide, Fungicide, and Rodenticide Act, 7 U.S.C.A. § 136 *et seq.* (1976 ed. and Supp. III).
2. Federal Noxious Weed Act of 1974, 7 U.S.C.A. § § 2801–2813.
3. Historic Sites, Buildings, and Antiquities Act, 16 U.S.C.A. § § 461–467 (1976 ed. and Supp. III).
4. Fish and Wildlife Coordination Act, 48 Stat. 401, as amended, 16 U.S.C.A. § § 661–666c.
5. Anadromous Fish Conservation Act, 16 U.S.C.A. § § 757a–757d (1976 ed., Supp. III).
6. Wild Free-Roaming Horses and Burros Act, 16 U.S.C.A. § § 1331–1340 (1976 ed. and Supp. III).
7. Marine Mammal Protection Act of 1972, 16 U.S.C.A. § § 1361–1407 (1976 ed. and Supp. III).
8. Wagner-Peyser National Employment System Act, 29 U.S.C.A. § 49 *et seq.*
9. Surface Mining Control and Reclamation Act of 1977, 30 U.S.C.A. § 1201 *et seq.* (1976 ed., Supp. III).
10. Interstate Commerce Act, 49 U.S.C.A. § 11502(a)(2) (1976 ed., Supp. III).

B. Resource Management

1. Laws involving the administration and management of national parks and scenic areas: e.g., Act of May 15, 1965, 16 U.S.C.A. § 281e (Nez Perce National Historical Park); Act of Sept. 21, 1959, 16 U.S.C.A. § 410u (Minute Man National Historical Park); Act of Oct. 27, 1972, 16 U.S.C.A. § 460bb–3(b) (Muir Woods National Monument).
2. Laws involving the administration of forest lands: e.g., Act of Mar. 1, 1911, 16 U.S.C.A. § 563; Act of Aug. 29, 1935, 16 U.S.C.A. § § 567a–567b.
3. Laws involving the construction and management of water projects: e.g., Water Supply Act of 1958, 43 U.S.C.A. § 390b; Boulder Canyon Projects Act, 43 U.S.C.A. § § 617c, 617g; Rivers and Harbors Appropriation Act of 1899, 33 U.S.C.A. § 401.
4. National Trails System Act, 16 U.S.C.A. § § 1241–1249 (1976 ed. and Supp. III).
5. Outer Continental Shelf Lands Act Amendment of 1978, 43 U.S.C.A. § 1345 (1976 ed., Supp. III).

C. Grant Programs

In addition to the familiar welfare, unemployment, and medical assistance programs established by the Social Security Act, these may include:

1. Food Stamp Act of 1964, 7 U.S.C.A. § § 2011–2026 (1976 ed. and Supp. III).
2. Small Business Investment Act of 1958, 15 U.S.C.A. § 636(d) (1976 ed., Supp. III).
3. Education Amendments of 1978, 20 U.S.C.A. § 2701 *et seq.* (1976 ed., Supp. III).
4. Federal-Aid Highway Act legislation, e.g., 23 U.S.C.A. § § 128, 131 (1976 ed., and Supp. III).
5. Comprehensive Employment and Training Act Amendments of 1978, 29 U.S.C.A. § 801 *et seq.* (1976 ed., Supp. III).
6. United States Housing Act of 1937, 42 U.S.C.A. § 1437 *et seq.* (1976 ed. and Supp. III).
7. National School Lunch Act, 42 U.S.C.A. § 1751 *et seq.* (1976 ed. and Supp. III).
8. Public Works and Economic Development Act of 1965, 42 U.S.C.A. § 3121 *et seq.*
9. Justice System Improvement Act of 1979, 42 U.S.C.A. § 3701 *et seq.* (1976 ed., Supp. III).
10. Juvenile Justice and Delinquency Prevention Act of 1974, 42 U.S.C.A. § 5601 *et seq.* (1976 ed. and Supp. III).
11. Energy Conservation and Production Act, 42 U.S.C.A. § 6801 *et seq.* (1976 ed. Supp. III).
12. Developmentally Disabled Assistance and Bill of Rights Act, 42 U.S.C.A. § 6000 *et seq.* (1976 ed. and Supp. III).
13. Urban Mass Transportation Act of 1964, 49 U.S.C.A. § 1601 *et seq.* (1976 ed. and Supp. III).

Notes

1. Although section 1983 is couched in sweeping language, as Justice Powell notes, it was very rarely invoked during the 90 years following its passage. This disinterest can partly be attributed to the Supreme Court's early narrow construction of the rights protected by the Fourteenth Amendment. In *The Slaughter-House Cases*, 83 U.S. (16 Wall.) 36 (1873), the Court held that the guarantee of section 1 against abridgments of "the privileges or immunities of citizens of the United States" embraced only those rights that arose immediately from an individual's relationship with the central government. These included the right to vote in federal elections, the right to travel from state to state, the right to be free from slavery, and the right to peaceably assemble and petition the federal government. But, the Court made clear, these "privileges or immunities" did not include such basic civil rights as the right to own or hold property, the right of free speech, the right to privacy, or rights relating to fair trial in state criminal proceedings. These were state creations and protected, if at all, by state law. See also *United States v. Williams*, 341 U.S. 70 (1951); *Twining v. New Jersey*, 211 U.S. 78 (1908).

At the time of *The Slaughter-House Cases*, the Fourteenth Amendment's assurance of "due process" was not yet perceived as a limitation on the substance of state legislation. Furthermore, as a guarantee of fair procedure in state proceedings its content was still narrowly, if dimly, viewed. The numerous Supreme Court decisions of the mid-twentieth century that interpreted "due process" as a constitutional shorthand for the procedural safeguards guaranteed against the federal government by the Bill of Rights (e.g., right to jury trial, right to counsel) were several decades in the future.   See, e.g., *Mapp v. Ohio*, 367 U.S. 643 (1961) (due process incorporates fourth amendment guarantee against unreasonable searches and seizures); *Gideon v. Wainwright*, 372 U.S. 335 (1963) (sixth amendment right to counsel).   Moreover, the amendment's equal protection guarantee was for many decades viewed exclusively as prohibiting discriminations based on race.   In short, in the years immediately following the passage of section 1983, citizens had no basis for anticipating the expansive reading recent decisions have given the rights protected against state interference by the Fourteenth Amendment and, thus, by the language of the statute itself.

2. Interest in section 1983 was rekindled in 1961 when the Supreme Court decided *Monroe v. Pape*, 365 U.S. 167.   In *Monroe* the complaint alleged (id. at 169):

> * * * that 13 Chicago police officers broke into petitioners' home in the early morning, routed them from bed, made them stand naked in the living room, and ransacked every room, emptying drawers and ripping mattress covers. * * * Mr. Monroe was then taken to the police station and detained on "open" charges for 10 hours, while he was interrogated about a two-day-old murder, that he was not taken before a magistrate, though one was accessible, that he was not permitted to call his family or attorney, that he was subsequently released without criminal charges being preferred against him.   It is alleged that the officers had no search warrant and no arrest warrant and that they acted "under color of the statutes, ordinances, regulations, customs and usages" of Illinois and of the City of Chicago. * * *

Responding to these outrageous allegations the Supreme Court, *per* Mr. Justice Douglas, held that section 1983 provided a damage remedy, notwithstanding the statute's rather special history and the possibility that it would provide federal "constitutional tort" remedies where conventional state law remedies already existed (id. at 183):

> Although the legislation was enacted because of the conditions that existed in the South at that time, it is cast in general language and is as applicable to Illinois as it is to the States whose names were mentioned over and again in the debates.   It is no answer that the State has a law which if enforced would give relief.   The federal remedy is supplementary to the state remedy, and the latter need not be first sought and refused before the federal one is invoked.   Hence the fact that Illinois by its constitution and laws outlaws unreasonable searches and seizures is no barrier to the present suit in the federal court.

Justice Frankfurter, in dissent, agreed with the majority that the Fourth Amendment created rights cognizable under section 1983; that plaintiffs need not allege specific intent to deprive them of constitutional rights; and that the Court in earlier criminal cases had read "under color of state law" expansively in the context of the similar criminal provision of the Civil Rights Act.   However, Frankfurter thought those decisions, in which he participated, ill-considered because the Court had not conducted a thorough analysis of the legislative history. Having made such an analysis he was convinced that Congress did not intend to substitute a federal remedy where state remedies were available (id. at 224–37):

> This case squarely presents the question whether the intrusion of a city policeman for which that policeman can show no such authority at state law as

could be successfully interposed in defense to a state-law action against him, is nonetheless to be regarded as "under color" or state authority within the meaning of § [1983]. Respondents, in breaking into the Monroe apartment, violated the laws of the State of Illinois. Illinois law appears to offer a civil remedy for unlawful searches; petitioners do not claim that none is available. Rather they assert that they have been deprived of due process of law and of equal protection of the laws under color of state law, although from all that appears the courts of Illinois are available to give them the fullest redress which the common law affords for the violence done them, nor does any "statute, ordinance, regulation, custom, or usage" of the State of Illinois bar that redress. Did the enactment by Congress of § 1 of the Ku Klux Act of 1871 encompass such a situation? * * *

The Court now says * * * that "It was not the unavailability of state remedies but the failure of certain States to enforce the laws with an equal hand that furnished the powerful momentum behind this 'force bill.' " Of course, if the notion of "unavailability" of remedy is limited to mean an absence of statutory, paper right, this is in large part true. Insofar as the Court undertakes to demonstrate—as the bulk of its opinion seems to do— that § [1983] was meant to reach some instances of action not specifically authorized by the avowed, apparent, written law inscribed in the statute books of the States, the argument knocks at an open door. No one would or could deny this, for by its express terms the statute comprehends deprivations of federal rights under color of any "statute, ordinance, regulation, *custom*, or *usage*" of a State. (Emphasis added.) The question is, *what* class of cases other than those involving state statute law were meant to be reached. And, with respect to this question, the Court's conclusion is undermined by the very portions of the legislative debates which it cites. * * * These statements indicate that Congress—made keenly aware by the post-bellum conditions in the South that States through their authorities could sanction offenses against the individual by settled practice which established state law as truly as written codes—designed § [1983] to reach, as well, official conduct which, because engaged in "permanently and as a rule," or "systematically," came through acceptance by law-administering officers to constitute "custom, or usage" having the cast of law. They do not indicate an attempt to reach, nor does the statute by its terms include, instances of acts in defiance of state law and which no settled state practice, no systematic pattern of official action or inaction, no "custom, or usage, of any State," insulates from effective and adequate reparation by the State's authorities.

Rather, all the evidence converges to the conclusion that Congress by § [1983] created a civil liability enforceable in the federal courts only in instances of injury for which redress was barred in the state courts because some "statute, ordinance, regulation, custom, or usage" sanctioned the grievance complained of. This purpose * * * accords with the presuppositions of our federal system. The jurisdiction which Article III of the Constitution conferred on the national judiciary reflected the assumption that the state courts, not the federal courts, would remain the primary guardians of that fundamental security of person and property which the long evolution of the common law had secured to one individual as against other individuals. The Fourteenth Amendment did not alter this basic aspect of our federalism.

3. The "rediscovery" of section 1983 in *Monroe* generated the flood of litigation against state and local officials noted by Justice Powell in *Maine v. Thiboutot*,

and called forth a substantial number of Supreme Court decisions developing both the contours of the section 1983 cause of action and the availability of various immunities, both official and governmental, from liability.   These developments are summarized briefly in P. SCHUCK, SUING GOVERNMENT, Appendix 2 (1983); and more extensively in Kupfer, *Restructuring the* Monroe *Doctrine: Current Litigation Under Section 1983*, 9 Hastings Const. L.Q. 463 (1982).

Much of the ensuing litigation has involved Fourth, Fifth and Sixth amendment claims against law enforcement personnel, although these are hardly the only constitutional provisions that have formed the basis for section 1983 suits. Indeed, the capacious language of the Fourteenth Amendment's Due Process and Equal Protection Clauses might, with modest creativity, cover virtually any offending act by a state or local official.   See, *e.g., Parratt v. Taylor*, 451 U.S. 527 (1981); *Paul v. Davis*, 424 U.S. 693 (1976).   These officials are protected by a range of immunities, see generally *Scheuer v. Rhodes*, 416 U.S. 232 (1974), "predicated upon a considered inquiry into the immunity historically accorded the relevant official at common law," *Imbler v. Pachtman*, 424 U.S. 409, 421 (1976) (public prosecutor absolutely immune), but tempered by the need to effectuate the policies of section 1983.   See *Tower v. Glover*, ___ U.S. ___, 104 S.Ct. 2820 (1984) (no immunity for a public defender accused of intentional misconduct).   Many of the more important cases on official immunity are rehearsed in *Butz v. Economu*, supra p. 827.

States retain their Eleventh Amendment immunity, to which we shall shortly return, but other political subdivisions, *Lake Country Estates v. Tahoe Regional Planning Agency*, 440 U.S. 391 (1979), including cities and towns, do not share in that immunity, or indeed in any other where constitutional claims are involved.   *Owen v. City of Independence*, 445 U.S. 622 (1980).   Sub-state political entities thus face a risk of liability for constitutional torts more extensive than the analogous liability of the United States under the FTCA.   See supra p. 791 *et seq.*   See generally *Monell v. Department of Social Services of the City of New York*, 436 U.S. 658 (1978).

4. *Maine v. Thiboutot* obviously further expands the potential liability of state and local entities and their officials under section 1983.   Moreover, with the elimination of the $10,000 jurisdictional amount requirement in 28 U.S.C.A. § 1331(a), those statutory claims may proceed in federal court without the requirement that they be "pendent to" a constitutional claim.   See *Chapman v. Houston Welfare Rights Organization*, 441 U.S. 600 (1979); *Hagans v. Lavine*, 415 U.S. 528 (1974).

Beyond increasing the paranoia that the threat of section 1983 suits has induced in state and local officials, *Maine v. Thiboutot* is of major importance in confirming the possibility for federal court review of the implementation of federal statutes by state and local administrative officials.   As Justice Powell's partial list of cooperative federal state arrangements suggests, the federal government, for various reasons, increasingly implements policy through state and local agencies.   See generally Mashaw and Rose-Ackerman, *Federalism and Regulation,* in G. EADS & M. FIX, Eds., THE REAGAN ADMINISTRATION'S REGULATORY RELIEF EFFORT 1 (1984).   Thus, while the federal government's expenditures have risen 500% since 1950 and its regulatory functions have increased exponentially, the number of federal employees has remained almost constant—indeed, as percentage of population has declined.   See Mosher, *The Changing Responsibilities and Tactics of the Federal Government,* in J.

FESLER, Ed., AMERICAN PUBLIC ADMINISTRATION: PATTERNS OF THE PAST 198 (1982).

Although Justice Powell laments that state and local employees face a "liability" that federal agents or regulatory personnel do not, the real significance of *Maine v. Thiboutot* may be in providing a rather conventional form of federal judicial review (injunction or declaratory judgment) of implementing decisions that would have been readily available had the Congress chosen to rely exclusively on federal employers for the concrete realization of its policies.   Indeed, that is the view of such beneficiary enforcement actions that the Court seems to have entertained when it decided *Rosado v. Wyman*, 397 U.S. 397 (1970), one of the cases upon which the majority principally relies.   For while Justice Powell analogizes the action in *Thiboutot* to "implied rights of action," the *Rosado* Court cited *Data Processing*, supra p. 645, as authority and referred to the question as one concerning the availability of judicial review.   397 U.S. at 420.   On the relationship between "standing," implied rights of action and section 1983 actions, see generally Mashaw, *"Rights" in the Federal Administrative State*, 92 Yale L.J. 1129 (1983); Stewart and Sunstein, *Public Programs and Private Rights*, 95 Harv. L. Rev. 1193 (1982).

PENNHURST STATE SCHOOL AND HOSPITAL v. HALDERMAN

Supreme Court of the United States, 1981.
451 U.S. 1, 101 S.Ct. 1531, 67 L.Ed.2d 694.

JUSTICE REHNQUIST delivered the opinion of the Court.

At issue in these cases is the scope and meaning of the Developmentally Disabled Assistance and Bill of Rights Act of 1975, 42 U.S.C.A. § 6000 *et seq.*   The Court of Appeals for the Third Circuit held that the Act created substantive rights in favor of the mentally retarded, that those rights were judicially enforceable, and that conditions at the Pennhurst State School and Hospital (Pennhurst), a facility for the care and treatment of the mentally retarded, violated those rights.   For the reasons stated below, we reverse the decision of the Court of Appeals and remand the case for further proceedings.

I

The Commonwealth of Pennsylvania owns and operates Pennhurst. Pennhurst is a large institution, housing approximately 1,200 residents. Seventy-five percent of the residents are either "severely" or "profoundly" retarded—that is, with an IQ of less than 35—and a number of the residents are also physically handicapped.   About half of its residents were committed there by court order and half by a parent or other guardian.

* * *

The District Court['s] * * * findings of fact are undisputed: Conditions at Pennhurst are not only dangerous, with the residents often physically abused or drugged by staff members, but also inadequate for the "habilitation" of the retarded.   Indeed, the court found that the physical, intellectual, and emotional skills of some residents have deteriorated at Pennhurst.

The District Court went on to hold that the mentally retarded have a federal constitutional right to be provided with "minimally adequate habilitation" in the "least restrictive environment," regardless of whether they were voluntarily or involuntarily committed. * * * In addition, it found that § 504 of the Rehabilitation Act of 1973, 29 U.S.C.A. § 794, and § 201 of the Pennsylvania Mental Health and Mental Retardation Act of 1966 provided a right to minimally adequate habilitation in the least restrictive environment.

Each of these rights was found to have been violated by the conditions existing at Pennhurst. * * *

The Court of Appeals for the Third Circuit substantially affirmed the District Court's remedial order. 612 F.2d 84 (1979) (en banc). Unlike the District Court, however, the Court of Appeals sought to avoid the constitutional claims raised by respondents and instead rested its order on a construction of the Developmentally Disabled Assistance and Bill of Rights Act, 42 U.S.C.A. § 6000 *et seq.* It found that § § 6010(1) and (2) of the Act, the "bill of rights" provision, grant to mentally retarded persons a right to "appropriate treatment, services, and habilitation" in "the setting that is least restrictive of * * * personal liberty." * * * As an alternative ground, the court affirmed the District Court's holding that Pennhurst residents have a state statutory right to adequate "habilitation."

The court concluded that the conditions at Pennhurst violated these federal and state statutory rights. * * *

We granted certiorari to consider petitioners' several challenges to the decision below. Petitioners first contend that 42 U.S.C.A. § 6010 does not create in favor of the mentally retarded any substantive rights to "appropriate treatment" in the "least restrictive" environment. Assuming that Congress did intend to create such a right, petitioners question the authority of Congress to impose these affirmative obligations on the States under either its spending power or § 5 of the Fourteenth Amendment. Petitioners next assert that any rights created by the Act are enforceable in federal court only by the Federal Government, not by private parties. Finally, petitioners argue that the court below read the scope of any rights created by the Act too broadly and far exceeded its remedial powers in requiring the Commonwealth to move its residents to less restrictive environments and create individual habilitation plans for the mentally retarded. Because we agree with petitioners' first contention—that § 6010 simply does not create substantive rights—we find it unnecessary to address the remaining issues.

II

We turn first to a brief review of the general structure of the Act. It is a federal-state grant program whereby the Federal Government provides financial assistance to participating States to aid them in creating programs to care for and treat the developmentally disabled. Like other federal-state cooperative programs, the Act is voluntary and the States are given the choice of complying with the conditions set forth in the Act or foregoing the benefits of federal funding. See generally *King v. Smith*, 392 U.S. 309 (1968); *Rosado v. Wyman*, 397 U.S. 397 (1970). The Commonwealth of Pennsylvania has elected to participate in the program. The Secretary of the Department of Health and Human Services (HHS), the agency responsible for administering the Act, has approved Pennsylvania's state plan and in 1976 disbursed to Pennsylvania approximately $1.6 million. Pennhurst itself receives no federal funds from Pennsylvania's allotment under the Act, though it does receive approximately $6 million per year in Medicaid funds.

The Act begins with an exhaustive statement of purposes. 42 U.S.C.A. § 6000(b)(1). The "overall purpose" of the Act, as amended in 1978, is:

> "[*T*]*o assist* [the] states to assure that persons with developmental disabilities receive the care, treatment, and other services necessary to enable them to achieve their maximum potential through a system which coordinates, monitors, plans, and evaluates those services and which ensures the protection of the legal and human rights of persons with developmental disabilities." (Emphasis supplied.)

As set forth in the margin, the "specific purposes" of the Act are to "assist" and financially "support" various activities necessary to the provision of comprehensive services to the developmentally disabled. § 6000(b)(2).[8]

The Act next lists a variety of conditions for the receipt of federal funds. Under § 6005, for example, the Secretary "as a condition of providing assistance" shall require that "each recipient of such assistance take affirmative action" to hire qualified handicapped individuals. Each State, in turn, shall "as a condition" of receiving assistance submit to the Secretary a plan to evaluate the services provided under the Act. § 6009. Each State shall also "as a condition" of receiving assistance "provide the Secretary satisfactory assurances that each program

---

8. Section 6000(b)(2) provides:

"The specific purposes of this chapter are—

"(A) to assist in the provision of comprehensive services to persons with developmental disabilities, with priority to those persons whose needs cannot be covered or otherwise met under the Education for All Handicapped Children Act, the Rehabilitation Act of 1973 * * * , or other health, education, or welfare programs;

"(B) to assist States in appropriate planning activities;

"(C) to make grants to States and public and private, nonprofit agencies to establish model programs, to demonstrate

innovative habilitation techniques, and to train professional and paraprofessional personnel with respect to providing services to persons with developmental disabilities;

"(D) to make grants to university affiliated facilities to assist them in administering and operating demonstration facilities for the provision of services to persons with developmental disabilities, and interdisciplinary training programs for personnel needed to provide specialized services for these persons; and

"(E) to make grants to support a system in each State to protect the legal and human rights of all persons with developmental disabilities."

* * * which receives funds from the State's allotment * * * has in effect for each developmentally disabled person who receives services from or under the program a habilitation plan." § 6011(a). And § 6012(a) conditions aid on a State's promise to "have in effect a system to protect and advocate the rights of persons with developmental disabilities."

At issue here, of course, is § 6010, the "bill of rights" provision. It states in relevant part:

> "Congress makes the following findings respecting the rights of persons with developmental disabilities:
>
> "(1) Persons with developmental disabilities have a right to appropriate treatment, services, and habilitation for such disabilities.
>
> "(2) The treatment, services, and habilitation for a person with developmental disabilities should be designed to maximize the developmental potential of the person and should be provided in the setting that is least restrictive of the person's personal liberty.
>
> "(3) The Federal Government and the States both have an obligation to assure that public funds are not provided to any institutio[n] * * * that—(A) does not provide treatment, services, and habilitation which is appropriate to the needs of such person; or (B) does not meet the following minimum standards * * * ."

Noticeably absent from § 6010 is any language suggesting that § 6010 is a "condition" for the receipt of federal funding under the Act. Section 6010 thus stands in sharp contrast to § § 6005, 6009, 6011, and 6012.

The enabling parts of the Act are the funding sections. 42 U.S.C.A. § § 6061–6063. Those sections describe how funds are to be allotted to the States, require that any State desiring financial assistance submit an overall plan satisfactory to the Secretary of HHS, and require that funds disbursed under the Act be used in accordance with the approved state plan. To be approved by the Secretary, the state plan must comply with several specific conditions set forth in § 6063. It, *inter alia*, must provide for the establishment of a State Planning Council, § 6063(b)(1), and set out specific objectives to be achieved under the plan, § 6063(b)(2)(A). Services furnished under the plan must be consistent with standards prescribed by the Secretary, § 6063(b)(5)(A)(i), and be provided in an individual manner consistent with § 6011, § 6063(b)(5)(B). The plan must also be supported by assurances that any program receiving assistance is protecting the human rights of the disabled consistent with § 6010, § 6063(b)(5)(C). Each State must also require its State Planning Council to serve as an advocate of persons with developmental disabilities. § 6067.

The Act further provides procedures and sanctions to ensure state compliance with its requirements. The Secretary may, of course, disapprove a state plan, § 6063(c). If a State fails to satisfy the requirements of § 6063, the Secretary may terminate or reduce the federal grant. § 6065. Any State dissatisfied with the Secretary's disapproval of the plan, or his decision to terminate funding, may appeal to the federal courts of appeals. § 6068. No other cause of action is recognized in the Act.

III

As support for its broad remedial order, the Court of Appeals found that 42 U.S.C.A. § 6010 created substantive rights in favor of the disabled and imposed an obligation on the States to provide, at their own expense, certain kinds of treatment. The initial question before us, then, is one of statutory construction: Did Congress intend in § 6010 to create enforceable rights and obligations?

In discerning congressional intent, we necessarily turn to the possible sources of Congress' power to legislate, namely, Congress' power to enforce the Fourteenth Amendment and its power under the Spending Clause to place conditions on the grant of federal funds. Although the court below held that Congress acted under both powers, the respondents themselves disagree on this point. The Halderman respondents argue that § 6010 was enacted pursuant to § 5 of the Fourteenth Amendment. Accordingly, they assert that § 6010 is mandatory on the States, regardless of their receipt of federal funds. The Solicitor General, in contrast, concedes that Congress acted pursuant to its spending power alone. Thus, in his view, § 6010 only applies to those States which accept federal funds.

Although this Court has previously addressed issues going to Congress' power to secure the guarantees of the Fourteenth Amendment, we have had little occasion to consider the appropriate test for determining when Congress intends to enforce those guarantees. Because such legislation imposes congressional policy on a State involuntarily, and because it often intrudes on traditional state authority, we should not quickly attribute to Congress an unstated intent to act under its authority to enforce the Fourteenth Amendment. * * * The case for inferring intent is at its weakest where, as here, the rights asserted impose *affirmative* obligations on the States to fund certain services, since we may assume that Congress will not implicitly attempt to impose massive financial obligations on the States.

Turning to Congress' power to legislate pursuant to the spending power, our cases have long recognized that Congress may fix the terms on which it shall disburse federal money to the States. Unlike legislation enacted under § 5, however, legislation enacted pursuant to the spending power is much in the nature of a contract: in return for federal funds, the States agree to comply with federally imposed conditions. The legitimacy of Congress' power to legislate under the spending power thus rests on whether the State voluntarily and knowingly accepts the terms of the "contract." There can, of course, be no knowing acceptance if a State is unaware of the conditions or is unable to ascertain what is expected of it. Accordingly, if Congress intends to impose a condition on the grant of federal moneys, it must do so unambiguously. By insisting that Congress speak with a clear voice, we enable the States to exercise their choice knowingly, cognizant of the consequences of their participation.

* * *

Applying those principles to these cases, we find nothing in the Act or its legislative history to suggest that Congress intended to require the States to assume the high cost of providing "appropriate treatment" in the "least restrictive environment" to their mentally retarded citizens.

There is virtually no support for the lower court's conclusion that Congress created rights and obligations pursuant to its power to enforce the Fourteenth Amendment. The Act nowhere states that that is its purpose. Quite the contrary, the Act's language and structure demonstrate that it is a mere federal-state funding statute. * * * Surely Congress would not have established such elaborate funding incentives had it simply intended to impose absolute obligations on the States.

Respondents nonetheless insist that the fact that § 6010 speaks in terms of "rights" supports their view. Their reliance is misplaced. * * * We are persuaded that § 6010, when read in the context of other more specific provisions of the Act, does no more than express a congressional preference for certain kinds of treatment. It is simply a general statement of "findings" and, as such, is too thin a reed to support the rights and obligations read into it by the court below. The closest one can come in giving § 6010 meaning is that it justifies and supports Congress' appropriation of money under the Act and guides the Secretary in his review of state applications for federal funds. As this Court recognized in *Rosado v. Wyman,* [397 U.S. 397 (1970)] "Congress sometimes legislates by innuendo, making declarations of policy and indicating a preference while requiring measures that, though falling short of legislating its goal, serve as a nudge in the preferred directions." This is such a case.

* * *

There remains the contention of the Solicitor General that Congress, acting pursuant to its spending power, conditioned the grant of federal money on the State's agreeing to underwrite the obligations the Court of Appeals read into § 6010. We find that contention wholly without merit. As amply demonstrated above, the "findings" in § 6010, when viewed in the context of the more specific provisions of the Act, represent general statements of federal policy, not newly created legal duties.

The "plain language" of § 6010 also refutes the Solicitor General's contention. When Congress intended to impose conditions on the grant of federal funds, as in § § 6005, 6009, 6011, 6012, 6063, and 6067, it proved capable of doing so in clear terms. Section 6010, in marked contrast, in no way suggests that the grant of federal funds is "conditioned" on a state funding the rights described therein. * * *

Equally telling is the fact that the Secretary has specifically rejected the position of the Solicitor General. The purpose of the Act, according to the Secretary, is merely "to improve and coordinate the provision of services to persons with developmental disabilities." 45 C.F.R. § 1385.1 (1979). The Secretary acknowledges that "[n]o authority was included in [the 1975] Act to allow the Department to withhold funds from States on the basis of failure to meet the findings [of § 6010]." 45 Fed. Reg. 31,006 (1980). If funds cannot be terminated for a state's failure to comply with § 6010, § 6010 can hardly be considered a "condition" of the grant of federal funds. The Secretary's interpretation of § 6010, moreover, is well supported by the legislative history. In reaching the compromise on § 6010, the Conference Committee rejected the Senate's proposal to terminate federal funding of States which failed to comply with the standards enumerated in Title II of the Senate's bill. By eliminating that sanction, Congress made clear that the provisions of § 6010 were intended to be hortatory, not mandatory.

The fact that Congress granted to Pennsylvania only $1.6 million in 1976, a sum woefully inadequate to meet the enormous financial burden of providing "appropriate" treatment in the "least restrictive" setting, confirms that Congress must have had a limited purpose in enacting § 6010. When Congress does impose affirmative obligations on the States, it usually makes a far more substantial contribution to defray costs. It defies common sense, in short, to suppose that Congress implicitly imposed this massive obligation on participating States.

* * *

IV

Respondents also suggest that they may bring suit to compel compliance with those conditions which are contained in the Act. Of particular relevance to these cases are § 6011(a) [see pp. 895–96 supra] and § 6063(b)(5)(C).*

That claim raises several issues. First, it must be determined whether respondents have a private cause of action to compel state compliance with those conditions. In legislation enacted pursuant to the spending power, the typical remedy for state noncompliance with federally imposed conditions is not a private cause of action for noncompliance but rather action by the Federal Government to terminate funds to the State. See § 6065. Just last Term, however, in *Maine v. Thiboutot*, we held that 42 U.S.C.A. § 1983 provides a cause of action for state deprivations of "rights secured" by "the laws" of the United States. Whether *Thiboutot* controls these cases depends on two factors. First, respondents here, unlike the plaintiffs in *Thiboutot*, who alleged that state law prevented them from receiving federal funds to which they were entitled, can only claim that the state plan has not provided adequate "assurances" to the Secretary. It is at least an open question whether an individual's interest in having a State provide those "assurances" is a "right secured" by the laws of the United States within the meaning of § 1983. Second, Jus-

---

*[Section 6063(b)(5)(C) requires each state plan to:

contain or be supported by assurances satisfactory to the Secretary that the human rights of all persons with developmental disabilities * * * who are receiving treatment, services, or habilitation, under programs assisted under this chapter will be protected consistent with § 6010 of this Title (relating to rights of the developmentally disabled). Eds.]

tice Powell in dissent in *Thiboutot* suggested that § 1983 would not be available where the "governing statute provides an exclusive remedy for violations of its terms." It is unclear whether the express remedy contained in this Act is exclusive.

Second, it is not at all clear that the Pennhurst petitioners have violated § 6011 and § 6063(b)(5)(C). Those sections, by their terms, only refer to "programs assisted" under the Act. Because Pennhurst does not receive federal funds under the Act, it is arguably not a "program assisted." Thus, there may be no obligation on the State under § 6011 to assure the Secretary that each resident of Pennhurst have a habilitation plan, or assure the Secretary under § 6063(b)(5)(C) that Pennhurst residents are being provided services consistent with § 6010.

Third, there is the question of remedy. Respondents' relief may well be limited to enjoining the Federal Government from providing funds to the Commonwealth. As we stated in *Rosado v. Wyman*, welfare claimants were "entitled to declaratory relief and an appropriate injunction by the District Court against the payment of *federal* monies * * * should the State not develop a conforming plan within a reasonable period of time." (Emphasis in original.) There, we rejected the suggestion that the courts could require the State to pay the additional sums demanded by compliance with federal standards. Relying on *King v. Smith*, 392 U.S. 309 (1968), we explained that "the State had alternative choices of assuming the additional cost" of complying with the federal standard "or not using federal funds." Accordingly, we remanded the case so that the State could exercise that choice.

In other instances, however, we have implicitly departed from that rule and have affirmed lower court decisions enjoining a State from enforcing any provisions which conflict with federal law in violation of the Supremacy Clause, e.g., *Carleson v. Remillard*, 406 U.S. 598 (1972). In still other cases, we have struck down state laws without addressing the form of relief, e.g., *Townsend v. Swank*, 404 U.S. 282 (1971). In no case, however, have we required a State to provide money to plaintiffs, much less required a State to take on such open-ended and potentially burdensome obligations as providing "appropriate" treatment in the "least restrictive" environment. And because this is a suit in federal court, anything but prospective relief would pose serious questions under the Eleventh Amendment. *Edelman v. Jordan*, 415 U.S. 651 (1974).

These are all difficult questions. Because the Court of Appeals has not addressed these issues, however, we remand the issues for consideration in light of our decision here. * * *

[Justice Blackmun's concurring opinion is omitted.]

Justice White, with whom Justice Brennan and Justice Marshall join, dissenting in part.

* * *

In essence, the Court concludes that the so-called "Bill of Rights" section of the Act, 42 U.S.C.A. § 6010, merely serves to establish guidelines which States should endeavor to fulfill, but which have no real effect except to the extent that the Secretary of Health and Human Services chooses to use the criteria established by § 6010 in determining funding under the Act. In my view, this reading misconceives the important purposes Congress intended § 6010 to serve. That section, as confirmed by its legislative history, was intended by Congress to establish requirements which participating States had to meet in providing care to the developmentally disabled. The fact that Congress spoke in generalized terms rather than the language of regulatory minutia cannot make nugatory actions so carefully undertaken.

[After extensive analysis of the statute and its legislative and administrative history, Justice White continued:]

Given my view that Congress intended § 6010 to do more than suggest that the States act in a particular manner, I find it necessary to reach the question whether these rights can be enforced in federal courts in a suit brought by the developmentally disabled. * * *

As a general matter, it is clear that the fact that a federal administrative agency has the power to oversee a cooperative state-federal venture does not mean that Congress intended such oversight to be the exclusive remedy for enforcing statutory rights. This Court is "most reluctant to assume Congress has closed the avenue of effective judicial review to those individuals most directly affected by the administration of its program[s]" even if the agency has the statutory power to cut off federal funds for noncompliance. *Rosado v. Wyman.* In part, this reluctance is founded on the perception that a funds cutoff is a drastic remedy with injurious consequences to the supposed beneficiaries of the Act. Cf. *Cannon v. University of Chicago.* In this litigation, there is no indication that Congress intended the funds cutoff, which, as the Court notes, the Secretary believed was not within the power of the agency, to be the sole remedy for correcting violations of § 6010 * * *.

I would vacate the judgment of the Court of Appeals and remand the cases for further proceedings. This litigation does not involve the exercise of congressional power to enforce the Fourteenth Amendment as the Court of Appeals held, but is an exercise of the spending power. What an appropriate remedy might be where state officials fail to observe the limits of their power under the United States Constitution or fail to perform an ongoing statutory duty imposed by a federal statute enacted under the commerce power or the Fourteenth Amendment is not necessarily the measure of a federal court's authority where it is found that a State has failed to perform its obligations undertaken pursuant to a statute enacted under the spending power. * * * [T]he courts in such cases must take account of the State's privilege to withdraw and terminate its duties under the federal law. Although the court may enjoin the enforcement of a discrete state statutory provision or regulation or may order state officials prospectively to perform their duties incident to the receipt of federal funds, the prospective force of such injunctions cannot survive the State's decision to terminate its participation in the program. Furthermore, there are cases in which there is no identifiable statutory provision whose enforcement can be prohibited. *Rosado v. Wyman* was such a case, and there, after finding that the State was not complying with the provisions of the Social Security Act, we remanded the case to the District Court to "afford [the State] an opportunity to revise its program in accordance with [federal requirements]" as we have construed them to be, but to retain jurisdiction "to review * * * any revised program adopted by the State, or, should [the State] choose not to submit a revamped program by the determined date, issue its order restraining the further use of federal monies. * * * "

It is my view that the Court of Appeals should have adopted the *Rosado* approach in these cases. It found the State to be in noncompliance with the federal statute in major respects and proceeded to impose a far-reaching remedy, approving the appointment of a Special Master to decide which of the Pennhurst inmates should remain and which should be moved to community-based facilities. More properly, the court should have announced what it thought was necessary to comply with the Act and then permitted an appropriate period for the State to decide whether it preferred to give up federal funds and go its own route. If it did not, it should propose a plan for achieving compliance, in which event, if it satisfied the court, a decree incorporating the plan could be entered and if the plan was unsatisfactory, the further use of federal funds could be enjoined. In any event, however, the court should not have assumed the task of managing Pennhurst or deciding in the first instance which patients should remain and which should be removed. * * *

Accordingly, I would vacate the judgment of the Court of Appeals and remand the cases for further proceedings.

The Eleventh Amendment

Justice Rehnquist's cryptic reference in *Pennhurst* to *Edelman v. Jordan*, and to the "difficult questions" that Eleventh Amendment immunity might pose, further obscures one of the darker corners of the jurisprudence of federal remedies. Adopted to overturn the Supreme Court's decision in *Chisholm v. Georgia*, 2 U.S. (2 Dall.) 419 (1793), the Eleventh Amendment imposes a special barrier to suits against state governments. The amendment provides that "The judicial power of the United States shall not be construed to extend to any suit in law or equity * * * against one of the United States by Citizens of another State. * * * " The Supreme Court has interpreted this language as also barring unconsented suits against a state by its own citizens. See, e.g., *Employees v. Department of Public Health and Welfare*, 411 U.S. 279 (1973). Private litigants have often sought to escape this bar by naming state officials, rather than the state itself, as defendants. *Cf. Larson v. Domestic & Foreign Commerce Corp.*, supra p. 627. In *Ex parte Young*, 209 U.S. 123 (1908), the Supreme Court held that the Eleventh Amendment did not bar a federal court injunction against a state officer who was acting unconstitutionally. In short, a plaintiff may claim not to be suing the state even where, as in *Ex parte Young*, the theory of the case requires that "state action" be the basis for the lawsuit. Yet later decisions have made clear that even though a plaintiff fails to include a state as a party, any action that would result in the recovery of money from the state is barred.

In *Ford Motor Co. v. Department of Treasury*, 323 U.S. 459, 463–64 (1945), for example, Ford brought suit in a federal district court against the Indiana Department of the Treasury and the individual members of its board for a refund of gross income taxes it claimed had been unlawfully collected. The Supreme Court concluded that the action was in substance one against the state and thus barred by the Eleventh Amendment. The action was based upon an Indiana statute authorizing suits to recover any refund, which, if due, would be paid "out of any funds in the state treasury." The individual defendants "were joined as the collective representatives of the state, not as individuals against whom a personal judgment is sought. * * * The petitioner's claim is for a 'refund,' not for the imposition of personal liability on individual defendants for sums illegally exacted."

Parden v. Terminal Railway, 377 U.S. 184, 192 (1964), opened a potentially broad chink in the armor provided by the Eleventh Amendment. In that case employees of a railroad operated in interstate commerce by the State of Alabama sued their employer under the Federal Employers Liability Act. The state resisted the suit on the basis of the Eleventh Amendment. In a murky opinion for the Court, Justice Brennan held that,

> By * * * ratifying the Commerce Clause, the States empowered Congress to create such a right of action against interstate railroads; by enacting the FELA * * * Congress conditioned the right to operate a railroad in interstate commerce upon amenability to suit in federal court as provided by the Act; by thereafter operating a railroad in interstate commerce, Alabama must be taken to have accepted that condition and thus to have consented to suit.

Some nine years later, however, the Supreme Court held that the Eleventh Amendment barred a suit against several state agencies by employees of the State of Missouri to recover overtime compensation guaranteed them by the Fair Labor Standards Act. *Employees v. Department of Public Health and Welfare*, 411 U.S. 279 (1973). Although Congress in 1966 had extended the Act's coverage to state-operated hospitals and schools while leaving unchanged the provision making covered employers subject to suit "in any court of competent jurisdiction," the Court was unwilling to conclude that Congress, in the exercise of its power to regulate interstate commerce, had intended to override the state's immunity. *Parden* was distinguished largely on the basis of the FELA's limited impact on states, few of which engaged in the essentially "private" enterprise of railroading. The Fair Labor Standards Act, by contrast, applied to the broad range of state governmental functions. The Court therefore required, but could not find, a specific indication in the statute that Congress meant to override state immunity.

Employees, although reaffirming the *Parden* "waiver" doctrine, exposed the weakness of that analysis. The waiver in any case would be implicit and would require a determination of whether the state had a real choice in undertaking the activity in question.   Ultimately that question requires that the Court distinguish between the "basic" or "mandatory" functions of government and those that are "discretionary" or "optional." Although this distinction may not be the same as the distinction between "governmental" and "proprietary" functions, it looks in the same direction and would likely produce similar conundrums.   Moreover, the prospect of federal courts deciding what are the "necessary" functions of state government conjures up precisely the image of federal judicial intervention in local affairs that the Eleventh Amendment was designed to erase.

The waiver theory was further restricted, and perhaps eviscerated, in *Edelman v. Jordan*, 415 U.S. 651, *rehearing denied* 416 U.S. 1000 (1974), which seems, with *Ex parte Young*, to have become the leading case on Eleventh Amendment immunity.   There the Court ordered dismissal of an action seeking an order directing the Director of Illinois' Department of Public Aid to pay out funds under the Aid to the Aged, Blind and Disabled program that had been withheld when the agency failed to process claims in accordance with the schedule prescribed by federal regulations.   The Court viewed this claim, styled as a claim for "equitable restitution," as essentially indistinguishable from a demand for damages against the state.   At the same time, however, it sustained the portion of the trial court's decree that ordered the *individual defendants* to comply with the federal regulations thereafter.

In his opinion for the Court, Justice Rehnquist rejected the suggestion that 42 U.S.C.A. § 1983 could be interpreted as supporting the plaintiffs' claim for retrospective monetary relief.   While § 1983 might support an action by public aid recipients to correct unlawful conduct of state officials, "a federal court's remedial power, consistent with the Eleventh Amendment, is necessarily limited to prospective injunctive relief, and may not include a retroactive award which requires the payment of funds from the state treasury."   415 U.S. at 677.   Four Justices dissented, arguing (in three separate opinions) that by participating in the AABD program—a voluntary program of federal grants-in-aid to the states—Illinois had waived its immunity from suit.   The majority's response was simply that it could not lightly presume waiver of a constitutional right.

A request for damages against state officials does not, of course, necessarily implicate the Eleventh Amendment.   In *Scheuer v. Rhodes*, 416 U.S. 232 (1974), a suit by representatives of students killed at Kent State University in 1970, the Court overturned a lower court's dismissal of damage actions against the former governor of Ohio, the Adjutant General of the Ohio National Guard, his assistant, and various members of the Ohio National Guard.   The lower court had concluded that the suits "were, in substance and effect, against the State of Ohio."   Writing for the Court, Chief Justice Burger ruled that the plaintiffs should have had the opportunity to prove their claims that the defendants had "intentionally, recklessly, willfully and wantonly" caused the unnecessary deployment of the Ohio Guard and ordered the Guard members to perform illegal actions which resulted in the death of the students.   These claims, said the Chief Justice, "[f]airly read * * * allege that each of the named defendants * * * acted either outside the scope of his respective office or, if within the scope, acted in an arbitrary manner, grossly abusing the lawful powers of office." Id. at 235.   The plaintiffs were thus seeking to establish the personal liability of the named defendants and not to impose liability on the state.

Moreover, it appears that in the special circumstance when it is legislating pursuant to section 5 of the Fourteenth Amendment Congress may in determining what is "appropriate legislation" provide for suits against states or state officials that would otherwise be barred by the Eleventh Amendment.   See *Fitzpatrick v. Bizer*, 427 U.S. 445, 456 (1976).   See also *Hutto v. Finney*, 437 U.S. 678 (1978); *Maher v. Gagne*, 448 U.S. 122 (1980).   Thus the question in *Pennhurst*, whether Congress was acting under section 5 or under the Spending Clause, bore both on the existence of a "right" and the remedies that might be available were such a right found to exist.   Justice Rehnquist's cryptic reference may suggest that he at least would be prepared to view an equitable decree of the sort the lower court issued in *Pennhurst* as more in the nature of a claim on the state treasury *a la Ford Motor Co.* than an injunction analogous to the decree in *Ex parte Young*. But see *Youngberg v. Romeo*, 457 U.S. 307 (1982) (holding Pennsylvania had duty under Fourteenth Amendment to provide minimum "habilitation" at Pennhurst School with no mention of the Eleventh Amendment).   See also *Texas v. California*, 457 U.S. 164 (1982) (barring the administrator of Howard Hughes' estate from interpleading Texas and California in federal district court to determine Hughes' domicile at death).

These considerations shed new light on (or raise new questions concerning) the attorney's fee award in *Maine v. Thiboutot*.   Presumably 42 U.S.C.A. § 1988, codifying the Civil Rights Attorney's Fees Awards Act, was an exercise of the section 5 power and therefore was intended to override the Eleventh Amendment bar.   But presumptions concerning the Eleventh Amendment are dangerous.   The Court has previously held that section 1983 itself (or rather the statutes from which it was codified) indicate no congressional intent to abrogate state immunity, *Quern v. Jordan*, 440 U.S. 332 (1979), notwithstanding the peculiar disjunction this produces between the immunities of states and sub-state public entities after *Monell, Owen,* and *Lake Country Estates*.   In addition, under *Hutto v. Finney, supra,* attorney's fees have a special position *vis a vis* the Eleventh Amendment.   And finally, remember that the *Thiboutot* case was filed in a state court.   Thus in a footnote, not reproduced above, the *Thiboutot* majority said (448 U.S. at 9, n.7):

> The States appearing as *amici* suggest that *Hutto v. Finney*, 437 U.S. 678 (1978), left open the issue whether Congress, exercising its power under § 5 of the Fourteenth Amendment, could set aside the States' Eleventh Amendment immunity in statutory as opposed to constitutional cases.   *Hutto*, however, concluded alternatively that the Eleventh Amendment did not bar attorney's fee awards in federal courts because the fee awards are part of costs, which have 'traditionally been awarded without regard for the State's Eleventh Amendment immunity.'   No Eleventh Amendment question is

present, of course, where an action is brought in a state court since the Amendment, by its terms, restrains only '[t]he Judicial power of the United States.'

The "nice" distinctions available in the Eleventh Amendment jurisprudence perhaps reach their apogee in *Florida Department of State v. Treasure Salvors, Inc.*, 458 U.S. 670 (1982). There the court permitted the district court sitting in an *in rem* admiralty action to "arrest" certain artifacts in the possession of Florida officials and turn them over to the respondent, provided the district court did not at the same time adjudicate Florida's title to the disputed articles. Yet, to avoid Florida's Eleventh Amendment defense the Court had to find that Florida had no "colorable claim" to the property (because they lay outside Florida territorial waters) and to characterize their retention by the relevant Florida officials as completely outside their authority. Justice Stevens thus invoked the *Larson*, supra p. 627, *ultra vires* exception to sovereign immunity as an extension of the *Ex parte Young* means of avoiding the State's Eleventh Amendment immunity (458 U.S. at 696–97):

> As recognized in *Larson*, 'action of an officer of the sovereign (be it holding, taking or otherwise legally affecting the plaintiff's property)' that is beyond the officer's statutory authority is not action of the sovereign; a suit for specific relief against the officer is not barred by the Eleventh Amendment. This conclusion follows inevitably from *Ex parte Young*. If conduct of a state officer taken pursuant to an unconstitutional state statute is deemed to be unauthorized and may be challenged in federal court, conduct undertaken without any authority whatever is also not entitled to Eleventh Amendment immunity.

Only four justices joined the plurality opinion. Justice Brennan concurred on the ground that *Employees v. Department of Public Health and Welfare*, supra, should be overruled on the basis of the plain language of the Eleventh Amendment ("by citizens of *another* state" (emphasis added)). Justices White, Powell, Rehnquist and O'Connor found themselves unable to suspend their disbelief beyond the *Ex parte Young* fiction (id. at 703–04):

> Justice Stevens' plurality opinion rests precariously on two transparent fictions. First, it indulges in the fantasy that the enforcement of process by arrest of the res is somehow divorced from the action to determine the State's claim to the res. * * * That dubious proposition is parlayed by a second fiction—that Florida's Eleventh Amendment freedom from suit is meaningfully safeguarded by not formally rejecting the State's claim to the artifacts although federal agents may seize the contested property and federal courts may adjudicate its title. Neither of these novel propositions follows from *Ex parte Young*. The rule of *Ex parte Young* is premised on the axiom that state officials cannot evade responsibility when their conduct "comes into conflict with the superior authority of [the] Constitution." Today, the plurality dilutes the probative force behind that cornerstone decision by extrapolating it to allow federal courts to decide a property dispute between a State and one of its citizens, without the State's consent.

With the addition of the Chief Justice the four dissenters in *Treasure Salvors* became a majority when *Pennhurst* returned for a second time to the Supreme Court.   On remand the Third Circuit, 673 F.2d 647 (1982) (*en banc*), affirmed its original decree on a pendent state law ground made compelling by the intervening action of the Pennsylvania Supreme Court. *In re Schmidt*, 494 Pa. 86, 429 A.2d 631 (1981).   The Circuit Court rejected Pennsylvania's Eleventh Amendment defense on the authority of *Ex parte Young* and *Edelman* because the decree involved only prospective relief.   The Supreme Court reversed (___ U.S. ___, ___, ___, 104 S.Ct. 900, 909, 909–11, 915 (1984)):

> While the rule permitting suits alleging conduct contrary to 'the supreme authority of the United States' has survived, the theory of *Young* has not been provided an expansive interpretation.   Thus, in *Edelman v. Jordan,* the Court emphasized that the Eleventh Amendment bars some forms of injunctive relief against state officials for violation of federal law.   In particular, *Edelman* held that when a plaintiff sues a state official alleging a violation of federal law, the federal court may award an injunction that governs the official's future conduct, but not one that awards retroactive monetary relief. Under the theory of *Young,* such a suit would not be one against the State since the federal-law allegation would strip the state officer of his official authority.   Nevertheless, retroactive relief was barred by the Eleventh Amendment.   *   *   *
>
> *   *   * [T]he injunction in *Young* was justified, notwithstanding the obvious impact on the State itself, on the view that sovereign immunity does not apply because an official who acts unconstitutionally is "stripped of his official or representative character."   This rationale, of course, created the "well-recognized irony" that an official's unconstitutional conduct constitutes state action under the Fourteenth Amendment but not the Eleventh Amendment. Nonetheless, the *Young* doctrine has been accepted as necessary to permit the federal courts to vindicate federal rights and hold state officials responsible to "the supreme authority of the United States."   *   *   * Our decisions repeatedly have emphasized that the *Young* doctrine rests on the need to promote the vindication of federal rights.
>
> The Court also has recognized, however, that the need to promote the supremacy of federal law must be accommodated to the constitutional immunity of the States.   This is the significance of *Edelman v. Jordan.*   We recognized that the prospective relief authorized by *Young* "has permitted the Civil War Amendments to the Constitution to serve as a sword, rather than merely a shield, for those whom they were designed to protect."   But we declined to extend the fiction of *Young* to encompass retroactive relief, for to do so would effectively eliminate the constitutional immunity of the States.   Accordingly, we concluded that although the difference between permissible and impermissible relief "will not in many instances be that between day and night," an award of retroactive relief necessarily " 'fall[s] afoul of the Eleventh Amendment if that basic constitutional provision is to be conceived of as having any present force.' "   In sum *Edelman*'s distinction between prospective and retroactive relief fulfills the underlying purpose of *Ex parte Young* while at the same time preserving to an important degree the constitutional immunity of the States.

This need to reconcile competing interests is wholly absent, however, when a plaintiff alleges that a state official has violated *state* law. In such a case the entire basis for the doctrine of *Young* and *Edelman* disappears. A federal court's grant of relief against state officials on the basis of state law, whether prospective or retroactive, does not vindicate the supreme authority of federal law. On the contrary, it is difficult to think of a greater intrusion on state sovereignty than when a federal court instructs state officials on how to conform their conduct to state law. Such a result conflicts directly with the principles of federalism that underlie the Eleventh Amendment. We conclude that *Young* and *Edelman* are inapplicable in a suit against state officials on the basis of state law.

The contrary view of Justice Stevens' dissent rests on fiction, is wrong on the law, and, most important, would emasculate the Eleventh Amendment. Under his view, an allegation that official conduct is contrary to a state statute could suffice to override the State's protection under that Amendment. The theory is that such conduct is contrary to the official's "instructions," and thus *ulta vires* his authority. Accordingly, official action based on a reasonable interpretation of any statute might, if the interpretation turned out to be erroneous, provide the basis for injunctive relief against the actors in their official capacities. In this case, where officials of a major state department, clearly acting within the scope of their authority, were found not to have improved conditions in a state institution adequately under state law, the dissent's result would be that the State itself has forfeited its constitutionally provided immunity.

The theory is out of touch with reality. * * * The crucial element of the dissent's theory was also the plaintiff's central contention in *Larson.* It is that "[a] sovereign, like any other principal, cannot authorize its agent to violate the law," so that when the agent does so he cannot be acting for the sovereign. * * * It is a view of agency law that the Court in *Larson* explicitly rejected. *Larson* thus made clear that, at least insofar as injunctive relief is sought, an error of law by state officers acting in their official capacities will not suffice to override the sovereign immunity of the State where the relief effectively is against it.

Pennhurst State School and Hospital v. Halderman, ___ U.S. ___, 104 S.Ct. 900 (1984).

Additional Limitations on Section 1983 Claims

One possible technique for limiting section 1983 actions would have been to require a plaintiff first to exhaust available state remedies. But *Monroe v. Pape* afforded little support for such a requirement (365 U.S. at 183):

It is no answer that the State has a law which if enforced would give relief. The federal remedy is supplementary to the state remedy, and the latter need not be first sought and refused before the federal one is invoked.

In *McNeese v. Board of Education,* 373 U.S. 668, 674 (1963), a section 1983 suit challenging segregation in Illinois public schools, the Court quoted this language in rejecting the defendants' contention that the plaintiffs should first exhaust state administrative remedies. The import of this decision was obscured, however, by the Court's observation that "[I]t is by no means clear that Illinois law provides petitioners with an administrative remedy sufficiently adequate to preclude prior resort to a federal court. * * * "

In subsequent cases the Supreme Court has reiterated its ruling in *McNeese* without clarifying its rationale. In *Damico v. California*, 389 U.S. 416 (1967), the Court refused to require exhaustion by plaintiffs challenging California's welfare system. And in *Houghton v. Shafer*, 392 U.S. 639, 640 (1968), a suit by a state prisoner challenging confiscation of legal materials he had assembled to prepare his appeal, the Court refused to require the plaintiff to exhaust the administrative procedures for handling prisoner grievances. The Court again obscured its meaning by both emphasizing the futility of administrative appeal and at the same time stating: "In any event, resort to these remedies is unnecessary in light of our decisions in *Monroe*, *McNeese*, and *Damico*." The basic policies of section 1983 and recent congressional action prescribing one limited exhaustion requirement have convinced the Court to reject the continued attempts of the lower federal courts to develop some form of exhaustion limitation that would utilize state judicial or administrative machinery to winnow their ever-increasing caseload of section 1983 claims. See *Patsy v. Board of Regents*, 457 U.S. 496 (1982). On the other hand, where a claimant has had a full and fair opportunity to litigate a federal constitutional claim in state court, a subsequent section 1983 action may be barred by collateral estoppel. Compare *Haring v. Prosise*, 459 U.S. 1013 (1983), with *Allen v. McCurry*, 449 U.S. 90 (1980). See Note, *Collateral Estoppel in Section 1983 Actions Based on Fourth Amendment Claims in the Aftermath of* Stone v. Powell: Allen v. McCurry, 25 St. Louis U.L.J. 161 (1981).

A related theory that some courts have invoked to limit actions under section 1983 is the equitable doctrine of "abstention," under which a federal court may dismiss or defer an action where it appears that further state proceedings may afford adequate relief and will at least permit a state tribunal to resolve issues of local law. The doctrine originated with *Railroad Commission v. Pullman Co.*, 312 U.S. 496 (1941), where the Court abstained from passing on the legality of a state agency's action which appeared unlikely to withstand scrutiny under state law.

Although the Court's abstention decisions following *Pullman* are not easily reconciled, it does seem clear that federal courts have not been invited to reintroduce the requirement of exhaustion by another name. The mere existence of state remedies that might make a federal court decision unnecessary is an insufficient ground for abstention. Abstention may be suggested where state proceedings are underway, see *Younger v. Harris*, 401 U.S. 37 (1971), but the considerations of equity, comity and federalism that underlie the abstention doctrine "have little force in the absence of a pending state proceeding." *Lake Carriers' Association v.*

MacMullan, 406 U.S. 498, 509 (1972). Questions of the constitutionality of state laws whose meaning is disputed may be avoided by invocation of the abstention doctrine, *Harris County Commissioners Court v. Moore,* 420 U.S. 77 (1975), but abstention is not appropriate even then unless state law is "obviously susceptible of a limiting construction," *Zwickler v. Koota,* 389 U.S. 241, 251 n. 14 (1967). See generally *Hawaii Housing Authority v. Midkiff,* ___ U.S. ___, 104 S.Ct. 2321, 2327–28 (1984); Rosenfeld, *The Place of State Courts in the Era of Younger v. Harris,* 59 B.U.L. Rev. 597 (1979).

D. SUBSTITUTION OF PUBLIC FOR PRIVATE RIGHTS

1. PRIMARY JURISDICTION

NADER v. ALLEGHENY AIRLINES, INC.

Supreme Court of the United States, 1976.
426 U.S. 290, 96 S.Ct. 1978, 48 L.Ed.2d 643.

MR. JUSTICE POWELL delivered the opinion of the Court.

In this case we address the question whether a common-law tort action based on alleged fraudulent misrepresentation by an air carrier subject to regulation by the Civil Aeronautics Board (Board) must be stayed pending reference to the Board for determination whether the practice is "deceptive" within the meaning of § 411 of the Federal Aviation Act of 1958, 49 U.S.C.A. § 1381 (1970). We hold that under the circumstances of this case a stay pending reference is inappropriate.

I.

The facts are not contested. Petitioner agreed to make several appearances in Connecticut on April 28, 1972, in support of the fundraising efforts of the Connecticut Citizen Action Group (CCAG), a nonprofit public interest organization. * * * On April 25, petitioner reserved a seat on respondent's flight 864 for April 28. The flight was scheduled to leave Washington, D.C., at 10:15 a.m. and to arrive in Hartford at 11:15 a.m. * * *

Petitioner arrived at the boarding and check-in area approximately five minutes before the scheduled departure time. He was informed that all seats on the flight were occupied and that he, like several other passengers who had arrived shortly before him, could not be accommodated. * * *

Both parties agree that petitioner's reservation was not honored because respondent had accepted more reservations for flight 864 than it could in fact accommodate. One hour prior to the flight, 107 reservations had been confirmed for the 100 seats actually available. Such overbooking is a common industry practice, designed to ensure that each flight leaves with as few empty seats as possible despite the large number of "no-shows"—reservation-holding passengers who do not appear at flight time. * * * The chance that any particular passenger will be bumped is so negligible that few prospective passengers aware of the possibility would give it a second thought. * * * Nevertheless, the total number of confirmed ticket holders denied seats is quite substantial, numbering over 82,000 passengers in 1972 and about 76,000 in 1973.

Board regulations require each airline to establish priority rules for boarding passengers and to offer "denied boarding compensation" to bumped passengers. These "liquidated damages" are equal to the value of the passenger's ticket with a $25 minimum and a $200 maximum. Passengers are free to reject the compensation offered in favor of a common-law suit for damages suffered as a result of the bumping. Petitioner refused the tender of denied boarding compensation ($32.41 in his case) and, with CCAG, filed this suit for compensatory and punitive damages. His suit did not seek compensation for the bumping *per se* but asserted two other bases of liability: a common-law action based on fraudulent misrepresentation arising from respondent's alleged failure to inform petitioner in advance of its deliberate overbooking practices, and a statutory action under § 404(b) of the Act, 49 U.S.C.A. § 1374(b),[6] arising from respondent's alleged failure to afford petitioner the boarding priority specified in its rules filed with the Board under 14 CFR § 250.3 (1975).

The District Court entered a judgment for petitioner on both claims, awarding him a total of $10 in compensatory damages and $25,000 in punitive damages. Judgment also was entered for CCAG on its misrepresentation claim, with an award of $51 in compensatory damages and $25,000 in punitive damages.

The Court of Appeals for the District of Columbia Circuit reversed. * * *

The only issue before us concerns the Court of Appeals' disposition of the merits of petitioner's claim of fraudulent misrepresentation. Although the court rejected respondent's argument that the existence of the Board's cease-and-desist power under § 411 of the Act eliminates all private remedies for common-law torts arising from unfair or deceptive practices by regulated carriers, it held that a determination by the Board that a practice is not deceptive within the meaning of § 411 would, as a matter of law, preclude a common-law tort action seeking damages for injuries caused by that practice.[7] Therefore, the court held that the Board

---

6. Section 404(b) provides:

"No air carrier or foreign air carrier shall make, give, or cause any undue or unreasonable preference or advantage to any particular person, port, locality, or description of traffic in air transportation in any respect whatsoever or subject any particular person, port, locality, or description of traffic in air transportation to any unjust discrimination or any undue or unreasonable prejudice or disadvantage in any respect whatsoever."

7. Section 411 provides in full:

"The Board may, upon its own initiative or upon complaint by any air carrier, foreign air

carrier, or ticket agent, if it considers that such action by it would be in the interest of the public, investigate and determine whether any air carrier, foreign air carrier, or ticket agent has been or is engaged in unfair or deceptive practices or unfair methods of competition in air transportation or the sale thereof. If the Board shall find, after notice and hearing, that such air carrier, foreign air carrier, or ticket agent is engaged in such unfair or deceptive practices or unfair methods of competition, it shall order such air carrier, foreign air carrier, or ticket agent to cease and desist from such practices or methods of competition."

must be allowed to determine in the first instance whether the challenged practice (in this case, the alleged failure to disclose the practice of overbooking) falls within the ambit of § 411. The court took judicial notice that a rulemaking proceeding concerning possible changes in reservation practices in response to the 1973–1974 fuel crisis was already underway and that a challenge to the carriers' overbooking practices had been raised by an intervenor in that proceeding.[8] The District Court was instructed to stay further action on petitioner's misrepresentation claim pending the outcome of the rulemaking proceeding. The Court of Appeals characterized its holding as "but another application of the principles of primary jurisdiction, a doctrine whose purpose is the coordination of the workings of agency and court."

II.

The question before us, then, is whether the Board must be given an opportunity to determine whether respondent's alleged failure to disclose its practice of deliberate overbooking is a deceptive practice under § 411 before petitioner's common-law action is allowed to proceed. * * *

Section 1106 of the Act, 49 U.S.C.A. § 1506 (1970), provides that "[n]othing contained in this chapter shall in any way abridge or alter the remedies now existing at common law or by statute, but the provisions of this chapter are in addition to such remedies." The Court of Appeals found that "although the saving clause of section 1106 purports to speak in absolute terms it cannot be read so literally." In reaching this conclusion, it relied on *Texas & Pacific R. Co. v. Abilene Cotton Oil Co.*, 204 U.S. 426 (1907). * * *

In this case, unlike *Abilene*, we are not faced with an irreconcilable conflict between the statutory scheme and the persistence of common-law remedies. In *Abilene* the carrier, if subject to both agency and court sanctions, would be put in an untenable position when the agency and a court disagreed on the reasonableness of a rate. The carrier could not abide by the rate filed with the Commission, as required by statute, and also comply with a court's determination that the rate was excessive. The conflict between the court's common-law authority and the agency's ratemaking power was direct and unambiguous. The court in the present case, in contrast, is not called upon to substitute its judgment for the agency's on the reasonableness of a rate—or, indeed, on the reasonableness of any carrier practice. There is no Board requirement that air carriers engage in overbooking or that they fail to disclose that they do so. And any impact on rates that may result from the imposition of tort liability or from practices adopted by a carrier to avoid such liability

---

8. * * *

In April of 1976 the Board announced a [second] proposed rulemaking proceeding with respect to deliberate overbooking and oversales. * * * The Board has decided to re-evaluate existing practices in light of a recent "trend toward a higher rate of oversales" and in light of the fact that oversales "continue to be a significant cause of [consumer] complaints." Among the options to be considered is a requirement that the practice of deliberate overbooking, if allowed to continue, be disclosed to customers.

would be merely incidental. Under the circumstances, the common-law action and the statute are not "absolutely inconsistent" and may coexist, as contemplated by § 1106.

Section 411 of the Act allows the Board, where "it considers that such action * * * would be in the interest of the public," "upon its own initiative or upon complaint by any air carrier, foreign air carrier, or ticket agent," to "investigate and determine whether any air carrier * * * has been or is engaged in unfair or deceptive practices or unfair methods of competition. * * * " Practices determined to be in violation of this section "shall" be the subject of a cease-and-desist order. The Court of Appeals concluded—and respondent does not challenge the conclusion here—that this section does not totally preclude petitioner's common-law tort action. But the Court of Appeals also held * * * that the Board has the power in a § 411 proceeding to approve practices that might otherwise be considered deceptive and thus to immunize carriers from common-law liability.

We cannot agree. No power to immunize can be derived from the language of § 411. And where Congress has sought to confer such power it has done so expressly, as in § 414 of the Act, 49 U.S.C.A. § 1384, which relieves those affected by certain designated orders (not including orders issued under § 411) "from the operations of the 'antitrust laws.' " When faced with an exemptive provision similar to § 414 in *United States Navigation Co. v. Cunard S.S. Co.*, 284 U.S. 474 (1932), this Court dismissed an antitrust action because initial consideration by the agency had not been sought. The Court pointed out that the Act in question was "restrictive in its operation upon some of the activities of common carriers * * * , and permissive in respect of others." Section 411, in contrast, is purely restrictive. It contemplates the elimination of "unfair or deceptive practices" that impair the public interest. Its role has been described in *American Airlines, Inc. v. North American Airlines, Inc.*, [351 U.S. 79 (1956)] at 85:

> " 'Unfair or deceptive practices or unfair methods of competition,' as used in § 411, are broader concepts than the common-law idea of unfair competition. * * * The section is concerned not with punishment of wrongdoing or protection of injured competitors, but rather with protection of the public interest."

As such, § 411 provides an injunctive remedy for vindication of the public interest to supplement the compensatory common-law remedies for private parties preserved by § 1106.

Thus, a violation of § 411, contrary to the Court of Appeals' conclusion, is not coextensive with a breach of duty under the common law. We note that the Board's jurisdiction to initiate an investigation under § 411 is expressly premised on a finding that the "public interest" is involved. * * * Indeed, individual consumers are not even entitled to initiate proceedings under § 411, a circumstance that indicates that congress did not intend to require private litigants to obtain a § 411 determination before they could proceed with the common-law remedies preserved by § 1106.

Section 411 is both broader and narrower than the remedies available at common law.   A cease-and-desist order may issue under § 411 merely on the Board's conclusion, after an investigation determined to be in the public interest, that a carrier is engaged in an "unfair or deceptive practice."   No findings that the practice was intentionally deceptive or fraudulent or that it in fact has caused injury to an individual are necessary. On the other hand, a Board decision that a cease-and-desist order is inappropriate does not represent approval of the practice under investigation.   It may merely represent the Board's conclusion that the serious prohibitory sanction of a cease-and-desist order is inappropriate, that a more flexible approach is necessary.   A wrong may be of the sort that calls for compensation in an injured individual without requiring the extreme remedy of a cease-and-desist order.   Indeed, the Board, in dealing with the problem of overbooking by air carriers, has declined to issue cease-and-desist orders, despite the determination by an examiner in one case that a § 411 violation had occurred.   Instead, the Board has elected to establish boarding priorities and to ensure that passengers will be compensated for being bumped either by a liquidated sum under Board regulations or by resort to a suit for compensatory damages at common law.

In sum, § 411 confers upon the Board a new and powerful weapon against unfair and deceptive practices that injure the public.   But it does not represent the only, or best, response to all challenged carrier actions that result in private wrongs.

The doctrine of primary jurisdiction "is concerned with promoting proper relationships between the courts and administrative agencies charged with particular regulatory duties." * * *

* * * In this case, however, considerations of uniformity in regulation and of technical expertise do not call for prior reference to the Board.

Petitioner seeks damages for respondent's failure to disclose its overbooking practices.   He makes no challenge to any provision in the tariff, and indeed there is no tariff provision or Board regulation applicable to disclosure practices.[13]   Petitioner also makes no challenge * * * to limitations on common-law damages imposed through exculpatory clauses included in a tariff.

Referral of the misrepresentation issue to the Board cannot be justified by the interest in informing the court's ultimate decision with "the expert and specialized knowledge" * * * of the Board.   The action brought by petitioner does not turn on a determination of the reasonable-

---

13. In 1965, the Board proposed a rule requiring carriers to notify individual passengers of overbooked conditions 12 hours prior to the scheduled departure time.   This proposal subsequently was abandoned after industry opposition on the ground that it was excessively rigid and unworkable.

The Board's abandonment of this proposal cannot be read as blanket approval of failure to make a public disclosure of overbooking practices.   The cost of an individual notification program in terms of expense, public relations, and passenger confusion could be prohibitive. But alternative means of disclosure may be significantly less disruptive.   Petitioner suggests, for example, that carrier overbooking practices be included in tariffs, which are required to be available for public inspection. And the Board has approved an innovative approach suggested by Eastern Air Lines, which provides for a system of limited overbooking in which passengers subject to possible denial of boarding are advised at the outset of their status.

ness of a challenged practice—a determination that could be facilitated by an informed evaluation of the economics or technology of the regulated industry.   The standards to be applied in an action for fraudulent misrepresentation are within the conventional competence of the courts, and the judgment of a technically expert body is not likely to be helpful in the application of these standards to the facts of this case.[14]

We are particularly aware that, even where the wrong sought to be redressed is not misrepresentation but bumping itself, which has been the subject of Board consideration and for which compensation is provided in carrier tariffs, the Board has contemplated that there may be individual adjudications by courts in common-law suits brought at the option of the passenger.   The present regulations dealing with the problems of overbooking and oversales were promulgated by the Board in 1967.   They provide for denied boarding compensation to bumped passengers and require each carrier to establish priority rules for seating passengers and to file reports of passengers who could not be accommodated.   The order instituting these regulations contemplates that the bumped passenger will have a choice between accepting denied boarding compensation as "liquidated damages for all damages incurred * * * as a result of the carrier's failure to provide the passenger with confirmed reserved space," or pursuing his or her common-law remedies.   The Board specifically provided for a 30-day period before the specified compensation need be accepted so that the passenger will not be forced to make a decision before "the consequences of denied boarding have occurred and are known." After evaluating the consequences, passengers may choose as an alternative "to pursue their remedy under the common law."

III.

We conclude that petitioner's tort action should not be stayed pending reference to the Board and accordingly the decision of the Court of Appeals on this issue is reversed.   The Court of Appeals did not address the question whether petitioner had introduced sufficient evidence to sustain his claim.   We remand the case for consideration of that question and for further proceedings consistent with this opinion.[19] * * *

MR. JUSTICE WHITE, concurring.

* * *

14. For example, if respondent's overbooking practices were detailed in its tariff and therefore available to the public, a court presented with a claim of misrepresentation based on failure to disclose need not make prior reference to the Board, as it should if presented with a suit challenging the reasonableness of practices detailed in a tariff.   Rather, the court could, applying settled principles of tort law, determine that the tariff provided sufficient notice to the party who brought the suit—as, indeed, petitioner suggests it would.

19. The Court of Appeals specifically remanded for reconsideration of the award of punitive damages on petitioner's claim of fraudulent misrepresentation.   The propriety of that ruling was not challenged in this Court.

As the issues of ultimate liability and damages are not before us, we express no opinion as to their merits.   We conclude above that mere compliance with agency regulations is not sufficient in itself under the Act to exempt a carrier from common-law liability.   We make clear, however, that this conclusion is not intended to foreclose the courts on remand from considering, in relation to other issues in the case, evidence that the Board was fully advised of the practice complained of, and that the carrier had cooperated with the Board.

It may be that under its rulemaking authority the Board would have power to order airline overbooking and to pre-empt recoveries under state law for undisclosed overbooking or for overselling. But it has not done so, at least as yet. It is also unnecessary to stay proceedings on the present state-law claim pending Board action under § 411. Neither an order denying nor one granting relief under that section would foreclose claims based on state law; and there is not present here the additional consideration that a § 411 proceeding would be helpful in resolving, or affecting in some manner, the state-law claim for compensatory and punitive damages. I seriously doubt that any pending or future § 411 case would reveal anything relevant to this case about the Board's view of the propriety of overbooking and of overselling that is not already apparent from prior proceedings concerning those subjects.

Origin and Rationale of Primary Jurisdiction

In the absence of a clear legislative directive that the imposition of public regulation is meant to abrogate private rights, courts historically have been reluctant to hold that longstanding judicial remedies have been abolished by implication. See generally O'Neil, *Public Regulation and Private Rights of Action*, 52 Calif. L. Rev. 231 (1964). Instead, they have sought ways of accommodating the legislature's objective of placing primary responsibility for regulatory decisions in administrative hands without precluding the assertion of preexisting private rights in the courts. The doctrine of primary jurisdiction is the result of judicial attempts "to resolve both the procedural and substantive conflicts inevitably created when there is carved out for an agency an area of original jurisdiction which impinges on the congeries of original jurisdictions of the courts." L. JAFFE, JUDICIAL CONTROL OF ADMINISTRATIVE ACTION 121 (1965). Yet, some cases make administrative jurisdiction effectively exclusive while suggesting that only "primary" jurisdiction is involved. See, e.g., *T.I.M.E., Inc. v. United States*, 359 U.S. 464 (1959).

Although the occasions for applying the doctrine of primary jurisdiction cannot be neatly defined, certain generalizations can be ventured. Generally, a court will focus on the issues raised by a litigant (not always the plaintiff) to determine whether they are of a kind that a particular regulatory agency should resolve. Factual issues, particularly if they require technical understanding or are likely to generate voluminous evidence, are more likely to be held within an agency's primary jurisdiction than are questions of law, unless the latter call for expert understanding. In *Far East Conference v. United States*, 342 U.S. 570, 574–75 (1952), the Supreme Court declared:

> * * * [I]n cases raising issues of fact not within the conventional experiences of judges or cases requiring the exercise of administrative discretion, agencies created by Congress for regulating the subject matter should not be passed over. This is so even though the facts after they have been appraised by specialized competence serve as a premise for legal consequences to be judicially defined. Uniformity and consistency in the regulation of business

entrusted to a particular agency are secured, and the limited functions of review by the judiciary are more rationally exercised, by preliminary resort for ascertaining and interpreting the circumstances underlying legal issues to agencies that are better equipped than courts by specialization, by insight gained through experience, and by more flexible procedure.

A series of well-known cases involving railroads subject to regulation by the ICC depicts the development of the doctrine in the Supreme Court. *Texas and Pacific Railway Co. v. Abilene Cotton Oil Co.*, 204 U.S. 426 (1907), is regularly cited as the foundation of the primary jurisdiction doctrine. The oil company, claiming that the carrier's published rate on file with the Interstate Commerce Commission was "unreasonable," sued in a state court to recover the excess. Section 22 of the Interstate Commerce Act provided that nothing in the Act "shall in any way abridge or alter the remedies now existing at common law or by statute," and it was undisputed that at common law a shipper had a right of action for any "unreasonable" charges exacted by a common carrier. Furthermore, section 9 provided that any person "claiming to be damaged by any common carrier * * * may either make complaint to the Commission * * * or may bring suit * * * for the recovery of the damages for which such common carrier may be liable under the provisions of this act. * * * " In the face of these provisions the Supreme Court held that the shipper's action would not lie. The central ground of its decision was that the congressional scheme for regulating railroad rates was incompatible with numerous and inconsistent judicial determinations of "reasonableness" that would result if shippers could bring suit "without previous action by the Commission."

This latter language, repeated several times in the Court's opinion, misleadingly suggests a qualification of its holding. The Court in substance held that the Act had extinguished the shipper's common law right to sue for unreasonable rates. It did not contemplate a situation in which a shipper might seek an initial ICC determination of reasonableness before proceeding to court to recover damages, for it construed section 9 as authorizing judicial redress only "of such wrongs as can, consistently with the content of the act, be redressed by courts without previous action by the Commission. * * * " The language in section 22 saving common law remedies was in effect repealed *pro tanto*, for the Act "cannot be held to destroy itself."

Several features of *Abilene Cotton* are noteworthy. While the Court did hold that the shipper's common law right had been extinguished (and, impliedly, that section 9 afforded no right to judicial relief), it did so realizing that the Interstate Commerce Act afforded a statutory reparations remedy before the ICC for rates the agency found unreasonable. Thus, the Court in substance concluded that the ICC's jurisdiction to remedy unreasonable rates was not simply "primary," but exclusive. There was obvious potential for inconsistent judicial rulings, as well as rulings contrary to ICC policy if shippers could sue for damages. Moreover, a court determination that a railroad's rates were too high would confront the carrier with a serious dilemma, for under the Act no carrier could lawfully depart from rates on file with the ICC. The Court's reading of section 9 did not erase that provision, because later decisions made clear that shippers could still sue carriers in court for practices, such as charging more than the applicable rate, that ordinarily did not call for an initial ICC determination of legality.

In *Great Northern Railway v. Merchants Elevator Co.*, 259 U.S. 285 (1922), the Supreme Court added a new dimension to the "uniformity" rationale of *Abilene Cotton*. There a shipper brought suit, claiming that the railroad had improperly exacted a special charge for reconsignment of its goods. The Court held that *Abilene* did not preclude suit, because the construction of a written instrument, the carrier's published tariff, presented only a question of law when the words in the instrument "are used in their ordinary meaning." Uniformity of interpretation was assured by the availability of Supreme Court review. Moreover, Justice Brandeis for the Court observed: "Here no fact, evidential or ultimate, is in controversy; and there is no occasion for the exercise of administrative discretion." Id. at 294. Since *Merchants Elevator*, the federal courts have regularly cited the need for administrative expertise as a principal reason for deferring to an agency's primary jurisdiction—witness the Supreme Court's treatment of the "new drug" issue in the *Bentex* case, supra p. 194.

In *United States v. Western Pacific Railway* 352 U.S. 59 (1956), the Court, on its own motion, held that a suit by carriers to recover charges unpaid by the United States (as shipper) should be referred to the ICC. The issue in the case was whether incendiary bombs without fuses were properly billed at the rate for "incendiary bombs"; the government contended that a lower rate for gasoline in drums should apply. Writing for the Court, Justice Harlan concluded that interpretation of the tariff might require appreciation of the cost or other "transportation" factors that the ICC had relied on in recognizing a special rate for incendiary bombs. He suggested that a claim that a tariff should not be interpreted as covering a commodity because of lower costs of carriage was not fundamentally distinguishable from a claim that an applicable rate was "unreasonable," which, under *Abilene Cotton* and *Merchants Elevator*, was clearly for the Commission. (For a recent review of the ICC jurisprudence and the determination that ICC jurisdiction to permit abandonment of the rail lines precludes state law claims for damages for failure to provide service, see *Chicago & Northwestern Transportation Co. v. Kalo Brick & Tile Co.*, 450 U.S. 311 (1981).)

A court's deferral to a regulatory agency's primary jurisdiction may amount to a holding that the agency has exclusive authority to determine the merits of a litigant's claim and afford relief—as in *Abilene Cotton*—or it may simply postpone judicial proceedings until the agency has had an opportunity to pass on one or more questions on which its expert judgment is sought. The cases, moreover, demonstrate that an agency need not have authority to afford the plaintiff complete or indeed any relief for a court to accord it primary jurisdiction. Where the agency lacks authority to grant requested relief, such as money damages, a court may simply stay the case while the plaintiff seeks an administrative determination of issues within agency competence, remaining ready to afford full relief if warranted by the agency's determination and applicable legal principles. See, *e.g.*, *Israel v. Baxter Laboratories, Inc.*, 466 F.2d 272 (D.C. Cir. 1972) (FDA has primary jurisdiction to determine approvability of plaintiff's new drug, but court will decide whether an unlawful conspiracy existed between competitors and FDA officials to prevent its marketing).

In the federal arena, generally speaking, any antitrust action against a regulated common carrier, whether brought by the Department of Justice or by a private plaintiff, will be referred to the responsible regulatory agency. E.g., *Far East Conference v. United States*, supra; *Pan American World Airways, Inc. v. United States*, 371 U.S. 296 (1963); *Laveson v. Trans World Airlines*, 471 F.2d 76 (3rd Cir. 1972). Even in the absence of authority to immunize anticompetitive activity, courts find referral justified either because it is thought appropriate to afford the agency an opportunity initially to assess the competing policies of competition and regulation, or because the regulatory legislation is read as impliedly limiting the operation of the antitrust laws. See generally L. JAFFE, JUDICIAL CONTROL OF ADMINISTRATIVE ACTION 141–51 (1965). Indeed, any antitrust suit against an enterprise whose activities are subject to broad federal regulation may founder initially on primary jurisdiction. See *Ricci v. Chicago Mercantile Exchange*, 409 U.S. 289 (1973) (suit by plaintiff claiming deprivation of seat on exchange violated exchange rules and antitrust laws held within primary jurisdiction of Commodity Exchange Commission). See also *Huron Valley Hospital v. City of Pontiac*, 666 F.2d 1029 (6th Cir. 1981); *Hansen v. Norfolk & Western Railway*, 689 F.2d 707 (7th Cir. 1982).

Primary jurisdiction has also been a recurrent issue in suits by unions or employers to enforce collective agreements falling generally within the ambit of the National Labor Relations Act and, thus, under the aegis of the NLRB. In most such cases, the Board's authority has not been held to preclude immediate resort to judicial enforcement. The numerous exceptions to this generalization, however, should caution against ready acceptance. See, e.g., Cox, *Labor Law Preemption Revisited*, 85 Harv. L. Rev. 1337 (1972); Note, *NLRB Primary Jurisdiction and Hot Cargo Issues Arising in Section 301(a) Actions*, 48 U. Chi. L. Rev. 992 (1981).

Although typically the agency whose jurisdiction is primary has had previous dealings with the defendant's activities, it is the power to regulate rather than past approval of activity that seems determinative. In *Port of Boston Marine Terminal Association v. Rederiaktiebolaget Transatlantic*, 400 U.S. 62 (1970), shipowners challenged the association's shift of demurrage charges for cargo remaining portside beyond five days from consignees to the owners of vessels. While the association itself had received approval from the Federal Maritime Commission in 1964, the new charges had been imposed without notice to or approval by it. And, in *Ricci v. Chicago Mercantile Exchange*, supra, the Commodity

Exchange Commission had not previously evidenced any interest in the plaintiff's claim that the defendants had unlawfully deprived him of his seat on the exchange. The transportation field has produced many leading primary jurisdiction decisions in the context of suits charging unlawful rates, but typically the rates attacked, though on file with the regulatory agency, have not been formally examined or approved. See also *United States v. Joseph G. Moretti, Inc.*, 478 F.2d 418 (5th Cir. 1973), in which the Court dismissed a prosecution for dredging without a permit under the Rivers and Harbors Act and instructed the Corps of Engineers first to dispose of the pending permit application that the defendant had filed many months after dredging had begun. Some of these cases reflect a judicial unwillingness to rule on the legality of activity the agency could later immunize, but as often the court's primary concern is to secure the views of the agency before making its own judgment.

It is unclear whether a litigant must have a *right* to an agency decision before a court will hold that he must first seek an administrative determination. In *Rosado v. Wyman*, 397 U.S. 397 (1970), welfare recipients challenged portions of New York's public assistance laws as inconsistent with the federal Social Security Act. The Department of HEW had already commenced an administrative review of the laws' compatibility, but had reached no decision. The Department declined the district court's invitation to make its views known by participating in the litigation. The Supreme Court rejected the defendants' suggestion that the matter fell within the Department's primary jurisdiction. In refusing to defer action, the Court emphasized that neither the Social Security Act nor HEW regulations authorized the Department to grant relief to recipients of assistance harmed by illegal state action, or, indeed, permitted them to trigger or participate in departmental proceedings to determine compliance. In *Ricci v. Chicago Mercantile Exchange*, supra, by contrast, the Court dismissed the plaintiff's suit in favor of the primary jurisdiction of the Commodity Exchange Commission, even though it acknowledged that the plaintiff could not force the Commission to institute proceedings to inquire into the propriety of the deprivation of his seat and that no statutory or regulatory provision guaranteed him the right to intervene in any proceedings that the Commission chose to initiate. All he could do was report to the Commission his belief that its rules had been violated. The Court's opinion, however, reflects an expectation that the Commission would institute appropriate proceedings if it found any basis for his charges. See also *Weinberger v. Bentex*, supra p. 194.

2. LEGISLATIVE SUPERSESSION OF COMMON LAW RIGHTS

MIDDLESEX COUNTY SEWERAGE AUTHORITY v. NATIONAL SEA CLAMMERS ASSOCIATION

Supreme Court of the United States, 1981.
453 U.S. 1, 101 S.Ct. 2615, 69 L.Ed. 2d 435.

JUSTICE POWELL delivered the opinion of the Court.

In these cases, involving alleged damage to fishing grounds caused by discharges and ocean dumping of sewage and other waste, we are faced with questions concerning the availability of a damages remedy, based either on federal common law or on the provisions of two Acts—the Federal Water Pollution Control Act (FWPCA), as amended, 33 U.S.C. § 1251 *et seq.*, and the Marine Protection, Research, and Sanctuaries Act of 1972 (MPRSA), as amended, 33 U.S.C.A. § 1401 *et seq.*

I

Respondents are an organization whose members harvest fish and shellfish off the coast of New York and New Jersey, and one individual member of that organization.   In 1977, they brought suit in the United States District Court for the District of New Jersey against petitioners— various governmental entities and officials from New York, New Jersey, and the Federal Government.[3]   Their complaint alleged that sewage, sewage "sludge," and other waste materials were being discharged into New York Harbor and the Hudson River by some of the petitioners.   In addition it complained of the dumping of such materials directly into the ocean from maritime vessels.   The complaint alleged that, as a result of these activities, the Atlantic Ocean was becoming polluted, and it made special reference to a massive growth of algae said to have appeared offshore in 1976.   It then stated that this pollution was causing the "collapse of the fishing, clamming and lobster industries which operate in the waters of the Atlantic Ocean."

Invoking a wide variety of legal theories,[6] respondents sought injunctive and declaratory relief of $250 million in compensatory damages, and $250 million in punitive damages.   The District Court granted summary judgment to petitioners on all counts of the complaint.

In holdings relevant here, the District Court rejected respondents' nuisance claim under federal common law, see *Illinois v. Milwaukee*, 406 U.S. 91 (1972), on the ground that such a cause of action is not available to private parties.   With respect to the claims based on alleged violations of the FWPCA, the court noted that respondents had failed to comply with the 60-day notice requirement of the "citizen suit" provision in § 505(b)(1)(A) of the Act.   This provision allows suits under the Act by private citizens, but authorizes only prospective relief, and the citizen plaintiffs first must give notice to the EPA, the State, and any alleged violator.[9] Because respondents did not give the requisite notice, the court re-

---

3. The federal defendants were the Environmental Protection Agency; Russell E. Train, individually and as EPA Administrator; the Army Corps of Engineers; and Martin R. Hoffman, individually and as Secretary of the Army.

6. Respondents based claims on the FWPCA; the MPRSA; federal common law; § 13 of the Rivers and Harbors Appropriation Act of 1899, 33 U.S.C.A. § 407; the National Environmental Policy Act of 1969, 42 U.S.C.A. § 4321 *et seq.*; New York and New Jersey environmental statutes; the Fifth, Ninth, and Fourteenth Amendments to the United States Constitution; 46 U.S.C.A. § 740;

the Federal Tort Claims Act, 28 U.S.C.A. § § 1346(b), 2671 *et seq.*; and state tort law.

9. Section 505 provides, in part:

"(a) Except as provided in subsection (b) of this section, any citizen may commence a civil action on his own behalf—

"(1) against any person (including (i) the United States, and (ii) any other governmental instrumentality or agency to the extent permitted by the eleventh amendment to the Constitution) who is alleged to be in violation of (A) an effluent standard or limitation under this chapter or (B) an order issued by the Adminis-

fused to allow them to proceed with a claim under the Act independent of the citizen-suit provision and based on the general jurisdictional grant in 28 U.S.C.A. § 1331. The court applied the same analysis to respondents' claims under the MPRSA, which contains similar citizen-suit and notice provisions. Finally, the court rejected a possible claim of maritime tort, both because respondents had failed to plead such claim explicitly and because they had failed to comply with the procedural requirements of the federal and state Tort Claims Acts.

*   *   *

The United States Court of Appeals for the Third Circuit reversed as to the claims based on the FWPCA, the MPRSA, the federal common law of nuisance, and maritime tort. 616 F.2d 1222 (1980). With respect to the FWPCA, the court held that failure to comply with the 60-day notice provision in § 505(b)(1)(A), does not preclude suits under the Act in addition to the specific "citizen suits" authorized in § 505. It based this conclusion on the saving clause in § 505(e), preserving "any right which any person (or class of persons) may have under any statute or common law to seek enforcement of any effluent standard or limitation or to seek any other relief." The Court of Appeals then went on to apply our precedents in the area of implied statutory rights of action, and concluded that "Congress intended to permit the federal courts to entertain a private cause of action implied from the terms of the [FWPCA], preserved by the savings clause of the Act, on behalf of individuals or groups of individuals who have been or will be injured by pollution in violation of its terms."

The court then applied this same analysis to the MPRSA, concluding again that the District Court had erred in dismissing respondents' claims under this Act. *   *   *

---

trator or a State with respect to such a standard or limitation, or

"(2) against the Administrator where there is alleged a failure of the Administrator to perform any act or duty under this chapter which is not discretionary with the Administrator.

"The district courts shall have jurisdiction, without regard to the amount in controversy or the citizenship of the parties, to enforce such an effluent standard or limitation, or such an order, or to order the Administrator to perform such act or duty, as the case may be, and to apply any appropriate civil penalties under section 1319(d) of this title.

"(b) No action may be commenced—

"(1) under subsection (a)(1) of this section—

"(A) prior to sixty days after the plaintiff has given notice of the alleged violation (i) to the Administrator, (ii) to the State in which the alleged violation occurs, and (iii) to any alleged violator of the standard, limitation, or order, or

"(B) if the Administrator or State has commenced and is diligently prosecuting a civil or criminal action in a court of the United States, or a State to require compliance with the standard, limitation, or order, but in any such action in a court of the United States any citizen may intervene as a matter of right.

"(2) under subsection (a)(2) of this section prior to sixty days after the plaintiff has given notice of such action to the Administrator, except that such action may be brought immediately after such notification in the case of an action under this section respecting a violation of sections 1316 and 1317(a) of this title. Notice under this subsection shall be given in such manner as the Administrator shall prescribe by regulation." § 505(C)(2), 33 U.S.C.A. § 1365(C)(2).

*   *   *

With respect to the federal common-law nuisance claims, the Court of Appeals rejected the District Court's conclusion that private parties may not bring such claims. * * *

* * * We granted these petitions, limiting review to three questions: (i) whether FWPCA and MPRSA imply a private right of action independent of their citizen-suit provisions, (ii) whether all federal common-law nuisance actions concerning ocean pollution now are pre-empted by the legislative scheme contained in the FWPCA and the MPRSA, and (iii) if not, whether a private citizen has standing to sue for damages under the federal common law of nuisance. We hold that there is no implied right of action under these statutes and that the federal common law of nuisance has been fully pre-empted in the area of ocean pollution.

II

The Federal Water Pollution Control Act was first enacted in 1948. It emphasized state enforcement of water quality standards. When this legislation proved ineffective, Congress passed the Federal Water Pollution Control Act Amendments of 1972, 33 U.S.C.A. § 1251 *et seq*. The Amendments shifted the emphasis to "direct restrictions on discharges" and made it "unlawful for any person to discharge a pollutant without obtaining a permit and complying with its terms." While still allowing for state administration and enforcement under federally approved state plans, the Amendments created various federal minimum effluent standards.

The Marine Protection, Research, and Sanctuaries Act of 1972 sought to create comprehensive federal regulation of the dumping of materials into ocean waters near the United States coastline. Section 1019(a) of the Act requires a permit for any dumping into ocean waters, when the material is transported from the United States or on an American vessel or aircraft. In addition, it requires a permit for the dumping of material transported from outside the United States into the territorial seas or in the zone extending 12 miles from the coastline, "to the extent that it may affect the territorial sea or the territory of the United States."

The exact nature of respondents' claims under these two Acts is not clear, but the claims appear to fall into two categories. The main contention is that the EPA and the Army Corps of Engineers have permitted the New Jersey and New York defendants to discharge and dump pollutants in amounts that are not permitted by the Acts. In addition, they seem to allege that the New York and New Jersey defendants have violated the terms of their permits. The question before us is whether respondents may raise either of these claims in a private suit for injunctive and monetary relief, where such a suit is not expressly authorized by either of these Acts.

It is unnecessary to discuss at length the principles set out in recent decisions concerning the recurring question whether Congress intended to create a private right of action under a federal statute without saying so explicitly. The key to the inquiry is the intent of the Legislature. * * *

These Acts contain unusually elaborate enforcement provisions, conferring authority to sue for this purpose both on government officials and private citizens. The FWPCA, for example, authorizes the EPA Administrator to respond to violations of the Act with compliance orders and civil suits. He may seek a civil penalty of up to $10,000 per day, and criminal penalties also are available. States desiring to administer their own permit programs must demonstrate that state officials possess adequate authority to abate violations through civil or criminal penalties or other means of enforcement. In addition, under § 509(b) "any interested person" may seek judicial review in the United States courts of appeals of various particular actions by the Administrator, including establishment of effluent standards and issuance of permits for discharge of pollutants. * * *

These enforcement mechanisms, most of which have their counterpart under the MPRSA, are supplemented by the express citizen-suit provisions in § 505(a) of the FWPCA and § 105(g) of the MPRSA. These citizen-suit provisions authorize private persons to sue for injunctions to enforce these statutes. Plaintiffs invoking these provisions first must comply with specified procedures—which respondents here ignored— including in most cases 60 days' prior notice to potential defendants.

In view of these elaborate enforcement provisions it cannot be assumed that Congress intended to authorize by implication additional judicial remedies for private citizens suing under MPRSA and FWPCA. As we stated in *Transamerica Mortgage Advisors*, "it is an elemental canon of statutory construction that where a statute expressly provides a particular remedy or remedies, a court must be chary of reading others into it." In the absence of strong indicia of a contrary congressional intent, we are compelled to conclude that Congress provided precisely the remedies it considered appropriate.

As noted above, the Court of Appeals avoided this inference. Discussing the FWPCA, it held that the existence of a citizen-suit provision in § 505(a) does not rule out implied forms of private enforcement of the Act. It arrived at this conclusion by asserting that Congress intended in § 505(a) to create a limited cause of action for "private attorneys general"— "non-injured member[s] of the public" suing to promote the general welfare than to redress an injury to their own welfare. It went on to conclude:

> "A private party who is *injured* by the alleged violation, as these plaintiffs allege they were, has an alternate basis for suit under section 505(e) and the general federal question jurisdiction of the Judicial Code, 28 U.S.C. § 1331 (1976). Section 505(e) is a savings clause that preserves all rights to enforce the Act or seek relief against the Administrator. Coupled with the general federal question jurisdiction it permits this suit to be brought by these parties."

There are at least three problems with this reasoning. First, the language of the saving clause on which the Court of Appeals relied is quite ambiguous concerning the intent of Congress to "preserve" remedies under the FWPCA itself.   It merely states that nothing in the citizen-suit provision "shall restrict any right which any person * * * may have under any statute or common law to seek enforcement of any effluent standard or limitation or to seek any other relief."   It is doubtful that the phrase "any statute" includes the very statute in which this statement was contained.

Moreover, the reasoning on which the Court of Appeals relied is flawed for another reason.   It draws a distinction between "non-injured" plaintiffs who may bring citizen suits to enforce provisions of these Acts, and the "injured" plaintiffs in this litigation who claim a right to sue under the Acts, not by virtue of the citizen-suit provisions, but rather under the language of the saving clauses.   In fact, it is clear that the citizen-suit provisions apply only to persons who can claim some sort of injury and there is, therefore, no reason to infer the existence of a separate right of action for "injured" plaintiffs.   "Citizen" is defined in the citizen-suit section of the FWPCA as "a person or persons having an interest which is or may be adversely affected."   It is clear from the Senate Conference Report that this phrase was intended by Congress to allow suits by all persons possessing standing under this Court's decision in *Sierra Club v. Morton*, 405 U.S. 727 (1972).   See S. Conf. Rep. No. 92–1236, p. 146 (1972).   This broad category of potential plaintiffs necessarily includes both plaintiffs seeking to enforce these statutes as private attorneys general, whose injuries are "non-economic" and probably noncompensable, and persons like respondents who assert that they have suffered tangible economic injuries because of statutory violations.

Finally, the Court of Appeals failed to take account of the rest of the enforcement scheme expressly provided by Congress—including the opportunity for "any interested person" to seek judicial review of a number of EPA actions within 90 days.

The Court of Appeals also applied its reasoning to the MPRSA.   But here again we are persuaded that Congress evidenced no intent to authorize by implication private remedies under these Acts apart from the expressly authorized citizen suits.   The relevant provisions in the MPRSA are in many respects almost identical to those of the FWPCA.   Although they do not expressly limit citizen suits to those who have suffered some injury from a violation of the Act, we are not persuaded by this fact alone that Congress affirmatively intended to imply the existence of a parallel private remedy, after setting out expressly the manner in which private citizens can seek to enjoin violations.

In *Cort v. Ash*, the Court identified several factors that are relevant to the question of implied private remedies.   These include the legislative history.   This history does not lead to a contrary conclusion with respect to implied remedies under either Act.   Indeed, the Report and debates provide affirmative support for the view that Congress intended the limitations imposed on citizen suits to apply to all private suits under these Acts.   Thus, both the structure of the Acts and their legislative history lead us to conclude that Congress intended that private remedies in addition to those expressly provided should not be implied. Where, as here, Congress has made clear that implied private actions are not contemplated, the courts are not authorized to ignore this legislative judgment.

Although the parties have not suggested it, there remains a possible alternative source of *express* congressional authorization of private suits under these Acts. Last Term, in *Maine v. Thiboutot*, 448 U.S. 1 (1980), the Court construed 42 U.S.C.A. § 1983 as authorizing suits to redress violations by state officials of rights created by federal statutes. Accordingly, it could be argued that respondents may sue the municipalities and sewerage boards among the petitioners under the FWPCA and MPRSA by virtue of a right of action created by § 1983.

It is appropriate to reach the question of the applicability of *Maine v. Thiboutot* to this setting, despite the failure of respondents to raise it here or below. This litigation began long before that decision. Moreover, if controlling, this argument would obviate the need to consider whether Congress intended to authorize private suits to enforce these particular federal statutes. The claim brought here arguably falls within the scope of *Maine v. Thiboutot* because it involves a suit by a private party claiming that a federal statute has been violated under color of state law, causing an injury. The Court, however, has recognized two exceptions to the application of § 1983 to statutory violations. In *Pennhurst State School and Hospital v. Halderman*, 451 U.S. 1 (1981), we remanded certain claims for a determination (i) whether Congress had foreclosed private enforcement of that statute in the enactment itself, and (ii) whether the statute at issue there was the kind that created enforceable "rights" under § 1983. In the present case, because we find that Congress foreclosed a § 1983 remedy under these Acts, we need not reach the second question whether these Acts created "rights, privileges, or immunities" within the meaning of § 1983.

When the remedial devices provided in a particular Act are sufficiently comprehensive, they may suffice to demonstrate congressional intent to preclude the remedy of suits under § 1983. * * * As discussed above, the FWPCA and MPRSA do provide quite comprehensive enforcement mechanisms. It is hard to believe that Congress intended to preserve the § 1983 right of action when it created so many specific statutory remedies, including the two citizen-suit provisions. We therefore conclude that the existence of these express remedies demonstrates not only that Congress intended to foreclose implied private actions but also that it intended to supplant any remedy that otherwise would be available under - § 1983.

III

The remaining two issues on which we granted certiorari relate to respondents' federal claims based on the federal common law of nuisance. The principal precedent on which these claims were based is *Illinois v. Milwaukee*, 406 U.S. 91 (1972), where the Court found that the federal courts have jurisdiction to consider the federal common-law issues raised by a suit for injunctive relief by the State of Illinois against various Wisconsin municipalities and public sewerage commission, involving the discharge of sewage into Lake Michigan.   In these cases, we need not decide whether a cause of action may be brought under federal common law by a private plaintiff, seeking damages.   The Court has now held that the federal common law of nuisance in the area of water pollution is entirely pre-empted by the more comprehensive scope of the FWPCA, which was completely revised soon after the decision in *Illinois v. Milwaukee*. See *Milwaukee v. Illinois*, 451 U.S. 304 (1981).

This decision disposes entirely of respondents' federal common-law claims, since there is no reason to suppose that the pre-emptive effect of the FWPCA is any less when pollution of coastal waters is at issue.   To the extent that this litigation involves ocean waters not covered by the FWPCA, and regulated under the MPRSA, we see no cause for different treatment of the pre-emption question.   The regulatory scheme of the MPRSA is no less comprehensive, with respect to ocean dumping, than are analogous provisions of the FWPCA.

We therefore must dismiss the federal common-law claims because their underlying legal basis is now pre-empted by statute.   As discussed above, we also dismiss the claims under the MPRSA and the FWPCA because respondents lack a right of action under those statutes.   We vacate the judgment below with respect to these two claims, and remand for further proceedings.

It is so ordered.

JUSTICE STEVENS, with whom JUSTICE BLACKMUN joins, concurring in the judgment in part and dissenting in part.

* * *

Although I agree with the Court's disposition of the implied-private-right-of-action question in these cases * * * I believe that the Court's appraisal of the intent expressed by Congress in the Federal Water Pollution Control Act Amendments of 1972 and the Marine Protection, Research, and Sanctuaries Act of 1972, with respect to the availability of private remedies under other federal statutes or the federal common law is palpably wrong.

* * *

The Court's holding that Congress decided in the Clean Water Act and the MPRSA to withdraw the express remedy provided by 42 U.S.C.A. § 1983 seems to rest on nothing more that the fact that these statutes provide other express remedies and do not mention § 1983.   Because the enforcement mechanisms provided in the statutes are "quite comprehensive," the Court finds it "hard to believe that Congress intended to preserve the § 1983 right of action. * * * "   There are at least two flaws in this reasoning.   First, the question is not whether Congress "intended to preserve the § 1983 right of action," but rather whether Congress intended to withdraw that right of action.   Second, I find it not at all hard to believe that Congress intended to preserve, or, more precisely, did not intend to withdraw, the § 1983 remedy because Congress made this intention explicit in the language of both statutes and in the relevant legislative history.

I agree with the Court that the remedial provisions of the Clean Water Act and the MPRSA are "quite comprehensive." I cannot agree, however, with the Court's implicit conclusion that this determination ends the inquiry under *Maine v. Thiboutot.* The question that must be answered in determining whether respondents may pursue their claims under § 1983 is whether Congress intended that the remedies provided in the substantive statutes be exclusive. * * * I have no quarrel as a general matter with the proposition that a comprehensive remedial scheme can evidence a congressional decision to preclude other remedies. However, we must not lose sight of the fact that our evaluation of a statute's express remedies is merely a tool used to discern congressional intent; it is not an end in itself. No matter how comprehensive we may consider a statute's remedial scheme to be. Congress is at liberty to leave other remedial avenues open. Express statutory language or clear references in the legislative history will rebut whatever presumption of exclusivity arises from comprehensive remedial provisions. In my judgment, in these cases we are presented with both express statutory language and clear references in the legislative history indicating that Congress did not intend the express remedies in the Clean Water Act and the MPRSA to be exclusive.

Despite their comprehensive enforcement mechanisms, both statutes expressly preserve all legal remedies otherwise available. * * * Respondents' right to proceed under § 1983 in light of these statutory provisions could have been made more plain only had Congress substituted the citation "42 U.S.C.A. § 1983" for the words "any statute" in the saving clauses.

The legislative history of both statutes makes it clear that the saving clauses were intended to mean what they say. The Senate Report on the Clean Water Act states:

> "It should be noted, however, that the section would specifically preserve any rights or remedies under any other law. Thus, if damages could be shown, other remedies would remain available. Compliance with requirements under this Act would not be a defense to a common law action for pollution damages." S. Rep. No. 92–414, 92d Cong., 1st Sess. 81 (1971).

* * * And the corresponding Report on the MPRSA similarly states that the authorization of citizen suits shall not restrict or supersede "any other right to legal action which is afforded the potential litigant in any other statute or the common law." S. Rep. No. 92–451, 92d Cong., 1st Sess. 23–24 (1971). * * *

In my judgment, the Court has failed to uncover "a clear congressional mandate" to withdraw the § 1983 remedy otherwise available to the respondents. Moreover, the statutory language and the legislative history reveal the exact opposite: a clear congressional mandate to preserve all existing remedies, including a private right of action under § 1983.   I therefore respectfully dissent from this portion of the Court's decision.

The effect of the Court's holding in *Milwaukee v. Illinois* was to make the City of Milwaukee's compliance with the requirements of the Clean Water Act a complete defense to a federal common-law nuisance action for pollution damage.   It was, and still is, difficult for me to reconcile that holding with the excerpts from the statutes and the Senate Reports quoted above—particularly the statement:

> "Compliance with requirements under this Act would not be a defense to a common law action for pollution damages."   S. Rep. No. 92–414, 92d Cong., 1st Sess., 81 (1971).

Today the Court pursues the pre-emption rationale of *Milwaukee v. Illinois* to its inexorable conclusion and holds that even noncompliance with the requirements of the Clean Water Act and the MPRSA is a defense to a federal common-law nuisance claim.   Because Justice BLACKMUN has already exposed in detail the flaws in the Court's treatment of this issue, see *Milwaukee v. Illinois*, supra, at 333–347 (dissenting opinion), I merely note that the reasoning in his dissenting opinion in *Milwaukee* applies with special force in this case.

Notes

1. Both the majority and dissenting opinions in *Sea Clammers* rely importantly on *Milwaukee v. Illinois*, 451 U.S. 304 (1981).   There, original proceedings were brought by the State of Illinois, alleging that petitioners—the City of Milwaukee, its Sewerage Commission, Milwaukee County's Metropolitan Sewerage Commission, and other Wisconsin cities—were polluting Lake Michigan.   That pollution resulted from overflows of untreated sewage from petitioners' sewer systems and discharges of inadequately treated sewage from their treatment plants.   In *Illinois v. Milwaukee*, 406 U.S. 91 (1972), the Supreme Court recognized the existence of a federal "common law" which could give rise to a claim for abatement of a nuisance caused by interstate water pollution, but declined to exercise original jurisdiction because of the availability of a lower court action. Accordingly, Illinois filed suit in district court (in which respondent State of Michigan intervened) seeking abatement, under federal common law, of the public nuisance were allegedly created by the petitioners' discharges.   Five months later, Congress passed the Federal Water Pollution Control Act Amendments of 1972, which established a new system of regulation making it illegal to discharge pollutants into the Nation's waters except pursuant to a permit that incorporated as conditions EPA regulations establishing specific effluent limitations.   (Permits are issued either by the EPA or a qualifying state agency, and petitioners operated their sewer systems under permits issued by the Wisconsin Department of Natural Resources (DNR).)

While the federal-court action was pending, DNR brought an action in a Wisconsin state court to compel compliance with the permits' requirements.   The state court entered a judgment requiring discharges from the treatment plants to meet effluent limitations in the permits and establishing a timetable for additional construction to control sewage overflows.   Thereafter, the district court found that the existence of a federal common-law nuisance had been proved and entered a judgment specifying effluent limitations for treated sewage and a construction timetable to eliminate overflows that went considerably beyond the terms of petitioners' permits and the state court's enforcement order. The court of appeals, ruling that the 1972 FWPCA Amendments, Pub. L. No. 92–500, 86 Stat. 816, had not preempted the federal common law of nuisance, upheld the district court's order as to elimination of overflows, but reversed insofar as the district court's effluent limitations on treated sewage were more stringent than those in the petitioners' permits and applicable EPA regulations. 599 F.2d 155 (7th Cir. 1979).

The Supreme Court held that any federal common law right of action had been extinguished by the 1972 Amendments. In his opinion for the Court, Justice Rehnquist emphasized the distinction between decisions concerning the preemption of state law by federal statute and decisions concerning congressional preemption of federal common law (451 U.S. at 316–17):

> Contrary to the suggestions of respondents, the appropriate analysis in determining if federal statutory law governs a question previously the subject of federal common law is not the same as that employed in deciding if federal law pre-empts state law. In considering the latter question " 'we start with the assumption that the historic police powers of the States were not to be superseded by the Federal Act unless that was the clear and manifest purpose of Congress.' " While we have not hesitated to find preemption of state law, whether express or implied, when Congress has so indicated, or when enforcement of state regulations would impair "federal superintendence of the field," our analysis has included "due regard for the presuppositions of our embracing federal system, including the principle of diffusion of power not as a matter of doctrinaire localism but as a promoter of democracy." Such concerns are not implicated in the same fashion when the question is whether federal statutory or federal common law governs, and accordingly the same sort of evidence of a clear and manifest purpose is not required. Indeed, as noted, in cases such as the present "we start with the assumption" that it is for Congress, not federal courts, to articulate the appropriate standards to be applied as a matter of federal law.

After calling attention to the self-consciously comprehensive nature of the 1972 FWPCA Amendments and to the DNR permits which addressed both the general effluent quality and overflow problems that had prompted the lawsuit, Justice Rehnquist's opinion continued (id. at 325):

> The invocation of federal common law by the District Court and the Court of Appeals in the face of congressional legislation supplanting it is peculiarly inappropriate in areas as complex as water pollution control. As the District Court noted:
>
> > "It is well known to all of us that the arcane subject matter of some of the expert testimony in this case was sometimes over the heads of all of us to one height or another. I would certainly be less than candid if I did not acknowledge that my grasp of some of the testimony was less complete than I would like it to be. * * * * "
>
> Not only are the technical problems difficult—doubtless the reason Congress vested authority to administer the Act in administrative agencies possessing the necessary expertise—but the general area is particularly unsuited to the approach inevitable under a regime of federal common law. Congress criticized past approaches to water pollution control as being "sporadic" and "ad hoc," apt characterizations of any judicial approach applying federal common law.

Nor was the Court impressed by arguments based on section 505(e)'s "savings clause," quoted in *Sea Clammers* (id. at 328–29):

Subsection 505(e) is virtually identical to subsections in the citizen-suit provisions of several environmental statutes. The subsection is common language accompanying citizen-suit provisions and we think that it means only that the provision of such suit does not revoke other remedies. It most assuredly cannot be read to mean that the Act as a whole does not supplant formerly available federal common-law actions but only that the particular section authorizing citizen suits does not do so. No one, however, maintains that the citizen-suit provision pre-empts federal common law.

Justice Blackmun, joined by Justices Marshall and Stevens, dissented both from the majority's holding and from its approach (id. at 333–36):

The court's analysis of federal common-law displacement rests, I am convinced on a faulty assumption. In contrasting congressional displacement of the common law with federal pre-emption of state law, the Court assumes that as soon as Congress "addresses a question previously governed" by federal common law, "the need for such an unusual exercise of lawmaking by federal courts disappears." This "automatic displacement" approach is inadequate in two respects. It fails to reflect the unique role federal common law plays in resolving disputes between one State and the citizens or government of another. In addition, it ignores this Court's frequent recognition that federal common law may complement congressional action in the fulfillment of federal policies.

It is well settled that a body of federal common law has survived the decision in *Erie R. Co. v. Tompkins. Erie* made clear that federal courts, as courts of limited jurisdiction, lack general power to formulate and impose their own rules of decision. The Court, however, did not there upset, nor has it since disturbed, a deeply rooted, more specialized federal common law that has arisen to effectuate federal interests embodied either in the Constitution or an Act of Congress.[3] Chief among the federal interests served by this common law are the resolution of interstate disputes and the implementation of national statutory or regulatory policies.

Both before and after *Erie,* the Court has fashioned federal law where the interstate nature of a controversy renders inappropriate the law of either State. When such disputes arise, it is clear under our federal system that laws of one State cannot impose upon the sovereign rights and interests of another. The Constitution, by Art. III, § 2, explicitly extends the judicial power of the United States to controversies between a State and another State or its citizens, and this Court, in equitably resolving such disputes, has developed a body of "what may not improperly be called interstate common law."

Long before the 1972 decision in *Illinois v. Milwaukee,* federal common law enunciated by this Court assured each State the right to be free from unreasonable interference with its natural environment and resources when the interference stems from another State or its citizens. The right to such federal protection is a consequence of each State's entry into the Union and its

---

3. See generally Hill, The Law-Making Power of the Federal Courts: Constitutional Preemption, 67 Colum. L. Rev. 1024, 1026–1042 (1967); Friendly, In Praise of *Erie*—and of the New Federal Common Law, 39 N.Y.U. L. Rev. 383, 405–422 (1964). See also Leybold, Federal Common Law: Judicially Established Effluent Standards as a Remedy in Federal Nuisance Actions, 7 B.C. Env. Aff. L. Rev. 293 (1978).

commitment to the Constitution.   In the words of Justice Holmes, speaking for the Court:

> "When the States by their union made the forcible abatement of outside nuisances impossible to each, they did not thereby agree to submit to whatever might be done.   They did not renounce the possibility of making reasonable demands on the ground of their still remaining *quasi*-sovereign interests; and the alternative to force is a suit in this court."
> *Georgia v. Tennessee Cooper Co.*, 206 U.S. [230, 237 (1907)].

This Court also has applied federal common law where federally created substantive rights and obligations are at stake.   Thus, the Court has been called upon to pronounce common law that will fill the interstices of a pervasively federal framework, or avoid subjecting relevant federal interests to the inconsistencies in the laws of several States.   *Textile Workers v. Lincoln Mills*, 353 U.S. 448 (1957).   If the federal interest is sufficiently strong, federal common law may be drawn upon in settling disputes even though the statute or Constitution alone provides no precise answer to the question posed.

Beyond these general propositions, the dissenters believed that Congress had in the 1972 Amendments evinced an intent not to fully occupy the field of water pollution abatement (451 U.S. at 339–41):

> In my view, the language and structure of the Clean Water Act leave no doubt that Congress intended to preserve the federal common law of nuisance. Section 505(e) of the Act reads:

> > "Nothing in this section shall restrict any right which *any person* (or class of persons) may have under *any statute or common law* to seek enforcement of any effluent standard or limitation *or to seek any other relief* (including relief against the Administrator of a State agency)."   (emphasis added).

The Act specifically defines "person" to include States, and thus embraces respondents Illinois and Michigan.   It preserves their right to bring an action against the governmental entities who are charged with enforcing the statute. Most important, as succinctly stated by the Court of Appeals in this case: "There is nothing in the phrase 'any statute or common law' that suggests that this provision is limited to state common law."   To the best of my knowledge, every federal court that has considered the issue has concluded that, in enacting § 505(e), Congress meant to preserve federal as well as state common law.

> Other sections of the Clean Water Act also support the conclusion that Congress in 1972 had no intention of extinguishing the federal common law of nuisance.   Although the Act established a detailed and comprehensive regulatory system aimed at eliminating the discharge of pollutants into all navigable waters, it did not purport to impose a unitary enforcement structure for abating water pollution.   In particular, Congress expressly provided that the effluent limitations promulgated under the Act do not preclude any State from establishing more stringent limitations.   It also made clear that federal officers or agencies are not foreclosed from adopting or enforcing stricter pollution controls and standards than those required by the Act.

2. The "comprehensive statutory scheme" rationale also extends to the preclusion of *Bivens*-style constitutional claims. In *Bush v. Lucas*, ___U.S.___, 103 S.Ct. 2404 (1983), the Supreme Court held that a NASA employee could not seek damages under the First Amendment for a demotion premised on his publicly critical statements concerning the operations of the George C. Marshall Space Flight Center. Writing for the Court, Justice Stevens noted (103 S.Ct. at 2411):

> This much is established by our prior cases. The federal courts' statutory jurisdiction to decide federal questions confers adequate power to award damages to the victim of a constitutional violation. When Congress provides an alternative remedy, it may, of course, indicate its intent, by statutory language, by clear legislative history, or perhaps even by the statutory remedy itself, that the Court's power should not be exercised. In the absence of such a congressional directive, the federal courts must make the kind of remedial determination that is appropriate for a common-law tribunal, paying particular heed, however, to any special factors counselling hesitation before authorizing a new kind of federal litigation.

He then went on to find those "special factors" determinative of the result in the case before him (id. at 2416–17):

> Given the history of the development of civil service remedies and the comprehensive nature of the remedies currently available, it is clear that the question we confront today is quite different from the typical remedial issue confronted by a common-law court. The question is not what remedy the court should provide for a wrong that would otherwise go unredressed. It is whether an elaborate remedial system that has been constructed step by step, with careful attention to conflicting policy considerations, should be augmented by the creation of a new judicial remedy for the constitutional violation at issue. That question obviously cannot be answered simply by noting that existing remedies do not provide complete relief for the plaintiff. The policy judgment should be informed by a thorough understanding of the existing regulatory structure and the respective costs and benefits that would result from the addition of another remedy for violations of employee's First Amendment rights.
>
> The costs associated with the review of disciplinary decisions are already significant—not only in monetary terms, but also in the time and energy of managerial personnel who must defend their decisions. The Government argues that supervisory personnel are already more hesitant than they should be in administering discipline, because the review that ensues inevitably makes the performance of their regular duties more difficult. Whether or not this assessment is accurate, it is quite probable that if management personnel face the added risk of personal liability for decisions that they believe to be a correct response to improper criticism of the agency, they would be deterred from imposing discipline in future cases. In all events, Congress is in a far better position than a court to evaluate the impact of a new species of litigation between federal employees on the efficiency of the civil service. Not only has Congress developed considerable familiarity with balancing governmental efficiency and the rights of employees, but it also may inform itself through fact-finding procedures such as hearings that are not available to the courts.

Nor is there any reason to discount Congress' ability to make an even-handed assessment of the desirability of creating a new remedy for federal employees who have been demoted or discharged for expressing controversial views.   Congress has a special interest in informing itself about the efficiency and morale of the Executive Branch.   In the past it has demonstrated its awareness that lower-level government employees are a valuable source of information, and that supervisors might improperly attempt to curtail their subordinates' freedom of expression.

Appendix A

THE CONSTITUTION OF THE UNITED STATES OF AMERICA

ARTICLE I

Section 1. All legislative Powers herein granted shall be vested in a Congress of the United States, which shall consist of a Senate and House of Representatives. * * *

Section 7. All Bills for raising Revenue shall originate in the House of Representatives; but the Senate may propose or concur with Amendments as on other Bills.

Every Bill which shall have passed the House of Representatives and the Senate, shall, before it become a Law, be presented to the President of the United States; If he approve he shall sign it, but if not he shall return it, with his Objections to that House in which it shall have originated, who shall enter the Objections at large on their Journal, and proceed to reconsider it. If after such Reconsideration two thirds of that House shall agree to pass the Bill, it shall be sent, together with the Objections, to the other House, by which it shall likewise be reconsidered, and if approved by two thirds of that House, it shall become a Law. * * * If any Bill shall not be returned by the President within ten Days (Sunday excepted) after it shall have been presented to him, the Same shall be a Law, in like Manner as if he had signed it, unless the Congress by their Adjournment prevent its Return, in which Case it shall not be a Law.

Every Order, Resolution, or Vote to which the Concurrence of the Senate and House of Reprensentatives may be necessary (except on a question of Adjournment) shall be presented to the President of the United States; and before the Same shall take Effect, shall be approved by him, or being disapproved by him, shall be repassed by two thirds of the Senate and House of Representatives, according to the Rules and Limitations prescribed in the Case of a Bill.

Section 8. The Congress shall have Power To lay and collect Taxes, Duties, Imposts and Excises, to pay the Debts and provide for the common Defense and general Welfare of the United States; * * *

To regulate Commerce with foreign Nations, and among the several States, and with the Indian Tribes;

935

To establish an uniform Rule of Naturalization, and uniform Laws on the subject of Bankruptcies throughout the United States; * * *

To constitute Tribunals inferior to the supreme Court; * * *

To make all Laws which shall be necessary and proper for carrying into Execution the foregoing Powers, and all other Powers vested by this Constitution in the Goverment of the United States, or in any Department or Officer thereof. * * *

ARTICLE II

Section 1. The executive Power shall be vested in a President of the United States of America. * * *

Section 2. The President shall be commander in Chief of the Army and Navy of the United States * * * ; he may require the Opinion, in writing, of the principal Officer in each of the executive Departments, upon any Subject relating to the Duties of their respective Offices * * * .

He shall have Power, by and with the Advice and Consent of the Senate, to make Treaties, provided two thirds of the Senators present concur; and he shall nominate, and by and with the Advice and Consent of the Senate, shall appoint Ambassadors, other public Ministers and Consuls, Judges of the Supreme Court, and all other Officers of the United States, whose Appointments are not herein otherwise provided for, and which shall be established by Law: but the Congress may by Law vest the Appointment of such inferior Officers, as they think proper, in the President alone, in the Courts of Law, or in the Heads of Departments.

The President shall have Power to fill up all Vacancies that may happen during the Recess of the Senate, by granting Commissions which shall expire at the End of their next Session.

Section 3. He shall from time to time give to the Congress Information of the State of the Union, and recommend to their Consideration such Measures as he shall judge necessary and expedient; * * * he shall take Care that the Laws be faithfully executed, and shall Commission all the Officers of the United States.

Section 4. The President, Vice President and all Civil Officers of the United States, shall be removed from Office on Impeachment for, and Conviction of, Treason, Bribery, or other high Crimes and Misdemeanors.

ARTICLE III

Section 1. The judicial Power of the United States, shall be vested in one supreme Court, and in such inferior Courts as the Congress may from time to time ordain and establish. The Judges, both of the supreme and inferior Courts, shall hold their Offices during good Behaviour, and shall, at stated Times, receive for their Services, a Compensation, which shall not be diminished during their Continuance in Office.

Section 2. The judicial Power shall extend to all Cases, in Law and Equity, arising under this Constitution, the Laws of the United States, and Treaties made, or which shall be made, under their Authority;—to all Cases affecting Ambassadors, other public Ministers and Consuls;—to all

Cases of admiralty and maritime Jurisdiction;—to Controversies to which the United States shall be a Party;—to Controversies between two or more States;—between a State and Citizens of another State;—between Citizens of different States;—between Citizens of the same State claiming Lands under Grants of different States, and between a State, or the Citizens thereof, and foreign States, Citizens or Subjects.

In all Cases affecting Ambassadors, other public Ministers and Consuls, and those in which a State shall be Party, the Supreme Court shall have original Jurisdiction. In all the other Cases before mentioned, the supreme Court shall have appellate Jurisdiction, both as to Law and Fact, with such Exceptions, and under such Regulations as the congress shall make. * * *

ARTICLE V

The Congress, whenever two thirds of both Houses shall deem it necessary, shall propose Amendments to this Constitution, or, on the Application of the Legislatures of two thirds of the several States, shall call a Convention for proposing Amendments, which, in either Case, shall be valid to all Intents and Purposes, as Part of this Constitution, when ratified by the Legislatures of three fourths of the several States, or by Conventions in three fourths thereof, as the one or the other Mode of Ratification may be proposed by the Congress; Provided that no Amendment which may be made prior to the Year One thousand eight hundred and eight shall in any Manner affect the first and fourth Clauses in the Ninth Section of the first Article; and that no State, without its Consent, shall be deprived of its equal Suffrage in the Senate.

ARTICLE VI

* * *

This Constitution, and the Laws of the United States which shall be made in Pursuance thereof; and all Treaties made, or which shall be made, under the Authority of the United States, shall be the supreme Law of the Land; and the Judges in every State shall be bound thereby, any Thing in the Constitution or Laws of any State to the Contrary notwithstanding.

* * *

AMENDMENT I [1791]

Congress shall make no law respecting an establishment of religion, or prohibiting the free exercise thereof; or abridging the freedom of speech, or of the press; or the right of the people peaceably to assemble, and to petition the Government for a redress of grievances.

* * *

AMENDMENT IV [1791]

The right of the people to be secure in their persons, houses, papers, and effects, against unreasonable searches and seizures, shall not be violated, and no Warrants shall issue, but upon probable cause, supported by oath or affirmation, and particularly describing the place to be searched, and the persons or things to be seized.

AMENDMENT V [1791]

No person shall be held to answer for a capital, or otherwise infamous crime, unless on a presentment or indictment of a Grand Jury, except in cases arising in the land or naval forces, or in the Militia, when in actual service in time of war or public danger; nor shall any person be subject for the same offence to be twice put in jeopardy of life or limb; nor shall be compelled in any criminal case to be a witness against himself, nor be deprived of life, liberty, or property, without due process of law; nor shall private property be taken for public use, without just compensation.

AMENDMENT VI [1791]

In all criminal prosecutions, the accused shall enjoy the right to a speedy and public trial, by an impartial jury of the State and district wherein the crime shall have been committed, which district shall have been previously ascertained by law, and to be informed of the nature and cause of the accusation; to be confronted with the witnesses against him; to have compulsory process for obtaining Witnesses in his favor, and to have the Assistance of Counsel for his defense.

AMENDMENT IX [1791]

The enumeration in the Constitution, of certain rights, shall not be construed to deny or disparge others retained by the people.

AMENDMENT X [1791]

The powers not delegated to the United States by the Constitution, nor prohibited by it to the States, are reserved to the States respectively, or to the people.

AMENDMENT XI [1798]

The Judicial power of the United States shall not be construed to extend to any suit in law or equity, commenced or prosecuted against one of the United States by Citizens of another State, or by Citizens or Subjects of any Foreign State.

AMENDMENT XIV [1868]

Section 1. All persons born or naturalized in the United States, and subject to the jurisdiction thereof, are citizens of the United States and of the State wherein they reside. No State shall make or enforce any law which shall abridge the privileges or immunities of citizens of the United States; nor shall any State deprive any person of life, liberty, or property, without due process of law; nor deny to any person within its jurisdiction the equal protection of the laws.

* * *

Section 5. The Congress shall have power to enforce, by appropriate legislation, the provisions of this article.

Appendix B

SELECTED PROVISIONS OF TITLE 28, U.S.C.

---

§ 1331. Federal Question; Amount in Controversy; Costs

The district courts shall have original jurisdiction of all civil actions arising under the Constitution, laws, or treaties of the United States.

§ 1343. Civil Rights and Elective Franchise

(a) The district courts shall have original jurisdiction of any civil action authorized by law to be commenced by any person:

(1) To recover damages for injury to his person or property, or because of the deprivation of any right or privilege of a citizen of the United States, by any act done in furtherance of any conspiracy mentioned in section 1985 of Title 42;

(2) To recover damages from any person who fails to prevent or to aid in preventing any wrongs mentioned in section 1985 of Title 42 which he had knowledge were about to occur and power to prevent;

(3) To redress the deprivation, under color of any State law, statute, ordinance, regulation, custom or usage, of any right, privilege or immunity secured by the Constitution of the United States or by any Act of Congress providing for equal rights of citizens or of all persons within the jurisdiction of the United States;

(4) To recover damages or to secure equitable or other relief under Act of Congress providing for the protection of civil rights, including the right to vote.

* * *

§ 1346. United States as Defendant

(a) The district courts shall have original jurisdiction, concurrent with the Court of Claims, of:

(1) Any civil action against the United States for the recovery of any internal-revenue tax alleged to have been erroneously or illegally assessed or collected, or any penalty claimed to have been collected without authority or any sum alleged to have been excessive or in any manner wrongfully collected under the internal-revenue laws;

939

(2) Any other civil action or claim against the United States, not exceeding $10,000 in amount, founded either upon the Constitution, or any Act of Congress, or any regulation of an executive department, or upon any express or implied contract with the United States, or for liquidated or unliquidated damages in cases not sounding in tort. * * *

(b) Subject to the provisions of chapter 171 of this title, the district courts, together with the United States District Court for the District of the Canal Zone and the District Court of the Virgin Islands, shall have exclusive jurisdiction of civil actions on claims against the United States, for money damages, accruing on and after January 1, 1945, for injury or loss of property, or personal injury or death caused by the negligent or wrongful act or omission of any employee of the Government while acting within the scope of his office or employment, under circumstances where the United States, if a private person, would be liable to the claimant in accordance with the law of the place where the act or omission occurred.

(c) The jurisdiction conferred by this section includes jurisdiction of any set-off, counterclaim, or other claim or demand whatever on the part of the United States against any plaintiff commencing an action under this section.

* * *

(f) The district courts shall have exclusive original jurisdiction of civil actions under section 2490a to quiet title to an estate or interest in real property in which an interest is claimed by the United States. * * *

§ 1361. Action to Compel an Officer of the United States to Perform His Duty

The district courts shall have original jurisdiction of any action in the nature of mandamus to compel an officer or employee of the United States or any agency thereof to perform a duty owed to the plaintiff. * * *

§ 1391. Venue Generally

(a) A civil action wherein jurisdiction is founded only on diversity of citizenship may, except as otherwise provided by law, be brought only in the judicial district where all plaintiffs or all defendants reside, or in which the claim arose.

(b) A civil action wherein jurisdiction is not founded solely on diversity of citizenship may be brought only in the judicial district where all defendants reside, or in which the claim arose, except as otherwise provided by law.

(c) A corporation may be sued in any judicial district in which it is incorporated or licensed to do business or is doing business, and such judicial district shall be regarded as the residence of such corporation for venue purposes.

(d) An alien may be sued in any district.

(e) A civil action in which a defendant is an officer or employee of the United States or any agency thereof acting in his official capacity or under color of legal authority, or an agency of the United States, or the United States, may, except as otherwise provided by law, be brought in any judicial district in which (1) a defendant in the action resides, or (2) the cause of action arose, or (3) any real property involved in the action is situated, or (4) the plaintiff resides if no real property is involved in the action. Additional persons may be joined as parties to any such action in accordance with the Federal Rules of Civil Procedure and with such other venue requirements as would be applicable if the United States or one of its officers, employees, or agencies were not a party.

The summons and complaint in such an action shall be served as provided by the Federal rules of Civil Procedure except that the delivery of the summons and complaint to the officer or agency as required by the rules may be made by certified mail beyond the territorial limits of the district in which the action is brought. * * *

§ 2674. Liability of United States

The United States shall be liable, respecting the provisions of this title relating to tort claims, in the same manner and to the same extent as a private individual under like circumstances, but shall not be liable for interest prior to judgment or for punitive damages.

§ 2680. Exceptions

The provisions of this chapter and section 1346(b) of this title shall not apply to—

(a) Any claim based upon an act or omission of an employee of the Government, exercising due care, in the execution of a statute or regulation, whether or not such statute or regulation be valid, or based upon the exercise or performance or the failure to exercise or perform a discretionary function or duty on the part of a federal agency or an employee of the Government, whether or not the discretion involved be abused.

* * *

(h) Any claim arising out of assault, battery, false imprisonment, false arrest, malicious prosecution, abuse of process, libel, slander, misrepresentation, deceit, or interference with contract rights: *Provided*, That, with regard to acts or omissions of investigative or law enforcement officers of the United States Government, the provisions of this chapter and section 1346(b) of this title shall apply to any claim arising, on or after the date of the enactment of this provisco, out of assault, battery, false imprisonment, false arrest, abuse of process, or malicious prosecution.   For the purpose of this subsection, "investigative or law enforcement officer" means any officer of the United States who is empowered by law to execute searches, to seize evidence, or to make arrests for violations of Federal law. * * *

*

Appendix C

ADMINISTRATIVE PROCEDURE ACT
5 U.S.C., Chapter 5

§ 551. Definitions

For the purpose of this subchapter—

(1) "agency" means each authority of the Government of the United States, whether or not it is within or subject to review by another agency, but does not include—

    (A) the Congress;

    (B) the courts of the United States;

    (C) the governments of the territories or possessions of the United States;

    (D) the government of the District of Columbia, or except as to the requirements of section 552 of this title—

    (E) agencies composed of representatives of the parties or of representatives of organizations of the parties to the disputes determined by them;

    (F) courts martial and military commissions;

    (G) military authority exercised in the field in time of war or in occupied territory; or

    (H) functions conferred by sections 1738, 1739, 1743, and 1744 of title 12; chapter 2 of title 41; or sections 1622, 1884, 1891-1902, and former section 1641(b) (2), of title 50, appendix;

(2) "person" includes an individual, partnership, corporation, association, or public or private organization other than an agency;

(3) "party" includes a person or agency named or admitted as a party, or properly seeking and entitled as of right to be admitted as a party, in an agency proceeding, and a person or agency admitted by an agency as a party for limited purposes;

(4) "rule" means the whole or a part of an agency statement of general or particular applicability and future effect designed to implement, interpret, or prescribe law or policy or describing the organization, procedure, or practice requirements of an agency and includes the approval or prescription for the future of rates, wages, corporate or financial structures

943

or reorganization thereof, prices, facilities, appliances, services or allowances therefor or of valuations, costs, or accounting, or practices bearing on any of the foregoing;

(5) "rule making" means agency process for formulating, amending, or repealing a rule;

(6) "order" means the whole or a part of a final disposition, whether affirmative, negative, injunctive, or declaratory in form, of an agency in a matter other than rule making but including licensing;

(7) "adjudication" means agency process for the formulation of an order;

(8) "license" includes the whole or a part of an agency permit, certificate, approval, registration, charter, membership, statutory exemption or other form of permission;

(9) "licensing" includes agency process respecting the grant, renewal, denial, revocation, suspension, annulment, withdrawal, limitation, amendment, modification, or conditioning of a license;

(10) "sanction" includes the whole or a part of an agency—

(A) prohibition, requirement, limitation, or other condition affecting the freedom of a person;

(B) withholding of relief;

(C) imposition of penalty or fine;

(D) destruction, taking, seizure, or withholding of property;

(E) assessment of damages, reimbursement, restitution, compensation, costs, charges, or fees;

(F) requirement, revocation, or suspension of a license; or

(G) taking other compulsory or restrictive action; (11) "relief" includes the whole or a part of an agency—

(A) grant of money, assistance, license, authority, exemption, exception, privilege, or remedy;

(B) recognition of a claim, right, immunity, privilege, exemption, or exception; or

(C) taking of other action on the application or petition of, and beneficial to, a person;

(12) "agency proceeding" means an agency process as defined by paragraphs (5), (7), and (9) of this section;

(13) "agency action" includes the whole or a part of an agency rule, order, license, sanction, relief, or the equivalent or denial thereof, or failure to act; and

(14) "ex parte communication" means an oral or written communication not on the public record with respect to which reasonable prior notice to all parties is not given, but it shall not include requests for status reports on any matter or proceeding covered by this subchapter.

§ 552. Public Information; Agency Rules, Opinions, Orders, Records, and Proceedings [Freedom of Information Act]

(a) Each agency shall make available to the public information as follows:

(1) Each agency shall separately state and currently publish in the Federal Register for the guidance of the public—

(A) descriptions of its central and field organization and the established places at which, the employees (and in the case of a uniformed service, the members) from whom, and the methods whereby, the public may obtain information, make submittals or requests, or obtain decisions;

(B) statements of the general course and method by which its functions are channeled and determined, including the nature and requirements of all formal and informal procedures available;

(C) rules of procedure, descriptions of forms available or the places at which forms may be obtained, and instructions as to the scope and contents of all papers, reports, or examinations;

(D) substantive rules of general applicability adopted as authorized by law, and statements of general policy or interpretations of general applicability formulated and adopted by the agency; and

(E) each amendment, revision, or repeal of the foregoing.

Except to the extent that a person has actual and timely notice of the terms thereof, a person may not in any manner be reuqired to resort to, or be adversely affected by, a matter required to be published in the Federal Register and not so published. For the purpose of this paragraph, matter reasonably available to the class of persons affected thereby is deemed published in the Federal Register when incorporated by reference therein with the approval of the Director of the Federal Register.

(2) Each agency, in accordance with published rules, shall make available for public inspection and copying—

(A) final opinions, including concurring and dissenting opinions, as well as orders, made in the adjudication of cases;

(B) those statements of policy and interpretations which have been adopted by the agency and are not published in the Federal Register; and

(C) administrative staff manuals and instructions to staff that affect a member of the public;

unless the materials are promptly published and copies offered for sale. To the extent required to prevent a clearly unwarranted invasion of personal privacy, an agency may delete identifying details when it makes available or publishes an opinion, statement of policy, interpretation, or staff manual or instruction. However, in each case the justification for the deletion shall be explained fully in writing. Each agency shall also maintain and make available for public inspection and copying current indexes providing identifying information to the public as to any matter issued, adopted, or promulgated after July 4, 1967, and required by this paragraph to be made available or published. Each agency shall promptly publish, quarterly or more frequently, and distribute (by sale or otherwise) copies of each index or supplements thereto unless it determines by order published in the Federal Register that the publication would be unnecessary and impracticable, in which case the agency shall nonetheless provide copies of such index on request at a cost not to exceed the direct cost of duplication. A final order, opinion, statement of policy, interpretation, or staff manual or instruction that affects a member of the public may be relied on, used, or cited as precedent by an agency against a party other than an agency only if—

> (i) it has been indexed and either made available or published as provided by this paragraph; or

> (ii) the party has actual and timely notice of the terms thereof.

(3) Except with respect to the records made available under paragraphs (1) and (2) of this subsection, each agency, upon any request for records which (A) reasonably describes such records and (B) is made in accordance with published rules stating the time, place, fees (if any), and procedures to be followed, shall make the records promptly available to any person.

(4) (A) In order to carry out the provisions of this section, each agency shall promulgate regulations, pursuant to notice and receipt of public comment, specifying a uniform schedule of fees applicable to all constituent units of such agency. Such fees shall be limited to reasonable standard charges for document search and duplication and provide for recovery of only the direct costs of such search and duplication. Documents shall be furnished without charge or at a reduced charge where the agency determines that waiver or reduction of the fee is in the public interest because furnishing the information can be considered as primarily benefiting the general public.

(B) On complaint, the district court of the United States in the district in which the complainant resides, or has his principal place of business, or in which the agency records are situated, or in the District of Columbia, has jurisdiction to enjoin the agency from withholding agency records and to order the production of any agency records improperly withheld from the complainant. In such a case the court shall determine the matter de novo, and may examine the contents of such agency records in camera to determine whether such records or any part thereof shall be withheld under any of the exemptions set forth in subsection (b) of this section, and the burden is on the agency to sustain its action.

(C) Notwithstanding any other provision of law, the defendant shall serve an answer or otherwise plead to any complaint made under this subsection within thirty days after service upon the defendant of the pleading in which such complaint is made, unless the court otherwise directs for good cause shown.

(D) Except as to cases the court considers of greater importance, proceedings before the district court, as authorized by this subsection and appeals therefrom, take precedence on the docket over all cases and shall be assigned for hearing and trial or for argument at the earliest practicable date and expedited in every way.

(E) The court may assess against the United States reasonable attorney fees and other litigation costs reasonably incurred in any case under this section in which the complainant has substantially prevailed.

(F) Whenever the court orders the production of any agency record, improperly withheld from the complainant and assesses against the United States reasonable attorney fees and other litigation costs, and the court additionally issues a written finding that the circumstances surrounding the withholding raise questions whether agency personnel acted arbitrarily or capriciously with respect to the withholding, the Special Counsel shall promptly initiate a proceeding to determine whether disciplinary action is warranted against the officer or employee who was primarily responsible for the withholding.   The Special Counsel, after investigation and consideration of the evidence submitted, shall submit its findings and recommendations to the administrative authority of the agency concerned and shall send copies of the findings and recommendations to the officer or employee or his representative.   The administrative authority shall take the corrective action that the Special Counsel recommends.

(G) In the event of noncompliance with the order of the court, the district court may punish for contempt the responsible employee, and in the case of a uniformed service, the responsible member.

(5) Each agency having more than one member shall maintain and make available for public inspection a record of the final votes of each member in every agency proceeding.

(6) (A) Each agency, upon any request for records made under paragraph (1), (2), or (3) of this subsection, shall—

(i) determine within ten days (excepting Saturdays, Sundays and legal public holidays) after the receipt of any such request whether to comply with such request and shall immediately notify the person making such request of such determination and the reasons therefor, and of the right of such person to appeal to the head of the agency any adverse determination; and

(ii) make a determination with respect to any appeal within twenty days (excepting Saturdays, Sundays, and legal public holidays) after the receipt of such appeal.   If on appeal the denial of the request for records is in whole or in part upheld, the agency shall notify the person making such request of the provisions for judicial review of that determination under paragraph (4) of this subsection.

(B) In unusual circumstances as specified in this subparagraph, the time limits prescribed in either clause (i) or clause (ii) of subparagraph (A) may be extended by written notice to the person making such request setting forth the reasons for such extensison and the date on which a determination is expected to be dispatched. No such notice shall specify a date that would result in an extension for more than ten working days. As used in this subparagraph, "unusual circumstances" means, but only to the extent reasonably necessary to the proper processing of the particular request—

(i) the need to search for and collect the requested records from field facilities or other establishments that are separate from the office processing the request;

(ii) the need to search for, collect, and appropriately examine a voluminous amount of separate and distinct records which are demanded in a single request; or

(iii) the need for consultation, which shall be conducted with all practicable speed, with another agency having a substantial interest in the determination of the request or among two or more components of the agency having substantial subject-matter interest therein.

(C) Any person making a request to any agency for records under paragraph (1), (2), or (3) of this subsection shall be deemed to have exhausted his administrative remedies with respect to such request if the agency fails to comply with the applicable time limit provisions of this paragraph. If the Government can show exceptional circumstances exist and that the agency is exercising due diligence in responding to the request, the court may retain jurisdiction and allow the agency additional time to complete its review of the records. Upon any determination by an agency to comply with a request for records, the records shall be made promptly available to such person making such request. Any notification of denial of any request for records under this subsection shall set forth the names and titles or positions of each person responsible for the denial of such request.

(b) This section does not apply to matters that are—

(1) (A) specifically authorized under criteria established by an Executive order to be kept secret in the interest of national defense or foreign policy and (B) are in fact properly classified pursuant to such Executive order;

(2) related solely to the internal personnel rules and practices of an agency;

(3) specifically exempted from disclosure by statute (other than section 552b of this title), provided that such statute (A) requires that the matters be withheld from the public in such a manner as to leave no discretion on the issue, or (B) establishes particular criteria for withholding or refers to particular types of matters to be withheld;

(4) trade secrets and commercial or financial information obtained from a person and privileged or confidential;

(5) inter-agency or intra-agency memorandums or letters which would not be available by law to a party other than an agency in litigation with the agency;

(6) personnel and medical files and similar files the disclosure of which would constitute a clearly unwarranted invasion of personal privacy;

(7) investigatory records compiled for law enforcement purposes, but only to the extent that the production of such records would (A) interfere with enforcement proceedings, (B) deprive a person of a right to a fair trial or an impartial adjudication, (C) constitute an unwarranted invasion of personal privacy, (D) disclose the identity of a confidential source and, in the case of a record compiled by a criminal law enforcement authority in the course of a criminal investigation or by an agency conducting a lawful national security intelligence investigation, confidential information furnished only by the confidential source, (E) disclose investigative technique and procedures, or (F) endanger the life or physical safety of law enforcement personnel;

(8) contained in or related to examination, operating, or condition reports prepared by, on behalf of, or for the use of an agency responsible for the regulation or supervision of financial institutions; or

(9) geological and geophysical information and data, including maps, concerning wells.

Any reasonably segregable portion of a record shall be provided to any person requesting such record after deletion of the portions which are exempt under this subsection.

(c) This section does not authorize withholding of information or limit the availability of records to the public, except as specifically stated in this section. This section is not authority to withhold information from Congress.

(d) On or before March 1 of each calendar year, each agency shall submit a report covering the preceding calendar year to the Speaker of the House of Representatives and President of the Senate for referral to the appropriate committees of the Congress. The report shall include—

(1) the number of determinations made by such agency not to comply with requests for records made to such agency under subsection (a) and the reasons for each such determination;

(2) the number of appeals made by persons under subsection (a)(6), the result of such appeals, and the reason for the action upon each appeal that results in a denial of information;

(3) the names and titles or positions of each person responsible for the denial of records requested under this section, and the number of instances of participation for each;

(4) the results of each proceeding conducted pursuant to subsection (a)(4)(F), including a report of the disciplinary action taken against the officer or employee who was primarily responsible for improperly withholding records or an explanation of why disciplinary action was not taken;

(5) a copy of every rule made by such agency regarding this section;

(6) a copy of the fee schedule and the total amount of fees collected by the agency for making records available under this section; and

(7) such other information as indicates efforts to administer fully this section.

The Attorney General shall submit an annual report on or before March 1 of each calendar year which shall include for the prior calendar year a listing of the number of cases arising under this section, the exemption involved in each case, the disposition of such case, and the cost, fees, and penalties assessed under subsections (a)(4)(E), (F), and (G). Such report shall also include a description of the efforts undertaken by the Department of Justice to encourage agency compliance with this section.

(e) For purposes of this section, the term "agency" as defined in section 551(1) of this title includes any executive department, military department, Government corporation, Government controlled corporation, or other establishment in the executive branch of the Government (including the Executive Office of the President), or any independent regulatory agency.

[5 U.S.C.A. § 552a, The Privacy Protection Act, is omitted.]

§ 552b. Open Meetings [Government in the Sunshine Act]

(a) For purposes of this section—

(1) the term "agency" means any agency, as defined in section 552(e) of this title, headed by a collegial body composed of two or more individual members, a majority of whom are appointed to such position by the President with the advice and consent of the Senate, and any subdivision thereof authorized to act on behalf of the agency;

(2) the term "meeting" means the deliberations of at least the number of individual agency members required to take action on behalf of the agency where such deliberations determine or result in the joint conduct or disposition of official agency business, but does not include deliberations required or permitted by subsection (d) or (e); and

(3) the term "member" means an individual who belongs to a collegial body heading an agency.

(b) Members shall not jointly conduct or dispose of agency business other than in accordance with this section. Except as provided in subsection (c), every portion of every meeting of an agency shall be open to public observation.

(c) Except in a case where the agency finds that the public interest requires otherwise, the second sentence of subsection (b) shall not apply to any portion of an agency meeting, and the requirements of subsections (d) and (e) shall not apply to any information pertaining to such meeting otherwise required by this section to be disclosed to the public, where the agency properly determines that such portion or portions of its meeting or the disclosure of such information is likely to—

(1) disclose matters that are (A) specifically authorized under criteria established by an Executive order to be kept secret in the interests of national defense or foreign policy and (B) in fact properly classified pursuant to such Executive order;

(2) relate solely to the internal personnel rules and practices of an agency;

(3) disclose matters specifically exempted from disclosure by statute (other than section 552 of this title), provided that such statute (A) requires that the matters be withheld from the public in such a manner as to leave no discretion on the issue, or (B) establishes particular criteria for withholding or refers to particular types of matters to be withheld;

(4) disclose trade secrets and commercial or financial information obtained from a person and privileged or confidential;

(5) involve accusing any person of a crime, or formally censuring any person;

(6) disclose information of a personal nature where disclosure would constitute a clearly unwarranted invasion of personal privacy;

(7) disclose investigatory records compiled for law enforcement purposes, or information which if written would be contained in such records, but only to the extent that the production of such records or information would (A) interfere with enforcement proceedings, (B) deprive a person of a right to a fair trial or an impartial adjudication, (C) constitute an unwarranted invasion of personal privacy, (D) disclose the identity of a confidential source and, in the case of a record compiled by a criminal law enforcement authority in the course of a criminal investigation, or by an agency conducting a lawful national security intelligence investigation, confidential information furnished only by the confidential source, (E) disclose investigative techniques and procedures, or (F) endanger the life or physical safety of law enforcement personnel;

(8) disclose information contained in or related to examination, operating, or condition reports prepared by, on behalf of, or for the use of an agency responsible for the regulation or supervision of financial institutions;

(9) disclose information the premature disclosure of which would—

(A) in the case of an agency which regulates currencies, securities, commodities, or financial institutions, be likely to (i) lead to significant financial speculation in currencies, securities, or commodities, or (ii) significantly endanger the stability of any financial institution; or

(B) in the case of any agency, be likely to significantly frustrate implementation of a proposed agency action,
except that subparagraph (B) shall not apply in any instance where the agency has already disclosed to the public the content or nature of its proposed action, or where the agency is required by law to make such

disclosure on its own initiative prior to taking final agency action on such proposal; or

(10) specifically concern the agency's issuance of a subpoena, or the agency's participation in a civil action or proceeding, an action in a foreign court or international tribunal, or an arbitration, or the initiation, conduct, or disposition by the agency of a particular case of formal agency adjudication pursuant to the procedures in section 554 of this title or otherwise involving a determination on the record after opportunity for a hearing.

(d)(1) Action under subsection (c) shall be taken only when a majority of the entire membership of the agency (as defined in subsection (a)(1)) votes to take such action.   A separate vote of the agency members shall be taken with respect to each agency meeting a portion or portions of which are proposed to be closed to the public pursuant to subsection (c), or with respect to any information which is proposed to be withheld under subsection (c).   A single vote may be taken with respect to a series of meetings, a portion or portions of which are proposed to be closed to the public, or with respect to any information concerning such series of meetings, so long as each meeting in such series involves the same particular matters and is scheduled to be held no more than thirty days after the initial meeting in such series.   The vote of each agency member participating in such vote shall be recorded and no proxies shall be allowed.

(2) Whenever any person whose interests may be directly affected by a portion of a meeting requests that the agency close such portion to the public for any of the reasons referred to in paragraph (5), (6), or (7) of subsection (c), the agency, upon request of any one of its members, shall vote by recorded vote whether to close such meeting.

(3) Within one day of any vote taken pursuant to paragraph (1) or (2), the agency shall make publicly available a written copy of such vote reflecting the vote of each member on the question.   If a portion of a meeting is to be closed to the public, the agency shall, within one day of the vote taken pursuant to paragraph (1) or (2) of this subsection, make publicly available a full written explanation of its action closing the portion together with a list of all persons expected to attend the meeting and their affiliation.

(4) Any agency, a majority of whose meetings may properly be closed to the public pursuant to paragraph (4), (8), (9)(A), or (10) of subsection (c), or any combination thereof, may provide by regulation for the closing of such meetings or portions thereof in the event that a majority of the members of the agency votes by recorded vote at the beginning of such meeting, or portion thereof, to close the exempt portion or portions of the meeting, and a copy of such vote, reflecting the vote of each member on the question, is made available to the public.   The provisions of paragraphs (1), (2), and (3) of this subsection and subsection (e) shall not apply to any portion of a meeting to which such regulations apply: *Provided*, That the agency shall, except to the extent that such information is exempt from disclosure under the provi-

sions of subsection (c), provide the public with public announcement of the time, place, and subject matter of the meeting and of each portion thereof at the earliest practicable time.

(e)(1) In the case of each meeting, the agency shall make public announcement, at least one week before the meeting, of the time, place, and subject matter of the meeting, whether it is to be open or closed to the public, and the name and phone number of the official designated by the agency to respond to requests for information about the meeting. Such announcement shall be made unless a majority of the members of the agency determines by a recorded vote that agency business requires that such meeting be called at an earlier date, in which case the agency shall make public announcement of the time, place, and subject matter of such meeting, and whether open or closed to the public, at the earliest practicable time.

(2) The time or place of a meeting may be changed following the public announcement required by paragraph (1) only if the agency publicly announces such change at the earliest practicable time. The subject matter of a meeting, or the determination of the agency to open or close a meeting, or portion of a meeting, to the public, may be changed following the public announcement required by this subsection only if (A) a majority of the entire membership of the agency determines by a recorded vote that agency business so requires and that no earlier announcement of the change was possible, and (B) the agency publicly announces such change and the vote of each member upon such change at the earliest practicable time.

(3) Immediately following each public announcement required by this subsection, notice of the time, place, and subject matter of a meeting, whether the meeting is open or closed, any change in one of the preceding, and the name and phone number of the official designated by the agency to respond to requests for information about the meeting, shall also be submitted for publication in the Federal Register.

(f)(1) For every meeting closed pursuant to paragraphs (1) through (10) of subsection (c), the General Counsel or chief legal officer of the agency shall publicly certify that, in his or her opinion, the meeting may be closed to the public and shall state each relevant exemptive provision. A copy of such certification, together with a statement from the presiding officer of the meeting setting forth the time and place of the meeting, and the persons present, shall be retained by the agency. The agency shall maintain a complete transcript or electronic recording adequate to record fully the proceedings of each meeting, or portion of a meeting, closed to the public, except that in the case of a meeting, or portion of a meeting, closed to the public pursuant to paragraph (8), (9)(A), or (10) of subsection (c), the agency shall maintain either such a transcript or recording, or a set of minutes. Such minutes shall fully and clearly describe all matters discussed and shall provide a full and accurate summary of any actions taken, and the reasons therefor, including a description of each of the views expressed on any item and the record of any rollcall vote (reflecting the vote of each member on the question). All documents considered in connection with any action shall be identified in such minutes.

(2) The agency shall make promptly available to the public, in a place easily accessible to the public, the transcript, electronic recording, or minutes (as required by paragraph (1)) of the discussion of any item on the agenda, or of any item of the testimony of any witness received at the meeting, except for such item or items of such discussion or testimony as the agency determines to contain information which may be withheld under subsection (c). Copies of such transcript, or minutes, or a transcription of such recording disclosing the identity of each speaker, shall be furnished to any person at the actual cost of duplication or transcription. The agency shall maintain a complete verbatim copy of the transcript, a complete copy of the minutes, or a complete electronic recording of each meeting, or portion of a meeting, closed to the public, for a period of at least two years after such meeting, or until one year after the conclusion of any agency proceeding with respect to which the meeting or portion was held, whichever occurs later.

(g) Each agency subject to the requirements of this section shall, within 180 days after the date of enactment of this section, following consultation with the Office of the Chairman of the Administrative Conference of the United States and published notice in the Federal Register of at least thirty days and opportunity for written comment by any person, promulgate regulations to implement the requirements of subsections (b) through (f) of this section. Any person may bring a proceeding in the United States District Court for the District of Columbia to require an agency to promulgate such regulations if such agency has not promulgated such regulations within the time period specified herein. Subject to any limitations of time provided by law, any person may bring a proceeding in the United States Court of Appeals for the District of Columbia to set aside agency regulations issued pursuant to this subsection that are not in accord with the requirements of subsections (b) through (f) of this section and to require the promulgation of regulations that are in accord with such subsections.

(h)(1) The district courts of the United States shall have jurisdiction to enforce the requirements of subsections (b) through (f) of this section by declaratory judgment, injunctive relief, or other relief as may be appropriate. Such actions may be brought by any person against an agency prior to, or within sixty days after, the meeting out of which the violation of this section arises, except that if public announcement of such meeting is not initially provided by the agency in accordance with the requirements of this section, such action may be instituted pursuant to this section at any time prior to sixty days after any public announcement of such meeting. Such actions may be brought in the district court of the United States for the district in which the agency meeting is held or in which the agency in question has its headquarters, or in the District Court for the District of Columbia. In such actions a defendant shall serve his answer within thirty days after the service of the complaint. The burden is on the defendant to sustain his action. In deciding such cases the court may examine in camera any portion of the transcript, electronic recording, or minutes of a meeting closed to the public, and may take such additional evidence as it deems necessary. The court, having due regard for orderly administration and the public interest, as well as the interests of the parties, may grant such equitable relief as it deems appropriate, including granting an injunction against future violations of this section or ordering the agency to make available to the public such portion of the transcript, recording, or minutes of a meeting as is not authorized to be withheld under subsection (c) of this section.

(2) Any Federal court otherwise authorized by law to review agency action may, at the application of any person properly participating in the proceeding pursuant to other applicable law, inquire into violations by the agency of the requirements of this section and afford such relief as it deems appropriate. Nothing in this section authorizes any Federal court having jurisdiction solely on the basis of paragraph (1) to set aside, enjoin, or invalidate any agency action (other than an action to close a meeting or to withhold information under this section) taken or discussed at any agency meeting out of which the violation of this section arose.

(i) The court may assess against any party reasonable attorney fees and other litigation costs reasonably incurred by any other party who substantially prevails in any action brought in accordance with the provisions of subsection (g) or (h) of this section, except that costs may be assessed against the plaintiff only where the court finds that the suit was initiated by the plaintiff primarily for frivolous or dilatory purposes. In the case of assessment of costs against an agency, the costs may be assessed by the court against the United States.

(j) Each agency subject to the requirements of this section shall annually report to Congress regarding its compliance with such requirements, including a tabulation of the total number of agency meetings open to the public, the total number of meetings closed to the public, the reasons for closing such meetings, and a description of any litigation brought against the agency under this section, including any costs assessed against the agency in such litigation (whether or not paid by the agency).

(k) Nothing herein expands or limits the present rights of any person under section 552 of this title, except that the exemptions set forth in subsection (c) of this section shall govern in the case of any request made pursuant to section 552 to copy or inspect the transcripts, recordings, or minutes described in subsection (f) of this section. The requirements of chapter 33 of title 44, United States Code, shall not apply to the transcripts, recordings, and minutes described in subsection (f) of this section.

(l) This section does not constitute authority to withhold any information from Congress, and does not authorize the closing of any agency meeting or portion thereof required by any other provision of law to be open.

(m) Nothing in this section authorizes any agency to withhold from any individual any record, including transcripts, recording, or minutes required by this section, which is otherwise accessible to such individual under section 552a of this title.

§ 553. Rule Making

(a) This section applies, accordingly to the provisions thereof, except to the extent that there is involved—

(1) a military or foreign affairs function of the United States; or

(2) a matter relating to agency management or personnel or to public property, loans, grants, benefits, or contracts.

(b) General notice of proposed rule making shall be published in the Federal Register, unless persons subject thereto are named and either personally served or otherwise have actual notice thereof in accordance with law.   The notice shall include—

(1) a statement of the time, place, and nature of public rule making proceedings;

(2) reference to the legal authority under which the rule is proposed; and

(3) either the terms or substance of the proposed rule or a description of the subjects and issues involved.

Except when notice or hearing is required by statute, this subsection does not apply—

(A) to interpretative rules, general statements of policy, or rules of agency organization, procedure, or practice; or

(B) when the agency for good cause finds (and incorporates the finding and a brief statement of reasons therefor in the rules issued) that notice and public procedure thereon are impracticable, unnecessary, or contrary to the public interest.

(c) After notice required by this section, the agency shall give interested persons an opportunity to participate in the rule making through submission of written data, views, or arguments with or without opportunity for oral presentation.   After consideration of the relevant matter presented, the agency shall incorporate in the rules adopted a concise general statement of their basis and purpose.   When rules are required by statute to be made on the record after opportunity for an agency hearing, sections 556 and 557 of this title apply instead of this subsection.

(d) The required publication or service of a substantive rule shall be made not less than 30 days before its effective date, except—

(1) a substantive rule which grants or recognizes an exemption or relieves a restriction;

(2) interpretative rules and statements of policy; or

(3) as otherwise provided by the agency for good cause found and published with the rule.

(e) Each agency shall give an interested person the right to petition for the issuance, amendment, or repeal of a rule.

§ 554. Adjudications

(a) This section applies, according to the provisions thereof, in every case of adjudication required by statute to be determined on the record after opportunity for an agency hearing, except to the extent that there is involved—

(1) a matter subject to a subsequent trial of the law and the facts de novo in a court;

(2) the selection or tenure of an employee, except an administrative law judge appointed under section 3105 of this title;

(3) proceedings in which decisions rest solely on inspections, tests, or elections;

(4) the conduct of military or foreign affairs functions;

(5) cases in which an agency is acting as an agent for a court; or

(6) the certification of worker representatives.

(b) Persons entitled to notice of an agency hearing shall be timely informed of—

(1) the time, place, and nature of the hearing;

(2) the legal authority and jurisdiction under which the hearing is to be held; and

(3) the matters of fact and law asserted.

When private persons are the moving parties, other parties to the proceeding shall give prompt notice of issues controverted in fact or law; and in other instances agencies may by rule require responsive pleading.   In fixing the time and place for hearings, due regard shall be had for the convenience and necessity of the parties or their representatives.

(c) The agency shall give all interested parties opportunity for—

(1) the submission and consideration of facts, arguments, offers of settlement, or proposals of adjustment when time, the nature of the proceeding, and the public interest permit; and

(2) to the extent that the parties are unable so to determine a controversy by consent, hearing and decision on notice and in accordance with sections 556 and 557 of this title.

(d) The employee who presides at the reception of evidence pursuant to section 556 of this title shall make the recommended decision or initial decision required by section 557 of this title, unless he becomes unavailable to the agency.   Except to the extent required for the disposition of ex parte matters as authorized by law, such an employee may not—

(1) consult a person or party on a fact in issue, unless on notice and opportunity for all parties to participate; or

(2) be responsible to or subject to the supervision or direction of an employee or agent engaged in the performance of investigative or prosecuting functions for an agency.

An employee or agent engaged in the performance of investigative or prosecuting functions for an agency in a case may not, in that or a factually related case, participate or advise in the decision, recommended decision, or agency review pursuant to section 557 of this title, except as witness or counsel in public proceedings. This subsection does not apply—

(A) in determining applications for initial licenses;

(B) to proceedings involving the validity or application of rates, facilities, or practices of public utilities or carriers; or

(C) to the agency or a member or members of the body comprising the agency.

(e) The agency, with like effect as in the case of other orders, and in its sound discretion, may issue a declaratory order to terminate a controversy or remove uncertainty.

§ 555. Ancillary Matters

(a) This section applies, according to the provisions thereof, except as otherwise provided by this subchapter.

(b) A person compelled to appear in person before an agency or representative thereof is entitled to be accompanied, represented, and advised by counsel or, if permitted by the agency, by other qualified representative. A party is entitled to appear in person or by or with counsel or other duly qualified representative in an agency proceeding. So far as the orderly conduct of public business permits, an interested person may appear before an agency or its responsible employees for the presentation, adjustment, or determination of an issue, request, or controversy in a proceeding, whether interlocutory, summary, or otherwise, or in connection with an agency function. With due regard for the convenience and necessity of the parties or their representatives and within a reasonable time, each agency shall proceed to conclude a matter presented to it. This subsection does not grant or deny a person who is not a lawyer the right to appear for or represent others before an agency or in an agency proceeding.

(c) Process, requirement of a report, inspection, or other investigative act or demand may not be issued, made, or enforced except as authorized by law. A person compelled to submit data or evidence is entitled to retain or, on payment of lawfully prescribed costs, procure a copy or transcript thereof, except that in a non-public investigatory proceeding the witness may for good cause be limited to inspection of the official transcript of his testimony.

(d) Agency subpoenas authorized by law shall be issued to a party on request and, when required by rules of procedure, on a statement or showing of general relevance and reasonable scope of the evidence sought. On contest, the court shall sustain the subpoena or similar process or demand to the extent that it is found to be in accordance with law. In a proceeding for enforcement, the court shall issue an order requiring the appearance of the witness or the production of the evidence or data within a reasonable time under penalty of punishment for contempt in cases of contumacious failure to comply.

(e) Prompt notice shall be given of the denial in whole or in part of a written application, petition, or other request of an interested person made in connection with any agency proceeding. Except in affirming a prior denial or when the denial is self-explanatory, the notice shall be accompanied by a brief statement of the grounds for denial.

§ 556. Hearings; Presiding Employees; Powers and Duties; Burden of Proof; Evidence; Record as Basis of Decision

(a) This section applies, according to the provisions thereof, to hearings required by section 553 or 554 of this title to be conducted in accordance with this section.

(b) There shall preside at the taking of evidence—

(1) the agency;

(2) one or more members of the body which comprises the agency; or

(3) one or more administrative law judges appointed under section 3105 of this title.

This subchapter does not supersede the conduct of specified classes of proceedings, in whole or in part, by or before boards or other employees specially provided for by or designated under statute. The functions of presiding employees and of employees participating in decisions in accordance with section 557 of this title shall be conducted in an impartial manner. A presiding or participating employee may at any time disqualify himself. On the filing in good faith of a timely and sufficient affidavit of personal bias or other disqualification of a presiding or participating employee, the agency shall determine the matters as a part of the record and decision in the case.

(c) Subject to published rules of the agency and within its powers, employees presiding at hearings may—

(1) administer oaths and affirmations;

(2) issue subpoenas authorized by law;

(3) rule on offers of proof and receive relevant evidence;

(4) take depositions or have depositions taken when the ends of justice would be served;

(5) regulate the course of the hearing;

(6) hold conferences for the settlement or simplification of the issues by consent of the parties;

(7) dispose of procedural requests or similar matters;

(8) make or recommend decisions in accordance with section 557 of this title; and

(9) take other action authorized by agency rule consistent with this subchapter.

(d) Except as otherwise provided by statute, the proponent of a rule or order has the burden of proof. Any oral or documentary evidence may be received, but the agency as a matter of policy shall provide for the exclusion of irrelevant, immaterial, or unduly repetitious evidence. A sanction may not be imposed or rule or order issued except on consideration of the whole record or those parts thereof cited by a party and supported by and in accordance with the reliable, probative, and substantial evidence. The agency may, to the extent consistent with the interests of justice and the policy of the underlying statutes administered by the agency, consider a violation of section 557(d) of this title sufficient grounds for a decision adverse to a party who has knowingly committed such violation or knowingly caused such violation to occur. A party is entitled to present his case or defense by oral or documentary evidence, to submit rebuttal evidence, and to conduct such cross-examination as may be required for a full and true disclosure of the facts. In rule making or determining claims for money or benefits or applications for initial licenses an agency may, when a party will not be prejudiced thereby, adopt procedures for the submission of all or part of the evidence in written form.

(e) The transcript of testimony and exhibits, together with all papers and requests filed in the proceeding, constitutes the exclusive record for decision in accordance with section 557 of this title and, on payment of lawfully prescribed costs, shall be made available to the parties. When an agency decision rests on official notice of a material fact not appearing in the evidence in the record, a party is entitled, on timely request, to an opportunity to show the contrary.

§ 557. Initial Decisions; Conclusiveness; Review by Agency; Submissions by Parties; Contents of Decisions; Record

(a) This section applies, according to the provisions thereof, when a hearing is required to be conducted in accordance with section 556 of this title.

(b) When the agency did not preside at the reception of the evidence, the presiding employee or, in cases not subject to section 554(d) of this title, an employee qualified to preside at hearings pursuant to section 556 of this title, shall initially decide the case unless the agency requires, either in specific cases or by general rule, the entire record to be certified to it for decision. When the presiding employee makes an initial decision, that decision then becomes the decision of the agency without further proceedings unless there is an appeal to, or review on motion of, the agency within time provided by rule. On appeal from or review of the initial decision, the agency has all the powers which it would have in making the initial decision except as it may limit the issues on notice or by rule. When the agency makes the decision without having presided at the reception of the evidence, the presiding employee or an employee qualified to preside at hearings pursuant to section 556 of this title shall first recommend a decision, except that in rule making or determining application for initial licenses—

(1) instead thereof the agency may issue a tentative decision or one of its responsible employees may recommend a decision; or

(2) this procedure may be omitted in a case in which the agency finds on the record that due and timely execution of its functions imperatively and unavoidably so requires.

(c) Before a recommended, initial, or tentative decision, or a decision on agency review of the decision of subordinate employees, the parties are entitled to a reasonable opportunity to submit for the consideration of the employees participating in the decisions—

(1) proposed finding and conclusions; or

(2) exceptions to the decisions or recommended decisions of subordinate employees or to tentative agency decisions; and

(3) supporting reasons for the exceptions or proposed findings or conclusions.

The record shall show the ruling on each finding, conclusion, or exception presented. All decisions, including initial, recommended, and tentative decisions, are a part of the record and shall include a statement of—

(A) findings and conclusions, and the reasons or basis therefor, on all the material issues of fact, law, or discretion presented on the record; and

(B) the appropriate rule, order, sanction, relief, or denial thereof.

(d)(1) In any agency proceeding which is subject to subsection (a) of this section, except to the extent required for the disposition of ex parte matters as authorized by law—

(A) no interested person outside the agency shall make or knowingly cause to be made to any member of the body comprising the agency, administrative law judge, or other employee who is or may reasonably be expected to be involved in the decisional process of the proceeding, an ex parte communication relevant to the merits of the proceeding;

(B) no member of the body comprising the agency, administrative law judge, or other employee who is or may reasonably be expected to be involved in the decisional process of the proceeding, shall make or knowingly cause to be made to any interested person outside the agency an ex parte communication relevant to the merits of the proceeding;

(C) a member of the body comprising the agency, administrative law judge, or other employee who is or may reasonably be expected to be involved in the decisional process of such proceeding who receives, or who makes or knowingly causes to be made, a communication prohibited by this subsection shall place on the public record of the proceeding:

(i) all such written communications;

(ii) memoranda stating the substance of all such oral communications; and

(iii) all written responses, and memoranda stating the substance of all oral responses, to the materials described in clauses (i) and (ii) of this subparagraph;

(D) upon receipt of a communication knowingly made or knowingly caused to be made by a party in violation of this subsection, the agency, administrative law judge, or other employee presiding at the hearing may, to the extent consistent with the interests of justice and the policy of the underlying statutes, require the party to show cause why his claim or interest in the proceeding should not be dismissed, denied, disregarded, or otherwise adversely affected on account of such violation; and

(E) the prohibitions of this subsection shall apply beginning at such time as the agency may designate, but in no case shall they begin to apply later than the time at which a proceeding is noticed for hearing unless the person responsible for the communication has knowledge that it will be noticed, in which case the prohibitions shall apply beginning at the time of his acquisition of such knowledge.

(2) This subsection does not constitute authority to withhold information from Congress.

§ 558. Imposition of Sanctions; Determination of Applications for Licenses; Suspension, Revocation, and Expiration of Licenses

(a) This section applies, according to the provisions thereof, to the exercise of a power or authority.

(b) A sanction may not be imposed or a substantive rule or order issued except with jurisdiction delegated to the agency and as authorized by law.

(c) When application is made for a license, required by law, the agency, with due regard for the rights and privileges of all the interested parties or adversely affected persons and within a reasonable time, shall set and complete proceedings required to be conducted in accordance with sections 556 and 557 of this title or other proceedings required by law and shall make its decision. Except in cases of willfulness or those in which public health, interest, or safety requires otherwise, the withdrawal, suspension, revocation, or annulment of a license is lawful only if, before the institution of agency proceedings therefor, the licensee has been given—

(1) notice by the agency in writing of the facts or conduct which may warrant the action; and

(2) opportunity to demonstrate or achieve compliance with all lawful requirements.

When the licensee has made timely and sufficient application for a renewal or a new license in accordance with agency rules, a license with reference to an activity of a continuing nature does not expire until the application has been finally determined by the agency.

§ 559. Effect on Other Laws; Effect of Subsequent Statute

This subchapter, chapter 7, and sections 1305, 3105, 3344, 4301(2)(E), 5372 and 7521 of this title, and the provisions of section 5335(a)(B) of this title that relate to administrative law judges, do not limit or repeal additional requirements imposed by statute or otherwise recognized by law. Except as otherwise required by law, requirements or privileges relating to evidence or procedure apply equally to agencies and persons.

Each agency is granted the authority necessary to comply with the requirements of this subchapter through the issuance of rules or otherwise. Subsequent statute may not be held to supersede or modify this subchapter, chapter 7, sections 1305, 3105, 3344, 4301(2)(E), 5372 or 7521 of this title, or the provisions of section 5335(a)(B) of this title that relate to hearing examiners, except to the extent that it does so expressly.

CHAPTER 7—JUDICIAL REVIEW

§ 701. Application; Definitions

(a) This chapter applies, according to the provisions thereof, except to the extent that—

(1) statutes preclude judicial review; or

(2) agency action is committed to agency discretion by law.

[handwritten margin note: NOT SHARP DISTINCTION]

(b) For the purpose of this chapter—

(1) "agency" means each authority of the Government of the United States, whether or not it is within or subject to review by another agency, but does not include—

(A) the Congress;

(B) the courts of the United States;

(C) the governments of the territories or possessions of the United States;

(D) the government of the District of Columbia;

(E) agencies composed of representatives of the parties or of representatives of organizations of the parties to the disputes determined by them;

(F) courts martial and military commissions;

(G) military authority exercised in the field in time of war or in occupied territory; or

(H) functions conferred by sections 1738, 1739, 1743, and 1744 of title 12; chapter 2 of title 41; or sections 1622, 1884, 1891-1902, and former section 1641(b)(2), of title 50, appendix; and

(2) "person", "rule", "order", "license", "sanction", "relief", and "agency action" have the meanings given them by section 551 of this title.

§ 702. Right of Review

A person suffering legal wrong because of agency action, or adversely affected or aggrieved by agency action within the meaning of a relevant statute, is entitled to judicial review thereof. An action in a court of the United States seeking relief other than money damages and stating a claim that an agency or an officer or employee thereof acted or failed to act in an official capacity or under color of legal authority shall not be dismissed nor relief therein be denied on the ground that it is against the United States or that the United States is an indispensable party. The United States may be named as a defendant in any such action, and a judgment or decree may be entered against the United States: *Provided,* That any mandatory or injuctive decree shall specify the Federal officer or officers (by name or by title), and their successors in office, personally responsible for compliance. Nothing herein (1) affects other limitations on judicial review or the power or duty of the court to dismiss any action or deny relief on any other appropriate legal or equitable ground; or (2) confers authority to grant relief if any other statute that grants consent to suit expressly or impliedly forbids the relief which is sought.

§ 703. Form and Venue of Proceeding

The form of proceeding for judicial review is the special statutory review proceeding relevant to the subject matter in a court specified by statute or, in the absence or inadequacy thereof, any applicable form of legal action, including actions for declaratory judgments or writs of prohibitory or mandatory injunction or habeas corpus, in a court of competent jurisdiction. If no special statutory review proceeding is applicable, the action for judicial review may be brought against the United States, the agency by its official title, or the appropriate officer. Except to the extent that prior, adequate, and exclusive opportunity for judicial reivew is provided by law, agency action is subject to judicial review in civil or criminal proceedings for judicial enforcement.

§ 704. Actions Reviewable

Agency action made reviewable by statute and final agency action for which there is no adequate remedy in a court are subject to judicial review. A preliminary, procedural, or intermediate agency action or ruling not directly reviewable is subject to review on the review of the final agency action. Except as otherwise expressly required by statute, agency action otherwise final is final for the purposes of this section whether or not there has been presented or determined an application for a declaratory order, for any form of reconsideration, or, unless the agency otherwise requires by rule and provides that the action meanwhile is inoperative, for an appeal to superior agency authority.

§ 705. Relief Pending Review

When an agency finds that justice so requires, it may postpone the effective date of action taken by it, pending judicial review. On such conditions as may be required and to the extent necessary to prevent irreparable injury, the reviewing court, including the court to which a case may be taken on appeal from or on application for certiorari or other writ to a reviewing court, may issue all necessary and appropriate process to postpone the effective date of an agency action or to preserve status or rights pending conclusion of the review proceedings.

§ 706. Scope of Review

To the extent necessary to decision and when presented, the reviewing court shall decide all relevant questions of law, interpret constitutional and statutory provisions, and determine the meaning or applicablility of the terms of an agency action. The reviewing court shall—

Substantial Evidence – Evidence that is accurately a substantial basis of fact from which a fact in issue can be reasonably inferred.

(1) compel agency action unlawfully withheld or unreasonably delayed; and

(2) hold unlawful and set aside agency action, findings, and conclusions found to be—

(A) arbitrary, capricious, an abuse of discretion, or otherwise not in accordance with law;

(B) contrary to constitutional right, power, privilege, or immunity;

(C) in excess of statutory jurisdiction, authority, or limitations, or short of statutory right;

(D) without observance of procedure required by law;

(E) unsupported by substantial evidence in a case subject to section 556 and 557 of this title or otherwise reviewed on the record of an agency hearing provided by statute; or

(F) unwarranted by the facts to the extent that the facts are subject to trial de novo by the reviewing court.

In making the foregoing determinations, the court shall review the whole record or those parts of it cited by a party, and due account shall be taken of the rule of prejudicial error.

------

§ 3105. Appointment of Administrative Law Judges

Each agency shall appoint as many administrative law judges as are necessary for proceedings required to be conducted in accordance with sections 556 and 557 of this title. Administrative law judges shall be assigned to cases in rotation so far as practicable, and may not perform duties inconsistent with their duties and responsibilities as administrative law judges.

§ 7521. Actions Against Administrative Law Judges

(a) An action may be taken against an administrative law judge appointed under section 3105 of this title by the agency in which the administrative law judge is employed only for good cause established and determined by the Merit Systems Protection Board on the record after opportunity for hearing before the Board.

(b) The actions covered by this section are—

(1) a removal;

(2) a suspension;

(3) a reduction in grade;

(4) a reduction in pay; and

(5) a furlough of 30 days or less;

but do not include—

(A) a suspension or removal under section 7532 of this title;

(B) a reduction-in-force action under section 3502 of this title; or

(C) any action initiated under section 1206 of this title.

§ 5372. Administrative Law Judges

Administrative law judges appointed under section 3105 of this title are entitled to pay prescribed by the Office of Personnel Management independently of agency recommendations or ratings and in accordance with subchapter III of this chapter and chapter 51 of this title.

§ 3344. Details; Administrative Law Judges

An agency as defined by section 551 of this title which occasionally or temporarily is insufficiently staffed with administrative law judges appointed under section 3105 of this title may use administrative law judges selected by the Office of Personnel Management from and with the consent of other agencies.

§ 1305. Administrative Law Judges

For the purpose of sections 3105, 3344, 4301(2)(D), and 5372 of this title and the provisions of section 5335(a)(B) of this title that relate to administrative law judges, the Office of Personnel Management may, and for the purpose of section 7521 of this title, the Merit Systems Protection Board may investigate, require reports by agencies, issue reports, including an annual report to Congress, prescribe regulations, appoint advisory committees as necessary, recommend legislation, subpoena witnesses and records, and pay witness fees as established for the courts of the United States.

Index

References are to Pages

ADMINISTRATIVE ADJUDICATION
Generally, 174–175.
Bureaucracy and formal decisionmaking, 224–250.
Conflict with prosecutorial function, 296–298.
Exhaustion before judicial review, 769–782.
Findings of fact, circumventing judicial review with, 261–267.
Formality as restraint on policy formulation, 282–283.
Impartiality, 232–239, 489.
Judicial review, 250–273.
Judicial trial model, applicability of, 174–175.
Limited by rulemaking, 273–316.
Minimum safeguards, 224.
Policy formulation, 387–399.
Rulemaking or, choice of, 385–413.
Separation of functions, 232–239.

ADMINISTRATIVE AGENCIES
See also Bureaucracy; Independent Regulatory Commissions.
Administrative law judge decisions, deference to, 230–232.
Agency agenda, determinants of, 447–450, 710–712.
Agency policy, methods for implementing, 406–408.
Compatibility of functions, 72, 232–239.
Compliance with own rules required, 408–413, 434, 793–800, 803.
Conflicting demands on, 285–316.
Decisionmaking models, 103–109, 381–383.
Decisionmaking process within, 224–250, 455–458.
Delegated authority, 69–71.
Executive branch agencies, 64–74, 110–111.
Ex parte contacts, 83, 470–489.
Functions, 7, 233–236, 273–274, 278, 296–298.
Independence, 65–70.
Interpretation of statutes, judicial deference to, 255–256, 754–769.
Legislative objectives, ability to undermine, 192–193.
Litigation authority, 71, 163–172, 285, 523.

ADMINISTRATIVE AGENCIES—Cont'd
Location, 64–74.
Outside experts, use of, 15, 288–294, 453–458, 795–796.
Reorganization, 44–65, 155–160.
Structure, 64–74.

ADMINISTRATIVE LAW JUDGES
Administrative Procedure Act provisions, 242–245.
Comparability of decisions, 240–241.
Deference to decisions of, 230–232.
Independence, 239–250.
Removal, 176.
Social Security Administration, 239–250.

ADMINISTRATIVE OFFICIALS
See also Administrative Law Judges; Attorney General.
Appointment and removal, 112–132.
Disqualification for bias or prejudgment, 78–83, 237–239, 489–498.
Duties owed to public at large, 623–624, 643.
Future employment, restrictions on, 61–63.
Gifts, restrictions on, 61–62.
Liability to suit, see Official Immunity.

ADMINISTRATIVE PROCEDURE ACT
See also Freedom of Information Act; Government in the Sunshine Act; Privacy Act.
Generally, 49–51.
Adjudication and rulemaking distinguished, 387–399.
Administrative law judges, 242–245.
Administrative procedure provisions, 14, 19, 323–328, 333–335, 338, 414–470, 498–507.
Agency adjudication, formal model, 176.
Agency compliance with own rules, 410–412.
"Aggrieved" party, 646–648.
Bumpers amendment (proposed), 383–385.
"Committed to agency discretion," 630–631.
Contemporaneous record required, 634, 637–638.
Findings, necessity of, 632–635, 714–718.

ADMINISTRATIVE PROCEDURE ACT—
Cont'd
Formal versus informal rulemaking, 323–335, 415–432, 468–469.
Judicial review presumed, 629–633, 754–755.
Judicial review provisions, 14, 322–385, 627–633, 645–658, 688, 698–706, 712–739, 754–766, 769–776.
Mental processes of decisionmakers, 633.
"Post hoc rationalizations," 633, 637–638.
Presidential oversight authority (proposed), 161–163.
Sovereign immunity waiver, 627–628.
Standards for judicial review, 631–633.

ADMINISTRATIVE STATE
See also Non-Delegation Doctrine.
Historically, 180–182.
Legislative voting paradox, 29–31.
Origins, 6–15, 24–31, 44–45.
Public law remedial system, 619–622.
Right to hearing issue, impetus for, 175, 180–182.
Rule of law, 619–620, 692.

ADMINISTRATIVE SUMMARY JUDGMENT
See also Food and Drug Administration.
By rulemaking, 291–311, 501–502.
Limiting right to a hearing, 291–316.
Without rulemaking, 313–316.

AGENCY EXPERTISE
Agency authority enhanced by, 304–305.
Food additive safety policy, 92–103.
Judicial review of complex decisions, 354–381, 458–461.
Outside experts supplement, 54, 453–458.
Preclusion of review, 720, 736, 780.
Primary jurisdiction doctrine, 914–918, 930.
Reliance on regulatees, 453–454.
Value in decisionmaking, 381–383.

AGENCY LOCATION
Historically, 65–67.
Independence from President, 64–69.
Reorganization, see Executive Reorganization.

AGENCY STRUCTURE
Collegial form, 69.
Incompatible programs split, 72.
Inefficient by design, 73–74.
Political ramifications, 64–65.
Separation of functions, 232–239.
Technical expertise, 73.

ATTORNEY GENERAL
Alien deportation authority, 31–43, 402–403, 409.

ATTORNEY GENERAL—Cont'd
Election procedures, approval of, 693–694.
Freedom of Information Act disclosure, control over, 164–166.
Liability for malicious prosecution, 808.
Litigation authority precluding private suits, 855–861.
Policy influence, 163–172, 523.
President's ally, 125.
Responsibility for government litigation, 71, 163–172, 523.
Settlement of tort actions, 804.
Special prosecutor, appointment of, 63, 125–128.

BENEFICIARY ENFORCEMENT SUITS
Bivens-style suits, 933–934.
Coexistence of statutory and common law remedies, 912–914, 916.
Comprehensive statutory enforcement schemes, 920–934.
Dangers of private enforcement of public law, 846–847.
Environmental citizen suits, 845–847, 921–926, 931.
Explicit remedies, 844–847.
Implied rights of action, see Implied Private Rights of Action.
Legislative preemption of common law, 920–934.
Primary agency jurisdiction, 910–920.
Public prosecutor, 844.
Qui tam (informer) suits, 844–845.
Section 1983, see Section 1983 Suits.
Statutory immunization from private liability, 913.
Supplementing agency enforcement, 849–850.

BUREAUCRACY
Bureaucratic rationality, 225–228.
Changes in policy priorities, 312–313.
Errors, effect on rights, 193–195, 202–203, 210–211.
Institutional decisions, 228–229.
Judicial review and bureaucratization, 634, 699.
Moral judgment distinguished, 226–228.
Rationality model of decisionmaking, 635–637.
Regulatory delay, effects, 313.
Welfare administration, 192–195.

CIVIL SERVICE
See also Administrative Officials.
Generally, 60–64, 128–132.
Civil Service Act, 60–61, 128–131.
Civil Service Reform Act, 61, 131–132.
History, 128–131.
Pendleton Act, 60–61, 128–131.

CIVIL SERVICE—Cont'd
Remedies for wrongful discipline, 933–934.
"Whistleblowers," 63–64, 131–132.

CONGRESSIONAL CONTROLS OVER ADMINISTRATION
Agency agenda, influence over, 449–450.
Agency impartiality, interference with, 78–83.
Agency location, choice of, see Agency Location.
Agency structure, choice of, see Agency Structure.
Budgetary controls, 1, 71.
Casework, 76.
Committee chairmen, powers of, 77–78, 449.
Ex parte contacts with agency decisionmakers, 488–489.
Legislative veto, see Legislative Veto.
Oversight, 74–78, 770–771.
Preclusion of judicial review, 688–698.
Standing, conferral to check agency discretion, 644–645.
Statutory controls, see Statutory Controls Over Administration.

CONSTITUTION
Bicameral requirement, 34–41.
Bill of rights, 179, 321, 817.
"Case or controversy" requirement, 644–646, 663–664, 670–671.
Due Process Clause, see Due Process.
Eleventh amendment, 892, 902–908.
Equal Protection Clause, 321, 410–412.
Establishment Clause, 672–676.
Executive branch, 110–111.
Fifth amendment, 521–522, 526–533, 668–673.
First amendment, 563.
Fourteenth amendment, 889, 893–902, 905.
Fourth amendment, 510–514, 532–533, 538–561, 818–826.
Presentment Clauses, 33–34, 38–41.
Property Clause, 673–675.
Speech and Debate Clause, 833, 841.
Taxing and spending power, 672–673.
Text (partial), 935–938.

CONSUMER PRODUCT SAFETY COMMISSION
Advisory committees required, 54–55, 73, 458.
Litigation authority, 168.
Negotiation, 407–408.
Outside experts, reliance on, 454.
Rulemaking by, 342, 453–454, 498–500.
Statutory deadlines, 448–449.

DAMAGE SUITS AGAINST GOVERNMENT
Generally, 783–843.
Administrative claim requirement, 804.
Bivens-style suits, 817–827.
Breach of trust action, 785–791.
Constitutional torts, 803–804, 817–843.
Court of Claims jurisdiction, 784–791.
Discretionary function exception, 791–792, 796–803.
District court jurisdiction, 791.
Good faith defense, 842.
"Good Samaritan" doctrine, 793–794, 799, 801.
Government versus official, suits against, 805–806.
Governmental functions exception, 791–792, 797–799.
Libel, 809–815.
Negligence, 801–802.
Official immunity defense, see Official Immunity.
Planning versus operational activities, 802–803.
Private law analogous actions, 783, 792, 801.
Private statutory relief as alternative, 804.
Section 1983, see Section 1983 Suits.
Sovereign immunity, see Sovereign Immunity.
State law in federal tort actions, 791–792, 801, 803–804, 818–819.
Substantive rights distinct from jurisdiction, 784–790.
Tort claims, 791–804.
Wrongful conduct, 802.

DELANEY CLAUSE
Generally, 92–103, 314–316.
Administrative discretion limited, 92–93.
History, 95–96.
Saccharin ban moratorium, 92–99.
Scientific judgments under, 93–97.

DEPARTMENT OF AGRICULTURE
Decisionmaking process within, 228–229.
Employee liability for enforcement actions, 827–840.
Food stamp program, 83–88.
Judicial review, 702.
Pesticide regulation, 746–753.
Reporting requirements, 536–537.
Rulemaking by, 438, 459.
Standing to challenge regulations of, 648–652, 686–688.
Subpoena power, 515–516.

DEPARTMENT OF LABOR
Including Occupational Safety and Health Administration.
Combination of functions within, 72–73, 118.
Enforcement discretion, 712–721.

DEPARTMENT OF LABOR—Cont'd
Field sanitation standards, 742–744.
Formal rulemaking by, 418–423.
Informal rulemaking by, 342, 500–502.
Information disclosure rules, 600–606.
Inspection power, 546–560.
Judicial review, 767–768.
Negotiation, 504.
Occupational safety and health standards, 5–6, 25–26, 354–381, 500–502.
Outside experts, use of, 455–457.
Private standards adopted, 506.
Standing to challenge orders of, 642.
Statutory deadlines and judicial oversight, 741–742.
Subpoena power, 511–514.

DEPARTMENT OF THE INTERIOR
Bureau of Indian Affairs, 399–401, 406, 433–434.
Compliance with own rules required, 409–410, 434.
Disclosure of commercial information, 607.
Ex parte contacts, 475–476.
Internal manual and rulemaking, 399–401, 406.
Liability for Indian lands, 785–791.
National parks, development of, 653–658.
Rulemaking, avoidance of, 397–401, 406.
Standing to challenge orders of, 653–657.

DEPARTMENT OF THE TREASURY
Including Internal Revenue Service.
Compliance with own rules, 411–412.
Inspection power, 542–543.
Nonprofit hospital charitable status, 660–665.
Racially discriminatory schools, tax-exempt status, 682–686.
Reporting requirements, 529–533, 536–537.
Standing to challenge rulings of, 660–665, 682–686.
Subpoena power, 515–517, 521–523.

DEPARTMENT OF TRANSPORTATION
Including National Highway Traffic Safety Administration.
Auto safety standards, 323–354, 450–453.
Congressional influence over, 80–81.
Federal aid highway program, 629–637.
Reporting requirements, 536–537.
Withdrawal of proposed rule, judicial review of, 343–354, 740–741.

DUE PROCESS
Generally, 176–224.
Administrative summary judgment, 304.
Agency compliance with own rules, 410–413.
Agency investigations, 520.
Combination of functions, 236–239.

DUE PROCESS—Cont'd
Dignitary theory, 184, 211–212.
Historically, 179–182.
Interest balancing theory, 179, 197–205.
"Life, liberty or property," 178–179, 197, 213–224, 668–673.
Minimum procedural requirements, 185–187, 249.
Natural rights theory, 178–179.
Official bias, 492–494.
Right to judicial review, 695–696, 700–702.
Rulemaking requirements, 319–321, 347, 414, 430.
Substantive, see Irrebuttable Presumption Doctrine.
Tradition theory, 177–178.

ECONOMIC STABILIZATION ACT OF 1970
Partial text, 15–16.
Upheld over non-delegation challenge, 6–15.

ENVIRONMENTAL PROTECTION AGENCY
Citizen suits, 845–846.
Clean Air Act, 271–273, 436–438, 476–489, 696–697.
Creation, 68–70.
Ex parte contacts, 472–473, 476–489.
Independent status, 68–69.
Judicial review limited, 696–698, 920–932.
Negotiation, 272, 408, 461, 504, 744.
Policy discretion, 5, 26–27, 449–450.
Rulemaking by, 439, 451–452, 458–459.
Scientific expertise, 73.
Water pollution control, 920–932.

EXECUTIVE ORDERS
Generally, 140–155.
Effects on private parties, 142–143.
Emancipation Proclamation, 140.
Executive Order No. 12291, 143–155, 439.
Legislative function, 6–7.

EXECUTIVE REORGANIZATION
Congressional acquiescence, 157–158.
History, 156–158.
Presidential control, 155–160.
Proposals concerning, 158–160.
Separation of powers, effect on, 65.
Tied to legislative veto, 44, 159–160.

FEDERAL ADVISORY COMMITTEE ACT
Generally, 54–55.
Agency-industry cooperation distinguished, 745.
Secrecy of committee deliberations, 457–458.

FEDERAL AVIATION ADMINISTRATION
Creation, 72.
Liability for aircraft certification, 792–801.
Pilot age rule, 307.

FEDERAL COMMUNICATIONS COMMISSION
Compliance with own rules required, 412.
Ex parte contacts, 470–474.
Judicial review, 231.
Limiting hearings, 276.
Litigation authority, 167.
Pre-enforcement judicial review of regulations, 754–766.
Primary jurisdiction, 861–865.
Rulemaking power, 276.
Standing to challenge orders of, 643–644.

FEDERAL ELECTION COMMISSION
Appointment of commissioners, 119–125.
Creation, 861–862.
Primary jurisdiction over campaign contribution laws, 862.

FEDERAL ENERGY REGULATORY COMMISSION
Independent status, 67–68.
Litigation authority, 170.
Rulemaking, avoidance of, 398.

FEDERAL POWER COMMISSION
Congressional influence over, 81–83.
Litigation authority, 167.
Rulemaking by, 459–460.

FEDERAL REGISTER ACT
Generally, 51.
Impetus for, 4, 15.

FEDERAL TRADE COMMISSION
Appointment and removal of commissioners, 112–116.
Compliance with own rules required, 413.
Congressional oversight, 77.
Disclosure of internal memoranda, 580–581, 589.
Disqualification of commissioners, 78–80, 237–239, 489–498.
Enforcement discretion, 727.
Enforcement proceedings, 282–283.
Formal adjudication required, 176.
Issuance of complaints, judicial review of, 769–776.
Litigation authority, 167–170.
Magnuson-Moss Amendments, 283–285, 454, 510.
Negotiated settlements, 718–719.
Reporting requirements, 524–526, 533–534.

FEDERAL TRADE COMMISSION—Cont'd
Rulemaking, avoidance of, 403–404.
Rulemaking power, 274–285.
Subpoena power, 509–511, 516, 518–519.
Trade regulation rules, 283–285.

FOOD AND DRUG ADMINISTRATION
See also Administrative Summary Judgment; Delaney Clause
Cosmetic ingredients regulation, 745–746, 761–766.
Disclosure of commercial information, 607–608.
Disclosure of internal memoranda, 590.
Drug regulation, 285–316, 723–733, 754–761.
Employee ethics rules, 61–62.
Enforcement discretion, 712, 723–733.
Enforcement impact, 711–712.
Ex parte contacts, 83, 474–475.
Food additive regulation, 92–103.
Formal rulemaking, 417, 424.
Independent status, 69–70.
Inspection powers, 761–766.
Leverage in field inspections, 406–407.
Liability for inspection errors, 802.
Litigation authority, 285.
Negotiation, 288, 407, 607, 745–746.
Outside experts, use of, 288–294.
Policy implementation by field inspectors, 406–407.
Possible regulatory approaches, 103–109.
Pre-enforcement judicial review of regulations, 754–766.
Primary jurisdiction, 919.
Private standards encouraged, 505.
Public participation, agency-funded, 454.
Rulemaking by, 291–311, 434, 440–447.
Scientific judgment, 93, 96–97.
Statutory deadlines, 741.

FREEDOM OF INFORMATION ACT
Generally, 51–52, 564–617.
Agency enforcement criteria, disclosure of, 712.
Attorney General control over, 164–166.
Effects, 610–614, 616–617.
Executive privilege, 585–587, 615–616.
Exemption 4, commercial records, 602–608, 615.
Exemption 5, intra-agency memoranda, 569–587.
Exemption 6, personal privacy, 608–610.
Exemption 7, investigatory files for enforcement, 578–579, 591–599.
Exemptions generally, 52, 457–458, 566–568, 589–590.
In camera judicial inspection, 587–589.
Judicial discretion under, 589–591, 608–610.
Privacy Act, 608–610.
Proprietary information, 606–608.
Purpose, 597.

FREEDOM OF INFORMATION ACT—
Cont'd
Standing under, 660, 682.
Trade Secrets Act, 603–606.

GOVERNMENT IN THE SUNSHINE ACT
Generally, 53–54.
Advisory committee meetings, 458.

IMPLIED PRIVATE RIGHTS OF ACTION
Generally, 847–878.
Borak doctrine, 847–851.
Congressional intent, 852–853, 857, 865, 878.
Cort v. Ash test, 862–866.
English law origins, 853–855.
Remedial purpose, 852.
State law, effect on, 851–852.

INDEPENDENT REGULATORY COMMIS-SIONS
See also Administrative Agencies.
Abolition urged, 232.
Appointment and removal of commissioners, 112–125.
Collegial form, 69.
Executive orders, effect on, 152–155.
Identifying, 67–69.
Information requirements, 533–537.
Legislative function, 67.
Presidential control, 66–69, 112–125.

INFORMATION
Generally, 508–617.
Government access, see Inspections; Investigation and Discovery.
Private access, see Freedom of Information Act.
Purposes of disclosure demands, 508, 561–564.

INSPECTIONS
See also Investigation and Discovery.
Generally, 537–561.
Consent as waiver of rights, 542–546.
Exceptions to warrant requirement, 542–546, 560–561.
General administrative plan as "probable cause," 546–557.
Warrant required, 538–542, 546–557.

INTERNAL REVENUE SERVICE
See Department of the Treasury.

INTERSTATE COMMERCE COMMISSION
Compliance with own rules, 410–411.
Hearings required, 416, 425–431.
Independent status, 66–67.
Interpretative rules, 434–436.
Litigation authority, 166–167.

INTERSTATE COMMERCE COMMIS-SION—Cont'd
Primary jurisdiction, 917–918.
Standing to challenge orders of, 639–641, 657–658.

INVESTIGATION AND DISCOVERY
Generally, 508–561.
Corporate or individual subject, 512–513, 521, 525–526, 539–540.
Enforcement power, 514–523.
Physical inspections, see Inspections.
Privileges to resist agency demands, 521–523, 532–533.
Record-keeping and reporting requirements, 523–537.
Subpoena power, see Subpoena Power.
Unlawful activity, 529–533.
Voluntary compliance, 509, 548.

IRREBUTTABLE PRESUMPTION DOC-TRINE
Generally, 83–92.
Constraining legislative choice, 83–92, 404.
Due process rationale, 84–92.
Equal protection rationale, 86–90.
Substantive rationality review, substitute for, 91–92.

JUDICIAL REVIEW
Generally, 250–252, 623–638.
Agency recalcitrance, 268–269.
Agency subpoenas, 514–521.
"Arbitrary and capricious" standard, 333–334, 341–342.
Complex or technical issues, 354–377, 458–461.
Constitutional review of agency rules, 319–322.
Effects, 270–273.
Evidence, standard of review of, 252–267.
Functions, 269–270.
Jurisdiction, see Jurisdiction.
Legislation by legislature or agency, 14, 319–322, 337–338, 404.
Limit on agency discretion, 267–273.
Modes of, 619–621, 624–628.
Non-statutory review, 625.
"On the record as a whole" standard, 257–260.
Presumptively available, 628–634.
Procedural review as substitute for substantive review, 413–414.
Public versus private law, 623–624.
Record for, 439–447, 632–638, 747–748, 752–753.
Reviewability, see Reviewability.
Ripeness, see Ripeness.
Rule precision, judicial control of, 404–406.

JUDICIAL REVIEW—Cont'd
Rulemaking, post-APA review, 322–385, 415–502.
Rulemaking, pre-APA review, 417–418.
Sovereign immunity, see Sovereign Immunity.
Standing to obtain, see Standing.
"Substantial evidence" standard, 230–231, 250, 256–261, 300–304, 333, 341–342, 631–632.

JUDICIARY
Accelerate agency action, 298–300, 741–745.
Administrative role assumed, 228, 656, 699–700.
Interference with public administration, 627.
Liability of judges, 806–807, 836–837.
Oversight of agency rulemaking priorities, 733–746.
Partner with agencies, 251, 270–273, 342, 912.

JURISDICTION
Amount in controversy requirement, 626.
Federal question, 626.
Non-statutory review, 625–626.
Pendent, 626.
Subject matter, 626.
Text, general jurisdictional statutes, 939–942.

LEGISLATIVE VETO
Generally, 31–48.
Alternatives, 46–48.
Constitutionality, 31–47.
Independent regulatory commissions, 45–46.
Severability, 43, 47.
Trade regulation rules, 284.
Types, 43–44.

NATIONAL ENVIRONMENTAL POLICY ACT
Generally, 56–58.
Reviewability, effect on, 703–704.
Rulemaking, effect on, 467–468, 635.
Standing in environmental litigation, 658, 675–676.

NATIONAL HIGHWAY TRAFFIC SAFETY ADMINISTRATION
See Department of Transportation.

NATIONAL LABOR RELATIONS BOARD
Disclosure of internal records, 569–579, 581–582, 591–599.
Enforcement discretion, 706–710, 718.
Exhaustion of remedies, 775–777.
Formal adjudication required, 176.
General Counsel's role, 72, 386, 569–572.

NATIONAL LABOR RELATIONS BOARD— Cont'd
Judicial review of decisions, 230–231, 252–268, 706–710.
Primary jurisdiction, 919.
Rulemaking, avoidance of, 385–399.
Subpoena power, 519.

NON–DELEGATION DOCTRINE
Administrative flexibility, 7–11.
Agency standards, need for, 12–13, 19–24, 274, 401–402, 408–413.
APA as alternative limit on agency discretion, 14, 19.
Democratic values, effect on, 24–31, 44–45.
Historical development, 2–6.
Ineffectual restraint on legislative choices, 404.
Judicial review, safeguard for, 12–14, 17–18, 23.
Legislative standards, need for, 3–15, 18–19, 317–318, 369–370, 381.
Policy choice and implementation, 27–28.
Political nature, 6.
Statutory context as standard, 9–10, 18–19.
Wage and price controls example, 6–19.

NUCLEAR REGULATORY COMMISSION
Creation, 72, 117.
Power plant licensure, 461–469, 668–671.
Price-Anderson Act, constitutionality of, 668–671.
Rulemaking procedures, 461–468.

OCCUPATIONAL SAFETY AND HEALTH ADMINISTRATION
See Department of Labor.

OFFICE OF MANAGEMENT AND BUDGET.
Budgetary oversight function, 71, 160–163.
Executive order review, 141.
Executive Order No. 12291, 145, 154–155.
History, 147–148.
Information requirements of agencies, 60, 533–537.
Integration of policies, 635.
Policy influence, 160–161.
Private standards encouraged, 506–507.
Regulatory impact analyses, 144–145.

OFFICIAL IMMUNITY
Absolute versus qualified, 811–815, 829–843.
Adjudicatory function, 836–838.
Constitutional violations, 829–843.
Extended to private persons, 816.
"Good faith" immunity, 842.
History, 806–815.

OFFICIAL IMMUNITY—Cont'd
Legislative function, 840–841.
Ministerial duties, 842–843.
Prosecutory function, 838–839.
Ultra vires acts, 806–813, 831–843, 906, 908.

PAPERWORK REDUCTION ACT
Generally, 60.
Record-keeping and reporting requirements, 534–537.

PRESIDENTIAL CONTROLS OVER ADMINISTRATION
Agency policy, authority to direct, 132–172.
Appointment and removal of officers, 112–132.
Civil service, 128–132.
Emergency powers, 132–141.
Ex parte contacts with agency decisionmakers, 475–499.
Executive orders, 140–155.
Managerial authority, 155–160.
Reorganization power, 156–160.
Through Attorney General, see Attorney General.
Through Office of Management and Budget, see Office of Management and Budget.

PRIVACY ACT
Generally, 55.
Disclosure of trade secrets, 600.
Freedom of Information Act, 609–610.

PUBLIC LAW REMEDIES
See also Administrative State; Separation of Powers.
Beneficiary enforcement, see Beneficiary Enforcement Suits.
Injunctions generally, 619–620.
Interrelationship of remedies, 619–622.
Public versus private law concerns, 620–621, 642–643.
Relief from officially inflicted injuries, see Damage Suits Against Government.
Review of legality of official action, see Judicial Review.

REGULATORY FLEXIBILITY ACT
Generally, 58–60.
Preclusion of judicial review, 688–689.

REVIEWABILITY
Generally, 688–746.
Administrative finality as preclusion, 692.
Agency inaction generally, 706–746.
"Committed to agency discretion," 630–631, 698–706, 722–723, 726–728, 736–738.

REVIEWABILITY—Cont'd
Constitutionality of statutory limits, 690–696.
Discretionary grants and government contracts, 701–703.
Enforcement discretion generally, 706–733.
Exclusive routes of judicial review, 688, 693, 696–698, 754–755, 764, 767, 779–780.
Foreign policy issues, 704–705.
Informal negotiation avoids, 744–745.
Judicial resistance to preclusion, 689–692.
Judicial self-restraint, 701.
"Jurisdictional fact" doctrine, 695–696.
Justiciability, 639.
Labor union certifications, 705–706.
Managerial nature of challenged action, 699–700.
Military decisions, 704.
Negotiated settlements, 714, 718–721.
"Political question" doctrine, 705.
Preclusion implied, 693–694.
Presumptive reviewability, 689, 728–729.
Public land management, 703–704.
Reasons for nonenforcement, 709–710, 718, 723–729.
Reasons for nonregulation, 738–739.
Regulatory discretion generally, 733–746.
Scope of judicial review, 714–717.
Statutory deadlines, compliance with, 741–742.
Statutory preclusion, 688–698.

RIGHT TO A HEARING
See also Due Process; Trial-Type Hearing.
Generally, 175–224.
Accuracy of determinations enhanced, 201–211.
Agency recalcitrance, 192–193.
Alternative remedies available, 206.
Credibility factor, 210–211.
Disability benefits, pretermination hearing, 195–204.
Disability benefits, recoupment of overpayments, 207–211.
Hardship factor, 183–184, 191–192, 199–201, 213–214, 218–219.
Hybrid hearings, 309–311.
Limited by administrative summary judgment, 291–316.
Limited by rulemaking, 246–250, 273–316.
Public employee dismissals, 220–223.
Statutory guarantees, 176, 221–224.
Welfare, pretermination hearing, 182–195.
Witness credibility, need for assessing, 210–211.

RIPENESS
Constitutional challenges to agency appeal procedures, 778–779.
Criminal cases, 780–782.
Delay as refusal to act, 747–748.
Exhaustion of administrative remedies, 769–782.
Exhaustion versus finality, 773.
"Final agency action," 757–759, 762, 766–767, 772–776.
"Final order" doctrine, 746–753.
Inaction, reviewability of, 740, 746–787.
Interim relief, 747–753.
Justiciability, 639.
Opinion letters, judicial review of, 767, 768–769.
Pre-enforcement judicial review, 14, 754–769, 777.
Record required for judicial review, 748–749, 752–753.
Ultra vires acts, 777–778.

RULEMAKING
Adjudication or, choice of, 385–413.
Administrative summary judgment, 285–316.
Agency agenda, determinants of, 447–450.
Agency authority to make rules, 274–316.
Agency freedom to fashion procedures, 461–469.
Contemporaneous explanation, 334–335, 442–447.
Ex parte contacts, 470–489.
Exemptions from procedural requirements, 432–439.
Formal rulemaking, 418–431.
Formal versus informal procedures, 323–335, 415–432, 468–469.
Informal rulemaking, 333–334, 432–507.
Legislating, similarity to, 281, 317–318.
Limiting right to a hearing, 273–316.
Negotiation as alternative, 502–505.
Notice, 400–401, 450–452.
Official bias and prejudgment, 489–498.
Oral hearings required, 458–461.
Pre-APA procedural requirements, 416–418.
Private standards, 505–507.
Procedural as substantive requirements, 413–414, 446.
Public participation, 452–458.
Record for judicial review, 439–447.
Reform proposals, 498–507.
Revocation of rule, 343–354.
Standards of judicial review, 323–385.
Waiver of general rules, 306–307.

SECTION 1983 SUITS
Generally, 621–622.
Abstention doctrine, 909–910.
Attorney's fees awards, 881, 905–906.

SECTION 1983 SUITS—Cont'd
Congressional creation of rights against states, 893–902, 905.
Exhaustion of state law remedies, 908–909.
History, 889–890.
Immunity of local governments, 892, 902–908.
Injunctive versus monetary relief, 907–908.
Official immunity, 834–835, 892.
Preclusion inferred from statutory enforcement schemes, 926–929.
Relief available, 890, 907–908.
State law remedies, 890–891.
State waiver of immunity, 903–904.
Statutory violations, 878–889.

SECURITIES AND EXCHANGE COMMISSION
Litigation authority, 169.
"No action" letters, judicial review of, 710.
Policymaking by adjudication, 393–394.
Private enforcement suits, 849–850.
Rulemaking discretion, 733–739.
Subpoena power, 520–521.

SEPARATION OF POWERS
See also Administrative State; Non-Delegation Doctrine
Generally, 110–111.
Appointment and removal power, 112–132.
Executive privilege, 585–587.
Implied rights of action as judicial lawmaking, 872–876.
Judicial recognition of damages actions, 820–826.
Legislative function, 2–24, 132–139.
Legislative veto, 31–46.
Preclusion of judicial review, 628, 694–696, 861.
Public law remedies, 619–621.
Standing doctrine, 683–684.

SOCIAL SECURITY ADMINISTRATION
Administrative law judges, 239–250.
Caseload, 267.
Disability benefits, 195–211, 239–240, 270–271, 778–779.
Exhaustion of administrative adjudication, 778–779.
Formal adjudication required, 176.
Grid regulations, 246–250.
Information-gathering ability, 508.
Judicial precedent, adherence to, 268.
Judicial review precluded by statute, 692–693.

SOVEREIGN IMMUNITY
Administrative Procedure Act waiver, 628.

SOVEREIGN IMMUNITY—Cont'd
Diminished importance, 624, 628.
Discretionary function exception, 791–792, 796–801.
Federal Tort Claims Act, 783, 791–804.
Government versus official, suits against, 627, 902, 904–905.
Governmental function exception, 791–792, 801.
History of doctrine, 626–628.
Misrepresentation exception, 802.
Specific statutory waivers, 625, 791.
Tucker Act, 783, 791–804.
Ultra vires acts, 627, 906, 908.
Waiver generally, 783.

STANDING
Generally, 623–624.
"Abstract stigmatic injury" not cognizable, 683–684.
"Aggrieved" party, 646–650, 655–656, 689.
Beneficiary of statute, 651–652.
Causal nexus requirement, 659–660, 665–666, 669–671, 684–687.
Economic versus non-economic injury, 643–644, 647, 654–658.
Enforcement discretion challenges, 686.
Injury-in-fact requirement, 646, 651, 654–658, 664–665, 669–670, 677–682, 687.
Jus tertii claims, 666–667.
Justiciability, 639, 650, 685–686.
"Legal right" test, 641–646, 658.
Merits and standing distinguished, 646, 650–652, 671.
Organizational standing, 680, 682, 687.
Party "aggrieved in fact," 641–642.
Personal direct stake necessary, 649–651, 655–656.
Post-APA doctrine generally, 645–658.
Pre-APA doctrine generally, 639–645.
Private attorney general rationale, 645, 647.
Redressability, 640, 663–665, 687.
Separation of powers, 683–684.
Statutory preclusion, 687–688.
Statutory versus constitutional interests, 675–676.
Subject matter nexus, 669–670.
Taxpayers' standing, 646, 659–666, 669–675.
Zone of interests test, 646–647, 649–650, 652, 671, 686–687.

STATUTORY CONTEXT OF ADMINISTRATION
See also statute by name.
Administrative Procedure Act, 49–51.
Civil Service Reform Act, 61–64.
Ethics in Government Act, 62–63.
Federal Advisory Committee Act, 54–55.
Federal Register Act, 51.
Freedom of Information Act, 51–52.
Government in the Sunshine Act, 53–54.
Intergovernmental Cooperation Act of 1968, 635.
Organic statutes, 176, 322–323.
Paperwork Reduction Act, 60.
Privacy Act, 55.
National Environmental Policy Act, 56–58.
Regulatory Flexibility Act, 58–60.
Saccharin ban moratorium, 92–103.
Special Prosecutor Act, 63.

SUBPOENA POWER
Generally, 509–523.
Authorized by statute, 514–517.
"Bad faith" defense, 516–517.
Corporate or individual subject, 512–513, 521.
Issued by proper official, 519.
Notice to "target" of third-party subpoena, 520–521.
Privileges not to comply, 521–523.
Reasonable demand, 515, 518–519.
Relevant information only, 515, 517–518.

TRIAL–TYPE HEARING
Characteristics, 176, 185–187, 224.
Counsel, right to, 187, 189.
Cross-examination, 186–187.
Decision on the record, 187.
Notice, 185–186.
Opportunity to be heard, 185–187.
Right to, see Right to a Hearing.

VETERANS ADMINISTRATION
Benefits decisions, judicial review of, 689–691.
Disciplinary actions, judicial review of, 701.
Disclosure of internal memoranda, 590.

†